Deviance and Social Control

2nd Edition

Deviance and Social Control

A Sociological Perspective

2nd Edition

Michelle Inderbitzin
Oregon State University

Kristin A. Bates
California State University San Marcos

Randy R. Gainey
Old Dominion University, Norfolk

Los Angeles | London | New Delhi
Singapore | Washington DC | Melbourne

FOR INFORMATION:

SAGE Publications, Inc.
2455 Teller Road
Thousand Oaks, California 91320
E-mail: order@sagepub.com

SAGE Publications Ltd.
1 Oliver's Yard
55 City Road
London, EC1Y 1SP
United Kingdom

SAGE Publications India Pvt. Ltd.
B 1/I 1 Mohan Cooperative Industrial Area
Mathura Road, New Delhi 110 044
India

SAGE Publications Asia-Pacific Pte. Ltd.
3 Church Street
#10-04 Samsung Hub
Singapore 049483

Acquisitions Editor: Jerry Westby
eLearning Editor: Nicole Mangona
Editorial Assistant: Laura Kirkhuff
Production Editor: Jane Haenel
Copy Editor: Jared Leighton
Typesetter: C&M Digitals (P) Ltd.
Proofreader: Scott Oney
Indexer: Karen Wiley
Cover Designer: Michael Dubowe
Marketing Manager: Amy Lammers

Printed in the United States of America

Library of Congress Cataloging-in-Publication Data

Names: Inderbitzin, Michelle Lee, author. | Bates, Kristin Ann, author. | Gainey, Randy R., author.

Title: Deviance and social control : a sociological perspective / Michelle Inderbitzin, Oregon State University, Kristin A. Bates, Cal State University, San Marcos, Randy R. Gainey, Old Dominion University, Norfolk.

Description: 2nd edition. | Los Angeles : SAGE, [2016] | Includes bibliographical references and index.

Identifiers: LCCN 2016005364 | ISBN 978-1-5063-2791-4 (pbk. : alk. paper)

Subjects: LCSH: Deviant behavior. | Social control.

Classification: LCC HM811 .I53 2016 | DDC 302.5/42—dc23
LC record available at http://lccn.loc.gov/2016005364

This book is printed on acid-free paper.

SUSTAINABLE FORESTRY INITIATIVE

Certified Chain of Custody
Promoting Sustainable Forestry
www.sfiprogram.org
SFI-01268

SFI label applies to text stock

16 17 18 19 20 10 9 8 7 6 5 4 3 2 1

Brief Contents

Detailed Contents

Chapter 13. Global Perspectives on Deviance and Social Control   527

READINGS

Foreword

By the time sociology came to universities at the beginning of the 20th century, all the "good" topics had been snatched up by earlier arrivals: Historians got to write about wars and kings and queens, economists acquired the market as their special turf, and political science took control of the state and government. Sociology was left with whatever topics were left over, especially (chief among these less desirable subjects) the "bad behavior" nice people didn't like in the increasingly urbanized society they lived in: slums, gangs, prostitution, alcoholism, and crime. No one had to worry, then, about defining this field or justifying all these disparate topics being treated under one heading. It seemed obvious to all right-thinking people that these things were problems that needed looking into. Sociologists took them over as their own, and the nature of these problems (and the solutions to them everyone hoped the new science would provide) defined the nature of the field.

Since university disciplines like to make sense of what they are doing, sociologists soon began to look for a unifying thread, for what all these things had in common that justified calling studying them a scientific field. Once you question the commonsense idea that they all simply exemplified "bad behavior" or "social problems," you commit yourself to finding a more logical and scientifically defensible description of what you're doing. Sociologists worked hard to come up with that definition. What they came up with, in the end, was not a definition but definitions, lots of them. Because to go beyond saying these were all simply differing versions of badness, to define what made bad people's behavior bad, created great difficulties because people don't agree on that kind of definition. The commonsense understanding of "badness" included a mixture of very different things: drunkenness, stealing, craziness—the definition really consisted of nothing more than a list of activities that the law banned. Because legislatures don't make laws to define the subject matter of a science but rather to satisfy constituents, the science part comes hard.

For many years, taking commonsense ideas of bad behavior at face value and accepting conventional definitions of what "bad" was, sociologists tried to make science by accepting and trying to prove and improve upon equally commonsense explanations of why people behaved badly. They mostly relied on one of two ideas. On one hand, some theories said that people did bad things because they were inherently bad—there were plenty of genetic theories in the early history of criminology, identifying potential criminals by physical markers of bad heredity—similar to the markers of feeblemindedness, another topic that sociology and criminology had on their hands—or because they lived in bad circumstances, which turned otherwise normal children into delinquents, sane people into the mentally ill, and healthy people into alcoholics and drug addicts.

These general ideas, scarcely worth being dignified as general theories, for many years dominated the classes taught under such titles as "Social Disorganization" or "Social Problems." Textbooks and lectures proceeded along a well-marked path of problems, dominated by well-known kinds of crimes—starting with juvenile delinquency and following criminal types through more adult crimes like robbery, theft, burglary, and murder—and equally familiar kinds of personal pathologies, revolving around pleasurable forms of behavior that right-thinking people thought were wrong—sex, drugs, and alcohol, all three leading to mental illness. Teachers and books rehearsed the numerous and varied things that had been found to be correlated with bad behaviors and presumably to cause them: living in a slum neighborhood, coming from a broken home (that is, a household not headed by a married heterosexual couple), low educational achievement, and a long list of other phenomena usually correlated with some measure of social class so that, in some fundamental sense, the cause of all this pathology seemed to be being poor.

Such an approach did not produce a lot of results. What one study found was often contradicted by another study, and eventually, some sociologists and criminologists began to take a more neutral approach to these subject matters, seeing them not as signs of bad character or heredity but rather as signs of a mixed-up society, whose operations and organization made it likely that some sizable number of people would find it attractive and/or profitable to engage in behavior that led them into conflict with the law (as the gang members in *West Side Story* sang, "We're not depraved, we're deprived!").

Since finding the causes of bad behavior in society did not produce reliable results any more than genetic and psychological theories had, some sociologists began to look further. They asked about a larger spectrum of things and focused on what we might call "the crime industry," the agencies and organizations that made laws that defined what things were crimes, that devoted themselves to finding people who had violated these laws, adjudicating their cases and administering the punishments and forms of supervision the resolution of those cases dictated: the legislatures that made the laws, the police who found the guilty parties, the courts where their cases were decided, the jails and prisons where they served their sentences, and the parole offices and officers that oversaw those who came out at the other end of this process.

All this research is best summarized, as the authors of this book have done, by considering the variety of theories that sociologists and criminologists have created to make sense of this confusing mass of ideas and of the research the variety of ideas has engendered. Reading their crisp, informative summaries of so many conflicting ideas and then the wisely chosen illustrative examples of what you get from each approach will give students the best possible introduction to a lively and still developing field of research.

Howard S. Becker

Preface

While there are many textbooks and readers on deviant behavior currently on the market, this book is unique for two reasons. First, it is framed within and written entirely from a sociological perspective. We explain the development of major sociological theoretical perspectives and detail how those theories have been used to think about and study the causes of deviant behavior and the reactions to it. We find the theories fascinating, and we think you will, too. We have provided many specific examples of deviant behavior and social control within the text so that students will have numerous opportunities to apply the concepts and theories and make connections to their everyday lives. The second unique aspect of this book is that as a text-reader, it is a true hybrid, offering both original text and primary readings. It includes both substantial original chapters that give an overview of the field and the theories as well as carefully selected articles on deviance and social control that have previously appeared in leading academic journals and books. In the following, we describe how *Deviance and Social Control: A Sociological Perspective, 2nd Edition,* differs from existing texts on the market.

While the widely used textbooks on deviant behavior have strong points, our book provides a very different experience for students by combining original text with existing studies. Professors will be able to assign one book (rather than a textbook and accompanying reader) and will be assured that their students are presented with both clear explanations of sociological perspectives on deviance and some of the best examples of research from the field. While some classic research articles are included, most of the primary readings were chosen because they are excellent, cutting-edge, contemporary examples of the use of theory to explain deviance. They offer the opportunity to explore a deviant topic more thoroughly yet still with an eye toward the importance of theory in that exploration.

In contrast to most of the popular readers and textbooks on deviant behavior, this book is primarily organized around theories and perspectives of deviance, rather than types of deviant behavior or a singular approach to understanding deviance. We have aimed for a combination of both depth and breadth in this book; in taking a broad sociological perspective, we focus on theory but also include full chapters on researching deviance, the social control of deviance, deviant careers, and deviance and social control in a global context.

We hope this book will serve as a guide to students delving into the fascinating world of deviance and social control for the first time, offering clear overviews of issues and perspectives in the field as well as introductions to classic and current research. *Deviance and Social Control: A Sociological Perspective, 2nd Edition,* is intended to replace standard deviance textbooks or readers; it can be used in both undergraduate and graduate deviance courses.

◈ Overview of Features

Deviance and Social Control: A Sociological Perspective, 2nd Edition, includes topics generally found in textbooks on deviant behavior, with significant focus on the major sociological theories of deviance and discussion of rule-making and societal reaction to deviance. This book offers clear explanations and discussion of concepts and theories and carefully selected examples to illustrate relevant topics. This book features the following:

1. An introductory section explaining the sociological perspective on deviance and social control. This section provides an overview on the organization and content of the book and also introduces relevant themes, issues, and concepts to assist students in understanding the different perspectives. Along with the introduction, we have full chapters on the diversity of deviance and methods of researching deviance to introduce students to the broader issues in the field.

2. Each chapter includes four different features or sections that prompt students to engage with the material, apply the concepts, and learn more about current research. These features include the following:

   a. *Deviance in Popular Culture*—offers several examples of films and/or television shows and encourages students to apply the concepts and theories to the behavior depicted in these examples

   b. *Explaining Deviance in the Streets and Deviance in the Suites*—explores the impact of social class and status on different types of deviance and the reactions to such behavior

   c. *Ideas in Action*—highlights examples of current policies or programs designed to address deviant behaviors from the perspective(s) covered in each chapter

   d. *Now YOU . . .*—asks students to apply the material they learned in the chapter to specific questions or examples

3. Each chapter includes discussion questions and exercises or assignments that will give students a chance to test and extend their knowledge of the material.

4. The book contains a glossary of key terms.

◈ Structure of the Book

We chose very deliberately to organize our book around sociological theories rather than around types of deviance. This is in direct opposition to most of the competing texts on the market, and it is one of the reasons you might consider using our book. We believe the theoretically based approach offers students fertile ground for learning and exploring the realm of deviant behavior and social control. Once they learn the different theoretical perspectives, students will be able to apply the different theories to virtually any type of deviant behavior and, furthermore, be able to compare and contrast the theoretical models and decide for themselves which offers the most compelling explanation for the behavior. This is the kind of understanding and flexibility we hope our students achieve; while studying types of deviance is certainly interesting, being able to consider both individual and macrolevel causes and explanations seems to us the larger and more important goal.

The book is divided into 13 chapters that cover an overview of the field of deviance and social control, methods and examples of researching deviance, the major theoretical traditions used in studying deviance, a glimpse into the social control of deviance and deviant careers, and a discussion of deviance and social control in a global context. The theory chapters each provide an overview of a theoretical perspective and its development, critiques of the perspective, and examples of current developments and research in that theoretical tradition. The chapters are as follows:

Chapter 1. Introduction to Deviance: We first provide the basic building blocks for studying deviant behavior from a sociological perspective. Different conceptions of deviance are described, and students are encouraged to develop and use their sociological imagination in studying deviant behavior. We explain the organization of the book and why we believe theory is so critical to understanding and researching deviance.

Chapter 2. The Diversity of Deviance: In this chapter, we offer an overview of some of the many types of deviance and show how our conceptions of deviance vary widely and change over time. We encourage students to think broadly about deviance and to always consider the culture, context, and historical period in which the "deviant" act takes place.

Chapter 3. Researching Deviance: This chapter addresses the many ways one might go about researching deviant behavior and social control. We highlight different research methods and the strengths and weaknesses of each approach. Examples are used throughout to make abstract concepts concrete for students.

Chapter 4. Anomie/Strain Theory: This chapter looks at one of the first sociological theories of deviance and traces the development of anomie and strain theories from Durkheim's, Merton's, and Cloward and Ohlin's macrolevel ideas on how the very structure of society contributes to deviant behavior to Agnew's general strain theory and Messner and Rosenfeld's institutional strain theory, which offer contemporary views on individual and institutional strain and the resulting deviance.

Chapter 5. Social Disorganization Theory: We discuss another early sociological perspective on deviance in this chapter: social disorganization theory, developed from early research on Chicago to explain patterns of deviance and crime across social locations, such as neighborhoods. We offer an overview of the perspective and show how it is being used today to explain high levels of deviance and violence in particular neighborhoods.

Chapter 6. Differential Association and Social Learning Theories: How do individuals learn to become deviant? This chapter covers ideas and research that try to answer that exact question. We explain the key ideas of Sutherland's differential association and Akers's social learning theories and offer an overview of the development of a sociological perspective that argues that deviance is learned through communication with intimate others.

Chapter 7. Social Control Theories of Deviance: Social control theories begin by flipping the question; rather than asking why individuals deviate, social control theories ask, If we are born prone to deviance, what keeps us from committing deviant acts? In this chapter, we trace the development of social control and life course theories and look at the importance of the individual's social bonds to conforming society.

Chapter 8. Labeling Theory: In this chapter, we look at the importance of being labeled deviant. We begin with a brief overview of symbolic interactionism, which then leads to a discussion of the labeling process and how it can affect individuals' self-concepts and life chances.

Chapter 9. Marxist and Conflict Theories of Deviance: Within the conflict perspective, power and inequality are key considerations in defining who and what is deviant in any given society. In this chapter, we begin with the ideas of Karl Marx and go on to show how Marxist perspectives have been used to study lawmaking and how the process of defining and creating deviant behavior is used to maintain positions of power in society.

Chapter 10. Critical Theories of Deviance: In this chapter, we focus on theories that examine deviance from a perspective that questions the normative status quo. We offer brief overviews of peacemaking criminology, feminist criminology, and critical race theory as alternative perspectives for studying deviance and social control.

Chapter 11. Social Control of Deviance: In this chapter, we offer a brief look into informal and formal social control of deviance. We discuss the medicalization (and medication) of deviance, mental hospitals, prisons and juvenile correctional facilities, felon disenfranchisement, and general effects of stigma on those labeled deviant.

Chapter 12. Deviant Careers and Career Deviance: While much attention is focused on getting into deviance, in this chapter, we consider the full deviant career, including desistance, or the process of exiting deviance.

Chapter 13. Global Perspectives on Deviance and Social Control: For our final chapter, we move beyond the United States to consider how deviance is defined and researched in other countries. Further, we briefly consider and discuss the many different forms of social control across the globe.

Each chapter offers original material that introduces students to the issues, concepts, and theories covered in that chapter and contextualizes the selected readings. Each chapter also includes two or three primary source readings that will offer students the chance to learn about current research on deviance and social control from some of the top theorists and researchers in the field.

◈ Ancillaries

To enhance the use of this text and to assist those using this book, we have developed high-quality ancillaries for instructors and students.

Instructor Resource Site. A password-protected site, available at study.sagepub.com/inderbitzindeviance2e, features resources that have been designed to help instructors plan and teach their course. These resources include the following:

- An extensive test bank that includes multiple-choice, true/false, short-answer, and essay questions for each chapter

- Chapter-specific PowerPoint slide presentations that highlight essential concepts and figures from the text

- Access to recent, relevant full-text SAGE journal articles and accompanying article review questions

- Class activities that can be used in conjunction with the book throughout the semester

- Multimedia resources for use in class to jump-start lectures and emphasize key topics of your discussions

Student Study Site. An open-access study site is available at study.sagepub.com/inderbitzindeviance2e. This site provides access to several study tools, including the following:

- Web quizzes for student self-review and for independent progress assessment

- Access to relevant full-text SAGE journal articles that support and expand on chapter concepts

- Multimedia resources for a more in-depth understanding of the material covered in class and in the text

◈ Acknowledgments

First, we thank Jerry Westby for choosing to work with us yet again and for shepherding our stubborn ideas for a different kind of book on deviance and social control through the publication process. Jerry's faith in this book and our vision and ideas for improving the second edition helped to sustain the project through difficult patches and busy schedules.

We would also like to thank our graduate school mentors and friends; our time with these people in the University of Washington sociology program contributed a great deal to our lasting understanding of deviant behavior and social control: Bob Crutchfield, George Bridges, Joe Weis, Charis Kubrin, Sara Steen, Rod Engen, Edie Simpson, Ed Day, and Tim Wadsworth—thanks to you all! We hope you recognize your influence in this book, and we hope that we have made you proud. We also thank Howie Becker for being a powerful figure in the field of deviance and social control generally, a supportive mentor for Michelle specifically, and for writing the foreword to this book.

Michelle would like to thank Kristin Bates and Randy Gainey for being wonderful coauthors and friends. It's a continuing joy to have colleagues who are like family and who even manage to make working on endless revisions enjoyable. Sincerest appreciation to you both for sharing ideas and laughs and for being there for every step of this journey. She also offers particular thanks to friends and colleagues Charis Kubrin, Chris Uggen, Scott Akins, Kristin Barker, Becky Warner, and Debbie Storrs for many, many thought-provoking conversations about teaching and writing. And finally, she is endlessly thankful to her parents and sisters for giving her a strong and loving start to life and for their continuing support.

Kristin would like to thank her colleagues in the Department of Sociology at California State University, San Marcos, for sharing their critical perspectives, their intellectual energy, and their friendship. A special thank you to Sharon Elise, Richelle Swan, and Marisol Clark-Ibañez. The work isn't work when I get to do it with all of you. To my students who remind me every day why I love what I do. And all my love to my parents and sisters who taught, fostered, and lived relativist/social constructionist/critical perspectives of deviance long before the livin' was cool.

Randy would like to thank his colleagues at Old Dominion University, where going to work is like going out and "playing with friends." He would also like to thank all of the students who have kept him engaged in social science research, always asking great questions and offering unique solutions. Much love to my family and friends—you rock!!!

And Randy and Kristin would like to thank Michelle for her leadership and hard work and for asking them to take this adventure with her. We always have fun with you!

We would also like to thank the reviewers of the first edition:

Keith J. Bell, *West Liberty University, West Virginia*

Cindy Brooks Dollar, *North Carolina State University*

Angela Butts, *Rutgers University*

Seth Crawford, *Oregon State University*

Joseph Gallo, *Sam Houston State University*

George Guay, *Bridgewater State University*

Abdy Javadzadeh, *Florida International University*

Eric Jorrey, *Ohio University*

Lutz Kaelber, *University of Vermont*

Joachim Kibirige, *Missouri Western State University*

Ross Kleinstuber, *University of Delaware, Newark*

Carol Cirulli Lanham, *University of Texas at Dallas*

Timothy O'Boyle, *Kutztown University of Philadelphia*

Robert Peralta, *University of Akron*

Andrew Rochus, *West Virginia University at Parkersburg*

Julia So, *University of New Mexico at Valencia*

Lindsey Upton, *Old Dominion University*

Brenda Vollman, *Loyola University New Orleans*

Lisa Weinberg, *Florida State University*

Lester Howard Wielstein, *California State University at Sacramento*

Janelle Wilson, *University of Minnesota Duluth*

And finally, we thank the reviewers for the second edition:

Helen Brethauer-Gay, *Florida A&M University*

Heather Griffiths, *Fayetteville State University*

Kimberly Lancaster, *Coastal Carolina Community College*

Carol Cirulli Lanham, *University of Texas at Dallas*

Shanell K. Sanchez-Smith, *Colorado Mesa University*

Matthew P. Sheptoski, *Grambling State University*

Julia W. So, *University of New Mexico at Valencia*

Mathilda Spencer, *University of Pittsburgh at Titusville*

Richard Tardanico, *Florida International University*

How to Read a Research Article

A s you travel through your studies of deviance and social control, you will soon learn that some of the best known and/or emerging explanations of deviance come from research articles in academic journals. This book has research articles included as part of the readings with most chapters, but you may be asking yourself, "How do I read a research article?" It is our hope to answer this question with a quick summary of the key elements of any research article, followed by the questions you should be answering as you read through the assigned sections.

Research articles published in social science journals will generally include the following elements: (1) introduction, (2) literature review, (3) methodology, (4) results, and (5) discussion/conclusion.

In the introduction, you will find an overview of the purpose of the research, and you will often find the hypothesis or hypotheses. A hypothesis is most easily defined as an educated statement or guess. In most hypotheses, you will find the following format: If X, Y will occur. For example, a simple hypothesis may be: "If the price of gas increases, more people will ride bikes." This is a testable statement that the researcher wants to address in his or her study. Usually, authors will state the hypothesis directly, but not always. Therefore, you must be aware of what the author is actually testing in the research project. If you are unable to find the hypothesis, ask yourself what is being tested, observed, and/or manipulated, and what are the expected results?

The next section of the research article is the literature review. At times the literature review will be separated from the text in its own section, and at other times it will be found within the introduction. In any case, the literature review is an examination of what other researchers have already produced in terms of the research question or hypothesis. For example, returning to my hypothesis on the relationship between gas prices and bike riding, we may find that five researchers have previously conducted studies on the effects of increases in gas prices. In the literature review, I will discuss their findings and then discuss what my study will add to the existing research. The literature review may also be used as a platform of support for my hypothesis. For example, one researcher may have already determined that an increase in gas prices causes more people to Rollerblade to work. I can use this study as evidence to support my hypothesis that increased gas prices will lead to more bike riding.

The methods used in the research design are found in the next section of the research article. In the methodology section you will find the following: who/what was studied, how many subjects were studied, and how the data were collected and processed. The methods section is usually very concise, with every step of the research project recorded. This is important because a major goal of the researcher is "reliability," or, if the research is done over again the same way, discovering if the results are the same.

The results section is an analysis of the researcher's findings. If the researcher conducted a quantitative study (using numbers or statistics to explain the research), you will find statistical tables and analyses that explain whether or not the researcher's hypothesis is supported. If the researcher conducted a qualitative study (non-numerical research for the purpose of theory construction), the results will usually be displayed as a theoretical analysis or interpretation of the research question.

Finally, the research article will conclude with a discussion and summary of the study, examining the implications of the research and what future research is still needed.

Now that you know the key elements of a research article, let us examine a sample article from your text.

From Chapter 2: "The 'Simmie' Side of Life: Old Order Amish Youths' Affective Response to Culturally Prescribed Deviance," by Denise M. Reiling

1. What is the thesis or main idea from this article?

   The thesis or main idea is found in the introduction of this article. At the beginning of the fifth paragraph, Reiling states, "Within this article, the special case of the Old Order Amish, a predominately North American Christian subculture, has been offered through which to examine selected propositions of TMT." Terror Management Theory suggests that, as youth realize that they are "mortal" (as the concept of death becomes more concrete for them), they will rely on youth culture to make this dawning notion of their mortality more bearable. Reiling goes on to explain that the unique context of Amish culture is a rare opportunity to explore the Terror Management Theory, agency, and social competence.

2. What is the hypothesis?

   Specifically, Reiling wants to know how the "simmie" period (the time during which Amish youth must engage in deviance in order to determine whether they will make "good" Amish adults) affects Amish youth.

3. Is there any prior literature related to the hypothesis?

   Reiling offers two discussions of the literature. The first discussion of literature sets the stage for her research study. It appears in the first three pages of the paper, offering a brief discussion of Terror Management Theory and youth culture. However, because this is a qualitative study on a very specific population that the general public probably does not have much familiarity with, Reiling offers a second review of literature in the Setting section of the paper that gives background on the Amish culture specifically.

4. What methods are used to support this hypothesis?

   In the Methods and Setting section, Reiling goes into great detail as to how she has collected her data. She engaged in 60 in-depth interviews (averaging 5 hours in length) of three Amish groups—Amish youth, Amish adults who had accepted the Amish culture and been baptized as adults, and adults who had been born Amish but had decided after their simmie period not to return to the Amish life.

5. Is this a qualitative study or a quantitative study?

   To determine whether a study is qualitative or quantitative, you can look at either the methods section, which may often tell you whether quantitative or qualitative methods are being used, or look at the results section. If the results are presented numerically, it is a quantitative study; if they are presented non-numerically (an analysis of quotes from interviews, for example), it is a qualitative study. Reiling states specifically that her study is qualitative; her results are presented non-numerically, in the form of analysis of interview quotes.

6. What are the results and how does the author present the results?

Reiling found that Amish youth forced into deviance or encouraged to engage in deviance during their simmie period experienced a great deal of anxiety and depression because many feared for their souls should they die before they got a chance to be baptized after this stage. Because of this unique cultural stage, most simmie youth actually reported a greater preference for adult culture rather than the simmie youth culture (contrary to the predictions of TMT).

7. Do you believe that the authors provided a persuasive argument? Why or why not?

The answer to this question is ultimately up to the reader, but a reader should think about the questions (research question and hypotheses) being asked, the theoretical framework being applied, and the methods used while answering this question.

8. What does the article add to your knowledge of the subject?

Again, this question is specific to each reader, and we suspect that you won't all respond the same to the same articles. In other words, an article that really excites one of you and gets you thinking about deviance may not be the article that excites someone else. But in general, when thinking about this question, you may want to ask yourself whether it effectively answers the question, So what?

We think that this article does add value. It is a fascinating examination of a specific culture that shows us that the context of the culture we grow up in has an effect on how we respond to deviance and our growing awareness of our mortality. We think that is useful for our understanding of deviance.

9. What are the implications for public policy (or social change) concerning deviance that can be derived from this article?

Not all articles will be equally good at addressing public policy. Some articles may be more about our cultural understanding of difference (as is the case with this article), and a formal public policy response would be inappropriate given how deviance is being framed.

This study, however, does point out that Amish youth experience a great deal of anxiety and depression while engaging in their simmie experience. While a formal public policy may be inappropriate, we can argue that the Amish may want to be aware of this anxiety and depression in order to make available some systematic help for youth after their experiences.

Now that we have gone through the elements of a research article, you should continue to answer these questions as you read the other articles in this textbook. The questions may be easier to answer for some of the articles than for others, but do not give up! You will benefit the most from answering these questions with the hardest articles.

CHAPTER 1

Introduction to Deviance

Founded in 1972, the Fremont Fair is one of Seattle's most beloved neighborhood street festivals, featuring a weekend of eclectic activities that celebrate the quirky community of Fremont, the self-proclaimed "center of the universe." Held annually in mid-June to coincide with the Summer Solstice, the event draws more than 100,000 people to shop, eat, drink, mingle, groove, and enjoy all manners of creative expression. Artistic highlights include craft and art booths, street performers, local bands, wacky decorated art cars, the free-spirited Solstice Parade produced by the Fremont Arts Council, and many other oddities that personify Fremont's official motto "Delibertus Quirkus"—Freedom to be Peculiar.

—Fremont Fair (2010)

The Fremont Arts Council (FAC) is a community-based celebration arts organization. We value volunteerism; community participation; artistic expression; and the sharing of arts skills. The Fremont Solstice Parade is the defining event of the FAC. We celebrate the longest day of the year through profound street theater, public spectacle, and a kaleidoscope of joyous human expressions. We welcome the participation of everyone regardless of who they are, or what they think or believe. However, the FAC reserves the right to control the content presented in the Fremont Solstice Parade.

The rules of the Fremont Solstice Parade, which make this event distinct from other types of parades, are:

- No written or printed words or logos
- No animals (except guide dogs and service animals)
- No motorized vehicles (except wheelchairs)
- No real weapons or fire

—Fremont Arts Council (2010)

(Continued)

(Continued)

It is true that a parade with no logos, animals, or motorized vehicles is different from most parades that we experience in the United States. But one more thing sets the Fremont Solstice Parade apart from other parades: the public displays of nudity. Every year at the parade, a contingent of nude, body-painted bicyclists (both men and women) ride through the streets of Fremont as part of the parade. Rain or shine (and let's face it, in June in Seattle, there can be a lot of rain), a large group of naked adults cycle down the street as the crowds cheer and wave. The Fremont City Council estimates that more than 100,000 people visit the weekend fair, and pictures show that the streets are crowded with parade watchers, from the very young to elderly.

Contrast this event to the following story of a flasher in San Diego County. Between the summer of 2009 and the summer of 2010, there were numerous reports of an adult man flashing hikers and runners on Mission Trails near Lake Murphy in San Diego. An undercover operation was set in motion to catch this flasher, and on July 19, 2010, an adult man was apprehended while flashing an undercover officer who was posing as a jogger in the park. The man was held on $50,000 bail while waiting for arraignment (KFMB-News 8, 2010).

While both these events center on public displays of nudity, one is celebrated while the other is vilified. Why?

Photodisc/ThinkStock

©JMW Scout/iStockphoto

▲ **Photos 1.1 & 1.2**   When is a public display of nudity considered deviant? When is it celebrated?

◈ Introduction

You might expect that a book about deviance would start with a definition of what deviance is. But like all things worth studying, a simple definition does not exist. For example, in the stories above, one public display of nudity was not only welcomed but celebrated by 6-year-olds and grandmothers alike, but another display led to arrest and possible jail time. Why? This chapter and this book explore how it can be that the Fremont Summer Solstice Parade can be celebrated in the same summer that a flasher is arrested and held on $50,000 bail until charged.

◇ Conceptions of Deviance

All deviance textbooks offer their "conceptions of deviance." Rubington and Weinberg (2008) argue that there are generally two conceptions of deviance as either "objectively given" or "subjectively problematic." Clinard and Meier (2010) also suggest two general conceptions of deviance, the reactionist or **relativist conception** and the **normative conception**. Thio (2009) argues that we can view deviance from a **positivist perspective** or a constructionist perspective.

While none of these authors are using the same language, they are defining similar conceptions of deviance. The first conception—that of an "objectively given," normative, or positivist conception of deviance—assumes that there is a general set of norms of behavior, conduct, and conditions on which we can agree. **Norms** are rules of behavior that guide people's actions. Sumner (1906) broke norms down into three categories: folkways, mores, and laws. **Folkways** are everyday norms that do not generate much uproar if they are violated. Think of them as behaviors that might be considered rude if engaged in, like standing too close to someone while speaking or picking one's nose. **Mores** are "moral" norms that may generate more outrage if broken. In a capitalist society, homelessness and unemployment can elicit outrage if the person is considered unworthy of sympathy. Similarly, drinking too much or alcoholism may be seen as a lapse in moral judgment. Finally, the third type of norm is the **law**, which is considered the strongest norm because it is backed by official sanctions (or a formal response). In this conception, then, deviance becomes a violation of a rule understood by the majority of the group. This rule may be minor, in which case the deviant is seen as "weird but harmless," or the rule may be major, in which case the deviant is seen as "criminal." The obvious problem with this conceptualization goes back to the earlier examples of reactions to public nudity, where we see that violation of a most "serious" norm (law) can receive quite different reactions. This leads to the second conception.

The second conception of deviance—the "subjectively problematic," reactionist or relativist, **social constructionist conception**—assumes that the definition of deviance is constructed based on the interactions of those in society. According to this conception, behaviors or conditions are not inherently deviant; they become so when the definition of deviance is applied to them. The study of deviance is not about why certain individuals violate norms but, instead, about how those norms are constructed. Social constructionists believe that our understanding of the world is in constant negotiation between actors. Those who have a relativist conception of deviance define deviance as those behaviors that elicit a definition or label of deviance:

> Social groups create deviance by making the rules whose infraction constitutes deviance, and by applying those rules to particular people and labeling them as outsiders. For this point of view, deviance is not a quality of the act the person commits but rather a consequence of the application by others of rules and sanctions to an "offender." The deviant is one to whom that label has successfully been applied; deviant behavior is behavior that people so label. (Becker, 1973, p. 9)

This is a fruitful conceptualization, but it is also problematic. What about very serious violations of norms that are never known or reacted to? Some strict reactionists or relativists would argue that these acts (beliefs or attitudes) are not deviant. Most of us would agree that killing someone and making it look like he or she simply skipped the country is deviant. However, there may be no reaction.

A third conception of deviance that has not been advanced in many textbooks (for an exception, see DeKeseredy, Ellis, & Alvi, 2005) is a critical definition of deviance (Jensen, 2007). Those working from a **critical conception** of deviance argue that the normative understanding of deviance is established by those in power to maintain and enhance their power. It suggests that explorations of deviance have focused on a white, male, middle- to upper-class understanding of society that implies that people of color, women, and the working poor are by definition deviant.

Instead of focusing on individual types of deviance, this conception critiques the social system that exists and creates such norms in the first place. This, too, is a useful and powerful approach, but there are still some things that the vast majority of society agrees are so immoral, unethical, and deviant that they should be illegal and that the system can serve to protect our interests against these things.

Given that each of these conceptualizations is useful but problematic, we do not adhere to a single conception of deviance in this book because the theories of deviance do not adhere to a single conception. You will see that several of our theories assume a normative conception, whereas several assume a social constructionist or critical conception. As you explore each of these theories, think about what the conception of deviance and theoretical perspective mean for the questions we ask and answer about deviance (Table 1.1).

Be Careful Who You Are Calling Deviant: Body Ritual Among the Nacirema

In 1956, Horace Miner published an article on the Nacirema, a poorly understood culture that he claimed engaged in body rituals and ceremonies that were unique, obsessive, and almost magical. He highlighted several of these beliefs and actions:

- The fundamental belief of the Nacirema people is that the human body is ugly and prone to "debility and disease."
- The people engage in rituals and ceremonies in a "ritual center" considered to be a shrine. Affluent members of society may have more than one shrine devoted to these rituals and ceremonies.
- Each shrine has, near its center point, a box or chest filled with magical potions. Many believe they cannot live without these magical potions and so collect to the point of hoarding them, afraid to let them go even when it is determined they may no longer hold their magic.
- The people have an "almost pathological horror and fascination with the mouth, the condition of which is believed to have a supernatural influence on all social relationships. Were it not for the rituals of the mouth, they believe that their teeth would fall out, their gums bleed, their jaws shrink, their friends desert them, and their lovers reject them" (p. 505).

Miner never lets on that this fascinating culture that believes magic will transform its members' ugly, diseased bodies is actually American (Nacirema spelled backward) culture. But his point is made: Our understanding and interpretation of events and behaviors is often relative. If we step back from the everyday events in which we engage with little thought, our most accepted practices can be made to seem deviant.

Take a moment to examine some everyday activity that you engage in from the perspective of an outsider. What might watching television, going to a sporting event, babysitting, or surfing look like to those who have never experienced it? Can you write a description of this everyday event from an outsider's point of view?

Source: Miner (1956).

Table 1.1 Conceptions of Deviance

Conceptions of Deviance	Assumptions	Definition of Deviance	Example Research Question
Positivist or Normative	There is a general set of norms of behavior, conduct, and conditions on which we can agree.	A violation of a rule understood by the majority of the group	"What leads an individual to engage in deviant behavior?"
Relativist/Social Constructionist	Nothing is inherently deviant; our understanding of the world is in constant negotiation between actors.	Deviance is any behavior that elicits a definition or label of deviance.	"What characteristics increase the likelihood that an individual or a behavior will be defined as deviant?"
Critical	The normative understanding of deviance is established by those in power to maintain and enhance their power.	Instead of focusing on individual types of deviance, this conception critiques the social system that exists and creates such norms in the first place.	"What is the experience of the homeless, and who is served by their treatment as deviant?"

HOW DO YOU DEFINE DEVIANCE?

As Justice Potter Stewart of the Supreme Court once famously wrote about trying to define obscene materials, "I shall not today attempt further to define the kinds of material I understand to be embraced within that shorthand description; and perhaps I could never succeed in intelligibly doing so. But I know it when I see it" (*Jacobellis v. Ohio,* 1964). Those who do not study deviance for a living probably find themselves in the same boat; it may be hard to write a definition, but how hard could it be to "know it when we see it"?

Choose a busy place to sit and observe human behavior for one hour. Write down all the behaviors that you observe during that hour. Do you consider any of these behaviors to be deviant? Which conception of deviance are you using when you define each as deviant? Might there be some instances (e.g., places or times) when that behavior you consider to be nondeviant right now might become deviant? Finally, bring your list of behaviors to class. In pairs, share your list of behaviors and your definitions of deviant behaviors with your partner. Do you agree on your categorization? Why or why not?

DEVIANCE IN POPULAR CULTURE

Many types of deviance are portrayed and investigated in popular culture. Films and television shows, for example, illustrate a wide range of deviant behavior and social control. There are often several interpretations of what acts are deviant in each film. How do you know when an act or person is deviant? One way to develop your sociological imagination is to watch films and television shows from a critical perspective and to think

(Continued)

(Continued)

about how different theories would explain the deviant behavior and the reactions portrayed. To get you started, we've listed a number of films and television shows that you might watch and explore for examples of cultural norms, different types of deviant behavior, and coping with stigma.

Films

Trekkies—A documentary following the stories of individuals who are superfans of *Star Trek*. Known as Trekkies, these individuals have incorporated *Star Trek* into their everyday lives. Some wear the uniforms or speak and teach the various languages from the show, one has considered surgery to alter the shape of his ears, and some have legally changed their names and incorporated *Star Trek* into their businesses and workplaces. The movie documents their fandom and experiences navigating these consuming obsessions while in mainstream society.

Crumb—A movie about the cartoonist Robert Crumb, who was a pioneer of the underground comix. This movie offers a dark portrait of an artist besieged with personal and family demons.

The Usual Suspects—A story of five men who are brought in for questioning for a crime they did not commit. While being held on suspicion of that crime, they agree to work together on another crime. They soon realize they are being set up by someone they had wronged in the past.

Fourteen Days in May—A BBC documentary of the fourteen days before Edward Earl Johnson's execution date in a Mississippi gas chamber. The film follows Johnson's allegations that his confession had been made under duress and that he was innocent and the reactions from other death row inmates, prison guards, and the warden.

Television

Television, reality shows and the TLC channel, in particular, features a number of programs offering an inside view of people perceived as deviant or different in some way and showing how they deal with stigma from various sources.

Sister Wives—A look inside the world of a polygamist marriage. This reality show introduces viewers to a man, his four wives, and his 16 children. His motto: "Love should be multiplied, not divided."

My Strange Addiction—A reality show that highlights potentially deviant obsessions of individuals with addictions such as eating glass, plastic bags, household cleaners, or makeup; having dozens of surgeries in order to look like a living doll; and living as husband and wife with a synthetic doll.

Seinfeld—A situation comedy that is simply masterful at focusing on small behaviors or characteristics that break norms and are perceived as deviant. Episodes on the close talker, the low talker, and the high talker, for example, all illustrate unwritten norms of interpersonal communication.

The Internet/Podcasts/Social Media

The Internet may be one of the best places to go for our examples of deviance and social control. It is all right at our fingertips all the time.

Dr. Pimple Popper, aka Dr. Sandra Lee. There are many YouTube videos dedicated to the oddities of the body, but one of our favorites is Dr. Pimple Popper, a board certified dermatologist who tapes some of her "extractions" for the popaholics who like to tune in to watch blackheads and pimples get popped.

In each of the chapters that follow, we will offer suggestions of one or more features of pop culture for you to watch from the theoretical perspective outlined in the chapter. We think you'll soon agree: Deviance is all around us.

◈ The Sociological Imagination

Those of us who are sociologists can probably remember the first time we were introduced to the concept of the **sociological imagination**. Mills argues that the only way to truly understand the experiences of the individual is to first understand the societal, institutional, and historical conditions that individual is living under. In other words, Mills believes that no man, woman, or child is an island. Below is an excerpt from C. Wright Mills's (1959/2000) profound book, *The Sociological Imagination*.

Men do not usually define the troubles they endure in terms of historical change and institutional contradiction. The well-being they enjoy, they do not usually impute to the big ups and downs of the societies in which they live. Seldom aware of the intricate connection between the patterns of their own lives and the course of world history, ordinary men do not usually know what this connection means for the kinds of men they are becoming and for the kinds of history-making in which they might take part. They do not possess the quality of mind essential to grasp the interplay of man and society, of biography and history, of self and world. They cannot cope with their personal troubles in such ways as to control the structural transformations that usually lie behind them. . . .

The sociological imagination enables its possessor to understand the larger historical scene in terms of its meaning for the inner life and the external career of a variety of individuals. It enables him to take into account how individuals, in the welter of their daily experience, often become falsely conscious of their social positions. With that welter, the framework of modern society is sought, and within that framework the psychologies of a variety of men and women are formulated. By such means the personal uneasiness of individuals is focused upon explicit troubles and the indifference of publics is transformed into involvement with public issues.

The first fruit of this imagination—and the first lesson of the social science that embodies it—is the idea that the individual can understand his own experience and gauge his own fate only by locating himself within his period, that he can know his own chances in life only by becoming aware of those of all individuals in his circumstances. In many ways it is a terrible lesson; in many ways a magnificent one. . . .

In these terms, consider unemployment. When, in a city of 100,000, only one man is unemployed, that is his personal trouble, and for its relief we properly look to the character of the man, his skills, and his immediate opportunities. But when in a nation of 50 million employees, 15 million men are unemployed, that is an issue, and we may not hope to find its solution within the range of opportunities open to any one individual. The very structure of opportunities has collapsed. Both the correct statement of the problem and the range of possible solutions require us to consider the economic and political institutions of the society, and not merely the personal situation and character of a scatter of individuals. . . .

What we experience in various and specific milieux, I have noted, is often caused by structural changes. Accordingly, to understand the changes of many personal milieux we are required to look beyond them.

And the number and variety of such structural changes increase as the institutions within which we live become more embracing and more intricately connected with one another. To be aware of the idea of social structure and to use it with sensibility is to be capable of tracing such linkages among a great variety of milieux. To be able to do that is to possess the sociological imagination. (*The Sociological Imagination* by C. Wright Mills [2000] pp. 3–11. By permission of Oxford University Press, USA.)

One of our favorite examples of the sociological imagination in action is the "salad bar" example. In the United States, one of the persistent philosophies is that of individualism and personal responsibility. Under this philosophy, individuals are assumed to be solely responsible for their successes and failures. This philosophy relies heavily on the notion that individuals are rational actors who weigh the costs and benefits of their actions, can see the consequences of their behavior, and have perfect information. The salad bar example helps those who rely heavily on this conception of the individual to see the importance of social structure to individual behavior.

No one doubts that when you order a salad bar at a restaurant, you are responsible for building your own salad. Every person makes his or her own salad, and no two salads look exactly alike. Some make salads with lots of lettuce and vegetables, very little cheese, and fat-free dressing. Others create a salad that is piled high with cheese, croutons, and lots and lots of dressing. Those who are unhappy with their choices while making their salad have only themselves to blame, right? Not necessarily.

A salad is only as good as the salad bar it is created from. In other words, individuals making a salad can only make a salad from the ingredients supplied from the salad bar. If the restaurant is out of croutons that day or decided to put watermelon out instead of cantaloupe, the individual must build his or her salad within these constraints. Some individuals with a great sense of personal power may request additional items from the back of the restaurant, but most individuals will choose to build a salad based on the items available to them on the salad bar. In other words, the individual choice is constrained by the larger social forces of delivery schedules, food inventory, and worker decision making. The sociological imagination is especially important to understand because it is the building block for our understanding of deviance and sociological theory.

The sociological imagination helps us understand the impact of social forces on both engaging in and reacting to deviance. One of the easiest reactions to or assumptions about someone who engages in deviance is that they are "sick" or "mentally ill." This assumption is what we refer to as **pathologizing** an individual. It puts all the responsibility for their actions onto them without asking what impact the social forces and social structures around them might have. The sociological imagination reminds us that individuals exist in a larger social system, and they impact that larger social system just as it impacts them. One of the ways to systematically understand these impacts is to understand sociological theory.

Comstock/Thinkstock

▲ **Photo 1.3**   The salad bar can represent the restriction on choices that individuals have. We can only make our salad with the ingredients offered to us on the salad bar.

◈ The Importance of Theory

The three of us (the authors of this book) spent many hours discussing the importance of **theory** as we wrote this book. Why did we choose to write a textbook about deviance with theory as the central theme? Many of you may also be asking this question and worrying that a book about theory may suck the life right out of a discussion about deviance. Really, who wants to be thinking about theory when we could be talking about "nuts, sluts, and preverts" (Liazos, 1972)? But this is precisely why we must make theory central to any discussion of deviance—because theory helps us *systematically* think about deviance. If it weren't for theory, classes about deviance would be akin to watching MTV's *Jersey Shore* or Bravo's *The Real Housewives of New Jersey* (Why is New Jersey so popular for these shows?)—it may be entertaining, but we have no clearer understanding of the "real" people of New Jersey when we are done watching.

Theory is what turns anecdotes about human behavior into a systematic understanding of societal behavior. It does this by playing an intricate part in research and the scientific method.

The **scientific method** is a systematic procedure that helps *safeguard against researcher bias* and the power of anecdotes by following several simple steps (Figure 1.1). First, a researcher starts with a research question. If the researcher is engaging in deductive research, this question comes from a theoretical perspective. This theory and research question help the researcher create hypotheses (testable statements) about a phenomenon being studied. Once the researcher has created hypotheses, he or she collects data to test these hypotheses. We discuss data and data collection methods for deviance research in detail in Chapter 3. The researcher then analyzes these data, interprets the findings, and concludes whether or not his or her hypotheses have been supported. These findings then inform whether the theory the researcher used helps with our understanding of the world or should be revised to take into consideration information that does not support its current model. If a researcher is engaging in inductive research, he or she also starts with a research question, but in the beginning, the researcher's theory may be what we call "grounded theory." Using qualitative methods, such as participant observation or in-depth interviews, the researcher would collect data and analyze these data, looking for common themes throughout. These findings would be used to create a theory "from the ground up." In other words, while a deductive researcher would start with a theory that guides every step of the research, an inductive researcher might start with a broad theoretical perspective and a research question and, through the systematic collection of data and rigorous analyses, would hone that broad theoretical perspective into a more specific theory. This theory would then be tested again as the researcher continued on with his or her work, or others, finding this new theory to be useful and interesting, might opt to use it to inform both their deductive and inductive work.

If we go back to our example of reality shows about people from New Jersey, we may see the difference between an anecdote and a more theoretically grounded understanding of human behavior. After watching both *Jersey Shore* and *The Real Housewives of New Jersey,* we may conclude that people from New Jersey are loud, self-absorbed, and overly tan (all three of which might be considered deviant behaviors or characteristics). However, we have not systematically studied the people of

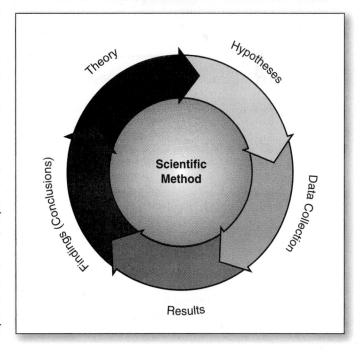

Figure 1.1 The Scientific Method Allows Us to Systematically Examine Social Phenomena Such as Deviance

Theory

Hypotheses

Scientific Method

Data Collection

Findings (Conclusions)

Results

New Jersey to arrive at our conclusion. Using inductive reasoning, based on our initial observation, we may start with a research question that states that because the people of New Jersey are loud, self-absorbed, and overly tan, we are interested in knowing about the emotional connections they have with friends and family. (We may suspect that self-absorbed people are more likely to have relationships with conflict.) However, as we continue along the scientific method, we systematically gather data from more than just the reality stars of these two shows. We interview teachers, police officers, retired lawyers, and college students. What we soon learn as we analyze these interviews is that the general public in New Jersey is really not all that tan, loud, or self-absorbed, and they speak openly and warmly about strong connections to family and friends. This research leads us to reexamine our initial theory about the characteristics of people from New Jersey and offer a new theory based on systematic analysis. This new theory then informs subsequent research on the people of New Jersey. If we did not have theory and the scientific method, our understanding of deviance would be based on wild observations and anecdotes, which may be significantly misleading and unrepresentative of the social reality.

In addition to being systematic and testable (through the scientific method), theory offers *solutions to the problems* we study. One of the hardest knocks against the study of deviance and crime has been the historically carnival sideshow nature (Liazos, 1972) of much of the study of deviance. By focusing on individuals and a certain caste of deviants (those without power) and using less-than-systematic methods, deviance researchers were just pointing at "nuts, sluts, and preverts" and not advancing their broader understanding of the interplay of power, social structure, and behavior. Theory can focus our attention on this interplay and offer solutions beyond the individual and the deficit model, which is a model that focuses on the individual (or group) in question and blames the deviance on something broken, lacking, or deficient in him or her. Bendle (1999) also argued that the study of deviance was in a state of crisis because researchers were no longer studying relevant problems or offering useful solutions. One of Bendle's solutions is to push for new theories of deviant behavior.

Theoretical solutions to the issue of deviance are especially important because many of our current responses to deviant behavior are erroneously based on an individualistic notion of human nature that does not take into account humans as social beings or the importance of social structure, social institutions, power, and broad societal changes for deviance and deviants.

The Poverty of the Sociology of Deviance: Nuts, Sluts, and Preverts

Liazos argues that the study of deviance used to be the study of "nuts, sluts, and preverts," a sensationalistic ritual in finger-pointing and moralizing. The focus was on individuals and their "aberrant" behavior. This meant that the most harmful behaviors in society—the ones that affected us most thoroughly—were ignored and, in ignoring them, normalized. Liazos referred to these forms of deviance as *covert institutional violence.*

According to Liazos, the poverty of the study of deviance was threefold: First, even when trying to point out how normal the "deviance" or "deviant" is, by pointing out the person or behavior, we are acknowledging the difference. If that difference really were invisible, how and why would we be studying it? This meant by even studying deviance, a moral choice had already been made—some differences were studied; some were not. Second, by extension, deviance research rarely studied elite deviance and structural deviance, instead focusing on "dramatic" forms of deviance, such as prostitution, juvenile delinquency, and homosexuality. Liazos argues that it is important to, instead, study covert institutional violence, which leads to such things as poverty and exploitation. Instead of studying tax cheats, we should study unjust tax laws; instead of studying prostitution, we should study racism and sexism as deviance. Finally, Liazos argues that even those who profess to study the relationship between power and deviance do not really acknowledge the importance of power. These researchers still give those in positions of power a pass to engage in harmful behavior by not defining much elite deviance as deviance at all.

The implication of this is that those who study deviance have allowed the definition of deviance to be settled for them. And this definition benefits not only individuals in power but also a system that has routinely engaged in harmful acts. While Liazos wrote this important critique of the sociology of deviance in 1972, much of his analysis holds up to this day. In this book, we examine theories expressly capable of addressing this critique.

As you explore each of the theories offered to you in this book, remember Liazos's critique. Which theories are more likely to focus on "nuts, sluts, and preverts"? Which are more likely to focus on elite deviance and new conceptions of deviance?

Compiled from Alexander Liazos, 1972, in *Social Problems, 20*(1), 103–120.

◈ Explaining Deviance in the Streets and Deviance in the Suites

We have included a section in each chapter that discusses a "street" deviance and juxtaposes it against an "elite" or "suite" deviance. We have chosen to do this because, in many instances, street deviance is the focus of examinations. (Again, we gravitate to conversations of "nuts, sluts, and preverts" if we aren't systematic.) We wanted to make sure for each street deviance we explored that we offered an exploration of an elite deviance, too. Depending on the chapter, we have chosen to do this in one of two ways. Some chapters focus on a single deviance that, while engaged in by a variety of individuals, is interpreted differently depending on the characteristics of who is engaging in it. For example, in Chapter 6, we focus on social learning theory and drug use and examine how class neighborhood characteristics impact drug use. In Chapter 8, we focus on labeling theory and how the class characteristics of individuals impact the likelihood that they will be labeled a person with a drinking problem. Both of these approaches show that a single behavior is impacted by class—by affecting either the likelihood of engaging in the behavior or the likelihood that the behavior will be perceived as deviant. Finally, in some of our chapters, we choose to examine two separate forms of deviance, highlighting how a street deviance (one that often receives more attention, is perceived as more detrimental, or is perceived as likely to be engaged in by the poor) compares with an elite or suite deviance (often an action or behavior that many cannot agree is deviant or that is engaged in by those who have substantial amounts of power). For example, in Chapter 10, we use critical theories to discuss how changing technologies have affected pornography (our example of street deviance) and illegal government surveillance (our example of suite deviance). In chapters such as this, we want to highlight how a single theory may address behaviors that are often on very different ends of the power and class spectrum. In all of the chapters, we first offer a substantive discussion of the deviance before we analyze it from the perspective of the chapter.

◈ Ideas in Action

For the purposes of this book, we are expanding the discussion of public policy to include public and private programs, which is why we have titled this section in each chapter "Ideas in Action." While a single, concrete definition of public policy is elusive, there is general agreement that public policy is the sometimes unwritten actions taken by the city, state, or federal government. These actions may be as formal as a law or regulation or be more informal in nature, such as an institutional custom. While public policy is often associated with government guidelines or actions, we also find it important to highlight the work of public and private programs, nonprofits, and nongovernmental organizations (NGOs). For this reason, our "Ideas in Action" section may highlight a private program or entity or a public (state or federal) guideline, rule, or law that affects our understanding or control of deviance.

Some argue that tension exists between public policies and private programs created to address deviance, crime, and public well-being. These tensions are twofold. The first argument involves what some argue is a movement of public well-being out of the public realm (the government) to a private and more likely profit-motivated industry (private programs). This shift is often referred to as neoliberalism.

> The term neoliberalism refers to a political, economic, and social ideology that argues that low government intervention, a privatization of services that in the past have predominately been the domain of government, an adherence to a free-market philosophy, and an emphasis on deregulation (Frericks, Maier, & de Graaf, 2009) is "the source and arbiter of human freedoms" (Mudge, 2008, p. 704). What may be one of the most important aspects of neoliberalism from the standpoint of those focused on social justice, then, is this link between the free markets and morality. While free markets have proven time and again to place the utmost emphasis on the profit motive (because this is what the free market is: an adherence to the notion of supply and demand)—this connection between free markets and "freedom" seems to intrinsically suggest that free markets, and, therefore, neoliberalism, have individual well-being as their focus.
>
> However, individual well-being in the form of a guarantee that individuals will have access to the basic human needs of shelter, food, clothing, good health care, and safety from harm is not always produced by two of the most central components of neoliberalism—privatization and deregulation. In some ways, privatization and deregulation are opposite sides of the same coin. Privatization means the "opening up of the market" and the loosening of the rules (regulations) that are often the purview of the government. But privatization, at its core, is also the introduction of the profit motive into services that, at *their* core, are about protecting the human condition. A reliance on a neoliberal philosophy and free market economy means that we begin to evaluate everything through the lens of profit and cost-benefit analyses. We abdicate the responsibility of the state to private companies and then feign surprise when those companies defer to the profit motive. . . . In addition to the increased preference for free markets and profits, privatization both reduces state responsibility for the care of its citizens and masks the lack of preparation of the government to care for its citizens that quickly develops (Mitchell, 2001). (Bates & Swan, 2010, p. 442)

As you read and evaluate the policies and programs we have chosen, keep this argument in mind. Does it play out with the programs we discuss?

The second argument is that public programs may more likely focus on **suppression** (the social control of deviance), whereas private programs may more likely focus on rehabilitation and prevention. In general, suppression policies are those that focus on the punishment and social control of behavior deemed deviant. **Rehabilitation programs** focus on groups or individuals who are deemed likely deviant and involve attempts to change this assumed deviant behavior. **Prevention programs** may be focused on groups or individuals who are assumed to be more "at risk" for deviant behavior, or they may be focused on decreasing the likelihood of deviance in all groups equally. Many argue that there has been a buildup of suppression policies in the state and federal governments at the expense of rehabilitation and prevention programs. Meranze (2009) argues,

> From the recently repealed Rockefeller drug laws through the expansion of the prison systems in Texas and Florida, onto the increasingly punitive response to poverty in the Clinton years, and the continuing disparity in sentencing laws, states and the federal government have chosen the Iron State over the Golden State. And whatever arguments there may be about the relative effectiveness of imprisonment in affecting crime

rates (a topic of great controversy amongst scholars and analysts), one thing seems certain: a policy that exacerbates the brutalization of society is not one that will make us safer. Investing in prisons means investing in institutions that produce neither goods nor new opportunities (aside from the limited jobs available for prison employees and the one-time opportunities in construction); money spent on imprisonment is money taken from rebuilding our worn out infrastructure, our schools, our communities, and our economic future. Insofar as corrections remains at the heart of our social policy—rather than as a supplemental or marginal support as it was throughout most of United States history—it is the Iron State stealing from the future of the Golden State. (n.p.)

Finally, according to Barlow and Decker (2010), "Policy ought to be guided by science rather than by ideology" (p. xi). As we have already briefly discussed, a central part of the scientific method is theory. Therefore, a book whose primary focus is a theoretical examination of deviance and social control should have as one of its central themes an examination of public policy from the viewpoint of each of these theories.

The reaction to deviance has often been spurred by interests well beyond science. Barlow and Decker (2010) point out,

The pen remains firmly in the hands of politicians and legislators, whose allegiance is less to the products of science—for example, how to deal with the AIDS pandemic, warnings about global warming, and the ineffectiveness of the Strategic Defense Initiative, or SDI (otherwise known as "Star Wars")—than to the whims of voters and the personal agendas of their counselors and financial supporters. (pp. xi–xii)

This means the reactions to deviance have often focused on the stigmatization and criminalization of a variety of behaviors and, in many instances, on the harsh punishment of those behaviors.

We offer a wide variety of public policies, or "ideas in action," that were designed to address deviant behaviors. It will be your job to evaluate these programs and policies for their intents and subsequent success.

NOW YOU . . . USE YOUR SOCIOLOGICAL IMAGINATION

In his 1972 article, "The Poverty of the Sociology of Deviance: Nuts, Sluts, and Preverts," Alexander Liazos argues that the sociology of deviance focuses too much attention on individual idiosyncrasies and not enough attention on structural dynamics and the deviance of the powerful. One of the areas that we might examine for examples of individual, organizational, and global deviance is the consumption of energy and the impact on climate change. While in certain segments of the population there is still an argument, there is a growing acceptance of the detrimental impact of industrialization on climate change. The following are several examples of individual and national behavior in response to this growing concern:

- In 1997, 192 out of 195 countries signed the Kyoto Protocol, pledging to lower greenhouse gas emissions. The agreement required that developed countries commit to lowering their emissions while developing countries were asked to *try* to lower emissions. The United States was one of the three countries that did not sign.
- In the summer of 2015, Shell Oil pulled its drilling rig into Puget Sound on the way up to the remote waters of the Chukchi Sea, off the coast of Alaska. Environmental activists known as kayaktivists protested the deep-sea drilling and the use of the Port of Seattle as a way station for drilling materials by

(Continued)

(Continued)

surrounding the drilling rig with kayaks, thus blocking the movement of the rig, and later by blocking a Shell icebreaker headed to Alaskan waters by dangling from the St. John's Bridge over the Willamette River while more kayaktivists surrounding the large vessel below (Brait, 2015).

- On December 12, 2015, in Paris, 195 countries adopted the Paris Agreement. In contrast to the Kyoto Protocol, this pact required that all countries address greenhouse emissions in some way. Some of the elements, like target reductions in carbon emissions, are voluntary, whereas other elements, such as verifying emissions, are legally binding (Davenport, 2015).

Figure 1.2 is taken from a webpage from the U.S. Energy Information Administration (part of the Department of Energy) explaining the U.S. energy consumption by sector for 2012. Following this chart on the webpage is

Figure 1.2   Primary Energy Consumption by Source and Sector, 2012 (Quadrillion BTU)

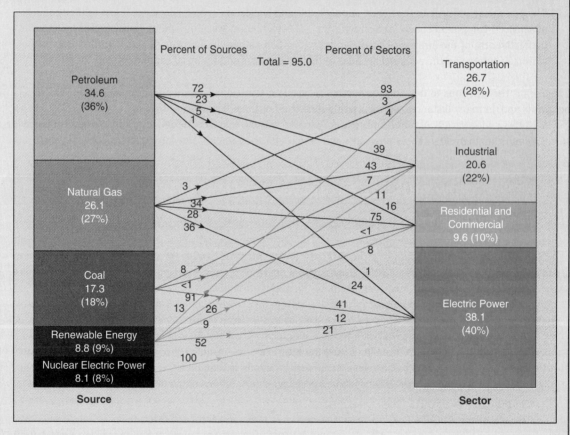

Source: U.S. Energy Information Administration, *Annual Energy Review 2012*, 2.0 Primary Energy Consumption by Source and Sector, 2012.

Note: Sum of components may not equal 100% due to independent rounding.

a section taken from the Environmental Protection Agency (also a federal agency) explaining the effects of fossil fuels on climate change.

Using your sociological imagination, how might you discuss the figures and examples as indicators of deviance? How might the relationship between the U.S. government, lobbyists, and oil companies affect the conversation around climate change? Pretend you are an oil executive. Which might be more deviant in your view: the breakdown of U.S. energy consumption, the research on climate change, or the Paris Agreement? Why? Now pretend that you are an oceanographer studying changes in the Gulf of Mexico, a zoologist studying polar bear migration, or an activist hanging off a bridge. What might you define as deviant? Why? Would these groups define the same information as deviant? Do you consider either the breakdown of the U.S. consumption of energy or the discussion of climate change to be deviant? Why or why not?

For over the past 200 years, the burning of fossil fuels, such as coal and oil, and deforestation have caused the concentrations of heat-trapping "greenhouse gases" to increase significantly in our atmosphere. These gases prevent heat from escaping to space, somewhat like the glass panels of a greenhouse.

Greenhouse gases are necessary to life as we know it, because they keep the planet's surface warmer than it otherwise would be. But, as the concentrations of these gases continue to increase in the atmosphere, the earth's temperature is climbing above past levels. According to NOAA and NASA data, the earth's average surface temperature has increased by about 1.2°F to 1.4°F in the last 100 years. The eight warmest years on record (since 1850) have all occurred since 1998, with the warmest year being 2005. Most of the warming in recent decades is very likely the result of human activities. Other aspects of the climate are also changing, such as rainfall patterns, snow and ice cover, and sea level.

If greenhouse gases continue to increase, climate models predict that the average temperature at the earth's surface could increase from 3.2°F to 7.2°F above 1990 levels by the end of this century. Scientists are certain that human activities are changing the composition of the atmosphere, and that increasing the concentration of greenhouse gases will change the planet's climate. But they are not sure by how much it will change, at what rate it will change, or what the exact effects will be. (Environmental Protection Agency, 2011)

◈ Conclusion: Organization of the Book

We start your introduction to deviance by examining the diversity of deviance, how our definitions of deviance change over time, and how we research deviance. Then, we focus on theories of deviance, starting with the traditional, positivist theories of deviance and moving to social constructionist and critical theories of deviance. We also try to present the theories in a fairly chronological manner. While all these theories are still in use in the study of deviance, some have been around longer than others. Positivist theories have been around longer than social constructionist theories, and within positivist theories, anomie has been around longer than social disorganization. We think this offers you a general road map of how thinking and theories have developed about deviance. In each of these chapters, we present the classical versions of each theory and then the contemporary version, and along the way, we explore several types of deviance that may be explained by each given theory. Then, in our final chapters, we examine our individual and societal responses to deviance and end with an exploration of global deviance, reactions, and social control.

This book has been written with a heavy emphasis on theory. In seven chapters, we explore nine theories. Anomie and strain theory, among the first of the truly sociological explanations of the causes of deviant behavior, seek to understand deviance by focusing on social structures and patterns that emerge as individuals and groups react to conditions they have little control over. Social disorganization theory was developed to explain patterns of deviance and crime across social locations, such as neighborhoods, schools, cities, states, and even countries. In Chapter 6, we focus on differential association and social learning theory. These theories focus on the importance of learning in the development of deviance. Social control theory is our last traditional or normative theory. Control theorists assert that human beings are basically antisocial and assume that deviance is part of the natural order in society; individuals are motivated to deviate. Our first social constructionist theory is labeling theory. Labeling theorists examine the social meaning of deviant labels, how those labels are understood, and how they affect the individuals to whom they are applied. Our next theories are Marxist and conflict theory. These theories focus on the effect of power on the creation and maintenance of laws (and policies) that benefit one group over another. For a book on deviance, then, we might say that Marxist and conflict theorists are interested in why and how some groups are defined as deviant and how their behavior, now defined as deviant, gets translated into illegal behavior through the application of the law. Finally, our last theory chapter focuses on critical theories. Critical theories question the status quo, examining societal responses to deviance often from the perspective of those with less societal power. While there are quite a few critical theories, we have decided to share critical race theory, feminist theory, and peacemaking theory.

We think you will agree, as you read the book, that these theories are an important organizational tool for understanding (1) why deviance occurs, (2) why some behavior may or may not be defined as deviant, and (3) why some individuals are more likely to be defined as deviant. It is important to note that you probably won't have the same level of enthusiasm for every theory offered here. Some of you will really "get" anomie theory, whereas others might be drawn to labeling or feminist theory. Heck, we feel the same way. But what is important to remember is that *all* of these theories have been supported by research, and all help answer certain questions about deviance.

Along the way, we present examples of specific acts that may be considered deviant in both the research and pop culture. You will be introduced, at the beginning of each chapter, to a vignette that discusses a social phenomenon or behavior. As you learn more about theory, you can decide for yourself how and why these acts and actors may be defined as deviant. One of our goals for you is to help you start to think sociologically and theoretically about our social world and the acts we do and do not call deviant.

EXERCISES AND DISCUSSION QUESTIONS

1. Choose a behavior, action, or group that you consider to be deviant. Explain why you consider your example to be deviant, and then explain which conception of deviant you are using when you make your determination.

2. Choose any half-hour sitcom. While watching the show, examine its treatment of "deviant" behavior. Is there a character that others treat as different or deviant? Why do others treat him or her this way? Is there a character that you would describe as deviant? Is he or she treated this way by others in the show? What conception of deviance are you using to determine the deviant behavior on the show?

3. Why is theory important to our understanding of deviance?

KEY TERMS

Critical conception

Folkways

Laws

Mores

Normative conception

Norms

Pathologizing

Positivist perspective

Prevention programs

Rehabilitation programs

Relativist conception

Scientific method

Social constructionist conception

Sociological imagination

Suppression

Theory

READING 1

Thomas examines the art of nonmainstream body modification and how "Mods" live their everyday lives as stigmatized individuals. Mods see their choices in body modification as a direct challenge of society's expectations of health and beauty. Finally, Thomas argues that body modification is perceived as outside the mainstream and so often incites a fear or panic response from members of the dominant culture.

Sick/Beautiful/Freak

Nonmainstream Body Modification and the Social Construction of Deviance

Morgen L. Thomas

 Introduction

Contemporary Western culture views the practice of nonmainstream (extreme) body modification as, alternately, an attention-seeking trend, the sign of a masochistic or sadistic personality, a symbol of affiliation with a deviant group, or a symptom of psychological instability. Therefore, dominant society often questions the motivations and mental capacity of individuals who engage in nonmainstream body modification and, in the process, ascribes labels of social deviance, personality disorder, and/or psychopathology to those who modify their bodies in unconventional ways. Although some individuals who engage in body modification activities do exhibit outstanding psychological comorbidity, research shows that body modifiers are not at any higher risk of mental illness than the general population (Favazza, 1996; Larratt, 2003; Musafar, 1996).

To interrogate these and other common assumptions, my research focuses on the individual as the agented subject of social action rather than the passive object onto which society projects meaning. Because nonmainstream body modifiers actively demonstrate a confounding agency that often results in the stigmatization of their physical characteristics, their moral constitution, and their behavior, my assertion is that it is through the conscious process of reappropriating and redefining *controlling images* (Collins, 2000) that nonmainstream body modifiers (perceived as insane, ugly, monstrous) recapture a measure of power from dominant society and, in the process, prove their humanity to others. Furthermore, I suggest that by inscribing meaning and identity in visible ways rather than allowing society to project expectations onto them based on their gender, age, race, sexual orientation, and so on, nonmainstream body modifiers present a unique challenge to American conceptions of what is healthy, what is beautiful, and what is human. In addition, because of the highly stigmatizing and discrediting effects of possessing nonmainstream body modifications ("mods"), body modification practitioners ("Mods") themselves are often labeled by dominant culture as monsters, curios, and sick freaks in desperate need of mental health intervention. Because of the deep social implications of such labels, this article examines the concept of *freakery/monstrosity* as a salient theme found through

Source: Thomas, M. L. (2012, October–December). Sick/beautiful/freak: Nonmainstream body modification and the social construction of deviance. *SAGE Open*, 1–12.

analysis of adult respondents' surveys, and examines dominant culture's tendency to conflate bodily appearance with psychopathology and Western beauty norms with definitions of masculinity and femininity.

◈ Review of the Literature

The literature describes myriad themes when it comes to the motivations behind and social implications of body modification, from the personal to the political, the social to the pathological (Bensler & Paauw, 2003; Favazza, 1996; Featherstone, 2000; Larratt, 2003; Musafar, 2002; Pitts, 2003; Sweetman, 1999; Vale & Juno, 1989). However, five main themes seem apparent in the literature.

The first theme is *tribal ritual/identification with an indigenous culture* (Camphausen, 1997; Gay & Whittington, 2002; Mercury, 2000; Musafar, 2002; Rush, 2005; Vale & Juno, 1989). As technology advances, so does our human need for connection and identification. The "modern primitive" movement remains in full force as individuals seek group affiliation with others who share their cross-cultural interests in body rites and intentional ordeals, characterized as "physically, emotionally, and spiritually challenging activities that are pursued for their potential psychological, social, and spiritual benefits" (Dryer, 2007).

The second theme is *reclamation of the body* (Orlan, 2005; Pitts, 2000, 2003; Sweetman, 1999). Many Western body modifiers view the physical body as a potential landscape for representation and inscription, a site of political and personal negotiation. These themes are not new, however, as noted by contemporary body theorists Bryan S. Turner (1984), Arthur W. Frank (1991), Chris Shilling (2003), Victoria Pitts (2003), Anthony Synnott (1993), John O'Neill (1985), Elizabeth Grosz (1994), and Mike Featherstone (1982). Across time and space, the corporeal body has been a site of discursive debate for, as these theorists suggest, embodiment is key to such systemic phenomena as sexism, racism, ageism, and other sociocultural concerns. Without a physical body to oppress, abuse, and subordinate, such acts as lynching and rape, for example, would be impossible. Thus, the very fact of our physical embodiment, and the explicit auto-manipulation of the corporeal landscape by

self and other, calls into question the status quo of body politics, beauty ideals, race relations, and gender norms as well as many other sociological discussions (Bogdan, 1988; Grosz, 1994; Pitts, 2000, 2003; Terry & Urla, 1995; Thomson, 1996).

The third theme is *sexual enhancement/body adornment.* With the sexual revolution of the 1960s and 1970s, the body became a focal point for inscribing sexual preferences and freedoms, a site of pleasure and pain, as well as a particular kind of sexual ownership—via adornment—and decoration (Larratt, 2003; Musafar, 2002; Vale & Juno, 1989).

The fourth theme is *self-expression/identity construction* (Camphausen, 1997; Gay & Whittington, 2002; Larratt, 2003; Mercury, 2000; Musafar, 2002; Pitts, 2000, 2003; Vale & Juno, 1989). Some writers have noted that by modifying their appearance in what some label *monstrous* ways, body modifiers are in fact reifying the stereotypes and associated behavioral expectations they claim to be resisting through their body modification practices (Adams, 1996; Bogdan, 1988; Edelman, 2000; Pitts, 2003). One example of this proposed reification is the modern day "freak" show, in which individuals with anomalous bodies put themselves on display in performance settings for the entertainment of "normals" (Bogdan, 1988; Cook, 1996; Goffman, 1963). Another example is the association of tattoos with a criminal stereotype, that is, prison tattoos. The concept of "monstrosity" is particularly salient when considering body practices that, because of their overt unconventionality, lie far outside what mainstream society deems acceptable for male and female bodies as far as gender, sexuality, and appearance norms.

The fifth theme prevalent in the literature is *pathology/mental illness* (Bensler & Paauw, 2003; Favazza, 1996). This theme is common to psychological discussions of body modification. Body modification—also known as body alteration, body invention, body adornment, body technology, body aesthetics, body projects, and body customization—has been a means of personal, social, and political expression in American society since the early 1970s (Vale & Juno, 1989; Musafar, 2002). Although forms of body modification such as tattooing have been prevalent among the American working class since the turn of the last century, and was used to indicate group membership status or familial connections, by mid-20th century, this type of body mark had become more closely associated with counterculture groups such as motorcycle and street gangs as well as those who had spent time in prison (Edelman, 2000; Mercury, 2000; Myers, 1992; Pitts, 2003). This visual signifier of affiliation officially relegated members of these subcultures to the socially constructed category of *deviant* in the public consciousness, a problem currently faced by many contemporary body modifiers. Today, body modifiers cite many reasons other than social affiliation when discussing their particular forms of body alteration, and claim that their actions are in no way an indication of an unstable mind, as some literature suggests (Bensler & Paauw, 2003; Favazza, 1996) but rather a process of expression, invention, and reception (Larratt, 2003; Musafar, 2002; Myers, 1992; Orlan, 2005; Pitts, 2003; Sweetman, 1999).

In rebuttal to mainstream society's ascriptions of monstrosity, deviance, and mental illness, Mods point out that in fact *all* people modify their bodies, whether by means of commercial cosmetic application, hair dye, aerobic exercise and weight-lifting, dieting, or plastic surgery (Featherstone, 1982; Gimlin, 2002; Pitts, 2006; Sweetman, 1999; Thesander, 1997). They assert that body modification—in particular, the signification of the corporeal body as a symbolic landscape to be used and manipulated as a means to reinforce or dismantle common cultural assumptions, reinforce societal norms, create identity and/or status, or influence the larger social body—has been practiced in one form or another for centuries and is evident across gender, class, and racial lines, transcending socioeconomic and cultural boundaries (Favazza, 1996; Mills, 2005; Musafar, 2002; Rosenblatt, 1997).

◇ Theoretical Considerations

Because this article examines constructions of bodily deviance, the term *deviant* warrants clarification. Erich Goode, following Lemert's (1951) discussion of *primary* and *secondary deviation*, defines extreme deviance in terms of "behavior, beliefs, or physical traits that are so far outside the norm that they elicit extremely negative reactions" (Goode, 2008, p. ix). Whereas *primary deviation* refers to simple nonnormative behavior that may

or may not elicit punishment, condemnation, or scorn from the members of any given group, *secondary deviation* refers to the more serious and pervasive acts of deviance that can result in deviance labeling on the part of mainstream society, or what Goode calls "the audience." Deviance labeling is a process whereby members of the in-group begin to view the rule violator as a deviant rather than viewing the act itself as deviant. The result is the internalization of the *deviant* label on the part of the norm violator, whereby the violator begins to view himself or herself *as* a deviant rather than simply someone who committed a deviant act. The label, in essence, becomes an important component of his or her actual identity. Both *primary* and *secondary deviance* definitions are crucial to understanding how Mods view themselves, how they view society-at-large, and how they think mainstream society views them. It is worth noting here that *deviance* is not inherent to the individual committing the norm violation. Rather it is a label imposed on the norm-breaker based on the reactions of those around him or her, and is a product of commonly understood and widely accepted cultural norms and their perceived violation.

Hand-in-hand with acts of social deviation is the concept of *stigma* or disgrace. Erving Goffman (1963) proposes three sources of stigma. The first, an *abomination of the body*, is defined as a physical characteristic or trait that is either an aesthetic violation or a physical impairment. The second is *a blemish of individual character*, defined as a weak will or unnatural passions. The third source of stigma is *that which is transmitted through lineage*, such as race or religion. For analysis purposes, this article largely incorporates Goffman's first and second sources of stigma—an abomination of the body (violations of normative appearance) and a blemish of individual character (pursuit of unnatural passions), which often earn Mods a deviant identity in the eyes of mainstream Western society. In addition, Goffman's term *normal(s)* is used to indicate members of mainstream (conventional) society as compared with individuals who occupy a stigmatized status, such as those who practice nonmainstream body modification.

To illustrate the interpersonal strategies many Mods use to neutralize potentially negative reactions within specific social environments, Arthur W. Frank's (1991) *styles of body usage typology* will also be

Figure 1   Arthur W. Frank's Styles of Body Usage

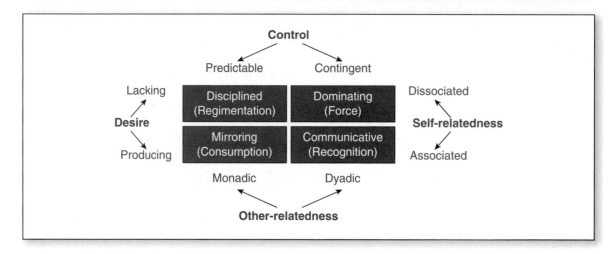

referred to. For Frank, the corporeal body is an essential component in how individuals experience their bodies not only as active agents but also as socially constructed and constituted entities whose contingency is part and parcel of the social process. Frank offers four dimensions, or "action problems," that a body must confront in social interaction with other bodies: control (predictable or contingent), desire (lacking or producing), other-relatedness (monadic or dyadic), and self-relatedness (alienation from or association with corporeality). Furthermore, Frank argues that individuals, as social actors, employ a primary style of body usage to accomplish tasks and reach their goals regarding specific action problems. The four styles of body usage are the disciplined body, the dominating body, the mirroring body, and the communicative body (Figure 1).

◈ Method

The primary research instrument was a qualitative survey questionnaire, the URL link to which was posted on the foremost website designed specifically for nonmainstream body modifiers (www.bmezine.com). The questionnaire included an informed consent page, 6 demographic questions, and 15 open-ended questions concerning motivation, social resistance, family, and views of mainstream society's perceptions concerning gendered bodies and nonmainstream body modifications. Only adult participants (age 18 and above) who met the operational definition of nonmainstream body modification were considered (see Table 1). Respondents ranged in age from 18 to 47 with an almost even split between being employed and being a student. The total number of self-reported males was 20, with a total of 55 respondents self-reporting as female. One respondent reported being female-to-male transgender, 2 respondents identified as androgynous, and 1 respondent declined to answer. Twenty-three females reported being married or in a relationship; 25 females reported being single. Nine males reported being married or in a relationship; 10 males reported being single. Five females and 1 male reported being gay, bisexual, or queer. One female respondent reported being in a long-term slave/master relationship. A qualitative content analysis was conducted using an inductive approach. Confidentiality and anonymity issues were handled in accordance with institutional review board (IRB) protocol and per the informed consent page indicating that actual names would not be used. To completely avoid the potential identification of respondents, any reference to a specific respondent or direct quote taken from a questionnaire is acknowledged only by the first

Table 1	Nonmainstream Body Modifications

Gauging/elongation: Earlobes, anal, nipple, penile, scrotal, labial
Skin: Branding, cutting, scarring, keloiding
Chiseling/scalpeling: Bone, cartilage
Tattooing: Facial, full body, ocular, anomalously placed
Piercing: Genital, facial, anomalously placed
Genital: Bifurcation (splitting), saline/silicone injection/pumping, inversion, excision, penile subincision (cutting underside of the penis), superincision (cutting both the underside and top of the penis), incision, bisection, labial or penile frenectomy (removal of restricting ligament), meatotomy (splitting of underside of the glans penis)
Implants: Genital, ocular, subdermal, microdermal, transdermal, beading, teeth
Nullification/negation: Genital, extremity, phalange, carpal, ocular, nipple, teeth
Oral: Teeth filing, tongue bifurcation (splitting), lingual frenectomy (removal of restricting ligament), piercing, tattooing
Other: Any other body modification that would be considered *nonmainstream* by Western societal standards

letter of the first name provided by the respondent, followed by his or her survey number. For example, if the respondent provided the name "Chris" and Chris was the 23rd respondent, the attribution shown would be "Mod C23."

Although some scholars may consider the Internet a questionable and unreliable venue for gathering social scientific data, the nature of this research, with regards to discreditable identities, mandated that the population researched for this study be assured a level of anonymity so as not to stigmatize them further. Therefore, approaching potential respondents via online forums that already offered a level of control to their members over issues of impression management seemed the most efficacious method for gathering transparent data, offering respondents the freedom to express themselves without fear of negative sanctions and public exposure. An unanticipated result of posting an open link on a web forum was that it allowed Mods from outside the United States to respond. In the end, this served to broaden the scope of perspectives concerning nonmainstream body modification in Western societies.

Operational Definitions

There are numerous definitions of *body modification*, so it is necessary to define this term. *Body modification* is generally defined as any permanent or semipermanent, voluntary alteration of the human body that is not medically mandated. Bodily alterations that are commonly accepted under the plastic surgery umbrella, diet and exercise regimes, and procedures such as permanent and nonpermanent cosmetic application fall under this definition of body modification. *Nonmainstream body modification* in my research is defined as any permanent or semipermanent, voluntary alteration of the human body that is not medically mandated and that transgresses and challenges common assumptions and expectations of bodily presentation and/or aesthetic, and therefore may be considered extreme and/or deviant by members of mainstream Western society. Therefore, conventional plastic surgery, while permanent/semipermanent and presumably voluntary, is not included in my definition of nonmainstream body modification. Tattoos and piercings, in general, are not considered. There is an exception to this exclusion, however. Full-body tattoos/piercings, genital tattoos/piercings, facial tattoos/piercings, and tattoos/piercings that may be considered within mainstream society's standards as egregiously norm-breaking, unconventionally placed, and/or excessive may fall under the definition of nonmainstream body modification. This definition therefore excludes conventional earlobe, tongue, nose, navel, and eyebrow piercings, traditional male circumcision, and the practice of genital mutilation on female children in some African and Middle Eastern societies (see Table 1).

◈ Sick/Beautiful/Freak: Confronting Controlling Images

Through detailed content analysis of the returned surveys, several themes emerged, highlighting the pervasiveness of specific controlling images that nonmainstream body modifiers must confront in their daily interactions with normals. The first is the attribution of psychopathology, or a "sick" mind. The second is the normative perception of modified bodies as being less beautiful because they fall outside conventional gender norms and beauty ideals, and the third is the attribution of monstrosity, or "freak," which implies a normative view of nonmainstream body modifiers as being less than human. The following section examines these controlling images and the impact they have not only on the social interactions Mods have with normals in daily life but also on identity construction processes and interpersonal communication styles.

Sick

Skin—as private canvas and public target—has played a role in every aspect of social interaction and construction of self since the dawn of humanity. As such, the highly visible sensorial human exterior is vulnerable to what Patricia Hill Collins (2000) terms *controlling images*—symbols of inscription that are projected by dominant society onto the bodyminds[1] of people, individually and collectively, to create and promote stereotypes. According to Collins, stereotypes serve two primary functions: (a) They serve to conceal or normalize oppression by making it seem like something

the subjugated person wants or something that is fundamental to the subjugated person's inherent nature and (b) they serve to influence people, consciously and subconsciously, into behaving in certain ways (Collins, 2000). In Collins's view, controlling images entail the conjoining of different features (i.e., race, class, gender, sexuality) and complicate the dynamic between acts of oppression and acts of resistance.

One controlling image that Mods directly challenge is the notion that skin (particularly female skin), the body's protective external barrier, should never be breached, marked, or otherwise "damaged," unless these practices serve to move an individual closer to a dominant ideal of attractiveness. Mods, by virtue of their overtly marked appearance and pursuit of "unnatural passions," do not meet the standards of *health* as defined by dominant culture. Therefore, because Western society continues to create and perpetuate arbitrary dualisms in every aspect of human behavior, there is only one other category available to normals in which to locate Mods—that of the unwell, the sick, physically and psychologically. According to the comments made by many survey respondents, Mods are regularly judged by mainstream Western society as psychologically unsound (i.e., mentally ill) and therefore potentially dangerous to themselves and others. Elaborating on the illness motif, Mod M20 notes that Mods are viewed as "freaks, sadists, dirty, worthless, and insane."

The language used in psychological literature implies, not so covertly, that individuals who intentionally cut themselves, burn themselves, or otherwise inflict pain on themselves, for whatever reason, suffer from some inherent mental defect or have experienced some type of emotional trauma in their lives that drives them to harm themselves. The implication is that these individuals are in need of intensive treatment to "correct" the disorder (Favazza, 1996; Pitts, 2003). Medical institutions, in particular, seem to have categorization and pathologization of *difference* as their primary goals, whether that difference manifests in "deviant" sexuality, transgression from the White male norm (i.e., the pathologization and subsequent medicalization of gynecological processes) or seeking a nonnormative appearance by having silicone horns subdermally implanted in one's head. Mod R63 elaborates on normals' tendency to connect body modification with emotional trauma: "Someone once asked me if I was abused as a child and if that was the reason I hated my body enough to do everything I do to it," and Mod H31 notes that "mainstream Western people automatically assume that if you have an 'extreme' mod there's something wrong with you."

When confronted with others' assumptions of illness or emotional trauma, Mods are quick to defend their body practices, differentiating themselves from "self-mutilators" and those who exhibit some type of documented psychological infirmity. Analyzing nonmainstream body modification within the context of the illness motif and the communicative style of body usage (see Figure 1) sheds light on how Mods reappropriate the controlling image of mental illness, turning this image and its social implications into possibility rather than limitation.

One goal of the communicative body, particularly the communicative body in illness, is to free itself from societal codes that constrain expression so that it can seek out new codes of its own invention (Frank, 1991). One way the communicative body does this is by sharing the personal story of its corporeal journey. In doing so, the individual has the opportunity to neutralize the fear, confusion, shock, anger, and despair that often accompany a diagnosis. In the case of nonmainstream body modification, it is mainstream society (normals) that diagnose and ascribe illness to the bodyminds of Mods.

Many Mods employ interactive strategies in an attempt to actively neutralize the fear, confusion, and shock their appearance sometimes elicits. One way Mods mediate others' reactions to them and reappropriate the controlling image of illness—thus creating new narratives surrounding mental and physical health—is by responding in an unanticipated manner, interrupting a potentially negative social exchange by calling out in the normal a wholly novel response that forces the normal's recognition of the Mod as *human*. Mod H29 illustrates this transactive approach: "I get asked questions which I wouldn't mind if people were polite about it. But just because they're not polite doesn't mean I'm not going to be," and Mod S42 writes, "I've never been rude to someone asking about mods, and I think that can influence their reactions." Mod M01 writes, "Some [people] seem weirded out at first,

but most are understanding after they meet me and find out I'm not an asshole." Mod S49 uses humor to neutralize the encounter: "I get a lot of people asking me if it hurt, how I got them done and stuff. I just tell younger teenagers that I got a giant hole punch and they actually believe me most of the time." Mod H31 notes the efforts of some normals to establish a familiar kinship: "Most often than not I get curiosity. 'Wow, did that hurt?' 'How many tattoos do you have?' 'I have a tattoo! Wanna see?' It's nice because 5 years ago that almost never happened." Elaborating on the curiosity of normals, Mod S50 writes,

> Generally, I don't have any issues with people . . . children are honest though. I see children staring at me as their parents try to drag them along. Children want to look at someone that looks different, but parents don't want to be caught staring. I've caught a few people trying to surreptitiously take my picture.

And Mod M02 highlights how Mods, as a stigmatized group, feel they have to employ certain tactics to prove their mental stability:

> To me the mods feel natural and normal so I'm not going to announce them, but on the other hand, I do take my time explaining them because I don't want [people] to think there's anything mentally wrong with me.

Mod H23 demonstrates personal agency (with a hint of social resistance) in her interactions: "The general public believes I am over the edge, crazy, not in the right mind, and I enjoy every moment that I can prove their shallow outlooks false."

In terms of the (ill) communicative body in nonmainstream body modification, this process of story sharing serves to create social cohesion rather than the monadic isolation that many Mods experience as a result of their deviance label. Furthermore, a dyadic other-relatedness and an associated self-relatedness are achieved when Mods actively pursue interactions that result in the healthy establishment of their humanity and their sanity because "when illness is told, its lack becomes producing, and as desire becomes producing, contingency becomes possibility" (Frank, 1991, p. 88). This narrative sharing opens new possibilities for normals and Mods alike to realize their own bodies in relation to others who share the corporeal story not only of weakness and affliction but also of pleasure and imagination. Among the unwell and infirm, as among performance artists who use their bodies as a means to communicate dissent and resistance, narratives are fundamentally embodied and therefore vital to the mutual recognition of bodies and lives as interwoven with the bodies and lives of others (Frank, 1991).

Cultural psychiatrist Armando Favazza (1996) emphasizes the need of psychological and psychiatric institutions to have a more inclusive, holistic view of "self-mutilative" behaviors, asserting that reducing these acts to nothing more than a passive attempt at suicide, a cry for help, the sign of an afflicted mind, or an attention-seeking scheme is a gross oversimplification of a very complex aspect of human behavior.

> It is clear that the individual human body mirrors the collective social body, and each continually creates and sustains the other. Misperceptions of reality, feelings of guilt, negative self-images, antisocial acts, and all the other symptoms we associate with personal mental illness defy understanding without reference to the psychological, social, cultural, and physical integrity of the communal "body." (Favazza, 1996, p. xiii)

In other words, situating the individual behavior within a broader social context is crucial to understanding the motivation behind phenomena such as nonmainstream body modification. Mods are not chronically, terminally, or psychologically ill simply because they choose to modify their bodies in nonnormative ways. However, mainstream society, in its quest for continued binary categorization opportunities, ascribes illness to heavily modified bodies in an attempt to understand what is healthy and what is not. *Healthy*, within the context of corporeal bodies, is defined as a pristine, smooth, firm, youthful, capable presentation. *Unhealthy*, by dual opposition then, is defined at the opposite end of the dichotomous framework that bodies are often forced into—in this case deficient, blemished,

flabby, old, and incapable. By restructuring the illness motif, one of many controlling images constructed around Western ideas of ableness, and creating new narratives surrounding health and ability, Mods actively and tacitly attempt to counteract society's projection of pathology onto their bodyminds. In this process, Mods inscribe new meanings and create new codes that assert not only their humanity but their mental and physical health as well.

Beautiful

Like such body practices as pumping iron, dieting, using hair dye and applying cosmetics, as well as socially acceptable plastic surgery techniques, some nonmainstream body modifications reflect an individual's desire to achieve a perfected version of himself or herself. However, what is considered the "perfect" or "beautiful" body is greatly dependent on cultural definitions of feminine and masculine bodies and how they may or may not digress from the characteristics and expectations of gendered behavior and appearance.

Mods who cite aesthetics as a primary motivating factor behind their body modification practices enjoy adorning and decorating their bodies in unique ways because they find the end result aesthetically and artistically pleasing (i.e., beautiful), despite the social ramifications of their body practices. Demonstrating this confounding agency, Mod A64 explains,

> I find body modifications of all types to be aesthetically enhancing. I like the way you can accentuate a particular feature of your body with a modification, or draw attention away from a part of your body you find less desirable.

Contemporary media outlets reproduce depictions of the young, hypersexual, and/or infantilized female body and the youthful, hypermasculinized male body, constantly messaging through these images how men and women, girls and boys, should *want* to look. Any physical presentation that transgresses these normalized (controlling) images, whether it's the morbidly obese woman or the effeminate man, is met with disdain, judgment or, in some cases, outright aggression on the part of normals. These controlling images are often associated, overtly and covertly, with relevant messages regarding marriageability, fertility, strength, youth, vibrancy, and healthy body integrity—all of which are symbolic indicators of successful bodily presentation according to Western beauty and gender norms.

Accepted body modification procedures such as breast implants, liposuction of fat cells, relocation and tightening of facial tissue, and silicone implants designed for the cheeks, buttocks, and pectoral areas of men's bodies are just a few examples of Frank's mirroring style of body usage. Not only do these practices make the body predictable in many ways but they also help to recursively reproduce unconscious desire, which manifests in isolated monadic consumerist behavior. By ceaselessly producing in individuals a superficial desire aimed at the materiality of things that consumer culture promotes as necessary (youthful appearance, on-demand sexual function, etc.), certain capitalist institutions and the values they promote become more firmly rooted in the collective consciousness regarding what is available for immediate consumption—physically, emotionally, spiritually, and mentally. Because of this, the mirroring body style is of particular interest when considering the divergent consumer practices of Mods and the predictability they seek through a contradictory form of consumption that they find beautiful and make apparent to others through their highly visible modified appearance, the presentation of which causes an expected outcome, thus offering the Mod a measure of control in social encounters.

As noted, Goffman's (1963) first source of stigma (an abomination of the body) is particularly relevant to nonmainstream body modifiers and their lived experience, as any perceived violation of the corporeal landscape forces a reconfiguring of common assumptions about body integrity, appearance, and function not only for the modifying individual but for conventional society as well. Many Mods implicate the American beauty ideal of smooth, pristine, firm skin as one source of their discreditable status and their rebellion, whether social or personal, against it.

Illustrating the perceived hypocrisy of normals who differentiate between mainstream and nonmainstream body modification, positively sanctioning one practice while demonizing the other, Mod H31 writes,

No one looks twice if you've got a nose job or boob implants, or if you get botox once a week ... choosing to be modified does not make someone sick, twisted, insane, a satanist, or any other negative attribute. [Mods] should be given the same respect and opportunities as anyone else.

Speaking to the automatic assumption of bad character, Mod L11 writes, "Having visible modifications does not make me a worse student, human being, etc. I can't wait for the day when I stop being judged based solely on my appearance," and Mod A62 shares, "I don't have a motorcycle or breed snakes in my parents' basement or do drugs. Body modification is not about bikers and rappers. It's a very personal choice." Addressing the manufactured connection between health and beauty, Mod E75 writes,

I do think we should try to be healthier, but not aspire to a prototype of beauty, but one that makes US feel beautiful and confident. Me and my body mods make me feel enough confidence to feel extremely attractive, and in my experience that makes me attractive.

Mainstream society defines as abhorrent such modifications as facial or genital piercings, scarring, cutting, branding, burning, and tattooing of the skin. The perception of abhorrence on the part of normals is what makes these acts deviant, not the act itself, especially when compared with more conventional body enhancement practices that reify and reproduce the American beauty ideal, rewarding and privileging those who strive *toward* the positively sanctioned representations of what a woman or a man "should" look like. As Mods show through the deliberate cutting, burning, marking, and scarring of their flesh, definitions of beauty do not always follow social protocol. These forms of appearance normbreaking can and do result in scorn and ostracism. Mod J34 illustrates this point: "Society in general is quite hateful, and I've yet to figure out why some color on one's skin or a few pieces of metal alter who a person is in the eyes of another." Mod J19, also noting Western society's emphasis on appearance and the consequences of having a nonnormative physical presentation, writes, "[Mods] are often stared at and cast aside because they look different from everyone else. I find it sickening that [Mods] are not treated with respect or like a human being, they are treated like an animal." The concept of humanness and the desire of the bodymind to not only comprehend but also to prove its humanity is an interesting component of the interactive social strategies used by individuals who practice nonmainstream body modification.

By marking their bodies in highly visible and potentially discrediting ways, as opposed to adopting routines that validate and reward aesthetic conformance, Mods seemingly move *away* from the American beauty ideal of pristine, unblemished, youthful skin and body presentation, and *toward* what dominant society deems an unacceptable appearance and body presentation. In showing a unique kind of agency when it comes to their consumer habits and tastes—an agency that could be interpreted as blatant rejection of bodily conformance—these Mods directly challenge Frank's construct of the mirroring body as a purely passive and oblivious receptor of dominant consumerist ideals.

Beautiful Girl, Handsome Boy

As noted, the negative comments and reactions of others do little to stop a Mod from modifying. Mods will engage in a variety of strategies, including covering, passing, information control, and impression management (Goffman, 1963) to avoid and/or neutralize normals' gestural and verbal condemnation of their body practices, practices that actively violate the American beauty ideal of what male and female bodies should (want to) look like. However, nowhere is the disapproval Mods experience more egregious than in the family milieu.

In answering the question concerning how family and friends react to their body modifications, many Mods noted the negative responses of their parents and relatives, while stating that their friends are more accepting of their body practices. Mod S08 writes, "My family has never understood the reasoning behind my modifications and have been unsupportive of my decisions," and Mod T48 writes, "My parents have not been so accepting of my modifications. My mom even said to me once, 'How many holes are enough?!'" Mod S42 shares,

"I've not told my family about [my tattoos] to avoid confrontation. I'd rather my short visits home are happy rather than end up with me being shouted at."

Differential socialization of boys and girls is a given. Examples of body control tactics abound in literature and popular media, reinforcing not only strict gender roles but also the expectation of conformance to a cultural ideal, whether that ideal be aesthetic (beauty), material (status), cognitive (beliefs), or expressive, as in the case of socially acceptable demonstrations of masculine and feminine behavior. While my questionnaire did not include the parents of Mods as potential respondents, parents—as socially and historically situated members of dominant culture—appear to share the attitudes of mainstream normals when it comes to unconventional bodily alterations. In particular, the comments female Mods relayed concerning their parents' reactions indicate an anxiety on the part of mothers and fathers that seems to stem from a fear that their daughter will, through her alternative body practices, alienate a potential life partner. Mod S49 illustrates this point: "My dad always got angry at me and told me I'd never meet a good guy that did anything useful because of my stretched lobes and my tattoos," and Mod C17 writes, "[The main question is] 'Don't you have a hard time dating looking like that?'" Mod A64 writes, "My mother does not know I have [mods]. She would go nuts." Mod M02 shares a deep frustration when it comes to communicating any aspect of her modifications to her family: "I try to make [my family] understand what it means to me. No matter how much they love me, they will not understand. They've drawn a line and I've crossed it."

As in most aspects of social life, embodied experience can be understood in terms of gendered experience. Nonmainstream body modification—as an embodied, agented endeavor—is no different. As the above statements suggest, how bodies are perceived and treated by conventional society depends greatly on how that body looks and behaves in accordance with social norms, including acceptable expressions of masculinity and femininity. Survey respondents had much to say when answering the question concerning how male and female bodies are perceived by society, with many of them again pointing to the American beauty ideal and (controlling) media images as sources of discontent regarding acceptable bodies. Exemplifying the power and cultural scope of these controlling images in contemporary society, Mod E75, a male Mexican national, writes,

> Most people are surprised that someone "like me" (professional, business owner, commercial director, come from a good family) has body modifications. We make way too much preconceptions and the media tries to sell us this image of rockers or actors that we should pursue.

Mod M20 addresses the increasing pressure young men are experiencing as the target of media images that create and reproduce the ideal masculine body: "Men should be straight-laced muscle bound healthy clean cut and professional and girls should all look like models, if not you suck and you're not accepted." Taking this notion a step further, Mod K22 writes,

> [We are] fed the thought that you should be a provocative, skinny, smart but ditsy, pink plaid wearing college graduate that drives a BMW or a clean cut businessman. There is a fine line between what is okay and what isn't.

Mod H23 notes how controlling images concerning ideal bodies can be internalized and thus affect a person's self-concept:

> Male and female bodies seem to be set in a narrow view of what is beautiful and what is not. Females must be thin, decently breasted, and have a pretty face. Males have a broader range on how they may look to be acceptable. Plastic and cosmetic surgery is becoming widely acceptable but it's shoving people through a narrow viewfinder on what they think of themselves.

Confronting the conformist mentality expected by normals, Mod K30 writes, "There is too much pressure on men and women to keep their bodies looking a certain way in our society. Tall, thin, muscular, blonde, tanned . . . all of these make people look like sheep."

One particular comment, by Mod S50, stood out because it is a profound observation concerning attitudes toward gendered appearance:

> Western society is still very male oriented; maybe being part of the group that largely has power confers partial immunity towards body objectification? Women seem to end up more concerned with whether they have the "right" appearance than men do. I catch female students complaining about breast size regularly (too small, too big), but I have yet to find any group of male students complaining about muscle mass, body fat composition, height issues, penis size.

This comment by Mod S50, who identifies himself as a heterosexual male, warrants special attention because it implies the differential judgments male and female Mods experience. Some body practices are more acceptable for men than they are for women, and vice versa. For example, being a heavily tattooed and/or pierced woman elicits more comments from normals about sexual promiscuity, attractiveness, childbearing, and marriage than it does for male Mods, who are often grouped under the "criminal" label. Mod T82 elaborates this point: "Women with piercings are still looked upon as wild women who are too overtly sexual. Men with modifications are often grouped with White trash or gangsters or other degenerates of society," and Mod M79 writes, "Females are definitely looked down upon when they are modified. Men can be a little dirty with a few tattoos, but girls are seen as downright skanky gang-related bitches." Mod S42 shares,

> Some people have even had the reaction "you'd be so much prettier without all that" when talking about my modifications and yet made no comment about my boyfriend's tattoos and piercings, which also gives me the impression it's okay for males to heavily modify themselves and yet women should only have their ears pierced.

These comments support tattoo and body-play artist Sheree Rose's assertion that "tattoo is one of those big taboos for women, although it's always been something that men could do when they get drunk" (Vale & Juno, 1989, p. 109). In sum, by consciously moving *away* from conventional ideas surrounding ideal (i.e., gendered) bodily appearance and behavior and *toward* the perceived opposite, Mods directly confront the social constructs and institutions that demand a very narrow definition of attractiveness and gendered behavior. Mods do this by reappropriating, overtly and covertly, the controlling images Western society produces, reproduces, promotes, and expects—the positively sanctioned images of smooth, pristine, unblemished, youthful bodies that operate at a high functionality (defined as beautiful) and the demonized images of criminal, insane, defect, and monstrous (defined as ugly).

Freak

When asked how individuals with nonmainstream body modifications are perceived by mainstream Western society, and what the general public's reaction to their specific body modifications is, an overwhelming majority of Mods made reference to the term *freak* and how having nonnormative physical characteristics can result in this disparaging, dehumanizing label. This is nothing new. Ascribing the *freak* term to individuals who exhibit "monstrous" or "abnormal" physical traits has deep roots in antiquated ideologies concerning race, experimentation in the name of medical science, and strict binary categorizations of gender (Bogdan, 1988; Cook, 1996; Terry & Urla, 1995). Some general characteristics that could earn someone a *freak* label included possessing too many or too few body parts, having a distorted or "monstrous" form, being much larger/smaller/thinner/fatter/hairier than the average person, possessing hair or skin of an anormative color with regard to sex/race/age, or having two or contradictive genders. Historically, individuals with some type of abomination of the body were systematically studied, exploited, exhibited, and feared (Bogdan, 1988; Cook, 1996; Terry & Urla, 1995). Grotesques of days past were, alternately, targets of derision and objects of reverence.

Researcher Robert Bogdan (1988) explains the origins of two types of *freak*, each of them historically, geographically, physically, and metaphorically dislodged from their own social milieus and then systematically relocated and resituated within a Western context as *other*. The first type of freak—the "exotic freak"—is directly connected to the exploration of the non-Western world in the 18th and 19th centuries. As explorers and natural scientists struck out over the oceans and tributaries to investigate new worlds, they returned with not only countless—albeit exaggerated—stories of bizarre people and unusual cultures but also actual specimens of these cultures, sparking intense curiosity in the American public that provided an opportunity for the showmen of the age to capitalize on the differentness of these specimens.

> Tribal people, brought to the United States with all the accoutrements of their culture out of context, stimulated the popular imagination and kindled belief in races of tailed people, dwarfs, giants, and even people with double heads that paralleled creatures of ancient mythology. The interest thus spawned was an opportunity, a platform, and a backdrop for showmen's creations. (Bogdan, 1988, p. 6)

The second category of freak consists of those individuals who met all the criteria to be labeled under the medical term for people with obvious and, oftentimes, extreme bodily difference—the monster, the *lusus naturae*, the "freak of nature." These were people born with a physical anomaly so severe that they were touted as "born freaks" (Bogdan, 1988), individuals who not only piqued the interest of the medical community but also aroused the curiosity of normals. Born freaks elicited reactions of pity and stunned horror, and showmen of the age played on audience members' fears of bodily invasion, dysfunction, and disfigurement to entice them inside the mysterious tent in which the freak was housed. A widely known example of a born freak who was put on display and marketed for the sole benefit of curiosity seekers is Joseph Carrey Merrick, the "elephant man."

Rachel Adams (1996) suggests the social construction of a third type of freak, the "normal freak," a person of normal bodily constitution who emphasizes his or her difference from the average person by appropriating a special skill or by becoming a "made freak," someone who does something to himself or herself to become unusual enough in appearance or ability to warrant exhibition. This freak can be found in the strongman, the snake charmer, the sword swallower, and the heavily tattooed man or woman. For obvious reasons, the concept of the made freak is especially relevant in discussions of nonmainstream body modification.

While no less than 43 comments appeared in the questionnaires regarding the *freak* attribution to those who possess a nonnormative physical appearance, the following statement from Mod H31 profoundly sums up the thoughts of the majority of survey respondents.

> Mainstream Western people automatically assume that if you have an "extreme" mod there's something wrong with you. That you're a criminal, a freak, the dregs of the dregs. Right up there with fags, drag spics, niggers, or any other minority that is full of people that the "mainstream" don't want to understand or know, because hating someone for something silly gives them something to feel better about. They can get up in the morning, look in the mirror, and say "gee at least I'm not fat/gay/Black/have horns implanted in my forehead."

Many Mods undertake body projects as a means of outwardly projecting an internal self-image by inscribing their bodies with symbolic signifiers that indicate how they perceive themselves and how they wish to be perceived by others. Some Mods feel that their "normal" exterior presentation does not match their internal perception of how they "should" look. Several go so far as to say they view their bodies as anomalous or incomplete without body modifications, at times using language that implies aesthetic defect or impaired function. As a made freak, Mod A64 elaborates the related concepts of self-expression and identity this way:

> Body modification enables me to express the person that I truly am. I feel it is a form of art and flesh is my medium. I wouldn't say that body modification makes me who I am, but if for some reason I take out my jewelry . . . I feel uncomfortable, I feel naked and I feel as if a crucial part of me is missing.

Mod J19 writes, "I will always be changing different parts of [my body] to complete it or to make it look more like who I am on the inside and express my values, scene, culture, opinions, etc." Mod K22 expands on this point: "[I modify] to be myself the way I see myself. I like feeling free. Expressing myself this way and telling stories on my skin is my way of growing," and Mod H23 writes, "It's purely become an expansion on a personal outlook of myself . . . it's an exciting experience and makes me someone of my own making." Mod J34 notes simply, "[body modification] allows me to feel as if I'm bringing what's inside me out."

Several interesting observations are made when analyzing the made freak within the framework of Frank's communicative style of body usage. The primary mode of action undertaken by the communicative body in social interaction is *recognition*. Self-expression (in this case narrative sharing in the form of visible symbolic inscription) and a desire that is conscious and producing in its pursuit of dyadic other-relatedness and an associated self-relatedness are the main characteristics of the communicative body in nonmainstream body modification. These bodyminds confront contingencies and the action problem of predictability in their everyday encounters with normals. However, made freaks tend to be individuals who enjoy the narrative process, engaging normals in a dyadic exchange, thus helping the normal perceive the Mod as just one more human who has a story to share; they simply share it through unconventional means. In true communicative body form, Mod J34 eloquently clarifies this concept: "No matter our color or religion or wealth or sexuality or body appearance . . . we have a story to tell. Everyone else should be willing to listen," and Mod S08 shares, "I believe that human expression is one of the most beautiful and responsible things for a person to do."

As the statements of these made freaks illustrate, in using their bodies to personify identity through the inscriptive expression of the internal landscape, a declaration of body ownership becomes evident. In sharing its narrative, the communicative bodymind in nonmainstream body modification actively dictates how its physicality is to be understood and evaluated rather than allowing society to ascribe meaning to it. Furthermore, knowing the automatic assumptions of normals, many made freaks allow themselves to be viewed initially within a context of deviance (monstrous, criminal, insane) but then challenge those same assumptions through innovative bodily expression and dyadic social exchange. It is during this transactive exchange that the expressive, communicative bodymind turns the expected encounter inside out, forcing the normal to not only look at, but also really see, dominant culture's contradictions and dualities. Mod L41 illustrates this interactive strategy:

> When my face was more full of metal I had a lot of people stare at me and little kids nearby would try and touch them. If I get a glare, I can be rude. If they are curious (you can obviously tell the difference) I usually say hi to let them know it is obvious they are staring at me and any questions they have I would be happy to answer.

Deeply rooted in history, the term *freak* certainly has a controlling aspect to it. The term is employed by normals to communicate to Mods that their bodyminds lie far outside the accepted appearance and behavioral norms of Western society, and that there are consequences for these transgressions, such as being stigmatized as less-than-human and/or ostracism in the form of social isolation. Mod J15 shares, "I see 'normal' people's reactions and feel alone, ugly and like a freak," and Mod J12 notes, "It's like the days of the old circus sideshow."

As these comments illustrate, controlling images affect not only the subordinated individual or group but also dominant culture as the images are disseminated in everyday media accounts and common discourses. However, as Collins asserts, controlling images can not only be created and used to dominate a specific group, promoting stereotypes and limiting the subjugated group's access to potentially liberating symbols, but they can also be reappropriated by the stigmatized group and turned into powerful symbols of liberation, resistance, and reclamation. As Mod A62 shares, "It's very important to me that I have this kind of strength/power represented on my body because it is everything I want to be in life." Bringing the ideas of spiritual identity, ritual, humanness, and body ownership together, Mod C32 writes,

> I wanted to be happy with the skin I was in, so I made myself what I am. It's very spiritual to

have that power. I also have strong beliefs in the significance of modification throughout human history. I feel that it is a part of what makes us human to modify ourselves. I like the feeling of having that connection to the rest of the world, past and present. It's very grounding to know that while we may be going off the deep end as a culture, I can still have a small link to the people who lived with the land instead of against it.

 ## Conclusion

This article explores the ways in which contemporary nonmainstream Mods facilitate daily social interaction as a stigmatized *other*. Mods, as social agents, act on their environment as well as allow their environment to act on them. As a result, they are highly aware of the unique contingencies presented in social encounters due to their anormative appearance, demonstrating a deep awareness of how conventional society views them—as the mentally unstable nut, the ugly man or woman, the monstrous freak.

Because dominant society messages through controlling images what men and women should (want to) look like, the comments of Mods demonstrate that their unconventional body practices directly challenge society's expectations of beauty and health norms, gender expression and roles, corporeal presentation, and symbolic inscription simply by moving *away* from Western appearance ideals (beauty) and *toward* its perceived opposite (monstrosity). By blatantly opening, puncturing, excising, scarring, stretching, burning, nullifying, implanting, and tattooing various body parts, Mods defy accepted notions of skin as something pristine, pain as something to be avoided, body integrity as something to be preserved, and self as a fixed and rigid concept. As the testimonials of Mods show, their nonconformance to these normative notions has earned them the label of *deviant*—the dangerous and discreditable outsider, the freak that escapes definition and categorization, the perplexing oddity that challenges what it means in Western society to be a man or a woman, indeed what it means to be *human*.

Furthermore, as the self-statements of Mods show, images that are perceived as lying outside the realm of commonly shared experiences can incite a fear response in members of dominant culture, resulting in pathologization and stigmatization of the offending individual, effects that could greatly influence that individual's sense of self and his or her continuing formation of identity, both group and individual. By showing agency in altering their physical appearance and/or function, however, Mods, like all people, stake a claim on their own corporeal presentation, declaring ownership of their bodies as well as their individual, social, and political identity. In doing so, Mods make the tacit claim that dominant Western social institutions do not—will not—dictate their public presentation or definition of self. If Armando Favazza (1996) is correct in his analysis of cross-cultural body modification practices, and if these practices are indeed the embodied expression of universal archetypes residing in our collective consciousness, nonmainstream body modification can be viewed simply as one more manifestation of a cross-culturally shared curiosity about the human body and its limits.

In sum, by inscribing their bodies with symbols that communicate entire biographies and ideologies, Mods and their embodied practices lend support to various theories of the body while challenging common assumptions about the body. Indeed, it could be argued that Mods are simply undertaking the most profound human endeavor—the enduring search for identity and meaning, the embodied quest for connection and recognition.

◈ Note

1. To challenge Descartes's assertion that the body and the mind are distinctly separate aspects of self, I use the term *bodymind* to illustrate the obvious connections between the two.

◈ References

Adams, R. (1996). An American Tail: Freaks, gender, and the incorporation of history in Katherine Dunn's Geek Love. In R. G. Thomson (Ed.), *Freakery: Cultural spectacles of the extraordinary body* (pp. 277–290). New York: New York University Press.

Bensler, J., & Paauw, D. (2003). Apotemnophilia masquerading as medical morbidity. Retrieved from http://www.medscape.com/viewarticle/459183

Bogdan, R. (1988). *Freak show: Presenting human oddities for amusement and profit*. Chicago, IL: University of Chicago Press.

Camphausen, R. C. (1997). *Return of the tribal: A celebration of body adornment*. Rochester, NY: Park Street Press.

Collins, P. H. (2000). *Black feminist thought: Knowledge, consciousness, and the politics of empowerment*. New York, NY: Routledge.

Cook, J. W. (1996). Of men, missing links, and nondescripts: The strange career of P. T. Barnum's "What is it?" exhibition. In R. G. Thomson (Ed.), *Freakery: Cultural spectacles of the extraordinary body* (pp. 139–157). New York: New York University Press.

Dryer, D. C. (2007). Characterizing intentional ordeals. Available from www.networkedblogs.com

Edelman, D. (2000). The thin red line: Social power and the open body. Retrieved from http://www.csa.com/discoveryguides/redline/overview.php

Favazza, A. R. (1996). *Bodies under siege: Self-mutilation and body modification in culture and psychiatry*. Baltimore, MD: Johns Hopkins University Press.

Featherstone, M. (1982). The body in consumer culture. In M. Featherstone, M. Hepworth, & B. Turner (Eds.), *The body: Social process and cultural theory* (pp. 170–196). London, England: SAGE.

Featherstone, M. (Ed.). (2000). *Body modification*. London, England: SAGE.

Frank, A. W. (1991). For a sociology of the body: An analytical review. In M. Featherstone, M. Hepworth, & B. Turner (Eds.), *The body: Social process and cultural theory* (pp. 36–102). London, England: SAGE.

Gay, K., & Whittington, C. (2002). *Body marks: Tattooing, piercing, and scarification*. Brookfield, CT: Millbrook Press.

Gimlin, D. L. (2002). *Body work: Beauty and self-image in American culture*. Berkeley: University of California Press.

Goffman, E. (1963). *Stigma: Notes on the management of spoiled identity*. New York, NY: Simon & Schuster.

Grosz, E. (1994). *Volatile bodies: Toward a corporeal feminism*. Bloomington: Indiana University Press.

Larratt, S. (2003). *ModCon: The secret world of extreme body modification*. Canada: BME Books.

Lemert, E. M. (1951). *Social pathology: A systematic approach to the theory of sociopathic behavior*. New York, NY: McGrawHill.

Mercury, M. (2000). *Pagan fleshworks: The alchemy of body modification*. Rochester, VT: Park Street Press.

Mills, R. (2005). *Suspended animation: Pain, pleasure and punishment in medieval culture*. London, England: Reaktion Books.

Musafar, F. (1996). Body play: State of grace or sickness? In A. Favazza (Ed.), *Bodies under siege: Self-mutilation and body modification in culture and psychiatry* (pp. 325–334). Baltimore, MD: Johns Hopkins University Press.

Musafar, F. (2002). *Spirit flesh*. Santa Fe, NM: Arena Editions.

Myers, J. (1992). Nonmainstream body modification: Genital piercing, branding, burning, and cutting. *Journal of Contemporary Ethnography, 2*, 267–306.

O'Neill, J. (1985). *Five bodies: The human shape of modern society*. Ithaca, NY: Cornell University Press.

Orlan. (2005). I do not want to look like . . . In M. Fraser & M. Greco (Eds.), *The body: A reader* (pp. 312–315). New York, NY: Routledge.

Pitts, V. (2000). Visibly queer: Body technologies and sexual politics. *Sociological Quarterly, 41*, 443–463.

Pitts, V. (2003). *In the flesh: The cultural politics of body modification*. New York, NY: Palgrave Macmillan.

Pitts, V. (2006). The body, beauty, and psychosocial power. In N. Chen & H. Moglen (Eds.), *Bodies in the making: Transgressions and transformations* (pp. 28–46). Santa Cruz, CA: New Pacific Press.

Rosenblatt, D. (1997). The antisocial skin: Structure, resistance, and "Modern Primitive" adornment in the United States. *Cultural Anthropology, 12*, 287–334.

Rush, J. A. (2005). *Spiritual tattoo: A cultural history of tattooing, piercing, scarification, branding, and implants*. Berkeley, CA: Frog.

Shilling, C. (2003). *The body and social theory*. London, England: SAGE.

Sweetman, P. (1999). Anchoring the (postmodern) self? Body modification, fashion and identity. In M. Featherstone (Ed.), *Body and society: Body modification* (pp. 51–76). Thousand Oaks, CA: SAGE.

Synnott, A. (1993). *The body social: Symbolism, self, and society*. New York, NY: Routledge.

Terry, J., & Urla, J. (Eds.). (1995). *Deviant bodies*. Bloomington: Indiana University Press.

Thesander, M. (1997). *The feminine ideal*. London, England: Reaktion Books.

Thomson, R. (Ed.). (1996). *Freakery: Cultural spectacles of the extraordinary body*. New York: New York University Press.

Turner, B. S. (1984). *The body and society*. Oxford, UK: Basil Blackwell.

Vale, V., & Juno, A. (1989). *Re/Search #12: Modern Primitives*. Eugene, OR: Re/Search Publications.

READING 2

In this article, Wahrman points to three concepts common to the student of deviance: "status," "norms," and "sanctions." These are common sociological concepts, but they are at best fuzzy and in need of deep contemplation if we are to advance our understanding of some basic issues in the study of deviance. The concept of status, for example, is multidimensional and may refer to "esteem," "admiration," or "prestige." In the study of deviance, we tend to think that these concepts are associated with power and the ability to "get away with stuff." Wahrman reminds us that both the conceptualization and the context may affect how status affects behavior and reaction to behavior. Similarly, one of the most common definitions of deviance is "the violation of group norms." Wahrman discourages us from oversimplifying the term and uses experimental studies to show just how complicated the concept can be. Finally, the term *sanctions,* which is so common in the study of deviance, is no more clear. Wahrman makes a strong case that experimental studies of sanctions have been far too narrow for the student of deviance to make much use of them. Two important things can be taken from this article. First, it seems to us that Wahrman makes clear the overlapping and interacting nature of these key concepts and how, taken together, we find ourselves in quite murky waters. Second, he argues against the overly simplistic notion that status is simply a measure of power that protects certain persons who violate norms; to illustrate his claim, he points to contexts where high-status persons may be particularly subject to sanctions and low-status persons may be less sanctioned than those holding power.

Source: Wahrman, R. (2010). Status, deviance, and sanctions: A critical review. *Small Group Research, 41*, 91–105. Reprinted with permission of SAGE Publications, Inc.

Status, Deviance, and Sanctions

A Critical Review

Ralph Wahrman

◈ Groups Have Norms

Group members abide by the norms because they believe the norms are proper or because they fear that sanctions will be applied by other group members who *do* believe in the norms. High-status members apparently have less to fear. We frequently find that nonconforming high-status members of a group are not sanctioned (Wahrman, 1970a). On those rare occasions when they do receive sanctions, those who possess high status may be more severely sanctioned than lesser members (Wahrman, 1970b).

There are two schools of thought about the reasons high status so often enables people to avoid sanctions. One approach suggests that nonconformity is perceived as deviant regardless of who performs it. Because high status and high power often go together, less powerful members of the group fear retaliation and therefore do not act on their perceptions (Blau, 1964a; McGrath, 1964; Homans, 1961).

The other approach suggests that behavior is perceived differently depending on who the actor is and that nonconformity by high-status group members is not seen as deviance but as innovation, tolerable idiosyncrasy, occasion for changing the norm or broadening its limits, and so on. In other words, what strikes an outside observer as "deviance" appears to the group as an event which does not call for sanctions (Hollander, 1961).

Disentangling the circumstances under which each approach is correct and the circumstances under which certain levels and types of status do or do not make it possible to violate certain types of norms is the sort of problem for which field and laboratory experiments are eminently suitable. Therefore, this review concentrates on experimental studies of status and deviance. The literature is not a large one, but the issues and their implications are not only significant for understanding abstract questions about the dynamics of social control in informal groups but are also of relevance for students

of delinquency (Black & Reiss, 1970) and adult crime (Wolfgang et al., 1962), for students of social change (e.g., Putney & Putney, 1962; Fathi, 1968), students of intergroup relations (Sherif, 1962; Julian et al., 1969), and for students of leadership (Hollander, 1964).

Although the literature is not generally thought of as a large one, it is much smaller than we usually admit. I exclude from this review studies which have asked about the *willingness* of high-status people to violate norms. These are generally inaccurately cited in social psychology texts as supplying evidence for the *ability* of high-status people to get away with deviance. Willing and able are not the same things.

I exclude here also studies of credibility (Berlo et al., 1969; Griffin, 1967; Simons et al., 1970) for several reasons. First, they tend not to study normative issues but rather issues on which subjects tend to have quite weak personal opinions (Hovland, 1959). Second, the speakers tend not to be members of groups of which subjects are members. Space limitations suggest that I focus here on situations in which subjects and deviants, if only temporarily, are members of the same group, and the deviant has some reason to be aware of the existence of the group and its norms.

Although this review examines limitations of existing research, my basic intention is to suggest research possibilities for the future. Let us first examine the basic concepts "status," "norms," and "sanctions" as utilized in studies which attempt to combine all three.

◈ Status

Groups do not value all members equally. Abstractly, we can say that some members have higher value to the group because they possess rewarding (or potentially rewarding) qualities and abilities, and their fellow members reward them in turn by according them "status" or social approval (Secord & Backman, 1964; Homans, 1961; Thibaut & Kelley, 1959).

The particular qualities for which one is accorded varying levels of status vary with the nature and purpose of the group, and depending on the circumstances, a group may have more than one status hierarchy. Researchers studying the effects of status on deviance have not been clear about whether their studies were addressed to studying "status," "prestige," "esteem," or "admiration" (cf. Ellis, 1962; Ellis & Keedy, 1960), which should be thought of as different kinds of rankings with potentially different consequences for the possessor. Although these terms tend to be used mainly by sociologists who wish to refer to responses to one's possession of formal roles separately from personal reactions to the role incumbent, students of informal groups have utilized similar distinctions and supplied an additional vocabulary related to roles and dimensions of behavior in informal groups. "Status" may have reference to a task or social-emotional activity hierarchy (Slater, 1955) or to attractiveness as a workmate or roommate (Jennings, 1943), to private or public popularity (Taylor, 1954), to integration (Blau, 1960), or to whatever shows up on some global observational measure like Sherif and Sherif's (1969) "effective initiative" or a global question such as "who are your most valued members?" or "who would you select to represent this group at a conference?" All of these are presumably valid measures of some of the kinds of things referred to as "status," but there is no evidence that behavior permitted to or forbidden people who score high on one measure applies to someone who scores high on another. Although most of these conceptions of status are represented in studies cited below, I am not aware of a single study which attempted to compare reactions to the deviance of people who scored high on different measures of status. Perhaps this is only another way of saying that our research on status and deviance is not systematic and tends not to represent attempts to formulate and test theories about status. Rather, the theoretical discussion sections of most of the studies cited below appear to be plausible justifications of hunches about the circumstances under which a high-status deviant will elicit a certain kind of reaction rather than strict derivations from any kind of theory.

Whether we choose to study status one dimension at a time or to use a global measure, we will ultimately have to start studying complex variables (group characteristics) such as status congruence, consensus on status, and the distances between ranks as suggested by Videbeck (1964). We must go beyond oversimplified problem formulations which ask only if high status (nature unspecified) always (or ever) protects one from sanctions.

The typical approach to status manipulation is to utilize extreme dimensions of competence or socioeconomic status or academic rank—that is, highly competent versus incompetent, professor versus department store clerk, graduate student versus freshman, and so on. Although these extreme differences may be necessary for a strong manipulation, they neglect an important consideration. People at both extremes may be treated quite differently from the way anyone in the middle ranks is treated.

Responses may follow a curvilinear pattern. Furthermore, even close to the extremes, people may be responded to differently: Leading members may not receive the same response as *the leader* who has not only high status but a role which may have to be taken into account in understanding reactions to his deviance (see Hollander, 1964). The leader, for example, is expected to innovate even if it means disregarding certain norms. A high-status nonleader's innovation may be responded to with "who asked you?"

The issue of roles and status enters into consideration in another way. We have tended to utilize a somewhat simple model of status in our research and assumed that what one high-status person will be permitted or forbidden to do will be also permitted or forbidden to every other person of equally high status. This may not be so. For example, a task leader and a social-emotional leader may be equally valued, but each may find himself with freedom or restraints on deviation in quite different realms of behavior (Wahrman, 1970b). This may appear obvious and trivial, but it bears on an important point in interpreting research findings: Groups *may* be misperceiving or inventing excuses or good motives by which they excuse a high-status person for violating a norm which is applicable to all members *or* it may be that it was never intended or expected that a certain norm be applicable to that particular actor (see Sampson, 1963).

◈ Norms

If the nature of "status" is something on which there is low consensus, "norms" are no less confusing (see Gibbs, 1965, 1968).

Norms may be thought of as a range of permitted behaviors (Jackson, 1965; Sherif & Sherif, 1969) or as a single permissible behavior. They may be seen as matters of high consensus, or amount of consensus may be thought of as a contingent attribute of norms rather than part of their definition (Gibbs, 1965, 1968). Research on status and deviance has tended to utilize the single-behavior model, and laboratory studies have attempted to find behaviors on which virtually all subjects could be expected to agree. As was suggested for status earlier, research should consider amounts of consensus on norms and other qualities of norms as variables. One can see in descriptions of status manipulations some understanding that there may be different types of status: The conceptions are more or less standard distinctions and dichotomies—e.g., liking versus working, respect versus affection. In the study of norms, there are no commonly accepted classifications or typologies. Procedures for scaling norms in terms of relevance or importance, such as that of Mudd (1968), or for tapping dimensions, such as those suggested by Jackson (1965), have not been introduced into the study of status and deviance in the laboratory or outside. This makes it difficult to specify the types of norms to which the study is an attempt to generalize.

Again, this may be considered a reflection of the unsystematic nature of research on status and deviance. Although, as noted, we have never had a high degree of consensus on which phenomena to reserve the concept "norm" for, one difference between the way social psychologists and sociologists tend to use the word involves the issue of "sharedness." Homans (1961), Newcomb et al. (1965), and others have argued that what makes a norm different from any old garden-variety belief about appropriate behavior held by a given individual is that they would reserve the term for a belief which a certain number of members of a group share, are aware they share, and believe they have a right to demand that other people abide by. Homans (1961) further suggests that a norm effectively exists when the people who believe in it can effectively apply sanctions more or less freely; i.e., others who are not particularly committed to the norm will permit those who do care to enforce it.

Studies in which a deviant performs in the presence of more than one subject are unusual (Sampson & Brandon, 1964; Alvarez, 1968; Sabath, 1964; Harari & McDavid, 1969). This is unfortunate, not only because knowledge that other people share a belief about proper behavior gives norms their character, but also because the response to a deviant may not be a simple function of individual reactions but may be the result of a *collective* interpretation of what the act represents, and some people's opinions may carry more weight than the opinions of others. Studying individual responses has its advantages, but the question of who stands up to tell the deviant to stop doing whatever he is doing, or of what happens if the lower-status members disapprove while the high-status members back the alleged deviant, and other questions about social control as a dynamic process are ignored if we limit ourselves to considering individual responses to an esteem questionnaire as the sole dependent variable. The aforementioned studies, which have utilized group situations, have presumably produced overt responses in other subjects; i.e., the other subjects must have glared, questioned the deviant, or asked him to stop whatever it was that he was programmed to do, but with the exception of Sampson and Brandon's Interaction Process Analysis (Bales, 1950), this dialogue remains unreported and unacknowledged.

With one exception (Hollander, 1961), no study has attempted to use the same stimulus person to study more than one norm. Hollander asked each of his subjects to imagine a hypothetical person of high or low status and then to imagine that this person had performed eight behaviors and to indicate how much they disapproved of each of these eight acts. Hollander apparently formulated no hypotheses, but he reports that several of these behaviors elicited statistically significant differences in disapproval. Although, as Doob and Gross (1968) note, the sanctions one says he would hypothetically give and what he actually does may be quite different; the hypothetical situation may be the only feasible way to compare reactions in a group to violations of different norms by the same person.

The area is still in its infancy, which perhaps explains why many researchers tend to ask their confederates to violate several norms *simultaneously*. Hollander (1960), for example, asked his confederate to violate several procedural norms. Sabath (1964) had his confederate violate several procedural and courtesy norms, and so did Alvarez. As one reads the descriptions of the manipulations, it is clear that these researchers have achieved great spontaneity and realism at the cost of replicability (see Wahrman & Pugh, 1971), as well as understanding of the norms to which subjects were responding.

Only one study in this literature has attempted to work without a confederate. Videbeck (1964) set up three-man discussion groups and instructed the members privately about the best way to perform in a discussion group, always instructing one differently from the other two. He found a positive relationship between amount of nonconformity and status assigned by others at the end of the discussion. The basis for assigning status is not described. Videbeck's study appears to me to confuse the processes involved in gaining status with those involved in maintaining status (Hollander, 1960). This is the only study in this literature that has considered consensus on norms and consensus on status as variables.

Thibaut and Riecken (1955) had two confederates, one of high status and one of low status, simultaneously first refuse to share certain materials with the subject and then simultaneously agree to share these materials. Thibaut and Riecken then asked subjects for their interpretations of the sudden generosity of each confederate. They did not ask about subject interpretations of the confederates' selfishness. This is the only study that exposed subjects to high- and low-status people simultaneously violating the same norm.

◈ Sanctions

"Sanctions" are no less fuzzy a concept than "norms" and "status." Gibbs (1966) points out that we cannot seem to agree on such basic issues as whether a sanction must be a response to deviance that is intended to punish the deviant or whether it must be intended to prevent future occurrences of the behavior, whether it must be perceived by the deviant or it must merely be the sort of internal response that would distress the deviant if he were aware of it.

At least, among the researchers cited here, there seems to be consensus that some measure of loss of esteem is a minimal if not completely adequate measure of sanctioning.

Nonetheless, there is some question of what responses should be considered sanctions. For example, Sampson and Brandon (1964) had a liberal confederate take a somewhat reactionary position on the appropriate treatment for a Negro delinquent. Although, on sociometric measures, the confederate appeared not to suffer a loss of esteem, during the discussion significantly more questions and hostile comments were directed to her than to a bigot who scored low on the esteem measures. Should Sampson and Brandon have considered the questions and hostility to be sanctions, as does Israel (1956)?

Hollander (1960) found that a confederate who was highly competent but who violated procedural norms early in the course of a meeting temporarily lost influence over the group's decisions. A confederate who waited until later in the session to violate these norms did not suffer such influence loss. Shall we assume that this patient deviant did not suffer a loss of esteem (Hollander did not ask esteem questions), or shall we go along with Hollander and argue that the only relevant sanction is the one he chose to utilize—actual loss of influence? Doob and Gross (1968) had confederates in either new, expensive cars or old, inexpensive cars remain at traffic lights after the signals had changed. People blocked by the old car honked their horns sooner and more frequently. Is it possible that the new car owner was cursed more vehemently in the privacy of the honkers' cars (male students in a classroom situation claimed they would have honked faster at the newer car than the field data indicated they probably would have)? Or does it not matter? Harari and McDavid (1969) suborned high- and low-status classroom and club members, had the children in class steal money from the teacher's desk, and had the club members break the club leader's tape recorder. When interrogated in the presence of another child (witness), peers turned in high-status children. When interrogated alone, peers did not turn them in. Low-status children were turned in whether the "fink" was interrogated alone or in the presence of another. Shall we say that if the child was not turned in he was not therefore sanctioned—e.g., peers did not lose respect for him? Or shall we say that if others did not blow the whistle on him he was unsanctioned? This is the only study of status and deviance I am aware of which utilized an actual group member as a confederate rather than using a trained confederate.

Evan and Zelditch (1961) found, in the simulated organization they set up, subjects privately disobeyed an incompetent supervisor and ignored his instructions. Shall we say that because there was no overt defiance, the supervisor is unsanctioned?

The answers to these questions depend on how one chooses to utilize the term *sanction.* In the case of sanctions, perhaps more than in the case of norms and status, the question represents more than semantic quibbling. Although the majority of studies cited here have been limited to studying individual responses on various paper-and-pencil esteem measures, in the world outside the laboratory, overt responses are important cues for letting other group members know whether the norm is still in effect for the deviant or for other members of the group.

One can possibly make equally valid arguments for the relative importance of covert or overt responses, but if the reader decides to limit his consideration only to studies of overt sanctions, he remains with a quite tiny experimental literature using quite nonequivalent sanctions. On what scale does one equate, let us say, "finking" to the teacher with horn-honking, or refusal to follow a deviant across the street against the light (Lefkowitz et al., 1955), particularly in terms of other possible overt responses within those experimental situations. Mudd (1968) is the only one I am aware of who attempts to scale overt behaviors and sanctions, but this technique has not been used in the context of status, deviance, and sanctions.

As noted earlier, some theorists have interpreted an absence of overt sanctions to mean that the group must have been intimidated by high-status people into withholding sanctions that would otherwise have been applied. The vast majority of the studies cited here appear to lend little support to this interpretation. Most of them find that the high-status person's behavior is interpreted quite generously. Certainly there are occasions when high-status people are perceived as deviant and do intimidate the group into withholding sanctions.

This body of literature is not helpful in understanding such situations, not only because subjects did not appear to disapprove of the high-status confederate, but because, even if they had disapproved, the situations were not structured in such a way as to enable them to actually react overtly to the deviant.

The few studies that do provide evidence of greater disapproval of the high-status deviant also restrict the sorts of responses subjects could make.

Iverson's (1964) subjects disapproved of a high-status person who was self-punitive but who praised his audience. Subjects were aware that they were rating a tape-recorded person and could only react by means of a rating scale.

Alvarez's (1968) subjects apparently withdrew esteem (4-point scales multiplied by 100 and presented without statistical tests are not strong evidence) from a high-status deviant, but nothing is reported about subject reactions in any of the four 1-hour meetings at which the deviant insulted subjects and violated rules of procedure.

Hollander's (1961) subjects would hypothetically have disapproved of certain behavior if the actor was of high status, but he does not explore what they would hypothetically have done about it.

Harari and McDavid's students presumably disapproved of the confederate's theft or vandalism. Since the researchers were not observing the act, but only the later willingness to identify the culprit, there is not much they can say about subject responses.

Thibaut and Riecken (1955) found that some of their subjects, not the majority, disapproved more of a high-status confederate who refused to share certain materials, but the subjects were in no position to do much about it. Wahrman's (1970b) subjects were more severe in their criticism of a high-status deviant, but again were not in a position to do anything about it.

Evan and Zelditch (1961) ran subjects individually, and although subjects were apparently willing to sanction by disobedience the confederate's violation of the normative expectation that supervisors ought to be competent, subjects were alone, and perhaps the absence of social support made it less likely than otherwise that they would openly rebel.

Apparently, we have not selected sufficiently strong manipulations to produce laboratory answers to such problems as the circumstances under which high-status deviance will both be disapproved and acted upon. Keeping subjects isolated from one another makes it easier to study individual responses uncontaminated by interaction with others, but it may, where subjects disapprove of the high-status deviant, underestimate the severity of responses which subjects in interaction would have produced.

◈ Explanations of Extreme Responses to High-Status Deviants

Many studies of criminal justice, anecdotes, field studies, and experiments back up the proposition that high status frequently enables the possessor to receive minimal or no sanctions for acts that would be harshly dealt with if the perpetrator were of middle or low rank.

Much less evidence exists for the proposition that penalties for certain acts of deviance may be more severe for those of high status than for those of lesser rank—e.g., indulgence of upper-rank behavior has limits.

Little attempt has been made to explain both kinds of response in the same theory (compare Hollander & Willis, 1967; Wahrman, 1967, 1970a, 1970b). Rather, many explanations have been offered for the mild response, and the more severe response has been barely acknowledged.

Mild Response

Let us first consider explanations of why high status often gives license to misbehave. As noted earlier, there are two schools of thought on this issue. Sociologists have tended to consider the prospect that power and status often go together. They suggest that the group may well perceive the act as equally deviant regardless of whether the actor has high or low status, but because group members of lesser rank may be intimidated by those of high rank, they do not act on their perceptions.

Psychologists have tended to ignore the prospect of power-blocking sanctions and have provided a good deal of evidence that the behavior is perceived differently when an actor has high status. The actor's power

is irrelevant if others see nothing wrong in his behavior. The experiments cited above have tended to provide support for this approach, although, as noted earlier, those instances where there was greater disapproval of the high-status deviant have not offered subjects much opportunity to express this to the deviant.

If one accepts for the moment the proposition that most of the time high-status nonconformity is not perceived as inappropriate and leaves for future research the question of what happens if and when it is, one still has the problem of explaining why this should be so. What *do* the subjects perceive? Why does what strikes the outside observer as deviance not strike the members this way?

The studies have offered a variety of explanations of what subjects might have perceived and why this should have been so. With very few exceptions (e.g., Iverson, 1964; Pepitone, 1958), the researchers *assumed* that certain thoughts were occurring to their subjects but neglected to ask for confirmation. Iverson (1964) reports that some of his subjects saw, in extrapunitive behavior by an expert on retardation, missionary zeal and concern for his fellow man, whereas they saw in identical behavior exhibited by a speaker described as a high school student, "impudence."

Pepitone (1958) reports that his subjects found justifications for the rudeness of a renowned expert toward an ignorant student. Hollander (1960) reports that when his competent confederate delayed his procedural nonconformity several groups changed the norms and followed his example. Thibaut and Riecken (1955) had low- and high-status deviants first simultaneously refuse and then simultaneously agree to share certain materials. They report no subject explanations for the original selfish acts. Asking subjects any kind of question about how they justified the deviance is clearly the exception rather than the rule.

There are a number of theories which can be offered to explain why an act is not perceived as deviant. The various consistency theories can be and have been offered as explanations for why it is uncomfortable to perceive "good" people as guilty of "bad" acts, though the various theories do not appear to be sufficiently developed to explain why one deviant act results in a complete change in the norm for all, another results in an excuse being made for the actor but the norm being retained, still another ends up with the norm's range being broadened for the deviant but no one else, while still another deviant act is denied to have occurred to begin with.

Berkowitz and Goranson (1964), Kelman and Eagly (1965), and Manis (1961) provide evidence that the act may be "assimilated" to fit the norm. Exchange theory can be invoked (Wahrman, 1970a) to explain why groups would prefer not to admit deviance is possible in people who have been granted status in exchange for conformity; i.e., this is to admit that they have foolishly given status to an unworthy person. Sherif and Hovland's (1961) conception of "latitudes of acceptance" may be invoked to suggest that the range of permissible behaviors can be widened to incorporate behavior previously not within the latitude of acceptance. One can argue for a primacy effect, earlier good behavior being weighted more heavily in judgments than more recent deviant behavior (Hendrick & Constantini, 1970; Petronko & Perin, 1970).

Asch's (1946) theory can be invoked to explain why the act has a different meaning if performed by different actors. It strikes me that what I am doing here is changing vocabularies rather than explaining anything. Nor has anyone attempted to test the utility of one of these perceptual explanations against another. Certainly there is a difference between attributing benevolent motives to the nonconformer and retaining the norm and changing the norm for the actor or for the whole group, but we do not know how these differences occur. It may help to ask subjects to explain their responses instead of inferring what they must have believed or perceived.

Hollander (1958) and Homans (1961) have both suggested "bank account" models of status from which group members draw for deviance. Homans implies that although a given act costs everyone the same number of units, those of high status have more to spare and therefore may retain their standing as the highest-ranked members even if they violate some norms.

Hollander suggests that the price of deviance is lower for those of high status; they lose fewer units per act of deviance than would lesser members and therefore suffer only mild drops in status for deviance.

Hollander's idea of sanctions is unclear. He suggests that one uses up "idiosyncrasy credits" by violating norms, but that, if one does not use up his credits, there will be no sanctions. In other portions of his theory, he suggests that one *needs* these credits to innovate. Unless I seriously misunderstand Hollander, losing these credits is in itself a sanction if it inhibits the actors' freedom to innovate at a later date.

In any case, neither Homans nor Hollander nor anyone else can supply us with acceptable measures of what such units or credits might be. How these units get translated into various interpretations of behavior is not yet known. The question of what happens when one has lost sufficient units so that the person who had been next ranking is suddenly one's superior remains to be explored.

Severe Response

The question of why and when—despite the aforementioned tendencies toward consistency, assimilation, benevolent motive attribution, and the like—groups not only decide the high-status people are deviant but are also worthy of more severe penalties than lesser deviants would have received remains unclear and unexplored. It is not clear whether the deviance is seen as *more* deviant and therefore worthy of more severe penalties or it is seen as equally deviant but, for some unclear reason, more severe penalties are applied.

Wahrman (1970b) found evidence that subjects found a psychology graduate who insisted on giving strict discipline to a delinquent (who clearly required warmth) a good deal more disturbing than they did a graduate biologist or undergraduate psychology major who espoused the same position.

Wiggins et al. (1965) found that a highly competent confederate whose violation of the experimenter's procedural rules resulted in the experimenter's penalizing the group severely was sanctioned more severely than a confederate of moderate competence who provoked the experimenter into equally harsh treatment of the group.

Walster et al. (1966); Rokeach and Rothman (1965); and Wyer (1970) also supply evidence of overreaction to those of high status.

This phenomenon may result from a calculation of what it takes to make a high-status deviant feel sanctioned—a one-dollar fine means less to a wealthy man than to a pauper—or may involve some less calculated process. Hollander and Willis (1967) suggest that high-status people are seen as more in control of their own behavior and therefore their deviance represents greater willfulness on their part. Perhaps, as Wahrman (1970a) suggests, extreme penalties should be thought of as a response to an exchange agreement which high-status people are seen as having betrayed. The excess esteem withdrawn is the psychological equivalent of interest; i.e., a penalty for betrayal is added to the normal penalty for deviance.

It may be that, as Sampson (1963) and Turner (1962) suggest, we cannot interact with people effectively unless we know how to anticipate their behavior, and it may be more important for people in important roles to live up to their expectations than those of less value to the group. The annoyance produced by deviance would, if this approach is correct, be less disturbing than the fact of unpredictability. The confusion surrounding interpretation of how to respond to the actor in the future would be more responsible for the severe penalties than the deviance itself.

Although one could invent other explanations in addition to these, we have not yet been in a position to test the explanations we already possess.

◆ Conclusions

We have reason to believe that high status tends to protect the possessors from sanctions. On those occasions when it does not protect them, it tends to make them more vulnerable than lesser members of the group would be. It is, apparently, rare for the same sanctions to be applied to high-status people as are applied to those of moderate or low status.

Future research will have to systematically vary types of status and types of norms. The available literature has tended to rely on individual responses to rating scales and has ignored both the process by which groups reach consensus on how to interpret the behavior and consensus on what overt responses to make to deviance.

Research on status and deviance has drawn on the vocabularies of a number of theories but has not been strictly derived from theory. There is need for theories which will clearly predict not only whether sanctions will be stronger or milder for those of high status but also which of a variety of mild or strong outcomes will occur.

◆ References

Bales, R. F. (1970) Personality and Interpersonal Behavior. New York: Holt, Rinehart & Winston.

——. (1955) "How people interact in conferences." Scientific Amer. 192, 3: 31–35.

——. (1954) "In conference." Harvard Business Rev. 32: 44–50.

——. (1953) "The equilibrium problem in small groups," pp. 111–161 in T. Parsons et al., Working Papers in Theory of Action. New York: Free Press.

——. (1952) "Some uniformities of behavior in small social systems," pp. 146–159 in G. E. Swanson et al. (eds.) Readings in Social Psychology. New York: Holt.

——. (1950) Interaction Process Analysis: A Method for the Study of Small Groups. Reading, Mass.: Addison-Wesley.

Bales, F. F. and A. P. Hare (1965) "Diagnostic use of interaction profile." J. of Social Psychology 67 (December): 239–258.

Bales, R. F. and F. L. Strodtbeck (1951) "Phases in group problem solving." J. of Abnormal Social Psychology 46: 485–495.

Bennis, W. G. and H. A. Shepard (1956) "A theory of group development." Human Relations 9: 415–437.

Bion, W. R. (1961) Experience in Groups: and Other Papers. New York: Basic Books.

Borgatt, A. E. F. (1963) "A new systematic interaction observation system: behavior cores system (BSS system)." J. of Psych. Studies 14: 24–44.

——. (1962) "A systematic study of interaction process scores, peer and self assessments, personality, and other variables." Genetic Psychology Monographs 65: 219–291.

Borgatt, A. E. F. and R. F. Bales (1953) "Task and accumulation of experience as factors in the interaction of small groups." Sociometry 16: 239–252.

Carter, L. F. (1954) "Recording and evaluating the performance of individuals as members of small groups." Personnel Psychology 7: 477–484.

Couch, A. S. (1960) "Psychological determinants of interpersonal behavior. Ph.D. dissertation. Harvard University.

Coyle, G. L. (1930) Social Process in Organized Groups. New York: Smith.

Dewey, J. (1933) How We Think. Lexington, Mass.: D. C. Heath.

Dunphy, D. C. (1964) "Social change in self-analytic groups." Ph.D. dissertation. Harvard University.

Effrat, A. (1968) "Editor's introduction." Soc. Inquiry 38 (Spring): 97–104.

Freud, S. (1949) Group Psychology and the Analysis of the Ego. New York: Liveright.

Hare, A. P. (1969) "Four dimensions of interpersonal behavior." (unpublished)

———. (1968) "Phases in the development of the Bicol Development Planning Board," in S. Wells and A. P. Hare (eds.) Studies in Regional Development. New York: Bicol Development Planning Board.

Hare, A. P., and A. Effrat (1969) "Content and process of interaction in Lord of the Flies." (unpublished)

Hare, A. P., N. Waxler, G. Saslow, and J. D. Matarazzo (1960) "Interaction process in a standardized initial psychiatric interview." J. of Consulting Psychology 24: 193.

Heinicke, C. and R. F. Bales (1953) "Developmental trends in the structure of small groups." Sociometry 16: 7–38.

Horsfall, A. B, and C. M. Arens Berg (1949) "Teamwork and productivity in a shoe factory." Human Organization 8, 1: 13–25.

Landsberger, H. A. (1955) "Interaction process analysis of the mediation of labor-management disputes." J. of Abnormal Social Psychology 51: 552–558.

Lanzetta, J. T., G. R. Wendt, P. Langham, and D. Haefner (1956) "The effects of an 'anxiety-reducing' medication on group behavior under threat." J. of Abnormal Social Psychology 52: 103–108.

Leary, T. (1957) Interpersonal Diagnosis of Personality. New York: Ronald.

Lennard, H. and A. Bernstein with H. C. Hendln and E. B. Palmore (1967) The Anatomy of Psychotherapy: Systems of Communication and Expectation. New York: Columbia Univ. Press.

Mann, R. D. (1967) Interpersonal Styles and Group Development. New York: John Wiley.

Matarazzo, J. D., G. Saslow, R. Matarazzo, and J. S. Phillips (1957) "Stability and modifiability of personality patterns during standardized interviews," in P. A. Hoch and J. Zubin (eds.) Psychopathology of Communication. New York: Grune & Stratton.

Mills, T. M. (1964) Group Transformation: An Analysis of a Learning Group. Englewood Cliffs, N.J.: Prentice-Hall.

Parsons, T. (1961) Article, pp. 30–79 in T. Parsons et al. (eds.) Theories of Society. New York: Free Press.

Parsons, T., et al. (1953) Working Papers in the Theory of Action. New York: Free Press.

Plank, R. (1951) "An analysis of a group therapy experiment." Human Organization 10, 3: 5–21; 4: 26–36.

Psathas, G. (1960) "Phase movement and equilibrium tendencies in interaction process in psychotherapy groups." Sociometry 23: 177–194.

Schutz, W. C. (1958) FIRO: A Three-Dimensional Theory of Interpersonal Behavior. New York: Holt.

———. (1955) "What makes groups productive?" Human Relations 8: 429–465.

Slater, P. E. (1966) Microcosm: Structural, Psychological, and Religious Evolution in Groups. New York: John Wiley.

Stock, D. and H. A. Thelen (1958) Emotional Dynamics and Group Culture: Experimental Studies of Individual and Group Behavior. New York: New York Univ. Press.

Stone, P. J., D. C. Dunphy, M. S. Smith, and D. M. Ogilvie (1966) The General Inquirer: A Computer Approach to Content Analysis. Cambridge, Mass.: MIT Press.

Talland, G. A. (1955) "Task and interaction process: some characteristics of therapeutic group discussion." J. of Abnormal Social Psychology 50: 105–109.

Theodorson, G. A. (1953) "Elements in the progressive development of small groups." Social Forces 31: 311–320.

Tuckman, B. W. (1965) "Developmental sequence in small groups." Psych. Bull. 63 (June); 384–399.

Van Zelst, R. H. (1952) "An interpersonal relations technique for industry." Personnel 29: 68–76.

READING 3

Ross examines the student loan and college tuition crisis in the United States, looking at both the transfer of fiscal responsibility for the funding of college from the state to individuals and the impact this shift has on the educational system and students who are left holding the bill. There are plenty of opportunities in this short piece to use one's sociological imagination to examine the impact of a changing economic system and philosophy on the students of today as well as the existence of deviance at both the state and individual level.

Source: Ross, A. (2012). Anti-social debts. *Contexts, 11*(4), 28–32.

Anti-Social Debts

Andrew Ross

Government is fast exiting the business of funding higher education. At state universities, tuition costs have risen by 500 percent since 1985, and the price gap between leading public institutions and private colleges is narrowing sharply. Lawmakers in Washington and state capitols across the nation are compelling student users—the would-be beneficiaries—to finance their education privately. And the federal government is committed to lend monies, at unjustifiable rates of interest, to facilitate that end, leading to a student debt crisis that has become impossible to ignore.

In the public mind, the "privatization of education" encompasses university–industry partnerships, intellectual property licensing agreements, corporate sponsorship of research, or "contract education"—whereby a firm will pay a community college to up-skill its trainees. But the quintessential act of education privatization is to shift responsibility for funding onto individuals.

This transfer of fiscal responsibility from the state has been proceeding for more than three decades. Even in the immediate pre-recessionary years, when debt was still considered a worthy asset and employment a plausible prospect, it was easy to predict that mounting levels of student debt were unsustainable over time. Today, in the face of chronic underemployment, we can safely conclude that a large portion of the 1 trillion dollars currently owed by debtors is unpayable in their lifetimes. Two-thirds of U.S. students graduate with loan debt, averaging $27,000, and then rapidly fall behind in their payments—41 percent of the class of 2005 is either delinquent or in default.

Increasingly, student debt is a topic of discussion at family dinner tables and even in the halls of Congress. Thanks in large part to the great public amplifier of the Occupy movement, this year's presidential contenders have been forced to embrace student loan reform as a talking point in their respective campaigns. But as student debt becomes the primary source of funding for American colleges and universities, it threatens the democratic ideal of a freethinking citizenry.

◈ How the Profits Flow

Universities are one of the few places where neoliberalism—the economic program of deregulation, financialization, and free enterprise that used to be known as the Washington Consensus—has not missed a beat since its death was prematurely declared. In 2010, the federal government disbanded the old Federal Family Education Loan Program (FFELP) lending system. FFELP had been an extremely lucrative program for private banks, which were subsidized for issuing government-guaranteed loans. As part of this reorganization, all federal loans now originate with the government, though service fees for administering the loans are still designated to Sallie Mae, Nelnet, and other industry giants. In taking this step, the federal government put its official stamp on the neoliberal funding formula that is now normative in U.S. higher education.

Today, at a time when lending rates are at a historic low, federal loans are offered at rates (3.4 percent for subsidized, and 6.8 percent for unsubsidized Stafford loans, and 7.9 percent for PLUS loans for parents) that far exceed those at which the government borrows money. The profits are extravagant: 120 percent of every defaulted loan is recovered. In the private sector, they are even higher. While banks now only issue 20 percent of all student loans, the rate of increase in loan issuance is greater than for federal loans, and so private lending is expected to surpass the government sector in 10 to 15 years.

Unlike almost every other kind of debt, student loans are non-dischargeable through bankruptcy, and, over time, collection agencies have been granted extraordinary powers to extract payments, including the right to garnish wages, tax returns, and social security. It's no wonder that student loans are among the most lucrative sectors of the financial industry. Nor is it any surprise to find a thriving market in securitized loans (almost a quarter—$234.2 billion—of the aggregate $1 trillion debt) known as SLABS (Student Loans Asset-Backed Securities). Given the predatory nature of student lending, many commentators have compared SLABS to the subprime mortgage securitization racket that inflated the housing bubble and triggered the financial crash. Since SLABS are often bundled with other kinds of loans and traded on secondary debt markets, investors are not only speculating on the risk status of student loans, but also profiting from resale of the loans though collateralized derivatives. In the meantime, creditors stand to profit most from defaults, when additional fees and penalties kick in, and so they often seek out high-risk borrowers just as subprime lenders did during the housing bubble.

This is not the only way debt-based profit is mined from the daily business of higher education. As low-income families get priced out of public colleges, they are pushed into the for-profit system, whose mercurial rise has been fueled by the ready availability of federal loans. For families with a multigenerational experience of college, the staggering array of higher education choices can be confusing. But first-generation students, with limited access to information about their choices, are especially easy prey for the "admissions counselors" of for-profit colleges that act as a conduit for the lending industry.

In the for-profit sector, 95 percent of students graduate with debt (versus 58 percent of students at all institutions), and graduation rates, already low, are falling. While the largest proportion of student debt is racked up by students from middle-income families seeking a private university degree, the overall impact of debt is magnified among low-income families. African Americans, among all racialized groups, graduate with the highest debt on average, and those in Deep South states, where community colleges do not participate in the federal loan system, are most disadvantaged of all.

 Indenture or Investment?

With wealth now diverted more exclusively to the 1 percent (bypassing the top quintile to which most college graduates aspire), the belief that education debt is a smart investment in a high-income future has eroded. Should we, instead, compare student debt to a form of indenture? The analogy has served as a useful provocation. In a knowledge economy, where a college degree is considered a passport to a decent livelihood, workforce entrants must go into debt in return for the right to labor. This kind of contract is the essence of indenture. Moreover, for the traditionally indentured, employment has usually been guaranteed or is readily available, and the bonds are paid off in a relatively timely manner. By contrast, student debt can endure for decades, and employment prospects are more and more precarious. A damaged credit score—triggered by two delayed payments—will generate additional obstacles to finding employment, since many employers consult the student debt payment schedules of applicants to gauge their reliability. The emerging pattern for those who want to preserve their credit record is to put their preferred career paths on hold for several years, and therefore risk abandoning them, until they have paid off their loans through employment options that are much less desirable. Ironically, the quickest pathway toward discharging debts is to find work in the finance industry, issuing loans, or speculating on derivatives. For those caught in the limbo of more precarious labor, the burden of finding the means to pay off student debt may drastically reduce the choices traditionally available to the college-educated workforce. The outcome is a nightmare to national economic managers struggling to keep the standard elements of the American Dream in place—homeownership, family formation, upwardly mobile consumer behavior.

Practically speaking, no reform program of any substance is on the legislative horizon, least of all one that would regulate the predatory lending practices of Wall Street banks. Congressional members have proposed the Student Loan Forgiveness Act (H.R. 4170)—which allows for loan forgiveness after 10 years of appropriate debt service—and the Private Student Bankruptcy Fairness Act (H.R. 2028)—which seeks to restore the ability to discharge private student loans through bankruptcy. But these bills have no chance of passing in their current form.

The debt relief being pushed by the Obama administration this year is a token gesture, aimed at getting some traction on the youth vote—especially the more disillusioned or alienated student constituencies. GOP interest in blocking any Obama competitive advantage ensured that, in June, the House approved a bill extending the temporary lower rate (3.4 percent) on subsidized Stafford loans for another year. Hailed as a major victory in the Obama camp, the relief amounted to a mere $9 in savings per month for a handful of borrowers. At the same time, and with much less public attention, graduate students lost the federal subsidy by which the government paid the interest accrued on subsidized loans while in school and for six months after graduation.

Nor should we expect enlightened responses from university leaders, for whom debt-financed education has lavishly serviced their own bank accounts. The salaries of senior administrators have risen in tandem with tuition costs and student debt. Faculty have established their own wall of denial around the issue, which may take some time to breach. Since their salaries have been stagnant or rising at rates below the cost of living increases, they (quite rightly) don't feel responsible for skyrocketing college costs. Nor are they keen to inflame public sentiment that may further destabilize the fragile state of their profession.

Student debtors have begun to break the silence. At Occupy locations around the country, those confronting chronic underemployment while being saddled with crushing debt burdens offered eloquent testimony. Tumblr and other websites swelled with the stories of students who felt too constrained by guilt to stand up in the face-to-face agora of Occupy. The act of casting aside the shame and humiliation that accompanies debt, especially for those aspiring to join the middle class, was an important kind of "coming out" for student debtors. It seemed to herald a decisive political moment, and may now be blossoming into a movement all of its own (see www.strikedebt.org). The alternative—suffering the consequences of debt and default in private—is a thinly documented trail of tears, leading to depression, divorce, and suicide in ever increasing numbers.

Analysts who have investigated Occupy's claims about the 1 percent have concluded that, of all the factors responsible for the upward redistribution of wealth, financial manipulation of debt ranks very high. But the imposition of debt is not just a mode of wealth accumulation, it is also a form of social control, with acute political consequences.

This was most notable in the case of the International Monetary Fund (IMF) "debt trap" visited upon so many postcolonial countries as part of Cold War client diplomacy. In the global North, debt has been institutionalized for so long as a "good" consumer asset that we forget how homeownership was promoted as an explicitly anti-socialist policy in the United States in the 1920s. Subsequently, the long-term mortgage loan became the basis of anti-communist citizenship; William Levitt, the master merchant builder, pronounced that "no man can be a homeowner and a Communist." In the postwar decades, the threat of a ruined credit score effectively limited the political agility of our "nation of homeowners."

Can the same be said of student debt? Protest is no longer a rite of passage for students. The rising debt burden has played no small part in stifling the optional political imagination of students in the decades since the 1960s. Now typically saddled with debts on day one of college, they are obliged to seek out low-paying jobs to stave off further debt; they are compelled to think of their degree as a bargain for which their future wages have been traded. These are not conditions under which a free critical mind is likely to be cultivated. This is one of the reasons why student debt abolition might be more effectively approached as the target of a political movement than one aimed at limited economic reforms.

◈ Real Debt Relief

Most of the initiatives that have sprung up in response to the student debt crisis are aimed at limited economic reforms, such as restoring bankruptcy provisions and other protections that are enjoyed by consumer debtors.

But paying for education is not like buying a flat-screen TV, and student loans should not be packaged in the same way.

Real change will alter the customary neoliberal practice of treating public goods, like education, as a profit center. The long list of developed and developing countries—none of them as affluent as the United States—which provide free public education demonstrate how different national priorities are elsewhere. The United States is an outlier in this regard, and efforts to export the pay-per model have met with strong student resistance, most recently, in Chile, England, and Quebec. In response to efforts by states to pay off their sovereign debt by slashing education budgets, the European student resistance crystallized around the slogan, "We Won't Pay for Your Crisis." In college towns across the United States, the red square, symbol of the Quebec movement (*carrement dans le rouge*), recently became the summer clothing accessory of choice.

Debt relief is sorely needed, and a write-off of all current student debt would be a noble, and appropriate, contribution to the jubilee tradition, whereby elites periodically forgive unsustainable debt burdens. But this single corrective act by itself won't alter the formula for the debt financing of education. An affordable education system needs to be reestablished.

As part of our Occupy Student Debt Campaign, we argued that for $70 billion a year, the federal government could, and should, cover the tuition of all students enrolled in two and four year public colleges. In the twentieth century, the decision to properly fund K–12 education was a prerequisite for a society that wanted a stable middle class. If the American middle class has any future in this century, then a decision will have to be made to extend the guarantee to tertiary education. Loans should be interest-free—no one should profit from them. So, too, private universities, which benefit from public largesse in all sorts of ways, but not least through the federal loan program, should adopt fiscal transparency. Students and their families surely have a right to know how colleges spend and allocate their tuition fees.

Top university administrators and trustees have had little to say about the rapid escalation of tuition costs over the last two decades. They seem content to weather the current storm. It is unlikely that costs will stabilize until demand falls off, and even if this were to happen nationally, the growth in overseas demand—fueled by the desire of the swelling middle class in the global South for brand-name degrees—would more than make up the deficit.

Analysts put the global growth rate at 80 percent over the next decade, and that figure may well dictate how college administrators, faced with weakening political will on the part of their state legislatures, react to budgetary dilemmas. The rush to establish online and offshore programs, and branch campuses is a tell-tale symptom of their response. There are many risks involved in such ventures, especially those hosted by authoritarian states. But the prospect of adding overseas revenue streams will continue to attract higher education's fiscal managers, driven by desperation or ambition or simply by their training in neoliberal economics.

The struggle over wages was a defining feature of the industrial era. Will the struggle over debt play a similar role in the postindustrial economy? Given the centrality of higher education to the formation of knowledge capitalism, the growing conflict around student debt seems to fit the bill. Bargaining over the outcome will take many forms. Just as industrial elites once recognized that wages had to be raised to stimulate consumer purchasing, so too, they will entertain the reduction of debt burdens to facilitate the re-entry of middle-class debtors into the circuits of big-ticket consumption.

Some are already contemplating debt strikes and other methods of debt refusal. For these tactics to gain legitimacy in the public mind, the moral ideology of honoring debts, however unjustly incurred, will need to be challenged and eroded. The track record of the finance sector before and after 2008 shows that this morality does not apply to Wall Street. Loans are no more than electronic figures on a computer screen. They are new forms of money and credit that did not exist hitherto and they are created ex nihilo for the use of the borrower. Financiers know this, and so they treat debts accordingly, as matters to be renegotiated or written off at will. Only the little people are expected to actually pay off their debts.

Recommended Resources

Collinge, Alan Michael. *The Student Loan Scam: The Most Oppressive Debt in U.S. History—and How We Can Fight Back* (Beacon, 2009). A survey of how private banks have profited lavishly from student loans.

Graeber, David. *Debt: The First 5000 Years* (Melville Press, 2011). A comprehensive, iconoclastic history of the relationship between credit, debt, and state violence.

Meister, Robert. "Debt and Taxes: Can the Financial Industry Save Public Universities? Privatization Is Now the Problem—Not the Solution," *Representations* (2000), 116: 128–155. Persuasive analysis of how the UC system relies on debt financing.

Williams, Jeffrey J. "Student Debt and the Spirit of Indenture," *Dissent* (2008), 55: 73–78. A provocative account of the analogy of student debt with indenture.

The open-access Study Study Site, available at
study.sagepub.com/inderbitzindeviance2e,
provides useful study materials including SAGE journal
articles and multimedia resources.

CHAPTER 2

The Diversity of Deviance

What would you think if you were walking down the street and passed a man covered entirely in leopard spots? It would definitely make you look twice and would qualify as a deviant appearance. Would you wonder what he was thinking, how it felt to live within those spots, and why he would choose such a visible form of body modification? Tom Leppard once held the title of the most tattooed man in the world, with 99% of his body covered in tattooed leopard spots. For more than 20 years, Leppard lived as something of a hermit in a shack with no electricity or furniture on the Scottish island of Skye. Despite his solitary lifestyle, Leppard clearly enjoyed the attention of strangers, at least to some degree. He spoke of choosing his leopard appearance and his visible status: "I've loved every minute and when you're covered in leopard tattoos you certainly get noticed— I became a bit of a tourist attraction on Skye" (Irvine, 2008).

▲ **Photo 2.1** What would you think if you were at the grocery store and ran into Tom Leppard, who has tattooed leopard spots over 99% of his body?

©Murdo McLeod/The Guardian

◈ Introduction

Now that you've been introduced to the concept of deviance and the importance of understanding deviant behavior from a theoretical perspective, we want to spend some time exploring the various forms that deviance can take. When you think about deviance, what do you typically think about? Take a moment to quickly think of five types of deviant behavior. What immediately comes to mind? You probably came up with examples that reflect criminal behavior, such as drug dealing, assault, robbery, or homicide. These are quite common responses, especially given the way the media cover crime and deviance. Yet deviance is not always criminal in nature. Nor does it always reflect an act or a behavior. There is a much broader array of what constitutes deviance in our society. In short, deviance can take many forms.

In this chapter, we discuss the diversity and relativity of deviance and explore its many manifestations in American society. It is our hope that by introducing you to deviance in its varied forms, you'll gain a deeper understanding of its nature before we move on to learning about how deviance is researched (Chapter 3), explained (Chapters 4–10), and responded to in American society (Chapters 11–12) and in a global context (Chapter 13). This chapter on the different types of deviance is a good place to begin an analysis of the sociological field of deviance and the phenomena it investigates.

A chapter on types of deviance is difficult to write because deviance as a field of study is very subjective. Many textbooks offer a survey or overview of different types of deviant behavior, devoting entire chapters to such topics as **physical deviance**, **sexual deviance**, drug use, mental disorders, and corporate deviance. As authors of this text, we do not necessarily agree with those categories or characterizations of different behaviors, attitudes, and physical attributes as deviant. Rather than writing simply from our own points of view and trying to persuade you to adopt our perspectives, however, in this chapter, we offer a glimpse into the field of deviance as it has been defined, studied, and treated throughout the years.

◈ Deviance and Its Varied Forms

While deviant behavior and crime certainly overlap, deviance encompasses much more than crime. Sociologists who have studied deviance have researched and written about a range of topics, including the disabled (Goffman, 1963), the mentally ill (Link, Phelan, Bresnahan, Stueve, & Pescosolido, 1999), the voluntarily childless (Park, 2002), the homeless (L. Anderson, Snow, & Cress, 1994), Jewish resisters during the Holocaust (Einwohner, 2003), topless dancers (Thompson, Harred, & Burks, 2003), bisexuals (Weinberg, Williams, & Pryor, 2001), anorexics and bulimics (McLorg & Taub, 1987), self-injurers (P. A. Adler & P. Adler, 2007), and gay male Christian couples (Yip, 1996), to name just a few. This research is in addition to the many studies of criminal deviance, too numerous to list here. You can get a sense of the range of deviant behavior and how it has been studied simply by exploring the contents of the academic journal that is devoted to this very topic: *Deviant Behavior*. In addition to this introductory chapter exploring the many forms of deviance, we include short summaries of recent research on different types of deviant behavior in each chapter of this book.

The diversity of deviance and how drastically norms and attitudes may change over time is attested to in research conducted by J. L. Simmons (1965), who, several decades ago, surveyed 180 individuals, asking them to "list those things or types of persons whom you regard as deviant." More than 250 different acts and persons were listed. The range of responses not only included expected items such as prostitutes, drug addicts, and murderers but also liars, Democrats, reckless drivers, atheists, the self-pitied, career women, divorcees, prudes, pacifists, and even know-it-all professors! The most frequent survey responses are listed in Table 2.1.

Imagine conducting a similar survey today. Which responses from this list might still occur with some frequency? Which might be less frequent? Whatever you imagined, there is little doubt that the list would look different today compared with 1965, reflecting the key point that what constitutes deviance changes depending on the historical context, something we discuss more later on in this chapter. For now, we want you to simply recognize the sheer range of deviance and its diversity.

It would be nearly impossible to describe deviance in *all* its varied forms. Rather than try to provide an exhaustive list of the different realms of deviance, we have chosen to highlight a few to illustrate the broad spectrum of behaviors, attitudes, and characteristics that have been deemed deviant by at least some segments of the larger society.

Table 2.1 Most Frequent Responses to the Question, "What Is Deviant?"

Response	Percentage
Homosexuals	49
Drug addicts	47
Alcoholics	46
Prostitutes	27
Murderers	22
Criminals	18
Lesbians	13
Juvenile delinquents	13
Beatniks	12
Mentally ill	12
Perverts	12
Communists	10
Atheists	10
Political extremists	10

Source: Simmons (1965).

THINKING LIKE A SOCIOLOGIST—STRICT CONFORMITY AS DEVIANCE

A student film, *55: A Meditation on the Speed Limit,* which can be viewed on YouTube (www.youtube.com/watch?v=1B-OxOZmVIU), illustrates a potential problem with strict conformity. In the 5-minute video, college students filmed an experiment where they managed to have cars in every lane of the freeway driving exactly the speed limit. This created a wall of traffic and frustrated drivers in the cars behind them, leading to visible road rage. Do you think strict conformity can also be a form of deviance? Why or why not? Can you think of other circumstances in which strict conformity might be considered deviant?

◈ Physical Deviance and Appearance: Ideals of Beauty and Everyone Else

Physical deviance is perhaps the most visible form of deviance, and it can evoke stereotypes, stigma, and discrimination. Sociologists have described two types of physical deviance: (1) violations of aesthetic norms (what people should look like, including height, weight, and the absence or presence of disfigurement) and (2) physical incapacity, which would include those with a physical disability (Goode, 2005).

Erving Goffman (1963) opens his book *Stigma* with a letter a 16-year-old girl wrote to Miss Lonelyhearts in 1962. The young girl writes about how she is a good dancer and has a nice shape and pretty clothes, but no boy will take her out. Why? Because she was born without a nose.

> I sit and look at myself all day and cry. I have a big hole in the middle of my face that scares people even myself. . . . What did I do to deserve such a terrible bad fate? Even if I did do some bad things, I didn't do any before I was a year old and I was born this way. . . . Ought I commit suicide? (reprinted in E. Goffman, 1963, first page)

As suggested by the letter to Miss Lonelyhearts, physical deviance may be viewed as a marker of other forms of deviance. In other words, passersby may notice people with numerous tattoos, heavily muscled female bodybuilders, or those with visible physical disabilities and may attribute other characteristics to those individuals. You may notice, for example, when talking to a person who is hard of hearing that others in the conversation may slow their speech considerably and use smaller words, as well as speaking louder than usual; this suggests an implicit assumption that the individual has difficulty understanding as well as hearing.

Our ideas of what is acceptable or desirable in terms of physical appearance vary widely, depending on the context. You can get a sense of this by visiting a local museum or simply flipping through an art book showing paintings and photographs of women thought to be very beautiful in their time. From the rounded curves of the women painted by Peter Paul Rubens in the 1600s (which is where the term "Rubenesque" originated to describe an hourglass figure) to the very thin flappers considered ideal in the 1920s to Marilyn Monroe in the 1950s, Twiggy in the 1960s, Cindy Crawford in the 1980s, Kate Moss in the 1990s, and Kim Kardashian in 2010, our ideals of beauty and the most desired body types clearly change and evolve over time.

Along with professionally styled hair and makeup and the use of meticulous lighting and camera angles, editors can now touch up photographs to remove wrinkles and traces of cellulite and to make beautiful models' already thin limbs and waists trimmer and more defined. This is of concern to sociologists because setting a truly unattainable standard for the ideal physical appearance can lead to deviant behavior, including harmful eating disorders, such as anorexia nervosa or bulimia, or unnecessary plastic surgeries.

Another form of physical deviance is **self-injury**—cutting, burning, branding, scratching, picking at skin or reopening wounds, biting, hair pulling, and bone breaking. Adler and Adler (2007) found that most self-injurers never seek help from mental health professionals and that most of the self-incurred wounds do not need medical attention; thus, the majority of self-injurers remain hidden within society. Why would anyone purposely hurt him- or herself? Adler and Adler explain the reasoning behind this.

> Although self-injury can be morbid and often maladaptive, our subjects overwhelmingly agree that it represents an attempt at self-help. They claim that their behaviors provide immediate but short-term release from anxiety, depersonalization, racing thoughts, and rapidly fluctuating emotions. . . . It provides a sense of control, reconfirms the presence of one's body, dulls feelings, and converts unbearable emotional pain into manageable physical pain. (p. 540)

Adler and Adler (2007) suggest that self-injury is currently being "demedicalized"—shifted out of the realm of mental illness and categorized instead as deviance, characterized by the voluntary choice of those involved. We will return to the idea of the medicalization—or demedicalization—of deviance in our discussion of the social control of deviance in Chapter 11.

Adler and Adler's argument that self-injury is now viewed as a form of personal expression was supported in a recent study of nonsuicidal women in a small, liberal arts women's college. Kokaliari and Berzoff (2008) found that 91 of the 166 participants in their survey—more than 50% of respondents—reported purposely injuring themselves, including scratching themselves, cutting, burning, self-hitting, and self-biting. The researchers conducted interviews with 10 of the college women and found that the women had been raised to be self-sufficient, independent, and in control. Emotions were often discouraged in their families. Many of the women described their use of self-injury as a "quick fix" to alleviate difficult or painful emotions and allow them to continue being productive in their daily lives.

While there are certainly other forms of physical deviance, **body modification** is the last example we will discuss. Body modification includes extreme tattooing, like Mr. Leppard from the opening story, who paid to have more than 99% of his body covered in inked leopard spots. It also includes piercings, scarification, and reconstructive and cosmetic surgery. The reasons for body modification vary, but more than 3,500 people have joined the Church of Body Modification and view their physical changes as a way to spiritually strengthen the connection between body, mind, and soul.

Individuals choose to engage in body modification, but the choice may not be respected by the larger society. In September 2010, a 14-year-old freshman girl, Ariana Iocono, was suspended from school for wearing a small stud in her nose and thus violating the school's dress code, which forbids piercings. The girl and her mother were members of the Church of Body Modification and claimed that the nose ring was a religious symbol, but school administrators were unsympathetic, arguing that Ariana had not met the criteria for a religious exemption (Netter, 2010).

DEVIANCE IN POPULAR CULTURE

A wide variety of deviance can be examined by paying careful attention to popular culture. Below are a number of documentary films and television shows that offer concrete examples of specific cultural norms, different types of deviant behavior, and how individuals cope with stigma. What messages about norms and acceptable behavior are portrayed in each of these examples? What is the deviant behavior in each film or episode? What does the reaction to the deviant behavior tell you about the larger culture?

Films

Devil's Playground (2002)—A documentary following four Amish teenagers through the experience of Rumspringa, during which they are given freedom to experience the outside world before deciding whether or not to commit to a lifetime in the Amish community.

Enron: The Smartest Guys in the Room—A documentary investigating white-collar crime and the greed that toppled what was once the seventh-largest corporate entity in the United States and left 20,000 employees without jobs.

Deliver Us From Evil (2006)—A documentary investigating sexual abuse within the Catholic Church. The focus is on Father Oliver O'Grady, a pedophile who sexually assaulted dozens of children.

Dark Days—A documentary featuring people living in the tunnels under the subway system in New York City. Filmed in black-and-white, it shows how one segment of the homeless population built homes and a community under the city.

(Continued)

(Continued)

Citizenfour—A documentary film offering an inside look at Edward Snowden's decision to hand over classified documents showing massive and illegal invasions of privacy by the National Security Agency. Viewers can decide whether Snowden is a hero or a criminal.

Food, Inc.—An investigation into the global food production system, showing that a handful of multinational corporations largely control our food supply, with a clear focus on profit rather than health.

Television

Reality television and the TLC channel, particularly, feature a number of programs offering an inside view of people perceived as deviant or different in some way and showing how these people deal with stigma from various sources. Older shows include *Hoarders*; *Little People, Big World*; and *My Five Wives*. Current shows include the following:

The Little Couple—Follows Bill Klein and Jen Arnold. The TLC website proclaims that they're "just like your average couple—except for the fact that they are both under 4 feet tall!"

My Strange Addiction—Focuses on individuals with unusual food addictions (such as eating bricks or drinking air freshener) and fantasy or celebrity addictions.

In paying attention to popular culture and how different subcultures and characteristics are portrayed, we can easily see that deviance is all around us.

◈ Relationships and Deviance

Sexually unconventional behavior is another central topic of discussion when it comes to deviance. As a society, we are generally intrigued with others' intimate relationships and sexual practices. Goode (2005, p. 230) asks, Why are there so many norms about sexual behavior? And why are the punishments for violating sexual norms so severe? Concerning the first question, Goode rightly claims the ways that we violate mainstream society's norms by engaging in variant sexual acts are almost infinite. The realm of sexual deviance may include exotic dancers, strippers, sex tourism, anonymous sex in public restrooms, bisexuality, online sexual predators, prostitutes, premarital chastity, and many others. As with virtually every kind of deviance, sexual deviance is largely determined by the community, culture, and context.

Even within the United States, there is considerable disagreement about what sexual activities should and should not be allowed. The issue of gay marriage is one current example where community values are being tested and defined on political ballots across the country. Another example where context matters is prostitution. While considered a crime in most of the country, prostitution is legal in many areas of Nevada. Certain counties in Nevada are allowed to regulate and license brothels, a multimillion-dollar industry based on legalized prostitution.

While societal norms shape our conceptions of appropriate sexual behavior, those boundaries are regularly tested by new fads and businesses and by many different **subcultures** making up their own rules as they go along. The Ashley Madison Agency, for example, bills itself as the world's premiere discreet dating service; it is marketed to those who are married and wish to have affairs. The agency's slogan captures the intent succinctly: "Life is short.

Have an affair." The Ashley Madison Agency courts publicity, advertising widely on billboards, in magazines, and on television commercials. Interested adults can go on the website and purchase the "Affair Guarantee" package; if they do not find a suitable partner within three months, they can get a refund. With more than 7 million anonymous members, it is clear that there is widespread interest in relationships outside of marriage. The need for anonymity and discretion also suggests that there is still enough stigma attached to such relationships that it is preferable to shop for a partner before identifying oneself.

This need for privacy was tested when the Ashley Madison Agency was hacked in August 2015, and an estimated 37 million users' information was breached. Some subscribers received extortion letters, demanding payment lest the blackmailers share the information with the individual's family, friends, and social networks (Ridley, 2015). At least one man, a married pastor and seminary professor, killed himself after he was identified as an Ashley Madison client (Segall, 2015). Ashley Madison's parent company expressed condolences for the pastor's death while placing the blame squarely on the hackers, releasing a statement that read: "Dr. Gibson's passing is a stark, heart-wrenching reminder that the criminal hack against our company and our customers has had very real consequences for a great many innocent people" (Segall, 2015). While the lines of exactly which behaviors one might consider deviant may be blurred in this case, it is clear that it ended in tragedy.

Polygamy is another frequently discredited form of relationship. In the United States, monogamy is the legal norm, yet some religions and subcultures still allow and encourage men to take multiple wives. The conflict between a subculture's values and the larger societal norms came vividly into play in 2008 when the State of Texas conducted a military-style raid on the Yearning for Zion Ranch, a polygamous religious sect of the Fundamentalist Church of Jesus Christ of Latter-day Saints.

Warren S. Jeffs, the leader of the Fundamentalist Church of Jesus Christ of Latter-day Saints, had been convicted a year earlier on felony charges as an accomplice to rape for his role in coercing the marriage of a 14-year-old girl to her 19-year-old cousin. When the raid on the Yearning for Zion Ranch took place, Jeffs was in the early phases of a 10-year-to-life sentence while awaiting trial on other sex charges in Arizona.

On the basis of an accusation of sexual abuse from an anonymous 16-year-old girl, SWAT teams raided the Yearning for Zion Ranch and forcibly removed more than 400 children from their homes and families. Texas child welfare officials believed that the children were in danger; they suspected young girls were being made into child brides, among other physical and sexual abuse occurring within the polygamous community.

This clash of cultures and values played out dramatically in the media. After being removed from their homes and the insular community in which they were raised, the children of the ranch were suddenly exposed to many strangers, different foods, varied styles of dress, and a new set of norms. When some of their mothers voluntarily left the ranch to be with the children, they were visibly out of their element in their prairie dresses and old-fashioned hairstyles, forced to move to the suburbs and shop at Walmart, rather than tend to their gardens and livestock on the ranch.

In the end, the telephone calls that set the raid in motion may have been a hoax or a setup, but the damage was irreparably done. The children of the Yearning for Zion Ranch were returned to their parents approximately two months later, but the trauma inflicted on the families from such a forced separation could not be

▲ **Photo 2.2** Community members from the Yearning for Zion Ranch react after the state of Texas forcibly removed more than 400 children from their homes and families.

taken back. While this was clearly a difficult situation for everyone involved, it presents sociologically interesting questions about what is deviant and who gets to decide this. Those living at the Yearning for Zion Ranch were nearly self-sufficient and seemed to live quietly by their own rules and norms within its bounds. At what point do you think it would be appropriate for the state of Texas to step in and take the children away from their families? Who should ultimately decide? Who are the deviants in this case—the polygamous families or the state of Texas for breaking up those families and traumatizing a whole community? These are interesting and complex questions without easy answers, which is part of what makes deviance such a fascinating—and ever-changing—field of study.

◈ Deviance in Cyberspace: Making Up the Norms as We Go

One way to clearly see that our ideas about deviance and deviant behavior change over time is to consider the creation of whole new categories of deviant behavior. As new technology has developed, brand-new forms of deviance have also taken shape. Cyberdeviance, for example, is a relatively new phenomenon, but it already has many different forms, including the online pedophile subculture, cyberbullying, online misbehavior of college students, sexting, and the illegal downloading of music, movies, and readings.

If such behavior is prevalent, particularly among younger people and hidden populations, should it still be considered deviant? That question is difficult to answer; norms and laws are being created and modified all the time, even as technology improves and offers new possibilities for deviant behavior. Here we offer a few examples of cyberbehavior; you can consider whether you believe such behavior is deviant or not.

Kristi Blevins and Thomas Holt (2009) conducted research into a subculture that crosses the boundaries between cyberdeviance and criminal deviance when they focused on the online subculture of "johns," or the male heterosexual clients of sex workers. Blevins and Holt (2009) explored Web forums in a number of U.S. cities in an attempt to identify the norms and values in the mostly hidden world of the client side of sex work. The authors analyzed Web forums where heterosexual johns shared questions and information while seeking to minimize exposure to law enforcement. Blevins and Holt (2009) particularly focused on the "argot," or specialized language, of the virtual subculture of johns, and they used extensive quotes to illustrate their points. Three themes related to argot emerged from their analysis. The first theme was "experience," which, among other things, categorized the johns across a hierarchy of novices or "newbies" to the more experienced "mongers, trollers, or hobbyists" (note that the derogatory term "john" was not used in the argot of the subculture). The second theme was "commodification"—the notion that the prostitutes themselves and the acts the johns wanted were a commodity that came with a cost. This issue raised a great deal of discussion over how much different prostitutes or different sexual acts were worth or likely to cost. Finally, a related theme of "sexuality," or the various sexual acts desired or experienced, was examined, along with the unique argot for a host of sexual activities. The language and subject matter are crude but offer a glimpse at the subcultural norms and values of these online communities or subcultures of johns.

Adler and Adler's study of self-injury, as described above, has also crossed into cyberspace. They explain,

> In the past, self-injurers suffered alone and in silence; today, the Internet has enabled the rise of safe subcultural spaces and helped facilitate the transformation of self-injury from a purely psychological phenomenon into something sociological. . . . In the early 2000s, the Internet offered a way for self-injurers to express hidden sides of themselves they could not share with friends or family members. . . . Isolated and stigmatized as suicidal or mentally ill, they sought to find people who might tell them that they weren't alone or crazy. (Adler and Adler, 2012, p. 60)

Adler and Adler found that the cybercommunities and Internet subcultures varied in their approach to self-injury, with some focused strictly on recovery and holding firm to "no trigger" policies and formal rules for participation, whereas other groups embraced and seemed to glorify self-injury. By the mid-2000s, most sites strove to mediate interaction without stifling communication. As Adler and Adler (2012) suggest,

> The cyber-world represents a new form of space that is both "out there" and "in here"—simultaneously public and social, while remaining private and solitary. . . . These spaces are fertile locations for the rise of virtual communities that challenge traditional notions of identity and community, and, as some suggest, radically alter our conceptions of community and the nature of our communities. (p. 61)

◈ Subcultural Deviance

The virtual subculture of johns is just one example of many subcultures that might be considered deviant by at least some segment of the population. While the johns are generally a hidden population, as you can see from the earlier example of the Yearning for Zion Ranch, some subcultures are easily identifiable and can be singled out for holding different norms and values than the larger society. That case is particularly dramatic as children were taken from their parents and homes, but many other subcultures also draw strong reactions from the outside community.

Research on subcultures has been wide-ranging. Hamm (2004) studied terrorist subcultures, examining the "complex ways in which music, literature, symbolism and style are used to construct terrorism" (p. 328). Others have written about "fat admirers," men who have a strong, erotic desire for obese women (Goode, 2008b); radical environmentalist organizations (Scarce, 2008); and the subculture of UFO contactees and abductees (Bader, 2008).

The Amish are another example of a subculture, but the question of deviance becomes quite complicated, particularly during the time when Amish youth are encouraged to go outside of the community and explore the "English" way of life. In this case, some types of deviant behavior are sanctioned for a short time before the teenagers choose their adult path and decide whether to be baptized and become an Amish adult in good standing or basically be ostracized from their parents and communities.

Reiling (2002) conducted a study on Amish youths' response to culturally prescribed deviance that presents a number of complex questions. Old Order Amish believe in nonassimilation with the dominant culture, in-group conformity, and a very disciplined lifestyle. Yet Amish teenagers are expected to engage in deviant behavior in the rite of passage known as the "simmie" period, when they explore the "English" lifestyle before choosing to either commit to their Amish culture or leave it forever. Reiling found that youth generally stayed in this decision-making period for two to three years, with 20% to 25% of youth in the settlement choosing to defect from the Amish, at which point they are excommunicated, cut off from their families, and ostracized. Even though Old Order Amish youth are encouraged to dabble in deviance, they are generally not able to do so openly. They must live between rules, and the question of what is deviant—and to whom—takes on a whole new meaning during this time frame and in this context. Reiling (2002) reports that

> virtually every participant reported that they experienced social isolation during this time, which generated a high level of depression and anxiety. Amish youth are caught in a double bind because even though they are culturally mandated to explore their identity, they are granted very little room to do so openly. First, it is believed to be necessary to emotionally distance themselves from their parents to fully explore English identity. Second, the youth are forced to quit school when they turn 16. These conditions create the ironic consequence of Amish youth's becoming socially isolated from English youth and emotionally isolated from their Amish parents at a time when they are deliberating which of those two identities they will adopt. (pp. 155–156)

◈ Elite Deviance, Corporate Deviance, and Workplace Misconduct

Elite deviance is an important topic but one that does not generally receive as much attention as the potentially more dramatic violent acts and property crimes ("street" crimes) that affect individuals on a personal level. While individuals tend to actively fear being victimized by street crimes, they probably do not realize the enormous impact elite deviance may have on their everyday lives. Mantsios (2010) offers a strong statement and indictment on how the corporate elite gain and maintain their status.

> Corporate America is a world made up of ruthless bosses, massive layoffs, favoritism and nepotism, health and safety violations, pension plan losses, union busting, tax evasions, unfair competition, and price gouging, as well as fast buck deals, financial speculation, and corporate wheeling and dealing that serve the interests of the corporate elite, but are generally wasteful and destructive to workers and the economy in general.
>
> It is no wonder Americans cannot think straight about class. The mass media is neither objective, balanced, independent, nor neutral. Those who own and direct the mass media are themselves part of the upper class. (pp. 240–241)

Elite deviance has been defined as "criminal and deviant acts by the largest corporations and the most powerful political organizations" (D. R. Simon, 2008, p. xi). In the introduction to his book on the topic, D. R. Simon (2008) explains that elite deviance refers to acts by elites or organizations that result in harm. He distinguishes between three different types of harm: physical harms, including death or physical injury; financial harms, including robbery, fraud, and various scams; and moral harms, which are harder to define but encourage distrust and alienation among members of the lower and middle classes (p. 35). Simon further breaks the topic of elite deviance down into three types of acts: economic domination, government and governmental control, and denial of basic human rights.

Bandura, Caprara, and Zsolnai (2000) explored corporate transgressions—the exercise and abuse of power closely linked to the legitimate conduct of business—through moral disengagement. Their study offers an interesting analysis of how corporations may adopt institutional practices that violate laws and harm the public. The authors briefly highlight four famous cases: an industrial disaster in Bhopal, India; the Ford Pintos that burst into flame on impact; Nestle's selling of infant formula to developing countries—a practice that led to the malnutrition of babies in Third World countries; and the Three Mile Island case, the most severe accident in U.S. commercial nuclear power plant history. Unlike most elite deviance, these cases garnered widespread public attention and brought notice—at least temporarily—to harmful corporate practices. Bandura and colleagues identified a number of disengagement mechanisms that led to these tragic cases, including moral justification, euphemistic labeling, displacement of responsibility, diffusion of responsibility, disregarding consequences, dehumanization of those affected, and attribution of blame to others or circumstances outside of themselves. Bandura et al. (2000) concluded that

> what is informative in these cases is that the moral collusion can end in justifying actions whose outcomes continue to be disapproved. The belief system of the corporation may remain unaffected for a long time by practices that are detrimental to it as well as to the general public. Selective disengagement mechanisms are deployed to mask such a contradiction and to perpetuate harmful corporate practices. (p. 63)

A much more common and smaller scale form of deviance is workplace deviance. Employee misconduct undoubtedly leads to business failures and higher consumer costs; studies estimate that as many as two thirds of workers are involved in employee theft or other forms of employee deviance. Table 2.2 documents the percentage of employees taking part in the "invisible social problem" of workplace misconduct (Huiras, Uggen, & McMorris, 2000).

Table 2.2 Employee Deviance in the Previous Year

Behavior	Percentage Reporting Act
Got to work late without a good reason	51.0
Called in sick when not sick	47.9
Gave away goods or services	32.7
Claimed to have worked more hours than really did	9.7
Took things from employer or coworker	9.1
Been drunk or high at work	7.2
Lied to get or keep job	5.8
Misused or took money	2.5
Purposely damaged property	2.1

Source: Huiras, Uggen, and McMorris (2000).

◈ Positive Deviance

Even within sociology, there is some debate as to whether such a thing as **positive deviance** exists. Goode (1991), for example, believes that positive deviance is a contradiction in terms, or an oxymoron. Jones (1998) and others disagree. We encourage you to try the exercise on random acts of kindness in the "Now YOU . . ." box at the end of the chapter and compare your results with your classmates. In conducting your own small research project, you are addressing a research question (Does positive deviance exist?), collecting data (observing your own feelings and the reactions of others), and drawing conclusions. As a social scientist, what are your thoughts on positive deviance? Which side do you land on in the debate?

While the exercise on random acts of kindness gives you a chance to think about positive deviance on an individual level, scholars have recently been studying the idea of positive deviance at the organizational or corporate level. Spreitzer and Sonenshein (2004) define positive deviance as "intentional behaviors that significantly depart from the norms of a referent group in honorable ways" (p. 841). The following example from Spreitzer and Sonenshein's article helps to clarify the concept:

In 1978, Merck & Co., one of the world's largest pharmaceutical companies, inadvertently discovered a potential cure for river blindness, a disease that inflicts tremendous pain, disfigurement, and blindness on its victims. The medication was first discovered as a veterinarian antibiotic, but it quickly created a major dilemma for Merck when its scientists realized the medication could be adapted to become a cure for river blindness. Because river blindness was indigenous to the developing world, Merck knew that it would never recover its research or distribution expenses for the drug. In addition, the company risked bad publicity for any unexpected side effects of the drug that in turn could damage the drug's reputation as a veterinary antibiotic (Business Enterprise Trust, 1991). Departing from norms in the pharmaceutical industry, Merck decided to manufacture and distribute the drug for free to the developing world, costing the company millions of dollars. Consequently, Merck helped eradicate river blindness, at its own expense. (pp. 834–835)

▲ **Photo 2.3**   Would you consider the "Free Hugs" movement a form of positive deviance? Why or why not?

http://www.flickr.com/photos/eelssej_; licensed under the Creative Commons Attribution 2.0 Generic license at https://creativecommons.org/licenses/by/2.0/deed.en

Spreitzer and Sonenshein (2004) argue that Merck's action in this case is an excellent example of positive deviance. The organization faced great cost and risk to develop, manufacture, and distribute the drug, yet Merck chose to depart from corporate norms prioritizing profit and gains and, in doing so, prevented further suffering from river blindness.

Sometimes the line between positive deviance and crime is extremely hard to define. Edward Snowden, for example, is an individual who went against all corporate and government norms to expose thousands of top-secret government documents. His leaking of these documents was viewed by a former Central Intelligence Agency (CIA) deputy director as "the most serious compromise of classified information in the history of the U.S. intelligence community" (Reitman, 2013). Snowden was a reportedly brilliant high school dropout who began working as a computer technician with the CIA and became increasingly disturbed by "a continuing litany of lies from senior officials to Congress—and therefore the American people" (Reitman, 2013). Snowden eventually downloaded more than 50,000 documents and intelligence reports; he chose to become a whistleblower and outlaw when he leaked those documents to the press. Just two days after the first stories were printed, President Barack Obama admitted that the National Security Agency (NSA) was collecting enormous amounts of intelligence on ordinary citizens; two weeks later, the Obama administration brought criminal charges against Edward Snowden under the Espionage Act, and a number of U.S. officials labeled Snowden a traitor (Reitman, 2013). Snowden was granted temporary asylum in Russia, where he went into hiding. While demonized by the U.S. government, others consider Snowden a hero who risked his life to get the public vital information. History will ultimately be the judge of whether Snowden is remembered as an individual bravely practicing positive deviance for the greater good or a traitor committing crimes against his country.

The idea of positive deviance is growing at the individual, organizational, and community levels, and new research continues to stretch the concept and add to our understanding of how this "oxymoron" may play out in everyday life. Tufts University even hosts its own Positive Deviance Initiative. The initiative takes the following as its starting point:

> Positive Deviance is based on the observation that in every community there are certain individuals or groups whose uncommon behaviors and strategies enable them to find better solutions to problems than their peers, while having access to the same resources and facing similar or worse challenges. (http://www.positivedeviance.org)

◈ Explaining Deviance in the Streets and Deviance in the Suites: The Cases of Addiction, Prostitution, and Graffiti

When deciding whether an act or a characteristic is deviant, the social class and status of the actor(s) can make all the difference. Already in this book, we have covered examples of elite deviance and what is colloquially referred to as "street" crime and deviance. Above, we considered corporate deviance versus workplace misconduct. A few other examples of street versus elite deviance—and the very different reactions they may receive—follow.

Addiction

Amy Winehouse famously sang about how "they tried to make me go to rehab," but she was one celebrity who declined treatment (saying "no, no, no"), and she tragically died at age 27, cutting short an incredibly promising musical career. Recently, it seems, more and more celebrities are choosing to go to rehab, checking themselves into treatment facilities for a variety of ailments, including addictions to prescription pills, alcohol, and cocaine. It is frequently reported that stars have checked into hospitals or treatment centers for personal and health reasons, with the details left to the imagination. The act of celebrities checking themselves into treatment has lost much of its stigma. While some stars, such as Lindsay Lohan, are sent to inpatient rehabilitation as part of a court order, celebrities who voluntarily choose inpatient treatment are often applauded for attempting to take control of their lives and work through their particular issues. They are fortunate that they have the resources to go to expensive facilities where their privacy and care is closely guarded. Poor and working-class addicts face a much different reality. Many local rehab centers work with community drug courts and jail and prison diversion programs, receiving clients that are sent to them through force rather than choice. A recent study focusing on rehab facilities with strong ties to drug courts, probation, and parole calls such institutions "strong-arm rehab" and identifies "a particular type of court-mandated rehabilitation emphasizing long residential stays, high structure, mutual surveillance, and an intense process of character reform. Strong-arm rehab also tends to be a highly racialized form, consistently linked to poor African American drug offenders" (Gowan & Whetstone, 2012, p. 70). There is nothing glamorous about these facilities; if the clients do not follow the treatment program, their lack of cooperation can lead to criminal sanctions. The treatment received by these addicts is very different than the treatment and response afforded to their celebrity counterparts.

Prostitution

Media images of prostitution range from the hardened streetwalker working the corner to the expensive and exclusive call girls working to satisfy their wealthy clients. While legal in some states, prostitution is generally a criminal act that draws both workers and clients from across the entire spectrum of social classes and cultures. The demand is high, and prostitutes and johns—or call girls and their clients, as the more upscale agencies may refer to them—can meet in many different ways, including through the use of a wide array of websites. One such website, SeekingArrangement.com, recently advertised a "college tuition sugar daddy," enticing heavily indebted college students to consider setting up profiles as "sugar babies" to arrange for them to have sex with older men to pay their bills. The founder of Seeking Arrangement estimates that 35% of his 800,000 members are students. The nearly 180,000 college sugar babies attend universities that include New York University, Harvard, UCLA, and the University of Southern California (Fairbanks, 2012). Seeking Tuition (seekingtuition.com) is another website that specifically targets young women who are considering selling themselves to pay for their education; it promotes itself as "providing mutually beneficial arrangements to college girls and wealthy benefactors." Even as they trade sex for money, the college women looking for sugar daddies and using these websites generally resist the label and do not consider themselves prostitutes. They often lead two lives—keeping secret their identities as sugar babies for fear of being labeled and stigmatized as they continue their college educations and conforming careers. One young woman involved in a sugar daddy relationship explained her thoughts on her boundaries and her framing of her own identity.

> I'm not a whore. Whores are paid by the hour, can have a high volume of clients in a given day, and it's based on money, not on who the individual actually is. There's no feeling involved and the entire interaction revolves around a sexual act. . . . I don't engage with a high volume of people, instead choosing one or two men I actually like spending time with and have decided to develop a friendship with them. And while sex is involved, the focus is on providing friendship. It's not only about getting paid. (Fairbanks, 2012)

© jvdwolf/istockphoto

▲ **Photo 2.4**   Why is graffiti sometimes considered art and sometimes considered vandalism? Which would you consider this piece by Banksy to be? Why?

Graffiti

Why is defacing public property sometimes considered vandalism and sometimes considered art? Some graffiti writers set out to offend people in the community, viewing their practice as a key aspect of a rebel lifestyle and describing graffiti "as the space that allowed them to be the assholes they wanted to be" (Monto, Machalek, & Anderson, 2013, p. 273). Illegal graffiti can be viewed as a subcultural activity, offering risk and thrills to the graffiti writers. These writers often lead double lives, hiding their conventional identities behind their chosen graffiti tags (Campos, 2012). "Graffiti elders" such as Andrew "Zephyr" Witten continue wielding the spray-paint can into middle age, balancing parenthood and conforming careers with the illicit thrills of "train-bombing," or illegally painting trains or other people's property (Ghosh, 2012). Yet some murals by graffiti writers have been heralded as public art, and British artist Banksy—described in *Smithsonian* magazine as "graffiti master, painter, activist, filmmaker and all-purpose provocateur"—was named to *Time* magazine's list of the world's most influential people in 2010. The *Smithsonian* article describes Banksy's remarkable success as an "upward trajectory from the outlaw spraying—or, as the argot has it, 'bombing'—walls in Bristol, England, during the 1990s to the artist whose work commands hundreds of thousands of dollars in the auction houses of Britain and America" (Ellsworth-Jones, 2013). Even as his fame and fortune has grown, Banksy has worked hard to remain anonymous, continuing to create memorable street art both in public spaces and in formal art exhibits around the world. When should we consider graffiti a criminal act and a public nuisance, and when should we think of it as art? Is Banksy deserving of his success? Will any of today's young graffiti writers have the same kind of artistic success? At what point does the transition from vandal to celebrated artist occur?

◈ Ideas in Action: Guerrilla Gardening in Low-Income Areas

Ron Finley has gained fame for his crusade to plant edible gardens in urban areas, allowing those living in low-income communities access to fresh vegetables and produce. He cofounded L.A. Green Grounds, a nonprofit volunteer group that helps people to set up edible community gardens, teaching them to grow and maintain their own organic fruits, vegetables, and herbs in their neighborhood (Gunther, 2011).

Finley's work began when he planted a community garden in the narrow strip of land between the sidewalk and the curb in front of his house in Crenshaw, California. As his organic tomatoes, onions, peppers, and eggplants grew, he garnered attention from both neighbors and the city. The strip of land in front of his house is known as a "parkway"; parkways are managed by the city, and Finley's garden was in violation of city regulations. Finley chose to challenge the rules, and he mobilized the community and the media to support his cause. Los Angeles officials backed off and opened the door to the growth of urban farming.

Finley gave a dynamic, challenging, and inspiring TED talk in 2013 that quickly gained more than 1.5 million views. In it, he paints a vivid picture of living in a "food desert," an area where there are plenty of liquor stores, fast food restaurants, and vacant lots but little access to healthy foods. He claims that Los Angeles owns 26 square miles of vacant lots, which he suggests is enough space to plant 700 million tomato plants. "It's like my gospel: I'm telling people, grow your own food. Growing your own food is like printing your own money" (Finley, 2013).

Finley calls on audience members to become "ecolutionaries, renegades, gangsters, gangster gardeners," to pick up shovels. Finley sees gardens as a tool for transformation. He asserts that gardening is "the most therapeutic and defiant act you can do—especially in the inner cities." He believes young people want to work and that kids can be taken off the streets and trained to "take over their communities and have a sustainable life." He wants to "flip the script on what a gangster is . . . if you ain't a gardener, you ain't gangster. Get gangster with your shovel and let that be your weapon of choice" (Finley, 2013).

A 2013 *New York Times* story allowed Finley to share his vision for the future. He said, "I want to plant entire blocks of vegetable beds. . . . I want to turn shipping containers into healthy cafes where customers can pick their salad and juice off the trees. I want our inner-city churches to become ministries of health instead of places that serve up fried, fattening foods. I want to clean up my yard, my street and my 'hood" (Hochman, 2013).

Finley and his L.A. Green Grounds organization are another example of positive deviance—they are acting altruistically and outside of the norms. They have challenged city regulations about the use of parkways and vacant lots, and they are literally transforming low-income areas of Los Angeles from the ground up, providing healthy activities and organic food for community members.

▲ **Photo 2.5**   Ron Finley has challenged people to be "gangster gardeners" and to grow edible gardens in urban areas.

NOW YOU . . . TRY AN EXPERIMENT IN POSITIVE DEVIANCE!

One way to explore the idea of positive deviance is to conduct your own small-scale experiment and then decide whether you think positive deviance exists. For this exercise, your task is to go out and commit random acts of kindness—arguably a form of positive deviance.

Many introductory sociology classes ask students to conduct a breaching experiment by breaking a norm and then observing the reactions of those around them. In this case, the goal is to perform a face-to-face act of kindness for a *stranger* and to take note of the reaction to your behavior.

Think about the following questions in completing your act(s) of kindness (you may find it helpful, necessary, or interesting to repeat the act more than once):

1. Why did you choose to do this particular act of kindness?

2. How did you feel while doing the random act of kindness, and why do you think you felt this way?

3. How did the recipient—and any others who witnessed the kindness—react? Speculate as to why they reacted the way they did. If the situation was reversed, do you think you would have reacted differently?

(Continued)

(Continued)

Be safe and smart in your choice of kindnesses, be careful not to inflict trauma on yourself or the recipient, and be certain that you do not put yourself in a dangerous position. After conducting your experiment, reflect on how you felt and what the reactions to your act of kindness were. Did you take age or gender into consideration in choosing your "target"? Did you feel the need to explain that your act was an experiment or assignment for class? Based on this data, do you think positive deviance exists? Why or why not?

Source: Adapted from Jones (1998).

◈ Question: So Who Are the Deviants? Answer: It Depends on Whom You Ask

We cannot emphasize enough how much context matters in any discussion or explanation of deviant behavior. You simply can't discuss forms of deviance without some reference to culture, context, and historical period. What some people regard as deviant, others regard as virtuous. What some might praise, others condemn. To say that deviance exists does not specify which acts are considered deviant by which groups, in what situations, and at any given time.

◈ Conclusion

We hope that after reading this chapter—and delving further into this book—your ideas about deviant behavior and social control will have greatly expanded. The more commonly studied types of deviant behavior, such as criminal deviance (including street crime) and elite deviance (including corporate and white-collar crimes), are explored further throughout the book. Our goal in this chapter is simply to help broaden your understanding of what constitutes deviance and to realize the question What is deviance? must be followed by the qualifier According to whom? We realize that this chapter and this book will not resolve these issues for you and may very well raise more questions than answers. Still, our goal is to broaden your understanding of deviance and its many forms.

With that goal in mind, we provide a few extra exercises and discussion questions in this chapter to help you explore boundaries, conduct your own experiments, form your own analyses, and begin to think about deviance and social control very broadly. Chapter 3 delves much more specifically into the art and science of researching deviance. You'll soon see that deviance is a very interesting topic to study and research. For now, we hope you will take a close look at the norms and behavior of your community and the larger society. We think you will soon discover an enormous amount of diversity in the deviance that is all around you.

EXERCISES AND DISCUSSION QUESTIONS

1. Look again at Table 2.1, compiled by Simmons in 1965. Give several friends or family members the same instruction that Simmons used, "List those things or types of persons whom you regard as deviant," and compile the responses. Do any of the categories from your small study overlap with those that Simmons found? Do any of the categories from 1965 disappear entirely? How would you explain this?

2. Pay attention over the next 24 hours, and see what kinds of deviant behavior you notice. It can be behavior you witness, you commit (hopefully nothing that will get you

in trouble!), or you hear about on the news or media. What did you notice? How many different types of deviance were you exposed to in one day?

3. To explore the idea of stigma and how a physical trait can deeply affect an individual's life, you might try imagining a day with a disability. This exercise will begin with a diary entry: Record a typical day (e.g., what you did, the interactions you had, etc.), and then assign yourself a visible attribute typically associated with deviance (e.g., being blind, obese, or missing a limb). Rewrite your diary entry to reflect what you imagine would be different that

day given your stigma. What obstacles would you face? Would people treat you differently? What did you learn about deviance, social norms, stigma, and coping by completing this exercise?

4. In a recent example of a polygamous lifestyle, the reality television show *Sister Wives* portrays a polygamist family and begins at the point where the husband is courting his fourth wife. His motto is, "Love should be multiplied, not divided." Do you think this kind of polygamy—where the relationships are consensual and the brides are all adults— is deviant? Why or why not?

KEY TERMS

Body modification

Elite deviance

Physical deviance

Polygamy

Positive deviance

Self-injury

Sexual deviance

Stigma

Subcultures

READING 4

This fascinating article presents a number of complex questions regarding the nature of deviance, the social contexts that determine what is and what is not deviance, and the social and emotional consequences that explorations into deviance can cause. The researcher observed and interacted with a particular settlement of the Old Order Amish, a unique Christian and collectivist subculture largely guarded from "conventional American society." Among this settlement, it is common (to some extent, expected and tolerated) for youth in American society to deviate in their teenage years from the controlled childhood from which they recently emerged and prior to becoming an adult and fulfilling the roles of an adult. In the Amish subculture, the staging of the life course is taken to an extreme. Childhood is far more guarded and controlled than it is in conventional American society, with very little deviance tolerated. However, beginning with their 16th birthday and ending only when they are baptized and accept the Amish religion and subcultural practices or they leave the settlement, the youth are expected to engage in deviant behaviors. In this "simmie" period, youth are almost forced to explore American lifestyles (referred to as "English" lifestyle) before choosing to either commit to their Amish culture or leave it forever. The ritualized "simmie" period is characterized by a number of deviant behaviors (especially deviant for the very conservative Amish people), including alcohol consumption, bedding (sleepovers with the opposite sex where although intercourse is not permitted, it happens, as do other forms of sexual behavior), and other deviances actually quite common and viewed

Source: Reiling, D. M. (2002). The "simmie" side of life: Old Order Amish youths' affective response to culturally prescribed deviance. *Youth & Society,* *34*(2), 146–171. Reprinted with permission.

as less deviant in American culture. The "simmie" period is psychologically and emotionally difficult for the Amish youth because they are expected to do things they have been told are wrong and that can literally send them to hell for all of eternity. That is, they believe that the baptism that occurs when they accept the Amish way of life does not necessarily wipe away their sins, even during a time when they are expected to deviate (sin). The description of the Old Order Amish youth culture is interesting and useful; they are living between rules, and the question of what is deviant—and to whom—takes on a whole new meaning during this time frame.

The "Simmie" Side of Life*

Old Order Amish Youths' Affective Response to Culturally Prescribed Deviance

Denise M. Reiling

Until fairly recently, youth culture has not been viewed as a sufficiently important sociological phenomenon to be worthy of separate study. It can be argued that this stance is a direct reflection of the marginalized status of youth in the larger social context (Adler & Adler, 1998; Hutchby & Moran-Ellis, 1998). The prevailing understanding of youth culture within society, as well, has been that youth culture is simply a phase or a stage that adolescents pass through on their way to becoming an adult.

Others, however, describe youth culture as a highly vital and dynamic process that is instrumental and productive to the formation of the adult individual, particularly as it influences the development of identity (Adler & Adler, 1998; Baumeister & Muraven, 1996; Corsaro & Eder, 1990; Danielsen, Lorem, & Kroger, 2000; Hutchby & Moran-Ellis, 1998). According to this view, children and youth are separate, autonomous social actors, capable of demonstrating fairly high levels of social competence and agency (Adler & Adler, 1998; Hutchby & Moran-Ellis, 1998).

Terror Management Theory (TMT) (Pyszczynski, Greenberg, & Solomon, 1997; Solomon, Greenberg, & Pyszczynski, 1991) provides a theoretical framework through which to examine social competence and agency during the youth period. One of the primary tenets of TMT is that youth culture develops as a "cultural-anxiety buffer" against the reality of mortality. Accordingly, one would expect that as one's own death becomes salient through conscious reminders of death, defense of one's culture would increase. As we contemplate our own mortality, we depend on our culturally constructed worldview to make life and death more rational and bearable. Therefore, if reminded of death during the youth period, allegiance to and defense of youth culture should be high (Greenberg et al., 1990; Janssen, Dechesne, & Van Knippenberg, 1999).

Janssen et al. (1999) found support for TMT, in that they discovered that youth culture did function as a specialized cultural-anxiety buffer, in that reminding youth of death caused them to more greatly identify with and defend their youth culture. As with adult culture, youth culture constructs a worldview that provides youth with an explanation for life, death, and the after-life experience. Youth culture also influences an adolescent's self-esteem, functioning as a measuring rod for their social performance (Janssen et al., 1999).

Within this article, the special case of the Old Order Amish, a predominately North American Christian sub-culture, has been offered through which to examine selected propositions of TMT. Several unique cultural dynamics found among the Amish make them a valuable research population. Of particular importance is that Amish youth enter a decision-making period,

---

* Some text and accompanying references have been omitted. Please consult the original source.

beginning on their 16th birthday and lasting for potentially several years, within which they are to contemplate whether they will retain or repudiate Amish identity (Hostetler, 1993). During this "simmie" period, Amish youth must respond to implicit cultural prescriptions for deviance that have been constructed by adult Amish culture. Because most Amish parents do not openly object to this deviance (Hostetler, 1993) the deviance is implicitly sanctioned.

The Amish believe that exposing their youth to deviance functions to select out those who would not be adult Amish people. The Amish articulate a Social Darwinist analysis, wherein to assure the cohesion of their group, it is necessary for those not suitable to be "weeded out early lest they infect the rest of the group." As they explain, for this selection process to be fully effective, the individual must have the opportunity to deny the profane by being exposed to temptation. This belief prevents Amish parents from acting against, and in many cases causes them to condone and even encourage, the more serious forms of deviance, such as the consumption of alcohol.

Engaging in this deviance, however, creates an extraordinary and complex dilemma for Amish youth. The Amish believe that engaging in this culturally prescribed deviance endangers the individual's salvation, making their fate after death, at best uncertain, and at worst, condemnation to Hell. As such, this decision-making period instigates a search for existential meaning. But, to not engage in the culturally prescribed deviance during the simmie period would be a deviant act that would not be culturally sanctioned. Conforming to youth culture necessitates engaging in deviance to test their suitability as adult Amish people. Thus, Amish youth must negotiate the dilemma of being damned if they do and damned if they don't. This cultural dynamic provides an excellent and rare opportunity for social competence, agency, and TMT to be explored in a natural setting.

◈ Methods and Setting

The setting for this research was a nonmetropolitan county, located in a north-central state within the United States. This particular Amish settlement has an approximate population size of 12,500 members, around 40% of the county's total population. The research findings emerged as part of a larger, ethnographic study of Old Order Amish culture, with the primary data collection techniques being in-depth interviews and participant observation.

Observational data were collected over a period of 10 years, during which time the Amish extended to me as "complete membership" (Alder & Adler, 1987) as possible for a non-Amish person, spending summers, many weekends, and academic recess in one particular Amish home. Entrée was facilitated by three important factors, the first of which was the investment of time. As one Bishop noted, he respected the fact that I simply observed patiently for more than a year before asking direct questions. The second factor was that my having been raised on a farm allowed me a respectable level of cultural competence within this agrarian culture.

The third factor that facilitated entrée was that I quickly assumed the role "fieldworker as resource" (Emerson & Pollner, 2001), which, as collectivists, the Amish appreciated for the reciprocal relationship that being a resource created. I was known as someone who "takes down stories," but I was also known as someone who gave two highly valued things in return: information and confidentiality. As a medical sociologist, I became a resource for information concerning health, particularly mental health. As a researcher, I became a trusted confidant because of the confidentiality that I could promise them in that role. Amish people could say things to me that their cultural prescription against the expression of negative emotion and their cultural prescription for gossip prevented them from saying to each other.

In addition to the observational data collected through my unique position and length of time within the Amish settlement, more than 60 in-depth interviews on the particular topic of the youth decision-making period were conducted with Amish participants, within the last year of the research endeavor. The average length of the interviews was 5 hours. Interviews were also collected from non-Amish mental health professionals and non-Amish criminal justice agents. Non-Amish public school officials were also interviewed because it had been reported that approximately 80% of the Amish children in this settlement attend public rather than parochial schools.

Twenty interviews were gathered from participants within each of the three Amish participant pools that were constructed: prebaptism Amish, postbaptism Amish, and defected coethnics. Prebaptism Amish were defined as Amish youth who were in the culturally mandated decision-making period concerning the adoption or repudiation of Amish identity, between the ages of 16 and approximately 25. Postbaptism Amish were defined as Amish adults who had passed through the decision-making period and had formally adopted Amish identity by publicly taking adult baptism. Defected coethnics were defined as adults who had been born Amish, had passed through the decision-making period, but had repudiated Amish identity by publicly refusing to take adult baptism. They had subsequently defected from the group and had adopted "English" identity (a label the Amish use to denote the non-Amish population living within the same geographic area).

Although not by design, the 40 interviews of the postbaptism Amish and the defected coethnics were actually interviews of couples, not individuals. Indicative of the interdependent relationship that develops within marriages in this context, almost every participant requested that their spouse participate in these interviews. This circumstance proved to be highly productive and did not appear to inhibit free and full disclosure.

Even though the youth period was the focus of this line of inquiry, those who had already passed through this period, the postbaptism Amish and the defected coethnics, were included as interview participants for three reasons. First, because the Amish go to extraordinary lengths to protect their children from outside influence, if I had asked to interview only the youth, this request would have been met with suspicion, and most likely, entrée to the youth would have been denied. Participants within the two adult groups were interviewed first to establish trust. The second reason was that because the Amish are a collectivist culture, it was imperative to seek what they would view as a fair and balanced voice, by allowing for representation of all group members, including those who had defected.

The third reason for the inclusion of adults was that adults had been part of the larger, ethnographic study. I had assumed prior to interviewing that the adult accounts would differ notably from those of the youth. I expected the accounts of the adults to be more introspective, as a reflection of the length of time that had passed. I also anticipated that their standpoint as an adult would make their retrospective accounts more negative than the concurrent accounts of the youth. This was not found to be true, however. The accounts of both adult groups were virtually indistinguishable from those of the youth. There was not a notable difference in perspective. The youth appeared to have given as much thought as the adults to the consequences of deviance on their lives, as well as the lives of their future children.

The problem of social desirability merits some comment. One could speculate that the Amish would have a high need to protect the construction of Amish culture as virtuous, so how much could their reports and portrayals be trusted? The ability to answer that question with a great deal of certainty is always limited, but one of the best ways to assess the impact of social desirability is to study over time. Throughout the past 10 years of knowing the Amish, I have become convinced that social desirability is not a significant concern. Among the Amish, social desirability would more likely function to prohibit participation, rather than taint the data. Chances are that if they feel they cannot be truthful they will not grant an interview. I was also not concerned that social desirability would result in respondent bias because I received nearly total compliance with my requests for an interview.

A random sampling design of all Amish households was used to pull the Amish samples, using the Amish Directory (a census that the Amish compile) as a population list. I was able to locate the defected coethnics using the Amish Directory, too, because the Amish continue to list their names and geographic locations in the Directory. Because of the shame attached to defection, the Amish believe that listing the names of those who defect will function to limit defection. The age of the resultant interview participants ranged from age 16 through age 76, although most participants were approximately age 16 to 40. The sex ratio was equal.

Assessment of the affective response to deviance was based solely on participants' qualitative self-reports and descriptions of their experiences. Qualifiers have been used in reporting the findings to illustrate the degree of the affective response and the representativeness of the reports, for example, "every subject," "most subjects," "very high anxiety," and so on. The text has been illustrated with excerpts from the interviews that were tape-recorded. Verbatim transcriptions of the tapes and my field notes were analyzed using the NUDIST program for qualitative data analysis.

It should be noted that most of the prebaptism Amish did not want their interview to be tape-recorded. These participants did not give an explanation for their refusal to be tape-recorded, and human participants constraints prohibited probing their decline. Based on observation, their wariness about having their voice tape-recorded was understood as reflective of the conflicted state that their ambiguous, interstitial identity was generating. These participants did not appear to be uncomfortable with my note-taking, however, so it is possible that having their voice tape-recorded, an act that would otherwise have been culturally prohibited, extended them beyond their already overextended deviance comfort zone.

◈ Description of Old Order Amish Youth Culture

The Old Order Amish can be defined as a Christian subculture for which "Amish" has developed as a non-racialized, ethnic identity. They are reportedly direct descendants of Anabaptists (Christians believing in adult rather than infant baptism) who emerged in Switzerland between 1525 and 1536 (Huntington, 1988), as part of a religious-based social movement throughout Europe (Nolt, 1992). Due to religious persecution in Europe, the Old Order Amish, what was to remain the most conservative faction of the original Anabaptist group, began immigrating to the United States in the 1700s, primarily into Pennsylvania (Huntington, 1988). Migration from Pennsylvania to Ohio and Indiana occurred primarily between 1815 and 1860 (Huntington, 1988). By 1991, Old Order Amish settlements had been located in 22 states within the United States (Nolt, 1992).

Each of the following practices that were advocated by the early Anabaptists are reportedly still in place today: adult baptism; nonassimilation with the dominant culture; in-group conformity; endogamy; nonproselytization; nonparticipation in military service;

high, unrestrained fertility; a disciplined lifestyle; conformity in dress and hairstyle; a prohibition against alcohol and drug use by adults; strong proscriptions against modernization and technology-based living; and strong prescriptions for reciprocity (Hostetler, 1993; Huntington, 1988; Nolt, 1992).

As with the early Anabaptist groups, the Amish settlement under study continues to represent a near ideal type of collectivist, or Gemeinschaft, society. Each of what Triandis (1990) has identified as the defining attributes of a collectivist society were evidenced within this particular settlement: in-group primacy; the maintenance of in-group harmony through consensus and face-saving; a lack of out-group memberships; an emphasis on obedience and conformity to the exclusion of creativity, competition, and individual achievement; gossip as a key mechanism of social control; and strong boundary maintenance practices, which result in an almost total exclusion of the out-group.

Among the Old Order Amish, the 16th birthday signifies that the "child" has entered a rite of passage, wherein the "youth" is to begin to deliberate his or her identity. During this time, the youth will decide whether they want to take adult baptism and become "Amish" or whether they want to defect from the Amish and become "English." The end of this period is signified by the child's announcement of his or her decision to either repudiate or adopt Amish identity (Hostetler, 1993). And indeed, approximately 20% to 25% of youths within this settlement do eventually defect from the Amish. Most youth remain in this decision-making period for only 2 to 3 years, whereas others do not make their decision for as much as 8 to 10 years. It was reported that those who remain for an extended period of time are generally those who know they will eventually defect (Reiling, 2000).

Upon defection, the youth immediately becomes excommunicated from the Amish church. In this context, excommunication also results in ostracism and, in almost every case, physical displacement from the family and from the entire Amish settlement. In essence, those who defect become outcasts for an indeterminate period of time, ranging from a few months to their entire lifetime. Varying degrees of estrangement remain, however, in those relationships where some level of communication is eventually reestablished. It was reported that defection is a permanent state, despite the fact that it was also reported that many in this particular settlement believe that defection from the Amish results in damnation to Hell (Reiling, 2000).

The Amish in this settlement have constructed a label for youth in this decision-making period. As explained, the label of "simmie" is applied to Amish youth to signify that they are "foolish in the head." Whereas a range of descriptors was given, all participants agreed that this label signifies that youth are immature and not yet ready to be adult Amish persons. As one Amish man explained, "What happens during this time is that they start joining the group, the young folks. They want to be top grade, but they're still greener than a colt. They aren't trained yet. But once they're trained and mature, then they'll act like the rest of us. But these young kids aren't broke yet. They want to try to do what the others do, and they make a lot of dumb moves. So we call them simmies."

The application of this label is not automatic, however, although most youth experience the application of this label for some period of time. It is expected that after an initial period of being particularly immature, the youth will begin to "gel" or "pull themselves together," "to get ahold on themselves a bit more." One Amish woman, who had exited the simmie period only within the last year, explained that "the young folk generally aren't simmies anymore once they turn 18. When they get to be around 18, for some reason they become a little more sensible. It's just natural. Then we don't call them simmies anymore."

The label of simmie came to be understood as a "black sheep" label (Marques, 1986) that is applied in a preemptive attempt to shame or warn the adolescent into keeping his or her culturally prescribed period of deviance within culturally prescribed boundaries. As one Amish woman explained, "You don't brag about it. It's a put-down. It means you're gullible, or you're dangerous, because you've broken loose." And indeed, it is important to note that not all forms of deviance have been positively sanctioned. It certainly is not a situation of "anything goes." As illustrated by the following quote given by a middle-aged Amish woman, it was reported by every participant that limits to deviance were well known: "I just knew that I was doing something that I wouldn't want them (parents) to know. They would not

have approved of how I was. I had gone too far outside of what's allowed for even a simmie."

Reports concerning deviant behavior during the simmie period should be kept in cultural perspective, however, as it is important to understand that constructions of normative behavior are numerous and rigid among the Amish. As such, the chance of being labeled as deviant is great. Granted, more serious forms of deviance, such as excessive consumption of alcohol and sexual exploration, do occur, but many of the behaviors that constitute deviance among the Amish would be considered quite benign in most other cultural contexts.

For example, because of the high standards that have been set for Amish behavior, being irresponsible, intentionally hurting another person's feelings, telling lies, being unkind by excluding another person from a group activity, or just acting in an unwise, reckless, or impractical fashion is considered deviant in the Amish context. As one Amish man remembered, "I did things that I know I shouldn't have, so I deserved the name simmie, I'm quite sure. I remember one time I left my flashlight at her (girlfriend's) place, but I didn't want to go back and admit I'd left it there, so I just went home without my flashlight. That was a simmie thing to do."

Identity during this decision-making period was reported to be highly ambiguous. Almost every participant's description depicted this decision-making period as one of limbo, wherein the child does not identify as Amish, even though continuing to live in an Amish home and to engage in Amish cultural practices. Nor does the child identify as English, even though many will wear English clothes outside of the home, cut their hair, drive cars, and engage in "worldly culture." This interstitial state resonates with the ambiguous identities of bisexuals, Christianized Jews, and light-skinned Blacks, as analyzed by Adam (1978). One Amish male, who was approximately 20 years old and had just taken adult baptism and formally adopted Amish identity 1 month prior to the interview, expressed this ambiguity: "During that time, I wouldn't have even admitted that I was Amish. I wouldn't have claimed it. I don't have a name for what I was during that period. We really don't think about what we were, just what we weren't—we weren't Amish kids. I wouldn't have a name for it, but I wouldn't have said I was an Amish person."

Virtually every participant reported that they experienced social isolation during this time, which generated a high level of depression and anxiety. Amish youth are caught in a double bind because even though they are culturally mandated to explore their identity, they are granted very little room to do so openly. First, it is believed to be necessary to emotionally distance themselves from their parents to fully explore English identity. Second, the youth are forced to quit school when they turn 16. These conditions create the ironic consequence of Amish youth's becoming socially isolated from English youth and emotionally isolated from their Amish parents at a time when they are deliberating which of those two identities they will adopt.

Every participant reported that their decision concerning whether to join or to defect from the Amish was made in relative isolation, without much discussion or deliberation with others. The explanation for this circumstance was that to consider defection was to consider committing a very serious sin, and as such, involving others in the deliberation would exacerbate the offense. Defection was considered sinful because defection dishonors parents' desires for the child to join the church, which is thought to violate the 5th commandment of their religious text, to honor one's mother and father (Book of Exodus 20, Holy Bible). Consequently, defection could possibly result in the individual's going to Hell for all of eternity. The following quote from a 25-year-old Amish man illustrates this belief: "We're taught that if we leave, if you don't stay with what you were raised in, and honor your parents, which they say is doing exactly as I tell you to, if you're not honoring me, then you'll go to Hell."

It was further reported that they did not discuss their deliberations out of concern for the stress this discussion would cause their parents. Even though parents knew that their child was to consider defection during the simmie period, the parents reportedly acted as if their particular child was not. Because of the suppression of discussion of the matter, a sense of shame accompanied this isolation. The youth reported that they saw the paradox inherent in this situation, that they were being required to explore and consider becoming what their parents would then be ashamed of. They could also clearly articulate the function of this practice. As one simmie youth stated, "It's like we have

to go through this period of feeling what it would feel like to suffer our parents' disappointment and rejection, so that we live right to avoid this pain. Even those of us who would never consider leaving the Amish have to feel what it would feel like to be turned away, 'cause when we are forced to think about it, we are much more likely to stay."

It was discovered in earlier research that, in this particular Amish settlement, approximately 80% of Amish youth attend public rather than parochial school. So until their 16th birthday, Amish children actually have a great deal of interaction with non-Amish youth within the school setting. But, it is not generally the case that English and simmie youth develop extensive friendship networks. Informants within the public schools gave the explanation that English youth do not want to publicly associate with simmies because of the high level of stigmatization that is applied to the Amish in general and Amish youth in particular. As evidence of this circumstance, the English youth have developed the slang term "jerked-over" to signify disdain for simmies whom they believe are attempting to jerk-over to the other side (Reiling, 2000).

It was reported by public school officials that much of the hostility that the English youth feel toward the simmies stems from their perception of Amish youth and adults as unfair economic competition, due to the construction of the Amish as superior workers. As validation of this perception, the county's Chamber of Commerce reported the presence of a large Amish workforce to be the greatest incentive to industry location. More specific to the youth experience, because withdrawing from school at age 16 is a cultural practice, non-Amish employers do not view Amish "dropouts" in a negative light (Reiling & Nusbaumer, 1997). At age 16, Amish youth are expected to join, and they are fully welcomed into, the adult, non-Amish, paid-labor workforce.

Despite the stigmatizing label, the social and emotional isolation, and the identity conflict that accompanied this period, it was reported by every participant that the 16th birthday was greatly anticipated because the youth was finally freed from the highly subjugated role of the child. For example, they would no longer need to be accompanied outside the home by one of their parents, and they were free to more fully develop relationships and to explore their social world. As one prebaptism Amish male, who had been in the decision-making simmie period for about a year, reported, "When I was 10, it seemed like 20 years from 10 to 16. That's how much you look forward to turning 16." Certainly, elation over this period of emancipation from parental control resonates quite well with the experience of youth within many other cultural contexts. As such, the positive affective response the Amish youth make to this changed circumstance necessitates no further comment or articulation.

It is more important to examine the discovery that this period was also greatly dreaded because of other affective responses that were negative, namely depression and anxiety. These affective states are not unheard of responses to this period of increasing independence and identity exploration, either, for we know that other youth experience adolescence as disruptive (Erikson, 1968; Rumbaut, 1996). However, the strength of the Amish youths' negative affective response and the source of their angst are certainly noteworthy.

Almost every participant interviewed reported that engaging in the culturally prescribed deviance generated fairly high levels of depression and anxiety because the youth judged this deviance to be a "morally wrong" practice, despite the fact that it was culturally sanctioned by adults. The strong affective response of these youth caused them to internally reject youth culture as an ideology, and internally identify with adult culture, even though they felt compelled to continue to engage in this period of deviance. The conflicted state that was generated and its consequences have been examined more closely below, along with implications of the application of the case of Amish youth to TMT (Pyszczynski et al., 1997).

◈ Findings Concerning the Affective Response to Deviance During the Simmie Period

The negative affective response made to culturally prescribed deviance during the simmie period was influenced heavily by two factors: the seriousness of the deviance that the youth engaged in and the length

of time the youth spent in the simmie period. In general, the more serious the deviance and/or the greater the length of time in this period, the more intense the contemplation of their mortality, and hence, the greater the rejection of youth culture. Virtually no Amish youth exited the simmie period without having committed numerous acts of the more innocuous deviance, such as being irresponsible, reckless, or disrespectful to their parents. But more strikingly, particularly because the interview sample was pulled in a random fashion, was the discovery that almost every participant had also engaged in the more serious forms of deviance, those they viewed as morally wrong practices, particularly drinking alcohol.

Most expressed high levels of anxiety over the presence of, or having felt forced, encouraged, or allowed to participate in, these more deviant acts. As an extension of this belief, many of the participants expressed having been afraid for their salvation during the simmie period, as they feared that they would be "caught out," meaning that because they were not yet baptized, they were afraid that they would die in a state of sin. In essence, they were concerned for their soul. The participants understood the function of this period of deviance, but even those currently in the simmie period expressed a greater belief in, and preference for, the norms of adult culture.

Anxiety did not automatically dissipate, however, upon taking adult baptism or upon defection. This is so because the Amish do not adhere to the "plan of salvation" (Book of John, verse 3:16, Holy Bible) as do most Christian churches (Hostetler, 1993; Reiling, 2000), wherein the acknowledgment of "Jesus Christ as the Son of God" and the acceptance of "Jesus Christ as Lord and Savior" through the taking of baptism guarantees acceptance into Heaven. Instead, the Amish believe that accepting "Jesus Christ as Lord and Savior" may be necessary to achieve salvation, but acceptance alone may not be sufficient. For the Amish, their God is continually judging whether they are "fit for Heaven," even after baptism.

As such, anxiety over transgressions committed during the simmie period did not diminish for most upon taking adult baptism because they believed that their God could still hold them accountable for these acts. Consequently, regret over their behavior was high. As evidence of the strength of this belief, almost every one of the defected coethnics reported still fearing for their salvation, even though they had subsequently joined a Christian church that did accept John 3:16 as the plan of salvation. New ideology did not totally supplant the old beliefs.

The following quote from a 25-year-old Amish man illustrates this belief, as well as the conviction that the risk was necessary for the survival of the group: "I'm very concerned about my children coming to the youth age and running with the crowd. I realize other youth, the English, aren't perfect and there's going to be problems, but that's different, 'cause the Amish say, you know, they sow their wild oats and they go out and do things for a while, but then they come back to the church. But then I'm thinking, but someday, somebody's children are going to be in that state and Jesus is coming. That is my greatest concern. That my children will be in that stage and caught out when Jesus comes. But that's a risk we've all had to take to get to be Amish, passing through that period."

High levels of anxiety were generated because the Amish apparently had not constructed, or had at least not been able to articulate, an explanation of what happens to an Amish youth who dies not only without having achieved adult baptism but while living in what they believed to be a morally wrong way. There was no definitive answer for them, other than a vague notion that "sinners probably go to Hell." Participating in this deviance caused youth to engage in a high level of contemplation of their mortality. More correctly, what they contemplated was not the fact that someday they would die, but the question of what would happen to them when they did. . . .

As one simmie girl explained, "I just hope Jesus understands that I'm just doing what I'm expected to do."

To more fully illustrate the experience, each of the four types of culturally prescribed deviance, or morally wrong practices, that were identified as particularly problematic will be discussed more fully below: differential norms, alcohol use, bedding, and parental complicity in deviance. . . .

It was reported that the amount and type of deviance that was allowed varied greatly by district. The lack of uniformity of norms was considered to be a morally wrong cultural practice because it left the youth uncertain as to their fate after death. Amish people attempt to live within their stated ideology, and as such,

it is imperative to have consensus concerning that ideology. The anomic state created by differential norms generated a high level of anxiety. As one Amish woman noted, "Each district being so different about what's right and wrong sends mixed messages to kids. That was one thing that was real hard for me, 'cause is there more than one way to be right?"

. . . .

◇ Discussion

The expression of angst and turmoil among the Amish youth must be put into perspective as a characteristic of most youth cultures and not necessarily Amish specific. The fact that they had identity crises, as such, was not surprising when considering that the youth period has long been theorized as disruptive, particularly in terms of identity (Erikson, 1968). Nor should the affective responses of anxiety and depression be unexpected, given that youth, in general, have been found to have higher rates of emotional distress (Rumbaut, 1996).

But what is context specific and therefore different for Amish youth is the complex nature of their deviance, and their negative affective response to that deviance, especially because the deviance is prescribed and sanctioned by adult culture. This circumstance is created by primarily four unique factors. First and foremost, on the child's 16th birthday, norms become immediately inverted. Amish youth literally wake up one morning and find themselves in an intense state of anomie. Even though the youth knows that change is coming, there is no transition period, no anticipatory socialization within which to prepare gradually.

Second, norms for the youth period are radically different from the adult norms the youth had been following. Unlike other cultural contexts, Amish youth are not engaging in anticipatory socialization when engaging in youth deviance. Learning to drink alcohol, for example, is not anticipatory socialization because drinking alcohol is not a part of adult culture. Neither are fornication (symbolic or literal), sanctioning deviant behavior, or sanctioning differential norms. The youth view these behaviors as morally wrong cultural practices because these behaviors are not part of adult cultural practice.

The third factor is that the norms that Amish adult culture prescribes for Amish youth vary so greatly from the norms that English adult culture prescribes for English youth living within their same geographic area. Because of this, Amish youth have a very difficult time dealing with the enormity of their lived contradictions, especially when comparing themselves to the English. The Amish way of life has been socially constructed as more virtuous, and yet many times Amish youth are more deviant than English youth, with the complicit permission of their "virtuous" parents. As such, self-discrepancy generates a level of depression and anxiety among Amish youth that would probably measure far higher than for youth in other cultural contexts.

The fourth and final factor that makes the youth period particularly disruptive is that, after 16 years of intense family socialization, Amish youth have very firmly internalized the more rigid adult norms. As such, having norms suddenly inverted, and to such an extraordinary degree, is experienced as tremendous culture shock. One could argue that the inversion of norms is a characteristic of most youth cultures, but a vital distinction must be made in that Amish youth are not choosing for the norms to be inverted. Adults, not youth, construct Amish youth culture.

. . . .

◇ References

Adam, B. D. (1978). *The survival of domination: Inferiorization and everyday life.* New York: Elsevier.

Adler, P., & Adler, P. (1987). *Membership roles in field research.* Newbury Park, CA: Sage.

Adler, P., & Adler, P. (1998). *Peer power: Preadolescent culture and identity.* New Brunswick, NJ: Rutgers University Press.

Baumeister, R. F., & Muraven, M. (1996). Identity as adaptation to social, cultural, and historical context. *Journal of Adolescence, 19*, 405–416.

Corsaro, W., & Eder, D. (1990). Children's peer culture. *Annual Review of Sociology, 76*, 197–220.

Danielsen, L. M., Lorem, A. E., & Kroger, J. (2000). The impact of social context on the identity-formation process of Norwegian late adolescents. *Youth & Society, 31*, 332–362.

Emerson, R., & Pollner, M. (2001). Constructing participant/observation relations. In R. M. Emerson (Ed.), *Contemporary field research: Perspectives and formulations* (pp. 239–259). Prospect Heights, IL: Waveland.

Erikson, E. H. (1968). *Identity: Youth and crisis.* New York: Norton.

Greenberg, J., Pyszczynski, T., Solomon, S., Rosenblatt, A., Veeder, M., Kirkland, S., et al. (1990). Evidence for terror management theory II: The effects of mortality salience on reactions to those who threaten or bolster the cultural worldview. *Journal of Personality and Social Psychology, 58*, 308–318.

Hostetler, J. A. (1993). *Amish society.* Baltimore: Johns Hopkins Press.

Huntington, G. E. (1988). *Ethnic families in America: Patterns and variations.* New York: Elsevier.

Hutchby, I., & Moran-Ellis, J. (1998). *Children and social competence: Arenas of action.* London: Falmer.

Janssen, J., Dechesne, M., & Van Knippenberg, A. (1999). The psychological importance of youth culture: A terror management approach. *Youth & Society, 31*, 152–167.

Marques, J. M. (1986). *Toward a definition of social processing of information: An application to stereotyping.* Doctoral dissertation.

Nolt, S. M. (1992). *A history of the Amish.* Intercourse, PA: Good Books.

Pyszczynski, T., Greenberg, J., & Solomon, S. (1997). Why do we need what we need? A terror management perspective on the roots of social motivation. *Psychological Inquiry, 8*, 1–21.

Reiling, D. M. (2000). *An exploration of the relationship between Amish identity and depression among the Old Order Amish.* Dissertation. UMI9985454.

Reiling, D. M., & Nusbaumer, M. R. (1997). The Amish Drug Task Force: A natural history approach to the construction of a social problem. *Journal of Multicultural Nursing & Health, 3*, 25–37.

Rumbaut, R. G. (1996). The crucible within: Ethnic identity, self-esteem, and segmented assimilation among children of immigrants. In A. Portes (Ed.), *The new second generation* (pp. 119–170). New York: Russell Sage.

Solomon, S., Greenberg, J., & Pyszczynski, T. (1991). A terror management theory of social behavior: The psychological functions of self-esteem and cultural worldviews. *Advances in Experimental Social Psychology, 24*, 93–159.

Triandis, H. C. (1990). Theoretical concepts that are applicable to the analysis of ethnocentrism. In R. W. Brislin (Ed.), *Applied cross-cultural psychology* (pp. 34–55). Newbury Park, CA: Sage.

READING 5

This article describes illness as an increasingly public experience as individuals access the Internet and share information through chat rooms, listservs, electronic support groups, and other online forums. The authors focus on celiac disease as an example for social media and health, viewing open-access Facebook posts where users shared personal information and experiences. They find the Internet is an important source of information, advice, and advocacy. The health-related Internet sites are available 24/7 and are globally accessible; the authors argue that this is a revolutionary change.

Illness and the Internet

From Private to Public Experience

Peter Conrad, Julia Bandini, and Alexandria Vasquez

Illness is a ubiquitous experience in all societies. Different cultures have different ways of responding to illness. Historically in Western cultures, illness is typically handled by self, kin, healers, or other specialized individuals. While the existence of illness may become a societal concern (e.g. various plagues, public health), the sufferers' experience and management of illness, while possibly culturally scripted, remain largely a private experience, until recently.

Sociologists have been studying the subjective experience of illness for nearly 50 years (Conrad and Stults, 2010). Until roughly the turn of this century, there were two consistent findings: (1) there were no illness subcultures, and (2) illness was a profoundly privatizing experience (with a few notable exceptions like the HIV/AIDS or breast cancer activist and support groups). As the sociological theorist Talcott Parsons observed, "illness usually prevents the individual from attaching himself to a solitary subculture of similarly oriented deviants" (Parsons and Fox, 1952: 137). French sociologist Claudine Herzlich (2004) notes, "It is difficult

to discern whether health and illness belong more in the private or public domain." The few studies available suggest that, even in institutions, illness experience remained individual and private, and even more so in the community (Conrad and Stults, 2010). As just one example, several decades ago, Schneider and Conrad (1983) interviewed 80 people with epilepsy and found that only 5 of the respondents had ever talked to anyone else who shared the same illness. For the overwhelming majority of people with chronic conditions, illness remained a private experience and shared only with family, medical personnel, and perhaps a few close friends. We are quite certain this would not be the case today. It would be an exaggeration to say that the Internet has changed everything, but it seems clear the Internet has revolutionized the interactive experience of illness, transforming illness experience for many people from a private to public experience. In this article, we will examine the role of the Internet in the facilitation of illness from a private to a public experience and the social consequences of the Internet in illness experience.[1]

Source: Conrad, P., Bandini, J., & Vasquez, A. (2016). Illness and the Internet: From private to public experience. *Health, 20*(1), 22–32. doi:10.1177/ 1363459315611941

The Internet, as we know it, with a browser for general use began in 1993 (e.g. Mosaic). Google, as an Internet search engine, appeared in 1998. This kind of potential access to online information and interconnectivity is the watershed event that made the Internet increasingly useful for obtaining information and connecting with others. There were about 360 million users in 2000, and by 2015, there are over 3 billion users worldwide (stastica.com). In the United States, 87 percent of US adults use the Internet, 72 percent of Internet users say they looked online for health information within the past year, 26 percent of Internet users have read or watched someone else's experience about health in the past year, and 18 percent of Internet users have gone online to find others who might have similar health concerns (Pew Internet Project, 2014). In short, there is a large and active number of people who use the Internet for health information and to interact with others about their illness or medical condition.

Based on their research, Ziebland and Wyke (2012) contend that there are seven health domains that drive the use of the Internet in peer-to-peer connections. The five major ones include finding information, feeling supported, maintaining relationships with others, affecting behavior, and experiencing health services. Not surprisingly, people with chronic illness and disability (or sometimes their caregivers) are among the largest users of health sites on the Internet.

As Ziebland and Wyke (2012) note, "the use of the Internet for peer-to-peer connection has been one of its most dramatic and transformational features" (p. 19). Whether people with illness go online for information, support, advocacy, or comparative experiences, the Internet becomes a route to connections, often forming an illness subculture. In the first decade of online communities, there were a range of online mechanisms to make peer-to-peer connections including websites, blogs, bulletin boards, chat rooms, news groups, listservs, electronic support groups (ESGs), and forums. Some of these were asynchronous, in which individuals need not be online at the same time, while others were synchronous in which online users participated in real time.

Some of these websites required signing on to their accounts or joining, some had moderators, while many others were open to the public. While these Internet modes of connection differed in some ways, they all were available 24/7, many were anonymous or used screen names, most were globally available, and were "free" to anyone who had access to the Internet. Together, they created a vehicle that produced new connections, lay knowledge, and often vibrant online communities. It is difficult to know how many people these sites affected since only some participants actually posted material, while many more were observers, termed "lurkers," who would view the discussions, but did not post or actively participate. It is both the anonymity and lurking that make the actual participation difficult to measure. It is hard to estimate participation. The 1 percent rule states that 90 percent of online users do not actively contribute to Internet posts, while 9 percent somewhat contribute, and only 1 percent are responsible for generating new content. A recent study (Van Mierlo, 2014) found that this 1 percent rule was consistent across digital health social networks (DHSNs) as 1 percent of users actively contributed to content on these sites. This suggests that there are far more individuals silently participating in the various sites than are visible on screen. A study of 3000 respondents found that one in four Internet users living with a chronic condition reported going online to find others with similar health conditions (Fox, 2011). The utility of the Internet as a knowledge base and interactive venue for various diseases has transformed the nature of the experience of illness. Virtually any illness or medical condition has multiple sites online, openly accessible to anyone interested. Without question, illness in the 21st century has moved from a private to a public experience.

◈ From Web 1.0 to Web 2.0

In the past two decades, we have seen an enormous expansion of the Internet both in the number of users and in the amount of information and connections available. In terms of this article, one can see two kinds of Internet experiences, called in retrospect Web 1.0 and Web 2.0 (Cornode and Krishnamurthy, 2008). In Web 1.0, the vast majority of users are seeking already created content, which can be searched and retrieved from existing websites. Here, communication is largely in one direction, where information sought and retrieved has been already produced, often by professionally created websites (e.g. WebMD, the Mayo Clinic). In a sense, these websites are "passive": they can be accessed but not modified or contributed to by users.

In what is often called Web 2.0, the emphasis is on user-generated content and visibility. Here is where users can be interactive and collaborative with one another. The users create much of the content. In the past decade, Web 2.0 has expanded with a range of interactive websites (blogs, ESGs) and especially what is called "social media" (e.g. Facebook, Instagram, Twitter). With social media, the participants create, share, or exchange information, experiences, and even photos and videos in user-defined virtual communities and networks. The numerous kinds of Internet-based social media are built on the capabilities of Web 2.0 technologies and have significantly expanded the ways in which people with special interests (e.g. in our case an illness or condition) can connect with one another as "friends," network connections on Facebook, or through specifically created "Facebook pages." Together, these groups facilitate the interaction and exchange of user-generated content, often to a specific group of friends. One major difference from previous Internet interaction modes, social media does not emphasize online "anonymity," as did previous vehicles such as bulletin boards and chat rooms. Yet, the Information Highway has been supplemented by the Interaction Highway.

◈ Web 2.0 and the Proliferation of Public Illness Experiences

Interaction on the Internet became the norm after 2000 or so. There were thousands of websites, representing virtually any illness, both well-known and unknown. For example, Barker (2008) examined an ESG for the contested illness, fibromyalgia. This was one of numerous sites that provided support, information, and advocacy for the treatment of fibromyalgia. The wide reach of illness on the Internet can be exemplified by two unusual and controversial conditions that have spawned interactive websites that are at the same time supportive, informative, and involved in advocacy. Conrad and Rondini (2010) described support groups that are depicted as

"proana" and "transabled." The proana websites claimed to provide support for anorexics, but in a particular way: claiming anorexia is a lifestyle and not a disease, providing advice on how to be a "better anorexic," and advocating for the demedicalization of anorexia. The second case Conrad and Rondini examined went under a number of names, including "amputees by choice" and "transabled." Subscribers who posted on these sites were individuals who believed that they were meant to be amputees (usually of some limb) and searched for others who shared the same orientation. They use a similar vocabulary as transgendered individuals: "I wasn't meant to be born with my 'left leg' or 'arm.'" Because the phenomenon of transabled is very rare, it seems likely that without the Internet, this phenomenon as a potential diagnosis would not exist, since each individual might believe only that he or she had these unusual desires. But with the Internet, there are a number of interactive websites that allow transabled individuals to exchange information, engender support for their condition, and advocate that their condition become medicalized as Body Image Identity Disorder (BIID) in the American Psychiatric Association's Diagnostic and Statistical Manual (DSM) with the hope that the medical profession will accept their disorder and thus provide the surgical amputation treatment they are seeking. (As of 2015, this condition is not a medically accepted diagnosis, nor are any surgeons willing to amputate healthy limbs.)

Most illnesses on the Internet are more common and have spawned many different websites, online support groups, and social networks. For example, if one googled "diabetes support group" in mid-2015, the results page tells us there are 13,300,000 hits. While it is likely the number is hugely exaggerated since there are probably hundreds of repeats, it gives an idea that there are at least "very many" diabetes support groups available on the Internet. To give another example, if one googled "celiac disease support group," one would see that there were 636,000 hits. As a comparison, "anorexia support groups" yielded about 1,490,000 hits and "transabled support groups" a mere 6130 hits. Such numbers indicate both a proliferation of opportunities to connect with similarly ill others and a redundancy from poorly filtered hits on the Internet search. It is unclear what these numbers mean except as comparative availability of potential "hits" of one illness relative to another.

We will use celiac disease, an autoimmune disorder in which the ingestion of gluten can cause damage in the small intestine, as our example for social media and health. It is treated by eliminating gluten from one's diet. Gluten-free diets and the diagnosis of celiac disease (and the more controversial claims to "gluten sensitivity") are issues that have come to the public forefront within the last two decades. Our choice of illness here lies partly on the currency of the publicity of gluten and celiac disease, with most of the Internet and social media interactions occurring in the past decade. Our focus is primarily on Facebook because it has the most users and overall activity of all social media platforms, it provides the most communication variation of all social media platforms (e.g. visual, textual, community pages), and because many social media users now have accounts on other social media platforms, such as Twitter, Instagram, Vine, Google+, to name a few, yet still consider Facebook to be their "home-base" platform (Duggan et al., 2015). This example will allow us to illustrate how individuals with celiac disease both create and interact using social media on the Internet.

◈ Social Media and Illness Experience: Celiac Disease

The advent of Web 2.0 and active media sites such as Facebook, Twitter, and Instagram is one avenue for exploring the experience of illness on the Internet. In particular, Facebook serves as a site in which people can both anonymously and visibly view a variety of Facebook pages devoted to particular diseases as well as engage in private or restricted Facebook groups. The case of celiac disease is a particularly interesting example for studying illness on the Internet because the treatment is a lifestyle change involving the gluten-free diet, rather than a medical regimen of prescription medications.

Viewers can anonymously view Facebook pages sponsored by national celiac disease or medical organizations, such as the Celiac Disease Foundation's Facebook page,[2] the National Foundation for Celiac Awareness,[3] Gluten Intolerance Group of North America,[4] and the University of Chicago Celiac Disease Center.[5] In addition to accessing basic information about celiac disease and recent medical updates, visitors to these public Facebook pages can view recent news articles about celiac disease, be alerted to product recalls for gluten-free products, watch videos for gluten-free recipes, and view photos of new gluten-free products and recipes. Public posts range from personal issues on how to talk to family members about screening for celiac disease to public announcements of upcoming gluten-free products by mainstream food companies. Regional support and advocacy groups for people with celiac disease have also created Facebook pages to facilitate local connectivity both online and offline through tips about new products and local gluten-free restaurants, as well as closed Facebook groups that are not accessible to the public that enable individuals to connect on a more personal and private basis. Individuals also post questions and comments on many public pages, which can be viewed by outside anonymous visitors from all over the United States and globally, and other online users post responses to these questions. For example, on the National Foundation for Celiac Awareness public Facebook page under a post to a video on the diagnostic delay of women with celiac disease, one woman comments on her own experience of diagnosis:

> Years and years and years! That's how long! And then, after my primary doctor got a positive on the blood test, the gastro doc didn't want to take the time for the intestinal biopsy during my colonoscopy, telling me, "you're not celiac, you're only sensitive. You're numbers aren't high enough to actually be celiac," which was news to me because my primary had actually diagnosed me as celiac. So, I tell my primary doc and she tells my gastro doc to DO THE BIOPSY. After years of suffering, guess what! The biopsy was positive! Always be your own advocate. Be your best supporter and never take no for an answer but more importantly, don't ever be discredited or talked down to by a doctor.

Another online user agrees and comments,

> My GI doctor was the same way! Argued with me about performing the endoscopy . . . When

he came into the recovery room (while I was still asleep but could hear everything he was saying) and said that everything was flattened and I needed to start a GF diet immediately . . . All I wanted was to sit up and scream I told you so. Lol.

These posts are not anonymous and can be easily accessed by viewing the group's Facebook page, yet online users post personal information related to their diagnosis, family history, and symptoms on these Facebook pages, demonstrating a type of support community for individuals with celiac disease facilitated by social media. These open-access Facebook pages exemplify the transformation of the experience of celiac disease from a private illness involving a change in diet to a public experience to which a community of online users contribute and provide suggestions and recommendations on the latest updates on the gluten-free diet. Unlike Web 1.0 and online support groups, the social media connectivity in these examples of celiac disease on Facebook represents the advance of Web 2.0 as they demonstrate the interactive and public nature of social media. They are indeed virtual communities creating an online subculture of celiac sufferers. Online posts about celiac disease also blur the boundary between medical treatment and food, as the medical regimen for celiac disease is a dietary change, and serve as an example of the transformation of the experience of illness from a private to public experience that is reinforced by an active community of online users.

◈ Implications and Consequences of Illness as a Public Experience

In considering the implications of the Internet in the experience of illness, Conrad and Stults (2010) note that "the Internet has changed the experience of illness" (p. 180), particularly through illness subcultures and public notions around illness. The Internet has served as a catalyst in transforming the experience of illness from a private experience to a public one, particularly through its variety of its characteristics: (1) in serving as an information source for patients, (2) in becoming

a repository of experiential knowledge, (3) in facilitating communication and support among individuals affected by a particular condition, (4) in shaping social movements (e.g. advocacy) around illnesses and collective illness identity, and (5) in playing a role in the changing nature of the doctor–patient relationship. We will comment briefly on all five aspects of social media and its impact on illness experience:

1. The Internet serves as a source of information for patients as well as for those who provide care to family members or others with an illness. Individuals can seek information online about their own condition and the recommended treatment rather than rely solely on the physician or standard medical sources as a resource of information about one's illness. This characteristic of the Internet is particularly notable for acute illnesses in which individuals may "self-diagnose" based upon symptoms described on the Internet. In addition, many aspects of Web 2.0 are interactive in that they bridge geographical spaces and time and allow illness peers to engage in online health communities (OHCs) and information seeking from their computers (or smart phones) 24/7. However, the notion of risk is an important consequence of seeking information related to health on the Internet and engaging in these OHCs, as patients may receive misinformation from other online users. Healthcare providers do not monitor online health forums and communities, and online users can post their own opinions and experiences around their condition and medical treatments they utilized, which is available to be read by all those who access the site. Advertisements to patients about specific medical treatments also appear online and may shape patients' ideas about their own health condition.

2. The Internet allows individuals to easily seek experiential knowledge. The Internet provides a different type of knowledge and empowerment to online users that they would otherwise not receive from a physician or other medical

sources. For example, online users share knowledge around particular physicians to consult, preferences for medications, and issues around one's lifestyle that they can receive online without a visit to a clinician. In addition, non-ill others, including caretakers, can learn about the illness experience from these sites. Goffman (1963) might have called this the knowledge of the "wise," individuals who understand insider meanings of living with the illness. This availability of experiential knowledge represents more of the "soft" subjective side of an illness rather than the clinical or biomedical information one may receive in a clinic visit. In a fashion, this is like joining an Internet club where individuals with an illness can interact with similar others.

3. The Internet also facilitates communication among other patients and families, particularly caregivers, dealing with illness. This function of the Internet resonates more clearly with those with chronic rather than acute illnesses. Glenn's (2015) recent article of mothers of children with rare genetic disorders demonstrates the ways in which patients or caregivers can engage and connect with other individuals who are confronted with the same illness via the Internet, especially in cases in which the condition is rare and in which the individual has never met anyone with the illness in person. OHCs in particular serve as a source of emotional support for online patient seekers, as they allow individuals to learn about and engage in their illness experience without the potential stigma present in face-to-face interactions through the anonymity of the Internet (Broom, 2005), particularly in cases of psychiatric conditions (Berger et al., 2005). OHCs also enable patients to engage in various activities of activism around a particular cause for a disease. For example, "Glu,"[6] an online health community for Type 1 diabetes (T1D), allows participants to connect and emphasize the importance of research on T1D, as their mission statement reads: "Glu is an active and diverse type 1 diabetes online community designed to accelerate research and amplify the collective voice of those living with T1D." Additionally, the weight-loss bloggers that Leggatt-Cook and Chamberlain (2012) study engaged in a more indirect method of activism through their comments on the meanings of being overweight in society and "offered critical commentary on fatness that went beyond individual struggles with weight" (p. 967). This article also points to the notion that blogs shift the private experience of weight loss to a public one, in which bloggers post their individual details, struggles, and experiences about their weight publicly.

4. The Internet has changed the notion of social movements and advocacy for various diseases and the collective identity around illness, as it facilitates the virtual connection of individuals through cyberspace. For example, the Internet has enabled connectivity and virtual interactions for parents of children with autism, aiding in the anti-vaccine movement as well as spawning the neurodiversity movement among some diagnosed with autism (Baker, 2006). Barker (2008) discusses such issues of collectivity in her piece on ESGs for patients with fibromyalgia, noting the ways in which ESGs provide the opportunity for patients to share information and become "experts" and advocates for their contested illness. Social movements surrounding certain diseases are possible with the Internet, as such a virtual place allows patients to collectively mobilize in cyberspace.

5. There is also a change in the doctor–patient relationship in which there is a resistance to the traditional hierarchy, as the patient becomes active in his or her disease management and lifestyle. Hardey's (1999) early notion when the Internet became more publicly available at the end of the 20th century that the Internet blurs the personal and professional aspects of illness remains true today, as patients are increasingly becoming active consumers of their own medical care and knowledge around health. Conrad

and Stults (2010) suggest that the Internet empowers patients and oftentimes "challenges physicians' expertise . . . which probably does erode physician authority to some degree, but to what extent and with what consequences are not yet understood" (p. 187).

Because the Internet is used among patients to seek information and learn about one's condition, it is important to recognize that there is no one term to describe the site at which online users gather to exchange information and share experiences. These terms are also followed by a certain acronym to shorten the phrase to describe these communities. Barker (2008) uses the term "electronic support groups," while others use the term "digital health social networks" (Van Mierlo, 2014) or "online health communities" (Glenn, 2015). The language of an OHC is a more neutral term to describe a location for the exchange of knowledge and information than solely a site for reasons of support. Similarly, it is important to consider the language we use to refer to these individuals who access the Internet for information and support around disease and illness. These individuals can be termed in different ways, including "patients," "visitors," "online users," and "online surfers," depending on their use of the Internet as a tool in illness experience. For example, the fact that the term to describe these individuals is unclear indicates that there are new ways of thinking about the experience of illness with advances in technology in our society and the ability to engage actively in one's own care.

◇ Concluding Remarks

As this article has argued, the availability and use of the Internet have transformed the experience of illness from a fundamentally private experience to an increasingly public one. This is a major transformation of the illness experience, one from which we believe there is no return. We expect that while there will of course always be private aspects of illness, the Internet-facilitated public faces of illness will remain and probably grow. There are just too many benefits for ill or disabled people for the interactive sites to fade away. These sites are convenient, accessible from the comforts of home, via computer, tablet, and smart phone. Not only can these interactive sites now always be with us, they are 24/7 and globally accessible by our ever-present mobile phone. It is likely that as new dimensions of the Internet are created, experiential illness-oriented websites will adapt to new technologies and find ways to maintain or even expand their interactive capabilities. In this sense, there was a smooth transition from the early interactive Web 2.0 websites to the current social media connections (e.g. Facebook). Future technological advances in the Internet through new media avenues, mobile apps, or innovations that we cannot yet even imagine may change the shape of the interactive experience, but the existence of the public face of illness will adapt and remain vibrant.

There are a few characteristics of the Internet experience of illness that bear watching to see how they develop in future years. The potential of anonymity (e.g. screen names, lurking) has always been part of the attraction of the Internet and is already somewhat challenged by social media, where one of the main characteristics is individual identity (e.g. Facebook pages). Will social media or some future form of connectivity erode the anonymity that remains an attractive feature of the illness interaction sites? Related to this, will many sites remain "open access" so that any interested party can join and participate? Will the Internet remain essentially "cost free" and globally available? The interactive illness websites have adapted as necessary for the past two decades, and one can only imagine that the demand is sufficient for continuing types of adaptation. The public face of illness, while recent in creation, is likely to remain a significant characteristic of illness well into the future.

◇ Notes

1. While there is a multitude of Internet technologies that play a role in illness experience including websites, listservs, online chat rooms, social media sites, and mobile apps, we include all of these as Internet facilitators for the public experience of illness. For social media, we focus on Facebook, the largest and most popular Internet site.
2. https://www.facebook.com/CeliacDiseaseFoundation
3. https://www.facebook.com/NFCeliacAwareness
4. https://www.facebook.com/GlutenIntoleranceGroup
5. https://www.facebook.com/CureCeliac
6. https://myglu.org/?gclid=COf_k7S3psYCFREoaQodILcA0Q

◈ References

Baker DL (2006) Neurodiversity, neurological disability and the public sector: Notes on the autism spectrum. *Disability and Society* 21(1): 15–29.

Barker KK (2008) Electronic support groups, patient-consumers, and medicalization: The case of contested illness. *Journal of Health and Social Behavior* 49(1): 20–36.

Berger M, Wagner TH and Baker LC (2005) Internet use and stigmatized illness. *Social Science & Medicine* 61(8): 1821–1827.

Broom A (2005) Virtually He@lthy: The impact of Internet use on disease experience and the doctor-patient relationship. *Qualitative Health Research* 15(3): 325–345.

Conrad P and Rondini A (2010) The internet and medicalization: Reshaping the global body and illness. In: Ettorre E (ed.) *Culture, Bodies and the Sociology of Health*. Farnham: Ashgate, pp. 107–120.

Conrad P and Stults C (2010) Internet and the experience of illness. In: Bird C, Conrad P, Fremont A, et al. (eds) *Handbook of Medical Sociology*. 6th ed. Nashville, TN: Vanderbilt University Press, pp. 179–191.

Cornode G and Krishnamurthy B (2008) Key differences between Web 1.0 and Web 2.0. *First Monday* 13: 6.

Duggan M, Ellison NB, Lampe C, et al. (2015) *Social Media Update 2014*. Pew Research Center: Internet, Science & Tech. Available at: http://www.pewinternet.org/2015/01/09/social-media-update-2014/ (accessed 8 September 2015).

Fox S (2011) *The Social Life of Health Information, 2011*. Pew Research Center: Internet, Science & Tech. Available at: http://www.pewinternet.org/2011/05/12/the-social-life-of-health-information-2011/ (accessed 23 July 2015).

Glenn AD (2015) Using online health communication to manage chronic sorrow: Mothers of children with rare diseases speak. *Journal of Pediatric Nursing* 30(1): 17–24.

Goffman E (1963) *Stigma: Notes on the Management of Spoiled Identity*. Englewood Cliffs, NJ: Prentice Hall.

Hardey M (1999) Doctor in the house: The Internet as a source of lay health knowledge and the challenge to expertise. *Sociology of Health & Illness* 21(6): 820–835.

Herzlich C (2004) Health and illness at the dawn of the 21st century: From private experience to public affair and back. *Michael* 1: 163–171.

Leggatt-Cook C and Chamberlain K (2012) Blogging for weight loss: Personal accountability, writing selves, and the weight-loss blogosphere. *Sociology of Health & Illness* 34(7): 963–977.

Parsons T and Fox R (1952) Illness, therapy and the modern urban American family. *Journal of Social Issues* 8(4): 31–44.

Pew Research Center: Internet, Science & Tech (2014) *Health Fact Sheet*. Available at: http://www.pewinternet.org/fact-sheets/health-fact-sheet/ (accessed 23 July 2015).

Schneider JW and Conrad P (1983) *Having Epilepsy: The Experience and Control of Illness*. Philadelphia, PA: Temple University Press.

Van Mierlo T (2014) The 1% rule in four digital health social networks: An observational study. *Journal of Medical Internet Research* 16(2): e33.

Ziebland S and Wyke S (2012) Health and illness in a connected world: How might sharing experiences on the internet affect people's health? *Milbank Quarterly* 90(2): 219–249.

READING 6

This brief article explores elite deviance or "corporate transgressions" through the concept of moral disengagement. The authors outline concepts and strategies that allow for corporate deviance to occur and why corporate deviants' consciences are not seemingly bothered. Strategies include moral justification (justifying the rightness of their actions), euphemistic labeling (changing the deviant status of an activity by changing its label to something innocuous or even positive), advantageous comparison (making something look better by comparing it to something much worse), displacement of responsibility (placing the blame elsewhere), diffusion of responsibility (taking less blame by placing it on the group), dehumanization (ascribing less-than-human qualities to the victims so they appear less deserving), and the attribution of blame (placing the blame on others or on certain circumstances). They then describe four famous case studies of elite deviance: (1) an industrial disaster in Bhopal, India, in 1984, where "at least

Source: Bandura, A., Caprara, G.-V., & Zsolnai, L. (2000). Corporate transgressions through moral disengagement. *Journal of Human Values*, 6(1): 57–64. Originally published in the *Journal of Human Values*, Indian Institute of Management, Kolkata. All rights reserved. Reproduced with the permission of the copyright holders and the publishers, SAGE Publications India Pvt. Ltd, New Delhi.

2,500 people were killed, 10,000 seriously injured, 20,000 partially disabled, and 180,000 others affected" in other ways; (2) the Ford Pinto case, in which faulty designs led to hundreds of burn deaths; (3) the Nestle case, in which the company sold infant formula to Third World countries where environmental and social conditions interacted with the formula so that it was not good for the babies' health; and (4) the Three Mile Island case involving a devastating accident at a nuclear power plant and how it was dealt with by those in charge. The case examples show how corporations were able to disregard the consequences of their negligent and harmful behavior.

Corporate Transgressions Through Moral Disengagement*

Albert Bandura, Gian-Vittorio Caprara, and Laszlo Zsolnai

In the past decades corporate transgressions have become a major socio-political problem both in developed and developing countries. The phenomenon of corporate deviance requires critical, cross-disciplinary studies that might illuminate the darker side of contemporary business practice. We have to acknowledge that one is dealing with institutional practices that are not easily examinable by conventional means. Study of corporate transgressions is highly reliant on scandals, the media, public inquiries, police investigations and whistle-blowers for glimpses of the concealed world of top management and its involvement in dirty tricks. Much research relies therefore on published secondary sources.[1]

Corporate transgression is about the exercise and abuse of power that is closely linked to the legitimate conduct of business. The essence of business is pursuit of legitimate interests of the parties involved in transactions circumscribed by rules that protect both the parties and their relationship to the interests of the public, society, state and regulatory agencies.[2]

Although a great deal of corporate transgression is never classified as crime and the law plays a minor role in its regulation, the greatest discrepancy between common and white-collar violations is that corporations have the power to mobilize resources to influence the rules that cover their own conduct. In many cases corporations actively defend their interests in ways that would normally be unthinkable for common law breakers.[3]

The most striking aspect of corporate transgression is that it is committed not by dangerous criminally-oriented mavericks, but by eminent members of the business community who break rules ostensibly in the interests of their companies and their own.[4] The challenging question is why otherwise good managers engage in dirty business and why their conscience never bothers them.[5] In this article we draw on the theory and empirical findings of moral psychology to shed some light on this paradox.

◈ Social Cognitive Theory of Moral Agency

Social cognitive theory addresses the exercise of moral agency.[6] In this explanatory framework personal factors in the form of moral thought and self-evaluative reactions, moral conduct and environmental influences operate as interacting determinants of each other. Within this triadic reciprocal causation, moral agency is exercised through self-regulatory mechanisms. Transgressive conduct is regulated by two sets of sanctions, social and personal. Social sanctions are rooted in the fear of external punishment, while self-sanctions operate through self-condemning

---

*Some text and accompanying endnotes have been omitted. Please consult the original source.

reactions to one's misconduct. After people adopt moral standards, self-sanctions serve as the main guides and deterrents that keep behaviour in line with moral standards.

The adoption of moral standards does not create a fixed control mechanism within the person. There are many psycho-social mechanisms by which moral control can be selectively engaged or disengaged from detrimental conduct.[7] The mechanisms of moral disengagement enable otherwise considerate people to commit transgressive acts without experiencing personal distress.

Moral Justification

People do not ordinarily engage in reprehensible conduct until they have justified to themselves the rightness of their actions. In this process of moral justification detrimental conduct is made personally and socially acceptable by portraying it in the service of valued social or moral purposes.

Euphemistic Labelling

Activities can take on markedly different appearances depending on what they are called. Euphemistic labelling provides a convenient tool for masking reprehensible activities or even conferring a respectable status upon them. Through sanitized and convoluted verbiage destructive conduct is made benign and those who engage in it are relieved of a sense of personal agency.

Advantageous Comparison

Behaviour can also assume very different qualities depending on what it is contrasted with. By exploiting advantageous comparison injurious conduct can be rendered benign or made to appear to be of little consequence. The more flagrant the contrasted activities, the more likely it is that one's own injurious conduct will appear trifling or even benevolent.

Displacement of Responsibility

Under displacement of responsibility people view their actions as springing from social pressures or dictates of others rather than as something for which they are personally responsible. Because they are not the actual agents of their actions, they are spared self-censuring reactions. Hence, they are willing to behave in ways they normally repudiate if a legitimate authority accepts responsibility for the effects of their actions.

Diffusion of Responsibility

The exercise of moral control is also weakened when personal agency is obscured by diffusion of responsibility for detrimental conduct. Any harm done by a group can always be attributed largely to the behaviour of others. People behave more cruelly under group responsibility than when they hold themselves personally accountable for their actions.

Disregarding or Distorting the Consequences

Additional ways of weakening self-deterring reactions operate by disregarding or distorting the consequences of action. When people pursue activities harmful to others for personal gain or because of social inducements they avoid facing the harm they cause or they minimize it. In addition to selective inattention and cognitive distortion of effects, the misrepresentation may involve active efforts to discredit evidence of the harm that is caused.

Dehumanization

Self-censure for injurious conduct can be disengaged or blunted by dehumanization that divests people of human qualities or attributes bestial qualities to them. Once dehumanized, they are no longer viewed as persons with feelings, hopes, and concerns, but as subhuman objects.

Attribution of Blame

Blaming one's adversaries or compelling circumstances is still another expedient that can serve self-exonerating purposes. In moral disengagement by attribution of blame, people view themselves as faultless victims driven to injurious conduct by forcible provocation. By fixing the blame on others or on circumstances, not only are one's own injurious actions excusable, but one can even feel self-righteous in the process.

Moral disengagement can affect detrimental behaviour both directly and indirectly. People have little reason to be troubled by guilt or to feel any need to make amends for harmful conduct if they construe it as serving worthy purposes or if they disown personal agency for it.

High moral disengagement is accompanied by low guilt, thus weakening anticipatory self-restraints against engagement in detrimental behaviour. Self-exoneration for harmful conduct and self-protective dehumanization of others and treating them as blameworthy spawn a low pro-social orientation. Low pro-socialness in turn contributes to detrimental conduct in two ways: having little sympathy for others both removes the restraining influence of empathetic consideration of others and activates little anticipatory guilt over injurious conduct; and under some circumstances effective moral disengagement creates a sense of social rectitude and self-righteousness that breeds ruminative hostility and retaliatory thoughts for perceived grievances.

◈ Moral Disengagement Strategies of Corporations

A corporation is similar to a person in some important respects. First, the reciprocal causation operates among corporate modes of thinking, corporate behaviour and the environment. Second, a corporation can be viewed both as a social construction and as an agentic system with the power to realize its intentions. Third, corporate identity is crucial for the development and functioning of a corporation. Moreover, the practices of a corporation operate through self-regulatory mechanisms. These mechanisms regulate the allocation of resources in the pursuit of the goals and objectives of the corporation in accordance with its values and standards. When corporations engage in reprehensible conduct they are likely to do so through selective disengagement of moral self-sanctions. The following brief analyses of famous business ethics cases illustrate the disengagement practices.

The Bhopal Case[8]

On 3 December 1984 the world's worst industrial disaster happened in Bhopal, India. Some 40 tonnes of methyl isocyanate (MIC) gas escaped from the Union Carbide India Limited (UCIL) pesticide production plant. At least 2,500 people were killed, 10,000 seriously injured, 20,000 partially disabled and 180,000 others affected in one way or another.

Very early in the morning of that day a violent chemical reaction occurred in a large storage tank at the Union Carbide factory. A huge amount of MIC—a chemical so highly reactive that a trace contaminant can set off a chain reaction—escaped from the tank into the cool winter's night air. A yellow-white fog, an aerosol of uncertain chemical composition, spread over the sleeping city of some 800,000. The mist, which hung close to the ground, blanketed the slums of Bhopal. Hundreds of thousands of residents were roused from their sleep, coughing, vomiting and wheezing.

The Bhopal plant was operated by UCIL, a subsidiary of the Union Carbide Corporation headquartered in Danbury, Connecticut. Despite Indian law limiting foreign ownership of corporations to 40 per cent, the US parent company was allowed to retain majority ownership (50.9 per cent) of UCIL because it was considered a 'high-technology' enterprise.

Union Carbide officials claimed that they did not apply a 'double standard' in safety regulation. Warren Anderson, chairman of Union Carbide Corporation, insisted that there were no differences between the Bhopal plant and Union Carbide's West Virginia plant. This argument was erroneous but served as an advantageous comparison for Union Carbide. In reality, the Bhopal plant had violated the company's safety standards and operated in a way that would not have been tolerated in the United States.

Two years before the disaster a three-member safety team from Union Carbide headquarters had visited the Bhopal plant and submitted a revealing report on the dangers of the MIC section. The report had recommended various changes to reduce the risks at the plant, but the recommendations were never implemented. Union Carbide's main strategy was to displace responsibility by blaming the Indian government for its failure to effectively regulate the plant and for allowing people to live nearby.

Union Carbide was allowed to locate its factory in the middle of Bhopal, just 2 miles from the Bhopal railway station. It was convenient for shipping, but proved to be disastrous for the people living nearby. For years the plant had been ringed with shantytowns, mostly populated by squatters. All three of the worst-affected communities in the disaster apparently existed before the Union Carbide plant opened. In court trials Union Carbide refused to pay anything to the Indian victims and their families, whose impoverished status made them easy to be dehumanized and disregarded.

The Ford Pinto Case[9]

On 10 August 1978 a tragic automobile accident occurred on US Highway 33 near Goshen, Indiana. Sisters Judy and Lynn Ulrich and their cousin Donna Ulrich were struck from the rear in their 1973 Ford Pinto by a van. The gas tank of the Pinto ruptured, the car burst into flames and the three teenagers were burnt to death.

This was not the only case when the Ford Pinto caused a serious accident by explosion. By conservative estimates Pinto crashes had caused at least 500 burn deaths. There were lawsuits against Ford because it had been proven that the top managers of the company were informed about the serious design problem of the model. Despite the warnings of their engineers, the Ford management decided to manufacture and sell the car with the dangerously defective design.

Ford used different moral disengagement strategies to defend its highly controversial decision. First, Ford continuously claimed that the 'Pinto is safe,' thus denying the risk of injurious consequences. Ford managers justified their claim by referring to the US safety regulation standards in effect till 1977. In doing so they displaced their responsibility for a car that caused hundreds of deaths to the driving practices of people who would not have been seriously injured if their Ford Pinto had not been designed in a way that made it easily inflammable in a collision.

Ford engineers concluded that the safety problem of the Pinto could be solved by a minor technological adjustment. It would have cost only $11 per car to prevent the gas tank from rupturing so easily. Ford produced an intriguing and controversial cost–benefit analysis study to prove that this modification was not cost effective to society. The study provided social justification for not making that option available to customers.

Ford convinced itself that it was better to pay millions of dollars in Pinto jury trials and out-of-court settlements than to improve the safety of the model. By placing dollar values on human life and suffering, Ford simply disregarded the consequences of its practice relating to the safety of millions of customers.

The Nestle Case[10]

Nestle has been the largest producer and seller of infant formula products in Third World countries. Its marketing practices received worldwide criticism during the seventies and eighties. Infant formula is not harmful to the consumer when used properly under appropriate conditions. However, it is a demanding product that can be harmful to users when risk conditions are present. Nestle sold its infant formula to mothers in Africa, Latin America and South Asia, many of whom lived under circumstances that made the use of such products a highly risky practice.

First, infant formula must be sold in powdered form in tropical environments, requiring that mothers mix the powder with locally available water. When water supplies are of poor quality, as they are in many developing countries, infants are exposed to disease. Second, since the product must be mixed, preparation instructions are important and mothers must be able to read them. However, the rate of female illiteracy is very high in many developing nations. Third, since infant formulas are relatively expensive to purchase there is a temptation to overdilute the powder with water. Unfortunately, overdiluted formula preparations provide very poor nutrition for infants. Having decided to bottle-feed their babies in order to increase their chances for a healthy life many mothers discovered to their horror that they had actually been infecting and starving their infants.

During the late seventies the infant formula controversy became increasingly politicized in Europe and the United States. A Swiss public action group labelled Nestle as the 'baby killer.' Others claimed that Nestle causes 'commerciogenic malnutrition' in Third World countries—malnutrition brought about because of its commercial practices. In 1978 a powerful consumer boycott of Nestle and its products was begun in the United States.

The company's representatives charged that the boycott was a conspiracy of religious organizations and an indirect attack on the free enterprise system. Nestle tried to defend and morally justify its questionable marketing practice by referring to the freedom of production and marketing. The Nestle statement was a political disaster. The company was denounced for its foolishness in the US media.

Companies may not close their eyes once their product is sold. They have a continuing responsibility to monitor the product's use, resale and consumption to determine who are actually using the product and how they are using it. Post-marketing reviews are a necessary step in this process. In 1978 Nestle confessed that like other companies in the industry it did no such research and did not know who actually used its products and the manner in which they did so. In this negligent attitude towards learning about the effects of its product, Nestle was acting on the strategy of disregarding the harmful consequences of its practice in developing countries.

In 1984 Nestle's self-discrediting experience with the controversy over its infant formula finally came to an end by adopting the policy recommendations of the WHO international marketing code. However, the company and the morale of its employees suffered a major blow. It is difficult to say how long it will take for Nestle to regain its good name and for the public to regard the company once again as a good corporate citizen.

The Three Mile Island Case[11]

The most severe accident in US commercial nuclear power plant history occurred at the Three Mile Island Unit 2 in Harrisburg on 28 March 1979. People were told to stay indoors and pregnant mothers and small children were advised to leave the area. There were widespread rumours of a general evacuation. Indeed, some 100,000 people simply voted with their feet and got up and left the area. Although there were no direct deaths or injuries, there was talk of a possible explosion equivalent to a 1-megaton bomb. There were 4 million litres of contaminated water blown out of the system. Figures for the clean-up were initially set at somewhere between $200 and $500 million. Ten years later the cleaning was still continuing.

Babcock and Wilcox built the reactor, General Public Utilities ran Three Mile Island and Metropolitan Edison owned it. During and after the event Metropolitan Edison simply refused to face up to the seriousness of the situation. The company tried to distort consequences by continually issuing denials and minimizing the accident. In effect, the public was told there was no problem, no danger and everything was routine. They also used euphemisms and displacement of responsibility to 'operator error' in providing a public explanation that tended to play down the seriousness of the accident.[12]

Later on Metropolitan Edison made strong efforts to diffuse responsibility among the other main actors involved, namely, Babcock and Wilcox, General Public Utilities and the Nuclear Regulatory Commission. All endeavoured to avoid blame for the accident in which the United States had just narrowly escaped its Chernobyl.

Table 1 shows the moral disengagement mechanisms used in the analyzed cases. The listed ones probably underestimate the scope of the mechanisms employed because they are confined to publicly observable manifestations of moral disengagement. The enlistment of exonerative practices is often buried in corporate memos and surreptitious sanctioning practices rather than being publicly expressed.

What is informative in these cases is that the moral collusion can end in justifying actions whose outcomes continue to be disapproved. The belief system of the corporation may remain unaffected for a long time by practices that are detrimental to it as well as to the general public. Selective disengagement mechanisms are deployed to mask such a contradiction and to perpetuate harmful corporate practices. . . .

◈ Implications for Business Ethics

When the mechanisms of moral disengagement are at work in corporations, business ethics is difficult to manage, especially when the sanctioning practices are surreptitious and the responsibility for policies is diffused. Numerous exonerative strategies can be enlisted to disengage social and moral sanctions from detrimental practices with a low sense of personal accountability. A central issue is how to counteract moral disengagement strategies of corporations.

From the perspective of business ethics, there are several strategies for counteracting resort to moral disengagement. One approach is to monitor and publicize corporate practices that have detrimental human effects. The more visible the consequences are on the affected parties for the decision makers, the less likely it is that they can be disregarded, distorted or minimized for long. Another approach is to increase transparency of the discourse by which the deliberation of corporate policies and practices are born. The more public the discourse about corporate decisions and policies, the less likely are corporate managers to justify the reprehensible conduct of their organizations.

Diffused and ambiguous responsibility structures make it easy to discount personal contribution to harmful effects. Instituting clear lines of accountability

Table 1   Disengagement Mechanisms Used in Different Business Ethics Cases

Disengagement Mechanisms	Bhopal Case	Ford Pinto Case	Nestle Case	Three Mile Island Case
Moral justification		✓	✓	
Euphemistic labelling				✓
Advantageous comparison	✓			
Displacement of responsibility		✓		
Diffusion of responsibility				✓
Disregarding or distorting the consequences		✓	✓	✓
Dehumanization	✓			
Attribution of blame	✓			

curtail moral disengagement. Exposing sanitizing language that masks reprehensible practices is still another corrective. The affected parties often lack social influence and status that make it easy to dehumanize and disregard them. They need to be personalized and their concerns publicized and addressed.

 Notes and References

1. M. Punch, *Dirty Business: Exploring Corporate Misconduct* (London: Sage Publications, 1996).

2. M. Clarke, *Business Crime* (Cambridge: Polity Press, 1990).

3. Punch, *Dirty Business* (n. 1 above).

4. M. Levi, *Regulating Fraud: White-collar Crime and the Criminal Process* (London: Tavistock, 1987).

5. Punch, *Dirty Business* (n. 1 above).

6. A. Bandura, *Social Foundations of Thought and Action: A Social Cognitive Theory* (Englewood Cliffs, NJ: Prentice-Hall, 1986); and ibid., 'Social Cognitive Theory of Moral Thought and Action,' in W. M. Kurtines and J. L. Gewirtz, eds., *Handbook of Moral Behavior and Development* (Englewood Cliffs, NJ: Lawrence Erlbaum Associates, 1991), Vol. 1, 44–103.

7. A. Bandura, 'Mechanisms of Moral Disengagement,' in W. Reich, ed., *Origins of Terrorism: Psychology, Ideologies, States of Mind* (Cambridge: Cambridge University Press, 1990), 45–103; and ibid., 'Social Cognitive Theory of Moral Thought and Action' (n. 6 above).

8. D. Weir, *The Bhopal Syndrome* (San Francisco: Sierra Club Books, 1987).

9. M. W. Hoffman, 'The Ford Pinto,' in W. M. Hoffman and R. E. Frederick, eds., *Business Ethics: Readings and Cases in Corporate Morality* (New York: McGraw-Hill, 1984), 552–59.

10. K. E. Post, 'The Ethics of Marketing: Nestle's Infant Formula,' in W. M. Hoffman and R. E. Frederick, eds., *Business Ethics* (n. 9 above), 416–21.

11. Punch, *Dirty Business* (n. 1 above).

12. C. Perrow, *Normal Accidents* (New York: Basic Books, 1984).

CHAPTER 3

Researching Deviance

THREE RESEARCH-RELATED STORIES FROM THE AUTHORS

Story 1

I was working as an interviewer on a longitudinal research project to evaluate a treatment program for people with cocaine-related problems. This was a relatively small, experimentally designed project, and there were only two interviewers (me, male; the other, female). The participants were paid to complete the interviews, and the treatment was free. The interview instruments were somewhat complex, and certain items had to be carefully worded and the responses carefully recorded. So periodically, the interviewers would work in conjunction to assess reliability. I had already interviewed one male program participant at several time points when the other interviewer and I decided to do the interview together. The female interviewer was quite attractive and seemed to elicit far more positive responses (e.g., "Yes, I have used cocaine in the past month.") than did I in our previous encounters. There are many possible explanations, but one obvious interpretation is that the participant realized he could get through the interview quicker with me and get paid his nominal fee by responding "no" to certain items (i.e., if he answered "yes," then a slew of questions followed). Getting the interview over with quickly didn't seem to be an issue when my attractive female colleague was asking the questions.

Story 2

I am currently working on a project in which my colleague and I are examining the effect of policing practices on individuals and the community. Specifically, we are interested in finding out how civil gang injunctions affect alleged gang members, their families and friends, and the community in which the injunction is enacted. Before we are allowed to start interviewing participants, we must submit and be approved by our university's institutional review board (IRB; human subjects review). Given our population—alleged gang members and their families and friends—the IRB process has raised many questions. The IRB is designed to make sure that participants

(Continued)

87

(Continued)

are not harmed (psychologically, emotionally, or physically) by participating in a research study. While our study is not designed to ask questions about deviant or criminal behavior, given our potential sample, the IRB committee is very focused on the likelihood that our subjects might discuss their criminal behavior. What are the safeguards we have in place to protect the subjects? What are the safeguards we have in place to protect the community? What are we obligated to report should our subjects discuss deviant behavior?

Story 3

Ethnographers necessarily have a special relationship with data—we're immersed in it and interact continually with the people and places that we study. I have chosen to do most of my research in prisons and juvenile correctional facilities. This kind of work is certainly not as dangerous as researching crack dealers or gang members on the streets, but it does present its own challenges. You have to follow all of the rules of the institution, of course, always remembering that security is the first priority for staff members and administrators. You have to build trust with inmates, which can take time, patience, and an open mind. And you have to set clear boundaries for yourself and your research. Getting too close may compromise the research and your access to the institution. The hardest and most important lesson that I have learned in doing this kind of research is to find a way to keep emotional distance between myself and the people in the institution. There are people in prisons and juvenile facilities who have worked hard for second chances that they may never get. I get to know some very likable people who will never have the opportunity for a better life. These are difficult truths to accept, but as my wise adviser reminded me, as a researcher, I'm not where the action is in their lives, nor should I be. I can witness the process, share their stories, and analyze the system, but I probably can't make things substantially better or drastically change the life chances of any one individual. Once I was able to accept this painful reality, it got easier to take a step back and do my job as a researcher and a sociologist—giving others on the outside a chance to learn about and understand prison culture.

◈ Introduction

On one hand, studying deviant behavior is exciting, intellectually rewarding, and often quite fun. On the other hand, studying deviance can be stressful, heart wrenching, and plagued with difficulties that are extremely challenging to grapple with. Serious researchers must be armed with numerous tools necessary to help deal with problems encountered in the study of behaviors that are often shielded from public purview and/or forced underground by mainstream society. Researchers must also be cognizant of the ethical issues that plague the investigation of deviance. First, researchers must be aware that their influence on individuals through, for example, an experiment can have purely unintended consequences. Second, simply studying the attitudes and beliefs of people can be problematic because holding deviant attitudes and beliefs can be costly to individuals even if they never act on them. Indeed, we all probably hold certain attitudes and beliefs we would not like other people to know about. In this chapter, we discuss various issues that confront researchers of deviance and strategies to overcome those difficulties. Not all hurdles surrounding a full understanding of issues related to deviance can be overcome, but we argue that through persistence and the use of multiple methods, almost invariably a better understanding of deviance can be achieved.

The stories provided above by each of the authors of this book offer insights into several problems associated with researching deviance. The first story brings up issues of measurement and how different interviewers may elicit different responses from subjects. Research has shown that when conducting interviews, good interviewers can get almost anyone to discuss their deviant behavior, attitudes, and beliefs if they can get the subject to feel comfortable. However, a number of factors—most of which are unknown—will affect how good the information is that is collected. For example, in the first story related earlier, we suggested that the "attractive" woman was better able to get the respondent to talk, truthfully or not. However, it could have been that the respondent had simply recently relapsed and felt the need to talk about it. The male interviewer might have elicited the same or very similar responses. The story also relates to the utility and potential problems of paying respondents for their interview time. Paying or providing other incentives to respondents for their time and effort is relatively common-place today, though there are many who have advocated against the practice (e.g., Fleisher, 1995). More recently, Seddon (2005) discussed the ethical issues related to providing incentives to drug users (especially monetary incentives). Hanson, Letourneau, Olver, Wilson, and Miner (2012) have argued that providing "incentives to offenders is both practical and ethical" (p. 1391). Finally, for further investigation in the area, Singer and Ye (2013) have provided the most comprehensive overview of the effects of incentives in both cross-sectional and longitudinal research that we are aware of.

The second story introduces the existence of **human subjects institutional review boards** (IRBs), which are a part of virtually all universities and research organizations. IRBs are developed in an effort to protect human subjects, researchers, and the university or organization. Working with an IRB can be a painful process, and they can literally squelch research. Alternatively, they can be very helpful in thinking through the research process, and their questions and recommendations can actually make a research project better. We discuss human subjects and the IRB process in detail toward the end of the chapter.

The third story makes us critically aware that studying those who may be considered deviants—be they criminals, "street" people, or persons with severe illnesses such as AIDS—can be tremendously disturbing emotionally. Recognizing that there is often very little we can do to help deserving people is not easy. Furthermore, becoming emotionally involved with those we study, while not necessarily a bad thing, may be a slippery slope: It can lead to a loss of objectivity and potentially damage relationships with institutions or gatekeepers to the research. Although we may not be able to make drastic changes in a person's life, sometimes talking about one's life can be a rewarding experience, especially for those isolated from society. We return to these types of issues when we discuss **field research** (in particular, qualitative fieldwork) later in this chapter.

◈ Methodological Approaches to Studying Deviance

Experiments in the Study of Deviance

Experiments have been called the "gold standard" for determining causal relationships in the social sciences. In a true experimental design, subjects are randomly assigned to one of two or more conditions that are thought to affect some outcome, usually a behavior. Random assignment ensures that any differences following the intervention or "experimental" stimulus must have been caused by the intervention.

For example, Maass, Cadinu, Guarnieri, and Grasselli (2003) were interested in whether men exposed to an identity threat (e.g., exposure to a fictitious feminist versus traditional female interaction) might be more influenced to engage in sexual harassment as measured by sending pornography to a fictitious female through the computer when instigated by another fictitious male. (He was supposedly sending porn and encouraging the subject to do so as well.) So, in this case, participating males were randomly assigned to one of two conditions. The experimental subjects were presented with an interaction shown to act as an identity threat in previous studies (interaction with a female with a strong feminist stance) and then were encouraged by a confederate to send pornography to a fictitious female. The males in the control group were presented with an innocuous stimulus (interaction with a female with "traditional" gender values) and then encouraged to send porn to the traditional female confederate. The results of the experiment were consistent with the notion that threatening males' identity can lead to a heightened risk of engaging in a particular form of deviance: sexual harassment.

Studies such as the one described earlier are praised because of the high level of internal validity. That is, the subjects are randomly assigned, and the only difference between conditions is planned, controlled, and carried out consistently by the researcher. Hence, no other factor should explain the higher levels of sexual harassment in the experimental condition. Alternatively, such studies are often criticized because of concerns with external validity—that is, to what extent the results can be applied to other contexts, particularly "the real world." So, for example, in the sexual harassment study, the experimental subjects were encouraged by a fictitious confederate who was also sexually harassing the supposed or hypothetical victim. The results suggest that identity threats may increase sexual harassment but only in conditions where the potential victim is anonymous (no face-to-face or verbal contact) and there is considerable pressure from peers to engage in the deviant activity. Given the availability of pornography on the Internet, the situation is obviously possible, but the experiment was clearly contrived and may not be likely to occur in natural settings.

Problems with true experimental designs have led to a host of "not quite experimental designs" referred to as quasi-experiments (Campbell & Stanley, 1963). The breadth of these designs precludes a thorough discussion in this chapter. Suffice it to say that **quasi-experimental designs**, in general, lose points in terms of internal validity; the requirement of true random assignment is often relaxed. Alternatively, in many cases, external validity is enhanced—that is, oftentimes, quasi-experiments move to less contrived environments that may have more validity.

For example, suppose you are interested in examining the effectiveness of a school-based drug prevention program. You find two junior high schools that are interested, but you realize that you cannot randomly assign students in the schools to receive the intervention because the nature of the intervention needs to be in a particular type of class (e.g., health education), and it would be impossible to move students between the two schools. Furthermore, you suspect that even if you could move students around, they may come back to their home school and share what they had learned with control students, thus contaminating the manipulation. So the only real way to do this is to assign one school to the intervention, and let the other be the control. (You may even offer the control school to have the intervention a year or so later if they will participate in the research.) The problem, of course, is that the schools may be quite different in terms of faculty and resources, and the student body may be quite different in terms of demographics, exposure to risk factors for drug use, and actual proclivity to use drugs. Still, you may have a relatively large sample from each school to compare. In addition, you can do pretests in both schools to assess those differences and statistically adjust for those differences.[1] While still problematic, this may be a useful starting point and is actually a fairly common problem and solution in the prevention literature.

Another form of quasi-experiment useful in the study of crime and deviance takes advantage of "naturally occurring" events. For example, researchers might compare rates of "deviance" before and after a major event, such as a natural disaster (e.g., Hurricane Katrina or 9/11) or some other social or legal change (e.g., the implementation of a new law or policy). These types of studies can inform both theory and policy. For example, recently Chamlin (2009) theoretically considered the impact of a 2001 race riot in Cincinnati as a potential event to examine consensus or functionalist perspectives versus conflict theory explanations (see Chapter 9). The race riot emerged following the shooting and killing of Timothy Thomas, a 19-year-old black man who was wanted for several nonserious, nonviolent crimes, such as loitering and not wearing a seat belt (Chamlin, 2009, p. 545). In the prior six years, 15 other black males had been killed by the Cincinnati police; no whites had been killed by police during this time. Subsequently, and as a direct result of the shooting, three days of riots ensued. Chamlin thought that, from a conflict perspective (see Chapter 9), the riots might result in a heightened crackdown on robbery, which is a crime particularly more highly interracial than most crimes. Through a sophisticated statistical analysis, he showed that the riots (a challenge to authority) resulted in significantly higher levels of arrests for robbery. Although there are numerous challenges to Chamlin's interpretation, he supplemented his analyses in a variety of ways and provided unique insights into conflict and consensus perspectives.

In conclusion, although experimental and quasi-experimental designs have a long history in the sociological study of deviance, they are fairly rare compared with other research designs. Alternatively, there appear to be more and more experimental and quasi-experimental designs being conducted in criminology and criminal justice, hence the new publication of the *Journal of Experimental Criminology,* which began in 2005. Not all but much of this research focuses on prevention, early intervention, or treatment programs for criminals, juvenile delinquents, or at-risk youth, rather than on the etiology of deviance. Research on deviance is often descriptive or correlational, focused on factors associated with how deviance is distributed across different groups or factors thought to be causes or consequences of deviance. We now turn to other research designs more common among studies of deviance.

▲ **Photo 3.1**   Experiments are the gold standard for determining causal relationships but are often difficult in the study of deviance.

DEVIANCE IN POPULAR CULTURE

The documentary *Quiet Rage: The Stanford Prison Experiment* depicts one of the most famous and disturbing experiments in the history of psychology, deviant behavior, and social control. In 1971, Professor Philip Zimbardo set out to answer this question: "What happens when you put good people in an evil place?"

In an elaborate setup, Zimbardo and colleagues converted part of the basement of the Stanford Psychology Department into a simulated jail, complete with cells, solitary confinement ("the hole"), and standardized uniforms for both the prisoners and guards.

Zimbardo and colleagues recruited psychologically healthy male college students to participate in the study; individuals were randomly assigned to be either a guard or a prisoner. The experiment was planned to run for two weeks but was ended after only six days amid grave concerns about the psychological damage incurred by both prisoners and guards.

Watch the film, and consider the following questions:

1. What are the ethical considerations that emerged from the Stanford Prison Experiment? What are the potential problems with doing a study like this? The young men agreed to participate in the study and were compensated as agreed upon; what other responsibilities do researchers have to their subjects?

2. Do you think it would be possible to have learned the information garnered from the study in any other way? Why or why not?

3. Do you think the same patterns found in the Stanford Prison Experiment exist in real prison settings? Why do you think as you do?

Another popular, more recent film that portrays ethical issues in research is *Experimenter* (2015), which dramatizes Stanley Milgram's studies on obedience. His experiments are discussed at greater length later in the chapter.

Large-Scale Survey Research

If experimental designs are the "gold standard" for determining causality, then **survey** research might be considered a "gold mine" of information for the student of deviance. Ever since Kinsey and his colleagues' work in the 1930s and 1940s on human sexuality (something many believed one couldn't or shouldn't ask about), literally thousands of studies have used survey research techniques to better understand deviant behavior and its correlates—that is, how deviance is distributed across individual, social, and environmental conditions.

We assume that most readers are familiar with various forms of survey research. In fact, we are all bombarded with surveys, be they via phone, mail, or the Internet. We are queried by political scientists about who we will vote for; by sociologists about our family and household characteristics; by economists regarding our employment, income, and expenditures; and, of course, by businesses, which are interested in what we are attracted to buying or how their organization has served us so they can get feedback to modify their approach (or brag about their performance). So we will briefly discuss a few things that scientific surveys attempt to do and how; then we will examine the role that surveys have played in a better understanding of deviance as well as some of the limitations of survey research.

In general, for students of deviance, survey research involves asking a *sample* of a *target population* questions about their behaviors, attitudes, values, and beliefs. The two italicized words in the previous sentence bear some consideration. A target population is all units in some universe. The target population could be almost anything—for example, all adult residents of the United States in 2015, all fifth-grade students in a particular school district in a particular academic year, or all homeless families staying in homeless shelters between 9 p.m. and 8 a.m. in New York City on December 25, 2015. A **sample** simply refers to a subset of the target population. When dealing with people, it is usually quite difficult (if not impossible), time-consuming, and expensive to survey an entire target population. Unless one wished to define the target population, for example, as students who show up on time to an "Introduction to Sociology" class on Wednesday at 1:30 p.m., October 5, 2012, things tend to get tricky, and often, we are more interested in generalizing to larger populations. Typically, when people survey students in courses, we refer to the outcome as a convenience sample, indicating, perhaps, that the class is composed of many different kinds of students since most students take "intro soc" and "may reflect" the population of undergraduates, or at least freshmen and sophomores. Of course, in reality, we wish that the sample reflected an even larger population (e.g., the United States), but that is not very likely. Note that this is not a problem solely of survey research. Many experimental studies, especially in psychology, are studies of how manipulations affect college students because they are a convenient population but very different in many ways from the general population.

Survey researchers usually want a representative sample of the target population so that the sample provides a smaller but accurate description of the population, and the researchers can use statistical procedures to generalize to the larger population. There are many ways of obtaining a representative sample, but the simplest, in some ways, is a random sample. Unfortunately, garnering a random sample generally requires having data on the entire population so that a sample can be drawn from that population. That is, everyone in the population has an equal chance of being surveyed, although only a subset is actually drawn. Thus, for the social scientist, *random* has a very specific meaning that doesn't sound very "random" to the layperson, who might think "randomly approaching potential respondents in a mall" to be collecting a random sample. Such an approach produces *anything but* a random sample to the social scientist.

Suffice it to say that there are many strategies for surveying samples of large populations, but it is still an expensive process and usually conducted by large research agencies with considerable funding. Even well-funded projects have problems drawing adequate samples that are representative of the target population and often have to oversample certain populations that are hard to access. For example, most phone surveys of adults we have been involved in result in an older, more female sample and sometimes samples that over-reflect certain racial groups. It is likely that these groups are more likely to have adults at home, have a home phone, and be willing to answer a call and respond to the survey.

Hence, a major concern for social scientists is the **response rate** and how that might affect the results of a survey. If the response rate is low, the sample may still reflect the population, but this is highly unlikely and would occur only if the various demographic groups were equally likely to respond and those who responded versus those who did not respond were similar in all respects related to the study. Of course, this is highly unlikely, especially in the study of deviant behavior, where some may be less willing to provide information, especially to certain types of investigators (see Pruitt, 2008).

A somewhat related concern involves the appropriate sample size. To address many questions, relatively small samples (e.g., 100 to 200 cases and sometimes even much smaller) may be more than sufficient, and, of course, much qualitative research will use only a few subjects. One of the authors of this book recently published a research report concerning attitudes of residents in five Southeastern Virginia cites. A concerned reader e-mailed to ask how we could make generalizations to more than a million people with only around 850 cases. The full answer is beyond the scope of this paper, and there are plenty of textbooks to explain it more fully, but the simple answer is that generalizing from a sample to a population is more about the number of cases rather than the proportion of cases.

Garnering enough cases to obtain a nationally representative sample of registered voters' attitudes toward a presidential candidate or even their opinions on "deviant issues," such as abortion, pornography, or fear of being a victim of crime, may take a thousand or more cases. Indeed, the General Social Survey of the United States, which has been conducted since 1972, includes about 1,500 cases at each time point. Using a sample like this, we would feel quite confident in describing how the American population stands on various issues and how these attitudes and beliefs vary across groups and with other social variables. This is because the issues that surveys address are generally fairly common, and a significant proportion of the population is willing to express attitudes and beliefs about the subject. Alternatively, when events are very rare, much larger samples are required to garner enough respondents to accurately describe the population and how its members vary across subgroups. For example, contrary to popular belief, serious victimization (e.g., rape, robbery, aggravated assault) is fairly rare, and so the National Crime Victimization Survey requires approximately 12,000 respondents at each sampling. Similarly, studies such as the Monitoring the Future project, which focuses on involvement in serious drug use, including cocaine, heroin, and methamphetamine use among children and young adults, now includes approximately 50,000 respondents annually.

Field Research: Pure Observer to Full Participant

Field research, too, can be a gold mine for investigating various forms of deviance and especially deviant groups and subcultures. "Field research" is a term that brings to mind the anthropologist immersing himself or herself into some foreign, perhaps indigenous, society and learning the language, customs, beliefs, and behaviors of its members or the researcher of a religious cult who feigns being a believer and observes others, always under the dangerous possibility that his or her identity will be revealed, and he or she will, at best, be alienated from the study site or, worse, physically harmed or even killed. These are, of course, examples of real cases of fieldwork, but in our perspective, "fieldwork" is a more generic term, with several dimensions and polar extremes. True, the term clearly delineates fieldwork practices from the large-scale mail, phone, or Internet surveys that are indicative of much social survey research. Alternatively, at one polar end, we might include as field research going into a school district or a neighborhood and systematically surveying students or residents, even with short, close-ended survey questions about deviance. On the other extreme, taking a job as a stripper to better understand—indeed, truly empathize with—what the lives of these women (and men) are like and the social structures and relations that dictate a major part of their lives is more likely to be viewed as field research. So to some extent, unless one is studying the deviance of college students actually in the classroom, field research more generally means getting outside the "ivory tower"—getting one's hands dirty, so to speak—to better understand some form of deviance, be it behavior, attitudes, or beliefs.

Excluding our more structured example of handing out surveys to students, two types of fieldwork are sometimes viewed as two points on a continuum between **pure observation** and **participant observation**. Before distinguishing the two, it is important to recognize that both strategies typically involve extensive observation and recording of those observations. Historically, this has been done primarily in written form, although audio recording in various formats has been around for a long time.

Let's start with pure observations, which would theoretically entail observing people not only with them not knowing the researcher is observing them but also with them not observing the researcher whatsoever. Of course, this can be done; one can look through a peephole, through a one-way mirror, or down at a place of social interaction, such as observing a park from a higher building. A study at one of the authors' universities involved simply sitting at various intersections and documenting the running of red lights (Porter & England, 2000) and various characteristics of drivers and automobiles associated with the transgressions. Another study at one of our universities studied hand-washing behavior (or lack thereof) in public restrooms. This was about as close as it comes to pure observation, although usually it was clear that someone was in the stall doing something (Monk-Turner et al., 2005).

A more recent study by McCleary and Tewksbury (2010) used an almost pure observation strategy to study female patrons of sexually oriented book-video-novelty stores in three major counties in California over a two-year period. Trained researchers observed 33 stores and the customers who entered them, with a total of 271 observation periods spanning 162 hours. The researchers were trained to remain as unobtrusive as possible. McCleary and Tewksbury wrote that

> working from a common protocol, researchers observed customers from at least 250 feet away for 30 consecutive minutes. Researchers were allowed to break the 30-minute rule if necessary. Observation ended before 30 minutes in approximately 20 percent of the trials and lasted longer than 30 minutes in 60 percent of the trials. In every instance, researchers cited the need to remain unobtrusive as the rationale for breaking the 30-minute rule. (p. 212)

The authors found that women were much more likely than men to come to sexually oriented businesses with other females (46%), in mixed-sex groups (22%), or as a male–female couple (15%). In contrast, men were most likely to come alone (76%) or in same-sex groups (18%). Women also preferred "safer"-appearing stores with security guards, more employees, and more business traffic. They avoided stores with "viewing booths," which the authors argued are often viewed as places for male–male encounters. Interestingly, across all observations, approximately half of the store employees were female, but women were significantly less likely to patronize stores with a larger number of women employees.

As shown in this example, researchers often study various forms of deviance with no or very little interaction with the persons they are observing. The benefit of this approach is that the presence of the researcher is very unlikely to affect the behavior of the research subjects. This is similar to what medical researchers do in a double-blind study; in these studies, the medical researchers have very little potential to affect the results of the experiment because they don't know if they are administering a new drug or a placebo.

Let's move to the other extreme of the spectrum and examine the strategies of researchers who actively interact with and participate in the activities of the deviants they study. This method is called participant observation. In contrast to the "objective" pure observer, for other social scientists, active participation is the only way to truly understand the attitudes, beliefs, and behaviors of deviant actors and the factors that shape and affect deviance. Researchers have "become" nudists (Weinberg, 1966), panhandlers (Lankenau, 1999), erotic dancers (Ronai & Ellis, 1989), and "lookouts" for men engaging in homosexual acts in public restrooms (Humphreys, 1970), among many others. A classic study of high-level drug dealing and smuggling was conducted by Patricia Adler (1993). Although Adler was not a drug dealer herself, she revealed that she used marijuana and cocaine; she serendipitously came to know a major dealer, and deals were done in her presence and even in her home. Through this contact, she met many drug dealers and smugglers covertly (they assumed she was in the business) and overtly when she asked to interview them. Her research with drug dealers and smugglers continued for six years and resulted in a classic book in the field, *Wheeling and Dealing: An Ethnography of an Upper-Level Drug Dealing and Smuggling Community.* This research was dangerous, as many of the dealers obviously did not want others to know about their illegal enterprises. It also raised important ethical considerations. The author obviously knew about illegal behavior and did not report it. Of course, the research could not have been conducted if she reported the behavior, and indeed, reporting it would have harmed her subjects—something as researchers we should strive very hard not to do. Indeed, it is unlikely that this research would be approved by most university human subjects committees.

Mark Fleisher (1995) also gained entry into a community of street hustlers, drug addicts, and alcoholics in the Seattle area. Over the course of three years (1988–1990), Fleisher completed in-depth interviews of nearly 200 ($n = 194$) deviant street people of various ages, races, ethnicities, and genders. Unlike Patricia Adler, who clearly befriended her primary source and other dealers, Fleisher was skeptical of the responses of street hustlers, especially those based on short interviews on issues that could not be supported with other information.

> I distrust data gathered in a few interviews with informants whom I don't know well or for whom I can't verify the facts with reliable documents. Hustlers', inmates', and former inmates' self-reports are, until proven otherwise, just "folklore," simply informants' comments, opinions, and explanations often engineered to sound legitimate. After all, these informants have been shown to be untrustworthy, manipulative, and disingenuous. Why should they be otherwise with me? (p. 21)

This is not to say that there were not interviewees that he came to like and even felt concern for. Indeed, he tried to assist several to get the help they needed. However, his overall commentary on the street hustlers was not pretty or very sympathetic. Ultimately, Fleisher uses his field research to inform both theory and policy. In regard to theory, his work seems most consistent with Gottfredson and Hirschi's (1990) theory of low self-control (see Chapter 7) and the role certain parents play in not socializing their children appropriately. In fact, he argues that the hustlers' lives are largely shaped by abusive, drug- and alcohol-abusing parents. In terms of policy, his conclusions are conservative and emphasize incarceration and making offenders work. Overall, Fleisher's **ethnography** provides very powerful insights into the lives of "beggars and thieves" in the streets of Seattle and elsewhere.

Participatory observation, be it **covert** or **overt observation**, can be dangerous, emotionally and physically draining, and—quite simply—very hard work. It can also be intellectually and emotionally rewarding. Hands-on research of this type brings one much closer to the lives of the deviant and therefore enables a greater sense of empathy and a much closer sense of the experiences of those people shunned by society. Some have argued that this participant observation is the best, if not the only, approach to truly study deviance (Ferrell & Hamm, 1998). We would disagree and argue that yes, participant observation is a powerful methodology with many benefits, but like all methodologies, it has many limitations.

◈ Content Analysis

Content analysis may be a term less familiar to undergraduate students in general or students of deviance in particular. This research strategy, however, has a long history in the study of deviance and deviant behavior. Content analysis involves reviewing records of communication and systematically searching, recording, and analyzing themes and trends in those records. Sources of communication are virtually unlimited and often free or quite cheap, making content analysis another gold mine of opportunity, especially for the undergraduate student of deviance.

Sources of communication used for studying deviance include transcribed interviews or open-ended responses to surveys, historical documents, legal codes, newspapers, advertisements from many sources, song lyrics, movies, TV shows, books and magazines, and websites and chat rooms, among myriad others. Indeed, all of these have been the source of content analyses in the study of deviance. Keys to a successful content analysis include (1) a solid research question, (2) a reasonably good understanding of the population of the materials or sources of interest, (3) a strategy for sampling records of communication, and (4) a systematic approach to extracting and coding themes or looking for trends.

A solid research question is probably the best starting place, and it can come from many directions and levels. The most interesting questions tend to emerge from theory, previous research, debates and conflicts, or suspected myths that one may want to empirically examine to support or debunk. The research question(s) may be very exploratory, especially at first or when there is little or conflicting theoretical or empirical guidance. For example, Pruitt and Krull (2011) recognized that there was actually little systematic research on why males seek female prostitutes and exactly what they want; what little research was available was based on nonrepresentative samples. They argued that a content analysis of female-escort Internet advertisements might provide information on what men want from prostitutes, assuming that the escorts are accurate in their perceptions of what males want and, therefore, choose to advertise these options. Analyzing 237 female-escort advertisements, Pruitt and Krull found that ads focused on "girlfriend experiences, unrushed encounters, and escort-type services" were far more common than those focused on specific sex acts.

Alternatively, Tuggle and Holmes (1997) were interested in the politics surrounding a smoking ban in California and especially in Shasta County, where the debate included 105 letters to the editor, which the authors analyzed. It was no surprise—and even expected—that pro-ban supporters tended to be nonsmokers and anti-ban supporters smokers. The logic of the arguments might also have been expected, with the former focusing on health risks (especially the risks associated with secondhand smoke) and the latter focusing on individuals' right to smoke. What might not have been predicted was that the power, measured by personal property, held by the pro-ban moral crusaders was much greater than that of the smokers arguing for the status quo. Given the large disparity in power, the fact that the ban was successful was not terribly surprising.

As discussed earlier, developing a reasoned understanding of the population of interest and then crafting a strategy for sampling cases to study is not an easy task. If one is interested in the prevalence of "derogatory depictions of women" in pornography, are we talking about magazines, movies, Internet sites, and so on? Once this question has been answered and refined, the sampling process should most likely be determined by a systematic process that fits into one's time and budget constraints.

The final issue, developing a systematic approach to extracting and coding themes or looking for trends, is another important consideration in a quality content analysis. Sticking with the example above, consider how different people are in their perceptions of what is derogatory and what is innocuous or simply entertaining. Developing an **operationalization** of "derogatory depictions" that can be selected and categorized consistently and replicated by others can be a very difficult issue to grapple with.

Content analysis is an exciting research avenue for those interested in studying deviant behavior and reactions to deviance. As mentioned, because records of communication are often available for free or are accessible quite cheaply, this is an excellent research design for undergraduate students interested in conducting a class research project. Since the topic areas are largely unbounded, we simply offer a few recent examples to stir up interest and possibilities.

▲ **Photo 3.2** Measurement is critical to every scientific discipline but is especially interesting and important in the study of deviance.

◈ Secondary Data Sources

Very important data have already been collected and are readily available for the study of crimes and other forms of deviance. These sources all have limitations but can still be extremely useful for conducting research. In addition, sometimes different sources can be used in conjunction with each other to better understand the causes and consequences of various deviant phenomena. Here we discuss just four general sources of **secondary data**. Thus, we do not cover the entire spectrum of secondary sources but, rather, highlight just a few of the more useful ones for undergraduate students interested in deviant behavior.

The Uniform Crime Report and the National Incident-Based Reporting System

The Uniform Crime Report (UCR) was developed by the Federal Bureau of Investigation (FBI) in the 1930s. Data from nearly 17,000 police agencies are compiled by the bureau and presented online and in many published documents. Data is included on violent crimes (murder, forcible rape, robbery, and aggravated assault) and property crimes (burglary, larceny theft, and motor vehicle theft) known by the police. Data are generally provided in terms of numbers and rates and can be organized by region, state, and city and for longitudinal comparisons. With very little skill, figures such as the following can be created online. Figure 3.1 shows that, in contrast to popular opinion, the rate of violent crime dropped precipitously through the 1990s up to 2012. (This figure was created by the authors from data available from the FBI website.) The National Incident-Based Reporting System (NIBRS) was also developed by the FBI to provide more detailed information across jurisdictions. Focusing on the "crime incident," the NIBRS includes information on more crime types, weapon involvement, injuries that may have taken place, location of the event, property damage, and characteristics of victims and offenders.

A number of problems are associated with these data. For example, we don't know much about crimes known to police other than the type of offense and where it was detected or reported. Also, the gender, race, and age of the offender are often not known or not provided. However, data are also provided on arrests where we do have demographic information on the accused. Limitations of these data are fairly obvious. First, although they are important crimes, only certain offenses are recorded, and others are ignored, including both street crimes and white-collar offenses. Second, demographic data often used from arrest statistics may reflect not only crime but also activities of the police. That is, arrest statistics may provide a better picture of what the police do as opposed to what criminals do. Finally, there is what has come to be referred to as the "dark figure" of crime and deviance, which reminds us that these data do not take into account all of the crimes that the police never become aware of—and that figure would appear to be huge. Consider all the rapes, assaults, burglaries, and thefts that are never reported to the police or every joint or crack pipe smoked or every shoplifted item that was just listed as missing inventory. In fact, it is common knowledge among criminologists that the best statistics are probably for murder and motor vehicle theft because there is usually a body for the former, and insurance requires a police report for stolen vehicles. Still, these statistics can be very useful and are at the heart of a great deal of criminological research.

Substance Abuse and Mental Health Services Administration

The Substance Abuse and Mental Health Services Administration (SAMHSA) is an agency of the U.S. Department of Health and Human Services. This agency provides critical information on drug use and mental health, making it an excellent source for the student of deviance (Figure 13.2). In particular, it supports a public health surveillance system, the Drug Abuse Warning Network (DAWN). This system provides information from emergency rooms and medical examiner reports. It records "emergency room episodes" that involve one or more drugs, including overdoses,

Figure 3.1 Violent Crime Rate (1985–2012)

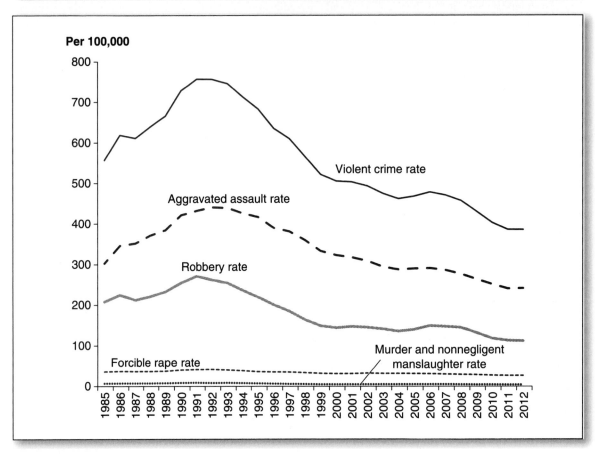

Source: Data from FBI.gov.

hallucinations, and suicide attempts, as well as incidents of people requesting help with drug addiction. It also collects data from medical examiners who report on drug-related causes of death through their autopsies. Medical examiners tabulate data for a variety of comparisons, particularly longitudinal analyses that allow us to evaluate trends in the types of drugs causing the most problems in terms of death and emergency room visits.

SAMHSA also supports and provides statistics from the National Survey on Drug Use and Health, which collects self-report data on alcohol and other drug use that better reflect general deviance not resulting in such serious consequences as emergency room episodes or death. The research is equally important, however, for many questions raised by the student of deviance. These statistics also can provide trend-level data and state-level comparisons, and maps of various indicators of drug use can be obtained.

SAMHSA also provides a wealth of data on mental health. For example, the Community Mental Health Services' (CMHS) Uniform Reporting System Output Tables provide demographic data (age, race, gender) on people receiving mental health services by state. Various comparisons can be made between states or between a particular set of states and national estimates.

Figure 3.2 Marijuana Use in Past Year Among Persons Aged 12 or Older, by State: Percentages, Annual Averages Based on 2006 and 2007 National Survey on Drug Use and Health

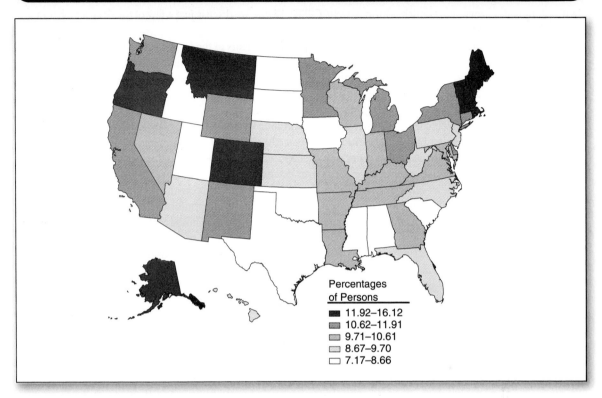

Percentages
of Persons

- ■ 11.92–16.12
- ■ 10.62–11.91
- ▨ 9.71–10.61
- ▢ 8.67–9.70
- ☐ 7.17–8.66

Source: SAMHSA, Office of Applied Studies, National Survey on Drug Use and Health, 2006 and 2007.

Monitoring the Future

Although related to SAMHSA, Monitoring the Future (MTF) is such a major, large-scale, longitudinal project that we discuss it separately. Using funding from the National Institutes of Health and the National Institute on Drug Abuse, MTF projects involve surveying students about their attitudes, behaviors, and beliefs concerning legal and illegal drug use (alcohol, tobacco, and other illegal drugs, such as marijuana, cocaine, and heroin). When it began in 1975, the project involved data collected from approximately 16,000 twelfth-graders in 133 high schools. In 1991, the study was expanded to include approximately 18,000 eighth-graders in 150 schools and 17,000 tenth-graders in 140 schools. So, in all, there are approximately 50,000 students in 420 schools surveyed in their classrooms annually. Behaviors can also be linked to large social contexts (e.g., school characteristics) for very interesting analyses. Some of the data are easily downloaded for analysis, and online mechanisms are available to analyze the data.

Archived Data: Inter-university Consortium for Political and Social Research

People who have been gathering data for a while sometimes are willing to share that data with other researchers for further analyses. The Inter-university Consortium for Political and Social Research (ICPSR) houses a great many data sets. While the majority of these data sets are not relevant to students of deviance, much data is available on crime and the criminal justice system as well as softer forms of deviance. Students working on class projects or senior theses are encouraged to see if their college or university is a member of the ICPSR and explore the many offerings the ICPSR provides (www.icpsr.umich.edu/icpsrweb/ICPSR). Below, we discuss just a few of the data sets that might be of interest to students of deviance.

Elaine Sharpe (2005) provided a data set on how 10 city governments in the United States responded to morality issues in the 1990s. The focus was on how municipalities reacted to deviant issues such as "gay rights, abortion rights, abortion clinic protests, needle exchange programs for drug users, hate speech, hate groups, gambling policies and regulations, animal rights, and regulations pertaining to the sex industry, which included pornography, prostitution, and adult entertainment" (n.p.). Martin Monto was the principal investigator on a project that examined characteristics of arrested clients of street prostitutes in four western cities (Portland, Oregon; San Francisco and Santa Clara, California; and Las Vegas, Nevada) between 1996 and 1999. Men arrested for soliciting prostitutes ("johns") were court-referred to client intervention workshops where they were anonymously surveyed. In addition to basic demographic information, clients were questioned extensively about various sexual behaviors and encounters (with prostitutes as well as other sexual relations), attitudes regarding women in general and prostitutes in particular, and beliefs about violence against women and the legality of prostitution. Estes and Weiner provided ICPSR data for the project Commercial Sexual Exploitation of Children in the United States (1997–2000). This project attempted to collect systematic data on "the nature, extent, and seriousness of child sexual exploitation (CSE) in the United States." The researchers surveyed staff in nongovernment and government organizations that were tasked with dealing with the transnational trafficking of children for sexual purposes. These are just three data sets focused on deviant behavior and social control.

◈ Ethical Considerations in Studying Deviance

As has been hinted at earlier in this chapter, there are serious ethical considerations in the study of deviance. Many experiments conducted not so long ago would no longer be allowed on college campuses or elsewhere. In the 1960s, Milgram created a study in which subjects were told to shock other participants when they provided an incorrect response to a question. The shocks supposedly got more intense with each wrong answer. What made this experiment potentially unethical was not causing pain to humans, as no one actually received the shocks. Rather, it was that people quite often continued to "shock" the confederate until it resembled torture, and it was quite likely that subjects experienced guilt and remorse over what they had just done.

Experimental studies are not the only methodology in which ethical concerns are raised. *Tearoom Trade*, a classic study of male homosexual encounters in public bathrooms, is often cited as unethical research. Laud Humphreys (1970) acted as a "lookout" in these venues. He did not disclose to the subjects that he was studying them, and more importantly, he collected license plate numbers and, through a police officer contact, obtained addresses to do "market research." He then interviewed these men under the guise that he was doing a social health survey. So several issues of **ethics in research** are raised. Observing behavior that is public, even if attempts are made to hide the behavior, is probably relatively innocuous, although some might question the ethics of acting as a "lookout" for cops and "straights." He lied to a police officer to access addresses, which certainly fractures the call for honesty and may even be illegal. Finally, he lied to the respondents when he interviewed them, not disclosing that he was actually interested in their homosexual acts.

Today, there are structured committees associated with universities and other research organizations that are set up to protect human subjects. These committees are referred to as institutional review boards (IRBs) and are generally composed of persons from different fields (e.g., scientists and nonscientists), an outside person from the community, and a legal representative, among others. These boards meet and review applications to conduct research. Many researchers have come to hold a dim and jaded view of IRBs. IRBs are often seen as gatekeepers prohibiting the researcher from engaging in important work that poses little to no risk to the human subjects involved, and the researchers' own exposure to risk is often seen as being their business, not that of "big brother." Indeed, some see IRBs as being "more concerned about preventing their parent institution from being sued than the rights of human subjects" (Goode, 2008a, p. 121). Furthermore, because of the bureaucratic nature of the beast, IRBs often seem more concerned that the appropriate boxes are checked than with any possible harm the research might present to human subjects. While these views may be accurate of IRBs in some institutions, many individuals on these committees are researchers themselves, and even those not directly involved in research generally have no interest in stifling the pursuit of knowledge.

There are several general concerns when considering the protection of human subjects. The first comes from the medical adage "First, do no harm." This is an especially problematic issue in experimental studies where subjects are asked to do things they wouldn't normally do. If there are risks, the subjects need to be aware of those risks and how the risks will be minimized. Even an anonymous survey that asks sensitive questions may invoke unpleasant emotions, especially among certain populations (e.g., victims of crimes or other abuses). These risks might be reduced by making the survey voluntary and letting respondents know they can stop at any time or ignore any question. If it is an especially vulnerable population, a referral might be provided to a common service provider. Research must be voluntary, which brings up how subjects are recruited, how they are asked to participate, and what sorts of incentives might be offered for their participation (which should not be coercive).

This gives rise to an interesting issue regarding informed consent. Subjects should be provided with sufficient information to make the decision to participate in various forms of research (e.g., surveys, interviews, experiments) if at all possible. We think, however, that often, formal consent forms, especially signed ones, can be off-putting to potential subjects and sometimes result in increased risk. Consider a 5-minute survey; do you really need to have respondents read a two- to three-page consent form? In most cases, probably not. In fact, a long consent form may thwart otherwise interested respondents from participating. Generally, a paragraph that requests participation and states that the research is voluntary and how the respondent's identity will be protected is plenty. Second, consider studies of many deviant populations in which others simply finding out that respondents are among a deviant population may put the employment and/or social relations of the respondents at risk or even lead to their arrest. If we required signed consent to study persons with AIDS, those who use drugs, or those who have been arrested for soliciting prostitution, we may find it very hard to get persons to agree to the research. More importantly, their signature on the form puts them at risk because it is basically a legal document with their signature saying that they have AIDS, use drugs, or have recently solicited prostitution. Thus, anonymity, rather than confidentiality, is often far safer for the individuals studied, and a consent form may be totally inappropriate.

⬥ Explaining Deviance in the Streets and Deviance in the Suites: In-Depth Research of Street Gangs and NASA

There is no "right way" to study deviance in the streets or in the suites, and most research strategies can be used to study deviance in either domain. That is, in-depth interviews can be just as useful for studying elite deviance as they are for studying street crime. Similarly, analyzing historical documents, surveying various populations, or using official records are all useful for studying deviance at every level of a society's economic and/or social hierarchy. Therefore, we have chosen just two illustrative examples in which researchers have studied deviance in the streets and in the suites that we hope you find interesting.

While much social science research is done using surveys and large data sets, some of the most intriguing work uses in-depth qualitative research to give an up-close look into the inner workings of organizations that are often a mystery to outsiders. Sudhir Venkatesh (2008) provides an example of this kind of research into street deviance in his popular book *Gang Leader for a Day*. A self-described "rogue sociologist," Venkatesh went to graduate school in Chicago and befriended a gang leader named J. T. in the city. Under J. T.'s protection and tutelage, he was able to spend years documenting the gang's efforts at selling crack cocaine and evading the law. Venkatesh (2008) explains his relationship with J. T. and J. T.'s view of his illegal industry:

> J. T. seemed to appreciate having the ear of an outsider who would listen for hours to his tales of bravado and managerial prowess. He often expressed how hard it was to oversee the gang, to keep the drug economy running smoothly, and to deal with the law-abiding tenants who saw him as an adversary. Sometimes he spoke of his job with dispassion, as if he were the CEO of some widget manufacturer—an attitude that I found not only jarring but, given the violence and destruction his enterprise caused, irresponsible.
>
> He fancied himself a philanthropist as much as a leader. He spoke proudly of quitting his mainstream sales job in downtown Chicago to return to the projects and use his drug profits to "help others." How did he help? He mandated that all his gang members get a high-school diploma and stay off drugs. He gave money to some local youth centers for sports equipment and computers. He willingly loaned out his gang members to Robert Taylor tenant leaders, who deployed them on such tasks as escorting the elderly on errands or beating up a domestic abuser. (pp. 114–115)

Venkatesh's research provides a provocative look at the lives of gang members and the drug trade in Chicago in the 1990s and provides a unique example and study of deviance in the streets. One must wonder how generalizable his research is—and how useful—now that the homes in the Robert Taylor area have largely been torn down by the city. One should also consider the ethical issues raised in this book; Venkatesh certainly knew a great deal about illegal activities operating in the city that he did nothing to stop.

Diane Vaughan took a much different approach in trying to understand the culture of NASA (National Aeronautical and Space Administration) that helped lead to the 1986 space shuttle *Challenger* disaster. A technical failure caused the *Challenger* to explode mere moments after takeoff. The presidential commission appointed to investigate the disaster found that there had been technical issues on previous shuttle missions and that engineers had objected to the launch the night before it took place. Information was suppressed and "NASA managers, experiencing extraordinary schedule pressures, knowingly took a chance, moving forward with a launch they were warned was risky, willfully violating internal rules in the process, in order to launch on time" (Vaughan, 2004, p. 316).

Vaughan conducted a historical ethnography of NASA and the *Challenger* launch decision, relying on documentary records—including 122,000 pages of NASA documents—to reconstruct history. Based on her own research, Vaughan concluded that the accident resulted from a mistake rather than misconduct (p. 316) and that standards of "acceptable risk" were commonplace at NASA and ruled all shuttle launches (p. 324). She argues that there was a normalization of deviance in the culture at NASA and that it was conformity to this organizational culture, rather than deviance, that caused the disaster. As Vaughan (2004) explains,

> This case was not an example of misconduct as I originally thought: rules were not violated. Still, harm was done. Moreover, NASA's actions were deviant in the eyes of outsiders, and, after the accident, also in the eyes of those who made decisions. (p. 341)

The two studies described above are, in some ways, as different as night and day. The former focuses on gang activity in the streets and relies purely on informal interviews and the researcher's observations and experiences with gang members. The latter involves a researcher's laborious efforts to review 100,000 pages of NASA documents to uncover the cause of a major catastrophe. However, it is interesting to note that, in both cases, deviance was an important issue for the deviants themselves. In the first case, J. T. (the gang leader), while clearly engaging in illegal activities, insisted that his gang members get an education and stay off drugs. In the second case, while no illegal behavior was technically uncovered, those involved came to recognize their behavior as "deviant." In both cases, much deviant behavior was conformity to the particular organizational culture.

◈ Ideas in Action: Evaluating Programs and Policy

There are some types of deviance that society wishes to control or eliminate, and policies are put into place or programs are developed to help deal with these "social problems." Social scientists are often interested in evaluating these programs and policies. Indeed, phrases such as "evidence-based decision making," "evidence-based practice," "research-based programs," and "cost–benefit analysis of programs and policy" have become quite popular across disciplines in recent years. Funding agencies now often require that the programs they subsidize must be "proven" or at least "promising" based on solid scientific research. And while government officials and other policymakers are often accused of making or changing policy based on whim, political pressure, or popular opinion, we suspect that many are actually trying to "do good"—or at least they are not trying to make things worse. The only proven way to assess the effectiveness of programs and policies to address deviance is with solid research invoking the tools we discussed earlier. Let us acquaint you with several programs and policies and how they have been evaluated.

In the mid-1930s, a juvenile delinquency prevention program known as the Cambridge-Somerville Youth Study was developed. This was a treatment program for boys aged 5 to 13 and their families. A variety of organizations (e.g., churches) and agencies (e.g., social welfare agencies) and the police recommended boys identified as "average" or "difficult" to the program. Beginning in 1939, boys were randomly assigned to the treatment program or to a control condition that only provided information to the study. The treatment included academic tutoring, medical and psychiatric treatment, counselors who visited the families to discuss problems, and involvement in various activities (e.g., Boy Scouts, YMCA, or summer camps). In a 30-year follow-up study of the intervention, McCord (1978) examined a great deal of information obtained on the boys over their life spans, including but not limited to court, mental health, and alcohol treatment records. Given the large amount of "help" offered the families, one might expect far more positive outcomes among the treated subjects. Actually, very few differences were found in terms of juvenile delinquency and adult criminal activity. Furthermore, there were at least seven negative "side effects." The treated men were more likely to have (1) committed a second offense, (2) shown greater signs of alcoholism, (3) shown greater evidence of mental illness, (4) died younger, (5) suffered from more stress-related diseases (e.g., high blood pressure), (6) held jobs with lower occupational prestige scores, and (7) reported less satisfaction with their jobs (McCord, 1978). Why were the outcomes of the treated men so poor compared with the outcomes of the control group? Unpacking that relationship is virtually impossible; the lesson to be learned, however, is that bad things can happen when we try to "do good" and, more importantly, when we assume we "do good."

More recently, the Drug Awareness Resistance Education (DARE) program has become very popular. Begun in 1983, DARE involves police officers teaching a standardized drug prevention curriculum in classrooms from kindergarten through high school (depending on the school or jurisdiction). While a few early studies suggested that the program may be effective (e.g., DeJong, 1987), larger, more rigorous studies have failed to find significant differences in drug use behaviors between those who experience the program and those who do not (e.g., Rosenbaum, 2007). Subsequently, numerous studies have examined the effectiveness of DARE, and these studies have been reviewed in two comprehensive meta-analyses (Ennet, Tobler, Ringwalt, & Flewelling, 1994; S. L. West & O'Neal, 2004). A meta-analysis is a systematic and statistical review of the literature on a particular issue and is composed mostly of experiments and, often, program evaluations. Both meta-analyses concluded that DARE programs were not reducing substance use among youth. Indeed, the bulk of evidence influenced one social scientist to borrow the now classic slogan "Just Say No to Drugs!" and modify it to read "Just Say No to DARE!" (Rosenbaum, 2007).

The point of these two examples is not that "nothing works" but, rather, that we often don't know *what* works, and we promote, at great costs, programs that are ineffective—or worse, that are negatively affecting participants. In the case of DARE, at one point, public funding for the program amounted to $200 million a year (Rosenbaum, 2007). This is a great societal cost for an ineffective program.

So are there programs that have been shown to be effective? The Office of Juvenile Justice and Delinquency Prevention (OJJDP) offers a website describing programs that are rated by experts to be either "effective" (solid studies show the program to be effective) or "promising" (studies suggest that the program may be effective, but stronger

NOW YOU . . . CONDUCT THE RESEARCH

The Southern Poverty Law Center documented 932 hate groups in the United States in 2010. Figure 3.3 provides a map showing the number of hate groups in each state. As a deviance researcher, you are interested in studying *white supremacy* groups, and you need to establish your research question, define your population, and determine your sample. Do you want to conduct macrolevel research on trends and characteristics of these hate groups in the United States? Or would you prefer to engage in microlevel research that examines participants in these groups? How will you conduct this research? How will you collect your data? What may some of the challenges be with a study on this topic?

Figure 3.3 Active U.S. Hate Groups

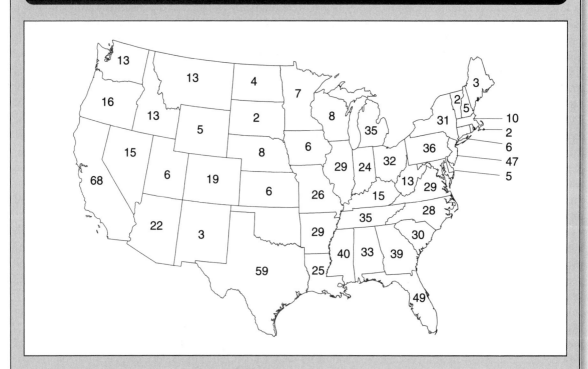

Source: Reprinted by permission of the Southern Poverty Law Center.

research designs are needed to confirm this) or to have "no effect," meaning, at least to date, the program has not been shown to be effective. Each program is rated by more than one expert, and any differences in scoring are reconciled. The website also includes programs on a number of social issues, including bullying, drug and alcohol use and abuse, and gang prevention, among others. The site also includes a list of useful program types, including family-based services, school-based and other academic programs, early intervention programs, and programs for courts and corrections.

Conclusion

In this chapter, we have presented the reader with several strategies to investigate and answer questions regarding deviance. We have not favored any particular approach, resting on the belief that the appropriate methodology comes after the research questions have been decided upon and the population of interest specified as well as the resources and skills of the researcher or research team spelled out. In fact, it would seem much more profitable to think about how different methodologies might work in concert to better understand the phenomenon at hand than immediately relegating the phenomenon to a specific methodology. A few in-depth interviews might snowball into a larger sample, or a survey might be developed based on the interviews to give to a larger, more representative sample. Alternatively, results of a large-scale survey may suggest a subpopulation of which more detailed investigation is warranted, or unexpected results might lead to a qualitative study. Given that these methodologies are not very conducive to tests of causal relationships, an experiment or quasi-experiment might be designed to aid in our knowledge of what factors affect some deviant attitude, belief, or behavior. In conclusion, we find that combining or triangulating research methods may be the only way to truly understand issues involving deviance.

ENDNOTE

1. While beyond the scope of this chapter, there are several ways of matching students across schools or to make statistical adjustments so that more reasonable comparisons can be made.

EXERCISES AND DISCUSSION QUESTIONS

1. Compare the similarities and differences between experimental and quasi-experimental designs. Give an example of one subject that might be best studied using each design.

2. Discuss survey research. What is the importance of sampling and response rates for a good representative sample?

3. What is the difference between being a "pure observer" of versus a "full participant" in social events?

4. What are official data? What are the strengths and weaknesses of official data?

5. Discuss the ethical concerns that come with studying deviance. In your opinion, how might we balance these ethical concerns with research on deviant behavior?

KEY TERMS

Content analysis	Ethics in research	Experiments
Covert observation	Ethnography	Field research

Human subjects	Participant observation	Sample
Institutional review board	Pure observation (nonparticipant)	Secondary data
Operationalization	Quasi-experimental designs	Survey
Overt observation	Response rate	

READING 7

In this provocative article, Ayella raises a number of problematic issues in the study of "cults," "new religious movements," "charismatic groups," or "world-rejecting groups." The study illustrates problems common to the study of many deviants: gaining and maintaining access and issues related to gatekeepers, including the decision of whether the researcher should let gatekeepers or followers know of the intention to conduct research or to act as a potential follower. Sampling what members to interact with (or simply realizing the potentially unique group that a gatekeeper sets the researcher up with) is complicated, especially if the time frame is relatively short. In addition to the sampling issues raised above, cults change and evolve over time with different leaders and followers. Researchers clearly leave with a snapshot, but what things will look like in the future is really unknown. Finally, researchers must confront the limitation of what information they are walking away with and how they will use it.

"They Must Be Crazy"

Some of the Difficulties in Researching "Cults"

Marybeth Ayella

This article examines some of the methodological difficulties encountered in researching "cults." The last 10 years have seen an enormous amount of research and writing on groups known variously as "cults," "new religious movements," "charismatic groups," or "world-rejecting groups," to name some of the most commonly used terms.[1]

In this article, I use the term "cult." What I am interested in exploring is how one does research on groups popularly labeled "cults." This labeling of a group as a cult makes this a sensitive topic to study, for given the public's predominantly negative assessment of cults,[2] one is researching a group considered by many to be deviant.

I will discuss some of the methodological problems which I think are particularly vexing in the study of cults, and I will point to some solutions suggested by researchers. My examination will be limited to one kind of research done by sociologists: field research.[3] I focus on this type of research because it seems to have been stimulated by cults. Robbins (1988) pointed to a virtual explosion of anthropological-like studies by sociologists

Source: Ayella, M. (1990). "They must be crazy": Some of the difficulties in researching "cults." *American Behavioral Scientist, 33,* 562–577. Reprinted with permission.

of religion. Field research seems to be an attempt to get behind the strangeness and controversial aspects of cults. This method provides the closest look at cult groups, and it thus has the potential to provide in-depth understanding of the group examined, as well as the group's self-understanding. This research has as its strong point debunking overly psychiatric or psychological "brainwashing" perspectives, in showing the interactional aspect of becoming and remaining a cult member. This humanizes cult members—they are portrayed as more than crackpots, psychological basket cases, or brainwashed robots.

◇ Gaining Access

Contingencies of Research

Mitchell, Mitchell, and Ofshe (1980, chap. 9), Wallis (1977a, 1977b), Bromley and Shupe (1979, Shupe & Bromley, 1980), and Barker's (1984, chap. 1) discussions of their research on Synanon, Scientology, and the Unification Church highlight the contingencies of research, which are those aspects of research over which the researcher has little or no control. One very important contingency is the group's present social reputation.

Richard Ofshe's research on Synanon began in the summer of 1972 with a chance visit to Synanon's Tomales Bay facilities. Ofshe's neighbor, a marine biologist, was asked by Synanon for help in setting up a lab for a sewage-treatment system. Ofshe accompanied him on a visit, and was given a trail-bike tour of the ranching facility. After the visit, Ofshe asked the ranch director if he could come back to do research. During the next year, Ofshe paid over 50 visits, during which he did participant observation, to the ranch and Synanon facilities in Oakland, San Francisco, and Santa Monica. In addition, five of his students did research on Synanon over a three-month period, joining the Oakland "game club" and participating in games and in Synanon community life to varying degrees.

Ofshe's and students' professional interests and intentions to observe and analyze were made known to management and community members from the initial contact. Ofshe's entry was welcomed. Two aspects of Synanon's history seem important in explaining his welcome: (a) in 1972, Synanon considered itself a social movement and an alternative society, and it welcomed middle-class professionals, hoping to recruit them as members; and (b) Ofshe followed three researchers who had visited Synanon and written books favorable to the organization. Synanon's openness seemed based on its changing self-conception and its good reputation, which grew largely out of its claims of unprecedentedly effective drug rehabilitation.

Roy Wallis offers a contrasting example. He presented himself at an introductory "Communications Course" in Scientology as an interested newcomer. He wanted "to learn how 'anyman' coming in off the street would be received, not how a visiting sociologist doing a thesis on Scientology would be treated" (Wallis, 1977b, p. 155). He arranged to stay in a Scientology "boarding house" during this course. Wallis left after two days because he found it too difficult to continue. He felt he would have been able to stay only if he were in agreement with what he was officially learning. Not feeling this agreement, Wallis felt it would have been dishonest to indicate agreement. When Wallis later officially requested help from the movement's leaders, this earlier abrupt exit, as well as the movement's knowledge that Wallis had surveyed (with a questionnaire) present and ex-members, needed to be explained. Scientologist David Gaiman commented in an appendix to Wallis' article that he "could not understand at that time, and still do not understand, the ethics of his failing to declare this to me in his initial approach" (Wallis, 1977b, p. 168).

Wallis had initially thought to do covert participant observation, because he anticipated a hostile reaction to an open request from a sociologist, given previous, critical investigations by the Food and Drug Administration (FDA) in the United States and by government bodies in Australia and New Zealand, and because he thought "that approaching the leaders and officials of such a public-relations-conscious social movement directly, for assistance with my research, was simply to invite public relations" (Wallis, 1977b, p. 152).

David Bromley and Anson Shupe's simultaneous participant observation of the Unification Church (UC) and the "anti-cult" movement seemingly originated in two chance events. While writing a conference paper on the enormous negative media coverage of the Unification Church, they requested information from the headquarters for the National Ad Hoc Committee—Citizens Engaged in Freeing Minds (CEFM)—and discovered that it was based in a nearby metropolitan area. At the same time, two high-ranking and 50 rank-and-file members of the Unification Church arrived in the area, seeking to recruit university students. One of the researchers was acting chair of his university's sociology department and he agreed, "on civil libertarian principles," to be faculty sponsor for a UC campus student organization. In exchange, Bromley and Shupe were permitted to conduct in-depth interviews and were allowed to observe the group.

Eileen Barker's research on the Unification Church is unique in that, after two years of negotiating with the Church to do research on her terms (e.g., receiving a list of all members, so that she might draw a random sample to interview), she seemed to have been granted relatively free access to the group. However, she did not search out the Unification Church; rather, she was in the favorable position of being sought out by the Church to do research on it. Being sought out may have put her in a more powerful position to negotiate for a favorable research "bargain."

The UC apparently sought her out as an established sociologist of religion. She participated in one conference which the UC sponsored, and in a "series of three residential weekend 'Roundtables on Science and Religion'" (Barker, 1984, p. 13) held at the UC's national headquarters in London, before she was asked if she would like to write about the Church. A Moonie she knew sought her out because he was worried about a sociologist of religion doing research on the group, based on negative reports. Barker replied that it was "hardly surprising that he had to rely on negative reports, as it was well-nigh impossible to get any other kind of information" (p. 14). She later found out that the UC agreed to let her do her research because she "had been prepared to listen to their side of the argument, and they could not believe that anyone who did that could write anything worse than what was already being published by people who had not come to find out for themselves" (p. 15). They felt she was open-minded enough to present a fair picture of them. This seeking her out, and her negotiating for certain conditions of research, allowed her free and long-term access to the group.

There are several points worth noting from these brief descriptions of extant research on cults. Most important, the researcher should be critical of access, asking the question of why the group has allowed the researcher in, looking to the recent history of the group and its present self-understanding in answering this question. One should question the kind of access one is being given, ever conscious of the possibility of sanitization or impression management. The researcher should not simply assume that the group he or she is studying understands and agrees with the unfettered pursuit of scientific inquiry. The researcher should learn as much as he or she can about the group—through newspaper/media accounts, public relations materials, or efforts such as open houses, and through interviews with ex-members or present members—before undertaking field research. These actions, however, may have unforeseen consequences.

Researcher as Person

Downes and Rock (1982, p. 30), in discussing research on deviance, made the point that "one will not be at ease everywhere. There are always likely to be certain social groups who defy research by certain sociologists. . . . Many of the barriers which divide people from one another in everyday life also keep the sociologist at bay." Field research highlights the researcher. Some researchers, like informants, are simply better able to establish rapport and to feel at ease in a new, let alone strange, setting. Wallis (1977b, p. 155) said of himself in his brief participant observation on Scientology: "Good participant observation required a particular personality or discipline which I did not possess. Outside a 'mass' context I felt uncomfortable in my role. It felt like spying and a little dishonest. In general, I tried to shift the situation to an 'open' interaction context as quickly as possible."

Among the problems relating to the researcher are: culture shock, handling emotional responses to the group (the chief difficulty here is that overrapport may hinder objectivity), handling conversion attempts of the group, and the stigma of investigating a group considered by many to be deviant.

Balch (1985, p. 24) emphasized that the authoritarian social worlds of cults may rub against the grain of researchers' views of reality, since researchers tend to be humanists. In addition, there is the question of dealing with bizarre behaviors. Balch stated his first reaction to the UFO cult which he and Taylor studied: "My gut reaction to this message was something like: 'They look normal to me, so how can they possibly believe this nonsense?'" (p. 24). Continued interaction with the group overcame these responses, in a way similar to anthropologists' dealing with culture shock.

Whose Perspective? Sampling Members

In researching any group, the question arises immediately as to who and what to sample. The problem of sampling interacts with that of brief field research. That is, if one is going to observe a group for a very short time, the question of who one interviews becomes more important. With longer time in the group, one can make efforts to gain a sampling of members to represent the various viewpoints that are present in the group.

Drawing a representative, random sample of a cult or of ex-cult members (of one group or of all groups) is very difficult. If the group presents a sample of members to a researcher, how does the researcher know if these members are representative? Perhaps they are more intelligent, more likely to be "true believers," or those thought more likely to present the group in a good light than other members. How does the researcher determine how they were selected? Given the high turnover in most cults, longitudinal analysis of a sample of members is also difficult, and such longitudinal analyses of conversion are few (Balch, 1985).

Different understandings within a group are a fact of life. These differences of perspective are the result of one's role and status in the group, one's length of time in the group, and analytical abilities, among other things. In studying any group, the researcher needs to get a sampling of views from all factions to come up with a complete picture of the "reality" of the group. One problem in identifying these factions is that cults often are precisely those organizations which brook no public dissent, so that the only view expressed is the official view. That is, the group presents the appearance of unanimous agreement to outsiders and insiders. Factions do not emerge as organized entities with a

recognized different point of view. Individuals remain in a state of pluralistic ignorance of discontent and doubt or criticism of the group. They do not know that others share doubts; they feel only they have doubts (Ayella, 1985; Bainbridge & Stark, 1980).

Yet, here too, "politics" are a fact of life, and it is important for the researcher to assume that members experience the group differently, even when confronted by apparent unanimity. As Rochford (1985, p. 41) concluded from his study of the Hare Krishnas, "First, many, if not most settings are characterized by local politics. To take on a membership role necessarily involves making choices about what sort of member the researcher wants to be." This role will then influence how other members treat the researcher. The researcher would be wise to accept Downes and Rock's (1982, p. 27) advice on researching deviant behavior: "It is only by taking a jaundiced perspective on the world that its disreputable life becomes apparent. Surfaces reveal little. They certainly do not point one at deviant populations." The deviance to be searched for here is doubt, uncertainty, and less than total commitment to the official group ideology.

An additional aspect of sampling remains. New religious movements (NRM) researchers have often described leavers of cult groups as "apostates," and they discount their accounts (of their entry, life, and exit from the group) as being valid sources of data on the group, as being biased—as being not more than "atrocity tales" cultivated in deprogramming sessions. On the other hand, they often accept accounts from current members as being acceptable sources of information on the group. Beckford (1985) is one NRM researcher who has criticized this approach to ex-members' accounts, asserting the desirability of taking ex-members' testimony as seriously as that of current members, and rejecting "the idea that ex-members' accounts can all be subsumed under the heading of 'atrocity tales'" (p. 146). Having made this statement, Beckford felt compelled to defend himself from the assumption that he is an anti-cultist (pp. 146–147).

If one sees only ex-members, one's sample is likely to be of people who were unhappy enough with the group to leave on their own, or people who were deprogrammed. The methodological question is how one interprets these ex-members' versions of the group and its effect on them. One way is to recognize the contextual construction of individual accounts of participation and leave-taking—that is, the fact that such accounts are strongly shaped by individuals' present reference groups. Thus a present member's account is shaped by other members' views, including the desirability of presenting the appearance of complete commitment.

Beckford (1978) and Rochford (1985) both emphasized how the group's ideology presents itself as a "screen" by which members can reinterpret their past and present. Balch (1985) also emphasized how retrospective reinterpretation must be taken into account in interviewing *both* members and ex-members. Recognizing that neither group, present members nor ex-members, can express the complete "truth" is a step toward resolving this problem. In addition, Wright (1987) and Solomon's (1981) research showed that individuals' modes of leaving the group shape their evaluation of the group. Solomon's questionnaire study of ex-Moonies suggested differences in adjustment between ex-cultists who have been deprogrammed and those who have not. She emphasized that we cannot generalize to all members or ex-members of cults from samples of ex-cultists who seek therapy, because we do not know how they compare to ex-cultists who do not seek therapy.

◈ Maintaining Access

Easy Access, Difficult Maintenance

Conversion-oriented groups provide a paradoxical research setting, where access may be easy, but continued presence or interaction is more difficult. This is the result of their expectation that one should accept the group's perspective—and convert—within some specified time period. This carries with it the expectation that one's behavior should change to reflect this conversion or commitment (e.g., living with the group, and giving up previous ties or jobs).

John Lofland, in his now-classic (and disguised) study of the early Unification Church, "assumed the standard seeker's posture, namely, interested and sympathetic but undecided" after he and two fellow graduate students decided in 1962 to study the group (Lofland, 1966, pp. 270–271). The group pressured the three to commit themselves to serious study of the

Divine Principle (the group's theology) and to move in with the group. Lofland then expressed interest in doing a sociological study of the group and met with enthusiastic approval from the group's leader. For 11 months, he did participant observation on the group: From February through October of 1962, he spent about 15 hours a week with the group; and from November 1962 through January 1963, he lived in the center four days a week. During this time, Lofland thought there was a shared understanding of his interest in the group, that "I was personally sympathetic to, and accepting of, them and desired to understand their endeavors, but I was not likely to be a convert" (p. 274). In January 1963, the leader told Lofland "that she was tired of playing the 'studying the movement' game" (p. 274). Given his apparent unlikeliness to convert, the leader saw no further reason for his presence, and Lofland left the group. However, a sociology undergraduate student who feigned conversion and joined the group provided information to Lofland until June 1963.

Lofland's experience highlights the problem of adopting a long-term, participant-observer stance to a conversion-oriented group. What happens if one does not convert after what the group considers a reasonable time? Robbins, Anthony, and Curtis (1973) also illustrated an unsuccessful resolution of this dilemma in Anthony's participant observation study of a Jesus Freaks group. When confronted by questions as to his religious beliefs, Anthony refused to discuss them, feeling that the religious beliefs he held would alienate group members and end his observation. This response brought strenuous pressure by the group on him to convert. Anthony responded to the pressure by gradual withdrawal.

Richardson, Stewart, and Simmonds (1978) suggested that this outcome of ejection from the group may be averted by the expression of honest difference of opinion, admitting (in their case, that of a fundamentalist commune) that one is aware of the necessity to be "saved," but that one rejects it. This strategy apparently was successful, for they had maintained a relationship with the group for almost seven years at the time of publication of this article. Gordon (1987), too, found this strategy to be successful in his research on two fundamentalist Jesus groups. He suggested that researchers in these groups cultivate distance in the interaction. Two methods of doing this are to be forthright about one's own, differing beliefs, and to emphasize one's research role. Doing so did not alienate members of the group he studied; paradoxically, he felt a sense of greater rapport. Gordon theorized that this open discussion and emphasized researcher role kept the group from feeling that their persuasion efforts had failed.

Shupe and Bromley's (1980; Bromley & Shupe, 1979) articles describing their research on both the Unification Church and the anticult movement also illustrated initially easy access and difficulty as interaction continued. Their role as sociologists was important in two ways in reducing the barriers between themselves and the groups: The role itself "carried a certain degree of legitimacy," and "each group was seeking some type of legitimation to which it was perceived we might contribute" (1980, p. 8). Underpinning both groups' welcome of the researchers was the understanding that "to 'really know' their respective positions was to come to believe in them" (1980, p. 12). The difficulties arose when this did not occur in each group with greater knowledge.

Each group knew that Bromley and Shupe were investigating both groups, and this presented one of the difficulties they faced. Neither group could understand why the researchers needed information from the other group, and Bromley and Shupe were continually forced to explain each dealing with the other group. When time passed and it was clear the researchers were no longer ignorant of the group, members of each group pressured them to take a public stand in support of their respective group, advocating for the group in the media and to other interest groups. Their delicate solution to this persistent dilemma was to "avoid interviews that seemed superficial, highly partisan, or exploitative" (1980, p. 13), and to present each group in its complexity when doing an interview or giving a public talk.

As their research proceeded, Bromley and Shupe sought more extensive and more sensitive information. In attempting to visit the UC's seminary, they became involved in a lengthy negotiation process. They feared this access would not be granted because "the authors' published work was perceived as not sufficiently 'objective' and sensitive to the uses to which the information might be put by others" (1980, p. 9). The UC scrutinized their written work, requested a list of the questions they wanted to ask, and a seminary faculty member visited their campus to "test fully our good

will, honesty, and neutrality" (1980, p. 14). Part of the UC's concern stemmed from the fact that they were unable to locate Bromley and Shupe on a supporter/opponent continuum, and they felt they had been harmed by previous researchers to whom they had granted access.

How can researchers cope with the pressures to adopt the group's perspective, to become a committed participant instead of a researcher concerned with objectivity? Richardson et al. (1978) emphasized the importance of maintaining a base camp at the research site to daily reinforce, through conversation with co-workers, one's alternative (to the group) reality. This may facilitate the handling of culture shock and prevent researcher conversion, but it also helps the researcher in other ways. Two (or more) researchers can share the moral dilemmas encountered during the research; they can correct each other's biases (Stone, 1978); and they can alleviate the loneliness of the "professional stranger" role. Barker (1984, pp. 21–22) described her reaction to a BBC producer who

> spent some time with me doing "joint participant observation" in preparation for the filming. Each time we ended a visit I would thrust a tape recorder into her hands and beg her to pour out whatever occurred to her. The fact that her impressions largely coincided with my own did not, of course, prove that we were right and everyone else wrong, but it was enormously reassuring to learn that I was not totally idiosyncratic.

The Researcher's Role in the Group

Groups vary in the kind of access they allow; "potential convert" may be the only way they conceptualize outsiders, in spite of the researcher's identification of self as researcher. In my three-week participant observation of the Unification Church (Ayella, 1977), I identified myself as a researcher from the start. I was told I could observe the group, but I was treated throughout more as a "potential convert" than as a researcher. When attempting to get background information on members or newcomers, I was repeatedly interrupted and asked to do something else. One night, when I chose to skip a lecture (I had learned that that week's set of lectures was virtually identical to the set of lectures given the previous week) to read and take notes, I was confronted with repeated requests from other members to attend. Finally, I decided to do so, thinking that the members would simply stay with me and request until the lecture was over. When I returned to the trailer in which I was staying, the article I had been reading (on Synanon) was gone, as were some notes. No one remembered seeing the article when I questioned members; neither article nor notes ever turned up. This incident was one of the events that destroyed my trust—I doubted the group really meant for me to do research. The consequence was that I stopped taking notes to the degree that I had previously.

In contrast, Rochford (1985) mentioned that at the time of his research on the Hare Krishnas, the movement was changing from an exclusionist group to more of an inclusionist group. As an exclusionist group, one was either an insider or an outsider. At the time of Rochford's research, the movement was developing a role for less committed individuals: that of movement sympathizer. This allowed him to continue participant observation beyond the stage allowed for in the "potential convert" role. This also illustrates some of the contingencies of research. That is, Rochford was in the right place at the right time to do long-term participant observation.

Rochford's reflections (1985, chap. 2) on his research on the Hare Krishna group also highlight the difficulties of long-term participant observation. The Hare Krishnas demanded high commitment and belief from members, so one problem was how much to participate in the group's activities. As Rochford stated, "Because of strong pressures to participate in the activities of the group, it often becomes difficult to work out a role that is acceptable both to the researcher and to those under study" (1985, p. 22). Rochford's role in the group evolved over the seven years of his research. After the first year, he became a "fringe" member of the group, and he was able to maintain this "fringe" devotee role in the group's Los Angeles community for the next several years. This status enabled him to research ISKCON (International Society for Krishna Consciousness) communities in other parts of the country: "I sent each of these communities a letter from a well-known and respected devotee, who showed his support for my

research and pointed out my general sympathies toward Krishna Consciousness and ISKCON" (1985, p. 29). In his own letter of request, Rochford emphasized his five years' involvement, his interest both sociologically and spiritually, and his involvement in the community school and the "bhakta" program for newcomers. He gained stronger support for his research in the form of a higher rate of questionnaire completion from the other communities. However, in his own (Los Angeles) community, Rochford's fringe devotee status resulted in the lowest rate of questionnaire completion.

Rochford pointed out other instances in which his being a fringe member made research personally difficult; for example, at times he was shown to be an "incompetent" member of the group by his repeated ignorance of Sanskrit. Reflecting on this, he realized that learning the language was of lesser importance to him than were other research occupations. In addition, he had "little or no access to the dynamics of recruitment," and he avoided asking questions when he was not sure of something, because he was "very sensitive not to appear ignorant in the eyes of devotees" (1985, p. 31).

◈ Leaving the Field

After successfully gaining access to a group and studying it in-depth, several important questions confront the researcher: To what, if anything, can one generalize from one's research? How representative of the group are one's observations? How representative of cults is this group? While field research may substantially increase our understanding of a particular group, it certainly complicates generalization.

The longer one is with the group, the more confident one may be that one has (a) pierced the public front of the group; (b) gained the trust of members, which often precedes the researcher's entry to back regions of a group; and (c) seen the difference between attitude and behavior. Cults, as social movements, change continually in response to both internal (e.g., in response to a charismatic leader's desires) and external events (e.g., a spate of negative media publicity); thus "snapshots" of the group may soon be outdated. Knowledge of the long-term development of the group may help to establish how representative a snapshot of the group is, but the difficulty is that one does not know at times whether one is at the beginning, the middle, or the end of the group's history. Lofland's (1966) *Doomsday Cult* portrayal of the early Unification Church would not have led one to predict its evolution into a larger and more successful group.

Very few researchers are going to be able to do many in-depth studies—for example, Barker had been studying the Moonies for six years before she published *The Making of a Moonie* (1984). At the time of publication of "Researching a Fundamentalist Commune" (1978), Richardson et al. had been doing research for almost seven years on this group. Rochford had studied the Hare Krishnas for about eight years before his *Hare Krishna in America* was published in 1985. Compounding the difficulty, Balch (1985, p. 24) argued that one cannot compare groups using other people's research, for "any secondary analysis of the current research is apt to get bogged down by ambiguous terms, incomplete data, and idiosyncratic research methods."

In addition to the question of what the researcher can generalize to after doing field research, there is the difficulty of getting published. Cults may attempt to prevent critical research from being published, or may respond to published critical research by litigation. Both Beckford (1983) and Horowitz (1981) pointed to the Unification Church's efforts to prevent their research from being published and distributed. Wallis's (1977b) account of his difficulty in getting his research on Scientology published is daunting. Synanon responded to the publication of Mitchell, et al.'s (1980) book, *The Light on Synanon,* with libel suits, necessitating countersuits by the defendants which dragged on for years.

◈ Conclusion

If politics are present at the level of the individual researcher and cult, they are also present at the level of scientific community and society. Jonestown seems to have been a watershed event in terms of public awareness and evaluation of cults. This event was widely publicized, and in its wake, greater credibility was given to those critical of cults, stimulating government investigations and legislation to regulate cult practices (Barker, 1986). As Barker (1986, p. 332) saw it:

After Jonestown they tended to be all lumped together under the now highly derogatory label "cult." Despite pleas from the movements themselves . . . , all the new religions were contaminated by association, the worst (most "sinister" and "bizarre") features of each belonging, by implication, to them all.

Applying Schur's (1980) concept of "deviantizing," cults are engaged in "stigma contests," or battles over the right to define what shall be termed deviant. The outcome of deviantization is the loss of moral standing in the eyes of other members of society. A negative assessment of a group by a researcher may be used in this stigma contest and may change public opinion significantly, making it more difficult for the group to mobilize resources of people and money to accomplish its goals. Conversely, a positive assessment may assist the cult in countering accusations of deviance (e.g., being labeled as an "unauthentic" religion). In Schur's analysis of the politics of deviance, the more powerful group usually has the edge in stigma contests. In this instance, the more powerful cults have the resources to use the courts to assert their rights. Robbins (1988, p. 181) described cults' reaction to the "anticult" movement: "However, the latter, buoyed by their initial 'institutionalized freedom' and insulation from routinized controls, stridently affirms their 'rights,' which are interpreted as granting to 'churches' freedom from all interference."

If the group studied is powerful, it can use its resources to hinder critical evaluations from being published. Scientology's wealth enabled it to successfully insist on changes in Wallis's manuscript, using the threat of an expensive libel suit, which neither Wallis nor his publisher wanted. Synanon is another group which used its considerable resources—the unpaid labor of its many lawyer members—to discourage journalists and other observers from making critical public comment. The group's use of lawsuits charging libel and seeking multi-million-dollar damages so deterred large newspapers and news magazines that the small newspaper, the *Point Reyes Light,* was the only one willing to publish the negative reports of Synanon (Mitchell et al., 1980).

Co-optation of the researcher can be a major problem for the unwary researcher, because he or she can become, without intent, a "counter" in the ongoing stigma contest between cult and anticult. Openness to social scientists (with their relativizing, "debunking" perspective) can be used as evidence to counter accusations of extreme authoritarianism or totalism of belief and practice. The researchers' participation in cult-sponsored conferences and publication in cult-printed publications can lend the prestige of social science to the group, fostering social respectability. Perhaps the most noteworthy example of this is the Unification Church's sponsorship of conferences and publication of the conference proceedings. The journal *Sociological Analysis* devoted a 1983 issue to discussion of a conference on the propriety of participation in such proceedings. Beckford (1983) emphasized that individual participation may have long-term "transindividual" negative consequences for social scientists specializing in the study of new religious movements. In this instance, Beckford worried that UC sponsorship of conferences and publications will restrict publication to those approved by the UC, and divide the academic specialist community.

The point here is that research has consequences: to generate favorable or unfavorable publicity; an increase or a loss of social prestige; funding or financial support or its loss; or an increase or loss of moral standing (in the case of people considered to be "cultists," they are not just regarded as less prestigious people, but as different kinds of people—as "nuts" or "crackpots"). The fact that many of the groups referred to as cults are social movements, which need an ongoing relationship with the society outside their doors to survive and to grow, means that they are particularly sensitive to public opinion. In the wake of Jonestown, however, I am arguing that "stigma contests" increased, making cults even more sensitive to public opinion.

Stigma contests over what is acceptable behavior continue to be fought by cults. It is inevitable that researchers will be caught up in these contests, because concerns with respectability and social power are ever-present concerns of cults, given the widespread perception of them as deviant. This fact of stigma contests can influence researchers' gaining and maintaining of access, their analysis of research, and their perceived credibility. The important point to emphasize here is that the researcher should not let his or her research agenda be set by the movement. Maintaining one's own agenda will undoubtedly cause various problems, not all of which can be determined in advance.

 Notes

1. It is impossible to explore here the range of theoretical and methodological issues involved in this research. Whichever term we use, these groups have been very controversial, and this is also true of the research done on the groups. The two predominant theoretical positions are those of the "new religious movements" and the "destructive cult" researchers. For the uninformed reader, I recommend Robbins's *Cults, Converts, and Charisma* (1988) for the most comprehensive and well-balanced analysis of the research. Beckford's *Cult Controversies* (1985) provides a compelling analysis of the controversiality of cults. Both of these are from the perspective of "new religious movements" researchers. For a statement of the issues from "destructive cult" researchers, I suggest Clark, Langone, Schecter, and *Daly's Destructive Cult Conversion: Theory, Research, and Treatment* (1981).

2. Barker (1984, p. 2) illustrated widespread public awareness and negative assessment of these groups and events by referring to a late 1970s survey in which a thousand Americans born between 1940 and 1952 were given a list of 155 names and asked how they felt about each of them. Only 3 per cent of the respondents had not heard of the Reverend Moon. Only 1 per cent admitted to admiring him. The owner of no other name on the list elicited less admiration, and the only person whom a higher percentage of respondents did not admire was the ritual killer Charles Manson.

Elsewhere, Barker (1986, p. 330) referred to a December 1978 Gallup Poll which found that "98% of the US public had heard or read about the People's Temple and the Guyana massacre—a level of awareness matched in the pollsters' experience only by the attack on Pearl Harbor and the explosion of the atom bomb."

3. I suggest the collection of papers edited by Brock K. Kilbourne, *Scientific Research and New Religions: Divergent Perspectives* (1985), as the best source of information on this research. Both "new religious movements" and "destructive cult" researchers are represented, so that one obtains a sampling of both perspectives as they influence analyses of research.

 References

Ayella, M. (1977). *An analysis of current conversion practices of followers of Reverend Sun Myung Moon.* Unpublished manuscript.

Ayella, M. (1985). *Insane therapy: Case study of the social organization of a psychotherapy cult.* Unpublished doctoral dissertation, University of California at Berkeley.

Bainbridge, W. S., & Stark, R. (1980). Scientology: To be perfectly clear. *Sociological Analysis, 41,* 128–136.

Balch, R. W. (1985). What's wrong with the study of new religions and what we can do about it. In B. K. Kilbourne (Ed.), *Scientific research and new religions: Divergent perspectives* (pp. 24–39). San Francisco: American Association for the Advancement of Science.

Barker, E. (1983). Supping with the devil: How long a spoon does the sociologist need? *Sociological Analysis, 44,* 197–206.

Barker, E. (1984). *The Making of a Moonie.* New York: Blackwell.

Barker, E. (1986). Religious movements: Cult and anticult since Jonestown. *Annual Review of Sociology, 12,* 329–346.

Beckford, J. A. (1978). Accounting for conversion. *British Journal of Sociology, 29,* 249–262.

Beckford, J. A. (1983). Some questions about the relationship between scholars and the new religious movements. *Sociological Analysis, 44,* 189–196.

Beckford, J. A. (1985). *Cult controversies.* New York: Tavistock.

Bromley, D. G., & Shupe, A. D. (1979). Evolving fool in participant observation: Research as an emergent process. In W. Shaffir, A. Turowitz, & R. Stebbins (Eds.), *Fieldwork experience: Qualitative approaches to social research* (pp. 191–203). New York: St. Martin's.

Clark, J. G., Jr., Langone, M. D., Schecter, R. E., & Daly, R. C. B. (1981). *Destructive cult conversion: Theory, research, and treatment.* Weston, MA: American Family Foundation.

Downes, D., & Rock, P. (1982). *Understanding deviance.* New York: Oxford University Press.

Gordon, D. (1987, August). *Getting close by staying distant: Field work on conversion-oriented groups.* Paper presented at the annual meeting of the American Sociological Association, New York City.

Horowitz, I. (1981). The politics of new cults. In T. Robbins & D. Anthony (Eds.), *In gods we trust* (pp. 161–170). New Brunswick, NJ: Transaction Books.

Kilbourne, B. K. (Ed.). (1985). *Scientific research and new religions: Divergent perspectives.* San Francisco: American Association for the Advancement of Science, Pacific Division.

Lofland, J. (1966). *Doomsday cult.* Englewood Cliffs, NJ: Prentice-Hall.

Mitchell, D., Mitchell, C., & Ofshe, R. (1980). *The light on Synanon.* New York: Seaview Books.

Richardson, J. T., Stewart, M. W., & Simmonds, R. B. (1978). Researching a fundamentalist commune. In J. Needleman & G. Baker (Eds.), *Understanding the new religions* (pp. 235–251). New York: Seabury.

Robbins, T. (1988). *Cults, converts, and charisma.* Newbury Park, CA: Sage.

Robbins, T., Anthony, D., & Curtis, T. (1973). The limits of symbolic realism: Problems of empathetic field observation in a sectarian context. *Journal for the Scientific Study of Religion, 12,* 259–272.

Rochford, E. B. (1985). *Hare Krishna in America.* New Brunswick, NJ: Rutgers University Press.

Schur, E. M. (1980). *The politics of deviance.* Englewood Cliffs, NJ: Prentice-Hall.

Shupe, A. D., Jr., & Bromley, D. G. (1980). Walking a tightrope: Dilemmas of participant observation of groups in conflict. *Qualitative Sociology, 2,* 3–21.

Solomon, T. (1981). Integrating the "Moonie" experience: A survey of ex-members of the Unification Church. In T. Robbins & D. Anthony (Eds.), *In gods we trust* (pp. 275–294). New Brunswick, NJ: Transaction Books.

Stone, D. (1978). On knowing how we know about the new religions. In J. Needleman & G. Baker (Eds.), *Understanding the new religions* (pp. 141–152). New York: Seabury Press.

Wallis, R. (1977a). *The road to total freedom.* New York: Columbia University Press.

Wallis, R. (1977b). The moral career of a research project. In C. Bell & H. Newby (Eds.), *Doing sociological research* (pp. 149–169). London: Allen & Unwin.

Wright, S. (1987). *Leaving cults: The dynamics of defection* (Monograph No. 7). Washington, DC: Society for the Scientific Study of Religion.

READING 8

Lee and Renzetti begin their introduction to a journal issue on "Legitimacy in the Modern World" by noting that a "sensitive topic" is actually a difficult and vague description that is not well defined in the literature, and they discuss various definitions to help us think through the problem. They make a very interesting point stating that results from studies concerning sensitive topics are likely to be accepted by the public regardless of how poorly the research was conducted. For example, we have heard Kinsey's research finding that about 10% of his sample was homosexual stated

Source: Lee, Raymond M., and Claire M. Renzetti. 1990. "The Problems of Researching Sensitive Topics." *American Behavioral Scientist 33,* 510–528. Reprinted with permission.

as fact and even exaggerated and extended to all cultures and societies. Kinsey's sample was a nonprobability sample and was not intended to represent the U.S. population (and certainly not all societies) even at the time of his publication. As other articles have emphasized, sampling is almost always a problem when dealing with sensitive topics, but the authors put a unique spin on the issue as they discuss legal issues surrounding sampling. Finally, the authors provide some especially interesting examples of ethical issues in the study of sensitive issues.

The Problems of Researching Sensitive Topics

An Overview and Introduction

Raymond M. Lee and Claire M. Renzetti

◈ Defining "Sensitive" Topics

One difficulty with the notion of a "sensitive topic" is that the term is often used in the literature as if it were self-explanatory. In other words, the term usually is treated in a commonsensical way, with no attempt at definition. Consider the substantive topics addressed by the articles in this issue. Child abuse, AIDS, and policing in Northern Ireland, for instance, are topics that most social scientists would generally regard without much reservation as sensitive. Why? What is it about these topics that makes them "sensitive," relative to other research topics?

A starting point for answering these questions is provided by Sieber and Stanley (1988). They define "socially sensitive research" as

> studies in which there are potential consequences or implications, either directly for the participants in the research or for the class of individuals represented by the research. For example, a study that examines the relative merits of day care for infants against full-time care by the mother can have broad social implications and thus can be considered socially sensitive. Similarly, studies aimed at examining the relation between gender and mathematical ability also have significant social implications. (p. 49)

A major advantage of defining sensitive research in this way is that it is broad in scope, thereby allowing for the inclusion of topics that ordinarily might not be thought of as "sensitive." In addition, it alerts researchers to their responsibilities to the wider society. This is entirely appropriate, given the ethical and professional issues which form the primary focus of Sieber and Stanley's article. The difficulty is that Sieber and Stanley do not specify the scope or nature of the kinds of consequences or implications, that they have in mind. As a result, their definition logically encompasses research that is consequential in any way. This would include presumably almost any kind of applied research, even where it had limited scope or was wholly beneficial. Therefore, the term "sensitive," as used by Sieber and Stanley, almost seems to become synonymous with "controversial." Moreover, while the importance of ethical issues should not be diminished, one needs to remember that research on sensitive topics raises a whole range of problems, including those of a more specifically technical or methodological kind. The definition proposed by Sieber and Stanley tends to draw attention away from these problems.

An alternative approach to defining sensitive topics would be to start with the observation that those topics which social scientists generally regard as sensitive are ones that seem to be threatening in some way to those being studied. Another way to put this is to say that sensitive topics present problems because research into them involves potential costs to those participating in the research. It is true, of course, that all research involves some cost to those who participate, if only in terms of time and possible inconvenience. While there are cases in which research makes demands on participants that are quite substantial, the potential costs in the case of sensitive topics go beyond the incidental or merely onerous. Thus, for a topic to be sensitive, the threat it poses should at least be moderate, although probably more often it is severe.

At the same time, sensitive topics seem to involve particular kinds of costs. On one hand, these may take the form of psychic costs, such as guilt, shame, or embarrassment. Alternatively, sensitive topics are threatening because participation in research can have unwelcome consequences. For instance, wrongdoing uncovered by the research might bring with it the possibility of discovery and sanction. As a result, the relationship between the researcher and the researched may become hedged with mistrust, concealment, and dissimulation. This, in turn, has obvious detrimental effects on levels of reliability and validity, and raises a concomitant need for ethical awareness on the part of the researcher.

Finally, it is important to remember that research can be threatening to the *researcher* as well as to the researched. Researchers may be placed in situations in which their personal security is jeopardized, or they may find themselves stigmatized by colleagues and others for having studied particular topics (e.g., sexual deviance).

This is an important point to which we will return shortly. Now, however, we are in a position to offer at least a preliminary definition of a sensitive topic. The threatening character of the research, and its potential consequentiality for both researcher and researched, suggests that

> a sensitive topic is one which potentially poses for those involved a substantial threat, the emergence of which renders problematic for the researcher and/or the researched the collection, holding, and/or dissemination of research data.

Although one could attempt to develop a comprehensive list of sensitive topics based on this definition, it seems more fruitful to look at the conditions under which "sensitivity" arises within the research process.

 ## Sensitive Topics and the Research Process

The sensitive nature of a particular topic is emergent. In other words, the sensitive character of a piece of research seemingly inheres less in the topic itself and more in the relationship between that topic and the social context within which the research is conducted. It is not uncommon, for example, for a researcher to approach a topic with caution on the assumption that it is a sensitive one, only to find that those initial fears had been misplaced. Nor is it unusual for the sensitive nature of an apparently innocuous topic to become apparent once research is underway. Just as Goyder (1987) hypothesized that different social groups attribute different meanings to requests for participation in research, it may well be that a study seen as threatening by one group will be thought innocuous by another.

It is probably possible for any topic, depending on context, to be a sensitive one. Experience suggests, however, that there are a number of areas in which research is more likely to be threatening than others. These include (a) where research intrudes into the private sphere or delves into some deeply personal experience; (b) where the study is concerned with deviance and social control; (c) where it impinges on the vested interests of powerful persons or the exercise of coercion or domination; and (d) where it deals with things sacred to those being studied which they do not wish profaned.

Intrusions into the private sphere need not always be threatening. Day (1985), for instance, concluded that there is no fixed private sphere. Topics and activities regarded as private vary cross-culturally and situationally. Commonly, however, areas of social life concerned with sexual or financial matters remain shielded from the eyes of nonintimates. Other areas of personal experience, such as bereavement, are not so much private as emotionally charged. Research into such areas may threaten those studied through the levels of emotional stress which they produce.

Research involving the investigation of deviant activities has frequently been regarded as having a sensitive character. Those studied are likely to fear being identified, stigmatized, or incriminated in some way. Areas of social life which are contentious or highly conflictual often produce topics for research which are sensitive. Normally, this is because in such situations research can be seen by those involved as threatening the alignments, interests, or security of those in a conflict, especially those who are in positions of relative power. Finally, the values and beliefs of some groups are threatened in an intrinsic way by research. Some religious groups—old-time fundamentalists, for example—quite literally regard research into their beliefs and activities as anathema (Homan, 1978; Homan & Bulmer, 1982).

Sensitivity, as we have used the term here, affects almost every stage of the research process from formulation through design to implementation, dissemination, and application (Brewer, this issue; Sieber & Stanley, 1988; Seigel & Bauman, 1986). Perhaps only the actual process of data analysis is likely to remain relatively untouched (although considerations relating to the confidentiality of data can add complexities even here). The problems that arise at each stage can take a variety of forms. Sensitive research raises methodological, technical, ethical, political, and legal problems, as well as having potential effects on the personal life of the researcher (Plummer, 1983), not least in some contexts at the level of personal security (Brewer, this issue).

Research on sensitive topics has tended to have two rather contradictory outcomes. First, the difficulties associated with sensitive research have tended to inhibit adequate conceptualization and measurement (Herzberger, this issue). However, the problems raised by sensitive topics have also led to technical innovation in the form of imaginative methodological advances (e.g., see Caplan, 1982). As a result, research on sensitive topics has contributed to methodological development in both the widest and the narrowest sense. Good examples here are the development of strategies for asking sensitive questions on surveys (Bradburn & Sudman, 1979) and technical means for preserving the confidentiality of research data (Boruch & Cecil, 1979).

Sensitive topics also raise wider issues related to the ethics, politics, and legal aspects of research. In recent years, the ethical and legal aspects of social research have become increasingly salient. In many countries, there has been a growing concern for individual rights, including those of research participants, and for the rights of social groups who may be affected by research. Such trends are likely to intensify as researchers move toward more complex research designs (Kimmel, 1988) and a greater involvement in applied research.

Such issues impinge on all research, whatever its character, but they may impinge most forcefully in the case of sensitive topics. In many cases, of course, neither the problems raised by sensitive research nor the issues involved can be dealt with in any simple way. However, the experiences of researchers studying sensitive topics, of the kind represented in this special issue, may serve to guide researchers embarking on sensitive research, and to sharpen debate about critical issues.

◈ Issues and Problems in Researching Sensitive Topics

Duelli-Klein (1983, p. 38) pointed out that "the 'what' to investigate must come prior to the decision of 'how' to go about doing one's research." In a number of important respects, what is studied can be constrained in significant ways by the sensitive character of the topic. For example, powerful gatekeepers can impose restrictions on researchers in ways that constrain their capacity to produce or report on findings that threaten the interests of the powerful. Funding agencies, it has been argued, tend to prefer research having a particular character: research that is relevant to the policymaking process (Abrams, 1981; Sjoberg & Nett, 1968); based on individualistic, rather than structural explanations (Galliher & McCartney, 1973; Hanmer & Leonard, 1984); and which is quantitative or positivistic in its methodology (Broadhead & Rist, 1976; Ditton & Williams, 1981). One lesson which some writers have drawn from this is that the organization of research funding tends to serve the interests of powerful groups in society by excluding support for research on topics which they might consider sensitive or detrimental to their interest. The institutional context within which researchers operate is also seen to abet this tendency since, it is argued, universities and research institutes dislike offending local elites or putting in jeopardy sources of possible funding (Broadhead & Rist, 1976; Moore, 1973; Record, 1967).

Sensitivity, as we have defined it, can also affect the "what to investigate" in other ways. According to Sieber and Stanley (1988, p. 50), the very fact that a researcher poses a particular theory or research question can have major social implications even if the research is never performed. Thus framing a specific research question about a sensitive topic presents an initial set of problems. Consider, for instance, research on domestic violence. The question that has dominated this area of inquiry for more than two decades has been, Why do battered women stay with partners who abuse them? Regardless of the answers generated, posing the question itself establishes the parameters of the problem of spouse abuse in terms of the behavior of battered women. Attention is deflected from batterers onto victims. It is battered women who are defined as deviant for remaining in abusive relationships, not their partners who are deviant for battering them (Loseke & Cahill, 1984). In short, asking "Why do battered women stay?"—rather than "What factors make it possible or even permissible for men to batter women?"—creates a scientific and popular milieu for blaming the victim. To paraphrase Sieber and Stanley (1988, p. 50), faulty ideas drawn from social science research may powerfully affect social conceptions of significant social problems and issues regardless of the adequacy of the research findings.

This is a point taken up in this issue in Sharon Herzberger's article on studying child abuse. Herzberger, a psychologist, examines the methodological difficulties that arise when studying this sensitive topic. She is especially concerned with empirical tests of the widely accepted "cyclical hypothesis," the notion that individuals who were physically abused by their parents tend to become child abusers themselves. Herzberger argues that research on child abuse has been plagued by four

major problems: inconsistent operational definitions, lack of control or comparison groups, failure to utilize multivariate analysis, and the limits of retrospective studies. Although these are problems that occur in many research areas, the deficiencies which Herzberger identifies can be generalized to research on other sensitive topics. For example, Renzetti (1988) noted in her research on homosexual partner abuse that vague and inconsistent definitions of the behavior in question make comparisons of findings across studies difficult at best and also give rise to disagreements and confusions over important "facts," such as the incidence of the behavior.

In the case of child abuse, Herzberger argues, the methodological flaws which she identifies seriously undermine many of the early studies of the cyclical hypothesis. Later, better designed research has provided only modest support for the proposition. As Sieber and Stanley (1988, p. 53) pointed out, "Sensitive research topics are more likely to have applications in the 'real' world that society will enthusiastically embrace, irrespective of the validity of the application." Perhaps for this reason many social scientists and lay people continue to treat the cyclical hypothesis as fact. Herzberger contends, however, that this has serious consequences: It provides a shaky foundation on which to build future research and inhibits accurate theory building by researchers; it misguides social service personnel and policymakers as they attempt to develop effective programs; and it arouses stress and fear in many formerly abused adults who are misled into believing that they will inevitably abuse their own children.

Problems deriving from the recruitment of study participants are especially acute for researchers investigating sensitive topics. In studies of relatively innocuous behavior or issues, complete sampling frames are often available which allow for random sampling and a sound estimate of sampling bias. This is rarely the case, however, in studies of sensitive topics. Indeed, the more sensitive or threatening the topic under examination, the more difficult sampling is likely to be, since potential participants have greater need or incentive to hide their involvement.

Systematic treatments of sampling issues related to deviant populations can be found in Becker (1970) and for rare populations in Sudman and Kalton (1986),

Sudman, Sirken, and Curran (1988), and Kish (1965). The major strategies that can be used, singly or in combination, for sampling "special" populations which are rare and/or deviant in some way are (a) the use of lists, (b) multipurpose surveys, (c) household screening procedures, (d) the location of locales within which sample members congregate as sites for the recruitment of respondents, (e) the use of networking or "snowballing" strategies, (f) advertising for respondents, and (g) obtaining sample participants in return for providing a service of some kind. In the study of deviant populations, probably the most common method used has been the "snowball" sample. Ironically, though, as qualitative researchers have begun to develop a more critical assessment of the limitations of this method (Biernacki & Waldorf, 1981), survey researchers have become more open to using similar network sampling methods in order to locate rare or elusive populations (Rothbart, Fine, & Sudman, 1982; Sudman & Kalton, 1986; Sudman et al., 1988).

Martin and Dean (this issue) had both ethical and technical reasons for rejecting screening procedures in order to generate a sample for their study of the impact of the AIDS epidemic on the emotional and behavioral functioning of gay men. They reasoned that the stigma attached to homosexuality, along with growing antigay harassment and violence, would likely bias the sampling frame toward gay men who were self-assured and open about their sexual preference. Neighborhood screening would also produce biases, since the logical choice—in this case, Greenwich Village—is a predominantly white, upper middle-class neighborhood of highly visible gay men. (In any case, as a number of researchers have recorded [Hope, Kennedy, & DeWinter, 1976; McRae, 1986], the costs of having to screen large populations to uncover individuals possessing relatively rare traits is a major limitation on such methods.)

Martin and Dean's choice was to use network sampling using a variety of sources to "seed" their initial sample. Sudman and Kalton (1986) recently demonstrated that lists which provide only partial coverage of some populations may still provide a useful starting point for the development of an adequate sample. Among the sources which Martin and Dean used to provide the base, or "generation zero" as they call it, for

their sample was the membership list of gay organizations in New York City. Although they tried to control for many of the difficulties inherent in network or snowball sampling, they were unable to determine precisely to what extent they had been successful in generating a reliable sample. Nevertheless, cross-group comparison and comparisons with two random samples of gay men indicate that they obtained a fairly representative sample of gay men who have not been diagnosed as having AIDS. Their article is likely to be helpful to researchers interested in developing a workable sampling strategy for a survey of a hidden population. Martin and Dean's work suggests that even in the absence of external validating criteria, it is possible to go a long way despite imperfect circumstances.

Perhaps because of its historical development, sampling has tended to be seen primarily as a technical matter. However, sampling decisions can rarely be divorced from theoretical issues, particularly those dealing with how populations are to be defined (for problems of this kind which arise in AIDS research, see Siegel & Bauman, 1986), or from ethical or political issues. Gillespie and Leffler (1987), for example, noted that controversy over the technical adequacy of samples can enter into political conflicts over the status of social science knowledge. In a similar way, as Hartley (1982) pointed out, ethical problems may arise because of the potential for invasions of privacy when lists are used for sampling purposes.

While research participants should, in general, expect their rights to privacy, anonymity, and confidentiality to be protected, maintaining confidentiality of research data is especially important where informants or respondents are being asked to reveal intimate or incriminating information. Recently, AIDS researchers have begun to be concerned about public health reporting laws and the power of courts to subpoena research data (Melton & Gray, 1988). This last is an issue which at various times has attracted considerable interest and concern among researchers involved in the study of deviant and criminal behavior. As Marybeth Ayella indicates in her article (this issue), the law also has impinged on scholars researching the plethora of "new" or "alternative" religious movements which emerged as a novel social phenomenon in the West in the 1960s and 1970s.

The legal system both regulates research and intervenes in the research process. The state, for instance, regulates the relationship which researchers have to those they study either, commonly in Europe, through data protection legislation (Akeroyd, 1988) or, to take the U.S. case, by compelling prior ethical review. There have been a number of suggestions that legal regulation can lead to research of a sensitive nature being inhibited or sanitized. Thus the Data Inspection Board in Sweden has required researchers to remove questions judged to be sensitive from questionnaires (Flaherty, 1979; Hammar, 1976; Janson, 1979), while researchers in the United States have charged that for a period in the 1970s, government regulations increased the difficulty of undertaking research on deviance or controversial topics (Ceci, Peters, & Plotkin, 1985; Hessler & Galliher, 1983; Reiss, 1979).

Although malpractice suits against researchers apparently remain only a theoretical possibility (Reiss, 1979; Useem & Marx, 1983), the law has intervened in the research process on a number of occasions. In the United States, legal intervention has been seen most commonly in attempts by prosecutors and courts to subpoena research data (Brahuja & Hallowell, 1986; Knerr, 1982). In contrast, legal threats in Britain usually have taken the form of actual or threatened libel actions (Braithwaite, 1985; Punch, 1986; Wallis, 1977). In both instances, the risks of legal intervention are felt most keenly by those researching sensitive topics. Thus attempts have been made to subpoena data relating to criminal activities, while powerful groups on occasion have been able to use the threat of libel litigation to suppress or substantially modify the accounts that social scientists give of their activities (Ayella, this issue; Braithwaite, 1985). In neither Britain nor the United States are research data legally privileged, although some limited protection does exist in the United States (Melton & Gray, 1988; Nelson & Hedrick, 1983). Again, few researchers will have the resources to fight cases or to pay the necessary penalties if they lose. This is particularly so in Britain where libel laws are stringent, and where libel damages can be substantial.[1]

Although she discusses the problems of sampling and some of the legal issues raised by research on new religious movements or "cults," the primary focus of Marybeth Ayella's article (this issue) is with the process of gaining entry to the group or setting one wants to study.

(In field research, concerns over sampling traditionally have been superseded by a preoccupation with problems of access.) Although there is a general assumption that deviant groups are difficult to study, Ayella points out that gaining initial access to some groups may be relatively easy, but that once inside, access may be difficult to sustain. Some cults, for instance, may welcome the researcher at first, perceiving him or her as an interested newcomer and potential convert. However, when conversion does not appear within a given period of time, the researcher may be ejected from the group and denied further access. Ayella notes that some researchers are able to maintain access by establishing a unique role or special category of membership for themselves, such as "fringe devotee." Others apparently handle this problem successfully by honestly expressing their disagreements with the group and by stressing their role as researcher rather than as member. Still others negotiate access by establishing a reciprocal relationship with the group, for example, by lending, in effect, legitimacy or respectability to the group in exchange for access, although Ayella rightly warns of the dangers of co-optation of the researcher in such situations. In line with Johnson (1975), who argued that access is not an initial phase of entry to the setting around which a bargain can be struck, but rather a continuing process of negotiation and renegotiation, Ayella advises researchers not to allow the groups which they wish to study to set the research agenda for them.

Ayella examines a number of other problems, such as culture shock and handling one's emotional responses to stressful research situations, that are related to sustaining a research project on deviant groups. John Brewer, from Queen's University of Belfast, elaborates on many of the points raised by Ayella in his discussion of the difficulties of conducting research in a setting that is politically, psychologically, and physically threatening to both researchers and study participants. One of the most significant aspects of Brewer's article is that it highlights the contextual nature of sensitive research. Although other field studies of police officers demonstrate that the police in general are a difficult group to study (Fielding, this issue; Hunt, 1984; Klockars, 1985; Van Maanen, 1988), the politically charged and conflict-ridden atmosphere of Northern Ireland renders a study of the police force there especially sensitive.

To conduct research on the Royal Ulster Constabulary (RUC), Brewer first had to obtain permission from the Chief Constable. This had the potential for severely restricting the research, since "gatekeepers" frequently impose explicit conditions on the way in which research may be conducted as well as on how the findings may be disseminated. Although this did not happen in Brewer's case, obtaining permission from the Chief Constable created other problems, not the least of which was the suspicion it produced among ordinary police officers about the researchers' and police managers' objectives and motives.

In short, although gaining initial access to the RUC proved fairly straightforward, Brewer and his research assistant had to pass through a second set of gatekeepers, the ordinary police officers. Since, as in organizational contexts generally, the RUC is characterized by what Dingwall (1980) called a "hierarchy of consent," it was assumed that superiors have the right to permit subordinates to be studied. However, this does not insure that the subordinates will be cooperative. As Brewer and others have discovered, people in research situations may intentionally undermine the research through obfuscation and deception. In addition, researchers may be subjected to repeated "trust tests" which force them to legitimate themselves in the eyes of study participants and, like some of the researchers cited by Ayella, they may have to construct or capitalize on a special identity.

During the research, the identity of Brewer's research assistant proved to be an important factor. She was a Catholic studying mostly Protestants, an innocuous element in other contexts, but in the context of Northern Ireland, it prompted the researchers to try (unsuccessfully) to conceal her religious identity from those studied. As the research proceeded, the fieldworker found herself being "culturally contextualized" (Warren, 1988), in terms of both her religion and her sex.

As other female fieldworkers have noted, women researchers may become "encapsulated in the stereotypical [gender] role designated by subjects" and consequently have limited access to data, especially data in such male-dominated groups as the police (Hunt, 1984, p. 286). However, Warren (1988) maintained that gender itself is a negotiated rather than an ascribed status in the field. Furthermore, she pointed out that researchers may

be able to capitalize on the sexism of study participants. For instance, while doing fieldwork in a drug rehabilitation center, Warren discovered that she had relatively free access to areas usually off-limits to outsiders and could even investigate the contents of file drawers because the male staff at the center often viewed themselves as too engaged in "important business" to worry about a harmless female (p. 18). Brewer's research assistant encountered a similar attitude among some RUC officers. Of course, Warren also noted that this trade-off of accepting sexism to obtain information often is both personally and politically repugnant to female researchers. In addition, she showed that while gender issues in the field have usually been most problematic for women, male researchers must deal with them at times. Johnson (1986), for example, reported that he encountered considerable resistance to his presence from the female elementary school teachers he was observing because these women typically had their professionalism and authority undercut by their male colleagues and supervisors. As Johnson interpreted it, the teachers needed to determine if he, as a man, could be trusted.

Brewer's article also raises the issue of the researcher's personal security. In the context of the kind of violent social conflict found in Northern Ireland, research can be a dangerous activity (Burton, 1978; Lee, 1981). Indeed, at various times, researchers have been forced into hiding or have had to leave Northern Ireland due to fears (apparently unfounded, it should be said) that research materials were finding their way to the security forces (Taylor, 1988). While many researchers are unlikely to face the stresses produced by research in a violent social situation, it should also be borne in mind that "researcher jeopardy" can take a number of forms. As we noted earlier, work with deviant groups also can lead to unwelcome consequences for researchers who may find themselves subject to "stigma contagion." This seems to be particularly true of research on human sexuality. Those involved in the study of sexual deviance have frequently remarked on their stigmatization by colleagues, university administrators, and students (Plummer, 1981; Troiden, 1987; Weinberg & Williams, 1972). In a similar way, research in controversial areas which produce findings unpopular among colleagues can lead to negative consequences for the researcher (Sieber & Stanley, 1988).

Brewer's research points to how research participants, at least in naturalistic settings, can be threatened and discomforted by research, as well as to some of the ways in which they may artfully deal with such threats. The threatening character of research and its implications for the relationship between researcher and researched form a focus for the articles by Bertilson and Fielding (this issue). Hal Bertilson, a social psychologist, addresses some of the ethical and methodological issues that arise in research on human aggression. As he remarks in his article, the study of human aggression is sensitive for reasons of methodology rather than of topic. This is because experimentally-based research on aggression in social psychology incorporates both aggressive behaviors in the form of electric shocks delivered to research subjects, as well as their deception about the purposes of the research. Research participants, it would seem, are therefore capable both of being harmed and of being wronged (Macintyre, 1982) by the research.

In responding affirmatively to the question, "Can aggression be [ethically] justified in order to study aggression?," Bertilson produces a number of justifications. Drawing in part on the ethical guidelines published by the American Psychological Association, he argues that research of the kind he describes can be ethically undertaken if three conditions are met: (a) if the potential benefits to society are great enough; (b) if the research is planned in a way that maximizes the yield of generalizable knowledge; and (c) if the risks to participants are controlled and minimized.

Ethical debates in the social sciences have tended to be conducted between those, on one hand, who espouse ideological conceptions of ethics, frequently based around a utilitarian calculus of costs and benefits, and those, on the other, whose underlying ethical conceptions are deontological in character (Kimmel, 1988). Pointing to the appalling human cost of aggression in terms of violence, Bertilson presents a robust defense of a position based on an essentially utilitarian conception. Readers will no doubt judge for themselves how compelling Bertilson's argument is in relation to aggression research. By its very nature, however, research on sensitive topics, because it sharpens ethical dilemmas, tends to reveal the limits of existing ethical theories.

Where sensitive topics are involved, utilitarianism can lead to a lessened rather than to a heightened ethical

awareness, while deontological theories may be too restrictive, replacing the sin of callousness with the sin of scrupulosity. Thus Macintyre (1982) argued that one difficulty with a utilitarian approach to ethical decision making is that there is no consensus among social scientists about what counts as a benefit. Moreover, apparently disinterested assertions about risks and rewards may actually be self-serving because researchers have greater power than research participants to define costs and benefits. One can also note that to assume that there are substantial benefits to society from a particular piece of research is also to assume that the relationship between the production of knowledge and its application is linear and nonproblematic with no scope for misuse.

If this argument is accepted, it becomes necessary to be careful before concluding, as Bertilson does, that experiments on aggression that incorporate aggressive behaviors and deception are "moral imperatives." (Bertilson is perhaps too dismissive of nondeceptive research procedures, such as the use of role-plays and simulation. It should be noted, though, that their use does not automatically prevent harm to research participants, as the Stanford prison experiment graphically demonstrated [Barnes, 1979; Zimbardo, 1973]). On the other hand, if one follows the kind of line taken by Macintyre, there is the danger of excluding as legitimate research a number of areas judged earlier to be sensitive. According to Macintyre (1982, p. 188):

> The study of taboos by anthropologists and of privacy by sociologists show how important it is for a culture that certain areas of personal and social life should be specially protected. Intimacy cannot exist where everything is disclosed, sanctuary cannot be sought where no place is inviolate, integrity cannot be seen to be maintained—and therefore cannot in certain cases be maintained—without protection from illegitimate pressures.

For Macintyre, to violate those sanctuaries is to do a wrong to those one studies. This is despite the fact that, as Macintyre acknowledges, research into the areas of human life which he wants to protect—he uses bereavement as an example—would lead to substantial good in terms of increasing knowledge. Whatever the benefits accruing from these gains, however, Macintyre insists that it cannot be right to do a wrong to anyone. One difficulty with Macintyre's position is that his assertion of the inviolability of the intimate sphere is justified by reference to empirical research by anthropologists and sociologists on the functions of privacy. However, if Macintyre's point of view is accepted, research of this kind would be unethical. It also would not be possible to assess Macintyre's own claims empirically. At the same time, permitting research on the private sphere might reveal that in many instances, particularly in sensitive areas, research participants desire catharsis rather than sanctuary (Lee, 1981). That is, research on sensitive topics may produce not only gains in knowledge, but also effects that are directly beneficial to research participants.

A complicating factor in all of this is that empirical studies of researchers' ethical decision making are surprisingly lacking (Stanley, Sieber, & Melton, 1987). One suspects, however, that relatively few researchers actually desist from research either because the costs involved exceed the benefits or on grounds of moral principle. Paradoxically, this may be especially true where research has a sensitive character. In sociology, for example, the sensitive nature of a study has frequently been used as a justification for the use of covert methods, a practice which many regard as ethically dubious. (A range of articles debating this issue may be found in Bulmer, 1982.) The argument is made that because the topic under investigation is sensitive, research into it can be conducted only in a covert way (see, for example, Humphreys, 1970).

The issue of the ethical character of the relationship between the researcher and the researched in ethnographic studies lies at the heart of Nigel Fielding's article (this issue). Fielding, a criminologist, is critical, on one hand, of the naturalistic approach to field research. This approach advocates that the researcher should take an "appreciative" stance (Matza, 1969) toward his or her informants and their accounts of events and behavior. Naturalism stresses rapport and empathic relations with informants in the field. Fielding notes that this is easier to accomplish in studies of non-threatening or non-threatened groups than in those of "unloved" groups, such as the police. Moreover, the naturalistic approach establishes a false dichotomy in relation to the accounts of the research given by those involved: Those of the study participants are viewed as complete and accurate, while those of the researcher are viewed as partial and flawed.

An alternative approach to research based on the appreciative stance involves "investigative research," or the use of "conflict methodologies" (Douglas, 1976; Galliher, 1973). Such approaches—involving the use of covert research, the analysis of publicly available data, the seeking out, for example, of dissatisfied former employees as informants, and so on—have the advantage in that they do not require the cooperation of powerful subjects. Fielding, however, is critical of the assertive skeptical role embodied in this kind of research, for he sees a danger that the researcher may become manipulative and deceitful with informants or that skepticism may turn into cynicism that prevents informants' accounts from being taken seriously by the researcher.

Instead, Fielding calls for field researchers to take an "intercalary role" in relation to study participants, an approach not unlike Maguire's (1987) participatory research model. Taking an intercalary role places the field researcher in a position between passive recipient of informants' accounts and skeptical investigator. In this model, fieldworker and study participants are simultaneously inquirers into the group's culture and educators of one another with respect to that culture. In this way, the researcher and the researched coproduce fieldwork. Fielding skillfully demonstrates the usefulness of the intercalary role for studying sensitive topics and groups through his discussion of an incident that occurred during his own field research on the criteria of competence in urban policing. One particularly valuable outcome of adopting the intercalary role is that it presents the opportunity to understand the issue of sensitivity from the point of view of the study participants, rather than solely from the perspective of the researcher.

The final article in this issue is by economist J. J. Thomas who focuses on the difficulties of studying the hidden or underground economy. There are many respects in which Thomas's article echoes the concerns about operationalization and measurement raised by Herzberger. He notes that disagreement over definitions of the underground economy has led to considerable confusion. More important, however, is his point that two factors have constrained research on this sensitive topic and have inhibited the development of a comprehensive understanding of it: the training of economists to analyze rather than collect data, and a lack of interest in criminal behavior among mainstream economists.

After reviewing several indirect measures of the underground economy using both macro- and micro-economic data sources, and delineating the strengths and weaknesses of each, Thomas suggests that an inter-disciplinary approach to the study of the underground economy may be more fruitful. While mindful of the problems involved, he urges economists to adopt various methods used by other social scientists, such as the use of surveys and participant observation techniques, and he encourages collaborative research between economists and other social scientists. It is this interdisciplinary emphasis which led us to conclude this issue with Thomas's article. We share his optimism that interdisciplinary research endeavors may generate higher quality data, not only in studies of the underground economy, but in studies of other sensitive topics as well.

At this point, it may appear to readers that researching sensitive topics is a daunting enterprise. Brewer (this issue) notes that the many problems which arise in studying a sensitive topic may indeed defeat the researcher unless he or she brings a tough, single-minded, tenacious but pragmatic attitude to the task. Moreover, the fact that sensitive topics pose complex issues and dilemmas for researchers does not imply that such topics should not be studied. As Sieber and Stanley (1988, p. 55) convincingly argued,

> Sensitive research addresses some of society's most pressing social issues and policy questions. Although ignoring the ethical issues in sensitive research is not a responsible approach to science, shying away from controversial topics, simply because they are controversial, is also an avoidance of responsibility.

Likewise, we argue that ignoring the methodological difficulties inherent in researching sensitive topics is also socially and scientifically irresponsible since this ignorance may potentially generate flawed conclusions on which both theory and public policy subsequently may be built. If social scientists are not to opt out of research on sensitive topics, they must confront seriously and thoroughly the problems and issues that these topics pose. This issue of *American Behavioral Scientist* is a step in that direction.

 Note

1. Of course, problems of confidentiality do not arise only in relation to raw data. What Boruch and Cecil (1979) referred to as "deductive closure" is also possible. Here, particular or distinctive combinations of attributes permit the identification of individuals by secondary analysts or the readers of published reports. For a range of strategies for preserving the confidentiality of research data, see Borneo and Cecil (1979), Boruch (1979), and Campbell, Boruch, Schwartz, and Steinberg (1977). There are some situations in which these strategies may not be useful, such as when the identity of research participants is itself sensitive information. It is also the case that it is more difficult to maintain the confidentiality of qualitative data by technical means than it is for quantitative data. Yet qualitative researchers are facing mounting pressure to protect the confidentiality of their data, both from the growth of field research in applied settings, where there may be greater likelihood of legal intervention (Broadhead, 1984), and from the increasing use of computers to analyze qualitative data (Tesch, 1988). This last advance, in particular, has come about at a time when national data protection laws are becoming increasingly common (Akeroyd, 1988).

References

Abrams, P. (1981). Visionaries and virtuosi: Competence and purpose in the education of sociologists. *Sociology, 15,* 530–538.

Akeroyd, A. V. (1988). Ethnography, personal data and computers: The implications of data protection legislation for qualitative social research. In R. G. Burgess (Ed.), *Studies in qualitative methodology: Vol. I. Conducting qualitative research* (pp. 179–200). Greenwich, CT: JAI.

Barnes, J. A. (1979). *Who should know what? Social science, privacy and ethics.* Harmondsworth: Penguin.

Becker, H. S. (1970). Practitioners of vice and crime. In R. Haberstein (Ed.), *Pathways to data* (pp. 30–49). Chicago: Aldine.

Biemacki, P., & Waldorf, D. (1981). Snowball sampling: Problems and techniques of chain referral sampling. *Sociological Methods and Research, 10,* 141–163.

Boruch, R. F. (1979). Methods of assuring personal integrity in social research: An introduction. In M. Bulmer (Ed.), *Censuses, surveys and privacy* (pp. 234–248). London: Macmillan.

Boruch, R. F., & Cecil, J. S. (1979). *Assuring the confidentiality of social research data.* Philadelphia: University of Pennsylvania Press.

Bradburn, N. M., & Sudman, S. (1979). *Improving interview method and questionnaire design.* San Francisco, Jossey-Bass.

Brailhwaite, J. (1985). Corporate crime research: Why two interviewers are needed. *Sociology, 19,* 136–138.

Brajuha, M., & Hallowell, L. (1986). Legal intrusion and the politics of fieldwork: The impact of the Brajuha case. *Urban Life, 14,* 454–478.

Broadhead, R. S. (1984). Human rights and human subjects: Ethics and strategies in social science research. *Sociological Inquiry, 54,* 107–123.

Broadhead, R. S., & Rist, R. C. (1976). Gatekeepers and the social control of social research. *Social Problems, 23*, 325–336.

Bulmer, M. (1982). *Social research ethics*. London: Macmillan.

Burton, F. (1978). *The politics of legitimacy: Struggles in a Belfast community*. London: Routledge & Kegan Paul.

Campbell, D. T., Boruch, R. F., Schwartz, R. D., & Steinberg, J. (1977). Confidentiality-preserving modes of access to files and interfile exchange for useful statistical analysis. *Evaluation Quarterly, 1*, 269–300.

Caplan, A. L. (1982). On privacy and confidentiality in social science research. In T. L. Beauchamp, R. R. Faden, R. J. Wallace, Jr., & L. Waters (Eds.), *Ethical issues in social science research* (pp. 315–325). Baltimore: Johns Hopkins University Press.

Ceci, S. J., Peters, D., & Plotkin, J. (1985). Human subjects review, personal values and the regulation of social science research. *American Psychologist, 40*, 994–1002.

Day, K. J. (1985). *Perspectives on privacy: A sociological analysis*. Unpublished doctoral dissertation, University of Edinburgh.

Dingwall, R. G. (1980). Ethics and ethnography. *Sociological Review, 28*, 871–891.

Ditton, J., & Williams, R. (1981). *The fundable versus the doable* (Occasional paper). Glasgow: University of Glasgow, Department of Sociology.

Douglas, J. D. (1976). *Investigative social research*. Beverly Hills, CA: Sage.

Duelli-Klein, R. (1983). How to do what we want to do: Thoughts about feminist methodology. In G. Bowles & R. Duelli-Klein (Eds.), *Theories of women's studies*. London: Routledge & Kegan Paul.

Flaherty, D. (1979). *Privacy and government data banks: An international comparison*. London: Mansell.

Galliher, J. F. (1973). The protection of human subjects: A reexamination of the Professional Code of Ethics. *American Sociologist, 9*, 93–100.

Galliher, J. F., & McCartney, J. L. (1973). The influence of funding agencies on juvenile delinquency research. *Social Problems, 21*, 77–90.

Gillespie, D. L., & Leffler, A. (1987). The politics of research methodology in claims-making activities: Social science and sexual harassment. *Social Problems, 34*, 490–501.

Goyder, J. (1987). *The silent minority: Non-respondents on sample surveys*. Cambridge: Polity.

Hammar, T. (1976). The political resocialization of immigrants project. In T. Dalenius & A. Klevamarken (Eds.), *Personal integrity and the need for data in the social sciences* (pp. 37–42). Stockholm: Swedish Council for Social Research.

Hanmer, J., & Leonard, D. (1984). Negotiating the problem: The OHSS and research on violence in marriage. In C. Bell & H. Roberts (Eds.), *Social researching: Politics, problems and practice* (pp. 32–65). London: Routledge & Kegan Paul.

Hartley, S. F. (1982). Sampling strategies and the threat to privacy. In J. E. Sieber (Ed.), *The ethics of social research: Surveys and experiments* (pp. 167–190). New York: Springer-Verlag.

Hessler, R. M., & Galliher, J. F. (1983). Institutional Review Boards and clandestine research: An experimental test. *Human Organization, 42*, 82–87.

Homan, R. (1978). Interpersonal communication in Pentecostal meetings. *Sociological Review, 26*, 499–518.

Homan, R., & Bulmer, M. (1982). On the merits of covert methods: A dialog. In M. Bulmer (Ed.), *Social research ethics* (pp. 105–121). London: Macmillan.

Hope, E., Kennedy, M., & De Winter, A. (1976). Homeworkers in North London. In D. L. Barker & S. Allen (Eds.), *Dependence and exploitation in work and marriage* (pp. 88–109). London: Longman.

Humphreys, L. (1970). *Tearoom trade: Impersonal sex in public places*. Chicago: Aldine.

Hunt, J. (1984). The development of rapport through the negotiation of gender in field work among police. *Human Organization, 43*, 283–296.

Janson, C. (1979). Privacy legislation and social research in Sweden. In E. Mochman & P. J. Mullaer (Eds.), *Data protection and social science research: Perspectives from ten countries* (pp. 27–47). Frankfurt: Campus Verlag.

Johnson, J. M. (1975). *Doing field research*. New York: Free Press.

Johnson, N. B. (1986). Ethnographic research and rites of incorporation: A sex- and gender-based comparison. In T. L. Whitehead & M. E. Conway (Eds.), *Self, sex and gender in cross-cultural fieldwork* (pp. 164–181). Urbana: University of Illinois Press.

Kimmel, A. J. (1988). *Ethics and values in applied social research*. Newbury Park, CA: Sage.

Kish, L. (1965). *Survey sampling*. New York: Wiley.

Klockars, C. (1985). *The idea of police*. Beverly Hills, CA: Sage.

Knerr, C. R. (1982). What to do before and after a subpoena of data arrives. In J. E. Sieber (Ed.), *The ethics of social research: Surveys and experiments* (pp. 191–206). New York: Springer-Verlag.

Lee, R. M. (1981). *Interreligious courtship and marriage in Northern Ireland*. Unpublished doctoral dissertation, University of Edinburgh.

Loseke, D. R., & Cahill, S. E. (1984). The social construction of deviance: Experts on battered women. *Social Problems, 31*, 296–310.

Macintyre, A. (1982). Risk, harm and benefit assessments as instruments of moral evaluation. In T. L. Beauchamp, R. R. Faden, R. J. Wallace, Jr., & L. Waters (Eds.), *Ethical issues in social science research* (pp. 175–189). Baltimore: Johns Hopkins University Press.

Maguire, P. (1987). *Doing participatory research: A feminist approach*. Amherst: Center for International Education, University of Massachusetts.

Matza, D. (1969). *Becoming deviant*. Englewood Cliffs, NJ: Prentice-Hall.

McRae, S. (1986). *Cross-class families*. Oxford: Clarendon.

Melton, G. B., & Gray, J. N. (1988). Ethical dilemmas in AIDS research: Individual privacy and public health. *American Psychologist, 42*, 735–741.

Moore, J. (1973). Social constraints on sociological knowledge: Academics and research concerning minorities. *Social Problems, 21*, 65–77.

Nelson, R. L., & Hedrick, T. E. (1983). The statutory protection of confidential research data: Synthesis and evaluation. In R. F. Boruch & J. S. Cecil (Eds.), *Solutions to ethical and legal problems in social research* (pp. 213–236). New York: Academic Press.

Plummer, K. (1981). Researching into homosexualities. In K. Plummer (Ed.), *The making of the modern homosexual* (pp. 211–230). London: Hutchinson.

Plummer, K. (1983). *Documents of life: An introduction to the problems and literature of a humanistic method.* London: Allen & Unwin.

Punch, M. (1986). *The politics and ethics of fieldwork.* Beverly Hills, CA: Sage.

Record, J. C. (1967). The research institute and the pressure group. In G. Sjoberg (Ed.), *Ethics, politics and social research* (pp. 25–49). Cambridge, MA: Schenckman.

Reiss, A. J. (1979). Government regulation in scientific inquiry: Some paradoxical consequences. In C. B. Klockars & F. W. O'Connor (Eds.), *Deviance and decency: The ethics of research with human subjects* (pp. 61–95). Beverly Hills, CA: Sage.

Renzetti, C. M. (1988). Violence in lesbian relationships: A preliminary analysis of causal factors. *Journal of Interpersonal Violence, 3,* 381–399.

Rothbart, G. S., Fine, M., & Sudman, S. (1982). On finding and interviewing the needles in a haystack: The use of multiplicity sampling. *Public Opinion Quarterly, 45,* 408–421.

Seigel, K., & Bauman, L. J. (1986). Methodological issues in AIDS-related research. In D. A. Feldman & T. M. Johnson (Eds.), *The social dimensions of AIDS* (pp. 15–39). New York: Praeger.

Sieber, J. E., & Stanley, B. (1988). Ethical and professional dimensions of socially sensitive research. *American Psychologist, 43,* 49–55.

Sjoberg, G., & Nett, R. (1968). *A methodology for social research.* New York: Harper & Row.

Stanley, B., Sieber, J. E., & Melton, G. B. (1987). Empirical studies of ethical issues in research: A research agenda. *American Psychologist, 42,* 735–741.

Sudman, S., & Kalton, G. (1986). New developments in the sampling of special populations. *Annual Review of Sociology, 12,* 401–429.

Sudman, S., Sirken, M. G., & Curran, C. D. (1988). Sampling rare and elusive populations. *Science, 240,* 991–996.

Taylor, R. (1988). Social, scientific research on the "troubles" in Northern Ireland. *Economic and Social Review, 19,* 123–145.

Tesch, R. (1988). Computer software and qualitative analysis: A reassessment. In G. Blank, J. L. McCartney, & E. Brent (Eds.), *New technology in sociology* (pp. 141–154). New Brunswick, NJ: Transaction Books.

Troiden, R. R. (1987). Walking the line: The personal and professional risks of sex education and research: *Teaching Sociology, 15,* 241–249.

Useem, M., & Mara, G. T. (1983). Ethical dilemmas and political considerations. In R. B. Smith (Ed.), *Handbook of social science methods: Vol. 1. An introduction to social research* (pp. 169–200). Cambridge: Ballinger.

Van Maanen, J. (1988). *Tales of the field.* Chicago: University of Chicago Press.

Wallis, R. (1977). The moral career of a research project. In C. Bell & H. Newby (Eds.), *Doing sociological research* (pp. 149–167). London: Allen & Unwin.

Warren, C. A. B. (1988). *Gender issues in field research.* Newbury Park, CA: Sage.

Weinberg, M., & Williams, C. J. (1972). Fieldwork among deviants: Social relations with subjects and others. In J. D. Douglas (Ed.), *Research on deviance* (pp. 165–186). New York: Random House.

Zimbardo, P. G. (1973). On the ethics of intervention in human psychological research: With special reference to the Stanford prison experiment. *Cognition, 2,* 243–256.

READING 9

"Reefer Normal" is an interesting substantive article that focuses on changes in attitudes toward marijuana use. Use of this substance was once considered quite deviant by many, and still is today, but currently it is more accepted, legalized in some states, and appears to be becoming "normalized." More important for this chapter is that Professor Linneman addresses his research questions with relatively basic statistics available to almost any undergraduate student and with the General Social Survey, a social survey of U.S. residents spanning nearly 40 years. His analyses are well crafted to provide very persuasive answers to the important questions he raises.

Source: Linneman, T. J. (2014). "Reefer normal." *Contexts, 13*(4), 71–73.

Reefer Normal

Thomas J. Linneman

This past spring, a Girl Scout made national news for selling her cookies outside a medical marijuana dispensary. While some adult members of the Girl Scouts were not amused by this tactic, the nature of the news coverage was revealing. The tenor of the coverage smacked not of "reefer madness" paranoia, but rather amazement at the girl's entrepreneurial ingenuity. Indeed, we seem to be entering a new age of marijuana acceptance.

While I'll claim indifference to marijuana itself, I cannot help but marvel at the skyrocketing support for its legalization. Typically, when public opinion shifts, it does so gradually. Support for marijuana legalization is an exception to this rule. Twenty years ago, only *High Times* readers (and a few others) favored legalization. Currently, nearly half of all Americans support it. Legislatively, a floodgate is opening. During the latest election cycle, two states (Colorado and Washington) approved legalization,

and state-regulated sale of marijuana has begun. What factors converged to get us to this point? To develop some potential answers, I turned to the General Social Survey (GSS), which has been asking a single question regarding marijuana legalization for nearly 40 years.

The GSS is one of the most longstanding and respected surveys of Americans' opinions on a wide variety of social issues. GSS researchers began collecting data in 1972, and very shortly thereafter started asking this question: "Do you think the use of marijuana should be made legal or not?" Given that it was the 1970s, the GSS researchers gave the resulting variable the name *grass*. Figure 1 illustrates the general opinion trend.

Support for "grass" climbed throughout the 1970s, peaking at nearly a third of the respondents. As the 1980s began, support diminished, sinking to a low of 17 percent in the 1990 GSS. Support then quickly grew to its current point of nearly 48 percent. This up-down trend differs

Figure 1   Support for Marijuana Legalization

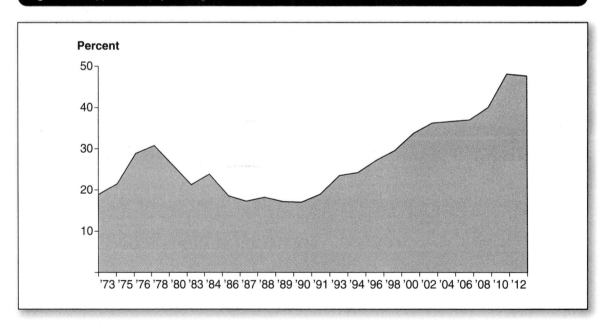

Source: General Social Survey

Figure 2   Support for Marijuana Legalization by Political Views

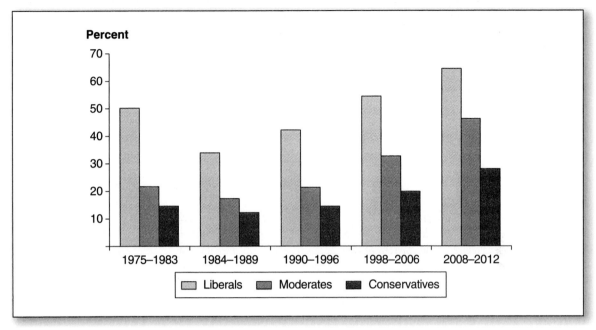

Source: General Social Survey

from that of most other social issues, for which support typically grows in a linear fashion. Could the decline in support occur again? I say no, for reasons I describe below.

◇ A Broadening of Support

Support for legalization is climbing, but it is important to realize that it is climbing in particular ways among particular groups. The figures illustrate this. Figure 2 shows how support has changed over time among three groups, as measured by the basic GSS political views variable: liberals, moderates, and conservatives.

The first year that the GSS included both the GRASS variable and the political views variable was 1975. In the early years, the vast majority of support for legalization came from liberals. Few moderates and conservatives favored legalization. Then, liberals' declining support significantly contributed to the overall decline illustrated in the chart above, left. In recent years, not only has liberals' support climbed, moderate support has also increased. Whereas these groups differed by 29 percent

in the early years, they now differ by only 18 percent. And nearly a third of conservatives also support legalization in recent years. Support, then, is no longer reliant only on the liberal members of the U.S. public.

The same is true of age, as Figure 3 shows. To create this chart, I divided the GSS respondents into quartiles by creating age groupings that each contained roughly a quarter of the respondents.

In the early years, most of the support for legalization came from the younger age groups (those crazy kids!). In contrast, ever since the nadir of 1990, older age groups have supported legalization at levels similar to that of the youngest respondents. Even among the oldest age group, over a third of the respondents now favor legalization. When one combines political views and age, an even more interesting story emerges: older liberals support legalization at the same level or even more so than younger liberals. Sixty-two percent of liberals aged 18 to 31 support legalization, 60 percent of liberals aged 32 to 43 support, support is at 71 percent among liberals aged 44 to 58, and 66 percent among liberals aged 59 and older. Perhaps the rise in support among older groups in recent years is a

Figure 3 Support for Marijuana Legalization by Age

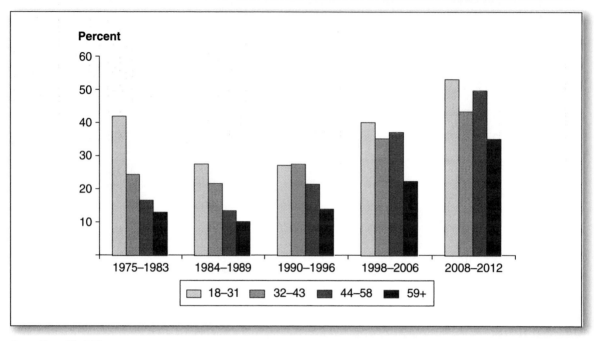

Source: General Social Survey

cohort effect: young people who favored legalization in the 1970s are now in older age groups forty years later. Given that the GSS is not longitudinal, we have no way of knowing from these data if specific individuals have changed their opinions over time. However, it is clear that support for legalization is no longer reliant on a single generation.

◈ It's My Body, I'll Do What I Want

Another reason support for marijuana may be here to stay is that it seems that these opinions have become part of a larger belief that control of one's own body is a human right. While marijuana concerns what one puts into one's body, other important social issues concern the body as well: abortion (who controls women's bodies?), euthanasia (should people be allowed to let their own bodies die?), and sex (should we legislate what people do with their bodies in their own bedrooms?). To examine this possibility, I cross-tabulated support for marijuana legal-

ization with these related GSS questions: abortion ("it should be possible for a woman to obtain a legal abortion if she wants it for any reason"), euthanasia ("when a person has a disease that cannot be cured, doctors should be allowed by law to end the patient's life by some painless means if the patient and his family request it"), premarital sex ("a man and a woman who have sex relations before marriage is not wrong at all"), and homosexuality ("sexual relations between two adults of the same sex is not wrong at all"). Figure 4 illustrates what I found.

The bars represent the percentage of respondents who support each issue *and* marijuana legalization. For example, in the early years, among those who supported a woman's right to abortion, only 40 percent supported marijuana legalization. Currently, 64 percent of those who support a woman's right to abortion also support marijuana legalization. The other social issues follow the same trend: support for these other social issues and marijuana legalization is now more likely to occur together. It seems that people may be viewing marijuana use as one of a series of body-related behaviors over which they feel

Figure 4 Support for Body-Related Issues

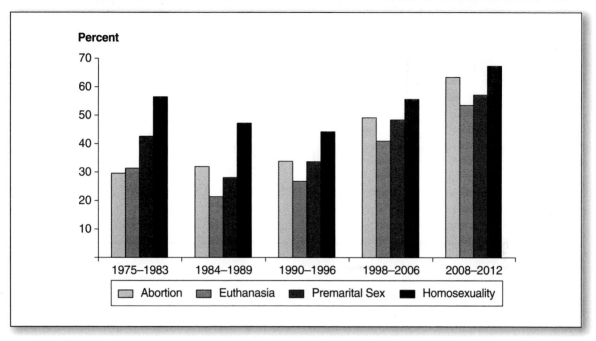

Source: General Social Survey

people should have control. This is yet another sign that support for legalization is likely to be permanent.

◈ High Time for New Data

Though opinions have shifted significantly, we must keep in mind that a slim majority of GSS respondents still believe marijuana should remain illegal, and support for legalization did not rise between 2010 and 2012.

Even though popular culture increasingly treats marijuana as a harmless pastime, many Americans remain skeptical of the drug. Though the days of "reefer madness" may be far behind us, many Americans still fear the potential gateway effect marijuana is reputed to have. Sociologists must keep a very close eye on Colorado and Washington State and carefully measure the effects of legalization over the next few years. Only with new data will we be able to make fully informed decisions regarding the possibility of legalization in other states.

❖   ❖   ❖

CHAPTER 4

Anomie/Strain Theory

In April 1992, a young man from a well-to-do East Coast family hitchhiked to Alaska and walked alone into the wilderness north of Mt. McKinley. Four months later his decomposed body was found by a party of moose hunters....

His name turned out to be Christopher Johnson McCandless. He'd grown up, I learned, in an affluent suburb of Washington, D.C., where he'd excelled academically and had been an elite athlete.

Immediately after graduation, with honors, from Emory University in the summer of 1990, McCandless dropped out of sight. He changed his name, gave the entire balance of a twenty-four-thousand-dollar savings account to charity, abandoned his car and most of his possessions, burned all the cash in his wallet. And then he invented a new life for himself, taking up residence at the ragged margin of society, wandering across North America in search of raw, transcendent experience. His family had no idea where he was or what had become of him until his remains turned up in Alaska.

— Jon Krakauer (1996), *Into the Wild*. Copyright ©1996
by Jon Krakauer. Published by Anchor Books, a division of Random House, Inc.

◈ Introduction

Christopher McCandless grew up in a conforming, upper-middle-class family and seemed to be on the fast track to success. He graduated from Emory University with a 3.72 grade point average, and he spoke of going to law school. Instead, he turned his back on his family, adopted the new name of Alexander Supertramp, and set out to make his way alone in the wilderness. How might we explain this drastic turnaround and McCandless's blatant rejection of societal norms and expectations?

Anomie and strain theories are among the first truly sociological explanations of the causes of deviant behavior. These theories seek to understand deviance by focusing on social structures and patterns that emerge as individuals and groups react to conditions they have little control over. The question these theories address is, How exactly does the structure of society constrain behavior and cause deviance?

Strain theories are generally macrolevel theories, and they share several core assumptions: first, the idea that social order is the product of a generally cohesive set of norms; second, that those norms are widely shared by community members; and third, that deviance and community reactions to deviance are essential to maintaining order.

◈ Development of Anomie/Strain Theory

Émile Durkheim and Anomie

Émile Durkheim's classic statement of anomie set the stage for one of the most important theoretical traditions in criminology. In one of his major works, Durkheim—often considered the father of sociology—studied suicide in 19th-century Europe. While suicide is generally viewed as a very individualistic and personal act, Durkheim effectively argued that characteristics of communities influence suicide rates, independent of the particular individuals living in those communities. He found that some countries had consistently high rates of suicide over several decades, while other countries had consistently low rates. How can we explain these macrolevel differences?

In brief, Durkheim argued that suicide was related to the amount of regulation in a society and the degree of group unity. For Durkheim, social integration and social change are key factors in deviant behavior. As a society undergoes rapid change, norms will be unclear, and a state of anomie will result. **Anomie** is a state of normlessness where society fails to effectively regulate the expectations or behaviors of its members; it occurs when aspirations are allowed to develop beyond the possibility of fulfillment. In better-functioning societies, ambitions are restrained and human needs and desires are regulated by the collective order.

Durkheim argued that "no living being can be happy or even exist unless his needs are sufficiently proportioned to his means" (Durkheim, 1897/1951, p. 246). In Durkheim's understanding, society alone held the moral power over the individual to moderate expectations and limit passions. Durkheim suggested that a state of anomie, or norm-lessness, results from a breakdown in the regulation of goals; with such lack of regulation, individuals' aspirations become unlimited, and deviance may result. Durkheim argued that in a stable society, individuals are generally content with their positions or, as later scholars interpreted, they "aspire to achieve only what is realistically possible for them to achieve" (Cloward & Ohlin, 1960, p. 78).

A macrolevel example may clarify the concept of anomie: Think back to what you know about the 1960s in the United States. What was happening nationally at that time? The country was undergoing enormous changes as the civil rights movement took hold, women became more liberated and fought for equal rights, and America sent its young men to war in Vietnam. There was rapid and significant social change. Imagine what it would have been like to be a college student in the 1960s—whole new worlds of opportunities and challenges were opening for women and minorities. What should young people expect? How high could they aspire to go? The answers simply were not clear; the old norms no longer applied. With norms and expectations unclear for a large segment of the society, anomie theory would lead us to expect higher rates of deviance.

Anomie might also be applied to the normative expectations for physical attractiveness. Think for a moment about the standard for female beauty in the United States. Is there one ideal type? Or are there common characteristics we can identify? One trait that has been idealized for decades is that female beauties are nearly always thin, sometimes dangerously thin. Fashion models in magazines and walking the runway are very tall and extremely thin. They spend hours being tended to by professional hair and makeup artists and photographed by the best photographers in the world, and, even so, their photos are often airbrushed and photoshopped to make the already beautiful absolutely perfect.

This vision of ideal beauty is pervasive in the media. Young women (and increasingly young men) are exposed to unrealistic expectations of how they should aspire to look. For a time, network television shows glorified improving one's looks through plastic surgery with "reality" shows like *The Swan* and *I Want a Famous Face*. To frame this in terms of the theory, society has failed to regulate the expectations of its members when it comes to physical attractiveness, and we see deviance in the form of eating disorders and extensive elective plastic surgery resulting.

◈ Robert Merton and Adaptations to Anomie/Strain

Informed by Durkheim's writing on anomie, Robert K. Merton narrowed the focus and extended the theory to the United States in his 1938 article "Social Structure and Anomie." Merton argued that anomie does not result simply from unregulated goals but, rather, from a faulty relationship between cultural goals and the legitimate means to access them. While we are all socialized to desire success, we do not all have the same opportunities to become successful. Thus, Merton defined several adaptations to anomie and strain.

Merton was born Meyer Schkolnick, the son of Eastern European Jewish immigrants. He grew up in poverty in a "benign slum" in south Philadelphia. He legally changed to the "Americanized" name of Robert King Merton after he earned a scholarship to Temple University and entered college; he went to Harvard for his PhD and became a professor at Columbia University and one of the most famous sociologists in the world. His own story seems to capture a piece of the "American Dream." Growing up in the pre-Depression era, there was, according to Merton, a sense of "limitless possibilities." As Cullen and Messner (2007) suggest, this sense of limitless possibilities is illuminating. It relates to Merton's view not simply that Americans were urged to pursue some rigidly defined goal of success but, rather, that there also was a broad cultural message that everyone—even those in Merton's impoverished circumstances—could seek social mobility and expect to enjoy a measure of success (p. 14).

Given this biographical background, Merton's ideas begin to come to life. In "Social Structure and Anomie" (1938), Merton focused on the needs, desires, and processes of cultural socialization. He argued that in the United States, we are all socialized to believe in the sense of limitless possibilities and to desire success on a large scale. These cultural goals are widespread; the problem, however, is that the social structure "restricts or completely eliminates access to approved modes of acquiring these symbols for *a considerable part of the same population*" (p. 680). In other words, **structural impediments** or obstacles exist for whole classes of people who wish to attain wealth using legitimate means. For those in the lower classes who share the cultural goals for success but have limited means to attain them, lack of education and job opportunities create a strain toward anomie, which may translate into deviance.

Merton argued that there are five general adaptations to anomie. The key to each is whether there is an acceptance or rejection of the cultural goal of success (or, to adopt a concept that is easier to measure, wealth attainment) and whether or not the choice is to strive for the goal via legitimate or conforming means (Figure 4.1).

Merton's Adaptations to Anomie

Conformity is the most common adaptation. Conformists have accepted the cultural goal of success or wealth attainment, and they are trying to achieve it via legitimate means. Most college students might be considered conformists as they work hard to earn degrees to get better jobs and have more success after graduation. For Merton, conformity was the only nondeviant adaptation to strain and anomie.

Figure 4.1   Robert K. Merton's Deviance Typology

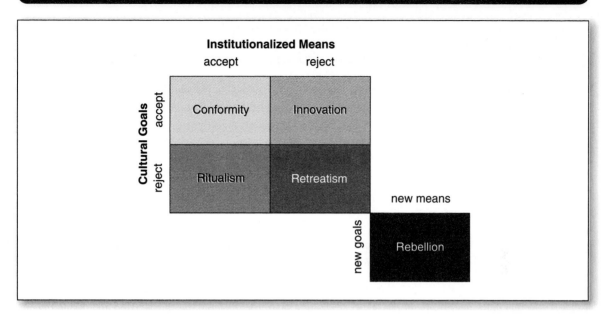

Innovation is the adaptation for those who have accepted the cultural goal of success/wealth attainment but are trying to achieve it via illegitimate means. Any crime for profit would be an example of innovation. Robbers, thieves, drug dealers, embezzlers, and high-priced call girls all would be classified as innovators in Merton's adaptations.

Ritualism is the category for those who have abandoned the cultural goal of success/wealth attainment but continue to use legitimate means to make their living. The dedicated workers who will never advance to management might be considered ritualists in Merton's typology.

Retreatism is the adaptation of those who have rejected the cultural goal of success/wealth attainment and have also rejected the legitimate means. Merton describes people who adapt in this way as "in the society but not of it. Sociologically, these constitute the true aliens" (Merton, 1957, p. 153). The chronically homeless and serious drug addicts might be considered retreatists in this model. Christopher McCandless, from this chapter's opening story, is a vivid individual example of a retreatist. He clearly rejected the conforming goals and lifestyle of his parents and the larger society;

▲ **Photo 4.1**   This photo might represent either conformity or ritualism in Merton's adaptations. Which concept do you think it best illustrates? Why do you think so?

DEVIANCE IN POPULAR CULTURE

Robert Merton's ideas on strain theory and particularly the adaptation of innovation can be easily seen in many movies dealing with the drug trade, audacious heists, kidnappers holding victims for ransom, or virtually any other crime for profit. Many examples are available, including the following:

Blow—A movie based on the true story of George Jung, a working-class kid who built an illegal empire and attained the cultural goal of wealth attainment, making a fortune via illegitimate means first by dealing marijuana and then importing cocaine.

Set It Off—A fictional story of four young African American women struggling to survive in Los Angeles. As their personal troubles mount, they begin robbing banks to solve their money woes.

Merton's other adaptations are less common in film, as they often make for less dramatic stories, but they are represented in popular culture.

Leaving Las Vegas—This story of an alcoholic man who has lost his wife and family and goes to Las Vegas to literally drink himself to death may be viewed as an example of Merton's retreatism.

Murder in Mississippi—A film based on the true story of the murder of three civil rights workers in Mississippi in 1964. The civil rights workers might be viewed as rebels in Merton's typology: They are working and risking their lives for social change. While this was clearly considered deviant in the South, it is another good illustration of how norms and boundaries change over time, perhaps in response to positive deviance and collective action.

As you watch films over the next few weeks and months, try to keep the sociological theories of deviance in mind. It may surprise you how many can easily be applied to the stories and perspectives on the screen.

he chose, instead, to exist in the margins, occasionally working low-level jobs, hitching rides, and ultimately attempting to live off the land in Alaska.

Rebellion is the category for political deviants—those who don't play by the rules but work to change the system to their own liking. Rebels reject the cultural goal of success/wealth attainment and replace it with another primary goal; they may use either legitimate or illegitimate means to achieve this goal—one way to think about it is that rebels will use whatever means necessary to reach their chosen goal. Perhaps the clearest example of rebellion would be terrorist groups, who often use violence in an attempt to achieve political goals.

Merton's 1938 article "Social Structure and Anomie" (SS&A) remains one of the most influential and referenced works in all of criminology and sociology. Reflecting on his seminal ideas in an interview five decades later, Merton observed that

it holds up those goals of success, especially economic, as a legitimate expectation for everybody. You do not have statements anywhere in the history of American aspirations that say: "You the poor, and you the ethnically subordinate—you can have no hopes or legitimate expectation of upward social mobility." You have never heard that said . . . call it rhetoric, call it ideology, call it myth, call it what you will, call it the

American Dream.... Now that is not typical of other cultural structures and other historical times and places. So it is a very powerful, if you will, theoretically sensitized observation.... SS&A '38 was saying what is universal for all is the legitimacy of striving to better yourself, to rise upward and onward.... That's the universal thing and that differs from other cultures ... in which you say: "Of course, you have no right; you are a servant class and you know your place." ... Now that's the dynamic new component of the cultural structure, and that is what is being said—what is common to all. (Cullen & Messner, 2007, p. 24)

◈ Richard Cloward and Lloyd Ohlin, Differential Opportunity

Richard Cloward was a student of Merton's and undoubtedly knew his work well. Cloward added an important dimension to anomie/strain theory by extending our focus to include the idea of illegitimate means. Cloward (1959) argued that just as not everyone has equal access to the legitimate means of attaining wealth, we cannot assume that everyone has access to illegitimate means either. This is a key point. Imagine that you wanted to become a successful drug dealer. Where would you begin? Would you know where to purchase your product? Would you know where to access customers and how to gain their trust and their business? Would you be able to keep your illicit business going without getting caught and punished? Cloward's point makes perfect sense in this context: Just because you might wish to gain wealth and success via illegitimate means does not mean that you will have the skills and connections to do so.

Cloward teamed up with Lloyd Ohlin in 1960 to write the book *Delinquency and Opportunity.* Just as Cloward was a student of Merton's, Ohlin was a student of Edwin Sutherland's, and he was well versed in the ideas of differential association and the importance of social learning (see Chapter 6 for more details on Sutherland and differential association). They found a research puzzle to be explored in Merton's work: While Merton may generally be accurate in describing pressures and motivations that lead to deviant behavior, the particular type of deviant behavior is unexplained. Cloward and Ohlin argued that we need to understand not just the motivations of individuals to commit deviant behavior but also the availability of opportunities to learn about and participate in illegal or deviant acts.

Cloward and Ohlin incorporated Sutherland's ideas into their theory and argued that criminal and deviant behavior is learned like any other behavior and, importantly, that not everyone has the same opportunities to learn criminal skills and have criminal careers. Their particular focus was on delinquent gangs and the circumstances under which different types of gangs emerged. They focused on neighborhood conditions (still a macrolevel theory) and the opportunities available to learn and practice legitimate or illegitimate skills. Ultimately, Cloward and Ohlin suggested that only neighborhoods in which crime flourishes as a stable institution are fertile criminal learning environments for the young.

To further clarify their ideas, Cloward and Ohlin argued that the different kinds of illegitimate opportunities available in poor urban neighborhoods lead to three types of criminal subcultures: criminal, conflict, and retreatist. Because the focus is on disadvantaged neighborhoods, the assumption is that most young people growing up in these conditions will have poor and limited legitimate opportunities for attaining wealth and success. Thus, the availability of illegitimate opportunities becomes extremely important in shaping the deviance that takes place in these neighborhoods and the types of adolescent gangs that develop.

Criminal subcultures develop among lower class adolescent boys in neighborhoods with open illegitimate opportunity structures. These neighborhoods are characterized by systematic, organized crime, and they provide an outlet in illegal employment for youths to attain wealth and "get paid" via illegitimate means. Successful criminals populate the neighborhood and become visible, serving as distinctive role models for children growing up in the community. For those young people who aspire to emulate these illegitimate role models, there is generally an age-graded criminal structure in place where young males may do low-level jobs and learn from the older criminals in the neighborhood. In this way, social learning takes place, and the young acquire the skills and norms to fully take advantage of the illegitimate opportunities available to them. Compared with alternative poor neighborhoods, those with criminal subcultures are very structured and are relatively safe places to grow up and live. There is an absence of violence in these neighborhoods because violence—and the attention it draws—would be considered disruptive to both criminal and conventional activities.

Conflict subcultures develop in disorganized communities where illegitimate opportunities are largely absent, and those that exist are closed to adolescents (see Chapter 5 for more information on social disorganization). Such neighborhoods are characterized by social instability, and youth growing up in these conditions are deprived of both conventional (legitimate) and criminal (illegitimate) opportunities. As Cloward and Ohlin (1960) explained it, "The disorganized slum . . . contains the outcasts of the criminal world . . . what crime there is tends to be individualistic, unorganized, petty, poorly paid, and unprotected" (pp. 173–174). With no real access to legitimate or illegitimate opportunities, adolescents growing up in disorganized neighborhoods suffer acute frustration and turn to violence to prove their personal worth. Social controls are weak in these areas, and violence for violence's sake is valued. With few role models and little chance at success, young men work to earn the toughest reputation and, through their physical prowess, to command some level of respect and deference from those around them.

Retreatist subcultures are associated with drug use and the drug culture among some lower class adolescents. Cloward and Ohlin characterized adolescents in retreatist subcultures as "double failures" who cannot find a place for themselves in either criminal or conflict subcultures. While this is closely related to Merton's concept of retreatists, Cloward and Ohlin directed attention to the social environment and the conditions that help to explain the formation of each type of deviant subculture. The "double failures" in poor neighborhoods may withdraw from the larger society and retreat into drug use and relative isolation.

It is important to remember that Cloward and Ohlin are still explaining deviance at the macrolevel. Criminal, conflict, and retreatist subcultures develop primarily because communities are organized differently and offer varying legitimate and illegitimate opportunities.

◈ Albert Cohen, *Delinquent Boys*

Similar to Cloward and Ohlin, Albert K. Cohen was an undergraduate student of Merton's and a graduate student of Sutherland's, so he, too, combined elements of Merton's anomie theory and Sutherland's ideas on social learning in his work. In his book *Delinquent Boys*, Cohen (1955) introduced the idea of delinquent subcultures. Cohen argued that a lower class or working-class boy may find himself at the bottom of the status hierarchy in middle-class schools and the larger middle-class world, and

> to the degree to which he values middle-class status, either because he values the good opinion of middle-class persons or because he has to some degree internalized middle-class standards himself, he faces a problem of adjustment and is in the market for a "solution." (Cohen, 1955, p. 119)

Cohen argues that this **status frustration** or strain may lead to the collective solution of forming a delinquent subculture in which middle-class norms and values are replaced with their antithesis—their very opposite. Cohen suggests that the delinquent subculture can be described as nonutilitarian—for example, stealing just "for the hell of it" and not because the boys need or even want what they steal; malicious, or being "just plain mean" and destructive; and negativistic, or taking the norms of the larger culture and turning them upside down. The delinquent subculture forms and is sustained because it offers alternative criteria that working-class boys can meet and excel at; attributes that are disvalued by the larger culture become status-giving assets within the subculture.

◈ Robert Agnew, General Strain Theory

Anomie and strain theories have a long history in sociology and criminology and have surged and waned in popularity over the years. Classic strain theories dominated criminological research in the 1950s and 1960s, and their relevance was marked in public policy of the time, particularly in strain theory's impact on the War on Poverty during the 1960s (Cullen & Agnew, 2006). Strain theory came under attack in the 1970s as relativist theorists shifted the focus to conflict and labeling theories (see Chapters 8 and 9), offering a new perspective on societal influences on both crime and punishment.

Robert Agnew (1992) breathed new life into the tradition with his **general strain theory (GST)**. Strain theory focuses on what circumstances lead individuals and groups within a society to engage in deviant behavior. Agnew suggests that they are "pressured into crime." Along with the failure to achieve valued goals, Agnew argues that strain may also result from negative relationships. Agnew specifies three major types of negative relations where others

1. Prevent or threaten to prevent the achievement of positively valued goals (for example, preventing monetary success or popularity with peers)

2. Remove or threaten to remove positive stimuli (for example, the death of a parent or the breakup of a romantic relationship)

3. Present or threaten to present negative stimuli (for example, physical assaults, failing grades, or public insults)

Such negative relations will likely lead to anger and frustration, which may then lead to deviant behavior, such as physical violence, running away from home, illicit drug use, or self-harming behavior.

Agnew (2006) argues that some types of strain are more likely to cause crime and deviance than others. He identifies the following characteristics as most likely to cause crime: The strain is high in magnitude, the strain is seen as unjust, the strain is associated with low self-control, and/or the strain creates some pressure or incentive for criminal coping. More specifically, examples of strains that are likely to cause crime include parental rejection, erratic or excessively harsh discipline, child abuse and neglect, negative school experiences, abusive peer relationships, chronic unemployment, marital problems, criminal victimization, residence in economically deprived neighborhoods, and discrimination based on characteristics such as race/ethnicity and gender.

Agnew is careful to point out that not all individuals respond to strains with crime and deviance, and in fact, most people cope in legal and conforming ways. There are many possible coping strategies, including behavioral coping, cognitive coping, and emotional coping (Agnew, 2006). The resources and social support available to the individuals are important: Do they have conforming friends and family they can turn to for help? Do they associate with criminal others? What is their level of self-control? Is the cost of criminal coping high or low? For some individuals, there is low risk in criminal or deviant coping because they have little to lose—they may not have jobs or close relationships that would be put at risk with criminal or deviant acts. While it is difficult to tease out the exact impact of each of these factors, Agnew argues that whether by personality traits, socialization, or learned attitudes and behavior, some individuals are simply more disposed to crime than are others.

◈ Messner and Rosenfeld, *Crime and the American Dream*—Institutional Anomie Theory

Messner and Rosenfeld (2007a) turn attention to the American Dream and how it contributes to crime and deviance. They write,

The essence of our argument is that the distinctive patterns and levels of crime in the United States are produced by the cultural and structural organization of American society. A strong emphasis on the goal of monetary success and a weak emphasis on the importance of the legitimate means for the pursuit of success characterize American culture. This combination of strong pressures to succeed monetarily and

▲ **Photo 4.2**   Do you agree with Messner and Rosenfeld that the American Dream fosters an "anything goes" attitude when pursuing monetary success?

weak restraints on the selection of means is intrinsic to the dominant cultural ethos: the American Dream. The "American Dream" refers to a cultural commitment to the goal of economic success to be pursued by everyone under conditions of open, individual competition. The American Dream contributes to crime directly by encouraging people to employ illegal means to achieve goals that are culturally approved. (p. x)

Messner and Rosenfeld argue that the American Dream fosters an "anything goes" mentality when pursuing personal goals. They go on to identify the values underlying the American Dream as follows: achievement, individualism, universalism, and materialism. Achievement is connected to personal worth; Messner and Rosenfeld argue that the cultural pressures to achieve are enormous, and failure to achieve is often perceived as a failure to make any sort of meaningful contribution to society. Individualism encourages everyone to find a way to "make it" on his or her own. Within this framework of intense competition to succeed, others in the society are viewed as competitors and rivals, and thus, general restraints on behavior are disregarded in the pursuit of personal goals. Universalism echoes Merton's ideas that virtually everyone in American society is encouraged to aspire to success and wealth attainment. Messner and Rosenfeld point out that while everyone may dream about success, "the hazards of failure are also universal" (p. 70). Materialism is the last value that underlies the American Dream. Money has special significance in American culture; it is the preeminent way in which we measure success and achievement.

At the institutional level, Messner and Rosenfeld argue that the major institutions in the United States, including the family, school, and political system, are all dominated by economic institutions. Noneconomic goals and accomplishments are valued much less than economic pursuits and gains, and economic norms have infiltrated and overpowered other important societal institutions.

Messner and Rosenfeld suggest that the American Dream leads to crime and deviance because of its exaggerated emphasis on monetary success and its resistance to restraint or limits on individual pursuit of success. Thus, they extend Merton's idea that the very fabric of American society promotes at least some level of deviance. Even as we all aspire to achieve great things and believe it is possible to realize our dreams, the social structure of American society constrains pathways to success; this, in turn, leads to deviance as some members of society pursue alternative success models by any means necessary.

◈ Application of Anomie and Strain Theories

Today, classic strain theory has renewed support, and it is used to examine group differences in crime rates, inequality, and **relative deprivation**, a perspective that suggests that socioeconomic inequality has a direct effect on community crime rates. At the micro level, Agnew continues to actively revise and refine his ideas on general strain theory. Many, many studies have tested pieces of Agnew's theory and offer limited support; there are still many hypotheses to be discovered, tested, and explained. While research on general strain theory is quite easy to find in the sociological and criminological literature, in the following, we high-light three studies that explore different aspects of anomie and strain.

Anomie and the Abuse at Abu Ghraib

A recent study analyzed the abuse at Abu Ghraib prison in Iraq in terms of Durkheim's concept of ano-mie (Mestrovic & Lorenzo, 2008). You may remember the vivid images of American soldiers torturing and humiliating Iraqi prisoners: Photos were published of soldiers threatening the nude men with snarling dogs, smiling over the bodies of dead Iraqis, forcing the prisoners to walk around and pose nude with hoods and blindfolds blocking their vision, and offering a thumbs-up to the cameras as they posed in front of literal piles of prisoners in humiliating positions.

▲ **Photo 4.3** American soldiers purposely degraded and humiliated Iraqi prisoners at Abu Ghraib. How does Durkheim's theory of anomie help to explain such abuse?

Mestrovic and Lorenzo (2008) argue that there were high levels of social disorganization or anomie at Abu Ghraib and within the social structures of the U.S. Army, other government agencies, civilian contractors, and others who interacted with and had responsibility for the prisoners at Abu Ghraib. The authors argue that the social system at Abu Ghraib was disorganized and anomic from the outset and grew progressively worse over time; this confusion produced widespread deviance among prisoners and U.S. personnel alike.

Mestrovic and Lorenzo (2008) identify several sources of confusion that contributed to the anomie and deviance, including confusion as to who was in charge, insufficient training, lack of social integration within the military units at Abu Ghraib, rapid changes in the social milieu, intense pressure to obtain intelligence, confusion as to which norms to follow, "unhealthy mystique," failure of self-correcting mechanisms, and cultural insensitivity. The authors go on to explain,

> The extent of social disorganization, social chaos, dysfunction, lack of coordination, and of a general state of *anomie* was so great at Abu Ghraib that abuse and the breaking of norms that are documented was the *inevitable* outcome and should have been expected. (p. 202)

We have included a longer excerpt from Mestrovic and Lorenzo's article in the readings for this chapter so that you can read the primary source and think more deeply about their claims as they relate to anomie.

The American Dream and Incarcerated Young Men

A study by Inderbitzin (2007) focused on boys in a juvenile prison who held deeply to the idea of the American Dream but had few legitimate means to achieve it. The decline of manufacturing jobs and their replacement with low-wage and unskilled work has made it difficult for young men, particularly those with poor educations, to be successful. The ongoing racism experienced by minorities in the labor market imposes an additional barrier to eco-nomic success through legitimate means. As such, the loss of viable work for young, poorly educated, minority males seems inextricably linked to their criminal behavior. Committing crimes for profit can help such young men meet their financial needs and counter threats to their self-perception as competent men.

The young men in the study followed the lure of money and status into illegal endeavors that led to confrontations with the law and conforming society. Profit or "getting paid" (M. L. Sullivan, 1989) was frequently cited as one of the main motivating factors in their crimes. They were examples of Merton's innovators—"men who hold fast to culturally emphasized goals while abandoning culturally approved ways of seeking them" (Merton, 1964, p. 218). Thus, Merton's ideas remain both useful and relevant some eight decades after the publication of "Social Structure and Anomie."

Inderbitzin (2007) goes on to argue that staff members in the juvenile facility explicitly encourage the young men in their care to shift their values and aspirations to conforming, less glamorous goals and to adopt new definitions of success and the American Dream. In this way, Durkheim's ideas on anomie are also found in the work that staff members of the juvenile correctional facility or "training school" are doing to resocialize the incarcerated adolescents to more prosocial goals and behavior.

A latent function of the juvenile prison is to work to normalize the young inmates, re-directing the aspirations of its charges, releasing them back into their communities with more realistic, but essentially deflated goals for their futures. In this way, the institution becomes an important agent of social control in its attempts to combat conditions of anomie and the resulting crime in the larger community. The training school graduates who go on to conforming futures have likely been at least partially normalized and resocialized to expect less from the world outside. (Inderbitzin, 2007, p. 236)

Institutional Anomie Theory and Student Cheating

One attempt to extend and refine Messner and Rosenfeld's (2007a) **institutional anomie theory** took their ideas and applied them to individual student cheating. Muftic (2006) sought to test the idea that the exaggerated emphasis on economic success in the United States has bled into other social institutions, including academia. She surveyed American and international undergraduate students and asked them about their cheating behavior and their economic goals. Results suggested that American students were more oriented to economic goals and were more likely to admit to cheating. "Students with higher adherence to the cultural values of universalism and the fetishism of money had a higher likelihood of cheating. . . . Location of birth (i.e., born in the United States) appeared to have the strongest impact on cheating" (Muftic, 2006, p. 648).

While she found some support for institutional anomie theory, Muftic also points out that adherence to the American Dream is not universal. Even in a fairly homogeneous sample, American students embraced the cultural ideal at varying levels. Muftic concluded her article by suggesting that both microlevel (neighborhood cohesiveness and levels of informal social control) and macrolevel (poverty, family disruption, racial heterogeneity, and social mobility) analyses be combined in future studies of institutional anomie theory.

◈ Critiques of Anomie and Strain Theories

Macrolevel components of Merton's theory have rarely been tested as it is difficult, if not impossible, to measure how whole societies focus on particular goals and means (Kubrin, Stucky, & Krohn, 2009, p. 127). Messner and Rosenfeld (2007a) discuss four primary critiques of Merton's argument and anomie theory. First, Merton assumes that value consensus exists in society and that the goal of monetary success is held above all. As Muftic (2006) pointed out, we should not assume those values are universal; other goals may be equally important—or more important—for many Americans. Second, Merton's theory and many versions of classical strain theory are class biased and have difficulty accounting for deviance among the privileged classes. Third, Merton seems to suggest that providing more equal opportunity offers a realistic solution to crime and deviance in the United States; Messner and Rosenfeld do not believe this to be the case. Finally, Merton never precisely defines anomie.

Messner and Rosenfeld (2007a) dispense with the first two critiques as being oversimplified readings of Merton's argument, suggesting that Merton never claimed complete value consensus but that monetary success is a particularly powerful benchmark in the United States. Furthermore, Merton's basic argument can be used to explain deviance and criminal behavior in the middle and upper classes as well, as the definition of success is relative and must still be achieved despite structural constraints.

◆ Explaining Deviance in the Streets and Deviance in the Suites: The Occupy Wall Street Movement

The Occupy Wall Street movement in New York in the fall of 2011 focused attention on inequality in the United States and the perceived crumbling of the American Dream. Protesters, embracing the slogan "We are the 99 percent," took over Zuccotti Park in Lower Manhattan, disrupting the work and daily life of wealthy financial traders for weeks and months. The message of the Occupy movement spread quickly, with protests taking root in cities and college campuses across the country. The protests were largely tolerated by local authorities, but law enforcement created headlines when college students protesting on the University of California campus in Davis were pepper-sprayed by campus police. The Occupy movement lasted for months. Eventually, hundreds of Occupy participants were displaced when they were evicted from Zuccotti Park and arrested for violations as simple as disorderly conduct or laying down in public.

Many of the activists of the Occupy movement were young, highly educated adults. Sociologists found that more than a third of the protesters lived in households with annual incomes over $100,000, and more than two thirds of them held professional jobs (Moynihan, 2013). And yet, their discontent was palpable and spurred them to action.

It seems education is no longer a guaranteed conforming route to a successful, fulfilling, and profitable career. Researchers found that nearly 80% of the Occupy participants had a bachelor's degree, and of those, about half had a graduate degree, yet a significant portion of the protesters had credit card or student loan debt and were underemployed, working less than 35 hours a week (Moynihan, 2013). Milkman (2012) describes the origin of the Occupy protesters' frustration and activism.

> They followed the prescribed path to prepare themselves for professional jobs or other meaningful careers. But having completed their degrees, they confronted a labor market bleaker than anytime since the 1930s. Adding insult to injury, many were burdened with enormous amounts of student debt.
>
> In this sense, Occupy might be seen as a classic revolution of rising expectations. But it is not only about blocked economic aspirations: The millennials were also seduced and abandoned *politically*. Their generation enthusiastically supported Barack Obama in 2008; some participated in "Camp Obama," and many were otherwise actively involved in the campaign. But here, too, their expectations were brutally disappointed. (pp. 13–14)

As economic, political, and social expectations are disappointed and new realities created, it might be argued that the United States is again experiencing a time of anomie as Durkheim described it, where society fails to regulate the expectations and behaviors of its members. Young people—who if they had been born into an earlier generation might have found their investment in education paying financial dividends—were so frustrated by the inequality and lack of good opportunities that they literally took to the streets in the Occupy movement, banding together and risking arrest in order to make a point and feel heard.

© CribbVisuals/iStockphoto

▲ **Photo 4.4** How might the Occupy movement be an example of both Deviance in the Streets and Deviance in the Suites?

Langman, a sociologist, explains how the Wall Street bailout, in which the federal government committed some $700 billion in taxpayer money to rescue Wall Street banks, showed power differences in the extreme, with wealthy corporations offered enormous financial assistance while middle- and working-class citizens lost their homes, their jobs, and their hope.

There was an explosion of "subprime" mortgages in which vetting applicants was negligent at best, criminal at worst. Eventually, the bubble burst, the rapidly expanding housing market crashed, the entire financial industry imploded and took the entire economy down. There followed a wave of bankruptcies, layoffs of workers, and subsequent economic stagnation, if not devastation for many in vulnerable positions, who have been dubbed the precariat. But while surely there was malfeasance, if not criminal behavior, this must be understood as a structural crisis in which the "steering mechanisms" failed.

A vast government bailout pumped trillions of dollars into the insolvent banks and "saved" the banking/financial system. The government rescue halted the plummet, saved the financial system and its elite prospered, yet ordinary people lost jobs, houses were foreclosed, people evicted, and many remain unemployed and/or underemployed. It was soon evident that thanks to "crony capitalism," the casino players won, the banking/finance industries had "recovered," indeed amassed more wealth than ever before. Its elites were well rewarded—thanks to the taxpayers.

Economic crises, implosions, and structural contradictions that threaten survival or the maintenance of living standards, or render social status, dignity and self-esteem problematic, lead to questions and challenges to the legitimacy of the economic system, political leadership, and legitimating ideologies. (Langman, 2013, pp. 511–512)

Even as its members protested extreme inequality in the United States, some controversy arose from within the Occupy movement when chronically homeless people moved into the Occupy camps in areas such as New York City, Boston, and Los Angeles. While some Occupy protesters embraced the homeless as epitomizing the very soul of arguments about inequality and the lack of resources of the 99%, others felt like the homeless population took advantage of the comparative luxury and safety of the camps and that their presence brought more stringent scrutiny from authorities and law enforcement.

The Occupy Wall Street movement is an interesting example of highly educated individuals literally taking to the streets to protest what they perceive as deviance in the corporate suites. We began this chapter with the example of Christopher McCandless, who, after graduating college, gave up all of his worldly possessions and struck out to make it on his own in the wilderness far away from the trappings of the larger society. He shared in common with the young people of the Occupy movement a deep frustration with the norms and expectations of American society. In responding to the conditions of anomie and strain, McCandless chose to retreat, whereas the Occupy participants chose to band together and rebel.

◈ **Ideas in Action: Defy Ventures—Transforming Innovation Into Legitimate Success**

In describing the adaptations to anomie, Robert Merton defined innovation as acceptance of the cultural goal of wealth attainment and the use of illegitimate means to work toward that goal. Thus, crimes committed for money or profit would generally fall under the heading of innovation. While illegal, there are often real skills involved in these illicit business pursuits, and individuals may become successful entrepreneurs selling drugs and services.

After visiting Texas prisons in a religious outreach program, Catherine Rohr discovered that many of the skills and talents prisoners developed and used as drug dealers and criminals—street smarts, resourcefulness, money management, risk taking, and the ability to manage employees—were exactly the traits needed to succeed in more conventional business endeavors. She started the Prisoner Entrepreneurship Program (n.d.), a nonprofit program that teaches Texas inmates an MBA-level curriculum and encourages them to translate their previous skills and work ethic into new and conforming ventures as they form plans to start their own businesses. The Prison Entrepreneurship Program has proven to be very successful in its first decade; it trains and socializes inmates to prepare them for conforming business opportunities, helps individuals with reentry and job placement upon release, and boasts a recidivism rate of less than 10%.

After a highly publicized scandal involving intimate (but not illegal) relationships with four graduates of her program after they were released from prison, Rohr resigned from her role with the Prison Entrepreneurship Program, but she did not give up on her belief that former prisoners could translate their skills into successful businesses. The following is an excerpt from a 2013 interview with Rohr.

"America puts these people in the trash pile," Rohr said. "They represent America's most overlooked talent pool: the underdogs." But, she says they are brilliantly equipped to be leaders because of their street-smart and entrepreneurial (albeit illegal) past activities. After going through 1,000 hours of character and business development, the former felons come out as business people ready to face the world. (Menardi, 2013, n.p.)

Rohr went on to found the New York–based Defy Ventures (n.d.), a nonprofit funded and managed by entrepreneurs and venture capitalists who believe that former drug dealers and gang members may share similar skills with top business leaders. A news story checked in with the first class of Defy students, describing the program and the students' evolution and practices:

These men are the inaugural class of Defy Ventures, a yearlong, M.B.A.-style program that Rohr created to teach former inmates how to start their own companies. For months, they have been meeting here for 14 to 16 hours a week to learn about things such as cash flow, balance sheets, intellectual property, accounting, and taxes. There are workshops on how to behave in professional settings, how to speak in public, and how to be a better parent. These men are also learning how to create business plans. In June, they will compete in a business-plan competition. The winners will split $100,000 in seed funding.

Rohr has an interesting theory about criminals. She says that many of the qualities that made these men good at being bad guys (until they got caught, of course) are the same qualities that make effective entrepreneurs. Some of the men in this class had up to 40 employees under management. Though their merchandise was illegal narcotics and not, say, office supplies, these men developed certain business skills—the ability to motivate a team, identify new markets, manage risk, and inspire loyalty and hard work. Rohr's goal is to help these students apply their abilities to legal endeavors. (Frieswick, 2012)

NOW YOU . . . USE THE THEORY

The following is a graph of the suicide rates in the United States between 1950 and 2003. Note that the data are broken down by age and gender. Using anomie or general strain theory, explain the following:

1. The overall trend (all ages, age adjusted) between 1950 and 2003. Start by describing the trend; then choose one of the two theories to explain it.

2. The trend, over time, for 45- to 64-year-olds between 1950 and 2003. Start by describing the trend; then choose one of the two theories to explain it.

3. The trend for male suicides and female suicides over time. According to one of the two theories, why might women always be less likely to engage in suicidal behavior than men?

Visit the website for the American Foundation for Suicide Prevention for additional facts and figures, updated through 2013, at https://www.afsp.org/understanding-suicide/facts-and-figures.

U.S. Suicide Rates, 1950–2003 (per 100,000 population)

	1950	1960	1970	1980	1990	1995	2000	2001	2002	2003
All ages, age adjusted	13.2	13.2	13.2	13.2	12.5	11.8	10.4	10.7	10.9	10.8
5–14 years	0.2	0.3	0.3	0.4	0.8	0.9	0.7	0.7	0.6	0.6
15–24 years	4.5	5.2	8.8	12.3	13.2	13.0	10.2	9.9	9.9	9.7
15–19 years	2.7	3.6	5.9	8.5	11.1	10.3	8.0	7.9	7.4	7.3
20–24 years	6.2	7.1	12.2	16.1	15.1	15.8	12.5	12.0	12.4	12.1
25–44 years	11.6	12.2	15.4	15.6	15.2	15.1	13.4	13.8	14.0	13.8
25–34 years	9.1	10.0	14.1	16.0	15.2	15.0	12.0	12.8	12.6	12.7
35–44 years	14.3	14.2	16.9	15.4	15.3	15.1	14.5	14.7	15.3	14.9
45–64 years	23.5	22.0	20.6	15.9	15.3	13.9	13.5	14.4	14.9	15.0
45–54 years	20.9	20.7	20.0	15.9	14.8	14.4	14.4	15.2	15.7	15.9
55–64 years	26.8	23.7	21.4	15.9	16.0	13.2	12.1	13.1	13.6	13.8
65 years and over	30.0	24.5	20.8	17.6	20.5	17.9	15.2	15.3	15.6	14.6
65–74 years	29.6	23.0	20.8	16.9	17.9	15.7	12.5	13.3	13.5	12.7
75–84 years	31.1	27.9	21.2	19.1	24.9	20.6	17.6	17.4	17.7	16.4

	1950	**1960**	**1970**	**1980**	**1990**	**1995**	**2000**	**2001**	**2002**	**2003**
85 years and over	28.8	26.0	19.0	19.2	22.2	21.3	19.6	17.5	18.0	16.9
Male, all ages	21.2	20.0	19.8	19.9	21.5	20.3	17.7	18.2	18.4	18.0
Female, all ages	5.6	5.6	7.4	5.7	4.8	4.3	4.0	4.0	4.2	4.2

Source: Graph from World Health Organization.

Graduates of Defy Ventures have started cleaning businesses, concierge services, construction companies, financial-planning services, repair businesses, a mobile barbershop, and other startup companies. In their quest to build new lives once they were released from prison, they recognized that Defy Ventures was offering legitimate, conforming opportunities, and they put in the work needed to translate their hard-earned skills and energy into new professional businesses.

Rohr and others working at and supporting Defy Ventures hope to eventually replicate the program in every urban community in the United States. If and when communities come together to support formerly incarcerated people who are trying to change their lives, there will be less strain, less need for innovation, and more opportunities for every member of society to conform and thrive.

◈ Conclusion

Anomie and strain theories have a more clearly developed history than other theoretical traditions. Nearly everyone can agree that these ideas began with Durkheim and Merton and were extended in important ways by Cloward and Ohlin and a handful of other theorists. One recent revision of the theory views strain as a function of relative deprivation. In this model, the reference group is a key element. Your own absolute success or wealth is less important than your position relative to those around you. Comparing yourself with those with more wealth and more material success may lead to strain and deviant behavior. Today, Messner and Rosenfeld's institutional anomie theory might be considered the leading version of anomie theory, and Agnew's general strain theory might be considered the leading version of strain theory (Cullen & Agnew, 2006).

Research continues on both anomie and strain theories. More sophisticated methods are allowing for analyses that bridge both macrolevel and microlevel variables, which will offer an ever-increasing understanding of how cultural goals and the social structure affect individuals and lead to deviant behavior.

EXERCISES AND DISCUSSION QUESTIONS

1. Provide another example of a state of anomie. How did it affect rates of deviance?

2. Give a specific example of each of Merton's five adaptations.

3. What are the policy recommendations you might make based on Cloward and Ohlin's ideas? In other words, using Cloward and Ohlin's ideas on delinquency and opportunity,

what programs might be put into place to prevent crime and deviance?

4. Institutional anomie theory argues that our economic goals and system have permeated and overrun other social systems and institutions in the United States. Do you think this is true? Can you think of examples from politics, education, and families?

5. Do you think that Agnew is correct that individuals are pressured into crime and deviance? Can you think of an example of a time when you were faced with a negative relationship but did not turn to deviant behavior? How did you react instead?

KEY TERMS

Anomie

Conflict subcultures

Criminal subcultures

General strain theory (GST)

Institutional anomie theory

Relative deprivation

Retreatist subcultures

Status frustration

Strain

Structural impediments

READING 10

Contreras argues in this brief piece that context is critically important in understanding how and why a group of young men became incredibly violent drug dealers. He frames Tukee's story through his learning to desire and believe in the American Dream, the criminal opportunities found in the rise—and fall—of crack cocaine, and the struggle Tukee and his friends went through to attain and maintain wealth and the "high life." Which version of anomie/strain theory do you think best fits the story of the young men in this reading?

Becoming a Stickup Kid

Randol Contreras

The South Bronx summer night was warm and moist, with that mild glow we always felt after it rained. The neighborhood residents slowly resumed their places on the streets, first standing next to building entrances, then next to wet cars, and then sitting on the cars after they'd dried. The neighborhood bodega, or grocery store, revitalized the block, blasting the 1980s salsa classics that brought bolero lyrics to the dance floor: *Y me duele a pensar, que nunca mia seras, De mi enamorate-e-e-e . . .*

Source: Contreras, R. (2015). Becoming a stickup kid. *Contexts, 14*(4), 20–25.

Dressed in large T-shirts, Nikes, and baggy shorts, some young Dominican men listened to the cool music alongside me. "Yo, that used to be the jam!"—we nodded our heads; "I used to dance to this shit!"—we tapped our feet; "*A si mi'mo!*"—one of us did a fancy salsa step; *Mira que e, e, e, e, e, e—el-l-l-l!*—some of us sang along, straining our voices with each rising octave. We were all in a good mood. Just chillin'. *Chilliando*, baby.

Then Jonah arrived. He pulled Gus aside for a furtive chat. Despite their low voices, we could hear them planning a drug robbery. After about ten minutes, they returned to the group, energized, and recounted stories of their past *tumbes* (drug robbery hits). Most of the young Dominican men joined in with their own tales of brutality and adventure.

Jonah and Gus recounted a drug robbery when they'd targeted a Dominican drug courier who always delivered five kilos of cocaine to a certain dealer on a certain day. For a share of the take, the dealer told Jonah and Gus where to intercept the courier as he walked out of an apartment building. At gunpoint, they led him to the building's rooftop, beat him, and stole $100,000 worth of drugs.

Tukee and Pablo told the group about a drug robbery where they had pretended to be undercover officers. With fake badges and real guns, they stopped a pair of drug dealers on the street: "Freeze! Don't move, motherfucker!" they yelled out. They faced the dealers against a wall and grabbed their suitcase, stuffed with $40,000 in cash. "Keep facing the wall!" they commanded before trotting around the corner to their getaway car. Neno and Gus told a third story, of a drug robbery that went wrong. They had tortured a drug dealer—punched and kicked him, choked and gagged him, mutilated and burned him—until he passed out. The victim, however, remained unconscious. Afraid, *se fueron volando*—they hurried out so if the victim died, they wouldn't be there.

Throughout my field research, I heard many of these robbery tales. In fact, I grew up with these stories and these men. As a young man, I had tried my hand at drug dealing. So I was used to seeing and hearing about drug market violence. Yet there were times when I questioned the humanity of the men next to me on front stoops and car hoods.

How could Pablo almost beat someone to death? How could Gus repeatedly burn someone with an iron? How could Tukee chop off someone's finger? How could Neno sodomize a dealer with an object? How could all of these men *torture*, a cruel and deplorable human act?

In trying to understand drug robbery violence, I realized how easy it was to fall into an individualistic, sociopathic-reasoning trap. Could one not argue that these men were sociopaths who enjoyed inflicting pain on others? Maybe they were evil and solely pursued the emotional thrills of crime?

As a sociologist, though, I took a step back to frame what seemed solely evil and sociopathic within larger historical and social forces, forces that sweep people in one direction or another, that shape "why" some people do violence or crime.

Everyone respects Tukee for his tremendous violence during drug robberies. It seems like he could chop off fingers and pistol-whip someone to the brink of death with no hesitation or thought. Sometimes, he even seemed to enjoy torture:

"I remember one time, we put a[n] iron on this dude's back," Tukee recounts, laughing. "I had told him, 'Just tell me where the shit is [the drugs and cash]. If you don't tell us, I'ma do some things to you, B[ro]. Things you won't like.' He ain't tell us so, boom, [we] took off his shirt and made the iron real hot. I put that shit on his back and the dude started screaming, B, ha-ha-ha! Then he was like, 'Alright, take it! It's inside the mattress!' That shit was funny, B! Ha-ha-ha!"

Taken out of the proper socio-historical context, the laughter and joy in Tukee's account make it seem like he's pure evil. Tukee, though, was born neither a drug robber nor torturer. His biography emerged within a particular social context: the rise and fall of crack cocaine in the abandoned and burned-out South Bronx.

Tukee's Story

Tukee was born to a Dominican father and a Puerto Rican mother in the South Bronx during the early 1970s. For reasons he never disclosed, his father abandoned the family, never to be seen or heard from again. His mother worked several informal jobs, mostly as a seamstress in a local sweatshop. Tukee went to underfunded public schools—when he went. A disengaged and unprepared student, he eventually dropped out of high school. He worked part-time, here and there, moving from one fast-food chain job to the next. But he wanted to make money, get rich.

Tukee's chances for upward mobility, though, were fading. Between 1947 and 1976, New York City lost about 500,000 factory jobs. That's half a million unionized jobs that, for about three-quarters of the twentieth century, had provided security and upward mobility for European immigrants and their children. By the time Blacks, Puerto Ricans, and, later, Dominicans, settled in the Bronx, the burgeoning service economy had taken hold. There were lower wages and less job security available to workers with little education, like Tukee.

Crack showed up right on time.

Crack had its origins in the powder cocaine craze of the 1970s. This was a time when professionals like doctors, Wall Street executives, and lawyers likened a line of cocaine to a sip of champagne. The federal government's hysteria over marijuana and its reduction of drug treatment funds further widened the demand for and use of cocaine. Later, in the early 1980s, when cocaine users reduced their intake, desperate cocaine dealers then turned to crack, a smokable form of the drug, to maintain profits. Instead, their profits soared: crack yielded more quantity than cocaine after preparation. More importantly, crack invited binging. Soon many users were consuming the drug around-the-clock.

Crack quickly proliferated in inner cities across the United States. For marginal urban residents, who suffered because of both a declining manufacturing sector and Reaganomics but still hoped to take part in the grandest version of the American Dream—crack was a Godsend. The start-up money for a crack business was low. And unlike the tightly knit heroin market, there was no need for pre-existing family or ethnic ties to edge your way in. Almost anyone could enter this market.

Tukee walked right in.

He and a friend started selling crack in his Highbridge neighborhood. He began earning between $300 and $500 per day, all profit. He purchased a salvaged luxury car and restored it to its former glory with stolen car parts. Along with his new expensive jewelry and clothes, the car made him a neighborhood celebrity. *Yo, here comes Tukee!* The sidewalk crowd flocked around. *What up Tuke', where you going?* The guys and gals wanted to cruise around in his ride.

Tukee also spent his *riquezas*, or riches, living the high life. He arrived at nightclubs *con estilo*, or in style, with an entourage-packed white limousine. Inside, he treated his broke neighborhood friends to over-priced bottles of liquor and bought attractive women expensive drinks. Afterward, if he was still around, the weed was on him, too. Everyone loved Tukee. He was a drug market star.

Of course, Tukee was also feared. As crack use rose, more dealers tried to squeeze into the now-saturated market. Tukee pulled his gun on several newcomers, warning them to stay away from his "spot." He became a legend after he shot a dealer for dealing drugs without his permission. After coming out of hiding (the police investigation lasted a few weeks), everyone deferred to him, greeting him with open arms and a smile. *Tukee—he's crazy!*

Then, after about a year, it was over. Tukee's lucrative crack business slowed down. His nightclubbing and largesse took a hit, and he limited his outings to the affordable Dallas BBQ restaurant. "That was the only place I could take girls to," he remembers. "They served these big-ass glasses of margaritas for real cheap. Those shits looked like they came in Cheerio [cereal] bowls, so I could get bitches drunk for real cheap. I'm telling you, B[ro], times were real hard."

Tukee wasn't alone. During the mid-1990s, crack dealing across New York City took a mighty hit. Unbeknownst to dealers, many crack users had reduced their intake because of the drug's stigma and frenetic, binging lifestyle. Also, the new generation of youth shunned crack because they had seen what it did to their family members, neighbors, and friends. Malt liquor beer and marijuana would become their recreational drugs of choice. The crack market shrank, bringing once-successful crack dealers to the lowest of the lows.

Riches and highlife—gone.

To maintain his dealing income, Tukee started transporting crack to Philadelphia, where he established a selling spot with a local. The money was decent, but it wasn't "Donald Trump" money. When he got word that the police were watching him, he returned to the South Bronx dejected and broke.

"I was sellin' all my guns, all my jewelry, everything B[ro], just to stay in the game," Tukee recounts. "I used that money to buy some dope [heroin] and sell that shit."

However, Tukee struggled to find an open dealing spot. The heroin dealers—who funded quasi-armies for protection—demanded a daily "rent" of $1,200 to $2,000 for the right to sell on their block. Tukee could not afford the rent. So he returned to Philadelphia to sell his heroin. No luck. Philly heroin users remained loyal to local brands. Defeated, Tukee again returned to the South Bronx.

Eventually, Tukee joined an auto theft crew that catered to the Crack Era's big-time drug dealers (the same crew that had sold him the stolen car parts for his own ride). But the stolen car business was no longer lucrative—the shrinking crack market lessened its need, too. Tukee hardly earned any money. He was at a loss: "I was like, 'This is it,'" Tukee recalls. "Nothing's workin' out. This is the end of me."

Like Tukee, other displaced drug dealers felt a financial strain because of the crack market's decline. Several of them responded by creating a lucrative new niche in drug robberies. Now they beat, burned, choked, and mutilated their drug-dealing victims. Now they committed horrific acts that they had never done before. Now they were Stickup Kids, the perpetrators of the worst violence in the drug world. Tukee joined their ranks.

A former drug dealing connection contacted Tukee for a drug robbery. They planned to rob a drug dealer for about eight kilos of cocaine and $30,000 in cash. Tukee had never done a drug robbery before, not even a street robbery. But he was handy with a gun. "I didn't even think twice about it," Tukee recalls. "I was like, 'Fuck it. Show me where the money's at.'"

It was an inside job, where a drug dealer *wanted* to get himself and his partner robbed. The dealer, of course, would be absent. But he gave the Stickup crew the best time to storm the stash apartment, where his partner sometimes stayed alone. If all went well, the treacherous dealer would get half the proceeds just for providing the information. The crew would split the other half: $95,000 in drugs and cash.

For the robbery, they brought along "The Girl," a young, attractive female accomplice. "We needed her 'cause we can't just knock on the door and the dude just gonna open," Tukee explained. "He don't know us and he's fuckin' holding drugs. He's gonna be like, 'These motherfuckers are cops or trying to rob my ass.' So we got her to knock on the door and get the door open."

It worked. She knocked. The dealer peeped through the peephole. She smiled and flirted and asked for help. When he opened the door to get a better sense of her needs, the drug robbers, crouched on either side of the door, guns in hand, exploded into action. Tukee's crew rushed the dealer, rammed him back into the apartment, slammed him onto the floor, kicked him, punched him, pistol-whipped him, threatened him to stay down, not to move, or they would stab him, shoot him, would do everything imaginable that would cause his death.

"The shit was crazy, son," Tukee recalls. "I was like watching at first. But then I had to make sure that niggas saw me do shit. Let niggas know that I ain't no slouch. [So] I started kickin' the dude—Bah! Bah! Then we tied him up with duct tape and I put my gun in his head [sic], I was like, 'Where's the shit at! You wanna die, nigga?'"

As Tukee and a partner terrified the dealer, the other two robbers frantically searched the apartment for the drugs and cash. After flipping mattresses, pulling out dresser drawers, and yanking out clothes from a closet, they found it. Everyone scrambled out of the apartment, leaving the dealer bloody, bruised, and bound on the living room floor.

There was no need for torture in this robbery. But the thrill energized Tukee. "I was amped up after that, like for awhile, B. I remember we was counting the money, weighing the drugs, splitting everything, giving this dude this much, me this much, him that much . . . I was like, 'I'm ready to do this again.' Let's go, B!"

According to Tukee, the robbery netted him about $30,000 worth of drugs and cash. This was more than he had earned in a year of stealing cars and selling heroin. So, for him, the violence was worth the money. He wanted to be rich again. Soon, he became a violence expert. He knew how to overcome resistant victims.

"I started doing all types of shit," Tukee explains. "Like I would tie them [the dealers] up and ask them, 'Where the fuck the kilos at?' If they don't tell me, or be like, 'I don't sell drugs. I don't know why you doing this,' then I pistol-whipped them. If they still don't say nothin', I choked them. If they still don't say nothin', then you bring the iron out and burn them. Or you could go to the kitchen and get a kitchen knife, some butcher-type shit, and chop-off one of their fingers. Then those dudes be like, 'Alright, alright, take it! It's over there!'"

Tukee, then, *learned* how to do one-on-one violence—fist-to-face, knife-to-neck, hands-to-throat violence—to someone vulnerable, tied up, who pled for mercy, to please, please leave them alone. Tukee felt he had to. *You gotta do what you gotta do*, he always said. Violence for money would become his way of life. *Tukee*—he's no joke.

◈ Social Context and Violence

Throughout his life, Tukee pursued meaning through the illegal drug market. And his words seem to support an evil and sociopathic understanding of his behavior. Did Tukee enjoy the emotional rush of a drug robbery—yes. Did Tukee enjoy doing violence—yes. But we must also ask: *Why* did he seek thrills as a drug robber rather than as a courtroom lawyer or a Wall Street executive? *Why* did he enjoy physically hurting people as a drug robber rather than as a hockey player, football player, or mixed-martial artist?

The answer lies in the social context, the South Bronx setting in which Tukee's life unfolded. He came of age during the Crack Era, which resulted from misguided drug policies, the decline of manufacturing, and the collapse of inner cities. If we add the daily cultural messages that try to make Americans pursue the ultimate, most gluttonous version of the American Dream, then we see marginal residents who not only used crack to exit poverty, but also to strike it rich. They wanted the material status symbols that Madison Avenue advertising agencies *taught* them to want and need.

Tukee was born into this world, a world not of his own creation, but one that influenced him first into crack dealing, then into drug robberies. If the Crack Era had not appeared, there is a great chance—though not absolute—that Tukee would have become neither a drug dealer nor drug robber. These lucrative criminal opportunities would have been unlikely, less abundant options. So to understand Tukee, we must understand how history and social structure intersects with his biography. Otherwise, the study of poverty-related brutality becomes a distorted enterprise in which Tukee and other marginal criminals are improperly portrayed.

◈ Recommended Resources

Timothy Black. 2009. *When a Heart Turns Rock Solid: The Lives of Three Puerto Rican Brothers on and off the Streets.* New York: Pantheon Books. A long-term ethnography that economically and politically contextualizes the criminal and legal life course of three Puerto Rican brothers in Springfield, Massachusetts.

Philippe Bourgois. 2003 [1995]. *In Search of Respect: Selling Crack in El Barrio.* New York: Cambridge University Press. A theoretically informed ethnography linking the declining manufacturing sector to the everyday lives of Puerto Rican crack dealers in New York City.

Randall Collins. 2008. *Violence: A Micro-sociological Theory.* Princeton, NJ: Princeton University Press. A theoretical examination of the emotional dynamics that produce violence during micro-interactions.

Jack Katz. 1988. *Seductions of Crime: Moral and Sensual Attractions of Doing Evil.* New York: Basic Books. An examination of how emotional thrills and other foreground factors are linked to the commission of crimes.

READING 11

As highlighted in the text, Mestrovic and Lorenzo used Durkheim's ideas on anomie to help explain the abuse at Abu Ghraib. They argue that the dysfunction and disorganization at Abu Ghraib was so great that the breaking of norms and abuse of prisoners was inevitable. The authors reframe, from a sociological perspective, an important

Source: Mestrovic, S. G., & Lorenzo, R. (2008). Durkheim's concept of *anomie* and the abuse at Abu Ghraib. *Journal of Classical Sociology, 8*(2), 179–207. Reprinted with permission.

government report documenting the abuse at Abu Ghraib. They highlight the following conditions leading to ano-mie and abuse: confusion as to who was in charge, insufficient training, lack of social integration within the military units at Abu Ghraib, rapid changes in the social milieu, intense pressure to obtain intelligence, cultural insensitivity, and confusion as to which norms to follow. The conclusion is especially interesting as the authors argue that the courts-martial at Fort Hood, Texas, were meant to bring justice to the abusees and restore the collective conscience. They further argue that this did not happen. Rather, a few "bad apples" were punished, which may not be nearly enough to "make things right" for those directly involved or for the worldwide audience. We think this piece is both useful and interesting for students, teachers, and researchers. It offers a vivid example of how "classic" sociological theories and ideas can still be used today to gain new insight into current examples of deviant behavior.

Durkheim's Concept of Anomie and the Abuse at Abu Ghraib

Stjepan G. Mestrovic and Ronald Lorenzo

The overall conclusion reached by the various US government reports on the abuse committed at Abu Ghraib prison in Iraq is that abuse did in fact occur; that no direct orders to commit the abuse were issued by officials high in the chain of command; and that some personnel low in the chain of command should be prosecuted for some of the abuse (Mestrovic, 2007; Strasser, 2004). These same reports also expose evidence of high levels of social disorganization and what sociologists call *anomie* at Abu Ghraib and within the social structure of the US Army and of other govern-ment agencies (OGA), among civilian contractors, and among others who were involved with policing, inter-rogating, and incarcerating prisoners at Abu Ghraib as well as in Afghanistan, Guantánamo, and elsewhere in Iraq. The occurrence of social disorganization and *ano-mie* ranges from the most microscopic level of analy-sis (such as the unauthorized merging of the roles of Military Intelligence and Military Police at Abu Ghraib, which led to the policy that MPs 'softened up' prison-ers for MI) through mid-levels of analysis (such as the question of who was the executive officer in charge at Abu Ghraib) to macro-levels of analysis (such as which interrogation procedures were approved by the US Army and the Department of Defense at which period of time and in which theater of action, as well as the ques-tion whether the Geneva Conventions apply in whole

or in part or in what specific aspect, and also what is the significance of the denial of findings contained in International Committee of the Red Cross reports).

Sociological theory and research holds that social disorganization and *anomie* inevitably cause what sociologists call deviance or the breaking of social norms. However, the government reports use meta-phors such as 'poisoned climate,' rather than the word *anomie*, to describe the social setting at Abu Ghraib. The authors of these reports prefer the word 'abuse' to the sociological concept of 'deviance.' The military judge allowed an expert witness in sociology to use and explain the concept '*anomie*' in open court during testimony at three of the courts-martial pertaining to Abu Ghraib that were held at Fort Hood, Texas, in 2005.[1] However, what appears to be a straightforward sociological representation of the chaotic social set-ting leading to abuse at Abu Ghraib as an anomic one actually involves intricate and complex interpretation. It raises questions for sociological theory that have been dormant for decades, including but not limited to the following: Is *anomie* a condition of *dérèglement*, as Durkheim taught, or is it a condition of 'normless-ness,' as conceptualized by structural functionalists and repeated in hundreds of textbooks? Is anomie primarily a 'deranged' state of disorganization involv-ing lack of coordination and other variations of social chaos that sets the stage for violence and abuse, as taught by Durkheim, or is it a 'normless' condition, as taught by the functionalists? One's assumptions in replying to these and related questions will have a profound impact on how one understands what caused the abuse and how one approaches the task of repairing the damage to social structure caused by abuse at Abu Ghraib and elsewhere. If Durkheim is correct, then the US Army needs to be put into a collective therapy of sorts, along the lines of the remedies that he proposed for healing the evil consequences of *anomie* (Durkheim, 1933 [1893], 1951 [1897], 1983b [1950]). These remedies include establishing fixed normative referents, promoting social integration, and ensuring that existing norms are coordinated, incorporated into policies, and function properly. If the functionalists are correct, then any working 'normative' solution is adequate to the task of restoring social order, even if the norms in question are out of sync with, say, the norms of the international community, such as the Geneva Conventions. In fact, functionalists assume that social systems self-correct automatically when it comes to fixing anomie: 'social life has a tendency to be and to remain a functionally integrated phenomenon' (Theodorson and Theodorson, 1969: 133).

These issues are important and have long-lasting consequences. As of this writing, strict adherence to the Geneva Conventions is *not* part of the discourse for fixing the damage to social relations caused by the abuse at Abu Ghraib. Instead, the US government has chosen to rely on the Army Field Manual as its standard, with the caveat that it can be changed at any time (and has been changed several times in the past six years). According to the Bush Administration, the Geneva Conventions did not and do not apply against Al-Qaida, but did and do apply in the war in Iraq (Danner, 2004). Yet policies from Guantánamo—where the Geneva Conventions were ruled to be irrelevant—were transferred to Abu Ghraib—where the Geneva Conventions were supposed to apply (see Falk et al., 2006). A Durkheimian sociological analysis would apprehend this 'migration' of unlawful policies and contexts as itself a confusing, chaotic, and *anomie*-producing process. Moreover, as the war in Iraq continues to be re-conceptualized as part of a global war against terror, the importance of the Geneva Conventions as an example of firm moral boundaries in the

Durkheimian sense is diminishing. New 'norms' relating to torture and warfare are being created, causing moral confusion among lawyers, officers, soldiers, and everyone else involved in this discourse.

For many decades, sociological theory pertaining to *anomie* and its relationship to deviance has been used by criminologists to study ordinary crime, but not war crimes, torture, and abuse. This vacuum in sociological theorizing has been filled by Philip Zimbardo, who draws upon the obedience-to-authority paradigm in social psychology. Zimbardo (2007) claims that his famous Stanford Prison Experiment explains the abuse at Abu Ghraib on the basis of 'good' people turning 'evil' as the result of 'situational' factors. Space does not permit a full analysis of *anomie* theory (further distinguishable into Durkheimian and functionalist versions) versus the obedience-to-authority paradigm in Zimbardo's book. Suffice it to say that facts and reports concerning Abu Ghraib suggest the opposite of what Zimbardo intends: an egregious lack of authority and leadership at Abu Ghraib seems to have been responsible for the abuse that ensued. Against Zimbardo's position, Durkheim's assumption seems to be that ordinary people (who exhibit a mixture of 'good' and 'bad' traits depending in part upon society's definitions) at Abu Ghraib behaved in ways that some—but not all—aspects of society label as 'evil.' Our purpose here is to clarify, deepen, and apply a genuinely sociological theory of *anomie* to the issue at hand.

Conceptualizing the Problem

The factual evidence for the presence of extreme social disorganization and *anomie* comes from the US government reports pertaining to Abu Ghraib as well as testimony from the courts-martial—described meticulously by Mestrovic (2007) based upon eyewitness accounts of the trials as well as participation in three of them as an expert witness in sociology—and includes, but is not limited to, the following:

- a systemic lack of accountability;

- a disorganized filing system;

- the fact that other government agencies (OGA), including the CIA, operated outside established rules and procedures established by the Army Field Manual as well as the Geneva Conventions;

- the fact that nobody was certain who was in charge of Abu Ghraib;

- overcrowding; a dysfunctional system for releasing prisoners;

- failure to screen detainees at the point that they were arrested as well as the point that they were brought to Abu Ghraib;

- the lack of screening for civilian contractors;

- the introduction of new elements (but not entire units) into the personnel structure (a process that the Army calls cross-leveling);

- failure to adequately train MPs and MIs in policing as well as in interrogation procedures;

- the fact that MPs did not know what they or MIs were not allowed to do;

- lack of military discipline;

- intense pressure to obtain information from a population of prisoners that was not capable of providing the desired information;

- lack of training; lack of familiarity with the Geneva Conventions; the fact that the US military upheld the Geneva Conventions while various attorneys for the White House opined that the Geneva Conventions did not wholly apply to the treatment of prisoners;

- poor paperwork procedures; and

- poor reporting procedures.

These facts, along with a host of others, suggest extreme social chaos. For example, the supply officer at Abu Ghraib, Major David DiNenna, testified that he begged the Army for adequate water, food, toilets, light bulbs, and generators, and that his pleas fell on deaf ears. He testified in open court that he felt 'abandoned' by the Army at Abu Ghraib (Mestrovic, 2007: 107).

The above findings of fact constitute evidence of egregious social disorganization, dysfunction, and anomie, which sets the stage for deviance. The term '*anomie*' was coined by Émile Durkheim in *The Division of Labor in Society* (1933 [1893]) and in *Suicide* (1951 [1897]). Durkheim refers specifically to *dérèglement* as the synonym for *anomie*: 'l'état de dérèglement ou d'anomie' (1983a [1897]: 287). *Anomie* is depicted by Durkheim as a general societal condition of *dérèglement* or derangement—literally, 'a rule that is a lack of rule' (1951 [1897]: 257), or in the original French: 'consciences déréglées et qui érigent en règle le dérèglement dont elles souffrent' (1983a [1897]: 287). Jean-Marie Guyau preceded Durkheim in using this concept in 1885: 'C'est l'absence de loi fixe, qu'on peut désigner sous le terme d'anomie' (1907 [1885]: 165). Note that Guyau referred to the lack of 'fixed' moral boundaries, but not a lack of laws or norms per se. French dictionaries such as the *Littré* refer to *dérèglement* as a state of corruption, evil, agitation, torment, impiety, and intemperance which leads to general suffering and torment.[2] All these terms can be applied to the social conditions at Abu Ghraib as revealed in testimony and reports, and are in line with Durkheim's general assumptions about *anomie*: that it is a disorganized social condition that leads to suffering and distress (see Mestrovic, 1988; Mestrovic and Brown, 1985; Orru, 1987). Durkheim treats *anomie* as acute and temporary as well as chronic and long-lasting. In *Suicide*, he also addresses several varieties of *anomie*, among them conjugal, marital, religious, political, military, and intellectual, pertaining to various social institutions. Durkheim's scaffolding for understanding *anomie* includes: Arthur Schopenhauer's philosophy, in which the imperious 'will' is unrestrained by rational categories or 'representations'; theological understandings of *anomia* as sin (Lyonnet and Sabourin, 1970); and the ideas of various other European philosophers (Mestrovic, 1985).

Durkheim's perspective was modified and changed considerably in its interpretation by the most influential American sociologist of the twentieth century, Talcott Parsons (1937). Parsons established what has come to be known as the Harvard School of Sociology, and elaborated *anomie* in relation to the Hobbesian meaning of 'the war of all against all' (Parsons, 1937: 407). His most famous disciple was Robert K. Merton, whose 'Social Structure and *Anomie*' (1957) became the most cited article in sociology. According to Merton: 'as initially developed by Durkheim, the concept of *anomie* referred to a condition of relative normlessness in a society or group' (1957: 161). Merton established that *anomie* will lead to crime and other forms of deviance when society—at any level of analysis, from the macrosociological to the microsociological—establishes agreed-upon *goals* but fails to provide for agreed-upon *means* for achieving those goals. Merton's theory has been applied in numerous studies of crime and deviance—but not to the phenomena of war crimes, torture, and abuse. At first glance, it seems to fit some aspects of the social state of affairs at Abu Ghraib that emerges from the US government reports: intense pressure was put on the military personnel at Abu Ghraib to reach the *goal* of obtaining information from prisoners, but the *means* for obtaining this information were unlawful, or, in Merton's words, 'innovative.' According to Merton's paradigm, this systemic discrepancy between socially approved goals and means is, by itself, sufficient to cause many sorts of deviance (the breaking of social norms), including, but not limited to, the type of abuse that has been documented at Abu Ghraib.

But is a Parsonian, or a Mertonian, conceptualization of the problem adequate? The government reports, as well as testimony at the courts-martial pertaining to Abu Ghraib at Fort Hood, Texas, show that abuse was not limited to seemingly rational interrogation techniques that involved goals and means. Some abuse occurred *ad hoc* in showers, hallways, stairwells, and other places not used for interrogation; some abuse was committed for sport and amusement, not for any official purpose at all; and most prisoners did not have the information the Army sought. Thus, the rationality of the goals in the goals–means equation can be called into question. The prosecutor at the courts-martial revealed in open court that 100 percent of the abused prisoners were not a threat to Americans and had no information to give them (Mestrovic, 2007: 11). In fact, it is highly irrational, chaotic, and 'deranged' to use torture for the sake of obtaining information on prisoners who had no information to give. Even if the soldiers who abused the prisoners did not always know that their victims did not have information to give them, the more important Durkheimian point is that there were

no established social mechanisms in place for ascertaining this important fact (for example, no screening, no judicial review boards, no assumption that prisoners were innocent until proven guilty, no implementation of the Geneva Conventions on processing and treating prisoners, and so on). As for the means, the reports, as well as testimony, suggest that nobody could discern whether the rational-legal authority for the approved techniques is to be found in the Army Field Manual, various memorandums, or the Geneva Conventions, none of which are consistent with each other.

From a Durkheimian point of view, the state of *anomie* and social chaos documented at Abu Ghraib was all-pervasive and fundamentally irrational in that it clouded soldiers' judgments concerning what constituted acceptable versus unacceptable thought, emotion, and behavior. Evidence for such a point of view is to be found in the numerous references to 'confusion' found in the reports and disclosed in testimony at the courts-martial (Danner, 2004; Mestrovic, 2007; Strasser, 2004). Soldiers could not discern the difference between normative versus abusive situations. For example, the Company Commander, Captain (CPT) Donald Reese, testified that when he inquired as to why prisoners were forced to wear women's panties on their heads, he was told by his superiors that it was 'a supply issue' or 'an MI thing.' There was no established social system in place to validate his concerns, and the same was true for scores of other whistleblowers at Abu Ghraib, who were routinely invalidated and in some cases threatened (Mestrovic, 2007). The new issues that are raised by this Durkheimian reading include, but are not limited to, the following: Who was responsible for causing, allowing, and failing to ameliorate the state of *anomie* or dysfunctional social organization at Abu Ghraib? What are the different levels of responsibility—sociologically speaking—for the abuse that occurred vis-à-vis the chain of command? Doctors, medics, lawyers, supply officers, and other professionals at Abu Ghraib were all responsible for limited and specific aspects of the division of labor, which was dysfunctional overall. In *Professional Ethics and Civic Morals*, Durkheim (1983b [1950]) suggests that the professional groups who govern the conduct of such individual professionals are ultimately responsible for the outcome. In the present case, this would mean that the American Medical

Association, the American Bar Association, and other professional groups share some of the responsibility for the abuse. Even if orders for the abuse were not given from positions high in the chain of command, why were the social conditions that led to the abuse not corrected? A Parsonian-inspired reply to the effect that officers could wait for or could trust in the system to self-correct seems inadequate.

The US government reports thus document not only abuse but also high levels of social disorganization and *anomie* at Abu Ghraib—but these reports lay the primary blame for specifically sexual and violent abuse on a 'few bad apples' (morally corrupt individuals) and neglect the question of blame for the state of social chaos that led to the abuse. Furthermore, these same reports document a systemic state of chaos in command, procedure, organization, and societal structure *vis-à-vis* the detainment and interrogation of prisoners at Guantánamo, in Afghanistan, and in Iraq. Logically, one is forced to draw the conclusion that a large segment of the 'apple orchard' was contaminated. It is important to determine the different levels of responsibility (international, national, local), sociologically speaking, not only for the abuse but also for the chaotic state of affairs that led to the abuse. A functionalist perspective might assume that social systems are self-correcting—but the dysfunctional military society at Abu Ghraib did not self-correct. In the words of CPT Jonathan Crisp, defense counsel for Lynndie England, the dysfunctional social system not only failed to self-correct, 'but was self-perpetuating' (Mestrovic, 2007: 175). Durkheim, however, assumes that *anomie* becomes chronic until self-conscious and deliberate remedies are sought from outside the dysfunctional system.

In general, functionalists who follow in the footsteps of Parsons and Merton tend to assume that society is a stable, self-maintaining, and self-correcting system made up of norms, values, beliefs, and sanctions.[3] All of these assumptions can be questioned with regard to the reality of abuse at Abu Ghraib. The functionalists typically do not address problems in synchronizing international with local dimensions of such units of analysis. In other words, there exist several layers of norms (international, national, local, and other finer distinctions), and the same holds true for the other system components (values, beliefs, and sanctions). But in the case of

Abu Ghraib, the international norms (exemplified by the Geneva Conventions) were sometimes out of sync with national norms (based upon the US Constitution as well as US Army field manuals) as well as local norms (memorandums and competing interpretations of permissible interrogation methods). US values concerning the importance of democracy, due process, and human rights were out of sync with the dehumanizing atmosphere established at Abu Ghraib. The collective belief that Americans were liberators was out of sync with the belief that Americans acted like tormentors at Abu Ghraib. The sanctions exemplified by courts-martial of low-ranking soldiers are out of sync with sanctions for 'grave breaches' of the Geneva Conventions which call for the prosecution of high-ranking leaders, or what is referred to as the doctrine of command responsibility (see Human Rights Watch, 2006).

The important point is that even though the doctrine of command responsibility exists as an international norm, and has been incorporated into the Uniform Code of Military Justice (UCMJ), it was dysfunctional at Abu Ghraib. It has been and continues to be applied at the tribunals at the Hague to punish high-ranking civilian as well as military officials, but has not been applied at the courts-martial at Fort Hood, where most of the blame for the abuse has been heaped onto low-ranking soldiers. Again, the problem seems to lie not in a lack of norms and moral boundaries, but in a lack of coordination, in confusion, and in dysfunction in implementing such norms and boundaries. From a Durkheimian perspective, all these factors and more constitute a widespread collective condition of *dérèglement*.

◈ **Cultural Frames of Reference**

An important development in social theory since Durkheim and Parsons has been the introduction of a variety of cultural perspectives. Every culture relies upon a frame of reference that is used to apprehend events ranging from natural disasters to wars and acceptable modes of leisure (see Cushman and Mestrovic, 1995; Goffman, 1986). Like a picture frame, a cultural frame excludes elements from discourse at the same time that it includes other elements. And some of these elements are contradictory. In part because of publicity given to the Abu Ghraib abuses, the image of the United States, too, has been framed by some members of the international community as the country that 'liberated' Iraq *and* as the country that became Iraq's brutal 'occupier.' The notorious prison that Saddam Hussein used to inflict torture, Abu Ghraib, served as a symbol of Arab oppression for Americans who framed themselves as liberators, but later became a symbol of American abuse and torture. One could multiply these and similar examples of how the popular consciousness changes the focus and frame of reference for perceiving events and their significance.

Sociological theory itself is not immune to the effects of cultural framing. There is no doubt that Durkheim's discussions of *anomie* are framed in a European context while Parsonian approaches are framed in an American context. Durkheim assumes a pessimism concerning human nature that is found in European cultural traditions. Parsons assumes a sunny-side-up American optimism. Perhaps it is significant that Durkheim comes from a cultural background including descent from several generations of German rabbis, and was a French Jew living in a deeply anti-Semitic France at the time. On the other hand, Parsons was the son of a Congregationalist minister whose writings bespeak the Puritan 'habits of the heart' described by Alexis de Tocqueville (2004 [1848])—specifically, Parsons seems to imply the doctrine of American exceptionalism (see Lipset, 1997). Durkheim was personally involved in the defense of Captain Alfred Dreyfus, a French Jewish officer from the German Alsace region (where Durkheim was also born) wrongly convicted of treason (see Lukes, 1985). Given these and other cultural and contextual differences between the USA and Europe, Parsons and Durkheim, it would not be surprising that Durkheim's and Parsons's understandings of *anomie* would differ despite overall similarities (Mestrovic, 1988). Writings such as Seymour Martin Lipset's *Continental Divide* (1990), which point to cultural differences that persist even between the United States and Canada, for example, serve to demystify some of the assumptions in functionalism which seem to reflect Protestant, American values from the 1930s. Perhaps because of these cultural differences, the European scholar André Lalande defines

anomie as 'absence d'organisation, de coordination' (1980 [1926]: 61) and refers to Durkheim, while the American writers Theodorson and Theodorson define it as 'a condition characterized by the relative absence or confusion of values in a society or group' (1969: 12) and refer to Parsons and Merton.

James Loewen's book *Lies My Teacher Told Me: Everything Your American History Textbook Got Wrong* (2007) exposes how facts about American history change in meaning when one questions one's assumptions and frames of reference in approaching these facts. We are approaching the meanings of *anomie* in a similar way, with the implied subtext: 'Lies My Social Theory Teacher Told Me: What Your Social Theory Textbooks Got Wrong Regarding *Anomie*.' While it is beyond the scope of this essay to review the many criticisms of Parsons and structural functionalism extant in the literature, the most important point, for this discussion, is that the Parsonian–Mertonian misinterpretation of *anomie* as 'normlessness' remains unseen and unchallenged.[4]

The conceptualization of cultural frames of reference also becomes significant when the sociologist addresses issues pertaining to law, crime, and justice. How and why do societies frame some acts as crimes in general and crimes of war in particular, yet exclude other similar acts from such frames of reference? How do societies distinguish between just laws and punishments versus inhumane punishment? How does the collective consciousness frame international war crimes tribunals as just versus 'victor's justice,' or as scapegoating? The concept of 'war crime' was not formally and legally conceptualized until the twentieth century and especially the end of World War II (Solis, 1998). Although massacres and mass killings are to be found throughout history, it is only in the post-Nuremberg era that genocide, persecution, and other war crimes came to be defined and distinguished from other crimes per se (Gutman and Rieff, 1999). The central focus of the relatively new conceptual frame regarding war crimes is that these sorts of crimes are typically depicted as being intentional, rational, planned from the top of a hierarchical organization, and widespread (Bauman, 1990). War crimes imply the existence of an organized bureaucracy and well-developed, modernist, state functions. This collective, cognitive shift—the ability to conceive of war crimes in a frame of reference that goes beyond the old adage that all wars are brutal—involves a fundamental ambiguity or ambivalence from the outset in conceptualizing war crimes as well as crimes committed during wars. It involves the forced conjunction of radically 'split' categories: that which is regarded highly (the many manifestations of modernism embodied in bureaucracy and the idea of the chain of command) and what is despicable (the passion and chaos of crime). The idea of a war crime conjoins numerous cultural refractions of highly idealized 'grand narratives of the Enlightenment' (Lyotard, 1984) with numerous cultural refractions of passionately devalued notions of crime. The inherent contradiction in depicting war crimes as intentional, rational, planned, and widespread is that modern, Western societies value highly the notions of agency, rationality, planning, and organization. Part of the shock of the Holocaust remains the fact that genocide was carried out in a cold, calculated, organized and almost business-like manner. It is as if the West's most esteemed virtues came to be twisted into the most hated vices. Additionally, contemporary Western societies seem to insist that international war crimes must be distinguished, conceptually, from crimes that are spontaneous and limited in scope, which is to say, distinguished from ordinary crimes of passion committed by a few corrupt individuals.

Nevertheless, it seems to be the case that regardless of how logically academics and jurists conceptualize war crimes in theory, an event or set of events comes to be regarded as criminal only when these events offend what Durkheim (1933 [1893]) called the collective consciousness. The so-called 'world community' responded in widely divergent ways to war crimes in the former Yugoslavia, Rwanda, Cambodia, Sierra Leone, and Abu Ghraib, among other sites. Reactions of the collective consciousness are emotional, unplanned, unscripted, and even disorganized—in Durkheim's (1995 [1912]) view, this is because they are based upon a spontaneous 'collective effervescence.' To be offended is to give in to passion. When one is discussing international war crimes, one needs to analyze which collective consciousness is offended, by which aspects of a given situation, at what time, and why. One also needs to ascertain whether a true, global, international collective consciousness exists or can exist. Can the international

community maintain a consistent frame of reference with respect to war crimes?

Durkheim pronounced in 1893 that an act—no matter how heinous—that is not punished by the collective consciousness is not a crime. Conversely, a punitive reaction by a collective consciousness transforms an event into a crime. Durkheim's counter-intuitive assessment has withstood the test of time and of rigorous research pertaining to crimes committed by individuals. A crime is that which offends the collective conscience in a strong and consistent manner, but not all acts that some people might deem criminal or immoral will necessarily offend a particular collective conscience in a specific cultural setting. In Durkheim's words, 'an act is criminal when it offends strong and defined states of the collective consciousness' (1933 [1893]: 80). And he elaborates:

> In other words, we must not say that an action shocks the common conscience because it is criminal, but rather that it is criminal because it shocks the common conscience. We do not reprove it because it is a crime, but it is a crime because we reprove it. (1933 [1893]: 81)

It seems that one could extend Durkheim's understanding of crime *vis-à-vis* a particular collective conscience to instances of *anomie vis-à-vis* an international collective conscience. We must not say that collective abuse shocks the international community because it is criminal, but rather that it is an international war crime because it shocks the international collective conscience. We do not reprove it because it is anomic, but it is anomic because the world reproves it. To put it another way, cultures vary greatly in their responses to collective abuse, ranging from the acts of the Pol Pot regime and various forces in the Balkans to the perpetrators of the Holocaust. The fact that the international community will respond to certain events and thereby transform them into crime is universal, but the acts which provoke this strong reaction are not universal. Yet the very concept of international war crimes seems to presuppose a universal standard for what is deemed criminal. In fact, as already noted, the world community responds in a politicized and inconsistent manner to war crimes—as defined by the Geneva Conventions—depending upon various factors and cultural frames of reference. For various reasons, a critical mass of the international community responded with passionate revulsion to the war crimes in Yugoslavia and Rwanda sufficient to establish international tribunals. Yet other sites of apparent international war crime failed to offend the international community's collective conscience strongly enough for it to react punitively, including the abuses at Abu Ghraib, in Afghanistan, and at Guantánamo. In general, Durkheim's insight regarding crime and its relationship to a collective conscience has not been extended into the domain of crimes committed upon an international stage, which range from acts labeled as war crimes to terrorism. But without the scaffolding of his sociological theory, the conceptualization of international war crimes can be reduced easily to explanations of vengeance, 'victor's justice,' scapegoating, and particularized politics (coercing some nation-states to hand over alleged war criminals to an international tribunal, while looking the other way for other nation-states).

The new millennium has raised the concept of international war crime to a much higher level of public consciousness than at any other time since World War II. However, the cultural frame of reference pertaining to the law that is being applied at Abu Ghraib constitutes a significant departure from the ways that crimes of war have been conceptualized since the Nuremberg era. If Zygmunt Bauman (1990) and others are correct that war crimes in general and genocide in particular are modernist phenomena (in that they necessarily involve rational planning, systematic procedures, and a chain of command with top-down hierarchy), then how can one conceptualize or prosecute crimes of war that are conceptualized primarily as irrational, chaotic, unsystematic, and as perpetrated by individuals who operate outside the chain of command? In other words, how does society understand a war crime as being *anomic* or disorganized and chaotic? This seems to constitute a gaping conceptual hole in sociological theory as well as in international law pertaining to war crimes.

In general, the law does not assume, as some other cultural institutions—for example, some religions—do, that everyone is a sinner, and that everyone deserves forgiveness. The law, as depicted by Durkheim, condemns the criminal and punishes him or her in the name of upholding social order and in the name of the 'sacred' and highly idealized symbolic status of the rest of society. Durkheim asserted that modern societies put more emphasis on restitution and less emphasis on extreme punishment (mutilation, torture, the death penalty, and so on) than do traditional societies, but in all human societies at every phase of development, the function of the law is to preserve the integrity of the group at the expense of the criminal, namely, he or she who dares to put him- or herself above the law. Foucault (1977) argued against Durkheim that in the punitive exercise of sovereignty, criminals were punished not because they had offended the collective conscience but because they had offended a particular 'sovereign' or symbolically charged political figure.[5] This divergence between Durkheim and Foucault on the role of society in punishment needs to be extended to the international stage and the concept of war crimes. How should the international community respond when a nation-state behaves as if it were above international law? Who or what is 'the sovereign' when it comes to 'the sovereignty of nations'?

In practice, at the Hague, contemporary international law has found culpable leaders in the chain of command who may not have pulled the trigger, who may not have known that crimes were committed low in the chain of command and who did not order crimes and abuse, but who laid out a policy that led to abuse and crime or who failed to prevent criminal and abusive acts (Hazan, 2004). Moreover, in all of the cases where the defendant was found guilty by the Tribunals for Yugoslavia and Rwanda, the Tribunal's judgments asserted that none of the guilty parties necessarily had to be 'an architect or the prime mover' of the established persecution in order to be deemed guilty of war crimes. Instead, the precedent established by the Tribunals is that the guilty war criminal could have known or *should* have known, and therefore prevented, the criminal actions of subordinates. The Tribunal's precedents have been reversed at the courts-martial pertaining to Abu Ghraib: the United States military chose to prosecute primarily low-ranking soldiers and not to prosecute officers high in the chain of command, in addition to accepting the excuse offered by many officers that they did not know about the abuse, without raising the issue that they should have known (see Karpinski, 2005).

In general, jurists and lawyers do not display what C. Wright Mills (1959) called the 'sociological imagination,' by which he meant grasping the interplay between a particular 'biography' and 'history.' For the most part, they act out their social roles without reflecting on the meaning of those roles and its attendant vocabulary. The commonly used legal terms 'widespread,' 'systematic,' 'planned,' 'command responsibility,' 'chain of command,' 'rational,' and other elements of judicial vocabulary are essential to lawyers who engage each other in verbal battle in various courtrooms that involve crimes of war, because without these concepts, given acts could not rise to the level of being framed as war crimes. Yet the 'biographies' of seven particular soldiers whom the government labeled as 'rotten apples' has been imperfectly linked to the sociological 'history' of the abuse at Abu Ghraib, which is connected to abuse at Guantánamo and elsewhere. Thus, opinion-makers, journalists, and some organizations such as the International Committee of the Red Cross (ICRC) and Amnesty International have noted that some acts committed by American soldiers and political leaders in both Gulf Wars qualify as war crimes, especially with regard to the abuse and torture inflicted upon prisoners in Abu Ghraib, Guantánamo Bay, and other American-run prisons around the world (Danner, 2004). But no one engaged in these discussions of alleged war crimes committed by Americans, or other Westerners such as Britons, seriously believes that an American or a Briton will be put on trial for war crimes at the Hague in the near future. Instead, the United States has put forth the argument that it will monitor and try American military lawbreakers under its Uniform Code of Military Justice (UCMJ). More significantly, some journalists as well as human rights groups claim to have uncovered evidence that leaders high in the 'chain of command' either knew or should have known and should have taken steps to prevent alleged abuses and war crimes committed by US troops in Iraq (Danner, 2004; Hersh, 2004). The ICRC, in particular, has labeled the abuses at Abu Ghraib as 'routine,' hence systematic, not as isolated incidents. A plethora of US government reports on abuses committed by American soldiers arrived at the general conclusion that abuse occurred, but offered competing and contradictory interpretations regarding who knew or ordered what sort of abuse or torture in the chain of command (Strasser, 2004). The discourse on this explosive subject avoids completely the subject of putting on trial Americans who are high in the chain of command and who should have known and should have taken steps to prevent the abuse even if they did not order it.

Thus, the sociologist must take seriously the general criticism leveled by postmodernists such as Baudrillard (1986) and other cultural theorists that Western institutions are self-privileging and regard themselves as exceptional in the world community; that: (1) the West in general and the United States in particular derive their cultural frame of reference from a specific cultural base, namely, Western Europe; (2) this Western European and American cultural base is depicted in terms of the grand narratives of the Enlightenment, which is considered unique to the West; and (3) the West is reluctant to apply this frame of reference to itself with regard to war crimes yet does sometimes apply it to cultural sites and actors which are labeled as non-Western. Put together, these assumptions seem to be part of what Lipset (1997) and others call American exceptionalism. Specifically, officials high in the chain of command in Yugoslavia and Rwanda were prosecuted and many were found guilty of war crimes even though several may not have known of and did not order crimes or abuse or other breaches of the Geneva Conventions. On the other hand, the Abu Ghraib torture scandal has been framed by the US government as a set of events that involved a small group of disorganized and unprofessional soldiers who were labeled as morally corrupt. The dominant frame of reference in the United States, namely, American exceptionalism, cannot tolerate the cognitive dissonance that an American (as the idealized representative of highly superior values) could engage in seemingly Balkan acts unless he or she was acting outside the American frame of reference. At the same time, some journalists in the information media and some organizations such as Human Rights Watch (2006) frame the abuses at Abu Ghraib as a set of events that flowed from a general 'climate' of disregard for the Geneva Conventions that was established at the highest levels of the United States military and political chain of command and that trickled down to the soldiers on the ground. The perspective taken in the present study supposes that it is a matter not of choosing between top-down versus bottom-up explanations, but of integrating both perspectives and finding a middle ground between them. Specifically, soldiers low in the chain of command clearly committed abuses, but officers high in the chain of command should have known and should have taken steps to prevent the abuse.

It is likely that the abuse at Abu Ghraib was not the result of direct orders that came top-down from high in the chain of command. But it is also unlikely that the abuse at Abu Ghraib was solely the result of a handful of unprofessional soldiers at the bottom of the chain of command. The most complete explanation must involve some middle-level explanation that includes elements of both the top-down and bottom-up explanations. In Major General (MG) Fay's words, an 'unhealthy mystique' developed at Abu Ghraib (Strasser, 2004: 53). Who is responsible for creating the unhealthy mystique? What effect did it have on the soldiers at Abu Ghraib? One can rephrase these questions in a sociological vocabulary: How did *anomie* develop at Abu Ghraib? What were its consequences for the soldiers as well as the relationship between the United States and the rest of the world? And how can it be remedied?

◈ A Socio-cultural Analysis of MG George R. Fay's Report

The most comprehensive US government report on the abuse at Abu Ghraib was written by MG Fay and is referred to as the Fay report.[6] In the remainder of this paper, we shall re-read portions of his report in a sociological and specifically Durkheimian context, with a particular focus on the relationship between 'confusion' and what Durkheim calls *anomie*. MG Fay writes:

This investigation found that certain individuals committed offenses in violation of international and US law to include the Geneva Conventions and the UCMJ and violated Army Values. Leaders in key positions *failed properly to supervise the interrogation operations at Abu Ghraib* and failed to understand *the dynamics created at Abu Ghraib*. (p. 7, emphasis added)

Note that several layers of normative structure are invoked (international, national, and local), and that MG Fay is treating Abu Ghraib as a social system, although he does not use this sociological term explicitly. MG Fay continues:

The *environment* created at Abu Ghraib contributed to the occurrence of such abuse and the fact that it remained undiscovered by higher authority for a long period of time. What started as nakedness and humiliation . . . carried over into sexual and physical assaults by a *small group of morally corrupt and unsupervised Soldiers and civilians.* (pp. 9–10, emphasis added)

Throughout his report, MG Fay makes the quasi-sociological and basically correct connection between the social 'environment' and abuse. Although he does not say it explicitly, he is clearly not writing about the environment and atmosphere as phenomena pertaining to meteorology. He is using these terms to refer to 'social environment' as a system of norms, values, sanctions, and beliefs, although he does not use this sociological vocabulary explicitly. First, he makes it clear that the sexual and physical abuse was part of the overall 'poisoned' or anomic atmosphere at Abu Ghraib. Second, he makes it clear that the sexual and physical abuse was part of an overall pattern of normative breakdown that includes other forms of abuse, including unauthorized use of dogs, the improper use of isolation, and humiliating and degrading forms of treatment. Third, he fails to explain how and why the social system at Abu Ghraib would have permitted morally corrupt individuals to perform acts of deviance or failed to properly sanction them after the initial acts of deviance. As stated at the outset, Parsons assumed that a healthy social system would correct itself, while Durkheim would have claimed that an unhealthy or anomic social system becomes increasingly anomic unless it is self-consciously corrected. Fourth, and finally, morally corrupt individuals (for example, persons who can be identified as sadists, perverts, or otherwise severely disturbed through psychological testing) exist in all social settings, but this does not mean that they are able to easily impose their deviant fantasies and behavior onto others. Under normal conditions, a healthy social system will keep morally corrupt individuals under control through a system of norms, values, sanctions, and beliefs (as postulated by Parsons) that regulates everyone, from the healthiest individuals to the most corrupt.

Before launching into an extended discussion of MG Fay's report, it is worth examining the sequence of logical steps he uses to arrive at his conclusion. On p. 71, he writes, regarding physical and sexual abuse at Abu Ghraib: 'They were perpetrated or witnessed by individuals or small groups.' Acts can only be perpetrated by individuals, acting alone or in small groups, but such individuals are always acting in the context of some social system. He continues: 'Such abuse can not be directly tied to a systemic US approach to torture or approved treatment of detainees' (p. 71). In this sentence, MG Fay leaps to the national level of normative discourse (the norms of the United States) and leaves open the possibility that the abuse might be *indirectly* tied to such a national level of norms. However, one should also note that MG Fay leaves out other logical possibilities, which he, in fact, supports with evidence in his report, namely that such abuse can be directly linked to a systemic approach at Abu Ghraib; that such abuse can be indirectly linked to a systemic approach at Abu Ghraib; that such direct as well as indirect links at Abu Ghraib are themselves linked in some fashion, through the chain of command, to national systems of norms, and to international systems of norms *vis-à-vis* the ICRC and information media coverage. By implication, MG Fay seems to take the position that there was a social environment or climate at Abu Ghraib for the very types of abuse (sexual and physical) that he attributes to morally corrupt individuals, as when he writes elsewhere in this same passage: 'The *climate* created at Abu Ghraib provided the opportunity for such abuse to occur and to continue undiscovered by higher authority for a *long period of time*' (p. 71, emphasis added). This claim begs the question: What was the state of dialogue between US Army and other US national organizations and the local 'climate' at Abu Ghraib? MG Fay leaves this question unanswered. He then makes the critical logical leap: 'What started as undressing and humiliation, stress and physical training (PT), *carried over* into sexual and physical assaults by a small group of morally corrupt and unsupervised Soldiers and civilians' (p. 71, emphasis added). Again, the sociologist must ask the question: How and

why did the unauthorized undressing and humiliation begin in the first place? What defect in the social system led to the initial breach of norms (primary deviance), and how did these breaches 'carry over' into systemic breaches of norms (secondary deviance)? This is the crux of the issue that needs to be explained. Based upon the facts that MG Fay reports, it seems that the social system at Abu Ghraib was disorganized and anomic from the outset; that this state of social disorganization and *anomie* grew progressively worse over time; and that these defects in the social system produced widespread forms of deviance among prisoners and US personnel alike. Abu Ghraib was a dangerous, stress-inducing, deviance-producing social setting for everyone who was forced to be there. There existed several specific sources of 'confusion' which contributed to this anomic state of affairs. We shall now consider these in more detail.

 ## Confusion as to Who Was in Charge

MG Fay notes that at Abu Ghraib, 'people made up their own titles as things went along' (p. 43). He adds that 'some people thought COL Pappas was the Director; some thought LTC Jordan was the Director' (p. 43). Can one imagine a sociology department or medical office or any other institutional setting in which people made up their own titles and did not know who was in charge? This fundamental confusion concerning roles and authority bespeaks extreme *anomie*.

 ## Confusion Between Approved and Abusive Activities

MG Fay writes: 'Theater Interrogation and Counter-Resistance Policies (ICRP) were found to be *poorly defined*, and *changed several times*. As a result, interrogation activities *sometimes crossed into abusive activity*' (p. 7, emphasis added). This state of affairs, alone, is sufficient to create the state of 'derangement' that is discussed by Durkheim. It is less a case of 'normlessness,' in that norms did exist, than it is a case of chaos and confusion regarding norms.

MG Fay notes that non-doctrinal approaches that were approved for use in Afghanistan and Guantánamo Bay ('GTMO') 'became *confused* at Abu Ghraib and were implemented without proper authorities or safeguards' and that 'soldiers were not trained on non-doctrinal interrogation techniques' (p. 8, emphasis added). One of these approaches involved the use of dogs, based on 'several documents that spoke of exploiting the Arab fear of dogs' (p. 10). MG Fay concludes that '[t]he use of dogs in interrogations to "fear up" detainees was utilized without proper authorization' (p. 10).

MG Fay returns to the improper use of dogs later in his report. He reports that as of 20 November 2003, 'abuse of detainees was already occurring and the addition of dogs was just one more abuse device' (p. 83). There arose controversy over who 'owned' the dogs and how they would be used. The presence of the dogs is mysteriously 'associated with MG G. Miller's visit,' but this link is not explored by MG Fay. MG Fay concludes this section: 'COL Pappas did not recall how he got the authority to employ dogs; *just that he had it*' (p. 83, emphasis added). In any bureaucracy based upon a hierarchical rational-legal authority, including the US Army, it is an indicator of *anomie* that a commanding officer would claim that he 'just had' authority without rational-legal justification.

Elsewhere MG Fay writes that '[e]ven with all the apparent *confusion over roles, responsibilities and authorities*, there were early indications that MP and MI personnel knew the use of dog teams in interrogations was abusive' (p. 84). If personnel knew that their use was abusive, at the same time that they engaged in abuse made possible and even encouraged by social disorganization, they were placed in what sociologists and psychologists call a 'double-bind' situation: one is damned if one does and damned if one does not engage in abuse. The double-bind situation has been researched thoroughly and found to be a causal factor in a plethora of forms of deviance, and mental breakdowns of various sorts.

◈ Insufficient Training

MG Fay writes: 'As pointed out clearly in the MG Taguba report, MP units and individuals at Abu Ghraib *lacked sufficient training on operating a detainment/interrogation facility*' and that 'MI units and individuals also *lacked sufficient, appropriate, training to cope with the situation encountered at Abu Ghraib*' (p. 46, emphasis added). In sociological terms, the MP and MI units were not able to internalize the proper and required norms, values, sanctions, and beliefs appropriate to their mission. This was, sociologically speaking, an invitation for abuse to occur.

The state of confusion was so great that MG Fay asserts that soldiers did not know what they were permitted to do or not do:

> Guard and interrogation personnel at Abu Ghraib were *not adequately trained or experienced and were certainly not well versed in the cultural understanding of the detainees*. MI personnel were *totally ignorant* of MP lanes in the road or rules of engagement. A common observation was that MI knew what MI could do and what MI couldn't do; but MI did *not know* what the MPs could or could *not* do in their activities. (p. 46, emphasis added)

In this passage MG Fay seems to imply that role confusion occurred such that MI did not know the role expectations for MPs. However, in another passage, MG Fay suggests that this role confusion was pervasive, and extended to the role expectations for MIs, MPs, and their perceptions of each other's role expectations: 'Again, who was allowed to do what and how exactly they were to do it was *totally unclear. Neither of the communities (MI and MP) knew what the other could and could not do*' (p. 70, emphasis added). The phrase 'totally unclear' refers to all of the personnel at Abu Ghraib, and constitutes a very powerful description of the drastic extent of *anomie* at Abu Ghraib. According to MG Fay: 'Most of the MPs were *never trained* in prison operations' (p. 46, emphasis added). From a sociological perspective, one could not expect even the minimal semblance of 'social order' and consensus in a social milieu which relied upon actors who were not trained in the normative expectations for their roles. This aspect of the social milieu at Abu Ghraib might be likened to a university whose professors were not trained in the subject areas they were teaching, or a clinic run by personnel untrained in medicine. Again, norms exist—but they are not coordinated or implemented properly.

Furthermore, according to MG Fay, 'approximately 35% of the contract interrogators lacked formal military training as interrogators' (p. 50). In addition: 'Proper oversight did not occur at Abu Ghraib due to a *lack of training and inadequate contract management and monitoring*' (p. 52, emphasis added).

◈ Lack of Social Integration Within the Military Units at Abu Ghraib

MG Fay writes: 'The JIDC [Joint Interrogation Detention Center] was created in a very short time period with *parts and pieces of various units. It lacked unit integrity, and this lack was a fatal flaw*' (p. 9, emphasis added). Elsewhere, MG Fay elaborates that 'cross-leveling' occurred with the 'disadvantage of inserting Soldiers into units shortly before deployment who had never trained with those units' (p. 32). In summary, 'The Soldiers did not know the unit' and 'the unit and the unit leadership did not know the Soldiers' (p. 32). COL Pappas had at his disposal 'disparate elements of units and individuals, including civilians, that had never trained together, but now were going to have to fight together' (p. 32). Later in the report, MG Fay emphasizes this point:

> It is important to understand that the MI units at Abu Ghraib were far from complete units. They were small elements from those units. Most of the elements that came to Abu Ghraib came *without their normal command structure*. The unit Commanders and Senior NCOs did *not* go to Abu Ghraib but stayed with the bulk of their respective units. (p. 41, emphasis added)

'JIDC interrogators, analysts, and leaders were unprepared for the arrival of contract interrogators and had no training to fall back on in the management, control, and discipline of these personnel' (p. 19). Moreover, the contract interrogators were supposed to be screened yet '[s]uch screening was not occurring' (p. 40).

In his conclusions, MG Fay explains:

> The JIDC was established in an ad hoc manner without proper planning, personnel, and

logistical support for the missions it was intended to perform. Interrogation and analyst personnel were quickly klu[d]ged together from a half dozen units in an effort to meet personnel requirements. Even at its peak strength, interrogation and analyst manpower at the JIDC was too shorthanded to deal with the large number of detainees at hand. (p. 113)

Lack of social integration among the individuals who make up a social system is one of the keystones of Durkheim's entire system of thought in the analysis of modern forms of social pathology. Lack of social integration has been found by sociologists to be consistently related to the breaking of norms. In his landmark study *The American Soldier*, Samuel Stouffer (1949) found that strongly integrated military units performed better than less cohesive units. It would be important to investigate in future theoretical and empirical work whether social integration is better understood in Durkheim's terms of a coordinated division of labor versus that functionalist view which tends to quantify integration in terms of instances of social interaction and bonding (Gibbs, 1982).

◈ Rapid Changes in the Social Milieu

MG Fay writes: 'By mid-October, interrogation policy in Iraq had changed three times in less than 30 days' (p. 28). Elsewhere he writes: 'There is no formal advanced interrogation training in the US Army' (p. 17). Furthermore, 'Most interrogator training that occurred at Abu Ghraib was on-the-job training' (p. 18). Rapid social and normative change is in itself a promoter of stress and contributes to social disorganization.

◈ Intense Pressure to Obtain Intelligence

MG Fay writes that 'as the *need for actionable intelligence rose*, the realization dawned that pre-war planning had not included planning for detainee operations' (p. 24, emphasis added). Later in the report, he elaborates: 'LTG

Sanchez did not believe significant pressure was coming from outside of CJTF-7 [Combined Joint Task Force Seven], but *does confirm that there was great pressure placed upon the intelligence system to produce actionable intelligence'* (p. 42, emphasis added). Elsewhere MG Fay writes: 'COL Pappas perceived *intense pressure for intelligence* from interrogations,' and that this pressure was passed 'to the rest of the JIDC leadership' (p. 45). MG Fay elaborates that '[p]ressure consisted in deviation from doctrinal reporting standards' and other ways (p. 45). Philip Zimbardo and others have found that intense pressure upon a police unit is one of the key components that lead to abuse, though without explaining the social structural reasons for this connection (see Huggins et al., 2002). Note that Fay volunteers the Durkheimian-sounding explanation that intense pressure may have led to a breaking of moral boundaries, which in turn led to abuse.

◆ Confusion as to Which Norms to Follow

MG Fay writes: 'Soldiers on the ground are confused about how they apply the Geneva Conventions and whether they have a duty to report violations of the conventions' (p. 19). Further confusion is documented on p. 28 of the Fay report, wherein the General discusses CPT Wood's chart on 'Interrogation Rules of Engagement.' MG Fay writes:

> The chart was confusing, however. It was not completely accurate and could be *subject to various interpretations.* . . . What was particularly confusing was that nowhere on the chart did it mention a number of techniques that were in use at the time: removal of clothing, forced grooming, hooding, and yelling, loud music and light control. Given the detail otherwise noted on the aid, the failure to list some techniques *left a question of whether they were authorized for use without approval.* (p. 28, emphasis added)

From a sociological point of view, the soldiers would have had a very difficult time making out the difference between what is normative versus what is not

if the commanding officer present could not. The commanding officer represents, in a Durkheimian sense, the values, norms, sanctions, and beliefs of the US Army and other, related organizations.

◆ 'Unhealthy Mystique'

MG Fay claims that the 'acronym "Other Government Agency" (OGA) referred almost exclusively to the CIA' and that 'CIA detention and interrogation practices *led to a loss of accountability, abuse, reduced interagency cooperation, and an unhealthy mystique* that further *poisoned the atmosphere* at Abu Ghraib' (pp. 52–3, emphasis added). MG Fay adds that 'the *systemic lack of accountability* for interrogator actions and detainees *plagued* detainee operations in Abu Ghraib' (p. 54, emphasis added). A 'systemic' lack of accountability suggests a social milieu that approximates social chaos much more than any semblance of social order. It is intriguing that MG Fay uses words such as 'unhealthy,' 'poisoned,' and 'plagued' when referring to the social milieu at Abu Ghraib. He repeatedly and explicitly describes a toxic social environment in terms similar to the vocabulary that Durkheim uses to describe an anomic social environment.

According to MG Fay, several abusive incidents 'were *widely known within the US community* (MI and MP alike) at Abu Ghraib' (p. 54, emphasis added). He adds: 'Speculation and *resentment* grew over the lack of personal responsibility, *of some people being above the laws and regulations.* The resentment contributed to the *unhealthy environment* that existed at Abu Ghraib' (p. 54, emphasis added). MG Fay refers again to a social 'atmosphere' at Abu Ghraib when he writes: 'According to COL Pappas, MG G. Miller said they, GTMO, used military working dogs, and that they were effective in *setting the atmosphere for interrogations'* (p. 58, emphasis added). Clearly, the 'social atmosphere' at Abu Ghraib was out of sync with Army Doctrine, the Geneva Conventions, and other systems of agreed upon social norms.

MG Fay implies that humiliating nudity was part of the social atmosphere at Abu Ghraib: 'Many of the Soldiers who witnessed the nakedness were told that this was an *accepted practice'* (p. 68, emphasis added). Because MG Fay lists nakedness as a form of abuse in his summary, he is implying that nudity was part of the deviant subculture that was created at Abu Ghraib. He does not address who told whom and with what regularity that this form of abuse was 'accepted practice.' Elsewhere he adds: 'MI interrogators started directing nakedness at Abu Ghraib as early as 16 September 2003 to humiliate and break down detainees' (p. 69). This observation gives one some indication of the long time-frame in which this form of abuse was practiced.

◈ Failure of Self-Correcting Mechanisms

MG Fay's report is replete with instances of soldiers objecting to or reporting abuse, and supervisors ignoring them, failing to take corrective action, or invalidating their morally correct observations. Consider incident #1 as an illustration: '1LT Sutton, 320th MP BN IRF intervened to stop the abuse and was told by the MI soldiers, "we are the professionals; we know what we are doing." They refused 1LT Sutton's lawful order to identify themselves' (p. 71). 1LT Sutton reported the incident 'to the CID [Criminal Investigation Command] who determined the allegation lacked sufficient basis for prosecution' (p. 71). Clearly, options other than prosecution were available, but were not pursued. In fact, '[t]his incident was not further pursued based on limited data and the absence of additional investigative leads' (p. 72). Incident #19 quotes an unnamed Colonel as responding as follows to a sergeant who cited the Geneva Conventions as objection to the abuse he witnessed: 'fine Sergeant, you do what you have to do, I am going back to bed' (p. 80). There is no need to go over the forty-plus other documented 'incidents' in detail here: taken as a whole, they suggest that a climate of abuse was prevalent at Abu Ghraib; that soldiers were not in a position to have their objections validated by superiors; and that officers high in the chain of command did not follow their role expectations to correct the abuse within the social system that was Abu Ghraib. The significance of this conclusion is that it contradicts MG Fay's interpretation that the abuse in question was the result of a few corrupt individuals. Clearly, using the facts in his own report, one may arrive at the conclusion that the abuse was widespread, systematic, and that

normative mechanisms which existed did not function as intended, so that soldiers were not validated by their superiors or the dysfunctional social system in objecting to the abuse.

In summary, the language used by MG Fay to describe the social environment at Abu Ghraib is remarkably similar to Durkheim's (1951 [1897]) descriptions of *anomie* as a social condition that is *déréglée*. MG Fay stops short of making the connection that an unhealthy environment of this sort inevitably leads to deviance, but this is precisely Durkheim's conclusion.

◈ Cultural Insensitivity

MG Fay writes that US soldiers at Abu Ghraib were 'certainly not well versed in the cultural understandings of the detainees' (p. 46). There is ample evidence to support this claim, but the problem goes far deeper than not being 'well versed.' A sociological reading of the US government reports on the abuse at Abu Ghraib suggests that the US Army failed to understand and predict the impact of forced nudity upon a specifically Muslim population. Moreover, this form of abuse seems to transcend the normative chaos at Abu Ghraib, to appear in other facilities. MG Fay writes: 'Removal of clothing was not a technique developed at Abu Ghraib, but rather a technique which was *imported and can be traced though Afghanistan and GTMO*' (p. 87, emphasis added).

'Removal of clothing is *not* a doctrinal or authorized interrogation technique but appears to have been directed and employed at various levels within MI as an "ego down" technique' (p. 88, emphasis added). Furthermore: 'It is apparent from this investigation that removal of clothing was *employed routinely* and *with the belief it was not abuse*' (p. 88, emphasis added). After an ICRC visit, CPT Reese is quoted as saying: 'We could not determine what happened to the detainee's original clothing' (p. 88). MG Fay makes the interpretation that '[t]he use of clothing as an incentive (nudity) is *significant* in that it likely *contributed to an escalating "de-humanization"* of the detainees and *set the stage for additional and more severe abuses to occur*' (p. 88, emphasis added). Note that this observation by MG Fay, and other ones like it, supports the sociological interpretation that an unhealthy, anomic social atmosphere was established at Abu Ghraib, which led to abuse. According to the anthropologist Akbar S. Ahmed (1992), nudity is a cardinal normative violation in Islamic culture because this culture puts a high premium on modesty.[7] Based on Ahmed's and other sociological and anthropological research into Islamic culture, one may conclude that forced nudity was a form of psychic abuse for most of the prisoners, due to its significance as an extreme form of humiliation in Islamic culture.

MG Fay writes:

The interrogators believed they had the authority to use clothing as an incentive, as well as stress positions, and were not attempting to hide their use. . . . It is probable that use of nudity was sanctioned at some level within the chain-of-command. If not, lack of leadership and oversight permitted the nudity to occur. (p. 90)

In general, MG Fay lists the following as organizational and sociological problems at Abu Ghraib:

- There was a lack of clear Command and Control of Detainee Operations at the CJTF-7 level.

- The JIDC was manned with personnel from numerous organizations and consequently lacked unit cohesion.

- Leaders failed to take steps to effectively manage pressure placed upon JIDC personnel.

- Some capturing units failed to follow procedures, training, and directives in the capture, screening, and exploitation of prisoners.

- The JIDC was established in an *ad hoc* manner without proper planning, personnel, and logistical support for the missions it was intended to perform.

- Interrogation training in the Laws of Land Warfare and the Geneva Conventions was ineffective.

- MI leaders did not receive adequate training in the conduct and management of interrogation operations.

- Critical records on detainees were not created or maintained properly, thereby hampering effective operations.

- OGA interrogation practices led to a loss of accountability at Abu Ghraib.

- ICRC recommendations were ignored by MI, MP, and CJTF-7 personnel.

But each and every one of these shortcomings also produced a cultural impact upon a primarily Islamic population of prisoners that was interpreted—by their cultural standards—as offensive, disrespectful, dehumanizing, uninterested in their cultural backgrounds, and hostile to their culture. In other words, the social disorganization among the American soldiers at Abu Ghraib promoted cultural suspicion and still more *anomie* from the point of view of Muslim culture. The results included riots by prisoners, which in turn led to vengeance by some American guards, which in turn escalated to more riots, and so on. Cultural insensitivity contributed to an initial state of *anomie*, which, left unchecked, contributed to a clash of cultures and still more *anomie*, which, in turn, set the stage for further abuse.

◈ Conclusions

The extent of social disorganization, social chaos, dysfunction, lack of coordination, and of a general state of *anomie* was so great at Abu Ghraib that abuse and the breaking of norms that are documented was the *inevitable* outcome and should have been expected. Moreover, because the social system at Abu Ghraib could not self-correct, as functionalists might claim to predict, its disintegration increased and it could not respond to corrective measures outside the system, including but not limited to the ICRC. Recent reports by journalists and human rights groups point to an increase in incidents of abuse at other military posts throughout Iraq, suggesting that the toxic or anomic state of affairs at Abu Ghraib has spread. All of this poses a challenge both to sociological theory and, practically, to the US Army.

Regarding social theory, sociologists need to re-examine the largely dormant understandings of anomie by Durkheim and by functionalists, compare and contrast them critically, and apply them appropriately to contemporary contexts, including but not limited to Abu Ghraib. Mountains of theory and research on the relationship of ordinary crime to *anomie* do not seem to be helpful in understanding international war crimes, abuse, and torture, which have become important global issues since World War II. Moreover, criticisms as well as applications of Parsonian or Mertonian functionalism have failed to settle the question whether *anomie* is a condition of normlessness that will correct itself. Durkheim seems more convincing in arguing that *anomie* is a grievous social evil characterized by genuine social 'derangement' that produces equally grievous and long-lasting negative consequences. In this case, the abuse at Abu Ghraib has stained American intentions of liberating Iraq, has contributed to a clash of civilizations between the West and Islamic cultures, and may have contributed to the insurgency movement. The Parsonian assumption that social systems can automatically self-correct thus seems to be off the mark. If Durkheim's classical perspective is the more correct one, then one should take seriously his proposed program for repairing anomic social systems.

This last point holds immediate consequences for the US Army and government. The Abu Ghraib courts-martial at Fort Hood, Texas, were supposed to repair the damage caused by the abuse, and restore justice. But if Durkheim is correct, the fact that the Army chose to shift all the blame onto a handful of low-ranking soldiers may not appease the collective conscience in the long run. In fact, Durkheim (1995 [1912]) introduced the concept of scapegoating to account for such instances of anomic miscarriage of justice, in which the 'sins' of a larger social group are displaced onto a few individuals, animals, or even objects.[8] In the case at hand, the Government's own reports, as well as the outcomes of the courts-martial, suggest a Durkheimian interpretation that the responsibility of American society as a whole and many of its institutions for the abuses at Abu Ghraib was displaced onto a handful of so-called 'rotten apples.' Durkheim's own public defense of Captain Alfred Dreyfus, also a target of collective scapegoating, lends further support to such a conclusion. In addition, Durkheim's concept of

scapegoating suggests that the prisoners at Abu Ghraib were themselves the scapegoats for American society's pain and rage in response to the terrorist event that has come to be known as 9/11. Durkheim writes:

> When society undergoes suffering, it feels the need to find someone whom it can hold responsible for its sickness, on whom it can avenge its misfortunes: and those against whom opinion already discriminates are naturally designated for this role. These are the pariahs who serve as expiatory victims. (in Lukes, 1985, p. 345)

No credible evidence has linked Iraq to 9/11, and MG Fay's as well as other reports and testimony make it clear that the prisoners at Abu Ghraib had no connection to 9/11 or any other sort of terrorist activity. In the final analysis, the abuse committed against the inmates at Abu Ghraib prison comes across as an exercise in irrationality and scapegoating, or what Durkheim called *dérèglement*.

 Notes

1. Matt Taibbi writes: 'Mestrovic described Abu Ghraib as a "state of *anomie*." "A what?" [Colonel] Pohl snapped, frowning. "A state of *anomie*," the doctor repeated. Pohl shuddered and sipped his coffee, seeming to wonder whether such a word was even legal in Texas' (2005: 48).

2. According the Littré *Dictionnaire de la langue française* ([1863], 1963 vol. 2, p. 1672), the principal meaning of *dérèglement* is derangement: '*Dérèglement, dérangement* are words expressing two nuances of moral disorder: What is *dérangé* is disarranged [*hors de son rang*] or is without place. What is *déréglé* is out of rule [*hors de la régle*]. The state of *dérèglement* is more serious than that of derangement.' One of the many sources that Litté cites is Jacques Bossuet, who describes *dérèglement* in the following terms, among others: *mal, égarement, péché, tourments, infini de miséres, maladie, désordre, dangereux, souffrir, impiété, intemperance, desséchement, miserable captivité* (Bossuet, [1731] 1836 pp. 43–79). It is interesting that many English equivalents of these words are used by soldiers and investigators to describe the social climate at Abu Ghraib.

3. These assumptions are ubiquitous and mostly unquestioned in literally hundreds of articles, treatises, and textbooks. However, one is at a loss to find any of these secondary interpreters quoting Durkheim in these regards.

4. The reader is free to consult any contemporary sociology text-book as evidence for this persistent misunderstanding. Thoughtful alternatives to functionalist misrepresentations of Durkheim's concept of *anomie* are also sidelined in sociological theory and text-books. For example, in *The Lonely Crowd*, David Riesman writes: 'Anomic is English coinage from Durkheim's *anomique* (adjective of *anomie*) meaning ruleless, ungoverned' ([1950] 1977 p. 242). But in his discussion, Riesman seems to imply that different types of *anomie* correspond to tradition-, inner-, and other-directed forms of social character. However, despite being acknowledged as one of sociology's most important writers, Riesman's analysis of *anomie* in the context of his overall theory has been largely ignored.

5. Foucault writes: 'The ceremony of punishment, then, is an exercise of "terror" . . . to make everyone aware, through the body of the criminal, of the unrestrained presence of the sovereign' (1977, p. 49).

6. It is also sometimes referred to as the Jones–Fay report, for internal, bureaucratic reasons within the structure of the US Army that need not be explored here. Reports by MG Antonio Taguba and James Schlesinger also exist (Strasser, 2004), along with other reports, but the Fay report is chosen here in the interest of conserving space. For a fuller discussion of the government reports on Abu Ghraib, see Danner (2004) and Mestrovic (2007).

7. It would be important to devote a separate study to Ahmed's observation about the relative meaning of nudity in American, Muslim, and other social contexts. Moreover, there are hints in the government reports, which cannot be pursued here, that American interrogators deliberately used this knowledge concerning nudity in Islamic culture to establish policies at Abu Ghraib. If true, such deliberate strategies are out of sync with the policies on interrogation that existed at the time of the abuse, and constitute yet another instance of *anomie*, specifically, lack of coordination with lawful Army policies on interrogation.

8. Durkheim writes: 'When the pain reaches such a pitch, it becomes suffused with a kind of anger and exasperation. One feels the need to break or destroy something. One attacks oneself or others. One strikes, wounds, or burns oneself, or one attacks someone else, in order to strike, wound, or burn him. Thus was established the mourning custom of giving oneself over to veritable orgies of torture. It seems to be probable that the vendetta and head hunting have no other origin. If every death is imputed to some magical spell and if, for that reason, it is believed that the dead person must be avenged, the reason is a felt need to find a victim at all costs on whom the collective sorrow and anger can be discharged. This victim will naturally be sought outside, for an outsider is a subject *minoris resistentiae*; since he is not protected by the fellow-feeling that attaches to a relative or a neighbor, nothing about him blocks and neutralizes the bad and destructive feelings aroused by the death. Probably for the same reason, a woman serves more often than a man as the passive object of the most cruel mourning rites. Because she has lower social significance, she is more readily singled out to fill the function of scapegoat' ([1912] 1995 p. 404).

 # References

Ahmed, Akbar S. (1992) *Postmodernism and Islam*. London: Routledge.

Baillot, Alexandre (1927) *Influence de la philosophie de Schopenhauer en France (1860—1900)*. Paris: J. Vrin.

Baudrillard, Jean (1986) *America*, trans. Chris Turner. London: Verso.

Bauman, Zygmunt (1990) *Modernity and the Holocaust*. Ithaca, NY: Cornell University Press.

Bossuet, Jacques (1836) *Traité de la concupiscence*. Paris: Éditeurs des Portes de France. (Orig. pub. 1731.)

Cushman, Thomas and Stjepan G. Mestrovic (eds) (1995) *This Time We Knew: Western Responses to Genocide in Bosnia*. New York: New York University Press.

Danner, Mark (2004) *Torture and Truth: America, Abu Ghraib and the War on Terror*. New York: New York Review of Books.

Durkheim, Émile (1933) *The Division of Labor in Society*, trans. Simpson. New York: Free Press. (Orig. pub. 1893.)

Durkheim, Émile (1951) *Suicide: A Study in Sociology*, trans. John A. Spaulding and George Simpson. New York: Free Press. (Orig. pub. 1897.)

Durkheim, Émile (1983a) *Le Suicide: Étude de sociologie*. Paris: Presses Universitaries de France. (Orig. pub. 1897.)

Durkheim, Émile (1983b) *Professional Ethics and Civic Morals*, trans. Cornelia Brookfield. Westport, CT: Greenwood Press. (Orig. pub. 1950.)

Durkheim, Émile (1995) *The Elementary Forms of Religious Life*, trans. Karen E. Fields. New York: Free Press. (Orig. pub. 1912.)

Falk, Richard, Irene Gendzier and Robert Jay Lifton (eds) (2006) *Crimes of War: Iraq*. New York: Nation Books.

Foucault, Michel (1977) *Discipline and Punish: The Birth of the Prison*, trans. Alan Sheridan. New York: Vintage. (Orig. pub. 1975.)

Gibbs, Jack P. (1982) 'Testing the Theory of Status Integration and Suicide Rates,' *American Sociological Review* 47: 227–37.

Goffman, Erving (1986) *Frame Analysis: An Essay on the Organization of Experience*. Boston: Northeastern University Press.

Gutman, Roy and David Rieff (1999) *Crimes of War*. New York: Norton.

Guyau, Jean-Marie (1907) *Ésquisse d'une morale sans obligation ni sanction*. Paris: Alcan. (Orig. pub. 1885.)

Hazan, Pierre (2004) *Justice in a Time of War: The True Story behind the International Criminal Tribunal for the Former Yugoslavia*. College Station, TX: Texas A&M University Press.

Hersh, Seymour M. (2004) *Chain of Command: The Road From 9/11 to Abu Ghraib*. New York: HarperCollins.

Huggins, Martha K., Mika Haritos-Fatouros and Philip G. Zimbardo (2002) *Violence Workers: Police Torturers and Murderers Reconstruct Brazilian Atrocities*. Berkeley: University of California Press.

Human Rights Watch (2006) 'By the Numbers: Findings of the Detainee Abuse and Accountability Project,' 18: 1–28.

Karpinski, Janis (2005) *One Woman's Army: The Commanding General of Abu Ghraib Tells Her Story*. New York: Hyperion.

Lalande, André (1980) *Vocabulaire technique et critique de la philosophie*. Paris: Presses Universitaires de France. (Orig. pub. 1926.)

Lipset, Seymour M. (1990) *Continental Divide: The Values and Institutions of the United States and Canada*. London: Routledge.

Lipset, Seymour M. (1997) *American Exceptionalism: A Double-Edged Sword*. New York: Norton.

Littré, Émile (1963) *Dictionnaire de la langue frangaise*. Vols. 1–9. Paris: Gallimard. (Orig. pub. 1863.)

Loewen, James (2007) *Lies My Teacher Told Me: Everything Your American History Textbooks Got Wrong*. New York: Touchstone Books.

Lukes, Steven (1985) *Émile Durkheim: His Life and Work*. Stanford: Stanford University Press. (Orig. pub. 1973.)

Lyonnet, Stanislas and Leopold Sabourin (1970) *Sin, Redemption and Sacrifice: A Biblical and Patristic Study*. Rome: Biblical Institute Press.

Lyotard, Jean-François (1984) *The Postmodern Condition*. Minneapolis: University of Minnesota Press.

Merton, Robert K. (1957) *Social Theory and Social Structure*. New York: Free Press.

Mestrovic, Stjepan G. (1985) '*Anomia* and Sin in Durkheim's Thought', *Journal for the Social Scientific Study of Religion* 24: 119–36.

Mestrovic, Stjepan G. (1988) *Émile Durkheim and the Reformation of Sociology*. Tottowa, NJ: Rowman & Littlefield.

Mestrovic, Stjepan G. (2007) *The Trials of Abu Ghraib: An Expert Witness Account of Shame and Honor*. Boulder, CO: Paradigm Publishers.

Mestrovic, Stjepan G. and Hélène M. Brown (1985) 'Durkheim's Concept of *Anomie* as *Dérèglement*', *Social Problems* 33: 81–99.

Mills, C. Wright (1959) *The Sociological Imagination*. New York: Oxford University Press.

Orru, Marco (1987) *Anomie: History and Meanings*. London: Allen & Unwin.

Parsons, Talcott (1937) *The Structure of Social Action*. Glencoe, IL: Free Press.

Riesman, David (1977) *The Lonely Crowd*. New Haven, CT: Yale University Press. (Orig. pub. 1950.)

Solis, Gary (1998) *Son Thang: An American War Crime*. New York: Bantam.

Stouffer, Samuel (1949) *The American Soldier: Adjustment during Army Life*. Princeton, NJ: Princeton University Press.

Strasser, Steven (2004) *The Abu Ghraib Investigations: The Official Reports of the Independent Panel and the Pentagon on the Shocking Prisoner Abuse in Iraq*. New York: Public Affairs.

Taibbi, Matt (2005) 'Ms. America', *Rolling Stone*, 20 October, pp. 47–8.

Theodorson, George A. and Achilles G. Theodorson (1969) *A Modern Dictionary of Sociology*. New York: Thomas Y. Crowell.

Tocqueville, Alexis de (2004) *Democracy in America*, trans. George Lawrence. New York: Library of America. (Orig. pub. 1848.)

Zimbardo, Philip G. (2007) *The Lucifer Effect: Understanding How Good People Turn Evil*. New York: Random House.

READING 12

While still using a version of strain theory, this article offers an alternative explanation for terrorism than the one just presented by Mestrovic and Lorenzo in Reading 11. In this piece, Agnew reviews terrorism research and offers a general strain theory of terrorism. Agnew argues that terrorism is most likely when people experience "collective strains," or strains that are experienced by an identifiable group such as a racial, ethnic, religious, class, or political group. Only a small percentage of collective strains increase the likelihood of terrorism, however. Agnew argues that such strains are (a) high in magnitude, with civilians affected; (b) perceived as unjust; and (c) inflicted by significantly more powerful *others*. These collective strains increase the likelihood of terrorism for several reasons, but they do not lead to terrorism in all cases. Agnew describes many factors that condition their effect.

Source: Agnew, R. (2010). A general strain theory of terrorism. *Theoretical Criminology*, 14(2), 131–153.

A General Strain Theory of Terrorism

Robert Agnew

It has been suggested that crime theories can shed much light on the causes of terrorism (Rosenfeld, 2002; LaFree and Dugan, 2004, 2008; Rausch and LaFree, 2007). Following that suggestion, this article applies general strain theory (GST) to the explanation of sub-state terrorism. The research on GST has focused almost exclusively on 'common crimes', such as interpersonal assault, theft, and illicit drug use (although see Agnew et al., 2009). But as argued below, GST can contribute much to the explanation of terrorism, although the theory needs to be extended to account for this type of crime.

The article is in three parts. First, it briefly reviews current strain-based explanations of terrorism. While promising, these explanations suffer from three major problems: they fail to describe the essential characteristics of those strains most likely to result in terrorism; they do not fully explain *why* such strains result in terrorism; and they do not explain why only a small percentage of those exposed to such strains turn to terrorism. Second, it provides a brief overview of GST, pointing to those key elements which can help address these problems. Third, it presents a general strain theory of terrorism, designed to explain why some people are more likely than others to form or join terrorist organizations and commit terrorist acts. In brief, this theory argues that terrorism is more likely when people experience 'collective strains' that are: (a) high in magnitude, with civilians affected; (b) unjust; and (c) inflicted by significantly more powerful *others*, including 'complicit' civilians, with whom members of the strained collectivity have weak ties. These collective strains increase the likelihood of terrorism because they increase negative emotions, reduce social control, reduce the ability to cope through legal and military channels, foster the social learning of terrorism, and contribute to a collective orientation and response. These collective strains, however, do not lead to terrorism in all cases. A range of factors condition their effect, with these factors influencing the subjective interpretation of these strains; the emotional reaction to them; and the ability to engage in, costs of, and disposition for terrorism.

Before applying GST to terrorism, however, it is first necessary to define terrorism. The many definitions of terrorism often disagree with one another, but several key elements are commonly mentioned (see National Research Council, 2002; LaFree and Dugan, 2004, 2008; Tilly, 2004; Goodwin, 2006; Hoffman, 2006; Post, 2007; Forst, 2009). Terrorism is defined as the commission of criminal acts, usually violent, that target civilians or violate conventions of war when targeting military personnel; and that are committed at least partly for social, political, or religious ends. Although not part of the formal definition, it is important to note that terrorist acts are typically committed by the members of sub-national groups (LaFree and Dugan, 2004; Pape, 2005).

◆ Current Strain-Based Explanations of Terrorism

Terrorism researchers commonly argue that strains or 'grievances' are a major cause of terrorism (e.g. Gurr and Moore, 1997; Blazak, 2001; National Research Council, 2002; de Coming, 2004; Bjorgo, 2005; Pape, 2005; Victoroff, 2005; Callaway and Harrelson-Stephens, 2006; Goodwin, 2006; Hoffman, 2006; Robison et al., 2006; Piazza, 2007; Post, 2007; Smelser, 2007; Stevens, 2002; Freeman, 2008; LaFree and Dugan, 2008; Forst, 2009). Rosenfeld (2004: 23), in fact, states that 'without a grievance, there would be no terrorism'. Researchers, however, differ somewhat in the strains they link to terrorism. Terrorism is said to result from:

- absolute and relative material deprivation;

- the problems associated with globalization/ modernization, such as threats to religious dominance and challenges to traditional family roles;

- resentment over the cultural, economic, and military domination of the West, particularly the United States;

- territorial, ethnic, and religious disputes resulting from postcolonial efforts at nation building and the breakup of the Soviet bloc;

- economic, political, and other discrimination based on race/ethnicity or religion;

- the problems encountered by certain immigrant groups, including unemployment, discrimination, and the clash between western and Islamic values;

- the denial of 'basic human rights', including political rights, personal security rights, and the right to the satisfaction of basic human needs;

- harsh state repression, including widespread violence directed at certain groups;

- severe challenges to group identity or what Post (2007) calls 'identicide';

- displacement or the loss of one's land/home;

- military occupation of certain types;

- threats to the status of working-class, white, male heterosexuals, including the loss of manufacturing jobs and the movements for civil, women's, and gay rights.

It should be noted that terrorists also explain their actions in terms of the strains they experience. This is apparent in the statements they make, the literature and videos they distribute, and on their websites (see Hoffman, 2006). The centrality of strain explanations for terrorists is frequently reflected in the names of their organizations, such as the Popular Front for the Liberation of Palestine and the Organization for the Oppressed on Earth (Hoffman, 2006: 21–2). Further, government figures frequently employ strain explanations when discussing terrorism. President George W. Bush, for example, stated that: 'We fight against poverty because hope is an answer to terror' (quoted in Piazza, 2006: 160; also see Atran, 2003; Krueger and Maleckova, 2003; de Coning, 2004; Hoffman, 2006; Newman, 2006).

Most of the academic research on strain and terrorism has involved case studies of terrorist groups. Such studies almost always conclude that strains played a central role in the formation of such groups (for overviews, see Callaway and Harrelson-Stephens, 2006; Hoffman, 2006; Post, 2007). It is possible, however, that similar strains do not lead to terrorism in other cases. Several quantitative studies have investigated this issue. Such studies should be interpreted with caution since they usually suffer from definitional, sampling, and other problems (Victoroff, 2005; Newman, 2007). Nevertheless, they provide the best test of the link between strain and terrorism. Surprisingly, such studies provide only mixed or weak support for strain explanations (see Gurr and Moore, 1997; Krueger and Maleckova, 2003; de Coning, 2004; Newman, 2006; Piazza, 2006; Robison et al., 2006; LaFree and Dugan, 2008).

Most research has focused on the relationship between terrorism and material deprivation (absolute and, to a lesser extent, relative). Studies suggest that this relationship is weak at best (Atran, 2003; de Coning, 2004; Turk, 2004; Maleckova, 2005; Merari, 2005; Pape, 2005; Victoroff, 2005; Krueger and Maleckova, 2003; Newman, 2006; Piazza, 2006; Smelser, 2007; Araj, 2008; Forst, 2009). This is true at the individual level. For example, poor and poorly educated Palestinians are *not* more likely to support terrorism or engage in terrorist acts (Krueger and Maleckova, 2003; also see Maleckova, 2005). In some regions, terrorists are more often drawn from the ranks of the middle class and educated— including college students (Maleckova, 2005; Victoroff, 2005; Post, 2007). The weak link between deprivation and terrorism is also true at the macro-level. Most studies suggest that measures of material deprivation are unrelated or weakly related to the number of terrorist acts that take place in or originate in a country (Maleckova, 2005; Pape, 2005: 17–19; Newman, 2006; Piazza, 2006).

It is a central contention of this article that this weak support stems from problems with the strain *explanations* that have been advanced, and not from the fact that strain plays a small role in terrorism. Drawing on GST, current strain explanations of terrorism suffer from three major problems. First, they fail to fully describe the core characteristics of strains likely to lead to terrorism. These theories typically focus on one or a few types of strain, such as material deprivation, threats to traditional values, and military occupation. But the characteristics of a given type of strain may differ greatly from situation to situation. For example, a type of strain such as material deprivation may differ in its magnitude (e.g. degree, duration, centrality, pervasiveness), perceived injustice, and source (e.g. is the source a more powerful *other*). Such differences, as argued below, have a major effect on whether the type of strain leads to terrorism.

Second, most strain-based explanations of terrorism fail to fully explain *why* certain strains increase the likelihood of terrorism. Such explanations most commonly argue that the strains are intensely disliked and terrorism represents a desperate attempt to end them or seek revenge. The connections between strain and terrorism, however, are far more complex; and the failure to fully describe them significantly diminishes the completeness and policy relevance of existing strain explanations (more below).

Finally, current strain explanations fail to explain why only a small portion of the individuals exposed to strains become involved in terrorism (see Victoroff, 2005: 19; Newman, 2006). For example, although 1.4 billion people lived in extreme poverty in 2005 (*New York Times*, 2008: A30), only a very small percentage turned to terrorism. The responses to strain are quite numerous, and include suffering in silence, legal challenge, common crime (e.g. theft, drug selling), political protest, and guerilla war. Current strain explanations of terrorism provide, at best, only limited information on those factors that influence or condition the response to strain.

In sum, three problems account for the mixed or weak support for current strain-based explanations of terrorism. General strain theory (GST) holds the potential to correct for these problems. In particular, GST has much to say about the characteristics of strains most conducive to crime, the intervening mechanisms between strains and crime, and the factors that condition the effect of strains on crime. With some modification, these arguments can be used to construct a general strain theory of terrorism.

◈ A Brief Overview of General Strain Theory (GST)

GST states that certain strains or stressors increase the likelihood of crime (for overviews, see Agnew, 1992, 2001, 2006a, 2006b). Strains refer to events or conditions that are disliked by individuals. They involve negative or aversive treatment by others (receive something bad); the loss of valued possessions (lose something good), and/or the inability to achieve goals (fail to get what is wanted). Those strains most likely to increase crime are high in magnitude, seen as unjust, associated with low social control, and create some pressure or incentive for criminal coping. Examples of such strains include parental rejection, harsh discipline, peer abuse, work in the secondary labor market, chronic unemployment, criminal victimization, discrimination based on ascribed characteristics, and the failure to achieve goals such as masculine status and monetary success.

A distinction is made between objective strains, which refer to events and conditions disliked by most people in a given group; and subjective strains, which refer to events and conditions disliked by the particular person or persons experiencing them. Much data suggest that people often differ in their subjective evaluation of the same events and conditions; for example, divorce may be a devastating event to some and a cause for celebration to others (see Wheaton, 1990). There is reason to believe that subjective strains may be more strongly related to crime than objective strains (Froggio and Agnew, 2007). Further, a distinction is made between strains that are personally experienced, those that are anticipated in the future, and those that are vicariously experienced (i.e. strains experienced by others around the individual, particularly close others such as family and friends). In certain cases, anticipated and vicarious strains may contribute to crime (Agnew, 2002; Eitle and Turner, 2002).

Strains of the above type increase the likelihood of crime for several reasons. Most notably, they lead to a range of negative emotions, including anger, frustration, humiliation, and fear. These emotions create pressure for corrective action; individuals feel bad and want to do something about it. Crime is one possible response. Crime may be a way to reduce or escape from strains. For example, individuals may steal the money they desperately desire or run away from abusive parents. Crime may be a way to seek revenge against the source of the strain or related targets. For example, individuals may assault those who have mistreated them. And crime may be a way to alleviate the negative emotions that result from strain. For example, individuals may use illicit drugs in an effort to make themselves feel better. Strains may also lead to crime for additional reasons; for example, the continued experience of strains may increase irritability or 'negative emotionality', reduce social control (e.g. emotional ties to parents), foster the belief that crime is excusable or justifiable, and lead to association with other criminals (more below).

Most strained individuals, however, do not cope through crime. They endure their strain and/or employ legal coping strategies, such as negotiation and exercise. Crime is more likely when people lack the ability to cope in a legal manner. In particular, they lack coping skills, such as problem-solving skills; they lack coping resources, such as money; and they are low in social support. Crime is more likely when the costs of crime are low. For example, people are in environments where crime is seldom sanctioned, they have little to lose if they are sanctioned, and they do not believe that crime is wrong. And crime is more likely when individuals are disposed to crime. For example, they possess personality traits conducive to crime, such as negative emotionality; they hold beliefs favorable to crime; and they associate with others who model and reinforce crime.

With some modification, these ideas can form the foundation for a more refined strain theory of terrorism.

◈ A General Strain Theory of Terrorism

Terrorism has certain special features that are in need of explanation. Terrorism is more extreme than most common crimes, since it often involves the commission of serious violence against civilians who have done nothing to directly provoke their victimization. Also, terrorists typically commit their acts with the support of sub-national groups, while most adult offenders act alone. Further, terrorism is committed wholly or in part for political, social, or religious reasons. Most common crimes, by contrast, are committed for reasons of self-interest. GST, then, must devote special attention to explaining the extreme and collective nature of terrorism.

Strains Most Likely to Contribute to Terrorism

Terrorism is most likely to result from the experience of 'collective strains', or strains experienced by the members of an identifiable group or collectivity, most often a race/ethnic, religious, class, political, and/or territorial group. Only a small percentage of collective strains increase the likelihood of terrorism, however. These strains are: (a) high in magnitude, with civilian victims; (b) unjust; and (c) caused by significantly more powerful *others*, including complicit civilians, with whom members of the strained collectivity have weak ties. These arguments draw on GST (Agnew, 1992, 2001, 2006a, 2006b), but also take special account of the characteristics of and literature on terrorism (see especially Senechal de la Roche, 1996; Gurr and Moore, 1997; Black, 2004; Goodwin, 2006; Smelser, 2007).

Are High in Magnitude, With Civilian Victims (Nature of the Strain)

Collective strains are high in magnitude to the extent that they have the following characteristics: they involve acts which cause a *high degree of harm*, such as death, serious physical and sexual assault, dispossession, loss of livelihood, and major threats to core identities, values, and goals. They are *frequent, of long duration, and expected to continue into the future*. (However, strainful events—experienced in the context of persistent strains—may increase support for terrorism and precipitate terrorist acts [see Hamm, 2002; Oberschall, 2004: 28; Bjorgo, 2005; Newman, 2006; Post, 2007; Smelser, 2007: 34–5].) And they are *widespread*, affecting a high absolute and/or relative number of people in the strained collectivity, including *many civilians* (defined as individuals not directly involved in hostile actions against the source of the collective strain).

Case studies of terrorist organizations provide preliminary support for these arguments. Consider those strains associated with the emergence of several major terrorist groups: the Tamil Tigers, Basque Homeland and Liberty, Kurdistan Workers Party, Irish Republican Army, Shining Path, Hezbollah, Hamas,

Revolutionary Armed Forces of Colombia, and al Qaeda. Such strains involved serious violence—including death and rape, major threats to livelihood, dispossession, large scale imprisonment or detention, and/or attempts to eradicate ethnic identity. Further, these strains occurred over long periods and affected large numbers in the collectivity, including many civilians (Callaway and Harrelson-Stephens, 2006; Hoffman, 2006; Post, 2007).

There are certain terrorist groups that do not seem to have experienced strains of high magnitude. Examples include the Red Brigades in Italy and the Red Army Faction in West Germany, which included current and former university students; many left and right-wing terrorist groups in the United States; and certain groups made up of Muslim immigrants in western countries. Case studies of these groups, however, suggest that the group members believe that they or those they identify with are experiencing strains of the highest magnitude (Hoffman, 2006; Post, 2007). For example, many right-wing terrorists in the USA believe that the 'Zionist Occupation Government' and others pose a fundamental threat to all that they value, including their livelihood, status, and freedom (Blazak, 2001; Hamm, 2002). There is, of course, good reason to believe that these threats are imagined or greatly exaggerated. Nevertheless, it is *perception* of strain that is critical in motivating action (see Agnew, 2006a; Froggio and Agnew, 2007). Further, there is evidence that the members of these groups were in fact under significant *objective* strain. For example, the Red Brigades and Red Army Faction emerged at a time when university students typically found that only unskilled factory work was available to them (see Post, 2007: 129). Also, students in both Germany and Italy were subject to harsh government crackdowns and other strains (see Post, 2007). Blazak (2001) and Hamm (2002) provide excellent discussions of those strains contributing to the emergence of contemporary right-wing groups in the USA, including threats to the employment prospects and social standing of working-class, white, heterosexual males. At the same time, the existence of these groups does raise critical questions about the relationship between objective and subjective strains, a topic discussed below.

Are Seen as Unjust, Involving the Voluntary and Intentional Violation of Relevant Justice Norms by an External Agent (Reason for the Strain)

Collective strains may result from several sources other than the voluntary and intentional acts of an external agent. For example, they may result from the acts of members of the strained collectivity (e.g. some lower-class individuals victimize other lower-class individuals), from natural disasters (e.g. hurricanes, epidemics), or from 'reasonable' accidents (e.g. airplane crashes, fires). In addition, collective strains may be seen as the result of 'bad luck' (Merton, 1968) or supernatural forces, such as an angry God (see Smelser, 2007: 65). Terrorism is much less likely in these cases, even though the collective strain may be high in magnitude.

Further, the voluntary and intentional infliction of collective strain by an external agent is unlikely to result in terrorism unless it also involves the violation of relevant justice norms. Several such norms appear to be applicable across a wide range of groups and cultures (Agnew, 2001, 2006a). In particular, the voluntary and intentional infliction of collective strain is more likely to be seen as unjust if:

(a) The strain is seen as undeserved. Strains are more likely to be seen as deserved if they result from the negatively valued behavior or characteristics of members of the strained collectivity that are deemed relevant in the particular situation. Further, the strain must not be seen as excessive given the behaviors or characteristics. To illustrate, members of a particular group may receive low pay for their work, but they may not view this as unjust if they believe they work in less demanding jobs and/or they have lower levels of education.

(b) The strain is not in the service of some greater good. Members of a collectivity, for example, may experience much loss of life during a war, but not view this as unjust if the war is seen as necessary.

(c) The process used to decide whether to inflict the strain is unjust. Among other things, victims are more likely to view the process as unjust if they have no voice in the decision to inflict the strain, they do not respect and trust those inflicting the strain, and no rationale is provided for the infliction of the strain.

(d) The strain violates strongly held social norms or values, especially those embodied in the criminal law.

(e) The strain that members of the collectivity experience is very different from their past treatment in similar circumstances and/or from the treatment of similar others (i.e. members of the collectivity are subject to discriminatory treatment).

Collective strains are likely to be viewed as unjust if conditions (a) and (b) are satisfied or if one of the other conditions is satisfied.

Explanations of terrorism commonly make reference to the perceived injustice of the strains that are experienced. For example, Ahmed's (2005: 95) account of Palestinian terrorism states that: 'The fact is unmistakable and the message comes over loud and clear: a deep sense of injustice beyond the stage of profound frustration and despair stands at the heart of the issue.'

Are Caused by More Powerful Others, Including 'Complicit' Civilians, With Whom Members of the Strained Collectivity Have Weak Ties (The Relationship Between Those in the Strained Collectivity and the Source of Strain)

These 'others' most commonly differ from members of the strained collectivity in terms of some salient social dimension, such as religion, race/ethnicity, class, territorial location, nationality, and/or political ideology. They are more powerful because of their greater resources, including numbers, military equipment and skills, and/or

support from others. The strain they inflict may be partly attributed to civilians for several reasons (see the excellent discussion in Goodwin, 2006). Civilians may play a role in creating the Government or organization that inflicts the strain (e.g. through voting); they may support the Government/organization through acts such as paying taxes, public expressions of support, and service in government agencies; they may benefit from the infliction of the strain (e.g. occupying land formerly held by those in the strained collectivity); and they may fail to take action against those who inflict strain when such action is seen as possible (also see Pape, 2005: 137). Goodwin (2006) roughly measures civilian complicity in terms of whether the source of strain is a democratic state; the argument being that terrorists are more likely to believe that civilians in democratic states play major roles in electing and influencing their governments. Finally, members of the strained collectivity have weak emotional and material ties to the source of strain. These weak ties may stem from lack of contact, strong cultural differences (e.g. differences in language, values, beliefs, norms), and/or large differences in wealth/status/power, which tend to limit positive interaction and mutually beneficial exchange (Senechal de la Roche, 1996; Black, 2004; Goodwin, 2006).

In sum, several characteristics related to the nature of the collective strain, reason for the strain, and the relationship between the recipients and source of strain influence the likelihood of terrorism. Most of these characteristics vary even when the focus is on a particular type of strain, such as material deprivation. Researchers sometimes take account of certain of these characteristics, but rarely consider all of them. And this is a major reason for the weak quantitative support for strain theories of terrorism.

◈ Why Do Strains of the Above Type Increase the Likelihood of Terrorism?

This section describes the intervening mechanisms between collective strains and terrorism. Examining such mechanisms not only provides a fuller explanation of terrorism, but suggests additional ways to prevent terrorism. Terrorism can be prevented not only by reducing or altering the strains that contribute to it, but also by targeting the intervening mechanisms below.

The Above Collective Strains Lead to Strong Negative Emotional States and Traits—Including Anger, Humiliation, and Hopelessness—Which Are Conducive to Terrorism

Strains of the above type contribute to a range of negative emotional *states*, and the persistent experience of these strains contributes to a heightened tendency to experience negative emotional states (referred to as an emotional *trait*). Negative emotions create much pressure for corrective action; individuals feel bad and want to do something about it. These emotions also reduce the ability to cope in a legal manner. Angry individuals, for example, are less able to accurately [assess] their situation and effectively communicate with others. Further, these emotions lower inhibitions, reducing both the awareness of and concern for the consequences of one's behavior. Finally, certain of these emotions create a strong desire for revenge, with individuals feeling they must 'right' the wrong that has been done to them (see Agnew, 2006a for an overview).

There is much anecdotal data suggesting that negative emotions play a key role in the explanation of terrorism (Stern, 2003; Victoroff, 2005; Moghadam, 2006a, 2006b; Newman, 2006; Forst, 2009). A member of the Tamil Tigers, for example, stated that:

> In the late '90s when I was in school, the Sri Lanka military bombed my village. An elderly woman lost both legs, one person dies and two students were injured. I was angry with the [military] and joined the Tigers one year later. (Post, 2007: 92)

Related to this, many terrorists state that revenge is a major motive for their acts. Araj (2008), in fact, argues that the desire for revenge is so strong that individuals will sometimes commit terrorist acts even when they believe that doing so will impede the achievement of their ultimate goals.

These Strains Reduce the Ability to Legally and Militarily Cope, Leaving Terrorism as One of the Few Viable Coping Options

The above strains reduce the ability of those in the strained collectivity to effectively employ such coping strategies as negotiation, lobbying, protest, appeals to external agents such as the United Nations, and insurgency. These strains frequently involve the massive loss of material and other resources, which facilitate these forms of coping. The weak ties between members of the strained collectivity and the source of strain further reduce the likelihood that many of these coping strategies will be effective, since the source has little emotional or material incentive to respond to the requests of those in the strained collectivity. In addition, these strains often involve exclusion from the political process and the brutal suppression of protest movements (Callaway and Harrelson-Stephens, 2006; Post, 2007). Finally, the significantly greater power of the source of strain reduces the effectiveness of these coping options (e.g., military campaigns by those in the strained collectivity are unlikely to be successful).

Those in the strained collectivity may turn to common crimes in an effort to cope; for example, they may engage in theft to reduce their material deprivation. Common crimes, however, do little to end the collective strain and frequently do little to alleviate individual suffering. Common crimes, for example, are not an effective remedy for those collective strains involving violence or displacement. Further, common crime may not be a viable option in circumstances of massive deprivation. Terrorism, then, is often one of the few remaining coping options. While those in the strained collectivity may not have the resources to mount an effective military campaign, it is usually the case that they can easily target civilians. Civilians are generally more accessible and less able to resist attack than military targets. Further, there is some evidence that terrorism is an effective coping strategy in certain cases, ending or alleviating collective strain (see Pape, 2005; Victoroff, 2005; Hoffman, 2006; Moghadam, 2006b; Smelser, 2007). Also, terrorism serves other important functions for members of the strained collectivity (more below).

These Strains Reduce Social Control

In addition to reducing the ability to effectively cope through legal and military channels, the above strains also reduce most of the social controls that prevent terrorism (see Agnew, 2006a). In particular, these strains further weaken the emotional ties between members of the strained collectivity and the source of strain. They rob those in the strained collectivity of valued possessions, as well as hope for the future, leaving them with little to lose if they engage in terrorism. They weaken the belief that terrorism is wrong (more below). And they reduce the likelihood that members of the strained collectivity will sanction terrorists, since the experience of these strains tends to create tolerance, sympathy, or even support for terrorism. Again, there is much anecdotal evidence for these arguments in the terrorism literature, with terrorists frequently stating that they have weak/hostile ties to the source of their strain, that their strain has left them with little to lose, and that they no longer condemn terrorism (e.g. Post, 2007; Araj, 2008).

These Strains Provide Models for and Foster Beliefs Favorable to Terrorism

Collective strains of the above type frequently involve violent acts against civilians, thereby providing a model for terrorism. To illustrate, an aide to Arafat stated that Israeli civilians 'are no more innocent than the Palestinian women and children killed by Israelis' (Hoffman, 2006: 26). These strains also foster beliefs that excuse, justify, or even require terrorism. Recall that these strains are high in magnitude, involve civilian victims, are seen as unjust, and are inflicted by more powerful *others*, including complicit civilians, with whom those in the strained collectivity have weak ties. Given these circumstances, it is not difficult for those in the strained collectivity to employ such techniques of neutralization as denial of the victim (the source of strain deserves punishment), appeal to higher loyalties (terrorism is necessary to protect those in the collectivity), and condemnation of the condemners (terrorism is no worse than the acts committed by the source of strain) (see Gottschalk and Gottschalk, 2004; Bloom, 2006; and Post, 2007 for examples).

These Strains Foster a Collective Orientation and Response

Members of the strained collectivity believe they are under serious assault by more powerful others with whom they have weak ties. This does much to foster a heightened sense of collective identity (see Hogg and Abrams, 2003; Stevens, 2002; Post, 2007). This identity amplifies the experience of vicarious strains, since we care more about those we closely identify with (Agnew, 2002). It creates a sense of 'linked fate', or an 'acute sense of awareness (or recognition) that what happens to the group will also affect the individual member' (Simien, 2005: 529). And it creates a sense of obligation to protect others in the collectivity, at least among those traditionally cast in the protector role. This collective orientation helps explain the terrorism of those who have not personally experienced severe strain. Such individuals strongly identify with others in the collectivity and, through this identification, they vicariously experience, feel personally threatened by, and feel responsible for alleviating the strain experienced by these others (see McCauley, 2002: 9). The literature on terrorism provides numerous illustrations of these points (e.g. McCauley, 2002; Gupta, 2005; Pape, 2005; Post, 2005; Victoroff, 2005: 21–2, 30; Loza, 2006; Forst, 2009). A Palestinian terrorist, for example, stated that she grieves for the loss of her

> homeland, for the loss of a whole people, the pain of my entire nation. Pain truly affects my soul; so does the persecution of my people. It is from pain that I derive the power to resist and to defend the persecuted. (Post, 2007: 26)

This collective orientation is also important because it contributes to the formation of 'problem solving' groups that respond to the collective strain. When individuals confront shared problems that they cannot solve by themselves, they may develop a collective solution to their problems—one that sometimes takes the form of a criminal group (Cohen, 1955; Cloward and Ohlin, 1960). The Internet and media have come to play a critical role in facilitating the formation of such groups, since they publicize strains, allow strained individuals to (virtually) interact with one another, and facilitate the recruitment of individuals by terrorist groups (see especially Hoffman, 2006; Moghadam, 2006b; Forst, 2009).

Terrorist Groups, Once Formed, Promote Terrorism in a Variety of Ways

For reasons suggested above, those problem-solving groups that develop in response to collective strains of the above type are often disposed to terrorism. These groups, in turn, play a critical role in the promotion of terrorism (Caracci, 2002; Hamm, 2002; McCauley, 2002; National Research Council, 2002; Victoroff, 2005: 30–1; Smelser, 2007). The members of such groups model terrorism; differentially reinforce terrorism—usually with social approval/status; promote the adoption of beliefs favorable to terrorism; and diffuse responsibility for terrorist acts. These effects are often heightened by isolating group members from others who might challenge the aims of the terrorist group. On a more practical level, terrorist groups provide informational, material, and other support necessary for the commission of many terrorist acts.

It is important to note that while collective strains contribute to the development of terrorist groups that pursue collective goals, such groups also alleviate a range of individual strains. As suggested above, collective strains embody a host of individual strains; including feelings of anger, humiliation, and hopelessness; identity threats; and the loss of material possessions. Participation in terrorist groups allows for the alleviation of these strains (e.g. McCauley, 2002; Stevens, 2002; Stern, 2003; Vicoroff, 2005; Moghadam, 2006a; Post, 2007; Forst, 2009). In particular, participation provides an outlet for one's rage, a sense of self-worth, and status. A Palestinian terrorist, for example, stated that: 'An armed action proclaims that I am here, I exist, I am strong, I am in control, I am in the field, I am on the map' (Post, 2007: 61). Further, participation may alleviate material deprivation, since terrorist organizations frequently provide material aid to terrorists and their families (Hoffman, 2006). In addition, participation may address individual strains not directly linked to the collective strain. Abrahms (2008), for example, argues that many terrorists are socially alienated and

that participation in terrorist groups allows them to develop close ties to others. Terrorist organizations, then, allow for the alleviation of a range of individual strains; some linked to the collective strain and some not. This fact helps explain the persistence of such organizations in the face of both repeated failure and full success (see Victoroff, 2005; Abrahms, 2008).

Factors That Condition the Effect of Collective Strains on Terrorism

While collective strains of the above type are conducive to terrorism, they do not guarantee terrorism. The members of certain collectivities experiencing these strains have not turned to terrorism or have only turned to terrorism after many years (Gupta, 2005; Pape, 2005; Bloom, 2006; Moghadam, 2006a; Goodwin, 2007; Post, 2007). This is not surprising given the extreme nature of terrorism and its mixed effectiveness (see Victoroff, 2005; Hoffman, 2006; Moghadam, 2006b; Smelser, 2007; and Abrahms, 2008 for discussions on the effectiveness of terrorism). This section draws on GST and the terrorism literature to describe those factors that influence or condition the effect of strains on terrorism. These factors influence the *subjective* interpretation of strains; that is, the extent to which given strains are seen as high in magnitude and due to the unjust acts of others, including civilians. They also influence the emotional reaction to strains, the ability to engage in both non-terroristic and terroristic coping, the costs of terrorism, and/or the disposition for terrorism. It is important to note that while these factors are to *some* extent independent of the collective strains experienced, collective strains may alter them in ways conducive to terrorism. For example, the continued experience of collective strains may alter individual and group beliefs such that they come to excuse, justify, or require terrorism (see above).

Coping Resources, Skills, and Opportunities

The members of some collectivities may be better able to cope through non-terroristic means. This includes collectivities with extensive financial resources and legal and political skills. Also critical are the opportunities for coping provided by the larger political environment. In this area, some argue that terrorism is less likely in democratic states since there are more opportunities for legal coping (Crenshaw, 1995; National Research Council, 2002; Callaway and Harrelson-Stephens, 2006; Krueger and Maleckova, 2006; Piazza, 2007; Freeman, 2008). The research on the relationship between democracy and terrorism, however, is mixed (see the overview in Maleckova, 2005; also see Newman, 2006; Robison et al., 2006; Piazza, 2007; Abrahms, 2008; Freeman, 2008). This may reflect the fact that while democracies provide more opportunities for legal coping, they also provide more opportunities for terrorists—with democracies being less willing to harshly repress terrorists and more willing to negotiate with them (see Piazza, 2007).

In addition to the ability and opportunity to engage in non-terroristic coping, it is important to consider the ability/opportunity to engage in terrorism. At the individual level, this ability includes certain physical skills and a willingness to engage in risky behavior; attributes which tend to favor the young males who most often engage in terrorism (LaFree and Dugan, 2004: 56; Forst, 2009: 22–3). At the group/collectivity level, this ability involves the knowledge, material resources (e.g. money, munitions), and organization to commit terrorist acts (see Gurr and Moore, 1997; Oberschall, 2004). It has been argued that there are more opportunities for terrorism in 'failed states', since such states are less able to repress terrorist groups and often provide a base for such groups to operate. There is limited support for this view (Newman, 2007; Piazza, 2007; Forst, 2009: 409).

Social Support

Individuals, groups, and the collectivity itself may receive support for non-terroristic coping. Other individuals and groups, including foreign nations, may attempt to alleviate strain through the provision of such things as food, shelter, medical care, and military protection. They may attempt to end the strain through persuasion, sanction, and military intervention. And they may provide information, material assistance, and moral support in an effort to help those in the strained collectivity cope through non-terroristic means. Such support should

reduce the likelihood of terrorism, particularly if it is believed to be effective and that terrorism will jeopardize it. For example, Goodwin (2007) argues that the African National Congress avoided terrorism partly because it feared alienating supportive groups.

Individuals, groups, and collectivities may also receive support for terroristic coping, including information, moral support, material resources, and direct assistance (e.g. the provision of outside fighters). Such support may come from outside groups, including governments and foreign terrorist organizations. For example, the PLO and other terrorist organizations helped train members of the Tamil Tigers in the late 1970s and early 1980s (Pape, 2005: 73). And such support may come from internal sources. Individuals may receive support for terrorism from friends and family, terrorist groups, and members of the larger collectivity. And terrorist groups may receive support from members of the larger collectivity. Some researchers argue that it is unlikely that individuals and groups will engage in terrorism without such support (e.g. Merari, 2005; Pape, 2005; Smelser, 2007). There are rare cases of lone terrorists, but such terrorists are often loosely affiliated with others who support terrorism (see Hamm, 2002; McCauley, 2002; Smelser, 2007).

Social Control

While collective strains of the above type reduce most forms of social control, there may nevertheless be some independent variation in the control experienced by those in the strained collectivity. In particular, the source of strain may exercise high direct control over individuals and groups in the strained collectivity, thus reducing the likelihood of terrorism (see Gupta, 2005; Bloom, 2006; Callaway and Harrelson-Stephens, 2006; Robison et al., 2006; Smelser, 2007; Abrahms, 2008; Araj, 2008). This was the case in Cambodia under the Khmer Rouge, in Iraq under Saddam Hussein, and in Germany under Hitler. Also, some strained individuals and groups may maintain their bonds with selected individuals associated with the source of the strain, again reducing the likelihood of terrorism. This is said to partly explain why the African National Congress avoided terrorism against white civilians; there were close ties between the ANC and whites involved in the antiapartheid movement (Goodman, 2007). Further, some strained individuals and groups may have valued possessions—including both material possessions and reputations—that would be jeopardized by terrorism.

Finally, individuals and groups within the collectivity are less likely to engage in terrorism when it is condemned and sanctioned by others in the collectivity (see Pape, 2005).

Individual Traits

Terrorists are no more likely than comparable controls to suffer from psychopathology (McCauley, 2002; Atran, 2003; Pape, 2005; Victoroff, 2005; Post, 2007). Certain other traits, however, may increase the disposition for terrorism. Such traits include negative emotionality, low constraint, and cognitive inflexibility (Gottschalk and Gottschalk, 2004; Post, 2005; Victoroff, 2005: 27; Loza, 2006). Individuals with these traits are especially sensitive to strains, inclined to aggressive coping, attracted to risky activities, and prone to view the world in 'black and white' terms. Also, those who are alienated and socially marginalized may be more inclined to terrorism, since they have less to lose through terrorism, terrorist groups may provide them with a sense of belonging, and terrorism may be seen as a solution to certain of their problems. Such individuals include young, unmarried males; widows; those not gainfully employed, and unassimilated immigrants (see National Research Council, 2002; Merari, 2005; Post, 2005; Smelser, 2007; Abrahms, 2008; Forst, 2009; see Victoroff, 2005 for a discussion of other traits that may contribute to terrorism).

Association With Close Others Who Support Terrorism

Associating with close others who support terrorism has a major effect on the disposition for terrorism. As indicated above, such others may model terrorism, reinforce terrorism, teach beliefs favorable to terrorism, and provide the training and support necessary for many terrorist activities. Anecdotal accounts and some research suggest that individuals whose family members and friends are involved in terrorism are much more likely to

be involved themselves (Sageman, 2005; Victoroff, 2005; Post, 2007; Smelser, 2007; Abrahms, 2008; Forst, 2009).

Beliefs Favorable to Terrorism

The beliefs/ideology of those experiencing collective strains also influence the disposition for terrorism. Such beliefs may be learned from family members, friends, schools, neighbors, religious figures, and a variety of media sources (National Research Council, 2002; Victoroff, 2005: 18; Post, 2007; Forst, 2009). Beliefs favorable to terrorism have at least some of the following features: they emphasize the importance of collective identity (e.g. religious affiliation, ethnicity); increase the sensitivity to certain strains by, for example, placing much emphasis on 'honor' and 'masculinity'; claim that the collective strain being experienced is high in magnitude; provide an explanation for the strain, attributing it to the unjust acts of more powerful others, including complicit civilians; provide guidance on how to feel in response to the strain, with negative emotions such as rage and humiliation being emphasized; depict the source of strain as evil, subhuman, and otherwise deserving of a harsh response; encourage little or no contact with the source of strain; depict the source as both powerful but vulnerable to attack; point to the special strengths of those in the strained collectivity; excuse, justify, or require a terroristic response; provide a vision of a more positive, often utopian future that will result from such a response; promise rewards to those who engage in terrorism, including martyrdom and rewards in the afterlife; and create a history to support these views (e.g. emphasize the past victories of the collectivity over similar injustices) (Gupta, 2005; Loza, 2006; Moghadam, 2006a; Post, 2007; Smelser, 2007).

While such beliefs are fostered by the experience of collective strains of the above type, they are also a function of other factors (see Smelser, 2007). As a result, some groups experiencing the above collective strains hold beliefs that discourage terrorism. For example, Goodwin (2007) argues that the emphasis of the African National Congress on nonracialism helped discourage terrorism against white South Africans. And the Dalai Lama's advocacy of the 'middle way' has likely done much to prevent terrorism by the Tibetans against the Chinese (see Wong, 2008).

Anticipated Costs and Benefits of Terrorist Acts

Estimates of costs/benefits are partly a function of the success of prior terrorist acts, both those committed by the collectivity in question and by others (Gurr and Moore, 1997; Pape, 2005; Hoffman, 2006; Sedgwick, 2007). It is important to note, however, that it is difficult to objectively define 'success' (see Pape, 2005; Goodwin, 2006; Hoffman, 2006; Moghadam, 2006a; Abrahms, 2008; Newman and Clarke, 2008). Terrorist acts seldom result in the end of the collective strain experienced. Such acts, however, may be deemed successful if they call greater attention to the collective strain, gain recruits or other support for the terrorist organization, boost the morale of those in the organization and sympathizers, inflict significant damage on the source of the collective strain, or result in the partial alleviation of the strain. Researchers must therefore consider the subjective views of those involved in terrorism when assessing success. Further, the anticipated costs and benefits of terrorism are influenced by a host of more immediate factors, including those having to do with the availability of attractive targets and the absence of capable guardians (Newman and Clarke, 2008).

◈ Conclusion

The general strain theory of terrorism presented in this article builds on current strain-based explanations of terrorism in three ways. First, it better describes the core characteristics of strains that contribute to terrorism. Terrorism is most likely in response to collective strains that are high in magnitude, with civilian victims; unjust; and caused by more powerful others, including complicit civilians, with whom members of the strained collectivity have weak ties. Second, it more fully describes the reasons why such strains increase the likelihood of terrorism. In particular, such strains lead to negative emotional states and traits; reduce the ability to effectively cope through legal channels, common crime, and military means; reduce social control; provide models for and contribute to beliefs favorable to terrorism; and foster a collective orientation and response to the strain. Third, it provides the most complete description of those factors that condition the effect of the above strains on terrorism. Such factors include a range of coping resources, skills, and opportunities; various types of social support; level of social control; selected individual traits; association with others who support terrorism; beliefs related to terrorism, and the anticipated costs and benefits of terrorism. The general strain theory of terrorism extends GST in important ways; pointing to new strains, intervening mechanisms, and conditioning variables that are especially relevant to terrorism.

It is important to note, however, that the general strain theory of terrorism is not a complete explanation of terrorism. Being a social psychological theory, it does not describe the larger social forces that contribute to the development of the above strains and help shape the reaction to them. Also, collective strains of the above type are likely only one of several causes of terrorism. Indeed, the final section of this article lists several factors that have been said to directly affect terrorism, such as social controls, beliefs/ideologies, association with others who support terrorism, and the anticipated costs and benefits of terrorism. A complete explanation of terrorism will require that we draw on a range of theories and describe the complex relations between them. The development of such an explanation is beyond the scope of this article, but this article does describe what will likely be a central variable in this explanation—collective strains of a certain type.

In addition to shedding light on the causes of terrorism, the general strain theory has important policy implications. The most obvious is to end or reduce collective strains of the above type. For example, the source of strain may attempt to reduce civilian causalities. In addition, it may be possible to target those intervening mechanisms that link collective strains to terrorism. For example, governments may make it easier to address grievances via legal channels. Further, conditioning variables may be targeted. Outside groups, for example, may provide social support to members of the strained collectivity. These multiple points for intervention provide some hope for efforts to reduce terrorism.

At the same time, it is important to note that collective strains of the above type often set in motion a self-perpetuating process that is hard to interrupt. These strains gradually change members of the strained collectivity in ways that increase the likelihood of a terroristic response. Among other things, these strains foster individual traits conducive to terrorism, such as negative emotionality; further reduce social control, including ties to the source of strain; lead to the adoption of beliefs that favor terrorism; and contribute to the development of terroristic organizations. In addition, the terrorism carried out by such organizations frequently provokes a harsh response, which further increases support for terrorism in the strained collectivity (see Hamm, 2002; Smelser, 2007: 80–1; Araj, 2008; LaFree and Dugan, 2008). And, to further complicate matters, concessions by the source of strain may be seen as a success for terrorism—also prompting further terrorist acts. As LaFree and Dugan (2008) point out, however, it may be possible to escape this cycle of violence with a very carefully calibrated response to terrorism—one that does not reinforce terrorism or provoke a harsh reaction—along with efforts to address the types of root causes described above.

Before proceeding further, however, it is critical to test the general strain theory. As indicated, most current tests of strain-based explanations are far too simplistic. They fail to measure the key dimensions of strain, including magnitude, injustice, and the nature of the source. Further, these tests do not examine intervening mechanisms, the subjective interpretation of strain, or conditioning variables. Unfortunately, most existing data sets do not permit anything close to a full test of the general strain theory. Agnew (2001, 2006a) provides suggestions on how to obtain both 'objective' and subjective measures of many of the dimensions of strain that were listed, as well as measures of many of the intervening and conditioning variables. In the interim, researchers can draw on the theory to conduct better tests of strain explanations. One example of an approach that might be taken is provided by the cross-national research on criminal homicide (Agnew, 2006a). Material deprivation is often unrelated to violence in such research. Certain researchers, however, have attempted to roughly measure the perceived injustice of such deprivation. For example, they have estimated whether such deprivation is due to race/ethnic or religious discrimination (Messner, 1989; also see Gurr and Moore, 1997). Deprivation resulting from discrimination is strongly related to violence.

If the general strain theory is supported, it is critical to note that while collective strains may help *explain* terrorism, they do not *justify* terrorism. First, it is important to distinguish between the objective nature and subjective interpretation of such strains. In certain cases, there is good reason to believe that the members of terrorist groups exaggerate—often greatly—the strains they experience (e.g. members of certain white supremacist groups in the USA who claim they are being oppressed by the Zionist Occupation Government). Second, it is important to recognize that the members of the strained collectivity may sometimes contribute to the strains they experience through such things as attacks on the source of strain. Finally, the argument that collective strains contribute to terrorism is a causal one, not an ethical one. There are many responses to strain, some ethical and some not; being subject to strain does *not* justify any response to it.

◈ References

Abrahms, Max (2008) 'What Terrorists Really Want', *International Security* 32(4): 78–105.

Agnew, Robert (1992) 'Foundation for a General Strain Theory of Crime and Delinquency', *Criminology* 30(1): 47–87.

Agnew, Robert (2001) 'Building on the Foundation of General Strain Theory: Specifying the Types of Strain Most Likely to Lead to Crime and Delinquency', *Journal of Research in Crime and Delinquency* 38(4): 319–61.

Agnew, Robert (2002) 'Experienced, Vicarious, and Anticipated Strain: An Exploratory Study Focusing on Physical Victimization and Delinquency', *Justice Quarterly* 19(4): 603–32.

Agnew, Robert (2006a) *Pressured into Crime: An Overview of General Strain Theory*. New York: Oxford.

Agnew, Robert (2006b) 'General Strain Theory: Current Status and Directions for Further Research', in Francis T. Cullen, John Paul Wright, and Michelle Coleman (eds) *Taking Stock: The Status of Criminological Theory, Advances in Criminological Theory*, Vol. 15, pp. 101–23. New Brunswick, NJ: Transaction.

Agnew, Robert, Nicole Leeper Piquero, and Francis T. Cullen (2009) 'General Strain Theory and White-Collar Crime', in Sally S. Simpson and David Weisburd (eds) *The Criminology of White-Collar Crime*, 35–60. New York: Springer.

Ahmed, Hisham H. (2005) 'Palestinian Resistance and "Suicide Bombing"', in Tore Bjorgo (ed.) *Root Causes of Terrorism*, pp. 87–101. London: Routledge.

Araj, Bader (2008) 'Harsh State Repression as a Cause of Suicide Bombing: The Case of the Palestinian–Israeli Conflict', *Studies in Conflict & Terrorism* 31(4): 284–303.

Atran, Scott (2003) 'Genesis of Suicide Terrorism', *Science* 299(5612): 1534–5, 1538.

Bjorgo, Tore (2005) 'Introduction', in Tore Bjorgo (ed.) *Root Causes of Terrorism*, pp. 1–15. London: Routledge.

Black, Donald (2004) 'Terrorism as Social Control', *Sociology of Crime, Law and Deviance* 5: 9–18.

Blazak, Randy (2001) 'White Boys to Terrorist Men', *American Behavioral Scientist* 44(6): 982–1000.

Bloom, Mia (2006) 'Dying to Kill: Motivations for Suicide Terrorism', in Ami Pedahzur (ed.) *Root Causes of Suicide Terrorism*, pp. 25–53. London: Routledge.

Callaway, Rhonda L. and Julie Harrelson-Stephens (2006) 'Toward a Theory of Terrorism: Human Security as a Determinant of Terrorism', *Studies in Conflict & Terrorism* 29(7): 679–702.

Caracci, Giovanni (2002) 'Cultural and Contextual Aspects of Terrorism', in Chris E. Stout (ed.) *The Psychology of Terrorism, Volume III: Theoretical Understandings and Perspectives*, pp. 57–81. Westport, CT: Praeger.

Cloward, Richard and Lloyd Ohlin (1960) *Delinquency and Opportunity*. Glencoe, IL: Free Press.

Cohen, Albert K. (1955) *Delinquent Boys*. Glencoe, IL: Free Press.

Crenshaw, Martha (1995) 'Thoughts on Relating Terrorism to Historical Contexts', in Martha Crenshaw (ed.) *Terrorism in Context*, pp. 3–26. University Park, PA: Pennsylvania State University Press.

De Coning, Cedric (2004) 'Poverty and Terrorism: The Root Cause Debate?', *Conflict Trends* 3/2004: 20–9.

Eitle, David J. and R. Jay Turner (2002) 'Exposure to Community Violence and Young Adult Crime: The Effects of Witnessing Violence, Traumatic Victimization, and Other Stressful Life Events', *Journal of Research in Crime and Delinquency* 39(2): 214–37.

Forst, Brian (2009) *Terrorism, Crime, and Public Policy*. Cambridge: Cambridge University Press.

Freeman, Michael (2008) 'Democracy, Al Qaeda, and the Causes of Terrorism: A strategic Analysis of U.S. Policy', *Studies in Conflict and Terrorism* 31(1): 40–59.

Froggio, Giancinto and Robert Agnew (2007) 'The Relationship between Crime and "Objective" versus "Subjective" Strains', *Journal of Criminal Justice* 35(1): 81–7.

Goodwin, Jeff (2006) 'A Theory of Categorical Terrorism', *Social Forces* 84(4): 2027–46.

Goodwin, Jeff (2007) '"The Struggle Made Me a Nonracialist": Why There Was So Little Terrorism in the Antiapartheid Struggle', *Mobilization: An International Quarterly Review* 12(2): 193–203.

Gottschalk, Michael and Susan Gottschalk (2004) 'Authoritarianism and Pathological Hatred: A Social Psychological Profile of the Middle Eastern Terrorist', *American Sociologist* Summer: 38–59.

Gupta, Dipak K. (2005) 'Exploring Roots of Terrorism', in Tore Bjorgo (ed.) *Root Causes of Terrorism*, pp. 16–32. London: Routledge.

Gurr, Ted Robert and Will H. Moore (1997) 'Ethnopolitical Rebellion: A Cross-Sectional Analysis of the 1980s with Risk Assessment for the 1990s', *American Journal of Political Science* 41(4): 1079–103.

Hamm, Mark S. (2002) *In Bad Company: America's Terrorist Underground*. Boston, MA: Northeastern University Press.

Hoffman, Bruce (2006) *Inside Terrorism*. New York: Columbia University Press.

Hogg, Michael A. and Dominic Abrams (2003) 'Intergroup Behavior and Social Identity', in Michael A. Hogg and Joel Cooper (eds) *The Sage Handbook of Social Psychology*, pp. 407–31. Los Angeles, CA: SAGE.

Krueger, Alan B. and Jitka Maleckova (2003) 'Seeking the Roots of Terrorism', B10–13, *Chronicle of Higher Education: The Chronicle Review* 6 June.

LaFree, Gary and Laura Dugan (2004) 'How Does Studying Terrorism Compare to Studying Crime?', *Sociology of Crime, Law and Deviance* 5: 53–74.

LaFree, Gary and Laura Dugan (2008) 'Terrorism and Counterterrorism Research', unpublished document.

Loza, Wagdy (2006) 'The Psychology of Extremism and Terrorism: A Middle-Eastern Perspective', *Aggression and Violent Behavior* 12(2): 141–55.

McCauley, Clark (2002) 'Psychological Issues in Understanding Terrorism and the Response to Terrorism', in Chris E. Stout (ed.) *The Psychology of Terrorism, Volume III: Theoretical Understandings and Perspectives*, pp. 3–30. Westport, CT: Praeger.

Maleckova, Kitke (2005) 'Impoverished Terrorists: Stereotype or Reality?', in Tore Bjorgo (ed.) *Root Causes of Terrorism*, pp. 33–43. London: Routledge.

Merari, Ariel (2005) 'Social, Organizational and Psychological Factors in Suicide Terrorism', in Tore Bjorgo (ed.) *Root Causes of Terrorism*, pp. 70–85. London: Routledge.

Merton, Robert (1968) *Social Theory and Social Structure*. New York: Free Press.

Messner, Steven F. (1989) 'Economic Discrimination and Societal Homicide Rates: Further Evidence of the Cost of Inequality', *American Sociology Review* 54(4): 597–611.

Moghadam, Assaf (2006a) 'The Roots of Suicide Terrorism: A Multi-Causal Approach', in Ami Pedahzur (ed.) *Root Causes of Suicide Terrorism*, pp. 81–107. London: Routledge.

Moghadam, Assaf (2006b) 'Suicide Terrorism, Occupation, and the Globalization of Martyrdom: A Critique of *Dying to Win*', *Studies in Conflict & Terrorism* 29(8): 707–29.

National Research Council (2002) *Terrorism: Perspectives from the Behavioral and Social Sciences*. Washington, DC: National Academies Press.

Newman, Edward (2006) 'Exploring the Root Causes of Terrorism', *Studies in Conflict & Terrorism* 29(8): 749–72.

Newman, Edward (2007) 'Weak States, State Failure, and Terrorism', *Terrorism and Political Violence* 19(4): 463–88.

Newman, Graeme R. and Ronald V. Clarke (2008) *Policing Terrorism: An Executive's Guide*. Washington, DC: Office of Community Oriented Policing Services, US Department of Justice.

New York Times (2008) 'Failing the World's Poor', *New York Times*, 24 September, p. A30.

Oberschall, Anthony (2004) 'Explaining Terrorism: The Contribution of Collective Action Theory', *Sociological Theory* 22(1): 26–37.

Pape, Robert A. (2005) *Dying to Win: The Strategic Logic of Suicide Terrorism*. New York: Random House.

Piazza, James A. (2006) 'Rooted in Poverty? Terrorism, Poor Economic Development, and Social Cleavages', *Terrorism and Political Violence* 18(1): 159–77.

Piazza, James A. (2007) 'Draining the Swamp: Democracy Promotion, State Failure, and Terrorism in 19 Middle Eastern Countries', *Studies in Conflict & Terrorism* 30(6): 521–39.

Post, Jerrold M. (2005) 'The Socio-Cultural Underpinnings of Terrorist Psychology: When Hatred Is Bred in the Bone', in Tore Bjorgo (ed.) *Root Causes of Terrorism*, pp. 54–69. London: Routledge.

Post, Jerrold M. (2007) *The Mind of the Terrorist*. New York: Palgrave Macmillan.

Rausch, Sharla and Gary LaFree (2007) 'The Growing Importance of Criminology in the Study of Terrorism', *The Criminologist* 32(6): 1, 3–5.

Robison, Kristopher K., Edward M. Crenshaw and J. Craig Jenkins (2006) 'Ideologies of Violence: The Social Origins of Islamist and Leftist Transnational Terrorism', *Social Forces* 84(4): 2009–26.

Rosenfeld, Richard (2002) 'Why Criminologists Should Study Terrorism', *The Criminologist* 27(6): 1, 3–4.

Rosenfeld, Richard (2004) 'Terrorism and Criminology', *Sociology of Crime, Law and Deviance* 5: 19–32.

Sageman, Marc (2005) *Understanding Terror Networks*. Philadelphia, PA: University of Pennsylvania Press.

Sedgwick, Mark (2007) 'Inspiration and the Origins of Global Waves of Terrorism', *Studies in Conflict & Terrorism* 30(2): 97–112.

Senechal de la Roche, Roberta (1996) 'Collective Violence as Social Control', *Sociological Forum* 11(1): 97–128.

Simien, Evelyn (2005) 'Race, Gender, and Linked Fate', *Journal of Black Studies* 35(5): 529–50.

Smelser, Neil J. (2007) *The Faces of Terrorism: Social and Psychological Dimensions*. Princeton, NJ: Princeton University Press.

Stern, Jessica (2003) *Terror in the Name of God: Why Religious Militants Kill*. New York: HarperCollins.

Stevens, Michael J. (2002) 'The Unanticipated Consequences of Globalization: Contextualizing Terrorism', in Chris E. Stout (ed.) *The Psychology of Terrorism, Volume III: Theoretical Understandings and Perspectives*, pp. 31–56. Westport, CT: Praeger.

Tilly, Charles (2004) 'Terror, Terrorism, Terrorists', *Sociological Theory* 22(10): 5–13.

Turk, Austin (2004) 'Sociology of Terrorism', *Annual Review of Sociology* 30: 271–86.

Victoroff, Jeff (2005) 'The Mind of the Terrorist: A Review and Critique of Psychological Approaches', *Journal of Conflict Resolution* 49(1): 3–42.

Wheaton, Blair (1990) 'Life Transitions, Role Histories, and Mental Health', *American Sociological Review* 55(2): 209–24.

Wong, Edward (2008) 'Tibetans Reaffirm a Conciliatory Approach to China', *New York Times*, 23 November, p. A13.

CHAPTER 5

Social Disorganization Theory

To LaJoe, the neighborhood had become a black hole. She could more easily recite what wasn't there than what was there. There were no banks, only currency exchanges, which charged up to $8.00 for every welfare check cashed. There were no public libraries, skating rinks, movie theaters, or bowling alleys to entertain the neighborhood's children. For the infirm there were two neighborhood clinics... both of which teetered on bankruptcy and would close by the end of 1989. Yet the death rate of newborn babies exceeded the infant mortality rates in a number of third world countries, including Chile, Costa Rica, Cuba, and Turkey. And there was no rehabilitation center, though drug abuse was rampant.

According to a 1980 profile of Twenty-seventh Ward—a political configuration drawn, ironically, in the shape of a gun and including Henry Horner and Rockwell Gardens, a smaller but no less forbidding housing complex—60,110 people lived here, 88 percent of them black, 46 percent of them lived below the poverty level. It was so impoverished that when Mother Teresa visited in 1982, she assigned nuns from her Missionaries of Charity to work at Henry Horner.

Source: Kotlowitz (1988, p. 12).

◈ Introduction

Kotlowitz's (1988) description of these Chicago neighborhoods provides an interesting introduction to **social disorganization theory**, a theory developed to explain patterns of deviance and crime across social locations, such as neighborhoods. Unlike many of the microlevel theories discussed in this book, which attempt to explain variation in deviant behavior across individuals, social disorganization theory is a macrolevel theory that focuses on larger units of analysis, such as neighborhoods, schools, cities, and even states or countries. This is a unique contribution because it is so clear that some places are safer than others and deviance is rare, controlled, or hidden and that all sorts of deviances flourish in other places. Rodney Stark (1987) accurately described a major problem in criminology stemming from the advent of self-report surveys.

This transformation soon led repeatedly to the "discovery" that poverty is unrelated to delinquency. . . . Yet, through it all, social scientists somehow knew better than to stroll the street at night in certain parts of town

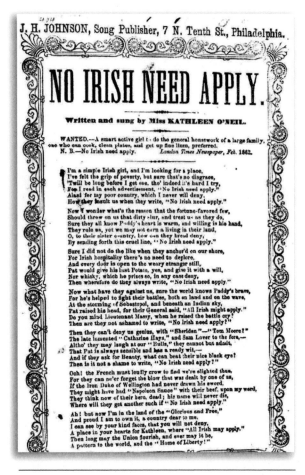

▲ Photo 5.1   Immigrants faced many problems when they arrived in the United States at the turn of the century, including discrimination.

© Library of Congress, Rare Book and Special Collections Division, *America Singing: Nineteenth-Century Song Sheets.*

or even to park there. And despite the fact that countless surveys showed that kids from upper and lower income families scored the same on delinquency batteries, even social scientists know that the parts of town that scared them were not upper-income neighborhoods. (p. 894)

Indeed, violence, drug use, prostitution, mental illness, and other forms of deviance are commonplace in neighborhoods such as Henry Horner and Rockwell Gardens. Other places seem to be able to control crime and deviance (or at least the deviance that does exist is far less visible). Social disorganization theory attempts to explain this variation. Why are certain neighborhoods able to control levels of deviance while others are unable to minimize it or eliminate it entirely? Social disorganization theory assumes that most people do not want to live in unsafe neighborhoods with high levels of delinquency, crime, and deviance. However, because of various structural conditions to be discussed, some people are not able to work together to achieve common goals.

In this chapter, we begin with some history behind the theory of social disorganization, including the creation of a major program in sociology at the University of Chicago toward the end of the 19th century and the social milieu of Chicago at that point in time. We then discuss the development of social disorganization theory and early empirical tests of the theory, which were focused primarily on juvenile delinquency. Historically, the theory was put on the back burner for many years only to come back strong in the 1980s. We discuss this revitalization as well as new advances of the theory. Today, social disorganization theory and variants of it are reasonably popular and are used quite often when investigating deviance at the aggregate level: neighborhoods, schools, cities, and even internationally.

DEVIANCE IN POPULAR CULTURE

When people are asked what causes crime and deviance, they tend to think in terms of individualistic causes of deviance. That is, they are looking to answer why certain individuals engage in crime and deviant behavior and others do not. Why do some people use hard drugs and others abstain? Why do some young males and females go into prostitution while other live "cleaner lives"? Why do some professionals "cheat" while others do not, even if they are pretty sure "cheating is lucrative," and they could get away with it? The social disorganization perspective asks a different question: Why is there more crime in certain areas than in others? *What community-level characteristics influence the rate of crime or deviance in any given area?*

The documentary film *Hoop Dreams* follows two young boys from inner-city Chicago as they are recruited into a private high school and different colleges in pursuit of their goal of basketball stardom. Watch the first 45 minutes of *Hoop Dreams* (freshman and sophomore years of high school), paying careful attention to the different environments that are captured on tape.

- What did you notice about the neighborhoods that Arthur and William grew up and lived in? What did the neighborhoods look like? What kinds of things went on there? What did people say about these areas?
- Now think about the neighborhood in which the high school, St. Joe's, is located. What did it look like? What did people say about it?
- Which neighborhood do you think had higher crime rates? Why do you think so? What are the important characteristics to consider?
- Think about the neighborhood that you grew up in. What was it like? What factors do you think contributed to the crime rates (high or low) in your neighborhood?
- If you were trying to lower crime or deviance rates in a given neighborhood, where would you start? What specifically would you target and try to improve?

Documentary films can sometimes tell us a great deal about deviance and social control, even if that is not the expressed intent of the story. The Chicago neighborhoods shown in *Hoop Dreams* have very different levels of social organization, which affect levels of crime and deviance and the life chances of individuals such as Arthur and William and their family members. Considering the neighborhood you grew up in as an additional case study can help to illustrate how social disorganization affects communities—and how it may have affected you and your friends, even though you may not have realized it at the time. Applying the theories to real examples helps to remind us that these are more than big ideas—deviance is all around us, and sociological theories can help us make sense of our own social worlds.

◈ Development of Social Disorganization Theory

To provide context for an understanding of the theory of social disorganization, we need to go back to the end of the 19th century and the transition to the 20th. Consider Chicago at the turn of the century (perhaps not so different in terms of deviance than it is today—plenty to go around!). Many of the new faculty members at the University of Chicago at that time were from rural and religious backgrounds. They were coming to Chicago, a city where crime and deviance were not hard to find—indeed, they were right in your face. Gambling, prostitution, alcohol consumption, violence, police abuse of power, and many other forms of deviance were common and well known to the citizens of Chicago. The question for these researchers was why these forms of deviance existed and seemed to flourish in certain areas of the city while other areas seemed to be able to control these "social problems."

Alternatively, how did people in general explain deviance at the turn of the century? In other words, what were the popular explanations of crime and deviance? Much like today, the explanations focused on individuals and groups—that is, "types of people" explanations. The criminals and deviants were the "new immigrants." Immigrants who brought their old traditions and who had not been appropriately socialized into the new world were seen as the causes of the social problems of the day. Of course, at different times, different groups felt the brunt of ethnic prejudice and were seen as the cause of various social ills. For example, Irish and Italian immigrants faced ethnic discrimination in

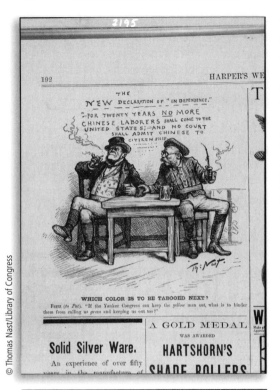

▲ **Photo 5.2** Which color is to be tabooed next?

the late 19th and early 20th centuries and were seen as a source of trouble. Indeed, in 1918, when labor was in high demand and employers were scrounging for workers, advertisements read "Italians and Coloreds" may apply, suggesting an ethnic stratification ranking of Italians as close to African Americans (Luhman, 2002). German Jews immigrating to the United States during the early to mid-1800s because of the repression and discrimination in Germany faced fewer legal restrictions here, but there were still some, including restrictions from "holding public office, becoming lawyers, and serving as officers in state militia" in certain regions (Luhman, 2002, p. 149). Immigration from China, beginning around 1850, also brought political and social reaction, leading to Chinese immigrants being viewed as deviant. Hispanics, too, have faced ethnic stereotyping and discrimination as evidenced by the editorials, discussion, and debate generated in the early 2000s that continued to be a major political issue throughout the 2016 presidential election. Finally, coming to America as slaves, African Americans have always faced prejudice and discrimination, but as they moved from the South to northern cities, they too became the scapegoat and the "cause" of social problems.

Fortunately, science was also making important discoveries and influencing how we thought about deviance and other social problems. The Chicago school was very familiar with scientific strides being made in plant and animal biology. For example, Darwin's *Origin of Species,* published in 1859, was well known to Chicago sociologists and influenced how they approached the study of human behavior. In contrast to the classical school of criminology, which focused on free will and the role of the government in controlling free will, the Chicago perspective did not ask whether plants "willed" themselves to do better in certain environments than others or whether animals "willed" themselves to reproduce and thrive in certain areas versus others. Rather, its proponents believed that environmental factors affected where certain plants and animals would thrive, and other plants and animals would flourish in others. The early Chicago researchers believed that they could find the causes of crime in the structure of the environment. Much like today, thanks to the explosion of information and analysis provided by geographic information systems, such as MapQuest, Google Earth, and a host of statistical software programs for analyzing geography, the principle of the Chicago school was that if you want to understand something, *map it!* Through this process of mapping social deviance, researchers were able to demonstrate that "types of people" explanations were often limited, if not downright wrong. Indeed, certain types of deviance seemed to flourish in some areas over time, even though the "types of people" (racial and ethnic groups) who lived there changed dramatically.

◈ Shaw and McKay's Study of Juvenile Delinquency and Urban Areas

Based on Park and Burgess's human ecology approach, the origin of social disorganization theory is generally attributed to Clifford Shaw and Henry McKay's (1942/1969) seminal work, *Juvenile Delinquency and Urban Areas,* in which they plotted on maps the home addresses of (1) boys brought to court for an alleged delinquent activity, (2) boys committed by the court to a correctional facility, and (3) "boys dealt with by the police probation officers with or without court appearance" (p. 44). Data on court cases and commitments were available for 1900, 1920, and 1930, and police contacts centered around 1930. As the authors noted, "The distribution of delinquents at different periods of time afford the basis for comparison and for analysis of long-term trends and processes that could not be made for a single period" (Shaw & McKay, 1942/1969, p. 45). Their maps clearly show three things. First, delinquency did not appear to be distributed randomly across the neighborhoods of Chicago. Second, rates of delinquency appeared to cluster in certain neighborhoods and appeared highest close to the **central business district** (CBD). Shaw and McKay noted that in addition to the high rates of delinquency near the CBD, delinquency was highest in neighborhoods in or around business and industrial areas, often referred to as mixed land use. Third, delinquency, by and large, tended to decline as one moved away from the CBD. Indeed, their analyses clearly showed that rates of delinquency as measured by juvenile commitments across five **concentric zones** around 1900, 1920, and 1930 fell precipitously as one moved away from the CBD.

Shaw and McKay (1942/1969) examined these zones and characterized Zone II, the one closest to the CBD, as a **zone in transition**. Here resided the most recent immigrants to the city, the poorest and least educated citizens, and those who needed to live close to the CBD for work—when they could find it. Shaw and McKay found that as one moved away from the zones in transition, one would find residents from earlier waves of immigrants. These were people who had learned English, had received more education, had better jobs, and could afford to get out of the impoverished inner city where only those who had no other choice lived. What was most interesting was that the people who lived in the zone in transition changed. Indeed, no one really wanted to live there, and immigrants quickly left the high-crime-rate and deviant areas for safer neighborhoods as soon as they could afford to, only to be replaced by another group of immigrants who were forced to live in the zone in transition.

To better understand why crime rates declined as one moved out from the inner city, Shaw and McKay (1942/1969) looked to other social factors that characterized these areas. So other than high rates of delinquency, what characterized these neighborhoods? Shaw and McKay highlighted three factors that characterized neighborhoods with high rates of delinquency: **poverty**, **population turnover**, and **racial/ethnic heterogeneity**. Shaw and McKay did not emphasize a direct link between poverty and delinquency (Bursik, 1988). Rather, they found that poor neighborhoods were characterized by population turnover and racial/ethnic heterogeneity. Bursik argues that "in its purest formulation, social disorganization refers to the inability of local communities to realize the common values of their residents or solve commonly experienced problems" (p. 521). When the primary goal of the residents is to move out of the neighborhood, there is little incentive to try to make it a better place. These people were poor and did not own their own residences, and the landlords ("slumlords") had little interest in making these neighborhoods better places to live. In fact, it was in their best interest to invest as little as possible in their apartment buildings and other structures because, as the city expanded, they would be bought out and their buildings torn down and replaced with industrial structures. Similarly, because the populations were changing and composed of people with different ethnic and/or racial backgrounds, further barriers existed, such as limited motivation to work together to reduce the crime and other deviance that characterized the area. These structural factors (poverty, population turnover, and racial/ethnic heterogeneity) consistently characterized high delinquency areas, even though the specific "types of people" changed over the decades studied.

◇ Critiques of Social Disorganization Theory

Shaw and McKay's (1942/1969) pioneering work in social disorganization theory was sharply criticized on a number of grounds and then waned in popularity and importance for several reasons, as described in a review by Bursik (1988). First, the field of criminology shifted and became far more focused on individuals as opposed to groups, and macrolevel theories such as social disorganization rarely have anything to say about individuals, only groups and places. Second, **longitudinal data** (data collected over time) are expensive and sometimes impossible to collect, and later studies typically were restricted to **cross-sectional designs** (data collected at only one point in time). Cross-sectional designs are problematic in the study of deviance, especially studies of a theory based on longitudinal data, because they typically assume a static view of urban life that seems inconsistent with history. Finally, there was considerable confusion about what social disorganization actually was and how it should be measured. In particular, there seemed to be some confusion in distinguishing social disorganization from delinquency itself, resulting in criticisms that the theory was tautological—that is, true by definition, circular, and, therefore, not testable. However, a number of important works in the late 1970s and 1980s gave social disorganization theory a rebirth.

◈ Rebirth of Social Disorganization Theory

In her classic work, *Social Sources of Delinquency*, Ruth Kornhauser (1978) divided the classic theories of juvenile delinquency into three basic types: cultural deviance (e.g., differential association and social learning; see Chapter 6), strain (see Chapter 4), and social disorganization. She clearly puts social disorganization as a macrolevel control theory whereby residents of certain neighborhoods are able to control and minimize unwanted deviance while residents in other neighborhoods, characterized by poverty, population turnover, and racial/ethnic heterogeneity, cannot control their environments and achieve common goals. Although Shaw and McKay (1942/1969) discussed the subculture found in socially disorganized neighborhoods, Kornhauser and others who followed tended to focus solely on the structural aspects of the theory. Following this important work, a number of scholars began reflecting on and promoting the potential of the theory. Stark (1987), for example, used social disorganization theory along with 100 years' worth of theorizing and empirical research on social ecology to develop 30 propositions linking neighborhood characteristics to high rates of deviance, including "(1) density; (2) poverty; (3) mixed [land] use; (4) transience; and (5) dilapidation" (p. 895).

In turn, Bursik (1988) documented the reasons for the decline in the popularity of the social disorganization theory and suggested several lines for pursuing the theory, including (1) thinking about the neighborhood as a social context for individual behavior, (2) focusing on measures of deviance, such as self-reported behavior and victimization surveys, that are not the result of official responses by law enforcement, and (3) considering the possible feedback effects of crime and delinquency on social disorganization (the ability to control the environment). Finally, several studies were conducted that empirically tested the validity of the theory.

◈ Empirical Tests of Social Disorganization Theory

One of the first innovations and empirical tests of the social disorganization theory involved consideration of the mediating factors hypothesized between the social structural variables identified by Shaw and McKay (1942/1969) and crime and delinquency. Sampson and Groves (1989) argued that sparse friendship networks, unsupervised teen peer groups, and low organizational participation should largely explain the relationship between poverty, ethnic heterogeneity, population turnover, family disruption, and urbanization. That is, neighborhoods characterized by these factors would be less able to control certain forms of deviance because residents were not communicating with one another and allowed teens to roam the streets unsupervised. The model is described in Figure 5.1.

Sampson and Groves (1989) analyzed data from the 1982 British Crime Survey (BCS), which included data on more than 10,000 respondents across 238 localities in England and Wales, and then they replicated the analyses using data from a slightly larger number of individuals residing in 300 British communities. They found that neighborhoods with sparse friendship networks, unsupervised teenage peer groups, and low organizational participation were associated with higher rates of victimization and self-reported offending (violence and property crimes) and that these variables explained much of the effect of the standard structural variables generally used to test social disorganization theory.

About a decade later, Veysey and Messner (1999) replicated these analyses using slightly more sophisticated statistical modeling techniques. They were more cautious in their interpretation of the results of their analyses

Figure 5.1 Sampson and Groves's Model of Social Disorganization

Low Socioeconomic Status		
Ethnic Heterogeneity	Sparse Networks	
Residential Mobility ⟶	Unsupervised Youth ⟶	Crime and
Family Disruptions	Organizational Participation	Delinquency
Urbanization		

in terms of the theory. They found that the mediating social disorganization variables (sparse friendships, unsupervised teens, and organizational participation) only partially explained the effects of the structural variables and argued that the results were only partially consistent with social disorganization theory but were also consistent with theories focused on peer affiliation, such as differential association theory (see Chapter 6). Again using the British Crime Survey but this time with data from 1994 (more than a decade later), Lowenkamp, Cullen, and Pratt (2003) replicated Sampson and Groves's (1989) model using similar measures. The results were largely consistent, and the authors argued that the consistency of the findings suggests that Sampson and Groves's model was not an idiosyncratic result of the timing of the original study but that the theoretical model is generalizable across time.

Classic social disorganization theory has continued to be tested in other environments. For example, given that Shaw and McKay and many others have focused on urban environments, some have questioned whether the theory is applicable to nonurban areas. Osgood and Chambers (2000) examined the structural correlates of juvenile homicide, rape, weapon offenses, and simple-assault arrest rates across 264 nonmetropolitan counties in Florida, Georgia, South Carolina, and Nebraska. They found that population turnover, family disruption, and ethnic heterogeneity were all related to most juvenile arrest statistics.

Most recently, Moore and Sween (2015) provided a partial replication of Osgood and Chambers's (2000) work, except they expanded the sample to all (n = 2,011) nonmetropolitan counties in fully 48 states (excluding Alaska and Hawaii); a few of the independent variables were slightly different, and the statistical analyses were slightly different as well. They, too, found that residential instability and ethnic heterogeneity were consistent predictors across juvenile crimes. Family disruption was related to total violent crimes and robbery; population density was related to homicide and robbery; and poverty was related to homicide. These studies suggest that social disorganization variables shown to "work" in urban areas can also predict juvenile crime in rural counties. Residential instability and ethnic heterogeneity appeared to be the most consistent predictors of each of the violent crimes measured, as Shaw and McKay would have hypothesized, but there is some evidence that poverty and population density play some role in predicting some juvenile crime.

A criticism raised against Shaw and McKay's (1942/1969) original analyses and many other analyses is the focus on official measures of crime. However, Sampson and Groves's (1989) classic analysis as well as replications (Lowencamp et al., 2003; Veysey & Messner, 1999) with self-reported offending and victimization with the British Crime Survey clearly show the generalizability of the theory. In an interesting approach, Warner and Pierce (1993) used calls to police, rather than reactions by the police (e.g., arrests), across 60 Boston neighborhoods in 1980 and found support for social disorganization theory. Finally, while most studies have focused on juvenile delinquency and street crimes, Benson, Wooldredge, and Thistlethwaite (2004) found that neighborhood factors associated with social disorganization theory affect both black and white rates of domestic violence.

As the reader might surmise, the theory of social disorganization has largely focused on delinquency and street crimes, especially violent street crimes, rather than on other forms of deviance, especially what might be seen as "soft deviance." This is not entirely the case, however, as even early researchers were interested in how social disorganization theory might help us understand the geographic concentration of mental illness, prostitution, gambling, alcoholism, and drug use. Some recent research continues in this tradition.

Eric Silver (2000) examined the structural correlates of violence, but his focus was on the mentally ill, whereas most research had previously only examined individual-level variables, such as gender, race, and socioeconomic status. He obtained data on 270 psychiatric patients discharged from the Western Psychiatric Institute and Clinic in Pittsburgh, Pennsylvania. The patients had been treated for a variety of mental disorders, including schizophrenia, depression, mania, and alcohol or drug dependence, among others. Violence was measured via self-report, "collateral" reports (i.e., reports from someone who knew the respondent well and had frequent interactions), and official records. Neighborhood-level variables included a composite measure of socioeconomic disadvantage and population turnover. Although population turnover was unrelated to violence, socioeconomic disadvantage was related to violence in bivariate analyses as well as in multivariate models controlling for a host of individual-level characteristics.

Another study by Hayes-Smith and Whaley (2009) focused on social disorganization and methamphetamine use. While the Silver study above focused on individuals and the neighborhoods around their homes, Hayes-Smith and Whaley studied school districts in Michigan. Self-reported data collected via an anonymous survey of eighth-, tenth-, and twelfth-grade students, about a third from each grade, were aggregated to the school district ($n = 202$). District characteristics included low socioeconomic status, residential instability, racial composition, and family disruption, among others. Findings showed that—consistent with social disorganization theory—methamphetamine use was consistently and positively related to low socioeconomic status and population instability. Interestingly, in contrast to social disorganization theory, racial/ethnic heterogeneity was negatively related to methamphetamine use, whereas the percentage of whites was positively related to it, suggesting that methamphetamine use may be more common among whites than racial minorities. The suburban, urban, and rural variables were significant in some models but not others. When significant, the results seemed to suggest that methamphetamine use may be higher in suburban and rural areas. Overall, the data largely support social disorganization theory, and this study adds to the literature by focusing on a relatively new and disturbing form of substance use across urban and rural school districts. Edwards (2010) examined neighborhood characteristics in urban counties in Texas where three types of sexually oriented businesses existed: adult sexuality boutiques, adult entertainment clubs, and adult bookstores. Using social disorganization theory, she critiqued the placement of these different businesses and the impact of race, class, and gender on their placement.

She determined the existence of the three types of sexually oriented businesses using a generally agreed-upon definition of each type of business. First, adult sexuality boutiques are more likely to be run by women and often emphasize "party favors," erotic clothing, and even female sexual health. Second, adult entertainment clubs are usually clubs that specialize in nude or topless dancing by females and usually cater to men. Finally, adult bookstores also sell sexual paraphernalia like adult sexuality boutiques, but these stores usually specialize in the sale or rental of pornographic videos and magazines and cater to male clientele.

Edwards found that adult sexuality boutiques are more likely to be in socially organized and cohesive neighborhoods, whereas adult entertainment clubs and bookstores are more likely to be in socially disorganized neighborhoods. While white men are the predominant clientele of both adult entertainment clubs and adult bookstores, the disorganized neighborhoods the businesses are in are more likely to be lower income neighborhoods with higher rates of minority residents. This suggests that "certain groups are able to keep their neighborhoods separated from [certain] sexually oriented businesses, while also maintaining anonymity if they choose to visit these businesses" (p. 155).

◈ More Theoretical and Empirical Advances and Divergences: Social and Physical Disorder

Minor misbehavior (e.g., prostitution and public rowdiness or drunkenness) and signs of **physical disorder** (e.g., litter, graffiti, and broken windows) and their relationship to crime has been a concern at least since the 1800s. Nearly 35 years ago, Wilson and Kelling (1982) published an essay titled "Broken Windows: The Police and Neighborhood Safety" in the *Atlantic Monthly* that brought these issues back into the public limelight as well as to the attention of scholars interested in crime and deviance. Basically, the authors argued that disorder leads to greater disorder and attracts and promotes more serious forms of deviance. The notion is simple to young men living in an area characterized by graffiti and broken windows: Why not break another window? It is fun, and what's the harm? Signs of disorder lead to further disorder. This led to the policy implication that police (and other agents of social control) attack crime at its roots and target physical and minor forms of **social disorder** deviance that seem to be critical causes of the escala-

▲ **Photo 5.3**   Can broken windows actually encourage crime and other forms of deviance?

tion of crime and further deviance (public drinking, rowdiness, crowds of teens, etc.). In other words, focus on less serious forms of deviance, and you may deter more serious forms of crime.

Although the two are clearly unique (see Kubrin, 2008), the parallels between the disorder theory and social disorganization theory are fairly obvious. The key to social disorganization theory is the ability of residents to control delinquency and crime, things that most everyone would like to minimize. Similarly, there are some areas where residents are able to minimize social and physical disorder (e.g., adults drinking, unsupervised youth, trash, and graffiti) and other areas where residents have difficulty minimizing disorder. Physical and social disorder are presumably things that most people would like to avoid if they had the ability to control them or could afford to live in "better" neighborhoods.

Considerable research links physical and social disorder with more serious street crimes. Skogan's (1990) *Disorder and Decline: Crime and the Spiral of Decay in American Neighborhoods*, for example, provides a compelling argument and data detailing that disorder is a major root cause of urban crime. His later work, "Disorder and Decline: The State of Research" (2015), provides an up-to-date overview of the progress made since Wilson and Kelling's seminal article. Obviously a proponent, he states that disorder has broad implications for public health and safety and that it is deeply implicated in the dynamics of neighborhood stability and change. Further, there is evidence that—directly and via its impact on other features of community life—disorder stimulates conventional crime. The theory is not without critics. For example, Harcourt (2001) argues that not enough empirical attention has been given to the causal link between disorder and crime, and he claims the policies (e.g., zero-tolerance policies) drawn from the "theory" are often inappropriate and/or ineffective. Sampson and Raudenbush (2004) are also less optimistic of the potential of the theory. They provided a very unique empirical test of the relationship between disorder and crime and found that while the two are correlated, factors including poverty and the concentration of minority groups are even stronger predictors of crime than social and physical disorder. Because it is simple and appealing to the public and public officials, Wilson and Kelling's (1982) **broken windows theory** will likely remain active and persuasive in terms of policies and practices. Why not focus on problems residents are concerned with, even if they don't have a causal link to more serious crime? In fact, social and physical disorder may really simply be "less serious" crime and deviance.

Collective Efficacy

Another advance in social disorganization theory came from Robert Sampson and his colleagues (Sampson, Raudenbush, & Earls, 1997), who drew an analogy between **individual efficacy** (i.e., an individual's ability to accomplish a task) and neighborhood or **collective efficacy** (i.e., a neighborhood's ability to recognize common goals of a safe environment that is largely free from crime and deviance). They defined collective efficacy as "social cohesion among neighbors combined with their willingness to intervene on the behalf of the common good" (p. 918). **Social cohesion** and trust between neighbors are seen as necessary conditions for residents to be willing to intervene for the common good. Basically, the authors made the argument that collective efficacy is an important mediating effect between structural factors associated with social disorganization and deviant behavior, particularly violent behavior.

Sampson et al. (1997) examined data from the Project on Human Development in Chicago Neighborhoods. Government-defined census tracts are often used as the unit of analysis to characterize neighborhoods. This is a reasonable strategy but nowhere near perfect as they often have arbitrary borders that do not reflect what residents perceive to be "their neighborhood." To get a better measure of neighborhoods, the researchers combined 847 Chicago census tracts into 343 neighborhood clusters in an attempt to create a unit of analysis that made meaningful sense in terms of composition and geographic boundaries (e.g., roads and waterways). They interviewed 8,782 residents across all neighborhood clusters in the residents' homes. They measured "informal social control" by asking respondents how likely their neighbors could be counted on to intervene in various ways if

- children were skipping school and hanging out on a street corner,
- children were spray-painting a building,
- children were showing disrespect to an adult,
- a fight broke out in front of their house, or
- the fire station closest to the house was threatened with budget cuts.

Cohesion and trust were measured by asking respondents how strongly they agreed with the following:

- People around here are willing to help their neighbors.
- This is a close-knit neighborhood.
- People in this neighborhood can be trusted.
- People in this neighborhood generally don't get along with each other.
- People in this neighborhood do not share the same values.

The two scales were so highly correlated at the neighborhood level that they were combined into a single composite scale termed "collective efficacy."

Structural variables related to social disorganization theory included concentrated disadvantage, immigrant concentration, and a lack of residential stability. The dependent measures of violence included perceived violence in the neighborhood and violent victimization from the neighborhood survey and the homicide rate from official records. Sampson et al. (1997) were able to assess the influence of structural variables on collective efficacy and the mediating effect of collective efficacy on violence. The results were consistent and robust. The structural variables were clearly related to collective efficacy, and collective efficacy, in turn, affected each measure of violence. The results strongly supported this modified version of social disorganization theory.

Subsequent to this publication, numerous studies have examined the role that collective efficacy plays on violence and other forms of deviance as well as reactions to deviance (e.g., residents' fear of crime). For example, Bernasco and Block (2009) found that collective efficacy keeps robbers out of certain census tracts in Chicago while D. Martin (2002) found that social capital (politically active citizens) and collective efficacy (active community organizations) were negatively related to burglary across Detroit neighborhoods in the mid-1990s. Browning (2002) showed that the effects of collective efficacy extend beyond violence and street crime to affect intimate partner violence, and Cancino (2005) showed that collective efficacy not only is important in inner cities but applies to nonmetropolitan areas as well.

J. Wright and Cullen (2001) developed the analogous concept of **parental efficacy**, which is focused on parents' ability to control their children's behavior through parent–child attachment, rules, supervision, and also social support. B. H. Rankin and Quane (2002) linked these ideas directly to the community and examined how collective efficacy leads to greater parental efficacy, which leads to greater social competency and lower levels of problem behavior among children. More recently, Simons and his colleagues (Simons, Simons, Burt, Brody, & Cutrona, 2005) showed that collective efficacy promoted positive parenting strategies and that both were related to lower levels of deviant peer association and delinquency involvement. More interestingly, they found that authoritative parenting had pronounced effects in communities with higher levels of collective efficacy, suggesting that both factors are important in themselves but that in conjunction, the effects are even stronger.

In a more recent study, Berg and Rengifo (2009) focused on robbery and the role of informal social control in the presence of illicit drug markets. They too moved beyond a sole focus on structural characteristics emphasized in social disorganization theory and actually included measures of informal social control, very close to measures of collective efficacy, as critical mediating factors between structural variables and robbery. They argue that the structural factors discussed above negatively affect residents' ability to regulate behavior, keep out drug market activity, and control serious violent crimes, such as robbery.

Berg and Rengifo's study focused on 66 block groups purposively selected to obtain variation in drug activity in the Kentucky cities of Louisville and Lexington. Block groups are aggregations of several blocks and are smaller units than census tracts. In fact, census tracts are usually aggregations of two or more block groups. In some cities, block groups are even more accurate depictions of "neighborhoods" than census tracts, but this is not always the case. Survey data were collected from just over 2,300 residents of these neighborhoods to measure informal social control and perceptions of drug market activity. Perceptions of drug market activity were measured by two items that asked how often people bought or sold drugs in the neighborhood and how often people used drugs in the neighborhood. Informal social control was measured with a scale consisting of items similar to the intervention variables described above in Sampson and his colleagues' work (1997). These variables were aggregated to the block group level.

Structural variables came from the census and included residential instability (percentage of renters and the percentage of the population residing somewhere else five years earlier); concentrated disadvantage (e.g., percentage living in poverty, unemployment, and female-headed households); and population age structure (percentage aged 15–29, a high-risk age-group for criminal activity). Robbery data came from crimes known to the local city police agencies. The purposive sampling led to significant variation in neighborhood characteristics. For example, the percentage reporting that drug market activity occurred frequently ranged from 0% to 88%, and robbery rates ranged from 0 to 60 per 1,000 residents. Further, unemployment ranged from 0% to 57%, and population turnover (instability) ranged from 12% to 86%.

Structural equation modeling was employed, which allowed the researchers to tease out direct and indirect effects of structural characteristics, informal social control, and drug market activity on rates of robbery. The analyses began with bivariate correlations, and as expected, concentrated disadvantage and residential instability were negatively related to informal social control and positively related to drug market activity and robbery rates. More complex models suggest that the effect of concentrated disadvantage is indirect, working by negatively affecting informal social control and positively affecting the presence of drug market activity, which directly affects rates of robbery. Residential instability also appears to lower informal social controls, in turn affecting drug market activity, which has the strongest direct effect on rates of robbery.

Clearly, collective efficacy has proven to be an important concept that has extended and promoted thought on social disorganization theory and on factors that affect neighborhood deviance. For the most part, research in this area has been largely restricted to violence and other forms of crime, and little attention has been given to collective efficacy's potential implication for other forms of deviance. More research in this direction is clearly warranted.

◈ Explaining Deviance in the Streets and Deviance in the Suites With Social Disorganization Theory

The emphasis on economic deprivation, which encourages population turnover, can lead to racial and ethnic heterogeneity, and ultimately affects the ability to work together toward common community goals such as reducing crime and delinquency, is clearly evoked in virtually all versions of social disorganization theory. Indeed, the vast majority of research testing social disorganization theory has emphasized "crime in the streets." But can social disorganization be utilized to explain "deviance in the suites," or elite deviance? It would appear so.

In 1940, Edwin Sutherland published the article "White-Collar Criminality," and while in it he primarily emphasized his theory of differential association (see Chapter 6), he also alluded to social disorganization. Just as in socially disorganized, lower class neighborhoods, conflicting pressures exist in the business community. Sutherland argued that "a second general process is social disorganization in the community" (p. 11), which allows for differential association. He further argued that white-collar offenders can operate because the business community cannot confront the powerful business leaders, and the agencies that are commissioned to handle white-collar crime typically focus on lower level crimes (e.g., "street crime"), ignoring those at their own level.

More recently, Rothe and her colleagues (see Rothe & Kauzlarich, 2010; Rothe & Mullins, 2009) have incorporated social disorganization theory into various frameworks for understanding state crime. Rothe and Kauzlarich (2010) argue that

> essentially, when strong, functioning social institutions are not present, this creates both motivation and opportunity for organized criminal activity. . . . Weak institutions produce a vacuum of formal and informal social control. A nation unable to adequately police or subdue paramilitary force in its hinterlands creates a gap of institutional control that provides motivation and opportunity for the aris[ing] of organized criminal activity. (p. 169)

Their emphasis on social institutions, such as the family, education, and religion, and on the ability or inability to control behavior at the state level is clearly in line with the social disorganization tradition. Can you think of other forms of elite deviance that might be enabled by the presence of weak institutions and a lack of informal social controls?

◈ Ideas in Action: Programs and Policy From Social Disorganization and Broken Windows Perspectives

A number of programs and policies have come out of social disorganization theory and variations on it, especially Wilson and Kelling's broken windows theory. Regarding the former, probably the largest program that has become institutionalized is the Chicago Area Project (CAP), which began in the 1930s. Based directly on social disorganization theory and led by sociologist and major contributor to social disorganization theory Clifford Shaw, the CAP sought the following:

1. The development of youth welfare organizations among residents of delinquency areas

2. Employment of so-called indigenous workers wherever possible

3. The fostering and preservation of the independence of these groups (Kobrin, 1959, p. 24)

The CAP emphasized the individual delinquent in the social context that created the delinquency. In contrast to psychological and psychiatric approaches, the CAP was sociological in nature and emphasized the social milieu that encouraged (or at least did not *dis*courage) delinquency in certain parts of the city. It also emphasized the lack of social organizations (i.e., organized sports with adult supervision) in certain areas of the city that were readily available to middle-class adolescents. Although solid statistical evidence of the effectiveness of the CAP to reduce delinquency remains evasive (see Schlossman & Sedlak, 1983, for a detailed discussion of these issues), most researchers agree that there were many benefits of the intervention. Kobrin (1959) makes three important points in this regard. First, the project showed that youth welfare organizations could be developed even in the most impoverished areas of the city with the highest rates of delinquency. Second, the project showed that citizens in high-crime areas could be made aware of the common problems shared by residents and mobilized to take action to confront delinquency and other social problems. Additionally, many of the neighborhood programs created remained stable and active over time. Third, it has been argued that

in all probability, the Area Project was the first organized program in the United States to use workers to establish direct and personal contact with "unreached" boys to help them find their way back to acceptable norms of conduct. The adoption of this pattern in many cities during recent years may be regarded as in part, at least, a contribution of the Area Project. (Kobrin, 1959, p. 25)

Other programs that are somewhat consistent with social disorganization theory are community policing and neighborhood watch programs. Community-policing policies and programs attempt to bring law enforcement into the community to work directly with residents to help solve problems and prevent crime and other forms of deviance. The shift from a "paramilitary-bureaucratic" organizational structure to a "friendlier" community-based model of crime prevention has been uneven at best. Chappell and Lanza-Kaduce (2010) argue that even though police academies often espouse community ideals, the training and socialization that takes place in them actually emphasizes and reinforces the paramilitary ideals advocated in earlier decades.

Neighborhood watch programs, often associated with civic leagues, attempt to bring residents together to solve problems themselves. They link often dissimilar residents (based, for example, on race, ethnicity, and/or social class) who might not normally interact together to work to solve common problems, such as crime and other forms of deviance. Bennett, Holloway, and Farrington (2006) conducted a meta-analysis and concluded that 15 of the 18 studies they reviewed showed at least some evidence of these programs' effectiveness. They did raise several questions about the quality of the studies, however, and recommend that more rigorous evaluations be conducted.

Finally, policies and programs related to broken windows theory generally focus on stopping low-level criminal activity before it escalates. This might involve enforcement of city code violations related to broken or abandoned vehicles, litter, graffiti, loud music, and the consumption of alcohol in public. Often there is an emphasis on zero-tolerance police policies. O'Shea (2006) offers a unique and important analysis of Wilson and Kelling's broken windows argument. He argues that the relationships between physical deterioration, disorder, and crime are not straightforward or additive. Rather, physical deterioration interacts with social disorder to affect levels of crime. Another way of thinking about this is that the effect of disorder on crime is dependent on levels of physical disorder (or vice versa). O'Shea finds

NOW YOU . . . USE THE THEORY

The map below is of Norfolk, Virginia. The dots represent prostitution arrests, and the shaded areas represent different levels of social disorganization as measured by a scale based on the level of racial heterogeneity, number of female-headed households, level of unemployment, and level of poverty in a certain area. The top of the map represents the section of the city next to the bay. This section was very popular many years ago but fell into disrepute. Since it is on the water, there has been some gentrification recently, and wealthier individuals and business owners have moved back and reclaimed the space as a desirable area. The southern end of the map is where the central business district is located.

Using social disorganization theory, explain the location of prostitution arrests in Norfolk. Can you use the theory to help explain how these arrests are clustered in the city? Why might these arrests be clustered on the edge of the most disorganized areas of the city?

Arrests of Female Prostitutes Over Social Disorganization

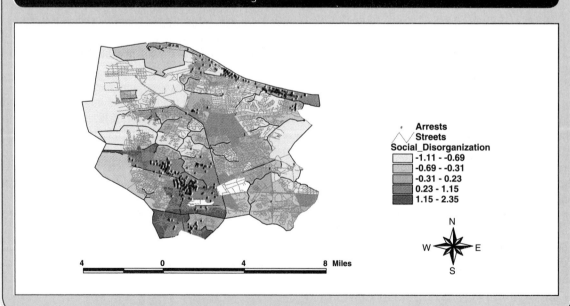

statistical support for this hypothesis that leads him to be skeptical of simple zero-tolerance policies. He argues that "simple arrests of the disorderly (however broadly defined) and citation of negligent property owners . . . may not be the most efficient use of those scarce law enforcement resources" (p. 185).

◈ Conclusion

The original work of Shaw and McKay (1942/1969) was clearly groundbreaking in its day and continues to influence the study of deviance. The major contribution of the original work was showing how crime, deviance, and other social problems cannot be understood, at least at the aggregate level, by using "types of people" explanations. Shaw and McKay found that crime and deviance were consistently located in particular parts of Chicago, even though the types of people who resided there changed across several decades. New versions of the theory continue to help us understand the factors that limit social control in certain neighborhoods.

Places such as Henry Horner in Alex Kotlowitz's (1988) *There Are No Children Here* continue to have high rates of crime and deviance because (1) the residents there do not have the resources (political or economic) to control these activities; (2) there is high residential instability or population turnover, resulting in limited social networking, which might lead to decreased social control; and (3) there is very little collective efficacy in that residents lack the willingness and ability to intervene when problems confront them. Most people residing in truly disadvantaged neighborhoods do not engage in a great deal of crime and deviance, and most would love to live in less dangerous places where they could raise their children safely without the opportunities and pressures to deviate. They stay because their opportunities are strictly limited.

EXERCISES AND DISCUSSION QUESTIONS

1. Explain how Shaw and McKay's theory moved us away from "types of people" explanations.

2. Why do you think we are so focused on individual-level explanations rather than on characteristics of social contexts?

3. How does the work of Sampson and his colleagues expand our understanding of social disorganization theory?

4. How does Wilson and Kelling's broken windows theory relate to social disorganization?

5. Consider the city you live in and where the safe areas are as well as where one might likely go to buy drugs or find a prostitute. What other factors characterize those areas of the city?

6. Go to www.youtube.com/watch?v=niJ3IiURCnE for a presentation of Chicago's deadliest neighborhoods, and write a personal reaction to the video.

KEY TERMS

Broken windows theory

Central business district

Collective efficacy

Concentric zones

Cross-sectional designs

Individual efficacy

Longitudinal data

Parental efficacy

Physical disorder

Population turnover

Poverty

Racial/ethnic heterogeneity

Social cohesion

Social disorder

Social disorganization theory

Zone in transition

READING 13

In Chapter 5, we discussed the early Chicago school and Shaw and McKay's empirical analysis of delinquency across neighborhoods. Their version of social disorganization linked poverty, population turnover, and racial/ethnic diversity. While immigration was part of the picture, it was not necessarily considered a major causal factor. Recent debates have centered on immigration (legal and illegal), especially of Hispanics, as an evil to be stopped. Professor Sampson provides a very different picture, showing, with data on individuals, neighborhoods, and cities, some very positive effects of Hispanic immigration. His arguments are very persuasive but have brought a barrage of "not so nice" criticisms—often with data to refute his arguments.

Rethinking Crime and Immigration

Robert J. Sampson

The summer of 2007 witnessed a perfect storm of controversy over immigration to the United States. After building for months with angry debate, a widely touted immigration reform bill supported by President George W. Bush and many leaders in Congress failed decisively. Recriminations soon followed across the political spectrum.

Just when it seemed media attention couldn't be greater, a human tragedy unfolded with the horrifying execution-style murders of three teenagers in Newark, N.J., attributed by authorities to illegal aliens.

Presidential candidate Rep. Tom Tancredo (R–Colorado) descended on Newark to blame city leaders for encouraging illegal immigration, while Newt Gingrich declared the "war at home" against illegal immigrants was more deadly than the battlefields of Iraq. National headlines and outrage reached a feverish pitch, with Newark offering politicians a potent new symbol and a brown face to replace the infamous Willie Horton, who committed armed robbery and rape while on a weekend furlough from his life sentence to a Massachusetts prison. Another presidential candidate, former Tennessee senator Fred Thompson, seemed to capture the mood of the times at the Prescott Bush Awards Dinner: "Twelve million illegal immigrants later, we are now living in a nation that is beset by people who are suicidal maniacs and want to kill countless innocent men, women, and children around the world."

Now imagine a nearly opposite, fact-based scenario. Consider that immigration—even if illegal—is associated with *lower* crime rates in most disadvantaged urban neighborhoods. Or that increasing immigration tracks with the broad *reduction* in crime the United States has witnessed since the 1990s. Well before the 2007 Summer of Discontent over immigration, I proposed we take such ideas seriously. Based on hindsight I shouldn't have been surprised by the intense reaction to what I thought at the time was a rather logical reflection. From the right came loud guffaws, expletive-filled insults, angry web postings, and not-so-thinly veiled threats. But the left wasn't so happy either, because my argument assumes racial and ethnic differences in crime not tidily attributable to material deprivation or discrimination—the canonical explanations.

Although Americans hold polarizing and conflicting views about its value, immigration is a major social force that will continue for some time. It thus pays to reconsider the role of immigration in shaping crime,

Source: Sampson, R. J. (2008). Rethinking crime and immigration. *Contexts, 7*(1), 28–33.

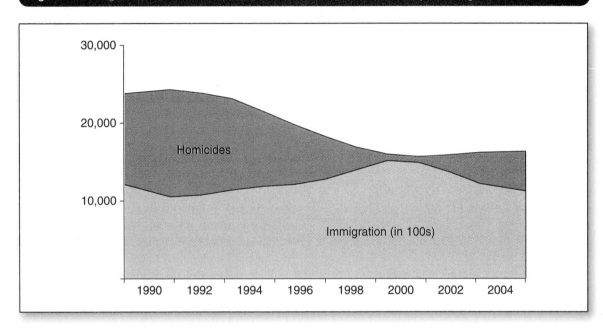

Figure 1 Immigration Flows and Homicide Trends: U.S. Total, 1990–2004 (three-year average)

cities, culture, and societal change writ large, especially in this era of social anxiety and vitriolic claims about immigration's reign of terror.

◈ Some Facts

Consider first the "Latino Paradox." Hispanic Americans do better on a wide range of social indicators—including propensity to violence—than one would expect given their socioeconomic disadvantages. To assess this paradox in more depth, my colleagues and I examined violent acts committed by nearly 3,000 males and females in Chicago ranging in age from 8 to 25 between 1995 and 2003. The study selected whites, blacks, and Hispanics (primarily Mexican-Americans) from 180 neighborhoods ranging from highly segregated to very integrated. We also analyzed data from police records, the U.S. Census, and a separate survey of more than 8,000 Chicago residents who were asked about the characteristics of their neighborhoods.

Notably, we found a significantly lower rate of violence among Mexican-Americans compared to

blacks and whites. A major reason is that more than a quarter of those of Mexican descent were born abroad and more than half lived in neighborhoods where the majority of residents were also Mexican. In particular, first-generation immigrants (those born outside the United States) were 45 percent less likely to commit violence than third-generation Americans, adjusting for individual, family, and neighborhood background. Second-generation immigrants were 22 percent less likely to commit violence than the third generation. This pattern held true for non-Hispanic whites and blacks as well. Our study further showed living in a neighborhood of concentrated immigration was directly associated with lower violence (again, after taking into account a host of correlated factors, including poverty and an individual's immigrant status). Immigration thus appeared "protective" against violence.

Consider next the implications of these findings when set against the backdrop of one of the most profound social changes to visit the United States in recent decades. Foreign immigration to the United States rose sharply in the 1990s, especially from Mexico and especially to immigrant enclaves in large cities. Overall, the foreign-born population increased by more than 50 percent in 10 years, to 31 million in 2000. A report by the Pew Hispanic Center found immigration grew most significantly in the mid-1990s and hit its peak at the end of the decade, when the national homicide rate plunged to levels not seen since the 1960s. Immigrant flows have receded since 2001 but remain high, while the national homicide rate leveled off and seems now to be creeping up. Both trends are compared over time [in Figure 1].

The pattern upends popular stereotypes. Among the public, policy makers, and even many academics, a common expectation is that the concentration of immigrants and the influx of foreigners drive up crime rates because of the assumed propensities of these groups to commit crimes and settle in poor, presumably disorganized communities. This belief is so pervasive that in our Chicago study the concentration of Latinos in a neighborhood strongly predicted perceptions of disorder no matter the actual amount of disorder or rate of reported crimes. And yet immigrants appear in general to be less violent than people born in America, particularly when they live in neighborhoods with high numbers of other immigrants.

We are thus witnessing a different pattern from early 20th century America, when growth in immigration from Europe, along with ethnic diversity more generally, was linked with increasing crime and formed a building block for what became known as "social disorganization" theory. New York today is a leading magnet for immigration, yet it has for a decade ranked as one of America's safest cities. Crime in Los Angeles dropped considerably in the late 1990s (45 percent overall) as did other Hispanic influenced cities such as San Jose, Dallas, and Phoenix. The same can be said for cities smack on the border like El Paso and San Diego, which have long ranked as low-crime areas. Cities of concentrated immigration are some of the safest places around.

◈ Counterpoint

There are criticisms of these arguments, of course. To begin, the previous figure juxtaposes two trends and nothing more—correlation doesn't equal causation. But it does demonstrate the trends are opposite of what's commonly assumed, which is surely not irrelevant to

the many, and strongly causal, claims that immigration increases crime. Descriptive facts are at the heart of sound social science, a first step in any causal inquiry.

Perhaps a bigger concern is that we need to distinguish illegal from legal immigration and focus on the many illegal aliens who allegedly are accounting for crime waves across the country—the "Newark phenomenon." By one argument, because of deportation risk illegal immigrants are afraid to report crimes against them to the police, resulting in artificially low official estimates in the Hispanic community. But no evidence exists that reporting biases seriously affect estimates of the homicide victimization rate—unlike other crimes there is a body. At the national level, then, the homicides committed by illegal aliens in the United States are reflected in the data just like for everyone else. The bottom line is that as immigrants poured into the country, homicides plummeted. One could claim crime would decrease faster absent immigration inflows, but that's a different argument and concedes my basic point. There is also little disputing that in areas and times of high legal immigration we find accompanying surges of illegal entrants. It would be odd indeed if illegal aliens descended on areas with no other immigrants or where they had no pre-existing networks. And so it is that areas of concentrated immigration are magnets for illegal concentration. Because crime tends to be negatively associated with undifferentiated immigration measures, it follows that we can disconfirm the idea that increasing illegal immigration is associated with increasing crime.

Furthermore, our Chicago study did include both legal and illegal immigrants. I would estimate the illegal status at roughly a quarter—but in any case no group was excluded from the analysis. The other important point is that the violence estimates were based on confidential self-reports and not police statistics or other official sources of crime. Therefore, police arrest biases or undercounts can't explain the fact that first generation immigrants self-report lower violence than the second generation, which in turn reports less than the third generation.

So let us proceed on the assumption of a substantial negative association across individuals, places, and time with respect to immigration and violence. What potential mechanisms might explain the connections and are they causal? Thinking about these questions requires attention be paid to confounding factors and competing explanations.

Social scientists worry a lot about selection bias because individuals differ in preferences and can, within means, select their environments. It has been widely hypothesized that immigrants, and Mexicans in particular, selectively migrate to the United States on characteristics that predispose them to low crime, such as motivation to work, ambition, and a desire not to be deported. Immigrants may also come from cultures where violence isn't rewarded as a strategy for establishing reputation (to which I return below).

This scenario is undoubtedly the case and central to the argument—social selection is a causal mechanism. Namely, to the extent that more people predisposed to lower crime immigrate to the United States (we now have some 35 million people of foreign-born status), they will sharply increase the denominator of the crime rate while rarely appearing in the numerator. And in the neighborhoods of U.S. cities with high concentrations of immigrants, one would expect on selection grounds alone to find lower crime rates. Selection thus favors the argument that immigration may be causally linked to lower crime.

Another concern of social scientists is common sources of causation, or "competing" explanations. One candidate is economic trends. After all, potential immigrants respond to incentives and presumably choose to relocate when times are better in their destinations. Although a legitimate concern, economics can't easily explain the story. Depending on the measure, economic trends aren't isomorphic with either immigration or crime at either the beginning or end of the time series. Real wages were declining and inequality increasing in the 1990s by most accounts, which should have produced increases in crime by the logic of relative deprivation theory, which says that income gaps, not absolute poverty, are what matters. Broad economic indicators like stock market values did skyrocket but collapsed sharply while immigration didn't.

Scholars in criminology have long searched for a sturdy link between national economic trends and violence, to little avail. The patterns just don't match up well, and often they're in the opposite direction of deprivation-based expectations. The best example is the 1960s when the economy markedly improved yet crime shot up. Don't forget, too, the concentrated immigration and crime link remains when controlling for economic indicators.

Finally, the "Latino Paradox" in itself should put to rest the idea that economics is the go-to answer: Immigrant Latinos are poor and disadvantaged but at low risk for crime. Poor immigrant neighborhoods and immigrant-tinged cities like El Paso have similarly lower crime than their economic profile would suggest.

Competing explanations also can't explain the Chicago findings. Immigrant youths committed less violence than natives after adjustment for a rich set of individual, family, and neighborhood confounders. Moreover, there's an influence of immigrant concentration beyond the effects of individual immigrant status and other individual factors, and beyond neighborhood socioeconomic status and legal cynicism—previously shown to significantly predict violence. We estimated male violence by age for three types of neighborhoods [see Figure 2]:

- "Low-risk," where a very high percentage of people work in professional and managerial occupations (90th percentile), few people hold cynical attitudes about the law and morality (10th percentile), and there are no immigrants;

- "High-risk," where professional/managerial jobs are scarce, cynicism is pervasive, and there are also no immigrants;

- "High-risk, immigrant neighborhoods," defined by similarly low shares of professional/managerial workers and high legal cynicism, but where about one-half of the people are immigrants.

The estimated probability an average male living in a high-risk neighborhood without immigrants will engage in violence is almost 25 percent higher than in the high-risk, immigrant neighborhood, a pattern again suggesting the protective, rather than crime-generating, influence of immigrant concentration.

Finally, we examined violence in Chicago neighborhoods by a foreign-born diversity index capturing 100 countries of birth from around the world (Figure 3). In both high- and low-poverty communities, foreign-born diversity is clearly and strongly linked to lower violence. Concentrated poverty predicts more violence (note the high poverty areas above the prediction line) but violence is lower as diversity goes up for low- and high-poverty neighborhoods alike. Interestingly, the link

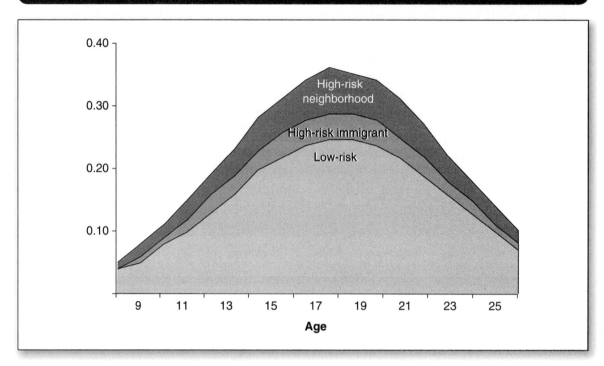

Figure 2   Estimated Probability of Violence by Third-Generation Males in Chicago Neighborhoods

between lower violence and diversity is strongest in the most disadvantaged neighborhoods.

◈ Crime Declines Among Non-Hispanics

A puzzle apparently remains in how immigration explains the crime decline among whites and blacks in the 1990s. One agitated critic, for example, charged that my thesis implies that for every Mexican entering America a black person would have to commit fewer crimes. But immigration isn't the only cause of the crime decline. There are many causes of crime—that declines ensued for blacks and whites doesn't in itself invalidate the immigration argument.

This critique also exposes a misconception about immigrant diversity. Immigration isn't just about Mexicans, it's about the influx of a wide range of different groups. The previous figure, for example, represents 100 countries, a conservative template for many places. In cities such as Los

Angeles and New York, immigrant flows are erasing simple black-white-brown scenarios and replacing them with a complex mixture of immigrant diversity.

Even the traditionally black-white city of Chicago reflects evidence of immigration's broad reach. When we looked at whites and blacks we still found surprising variation in generational status, with immigration protective for all racial/ethnic groups except Puerto Ricans/other Latinos. In fact, controlling for immigrant generation reduced the gap between African Americans and whites by 14 percent, implying one reason whites have lower levels of violence than African Americans is that whites are more likely to be recent immigrants. The pattern of immigrant generational status and lower crime is thus not just restricted to Latinos, and it extends to helping explain white-black differences as well.

Added to this is substantial non-Latino immigration into the United States from around the world, including Russia, Poland, India, and the Caribbean, to name just a few countries. Black and white populations are increasingly characterized by immigrants (Poles and

Figure 3　Violence and Diversity in Chicago Neighborhoods

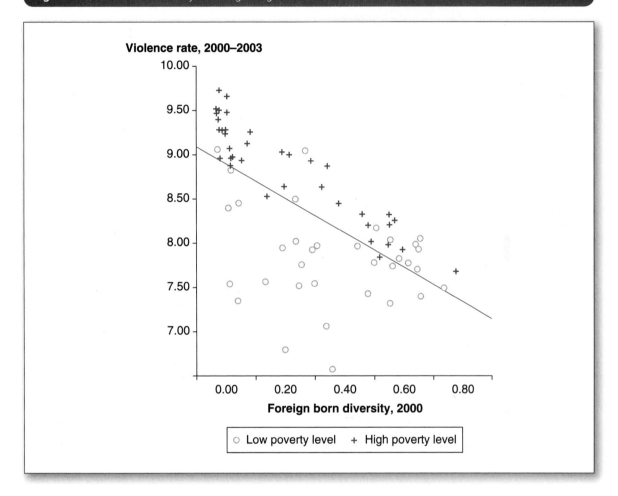

Russians among whites in Chicago, for example, and Caribbeans and West Africans among blacks in New York). According to Census 2000, the Chicago area has more than 130,000 Polish immigrants, so we aren't talking about trivial numbers.

Perhaps more important, focusing on the "what about whites and blacks" question misses the non-selection-based component of a broader immigration argument. We're so used to thinking about immigrant adaptation (or assimilation) to the host society we've failed to fully appreciate how immigrants themselves shape the host society. Take economic revitalization and urban growth. A growing consensus argues immigration

revitalizes cities around the country. Many decaying inner-city areas gained population in the 1990s and became more vital, in large part through immigration. One of the most thriving scenes of economic activity in the entire Chicagoland area, for example, second only to the famed "Miracle Mile" of Michigan Avenue, is the 26th Street corridor in Little Village. A recent analysis of New York City showed that for the first time ever, blacks' incomes in Queens have surpassed whites', with the surge in the black middle class driven largely by the successes of black immigrants from the West Indies. Segregation and the concentration of poverty have also decreased in many cities for the first time in decades.

Such changes are a major social force and immigrants aren't the only beneficiaries—native born blacks, whites, and other traditional groups in the United States have been exposed to the gains associated with lower crime (decreases in segregation, decreases in concentrated poverty, increases in the economic and civic health of central cities, to name just a few). There are many examples of inner-city neighborhoods rejuvenated by immigration that go well beyond Queens and the Lower West Side of Chicago. From Bushwick in Brooklyn to Miami, and from large swaths of south central Los Angeles to the rural South, immigration is reshaping America. It follows that the "externalities" associated with immigration are multiple in character and constitute a plausible mechanism explaining some of the variation in crime rates of all groups in the host society.

There are important implications for this line of argument. If it is correct, then simply adjusting for things like economic revitalization, urban change, and other seemingly confounding explanations is illegitimate from a causal explanation standpoint because they would instead be mediators or conduits of immigration effects—themselves part of the pathway of explanation. Put differently, to the extent immigration is causally bound up with major social changes that in turn are part of the explanatory process of reduced crime, estimating only the net effects of immigration will give us the wrong answer.

◈ Cultural Penetration and Societal Renewal

A related cultural implication, while speculative and perhaps provocative, is worth considering. If immigration leads to the penetration into America of diverse and formerly external cultures, then this diffusion may contribute to less crime if these cultures don't carry the same meanings with respect to violence and crime.

It's no secret the United States has long been a high-violence society, with many scholars positing a subculture or code of the streets as its main cause. In one influential version, shared expectations for demanding respect and "saving face" lead participants in the "street culture" of poor inner cities to react violently to perceived slights, insults, and otherwise petty encounters that make up the rounds of daily life. But

according to the logic of this theory, if one doesn't share the cultural attribution or perceived meaning of the event, violence is less likely. Outsiders to the culture, that is, are unlikely to be caught in the vicious cycles of interaction (and reaction) that promote violence.

The massive penetration of immigrant (particularly, but not only, Mexican) populations throughout the United States, including rural areas and the South, can properly be thought of as a diffusion-like process. One possible result is that over time American culture is being diluted. Some of the most voracious critiques of immigration have embraced this very line of argument. Samuel Huntington, in one well-known example, claims the very essence of American identity is at stake because of increasing diversity and immigration, especially from Mexico. He may well be right, but the diagnosis might not be so bad if a frontier mentality that endorses and perpetuates codes of violence is a defining feature of American culture.

A profound irony in the immigration debate concedes another point to Huntington. If immigration can be said to have brought violence to America, it most likely came with (white) Irish and Scottish immigrants whose cultural traditions emphasizing honor and respect were defended with violent means when they settled in the South in the 1700s and 1800s. Robert Nisbett and Dov Cohen have presented provocative evidence in favor of this thesis, emphasizing cultural transmission in the form of Scotch-Irish immigrants, descendants of Celtic herdsman, who developed rural herding communities in the frontier South. In areas with little state power to command compliance with the law, a tradition of frontier justice carried over from rural Europe took hold, with a heavy emphasis on retaliation and the use of violence to settle disputes, represented most clearly in the culture of dueling.

In today's society, then, I would hypothesize that immigration and the increasing cultural diversity that accompanies it generate the sort of conflicts of culture that lead not to increased crime but nearly the opposite. In other words, selective immigration in the current era may be leading to the greater visibility of competing non-violent mores that affect not just immigrant communities but diffuse and concatenate through social interactions to tamp down violent conflict in general. Recent findings showing the spread of immigration to all parts of America, including rural areas of the Midwest and South, give credence to this argument. The Willie Hortinization of illegal aliens notwithstanding, diversity and cultural conflict wrought by immigration may well prove healthy, rather than destructive, as traditionally believed.

 ## Recommended Resources

Richard Nisbett and Dov Cohen. *Culture of Honor: The Psychology of Violence in the South* (Westview, 1996). A fascinating take on the cultural roots of violence in the United States, including the culture of honor posited to afflict the South disproportionately and traced to European immigration.

Eyal Press. "Do Immigrants Make Us Safer?" *New York Times Magazine* December 3, 2006. A *New York Times* writer considers the questions raised in this article, taking to the streets of Chicago.

Rubén G. Rumbaut and Walter A. Ewing. "The Myth of Immigrant Criminality and the Paradox of Assimilation: Incarceration Rates among Native and Foreign-Born Men" (Immigration Policy Center, 2007). A recent synthesis of the empirical facts on immigration and crime, with a special focus on incarceration.

Thorsten Sellin. *Culture Conflict and Crime* (Social Science Research Council, 1938). Widely considered the classical account of immigration, culture, and crime in the early part of the 20th century.

READING 14

In this article, Professor Logan takes seriously notions of deviance and place linked to the theory of social disorganization, but he moves well beyond. He asks several quite illuminating questions. First, he is interested in the process that turns certain neighborhoods bad and in how certain neighborhoods are protected from negative characteristics. Second, he is interested in how certain types of people are found to live in these neighborhoods. Clearly, given the risks and quality of life characterizing these neighborhoods, most people would choose a better environment. His answers go well beyond the early Chicago school and the original theory of social disorganization.

Life and Death in the City

Neighborhoods in Context

John Logan

Everyone who has searched for a home knows that there are "good" neighborhoods and "bad" neighborhoods. Those differences occur neither by accident nor by design of their residents. The housing market and discrimination sort people into different neighborhoods, which in turn shape residents' lives—and deaths. Bluntly put, some neighborhoods are likely to kill you.

Source: Logan, J. (2003). Life and death in the city: Neighborhoods in context. *Contexts, 2*(2), 33–40.

According to the research tradition developed decades ago by sociologists at the University of Chicago, as neighborhoods age they naturally attract poorer and more troubled residents. These bad neighbors make bad neighborhoods. Another, more modern way of thinking about neighborhoods, however, suggests that this is far from a natural process. Public policies often accelerate a neighborhood's downward spiral, and areas with sufficient political clout protect themselves at the expense of poorer neighborhoods. Understanding this evolution in thinking about bad neighborhoods is critical to dealing with their problems.

◈ What Makes a Neighborhood Bad?

Sociologists for over a century have been compiling reams of statistics from censuses, school districts, health authorities, and police departments that distinguish "good" from "bad" neighborhoods—bad usually meaning disorderly and unsafe. Throughout, both scholars and the public have focused on one question: what's wrong with bad neighborhoods? We will see that this is the wrong question. Social reformers at the turn of the last century (like the well-known photographer of New York City, Jacob Riis) thought that the problem with bad neighborhoods was the environment, specifically the densely-packed tenements. Researchers at the University of Chicago in the 1920s broadened that interpretation to argue that certain areas of the city simply could not sustain wholesome family and neighborhood relations.

A report on juvenile delinquency in poor neighborhoods of New York City, prepared in the 1930s by researchers for the city's Housing Authority, illustrates this point of view and its implications for policy. "The same conditions which make slums," the authors wrote, "are often present in delinquent careers. Bad housing, low income levels or poverty itself, the weakened grip of regulatory institutions like the family, objectionable groupings, unwholesome or inadequate recreational outlets are but some [of these]." Scholars emphasized the way that "slum" neighborhoods undermined social relations: "Cultural levels and living standards are lower. There is neither neighborhood solidarity in the community sense, nor that strongly organized group opinion which frequently acts like a brake upon individual misbehavior. Attitudes, either of apathy or indifference, toward acceptable modes of behavior and individual delinquencies are common."

The solution for these authors was to eliminate the slums. Outside the ghetto, they argued, poor immigrants and minority families will shed ghetto behavior, making "slum clearance as effective an aid for crime control, as machine guns are for an infantry attack." This way of thinking infuses policies aimed at the inner city today. Massive public housing projects in some cities are being demolished. In Chicago, an experiment in public housing, the Gautreaux program, reverses decades of policy. Instead of concentrating the poor in housing projects, it moves residents into outer city and suburban neighborhoods, calling it "moving to opportunity." Such policies assume that to depopulate the ghetto, gentrify it, or blow it up is an effective solution to the problems concentrated in it.

This tradition of thought dominates current understandings of neighborhood disparities in crime and public health. But there is a better way to think about them.

◈ What Makes Some Neighborhoods Unsafe?

Both earlier scholars and modern ones focus on the quality of social life in neighborhoods to explain variations in crime among them. This sociological approach has its roots in work begun at the University of Chicago by Clifford Shaw in the 1920s and later continued by his collaborator and student Henry McKay. Their thesis was that juvenile delinquency occurred where there was physical deterioration and weak community ties. Regardless of who lives in a particular locality, they argued, some neighborhoods consistently lacked the institutions needed to control the behavior of local youth, such as trust among neighbors, intact families and recreational activities for children. "Traditions of delinquency" are passed on by neighborhood youth, families do not work well, residents are poor, and the

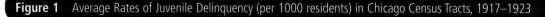
Figure 1   Average Rates of Juvenile Delinquency (per 1000 residents) in Chicago Census Tracts, 1917–1923

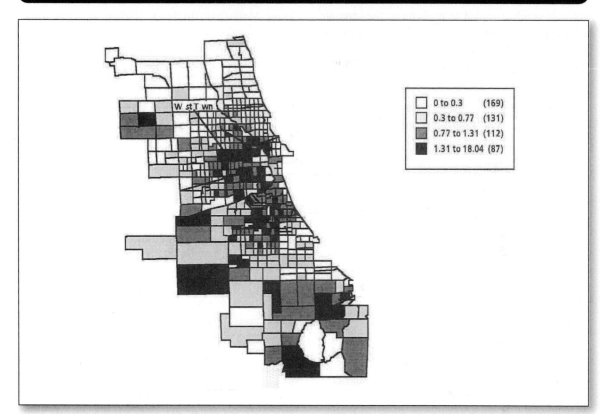

result is gangs. Some more recent scholars add on the problem of rapid urban change, noting that the northern neighborhoods that received waves of African-American migrants in the 1950s also experienced the highest rates of increase in delinquency.

An illustration of the neighborhood differences in crime that propelled Shaw and McKay's theories is presented in Figure 1. It depicts rates of juvenile delinquency by census tracts in Chicago in 1917–23. The areas that are more darkly shaded are those with higher rates of serious crimes. The densest cluster of delinquent tracts is to the west of the downtown Loop, including a mélange of neighborhoods, some largely African American at that time, and others of East European and Italian immigrants. To the south of the

Loop is the well-known Black Belt, the area of high African American in-migration, which also had high rates of delinquency. Finally, at the southern edge of the city—an industrial blue-collar district close to the steel mills—is another concentration of delinquents, variously African American or East European tracts. This geography of crime encouraged sociologists to think of it as the product of the neighborhoods themselves.

Current researchers seek to show that aspects of community "disorganization" really do stimulate crime. Robert Sampson used census data to show that the higher the proportion of divorced adults and the higher the proportion of households headed by a single woman in a neighborhood, the higher the proportion of residents who have been victims of crime. Family disruption, he believes, decreases a community's control over youths tempted to misbehave. For example, overburdened single mothers have little energy to watch out for their own teenagers, much less their neighbors' kids. Sampson has also studied local communities' ability to control their environments more directly, using surveys to ask residents about their ability to supervise teen peer groups, the strength of friendships in the neighborhood, and their participation in local organizations. He found that the more supervision, friendship, and participation in a neighborhood, the lower its crime rate.

Sampson's most recent research in Chicago combines video tapes of street activity, new surveys, census data and official crime reports. He finds that crime is higher where residents are both unattached to one another and do not expect neighbors to keep watch on the streets. The social arrangements within the neighborhood and the kinds of people who live there are what makes a neighborhood unsafe.

◈ What Makes Some Neighborhoods Unhealthy?

Concern over neighborhood differences in disease has even deeper roots than studies of crime and delinquency, and it, too, has led to looking inside the neighborhoods to explain their problems. Health officials have long pointed to variations among localities in mortality, infant deaths, and infectious disease to press for public policies such as water and sewer improvements, tenement law reform, and quarantine and vaccination programs. For example, U.S. Army Surgeon John Billings compiled information from death certificates of New York City and Brooklyn residents for the years 1884–1890. He found large differences in death rates among neighborhoods, which he attributed especially to physical features of the neighborhood itself. He showed that death rates were typically greatest for low-lying areas located on previously swampy or filled land, notably below 50th Street in Manhattan. Figure 2 presents a map of rates of infectious diseases in New York City in 1932. Four decades after Billings' study,

the spatial disparities that he noted remained strong. The highest disease rates were found in immigrant lower Manhattan, in black Harlem and the working-class Italian neighborhoods near it, in the South Bronx and in older sections of Brooklyn. Most districts with the lowest levels of disease were in areas that had been outside the city boundaries in 1890—the relatively undeveloped sections of South Brooklyn, Queens, Staten Island and the northern reaches of the Bronx. What are the sources of these disparities? The medical model of disease naturally led Billings to focus on the physical environment within the neighborhood. Sociologists today give more attention to social factors. One key hypothesis is that rapid community change creates stress in people which in turn lowers their resistance. There are many potential sources of chronic stress in disadvantaged neighborhoods: poor housing, few stores, a lack of health services and transportation, the threat of crime, a noxious physical environment, crowding and noise. While these stressors promote disease, other community characteristics make residents more vulnerable to stresses. Like criminologists, public health analysts point to variations in the extent to which residents talk to one another, agree on what is proper behavior, and lean on one another to conform. Where this tends not to happen, environmental stress is more likely to lead residents to aggression, risky behaviors, unhealthy coping patterns, such as smoking and alcohol or drug abuse, and individual isolation. Residents in cohesive neighborhoods foster better health by passing on information, encouraging preventative habits such as the use of condoms, and admonishing unhealthy ones such as smoking. Strong local ties also contribute to mental health by improving self-esteem and mutual respect.

Evidence is mounting that neighborhood social conditions do affect disease. Thomas LaVeist, for example, has shown that black infant mortality rates are higher in cities with higher levels of racial residential segregation (and conversely, white infant mortality rates are lower in those cities). Felecia LeClere and her colleagues found that adult men of whatever race ran a 10 percent greater chance of dying over a five-year period if they lived in a neighborhood that was more than about 3 percent black—even taking into

Figure 2   Rates of Infectious Disease (per 1000 residents) in New York City Health Areas, 1932

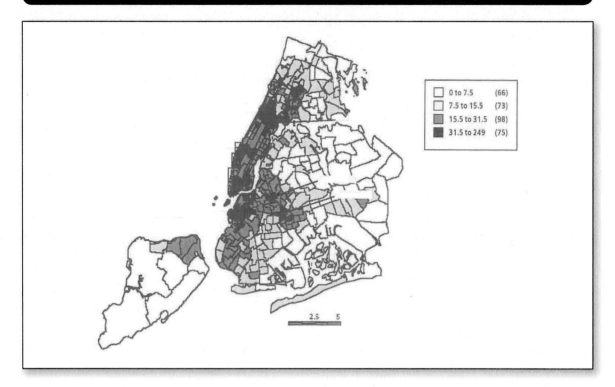

☐	0 to 7.5	(66)
☐	7.5 to 15.5	(73)
▨	15.5 to 31.5	(98)
■	31.5 to 249	(75)

account differences in age, income and the like. We do not yet have solid explanations for these patterns. Nonetheless, these studies illustrate that the current approach to understanding why some neighborhoods "go bad" is to look for sources of poor health in the neighborhood itself.

◈ Looking Beyond the Neighborhood

The most sophisticated research on neighborhood inequalities, as illustrated in criminology and medical sociology, is strongly focused on what is wrong with bad neighborhoods. But sociology teaches us to look farther, to look at the contexts of situations. Where should we look instead of within the neighborhoods to explain their conditions? I suggest that we try to answer two questions about the links between places and the world around them:

First, what happened to these places to create their conditions? All places have a history; currently troubled neighborhoods in Chicago and New York are much the same ones as those identified in the early maps. (The South Bronx, for example, had its problems long before it became a famous ghetto in the 1960s.) What forces protect the best neighborhoods over generations and leave others vulnerable to deterioration? Second, how and why do certain kinds of people come to live in places with such problems? Think of the delinquency and infectious disease maps as maps of the distribution of victims. Then the question to be answered is who, by virtue of where they live, is most exposed to these hazards? Who lives in an unsafe area or an unhealthy neighborhood, and why? Most observers ask why the crimes were committed or why the disease spread in particular places. It is an entirely different question to ask who is most successful in avoiding such areas altogether.

The traditional analysis posited that people were allocated to neighborhoods mainly by the market (their ability to pay vs. the costs of housing in different places). Where people lived was, in this sense, natural and expected. Of course poor people would be concentrated in certain neighborhoods. We could say more broadly, those who have least choice are most likely to live in the high-crime or high-disease district. But lacking choice is not only a matter of lacking money; because of discrimination, racial minorities, immigrants, non-English speakers, and people in unusual households also have less choice than others. In my own study of Cleveland, for example, I found that African Americans on average live in neighborhoods with violent crime rates four times higher than the neighborhoods whites live in. Even after adjusting this comparison for differences in age, household, income, and education, African Americans still have twice the exposure of whites to violent crime. Affluent blacks face higher risks than do lower-income whites.

If we focus on the places, rather than the people, we could ask—the first question I posed—why some neighborhoods have more resources, why these neighborhoods are protected over time, and why some even improve their relative standing compared to others. Conversely, why are other neighborhoods in a downward spiral?

Here again there is a standard view: The urban mosaic reflects the natural evolution of individual communities. As a neighborhood ages, its housing becomes less fashionable and more expensive to maintain, affluent residents begin to leave, homes are broken up into multiple family dwellings to accommodate more people at low rents, and the new residents are poorer than the old. It's just how the economy works.

Developments in urban theory in the past 25 years provide another view. New thinking emphasizes instead how "un-natural" processes, such as the exercise of political power and public protest, alter the operations of the housing market. Neighborhoods are targeted for preservation or change according to the interests of politically influential real estate and business organizations. Neither the opening up of new areas nor the gentrification or decline of old areas is accomplished without government action. From this point of view, the concentrations of crime and disease are created by decisions that are mainly taken outside the neighborhood itself. In the 1930s and 1940s, for example, the federal government contributed to racial segregation by its explicit policy against insuring home loans in racially mixed neighborhoods and its implicit policy of allowing housing authorities to locate public housing projects in minority areas (and to exclude minorities from public housing in white neighborhoods). The same government subsidies that encouraged the flight of middle class residents and industrial jobs to the suburbs—highway construction, home mortgage deductions, investment tax credits—equally undercut the inner city. It was taken for granted at the time that Robert Moses, the grand builder of New York's transportation infrastructure, would weave his Northern State Parkway around the borders of private estates on Long Island, but sink the Cross-Bronx Expressway right through the heart of working-class Tremont. Ameliorative public policy, at its best, simply puts health clinics and more police in the most troubled neighborhoods.

Market forces exacerbate the problems of particular neighborhoods. An increase in crime or disease or any hazard makes a neighborhood less desirable. People who can leave do and people who can avoid the neighborhood do. Eventually only those with the least choice live there, and it becomes a minority neighborhood of concentrated poverty, with high proportions of female-headed households and other types of residents with limited options. There is evidence that such social problems determine the residents, rather than the other way around. So, for example, areas of high crime tend to become more African American as whites leave. What many typically interpret as an effect of changing social composition may also be its cause.

◈ The Wider Problem

Neighborhood inequality seems to be a permanent feature of modern cities. It matters, because even in the era of cyberspace, most of us are affected by the risks in the places where we live. It matters more widely because the public as a whole pays a price when crime or disease is concentrated anywhere.

The old Chicago School tradition deserves great credit for paying attention to the question of why there are systematic and persistent differences among neighborhoods. They took us beyond studying delinquency only in terms of adolescents' personalities, social class, and family backgrounds, or studying disease in terms of genetic predispositions and individual risk behavior. They showed us that places, as social contexts, matter.

But we have to re-examine some of the assumptions in the Chicago School approach. Its key question, "What is wrong with bad neighborhoods?" is the obvious one only if we are willing to assume that impersonal market processes put people in their places and then the characteristics of those people determine the destinies of neighborhoods. These are erroneous assumptions.

Some people are unnaturally squeezed into risky places. The misdirection of state power contributes to the unequal fortunes of disparate neighborhoods. As long as our only question is what's wrong with bad neighborhoods, and we do not ask how those neighborhoods came to be and how people came to live there, we will not know what to do about them.

 Recommended Resources

Anderton, Douglas, Andy B. Anderson, J. M. Oakes, and M. Fraser. "Environmental Equity: The Demographics of Dumping." *Demography* 31 (1994):221–240. The environmental justice movement asks why some neighborhoods are made unsafe by outsiders.

Link, Bruce, and Jo Phelan. "Social Conditions as Fundamental Causes of Disease." *Journal of Health and Social Behavior* (1995):80–94. An innovative essay on the social origins of poor health.

Logan, John R., and Harvey Molotch. *Urban Fortunes: The Political Economy of Place.* Los Angeles: University of California Press, 1987. An overview of the political processes of neighborhood development and spatial inequality.

Logan, John R., and Brian Stults. "Racial Differences in Exposure to Crime: The City and Suburbs of Cleveland in 1990." *Criminology* 37 (1999):251–276. Explains how the color line continues to expose minorities to higher crime, regardless of their socioeconomic position.

Massey, Douglas S., and Nancy A. Denton. *American Apartheid: Segregation and the Making of the Underclass.* Cambridge, MA: Harvard University Press, 1993. The classic work on how segregation creates and reinforces inner city poverty.

Sampson, Robert, and Stephen Raudenbush. "Systematic Social Observation of Public Spaces: A New Look at Disorder in Urban Neighborhoods." *American Journal of Sociology* 105 (1999):603–51. A multi-method approach looking at neighborhood social problems from within.

Shaw, Clifford, and Henry McKay. *Juvenile Delinquency and Urban Areas.* Revised edition. Chicago: University of Chicago Press, 1969. The classic study of what's wrong with high-crime neighborhoods.

READING 15

Weisburd and colleagues begin their article lamenting the proliferation of articles focused on individuals and the pushes and pulls that lead them into crime and deviance and the lack of studies on types of places as contributors of crime and deviance. Importantly, they are concerned that since the development of social disorganization theory, the key focus has been on neighborhoods while smaller units of analysis, for example, the street blocks, have been largely ignored. They link social disorganization theory with opportunity theories (e.g., routine activity theory), among others, to argue that smaller units of analysis may be an important new direction for theories of place.

Source: Weisburd, D., Groff, E. R., & Yang, S.-M. (2014). The importance of both opportunity and social disorganization theory in a future research agenda to advance criminological theory and crime prevention at places. *Journal of Research in Crime & Delinquency, 51*(4), 499–508. doi:10.1177/0022427814530404

The Importance of Both Opportunity and Social Disorganization Theory in a Future Research Agenda to Advance Criminological Theory and Crime Prevention at Places

David Weisburd, Elizabeth R. Groff, and Sue-Ming Yang

Criminology has been primarily focused on people and why they commit crime. In an article in *Crime and Justice* that examined quantitative studies of criminological theory in *Criminology* (1968–2005), 60 percent of the articles identified focused on individuals (Weisburd and Piquero 2008). Just 15 (8 percent) of the studies examined communities or neighborhoods. Only one study examined a micro geographic unit such as that studied in our book, *The Criminology of Place*. While certainly the interest in small geographic units within neighborhoods and communities has grown over the last decade, the exploration of criminological theory at the level of small geographic units is new, and we would argue that it is an important area for criminological study. Braga and Clarke (Forthcoming) agree with us, and we think their thoughtful essay examining the implications of our work raises important issues regarding how to proceed with a research agenda on the criminology of place.

Behind recent interest in the criminology of place lies an empirical reality that fundamentally alters the ways in which we understand crime in urban areas. Starting with early studies of crime concentrations at addresses and extending to other micro geographic units (e.g., see Crow and Bull 1975; Pierce, Spaar, and Briggs 1986; Roncek 2000; Sherman, Bueger, and Gartin 1989; Weisburd et al. 2004; Weisburd and Green 1994), scholars began to identify what we call in our book a law of crime concentrations at places (Weisburd, Groff, and Yang 2012). Using the street segment as a micro geographic unit, there appears to be a consistent level of concentration across cities and across time (e.g., see Telep, Mitchell, and Weisburd Forthcoming; Weisburd and Amram 2014; Weisburd et al. 2004; Weisburd, Telep, and Lawton Forthcoming). About 5 percent of

streets account for 50 percent of crime and about 1 percent of streets accounts for 25 percent of crimes. In *The Criminology of Place*, we not only illustrate that concentration; we also show that there is strong street-to-street variability in crime levels. Our key concern was to answer the question of what factors seem to explain such variability.

We wanted our study to be theoretically informed, so we began by identifying the key theoretical perspectives that have been identified earlier by scholars to understand crime at place. Opportunity theories including routine activities theory (Cohen and Felson 1979), situational prevention (Clarke 1980, 1983), and crime pattern theory (Brantingham and Brantingham 1984, 1981 [1991]) have been seen by most of those who study micro geographic units as the key factors explaining crime patterns. But we also thought that it is important to consider the relevance of social disorganization theories (Bursik and Grasmick 1993; Sampson 2012; Sampson, Raudenbush, and Earls 1997; Shaw and McKay 1942), which have been dominant in understanding crime in studies of neighborhoods and communities.

Braga and Clarke (Forthcoming) question why we took this latter approach and did not stick to the core theories that have motivated study in this area. Our answer is that we began with a theory of life on street segments that seemed consistent with core elements of social disorganization theories at a higher geographic level. Our work was informed by behavior setting theory (Barker 1968; Wicker 1987:614) and its applications to criminology in earlier work (Taylor 1997; Taylor and Harrell 1996). Street segments in this context can be seen as micro communities. People who frequent a street segment get to know one another and become familiar with each other's routines. Residents develop certain roles they play in the life of the street segment (e.g., the busybody and the organizer). Norms about acceptable behavior develop and are generally shared. Blocks have "standing patterns of behavior" (Barker 1968, p. 18), for example, people whose routines are regular, like the mail carrier or the shop owner. Together, these elements support the cumulative familiarity that is the basis for the development of mutual trust, which supports the willingness to intervene and is necessary to the ability of a street segment's users to achieve their shared goals. In this context, street segments have many traits of communities that are prominent in social disorganization theory. These small spatial units function also as social units with specific routines. This led us to consider the implications of social disorganization theory at a micro level.

Reinforcing the potential importance of such social structural variables is the fact that they were concentrated in micro geographic hot spots and often varied tremendously street by street, just as crime varied across streets. For example, 50 percent of housing assistance (a measure of social disadvantage) is consistently found on about 0.4 percent of the street segments in Seattle. Within 800 feet of these public assistance hot spots, 84 percent of street segments do not have any public housing assistance recipients. The question is whether housing assistance and other possible indicators of social disorganization were strongly related to crime hot spots.

Braga and Clarke (Forthcoming) note that many of the most important variables we identify are associated with opportunity theories, and this is consistent with prior theorizing in the criminology of place. We acknowledge that our work provides confirmation of many of the elements of opportunity theories. But we also found that measures of poverty and collective efficacy were also key factors in understanding variability of crime at street segments. Braga and Clarke raise questions about our use of voting behavior as an indicator of collective efficacy. They argue that voting behavior is not a good measure of collective efficacy, pointing to Sampson's (2012) recent findings that voting patterns across neighborhoods were not strongly correlated with measures of collective efficacy. Importantly, our measure and Sampson's measure

are substantially different. Sampson examined the proportion of residents in the neighborhood who reported voting in the last mayoral election. We measure the proportion of active voters on a street, defined by voting patterns over two years. Voting once does not necessarily show strong commitment to involvement in public affairs, but voting consistently over time says more about an individual's commitment (see Coleman 2002; Putnam 2001). More important, it reflects a general propensity toward civic engagement that is likely to be even stronger on their home street segment. In turn, we found the same variability across street segments here as in many other of our measures. Within 800 feet of the hot spots of active voters (the top 10 percent), only 25 percent of neighboring street segments also evidenced such high levels of active voting.

Of course, we would have preferred to have a more direct measure of collective efficacy and indeed many of the other theoretical constructs in our study. A key theme of the article by Braga and Clarke (Forthcoming) relates to the need for more and better data, both on the nature of opportunities for crime at a micro geographic level and indicators of social disorganization. We agree wholeheartedly. The weakness of secondary data studies more generally is that they rely on information that is available. We were able to collect a wealth of data reflecting opportunities for crime and social disorganization at places using archival records for Seattle. Although our data are the most exhaustive available for examining crime trends at the street segment level, we could not measure directly some key dimensions of either opportunity or social disorganization. Like any study that explores new territory, our work is necessarily a first step. Weisburd with Brian Lawton, Justin Ready, and Amelia Haviland have recently embarked on a large study supported by the National Institutes of Health that will allow detailed information to be collected on opportunity, social and demographic factors at the street segment level, including detailed measures of collective efficacy.

We think that Braga and Clarke (Forthcoming) provide important suggestions for how to proceed, not only in terms of the identification of measures but also in examining dynamic models of how variables intersect in time and space. We would certainly have liked to model not just the presence in space and time of specific measures of opportunity and social disorganization but also the extent to which these measures overlap within more specific bands of time. For example, we show that increased opportunities for crime increase the likelihood of a street falling in a chronic crime pattern. This is a confirmation of routine activities theory (Cohen and Felson 1979). But a next generation of studies armed with more robust data will hopefully be able to model in a more dynamic way the specific moments of time when victims and offenders intersect in the absence of a capable guardian.

Finally, we comment on the strong reservations that Braga and Clarke (Forthcoming) have about our policy recommendations in the area of social prevention. We agree that the evidence for situational responses to crime have strong empirical support (e.g., see Guerette and Bowers 2009). This is particularly the case for hot spots policing, where a large number of randomized controlled trials have shown that police can prevent crime (Braga 2005; Braga, Papachristos, and Hureau Forthcoming; Sherman and Weisburd 1995). Our work helps us to understand why such interventions are effective. Opportunities for crime are key to understanding the variability of crime at a micro geographic level, and increasing police guardianship in that context can deter crime (Durlauf and Nagin 2011; Nagin Forthcoming). Such deterrence will not simply shift crime to areas nearby (Weisburd et al. 2006) because, as our study illustrates, areas nearby will often not have the same types of crime opportunities.

There is, in contrast, little evidence of the salience of social prevention at a micro geographic level as Braga and Clarke (Forthcoming) point out. But we disagree strongly that this means that we should not begin to consider social prevention at crime hot spots. When hot spots policing experiments began, there was little basic research literature beyond cross-sectional studies of crime at addresses (e.g., Pierce et al. 1986; Sherman et al. 1989). And much of what we know now about situational prevention comes from applied research (e.g., see Clarke 1980, 1995; Guerette and Bowers 2009). Our work provides empirical support for the idea that street segments are behavior settings and that the characteristics of such behavioral settings

vary across streets. Collective efficacy (as we measure it) and social disadvantage vary at a micro geographic level, and they are strongly related to crime at the street segment level. The question this raises is whether by altering these characteristics at a micro geographic level, we can do something about crime. We argue that directing social interventions at this level is more realistic, given the economic realities we face today, than trying to change whole neighborhoods or communities. In turn, just as hot spots policing has shown that the police must focus police patrol at the specific places where crime is concentrated (rather than wandering across large areas), we think that social interventions should be focused as well.

Braga and Clarke (Forthcoming) argue that social disorganization has been too amorphous a concept, seldom leading to direct proposals for action by police or other crime prevention agents. We think that the application of social prevention programs at the street segment level can help frame such approaches more sharply. Our suggested agenda would require clear and precise statements about what police or others might do to increase collective efficacy or reduce social disadvantage at specific places. Importantly, it will also require measurable mechanisms to be defined. For example, Weisburd and Gill are working with police in Brooklyn Park, Minnesota, to increase collective efficacy at hot spot streets (see Davis, Weisburd, and Gill 2013). Police will actively seek to meet with residents and encourage them to become involved with each other and the affairs of the streets more generally. They will try to identify key figures on the hot spot streets and work with them to get people on the block involved in crime prevention. Many community-policing programs have already taken similar approaches, without recognizing concepts of collective efficacy and informal social controls (Gill et al. 2014). Of course, as Braga and Clarke (Forthcoming) suggest, it will be difficult to distinguish these crime prevention gains from those that are due to the development of situational prevention approaches and deterrence through increased guardianship, by both the police and the public. We think that what is new here is the direct recognition that collective efficacy at the micro geographic level is relevant and important.

In some ways, our suggestions are more radical than simply taking into account both the social and physical environment of places, and perhaps this is what raises particular concern on the part of Braga and Clarke (Forthcoming). We are suggesting that street segment characteristics offer a stronger foundation for the targeting of social programs meant to address structural problems that lead to crime, such as employment and income inequality. We think that we should test the efficacy of economic and employment programs at the micro geographic level. And we argue that economies of scale make it feasible to develop such social interventions. Successful crime prevention can be seen as operating at two levels. One level responds to the immediate situational components of crime and often relies on deterrence and directly reducing crime opportunities as a method of reducing the likelihood of crime. At another, there are long-term social factors often relating to disadvantage and low collective efficacy. Our work suggests that it is time to experiment in this latter area at a micro geographic level. There will often be overlap, and we suspect that the most effective long-term crime prevention will focus on both approaches. Informal social controls that are encouraged by increased collective efficacy will also work to reduce opportunities for crime. Hot spots policing and situational prevention may, by reducing fear of crime and increasing quality of life on streets, also increase collective efficacy and reduce social disadvantage. It is time to examine these possibilities and mechanisms more carefully to develop a fuller repertoire of crime prevention at a micro geographic level. Accordingly, we would add to their proposed research agenda an emphasis on how social prevention at hot spots can be more carefully defined and systematically evaluated.

◈ References

Barker, R. G. 1968. *Ecological Psychology: Concepts and Methods for Studying the Environment of Human Behavior.* Stanford, CA: Stanford University Press.

Braga, A. A. 2005. "Hot Spots Policing and Crime Prevention: A Systematic Review of Randomized Controlled Trials." *Journal of Experimental Criminology* 1:317–42.

Braga, A. A. and R. V. Clarke. Forthcoming. "Explaining High-risk Concentrations of Crime in the City: Social Disorganization, Crime Opportunities, and Important Next Steps." *Journal of Research in Crime and Delinquency.* doi: 10.1177/ 0022427814521217

Braga, A. A., A. V. Papachristos, and D. M. Hureau. Forthcoming. "The Effects of Hot Spots Policing on Crime: An Updated Systematic Review and Meta-analysis." *Justice Quarterly.* doi:10 .1080/07418825.2012.673632

Brantingham, P. J. and P. L. Brantingham. (1981) 1991. *Environmental Criminology.* Prospect Heights, IL: Waveland Press.

Brantingham, P. J. and P. L. Brantingham. 1984. *Patterns in Crime.* New York: Macmillan.

Bursik, R. J. and H. G. Grasmick. 1993. *Neighborhoods and Crime: The Dimensions of Effective Community Control.* New York: Lexington.

Clarke, R. V. 1980. "Situational Crime Prevention: Theory and Practice." *British Journal Criminology* 20:136.

Clarke, R. V. 1983. "Situational Crime Prevention: Its Theoretical Basis and Practical Scope." Pp. 225–56 in *Crime and Justice: An Annual Review of Research,* edited by M. Tonry and N. Morris. Chicago: University of Chicago Press.

Clarke, R. V. 1995. "Situational Crime Prevention." Pp. 91–150 in *Crime and Justice: Vol. 19. Building a Safer Society: Strategic Approaches to Crime Prevention,* edited by M. Tonry and D. Farrington. Chicago: University of Chicago Press.

Cohen, L. E. and M. Felson. 1979. "Social Change and Crime Rate Trends: A Routine Activity Approach." *American Sociological Review* 44:588–608.

Coleman, S. 2002. "A Test for the Effect of Conformity on Crime Rates Using Voter Turnout." *The Sociological Quarterly* 43:257–76.

Crow, W. and J. Bull. 1975. *Robbery Deterrence: An Applied Behavioral Science Demonstration—Final Report.* La Jolla, CA: Western Behavioral Science Institute.

Davis, M., D. Weisburd, and C. Gill. 2013. *Increasing Collective Efficacy at Crime Hot Spots: A Patrol Force Approach in Brooklyn Park, Minnesota.* Grant proposal to the Bureau of Justice Assistance, U.S. Department of Justice. Fairfax, VA: Center for Evidence-Based Crime Policy, George Mason University.

Durlauf, S. N. and D. S. Nagin. 2011. "Imprisonment and Crime." *Criminology & Public Policy* 10:13–54.

Gill, C., D. Weisburd, C. Telep, Z. Vitter, and T. Bennett. 2014. "Community-oriented Policing to Reduce Crime, Disorder, and Fear and Increase Satisfaction and Legitimacy among Citizens: A Systematic Review." Unpublished manuscript.

Guerette, R. T. and K. J. Bowers. 2009. "Assessing the Extent of Crime Displacement and Diffusion of Benefits: A Review of Situational Crime Prevention Evaluations." *Criminology* 47:1331–68.

Nagin, D. Forthcoming. "Deterrence in the Twenty-first Century: A Review of the Evidence." *Crime and Justice: An Annual Review.*

Pierce, G., S. Spaar, and L. Briggs. 1986. *The Character of Police Work: Strategic and Tactical Implications.* Boston, MA: Center for Applied Social Research, Northeastern University.

Putnam, R. D. 2001. *Bowling Alone.* New York: Simon & Schuster.

Roncek, D. W. 2000. "Schools and Crime." Pp. 153–65 in *Analyzing Crime Patterns: Frontiers of Practice*, edited by V. Goldsmith, P. McGuire, G. J. H. Mollenkopf, and T. A. Ross. Thousand Oaks, CA: Sage.

Sampson, R. J. 2012. *Great American City: Chicago and the Enduring Neighborhood Effect*. Chicago: University of Chicago Press.

Sampson, R. J., S. W. Raudenbush, and F. Earls. 1997. "Neighbourhoods and Violent Crime: A Multilevel Study of Collective Efficacy." *Science* 277:918–24.

Shaw, C. R. and H. D. McKay. 1942. *Juvenile Delinquency and Urban Areas*. Chicago: University of Chicago Press.

Sherman, L. W., M. E. Bueger, and P. R. Gartin. 1989. *Repeat Call Address Policing: The Minneapolis RECAP Experiment*. Washington, DC: Crime Control Institute.

Sherman, L. W. and D. Weisburd. 1995. "General Deterrent Effects of Police Patrol in Crime 'Hot Spots': A Randomized, Controlled Trial." *Justice Quarterly* 12:625–48.

Taylor, R. B. 1997. "Social Order and Disorder of Street Blocks and Neighborhoods: Ecology, Microecology, and the Systemic Model of Social Disorganization." *Journal of Research in Crime and Delinquency* 34:113–55.

Taylor, R. B. and A. V. Harrell. 1996. *Physical Environment and Crime*. Washington, DC: U.S. Department of Justice.

Telep, C. W., R. J. Mitchell, and D. Weisburd. Forthcoming. "How Much Time Should the Police Spend at Crime Hot Spots? Answers from a Police Agency Directed Randomized Field Trial in Sacramento, California." *Justice Quarterly* 1–29.

Weisburd, D. and S. Amram. 2014. "The Law of Concentrations of Crime at Place: The Case of Tel Aviv-Jaffa." *Police Practice and Research* 15:101–14.

Weisburd, David, S. Bushway, C. Lum, and S. Yang. 2004. "Trajectories of Crime at Places: A Longitudinal Study of Street Segments in the City of Seattle." *Criminology* 42:283–322.

Weisburd, D. and L. Green. 1994. "Defining the Drug Market: The Case of the Jersey City DMA System." Pp. 61–76 in *Drugs and Crime: Evaluating Public Policy Initiatives*, edited by D. L. MacKenzie and C. D. Uchida. Newbury Park, CA: Sage.

Weisburd, D. L., E. R. Groff, and S. M. Yang. 2012. *The Criminology of Place: Street Segments and Our Understanding of the Crime Problem*. Oxford, England: Oxford University Press.

Weisburd, D. and A. R. Piquero. 2008. "How Well Do Criminologists Explain Crime? Statistical Modeling in Published Studies." *Crime and Justice* 37:453–502.

Weisburd, D., C. W. Telep, and B. A. Lawton. 2014. "Could Innovations in Policing Have Contributed to the New York City Crime Drop Even in a Period of Declining Police Strength? The Case of Stop, Question and Frisk as a Hot Spots Policing Strategy." *Justice Quarterly* 31:129–153.

Weisburd, D., L. A. Wyckoff, J. Ready, J. E. Eck, J. C. Hinkle, and F. Gajewski. 2006. "Does Crime Just Move around the Corner? A Controlled Study of Spatial Displacement and Diffusion of Crime Control Benefits." *Criminology* 44:549–92.

Wicker, A. W. 1987. "Behavior Settings Reconsidered: Temporal Stages, Resources, Internal Dynamics, Context." *Handbook of Environmental Psychology* 1:613–53.

CHAPTER 6

Differential Association and Social Learning Theories

The Internet is a hotbed of deviant information. Indeed, within a couple of minutes, we found various sites that encouraged a wide variety of deviant behavior and others that provided step-by-step guides offering the basic techniques to learn how to engage in deviance. You can learn how to grow the best marijuana indoors and out, or you can learn how to make crack cocaine or find peyote (a hallucinogenic drug found on San Pedro cacti). For the person considering bulimia, there are "Pro Bulimia Tips and Tricks." There are tips on building a bomb with typical household items. The would-be burglar can get instructions on how to pick locks. And amid all of the porn, there are now websites helping married men and women to have affairs. The World Wide Web is clearly a source for virtually any form of deviance.

◈ Introduction

The discussion of websites above suggests something that many sociologists of deviance believe today and study—the notion that much deviance, if not all deviant behavior, needs to be learned and that instruction is often required. All of these sites offer encouragement to engage in deviance as well as information to help people learn the techniques necessary to do so. It might not take much to learn to smoke pot or crack, but the drug needs to be made available, and—given its illegal status and the "war on drugs"—for many, it would require a certain amount of encouragement.

Of course, the Web is not the only way we learn about deviance. We learn it from family, friends, other media sources, and so on. In this chapter, we discuss two prominent sociological theories that emphasize the importance of learning in the development of deviance. The first, developed by Edwin Sutherland in the 1930s and still prominent today, is **differential association** theory. The second modifies and builds on differential association theory; it is widely known as social learning theory and is primarily associated with Ronald Akers. We also provide a brief description of a related theory focused on culture and subcultures—**cultural deviance theory**. Following a general overview and evaluation of the theories, we discuss how they have been useful in understanding a wide range of deviant behaviors from a sociological perspective.

◈ Development of Differential Association Theory

Edwin Sutherland (1883–1950) was a pioneer in sociological criminology who responded to and attacked many of the mainstream criminological ideas of his time and provided a solid sociological approach to understanding crime. While his focus was clearly on crime, his work has obvious implications for other noncriminal forms of deviant behavior. He was a prolific scholar who produced numerous scientific publications, was the president of the American Sociological Association, and was a mentor to many students who continued to advance the field of criminology and the study of deviance. Two of his books are of particular importance for this chapter: *White Collar Crime* (1949b) and a textbook from 1924 later titled *Principles of Criminology* (1934).

Sutherland titled his presidential address to the American Sociological Association "Is White Collar Crime, Crime?" challenging mainstream criminologists who focused almost exclusively (and to some extent still overly focus) on street crime. Here, Sutherland set the stage for his classic work, *White Collar Crime*, published four years later. Although white-collar crime has become an important area of inquiry and students today are generally familiar with highly exposed cases of white-collar crime, what is important here is what Sutherland brought to the proverbial table, that "conventional generalizations about crime and criminality are invalid because they explain only the crime of the lower classes" (Sutherland, 1949b, p. 217). He viewed crime as ubiquitous, occurring across dimensions of social class, race, gender, and other social conditions. This important work drew attention to crimes of the middle and upper classes whose perpetrators were obviously not suffering from poverty or biological predispositions.

Across editions, Sutherland modified and advanced *Principles of Criminology* to finally include, in 1947, his full-fledged theory of differential association, including his nine propositions of the theory. Sutherland's text continued to be updated even after his death in 1950, with Donald Cressey and later David Luckenbill as coauthors. But neither Sutherland nor his collaborators changed the wording or modified in any way the nine propositions. Given the history of the propositions, we list them as originally written in Table 6.1, but in our summary and examples, we use the term "deviance" and use noncriminological examples to better fit this text.

We will focus on the first seven propositions as the latter two are not terribly relevant for our discussion and were later discounted in subsequent formulations (see Akers, 1985; Burgess & Akers, 1966). The first proposition suggests that deviant behavior is learned and not inherited or the result of some biological trait. Today, even those interested in biological predictors of crime and deviance do not argue that *behavior* is inherited, but rather, they say that there may be *predispositions* that make some folks more likely to engage in behavior (see, e.g., Rowe, 2002; A. Walsh, 2000). The fact remains that the behavioral repertoire of babies is pretty limited. They hold few, if any, deviant (or nondeviant) thoughts. They don't know how to light a joint or why they would want to. They may have a predisposition for alcoholism, but they don't know why they would want to drink or where to find a bar. This may seem obvious to many, but Sutherland was responding to the early biological and psychological traditions that were fairly deterministic in nature. Even today, we speak of "crack babies" as if they are destined for a life of drug use. Furthermore, other schools of thought—in particular, certain social control theorists—still argue that for the most part, the learning necessary for most deviance is trivial and of little theoretical importance (Gottfredson & Hirschi, 1990).

From the second and third propositions, we can conclude that deviance is learned from other people, particularly intimate others—one's family and friends. Remember that Sutherland was writing during a time when people were not bombarded with mass media; current researchers have moved beyond intimate others in examining sources of deviance. However, even today, much learning takes place between parents and children and between friends and acquaintances. Much research suggests that early deviant behaviors are group activities. Underage drinking, smoking pot or using other drugs, vandalism, bullying, and so on are more often done in groups than in isolation, especially among adolescents and young adults (Warr, 2002).

The fourth proposition suggests that two things need to be learned. First, one must know how to engage in the deviant behavior, and this may be simple or complex. Little technique is needed to vandalize a building by breaking a window. Alternatively, picking locks, hot-wiring cars, and recognizing a drug-buying opportunity versus a police sting are more complex. Second, we need to know why people would want to engage in the behavior in the first place.

Sutherland believed that people need to learn the motivations, drives, rationalizations, and appropriate attitudes for engaging in deviant behavior. For example, given that smoking is illegal for minors, the massive ad campaigns on the hazards of smoking, and the fact that parents and teachers (even if they are smokers themselves) warn against the hazards of smoking, why do thousands of youngsters start smoking each year? There must be other sources of "information" that motivate youngsters to start smoking. Hence, the fifth proposition suggests that direction of the motives and drives varies and is learned from exposure to **definitions** (statements, attitudes, beliefs) that are favorable or unfavorable to engaging in particular behaviors.

The sixth proposition is the most important proposition to differential association theory and states that an excess of definitions favorable to deviant behavior over definitions unfavorable to deviant behavior increases the likelihood of committing deviant acts. Going back to the adolescent smoking example, with all of the definitions (laws, warnings of parents and teachers, ad campaigns) unfavorable to smoking, why would one smoke? For Sutherland, the likely answer is that many definitions favorable to smoking (via parents, peers, famous actors and actresses, and other influential people) make smoking appear "cool." Some young people come to hold more definitions favorable to smoking than to not smoking and begin the process of becoming a smoker.

The seventh proposition specifies this further and states that differential associations vary in terms of frequency (how often exposed), duration (length of exposure), priority (how early in life one is exposed), and intensity (the respect or admiration one holds for the person providing the definitions). Again, one can see that even in a society that rebukes smoking (at least symbolically via law, rules, and campaigns), some people are exposed to definitions favorable to smoking: frequently, for long durations of time, from an early age where youth are impressionable, and from people they are expected to respect (e.g., parents, an older sibling, or media figures), making them more likely to engage in the behavior themselves. It is important to note that Sutherland did not emphasize differential association with persons but, rather, differential exposure to definitions. Although the two variables may be related, they are clearly not the same thing. Smokers (and other deviants) can provide definitions that are favorable ("Smoking makes you look cool; try one") or unfavorable ("Hock, hock, wheeze, wheeze, I wish I could quit these!").

Table 6.1 Sutherland's (1947) Nine Propositions of Differential Association Theory

1. Criminal behavior is learned.

2. Criminal behavior is learned in interaction with other persons in a process of communication.

3. The principal part of the learning of criminal behavior occurs within intimate personal groups.

4. When criminal behavior is learned, the learning includes (a) techniques of committing the crime, which are sometimes very complicated, sometimes very simple, and (b) the specific direction of motives, drives, rationalizations, and attitudes.

5. The specific direction of motives and drives is learned from definitions of the legal code as favorable or unfavorable.

6. A person becomes delinquent because of an excess of definitions favorable to violation of law over definitions unfavorable to violation of the law.

7. Differential associations may vary in frequency, duration, priority, and intensity.

8. The process of learning criminal behavior by association with criminal and anticriminal patterns involves all of the mechanisms that are involved in any other learning.

9. Although criminal behavior is an expression of general needs and values, it is not explained by those general needs and values because noncriminal behavior is an expression of the same needs and values.

Sutherland's theory of differential association is perhaps the most long-standing and popular theory of deviance in terms of empirical evaluation, and it has made important inroads to policy and programs. It has been instrumental in studying a wide array of criminal and noncriminal deviant behaviors and has found much support. The theory has also been sharply criticized and challenged on a number of grounds (see Kubrin, Stucky, & Krohn, 2009, for a recent overview of the issues). However, it is still cited widely in the social sciences and has been modified and expanded by Ronald Akers and his colleagues.

DEVIANCE IN POPULAR CULTURE

Differential association holds that deviant behavior is learned behavior. Try to think of examples of behaviors that you have learned—deviant or not, the more specific, the better—and the specific processes that you went through to learn those behaviors. Did you learn them from people close to you? Did you learn both attitudes about the behavior and techniques to engage in the behavior?

If you are having a hard time thinking of examples, popular culture offers many films and television shows that illustrate the process of learning deviant attitudes and behaviors.

American History X—A disturbing film that explores the topic of learning hatred and racism, it chronicles the relationship of a neo-Nazi skinhead and his hero-worshipping younger brother.

GoodFellas—Based on a true story, this film chronicles the rise to power of gangster Henry Hill. The narration by Henry and his wife offers a perspective on life as part of the mob and how it all came to seem very normal to them.

The television series *Weeds* tells the fictional story of Nancy Botwin, a recently widowed white mother living in an affluent suburb in California. After the death of her husband, Nancy begins a career selling marijuana. As the seasons progress, she builds her customer base, expands her business, and deals with increasing risk to herself and her family.

◈ Development of Akers's Social Learning Theory

An early attempt at a serious reformulation of Sutherland's differential association theory came from Robert Burgess and Ronald Akers's (1966) "A Differential Association Reinforcement Theory of Criminal Behavior," which attempted to introduce the psychological concepts of operant conditioning to the theory. The notion behind operant conditioning is that learning is enhanced by both social and nonsocial **reinforcement**. Their collaboration led to a seven-proposition integration of differential association and operant conditioning concepts. We need not list all seven propositions for the reader to get the gist; therefore, we list the first three. (Note that Burgess and Akers used the term "criminal behavior," as did Sutherland. In a later work, Akers modified the propositions to reference "deviant behavior," recognizing the generality of the theory; see Akers, 1985.) They are as follows:

1. Deviant behavior is learned according to the principles of operant conditioning.

2. Deviant behavior is learned both in nonsocial situations that are reinforcing or discriminating and through that social interaction in which the behavior of other persons is reinforcing or discriminating for such behavior.

3. The principal part of the learning of deviant behavior occurs in those groups that comprise or control the individual's major source of reinforcements.

The attempt at integration was notable and important but never terribly popularized, except that Akers has continued to modify and advance his version of social learning theory (see Akers, 1998). His more recent work focuses on four specific concepts rather than on a larger number of propositions, but he still argues that his is not a new theory but an integration of ideas built around the important contributions of Sutherland. The four concepts are differential association, definitions, **differential reinforcement**, and **imitation**. Note that two of the four concepts come directly from Sutherland.

According to Akers (1998), "definitions" are attitudes, beliefs, and rationalizations that define a behavior as good or bad, right or wrong, or appropriate or inappropriate. Definitions can be general or specific. For example, a general definition that might endorse skipping school is the belief that "school rules are arbitrary and discriminatory." Alternately, a more specific definition might be the statement, "If I can get good grades and miss a few classes, why shouldn't I skip a few classes?" Definitions can also be favorable to a behavior, neutralizing, or reproachful of a behavior. For example, consider the following:

- *Favorable*—School is a waste of time and skipping school is cool!

- *Neutralizing*—Skipping school doesn't hurt anyone.

- *Reproachful*—Skipping school hurts not only the offender but also other members of the class.

So definitions—these beliefs, orientations, and rationalizations people hold—encourage deviance or neutralize restraints that conventional society might impose. The stronger these definitions favoring or encouraging deviance, the more likely a person is to engage in such behavior.

Definitions are important, but where do they come from? Like Sutherland, Akers argues that definitions are learned from "differential association" with the persons one interacts with. Early on, these contacts are primarily with the family—parents, siblings, and perhaps children of parental friends. Later, children meet other peers on their own in the neighborhood and in school. Then, eventually, people get jobs, find romantic relationships, and join new social networks, where new and different sorts of definitions and behaviors are modeled and encouraged (see Capaldi, Kim, & Owen, 2008; Warr, 1993).

Differential reinforcement is clearly a concept that Akers adds to Sutherland's original theory. The concept "refers to the balance of anticipated and actual rewards and punishments that follow or are the consequences of behavior" (Akers, 1998, pp. 66–67). Sutherland wrote a great deal about exposure to definitions but did not say much about how behavioral patterns are actually learned. Akers argues that to the extent it is likely that behaviors will be rewarded or punished (frequently and in terms of quantity), rewards and punishments will reinforce or diminish the behavior, respectively. Therefore, we see differential reinforcement as a factor that should largely predict the continuation or escalation of a behavior rather than initiation.

The final concept discussed by Akers (1998) is imitation, which is simply observing modeled behavior. Perhaps you may have seen children imitating cigarette smoking with a stick or straw (at least one of us remembers doing that as a child). Candy cigarettes, too, were once popular with children, allowing them

▲ **Photo 6.1** "It is all in the learning." Practicing smoking with candy cigarettes!

to imitate adult smokers. Whether candy cigarettes promote smoking or whether modeling is a strong predictor of anything is still debated, but the evidence is fairly clear that the tobacco industry has high hopes for both (Klein & St. Clair, 2000).

◈ Social Structure and Social Learning

The vast majority of Akers's theorizing and research, as well as that of other scholars interested in furthering and evaluating his theory, has focused on the four variables discussed above (definitions, differential association, differential reinforcement, and imitation)—that is, individual-level factors affecting various forms of deviant behavior. More recently, Akers (1998) has expanded his theory to incorporate characteristics of the **social structure** where the "learning" takes place, and he refers to this modified theory as social structure and social learning (SSSL) theory. He argues that characteristics of the social structure provide a context for social learning. Figure 6.1 depicts the causal sequence outlined by Akers and Sellers (2004, p. 97). Note that there are no direct links between the social structural variables and deviant and conforming behavior. This suggests that the social learning processes can fully explain the relationship between social structure and deviant and conforming behaviors.

Akers proposes four key characteristics of the social structure that might affect social learning: (1) differential social organization, (2) **differential location in the social structure**, (3) **theoretically defined structural variables**, and (4) **differential social location in groups**. Differential social organization refers to structural correlates of crime—in our case, deviance. These are "ecological, community, or geographic differences across social systems" (Akers, 1998, p. 332). They might include age or gender composition of the community, urban as opposed to rural or suburban communities, or the unemployment rate. Differential location in the social structure refers to social and demographic characteristics of individuals that define or influence one's position or role in the larger social structure. Social class, gender, race/ethnicity, and age are key variables that may influence who one is exposed to as well as the rewards and punishments for behaviors individuals may anticipate or receive. For example, young boys from poor neighborhoods may be differentially exposed to deviant definitions promoting various forms of deviance (gambling, alcohol and drug use, vandalism, or graffiti art). Theoretically defined structural variables might include "anomie, class oppression, social disorganization, group conflict, patriarchy," and others (Akers, 1998, p. 333). Socially disorganized communities, for example, because of scarce resources, racial/ethnic heterogeneity, and rapid population turnover, are said to be less able to control crime, delinquency, and other forms of deviance (see Chapter 5). These theoretical variables may also influence the types of people one is exposed to as well as the reinforcing patterns associated with various activities, including deviance. Finally, differential social location in groups refers to membership in various groups, such as the family, peer groups in the neighborhood, school or work, and sports or other recreational groups. An obvious example of group membership that might influence social learning is a gang in which various forms of crime and deviant behavior are learned. Alternatively, being the oldest sibling in a family with responsibility for taking care of younger siblings may be a membership that promotes conforming behavior.

The SSSL version of Akers's theory would appear to be a ripe area for sociological theorizing as it clearly attempts to incorporate social variables, at both the macro and micro levels. At the macro level, there is room to think about community characteristics, such as social disorganization or the prevalence of prosocial institutions and organizations, such as good schools and churches. At the societal level, we might consider linking patriarchy or class oppression to social learning. At a more micro level, we can think about how gender, race, or social class may affect association with deviant or conforming peers, which may affect the learning process. To date, there have been only limited theoretical or empirical advances in this direction, and in a symposium following the publication of *Social Learning and Social Structure* (Akers, 1998), all three reviewers of the book seemed to think the theory was underdeveloped (Krohn, 1999; Morash, 1999; Sampson, 1999). Still, the theory offers fertile ground for thinking about the social structural variables that may affect the social learning of deviant behavior.

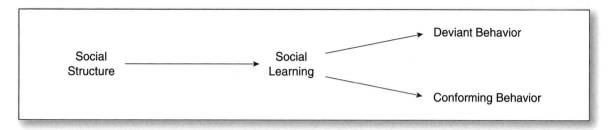

Figure 6.1 A Depiction of Akers's View of the Causal Effects of Social Structural Variables on Social Learning

◈ Application of Differential Association and Social Learning

Differential association and social learning theories have been among the most thoroughly investigated theories in the study of crime and deviance, and a wide variety of forms of crime and deviance have been investigated. Some have criticized this research because a great deal of it has come from Akers himself and his colleagues and students. For a variety of reasons, smoking has been a theme of this chapter, so we will start there. Smoking is clearly a deviant behavior as defined by at least three criteria: (1) It is illegal for certain segments of our society (those younger than age 18 in most, if not all, states) and in certain places (restaurants and bars in certain states and/or cities); (2) it is clearly a social and health harm in itself and is related to other forms of substance use; and (3) it is likely to bring negative reactions from at least certain segments of society. Akers himself was involved in a longitudinal study of teenage smoking in Iowa (see Akers, 1998). Each of the four key measures of Akers's standard social learning theory was included, and each of the learning variables contributed to the likelihood that teens would smoke cigarettes. Others have also tested the ability of social learning theory to explain smoking behavior among youth. For example, in a large nationwide study of 3,460 youth ages 11 to 19, Monroe (2004) found unique independent effects of measures of differential association, differential reinforcement, definitions, and imitation on having ever been a smoker.

Other types of substance use have also been studied via social learning theory. Akers and several of his colleagues (see Akers, 1998) were also involved in a large-scale study of drug and alcohol use. A novel aspect of this project was that it not only focused on use versus abstinence but also examined separately the effects of social learning variables on the onset, persistence/escalation, and desistance/cessation of the use of drugs and alcohol. The study involved a self-report study of just over 3,000 students in Grades 7 to 12 in the Midwest. The results showed that social learning variables were predictive of alcohol and marijuana use as well as problems associated with drug and alcohol use (Akers, 1998). In addition, Akers and Cochran (1985) were able to show that social learning variables were more powerful predictors of marijuana use than either social control theory (see Chapter 7) or strain theory (see Chapter 4).

Other researchers have shown that differential association and social learning variables are predictive of substance use. In a study of more than 4,846 male and 576 female juveniles committed to the Virginia Department of Juvenile Justice (1998–2003), peer substance use was one of the strongest factors affecting substance use for both males and females (Neff & Waite, 2007). In a study at four universities in Florida, Kentucky, Tennessee, and Virginia, Higgins and his colleagues found that peer associations were among the strongest factors affecting binge drinking at college sporting events (Higgins, Tewksbury, & Mustaine, 2007). Finally, Reed and Rountree (1997) found that direct peer pressure exerted little influence on substance use but that differential association and definitions favorable to substance use were important factors affecting substance use. Social learning would appear to be an important theory predictive of both substance use and abuse.

A large number of studies have focused on general or overall delinquency, so our review here focuses on some interesting and more recent findings. For example, Hochstetler, Copes, and DeLisi (2002) analyzed data from the National Youth Survey (NYS), a longitudinal data set, and showed that variables derived from differential association theory (e.g., friends' attitudes and beliefs) were moderately to strongly related to delinquent behavior and, more importantly, that these effects were not contingent on the presence of co-offenders. This provides support for both differential association and social learning theories and suggests that it is not just peer pressure but the socialization of deviant definitions and differential social reinforcement that leads to delinquent behavior. In another analysis of the NYS, Ploeger (1997) explored the often unanticipated positive correlation between employment and delinquent behavior among youth. He found that the positive correlation between employment and delinquency was largely explained by the deviant peers one encountered in the workplace.

In perhaps the most direct test of Sutherland's differential association theory, Dana Haynie (2002) provided a detailed examination of adolescent peer networks ($n = 2,606$) via the National Longitudinal Adolescent Health Survey (1995–1996). She found that peer networks were very heterogeneous (i.e., there was considerable variation within the networks), with a majority of youth having networks with both deviant and conforming associations. She found that "delinquent behavior is influenced by the ratio of definitions favorable to those unfavorable to law violation" and that the percentage of delinquent friends was the strongest factor affecting delinquent behavior (Haynie, 2002, p. 99).

Differential association and social learning theories have been criticized because they have largely focused on juvenile delinquency and other relatively minor forms of deviance (smoking, drinking, and less serious forms of drug use). However, the theories do have relevance for other, more serious forms of deviance. Akers himself, for example, has given a great deal of thought to the applicability of social learning theory on rape and sexual aggression (Akers, 1985). Boeringer, Shehan, and Akers (1991) asked a sample of male undergraduates about proclivities to engage in rape and sexual aggression (for example, "If you could be assured that you could in no way be punished for engaging in the following acts, how likely, if at all, would you be to force a female to do something sexual she didn't want to do?"). Social learning variables were important factors affecting self-reported proclivity to use force or commit rape. A second study of male undergraduate students was conducted with basically the same dependent variables, but there was the addition of another form of non-physical technique of sexual aggression, "plying a woman with alcohol or drugs with the intent of making her so intoxicated that she will be physically or mentally unable to refuse sexual intercourse" (Akers, 1998, p. 270). Again, social learning variables were important predictors of these forms of sexual deviance.

We have reviewed several empirical studies focusing on or at least including measures derived from differential association and social learning theories—often studies conducted by Akers himself and his colleagues. There are many studies beyond what is included here, but this review should provide the reader with evidence that the theories are quite versatile and large in terms of scope and are able to explain a wide variety of deviant behaviors. In addition, differential association theories are likely to explain what Goode (2008a) has come to refer to as "cognitive or intellectual deviance" (p. 270). He argues, for example, that in U.S. culture, being an atheist and not believing in God is a cognitive deviance. Indeed, a large number of political, religious, and social beliefs are considered deviant by mainstream society, and as the websites in the introductory story would indicate, there are thousands of sites where one can learn about various deviant beliefs.

Our review of differential association and social learning theories has been quite favorable, but we do recognize that there are limitations to them. The next section provides a short critique of these theories.

◈ Critiques of Differential Association and Social Learning Theories

We have argued that differential association and social learning theories are general theories that can explain a wide variety of deviant behaviors. In this regard, the theories can be described as wide in scope. There are, however, various forms of deviance that social learning theory would have a hard time explaining. Although today we are bombarded by images of serial killers in the popular media, historically, it would be difficult to argue that serial killers learn the techniques and motivations to kill through communication with intimate others (but see Castle & Hensley, 2002). Similarly, while there is good evidence to suggest that social factors have a great deal to do with how mentally ill patients are treated (see Krohn & Akers, 1977), the best evidence seems to suggest that the mentally ill are indeed mentally ill (Gove, 1975). All in all, however, differential association and social learning theories would appear to be robust in terms of scope.

Perhaps one of the greatest debates over differential association concerns the theoretical and empirical role of differential association, often measured as deviant behavior of one's peers. Some have argued that this measure is really a measure of one's own behavior, especially given that much criminal and delinquent behavior is done with peers. Control theorists, in particular, have charged that birds of a feather flock together and that there is no feathering necessary to understanding deviant behavior (Glueck & Glueck, 1950; Hirschi, 1969). There is probably something to this line of argument, and the correlations found between certain measures of differential association and deviance, especially in cross-sectional studies, are likely somewhat inflated. Alternatively, some good evidence from studies with careful measurement and with longitudinal designs seems to indicate that some of the learning (both motivation and techniques) does come from differential association with deviant others in which behavioral patterns are reinforced with rewards and punishments (see Capaldi et al., 2008; Haynie, 2002; Heimer & Matsueda, 1994) and that differential association affects not only group behavior but solo offending as well (Hochstetler et al., 2002). For example, in a longitudinal study of youth, Elliot and Menard (1996) found delinquent peer associations, more often than not, temporally precede—or come before—delinquent behavior. Furthermore, Thornberry and his colleagues (Thornberry, Lizotte, Krohn, Farnworth, & Sung Joon, 1994) hypothesized and found that association with delinquent peers leads to delinquency, which leads to exposure to other delinquent peers, which again encourages more delinquency. Warr (2002) has argued persuasively that criminologists have been misguided by a black/white or dichotomous conception of the role of peer influence versus selection (i.e., birds of a feather flock together) and that there is no reason why both can't be true (see also Akers, 1998).

◈ Cultural Deviance Theory and Subcultural Explanations of Deviance

Cultural deviance theories, in general, emphasize the values, beliefs, rituals, and practices of societies that promote certain deviant behaviors. Subcultural explanations then emphasize the values, beliefs, rituals, and practices of subgroups in society that distinguish those subcultures from the larger society. To answer the question "Why do some groups appear to behave in ways so different from mainstream society?" the cultural deviance theorist looks to the unique aspects of the culture or subculture to assess how people learn to tolerate, justify, and approve of deviant activities, at least in certain situations.

Cultural deviance, particularly subcultural explanations, has been very influential in the study of all kinds of deviance, and there is an interesting yet somewhat intractable debate over the relationship between cultural deviance theories and differential association and social learning theories. Thumbing through numerous databases, articles, and abstracts, you will often see cultural deviance theory linked to differential association or social learning theories as if they were one and the same. Similarly, numerous theorists (especially control theorists) link differential association and social learning theories under a cultural deviance label (see Hirschi, 1969; Kornhauser, 1978). Alternatively, Akers (1996) rejects the subcultural label for both Sutherland's differential association and his own social learning theory. He does, however, recognize that culture plays an important role in differential association theory and can play a role in social learning theory. The commonality, of course, is socialization and what one is exposed to and has reinforced in a given culture or subculture.

The linkages between cultural deviance theory and differential association and social learning theories are quite apparent, and this would appear to be an appropriate place for a brief discussion of the important role that theory has played in the study of deviance. The southern subculture of violence thesis (Gastil, 1971; Hackney, 1969) was an early subcultural explanation of deviance focused on the high rates of violence (especially lethal violence) in the South. The authors characterized the history and cultural tolerance of violence and the acceptance and availability of firearms as contributing factors to the high rates of violence in the South. Wolfgang and Ferrcuti (1967) also focused on subcultures of violence but shifted the focus to the high rates of homicide among young, minority males in inner cities. They formulated a subcultural theory that is clearly linked to differential association and social learning theories, as can be seen in their sixth proposition, which states that "the development of favorable attitudes toward, and the use of violence in a subculture usually involve learned behavior and the process of differential learning, association, or identification" (Wolfgang & Ferrcuti, 1967, p. 161).

Extending this line most recently, E. Anderson (1999) contrasts "decent" and "street" families, terms recognized and used by the residents he studied in a poor, inner-city, largely African American community. He argues that the child-rearing practices vary tremendously between the two groups—"decent" families are strict and focused on the values of mainstream society, and "street" families socialize their children to deal with problems aggressively and with violence that fits the environment of the "code of the streets." However, Anderson argues that the "code of the streets" subculture exists and promotes violent responses to signs of disrespect among inner-city African American youth regardless of whether they come from a "decent" or "street" family.

Subcultural explanations have been useful far outside the study of violence. Indeed, such explanations have historically been used to understand virtually any form of deviance. Recently, subcultural explanations have been used to understand, for example, computer hacking (Holt & Copes, 2010); online gaming (Downing, 2009); ecstasy use in a drug-using subculture (Gourley, 2004); corporate crime (Robinson & Murphy, 2009); excessive thinness and starvation among athletes (Atkinson, 2011; Atkinson & Young, 2008); bondage, discipline, and sadomasochism (Stiles & Clark, 2011); and Internet johns seeking prostitutes (Blevins & Holt, 2009), among many others.

One interesting example of a subcultural examination of deviance is Pamela Hunt's (2010) study of the jamband subculture. The jamband subculture is an extension of the Deadhead subculture that used to follow the Grateful Dead from venue to venue around the country for their concerts. Jambands follow such bands as Phish and the Dave Matthews Band, much the way the Deadheads followed the Grateful Dead. Jambands promote a countercultural philosophy of "kynd" behavior, which involves the sharing of resources; transitory, communal living; and an aversion to status and authority.

Hunt uses differential association theory to examine whether these countercultural behaviors (albeit considered prosocial) are learned the way other deviant behaviors are learned. In this manner, she is extending the use of differential association theory by examining within-group differences in prosocial and antisocial behavior. In other words, many might want to compare the jamband subculture with the larger society—asking why members might opt to follow a particular band across country—but Hunt, instead, examines why some jamband members espouse a stronger kynd philosophy than others in the subculture.

Hunt administered 379 surveys to participants in jamband concerts in the Midwest, Southeast, and Northeast. Her participants reported participating in between 1 and 150 jamband-related events per year—with an average of 18 events. Hunt found that those who attend more jamband events and are more emotionally connected to others in the subculture are more likely to believe in and promote kynd behaviors. In addition, those who became part of the jamband subculture at a younger age are also more likely to have a strong, positive belief in its philosophy. Those who might follow the subculture but not as closely or who came later in life to the subculture tend not to have a strong, positive belief in the philosophy.

◈ Explaining Deviance in the Streets and Deviance in the Suites: Teen Alcohol and Drug Use

There have been relatively few empirical tests of Akers's full social structure and social learning theory of deviance. Whaley, Smith, and Hayes-Smith (2011), however, provided such a test using a very large sample (~85,000 students) across 202 school districts. They focused on teen drug and alcohol use—specifically marijuana use, ecstasy use, methamphetamine use, and what they referred to as binge drinking (recent experience of having five or more drinks in a row). They were able to simultaneously examine the effects of both individual characteristics, including measures of differential association (peer approval of the use of each drug), and several other control variables as well as contextual-level (school district) variables, including a measure of low socioeconomic status of the areas. So while this was not a "street-level" study per se, one might argue that it is even better because it allowed the researchers to compare rates of drug use in wealthy and poorer areas and to see if the effect of differential associations varied across levels of socioeconomic status. Using relatively sophisticated statistical models, they found that socioeconomic status of the area predicted the use of alcohol and methamphetamines but not marijuana and ecstasy. More importantly, however, differential association was related to each form of drug use and actually mediated the effects of the socioeconomic status of the areas, thus providing pretty solid support for Akers's SSSL theory.

Sticking with substance use and Akers's SSSL theory, we now focus on college students—again, perhaps not the most elite group but, on average, still far above much of the population. In a cleverly titled article, "Liquor Is Quicker: Gender and Social Learning Among College Students," Lanza-Kaduce, Capece, and Alden (2006) examine the use of alcohol prior to sexual activity among male and female college students, some in sororities and fraternities, as well as others. They use secondary data, which leads to a relatively weak test of the theory because they could not design the questionnaire and thus relied on two measures of Akers's concepts. Students were asked about positive (e.g., "Alcohol makes me sexier") and negative (risks associated with drinking and sexual activity) aspects of combining alcohol and sex. These can be seen as definitions favorable and unfavorable to combining alcohol and sex.

Basically, Akers argues that social learning variables subsume other structural variables; that is, structural variables work through social learning variables to affect deviant behavior. Alternatively, feminist theories would disagree, suggesting that some measures should not work entirely through the socialization process. Lanza-Kaduce and his colleagues' basic goal, then, is to compare and contrast a feminist perspective with social learning theory. Some support for Akers's theory is found; for example, the effect of gender was mediated by the risk and rewards measures. Alternatively, the limited number of social learning variables did not mediate the "Greek effect" (the effect of fraternities), supporting the feminist perspective. In this regard, we are left with a quandary in which we can either stick with a feminist perspective or argue that we simply need more and better measures of social learning theory. As usual, we are left hoping for future research to help resolve these issues.

◈ Ideas in Action: Programs and Policy From a Social Learning Perspective

Differential association and social learning have long histories in terms of treatment and prevention programs and in policy, if policy includes the funding and/or implementation of particular programs (e.g., the large government funding of DARE, discussed in Chapter 3). The earliest programs based implicitly or explicitly on differential association focused on the treatment of juvenile delinquents. The key component, of course, was "differential association" of the delinquent with nondelinquent adults or other adolescents who would expose the delinquent to definitions unfavorable to deviance and favorable to prosocial behavior. In the early 1950s, the Highfield Project, for example, offered delinquent boys the opportunity to leave their residential treatment facility during the day to go to work or school and then return to what was referred to as "guided group interaction" (see Weeks, 1958). The group sessions were led by trained staff, and the boys could discuss problems they were experiencing with their families, in school, or in their jobs. The staff would offer solutions or strategies, but mostly they emphasized nondelinquent attitudes and behaviors. Heavy emphasis was placed on interactions between the youth. Although there were some methodological limitations with the evaluation of the program, most scholars appear to view the program as at least partially successful.

In the 1960s, two experimental treatment programs known as the Silver Lake Experiment were developed and tested first in Provo, Utah, and next in Los Angeles, California. The programs were based directly on differential association and borrowed from the guided group interaction approach. They again emphasized interactions between the youth. A classic quote from one participant began as follows:

> Boys know more about themselves than grownups do. The first couple of months [in this program] don't do any good. Then you find out that the meetin' knows you better than you know yourself. They can tell when you're lyin'. They can tell things about yourself an' find out what your problems are. . . . I jus' don't like listening to adults lecturing; . . . it is just boring as hell. All the help I got, I got from the other guys in the meetin'. (Empey & Erickson, 1972, p. 58)

Again, the programs seemed to meet with at least partial success but mostly only while the youth were involved in them. Once they left the programs, their rates of delinquency were comparable to other boys originally assigned to standard probation or periods of incarceration (Empey & Erickson, 1972; Empey & Lubeck, 1971).

Much has been learned since the 1950s and 1960s, and the programs based on social learning theories continue and often add in principles from other theories, such as social control and social bonding theories. Still, the group counseling approach has met with only marginal success, at best. Newer programs have moved to cognitive behavioral and social learning approaches that focus on risk and protective factors (Arthur et al., 2007). Some of the most successful programs that clearly emphasize principles of social learning theory come from the Oregon Social Learning Center. Researchers at the center apply the principles of social learning to the context of family, peers, and school. They contend that how children behave and interact with each other is learned in the family and that this extends into other arenas of life, such as interactions with peers and teachers (Patterson, Dishion, & Bank, 1984).

The center's Adolescent Transition Program targets at-risk youth and their parents and focuses on family management and disciplinary issues and how parents socialize their children. Parents in the program are trained in family management practices that emphasize skills to teach their children prosocial definitions and how to model and reinforce positive behaviors. Similarly, at-risk youth are provided training intended to promote positive peer associations and attitudes favorable to law-abiding and healthy behaviors (Dishion, Patterson, & Kavanagh, 1992). The program is promising, showing some improvement in family management skills among parents and less deviant behavior among youth.

The group extended its work to move beyond simply at-risk youth and focus on serious delinquents. Its researchers conducted an experiment that tested the effect of a program based on social learning principles for youth offenders who had already been adjudicated by the court as serious delinquents (see Eddy & Chamberlain, 2000). Offenders were randomly assigned either to standard group-based foster home care or to foster home parents that had been trained by staff at the Oregon Social Learning Center. The treated group showed significantly lower rates of both self-reported and officially recorded delinquency over an extended period.

Most recently, the center has extended its work on foster care training and, again using social learning principles, has been evaluating the Multidimensional Treatment Foster Care program for girls in the United States and England (Rhodes, Orme, Cox, & Buehler, 2003). In both cases, the focus of the studies were young females ages 12 to 17 who were referred to foster care due to chronic delinquency. The intervention showed improvements in violence, risky sexual behaviors, and school outcomes in both countries.

The Oregon Social Learning Center has too many programs, most showing at least moderate success, to thoroughly review here. Furthermore, a number of other programs based at least in part on social learning principles have been found to be successful as well. Suffice it to say that social learning theory clearly has the potential for working with at-risk youth to address a variety of deviant behaviors.

NOW YOU . . . USE THE THEORY

Texting has been declared one of the most dangerous activities to do while driving because it involves all three types of distraction—visual, manual, and cognitive. According to Madden and Lenhart (2009),

> 75% of all American teens ages 12–17 own a cell phone, and 66% use their phones to send or receive text messages. Older teens are more likely than younger teens to have cell phones and use text messaging; 82% of teens ages 16–17 have a cell phone and 76% of that cohort are cell texters. One in three (34%) texting teens ages 16–17 say they have texted while driving. That translates into 26% of all American teens ages 16–17. Half (52%) of cell-owning teens ages 16–17 say they have talked on a cell phone while driving. That translates into 43% of all American teens ages 16–17. 48% of all teens ages 12–17 say they have been in a car when the driver was texting. And, 40% say they have been in a car when the driver used a cell phone in a way that put themselves or others in danger. (p. 2)

> When asked about their experiences with texting while driving, one teen reported that "I don't really get worried because everyone does it. . . . And when my mother is texting and driving I don't really make a big deal because we joke around with her about it" (Madden & Lenhart, 2009, p. 7). Another stated, "[My dad] drives like he's drunk. His phone is just like sitting right in front of his face, and he puts his knees on the bottom of the steering wheel and tries to text" (Madden & Lenhart, 2009, p. 7).

Using social learning theory, explain the above statistics and quotes concerning texting while driving. Even though it has been declared one of the most dangerous behaviors to engage in while driving, why might teens continue to engage in this behavior in such alarmingly large numbers?

Source: Excerpt is reprinted with permission from Madden, M., and Lenhart, A. (2009). *Teens and Distracted Driving: Texting, Talking and Other Uses of the Cell Phone Behind the Wheel.* Pew Internet and American Life Project, Washington, D.C. Reprinted with permission of Pew Internet & American Life Project.

◈ Conclusion

In our reviews of differential association and social learning theories, we have emphasized studies that examine social learning through communication with intimate others—or at least persons known to the deviant. We have shied away from other sources of learning, such as music, movies, TV, video games, and the Internet. We did this for two reasons. First, both differential association and social learning theories have historically focused on learning from intimate others. Second, the research on the effects of the media on various behaviors is complex and far from conclusive.

Alternatively, we began this chapter with a list of websites from which people could learn both the techniques necessary to engage in a variety of deviances and the motivations and definitions favorable for doing so. It is clear that the Internet has changed our world and has become a viable source for those wishing to know more about almost any form of deviance and a source of support for those involved in various forms of deviant behavior. Indeed, the Internet is a place where one can be involved in a vast array of deviant activities, including such behaviors as online gambling, cyberporn and cybersex, political protests, and hate crimes, among many others. Many technologies provide us with mechanisms to learn deviant techniques, attitudes, and beliefs and to explore deviant (and nondeviant) relationships. Warr (2002) writes,

There is no evidence as yet that such virtual peer groups have replaced or supplanted real ones, but no one who visits the United States can fail to be struck by the remarkable similarity among adolescents who live thousands of miles apart in highly disparate communities and climates, or by teenagers who seem to include fictional characters in their real-life reference groups. (p. 87)

Clearly, physically present intimate others are no longer a necessary component of deviant learning.

EXERCISES AND DISCUSSION QUESTIONS

1. Explain the process of differential association. How might one learn to dump toxic waste according to this theory?

2. Explain the difference between favorable, neutralizing, and reproachful definitions of behavior.

3. What are the four key characteristics of the social structure that might affect social learning?

4. Discuss how prosocial behavior can be explained using social learning theory.

5. What are the similarities and differences between differential association and social learning theories?

6. As you continue on to read about social control theory (Chapter 7), think about the differences between how social control theory and differential association theory explain deviant behavior. Which explanation are you most convinced by?

KEY TERMS

Cultural deviance theory

Definitions

Differential association

Differential location in the social structure

Differential reinforcement

Differential social location in groups

Imitation

Reinforcement

Social structure

Theoretically defined structural variables

READING 16

As we mentioned previously, there have been few attempts to empirically test Akers's social structure and social learning theory. The following article does this and more. Granted, given data limitations, it is a somewhat weak test (as the authors themselves note), but it goes beyond including a single variable (gender) to explore differential location in the social structure. The authors use feminist theory (i.e., theoretically defined structural variables) to derive three hypotheses relating structural variables to their dependent variable—the use of alcohol prior to sexual activity among male and female college students, some in sororities and fraternities and others independent. They use secondary data, which leads to the relatively weak test of the theory as they could not design the questionnaire and thus

Source: Lanza-Kaduce, L., Capece, M., & Alden, H. (2006). Liquor is quicker: Gender and social learning among college students. *Criminal Justice Policy Review, 17*(2), 127–143. Reprinted with permission.

relied on two measures of Akers's concepts. Students were asked about positive (e.g., alcohol makes me sexier) and negative (e.g., risks associated with drinking and sexual activity) aspects of combining alcohol and sex. These can be seen as definitions favorable and unfavorable to combining alcohol and sex.

Basically, Akers argues that social learning variables subsume other structural variables—that is, they work through social learning theory. Alternatively, feminist theories would disagree, suggesting that some measures should not work entirely through the socialization process. The authors' basic goal, then, is to compare and contrast a feminist perspective with social learning theory. Some support for Akers's theory is found; for example, the effect of gender was mediated by the risk and rewards measures. Alternatively, the limited number of social learning variables did not mediate the "Greek effect" supporting the feminist perspective. In this regard, we are left with a quandary where we can either stick with a feminist perspective or argue that we simply need more and better measures of social learning theory. As usual, we are left hoping for future research to help resolve these issues.

Liquor Is Quicker

Gender and Social Learning Among College Students

Lonn Lanza-Kaduce, Michael Capece, and Helena Alden

Candy

Is dandy

But liquor

Is quicker

—Ogden Nash (1931/1992)

◈ Social Structure-Social Learning Theory and Feminism

Social Structure-Social Learning Theory (SS-SL) represents Akers's (1998) recent effort to integrate social structural elements with the social learning process that he has specified during the past three decades (Akers, 1973, 1977, 1985, 1994; Akers, Krohn, Lanza-Kaduce, & Radosevich, 1979; Burgess & Akers, 1966). His new general theory of crime and deviance was the subject of a symposium in which several critics raised questions about the integration. Krohn (1999), for example, argued that Akers seemed "content to add social structural dimensions as exogenous variables" (p. 473) rather than provide propositions relating social structure to the social learning process. Morash (1999) more specifically faulted SS-SL for failing to give adequate attention to gender and for ignoring theories and research on gender and crime or deviance.

Akers (1999) responded to Morash's criticism by explicitly including gender in his position that "the social learning process . . . mediate[s] a substantial portion of the relationship between most structural variables" and behavior (Akers, 1998, p. 340; also cited in Akers, 1999, p. 485). His position is that variables representing the social learning process (differential association, personal definitions, differential reinforcement and punishment contingencies, and imitation and modeling) will mediate rather than moderate or modulate the effects of social structure. Evidence of a moderating or modulating effect could be discerned by statistical interactions between structural variables, such as gender, and social learning variables (Baron & Kenny, 1986). The expectation of mediation rather than statistical interaction is one he and his colleagues have long held (Krohn, Lanza-Kaduce, & Akers, 1984).

Akers's response, however, is unlikely to silence those who insist that researchers "must begin to do more than consider gender as a variable. . . . We must theorize gender" (Chesney-Lind & Faith, 2001, p. 290). One of the specific foci of Chesney-Lind and Faith's (2001) argument is how sexual expression is sanctioned to regulate sexuality. Part of the challenge includes taking "feminist insights about gender and applying them to male behavior" (p. 294).

◈ Gender and Alcohol Use and Sex

This research examines Akers's mediation hypothesis in a context that incorporates structural variables that are suggested by feminist theory. The dependent variable—drinking before sexual intercourse among unmarried White heterosexual college students—is unusual in that it is neither clearly criminal nor deviant. It does, however, intersect two behaviors that implicate how people "do gender" or behave in gendered ways (Miller, 2000, p. 28). Inasmuch as Akers's general theory, in the tradition of Sutherland's (1947) exposition of differential association, purports to explain all behaviors (i.e., conforming and nonconforming ones), the choice of the dependent variable does not detract from scrutinizing the theoretical linkages between social structure and social learning.

Although Akers (1997, 1998, chap. 4) has insisted that social learning theory is not a theory of cultural deviance (which can only explain group differences), he readily accepts that culture is important to the learning process.

> Since the general conventional culture in modern society is not uniform and there are conflicts and variations among subgroups . . . , the individual is likely to be exposed to different and perhaps conflicting cultural definitions of specific acts as good or bad. The theory does not assume that one's own attitudes are a perfect replication of those cultural patterns. (Akers, 1998, p. 102)

In other words, the structural patterns that exist in society are incorporated into SS-SL—they are expected

to provide the contexts within which the learning processes operate. However, SS-SL does not provide a priori information about those larger structural arrangements.

Both alcohol, especially more frequent and heavier consumption, and its use in courtship and seduction are gendered (Boswell & Spade, 1996; Martin & Hummer, 1989). The adage "candy is dandy but liquor is quicker" may be dated but probably is not outdated. The subjective reasons for combining sex with alcohol are not the immediate concerns of behaviorist theories or of efforts to integrate behavior processes with structural patterns. What is important is that the intersection between alcohol and sex offers a strategic site for studying masculinist patterns within a given context or situation. In this sense, gender has import that transcends Akers's (1998) characterization of it as a "sociodemographic correlate" that represents "differential location in social structure" (p. 333).

Patterned use of alcohol in courtship reflects the kind of masculinity that is a common concern across feminist theories (Daly & Chesney-Lind, 1988). A feminist focus on structured masculinity leads to an expectation (one that would not surprise Akers but one that SS-SL does not generate): Males will report more use of alcohol before sex than females will even if only some of their efforts to seduce through alcohol are successful and even if some females employ a similar method. Because most students are assumed to be heterosexual, the difference probably will not be large. Akers (1999) anticipated this possibility; he insists that the

> question is the same whether there is a greater (as in the case of most crime and deviance) or smaller (as in the case of smoking, some other drug use, and some minor offenses) gender difference in the dependent variable. (p. 484)

His position, however, is clear: Gender differences will be mediated by social learning processes.

SS-SL is helpful in sensitizing scholars to the various levels of social structure through which factors such as gender can operate. It urges a consideration of institutional and other macrolevel social organizations as well as mesolevel primary, secondary, and reference groups (as distinguished from intimate family and friendship groups with which individuals are in differential association). The immediate challenge is to identify additional structured factors related to gender that would help explain male-female differences in alcohol use before sex.

One such structural variable in college contexts that comes immediately to mind is an affiliation with fraternities. Whether in popular renditions such as *Animal House* (Reitman, Simmons, & Landis, 1978) or in systematic research (Boswell & Spade, 1996; Martin & Hummer, 1989; Sanday, 1990), fraternity involvement is linked to alcohol consumption often in combination with sexual pursuit. The "brothers" use the fraternity at least as a reference group if not as a substitute primary group. The prediction that male campus Greeks will be more likely to drink alcohol before sex than will others can be more easily derived from feminist theorizing than from SS-SL.

The theorizing, however, may be double edged. Although fraternities are gender-linked social contexts that order the social life of their members, they are also linked to sororities in ways that help order gender relations for both fraternity men and sorority women. Fraternity men may be using alcohol in courtship, but they are probably drinking with and courting sorority women—a prediction that is easily derived from the differential association construct in social learning theory. Feminist theorists may be correct when they argue that gender ordering is a more important variable than gender, but the structural gender-ordered patterns that emerge may also be mediated by social learning processes, much as Akers posits.

Another school condition which may differentiate males from females is success or, perhaps more specifically, how the genders define success and deal with the lack of success. Feminist theorists have weighed in on this issue in a way that counters the position of SS-SL. "For White males (privileged by gender and race), the accomplishment of gender in school means either doing well . . . or if unsuccessful in the classroom, achievement elsewhere" (Simpson & Elis, 1995, p. 71). Simpson and Elis (1995) hypothesized that "adverse educational experiences . . . will increase delinquency among all youth, but effects will be more pronounced among females than among males" (p. 55). Although their focus was on students in secondary school and on violent and property crime, their hypothesis may extend to college

students and sex and alcohol behavior. They found some gendered differences (the relationships were also affected by race and class). This interaction between gender and school success is not predicted by Akers.

◆ Research Hypotheses

To this juncture, the Krohn (1999) and Morash (1999) criticisms of SS-SL have been used to go beyond Akers's integrative theory—beyond a mere absorption of structural variables by social learning processes. Feminist theory can be used to advance more precise predictions about differences between males and females in drinking before sex and to consider how gender orders the college context to explain that difference. Feminist theory's focus on masculinist patterns suggests the following hypotheses (Akers's arguments are used to present positions on the respective hypotheses):

1. Male students will be more likely than female students to drink before sex. (Akers would entertain the hypothesis to the extent that it reflects dominant cultural patterns but would argue that the impact of gender on conforming or deviant behaviors would be mediated by social learning processes.)

2. Male campus Greeks will be more likely to drink before sex than will male independents or female campus Greeks and independents. (Akers would entertain the hypothesis because it reflects general cultural patterns but would issue an important caveat: Fraternity men are likely to differentially associate with sorority women, so drinking before sex will also be high for sorority women.)

3. Adverse educational experiences, as indicated by low grades, will affect drinking and sex for both males and females but will affect females more. (Akers predicts no interaction by gender because the impact of school success should be mediated by social learning processes similarly for males and females.)

SS-SL theory does not generate or challenge any of these hypotheses. Akers does not provide a propositional integration between social learning and structural theories. Rather, he posits that the hypothesized relationships will be mediated to a large extent by social learning variables such as personal definitions and anticipated rewards or punishments. His assertion contains several implications that are amenable to empirical examination. First, the statistical significance and magnitude of relationships between the social structural variables (gender, Greek-system involvement, and academic success) and drinking before sex will be reduced substantially when social learning variables are entered with the structural ones in a multivariate analysis. That is, if the effects of the structural variables are mediated, then their relationships with the dependent variable should be attenuated when the social learning variables are entered into the analysis. Second, the social learning variables will relate to drinking before sex similarly for males and females, for Greek-system participants and independents and for those who earn high grades and those who earn low grades. If the effects of the structural variables are largely mediated by social learning variables, the structural variables should not interact statistically with the learning variables to explain the dependent variable.

A caveat is in order before proceeding. These issues are explored via secondary analysis. Consequently, the operationalizations for both the social structural and social learning variables are neither as extensive nor as exacting as would be desired. In particular, neither the definitions nor the differential association construct in social learning theory can be operationalized adequately. As such, this research represents a weak test of the hypotheses, especially Akers's mediation hypothesis. If this research has merit, it lies in the effort to show how other theories can be integrated via propositions into the SS-SL framework and to show how gender helps structure the learning process.

◈ Method

Sample, Data, and the Dependent Variable

The data used in this analysis were obtained from eight colleges where the long form of the Core Alcohol and Drug Survey was administered to students in the mid-1990s. Each of the colleges gave permission for the researchers to obtain its data from the Core Institute at Southern Illinois University, provided they did not identify any of the colleges. The Core survey consists of four pages of self-report questions that focus primarily on alcohol and drug use on campus. Unfortunately, many of the items contain double-barreled wording in that they ask about both alcohol and drugs in the same question. This practice limited the items that could be used.

The colleges varied markedly. They were spread throughout the United States from the Northeast to the Southeast to the Midwest and West. They included public and private institutions that varied in size. The majority of the student body in one school was African American, the plurality in another school was Asian American, and a third school had a mix of Hispanic, White, and Asian American students. Although no claims can be made that either the students in the study were representative of their respective colleges or the Core samples were representative of U.S. college students generally, the schools and the students were diverse enough to permit examining the theoretical linkages between social structural variables and social learning ones.

Because of the focus on gender, alcohol, and sex, additional sources of diversity could have complicated the effort to examine theoretical linkages. For example, feminist theorists note that gender plays out differently by race (Christian, 1985; Collins, 2000). Alcohol use (Goode, 2001) and sex patterns (Laumann, Gagnon, Michael, & Michaels, 1994) vary by race as well. Rather than trying to examine everything at once (including whether race interacts with gender; with other structural variables, such as Greek-system involvement; with social learning variables; and in various combinations), we simplified the research by using the subsample of White students. Subsequent analysis can be performed to see how different the findings are for students from other ethnic or racial backgrounds. Subsample selection was also used to control for other potential confounding effects, including marital status, age, prior alcohol use, and sexual activity. This analysis focused on White, single adult (18 years of age or older) students who reported both alcohol use and sexual activity in the preceding year. The important issue of how race and gender intersect (see Chesney-Lind & Faith, 2001) warrants separate treatment and can be joined later.

The dependent variable was whether students reported having drunk alcohol the last time they had sexual intercourse. This "alcsex" variable was coded 1 for yes and 0 for no. More than 75% of those in the original subsample indicated that they had not drunk before their last sexual encounter. The dichotomous dependent variable suggested the use of logistic regression, including its classification of cases, as the appropriate statistical analysis for such data. Unfortunately, classification analysis is altered by skewed distributions. If one predicted every case involved no alcohol use before sex, one would be right more than 75% of the time, leaving little room for the structural and learning variables to improve the accuracy of classifications. To obtain a more even split between students who recently had drunk before sex and those who had not, a 33% subsample, taken at random, of the cases in which drinking had not occurred before sex was pulled. These cases ($n = 349$) were joined with the total population of cases in which drinking had preceded sex ($n = 339$) to form the subsample used in the analyses.

Operationalization of Independent Variables

The integration of SS-SL and feminist theory identified three structural variables that were hypothesized to relate to whether drinking occurred before sex: gender, campus Greek-system involvement, and grades. Gender was dummy coded (0 for female and 1 for male). According to Akers, these variables locate individuals in social environments. Thus, they serve as rough indicators of social structural contexts.

Greek-system involvement (Greek) was also dummy coded. Students who reported being actively involved with or in a leadership position in social fraternities or sororities were coded as 1. All other students were coded as 0. Nearly as many female respondents in the subsamples were actively involved in campus Greek activities as were male respondents.

The survey also asked respondents to report their approximate cumulative grade average (ranging from A+ to F). A and B grades were coded together to indicate academic success (coded 1); lower grades were collapsed (coded 0) to indicate less success. Academic success locates students in the educational structure.

The Core survey contained only a few items that operationalized social learning constructs. One survey item asked students to anticipate the risk of harm (risk) involved when individuals "consume alcohol prior to being sexually active." The responses were categorized into *great risk (4), moderate risk (3), slight risk (2), and no risk (1)*. Males were less likely to anticipate as much harm as females.

Several items asked students to consider the anticipated positive consequences (rewards) of mixing alcohol and sex. Again, an index was constructed. One item asked whether (coded 1 or 0) alcohol "facilitates sexual opportunities." Another item asked whether (coded 1 or 0) alcohol "makes me sexier." A third item used in the index was whether alcohol made the opposite sex sexier. The survey did not distinguish heterosexuals from homosexuals or bisexuals, so for males, the response to whether alcohol makes females sexier was used, and for females, the response to whether alcohol makes males sexier was used. The rewards index ranged from 0 *(no anticipated positive consequences)* to 3 *(yes to all indexed items)*.

Data Analysis Strategy

The data analyses are driven by the respective hypotheses. For the first hypothesis, cross-tabular analysis is used to examine whether gender is related to using alcohol before sex (alcsex). Logistic regression is used to examine whether any gender effect (gender as a structural location) is mediated by social learning variables (risk and rewards).

The second hypothesis is examined via cross-tabular analysis. To see whether fraternity men are most likely to have drunk alcohol before having sex, we elaborate the cross-tabular relationship between Greek and alcsex by including gender. The differential association feature of SS-SL suggests that sorority women will also frequently use alcohol before sex. Unfortunately, no differential association measure is available in this data set to examine whether gender differences are mediated by differential association.

The third hypothesis looks for an interaction between gender and academic success. Feminist theorizing predicts that grades will relate to other behaviors more for females than for males; Akers does not expect an interaction. The analysis begins with elaborating the cross-tabulation between grades and alcsex by gender. If an interaction is found, a new variable will be constructed (with coding reversed so that females are coded 1) and incorporated into a logistic regression model to see whether its impact is mediated by social learning variables (risk and reward).

Finally, the relationships that emerged in the previous steps are incorporated into an overall model and logistic regression analysis is performed. This permits us to examine which variables (or interactions) relate to and help account for drinking before having sex.

◈ Results

Hypothesis 1

The beverage relationship between gender and drinking before sex (alcsex) is presented in Table 1. As feminist theory suggests, a masculinist pattern emerges. Males are somewhat more likely to report drinking before having sex (55.3%) than are females (42.6 %). The percentage difference is statistically significant (corrected $\chi^2 = 9.97$, $df = 1, p < .01$). The relationship is not strong ($F = .13$).

Next, gender is entered into the first block of a logistic regression analysis. The social learning variables (risk and rewards) are then entered on the second block. Gender is significantly related to having sex after drinking in Block 1 ($B = 0.50, SE = 0.16$, Wald $= 9.83$; $df = 1, p < .01$). The odds ratio is 1.65 (i.e., males are more than 1.5 times more likely to use alcohol before having

sex). When the social learning variables are entered in the second block, the gender relationship is no longer statistically significant ($B = 0.15, SE = 0.18$, Wald$=0.36$, $df = 1, p < .56$). Its odds ratio is reduced to 1.11. The masculinist pattern is mediated by social learning variables consistent with Akers's position. If gender is considered to be a mere locator in the larger social structure, its effects may operate almost entirely through social learning processes.

Hypothesis 2

The second hypothesis reflects feminist theorizing that gender is more than a variable—it comes into play in how social settings are structured or ordered. One structured context within which gender orders interactions and behaviors is the social Greek system on college campuses. The masculinist pattern that is expected is that fraternity men will be most likely to engage in drinking before having sex. The countervailing consideration derived from social learning theory's differential association construct is that fraternity men will be associating with sorority women, so sorority women will also be likely to drink before engaging in sex. Table 2 presents the relevant results from a cross-tabulation between Greek participation and alcsex, controlling for gender.

Table 2 presents the results. Consistent with masculinist patterns, fraternity men are most likely to report using alcohol before having sex (67.3%). But consistent with the differential association expectation, sorority women are next most likely to use alcohol before having

---

Table 1   Cross-Tabulation of Gender With Drinking Before Sex

Drank Before Sex?	Female		Male		Total		χ^2	P	
	n	%	n	%	n	%			
No	182	57.4	147	44.7	329	50.9			
Yes	135	42.6	182	55.3	317	49.1			
Total	317		329		646		9.97	.001	.13

Table 2   Cross-Tabulation of Greek Involvement With Drinking Before Sex, Controlling for Gender

Drank Before Sex?	Non-Greek		Greek		Total		χ^2	P	
	n	%	n	%	n	%			
Female									
No	147	62.8	35	42.2	182	57.4			
Yes	87	37.2	48	57.8	135	42.6			
Total	234		83		317		9.86	.001	.18
Male									
No	114	50	33	32.7	147	44.7			
Yes	114	50	68	67.3	182	55.3			
Total	228		101		329		7.82	.004	.16

sex (57.8%). Half of the independent males report drinking before sex, but only 37.2% of independent females do. The relationship between Greek and alcsex is significant for both females (corrected $\chi^2 = 9.86$, $df = 1$, $p < .01$) and males (corrected $\chi^2 = 7.82$, $df = 1$, $p < .01$).[1]

Hypothesis 3

The third hypothesis is derived from feminist research that expected and found that academic success related to crime differently by gender. Less academic success among females had a bigger impact than for males. This interaction is not predicted by Akers. Table 3 presents the cross-tabulation between grades and alcsex, controlling for gender. The results show that females with low grades (61.5%) are most likely to use alcohol before having sex. Females with high grades are least likely (38.5%). Males fall in between (about 55% of men drink before sex regardless of their grades). The chi-square tests of independence confirm the interaction. For females, grades are related to alcsex (corrected $\chi^2 = 9.62$, $df = 1$, $p < .01$); for males, they are not (corrected $\chi^2 = 0$, $df = 1$, $p = 1$).

An interaction term is computed (females with low grades and all males are coded 0, and females with high grades are coded 1). This interaction between two structural variables is entered in the first block of a logistic regression analysis. It is significant ($B = -0.77$, $SE = 0.17$, Wald $= 20.44$, $df = 1$, $p < .01$); the odds ratio is 0.46. When the social learning variables are entered in the second block of the logistic regression analysis, the interaction term remains significant at the .01 level ($B = -0.46$, $SE = 0.18$, Wald $= 6.35$, $df = 1$). The odds ratio changes a little (to a 0.63). Clearly, this gendered interaction is not mediated by the social learning variables that are available in this data set.

An Overall Model

To this point, the respective hypotheses have been dealt with individually. The variables that are implicated, however, can be used to advance a multivariate model that allows us to see what helps account for having sex after drinking. The complete model is examined via logistic regression with the significant structural variables that were identified previously entered in the first block

Table 3   Cross Tabulation of Grades With Drinking Before Sex, Controlling for Gender

Drank Before Sex?	C, D, and F		A and B		Total		χ^2	P	>
	n	%	n	%	n	%			
Female									
No	20	38.5	153	63.0	173	58.6			
Yes	32	61.5	90	37.0	122	41.4			
Total	52		243		295		9.62	.001	−.19
Male									
No	52	44.8	89	44.5	141	44.6			
Yes	64	55.2	111	55.5	175	55.4			
Total	116		200		316		.000	1.00	.003

(Greek and Grade × Gender interaction). The two social learning variables (risk and rewards) are entered in the second block. The relevant results are reported in Table 4.

In Block 1, both Greek involvement and the Grade × Gender interaction (females with high grades = 1 and all others = 0) are significantly related to alcsex. The unstandardized coefficient for Greek is 0.87 with a standard error of 0.19 (Wald = 21, $df = 1$, $p < .01$). Its odds ratio is 2.40. In other words, fraternity men and sorority women drink before engaging in sex 2.5 times more often than do independent students. The unstandardized coefficient for the Grade × Gender interaction is −0.75 with a standard error of 0.17 (Wald = 18.64, $df = 1$, $p < .01$). Its odds ratio is 0.47. In other words, females with high grades are less likely to report using alcohol before having sex. These two structural variables correctly predict 58.9% of the cases—an improvement over the 50–50 split between those who had reported drinking before sex and those who did not report drinking before sex.

The results for Block 2 show little change in the structural variables when the social learning variables are entered into the logistic regression analysis. The Greek variable continues to account for drinking before sex; students with Greek-system involvement use alcohol

before sex more often than other students. Greek showed virtually no change (it remained statistically significant and its odds ratio remained high at 2.40). The Grade × Gender interaction changed slightly. It is no longer significant at the .01 level but is significant at a .05 level. Its odds ratio moved to 0.64 (from 0.47). Block 2 shows that both learning variables also relate to drinking before sex. The unstandardized coefficient for risk (which had four ordinal categories) is −0.31 with a standard error of 0.08 (Wald = 13.38, $df = 1$, $p < .01$). The odds ratio is 0.74. The unstandardized coefficient for rewards (which had four interval categories) is 2.60 with a standard error of 0.09 (Wald = 8.73, $df = 1$, $p < .01$). The odds ratio is 1.30. The percentage of correctly classified cases increased to 63.9% (from 58.9%).

◆ Discussion and Conclusion

This research used feminist theory to advance three hypotheses relating structural variables to individual behaviors regarding the combination of alcohol and sex by unmarried White college students. These variables were used to determine if there are structural variables

Table 4 Having Sex After Drinking (Alcsex) Regressed on the Block of Social Structural (SS) Variables and the Block of Social Learning (SL) Variables

	Block 1					Block 2				
	B	*SE*	*P*	Wald	Exp(*B*)	*B*	*SE*	*P*	Wald	Exp(*B*)
SS variables										
Greek	.87	.19	.00	21.00	2.40	.86	.19	.00	19.77	2.40
Grade × Gender	−.75	.17	.00	18.64	0.47	.44	.19	.02	5.59	0.64
SL variables										
Rewards						.26	.09	.00	8.73	1.30
Risk						−.31	.08	.00	13.38	.074
Correct classifications										
No alcsex (%)			38.5					65.1		
Yes alcsex (%)			80.0					62.7		
Overall (%)			58.9					63.9		

that work independently of Akers's social learning process. The feminist perspective would not expect all group dynamics to be mediated by social psychological processes. Akers and his associates argue that such relationships will be substantially mediated by social learning variables, and they do not expect to find significant interactions. In this research, the Akers position and feminist theory both received partial support.

A masculinist effect was found for the structural variable gender. When gender was entered into a logistic regression with the social learning variables risk and reward, its effect was mediated by those social learning variables, as Akers predicts.

Greek-system males were most likely to use alcohol before having sex—a finding that would not surprise feminist theorists. We used Akers's arguments about differential association to predict that Greek-system females would also frequently drink before having sex. Greek-system males and females were more likely to drink before having sex than were independents, male or female. Unfortunately, there were no adequate measures

of differential association in these data to examine whether differential association would mediate the Greek effect. The logistic regression that was performed included two other social learning variables (risk and reward). Their inclusion did not reduce the effect of Greek-system involvement. Given that Akers et al. (1979) expect differential association to be correlated with the other leading variables, some mediation would have been expected. Without a differential association measure, conclusions about mediation need to remain tentative.

The analysis of the interactions produced the most interesting conclusions. Akers would predict no interactions because the effects of the structural variables would be mediated by the social learning process. Gender reemerged as an important theoretical consideration because it interacted with academic success as measured by grades. The logistic regression, which included Greek-system involvement, the Gender × Grade interaction, and the social learning variables risk and reward, indicate that Greek-system involvement and the Gender × Grade interaction were not mediated by the social learning variables. The inclusion of the social learning variables, however, did improve the percentage of cases correctly classified. The results indicate that structural variables can act independently of the mediating effects of the social learning process and that interactions may complicate our efforts to understand outcomes. Gender in particular may interact with other variables in ways that social learning processes do not mediate.

Finding structural effects that are not mediated by learning processes raises a basic philosophy of science issue: To what extent are group phenomena reducible? SS-SL assumes that group dynamics translate into social psychological processes to account for individual behavior. Durkheim (1893/1964) would have us believe that there are social facts—entities "out there"—that control and shape human behavior; these social facts would not be reduced or mediated by a social psychological process. The discontinuity between the group and the individual will not be completely bridged, and the search for additional processes or better measurements will be futile. Some groups may have higher rates of behavior, and we may not be able to predict which members engage in the behavior or why they do so using social psychological principles.

Akers deserves credit for staking out a clear position that is applicable to a broad array of structural arrangements and individual behaviors. His mediation hypothesis is one that can be empirically examined. His position was confirmed when gender was considered to be nothing more than a structural location; its effects were mediated. Hypotheses were advanced regarding how gender orders social relations (e.g., campus Greek life) and how it interacts with other social conditions (e.g., academic performance). The effects of Greek-system involvement and grades on drinking before having sex were not mediated by learning processes. Akers's theory can help us understand why sorority women also frequently engage in drinking before sex; they differentially associate with fraternity men, who are doing the same thing. The effect of Greek-system involvement may have been mediated had there been adequate measures of this theoretical construct. The interaction between gender and academic success (as measured by grades) is not anticipated by SS-SL. The finding points to the need to explicate ways in which we need to theorize gender. Why does academic performance operate differently for females than it does

for males? Suffice it to say that this research among unmarried, White college students found that there could be structural variables that are not mediated by the social learning process. Additional research is needed to identify which structural relationships are substantially mediated, which are not mediated, which interact, and which are population specific.

The conclusions in this research are to be viewed as tentative, given the limited measures of the social learning variables in this data set. The structural indicators are also not precise gauges of social contexts. Our findings need to be corroborated. To do that, data need to be collected that have adequate measures of both structural and social learning variables. The research also needs to go beyond the White college student sample we used. Future research should include race as a structural variable. Race has been shown to be a significant predictor of drinking behavior among college students (Capece, Schantz, & Wakeman, 2002) and has been linked to other problem behaviors of students (Simpson & Elis, 1995).

◈ Policy Implications

The problem with alcohol use, abuse, and associated problems on college campuses is well documented (Baer, Kiviahan, & Marlatt, 1995; Berkowitz & Perkins, 1986; Engs & Hanson, 1985). In the 1980s and 1990s, alcohol use increased among college women (Engs & Hanson, 1985, 1990; Harrington, Brigham, & Clayton, 1997), although college men generally still drink more frequently and more heavily than college women (Berkowitz & Perkins, 1987; Engs & Hanson, 1990; Perkins, 1999).

Racial patterns of alcohol use are less clear. Some earlier investigations reported that Black students drink more than (or at least as much as) White students (Blane & Hewitt, 1977; Maddox & Williams, 1968). In contrast, the recent studies report that Whites have higher rates of consumption than Blacks (Engs & Hanson, 1985; Haworth-Hoeppner, Globetti, Stern, & Morasco, 1989; Wechsler, 1996). Haworth-Hoeppner et al. (1989) account for lower consumption among Blacks because Black students, for the most part, do not participate in the White campus culture that encourages drinking.

Fraternity and sorority members, especially house residents, are more prone to heavy alcohol use. Wechsler, Kuh, and Davenport (1996) report from a national study that virtually all resident fraternity and sorority members drink: Ninety-nine percent of men and 98% of women, and 86% of fraternity house residents and 71% of fraternity nonresident members, engaged in binge drinking. This compares to 45% of nonfraternity men. In this same study, 80% of resident sorority members engaged in binge drinking at least once in the previous 2 weeks, compared to 35% of nonsorority members. Furthermore, nonmembers are most likely to abstain from alcohol: 16% of nonmember men and 17% of nonmember women. Additionally, even those without a history of binge drinking or heavy alcohol use became more likely to engage in it after joining a fraternity or sorority. Sorority members were the most likely to acquire heavy drinking behaviors when entering college and were more likely to experience alcohol-related problems. Lack of prior experience with drinking tends to place sorority members at greater risk to develop alcohol-related problems (Wechsler et al., 1996; Wechsler & Wuethrich, 2002).

Studies also examine problems related to drinking, including negative physical effects such as hangovers, vomiting, and injuries to self or others. Nonphysical effects include delinquent and/or criminal behavior (e.g., date rape, damage to property, fighting, drinking and driving), relationship troubles, and academic difficulties (Baer et al., 1995; Harrington et al., 1997).

Akers's (1998) SS-SL and the results of our research provide insight into how to change drinking behavior and related problems on college campuses; the drinking culture needs to be changed by altering the drinking climate, addressing drinking practices among both male and female Greek-system members, changing interaction and associational patterns, and encouraging administration, faculty, and staff to model appropriate drinking behavior. The expression *change the drinking culture* is now part of the college administrator's language when discussing the problem of alcohol use, abuse, and related problems on college campuses. The emphasis on changing the culture has prompted meetings between campus administration and political leaders, bar owners, and others in the community to discuss ways to work together to deal with student alcohol use and abuse ("Local Officials Discuss Alcohol Abuse," 2005). Consistent with Akers, there seems to be agreement that to change the drinking culture, change needs to take place on the structural and associational and interactional levels.

On the structural level, advertising of alcohol could be reduced significantly or eliminated from college campuses and college sporting events. This could also include advertising of drink specials by local bars on campus. We understand that there are significant economic considerations involved in this type of change. This effort would be an ongoing effort that would take place across a period of time. Additionally, the university could deemphasize the use of alcohol at official university events.

On the associational and interactional level, alcohol use and abuse among those in Greek-system organizations needs to be addressed. As past research seems to indicate, and as our research further substantiates, heavy drinking in Greek-system organizations may no longer be a male thing. Our results show that Greek-system women and men are both using alcohol before sex. It may no longer be an issue of men preying on women as much as it is a mutually reinforcing interaction between fraternity men and sorority women.

Changing the Greek-system drinking culture can also be addressed by the national Greek-system offices directly responsible for their respective members across the country. Responsibility could be shared between the national and regional Greek-system offices to implement drinking guidelines and consequences for underage drinking and/or drinking violations by their membership. Additionally, Greek-system members and the general student population might include group responsibility for drinking in addition to individual responsibility. Social controls could come from those around the drinker, much like "friends don't let friends drink and drive" has spread the responsibility for drinking and driving among bartenders, those hosting parties, and the friends of the drinker. Bartenders and those who own and operate package stores could also help with the social controls by doing what they can to combat underage purchasing of alcohol.

The drinking problem on college campuses would not be eliminated if we just address the Greek-system issue. Our research found that there was a relationship between females with low grades and drinking before sex. We assume that there are other subgroups of college students who are prone to inappropriate drinking. As these student subgroups are identified, interventions can be designed to address their particular needs.

The problem of excessive drinking on college campuses can be addressed by looking at the cultural context in which alcohol is used. Akers's theory and our research provide some valuable insight into how the problem can be viewed and confronted. The difficulty, of course, is that the college campus operates in a larger cultural context. If the larger cultural context is not willing to address this issue, it will be more difficult to affect change on campus.

◈ Note

1. Social learning theory led us to expect that many sorority women would report drinking before sex because of their differential association with fraternity men. A measure of differential association is not available in these data. Consequently, we can only begin to examine whether the impact of Greek would be mediated by social learning processes. A logistic regression was performed to see whether other social learning variables (risk and rewards) mediated the impact of Greek. They did not.

◈ References

Akers, R. L. (1973). *Deviant behavior: A social learning approach.* Belmont, CA: Wadsworth.

Akers, R. L. (1977). *Deviant behavior: A social learning approach (2nd ed.).* Belmont, CA: Wadsworth.

Akers, R. L. (1985). *Deviant behavior: A social learning approach (3rd ed.).* Belmont, CA: Wadsworth.

Akers, R. L. (1994). *Criminological theories: Introduction and evaluation.* Los Angeles: Roxbury.

Akers, R. L. (1997). *Criminological theories: Introduction and evaluation (2nd ed.).* Los Angeles: Roxbury.

Akers, R. L. (1998). *Social learning and social structure: A general theory of crime and deviance.* Boston: Northeastern University Press.

Akers, R. L. (1999). Reply to Sampson, Morash, and Krohn. *Theoretical Criminology, 3,* 477–493.

Akers, R. L., Krohn, M. D., Lanza-Kaduce, L., & Radosevich, M. (1979). Social learning and deviant behavior: A specific test of a general theory. *American Sociological Review, 44,* 635–655.

Baer, J. S., Kiviahan, D. R., & Marlatt, G. A. (1995). High-risk drinking across the transition from high school to college. *Alcoholism: Clinical and Experimental Research, 19,* 54–61.

Baron, R. M., & Kenny, D. A. (1986). The moderator-mediator variable distinction in social psychological research: Conceptual, strategic, and statistical considerations. *Journal of Personality and Social Psychology, 51,* 1173–1182.

Berkowitz, A. D., & Perkins, H. W. (1987). Recent research on gender differences in collegiate alcohol use. *Journal of American College of Heath, 36,* 123–129.

Berkowitz, A. D., & Perkins, H. W. (1986). Problem drinking among college students: A review of recent research. *Journal of American College of Health, 35,* 1–28.

Blane, H. T., & Hewitt, L. E. (1977). *Alcohol and youth: An analysis of the literature, 1960–1975.* Springfield, VA: National Institute on Alcohol Abuse and Alcoholism.

Boswell, A. A., & Spade, J. Z. (1996). Fraternities and collegiate rape culture. Why are some fraternities more dangerous places for women? *Gender and Society, 10,* 133–147.

Burgess, R. L., & Akers, R. L. (1966). A differential association-reinforcement theory of criminal behavior. *Social Problems, 14,* 128–147.

Capece, M., Schantz, D., & Wakeman, R. (2002). Fraternity and sorority alcohol use: Does race matter? *Journal of Applied Sociology, 19,* 9–21.

Chesney-Lind, M., & Faith, K. (2001). What about feminism? Engendering theory-making in criminology. In R. Paternoster & R. Bachman (Eds.), *Explaining criminals and crime* (pp. 287–302). Los Angeles: Roxbury.

Christian, B. (1985). *Black feminist criticism, perspectives on Black women writers.* New York: Pergamon.

Collins, P. H. (2000). *Black feminist thought.* New York: Routledge.

Daly, K., & Chesney-Lind, M. (1988). Feminism and criminology. *Justice Quarterly, 5,* 497–538.

Durkheim, E. (1964). *The division of labor in society* (G. Simpson, Trans.). New York: Free Press. (Original work published 1893)

Engs, R. C., & Hanson, D. J. (1985). The drinking-patterns and problems of college students: 1983. *Journal of Alcohol and Drug Education, 31,* 65–82.

Engs, R. C., & Hanson, D. J. (1990). Gender differences in drinking patterns and problems among college students: A review of the literature. *Journal of Alcohol and Drug Education, 35,* 36–47.

Goode, E. (2001). *Deviant behavior (6th ed.).* Englewood Cliffs, NJ: Prentice Hall.

Harrington, N. G., Brigham, N. L., & Clayton, R. R. (1997). Differences in alcohol use and alcohol-related problems among fraternity and sorority members. *Drug and Alcohol Dependence, 47,* 237–246.

Haworth-Hoeppner, S., Globetti, G., Stern, J., & Morasco, F. (1989). The quantity and frequency of drinking among undergraduates at a Southern university. *The International Journal of the Addictions, 24,* 829–857.

Krohn, M. (1999). Social learning theory: The continuing development of a perspective. *Theoretical Criminology, 3,* 462–476.

Krohn, M. D., Lanza-Kaduce, L., & Akers, R. L. (1984). Community context and theories of criminal behavior: An examination of social learning and social bonding theories. *Sociological Quarterly, 25,* 353–371.

Laumann, E. O., Gagnon, J. H., Michael, R. T., & Michaels, S. (1994). *The social organization of sexuality: Sexual practices in the United States.* Chicago: University of Chicago Press.

Local officials discuss alcohol abuse. (2005, January 20). *Gainesville Sun,* p. 1.

Maddox, G. L., & Williams, J. R. (1968). Drinking behavior of Negro collegians. *Quarterly Journal of Studies of Alcohol, 29,* 117–129.

Martin, P. Y., & Hummer, R. A. (1989). Fraternities and rape on campus. *Gender and Society, 3,* 457–473.

Miller, J. (2000). Feminist theories of women's crimes: Robbery as a case study. In S. S. Simpson (Ed.), *Of crime and criminality* (pp. 25–46). Thousand Oaks, CA: Pine Forge.

Morash, M. (1999). A consideration of gender in relation to social learning and social structure: A general theory of crime and deviance. *Theoretical Criminology, 3*, 452–461.

Nash, O. (1992). Reflections on ice breaking. In J. Kaplan (Ed.), *Bartlett's Familiar Quotations* (16th ed., p. 709). Boston: Little, Brown. (Original work published 1931)

Perkins, H. W. (1999). Stress-motivated drinking in collegiate and post-collegiate young adulthood: Life course and gender patterns. *Journal of Studies on Alcohol, 60*, 219–227.

Reitman, I., Simmons, M. (Producers), & Landis, J. (Director). (1978). *Animal house* [Motion picture]. United States: Universal Pictures.

Sanday, P. R. (1990). *Fraternity gang rape: Sex brotherhood and privilege on campus.* New York: New York University Press.

Simpson, S. S., & Elis, L. (1995). Doing gender: Sorting out the caste and crime conundrum. *Criminology, 33*, 47–81.

Sutherland, E. H. (1947). *Principles of criminology.* Philadelphia: J. B. Lippincott.

Wechsler, H. (1996). Alcohol and the American college campus: A report from the Harvard School of Public Health. *Change, 28*, 20–25, 60.

Wechsler, H., & Wuethrich, B. (2002). *Dying to drink: Binge drinking on college campuses.* Emmaus, PA: Rodale.

Wechsler, H., Kuh, G., & Davenport, A. E. (1996). Fraternities, sororities, and binge drinking: Results from a national study of American colleges. *National Association of Student Personnel Administrators Journal, 33*, 260–279.

READING 17

After arguing that prescription drug use (PDU) is on the rise and particularly dangerous, the authors argue that the initiation to prescription drug misuse is quite similar to the initiation to using street drugs, in particular that the initiation to both resembles a social process in that initiation begins with others. Although they start with Zinberg's theory that involves drugs (the pharmacology), the set (individual characteristics), and the setting (the social context) of drug use, they pay equal homage to Akers's social learning theory and suggest that the theories can be combined to provide a better explanation of PDU. The empirical part of the study involved interviews with 120 relatively serious nonmedical prescription drug users, defined as persons who have used prescription drugs a dozen times or more in the past six months. Focusing on initiation, they found a common trajectory, including "exposure to non-medical drug use, motivation to use, access to prescription drugs, and finally, the opportunity or setting to initiate use." They then provide qualitative data to elucidate these themes.

Everybody's Doing It

Initiation to Prescription Drug Misuse

Heather Z. Mui, Paloma Sales, and Sheigla Murphy

 Introduction

Young adults' nonmedical prescription drug use is a growing public health concern. Between 1992 and 2003, while the U.S. population grew 14%, the number of people misusing controlled prescription drugs increased 94% (Califano, 2005). In 2011, there were 6.1 million persons aged 12 or older who used prescription psychotherapeutic drugs nonmedically in the past month (Substance Abuse and Mental Health Services

Source: Mui, H. Z., Sales, P., & Murphy, S. (2014). Everybody's doing it: Initiation to prescription drug misuse. *Journal of Drug Issues, 44*(3), 236–253.

Administration [SAMHSA], 2012). And the three largest national epidemiological studies on nonmedical prescription drug use—National Survey on Drug Use and Health (NSDUH), Monitoring the Future (MTF), and National Epidemiological Survey on Alcohol and Related Conditions (NESARC)—indicate that 18- to 25-year-olds continue to have the highest prevalence rate of nonmedical prescription drug use (Kroutil et al., 2006; McCabe, Boyd, & Teter, 2009; SAMHSA, 2005, 2006, 2007, 2008, 2009, 2010, 2011, 2012). Among young adults between 18 and 25 years of age, the rate of past-year nonmedical use of prescription-type drugs in 2011 was 5.0%, compared with 2.8 among adolescents aged 12 to 17 and 1.9 among adults 26 years of age and older (SAMHSA, 2012).

In 2011, the number of new pain reliever users was 1.9 million, 1.2 million for tranquilizers, 670,000 for stimulants, and 159,000 for sedatives. Among recent initiates aged 12 to 49, the average age of first nonmedical use of any psychotherapeutics was 22.4 years. Specifically, the average age of initiation was 24.6 years for tranquilizers, 22.0 years for sedatives, 22.2 years for stimulants, and 21.8 years for pain relievers (SAMHSA, 2012). Not only did the 18- to 25-year-old age group have the highest rate of nonmedical prescription drug use, but the average age of first nonmedical use of any and all psychotherapeutics falls within that age cohort as well. Interviewing 18- to 25-year-olds focused our approach and provided important insights into their nonmedical prescription drug initiation process.

Various factors contribute to an individual's decision to use prescription drugs nonmedically for the first time. In this article, we explore how the interplay of individual factors and social context impact initiation of nonmedical prescription drug use. The questions we explore include the following: Where and when were participants exposed to nonmedical prescription drug use? What were their beliefs, expectations, and perceived attractions for initiation? How did they access the drug(s)? Where were they and what was the nature of the social situation during their first experience? There are various forms of exposure to prescription drugs and their effects, which may either deter or motivate individuals' prescription drug misuse. Then there

is the matter of access, the actual possession of the prescription pill that the individual is willing to try. And the final component is the physical and social environment in which an individual initiates nonmedical prescription drug use.

An individual's personal characteristics, experiences, and attributes interact with the external physical and social situation to shape the overall drug-using experience. Yet, most survey data collected on nonmedical prescription drug use convey the incidence and prevalence rates rather than understanding users' reasons for and implications of their behaviors. Studies that do focus on understanding nonmedical prescription drug use are scarce and limited, and often rely only on college student samples or focus on prescription opioids (Arria, Caldeira, Vincent, O'Grady, & Wish, 2008; Daniulaityte, Carlson, & Kenne, 2006; Daniulaityte, Falck, & Carlson, 2012; Lankenau et al., 2012; McCabe, Teter, & Boyd, 2006; Peralta & Steele, 2010; Quintero, 2009). Moreover, only a handful of recent studies have focused on the initiation of drugs, and those that do have mainly examined marijuana, heroin, methamphetamine, or Ecstasy.

For first-time methamphetamine users, researchers found that for the most part, friends and sometimes partners introduced them to the drug, often in social situations (Brecht, O'Brien, von Mayrhauser, & Anglin, 2004; Parsons, Kelly, & Weiser, 2007; Sheridan, Butler, & Wheeler, 2009). Exposure to drugs and drug users opens the door to the idea of individuals using themselves, increasing the probability that they will use as well. Exposure, most commonly through friends, allowed many of our study participants to become acquainted with the idea of nonmedical prescription drug use.

Similarly, Vervaeke, van Deursen, and Korf's (2008) study on Ecstasy initiation found that Ecstasy-using friends played an important role in their participants' decisions to use the drug. Our findings indicate that friends were not only the most common point of exposure but also often played a part in our participants' decisions to use prescription drugs nonmedically. Sometimes participants' friends were already using while other times they initiated nonmedical use together. There were various descriptions of motivating factors, but the most common were curiosity, a friend's suggestion to try it, to get high, and everybody seemed to be doing it.

We also found that access to prescription drugs often came from friends and peers, as well as family and doctors. Our own findings and those from other studies indicate that teenagers and young adults believe prescription drug use is more "responsible," "controlled," or "safe" compared with street drug use (Friedman, 2006; Manchikanti, 2007). Prescription drugs are not only available on the streets or through introductions from friends or family, like street drugs, but also through legitimate prescriptions from doctors. In fact, similar to Lankenau and colleagues' (2012) study on the initiation into prescription opioid misuse among young injection drug users, some of our participants reported legitimate prescriptions as one of their main sources for prescription drugs used nonmedically. Many had a prescription of their own or had a friend or family member with one, which made prescription drugs easily accessible.

In Best, Manning, and Strang's (2007) heroin initiation study, they found that there was at least one other person present when their participants initiated heroin use, and it was usually in a group setting. Likewise, the majority of our interviewees tried prescription drugs nonmedically for the first time in a social setting. Some initiated nonmedical prescription drug use in their own homes with a friend, while others had their first experience in a college dorm, and still others at a party.

In sum, most studies of initiation of illegal drug use found that initiation was a social process, which was also true for our study sample. The most prominent and commonly referenced factor for initiation was the influence of friends and peers. They were not only sources of exposure and access but also key influencers in the initiation process and present during the time of initiation. Our study of nonmedical prescription drug use points to the magnitude of peer influence, along with other social actors such as family, doctors, and communities. Thus, the social context in which exposure, motivation, access, and setting contribute to the initiation of nonmedical prescription drug use warrants further in-depth examination.

Theoretical Model

Zinberg's *Drug, Set, and Setting*

We explore nonmedical prescription drug initiation using Zinberg's (1984) theoretical model of drug, set, and setting. According to Zinberg, drug, set, and setting determine the nature of one's drug experience. He defines "drug" as the drug's actual pharmacological properties and actions. "Set" refers to the individual's psychology, meaning the personal characteristics and personality attributes the user brings to the experience, which includes the user's past experiences, mood, motivations, and expectations (Jansen, 1997; McElrath & McEvoy, 2002; Zinberg, 1984). "Setting" is the physical and social environment in which drug use occurs. The physical setting is the place, people, and things present during the time of use. And the social component encompasses the immediate social situation and "the set of other people present" (Jansen, 1997), the broader beliefs and values of the social group, which establishes the social and cultural milieu at that particular place and time (Moore, 1993; Zinberg, 1984).

The "drug" in question is prescription drugs used in a nonmedical manner. However, in this analysis, rather than examining the actual drug effects, we focus on how set and setting, the individual and environmental factors, interact in the process of initiating nonmedical prescription drug use. Zinberg emphasizes that an individual is not isolated from the society in which she or he lives; both personal characteristics and social context must be considered in understanding drug use initiation. People experience different events throughout their lives that shape their decisions and behaviors. These experiences build on existing beliefs, attitudes, and expectations, expanding one's set. Thus, one's set is dependent on the varying events in the life of an individual, and these experiences are dictated by the social milieu. As Zinberg (1984) notes, "Both individual personality structure and social setting must be included in any coherent explanation of the way in which the social learning process makes controlled intoxicant use possible" (p. 177). Thus, set and setting provide the analytic structure with which to consider the interconnected factors that lead to the initiation of nonmedical prescription drug use.

Akers's Social Learning Theory

We incorporate Social Learning Theory (Akers, 1985) to further our understanding of nonmedical prescription drug use initiation as a social learning process. Social Learning Theory describes how behaviors are learned within a social context through four major components: differential association, imitation, definitions, and differential reinforcement (Akers, 1985, 2009; Ford, 2008; Peralta & Steele, 2010). The most relevant component to our study is differential association, which states that the values, attitudes, techniques, and motives of deviant behavior are learned through interactions with others, such as family, friends, and peers (Peralta & Steele, 2010). The differential association, the frequent interactions with the behavior, impacts one's values and attitudes, and builds on one's experiences, contributing to an individual's overall set regarding that behavior. And the probability that someone will engage in a deviant behavior increases when they associate with others who model such conduct, which may lead to the imitation of these actions and the adaptation of desirable and justifiable definitions for the behavior (Akers, 2009). Differential association explains the normalization of deviant behavior, in this case, nonmedical prescription drug use. The more one associates with those who model such behavior, the more common and normal the behavior seems. More exposure to a behavior increases the chances of an individual learning and accepting the behavior as ordinary, normal, and conventional.

The social process of nonmedical prescription drug use can be understood with the combined framework of Zinberg's set and setting and Akers's Social Learning Theory. Both theories acknowledge the interaction of individual characteristics and sociocultural milieux. These theories provide a framework for understanding the impact of social context on individuals' constructions of nonmedical prescription drug use, cost-benefit analysis of use, and the social circumstances that facilitate the decisions and actions to initiate nonmedical prescription drug use.

 Method

Between September 2008 and February 2012, we recruited and interviewed 120 individuals between 18 and 25 years of age who had used prescription drugs nonmedically at least 12 times in the 6 months prior to the interview. We define "nonmedical prescription drug use" as follows: Prescription drugs, whether they were prescribed or not, used to get high, for the experience it caused, for self-medication, to enhance school/work performance, or to modify the effects of other drug or alcohol use. The study focused on the nonmedical use of pharmaceutical opioids, stimulants, and central nervous system (CNS) depressants because based on the research done by ourselves, other investigators, and the National Institute on Drug Abuse (NIDA), these are the three most popular categories of prescription drugs among nonmedical prescription drug users. For purposes of this study, opioids included OxyContin (oxycodone), Percocet (acetaminophen and oxycodone), Vicodin (acetaminophen and hydrocodone), Dilaudid (hydromorphone), Darvocet (acetaminophen and propoxyphene), codeine, morphine, and methadone. Stimulants reported were Adderall (amphetamine and dextroamphetamine), Dexedrine (dextroamphetamine), and Ritalin and Concerta (methylphenidate). CNS depressants included barbiturates and benzodiazepines, such as Xanax (alprazolam), Valium (diazepam), Klonopin (clonazepam), Ativan (lorazepam), and Soma (aspirin and carisoprodol). To be eligible, the individual had to be between the ages of 18 and 25, and had used prescription drugs nonmedically at least 12 times in the 6 months prior to the interview. We chose the criteria of 12 or more use episodes because we wanted to include new initiates, regular users, and bingers.

Our recruitment strategy included the use of key informants (Spradley, 1979), and snowball or chain referral sampling methods (Biernacki & Waldorf, 1981; Watters & Biernacki, 1989), proven techniques for accessing hard-to-reach populations. Key informants vouch for the authenticity of the research project and the staff's commitment to respectful treatment and confidentiality. Key informants were participants in previous studies, selected according to quality of knowledge, level of involvement with nonmedical prescription drug users, and contact with different communities throughout San Francisco. These informants were asked to refer people they knew to be nonmedical prescription drug users to project staff for screening, eligibility, and enrollment into the study sample. Then, employing the chain referral sampling method, we asked study participants, following the completion of the interview, to refer up to, but no more than three friends who were nonmedical prescription drug users, to ensure penetration into numerous social worlds.

After screening potential participants and upon receiving IRB approval, we obtained informed consent from those deemed eligible before beginning each interview. Eligibility criteria for initial recruits was very broad (age, number of times used) becoming more precise with subsequent interviews employing Targeted Sampling (Charmaz, 2006) as categories filled and we refined our emerging codes. Trained interviewers then proceeded to conduct recorded in-depth interviews and administer a questionnaire with participants at our offices in San Francisco, each lasting 2 to 3 hours. Our questions ranged from early life histories, school, employment, and personal relationships to medical histories, other drug use, current life, and the impact of nonmedical prescription drug use on health, lifestyle, and social relationships. More specifically, we inquired about their feelings, thoughts, expectations, and surroundings at the time they were first exposed to drugs and the first time they initiated drug use of each subsequent drug used, including prescription drugs. For their time, participants were provided a 50 dollar honorarium.

The recorded qualitative portions of the interviews were then transcribed, coded, and analyzed. We analyzed the qualitative data collected using a grounded theory methodology (Charmaz, 1983; Glaser & Strauss, 1967; Kuzel, 1992; Strauss & Corbin, 1990) to uncover emerging themes, utilizing QSR's Nvivo, a qualitative data analysis software, to facilitate these analyses. Although we had some pre-determined categories—based on our own and others' prior studies—we wanted to address that Grounded Theory methods gave us the flexibility to adjust our lines of inquiry to explore more in-depth any emerging themes. From the data, many themes emerged, including exposure to prescription drugs, medical prescription, access to prescription drugs, and initiation to prescription drugs, which became the codes in the code list used in our analyses.

 **Findings**

To date, nonmedical prescription drug use remains quite popular, especially among the 18- to 25-year-old age group. Interviewees expressed different motives and manners of initiation. They each brought their own set of beliefs, expectations, and attitudes to the experience, and were in varying physical and social settings at the time of initiation. But there were commonalities in thought, expectations, and settings, and it was most often the interaction of set and setting that had led to nonmedical prescription drug initiation. Set and setting were heavily influenced by peers and social learning, through observations and discussions around nonmedical prescription drug use. . . .

We had chosen to interview 60 (50%) men and 60 (50%) women to explore nonmedical prescription drug use among men and women of different racial and ethnic groups and social classes. The median age was 21. The majority of the sample had at least some college education, with 61.7% attending school full-time and 70.8% employed during the 12 months prior to the interview.

The interviewees were all active nonmedical prescription drug users. Nonmedical prescription drug use among our sample ranged from 1 to 14 different prescription drugs with a median of five different types used in the 6 months prior to the interview. The most prevalent prescription drug used was Vicodin, with 112 of the 120 interviewees reporting use of the drug in the 6 months prior to the interview. The next most prevalent prescription drug was Xanax (70 interviewees) followed by Adderall and oxycodone (57 each), Valium (49), Percocet (47), codeine (45), Klonopin (42), morphine (32), Soma (31), Ativan (21), Ritalin (13), and Dilaudid (12). While a few only used one prescription drug, most used several different varieties, often due to availability and access, and still others also used other drugs and alcohol in the 6 months prior to the interview. In fact, the majority of participants had reported trying other drugs and alcohol before initiating nonmedical prescription drug use, but a few did report prescription drugs to have been the first drug they ever used. The median age of nonmedical prescription drug initiation was 16, with a range of 5 to 24 years old. Many of our interviewees (35.0%) began regular nonmedical use of prescription drugs, defined as at least once a month, shortly after initiation, another 16.6% began using regularly within a year after initiation, while 48.4% began 1 to 7 years after their initiation. Of our 120 participants, 64 (53.3%) had initiated nonmedical prescription drug use with an opioid, 28 (23.3%) with a CNS depressant, and 22 (18.3%) a stimulant.

Our findings revealed a common trajectory for initiation characterized by exposure to nonmedical drug use, motivation to use, access to prescription drugs, and finally, the opportunity or setting to initiate use. Exposure to nonmedical prescription drug use normalized the behavior, impacting the individual's set, allaying fears about deviant aspects of nonmedical prescription drug use. Exposure led to an assessment of personal costs and benefits and motivations for use. Once the normalizing effects of exposure, coupled with assessed motivation for use were part of the set, access to prescription drugs was the next step toward the decision to initiate use. For most, prescription drugs were readily available, in the family's medicine cabinet, student health centers, or from friends. The final step was the proper setting in which to initiate use, not just the physical setting but also the social setting in which interviewees felt safe or ready to initiate use. In the following, we explore exposure, motivation, access, and setting within the context of set and setting and Social Learning Theory to better understand the initiation process of prescription drug misuse.

Exposure: Everybody's Doing It

Deviant behavior is learned through observation and consideration, followed by imitation. We learn by observing and examining others in given social contexts, then processing and giving meaning to that information. When we study others, our perception of their behaviors may be positive, negative, or neutral, but we are nonetheless processing what our observations are relaying to our brain in making sense of them. Our participants' exposure to nonmedical prescription drug use contributed to their set by expanding their understandings about and constructions of meaning around nonmedical prescription drug use.

Participants were exposed to prescription drugs at different stages in their life and in various social situations. The three main modes in which participants

recalled being exposed to prescription drugs were through parents, friends or peers, and doctors' prescriptions. Family and peers are the most direct social influencers to an individual, and have been considered the two most important social influences through childhood and adolescence (Kandel, 1996; Tang & Orwin, 2009). This is the time when many of our participants first became aware of the nonmedical use of prescription drugs.

As interviewees reflected on their childhoods, some remembered seeing their parents taking pills or finding their parents' pills in the house. Even when parents tried to hide their drugs and drug use from them, as children, participants were very observant and aware of their parents' actions. They knew that their mother and/or father had these substances and were using them. As was the case with a 20-year-old White female, who at 13 years of age initiated nonmedical prescription drug use:

> I didn't realize like, my dad was on heroin 'cause I always saw him taking other opiates. I like knew that he did it but I didn't know it was like serious . . . Like before school I could go in his room, walk past him, he'd be passed out, I'd grab like an eighth of weed, grab like a gram of coke, grab a few pills and go to school and like just do it during the day and like he would never notice. But then it was like three of us were doing that so he started to notice and then he got a safe but he had [methadone] on him which is like an opiate whatever and we never—we were just foolish it's like it gets us high, whatever . . . like you have no concept. So we would take his methadone and like snort lines with it which you're not supposed to do at all . . . we were like oh this is heroin, this is like synthetic heroin and it did have that effect it was like stronger than Oxycontin pretty much and we did it and um, and he would, he would absolutely lose his mind when there was no—and all his stuff is gone, he's like what the hell, what's going on? He's like in serious withdrawals and we didn't even connect it. We're just like oh he does this for fun but like it wasn't the case at all.

She lived with her father, who used drugs in the house, sometimes to the point where he would pass out, leaving his drugs available to the participant. She told us she and her siblings thought he was doing the drugs for fun. The participant saw her father's drug-using behavior and imitated it.

Another interviewee learned about nonmedical prescription drug use from his mother. He was initially exposed to prescription drugs through a legitimate prescription of his own, but his mother would ask him for the drugs to use nonmedically:

> Uh, believe it or not um, 'cause my mom used to always go crazy over Vicodin. She be like I need some Vikes, I need some Vikes. You got some drugs for me? And she called it drugs because like you know when I used to get prescribed my Vicodin and stuff like 'cause I caught a couple injuries skatin' a few of 'em broke my ankle one time, fucked up my elbow and I had to go get some uh, pills so like my mom would always like take a third of 'em like I'm a need these. (24-year-old male of mixed ethnicity; Age of Nonmedical Prescription Drug Initiation [AI]: 14)

Nonmedical prescription drug use was even more apparent and commonplace for others. A 21-year-old White male noticed his parents used prescription drugs quite often and freely:

> Vicodin? I mean my parents like I said take pills for everything . . . It's a pretty common drug. Even in high school people were talking about it, people know what it is, people can get it, probably stealing it from their parents or something. (AI: 14)

Vicodin was also a hot topic among his peers in high school. His attitude, his set, toward nonmedical prescription drug use was that it was normal because the behavior was so widespread in his social world. His parents were modeling nonmedical prescription drug use, and his peers were talking about using as well. As a matter of fact, peers and/or friends was the most frequent response to the question, "how were you first exposed to prescription drug use?" Peers and friends were important in shaping many participants' perceptions and expectations of drugs. When everybody around is talking about doing something and it seems everybody is in fact doing it, one might want to do it as well, such as the following 19-year-old White female, who first tried prescription drugs nonmedically at age 18:

> Yeah um, just from what my friends had told me that I met here because they had all done a lot of drugs in high school and so like they were like oh you have to try this, you have to try this it's so great and I'd be like alright.

Similarly, another participant, a 22-year-old Pacific Islander male, experienced persistent exposure to prescription drug misuse from his roommate. In fact, he regularly drove and made transactions for her. The continued exposure and contact, the differential association, with prescription drug use accompanied by his perception of his friend feeling and still looking good while using informed his set. His opinion of nonmedical prescription drug use was positive, and eventually led to his initiation at age 21:

> Um, the person that I lived with she takes [prescription drugs] every day and she would literally like she has the far, wake me up in the morning, drive me the Tenderloin, make me get out and get her some pills. She'd give me the money or whatever but after doing it 20, 30, 40 times you're like oh, I want some pills too . . . you're taking them all I see how you feel, you look great, you know what I'm saying? . . . That's how it really started for me.

Although the majority of our interviewees were exposed to drugs through family or friends, another major source of exposure was a legitimate prescription. Opioids were commonly prescribed to participants after wisdom teeth extraction. One participant had initially used for the pain as prescribed, but his use became recreational when he felt the additional effects and enjoyed the feeling of being high:

[O]ne month in March I got my wisdom teeth out and then like a week later I got um, toe surgery on two of my toes and so I was on bed rest for like two weeks or something with like three uh, refilled prescriptions of Percocets and so that's—I wasn't railing (snorting) them or something I was just popping them like you were supposed to . . . It's pretty much how I found out that you can get really high off prescription pills. (19-year-old male of mixed ethnicity; AI: 17)

And in a few cases, the neighborhood or school was identified as the initial exposure to prescription drugs:

INT: Okay, so where'd you get the idea of using Soma for fun?

081: Uh, 'cause like in Chinatown when I was little I used to hang out there and you'll see the older guys like probably like two, three years older they always at the playground called Chinese playground and then they always take it and then I would always see them and one of my friends hung out with them and he started taking it and that—I thought it was (unclear) back then and then I tried it once. (20-year-old Asian male; AI: 16)

Exposure alone did not always lead to prescription drug use but was a necessary step to initiation. For our study sample, who are active nonmedical prescription drug users, exposure contributed to their overall set, shaping their expectations and decisions to initiate nonmedical prescription drug use, but they also needed to feel a motivation to initiate use.

Motivation

Exposure taught our participants about nonmedical prescription drug use, but what were the reasons or factors behind their decisions to initiate? To answer this, we asked participants about their motivations to use prescription drugs nonmedically for the first time. Tang and Orwin (2009) found that the most consistent predictors of marijuana initiation for youth were experience

with alcohol and/or cigarettes, and marijuana offers. In our sample, the initiation of prescription drugs often occurred after experiences with alcohol, cigarettes, and/or marijuana, and sometimes even other illicit drugs, not because it was a natural progression in their drug use but because there was a desire to get high and experiment coupled with the opportunity that offers of prescription drugs presented. After experimenting with marijuana, a 22-year-old White male was open to trying other drugs, including prescriptions, which he did at the age of 15. In fact, he said he "would be down to try pretty much anything." Like many other participants, his decision to initiate nonmedical prescription drug use was influenced by his prior drug use experience. The positive experience he had with marijuana in addition to his desire to get high were part of his set when deciding to use prescription drugs nonmedically.

The more offers and suggestions to use prescription drugs, the more opportunities there are to consider and want to try pills. A majority of the young adults we interviewed reported being with someone who offered it to them or suggested they try the prescription drug, so they did:

My friend that got into a couple of car accidents, she like, she got [prescription drugs] and like abused them so much and she kept going back to the doctor to get more and more . . . she was like, "Holy crap this is coolest feeling! You have to try it!" So then I did and like after that like others were introduced and just . . . (19-year-old White male; AI: 17)

Other reported motives for use included curiosity, to get high, because others were doing it, or a combination of these factors. Many explicitly stated curiosity as their main motivation to initiate use:

Just curious . . . I was like, couldn't hurt. I heard good things about it, plus my roommate, he enjoyed it so much I was like it can't be that bad but uh it was just pure curiosity. (25-year-old White male; AI: 24)

For many, it seemed like everybody around them was using prescription drugs: their parents, siblings, neighbors, celebrities, classmates, and/or friends. It seemed that everyone in their immediate social network was engaging in nonmedical prescription drug use, and they wanted to know how it felt and to share in the experience. Such was the case with an 18-year-old Asian male, whose friends all used Somas:

> All my other friends were doing it so I thought it was okay. They said it was okay, it seemed like it was okay. They say it doesn't mess with your mind . . . it relaxes your muscles so I thought it was okay to take it you know so I started . . . it was safe . . . I never seen any of my friends OD, overdose on it or anything . . . (AI: 16)

Others felt overwhelmed by the pressure to achieve academically and wanted to keep up with other students whom they believed were using prescription drugs. They were motivated to initiate use for performance enhancement, and used a prescription stimulant as their first nonmedical prescription drug. White, Becker-Blease, and Grace-Bishop (2006) found the motives for stimulant use included to improve attention (69%), study habits (54%), grades (20%), and reducing hyperactivity (9%), with an additional 65% using for "partying." Other researchers have found additional motives such as to increase alertness, concentration, to get high, curiosity and experimentation, weight control, and athletic endurance (Barrett, Darredeau, Bordy, & Pihl, 2005; Boyd, McCabe, Cranford, & Young, 2006; Low & Gendaszek, 2002; Teter, McCabe, Cranford, Boyd, & Guthrie, 2005; Weiner, 2000). Several of our participants also mentioned the motivations found by other investigators to have played a part in their initiations. One particular participant felt overwhelmed and unmotivated to write a paper, so he used Ritalin to focus. He knew about the drug because other people were using it, and he had access to his brother's prescription:

> [U]sing Ritalin in college . . . pretty much exclusively to write papers . . . I knew for some time that other people had been doing it. And I think my brother had a prescription. He had, like, a legitimate prescription for Ritalin, and I got some from him . . . And I

just tried it one time because I was feeling really overwhelmed and unmotivated to write a paper. (22-year-old White male; AI: 18)

Still others may have been self-medicating. Many researchers have suggested that use may be an effort to self-medicate psychiatric symptoms (Chilcoat & Breslau, 1998; Dowling, Storr, & Chilcoat, 2006; Khantzian, 1997). A few of our participants were prescribed several medications at young ages for different diagnoses or symptoms, from depression to attention deficit hyperactivity disorder (ADHD) to bipolar, and felt like "guinea pigs." To feel normal or not to feel, they would use prescription drugs to help them function, sleep, forget, or to modify the effects of other drugs. Once exposed and motivated, our participants were mentally prepared to initiate nonmedical prescription drug use. However, to initiate use, the prescription drug had to be available. Access was another necessary component of initiation. For all of our participants, access to prescription drugs when they first used them nonmedically was easy and uncomplicated.

Access: The Power of Prescription

Over the years, prescription drugs have become increasingly more available to young adults in North America. The United States consumes 80% of the global supply of opioids and two thirds of the world's illegal drugs (Califano, 2007; Kuehn, 2007; Manchikanti, 2007). The NSDUH found that between 1992 and 2002, the U.S. population increased by 13% while prescriptions written for controlled drugs increased 154.3% (Califano, 2005). Not surprisingly, the majority of our interviewees had a legitimate prescription of their own, or knew a family member or friend with a prescription. A 22-year-old Middle Eastern female articulated just how powerful prescriptions can be:

> And then as far as drug use opening up more—I would say pills came after pot because it was just, you know, everyone's taken a pill in their life. So they're not scared of that so I wasn't necessarily scared of taking pills. And I think the first kind of pills it was definitely like a Vicodin kind of thing 'cause everyone kind of had access

to Vicodin. If someone got surgery or something, you know Vicodin was more apparent. So Vicodin, Valium, Percocet, Klonopin, SOMAs, Norcos, Xanax didn't come about until later and when it did, it's just crazy . . . (AI: 15)

Prescription drugs are prescribed by doctors for medical purposes, so most interviewees felt they were safe and socially acceptable to use. Other studies' findings have indicated that patients who take opioids for pain can progress from therapeutic use to misuse or dependence (Brands, Blake, Sproule, Gourlay, & Busto, 2004; Ives et al., 2006; Potter, Hennessy, Borrow, Greenfield, & Weiss, 2004). When a 25-year-old female of mixed ethnicity had her wisdom teeth removed at age 16, she recovered quickly and had some pills left over, so when her friend suggested taking it for fun, they did:

> I was prescribed Percocet when I had my wisdom teeth removed but at that time I was in so much pain that I don't think I—oh, okay I do remember sort of after the fact still having a few and then it hadn't occurred to me to use it recreationally but then other people were like, "ooh, you have this? You should you know have fun with it." . . . I remember being at a friend's house and her mom was where ever and we were drinking beer and I was taking it when I was drinking . . . It was fun.

Several participants referenced student health centers as places for easy prescription drug access. Interviewees reported that once someone discovered that a sore throat could result in a Vicodin prescription, "everybody" started going to the health center claiming to be sick to get prescription drugs:

> [W]hen you're going to [college], you get a free like health care kind of plan—well you pay for it but like um, you get to go to the health center for free and see doctors and what not. In like December and January, you know one kid gets sick and then it just sweeps the entire building and everybody is sick . . . And one girl went in and got a bottle of Vicodin for having a sore throat and we

were just like well—what the hell? And then more and more people started going in and everyone was getting like liquid Codeine and Vicodin just like [snaps] easy. You know like they wouldn't—"Oh you have a sore throat? Like here, get 2,500s." And it started from that. Like I took—the first thing I ever tried was Vicodin. (21-year-old White male; AI: 18)

And if participants did not have their own prescription, they often had friends or family who did. Similar to our findings, McCabe and Boyd (2005), who studied prescription drug use among undergraduate students, identified three different categories of prescription drug sources: peers, family, and other sources. They found that peers often shared their legitimately prescribed drugs. This was echoed by our own participants:

> I had a friend in college that had a lot of Vicodin and Norcos that he would just give me . . . He was prescribed them and he would just give 'em to me whenever I wanted. So I woke up with a hangover someday I'd just walk over there and he'd give me like 5 or something for free and then—you know can't beat that, you know? (21-year-old White male; AI: 19)

Family was the other major prescription drug source in McCabe and Boyd's (2005) study, which was also where a number of our interviewees obtained the prescription drug they first used nonmedically, mainly from parents. Parents were not only a source of exposure, but also for access. Again, some participants were exposed to prescription drugs in their homes as children or adolescents by their parents. This provided a source of prescription drugs for participants to use recreationally. In fact, the family medicine cabinet was a common place where participants accessed their parents' medications:

> Valiums and Xanax . . . They were in my mom's medicine cabinet. (24-year-old female of mixed ethnicity; AI: 15)

Other times, parents used pills openly. One participant mentioned that her mom trusted her with handling her prescriptions. When her mother switched prescriptions, she asked the interviewee to get rid of the remaining pills. She kept them for herself and later used the prescription drugs recreationally:

> My mom got into a car accident . . . I visited her for three weeks and I guess I was 16, 15. And, she gave me her pills to give 'em to her whenever she was in pain. And, I didn't take them then, I'm not that horrible . . . But, she decided that the OxyContin was too strong so she told me to throw 'em out and got Percocets instead so I kept the OxyContin. (18-year-old Latina female; AI: 16)

Access to prescription drugs was rather trouble-free for all of our interviewees. Rarely did our participants have to actively seek out prescription drugs for their initial use. However, three interviewees did report buying them. They knew someone who had a prescription and was selling or had a friend who knew somebody selling pills. But for most, there were numerous opportunities or offers from friends in social settings. We found that the drug was often suggested and supplied by others at no financial cost within the setting in which nonmedical prescription drug initiation took place, similar to the findings of Sheridan et al.'s (2009) methamphetamine initiation study and Daniulaityte et al.'s (2006) prescription opioid study. Once participants' set toward nonmedical prescription drug use was favorable and they had access to prescription drugs, all they needed was to be in an appropriate setting in which to initiate use.

Setting

Setting is not simply the physical location where the drug use occurs, but includes other dimensions, such as the people present and their social relationships and activities, which establish the social context. As Zinberg (1984) explained, an individual is not infinitely adaptive, but rather functions within a range of experiences, determined and structured by the physical and social environment that is one's setting. Initiation occurred when the individual felt comfortable doing so, usually with people they trusted, who had an open attitude

toward nonmedical prescription drug use. A trusted place where initiation often occurred was at a friend's house or with a friend in the participant's home:

> [F]irst time I tried Adderall was when one of my friends ended up coming over to my house and we were kinda just doing homework or whatever um, and we ended up getting like I don't know kind of restless and tired and then that's when she you know kinda brought the whole Adderall thing up and then kinda explained what it was. And in a way like I don't know it's kind of weird because it's like coming from the whole meth thing, like in a way it kind of is like the same little substances but it's like I don't know but in a way it's not even I don't know it's like different like I, I know like with meth it's like yeah during that time or whatever. But then it was like Adderall I'm looking at it more as like a positive thing like helping me through school even though you get kind of the same um, feelings or whatever you do with meth 'cause that's kind of what it is in a way. But it's like I don't know to me it's like different it feels different. (24-year-old African American female; AI: 23)

The combination of her set and setting influenced her decision to use. Although she believed Adderall to produce the same feelings as meth, her motivation and attitude about using the prescription pill was different. Factors such as her previous experience with meth, along with her trust in her friend, her positive feeling about the benefits for school work, and being in her own home were contributing components of her set and setting and ultimately her decision to initiate.

School settings often played a part in the initiation process. It was at school that some participants were exposed to prescription drugs, where friends and peers accessed prescription drugs, or the place where first use occurred, especially in college. College was not just an institution of higher academic learning but also the time and place for participants to explore, grow, and find their identity and niche in society. This was especially important during their dorm experience, where interviewees adapted to a new social milieu. In the dorms, some learned new behaviors, such as nonmedical prescription drug use, as some participants shared:

> [W]hen I came to college, all of a sudden I saw all these people around me always having pills. So it was when I moved here that I saw really saw those . . . cause I lived in the dorms freshman year so—yeah obviously it was on campus. (21-year-old Latina female; AI: 18)

The deviant behavior of nonmedical prescription drug use became normalized in college settings as part of a social learning process. It seemed everybody used prescription pills and they were readily available, thus the behavior was seen as a normal and popular activity. Prescription drug use was fairly common in the dorms and at social gatherings and those who used seemed to enjoy the effects. The curiosity and desire to be engaged in this component of peer bonding and belonging became increasingly attractive for some:

> It was my freshman year at the (academy) and it was in the dorms and I had met this group of people . . . from Alaska. And in Alaska, Oxycontin is extremely, extremely common that's like what all the people end up doing up here I don't know like certain towns it's like a meth town or a coke town or whatever up in (Alaskan city) specially Oxycontin is the drug of choice for everyone. So I met this group of people and this guy (name) . . . had been free-basing Oxycontin up in the dorm room and I had become friends with them 'cause they were all in my classes and stuff like that we hang out up there and at first they didn't even want me to touch the stuff like they didn't want me to do it with them and that was fine with me. But then I started getting curious. I was like come on what's one hit gonna do or what not? And like I don't snort or eat the pills, I smoke them. (21-year-old White female; AI: 16)

The dorms were a very social experience, an environment conducive for much interaction and imitation. And although the majority of our participants attended college full-time (61.7%), some may not have lived in dorms and there were others who did not attend college. Other settings for social encounters included parties and get-togethers, where active social roles were played and nonmedical prescription drug use initiated:

> I was at this party with some friends and then my other friend had these pills [Somas] like had 20 of them and then like he said take one and then I took it with soda and then it started hitting me but like the effect wasn't that strong so I took like two more and took it all at once. I started feeling relaxed but then I was just sitting there like I didn't really feel like moving but it was a good feeling though. Yeah, that's how I got started. (19-year-old Asian male; AI: 17)

Usually when someone goes to a party, he or she wants to have a good time. In these instances, as was the case with many interviewees, they associated the party setting with doing drugs and fun times, further contributing to the initiation process, as described by the following 24-year-old White female, who recalled her experience at age 17:

> 110: Xanax um, you know people would have at parties and we would take it when we're drinking so that was the first prescription drug that I was like around . . . I think the first time that I took the—that I took Xanax I 'member I was at a party um, this kid's parents were away maybe like 20 people were there everyone was sleeping over and we got like a lot of sushi and a lot of sake and we're taking shots of sake and I think like right before we sat down to eat I took a Xanax so I did my Xanax and they were taking like—
>
> INT: Only you took it or did everyone—
>
> 110: A lot of people, a lot of people.

A lot of people were doing it, so her perception of nonmedical prescription drug use was that it was probably not that bad, since it seemed to be a popular behavior that often accompanied drinking and having fun. An important factor that led to her initiation as well as that of many others was that everybody around her was doing it. However, there were also a few participants who used alone, usually in their own homes. They wanted to keep their use private and/or were more comfortable getting high on their own. But for most, nonmedical prescription drug use was a social experience. For our interviewees, initiation was a social process of learned behavior. They learned, through exposure to and interactions with nonmedical prescription drug users, how prescription drugs can be used in different ways and for different reasons. The behavior was first modeled and normalized by the people around them and then imitated by our interviewees. Drug-using peers reinforced the behavior, strengthening interviewees' sense of greater rewards than punishment for nonmedical prescription drug use. Interviewees' set and setting, through social learning, along with access, intertwined to facilitate their initiation of nonmedical prescription drug use.

◈ Discussion

During the course of their interviews, young adult nonmedical prescription drug users relayed their thoughts and feelings about their first experience using prescription drugs nonmedically and described the social contexts in which they initiated use. We have examined the social processes of initiation using Zinberg's theory of drug, set and setting, emphasizing the set and setting, along with Akers's Social Learning Theory, which further illuminates the social component of initiation and the ways in which deviant behavior is learned. The set refers to participants' thoughts, motivations, and expectations that are shaped by prior drug exposures and experiences. Social Learning Theory explicates the role of socialization to and normalization of nonmedical prescription drug use, particularly through peer influence, as a social learning process that shapes set and setting.

We learned from our participants' accounts that initiation of nonmedical prescription drug use followed a trajectory of exposure, motivation, access, and setting. Many reported being exposed through friends, family, doctors, or within their communities. Initial exposure to prescription drugs informed their set

about the perceived safety of using the drugs, since they are prescribed by doctors and used by parents, grandparents, siblings, and friends, even as children. Exposure to nonmedical use of prescription drugs awakened curiosity in some about possible alternative uses of the drugs. Some saw a benefit of using stimulants to enhance academic performance. Others became aware of the possibility of using prescription drugs to party and get high, and still others were exposed to widespread peer use and wanted to fit in with their friends. Once they had assessed the benefits of using nonmedically and felt motivated to use, then gaining access to the drugs was the next step. Most seized the opportunity to use nonmedically when pills were offered or prescribed to them, while others actively sought the drug, either from their parents' medicine cabinets, a friend, or purchasing from an acquaintance. Finally, the majority seemed to initiate use at social gatherings, be it in the college dorms, parties, or small gatherings. The settings were usually comfortable spaces, both physically and socially.

Nonmedical prescription drug use initiation was a social process, similar to findings in other drug initiation studies. However, unlike other drugs, prescription drugs were perceived to be safer than street drugs because they were used medically. As a participant noted, everybody had probably taken prescription drugs at some time in their life, thus further normalizing use. And for our study sample, there were no indications of gender differences in the initiation process. The median age of initiation for both males and females was 16, and there were no significant differences in the type of prescription drug used nonmedically for the first time. Regardless of gender and type of prescription drug participants initiated with, the initiation process involved the merging of exposure, motivation, access, and setting.

Understanding the initiation process of nonmedical prescription drug use can inform prevention and intervention strategies to address the increasing numbers of nonmedical prescription drug users. And although the data is retrospective, and subject to problems of recall, it is still important because it reveals participants' current set with which he or she describes and interprets past experiences. Their current understandings of what led to their own initiations of nonmedical prescription drug use are valuable for the design of efficacious intervention and prevention measures for problematic prescription drug misuse.

However, we do recognize the limitations of our study. We acknowledge that our sample is not representative of the general population, and findings cannot be generalized. Our study sample includes people from a specific age cohort in the San Francisco Bay Area, who had used prescription drugs nonmedically at least 12 times in the 6 months prior to their interview. The majority of our participants were attending college at the time of interview, and the ethnic breakdown does not properly represent that of the San Francisco Bay Area. In addition, this article focuses on prescription drugs as a whole, and disaggregating the different categories may provide deeper insights into the initiation process of each type of prescription drug to better inform and educate the public, medical professionals, and interventionists. Thus, we believe future research should focus on understanding initiation for each of the different categories of misused prescription drugs (opioids, stimulants, and CNS depressants) independently, particularly stimulants, for which there are limited data. Furthermore, there is a fine line between medical and nonmedical use of prescription drugs, and this complicates the kinds of prevention messages that are appropriate for specific populations. Further research is necessary to help determine the best approaches to address the problem.

◈ References

Akers, R. L. (1985). *Deviant behavior: A social learning approach.* Belmont, CA: Wadsworth.

Akers, R. L. (2009). *Social learning and social structure: A general theory of crime and deviance.* New Brunswick, NJ: Transaction Publishers.

Arria, A. M., Caldeira, K. M., Vincent, K. B., O'Grady, K. E., & Wish, E. D. (2008). Perceived harmfulness predicts nonmedical use of prescription drugs among college students: Interaction with sensation-seeking. *Prevention Science, 9,* 191–201.

Barrett, S. P., Darredeau, C., Bordy, L. E., & Pihl, R. O. (2005). Characteristics of methylphenidate misuse in a university student sample. *Canadian Journal of Psychiatry, 50,* 457–461.

Best, D., Manning, V., & Strang, J. (2007). Retrospective recall of heroin initiation and the impact on peer networks. *Addiction Research & Theory, 15,* 397–410.

Biernacki, P., & Waldorf, D. (1981). Snowball sampling: Problems, techniques and chain-referral sampling. *Sociological Methods & Research, 10,* 141–163.

Boyd, C. J., McCabe, S. E., Cranford, J. A., & Young, A. (2006). Adolescents' motivations to abuse prescription medications. *Pediatrics, 118,* 2472–2480.

Brands, B., Blake, J., Sproule, B., Gourlay, D., & Busto, U. (2004). Prescription opioid abuse in patients presenting for methadone maintenance treatment. *Drug and Alcohol Dependence, 73,* 199–207.

Brecht, M. L., O'Brien, A., von Mayrhauser, C., & Anglin, M. D. (2004). Methamphetamine use behaviors and gender differences. *Addictive Behaviors, 29,* 89–106.

Califano, J. A. (2005). *Under the counter: The diversion and abuse of controlled prescription drugs in the U.S.* New York, NY: The National Center on Addiction and Substance Abuse at Columbia University (CASA).

Califano, J. A. (2007). *High society: How substance abuse ravages America and what to do about it.* New York, NY: Perseus Publishing.

Charmaz, K. (1983). Contemporary field research. In R. Emerson (Ed.), *Contemporary field research* (pp. 109–126). Boston, MA: Little-Brown.

Charmaz, K. (2006). *Constructing grounded theory: A practical guide through qualitative analysis.* Thousand Oaks, CA: SAGE.

Chilcoat, H. D., & Breslau, N. (1998). Investigations of causal pathways between PTSD and drug use disorders. *Addictive Behaviors, 23,* 827–840.

Daniulaityte, R., Carlson, R. G., & Kenne, D. R. (2006). Initiation to pharmaceutical opioid and patterns of misuse: Preliminary qualitative findings obtained by the Ohio substance abuse monitoring network. *Journal of Drug Issues, 36,* 787–809.

Daniulaityte, R., Falck, R., & Carlson, R. G. (2012). "I'm not afraid of those ones just 'cause they've been prescribed": Perceptions of risk among illicit users of pharmaceutical opioids. *International Journal of Drug Policy, 23,* 374–384.

Dowling, K., Storr, C., & Chilcoat, H. D. (2006). Potential influences on initiation and persistence of extramedical prescription pain reliever use in the US population. *The Clinical Journal of Pain, 22,* 776–783.

Ford, J. (2008). Social learning theory and nonmedical prescription drug use among adolescents. *Sociological Spectrum, 28,* 299–316.

Friedman, R. A. (2006). The changing face of teenage drug abuse—The trend toward prescription drugs. *The New England Journal of Medicine, 354,* 1448–1450.

Glaser, B., & Strauss, A. (1967). *The discovery of grounded theory.* Chicago, IL: Aldine.

Ives, T. J., Chelminski, P. R., Hammett-Stabler, C. A., Malone, R. M., Perhac, J. S., Potisek, N. M., & Pignone, M. P. (2006). Predictors of opioid misuse in patients with chronic pain: A prospective cohort study. *BMC Health Services Research, 6,* 46.

Jansen, K. L. R. (1997). Adverse psychological effects associated with the use of Ecstasy (MDMA) and their treatment. In N. Saunders (Ed.), *Ecstasy reconsidered* (pp. 112–128). London, England: Neal's Yard.

Kandel, D. B. (1996). The parental and peer contexts of adolescent deviance: An algebra of interpersonal influences. *Journal of Drug Issues, 26*, 289–315.

Khantzian, E. J. (1997). The self-medication hypothesis of substance use disorders: A reconsideration and recent applications. *Harvard Review of Psychiatry, 4*, 231–244.

Kroutil, L. A., Brunt, D. L. V., Herman-Stahl, M. A., Heller, D. C., Bray, R. M., & Penne, M. A. (2006). Nonmedical use of prescription stimulants in the United States. *Drug and Alcohol Dependence, 84*, 135–143.

Kuehn, B. M. (2007). Opioid prescriptions soar: Increase in legitimate use as well as abuse. *The Journal of the American Medical Association, 297*, 249–251.

Kuzel, A. (1992). Sampling in qualitative inquiry. In B. Crabtree & W. Miller (Eds.), *Doing qualitative research* (pp. 31–45). Newbury Park, CA: SAGE.

Lankenau, S. E., Teti, M., Silva, K., Bloom, J. J., Harocopos, A., & Treese, M. (2012). Initiation of prescription opioid misuse amongst young injection drug users. *International Journal of Drug Policy, 23*, 37–44.

Low, K. G., & Gendaszek, A. E. (2002). Illicit use of psychostimulants among college students: A preliminary study. *Psychology, Health & Medicine, 7*, 283–287.

Manchikanti, L. (2007). National drug control policy and prescription drug abuse: Facts and fallacies. *Pain Physician, 10*, 399–424.

McCabe, S. E., & Boyd, C. J. (2005). Sources of prescription drugs for illicit use. *Addictive Behaviors, 30*, 1342–1350.

McCabe, S. E., Boyd, C. J., & Teter, C. J. (2009). Subtypes of nonmedical prescription drug misuse. *Drug and Alcohol Dependence, 102*, 63–70.

McCabe, S. E., Teter, C. J., & Boyd, C. J. (2006). Medical use, illicit use, and diversion of abusable prescription drugs. *Journal of American College Health, 54*, 269–278.

McElrath, K., & McEvoy, K. (2002). Negative experiences on ecstasy: The role of drug, set and setting. *Journal of Psychoactive Drugs, 34*, 199–208.

Moore, D. (1993). Beyond Zinberg's "social setting": A processual view of illicit drug use. *Drug and Alcohol Review, 12*, 413–421.

Parsons, J. T., Kelly, B. C., & Weiser, J. D. (2007). Initiation into methamphetamine use for young gay and bisexual men. *Drug and Alcohol Dependence, 90*, 135–144.

Peralta, R. L., & Steele, J. L. (2010). Nonmedical prescription drug use among US college students at a Midwest University: A partial test of social learning theory. *Substance Use & Misuse, 45*, 865–887.

Potter, J. S., Hennessy, G., Borrow, J. A., Greenfield, S. F., & Weiss, R. D. (2004). Substance use histories in patients seeking treatment for controlled-release Oxycodone dependence. *Drug and Alcohol Dependence, 76*, 213–215.

Quintero, G. (2009). Rx for a party: A qualitative analysis of recreational pharmaceutical use in a collegiate setting. *Journal of American College Health, 58*, 64–70.

Sheridan, J., Butler, R., & Wheeler, A. (2009). Initiation into methamphetamine use: Qualitative findings from an exploration of first time use among a group of New Zealand users. *Journal of Psychoactive Drugs, 41*, 11–17.

Spradley, J. (1979). *The ethnographic interview.* New York, NY: Holt, Rinehart and Winston.

Strauss, A., & Corbin, J. (1990). *Basics of qualitative research.* Newbury Park, CA: SAGE.

Substance Abuse and Mental Health Services Administration. (2005). *Results from the 2004 National Survey on Drug Use and Health: National findings* (Office of Applied Studies, NSDUH Series H-28, DHHS Publication No. SMA 05-4062). Rockville, MD: Author.

Substance Abuse and Mental Health Services Administration. (2006). *Results from the 2005 National Survey on Drug Use and Health: National findings* (Office of Applied Studies, NSDUH Series H-30, DHHS Publication No. SMA 06-4194). Rockville, MD: Author.

Substance Abuse and Mental Health Services Administration. (2007). *Results from the 2006 National Survey on Drug Use and Health: National findings* (Office of Applied Studies, NSDUH Series H-32, DHHS Publication No. SMA 07-4293). Rockville, MD: Author.

Substance Abuse and Mental Health Services Administration. (2008). *Results from the 2007 National Survey on Drug Use and Health: National findings* (Office of Applied Studies, NSDUH Series H-34, DHHS Publication No. SMA 08-4343). Rockville, MD: Author.

Substance Abuse and Mental Health Services Administration. (2009). *Results from the 2008 National Survey on Drug Use and Health: National findings* (Office of Applied Studies, NSDUH Series H-36, HHS Publication No. SMA 09-4434). Rockville, MD: Author.

Substance Abuse and Mental Health Services Administration. (2010). *Results from the 2009 National Survey on Drug Use and Health: Volume I. Summary of national findings* (Office of Applied Studies, NSDUH Series H-38A, HHS Publication No. SMA 10-4856). Rockville, MD: Author.

Substance Abuse and Mental Health Services Administration. (2011). *Results from the 2010 National Survey on Drug Use and Health: Summary of National Findings* (NSDUH Series H-41, HHS Publication No. SMA 11-4658). Rockville, MD: Author.

Substance Abuse and Mental Health Services Administration. (2012). *Results from the 2011 National Survey on Drug Use and Health: Summary of National Findings* (NSDUH Series H-44, HHS Publication No. SMA 12-4713). Rockville, MD: Author.

Tang, Z., & Orwin, R. (2009). Marijuana initiation among American youth and its risks as dynamic processes: Prospective findings from a National Longitudinal Study. *Substance Use & Misuse, 44*, 195–211.

Teter, C. J., McCabe, S. E., Cranford, J. A., Boyd, C. J., & Guthrie, S. K. (2005). Prevalence and motives for illicit use of prescription stimulants in an undergraduate student sample. *Journal of American College Health, 53,* 253–262.

Vervaeke, H., van Deursen, L., & Korf, D. (2008). The role of peers in the initiation and continuation of ecstasy use. *Substance Use & Misuse, 43,* 633–646.

Watters, J., & Biernacki, P. (1989). Targeted sampling: Options for the study of hidden populations. *Social Problems, 36,* 416–430.

Weiner, A. L. (2000). Emerging drugs of abuse in Connecticut. *Connecticut Medicine, 64,* 19–23.

White, B. P., Becker-Blease, K. A., & Grace-Bishop, K. (2006). Stimulant medication use, misuse, and abuse in an undergraduate and graduate student sample. *Journal of American College Health, 54,* 261–268.

Zinberg, N. E. (1984). *Drug, set, and setting: The basis for controlled intoxicant use.* New Haven, CT: Yale University Press.

READING 18

The article begins noting that digital piracy (copyright infringement) costs billions of dollars a year, though few people see it as a serious crime, and they ask, Can social learning theory help us understand the phenomenon? In fact, they provide a relatively detailed account of how social learning theory has and can be used to help explain and predict digital piracy. Using a college student sample, they ask about numerous types of digital piracy (frequency in the past six months) and various variables related to social learning theory, including skills, peer involvement, parental approval, reinforcement, and beliefs. This study finds considerable support for social learning and its ability to predict digital piracy.

*Piracy on the High Speeds**

A Test of Social Learning Theory on Digital Piracy Among College Students

Whitney D. Gunter

◇ Introduction

When one thinks of crime, violent street crime typically comes to mind. In more recent years, white collar crimes, environmental crimes, identity theft, and other crimes previously considered less important have at least shared the spotlight of America's interest with violent crime. Yet, the growing threat of digital piracy is still often overlooked by the general population. Though digital piracy is resulting in billions of dollars in losses each year, it is given little more consideration than jaywalking by most people. The effectiveness of efforts to combat this crime could be greatly enhanced if we simply knew which factors cause individuals to engage in electronic copyright piracy.

Source: Gunter, W. D. (2008). Piracy on the high speeds: A test of social learning theory on digital piracy among college students. *International Journal of Criminal Justice Sciences, 3*(1), 54–68. Reprinted with permission from IJCJS, www.ijcjs.co.nr.

*Some text and accompanying notes have been omitted. Please consult the original source.

This study assesses factors that potentially affect digital piracy among college students. Specifically, this study asks the question: Are social learning theories predictive of piracy behaviors? The importance of studying piracy has often been ignored in empirical studies. In 2005, copyright piracy in the United States software industry alone accounted for $6.8 billion in revenue lost (Business Software Alliance, 2006). Estimated losses in wages and tax revenue reflect similar importance. The music industry faces dire piracy problems as well. In 2004, the total amount of estimated sales for pirated music worldwide was $4.6 billion (International Federation of the Phonographic Industry, 2005). Moreover, this figure does not include the vast number of illegal files exchanged over the Internet without cost via peer-to-peer (P2P) file sharing programs. The total number of media files transferred through these programs has reached approximately 27.6 billion annually (House of Representatives, 2004a). Though the legality of such files cannot be ascertained due to the private nature of the exchanges, a large portion of the transfers is nonetheless illegitimate.

The violation of law and loss of potential revenue to "big business" are not, in and of themselves, considered harmful by the average citizen. The impact of digital piracy, however, still has a severe impact. First, governments worldwide are already spending millions of dollars to combat copyright piracy. These attempts often specifically outline goals consistent with deterrence-based law enforcement (e.g., House of Representatives, 2004a). Empirical evidence of the antecedents of digital piracy would undoubtedly assist in these efforts. Furthermore, tax revenue would increase if sales and the industry's taxable profits likewise increase. One study indicated that a ten percent decrease in the piracy rate would increase tax revenue by an estimated $21 billion in the United States alone (IDC, 2005).

Though using the word piracy to describe certain copyright violations has existed for over centuries, it is a relatively new concept as a widespread phenomenon. With the digital revolution came a new form of theft, digital piracy, which is unauthorized and illegal digital reproduction of intellectual property. Given its recent conception, few studies have addressed the causes of digital piracy and fewer still explicitly use a criminological theory as a foundation for research. The recent advancement of fast, easily accessible forms of electronic piracy has quickly outdated many of the few studies that have addressed this topic. More specifically, the rapid increase in popularity of P2P file sharing software since 1999 has dramatically increased the accessibility of music and video files. Presently, the average individual with minimal experience and broadband Internet access, which is common on virtually all college campuses, can download a music file in under a minute (Cooper & Harrison, 2001).

In light of this recent, rapid increase in accessibility, piracy has become more widespread than it ever has been. The technological access provided to college students and prevalence of piracy at universities is well documented and often the target of government actions (Cooper & Harrison, 2001; House of Representatives, 2004b). Using survey data from college students from two mid-Atlantic higher learning institutions, this study will empirically test whether variables derived from social learning theories affect digital Internet-based piracy among college students. More effective prevention strategies or the elimination of actions not consistent with the theoretical findings are some of the potential implications.

◈ Social Learning Theories of Digital Piracy

Differential association (Sutherland & Cressey, 1960), one of the first social learning theories specifically developed to explain crime, views crime as a product of social interaction. Crime, according to this theory, is learned and criminal actions are the end result of an individual's exposure to an excess of definitions favorable to the violation of law. Definitions include the motives, attitudes (rationalizations), and techniques (ability) that permit an individual to commit a crime, all of which are learned through association with others. According to the theory, the most powerful definitions come from intimate primary groups, such as family members and friends/peers. Secondary groups, such as government officials, entertainment industry representatives, university policies, and campaigns against piracy, generate less powerful definitions.

Modern social learning theories (Akers, 1985; Akers, 1998; Akers et al., 1979; Burgess & Akers, 1966) describe the social learning process in greater detail. Specifically, the social learning process is described as containing multiple concepts. The principle concepts of social learning include differential association, definitions, and differential reinforcement (Akers, 1985; Akers, 1998). The concept of differential association has remained quite similar to Sutherland's (Sutherland & Cressey, 1960) original description. Accordingly, differential association is the process by which people are exposed to normative definitions favorable or unfavorable to the violation of law. More specifically, this process usually involves direct contact with individuals engaging in deviant or criminal behaviors. Normative aspects such as moral approval or the absence of disapproval of deviant or criminal behavior, however, is also part of this process. Thus, the concept of differential association comprises both behavioral and attitudinal support for deviant or criminal acts.

In empirical studies of digital piracy, differential association has found some support relating to software piracy. Skinner and Fream (1997) tested differential association and found family and peer involvement to be predictive of piracy. These results, however, are quite dated and limited to only one distinct type of piracy. One other study from the pre-P2P era concluded that "social factors," which was defined as "norms, roles, and values at the societal level that influences an individual's intentions to pirate software" (Limayem, Khalifa, & Chin, 1999, p. 125), were similarly related [to] software piracy. The exact measure for this variable is unspecified, but implied to be peer activity and support of piracy. This study, however, was limited to business undergraduates at a Canadian university, so its generalizablility to the U.S., where piracy rates are significantly lower (Business Software Alliance, 2006), is questionable.

More recently, several studies by Higgins and colleagues have found additional support for differential association. Four of these studies (Higgins & Makin, 2004a; Higgins & Makin, 2004b; Higgins, 2005; Higgins & Wilson, 2006) included peer activity, measured using a six-item scale, and found statistical significance. In these studies, the behavior of study was again strictly limited to illegally copied software. All of these studies utilized various scenarios from a previous

study (Shore et al., 2001) to describe the behavior to participants. One of the studies (Higgins & Makin, 2004b), however, used a shareware-based scenario in which an individual is asked to send a registration fee to the author, but is not explicitly required to do so by law. Though scenarios about computer ethics are not uninteresting, they do not necessarily measure actual engagement in illegal activities rather than a more abstract willingness to do so. Despite this limitation, these studies indicated that differential association may be an antecedent of digital piracy.

The second concept of social learning theory is that of definitions. According to the theories (Akers, 1985; Akers, 1998; Akers et al., 1979; Burgess & Akers, 1966; Sutherland & Cressey, 1960), definitions represent a variety of attitudes or meanings by an individual toward a specific behavior. These can include rationalizations for deviant or criminal acts, a general orientation toward the behavior, or an overarching moral evaluation of the behavior. In other words, definitions form the general moral belief that one has or that pertains to a specific act. Definitions, not being an innate part of an individual, are learned through the differential association process. Thus, definitions are both an outcome of differential association and an influence over behavior.

Similar to differential association, definitions have also received empirical support as being relat[ed] to digital piracy. Moreover, studies have shown such a relationship holds true when definitions are operationalized as general moral beliefs toward piracy (Higgins, 2005; Higgins et al., 2005; Higgins & Wilson, 2006; Limayem et al., 1999), specific rationalizations for pirating behaviors (Higgins & Wilson, 2006; Skinner & Fream, 1997), and specific beliefs about crimes unrelated to piracy (Gopal, Sanders, Bhattacharjee, Agrawal, & Wagner, 2004). The relationship between differential association and definitions in the area of digital piracy, however, remains untested.

Another key concept of social learning theory is differential reinforcement. According to the theories (Akers, 1985; Akers, 1998; Akers et al., 1979; Burgess & Akers, 1966; Sutherland & Cressey, 1960), differential reinforcement refers to the anticipated rewards or punishments for a specific act or behavior. These hypothetical consequences serve to encourage or inhibit the likelihood of an individual engaging in deviant behavior. This concept is actually quite similar to that of deterrence (Beccaria, 1764/1985), especially when more recent rational choice theories (e.g., Cornish & Clarke, 1986) are considered. These views similarly predict that perceived certain and severe punishment is likely to prevent a person from engaging in a criminal behavior. Differential reinforcement can include informal rewards and punishments beyond the criminal justice system, such as a negative reaction by friends or family. In the case of piracy, however, such informal reactions seem unlikely given the low severity ascribed to the crime of piracy and the overall prevalence of digital piracy. It is unlikely that there is much variation in positive reinforcement, as pirating for personal use does not involve rewards beyond getting the sought item without cost.

Differential reinforcement has not often been tested in relation to digital piracy. In fact, the Skinner and Fream (1997) study was the only criminological test to explicitly relate the concept to a form of piracy. The results of the study noted only non-significant relationships between differential reinforcement variables and software piracy. This finding, however, is not entirely applicable to modern piracy. First, the vast changes in technology and subsequent increase in piracy over the last ten years would in and of themselves demand additional consideration before rejecting deterrence altogether. Second, the study defined the act being investigated as "knowingly used, made, or gave to another person a 'pirated' copy of commercially sold computer software" (p. 504). Thus, piracy in this study was strictly limited to the sharing or copying of software among peers. This variation of piracy occurs in a setting even more private than Internet-based digital piracy and could easily result in different perceptions of punishment. Additionally, it was unclear whether "pirated" was defined to the participants.

Though theories of general deterrence and differential reinforcement are clearly different in many vital aspects, the operationalization process in studies of digital piracy has resulted in both theories being tested through measures of punishment severity and certainty. Thus, while deterrence is not interchangeable with differential reinforcement, the research

applying these concepts to piracy is not unrelated. Unfortunately, despite an interest in applying deterrence to digital piracy (Sherizan, 1995), only one such study exists. In a test of software piracy (Higgins, Wilson, & Fell, 2005), empirical support for a link between deterrence and piracy was found for punishment certainty, but not severity. Similar to the Skinner and Fream (1997) study, Higgins and colleagues measured punishment and likelihood of pirating in terms of sharing a physical copy of software. As before, the private setting of in-person sharing radically changes the "chances of being caught" and will likely alter the potential offender's perceptions as well (Higgins, Wilson, & Fell, 2005, p. 173).

The Present Study

Using social learning theory, this study will investigate three hypotheses. First, given that social learning theory predicts that imitation is the result of differential association, belief, and differential reinforcement (Akers, 1985; Akers, 1998; Akers et al., 1979; Burgess & Akers, 1966), it is expected that (H1) individuals with differential association, belief and differential reinforcement supportive of piracy will be more likely to engage in piracy. More specifically, Sutherland and Cressey (1960) predict that primary groups, including family and peers, generate more powerful messages than do secondary groups, such as government officials. Thus, it is expected that differential association, which primarily involves family and peers, will have a greater impact than would differential reinforcement, which involves societal forces.

Second, Sutherland and Cressey (1960) postulate that the differential association process includes the transmission of definitions, motives, and abilities. Therefore, it is expected that (H2) the effects of differential association will partially be mediated through belief and technical ability. Third, primary groups may have influence over an individual's perceptions of rewards and punishments through the differential association process. Essentially, pirating friends may downplay the likelihood of getting caught and, therefore, (H3) differential association favorable to piracy will decrease perceptions of punishment.

◇ Methodology

Data Collection and Sample

Data used in this research were collected through student surveys from two mid-Atlantic higher-education institutions, one of which is a small, private, liberal-arts college and the other a moderately sized, public university. Prior research has postulated that perceptions of punishment and belief can best be ascertained through vignettes describing the criminal act being studied (Klepper & Nagin, 1989; Bachman, Paternoster, & Ward, 1992; Shore et al., 2001; Higgins & Makin, 2004a). Therefore, participants were presented with several vignettes each describing an individual committing a specific act of piracy. These vignettes were intentionally kept brief to minimize the introduction of mitigating circumstances in the hopes that the participant would respond to the crime, not specific events surrounding the particular scenario. Questions following each vignette addressed the morality of the act, likelihood of punishment, severity of punishment, similarity to peer behavior, technical ability to engage in the act, and parental approval of the behavior. To minimize confusion between piracy and legal downloading, participants were explicitly told prior to responding that the scenarios and questions in the questionnaire are not instances of legal downloading (e.g., iTunes, shareware, demos, etc.). Participants were reminded of this on the questionnaire itself as well.

The sample for this study was a non-random sample of undergraduate college students enrolled in various classes during the spring 2006 semester. Thirteen classes were selected for the sample primarily based on their large enrollment figures, but also for diverse topics and varying levels. From the 594 students asked to participate, seven students opted to not participate, resulting in a total response rate of about 98%.

The demographics of the sample are displayed in Table 1. Also displayed are the institution demographics from the larger public university. Unfortunately, enrollment statistics from the private college were unavailable. The gender, race, and class year demographics are roughly representative of the institutions from which the sample was drawn. The participants' majors, however, were over representative of the social sciences and under representative of the computer sciences, despite the fact that three introductory computer sciences classes were included in the sample.

Variables

The dependent variables for this study were measured using objective questions about the monthly average of piracy violations for three types of piracy: music, software, and movie. The available responses were ordinal, ranged from one to four and varied in description for each type of piracy. For music piracy, responses included: (1) Never, (2) 1–5 songs per month, (3) 6–15 songs per month, or (4) more than 15 songs per month. Movie piracy responses were: (1) Never, (2) 1–3 movies per month, (3) 4–6 movies per month, or (4) More than 7 movies per month. Finally, the software piracy questions contained the following categories: (1) Never, (2) 1–3 programs per year, (3) 4–6 programs per year, or (4) More than 7 programs per year.

The analysis will include six independent variables, each with three variations for each type of piracy in the vignette. The first independent variable, peer involvement, was measured similarly to previous studies (Skinner & Fream, 1997) by asking how many of the respondent's friends would do the described act (e.g., download music without paying for it). The possible responses were (1) none, (2) few, (3) about half, or (4) most or all. The second independent variable, parental approval, was measured with a Likert-like scale in response to asking if the respondent's parents would approve if they did the described act. The responses ranged from (1) strongly disapprove to (4) strongly approve. These first two measures comprise the differential association concept. Though a scale could theoretically be compiled from the two measures, the reliability of such a scale would be unacceptably low (<.50) and comparing peer and parent variables' independent effects will yield more interesting results.

Two variables were derived from concepts associated with differential reinforcement. Reinforcement certainty was measured by asking how likely it was that the described act would result in [the] individual being "caught and punished." Responses ranged from (1) extremely unlikely to (4) extremely likely. Reinforcement severity, on the other hand, asked what the punishment would be if the fictional individual in the vignette were "caught." Responses included: nothing, small fine, loss of Internet access, heavy fines/lawsuit, or jail/prison. These responses were later dichotomized to mild (0) for responses of nothing, small fine, or loss of Internet access and severe (1) for heavy fines/lawsuit or jail/prison.[1]

The measure for technical ability is a straightforward question about the respondent's ability (yes or no) to do the described act. The belief variable was measured using a question similar to Higgins's (2005) morality measure; "How morally wrong is this behavior?" with responses of (1) not wrong, (2) slightly wrong, (3) moderately wrong, and (4) very wrong (see Table 1 and Figure 1).

. . . .

◇ Discussion and Conclusion

This study investigated the empirical validity of differential association and deterrence as applied to multiple forms of digital piracy. As predicted by social learning theory (Akers, 1985; Akers, 1998; Akers et al., 1979; Burgess & Akers, 1966), differential association predicted digital piracy in that college students with peers engaging in piracy and parents supportive of piracy were more likely to engage in piracy themselves. This finding is consistent with several prior studies [that] have noted a strong relationship between peers and piracy (e.g., Higgins & Makin, 2004a; Higgins & Wilson, 2006; Limayem, Khalifa, & Chin, 1999; Skinner & Fream, 1997). However, this study has shown such an effect is not limited solely to peers and extends to parents as well. Furthermore, differential association theory (Sutherland & Cressey, 1960) also predicts the effects to be mediated through motives, beliefs, and ability. Though motives were beyond the scope of this study, significant indirect effects were observed through belief and ability. Additionally, it was hypothesized that perceptions of punishment would be influenced by differential association with pirating peers and parents supportive of piracy. The empirical evidence examined here is supportive of this postulation.

Conversely, the effects of differential reinforcement were statistically and substantively weak. The effects of

Table 1   Sample Demographics

Variables	Percent (*N*)	Population Percent
Gender		
Male	44.3 (*260*)	42.2
Female	55.7 (*327*)	57.8
Race/Ethnicity		
White	86.7 (*509*)	83.1
Black	5.3 (*31*)	5.3
Hispanic	4.1 (*24*)	4.4
Asian	2.2 (*13*)	3.8
Other/Mixed	1.7 (*10*)	3.3
Class Year		
Freshman	30.7 (*180*)	28.8
Sophomore	28.1 (*165*)	25.1
Junior	19.9 (*117*)	23.0
Senior	21.1 (*124*)	23.2
Other	0.2 (*1*)	
Major		
Business-related	12.4 (*73*)	
Computer sciences	0.9 (*5*)	
Criminal justice	27.4 (*161*)	
Natural sciences	8.0 (*47*)	
Psychology	8.70 (*51*)	
Sociology	5.8 (*34*)	
Other social science	9.4 (*55*)	
Other	26.6 (*156*)	

perceptions of severity and certainty of punishment only rarely were statistically significant and were consistently weak; a finding consistent with prior studies of deterrence and differential reinforcement (Higgins, Wilson, & Fell, 2005; Skinner & Fream, 1997). These mixed results

Figure 1 Theoretical Model

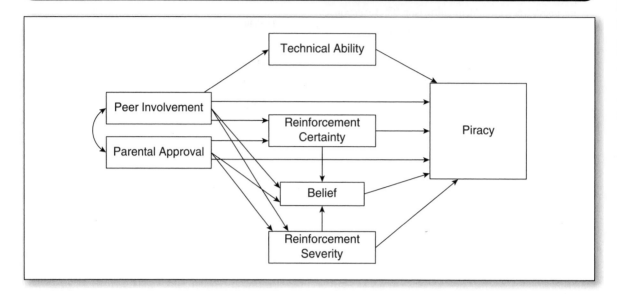

are obviously not enough to conclude there is an effect by reinforcement, but they are also not weak enough to definitively reject the notion that reinforcement may have some effect. With the simplicity of the measurement and analysis of this study, it is entirely possible that the poor relationships are the result of oversimplification in operationalizing severity and certainty.

Another noteworthy finding is the discrepancy between types of piracy. While the overall conclusion that differential association is a strong predictor of piracy and differential reinforcement variables are weak or non-predictors remains the same for all three types of piracy in this study, several differences were observed. Thus, different forms of piracy likely have similar causes and correlates. However, it would be erroneous to assume that such findings are identical without empirical verification.

The largest policy implication that can be derived from this study is the importance of social learning and belief. Obviously, the social learning process cannot be stopped altogether, but what is being learned can be altered if the environment changes. Attempting to sway the moral beliefs of college students to anti-piracy stances could result in exponentially growing anti-piracy beliefs. The effectiveness of programs designed to sway opinions is not guaranteed, but the data at least show that pro-social beliefs may prevent piracy.

Conversely, the deterrence factor so often discussed by government officials and the victimized industries did not receive much support. This is not necessarily a definitive conclusion though. The number of individuals who reported punishment being unlikely or extremely unlikely was consistently higher than the number of people engaged in the activity. If everyone believes punishment is unlikely, then the variance must be explained by other concepts. This data cannot predict what would happen should punishment become more certain. Rather, the data show that perceptions are presently so far removed from certain that a deterrent effect is not present even among most non-pirating students. In other words, deterrence theory cannot find empirical support, even if it is applicable to piracy, if the vast majority of respondents have correctly assessed the certainty and severity of punishment [to] be minuscule. Therefore, the policy implication for deterrence is that *if* a deterrence effect is possible, it will take a radical change in tactics to become powerful enough to actually deter.

There are several limitations to this study that must also be addressed. First, peer activity and parental support were measured using data reported by only the respondent. Given the number of cases involved and anonymity guaranteed, it was unfeasible to contact parents and peers to confirm the validity of the reported support and activity. While it is unlikely participants intentionally lied in their responses, it is entirely possible that their responses were inaccurate perceptions of parental support and peer activity. For parental support, students may be unaware of their parents' stance on what is typically considered to be a minor crime. Thus, they may have selected (guessed) an answer representative of their own philosophy. The same concern exists for peer activity, but at least here it would appear that popular answers for peer activity coincide with popular answers for self-involvement in piracy activities.

Second, the data used in this study were cross-sectional. Therefore, the results here cannot truly claim to explain causality without establishing time-order. While it seems unlikely one would select peers based on a relatively minor and typically considered secretive part of one's life, this data do[es] not disprove such a notion. Time-order would be a greater concern had punishment certainty and severity been significant predictors of piracy, as experimenting with piracy could increase awareness of the anonymity involved and become a reciprocal relationship. Finally, the items used to measure the variables were quite simplistic. Because a one-item measure is rarely as valid or reliable as a multiple-item measure, it may be more accurate to use scales or indices for more abstract concepts, such as belief.

Future research should attempt to overcome these limitations. In addition to using longitudinal data, assessing the validity of peer/parent measures, and importing more complex constructs, the theory should be expanded to go beyond the limited model used in this study. Modern and complete versions of social learning theory would be especially interesting to apply to Internet piracy and the learning process. Furthermore, research must distinguish between differing types of piracy. What may be true and well established for peers copying software may very well be undocumented and different for illegal, anonymous music downloads. Additionally, while P2P programs appear to be becoming a permanent part of technology, the Internet is ever changing and must be studied as such. The high number of individuals reporting having high-speed access and the technical ability to download music illegally are evidence of how theory can be impacted through technological evolution in even a relatively short period of time.

 Note

1. Multiple methods of coding the severity variable were attempted, including using it as an ordinal variable as originally collected. Severity's effect in the models remained similar regardless of the coding method. The dichotomous version was chosen because it seemed most consistent with general deterrence theory, which indicates that severity's effect should not increase once the severity becomes more severe than the crime, and because "nothing," "small fine" and "loss of Internet access" all appear to be considered insignificant punishments based on prior research of piracy (e.g., Cooper & Harrison, 2001).

 References

Akers, R. L. (1985). *Deviant behavior: A social learning approach.* Belmont, CA: Wadsworth.

Akers, R. L. (1998). *Social learning and social structure: A general theory of crime and deviance.* Boston: Northeastern University.

Akers, R. L., Krohn, M. D., Lanza-Kaduce, L., & Radosevich, M. (1979). Social learning and deviant behavior: A specific test of a general theory. *American Sociological Review, 44*, 636–655.

Bachman, R., Paternoster, R., & Ward, S. (1992). The rationality of sexual offending: Testing deterrence/rational choice conception of sexual assault. *Law & Society Review, 26*, 343–372.

Beccaria, C. (1985). *Essay on crimes and punishments* (H. Paolucci, Trans.). New York: Macmillan. (Original work published 1764)

Burgess, R. L., & Akers, R. L. (1966). A differential association-reinforcement theory of criminal behavior. *Social Problems, 14*, 128–147.

Business Software Alliance. (2006, May). *Third Annual BSA and IDC Global Software Piracy Study.* Retrieved February 11, 2007, from: http://www.bsa.org/globalstudy/upload/2005%20 Piracy%20Study%20-%20Official%20Version.pdf

Cooper, J., & Harrison, D. M. (2001). The social organization of audio piracy on the Internet. *Media, Culture & Society, 23*, 71–89.

Cornish, D., & Clarke, R. V. (1986). *The reasoning criminal: Rational choice perspectives on offending.* New York: Springer-Verlag.

Higgins, G. E. (2005). Can low self-control help with the understanding of the software piracy problem? *Deviant Behavior, 26*, 1–24.

Higgins, G. E., & Makin, D. A. (2004a). Does social learning theory condition the effects of low self-control on college students' software piracy? *Journal of Economic Crime Management, 2*, 1–22.

Higgins, G. E., & Makin, D. A. (2004b). Self-control, deviant peer association, and software piracy. *Psychological Reports, 95*, 921–931.

Higgins, G. E., & Wilson, A. L. (2006). Low self-control, moral beliefs, and social learning theory. *Security Journal, 19*, 75–92.

Higgins, G. E., Wilson, A. L., & Fell, B. D. (2005). An application of deterrence theory to software piracy. *Journal of Criminal Justice and Popular Culture, 12*, 166–184.

House of Representatives. (2004a). *Piracy deterrence and education act of 2004* (Report 108-700). Washington, DC: U.S. Government Printing Office.

House of Representatives. (2004b). *Peer to peer piracy on university campuses: An update* (Serial No. 112). Washington, DC: U.S. Government Printing Office.

IDC. (2005, December). *Expanding the frontiers of our digital future: Reducing software piracy to accelerate global IT benefits.* Retrieved on February 11, 2007, from http://www.bsa.org/idcstudy/pdfs/White_Paper.pdf

International Federation of the Phonographic Industry. (2005). *The recording industry 2005 commercial piracy report.* Retrieved on November 9, 2005, from http://www.ifpi.org/site-content/library/piracy2005.pdf

Klepper, S., & Nagin, D. (1989). Tax compliance and perceptions of the risks of detection and criminal prosecution. *Law & Society Review, 23,* 209–240.

Limayem, M., Khalifa, M., & Chin, W. W. (1999). Factors motivating software piracy: A longitudinal study. *International conference on information systems: Proceeding of the 20th international conference on Information Systems, 124–131.*

Sherizan, S. (1995). Can computer crime be deterred? *Security Journal, 6,* 177–181.

Shore, B., Venkatachalam, A. R., Solorzano, E., Burn, J. M., Hassan, S. Z., & Janczewski, L. J. (2001). Shoplifting and piracy: Behavior across cultures. *Technology in Society, 23,* 563–581.

Skinner, W. F., & Fream, A. M. (1997). A social learning theory analysis of computer crime among college students. *Journal of Research in Crime and Delinquency, 34,* 495–518.

Sutherland, E. H., & Cressey, D. R. (1960). *Principles of criminology* (6th ed.). Philadelphia: Lippincott.

CHAPTER 7

Social Control Theories of Deviance

Jamila Pleas and Rashod Bethany are siblings who grew up in Chicago in the 1980s and 1990s. Jamila remembers growing up close to her grandparents, who lived in a two-story house. She knew all of her neighbors, walked to school, and played in the nearby park. However, in the mid-1980s, the neighborhood began to change. Unemployment increased significantly in the area, drug sales increased, and homes were boarded up. Rashod, who was born four years after Jamila, came of age as the neighborhood began to deteriorate and opportunities began to dry up. Their mother became a drug addict. By the time Rashod was seven, he was required to bag marijuana as punishment when he got in trouble. Jamila and Rashod's grandparents permanently stepped in as guardians, but they died within a year of each other when the kids were 11 and 15 years old.

Without their grandparents' guidance, Jamila started to skip school and eventually dropped out. Rashod became more deeply involved in the drug trade and at age 12 was shot in the back.

A long-time family friend and the mother of Jamila's "childhood sweetheart" became aware of Jamila and her struggles and demanded that Jamila come to live with her family, saying that she had promised Jamila's grandmother that Jamila would go to college one day. The family didn't take Rashod in.

Jamila went to live with the family. She went to a new school, buckled down, made up her missed lessons, and applied to colleges. Rashod continued to live in the old neighborhood, getting his guidance from the drug dealers who took over his grandparents' house as a base of operations. After Rashod was shot, a social worker at the hospital noted he had "fallen through the cracks at several agencies" (Meisner, 2013, p. 2). By the time Rashod was in his late teens, he had risen in the ranks of the drug world and was known as "The Man," running two round-the-clock crack houses and cornering the area's drug racket.

Jamila finished college, became a nurse, and lives in a high-rise in Hyde Park; her brother Rashod was recently sentenced to 25 years in prison on drug charges. Jamila's memories of her old neighborhood have faded but continue to influence her, especially when she is dealing with young mothers-to-be caught in tough

(Continued)

(Continued)

situations. As for her brother, Jamila still remembers him as intelligent and industrious, the kid who at 6 would sneak down to the store and offer to push shopping carts or load grocery bags for change. "Sometimes I wonder if Rashod had been given another path, what he might have become," she said (Meisner, 2013, p. 3).

Source: Adapted from Meisner, J. (2013, April 14). Sister escaped "Trigger Town," but bleak fate snared brother. *Chicago Tribune.* Retrieved from http://articles.chicagotribune.com/2013-04-14/news/ct-met-brother-sister-trigger-town-20130414_1_grammar-school-drugs-family-friend

◈ Introduction

Jamila's and Rashod's stories are not unusual. And frankly, more than one theory could be used to explain their experiences and life trajectories. This chapter presents the perspective of several social control theories and will explain the behavior of Jamila and Rashod using these theories.

Social control theories of deviance got their start from the early classical theories usually associated with Beccaria. Both the classical school and the neoclassical school have as a basis a belief in the free will and rationalistic hedonism of the individual (Bernard, Snipes, & Gerould, 2009). Beccaria, writing in the 18th century, viewed the individual as a rational actor (the popular belief of the time) and sought, under this belief system, to reform the system of punishment (Bernard et al., 2009). Most important for modern control theories is Beccaria's overall support for the notion that being free actors, individuals need controls in their lives to keep them from hedonistic action (if that action was harmful to society).

Control theorists assert that human beings are basically antisocial and assume that deviance is part of the natural order in society; individuals are attracted to the idea of norm violation and thus motivated to deviate. This leads control theorists to assert that concern for deviant motivation alone does not account for the forces leading people to deviate—all people are capable of feeling a certain motivation to deviate. "The important question is not 'why do men not obey the rules of society,' but rather 'why do men obey the rules of society'" (Traub & Little, 1985, p. 241).

◈ Development of Social Control Theory

Our first theorist is important for two reasons. The first is that he is one of the earliest theorists to formulate the assumptions of the classical school into a sociological theory of deviance and social control. But more importantly, he is one of the first to articulate a distinction between *internal* and *external* social control. While later theorists do not always explicate their theories in the same dichotomy of internal and external, most accept the notion of internal social control (or a conversation with oneself—in other words, through thoughtful introspection, one decides not to engage in deviance) and **external control** (society places formal controls on the individual to keep him or her from engaging in crime).

Nye

F. Ivan Nye's (1958) position is that most deviant behavior is the result of insufficient social control. He offered four clusters of social control. The first cluster is internalized control exercised from within through our conscience. Nye argues that every society tries to instill its rules and norms in the conscience of its children. This cluster is the most powerful; in fact, Nye states that if internal controls were entirely effective, then there would be no need for the other three clusters of social control. Unfortunately, internal controls, for a variety of reasons, are never completely effective.

He argues that one reason for a variance in effectiveness is that the rules and norms of society are not always agreed upon at a level that allows for perfect socialization. Nye also argues that strong **internal control** can only be accomplished when the child completely accepts the parent; to the extent that the parent–child relationship is not a perfect one, internal control may not be as effective as necessary.

The second cluster Nye refers to as parents and indirect control. Nye argues that while parents are important to the internalizing of controls, they can also place indirect controls on juveniles. Nye sees these indirect controls as the disapproval the parent might show should the juvenile engage in deviant behavior. To the extent that the juvenile cares about the parent's disapproval, he or she will not engage in deviant behavior, thus being indirectly controlled through the parent's opinion of his or her behavior.

The third cluster is direct control imposed from without by means of restriction and punishment. Nye argues that no society relies solely on the individual to regulate his or her own behavior. Additional controls, in the form of punishment, disapproval, ridicule, ostracism, or banishment, are used by informal groups or society as a whole to control deviant behavior. These controls are often imposed by the police or other officials.

The final cluster is needed to give individuals reason not to engage in deviant behavior. Nye believes that alternative means to need satisfaction (goals and values) are necessary so that individuals do not have to engage in deviant behavior to get what they want. A readily available set of alternatives will mean that the above three clusters of social control will have a stronger influence on the likelihood of preventing deviant behavior.

Since all variations of social control theory assume that individuals *want* to engage in deviance and, therefore, the abnormal (or not expected) outcome is *not* engaging in deviance, we use social control theory to explain those instances when Jamila and Rashod are not engaging in deviance.

Given that Jamila never engaged in much deviance of a serious nature (she skipped school and dropped out, but did not engage in the drug trade like her brother did), Nye might argue that while not perfect, Jamila's internalized controls are fairly strong, but her indirect or direct controls were weakened when she lost her grandparents. Rashod, on the other hand, did not benefit from the stability of the family friend's household and lived under the unpredictability of his drug-addicted mother during a more influential time in his life.

Hirschi

The person most associated with control theories is Travis Hirschi. Hirschi's (1969) version of social control theory is often referred to as social bonding theory. This theory concentrates on indirect controls of behavior. Hirschi's social control theory suggests that deviance is not a response to learned behavior or stimuli or the strains surrounding an individual (as differential association theory or strain theory suggests); instead, social control theory assumes that deviant activity is a given and that it is the absence of deviance that needs to be explained. In fact, not only are we capable of it, but we are also willing creators and participants in it. The reason we do not engage in deviance or crime is because we have **social bonds** to conformity that keep us from engaging in socially unacceptable activities. This social bond comprises four parts: **attachment, commitment, involvement,** and **belief**.

Attachment is the "emotional" component of the bond. This component suggests that we do not engage in deviance because we care about what conforming others think about us. Hirschi argued that if we are strongly attached to others, we will contemplate what their reaction to our behavior will be before we engage in it. In other words, we will not engage in deviance if we think those we are attached to will be disappointed in us. This is the element of the social bond that may have us saying "What would Mom think?" or "Mom would be mad if she found out." Hirschi believed that our most important attachment is probably to our parents (and, by extension, other family members), but he also thought that attachments to friends (even if they were not always conforming themselves) and teachers would also keep us from deviating.

Commitment is the "rational" component of the bond. This component suggests that individuals will be less likely to engage in deviance when they have a strong commitment to conventional society. This commitment will

▲ **Photo 7.1**   In Hirschi's theory of social control, finding alternative activities for kids, such as music programs, may keep them from engaging in deviant behavior.

cause them to weigh the costs and benefits of deviant behavior. Those who have more to lose will be less likely to misbehave. Hirschi believed that conventional activities were most likely one's education and other school activities for juveniles and, for those who had successfully completed high school, work and occupational attainment. Hirschi actually believed that juveniles who entered adulthood too soon (for example, became young parents or worked while in high school) were more likely to become deviant, not less likely (Kubrin, Stucky, & Krohn, 2009).

Involvement is the component of the bond that suggests the more time spent engaged in conforming activities, the less time available to deviate. Hirschi (1969) characterized this bond as "idle hands are the devil's workshop" (p. 187). In other words, Hirschi argued that juveniles who spend their time in conventional activities, such as sports, homework, or band practice, have, literally, less time for deviant activities. The difference between commitment and involvement (since we have mentioned school and after-school activities when discussing both) is that commitment is the bond that focuses on not wanting to lose the benefits of the conventional activity one is engaging in. (For example, you don't want to be benched on the football team because you were caught drinking.) Involvement, however, refers specifically to the time you engage in a conventional activity. (For example, if you are at football practice, you cannot also be shoplifting at the same time.)

Finally, belief is the component of the bond that suggests the stronger the awareness, understanding, and agreement with the rules and norms of society, the less likely one will be to deviate. Given that social control is a normative theory (it assumes that there is societal agreement and understanding about the norms and rules of society), an individual with weakened norms is not thought to be completely unaware of the norms and rules; however, he or she is less accepting of the "moral validity of the law" (Kubrin et al., 2009, p. 172).

Hirschi would argue that Jamila benefitted from changing neighborhoods, schools, and families and increased her bonds to conformity while Rashod continued to live in an area that weakened his bonds to conformity because "conventional others" were in short supply.

◈ Techniques of Neutralization

Sykes and Matza (1957) offer an explanation for why individuals might engage in deviance even though they understand it is wrong. Asking, "Why would we violate the norms and laws in which we believe?" they suggest that we employ techniques of neutralization to rationalize away our understanding of the rules. They argue that society is organized for these sorts of rationalizations because much of our understanding of the rules comes with a certain flexibility already. In other words, they point out, while we understand the normative system, we also understand that under certain circumstances, those norms do not apply. For example, while killing someone is generally wrong, we know that during times of war or in self-defense, it is not. Under criminal law, an individual can avoid being guilty because of "non-age, necessity, insanity, drunkenness, compulsion, self-defense, and so on" (p. 666), in other words, if the individual can prove she or he did not *intend* to do harm. Sykes and Matza stated that it is our argument that much of delinquency is based on what is essentially an unrecognized extension of defenses to crimes, in the form of justifications for deviance that are seen as valid by the delinquent but not by the legal system or society at large. (p. 666)

Sykes and Matza (1957) argue that we can silence our internalized norms (what Nye refers to as our internalized controls) and external norms by using these techniques of neutralization. They suggest there are five such techniques:

1. *The Denial of Responsibility.* The first technique is used by individuals to argue that they are not responsible for their behavior. While some of this might be an argument that their behavior was a mistake or accident, Sykes and Matza (1957) argue that denial of responsibility goes well beyond just the claim that "it was an accident." This technique essentially is used to suggest that the individual is somehow compelled by forces beyond his or her control. The individual is "helplessly propelled" into bad behavior by unloving parents, a bad teacher, a boss, or a neighborhood.

2. *The Denial of Injury.* This technique focuses on whether the deviance is perceived to cause injury or harm to anyone. It might be symbolized by the statement, "But no one was hurt by it." It is probable that this technique is used frequently in the justification for deviant behavior since much behavior defined as deviant is not defined as harmful enough to be against the law. In these instances when the behavior may go against understood societal norms but not be very harmful to others, it is easy for individuals to argue that their behavior should be allowed and is not really all that bad because it isn't hurting anyone.

3. *The Denial of Victim.* An extension of the denial of injury is the rationalization that while a victim might exist, that person deserved the harm or "brought it on themselves." This technique of neutralization focuses on the fact that the victim deserves to be harmed because it is retaliation or punishment for some slight the victim has perpetrated on the deviant. The behavior becomes justified just as Robin Hood's behavior of stealing from the rich to give to the poor was justified. It may be against the rules to steal, but the rich brought it upon themselves by stealing from the poor first.

4. *The Condemnation of the Condemners.* This technique shifts the focus or blame to the individuals who are pointing the finger at the deviant's behavior. It is a diversionary tactic used to point out that others' behavior is also deviant, and therefore, those "condemners" have no right to call into question the behavior of the deviant individual. As with all diversionary tactics, the goal of this one is not to have a meaningful conversation about anyone's deviance but to deflect attention from the original assertion and help the deviant slip from view.

5. *The Appeal to Higher Loyalties.* The final technique of neutralization is one in which the wishes of the larger group (society) lose out to the wishes of a smaller, more intimate group. In other words, when an individual sees himself or herself as loyal to a group that demands behavior that violates the rules of society, he or she may argue that that loyalty requires breaking the rules for the good of the smaller group. In this instance, the individual may see himself or herself caught between the two groups. For example, a young man may know he should not fight another boy but may do it to protect his younger brother or because his friends demand he show loyalty to their group.

Sykes and Matza (1957) offer five phrases to sum up the five techniques of neutralization: "I didn't mean it, I didn't really hurt anybody, they had it coming to them, everybody's picking on me, and I didn't do it for myself" (p. 669). With these phrases comes the ability to rationalize away an individual's understanding of the normative behavior expected of him or her and an allowance for deviant behavior.

DEVIANCE IN POPULAR CULTURE

The ideas of social control theory can easily be applied to novels and films in popular culture. We offer two examples here but encourage you to think about the story lines of other books and films and see if you can apply the ideas of the theory to the different characters to explain their deviance and/or conformity.

The Outsiders is a book written by a 16-year-old girl, S. E. Hinton, in 1967 and made into a film in 1983 by Francis Ford Coppola. Hinton examines the experiences of two groups of juvenile delinquents divided by social class: the Greasers and the Socs. *The Outsiders* is narrated by 14-year-old Ponyboy Curtis, a Greaser, who lives with his two brothers, Darry and Sodapop, and considers the rest of the "gang"—Johnny, Dally, and Two-Bit—his family.

The Outsiders depicts a world without significant adults; the boys are accountable to each other more than anyone else. Johnny's parents are abusive, the Curtis brothers' parents were killed in a car accident, and the other boys' parents are rarely mentioned. Ponyboy is the only boy in his gang who is interested in school; Sodapop and Darry work full-time and try to stay out of trouble, attempting to hold their small family together after the death of their parents.

Social control theory can help to explain the relative conformity and deviance of each character. As an example, compare the social bonds of Ponyboy and Dally and see if the theory fits the outcome at the end of the novel/film.

For another example from a quite different era and setting, you might apply the ideas of social control theory to the film *Boyz N the Hood.* Set in South Central Los Angeles, the film focuses on the challenges of growing up in an extremely violent setting. The three main characters—Tre, Ricky, and Doughboy—are African American teenage boys with different backgrounds and opportunities.

Using Hirschi's theory, compare and contrast the social bonds of Tre, Ricky, and Doughboy. Do you think the relative strength of attachment, commitment, involvement, and belief explains their different levels of deviant behavior? Why or why not?

Finally, *Empire* is television drama depicting the hip-hop artist and CEO of Empire Entertainment, Lucious Lyon, and his ex-wife, Cookie, who took the fall for their drug-running business two decades ago, spending the last 17 years in jail while Lucious has built his empire. Now out, Cookie believes she is owed for her time in prison. Falling into the genre of nighttime soap opera, there is a lot of questionable behavior by many of the characters as they vie for a piece of the empire and an accumulation of power.

Can you see Hirschi's social bonds or the techniques of neutralization in play in this drama series as the characters jockey to take over the empire?

◈ Contemporary Additions to Social Control Theory

Power-Control Theory

Developed by Hagan, Gillis, and Simpson (Hagan, 1989; Hagan, Gillis, & Simpson, 1985, 1990; Hagan, Simpson, & Gillis, 1987), power-control theory combines class and control theories of deviance to explain the effects of familial control on gender differences in crime. Hagan et al. (1987) argue that parental positions in the workforce affect patriarchal attitudes in the household. Patriarchal attitudes, in turn, result in different levels of control placed on boys and girls in these households. Finally, differing levels of control affect the likelihood of the children taking risks and ultimately engaging in deviance. In other words, because of the greater levels of control placed on girls in patriarchal households, there are greater gender differences in delinquency in such households, with boys being more delinquent than girls.

Power-control theory begins with the assumption that mothers constitute the primary agents of socialization in the family. In households in which the mother and father have relatively similar levels of power at work—so-called balanced households—mothers will be less likely to differentially exert control upon their daughters. Thus, in balanced households, both sons and daughters will have similar levels of control placed upon them, leading them to develop similar attitudes regarding the risks and benefits of engaging in deviant behavior. This line of reasoning suggests that balanced households will experience fewer gender differences in deviant behavior. Power-control theorists further assume that households in which mothers and fathers have dissimilar levels of power in the workplace—so-called unbalanced households—are more patriarchal in their attitudes regarding gender roles. In such households, parents will place greater levels of control upon daughters than sons. Therefore, daughters will develop attitudes unfavorable toward deviance—higher levels of perceived risk and fewer perceived benefits for engaging in deviant acts. Thus, in unbalanced households, the theory predicts significant gender differences in deviant behavior, with male children being more likely than females to engage in deviant acts.

Initial tests of power-control theory suggested that these gender differences in crime come about because girls are differentially controlled in the household. In other words, female delinquency increases or decreases depending on the level of patriarchy and, thus, control in the household. Later tests of the theory (McCarthy, Hagan, & Woodward, 1999) suggest that gender differences in deviance and crime probably decrease because *both* male and female deviants are affected. Most importantly, McCarthy et al. (1999) demonstrate that in less patriarchal households, sons have more controls placed on them, decreasing their level of deviance.

Theory of Self-Control

Gottfredson and Hirschi introduced their general theory of crime in 1990, situating the theory in the classical school of criminology. Of all the theories discussed in this chapter (and, perhaps, in this book), this theory may be, arguably, the one best positioned to predict deviant behavior. This is because this theory was designed to be able to predict *all* behavior, not just criminal or delinquent behavior.

According to Gottfredson and Hirschi, crime and deviance are just like any other behaviors and should not be set apart as somehow different than, say, brushing one's teeth or listening to music. Using concepts from the classical school (Bentham, 1789/1970), they argue that people engage in all behavior to maximize pleasure and minimize pain. As rational creatures, humans will make choices in their lives that help them increase pleasure and avoid pain whenever they can. In this conception, deviance, then, is just like any other behavior—individuals freely choose to engage in that behavior when it is pleasurable to them.

Gottfredson and Hirschi (1990) define crime (and deviance) as "acts of force or fraud undertaken in pursuit of self-interest" (p. 15). Using the Uniform Crime Reports to illustrate the nature of crime, they argue that there is no difference between trivial and serious crime, between expressive and instrumental crime, between status offenses and delinquency, between victimizing and victimless crimes—the difference lies not in the behaviors but, to some extent, in the individual. While a strict classical theory would argue that all individuals are likely to make the decision to engage in deviance if it brings with it a reward for the individual and that the likelihood to not engage in deviance is based on that individual's social bond to society, Gottfredson and Hirschi argue that there may be a difference in individuals and their behavior that cannot be explained by the social bond. They write, "What classical theory lacks is an explicit idea of self-control, the idea that people also differ in the extent to which they are vulnerable in the temptations of the moment" (p. 87).

Gottfredson and Hirschi (1990) argue that self-control is a stable construct that develops early in the socialization process (or lack thereof) of an individual. Most likely, **low self-control** develops from an "absence of nurturance, discipline, or training" (p. 95). In other words, the major cause of low self-control is bad parenting or ineffective childrearing. But Gottfredson and Hirschi are emphatic in their assertion that low self-control is not actively created; it is what happens in the absence of socialization, not in the presence of socialization. In other words, Gottfredson and Hirschi believe that since deviant behavior "undermines harmonious group relations and the ability to achieve collective ends" (p. 96), no one would actively teach, learn, or promote deviant behavior.

Six elements make up the construct of low self-control, according to Gottfredson and Hirschi (1990):

1. Criminal acts provide *immediate gratification* of desires. A major characteristic of people with low self-control is therefore a tendency to respond to tangible stimuli in the immediate environment, to have a concrete "here and now" orientation. People with high self-control, in contrast, tend to defer immediate gratification for long-term goals.

2. Criminal acts provide *easy or simple* gratification of desires. They provide money without work, sex without courtship, revenge without court delays. People lacking self-control also tend to lack diligence, tenacity, or persistence in a course of action.

3. Criminal acts are *exciting, risky, or thrilling.* They involve stealth, danger, speed, agility, deception, or power. People lacking self-control therefore tend to be adventuresome, active, and physical. Those with high levels of self-control tend to be cautious, cognitive, and verbal.

4. Crimes provide *few or meager long-term benefits.* They are not equivalent to a job or a career. On the contrary, crimes interfere with long-term commitments to jobs, marriages, family, or friends. People with low self-control thus tend to have unstable marriages, friendships, and job profiles. They tend to be little interested in and unprepared for long-term occupational pursuits.

5. Crimes require *little skill or planning.* The cognitive requirements for most crimes are minimal. It follows that people lacking self-control need not possess or value cognitive or academic skills. The manual skills required for most crimes are minimal. It follows that people lacking self-control need not possess manual skills that require training or apprenticeship.

6. Crimes often result in *pain or discomfort for the victim.* Property is lost, bodies are injured, privacy is violated, trust is broken. It follows that people with low self-control tend to be self-centered, indifferent, or insensitive to the suffering and needs of others. It does not follow, however, that people with low self-control are routinely unkind or antisocial. On the contrary, they may discover the immediate and easy rewards of charm and generosity. (pp. 89–90)

Gottfredson and Hirschi argue that these traits are stable in individuals. In other words, they do not vary over time—once a person with low self-control, always a person with low self-control. What Gottfredson and Hirschi say may vary is the ability or opportunity for individuals to engage in deviance. So while individuals with low self-control might always be inclined to make an easy score, that easy score has to come along first.

Gottfredson and Hirschi would argue that Jamila and Rashod are an excellent contrast in self-control. While Jamila's formative years (according to the general theory, childhood until about age 8) were characterized by a safe, close-knit neighborhood; the strong influence of her grandparents; and the stability of working parents, by the time Rashod was 8 years old, the neighborhood was crime-ridden, his mother was an addict, and he was being used in the drug trade. Gottfredson and Hirschi would argue that these differing experiences affected each child's level of self-control, which, in turn, meant that Jamila could delay gratification to focus on finishing high school and attend and finish college while Rashod leaned toward more risky, self-centered pursuits (although critics of the notion of low self-control might point out that Rashod rose in the ranks of the drug trade at a very early age to run two crack houses and corner the drug market in the neighborhood, which some might argue takes quite a bit of organization).

Life Course Theory

While traditional social control or social bonding theories focus attention on the social bonds that juveniles and young adults maintain—attachment to parents and teachers, commitment to school, involvement in activities such as sports or band—life course theory extends this examination of social bonds from adolescents to adulthood (Sampson & Laub, 1993, 1995). Hirschi (1969) argued that bonds may be weak or broken (or may vary over time), but he never really explored the nature of that variance, whereas Gottfredson and Hirschi (1990) argue that life events (as they are related to social bonding) do not have an effect on deviant behavior because levels of self-control are set at an early age. Sampson and Laub (1993) argue that over the course of one's life, individuals are likely to go through stages that present them with social bonding opportunities and that while we may be able to see trajectories toward crime throughout the life course, these trajectories can change with changes in life events.

According to Sampson and Laub (1993), a **trajectory** is a "pathway or line of development over a life span . . . [that] refer[s] to long-term patterns of behavior and [is] marked by a sequence of transitions" (p. 8). A **transition**, then, is a shorter or specific life event that is embedded in a trajectory. For example, your life could be said to be on a working-class trajectory—born in a working-poor neighborhood to parents who had stable but low-paying employment, you received no schooling past high school and ended up working in the service sector. Then you married and got an entry-level position in your in-laws' furniture business (same pay as your other job but with significant room for advancement). It could be said you were on a trajectory for a working-poor lifestyle— barely making ends meet, most likely always working in the service sector, always worrying about the likelihood you might lose your job—but then your marriage (the transition) offered a sudden change from that earlier trajectory.

Sampson and Laub focus on an age-graded theory of informal social control. They argue that there are social bonds between (1) members of society and (2) wider social institutions, such as family, school, and work. As an age-graded theory, they argue that life events may have an effect on the likelihood to persist or desist with deviance (although it is the quality of these life events, not just the existence of them, that is important). They offer three components to their theory. The first is that during childhood and adolescence, social bonds to family and school are important for explaining the likelihood to engage in deviance. Those who hold strong bonds to family and school are less likely to engage in deviance than those with weak or broken bonds. The second component is the argument that there is a certain level of stability to the likelihood to engage in deviance. In other words, those who don't engage in deviance as adolescents are more likely to abstain from deviance as adults, and those who do engage in deviance as adolescents are more likely to engage in deviance as adults. Sampson and Laub argue this is so for two reasons: First, there are stable individual differences in the likelihood to engage in deviance (some people are just more likely to engage in deviance), but second, there is also a dynamic process by which the adolescent deviant behavior has an effect on later adolescent and adult social bonds. (For example, an individual who has been incarcerated or labeled a deviant may have less desirable job prospects.)

Finally, the third component, which is where Sampson and Laub spend a significant amount of explanatory time, is that important life events in adulthood have the likelihood of changing a trajectory. "In other words, we contend that trajectories of crime are subject to modification by key institutions of social control in the transition to adulthood" (Sampson & Laub, 1995, p. 146). These are likely to be such transitions as attachment to labor force participation or a particularly cohesive marriage. Sampson and Laub argue that it is not enough for these transitions to just happen; they must be quality transitions. (In other words, just getting married or committing to a partner is not enough; it must be a cohesive commitment.)

Moffitt (1993, 2003, 2006) makes an extended life course argument, claiming that there are two offender groups. The first is considered a life-course-persistent group whose deviance stems from neurodevelopmental processes; these individuals are predicted to be fairly consistent in their deviant behavior. In other words, over their lives, they are more likely to engage in crime. Moffitt considers this to be a fairly small group. The second group is called adolescence limited. This group is much larger. Its deviance stems from social processes, and over time, it is likely that most of its members will stop engaging in deviant behavior (Piquero, Daigle, Gibson, Leeper Piquero, & Tibbetts, 2007).

These variations on the life course theory are often used to explain the **age–crime curve**. The relationship between age and crime is so strong at the aggregate level that many believe it is invariant (meaning that it does not change over era or type of crime, for example). And while this is probably not the case (for two discussions on this, see Farrington, 1986; Piquero et al., 2007), it is a very strong relationship; we see, in general, that the likelihood for crime rises sharply as one ages into the teenage and late-teenage or early adult years and then not quite as swiftly drops off (see Figures 7.1 and 7.2). Steffensmeier, Allan, Harer, and Streifel (1989) found that the age–crime relationship was extremely strong but varied for type of crime. (For example, while the relationship between age and property crimes might peak at about 17, the relationship between age and violent crime peaks a bit later.)

Theorists who use the life course theory argue that this age–crime relationship exists because as people age, they go through stages that allow them to be more or less deviant. For example, as adolescents become teenagers, they are more likely to pull away from their parents' control, perhaps becoming less attached to their parents and more attached to their peers. Then, as individuals become even older, they enter new stages of their life in which deviant behavior may be less rewarding or available, and thus, they begin to engage in less and less deviance and more and more conformity—we call this "aging out of crime and deviance."

◈ Application of Social Control Theories

As you can tell, most versions of social control theory, both the classical and contemporary additions, have explanations for deviance that rely heavily on the socializing capacity of the family. In other words, social control theory, in all of its forms, points to the family as the primary controlling agent of deviance. While the family can be found as a component of many theories of deviance, it plays a central role in empirical works examining the predictive abilities of social control theory. Below is an example of the research examining the socializing abilities of families.

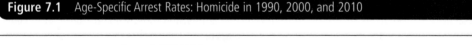

Figure 7.1   Age-Specific Arrest Rates: Homicide in 1990, 2000, and 2010

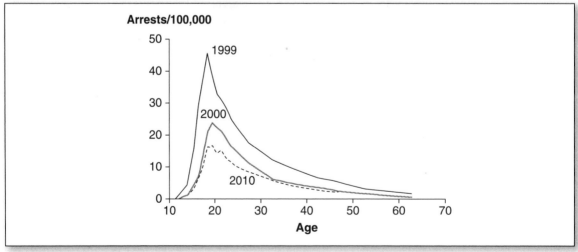

Source: Snyder (2012).

Figure 7.2   Age-Specific Arrest Rates: Robbery in 1990, 2000, and 2010

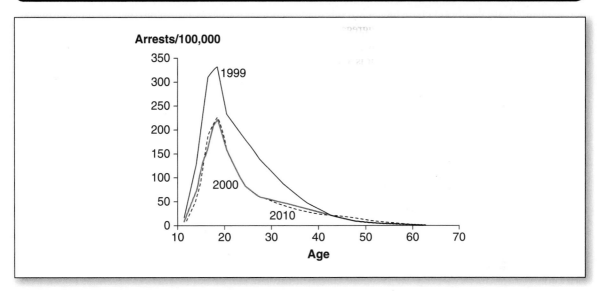

Source: Snyder (2012).

Instead of an intricate look at the structural characteristics of the single-parent family, some researchers have suggested that family process or family quality should also be a serious focus of examination (Patterson & Dishion, 1985; Rutter & Giller, 1984; Vazsonyi & Klanjsek, 2008) because structure may mask other processes or events in the juvenile's life (Haas, Farrington, Killias, & Sattar, 2004). Studies that have simultaneously examined family structure and family process have generally found that family structure is not a significant predictor of delinquency once family process has been added (Cernkovich & Giordano, 1987; Van Voorhis, Cullen, Mathers, & Garner, 1988) and that family structure, at most, had an indirect effect on delinquency through measures of family process (Laub & Sampson, 1988; Petts, 2009; Sampson & Laub, 1993).

▲ **Photo 7.2**   All of the theories connected to social control suggest that family relationships are an important factor in controlling deviant behavior.

Family process and/or family quality studies have been less systematic. Many of the studies examine the relationship between attachment and juvenile delinquency. However, the concept of attachment has been measured in a variety of ways—love or affection, interest or concern, support and help, caring and trust, encouragement, lack of rejection, parental conflict, and control and **supervision** (J. H. Rankin & Kern, 1994; see also J. H. Rankin & Wells, 1990). These measures of attachment could also be measures of other theoretical components.

In addition to attachment, other family quality measures include overall home quality, discipline, supervision, and level of conflict. For the most part, family process variables, no matter what they are called or how they are operationalized, are significant predictors of juvenile delinquency. Researchers have found that overall home quality (Van Voorhis et al., 1988), level of supervision (Cernkovich & Giordano, 1987), attachment to parents (Hirschi, 1969; Johnson, 1986; Warr, 1993), and type of discipline (Laub & Sampson, 1988; Sampson & Laub, 1993) are strong predictors of juvenile delinquency.

Levels of attachment in the family have long been linked to juvenile delinquency (Hirschi, 1969; J. H. Rankin & Kern, 1994). While much of this research has examined the direct effect of attachment on delinquency, some have taken a more extensive look at family processes, including such variables as family involvement, family conflict, and supervision (Sampson & Laub, 1993, 1994), and some have examined the effect that racial and ethnic diversity might have on the effect of attachment (Leiber, Mack, & Featherstone, 2012; Perez-McCluskey & Tovar, 2003), finding that there does seem to be a relationship between ethnicity and the effect of attachment. Levels of attachment in conjunction with structure have also been examined, with various findings. Some studies have shown that attachment is a better predictor of delinquency than structure (Sokol-Katz, Dunham, & Zimmerman, 1997), while others have found a relationship between attachment and structure (J. H. Rankin & Kern, 1994).

Supervision is a second extensively researched process within the family that is said to affect the likelihood of delinquency (Broidy, 1995; Jang & Smith, 1997; Junger & Marshall, 1997). Most of these studies show a relationship between levels of supervision and delinquency (Greenwood, 1992), although this relationship does depend on how family supervision is measured (Broidy, 1995; Wells & Rankin, 1988).

◈ Critiques of Social Control Theories

The earliest versions of social control theory were criticized for having underdeveloped constructs that could not be easily tested. This changed with Hirschi's version of social control theory. Not only did Hirschi present a test of his theory with his initial book (1969), but the theory may be one of the most tested in criminology today (Kubrin et al., 2009). Numerous researchers have found support for the theory using cross-sectional studies, although longitudinal studies show less support (Kubrin et al., 2009).

However, some theorists and researchers argue that traditional social control theory (specifically Hirschi's form of social bonding theory) is better at predicting minor forms of deviance and crime than more serious forms (Krohn & Massey, 1980) and that the four bonds do not really predict future deviance with any success at all (Agnew, 1985).

Contemporary versions of control theory have actually been critiqued by other control theorists; most notably, there is a robust exchange between Hirschi and Gottfredson (1995) and Sampson and Laub (1995) on the merits of the theory of self-control and life course theory. One of their central debates is whether control varies throughout a person's life or whether that control is set by a certain (young) age. Specifically, critics of self-control theory argue that self-control may be something that changes over time in one's life (as opposed to being set in someone by the time they are age 7 or 8).

Perhaps one of the most common and general critiques about all the theories that fall under the general heading of social control theory is that there is a background assumption that individuals are both rational and able to perceive the consequences of their behavior. These theories assume that people will weigh the costs and benefits of their behavior, and in instances in which they do not want to give up the connections they have made to society (attachment to their parents, benefits in school, a good job, a good marriage, or the esteem of their friends and colleagues), they will be less likely to deviate. However, as we know, when we engage in deviant behavior, often we do not take those things into consideration. For example, we know when we sit down with a pint of ice cream in the middle of the night to watch Spike TV's *The Ultimate Fighter* that this behavior is not good for us, but the consequences of these actions are far off (if perceived at all) while the benefits (a mindless night of chocolate chip mint ice cream and violent TV) are immediate.

◈ Explaining Deviance in the Streets and Deviance in the Suites: The Cases of Teenage Homelessness and Medical Deviance by Doctors

Teenage Runaways and Throwaways

There is no clear-cut way to estimate how many teenagers run away in a given year or how many teenagers are homeless at any given time. By definition, these are acts that are relatively invisible. Therefore, tracking and counting runaways is more of an art form than a science. When we talk about runaways, are we talking about youth who run away to become homeless? Or who just leave the house they are in for another, friendlier dwelling? Do we include youth who are forced to leave the family home because the parents demand it? (These youth are known as "throwaway kids.") For the purposes of our discussion, we will assume runaway and throwaway mean the child ends up on the streets. We only have estimates of the number of youth who run away or are thrown away, and those estimates often vary. Greene, Ringwalt, Kelley, Iachan, and Cohen (1995) reported that in 1992, approximately 2.8 million youth between the ages of 12 and 17 ran away from home. In 1999, the estimate was that approximately 1.7 million youth between the ages of 7 and 17 had had a runaway or throwaway experience (Hammer, Finkelhor, & Sedlak, 2002). And in 2013, the National Survey on Drug Use estimated that on any single night more than 6,000 youth between the ages of 12 and 17 had slept in the street, and 12.3% of those homeless in a single night are unaccompanied children (Office of Community Planning and Development, 2014). It is unlikely that the estimates vary so much from year to year because the incidence of running away varies that much; this is much more likely an illustration of exactly how hard it is to get an accurate account of youth who run away and sleep on the street.

While there are many reasons why youth run away from home, the most likely reason is family difficulties—most prevalently, child abuse and sexual abuse (Jencks, 1994; Tyler, Hoyt, Whitbeck, & Cauce, 2001). While both sexual and other abuse are strongly related to running away (Kaufman & Widom, 1999; Kempf-Leonard & Johansson, 2007), girls who have run away are more likely to report sexual abuse than runaway boys (Janus, Burgess, & McCormack, 1987; McCormack, Janus, & Burgess, 1986).

Chesney-Lind (1988, 1997) argues that this connection between the likelihood to be sexually abused and running away for girls is a gendered pathway to delinquency and continued victimization both on the streets and by the juvenile justice and adult justice systems. Calling this phenomenon *"the criminalization of girls' survival strategies"* (1988, p. 11), Chesney-Lind argues that the juvenile justice system heaps added problems onto the shoulders of girls just trying to escape their abuse by arresting them for running away after they have left home.

Besides the fact that runaway girls are more likely to report sexual abuse than runaway boys, why does this issue become a gendered one? A quick answer here is that studies tell us that the response to running away from society in general and the justice system in particular is a gendered one. While estimates suggest that both boys and girls are equally likely to run away (Kaufman & Widom, 1999), girls are more likely to be arrested and punished for doing so (Chesney-Lind & Shelden, 1998; Kempf-Leonard & Johansson, 2007). This means that girls who are merely looking to end their abuse are treated as delinquents, and running away becomes the first step in a long path through the juvenile and adult justice systems.

Teenage Runaways and Throwaways and Social Control Theory

Given that one of the strongest predictors of running away or becoming a throwaway is the presence of conflict—and often abuse—in the home, Hirschi's version of social control theory might be useful in explaining why a juvenile might run away and end up engaging in behaviors such as drug use that he or she wouldn't have under other circumstances. Hirschi argues that if the bonds to conformity are weakened, individuals will engage in deviant behavior. If the attachment bond to parents or other caregivers becomes weakened (even with a caregiver that is not engaging in abuse but that the youth sees as not helping to protect him or her), the youth may see running away as an acceptable alternative. Once homeless, with no daily commitment to a conventional lifestyle (the commitment bond) or to the usual conventional activities that the youth may have engaged in (the involvement bond), the youth may be more likely to engage in other deviant behaviors, such as drug use, that he or she would not have engaged in had he or she not run away or been thrown away. Homeless youth are reported to engage in many survival behaviors that extend from their homeless circumstances. Such behaviors include prostitution and pimping, stealing and selling stolen goods, dealing and using drugs, and conning others for goods (Greene, Ennett, & Ringwalt, 1999; Halcon & Lifson, 2004; Kipke, Unger, O'Connor, Palmer, & LaFrance, 1997). Many of these behaviors are engaged in for survival because homeless youth lack parental and other conventional support (Bender, Thompson, McManus, Lantry, & Flynn, 2007). This deviant behavior becomes a vicious circle because it further removes homeless youth from conventional relationships and institutions (Ferguson et al., 2011).

Medical Deviance by Doctors

Individuals who become doctors learn several ethical codes while studying medicine, the most well-known of which is the Hippocratic oath. While the Hippocratic oath has changed over time, at its essence, it is a promise by doctors and other medical professionals to practice medicine honestly. But while all doctors go through this training, some still behave in an unethical or criminal manner. There are many ways that doctors can act in a deviant manner while practicing their profession; some of these activities include fraud, unnecessary surgery, providing incompetent care, and overprescribing medications.

One of the better documented types of medical deviance is "fraud" because often the victim of that fraud is the government, and the government has established an extensive financial recovery system. Medicaid and Medicare fraud are the most pervasive forms of fraud. In general, fraud accounts for between 3% and 10% of health care spending, which means that each year somewhere between $68 billion and $226 billion is wasted on fraud (National Health Care Anti-Fraud Association, 2010, as cited in Payne, 2013). The following activities are all considered fraud:

- Phantom treatments: billing for services never provided

- Substitute provider: charging for services provided by an unauthorized employee

- Upcoding: billing for more expensive services than provided

- Falsifying records: providers change or lie on medical forms in order to be reimbursed by insurance

- Unbundling: billing separately for services that are considered one procedure

- Ping-ponging: unnecessarily moving patients from one medical provider to the next

- Ganging: billing for services provided to multiple family members when only one was treated

While "unnecessary surgery" is much less prevalent than fraud, the ramifications of this deviance can be much more severe. According to Black (2005), approximately 7.5 million unnecessary surgeries are performed annually (no, we didn't mistype that—it works out to about one surgery every four or five seconds), and approximately 12,000 people in the United States alone are killed each year because of these unnecessary surgeries and procedures. Many of the reasons for these procedures are not deviant themselves. Some of these procedures are done because there are differing opinions about the best course of action for many medical conditions; some doctors may have a more proactive approach, whereas others "wait and see." However, when it comes to certain types of medical conditions, often, patients are uncomfortable with a wait-and-see approach. For example, cancer has such a stigma that patients often think that invasive procedures are the only way to go, even when research suggests otherwise. But although many of these surgeries and procedures are the result of varying opinions, some occur because there is financial gain for doctors in performing surgeries (Black, 2005). In the United States in particular, many of these surgeries are quite expensive (G. Anderson, Hussey, Frogner, & Waters, 2005; Payne, 2013).

Medical Deviance by Doctors and Techniques of Neutralization

Looking at techniques of neutralization might be an especially fun way to examine how and why medical doctors engage in medical deviance. At first glance, medical doctors are not our first choice for a group that might engage in deviance. As people who we place immense trust in, they are an excellent example of white-collar crime or elite deviance because one of the main elements of their deviance is the violation of that trust. Remember that Sykes and Matza used the techniques of neutralization to explain how an individual can silence his or her internalized norms for conformity. These techniques may especially explain deviance among a group trained first to "do no harm." In many instances, the fraudulent practices are not aimed at doctors' patients but more likely at a third party, such as the government or an insurance company. But there are examples of doctors skirting Medicare limits by contracting separately with the patient for the patient to pay the remaining part of the bill, even though these are not the rules under Medicare. While critics argue that these contracts are coercive because they put patients in a position of having to agree to the arrangement to get the medical care they need, doctors involved justify these contracts and condemn Medicare as

> a tyrannical system that forbids wealthy citizens to pay more and that's unfair to doctors and patients. . . . Why should a patient lose the freedom to pay the doctor he wants for service he wants just because he turns 65? (Rosenthal, 1994, n.p.)

This quote can be interpreted as either a denial of injury—by focusing on wealthy patients it seems that no one is getting hurt by the behavior—or a condemnation of the condemners—the system itself is unfair and hurting patients by not letting them choose to pay the doctor an agreed-upon rate for agreed-upon services; thus, both the doctor and patient are the true victims of Medicare. A doctor might also appeal to higher loyalties by suggesting that in order to be able to remain in practice at all and treat patients, he or she must overbill Medicare or Medicaid. Thus, the care of the doctor's patients is more important than the rules of Medicare and Medicaid.

◈ Ideas in Action: Homeboy Industries

Homeboy Industries (Homeboy Industries, 2013a) may be one of the best existing examples of the tenets of social control theory in action (although, ironically, this program could be in the critical theories chapter, too, as an example of how when we critique existing policies, think of gang members as human beings instead of deviants, and decide to make changes, the resulting community programs and public policies can have transformative outcomes).

Homeboy Industries is the largest gang intervention and re-entry program in the country. It was founded by Father Gregory Boyle while he was the pastor of a parish in Boyle Heights (a neighborhood in Los Angeles). The program started in 1988 as Jobs for a Future (JFF), which was a small jobs program focused on decreasing gang violence. Over the years, JFF blossomed into what is known today as Homeboy Industries. Embracing the motto "Jobs Not Jails," Homeboy Industries now offers a variety of services and programs, including (1) tattoo removal; (2) employment services; (3) case management; (4) mental health, substance abuse, and domestic violence services; (5) legal services; (6) educational opportunities; and (7) a solar panel installation training and certification program (Homeboy Industries, 2013b).

▲ **Photo 7.3**   The Homeboy Industries' motto is "Jobs Not Jails," emphasizing both commitment to and involvement in a conventional lifestyle.

http://en.wikipedia.org/wiki/East_Side_Spirit_and_Pride; licensed under the GNU Free Documentation License on Wikipedia at https://commons.wikimedia.org/wiki/Commons:GNU_Free_Documentation_License,_version_1.2

In addition to these services and programs, Homeboy Industries has created seven job-training sites that are referred to as "social enterprises." These businesses offer both training and the opportunity for a social experience based on growing a business. These businesses include (1) Homegirl Café & Catering, (2) Homeboy Farmers Markets, (3) Homeboy Bakery, (4) Homeboy Diner, (5) the marketing and sale of Homeboy and Homegirl merchandise, (6) the inclusion of Homeboy grocery items in grocery chains such as Ralphs and Food 4 Less, and (7) Homeboy Silkscreen and Embroidery (Homeboy Industries, 2013b).

It might be argued that Homeboy Industries focuses on all four of Hirschi's social bonds to conformity. As a program that uses the skills and experiences of former gang members to guide new members, the program is emphasizing the importance of attachment and actively building the attachment bond between individuals at various stages of leaving gang life. The central focus on jobs and creating these social enterprises strengthens both the commitment bond and the involvement bond. Not only do jobs and the opportunity to help grow a business increase a commitment to a conventional lifestyle, but the sheer time that one spends on a job strengthens the involvement bond. According to testimonials about Homeboy Industries, "Small, perfect things happen every day at Homeboy. Amazing little happenings, human interactions that touch the soul. These moments are what makes this a place of healing and hope" (Homeboy Industries, 2012).

NOW YOU . . . USE THE THEORY

The University of Delaware takes copyright infringement of music, movies, and software very seriously. On their copyright guidelines page, the university explains, "While the University does not routinely monitor Internet activity, if you download or share copyrighted works over the Internet, your activity can be seen by the copyright owners. If the University receives notification of claimed infringement from a copyright owner or agent about your Internet activity, Federal law requires that the University take action. **You are responsible** for the activity associated with your IP address" (University of Delaware, 2013). Below are the copyright infringement statistics for the University of Delaware for the academic year 2009–2010. These statistics and the copyright violation policy are reprinted from the University of Delaware's security webpage (www.udel.edu/security/copyrightstats .html). Using social control theory and its variations, answer the following questions:

1. How might social control theory explain copyright infringement on a college campus?

2. How might social control theory explain the decrease in copyright infringement on the University of Delaware college campus?

3. In addition to the policies below, what might a social control theorist suggest as a policy to decrease copyright infringement on campuses?

Copyright Infringement Statistics Academic Year 2009–2010

This page shows the number of student computers that have been cited for copyright infringement and removed from the university's network in the [2009–2010] academic year. If you are a student, and you violate copyright laws, you:

1. Receive a *Copyright Violation Notice* with infringement specifics in your university e-mail account.
2. Have your network access disabled.
3. Must complete the Copyright Education course in Sakai.
4. Must schedule an appointment to have your computer examined by IT-Client Support & Services. You will be charged a fee for this service.
5. Will have your network access restored upon your completion of the Sakai course and examination of your system by IT-Client Support & Services.

Future incidents of alleged copyright infringement will be referred to the Office of Student Conduct.

Copyright Violations by Month

September '09	October '09	November '09	December '09	January '10	February '10	March '10	April '10	May '10	June '10	July '10	August '10
63	60	66	59	23	27	35	40	33	11	9	2

Copyright Violations Academic Year 2009–2010

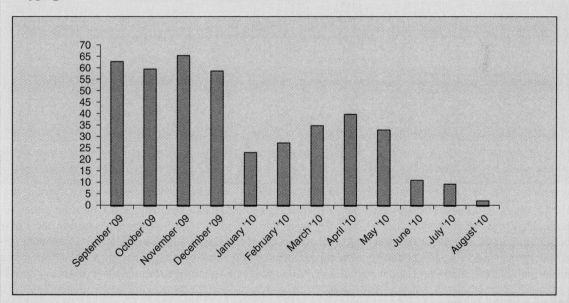

Conclusion

After discussing the theories above that traditionally fall under the heading of social control theory, it might be easy to suggest that they do not have much in common. The commonality between these theories, however, is their reliance on background assumptions that are based in the classical tradition of criminology—that is, the belief in a rational mind, an ability to make choices, and a belief that individuals want to maximize their pleasure and minimize their pain and must be restrained from engaging in deviance. And while many social control theories might engender robust disagreements among those who study deviant behavior, this is what makes this particular type of theory such a dynamic and central explanatory mechanism.

EXERCISES AND DISCUSSION QUESTIONS

1. Explain Sykes and Matza's techniques of neutralization. For each technique, give a real-world example of how that technique is in use today.

2. Watch a political exchange on CNN, MSNBC, or Fox News (preferably one in which two political parties are debating), or follow an exchange from an Internet news source. Can you identify techniques of neutralization in place to justify the behavior of either of the political parties?

3. Compare and contrast the theory of self-control (from *A General Theory of Crime* by Gottfredson and Hirschi, 1990) and the life course theory (from *Crime in the Making* by Sampson and Laub, 1993).

4. Explain the general difference between internal and external social controls. Choose one version of social control theory to illustrate the differences.

5. Explain Hirschi's four components of the social bond.

KEY TERMS

Age–crime curve

Attachment

Belief

Commitment

External control

Internal control

Involvement

Low self-control

Social bonds

Supervision

Trajectory

Transition

READING 19

Hirschi originally tested his theory with a sample of male high school students in Richmond, California, a community close to the University of California, Berkeley, where he attended graduate school. Subsequently, there have been numerous empirical tests of social control theory, primarily focusing on juvenile delinquency, with more representative samples of the U.S. population that also include females. However, most of the research has focused on adolescents in the United States, and few studies have attempted to assess the generalizability of the theory outside

Source: Cohen, B.-Z., & Zeira, R. (1999). Social control, delinquency, and victimization among kibbutz adolescents. *International Journal of Offender Therapy and Comparative Criminology, 43,* 503–513. Reprinted with permission.

the United States. Furthermore, while there are both theoretical and empirical reasons to believe that delinquency and victimization might be linked, few studies have examined the relationship between Hirschi's four bonds to society (attachment, commitment, involvement, and belief) and deviance. Here, Cohen and Zeira examine the relationship between an overall index of social control, including indicators of each of the four dimensions of social control developed by Hirschi and self-reported delinquency and victimization among high school students in the Kibbutzim of northern Israel. The Kibbutzim is a collective society originally based on an agricultural economy with socialist and Zionist ideals. The economy has expanded beyond agriculture and is much more capitalistic in nature. Still, the society is unique and provides a rare test of social control theory outside of mainstream American culture. The authors find that their measure of social control is negatively associated with unlicensed driving offenses and shoplifting as well as an index of victimization. Further multivariate analyses show that their measure of social control is not related to delinquency or victimization once gender and other measures are included. It is too bad that the analyses were not extended to examine the effects of social control separately for males and females as gender seemed to be the only variable associated with delinquency in the multivariate models. Still, this article does provide limited support that Hirschi's social control theory may be generalized outside the United States and to quite different societies and cultures.

Social Control, Delinquency, and Victimization Among Kibbutz Adolescents

Ben-Zion Cohen and Ruth Zeira

The kibbutz is one of the proudest accomplishments of Israeli society. For some six decades after the first kibbutz was founded at Degania in 1909, these collective settlements, although they rarely encompassed more than about 5% of the Israeli population, symbolized the pioneering spirit of the young Jewish state. The men and women of the kibbutz toiled long and hard to build and maintain their idealistic way of life, engaging in a wide range of physical labors and governing themselves with a unique system of members' committees and rotating executive assignments. The dominant branch of the kibbutz economy was agriculture and the workers were the members of the collective, although some kibbutzim even in the 1950s had developed industrial enterprises and many were employing limited numbers of salaried workers from the nearby towns in agriculture, industry, and services. The kibbutz raised and educated its children in the collective spirit and children lived with their peers in the children's houses until age 18 or 19 when they joined the army and were usually granted independent housing units. The kibbutzim, in most cases, maintained their own educational institutions with schools belonging jointly to several kibbutzim in the same area. During this period, with rare exceptions, the image of the kibbutz in Israeli society was untainted by images of corruption, delinquency, or deviance.

The kibbutzim entered into a series of radical changes in the 1960s. Industry and commerce became more important as agriculture became less labor intensive. Virtually all the kibbutzim conducted grand debates on child rearing and then moved the children into the parents' quarters for sleeping. Capitalist economics began to compete with socialist ideals in the workplace, and the Israeli media began to be more critical of kibbutz society, even reporting on such previously unheard-of topics such as alcohol, drugs, and delinquency in the kibbutz. Characteristically, social commentators tended to blame the first manifestations of deviant behavior in the kibbutzim on the young European and American volunteers who came to the kibbutzim after the 1967 Six Day War. Eventually, both the kibbutzim and their many urban supporters began to acknowledge the existence of such social problems as substance abuse and delinquent behavior in the indigenous kibbutz population.

The kibbutzim have a long-standing tradition of handling their problems internally and in many cases still prefer to cope with their own resources. Many kibbutz members considered calling on such outside agencies as the police or welfare authorities embarrassing, disloyal, and an admission of helplessness. In recent times, the kibbutzim have been more forthcoming about the presence of social problems, including delinquency, in their society. Kibbutz supporters have regarded the acknowledging of imperfections as a sign of resilience and as a cause for optimism about the survival of the kibbutz way of life. Today, there is enough openness in the system to allow studies such as the present research even if they do not guarantee complimentary results (Shoham, 1996).

The kibbutz is a self-contained, well-defined social system that has fought against economic inequality and promoted mutual responsibility among its members; even as the kibbutz economy has become more capitalistic in recent years, great effort has been invested in preserving these ideals (Oz, 1997). Similar to any complex social system, however, stratification proceeds along several dimensions, one of which is age. The norms of the older generation are quite different from those of the younger members, and the norms of the kibbutz adolescents are, as expected, considerably different from those of their parents. The adolescents are subject to a wide range of efforts by the adult establishment to reduce nonconformity and to induce the younger people to focus on becoming productive members of the kibbutz. Clearly, these efforts are not wholly successful. Some of the sons and daughters will not become members of the kibbutz at all; they will leave and go to the city. Others will become productive members; still others may become members but with imperfect motivation for productivity. The pressures to conform provide the backdrop for the study of kibbutz delinquency in the present study, which employs a theoretical framework derived from Hirschi's theory of social control (Hirschi, 1969). More than any other

theory in criminology, social control theory seeks to understand delinquency as the failure of the social system to generate conformist behavior.

The roots of social control theory, according to Kornhauser (1978), can be found in Thrasher's (1927) classic *The Gang*. Thrasher viewed both delinquent behavior and gang membership as results of ineffective social control. Shaw and McKay (1942) stressed the cultural transmission of delinquent norms but they too included the notion of controls in their theoretical formulations.

Additional early proponents of social control theories of delinquency include Reiss (1951), Toby (1957), Nye (1958), and Matza (1964). Reiss (1951) distinguished between personal and social controls and explained delinquency as the result of the failure of both types to direct behavior according to conventional norms. Toby (1957) regarded crime rates as reflecting social disorganization but his explanation of why certain persons in high-crime areas commit crimes (and others do not) referred to the individual's stake in conformity. Nye (1958) identified four different control factors: internalized control, or self-regulation; indirect control, which results from identification with noncriminals; needs satisfaction, which refers to the capacity to cope with the demands of school, work, friends, and so on; and direct control, which is the external system of rewards and punishments. Matza (1964) viewed delinquents as "drifting" between conventional commitments and criminal behavior patterns, with the drift into delinquency usually taking place when the naturally occurring bond between the individual and the moral order is temporarily weakened by the neutralization of conscience in the presence of temptation.

Building on the work of his predecessors, Hirschi (1969) articulated the most comprehensive social control explanation of delinquent behavior. His theory began with the assumption, found also in Nye (1958), that conformist behavior not delinquent behavior was the phenomenon requiring explanation. Hirschi explained conformist behavior as a consequence of the bond between society and individual. He also specified the elements of the social bond: attachment, commitment, involvement, and belief. *Attachment* has to do with sensitivity to the feelings and opinions of relevant others. *Commitment* refers to a person's investment of time and energy in a way of life. *Involvement* results from commitment; the choice of a way of life determines how an individual becomes involved in a delimited range of actions and relationships. *Belief,* according to Hirschi's theory, is the acceptance of the moral validity of conventional norms. Liska and Reed (1985) developed a nonrecursive version of social control theory, building on the assumption that the social bond not only affects delinquent behavior but is also affected by it. Their findings were consistent with their model of reciprocal influence.

Hirschi's (1969) study of 4,000 urban male junior and senior high school students in California confirmed the hypotheses derived from his theory of social control. Similar findings for rural male and female students in Grades 6 through 12 were presented by Hindelang (1973).

Krohn and Massey (1980) tested the elements of control theory on the self-report data of approximately 3,000 Grade 7 through 12 male and female students in the midwestern United States and found the components of social control theory differentially useful for explaining the delinquent behavior of subsamples of the participants in their study. Wiatrowski, Griswold, and Roberts (1981) constructed a more complex version of Hirschi's (1969) model and tested it on a large sample of 10th-grade boys from across the United States. Their findings supported control theory, as did those of Wiatrowski and Anderson (1987), who also studied a large national sample of adolescent males. Robbins (1984, 1985) explored the association of social control with delinquent behavior among American Indian youth living on reservations. The findings were somewhat ambiguous, but social control theory proved useful in explaining most of them. Social control variables were associated with all types of delinquent behavior in 12 of 13 countries (the single exception: vandalism in Holland) included in a collection of studies of self-report delinquency (Junger-Tas, Terlouw, & Klein, 1994).

Hirschi's more recent theoretical approach, developed with Gottfredson (Gottfredson & Hirschi, 1990), represents a shift of emphasis from social explanation of delinquent behavior to explanations based on individual differences. The theory of delinquency underlying the present research is Hirschi's earlier (1969) theory.

A classic tenet in the study of victimology (Hindelang, Gottfredson, & Garofalo, 1978; Lauritsen, Sampson, & Laub, 1991; Schafer, 1968) is the similarity of victim and offender in social status. From this proposition, it follows that if degree of social control predicts delinquent behavior within a given population, it should also be associated with delinquency victimizations within that population. Individuals with weaker ties to the social order should be more vulnerable. Moreover, previous research has found that in juvenile populations, involvement in delinquency is a predictor of victimization (Esbensen & Huizinga, 1991; Jensen & Brownfield, 1986; Thornberry & Figlio, 1974).

The present research is designed to test the utility of Hirschi's theory for understanding delinquent behavior and victimization in a sample of kibbutz adolescents. The hypothesis of this study is that the likelihood of both delinquency and victimization will be greater for those youth for whom the bonds of social control are weaker.

◈ Results

The first item of interest in the analysis is the prevalence of delinquent behavior in the sample. Table 1 displays the percentage of respondents reporting having committed each of the two focal offenses and the percentage reporting having committed either.

Thirty percent (132) of the respondents report never having committed either focal offense. Thus, a great majority (70%, 308) admit to having committed at least one of these offenses at least once. The offense of driving without a license is the more common of the two focal offenses, with 58.6% (258) reporting having done this at least once. Theft from the kibbutz mini-market was admitted by 34.4% (151) of the youth in the study.

The frequency of reported offenses, by gender, is presented in Table 2.

The distribution of offending among the male participants is very different from that of the females. Within the three-category breakdown of Table 2, the largest number of males (81.3%, 178) report having committed more than one offense, whereas the largest group of females (46.6%, 103) are those reporting no offenses. In the single-offense category, there are many more females (23.5%, 52) than males (5.5%, 12).

The first part of the hypothesis of this study predicted an association between social control and delinquency. The Pearson correlation coefficients for the associations between the 24-item index of social control and the number of reported offenses, by offense, and for all offenses, are presented in Table 3.

As seen in Table 3, the correlations of social control with unlicensed driving offenses ($r = -.18$), with mini-market thefts ($r = -.17$), and for total offenses ($r = -.16$), are weak but in the expected direction and statistically significant.

The second part of the study hypothesis predicted an association between social control and victimization. Table 4 displays the six types of victimizations investigated, the number of respondents reporting *never, once,* or *more than once* having been victimized in the past year, and the mean number of victimizations by type.

As seen in Table 4, the most common type of victimization is property damage ($M = 2.6$, $SD = 2.6$) and

Table 3   Correlations of Social Control With Delinquency

Correlation	R	P
Social control index with unlicensed driving offenses	−.18	<.001
Social control index with mini-market theft offenses	−.17	<.001
All offenses	−.16	<.001

Table 4   Type and Number of Reported Victimizations

Type of Victimization	Number of Victimizations				
	0	1	2+	M	SD
Taking of property	133	45	247	2.6	2.6
Damage to property	200	54	173	1.4	1.7
Violent threats	323	40	70	0.7	1.6
Nonviolent sexual harassment/abuse	411	10	10	0.1	0.8
Violent sexual abuse	427	1	3	0.02	0.3

Table 1   Offenses Reported by Repondent (N = 440)

Number of Offenses	Driving Without a License	Theft From Mini-Market	Either Offense
0	41.4%	65.6% (289)	30.0% (132)
1	12.7% (56)	13.9% (61)	14.5% (64)
2+	45.9% (202)	20.5% (90)	35.5% (244)

Table 2   Offenses Reported by Gender (N = 440)

Number of Offenses	Males	Females
0	13.2% (29)	46.6% (103)
1	5.5% (12)	23.5% (52)
2+	81.3% (178)	29.9% (66)
Totals	100.0% (219)	100.0% (221)

the least common is violent sexual abuse ($M = 0.02$, $SD = 0.3$). With the exception of property offenses, the majority of respondents reported no victimizations having occurred in the past year.

The Pearson correlation coefficient for the association between the 24-item index of social control and the number of reported victimizations is in the expected direction, of moderate strength ($r = -.18$), and statistically significant ($p < .001$).

To examine the influence of social control on delinquency with other relevant variables controlled, a multiple regression was performed. A series of independent variables likely to reflect social status of

Table 5 Multiple Regression on Total Offenses

Independent Variable	B	SE of B	Beta
Gender	−2.57	.22	−.50*
Age	0.24	.17	.09
Time spent with friends	0.08	.05	.06
Social control	−0.34	.22	−.06
Works as youth leader (0 = no, 1 = yes)	−0.27	.24	−.05
Born in kibbutz (0 = no, 1 = yes)	−0.02	.03	.02
Age moved into children's house	−0.05	.07	−.03
Mother born in kibbutz (0 = no, 1 = yes)	−0.12	.22	−.02
Father born in kibbutz (0 = no, 1 = yes)	0.13	.22	.03
Grade	−0.02	.21	−.10

Note: R^2(adj.) = .30.

*$p < .001$.

adolescents in the kibbutz were entered into the analysis. In addition to age, gender, and grade, these included whether the respondent and each of his or her parents were born in the kibbutz, how many hours per week are spent with friends, and whether the young person acts as a youth leader with younger children. The results of the multiple regression analysis appear in Table 5.

As indicated in Table 5, gender (beta = .50) is the strongest predictor of delinquent behavior; the delinquent acts are more likely to be committed by youth who are male. The contribution of the other independent variables, including social control, to the regression equation did not reach statistical significance. The variance in delinquent behavior explained by the independent variables in Table 5 reached 30%.

An additional multiple regression analysis, with the same independent variables and with number of victimizations as the dependent variable, explained only 7% of the variance and is not presented here.

◈ Discussion

The hypothesis of this study predicted that delinquent behavior and victimization among kibbutz youth would prove to be associated with social control as measured by the index developed here. The bivariate tests of the hypothesis yielded results that are, at best, ambiguous. The correlations of social control with each type of delinquency and with both in combination are in the expected direction and are statistically significant but they are too weak (< .20) to regard as confirmation of the hypothesis even at the bivariate level. The results of the multiple regression analyses lend no support to the hypothesis; only gender makes a statistically significant contribution to predicting delinquent behavior, social control does not. The association with gender is expected and virtually universal; boys reported more offenses than girls in all 13 countries included in a group of studies of self-reported delinquency (Junger-Tas et al., 1994). According to Heimer (1996), much research on the relationship of gender to delinquency attributes males' higher rates of offending to the weaker social controls usually exercised on boys. The present study, too, found the familiar pattern of higher delinquency rates for boys and also found a slightly higher degree of social control for girls ($M = 4.4$, $SD = 0.5$) than for boys ($M = 4.1$, $SD = 0.5$) in the kibbutz.

If social control was measured in a manner both valid and relevant to the social setting, and the authors believe it was, the results of this research indicate that the distribution of delinquent behaviors among kibbutz adolescents is consistent with but not strongly supportive of social control theory. One possible reason for this may be that with the influence of the peer group in the kibbutz so powerful, the social bonds to adult society have less direct impact on adolescent behavior.

The experience of adolescence in the kibbutz, even with the extensive changes the kibbutzim are undergoing in recent years (Oz, 1997), is quite different from adolescent experience in the urban settings of North America that have served as the test sites for the dominant theories of delinquency over the years. The patterns of relationships between different age groups in the kibbutz also differ significantly from those of urban families in Israel, as do the development of gender identities, and the residents of Israel are aware of the differences. A recent study, for example, found that urban Israeli adolescents perceived their male kibbutz counterparts as more masculine (Lobel & Bar, 1997). For kibbutz adolescents, the vast majority of whom grow to maturity in the very same communities where they were born, their daily routine and physical environment are safe, structured, and familiar. Within the community structure, they usually enjoy greater access to opportunities for academic, vocational, recreational, social, and sexual experimentation than their urban cousins. The disjointedness of contemporary adolescent lifestyles in the United States, as described by Felson (1998), and the delinquent career trajectories of the rural adolescents who participated in the recent study by Myner, Santman, Cappelletty, and Perlmutter (1998) are far removed from kibbutz life. Thus, these findings should be seen as evidence from a different culture as to the relevance of control theory. Multicultural evidence can enhance criminological understanding, but generalizing across cultures requires great caution.

If opportunities can be created for additional studies in the future, the authors would suggest building multiple theoretical models whose explanatory powers can be evaluated comparatively, and adding a sample of urban youth to explore the ways in which kibbutz youth differ from their urban counterparts.

◈ References

Binder, A., & Geis, G. (1983). *Methods of research in criminal justice and criminology.* New York: McGraw-Hill.

Brown, S. E., Esbensen, F.-A., & Geis, G. (1991). *Criminology: Explaining crime and its context.* Cincinnati, OH: Anderson.

Esbensen, F.-A., & Huizinga, D. (1991). Juvenile victimization and delinquency. *Youth and Society, 23,* 202–228.

Felson, M. (1998). *Crime and everyday life* (2nd ed.). Thousand Oaks, CA: Pine Forge Press.

Gold, M. (1966). Undetected delinquent behavior. *Journal of Research in Crime and Delinquency, 3,* 27–46.

Gottfredson, M. R., & Hirschi, T. (1990). *A general theory of crime.* Stanford, CA: Stanford University Press.

Heimer, K. (1996). Gender, interaction, and delinquency: Testing a theory of differential social control. *Social Psychology Quarterly, 59,* 39–61.

Hindelang, M. J. (1973). Causes of delinquency: A partial replication and extension. *Social Problems, 20,* 471–487.

Hindelang, M. J., Gottfredson, M. R., & Garofalo, J. (1978). *Victims of personal crime: An empirical foundation for a theory of personal victimization.* Cambridge, MA: Ballinger.

Hirschi, T. (1969). *Causes of delinquency.* Berkeley, CA: University of California Press.

Hood, R., & Sparks, R. (1970). *Key issues in criminology.* New York: McGraw-Hill.

Jensen, G., & Brownfield, D. (1986). Gender, lifestyles and victimization: Beyond routine activity. *Violence and Victims, 1,* 85–99.

Junger-Tas, J., Terlouw, G., & Klein, M.W. (Eds.). (1994). *Delinquent behavior among young people in the Western world: First results of the international self-report delinquency study.* Amsterdam: Kugler.

Kornhauser, R. R. (1978). *Social sources of delinquency: An appraisal of analytic models.* Chicago: University of Chicago Press.

Krohn, M. D., & Massey, J. L. (1980). Social control and delinquent behavior: An examination of the elements of the social bond. *Sociological Quarterly, 21,* 529–543.

Lauritsen, J. L., Sampson, R. J., & Laub, J. H. (1991). The link between victimization and offending among adolescents. *Criminology, 29,* 265–291.

Liska, A. E., & Reed, M. D. (1985). Ties to conventional institutions and delinquency: Estimating reciprocal effects. *American Sociological Review, 50,* 547–560.

Lobel, T. E., & Bar, E. (1997). Perception of masculinity and femininity of kibbutz and urban adolescents. *Sex Roles, 37,* 283–293.

Matza, D. (1964). *Delinquency and drift.* New York: John Wiley.

Myner, J., Santman, J., Cappelletty, G. G., & Perlmutter, B. F. (1998). Variables related to recidivism among juvenile offenders. *International Journal of Offender Therapy and Comparative Criminology, 42*, 65–80.

Nye, F. I. (1958). *Family relationships and delinquent behavior.* New York: John Wiley.

Oz, A. (1997). On social democracy and the kibbutz. *Dissent, 44,* 39–46.

Reiss, A. J., Jr. (1951). Delinquency as the failure of personal and social controls. *American Sociological Review, 16,* 196–207.

Robbins, S. P. (1984). Anglo concepts and Indian reality: A study of juvenile delinquency. *Social Casework, 65,* 235–241.

Robbins, S. P. (1985). Commitment, belief, and Native American delinquency. *Human Organization, 44,* 57–62.

Schafer, S. (1968). *The victim and his criminal.* New York: Random House.

Shaw, C. R., & McKay, H. D. (1942). *Juvenile delinquency and urban areas.* Chicago: University of Chicago Press.

Shoham, E. (1996). The attitude of kibbutz youth to rape: Myth versus reality. *International Journal of Offender Therapy and Comparative Criminology, 40,* 212–223.

Sutton, L. P. (1978). *Federal criminal sentencing: Perspectives of analysis and a design for research.* Washington, DC: Department of Justice.

Thornberry, T. P., & Figlio, R. M. (1974). Victimization and criminal behavior in a birth cohort. In T. P. Thornberry & E. Sagarin (Eds.), *Images of crime: Offenders and victims* (pp. 102–112). New York: Praeger.

Thrasher, F. M. (1927). *The gang.* Chicago: University of Chicago Press.

Toby, J. (1957). Social disorganization and stake in conformity: Complementary factors in the predatory behavior of hoodlums. *Journal of Criminal Law, Criminology, and Police Science, 48,* 12–17.

Wiatrowski, M., & Anderson, K. L. (1987). The dimensionality of the social bond. *Journal of Quantitative Criminology, 3,* 65–81.

Wiatrowski, M. D., Griswold, D. B., & Roberts, M. K. (1981). Social control theory and delinquency. *American Sociological Review, 46,* 525–541.

READING 20

It is rare that theories of deviance make their way into marketing journals, but researchers from the Warwick Business School did exactly that in this article focused on illegal Internet "misbehavior" and the techniques of neutralization that enable primarily conventional individuals to engage in this type of deviant behavior. Sykes and Matza began with five neutralizations: denial of responsibility, denial of injury, denial of the victim, condemnation of the condemners, and an appeal to higher loyalties. Others have unearthed such neutralization techniques as defense of necessity, claim to normalcy, and denial of negative intent, among others. These researchers interviewed a convenience sample of 54 informants who had engaged in illegal "peer-to-peer" downloading of CDs, DVDs, video games, or other software in the 2 weeks prior to the interview. The researchers found that these criminals used at least one and often several neutralizations, including denial of injury, claim of normalcy, claim of relative acceptability, appeal to higher loyalties, and denial of responsibility. We are sure the reader can imagine the types of neutralizations these offenders use; you may have used some yourself and will enjoy reading about them. Perhaps more interesting, the researchers find that some techniques are typically established prior to the act (perhaps indicative of a causal relationship) as well as after the fact (e.g., to neutralize guilt). Also interesting was that more than half (61%) were against legal and free downloading, which they believed would crush the entertainment industry as creators would not be compensated. Further, and consistent with Sykes and Matza, these deviants appear to understand that many consider their activities deviant, immoral, and illegal, but they believe the drift from conventional society can be justified in their cases.

Source: Harris, L. C., & Dumas, A. (2009). Online consumer misbehaviour: An application of neutralization theory. *Marketing Theory* 9, 379–402. Reprinted with permission.

Online Consumer Misbehaviour

An Application of Neutralization Theory

Lloyd C. Harris and Alexia Dumas

 Introduction

In recent years researchers have uncovered a range of diverse behaviors by consumers which disrupt otherwise functional exchange (see for example Withiam, 1998; Fullerton and Punj, 2004; Harris and Reynolds, 2004; Harris and Reynolds, 2006; Harris, 2008a). However, at the end of the 1990s, concordant with rapidly growing consumer internet use, a new type of consumer misbehaviour emerged. In 1999, Napster, the pioneer network of illegal downloading, was created and online digital piracy was popularized. Despite its closure two years later, peer-to-peer networks did not disappear; on the contrary they flourished. Neither a reinforcement of copyright, nor strengthened laws, nor the launch of online purchasing of digital media appeared able to prevent these illegal activities from becoming common practice. Indeed, the internet has become ever more convenient and user-friendly, making digital piracy easily available to consumers. Whether peer-to-peer activities involve copying music, movies, software or video games, the phenomenon affects the entertainment sector as a whole and costs the industry billions of pounds each year.

While a number of studies have explored online customer misbehaviour, typically focusing on a particular type of activity (see Hinduja, 2007), to date, broader theories regarding deviant human behaviour, such as neutralization theory (Sykes and Matza, 1957) have been neglected (see Cohn and Vaccaro, 2006; Hinduja, 2007). Sykes and Matza (1957) uncover five 'techniques of neutralization' which individuals employ to justify or rationalize their deviant behaviours. The application of the theory within criminology and broader sociology has subsequently extended these techniques and found strong support for cognitive deviance-neutralization as a justification or rationalization mechanism (e.g. Cromwell and Thurman, 2003; Fritsche, 2005). In customer-focused studies,

neutralization theory has been somewhat neglected, with the notable exceptions of a small number of insightful treatises into neutralization techniques and shoplifting (Strutton et al., 1994), consumer fraud (Rosenbaum and Kuntze, 2003), and generational differences (Strutton et al., 1997), all within offline retailing. This leads both Cohn and Vaccaro (2006) and Hinduja (2007) to argue that neutralization theory provides an insightful but neglected perspective from which to explore online consumer deviance and peer-to-peer deviance in particular.

The aim of this paper is to explore the extent to which peer-to-peer users employ techniques of neutralization to justify prior-to behaviour or rationalize their activities post behaviour. A particular emphasis is placed on the need to generate insights into the timing of neutralizations (that is, pre- or post-event) and in this way respond to the many studies that have called for more research into the sequencing of neutralization processes (e.g. Cromwell and Thurman, 2003; Maruna and Copes, 2005). This study is also intended to provide a better understanding of a phenomenon which increasingly troubles the entertainment industry, and can be viewed as a response to the calls by a number of researchers for more research into online consumers' neutralization practices (see Cohn and Vaccaro, 2006; Hinduja, 2007). Indeed, digital piracy, more than any other dysfunctional consumer behaviour, has significantly impacted on companies' business models.

This paper is structured in the following way. First, a review of online customer misbehaviour is provided, followed by an overview of existing research into the techniques of neutralization. Following a discussion of the research methods employed, findings regarding the peer-to-peer online misbehaviours and neutralization techniques are presented. The paper concludes with a series of implications for both theory and practice.

◈ Online Consumer Misbehaviour

Freestone and Mitchell (2004: 126) claim that the internet is the 'new environment for unethical behaviour'. Similarly to offline customers, who misbehave in a wide variety of ways (see Harris and Reynolds, 2003), online misbehaviours vary from digital piracy to fraud. These and other behaviours cost some industries billions of dollars in lost sales every year. For instance, in the music industry, the Recording Industry Association of America (RIAA) states 'global music piracy causes $12.5 billion of economic losses every year', while the Motion Picture Association of America (MPAA) declares: 'the worldwide motion picture industry [. . .] lost $18.2 billion in 2005 as a result of piracy'.

There are various types of online customer misbehaviour. Chatzidakis and Mitussis (2007: 306) state: 'Internet enables the proliferation of various ethically questionable consumer activities.' With the development of the internet, new kinds of dysfunctional consumer behaviour appear, taking advantage of this new technology: 'Love bug', a virus sent in May 2000 via an e-mail entitled 'I love you' and which infected tens of millions of computers (Foremski and Kehoe, 2000), software piracy, fraud (including Nigerian email fraud, cheque fraud, investment fraud, confidence fraud, auction fraud, non-delivery and credit/debit card fraud—see Mazur, 2007); piracy, illegal forms of pornography, cyber stalking, online pharmacies, organ sales and identity theft (Freestone and Mitchell, 2004). Indeed, in 2006, there were 207,492 internet crimes (or e-crimes) reported (Mazur, 2007). Simpson (2006: 14) defines 'e-crimes' as covering

> many different areas, including phishing, hacking, extortion, denial of service attacks, advanced fee fraud, money laundering; virus writing, distributing malicious code, botherding, grooming, distributing pedophile material, internet abuse in the work place, intellectual property theft, online piracy of copyright material, and spamming.

Freestone and Mitchell (2004) suggest a complete typology of deviant internet behaviour regarding five main activities. First are *illegal activities* such as using credit card numbers discovered on the internet or a stolen credit card; downloading child pornography; spreading viruses; selling counterfeit goods over the internet; or sending malicious e-mail, to name but a few (Freestone and Mitchell, 2004). Second are *questionable activities* which are not necessarily illegal and are usually victimless (for example purchasing potentially offensive products over the internet; online gambling; or accessing distasteful websites). Third are illegal hacking related activities such as changing hardware or software products. Fourth are *human internet trading activities* such as purchasing human organs. Finally is the issue of downloading material. This is related to the downloading of movies, music, games or software from the internet for free. These activities are found to be extremely common among young internet users and not necessarily perceived as being unethical.

It is the final category of online customer misbehaviour that is the focus of the current paper. Whether it is software piracy, also named 'softlifting' (for example Logsdon et al., 1994; Simpson et al., 1994; Gupta et al., 2004; Goles et al., 2008); peer-to-peer (P2P) file-sharing or music piracy (Gopal et al., 2004; Levin et al., 2004; Chiou et al., 2005; Chen et al., 2008); or digital piracy in general (Al-Rafee and Cronan, 2006; Hill, 2007; Cronan and Al-Rafee, 2008), this type of crime has been found to be widespread and, arguably, endemic to the internet.

In an effort to explore the reasons for the prevalence of these activities, researchers have generated some insights into the drivers of illegal downloading. Ingram and Hinduja (2008) determine that illegal downloaders are likely to be males, under 21 and white. Group influence, especially through online communities, is also significant (see for example Chiou et al., 2005; Sandulli, 2007). Such studies argue that peer groups may affect consumer behaviour on the internet even more than any other consumer behaviours, since the internet enables individuals easily to contact each other and renders the creation of communities easier.

Chatzidakis and Mitussis (2007) highlight the importance of the internet's scope on unethical internet behaviour. Not only does the internet permit the accomplishment of deviant consumer behaviour anonymously but it also makes it more difficult to identify unethical activities. First, individuals can remain 'faceless'. This makes the choice to engage in aberrant internet behaviour easier (Freestone and Mitchell, 2004; Rombel, 2004), while the impersonal side of the internet alleviates the guilt created by misconduct (Logsdon et al., 1994). This theory is also supported by the work of Reynolds and Harris (2005: 328), in which one of the informants declares: 'there is no face-to-face contact so you don't feel guilty . . . it definitely gives me more nerve'. Second, since individuals remain anonymous, deviant internet behaviours are difficult to detect and are more likely to go unpunished (Freestone and Mitchell, 2004; Chiou et al., 2005; Al-Rafee and Cronan, 2006). As Albers-Miller (1999: 275) highlights, 'when there is a lack of fear of punishment, people do engage in inappropriate behaviour'.

The ability to use virtual persona influences unethical internet behaviour all the more (Freestone and Mitchell, 2004). The internet's reproducibility makes deviant internet activities even more attractive. It is convenient (Sandulli, 2007) and permits the reproduction of CDs, software or DVDs very cheaply. In the case of music piracy for instance, illegally downloading enables individuals both to save money (Gopal et al., 2004; Cronan and Al-Rafee, 2008) and to end up with a 'burned' CD of virtually the same quality as a copyrighted CD (Sherman, 2000; Bhattacharjee et al., 2003).

In some regards, the internet offers an unprecedented opportunity to engage in aberrant behaviour. Ease of engaging (Gupta et al., 2004), ease of use (Sherman, 2000), access (Levin et al., 2004), flexibility (Sandulli, 2007), situational events (Simpson et al., 1994), internet speed and proficiency (Bhattacharjee et al., 2003; Levin et al., 2004; Rombel, 2004; Cronan and Al-Rafee, 2008; Ingram and Hinduja, 2008), the possibility to customize CDs or discover new talents (Gopal et al., 2004; Sandulli, 2007) are some of the reasons affecting internet users' behaviour.

Numerous studies suggest that some consumers believe that illegal downloading is ethically acceptable. Vitell and Muncy's (1992) study reveals that 46% of the 569 US heads of households interviewed believe that it is not wrong to record an album instead of buying it. Among the 71 informants of Fukukawa's (2002) research, 58% think that copying computer software or using unauthorized

software is acceptable and 32% actively softlift; furthermore, 71% claim that recording a tape or CD instead of buying a new copy in a shop is acceptable, with 52% already engaging in this deviant behaviour. Vitell and Muncy's (2005) survey discloses that 26% of informants strongly believe that downloading music from the internet instead of buying it is not wrong, against 11% who strongly believe that it is. Finally, Ingram and Hinduja (2008) unveil that 90% of their sample believes that downloading music illegally was an *appropriate* behaviour.

These results illustrate the problem intellectual property faces. Individuals do not give the same value to music, words or ideas that they confer to physical objects. This theory is significantly supported within the literature (Vitell and Muncy, 1992; Logsdon et al., 1994; Cheng et al., 1997; Kearns, 2001). Vitell and Muncy's (1992: 303) findings highlight that whereas 99% of informants (71% strongly) consider 'drinking a can of soda in a supermarket without paying for it' as wrong, only 34% (12% strongly) believe that 'recording an album instead of buying it' is unethical. These results are confirmed by Cheng et al. (1997: 56), who state: 'stealing a candy bar would not be tolerated while pirating software worth hundreds of dollars is generally condoned'.

In summary, illegal downloading by consumers is widespread and the nature of the internet greatly facilitates these behaviours. Moreover, many consumers appear tolerant and accepting of this misbehaviour and seem to rationalize or justify their illegal activities in some way. Given these insights, neutralization theory appears to provide an interesting perspective from which to analyse how online consumers reduce guilt or justify their actions (Cohn and Vaccaro, 2006; Hinduja, 2007).

◈ Techniques of Neutralization

The term 'techniques of neutralization' was first used in 1957 by Sykes and Matza in their article 'Techniques of neutralization: A theory of delinquency'. At that time, one of the main interests in criminology was the analysis of delinquency in order to understand such a deviant behaviour, especially among adolescents (Cromwell and Thurman, 2003). An investigation of juvenile delinquency led Sykes and Matza (1957) to propose five techniques of neutralization as an explanation of this misbehaviour (denial of responsibility, denial of injury, denial of victim, condemning the condemners and appealing to higher loyalties). Subsequently, Cohn and Vaccaro (2006: 71) note that techniques of neutralization have been employed to explain activities as diverse and numerous as shoplifting (Strutton et al., 1994; Cromwell and Thurman, 2003); marketing (Vitell and Grove, 1987); deer poaching (Eliason and Dodder, 2000); abortion (Brennan, 1974); genocide (Alvarez, 1997); religious dissonance (Dunford and Kunz, 1973); cheating in exams (Smith et al., 2004; Atmen and Al-Hadassah, 2008); hired killing (Levi, 1981); white-collar criminality (Pique et al., 2005); and finally, music piracy (Cohn and Vaccaro, 2006; Ingram and Hinduja, 2008).

According to Sykes and Matza (1957: 666), techniques of neutralization are used in order to 'protect [...] the individual from self-blame and the blame of others after the act'. They can be linked to what Mills (1940) names 'vocabularies of motive'. They enable individuals engaging in dysfunctional consumer behaviour to diminish the impact of their misconduct in their own eyes and those of others. As Chatzidakis et al. (2004: 528) state, the techniques of neutralization are 'ways in which consumers rationalize their behaviour in order to deal with the consequences of acting in ways that are not consistent with their core ethical values and beliefs'. Individuals use techniques of neutralization as 'guilt-reducing mechanisms' (Mitchell and Dodder, 1980: 241) in order to explain their misbehaviour and reduce both the consequences of their acts and their feelings of guilt. In the context of digital piracy, studies suggest that many (but far from all) illegal downloaders self-report their belief that their actions are ethically acceptable. This suggests five possible scenarios. First, such downloaders have rationalized or neutralized their actions to the extent that the ethical issues that were (presumably) initially encountered have been resolved (that is, neutralization has occurred and/or is occurring). Second, the psychological costs of norm violation in the form of social or legal chastisement are viewed as so improbably low as to be worth the cost/risk (a risk/cost which requires some neutralization). Third, self-reports of a belief that such actions are ethically acceptable may be reinforcing rationalizations in themselves (that is, denial

of ethical issue as a neutralization technique); or fourth, the public espousal of an ethical norm does not equate to cognitive acceptance (leading to the need for neutralization/ justification); or fifth, such behaviours are (and always have been) genuinely viewed as unethically unproblematic and that no neutralization or rationalization is required. Given the findings of Cohn and Vaccaro (2006) and Hinduja (2007), the first four scenarios seem eminently more probable than the fifth.

Originally, Sykes and Matza (1957) proposed five techniques of neutralization that can explain juvenile delinquency: denial of responsibility, denial of injury, denial of victim, condemning the condemners and appealing to higher loyalties.

1. *'Denial of responsibility'* enables individuals to cast the responsibility of their aberrant behaviour on someone else or on the circumstances. They are not really guilty since 'factors beyond their control' (Vitell and Grove, 1987: 434) cause their misbehaviour.

2. *'Denial of injury'* lessens the consequences of misconducts, emphasizing the lack of direct harm and therefore making the behaviour more acceptable.

3. *'Denial of victim'* is not used to refute the unethical side of the behaviour. It helps individuals to explain their motives by claiming that 'the violated party deserved whatever happened' (Vitell and Grove, 1987: 434).

4. *'Condemning the condemners'* enables individuals to shift the attention towards those who criticize them 'by pointing out that they engage in similar disapproved behaviour' (Vitell and Grove, 1987: 434).

5. *'Appealing to higher loyalties'* is used by individuals to explain that their aberrant behaviour is 'the by-product of their attempt to actualize a higher order ideal or value' (Vitell and Grove, 1987: 434).

Subsequently, researchers have identified other techniques, including: defence of necessity and metaphor of the ledger (Klockars, 1974; Minor, 1981); claim of normalcy, denial of negative intent and claim of relative acceptability (Henry, 1990); denial of the necessity of the law and the claim that everybody else is doing it (Coleman, 1994); and justification by comparison and postponement (Cromwell and Thurman, 2003).

1. *'Defence of necessity'* is argued by Minor (1981: 298) to mean that 'if an act is perceived as necessary, then one need not feel guilty about its commission, even if it is considered morally wrong in the abstract'. This technique corresponds to Coleman's (1994) denial of the *necessity of the law.*

2. *'Metaphor of the ledger'* implicates counterbalancing all the good and bad behaviours, thereby tolerating the aberrant behaviour in question.

3. *'Claim of normalcy'* insists that everybody engages in such activities, and thereby being commonplace, such behaviour cannot really be perceived as wrong (Coleman, 1994).

4. *'Denial of negative intent'* diminishes responsibility, since the behaviour was not supposed to cause any harm.

5. *'Claims of relative acceptability'* or 'justification by comparison' intend to minimize the consequences of the aberrant behaviour by drawing a comparison with other perpetrators or with more questionable forms of behaviour.

6. *'Postponement'* enables individuals to 'simply put the incident out of their mind' (Cromwell and Thurman, 2003: 547). Cromwell and Thurman (2003) observed that during the interviews, participants often use this technique in order to explain why they engage in shoplifting.

In summary, neutralization theory provides an insightful perspective from which to elucidate how aberrant human behaviours are justified or rationalized by participants. In the case of online customer misbehaviour and illegal downloading in particular, both Cohn and Vaccaro (2006) and Hinduja (2007) argue that focusing on online consumers' use of such techniques generates useful insights into how such consumers justify their illegal activities.

◈ Research Methodology

The aim of this paper is to explore the extent to which peer-to-peer users employ techniques of neutralization to justify prior-to behaviour or rationalize their activities post behaviour. While previous studies have generated insights into online misbehaviour the nature and dynamics of online consumers' application of neutralization techniques remains understudied (Cohn and Vaccaro, 2006; Hinduja, 2007). In particular, empirical insights into the sequencing of neutralizations are limited. While experimental or longitudinal studies are needed definitely to establish causality between cognitions and acts, in the current study an exploratory research design was deemed appropriate to generate insights into the sequencing of online consumer misbehaviour.

In order to develop a greater understanding of the core concepts within this area a qualitative interview-based approach was adopted, as in-depth interviews are particularly useful in generating 'rich' and 'deep' insights into complex phenomena (see Miller, 1991; Bryman, 2004). An advantage of in-depth interviews is the capture of the informant's perspective on key issues, using their own jargon and language; characteristics which are of particular value when the issues under research are sensitive or ethically questionable (Stainback and Stainback, 1988; Iacobucci and Churchill, 2006).

In order to achieve these goals, a central issue was identifying and gaining access to suitable informants (Crimp and White, 2000). As a result, this study adopted a 'discovery-oriented' design akin to that of Mahrer (1988). To produce a knowledgeable sample, a purposive sampling plan was utilized comparable to that used and recommended by Harris and Reynolds (2003) in their study of dysfunctional downloading and their knowledge of online service dynamics. All informants had participated in peer-to-peer downloading within the last two weeks. In total, 54 informants were interviewed, of which 34 were male. The ages of informants ranged from 18 to 48 years (the average age being 26.3). Males are more represented than females in the sample, since they download more through peer-to-peer networks, and informants are all relatively young since peer-to-peer file-sharers are composed mainly of young people (Gopal et al., 2004; Sandulli,

2007; Ingram and Hinduja, 2008). All 54 informants have at least once illegally downloaded music or movies; 34 of them have also pirated software and 17 of them have illegally copied video games. The informants engaged in illegal downloading activities twice a week on average (varying from once a month to several times each day).

All the interviews were conducted individually and typically lasted 50 minutes (although some lasted for as long as 90 minutes). Given the potentially illegal nature of the activities studied, and to reduce potential social desirability bias, informant confidentiality and anonymity were guaranteed. To ensure the accuracy of data collection, all interviews were audio-recorded and subsequently transcribed by the interviewer and annotated with notes taken during the interview. As recommended by Lindolf (1995), wherever appropriate, the interviewer took the opportunity to pursue potentially interesting lines of inquiry and to encourage elaboration of particular events or episodes. Interviews began with explicit confidentiality assurances in order to aid open discussion on the part of the informant. Particular emphasis was placed on noting informants' comments regarding the timing of neutralizations (pre-, during or post behaviour) and on critically exploring timing claims.

Data collection was terminated at the point which Strauss and Corbin (1998) label 'theoretical saturation' (the point at which no new insights are divulged). Subsequent data analysis followed a systematic process of transcript-based analysis following a form of the iterative stage process summarized by Turner (1981) and advocated by Reynolds and Harris (2005) as especially beneficial in the study of customer misbehaviour. The approach of Turner (1981) entails seven separate phases of analysis (generating categories, category saturation, abstract definition development, use of definitions, category explanation, category linkage and linkage evaluation) complemented by the iterative evaluation of the analysis after each phase. The analytical approach adopted is consistent with the suggestion of Dey (1993), in that the context of action and the social actors are described in such a way that facilitated the task of classifying and assessing the interconnectedness of themes. This approach has also been described as 'abductive reasoning' (Coffey and Atkinson, 1996). Nevertheless, it should be acknowledged that the method employed

(in part) evaluates an existing theoretical framework and therefore has a deductive element.

To improve the reliability and validity of the data collection, a systematic approach to data collection and analysis was adopted (Yin, 2003). Further, internal and external veracity checks of analyses were undertaken (see Price et al., 2000). Internally, coding procedures were reviewed by an experienced researcher, while externally, preliminary and final analyses were reviewed by five consumers during ex-post interviews. To maintain the anonymity of individuals and organizations, details encompassing informants' names and locations have been changed.

 ## Findings

Data analysis reveals that peer-to-peer file-sharers employ up to seven different techniques of neutralization in order to rationalize or justify their activities: denial of victim, denial of injury, denial of responsibility, claim of normality, claim of relative acceptability, justification by comparison and appeal to higher loyalties. The remainder of this section is devoted to the discussion of each of these neutralization techniques.

Denial of Victim

This technique of neutralization is one of the most exploited by peer-to-peer file-sharers to pre-justify their illegal activities. Informants often blame entertainment companies for their misbehaviour. It is mainly the case for record labels, in particular the Big Four (Warner Music, Universal Music Group, EMI Recorded Music, Sony/BMG Entertainment), since informants mostly illegally download music from the internet, but was also used against major software companies. Interestingly, this technique of neutralization appeared to be used mainly prior to the behaviour. Throughout the interviews, participants raised two main arguments to insist on denial of victim: unjustifiably high prices; and perceived exploitation by multinational firms.

None of the interviews were conducted without the informant reproaching the excessive prices set by the software, video game, DVD and music industries. For instance, one informant confesses:

I recently wanted to buy an album in a shop. The album is quite old so I expected it to be at a reduced price but it was actually more expensive than some brand new albums! If it had been in the shop for around 10 dollars, I would have bought it there but they set such a high price that they just encourage people to download. (Male, 26)

These findings confirm what has been previously highlighted in the literature review section: price can lead people to misbehave (see Levin et al., 2004; Al-Rafee and Cronan, 2006; Sandulli, 2007). All the participants believe that in setting high prices, companies deserve what happens with the development of peer-to-peer networks. One informant claims:

Prices are exorbitant. Companies just try to take advantage of us. If a lot of people are downloading today, they've only got themselves to blame. (Male, 27)

Microsoft Office costs $499.95, Photoshop costs $649; how can they really believe that people won't try to obtain them freely if possible.

I don't use Photoshop very often, but sometimes I enjoy using it to change or customize some pictures. There's no way I will spend so much on a software. I can't afford it. They should give it for free for individual use since they make so much profit with businesses. (Male, 28)

This opinion seems to be widely shared among peer-to-peer users, especially among the informants who download. According to them, the price of software is excessive, especially for individual use. Indeed, 30% of those interviewed believe that software should be free for personal use, since software companies can make their profits through their sales to businesses.

Some of the peer-to-peer file-sharers expressed feelings of being deceived by entertainment companies in order to justify their misconduct. This echoes the comments of both Levin et al. (2004) and Chen et al. (2008). Informants argue:

The music companies think that we're dumb. I mean, 99 cents per song but twelve bucks a CD? They're just trying to bleed us dry. They deserve all they get! (Male, 47)

In this regard, informants hold profitable multinationals responsible for their deviant behaviour. It is interesting to notice that all participants at one point during the interviews differentiated big labels from new and small ones, big and lucrative multinationals from small and medium companies, or famous and rich artists from new and unknown ones. These results confirm Fullerton and Punj's (2004) observation where they highlight 'pathological socialization' as a cause of dysfunctional behaviour. Indeed, informants engage in illegal activities when they consider companies deserving of it (see Wilkes, 1978).

Denial of Injury

Denial of injury is the second most common technique of neutralization used by informants to rationalize their deviant behaviour. However, in contrast to neutralization of guilt via denial of victim prior to acting, the denial of injury rationalization appeared most frequently to occur post behaviour. Of the 54 informants, 43 claim that their peer-to-peer activities do not harm anybody and that there is no direct financial impact on businesses involved. In order to illustrate their point of view, informants underline the wealth of multinationals. Moreover, they stress the non-lucrative side of their actions; they equate their downloadings with a complementary product and not a substitute one, and finally, they highlight the positive impact peer-to-peer networks may have on businesses.

The major argument used in such cases revolves around the idea that multinationals already make such a huge profit that several dollars fewer do not really matter or make a difference. These findings correspond to the 'attitude toward big businesses' cause observed by Fullerton and Punj (1993). One of the informants declares:

I'm sure the development of peer-to-peer networks doesn't have any impact on entertainment industries. They make a lot of money anyway. I also think artists could do without their huge profits. (Male, 19)

These views support Sykes and Matza's (1957) findings, where the latter noticed that delinquents distinguish between acceptable and unacceptable victims. This observation seems to apply to peer-to-peer users too. File-sharers mainly use peer-to-peer networks to download music from famous and wealthy artists and Hollywood movies, and in that case, they did not believe that their behaviour had negative consequences. Some of the informants even highlight the fact that businesses seem to cope extremely well with the situation:

> Some big CEOs from multinationals are complaining about peer-to-peer files sharing but I don't think they have really anything to worry about. Considering share prices of Universal, Fox, Lionsgate, Infogramme and Ubisoft, and their gigantic advertising they don't seem very miserable. (Male, 26)

It is interesting to notice that in the course of the interviews, participants often use denial of victim to reinforce their denial of injury. This finding supports Cromwell and Thurman (2003), who argue that customers may use more than one technique of neutralization to justify their deviant behaviour.

To justify their illegal behaviour, 85% of informants insist that they would not have bought the product (CD, DVD, software, or video game) anyway. Downloading through peer-to-peer networks does not represent a menace for companies since the latter cannot lose money on something they cannot sell in the first place, irrespective of peer-to-peer platforms. Some of the file-sharers thus rationalize their activities:

> I wouldn't have bought them [CDs and DVDs] anyway. [. . .] If I never intended to buy something in the first place there is no real loss to anyone. (Female, 22)

> I tend to download stuff that I would buy. If it is that good, I'd buy a copy but mostly I get programmes that I'll use every now and again. (Male, 34)

Some of the informants also insist that their downloading activities do not affect their consumption habits. Even if they do use peer-to-peer platforms to download some

music or films, that does not diminish their purchasing. These findings corroborate those of Azeez (2002), who claims that downloading does not impact on purchasing behaviour.

Claim of Normalcy

Data analysis reveals that three-quarters of informants seem to lessen their guilt post behaviour through the claim of normality. 'Everybody is doing it' seems to be a logical justification for peer-to-peer file-sharers to engage in their illegal behaviour. This technique pivots on claims that such actions are common to many other consumers and is distinct from the 'condemning the condemners' approach, wherein individuals accuse the other party in the conservation of undertaking similar or greater acts of deviance. Claims of normality appeared to be described by informants as occurring after the misbehaviour, enabling peer-to-peer users to rationalize the consequences of their activities.

Piracy, whether of music, films, software or more commonly video games, is often argued to be becoming commonplace. The significant number of people engaging in illegal downloading makes it easier for others to follow suit, confirming previous results (Cohn and Vaccaro, 2006; Hinduja, 2007; Bhal and Leekha, 2008). Since so many people use peer-to-peer networks in order to obtain the files they want, piracy does not seem so wrong, thereby assuaging the guilt of those using these platforms and offering them an excuse for their misbehaviour. Two informants state:

> Everybody is downloading. I mean if it was so wrong many people I know would never dare doing it. I would be an idiot not to do the same. (Female, 23)

> The world and their wife get free stuff from the Internet! I really doubt that anybody doesn't do it every now and again! (Male, 39)

These answers highlight the influence others can have on their close circle of acquaintances. Peer groups, as often observed within the literature (see Logsdon et al., 1994; Ingram and Hinduja, 2008), can influence their members, leading them to misbehave.

Claim of Relative Acceptability and Justification by Comparison

Individuals who engage in deviant behaviour may rationalize their misconduct by drawing a comparison with a more ethically questionable act (justification by comparison) or with other perpetrators whose behaviours are viewed as less acceptable (claiming relative acceptability). In this study, informants most commonly described incidents of these techniques after the online act of misbehaviour. Analysis of interviews revealed that nearly half of informants employed these techniques of neutralization in order to justify their illegal activities, each claiming that using peer-to-peer networks is nothing compared to crimes such as homicide, rape, or marital violence.

Consistent with Hinduja (2007), comparing a crime against one much more serious, even if there is no connection between them, seems a sufficient excuse for many informants to justify their illegal downloading. Indeed, when compared to homicide, downloading becomes a rather insignificant crime. A serial softlifter argues:

> Peer-to-peer networks have become one of the main sensitive issues today. Even governments get involved. Downloading won't kill anyone. Maybe they should concentrate their effort on something more important. I mean, violence is everywhere; why lose time with irrelevant stuff. (Male, 32)

Justification by comparison enables peer-to-peer file-sharers to make their activities almost acceptable to others, since they believe they do not really harm anyone.

It is interesting to notice that a small (but significant) minority of informants draw a comparison between online piracy and shoplifting in order to rationalize their deviant behaviour. Those against online piracy often associate it with shoplifting. However, peer-to-peer file-sharers claim that they are completely different. This last justification reinforces what has been previously highlighted in the literature review: intellectual property is not regarded as a physical good, thereby diminishing the guilt of illegally obtaining a copy of files (Vitell and Muncy, 1992; Logsdon et al.,

1994; Cheng et al., 1997; Kearns, 2001). An informant explains:

> That gets on my nerves when people say that downloading and shoplifting is the same thing. There is a huge difference. For example, to make a laptop you need raw material and man-hours to make it. While two laptops need twice as much material and twice as many man-hours, two copies of software don't. The cost could be covered by purchases made by companies and professionals, and there are lots of them, while clubs, radio stations, television etc. could cover the cost for music. Everybody downloads; maybe it's time now for companies to adapt themselves. (Male, 30)

The finding that peer-to-peer users do not believe that downloading is unethical is concurrent with a number of earlier studies (see Ingram and Hinduja, 2008).

Other participants use justification by comparison by claiming that they download much less than many other peer-to-peer users. They claimed they only download files occasionally, whereas some individuals pirate every day. This appears to be sufficient reason for them to continue downloading occasionally without feeling guilty about it. Those who engage in this behaviour much more than they do are the ones to blame for the possible harmful consequences. Informants declare:

> I'm not one of the big downloaders. I just download two or three items a month. It's not a big deal and compared to others, it's nothing. (Female, 27)

> I don't download night and day with several computers as some people do. (Female, 23)

As long as others are engaged in these activities much more than they themselves are, informants believe their behaviour can be forgiven.

Appeal to Higher Loyalties

The appeal to higher loyalties technique was most often described by informants as something they considered to occur before the downloading activity. Throughout the coding process, two main values stood out: discovery, and individual's rights and freedom (partly supporting similar findings in Cohn and Vaccaro, 2006).

In order to explain one of the reasons behind their illicit activities, 25 informants refer to the value of discovery. Peer-to-peer networks enable them to discover new songs, new artists, or new movies. For instance:

> When I use peer-to-peer networks I often discover new bands that I had no idea existed. (Male, 18)

> You can find some great new stuff online that you'd never hear about otherwise. (Female, 35)

The 'discovery' factor is especially important where music is concerned, confirming observations made in the literature (Gopal et al., 2004; Cohn and Vaccaro, 2006; Sandulli, 2007). Peer-to-peer networks allow informants to listen to new songs they would never have had the chance to do otherwise. When they have to pay for a CD, they are more cautious about their choice and usually go for the band or artist they know and are sure to enjoy. The safer way is then not to try anything new, thereby not discovering anything new. Even if the radio plays a significant role in the uncovering of novel bands, not every artist or song is broadcast. Moreover, sometimes one or two good songs do not justify the purchase of a CD:

> When I really like an album I would rather buy it instead of downloading it. However when I want only one or two songs on the CD I don't want to spend my money for nothing so I just download the tracks. (Female, 22)

The importance attached to the discovery value strengthens the last argument used by informants in order to deny injury as highlighted earlier. Peer-to-peer networks allow people to discover new things but they also help artists and companies to promote their products. File-sharing in this way is a novel way of sampling before buying the product. Peer-to-peer network advocates have mainly used this argument in order to justify their activities; however, some researches have questioned its accuracy (Blackburn, 2004; Michel, 2004;

Liebowitz, 2005). These results echo those of Jupiter Research's survey evoked in Azeez (2002: 14), who notes that peer-to-peer networks are just another way to *'try-before-you-buy'*.

Concordant with Cohn and Vaccaro (2006), consumer rights and freedom is the second value which a minority (20%) of informants mentioned in order to defend their actions, especially in the cases of music and film downloading. Informants associated music and film with culture and believe culture should be free and available to everybody:

> Music and movies are some kind of arts and should be free whoever the spectator. (Female, 23)

Peer-to-peer networks enable individuals to criticize and fight against the system. Thus, those employing this technique of neutralization argue that their engagement in such illegal behaviour is in order to defend their rights and those of others:

> It's the first time that culture and entertainment is available to everybody. Every civilisation has dreamt about it. It has happened and now everybody is outraged. Thanks to peer-to-peer networks, every individual, rich, and more importantly poor, have the ability to access liberally and free everything related to culture and entertainment. Why would someone, who is for equality between humans, want to prohibit it? (Male, 26)

Moreover, informants point out that usually they download files they were able to obtain freely. This is particularly the case for movies and television shows. When a film or programme is on television, it is easy to record it with a video tape and video player. Informants observed that they paid for the television, the tape and the video-tape recorder and that furthermore, multinational companies sell all the products necessary for this, thus facilitating consumers in recording what is transmitted on television. Thus, many informants argued that as long as a television show or movie has been broadcast on television, they believe they are entitled to use peer-to-peer networks to acquire them:

If a television show or a movie has been broadcast, I don't know why I can't download it since I was able to record it on television. If not, just explain to me why we can buy blank tapes and a video player? (Female, 30)

I like downloading series and even films already broadcast on television. I then consider that I don't have to pay for them since they have been already televized and I could have made a copy of them. (Female, 23)

Peer-to-peer networks are also a way to criticize the system as a whole and fight against an entertainment industry which is attracted more by profit than the will to promote the Arts. An informant contends:

The system for distributing artist's work to consumers is so backwards that I actually resent putting any money at all into it. Paying £35 for a television series that was just on television, when I know that most of that goes straight to the fat cat at the top, who uses it to fund things like Big Brother; I just can't believe it. (Male, 26)

Consumer rights and freedom are hence a value which peer-to-peer users endorse to neutralize guilt and rationalize their behaviour.

Denial of Responsibility

Denial of responsibility was depicted as a post-action process and was expressed by only 30% of informants, echoing Cohn and Vaccaro's (2006) findings. However, the informants who did use this technique of neutralization often brought up the argument of availability of peer-to-peer networks and their accessibility and ease of use.

Seven informants highlight the availability of peer-to-peer networks and the facility in engaging in illegal downloading due to the internet, its access and its ease of use, and thus neutralize their online misbehaviour by claiming that the conditions for illegal peer-to-peer are so favourable that their actions are justifiable. Interestingly, numerous informants argued that they do not create, develop or maintain these networks. Indeed, many informants did not share their own files with other peer-to-peer downloaders. However, since peer-to-peer file trading is available to them, they argue there is no reason for them not to use it and they cannot be held responsible for their behaviour since they have nothing to do with the creation and development of these networks. An informant declares:

Peer-to-peer networks exist and they're free. What should I do? Not use them because some people think it's wrong? I didn't create them. I don't even make my own files available for others. I just use peer-to-peer platforms, which are easily available to me. It's not as if I was the one at the origin of these networks. (Male, 18)

These answers are consistent with previous findings which contend that opportunity can cause aberrant behaviour (see Fukukawa, 2002; Levin et al., 2004).

Accessibility and ease of use are interlinked justifications employed by other informants to deny the responsibility of their behaviour. As highlighted earlier (see Cronan and Al-Rafee, 2008; Ingram and Hinduja, 2008), the internet has made deviant behaviour easier. People have ready access to the internet and it has become increasingly less difficult to use, therefore peer-to-peer file-sharers do not understand why they should not take advantage of peer-to-peer networks. An informant stresses:

With my broadband connection I can have access to the Internet whenever I want. In a few clicks, I can download music, films, software, and even video games. There is nothing difficult to do for that, it's available and free. It's the age of the Internet, you can't fight against it. (Male, 24)

This echoes Sherman's (2000) proposition concerning the ease of use of the internet facilitating dysfunctional behaviour.

◆ Implications

This paper attempts to explore the extent to which peer-to-peer users employ techniques of neutralization to justify their actions of prior-to behaviour or rationalize their activities post behaviour. Relatively few studies have taken an interest in both piracy and the justifications given by downloaders for engaging in such actions, at the same time (see Cohn and Vaccaro, 2006; Hinduja, 2007; Ingram and Hinduja, 2008; Bhal and Leekha, 2008). However, piracy has become a sensitive issue. Every day, billions of files are illegally downloaded throughout the world and despite the actions taken by entertainment companies and governments the movement does not seem to be slowing down.

The main contribution of this study lies not in the finding of neutralization during online consumer misbehaviour. While marketers may be surprised by such a statement (neutralization theory having received little attention by the marketing academy—see Harris, 2008b), other academics (such as criminologists) have long accepted neutralization of deviant actions to the extent that Maruna and Copes (2005) in their (already) seminal review note that such findings are not interesting in themselves. In contrast, the main contribution of the current study lies in the insights gained into the sequencing of neutralizations. This contentious aspect of neutralization theory finds many theorists divided into those that believe that neutralization occurs either pre- or post event (see Sykes and Matza, 1957; Hindelang, 1970); although Maruna and Copes (2005) extend Hirschi's (1969) 'hardening' conception into a theory of desistance. The current study contributes insights into these issues through finding evidence to support the view that both pre-event neutralizing justifications, as well as post-event ones, occur. Moreover, in this context, particular techniques appear linked to either pre- or post-event neutralization. Specifically, the denial of victims and appeal to higher loyalties techniques were found to be predominately used to justify actions prior to an event. In contrast, the denial of injury, claims of normalcy, claims of relative acceptability, justification by comparison and denial of responsibility techniques were found to be rationalizations of behaviour post-event. While the research design and methodology of this study prohibits definitive causal claims and precludes empirical generalizability, theoretical generalizability is possible and certainly the insights gained provide a good starting point for future studies (see below).

It is also worth noting here the differences between the techniques found in the current study and those found in similar studies. Hinduja (2007) observed that students engaging in softlifting particularly use denial of injury, appeal to higher loyalties, claim of relative acceptability and denial of negative intent to justify their behaviour; Bhal and Leekha (2008) state that their informants mainly employed appeal to higher loyalties and claim of normalcy. In contrast, the current study reveals that none of the participants use denial of negative intent to justify their activities, while only 30% employ claims of relative acceptability.

As Cromwell and Thurman (2003) observed, individuals engaging in misconduct tend to use more than one technique of neutralization to justify their behaviour; participants' answers confirm peer-to-peer users do the same. Moreover, in a similar way that delinquents differentiate acceptable from unacceptable victims (Sykes and Matza, 1957), peer-to-peer users distinguish multinationals from small and independent companies. Informants in the current study believe that multinational companies such as Universal, Fox and Microsoft cope perfectly with peer-to-peer networks and thus deserve the development and popularity of these platforms. However, as soon as downloading affects an entity other than a big [corporation], piracy becomes not-so-acceptable behaviour. This last point has never really been mentioned in previous literature on digital piracy and it may be interesting to investigate further in future research. Furthermore, contrary to Hinduja's (2007) findings, the 54 participants often use techniques of neutralization during the interviews. All of them used at least three of the techniques.

The fact that piracy becomes unacceptable behaviour when dealing with small and independent companies deserves particular attention. Many studies have found that piracy was not necessarily regarded as illegal or unethical (Vitell and Muncy, 1992; Logsdon et al., 1994; Simpson et al., 1994; Glass and Wood, 1996; Cheng et al., 1997; Kearns, 2001; Fukukawa, 2002; Cronan and Al-Rafee, 2008). However, the problem appears to be deeper than that. During the 54 interviews, peer-to-peer users claim that their downloading is acceptable and justified. Yet 61% of them are against legal and free downloading. They claim that if peer-to-peer networks are legalized, the entertainment industry will disappear, since artists and creators will not be compensated for their work. This is in total contradiction to the 'culture should be available and free to everybody' dogma. Informants, therefore, do not seem truly to question the illegal and unethical side of peer-to-peer networks, thereby acknowledging the social and conventional norms. However, they feel that these norms should not apply to their cases, echoing Sykes and Matza's (1957) findings. Even if participants, at least this 61%, do not consider piracy to be as unethical as shoplifting for instance, they do not deny the fact that some people can perceive peer-to-peer activities as morally wrong.

It may be particularly interesting and useful for the entertainment industry to further explore this last observation. Piracy is a real phenomenon, which will not disappear easily. On the contrary, the next generation is born with the internet and all the opportunities related to it. Some teenagers download on a daily basis but they have never bought a CD or a DVD in their life. As Sandulli (2007: 325) declares,

> in the words of John Kennedy, the Chairman and CEO of the [IFPI], the main problem of the recording industry is to 'persuade a young generation of music fans to pay for music that they have become used to acquiring for free'. (IFPI, 2006)

The movie, software and video games industries, one after the other, face the same crisis. New technologies will become ever more efficient; the next generation will become even more at ease with the internet; peer-to-peer systems will be increasingly expanded and difficult to control. There is no doubt multinationals will have to come up with a new business model (as suggested by some of the informants) if they want to face up to the situation. New strategies have already been adopted. Free game samples seem to reduce, if not eliminate, illegal downloading of video games. Free software such as Open Office seems to offer an alternative to expensive ones such as Microsoft Office. However, as long as no solution is recommended, the price of some software will continue to drive some individuals into softlifting. Online purchasing of digital media is getting closer to how it should be, and eventually will become the norm. More and more individuals consider CD and DVD support as obsolete and prefer mp3 files, since they take up less space and are more convenient both to download

and to keep. Laptops, mp3 players or bipods, to name but a few, have become commonplace in many people's lives, especially those of the next generation. However, before then, companies need to be realistic. The price they propose is too excessive for many people. Peer-to-peer users do not want to pay for extra 'hosting costs' because they buy a digital as opposed to a physical product. Companies will have to be very careful regarding the new business model and strategy they will adopt. Companies need to rethink their strategy and find new ways to make profits. Instead of considering peer-to-peer networks as opponents, multinationals should maybe try to use these networks to their advantage.

The fact that so many people are willing to download illegally may suggest an ignorance of the law by some consumers; or that legal loopholes may need tightening. Reinforced copyright of the products affected could be one solution. However, this may have unforeseen consequences. Consumers who actually buy the product (CD, DVD, software or videogame) may complain that they cannot make a copy of the product that they legally own. Moreover, there will always be hackers skilled enough to succeed in cracking the copyright. The legalization of such activities is likely to be infeasible. Thus, as noted by Fullerton and Punj (1997), potential solutions are likely to pivot on deterrence to reduce (but not eliminate) such behaviours.

Consequently, a prospective solution for policymakers could be to reinforce the law and implement tougher and stricter penalties. However, this does not ensure the problem will stop, as stricter laws will not convince people that engaging in digital piracy is truly wrong. This may only deter those individuals having the least impact on the problem. Staggering penalties and prison terms could really impact on digital piracy; however, these kinds of sentences would be quite improper for this type of crime. Furthermore, peer-to-peer users would create other sharing networks, which are less easily identified and devoid of proxies and data encoding.

This study highlights that the issue of software and music piracy is rooted deeper than was thought, whether digital piracy is illegal or not. The root causes of downloading should be analyzed in depth by the policymakers rather than their just hoping that increasing legal restrictions will solve the problem. Digital piracy is a sensitive issue which necessitates the generation of new ideas to tackle it. Policymakers have to rethink their strategy. However, peer-to-peer networks will not be easy to prevent or properly to legalize.

As with all studies of this nature, the findings and contributions of this study are constrained by the research design and methodology adopted; limitations which, in turn, suggest potentially fruitful avenues for future research. In particular, three issues appear especially important. First, this study explores an illegal activity. As such, interviews involve discussions of issues which could result in hefty fines or even imprisonment. These issues could constrain informant responses and interpretations. A virtual ethnography on forums related to file-sharing may allow researchers to gain more insights on the situation. Unlike face-to-face interviews, this method could anonymize responses and may generate interesting insights. Second, while the exploratory design and qualitative methods employed facilitate rich insights, the nature of the research design and methods limit the empirical (but not the theoretical) generalizability of the findings and contributions. In this regard, while the method adopted provides insights into the ordering of neutralization techniques (pre- or post actions), only experimental or longitudinal studies can definitively address the causal ordering question. Third, additional research could generate interesting insights through focusing on the conditions in which neutralizations are employed and on interpersonal differences during technique application.

◈ References

Al-Rafee, S. and Cronan, T.P. (2006) 'Digital Piracy: Factors that Influence Attitude toward Behavior', *Journal of Business Ethics* 63(3): 237–59.

Albers-Miller, N.D. (1999) 'Consumer Misbehavior: Why People Buy Illicit Goods', *Journal of Consumer Marketing* 16(3): 273–85.

Alvarez, A. (1997) 'Adjusting to Genocide: The Techniques of Neutralization and the Holocaust', *Social Science History* 21(2): 139–78.

Atmen, M. and Al-Hadassah, H. (2008) 'Factors Affecting Cheating Behavior among Accounting Students (Using the Theory of Planned Behavior)', *Journal of Accounting, Business & Management* 15:109–25.

Azeez, W. (2002) 'Music Downloads Used as Trial ahead of CD Purchase', *New Media Age*, 7 November, p. 14.

Bhal, K.T. and Leekha, N.D. (2008) 'Exploring Cognitive Moral Logics Using Grounded Theory: The Case of Software Piracy', *Journal of Business Ethics* 81(3): 635–46.

Bhattacharjee, S., Gopal, R.D. and Sanders, G.L. (2003) 'Digital Music and Online Sharing: Software Piracy 2.0?', *Communication of the ACM* 46(7): 107–11.

Blackburn, D. (2004) 'On-line piracy and recorded music sales', *Harvard Business School*, working paper, 1–60.

Brennan, W.C. (1974) 'Abortion and the Techniques of Neutralization', *Journal of Health and Social Behavior* 15(4): 538–65.

Bryman, A. (2004) *Social Science Research Methods*. Oxford: Oxford University Press.

Chatzidakis, A. and Mitussis, D. (2007) 'Computer Ethics and Consumer Ethics: The Impact of the Internet on Consumers' Ethical Decision-making Process', *Journal of Consumer Behaviour* 6(5): 305–20.

Chatzidakis, A., Hebert, S., Mitussis, D. and Smith, A. (2004) 'Virtue in Consumption?', *Journal of Marketing Management* 20(5): 526–43.

Chen, Y.C., Shan, R.A. and Lin, A.K. (2008) 'The Intention to Download Music Files in a P2P Environment: Consumption Value, Fashion, and Ethical Decision Perspectives', *Electronic Commerce Research and Applications* 1–12.

Cheng, H.K., Sims, R.R. and Teeter, H. (1997) 'To Purchase or to Pirate Software: An Empirical Study', *Journal of Management Information Systems* 13(4): 49–60.

Chiou, J.S., Huang, C.Y. and Lee, H.H. (2005) 'The Antecedents of Music Piracy Attitudes and Intentions', *Journal of Business Ethics* 57(2): 161–74.

Coffey, A.J. and Atkinson, P. A. (1996) *Making Sense of Qualitative Data: Complementary Research Strategies*. Thousand Oaks, CA: Sage.

Cohn, D.Y. and Vaccaro, V.L. (2006) 'A Study of Neutralization Theory's Application to Global Consumer Ethics: P2P File-trading of Musical Intellectual Property on the Internet', *Internet Marketing and Advertising* 3(1): 68–88.

Coleman, J.W. *Neutralization theory: An empirical application and assessment*. Stillwater, OK, PhD thesis, Oklahoma State University, Department of Sociology, 1994.

Crimp, M. and White, L.T. (2000) *The Market Research Process*. London: Prentice Hall.

Cromwell, P. and Thurman, Q. (2003) 'The Devil Made Me Do It: Use of Neutralizations by Shoplifters', *Deviant Behaviour* 24(6): 535–50.

Cronan, T.P. and Al-Rafee, S. (2008) 'Factors that Influence the Intention to Pirate Software and Media', *Journal of Business Ethics* 78(4): 527–45.

Dey, I. (1993) *Qualitative Data Analysis: A User-friendly Guide for Social Scientists*. London: Rutledge.

Dunford, F.W. and Kunz, P. R. (1973) 'The Neutralization of Religious Dissonance', *Review of Religious Research* 15(1): 2–9.

Eliason, S.L. and Dodder, R.A. (2000) 'Neutralization among Deer Poachers', *Journal of Social Psychology* 140(4): 536–8.

Foremski, T. and Kehoe, L. (2000) 'Love Bites: The Ease with which a Disruptive Computer Virus Sidestepped Elaborate Safety Systems this Week has Damaged Faith in the Internet', *Financial Times*, 6 May, p. 14.

Freestone, O. and Mitchell, V.W. (2004) 'Generation Y Attitudes towards e-ethics and Internet-related Misbehaviours', *Journal of Business Ethics* 54(2): 121–8.

Fritsche, I. (2005) 'Predicting Deviant Behaviour by Neutralization: Myths and Findings', *Deviant Behaviour* 26(5): 483–510.

Fukukawa, K. (2002) 'Developing a Framework for Ethically Questionable Behavior in Consumption', *Journal of Business Ethics* 41(1): 99–119.

Fullerton, R.A. and Punj, G. (1993) 'Choosing to Misbehave: A Structural Model of Aberrant Consumer Behaviour', *Advances in Consumer Research* 20: 570–4.

Fullerton, R.A. and Punj, G. (1997) 'Can Consumer Misbehavior be Controlled? A Critical Analysis of Two Major Control Techniques', *Advances in Consumer Research* 24: 340–4.

Fullerton, R.A. and Punj, G. (2004) 'Repercussions of Promoting an Ideology of Consumption: Consumer Misbehaviour', *Journal of Business Research* 57(11): 1239–49.

Glass, R.S. and Wood, W.A. (1996) 'Situational Determinants of Software Piracy: An Equity Theory Perspective', *Journal of Business Ethics* 15(11): 1189–98.

Goles, T., Jayatilaka, B., George, B., Parsons, L., Chambers, V., Taylor, D. et al. (2008) 'Softlifting: Exploring Determinants of Attitude', *Journal of Business Ethics* 77(4): 481–99.

Gopal, R.D., Sanders, G.L., Bhattacharjee, S., Agrawal, M. and Wagner, S.C. (2004) 'A Behavioral Model of Digital Music Piracy', *Journal of Organizational Computing and Electronic Commerce* 14(2): 89–105.

Gupta, P.B., Gould, S.J. and Pola, B. (2004) 'To Pirate or not to Pirate: A Comparative Study of the Ethical versus other Influences on the Consumer's Software Acquisition Mode Decision', *Journal of Business Ethics* 55(3): 255–74.

Harris, L.C. (2008a) 'Fraudulent Return Proclivity: An Empirical Analysis', *Journal of Retailing* 84(4): 461–76.

Harris, L.C. (2008b) 'Introduction to the Special Session: Customers Behaving Badly: A Tribute to Christopher Lovelock', paper presented at the American Marketing Association SERVSIG International Research Conference, University of Liverpool, June.

Harris, L.C. and Reynolds K.L. (2003) 'The Consequences of Dysfunctional Customer Behavior', *Journal of Service Research* 6(2): 144–61.

Harris, L.C. and Reynolds K.L. (2004) 'Jaycustomer Behavior: An Exploration of Types and Motives in the Hospitality Industry', *Journal of Services Marketing* 18(5): 339–57.

Harris, L.C. and Reynolds K.L. (2006) 'Deviant Customer Behavior: An Exploration of Frontline Employee Tactics', *Journal of Marketing Theory and Practice* 14(2): 95–111.

Henry, S. (1990) *Degrees of Deviance, Student Accounts of their Deviant Behavior*. Salem, WI: Sheffield Publishing.

Hill, C.W.L. (2007) Digital Piracy: Causes, Consequences, and Strategic Responses', Asia *Pacific Journal of Management* 24(1): 9–25.

Hindelang, M.J. (1970) 'The Commitment of Delinquents to their Misdeeds: Do Delinquents Drift?', *Social Problems* 17: 502–9.

Hinduja, S. (2007) 'Neutralization Theory and Online Software Piracy: An Empirical Analysis', *Ethics and Information Technology* 9(3): 187–204.

Hirschi, T. (1969) Causes of Delinquency. Berkeley, CA: University of California Press.

Iacobucci, D. and Churchill G. (2006) *Marketing Research: Methodological Foundations*. Cincinnati, OH: South Western Educational Publishing.

Ingram, J.R. and Hinduja, S. (2008) 'Neutralizing Music Piracy: An Empirical Examination', *Deviant Behavior* 29(4): 334–66.

International Federation of the Phonographic Industry (IFPI) (2006) *Digital Music Report*. London: IFPI

Kearns, D. (2001) 'Intellectual Property: Napster and Ethics', *Network World* 18(15): 18.

Klockars, C.B. (1974) *The Professional Fence*. New York: Free Press.

Levi, K. (1981) 'Becoming a Hit Man: Neutralization in a Very Deviant Career', *Urban Life* 10(1): 47–63.

Levin, A.M., Dato-on, M.C. and Rhee, K. (2004) 'Money for Nothing and Hits for Free: The Ethics of Downloading Music from Peer-to-Peer Web Sites', *Journal of Marketing Theory and Practice* 12(1): 48–60.

Liebowitz, S.J. (2005) 'Pitfalls in Measuring the Impact of File-sharing on the Sound Recording Market', CESifo *Economic Studies*, 51: 439–77.

Lindolf, T.R. (1995) *Qualitative Communication Research Methods*. Thousand Oaks, CA: Sage.

Logsdon, J.M., Thompson, J.K. and Reid, R.A. (1994) 'Software Piracy: Is it Related to Level of Moral Judgment', *Journal of Business Ethics* 13(11): 849–57.

Mahrer, A.R. (1988) 'Discovery-oriented Psychotherapy Research', *American Psychologist* 43(September): 694–702.

Maruna, S. and Copes, H. (2005) 'Excuses, Excuses: What Have we Learned from Five Decades of Neutralization Research?', *Crime and Justice: A Review of Research* 32: 221–320.

Mazur, M. (2007) 'Online Fraud Continues to Be a Concern', *Community Banker* 16(6):70.

Michel, N.J. (2004) 'Internet file sharing: The evidence so far and what it means for the future', *The Heritage Foundation*, working paper, 1790, 1–6.

Miller, D.C. (1991) *Handbook of Research Design and Social Measurement* (5th ed.). Newbury Park, CA: Sage.

Mills, C.W. (1940) 'Situated Actions and Vocabularies of Motive', *American Sociological Review* 5(6): 904–13.

Minor, W.W. (1981) 'Techniques of Neutralization: A Reconceptualization and Empirical Examination', *Journal of Research in Crime and Delinquency* 18(2): 295–318.

Mitchell, J. and Dodder, R.A. (1980) 'An Examination of Types of Delinquency through Path Analysis', *Journal of Youth and Adolescence* 9(3): 239–48.

Motion Picture Association of America (MPAA) (2008) *Who Piracy Hurts,* URL (consulted August 2009): http://www.mpaa.org/piracy_WhoPiracyHurts.asp

Piquero, N.L., Tibbetts, S.G. and Blankenship, M.B. (2005) 'Examining the Role of Differential Association and Techniques of Neutralization in Explaining Corporate Crime', *Deviant Behavior* 26(2): 159–88.

Price, L.L., Arnould, E.J. and Curasi, C.F. (2000) 'Older Consumers' Disposition of Special Possessions', *Journal of Consumer Research* 27(September): 179–201.

Recording Industry Association of America (RIAA) (2008) *Report Physical Piracy,* URL (consulted August 2009): http://www.riaa.com/physicalpiracy.php

Reynolds, K.L. and Harris, L.C. (2005) 'When Service Failure is not Service Failure: An Exploration of the Forms and Motives of "Illegitimate" Customer Complaining', *Journal of Services Marketing* 19(5): 321–35.

Rombel, A. (2004) 'Security and Fraud Become Top Tech Issue', *Global Finance* 18(4): 40–2.

Rosenbaum, M.S. and Kuntze, R. (2003) 'The Relationship between Anomie and Unethical Retail Disposition', *Psychology and Marketing* 20(12): 1067–93.

Sandulli, F.D. (2007) 'CD Music Purchase Behaviour of P2P Users', *Technovation* 27: 325–34.

Sherman, C. (2000) 'Napster: Copyright Killer or Distribution Hero?', *Online* 24(6): 16–28.

Simpson, C. (2006) 'Review of Computer Misuse Laws Essential to Keep up with Rapidly Developing Market', *Computer Weekly,* 14 February, p. 14.

Simpson, P.M., Banerjee, D. and Simpson, C.L., Jr. (1994) 'Softlifting: A Model of Motivation Factors', *Journal of Business Ethics* 13(6): 431–8.

Smith, K.J., Davy, J.A. and Easterling, D. (2004) 'An Examination of Cheating and its Antecedents among Marketing and Management Majors', *Journal of Business Ethics* 50(1): 63–80.

Stainback, S. and Stainback, W. (1988) *Understanding and Conducting Qualitative Research.* Dubuque, IA: Kendall/Hunt.

Strauss, A. and Corbin, J. (1998) *Basics of Qualitative Research: Techniques and Procedures for Developing Grounded Theory* (2nd ed.). London: Sage.

Strutton, D., Pelton, L.E. and Ferrell, O.C. (1997) 'Ethical Behavior in Retail Settings: Is there a Generation Gap?', *Journal of Business Ethics* 16: 87–105.

Strutton, D., Vitell, S.J. and Pelton, L.E. (1994) 'How Consumers May Justify Inappropriate Behaviour in Market Settings: An Application on the Techniques of Neutralization', *Journal of Business Research* 30(3): 253–60.

Sykes, G.M. and Matza, D. (1957) 'Techniques of Neutralization: A Theory of Delinquency', *American Sociological Review* 22(6): 664–70.

Turner, B.A. (1981) 'Some Practical Aspects of Qualitative Data Analysis: One Way of Organizing the Cognitive Processes Associated with the Generation of Grounded Theory', *Quality and Quantity* 15: 225–47.

Vitell, S.J. and Grove, S.J. (1987) 'Marketing Ethics and the Techniques of Neutralization', *Journal of Business Ethics* 6(6): 433–8.

Vitell, S.J. and Muncy, J. (1992) 'Consumer Ethics: An Empirical Investigation of Factors Influencing Ethical Judgments of the Final Consumer', *Journal of Business Ethics* 11(8): 585–97.

Vitell, S.J. and Muncy, J. (2005) 'The Muncy-Vitell Consumer Ethics Scale: A Modification and Application', *Journal of Business Ethics* 62(3): 267–75.

Wilkes, R.E. (1978) 'Fraudulent Behavior by Consumers', *Journal of Marketing* 42(4): 67–75.

Witham, G. (1998) 'Customers from Hell', *Cornell Hotel and Restaurant Administration Quarterly* 39(5): 11.

Yin, R.K. (2003) *Case Study Research: Design and Methods.* London: Sage.

READING 21

In this short reading, Amy Schalet compares the cultural differences in teenage sexuality between the Netherlands and the United States. Her work examines the impact of parent–child relationships on sexuality, love, and autonomy, finding that in a cultural setting in which sexuality is normalized, it is easier to communicate, whereas in settings in which sexuality is dramatized, it becomes harder for parents and teenagers to communicate.

Source: Schalet, A. (2010). Sex, love, and autonomy in the teenage sleepover. *Contexts, 9*(3), 16–21.

Sex, Love, and Autonomy in the Teenage Sleepover

Amy Schalet

Karel Doorman, a soft-spoken civil servant in the Netherlands, keeps tabs on his teenage children's computer use and their jobs to make sure neither interferes with school performance or family time. But Karel wouldn't object if his daughter Heidi were to have a sexual relationship.

"No," he explains. "She is sixteen, almost seventeen. I think she knows very well what matters, what can happen. If she is ready [for sex], I would let her be ready." Karel would also let his daughter spend the night with a steady boyfriend in her room, if the boyfriend had come over to the house regularly before-hand and did not show up "out of the blue." That said, Karel suspects his daughter might prefer a partner of her own sex. If so, Karel would accept her orientation, he says, though "the adjustment process" might take a little longer.

Karel's approach stands in sharp contrast to that of Rhonda Fursman, a northern California homemaker and former social worker. Rhonda tells her kids that premarital sex "at this point is really dumb." It's on the list with shoplifting, she explains, "sort of like the Ten Commandments: don't do any of those because if you do, you know, you're going to be in a world of hurt." Rhonda responds viscerally when asked whether she would let her fifteen-year-old son spend the night with a girlfriend. "No way, Jose!" She elaborates: "That kind of recreation . . . is just not something I would feel comfortable with him doing here." She might change her mind "if they are engaged or about to be married."

Karel and Rhonda illustrate a puzzle: the vast majority of American parents oppose a sleepover for high-school-aged teenagers, while Dutch teenagers who have steady boyfriends or girlfriends are typically allowed to spend the night with them in their rooms. This contrast is all the more striking when we consider the trends toward a liberalization of sexual behavior and attitudes that have taken place throughout Europe and the United States since the 1960s. In similar environments, both parents and kids are experiencing adolescent sex, gender, and relationships very

differently. A sociological exploration of these contrasts reveals as much about the cultural differences between these two countries as it does about views on adolescent sexuality and child rearing.

◆ Adolescent Sexuality in Contemporary America

Today, most adolescents in the U.S., like their peers across the industrialized world, engage in intercourse—either opposite or same-sex—before leaving their teens (usually around seventeen). Initiating sex and exploring romantic relationships, often with several successive partners before settling into long-term cohabitation or marriage, are now normative parts of adolescence and young adulthood in the developed world. But in the U.S., teenage sex has been fraught with cultural ambivalences, heated political struggles, and poor health outcomes, generating concern among the public, policy makers, scholars, and parents. American adolescent sexuality has been dramatized rather than normalized.

In some respects, the problems associated with adolescent sexuality in America are surprising. Certainly age at first intercourse has dropped in the U.S. since the sexual revolution, but not as steeply as often assumed. In a recent survey of the adult American population, sociologist Edward Laumann and colleagues found that even in the 1950s and '60s, only a quarter of men and less than half of women were virgins at age nineteen. The majority of young men had multiple sexual partners by age 20. And while women especially were supposed to enter marriage as virgins, demographer Lawrence Finer has shown that women who came of age in the late 1950s and early '60s almost never held to that norm. Still, a 1969 Gallup poll found that two thirds of Americans said it was wrong for "a man and women to have sex relations before marriage."

But by 1985, Gallup found that a slim majority of Americans no longer believed such relations were wrong. Analyzing shifts in public opinion following the sexual revolution, sociologists Larry Petersen and Gregory Donnenwerth showed that among Americans with a religious affiliation, only conservative Protestants who attended church frequently remained unchanged. Among all other religious groups, acceptance of pre-marital sex actually grew, although Laumann and colleagues reported a majority of the Americans continued to believe sex among *teenagers* was always wrong. Even youth agreed: six in ten fifteen to nineteen-year-olds surveyed in the 2002 National Survey for Family Growth said sixteen-year-olds with strong feelings for one another shouldn't have sex.

Part of the opposition to adolescent sexuality is its association with unintended consequences such as pregnancy and sexually transmitted diseases. In the U.S., the rate of unintended pregnancies among teenagers rose during the 1970s and '80s, dropping only in the early '90s. However, despite almost a decade and a half of impressive decreases in pregnancy and birth rates, the teen birth rate remains many times higher in the U.S. than it is in most European countries. In 2007, births to American teens (aged fifteen to nineteen) were eight times as high as in the Netherlands.

One would imagine the predominant public policy approach would be to improve education about, and access to, contraception. But "abstinence-only-until-marriage" programs, initiated in the early 1980s, have received generous federal funding over the past fifteen years, and were even written into the recent U.S. health reform law (which also supports comprehensive sex education). For years, schools funded under the federal "abstinence-only" policy were prohibited from educating teens about condoms and contraception and required to teach that sex outside of heterosexual marriage was damaging. A 2004 survey by NPR, the Kaiser Family Foundation, and Harvard University found that most parents actually thought that contraception and condom education should be included, but two thirds still agreed sex education should teach that abstinence outside of marriage is "the accepted standard for school-aged children." And

for most parents, abstinence means no oral sex or intimate touching.

While American parents of the post-Sexual Revolution era have wanted minors to abstain, few teens have complied. Many American teenagers have had positive and enriching sexual experiences; however, researchers have also documented intense struggles. Comparing teenage boys and girls, for example, University of Michigan sociologist Karin Martin found that puberty and first sex empowered boys but decreased self-esteem among girls. Psychologist Deborah Tolman found the girls she interviewed confronted dilemmas of desire because of a double standard that denies or stigmatizes their sexual desires, making girls fear being labeled "sluts." Analyzing the National Longitudinal Survey of Adolescent Health, researchers Kara Joyner and Richard Udry found that even without sex, first romance brings girls "down" because their relationship with their parents deteriorates.

Nor are American girls of the post-Sexual Revolution era the only ones who must navigate gender dilemmas. Sociologist Laura Carpenter found that many of the young men she interviewed in the 1990s viewed their virginity as a stigma which they sought to cast off as rapidly as possible. And in her ethnography, *Dude, You're a Fag,* C.J. Pascoe found boys are pressured by other boys to treat girls as sex objects and sometimes derided for showing affection for their girlfriends. But despite public pressures, privately boys are as emotionally invested in relationships as girls, found Peggy Giordano and her associates in a recent national study out of Toledo, Ohio. Within those relationships, however, boys are less confident.

In the 1990s, the National Longitudinal Study for Adolescent Health found that steady romantic relationships are common among American teenagers. Girls and boys typically have their first intercourse with people they are dating. But the Toledo group found that once they are sexually experienced, the majority of boys and girls also have sex in non-dating relationships, often with a friend or acquaintance. And even when they have sex in dating relationships, a quarter of American girls and almost half of boys say they are "seeing other people" (which may or may not include sexual intercourse).

◈ Teen Sexuality in the Netherlands

In a late 1980s qualitative study with 120 parents and older teenagers, Dutch sociologist Janita Ravesloot concluded that in most families, parents accepted that sexuality "from the first kiss to the first coitus" was part of the youth phase. In middle class families, teenagers reported that parents accepted their sexual autonomy, but didn't engage in elaborate conversations with them because of lingering feelings of shame. Working-class parents were more likely to use their authority to impose norms, including that sex belonged only in steady relationships. In a few strongly religious families—Christian or Islamic—parents categorically opposed sex before marriage: here there were "no overnights with steady boy- or girlfriends at home."[1] But such families remain a minority. A 2003 survey by *Statistics Netherlands* found that two thirds of Dutch fifteen to seventeen-year-olds with steady boy- or girlfriends are allowed to spend the night with them in their bedrooms, and that boys and girls are equally likely to get permission for a sleepover.

This could hardly have been predicted in the 1950s. Then, women *and* men typically initiated intercourse in their early twenties, usually in a serious relationship (if not engagement or marriage). In the late '60s, a national survey conducted by sociologist G.A. Kooy found most respondents still rejected premarital sex when a couple was not married or planning to do so very shortly. But by the early 1980s, the same survey found that six out of ten respondents no longer objected to a girl having intercourse with a boy as long as she was in love with him. Noting the shift in attitudes since the 1950s, Kooy spoke of a "moral landslide." His colleague, sociologist Evert Ketting, even went as far as to speak of a "moral revolution."

What changed was not just a greater acceptance of sex outside of the context of heterosexual marriage. There was also serious new deliberation among the general public, health professionals, and the media about the need to adjust the moral rules governing sexual life to real behavior. As researchers for the Guttmacher Institute later noted, "One might say the entire society has experienced a course in sex education." The new moral rules cast sexuality as a part of life that should be governed by self-determination, mutual respect, frank conversation, and the prevention of unintended consequences. Notably, these new rules were applied to minors and institutionalized in Dutch health care policies that removed financial and emotional barriers to accessing contraceptives—including the requirements for a pelvic examination and parental consent.

Indeed, even as the age of first sexual intercourse was decreasing, the rate of births among Dutch teenagers dropped steeply between 1970 and 1996 to one of the lowest in the world. What distinguished the very low Dutch teenage birth rate from, for instance, that of their Swedish counterparts, was that it was accompanied by a very low teen abortion rate. Despite the AIDS crisis, by the mid-1990s, funding agencies were so confident that, in the words of demographer Joop Garssen, youth were doing "wonderfully well," they decided further study of adolescent sexual attitudes and behavior wasn't warranted.

Sex education has played a key role. Sociologists Jane Lewis and Trudie Knijn find that Dutch sex education curricula are more likely than programs elsewhere to openly discuss female sexual pleasure, masturbation, and homosexuality. The Dutch curricula also emphasize the importance of self-reliance and mutual respect in negotiating enjoyable and healthy sexual relationships during adolescence.

A 2005 survey of Dutch youth, ages twelve to twenty-five, found the majority described their first sexual experiences—broadly defined—as well-timed, within their control, and fun. About first intercourse, 86 percent of women and 93 percent of men said, "We both were equally eager to have it." This doesn't mean that gender doesn't matter. Researcher Janita Ravesloot found that more girls than boys reported that their parents expected them to only have intercourse in relationships. Girls were also aware that they might be called sluts for having sex too soon or with too many successive partners. And although most of the 2005 respondents said they were (very) satisfied with the pleasure and contact they felt with their partner during sex, men were much more likely to usually or always orgasm during sex and less likely to report having experienced pain.

It also appears that having sex outside of the context of monogamous romantic relationships isn't as common among Dutch adolescents, especially older ones, as among their American counterparts. Again in the 2005 survey, two thirds of male youth and 81 percent of Dutch females had their last sex in a monogamous steady relationship, usually with a partner with whom they were "very much in love." Certainly, Dutch adolescents have "non-relational" sex—indeed, one in three males and one in five females had their last vaginal or anal sex outside of a monogamous romantic relationship. That said, relational sex seems to remain the norm, especially as young people age: two thirds of fifteen to seventeen-year-olds, and three quarters of those eighteen to twenty, had their last intercourse in a monogamous relationship. Among the oldest group—nineteen to twenty-four-year-olds—almost half of gay men surveyed, six in ten straight men and lesbians, and nearly three quarters of straight women were in long-term relationships.

◈ Explaining the Differences

So why do parents in two countries with similar levels of development and reproductive technologies have such different attitudes toward the sexual experiences of teenagers? Two factors immediately spring to mind. The first is religion. As the Laumann team found, Americans who do not view religion as a central force in their decision-making are much less likely to categorically condemn teenage sex. And devout Christians and Muslims in the Netherlands are more likely to exhibit attitudes towards sexuality and marriage that are similar to those of their American counterparts. That Americans are far more likely to be religiously devout than the Dutch, many of whom left their houses of worship in the 1960s and '70s, explains part of the difference between the two countries.

A second factor is economic security. Like most European countries, the Dutch government provides a range of what sociologists call "social" and what reproductive health advocates call "human" rights: the right to housing, healthcare, and a minimum income. Not only do such rights ensure access, if need be, to free contraceptive and abortion services, government supports make coming of age less perilous for both teenagers and parents. This might make the prospect of sex derailing a child's life less haunting. Ironically, the very lack of such rights and high rates of childhood poverty in the U.S. contributes to high rates of births among teenagers. Without adequate support systems or educational and job opportunities, young people are simply more likely to start parenthood early in life.

While they no doubt contribute, neither religion nor economics can solve the whole puzzle. Even Dutch and American families matched on these dimensions still have radically divergent views of teenage sexuality and the sleepover. After interviewing 130 white middle-class Dutch and American teenagers (mostly 10th graders) and parents, I became convinced that a fuller solution is to look at the different cultures of independence and control that characterize these two middle classes.

In responding to adolescent sexuality, American parents emphasize its dangerous and conflicted elements, describing it in terms of "raging hormones" that are difficult for young people to control and in terms of antagonistic relationships between the sexes (girls and boys pursue love and sex respectively and girls are often the losers of the battle). Moreover, American parents see it as their obligation to encourage adolescents' separation from home before accepting their sexual activity. Viewing sex as part of a larger tug of war between separation and control, the response to the question of the sleepover, even among many otherwise socially liberal parents is, "Not under my roof!"

Dutch parents, by contrast, downplay the dangerous and difficult sides of teenage sexuality, tending to normalize it. They speak of readiness (*er aan toe zijn*), a process of becoming physically and emotionally ready for sex that they believe young people can self-regulate, provided they've been encouraged to pace themselves and prepare adequately. Rather than emphasizing gender battles, Dutch parents talk about sexuality as emerging from relationships and are strikingly silent about gender conflicts. And unlike Americans who are often skeptical about teenagers' capacities to fall in love, they assume that even those in their early teens fall in love. They permit sleepovers, even if that requires an "adjustment" period to overcome their feelings of discomfort, because they feel obliged to stay connected and accepting as sex becomes part of their children's lives.

These different approaches to adolescent sexuality are part of the different cultures of independence and control. American middle-class culture conceptualizes the self and (adult) society as inherently oppositional during adolescence. Breaking away from the family is necessary for autonomy, as is the occasional use of parental control (for instance, in the arena of sexuality), until teenagers are full adults. Dutch middle-class culture, in contrast, conceptualizes the self and society as interdependent. Based upon the assumption that young people develop autonomy in the context of ongoing relationships of interdependence, Dutch parents don't see teenage sexuality in the household as a threat to their children's autonomy or to their own authority. To the contrary, allowing teenage sexuality in the home—"domesticating" it, as it were—allows Dutch parents to exert more informal social control.

◆ What It Means for Kids

The acceptance of adolescent sexuality in the family creates the opportunity for Dutch girls to integrate their sexual selves with their roles as family members, even if they may be subject to a greater level of surveillance. Karel's daughter, Heidi, for example, told me she knows that her parents would permit a boyfriend to spend the night, but they wouldn't be happy unless they knew the boy and felt comfortable with him By contrast, many American girls must physically and psychically bifurcate their sexual selves and their roles as daughters. Caroline's mother loves her boyfriend. Still, Caroline, who is seventeen, says her parents would "kill" her if she asked for a sleepover. They know she has sex, but "it's really overwhelming for them to know that their little girl is in their house having sex with a guy. That is just scary to them."

American boys receive messages ranging from blanket prohibition to open encouragement. One key message is that sex is a symbol and a threat—in the event of pregnancy—to their adult autonomy. Jesse has a mother who is against premarital sex and a father who

believes boys just want to get laid. But like Caroline, Jesse knows there will be no sleepovers: "They have to wait for me to break off from them, to be doing my own thing, before they can just handle the fact that I would be staying with my girlfriend like that," he says. By contrast, Dutch boys are, or anticipate being, allowed a sleepover. And like their female counterparts, they say permission comes with a social control that encourages a relational sexuality and girlfriends their parents like. Before Frank's parents would permit a sleepover, they would first have "to know someone well." Gert-Jan says his parents are lenient, but "my father is always judging, 'That's not a type for you.'"

These different templates for adolescent sex, gender, and autonomy also affect boys' and girls' own navigation of the dilemmas of gender. The category "slut" appears much more salient in the interviews with American girls than Dutch girls. One reason may be that the cultural assumption that teenagers can and do fall in love lends credence to Dutch girls' claims to being in love, while the cultural skepticism about whether they can sustain the feelings and form the attachments that legitimate sexual activity put American girls on the defensive. Kimberley, an American, had her first sex with a boy she loves, but she knows that people around her might discount such claims, saying "You're young, you can't fall in love." By contrast, in the Netherlands, Natalie found her emotions and relationship validated: her mother was happy to hear about her first intercourse because "she knows how serious we are."

In both countries, boys confront the belief and sometimes the reality that they are interested in sex but not relationships. But there is evidence in both countries that boys are often emotionally invested. The American boys I have interviewed tend to view themselves as unique for their romantic aspirations and describe themselves, as Jesse does, as "romantic rebels." "The most important thing to me is maintaining love between me and my girlfriend," while "most guys are pretty much in it for the sex," he says. The Dutch boys I interviewed did not perceive themselves as unusual for falling in love (or for wanting to) before having sex. Sam, for instance, believes that "everyone wants [a relationship]." He explains why: "Someone you can talk to about your feelings and such, a feeling of safety, I think that everyone, the largest percentage of people wants a relationship."

 ## Culture's Cost

How sexuality, love, and autonomy are perceived and negotiated in parent-child relationships and among teenagers depends on the cultural templates people have available. Normalization and dramatization each have "costs" and "benefits." On balance, however, the dramatization of adolescent sexuality makes it more difficult for parents to communicate with teenagers about sex and relationships, and more challenging for girls and boys to integrate their sexual and relational selves. The normalization of adolescent sexuality does not eradicate the tensions between parents and teenagers or the gender constructs that confine both girls and boys. But it does provide a more favorable cultural climate in which to address them.

 ## Note

1. This quote and subsequent quotes from Dutch sources are the author's translations. Names have been changed to protect anonymity.

 ## Recommended Resources

Michel Bozon and Osmo Kontula. "Sexual Initiation and Gender in Europe: A Cross-Cultural Analysis of Trends in the Twentieth Century." In M. Hubert, N. Bajos, and T. Sandfort (eds.), *Sexual Behaviour and HIV/AIDS in Europe: Comparisons of National Surveys* (UCL Press, 1998). Documents historical trends in sexual initiation in Europe during the last half of the 20th century.

Evert Ketting and Adriaan P. Visser. "Contraception in the Netherlands: The Low Abortion Rate Explained." *Patient Education and Counseling* (1994), 23:161–171. Describes various factors, including healthcare delivery and media education, which have contributed to the low teenage pregnancy rate in the Netherlands.

Jane Lewis and Trudie Knijn. "Sex Education Materials in the Netherlands and in England and Wales: A Comparison of Content, Use and Teaching Practice." *Oxford Review of Education* (2003), 29(1):113–132. Provides an analysis of the politics and content analysis of Dutch sex education as compared to programs in the U.K.

C.J. Pascoe. *Dude You're a Fag: Masculinity and Sexuality in High School* (University of California Press, 2007). An ethnographic study of a racially diverse working-class high school that shows American boys' pressures to "perform" masculinity.

Deborah L. Tolman. *Dilemmas of Desire: Teenage Girls Talk about Sexuality* (Harvard University Press, 2002). Illuminates how American girls grapple with the experience and articulation of their sexual desires in face of social and cultural pressures.

CHAPTER 8

Labeling Theory

Saturday, March 24, 1984. Shermer High School, Shermer, Illinois. 60062.

Dear Mr. Vernon, we accept the fact that we had to sacrifice a whole Saturday in detention for whatever it was that we did wrong . . . what we did was wrong, but we think you're crazy to make us write this essay telling you who we think we are. What do you care? You see us as you want to see us . . . in the simplest terms and the most convenient definitions. You see us as a brain, an athlete, a basket case, a princess and a criminal. Correct? That's the way we saw each other at seven o'clock this morning. We were brainwashed.

—From *The Breakfast Club*

http://karlgoestocoimbra.files.wordpress.com/2011/05/0251920 46186_bluray_ws_2d_ctr.jpg

▲ **Photo 8.1**   The film *The Breakfast Club* offers a great example of labeling, with each of the main characters representing a different high school clique. Can you recall five distinct student groups from your own high school experience?

◈ Introduction

The movie *The Breakfast Club* is a classic coming-of-age film that deals squarely with the issue of labeling and how labels can affect the quality of an individual's life. In the film, the group of students represents the popular kids, the jocks, the smart kids, the delinquents, and the outcasts. Think back to your own days in high school. . . . Can you identify several categories of students and a few specific traits associated with each of those groups? Were those groups treated differently by the school's staff members and the rest of the students? How so? Did that treatment then affect the way the individuals behaved and what was expected of them?

The impact of labeling has been a key idea in literature in works ranging from Hawthorne's Hester Prynne being branded with a scarlet letter for adultery in Puritan Boston to S. E. Hinton's story of the struggles of the teenage Greasers and Socs in 1960s Oklahoma in *The Outsiders*. In real life, as in these works, the way individuals are perceived and labeled can have important and long-lasting consequences for how they are treated by others and the opportunities that are available to them.

The labeling perspective is situated in the larger framework of social psychology and **symbolic interactionism** in sociology. This is a microlevel, relativist perspective that is focused on individuals and the meanings they attach to objects, people, and interactions around them. Symbolic interactionists advocate direct observation of the social world as it is experienced and understood by the individuals acting in it. Labeling theorists examine the social meaning of deviant labels, how those labels are understood, and how they affect the individuals to whom they are applied.

Labeling theorists argue that, to some extent, deviance is in the eye of the beholder. How others view us—or how we *believe* others view us—is key to our understanding of self and our place in society. Charles Horton Cooley (1902) offered the concept of the **looking-glass self**, explaining,

> So in imagination we perceive in another's mind some thought of our appearance, manners, aims, deeds, character, friends, and so on, and are variously affected by it. A self-idea of this sort seems to have three principal elements: the imagination of our appearance to the other person; the imagination of his judgment of that appearance, and some sort of self-feeling, such as pride or mortification. The comparison with a looking-glass hardly suggests the second element, the imagined judgment, which is quite essential. The thing that moves us to pride or shame is not the mere mechanical reflection of ourselves, but an imputed sentiment, the imagined effect of this reflection upon another's mind. This is evident from the fact that the character and freight of that other, in whose mind we see ourselves, makes all the difference with our feeling. (p. 152)

In defining deviance, the reaction to the behavior or the person is the key. Can you think of an act that is inherently deviant? An act that everyone would agree is and has always been deviant across cultures and across time? Chances are that any act you might initially think of has been accepted behavior in some cultures under some circumstances. For example, we generally consider taking the life of another to be a very serious criminal act; however, in times of war or acts of self-defense, taking a life can be viewed as acceptable and perhaps even laudable behavior. The relativist perspective reminds us that audience reaction is key in defining deviance—no act is thought to be inherently deviant; acts are judged depending on the context and the power of the individuals and groups involved. As Becker (1963/1973) makes clear,

> A major element in every aspect of the drama of deviance is the imposition of definitions—of situations, acts, and people—by those powerful enough or sufficiently legitimated to be able to do so. A full understanding requires the thorough study of those definitions and the processes by which they develop and attain legitimacy and taken-for-grantedness. (p. 207)

According to the labeling perspective, deviance is a status imposed on an individual or a group that may or may not be related to actual rule breaking. The focus is on reactions rather than norm violations; you could be falsely accused but still be labeled deviant and face the repercussions. When there are disagreements over when and whether an actor should be considered deviant, power is a key element through which the status of deviance is imposed. Individuals with power will be better able both to reject a label and to impose a deviant label on another. Matsueda (1992) makes this connection clear in the following excerpt:

> A hallmark of labeling theory is the proposition that deviant labels are not randomly distributed across the social structure, but are instead more likely to apply to the powerless, the disadvantaged, and the poor. . . . Moreover, the powerless, having fewer cultural and material resources at their disposal, may be more likely to accept deviant labels. Again, the result is a self-fulfilling prophesy: members of disadvantaged groups are labeled delinquent, which alters their self-conceptions and causes them to deviate, thus fulfilling the prophesy of their initial label. (p. 1558)

◈ Development of Labeling Theory

One of the earliest building blocks for the labeling perspective was developed in the work of Franklin Tannenbaum (1938). Tannenbaum suggested that police contact may turn relatively common acts of juvenile delinquency into a "dramatization of evil" that labels the individuals involved in a negative light. This societal reaction may lead to further deviant acts.

In his book *Social Pathology*, Edwin Lemert (1951) made the important distinction between primary and secondary deviation. **Primary deviance** refers to common instances where individuals violate norms without viewing themselves as being involved in a deviant social role. Primary deviance consists of incidental deviant acts—instances in which an individual breaks or violates norms but does not do so chronically. For example, teens may occasionally shoplift while with their friends, but they would not consider themselves delinquent.

With primary deviation, there is no engulfment in a deviant social role, but primary deviance can serve to trigger the labeling process. Individuals can be caught as they engage in deviant acts, and they may then be labeled delinquent, criminal, or mentally ill. Once labeled, they may move into secondary deviation. **Secondary deviance** occurs when a person begins to engage in deviant behavior as a means of defense, attack, or adjustment to the problems created by reactions to him or her. In some cases, when rules are broken, it elicits a reaction. In defense to the reaction, the individual may commit subsequent deviant acts and begin a more serious deviant career. Labeling someone deviant and treating that person as if he or she is "generally rather than specifically deviant produces a **self-fulfilling prophecy.** It sets in motion several mechanisms which conspire to shape the person in the image people have of him" (Becker, 1963/1973, p. 34).

For Lemert and other labeling theorists, the cause of the initial deviance is left unexplained. Rather than asking why someone commits a deviant act, the questions are these: who decides what is deviant, who is to be labeled deviant, and under what circumstances should someone be considered deviant? Howard S. Becker's (1963/1973) explanation of this view in his book *Outsiders* has become the classic interactionist or relativist statement of labeling and deviance. He writes,

> *Social groups create deviance by making the rules whose infraction constitutes deviance*, and by applying those rules to particular people and labeling them as outsiders. From this point of view, deviance is *not* a quality of the act the person commits, but rather a consequence of the application by others of rules and sanctions to an "offender." The deviant is one to whom that label has successfully been applied; deviant behavior is behavior people so label. (Becker, 1963/1973, p. 9)

◇ How the Labeling Process Works

If diagrammed in its simplest form, the labeling process would look something like this:

Deviance → reaction → role engulfment → secondary deviance

It's not that simple, of course, and the lines would not be so direct. In fact, there would be reciprocal or circular relationships as well, with lines going back and forth between deviance, reaction, secondary deviance, and role engulfment. Imagine that when you were a teenager, you were caught cheating on an exam. If it's your first offense (or the first time you were caught), there may be an informal reaction—a conference with your teacher and parents, a failing grade, and a strict warning. After this event, your teachers and parents may monitor your behavior more closely. You may commit more deviant or criminal acts to push the boundaries or because you are bored, or your friends are involved, and it looks like fun. If you are caught stealing from a store, the case begins to build that you are generally a troublemaker and a "bad kid" likely to cause further trouble. When treated this way and closely monitored, you may start to *feel* like a bad kid. If the reaction is severe enough (for example, being adjudicated delinquent in juvenile court), other parents may not want their children to spend time with you. You may start hanging out with the other "bad" kids (role engulfment) and committing more serious crimes (secondary deviance).

Labeling theory is an interactionist theory and does not suggest that once on the path to deviance, one must continue in that direction. As Becker (1963/1973) explains,

> Obviously, everyone caught in one deviant act and labeled a deviant does not move inevitably toward greater deviance . . . he may decide that he does not want to take the deviant road and turn back. If he makes the right choice, he will be welcomed back into the conventional community; but if he makes the wrong move, he will be rejected and start a cycle of increasing deviance. (pp. 36–37)

Labeling can lead to secondary deviance in three general and overlapping ways: by altering an individual's self-concept, by limiting conforming opportunities, and by encouraging involvement in a deviant subculture (Kubrin, Stucky, & Krohn, 2009, p. 203). Being labeled deviant may also lead to a deviant **master status,** a status that proves to be more important than most others. A deviant master status elicits strong reactions and shapes the perception and behavior of those around you. For example, being labeled a sex offender is often a master status; sex offenders may also be parents, spouses, employees, and friends, but once labeled a sex offender, that identity takes priority in the minds of others.

DEVIANCE IN POPULAR CULTURE

The process of labeling is a powerful theoretical concept and tool in studying deviant behavior. Can the way that others view you and react to you influence how you think of yourself and behave? If you cannot think of examples from your own life or family or friends, popular-culture films and television shows portray a wide variety of types of deviance and examples of labeling.

One Flew Over the Cuckoo's Nest—This is a classic film about life in a mental hospital. When R. P. McMurphy is sent to the state mental institution, he is not crazy; he has run afoul of the law and simply believes it will be

(Continued)

(Continued)

easier to serve his time in a mental hospital, rather than in a corrections facility or work camp. He does not, however, understand the power of the label as it relates to mental illness. Watch this film, and pay attention to how McMurphy and the other patients are treated by the hospital staff. How does it make the patients think about themselves? Why is McMurphy's presence so disruptive to the routine of the ward? How is he punished for not playing the expected role?

Girl, Interrupted—This film focuses on the experiences of young women inside a mental institution. Based on Susanna Kaysen's memoir detailing more than a year of voluntary institutionalization, the film is another strong example of labeling and mental illness.

Made—This MTV television show produced nearly 400 episodes, each one focused on teenagers working to change their labels—the shy boy who wants to become a ladies' man, the tomboy who aspires to be a beauty queen, or the artsy drama girl who wants to make the cheerleading squad. It's difficult to even describe the show without using labels as part of the description. What were some of your labels in high school? How do you think your life would have been different if you had a more positive or a more negative label? Do you think it's possible to re-create yourself—and the way others view you—in a relatively short amount of time as they did on *Made*? Why or why not?

The DUFF—When a high school senior finds out that the student body considers her the DUFF (Designated Ugly Fat Friend) to her attractive, popular friends, she works to reinvent herself and overthrow the school's label maker.

Divergent—The book(s) and film(s) portray a dystopian society where individuals are sorted into five factions based on their affinity for either selflessness (Abnegation), intellectualism (Erudite), honesty (Candor), peace (Amity), or bravery (Dauntless). The labels and factions are permanently applied and dramatically affect the development and lives of the characters.

◈ Labeling and Mental Illness

Scheff (1966) laid out a theory of labeling and mental illness that suggests most mental illness begins with a form of primary deviance he calls **residual rule breaking**. Residual rule breaking is essentially deviance for which there exists no clear category—it is not a crime, but it may be behavior that draws attention and makes the societal audience uncomfortable. Inappropriate dress, conversation, or interactions may be perceived as residual rule breaking. Consistent with other labeling theorists' ideas on primary deviance, Scheff is not particularly concerned with why people commit these acts in the first place; he argues that residual rule breaking comes from diverse sources. The acts may stem from biological, psychological, or situational conditions. Most residual rule breaking is denied and deemed insignificant, and the individuals get past it and move on with their lives.

Importantly, however, residual rule breaking can activate the labeling process. Say, for example, a college student breaks up with her boyfriend and stays in bed in her pajamas for a week. If she is left alone, this behavior might be written off as painful but temporary heartache and the incident might pass. If, however, her concerned parents take her to a doctor or a hospital, she may be given a diagnosis of clinical depression and labeled as mentally ill. If she is hospitalized for any time at all, her roommates and friends may start treating her as if she is fragile and cannot cope with difficult circumstances.

Scheff (1966) suggests that the symptoms and stereotypes of mental illness are inadvertently reaffirmed in ordinary social interactions. Friends and family may reward those labeled mentally ill for going along with their expectations and playing the stereotyped role. At the same time, labeled deviants may be punished or blocked when attempting to resume their regular activities and return to conventional lives.

While most residual rule breaking can be explained away and deemed insignificant, it can be the starting point for the labeling process. Once labeled, many individuals will have a difficult time continuing or resuming their conventional roles. Thus, Scheff (1966) argues that among residual rule breakers, labeling is a key factor leading to more serious and lengthy deviant careers.

David Rosenhan (1973) conducted a fascinating study of labeling and mental illness when he recruited eight sane citizens to act as "pseudopatients" and simulate symptoms of psychosis; they were admitted to 12 different mental hospitals across the United States over the course of the study. Once hospitalized, the pseudopatients immediately stopped simulating symptoms and began acting "normal" again, yet they had a difficult time proving themselves to be sane. Rosenhan begins his article with a provocative question: "If sanity and insanity exist, how shall we know them?" (p. 250), and he goes on to detail the treatment and medications received by the pseudopatients during their time in the mental hospitals. Real details of the pseudopatients' life histories were interpreted through the lens of their diagnoses; doctors and staff members assigned meaning to behaviors based on the individuals' diagnosis of schizophrenia. Throughout the experiment, the pseudopatients were issued nearly 2,100 pills, but only two of those were actually swallowed. As long as they were not causing trouble, hospital staff did not bother to ensure that the medication was taken as prescribed. The pseudopatients each entered the hospital without knowing when they would be discharged; they would only be released by convincing the staff that they were ready to return to the community. The length of hospitalization ranged from 7 to 53 days, with an average stay of 19 days. Ironically, when the pseudopatients were finally released from the hospital, each was discharged with a diagnosis of schizophrenia "in remission"; none were thought to be sane. Rosenhan concludes, "We now know that we cannot distinguish insanity from sanity . . . psychiatric diagnoses are rarely found to be in error. The label sticks, a mark of inadequacy forever" (1973, p. 257). You can read Rosenhan's full study in Reading 23 later in this chapter.

A more recent longitudinal study added depth to our understanding of the impact of being labeled mentally ill by exploring the stigma and social rejection experienced by mental patients once they return to the community (E. R. Wright, Gronfein, & Owens, 2000). The authors studied a cohort of 88 mental patients in a three-wave survey conducted while the individuals were institutionalized and in the two years following their discharge from a state hospital. They found that both institutionalization and community reactions affected the self-concept of former mental patients, concluding,

> Stigma is a powerful and persistent force in the lives of long-term mental patients . . . even for patients who have had extensive experience in the mental patient role, subsequent experiences of rejection increase and crystallize patients' self-deprecating feelings. . . . Our results demonstrate convincingly that exposure to stigmatizing experiences represents a potentially serious source of chronic or recurrent stress for mental patients who established identities as "mental patients." The fact that these effects persist over time and diminish feelings of mastery provides additional empirical support for modified labeling theory's claims that the impact of stigma on the self has long-term implications for a person's ability to function in society. (E. R. Wright et al., 2000, pp. 80–82)

◈ Labeling and Delinquency

Juvenile delinquency is another area where the labeling theory has been widely applied and used to create or change policies that affect the lives of young offenders. Although it predates any formal explication of the theory, the juvenile justice system itself was created in part because of a concern over the negative impact being labeled and treated as a criminal would have on a young person. The terminology used in juvenile court reflects this concern: Offenders in the juvenile system are "adjudicated delinquent," rather than convicted of a crime. One result of this gentler language is that delinquents processed through the juvenile system do not need to check the box on job applications that asks if they have been convicted of a felony. Another example that shows concern over labeling juveniles is that in many states, an offender's juvenile record may be sealed or expunged once he or she completes the sentence and stays out of trouble for a specified period of time. In effect, this offers juvenile offenders who pass through troubled times the possibility of a clean slate as adults.

William Chambliss (1973) offered a vivid example of delinquency, social power, and labeling in his article titled "The Saints and the Roughnecks." Chambliss began this research project by simply spending time "hanging out" with two different groups of high school boys—the working-class *Roughnecks* and the upper-middle-class *Saints*—from the same community. While both groups of boys were involved in similar levels and amounts of delinquency, the community reactions were quite different. The Saints were treated as good boys "sowing their wild oats" and were given the benefit of the doubt by teachers, police officers, and other community members. The Saints were never officially arrested for their behavior, and seven of the eight of them graduated from college and went on to lead successful, conforming lives. The Roughnecks, on the other hand, were viewed by the community as bad boys, troublemakers, and delinquents, and they were often in trouble with their teachers and the police. As adults, the Roughnecks had quite different outcomes than the Saints. While two of the Roughnecks went to college on athletic scholarships and later became high school teachers and coaches, two others committed murders and were sentenced to lengthy prison terms.

Chambliss was asked recently what surprised him in studying the Saints and Roughnecks; his response speaks to the impact of labels and how difficult it can be for those with less power to resist them.

▲ **Photo 8.2** From a labeling perspective, being hospitalized in a mental institution can be very damaging to the individual. If you were one of the pseudopatients in Rosenhan's study, how do you think institutionalization would have affected your self-image?

(1) How serious were the crimes of the Saints and how inconsequential were the crimes of the Roughnecks. (2) How readily the boys in each group accepted the labels attached to them even though the labels were incompatible with their actual behavior. (Inderbitzin & Boyd, 2010, p. 205)

Thinking about your own high school and adolescent experiences, you might be surprised at how familiar the story still sounds, long after it was written. Decades later, we see another case of a town's "golden boys" getting the benefit of the doubt even as they are accused of committing a horrific crime. The book *Our Guys*, by Bernard Lefkowitz (1997), chronicles a case in Glen Ridge, New Jersey, in which a group of well-to-do, popular athletes raped a 17-year-old mentally challenged girl with a baseball bat and a broomstick. When members of the community finally heard about this crime, their reaction was generally sympathy for the boys and concern for "our" guys' reputations—"They'll just be ruined by this." The boys had the power in this setting, and the girl, by virtue of her gender and her mental impairment, was easily labeled as the deviant. The boys in *Our Guys* are similar, in some way, to the Saints from Chambliss's study in that the community members did not see or chose to ignore years of the boys' escalating deviant behavior. The young men from Glen Ridge were obviously much more delinquent and destructive toward females in their community than the Saints, but they were able to get away with their bad behavior for a surprisingly long time, in part due to their positive label as the town's golden boys. Several of the Glen Ridge boys were eventually charged with the rape; Lefkowitz details the lengthy road to trial and, ultimately, the convictions of four of the boys for taking part in the sexual assault. Lefkowitz (1997) offers this overview of the case:

> A large group of charismatic athletes. A retarded young woman. The silence of the students and adults. The inclination to blame the woman and exonerate the men. These elements seemed to be linked by a familiar theme. . . . I began to frame Glen Ridge as a story of power and powerlessness: the power of young males and the community that venerated them, and the powerlessness of one marginalized young woman. (pp. 4–5)

As Lefkowitz's study in *Our Guys* makes clear, context matters when considering the impact of formal sanctioning and official labels of delinquency. You can read Chambliss's study, "The Saints and the Roughnecks," in its entirety later in this chapter.

While both the Saints and "our guys" benefitted from their privileged position in the larger community, stigma may also be deflected or denied in different ways in disadvantaged communities. Hirschfield (2008) conducted interviews with 20 minority youth from high-poverty urban neighborhoods and concluded that in the macrolevel context of severely disadvantaged neighborhoods, being arrested carries little stigma. Delinquent youth in his sample were quite concerned with being informally labeled by their family and friends, but arrest and processing by the justice system were viewed as relatively normal parts of adolescence in their neighborhoods and their experiences. Thus, labeling still matters and affects juvenile offenders in important ways, but researchers can work to better specify how macrolevel conditions affect perceptions of the label and community reaction.

▲ **Photo 8.3**   Being officially labeled delinquent may decrease the life chances of juvenile offenders; such labeling may lead to secondary deviance and more serious criminal careers.

© Stockbyte/Thinkstock

◈ Application of Labeling Theory

Braithwaite (1989), *Crime, Shame and Reintegration*

In *Crime, Shame and Reintegration,* John Braithwaite (1989) argues that societies will generally have lower crime rates if they can effectively communicate shame about crime. Importantly, however, Braithwaite makes a critical distinction between **reintegrative shaming** and stigmatization. With reintegrative shaming, the offender can be viewed as a good person who has done a bad deed; stigmatization, on the other hand, labels the offender a bad person. Put differently, "Stigmatization is unforgiving—the offender is left with the stigma permanently, whereas reintegrative shaming is forgiving" (Braithwaite, 2000, p. 282).

In Braithwaite's conceptualization of reintegrative shaming, an accused individual is expected to admit his or her offense, essentially accepting responsibility for the act and labeling the act as deviant, but then he or she is provided with an opportunity for reintegration back into society. In reintegration ceremonies, Braithwaite and Mugford (1994) argue that disapproval of a bad act is communicated while sustaining the identity of the actor as good. Shame is transmitted within a continuum of respect for the wrongdoer. Repair work is directed at ensuring that a deviant identity (one of the actor's multiple identities) does not become a master status trait that overwhelms other identities. (p. 142)

Braithwaite's work offers an alternative to simply labeling offenders deviant and creating new and harmful master statuses. The idea of reintegrative shaming has not been tested on a large scale in the United States as of yet, but it offers one promising alternative to punitive criminal justice policies that may engender serious deviant careers. According to Braithwaite's theory, while labeling makes things worse when it is stigmatizing, when done respectfully and focused on the act rather than the individual, labeling may actually reduce crime (Braithwaite, 2000, p. 288).

Matsueda (1992), "Reflected Appraisals, Parental Labeling, and Delinquency"

Building on the work of George Herbert Mead, Ross Matsueda (1992) developed an interactionist theory of the self and delinquency. In his study, Matsueda focused on informal labels made by an adolescent's parents and whether those parental appraisals affected delinquency by affecting the adolescent's own reflected appraisals (Matsueda, 1992, p. 1590). In essence, the idea is that labeling and the reflected appraisals of others can create a delinquent "self" that may lead the adolescent further into deviant behavior. Matsueda found that youths' reflected appraisals of themselves were strongly influenced by their parents' appraisals of them. As an example, if a boy perceives that his parents view him as a troublemaker, he may start to perceive himself that way, too, and may be more likely to act the part.

In a later study, Heimer and Matsueda (1994) explain secondary deviance as a "chain of events operating through labeling" (p. 381). According to them,

Youth who are older, nonblack, urban residents, and from nonintact homes commit more initial delinquent acts than others, which increases the chances that their parents will see them as rule-violators. In turn, labeling by parents increases the likelihood that these youth will affiliate with delinquent peers and see themselves as rule-violators from the standpoint of others, which ultimately increases the likelihood of future delinquent behavior. (pp. 381–382)

Rosenfield (1997), "Labeling Mental Illness"

A prominent study on labeling and mental illness centered on the concept and meaning of *stigma* (Rosenfield, 1997). Rosenfield (1997) suggests that stigma is an important point of disagreement for labeling theorists and their critics. For labeling theorists, the stigma attached to mental illness is a serious problem; in Goffman's words, "By definition, of course, we believe the person with a stigma is not quite human. On this assumption, we exercise varieties of discrimination, through which we effectively, if often unthinkingly, reduce his life chances" (Goffman, 1963, p. 5). Critics of labeling theory, on the other hand, suggest that stigma may be of little consequence to the mentally ill. Rosenfield designed a research project to compare the receipt of treatment and services versus the perception of stigma on the quality of life for people with chronic mental illness.

Rosenfield's (1997) research was conducted at a clubhouse-model program for people with chronic mental illness residing in the community. The club took an "empowerment approach" and offered a range of services, including psychiatric treatment, supervision, life skills, and vocational rehabilitation. Rosenfield found that "stigma is a problem for most people with chronic mental illness, and perceptions of stigma have a significant negative relationship with patients' quality of life. By contrast, services have a strong positive association with quality of life" (p. 669). As might be expected, then, Rosenfield concludes, "Life satisfaction is highest for those who experience little stigma and gain access to high quality services. Life satisfaction is lowest among those perceiving high levels of stigma and lacking such services" (p. 670).

Davies and Tanner (2003), "The Long Arm of the Law: Effects of Labeling on Employment"

A recent study on formal labeling by schools and the justice system suggests that labeling has long-term impacts on opportunities and employment. Davies and Tanner (2003) used a large, nationally representative sample to examine the effect that formal sanctions ranging from school suspension to incarceration during ages 15 to 23 had on subjects' occupational status, income, and employment 14 years later. While controlling for variables such as social background, prior deviant behavior, and family status, Davies and Tanner found that severe forms of labeling did have strong negative effects. They concluded, "The indirect effects of early encounters with teachers, police officers, courts, and prison systems upon the transition from adolescence to adult work roles are significant and cumulatively damaging" (p. 399). School-based sanctioning, such as being suspended or expelled, had a negative impact on later job outcomes for females but not for males. This finding reminds us of the complexity of the social world and how difficult it can be to tease out all of the relevant factors. While the Davies and Tanner study generally supports labeling theory, there is much work still to be done to fully understand all of the variables and interactions that affect the labeling process.

DEFINING ONESELF AS DEVIANT

How does one learn to define oneself as deviant? Terrell Hayes interviewed 46 individuals who attended Debtors Anonymous meetings to examine the process by which these individuals assumed the deviant status of "debtor." He examined the processes of both social labeling and self-labeling and found that most individuals went through several stages in which they slowly came to see themselves as a person with a problem.

Hayes (2010) found that social labeling involved "active cues" and "passive cues" in which the individual was confronted with the problem. The active cues involved informal interactions with close others (friends, spouses, relatives) who identified the individual's behavior as problematic.

(My husband) was saying that I was sick, sick, sick. I stayed in denial for a while saying (to him) you indulge yourself, I'm certainly entitled to indulge myself. . . . But then I began examining that finally agreeing with my husband (and others) that I overspend. (p. 281)

Passive cues, in the form of literature and other materials, can also be part of the self-labeling process. Finally, Hayes found that self-help groups contributed to the labeling process and likelihood that individuals would label themselves as debtors. Interestingly enough, these self-help groups were not limited to Debtors Anonymous. Several of his participants actually identified their time in other self-help groups as being a catalyst for their self-identification as debtors in need of help. Do you think labeling theorists would consider such groups as helping or hurting their participants?

◈ Impact of Labeling Theory

The labeling perspective caught hold in the United States during the 1970s and had a clear impact on public policy in two distinct areas: juvenile justice and the care of mental patients. As research showed the potential negative impact of being labeled delinquent (Chambliss, 1973) and being labeled mentally ill (Rosenhan, 1973), policymakers took notice and began to rethink how to best serve those populations.

Some change happened organically as individuals working in these systems strove for better and more humane results. Jerome Miller, the commissioner of the Department of Youth Services in Massachusetts, frustrated with the conditions in the juvenile correctional facilities in his agency, closed all of the state's training schools between 1970 and 1972 (Miller, 1998). Miller's original goal was to make the state's reform schools more humane, with more therapy and individualized treatment for incarcerated youth. But, as he tells it,

> Whenever I thought we'd made progress, something happened, a beating, a kid in an isolation cell, an offhand remark by a superintendent or cottage supervisor that told me what I envisioned would never be allowed. . . . The decision to close the institutions grew from my frustration at not being able to keep them caring and decent. (p. 18)

Over a two-year span, Massachusetts closed its secure reform schools and moved to a system of alternative community treatment and placements for youth considered the most dangerous in the state.

Miller's closing of Massachusetts's reform schools can be viewed in the larger context of **deinstitutionalization** that was occurring in the early 1970s. As Miller (1998) explained, "While we were moving a few hundred delinquents back to the community, state departments of mental health across the United States were deinstitutionalizing thousands of mental patients" (p. 20).

Edwin Schur (1973) suggested that a better way for our juvenile justice system to operate was to not institutionalize young offenders in the first place. Schur argued strongly for a policy of radical **nonintervention**—in other words, in dealing with delinquent youth, we should choose to "leave the kids alone wherever possible." Schur advocated a "hands-off" approach to juvenile misbehavior, which would purposely take moral judgment away from juvenile courts.

In 1974, the United States passed the Juvenile Justice Delinquency Prevention (JJDP) Act, which significantly altered the juvenile corrections system. Concerns over the labeling of minor offenders as delinquents and the potential for criminal learning in juvenile institutions led to widespread attempts to deinstitutionalize youth, tolerate minor misbehavior, and use community alternatives for youth who needed intervention. The JJDP Act offered states funding as an incentive to decriminalize status offenses (behavior such as truancy, disobedience, or running away that would not be crimes if committed by adults) and to deinstitutionalize status offenders. Reform schools and secure juvenile institutions became the agency of last resort, reserved for the most serious juvenile offenders.

Times have certainly changed since then, and while the juvenile justice system still exists and attempts to resocialize delinquent youth, the United States now incarcerates more people than in any other period in history. Punitive laws have largely replaced the goal of rehabilitation, and serious juvenile offenders are routinely tried and convicted as adults.

In recent years, scholars such as Braithwaite (2002) have endorsed a move to **restorative justice**. In a system of restorative justice, "The state functions as an arbiter or partner who works with the victim and the offender to reduce the harm associated with the criminal act that has been committed" (Cullen & Agnew, 2006, p. 270). Typically, restorative justice involves bringing the victims, offenders, and community members together in a mediated conference. The goal of these conferences is for the offenders to take responsibility for their actions and to reach consensus on a plan for them to restore the harm they have caused, often through restitution to the victim and service to the community.

◈ Critiques of Labeling Theory

Labeling theory has been widely critiqued as an explanation for why people commit deviant acts or crime. Rather than asking why individuals commit acts against the norms of society, this perspective focuses on how and under what circumstances the individual is judged as deviant and what impact that judgment may have on his or her self-concept, relationships, opportunities, and life chances. Early analyses of labeling did not show empirical support for the tenets of the theory, but those studies may have misinterpreted the claims of the impact of labeling.

Becker (1963/1973) suggested that labeling was never intended to be a full-blown theory of deviance, but instead, it offered a perspective that shifted the focus to the process of constructing deviance. Early proponents of the labeling perspective

> wanted to enlarge the area taken into consideration in the study of deviant phenomena by including in it activities of others than the allegedly deviant actor. . . . [O]ne of the most important contributions of this approach has been to focus attention on the way labeling places the actor in circumstances which make it harder for him or her to continue the normal routines of everyday life and thus provoke him or her to "abnormal" actions (such as when a prison record makes it harder to earn a living at a conventional occupation and so disposes its possessor to move into an illegal one). (Becker, 1963/1973, p. 179)

In discussing the development of labeling theory, Cullen and Agnew (2011) conclude that the ideas of labeling are likely helpful additions to the study of crime and deviance if used judiciously.

> Labeling theorists also often pay insufficient attention to how, independent of societal reaction, structural inequality and the concentration of disadvantage in inner-city communities might affect behavior. Nonetheless, scholars working in this tradition have identified a factor—stigmatizing, rejecting, nasty societal reactions—that rarely makes matters better and more often serves only to solidify an offender's commitment to a criminal career. It would be unwise, therefore, for criminologists to assume that "labeling has no effects," and more prudent for them to continue to specify the conditions under which societal reaction pushes offenders into, rather than out of, a life in crime. (Cullen & Agnew, 2011, p. 246)

◈ Explaining Deviance in the Streets and Deviance in the Suites: Considering Drinking—and Not Drinking—on College Campuses

Drinking alcohol is part of many rituals of college life, including fraternity parties and initiations and sporting events where universities allow tailgating and, implicitly, at least seem to encourage alcohol consumption. Young people in college are often away from home for the first time, and part of their college experience is testing boundaries and trying out their new freedoms. Many use alcohol to get over their own sense of shyness or awkwardness in social situations. Binge drinking and episodic drinking, or going beyond a "buzz," are part of the social life of many college students. Vander Ven (2011) argues that taking care of others who have imbibed to the point of illness offers some student drinkers their first real adult responsibility. Approximately 40% of young Americans between the ages of 18 and 25 reported that they had binged on alcohol (had five or more drinks on one occasion) in the last month, and that number has remained relatively constant for at least a generation (Szalavitz, 2012).

Binge drinking in college might be viewed as a form of elite deviance. Vander Ven suggests that heavy drinking emerged in the Ivy League and remains one way of showing status. He says,

There was a lot of heavy drinking in the big three Ivy League schools. It represented establishment privilege. If I go away to college and I spend most of my time just drinking, and not working hard, that sort of suggests to my audience that I don't need to work hard and that I'm one of the elite. Some of that still happens today. One way to demonstrate to your audience that you have a lot of money and status is to buy a round of drinks. And students today are jacking up their credit card debt by buying a lot of drinks for others and themselves. (Quoted in Rogers, 2011)

Many college towns bring together middle-class and elite students and working-class locals. Bars and other local establishments profit from and need the students' business, so they put up with a degree of unpleasant drunkenness in order to keep profits flowing. In a recent study of college students' "determined drunkenness" in England, the authors found that social class mattered in how such behavior was perceived. They observed,

There is a long history of ritualized drinking to excess amongst upper-class young men. However, this often takes place in the more secluded spaces of university colleges or private school grounds, and in the event of more public displays of drunken excess, this elite group have the money to buy themselves out of trouble (Ronay, 2008). The upper class as a whole is seldom subject to the same level of horrified moral outrage and disgust that has been directed at the drinking practices of white working-class youth. (Griffin, Bengry-Howell, Hackley, Mistral, & Szmigin, 2009, p. 460)

Among the study participants, binge drinking was viewed as a bonding activity that sometimes got out of control. There was a sense of escape and fun in student narratives about drinking with their friends, even as they told stories of going out, getting drunk, losing consciousness, and sometimes waking up in a hospital (Griffin et al., 2009). In spite of such serious consequences of binge drinking, the students appeared to suffer no long-term ill effects on their health or their status. Their drinking behavior was virtually ignored by their college administrators and local law enforcement, generally garnering no response or sanction.

College students are in a relatively privileged position, and their status likely offers some level of protection against negative labels. Drinking is often the norm on college campuses; in a recent study of nondrinkers on a "wet" campus or "party school," Herman-Kinney and Kinney (2013) found that only about 17% of students self-identified as nondrinkers. The nondrinkers reported that they were viewed as abnormal by their peers and "labeled deviant if you don't drink" (p. 72). Nondrinkers reported being stigmatized, harassed, and ostracized by their classmates. To avoid the negative labels and stigma, nondrinkers developed strategies to appear to be drinking, such as carrying around red plastic cups or nearly empty drinks and pretending to be getting drunk with their peers. Alternatively, they learned to simply stay away from parties and tailgating where heavy drinking was the norm. The authors concluded that

the drinkers as a group on the Keg State campus, and the social organizations (e.g., Greek, varsity athletics) of which they are a part, are essentially the ones with the power; the words that they use to stigmatize nondrinkers are fighting words—pussy, weanie, loser. In addition to the verbal warfare, we found instances of behavioral violence (e.g., showering with beer, damaging personal property). . . . [T]he drinkers may come to the realization that the nondrinkers are more likely to be successful adults because they are not spending time getting wasted and nursing hangovers, but focusing on what college is all about, preparing oneself for a successful future. (Herman-Kinney & Kinney, 2013, p. 95)

◈ Ideas in Action: The "I Have a Dream" Foundation—Instilling Positive Labels

In 1981, millionaire businessman Eugene M. Lang went back to give a speech to the graduating sixth-graders at the public elementary school he had attended in East Harlem. The future looked grim for many of those youth—Lang was told that three quarters of the students would likely never finish high school. As Lang took the stage, he made a surprising spur-of-the-moment decision: He promised the entire sixth-grade class that he would pay the college tuition for every student who stayed in high school and graduated. Lang built relationships with his Dreamers and made sure that they had the services and support they needed to succeed. He also began talking about the program and sharing his vision in the media. In 1986, Lang started the "I Have a Dream" Foundation in order to launch more "I Have a Dream" programs across the country.

The mission of the foundation is as follows:

> The "I Have A Dream" Foundation empowers children in low-income communities to achieve higher education and fulfill their leadership potential by providing them with guaranteed tuition support and equipping them with the skills, knowledge, and habits they need to gain entry to higher education and succeed in college and beyond.
>
> By helping our Dreamers gain access to college, we are putting our Dreamers on a different academic and life trajectory, while having a broader impact on the students' families and the generations that follow. (http://www.ihaveadreamfoundation.org/html)

There are now more than 200 "I Have a Dream" programs in 27 states, and more than 15,000 children have become Dreamers. The "I Have a Dream" approach is to sponsor a cohort of students in a lower income school or public housing development. The students are selected in the early years of elementary school and are given support and encouragement all the way through high school. If they decide to go to college, they are guaranteed that their tuition will be paid. While circumstances may vary by location, there are several common characteristics of "I Have a Dream" programs: (1) They are long term. Dreamers are selected in elementary school and followed and cared for until they enroll in college. (2) They are inclusive. Every child who is in a class at the time of sponsorship is given the same opportunity. They do not select the most promising or the most at-risk children to be Dreamers. All children are believed to be capable of succeeding if given the opportunity. (3) The programs are comprehensive. Along with focusing on education, the programs help Dreamers build life skills and cultural capital. The children are often taken on field trips to other parts of the country to expose them to careers and lifestyles they may aspire to. (4) The programs are leveraged. They work with local and national community partners to support their Dreamers and other children and families in similar circumstances.

Research on "I Have a Dream" programs has shown that Dreamers have improved school attendance and grades, have higher aspirations, and have more positive attitudes about the future. The Dreamers are better able to resist peer pressure, and they often graduate high school and attend college at double the rate of their peers.

Eugene Lang and the "I Have a Dream" Foundation have inspired other wealthy sponsors to create their own programs. Businessman Paul Tudor Jones started the Robin Hood Foundation to fight poverty in New York; the Robin Hood Foundation's board of directors personally pay for all operating costs, so every dollar that is donated goes directly to fighting poverty. Over the past 20 years, the Robin Hood Foundation has distributed more than a billion dollars to the most effective poverty-fighting programs.

The "I Have a Dream" Foundation offers children growing up in poor areas hope for a better future. Being labeled a Dreamer inspires positive deviance in the form of graduating high school and going to college, and it brings about a whole new set of expectations for the children's behavior and future. Children who were demographically at high risk of dropping out of school are given a reason to keep attending, keep working, and stay out of trouble. The positive label of "Dreamer" has certainly changed and improved the lives of many children. Just as negative labels can lead to stigma and negative responses from the individual, positive labels and opportunities can set youth on a trajectory for success.

NOW YOU . . . USE THE THEORY

In 1983, Edwin Schur published a book titled *Labeling Women Deviant: Gender, Stigma and Social Control*. One of Schur's arguments in the book is that women are more quickly and strongly labeled for their behavior if it falls outside of normative boundaries than men are. To highlight this gender imbalance in labeling, an often-used class exercise is one in which students are asked to think up all the derogatory labels that they can for men and women. Inevitably, that list is much longer for women than for men.

What are the normative expectations for women and men in society? Make a list of expected behaviors for each group. After making this list, make a list of positive labels associated with each group. Now make a list of negative labels associated with each group. How are these labels used in society? What is the relationship with power—both the use of power and the loss of power associated with these labels? According to the labels, which normative behaviors are most likely to produce a reaction if violated?

Was Schur right? Do his ideas still hold more than 30 years after the publication of his book? Are women more likely to be labeled for stepping outside the normative boundaries than men? What do you think has changed since 1983?

◈ Conclusion

Returning for a moment to the film *The Breakfast Club*, the letter that opened this chapter also opened the film. By the end of their day in detention—and the end of the film—the students have started to know each other and have learned to look beyond the labels of their high school cliques. They view and treat each other much differently at the end of the day than they did in the beginning. Each student contributes his or her voice to the final letter left for the principal when they are freed from detention.

Brian Johnson: Dear Mr. Vernon, we accept the fact that we had to sacrifice a whole Saturday in detention for whatever it was we did wrong . . . but we think you're crazy to make us write an essay telling you who we think we are. You see us as you want to see us . . . in the simplest terms and the most convenient definitions. But what we found out is that each one of us is a brain . . .

Andrew Clark: . . . and an athlete . . .

Allison Reynolds: . . . and a basket case . . .

Claire Standish: . . . a princess . . .

John Bender: . . . and a criminal.

Brian Johnson: Does that answer your question? Sincerely yours, the Breakfast Club.

If you pay attention to the world around you, you will see labels everywhere. They offer a convenient shorthand and can be helpful in categorizing complex relationships and interactions. But as the labeling perspective points out, being labeled deviant can have long-lasting, harmful impacts on an individual's self-concept and life chances. These issues will be further discussed in Chapter 11 (Social Control of Deviance) and Chapter 12 (Deviant Careers and Career Deviance), where we will explore the role of prisons, juvenile facilities, and mental hospitals as agents of social control and examine how they can affect the individual long after the original act and application of the deviant label.

In pointing to the larger ideas of the labeling perspective and to Howard Becker's work, in particular, as offering important sensitizing concepts for sociologists studying deviant behavior, Orcutt (1983) suggests that

> the impact of labeling theory on the field of deviance cannot be measured in strictly scientific terms alone. The work of the labeling theorists not only portrayed the definition and control of deviance as analytically problematic but also as morally and politically problematic. . . . This relativistic conception of labeling as a power game provides the basic ingredient for a political critique of the uses and abuses of social control by certain dominant groups in modern, complex societies. (pp. 241–242)

Certainly the relativist perspective broadened the way we think about deviant behavior and social control. Studies from labeling and conflict theories have highlighted the importance of power and inequality in defining deviance and in the differential enforcement of norms and laws. Chapter 9 will build on these ideas by introducing you to conflict theory, and Chapter 10 will provide an overview of critical theories of deviance.

EXERCISES AND DISCUSSION QUESTIONS

1. Imagine you were officially labeled deviant in junior high school. How do you think this would have affected your life and your opportunities? Would your parents, teachers, and peers have treated you differently? Where do you think you would be now if you had been labeled delinquent?

2. Based on the reading, what types of primary deviance do the Saints and the Roughnecks commit? Who goes on to commit secondary deviance? What are examples from the article of secondary deviance?

3. Another surprising finding Chambliss mentioned in studying the Saints and the Roughnecks was "how easily some of them [the two football players] changed their self image, their behavior and their lives" (Inderbitzin & Boyd, 2010). What do you think might have made the difference for those young men? What does that suggest for how we treat delinquents?

4. Why do you think the athletes from Glen Ridge (in *Our Guys*) were so difficult to label deviant? What affected the process? How might the victim's gender and mental challenges have contributed to the situation?

5. Can you imagine volunteering as a pseudopatient if we were going to replicate Rosenhan's study in "On Being Sane in Insane Places"? Why or why not? As a (presumably) sane person, how do you think being labeled as mentally ill and being hospitalized would affect your self-concept?

6. Sex offenders have been particularly demonized and feared in the United States. While ostensibly set up to provide important information to community members, sex offender registries have taken public labeling to a whole new level. There is real reason for fear when one's vital statistics, address, and photo are posted online on sex offender registries: Vigilantes killed two sex offenders in Washington state in 2005, and two more were shot to death in Maine in 2006 (Daniel, 2006; J. Martin & O'Hagan, 2005; O'Hagan & Brooks, 2005).

7. An important issue is that the label "sex offender" is a broad one, encompassing both predatory crimes and statutory ones. Take, for example, the case of Ricky Blackman, convicted as a sex offender for having intercourse with a 13-year-old girl when he was 16. The label and his place on a sex offender registry affected Blackman's life in many ways: He couldn't go to high school, couldn't attend sporting events, and couldn't even go into the public library (Grinberg, 2010). What do you think of sex offender registries? What are their strengths and weaknesses? How do you think society should deal with cases like Ricky Blackman?

KEY TERMS

Deinstitutionalization

Looking-glass self

Master status

Nonintervention

Primary deviance

Reintegrative shaming

Residual rule breaking

Restorative justice

Secondary deviance

Self-fulfilling prophecy

Symbolic interactionism

READING 22

For this piece, William Chambliss spent two years "hanging out" with two different groups of high school boys—the working-class "Roughnecks" and the upper-middle-class "Saints." While both groups were involved in similar levels and amounts of delinquency, the community reactions were quite different. The Saints were never officially arrested for their behavior, whereas the Roughnecks were often in trouble with the police. Chambliss poses two questions, the first dealing with why the community, school, and police reacted so differently to the two groups and the second dealing with why the two groups had such different outcomes following high school. Concerning the first question, Chambliss cites the differential visibility of the deviant behaviors, differences in demeanor toward authority figures, and bias among community residents, school officials, and the police. With regard to the second question, Chambliss kept in touch with these young men through early adulthood and was thus able to document the actual long-term outcomes of the boys. Because of the small sample size and other limitations of the data, Chambliss is cautious in answering the second question, but he clearly hints at the long-term effects of labels and community expectations on the life chances and adult careers of these two distinct groups of boys.

The Saints and the Roughnecks

William J. Chambliss

Eight promising young men—children of good, stable, white upper-middle-class families, active in school affairs, good pre-college students—were some of the most delinquent boys at Hanibal High School. While community residents knew that these boys occasionally sowed a few wild oats, they were totally unaware that sowing wild oats completely occupied the daily routine of these young men. The Saints were constantly occupied with truancy, drinking, wild driving, petty theft, and vandalism. Yet no one was officially arrested for any misdeed during the two years I observed them.

Source: Chambliss, W. J. (1973, November/December). The Saints and the Roughnecks. *Society*, pp. 24–31. With kind permission from Springer Science + Business Media.

This record was particularly surprising in light of my observations during the same two years of another gang of Hanibal High School students, six lower class white boys known as the Roughnecks. The Roughnecks were constantly in trouble with police and community even though their rate of delinquency was about equal with that of the Saints. What was the cause of this disparity? The result? The following consideration of the activities, social class, and community perceptions of both gangs may provide some answers.

◈ The Saints From Monday to Friday

The Saints' principal daily concern was with getting out of school as early as possible. The boys managed to get out of school with minimum danger that they would be accused of playing hooky through an elaborate procedure for obtaining "legitimate" release from class. The most common procedure was for one boy to obtain the release of another by fabricating a meeting of some committee, program, or recognized club. Charles might raise his hand in his 9:00 chemistry class and ask to be excused—a euphemism for going to the bathroom. Charles would go to Ed's math class and inform the teacher that Ed was needed for a 9:30 rehearsal of the drama club play. The math teacher would recognize Ed and Charles as "good students" involved in numerous school activities and would permit Ed to leave at 9:30. Charles would return to his class, and Ed would go to Tom's English class to obtain his release. Tom would engineer Charles's escape. The strategy would continue until as many of the Saints as possible were freed. After a stealthy trip to the car (which had been parked in a strategic spot), the boys were off for a day of fun.

Over the two years I observed the Saints, this pattern was repeated nearly every day. There were variations on the theme, but in one form or another, the boys used this procedure for getting out of class and then off the school grounds. Rarely did all eight of the Saints manage to leave school at the same time. The average number avoiding school on the days I observed them was five.

Having escaped from the concrete corridors the boys usually went either to a pool hall on the other (lower class) side of town or to a café in the suburbs.

Both places were out of the way of people the boys were likely to know (family or school officials), and both provided a source of entertainment. The pool hall entertainment was the generally rough atmosphere, the occasional hustler, the sometimes drunk proprietor and, of course, the game of pool. The café's entertainment was provided by the owner. The boys would "accidentally" knock a glass on the floor or spill cola on the counter—not all the time, but enough to be sporting. They would also bend spoons, put salt in sugar bowls and generally tease whoever was working in the café. The owner had opened the café recently and was dependent on the boys' business, which was, in fact, substantial since between the horsing around and the teasing they bought food and drinks.

◈ The Saints on Weekends

On weekends the automobile was even more critical than during the week, for on weekends the Saints went to Big Town—a large city with a population of over a million 25 miles from Hanibal. Every Friday and Saturday night most of the Saints would meet between 8:00 and 8:30 and would go into Big Town. Big Town activities included drinking heavily in taverns or nightclubs, driving drunkenly through the streets, and committing acts of vandalism and playing pranks.

By midnight on Fridays and Saturdays the Saints were usually thoroughly high, and one or two of them were often so drunk they had to be carried to the cars. Then the boys drove around town, calling obscenities to women and girls; occasionally trying (unsuccessfully so far as I could tell) to pick girls up; and driving recklessly through red lights and at high speeds with their lights out. Occasionally they played "chicken." One boy would climb out the back window of the car and across the roof to the driver's side of the car while the car was moving at high speed (between 40 and 50 miles an hour); then the driver would move over and the boy who had just crawled across the car roof would take the driver's seat.

Searching for "fair game" for a prank was the boys' principal activity after they left the tavern. The boys would drive alongside a foot patrolman and ask directions to some street. If the policeman leaned on the car in the course of answering the question, the driver would speed away, causing him to lose his balance. The Saints were careful to play this prank only in an area where they were not going to spend much time and where they could quickly disappear around a corner to avoid having their license plate number taken.

Construction sites and road repair areas were the special province of the Saints' mischief. A soon-to-be-repaired hole in the road inevitably invited the Saints to remove lanterns and wooden barricades and put them in the car, leaving the hole unprotected. The boys would find a safe vantage point and wait for an unsuspecting motorist to drive into the hole. Often, though not always, the boys would go up to the motorist and commiserate with him about the dreadful way the city protected its citizenry.

Leaving the scene of the open hole and the motorist, the boys would then go searching for an appropriate place to erect the stolen barricade. An "appropriate place" was often a spot on a highway near a curve in the road where the barricade would not be seen by an oncoming motorist. The boys would wait to watch an unsuspecting motorist attempt to stop and (usually) crash into the wooden barricade. With saintly bearing the boys might offer help and understanding.

A stolen lantern might well find its way onto the back of a police car or hang from a street lamp. Once a lantern served as a prop for a reenactment of the "midnight ride of Paul Revere" until the "play," which was taking place at 2:00 A.M. in the center of a main street of Big Town, was interrupted by a police car several blocks away. The boys ran, leaving the lanterns on the street, and managed to avoid being apprehended.

Abandoned houses, especially if they were located in out-of-the-way places, were fair game for destruction and spontaneous vandalism. The boys would break windows, remove furniture to the yard and tear it apart, urinate on the walls, and scrawl obscenities inside.

Through all the pranks, drinking, and reckless driving the boys managed miraculously to avoid being stopped by police. Only twice in two years was I aware that they had been stopped by a Big Town policeman. Once was for speeding (which they did every time they drove whether they were drunk or sober), and the driver managed to convince the policeman that it was simply an error. The second time they were stopped they had just left a nightclub and were walking through

an alley. Aaron stopped to urinate and the boys began making obscene remarks. A foot patrolman came into the alley, lectured the boys and sent them home. Before the boys got to the car one began talking in a loud voice again. The policeman, who had followed them down the alley, arrested this boy for disturbing the peace and took him to the police station where the other Saints gathered. After paying a $5.00 fine, and with the assurance that there would be no permanent record of the arrest, the boy was released.

The boys had a spirit of frivolity and fun about their escapades. They did not view what they were engaged in as "delinquency," though it surely was by any reasonable definition of that word. They simply viewed themselves as having a little fun and who, they would ask, was really hurt by it? The answer had to be no one, although this fact remains one of the most difficult things to explain about the gang's behavior. Unlikely though it seems, in two years of drinking, driving, carousing, and vandalism no one was seriously injured as a result of the Saints' activities.

◈ The Saints in School

The Saints were highly successful in school. The average grade for the group was "B," with two of the boys having close to a straight "A" average. Almost all of the boys were popular and many of them held offices in the school. One of the boys was vice president of the student body one year. Six of the boys played on athletic teams.

At the end of their senior year, the student body selected ten seniors for special recognition as the "school wheels"; four of the ten were Saints. Teachers and school officials saw no problem with any of these boys and anticipated that they would all "make something of themselves."

How the boys managed to maintain this impression is surprising in view of their actual behavior in school. Their technique for covering truancy was so successful that teachers did not even realize that the boys were absent from school much of the time. Occasionally, of course, the system would backfire and then the boy was on his own. A boy who was caught would be most contrite, would plead guilty and ask for mercy. He inevitably got the mercy he sought.

Cheating on examinations was rampant, even to the point of orally communicating answers to exams as well as looking at one another's papers. Since none of the group studied, and since they were primarily dependent on one another for help, it is surprising that grades were so high. Teachers contributed to the deception in their admitted inclination to give these boys (and presumably others like them) the benefit of the doubt. When asked how the boys did in school, and when pressed on specific examinations, teachers might admit that they were disappointed in John's performance, but would quickly add that they "knew that he was capable of doing better," so John was given a higher grade than he had actually earned. How often this happened is impossible to know. During the time that I observed the group, I never saw any of the boys take homework home. Teachers may have been "understanding" very regularly.

One exception to the gang's generally good performance was Jerry, who had a "C" average in his junior year, experienced disaster the next year, and failed to graduate. Jerry had always been a little more nonchalant than the others about the liberties he took in school. Rather than wait for someone to come get him from class, he would offer his own excuse and leave. Although he probably did not miss any more class than most of the others in the group, he did not take the requisite pains to cover his absences. Jerry was the only Saint whom I ever heard talk back to a teacher. Although teachers often called him a "cut up" or a "smart kid," they never referred to him as a troublemaker or as a kid headed for trouble. It seems likely, then, that Jerry's failure his senior year and his mediocre performance his junior year were consequences of his not playing the game the proper way (possibly because he was disturbed by his parents' divorce). His teachers regarded him as "immature" and not quite ready to get out of high school.

◈ The Police and the Saints

The local police saw the Saints as good boys who were among the leaders of the youth in the community. Rarely, the boys might be stopped in town for speeding or for running a stop sign. When this happened the boys were always polite, contrite and pled for mercy. As in school, they received the mercy they asked for. None ever received a ticket or was taken into the precinct by the local police.

The situation in Big Town, where the boys engaged in most of their delinquency, was only slightly different. The police there did not know the boys at all, although occasionally the boys were stopped by a patrolman. Once they were caught taking a lantern from a construction site. Another time they were stopped for running a stop sign, and on several occasions they were stopped for speeding. Their behavior was as before: contrite, polite and penitent. The urban police, like the local police, accepted their demeanor as sincere. More important, the urban police were convinced that these were good boys just out for a lark.

◈ The Roughnecks

Hanibal townspeople never perceived the Saints' high level of delinquency. The Saints were good boys who just went in for an occasional prank. After all, they were well dressed, well mannered and had nice cars. The Roughnecks were a different story. Although the two gangs of boys were the same age, and both groups engaged in an equal amount of wild-oat sowing, everyone agreed that the not-so-well-dressed, not-so-well-mannered, not-so-rich boys were heading for trouble. Townspeople would say, "You can see the gang members at the drugstore, night after night, leaning against the storefront (sometimes drunk) or slouching around inside buying cokes, reading magazines, and probably stealing old Mr. Wall blind. When they are outside and girls walk by, even respectable girls, these boys make suggestive remarks. Sometimes their remarks are downright lewd."

From the community's viewpoint, the real indication that these kids were in trouble was that they were constantly involved with the police. Some of them had been picked up for stealing, mostly small stuff, of course, "but still it's stealing small stuff that leads to big time crimes." "Too bad," people said. "Too bad that these boys couldn't behave like the other kids in town; stay out of trouble, be polite to adults, and look to their future."

The community's impression of the degrees to which this group of six boys (ranging in age from 16 to 19) engaged in delinquency was somewhat distorted. In some ways the gang was more delinquent than the community thought; in other ways they were less.

The fighting activities of the group were fairly readily and accurately perceived by almost everyone. At least once a month, the boys would get into some sort of fight, although most fights were scraps between members of the group or involved only one member of the group and some peripheral hanger-on. Only three times in the period of observation did the group fight together: once against a gang from across town, once against two blacks, and once against a group of boys from another school. For the first two fights the group went out "looking for trouble"—and they found it both times. The third fight followed a football game and began spontaneously with an argument on the football field between one of the Roughnecks and a member of the opposition's football team. Jack has a particular propensity for fighting and was involved in most of the brawls. He was a prime mover of the escalation of arguments into fights.

More serious than fighting, had the community been aware of it, was theft. Although almost everyone was aware that the boys occasionally stole things, they did not realize the extent of the activity. Petty stealing was a frequent event for the Roughnecks. Sometimes they stole as a group and coordinated their efforts; other things they stole in pairs. Rarely did they steal alone.

The thefts ranged from very small things like paperback books, comics, and ball-point pens to expensive items like watches. The nature of the thefts varied from time to time. The gang would go through a period of systematically lifting items from automobiles or school lockers. Types of thievery varied with the whim of the gang. Some forms of thievery were more profitable than others, but all thefts were for profit, not just thrills.

Roughnecks siphoned gasoline from cars as often as they had access to an automobile, which was not very often. Unlike the Saints, who owned their own cars, the Roughnecks would have to borrow their parents' cars, an event that occurred only eight or nine times a year. The boys claimed to have stolen cars for joy rides from time to time.

Ron committed the most serious of the group's offenses. With an unidentified associate the boy attempted to burglarize a gasoline station. Although this station had been robbed twice previously in the same month, Ron denied any involvement in either of the other thefts. When Ron and his accomplice approached the station, the owner was hiding in the bushes beside the station. He fired both barrels of a double-barreled shotgun at the boys. Ron was severely injured; the other boy ran away and was never caught. Though he remained in critical condition for several months, Ron finally recovered and served six months of the following year in reform school. Upon release from reform school, Ron was put back a grade in school, and began running around with a different gang of boys. The Roughnecks considered the new gang less delinquent than themselves, and during the following year Ron had no more trouble with the police.

The Roughnecks, then, engaged mainly in three types of delinquency: theft, drinking, and fighting. Although community members perceived that this gang of kids was delinquent, they mistakenly believed that their illegal activities were primarily drinking, fighting, and being a nuisance to passersby. Drinking was limited among the gang members, although it did occur, and theft was much more prevalent than anyone realized.

Drinking would doubtless have been more prevalent had the boys had ready access to liquor. Since they rarely had automobiles at their disposal, they could not travel very far, and the bars in town would not serve them.

Most of the boys had little money, and this, too, inhibited their purchase of alcohol. Their major source of liquor was a local drunk who would buy them a fifth if they would give him enough extra to buy himself a pint of whiskey or a bottle of wine.

The community's perception of drinking as prevalent stemmed from the fact that it was the most obvious delinquency the boys engaged in. When one of the boys had been drinking, even a casual observer seeing him on the corner would suspect that he was high.

There was a high level of mutual distrust and dislike between the Roughnecks and the police. The boys felt very strongly that the police were unfair and corrupt. Some evidence existed that the boys were correct in their perception.

The main source of the boys' dislike for the police undoubtedly stemmed from the fact that the police would sporadically harass the group. From the standpoint of the boys, these acts of occasional enforcement of the law were whimsical and uncalled for. It made no sense to them, for example, that the police would come to the corner occasionally and threaten them with arrest for loitering when the night before the boys had been out siphoning gasoline from cars and the police had been nowhere in sight. To the boys, the police were stupid on the one hand, for not being where they should have been and catching the boys in a serious offense, and unfair on the other hand, for trumping up "loitering" charges against them.

From the viewpoint of the police, the situation was quite different. They knew, with all the confidence necessary to be a policeman, that these boys were engaged in criminal activities. They knew this partly from occasionally catching them, mostly from circumstantial evidence ("the boys were around when those tires were slashed"), and partly because the police shared the view of the community in general that this was a bad bunch of boys. The best the police could hope to do was to be sensitive to the fact that these boys were engaged in illegal acts and arrest them whenever there was some evidence that they had been involved. Whether or not the boys had in fact committed a particular act in a particular way was not especially important. The police had a broader view: their job was to stamp out these kids' crimes; the tactics were not as important as the end result.

Over the period that the group was under observation, each member was arrested at least once. Several of the boys were arrested a number of times and spent at least one night in jail. While most were never taken to court, two of the boys were sentenced to six months' incarceration in boys' schools.

The Roughnecks in School

The Roughnecks' behavior in school was not particularly disruptive. During school hours they did not all hang around together, but tended instead to spend most of their time with one or two other members of the gang who were their special buddies. Although every member of the gang attempted to avoid school as much as possible, they were not particularly successful and most of them attended school with surprising regularity. They considered school a burden—something to be gotten through with a minimum of conflict. If they were "bugged" by a particular teacher, it could lead to trouble. One of the boys, Al, once threatened to beat up a teacher and, according to the other boys, the teacher hid under a desk to escape him.

Teachers saw the boys the way the general community did, as heading for trouble, as being uninterested in making something of themselves. Some were also seen as being incapable of meeting the academic standards of the school. Most of the teachers expressed concern for this group of boys and were willing to pass them despite poor performance, in the belief that failing them would only aggravate the problem.

The group of boys had a grade point average just slightly above "C." No one in the group failed either grade, and no one had better than a "C" average. They were very consistent in their achievement or, at least, the teachers were consistent in their perception of the boys' achievement.

Two of the boys were good football players. Herb was acknowledged to be the best player in the school and Jack was almost as good. Both boys were criticized for their failure to abide by training rules, for refusing to come to practice as often as they should, and for not playing their best during practice. What they lacked in sportsmanship they made up for in skill, apparently, and played every game no matter how poorly they had performed in practice or how many practice sessions they had missed.

Two Questions

Why did the community, the school, and the police react to the Saints as though they were good, upstanding, nondelinquent youths with bright futures but to the Roughnecks as though they were tough, young criminals who were headed for trouble? Why did the Roughnecks and the Saints in fact have quite different careers after high school—careers which, by and large, lived up to the expectations of the community?

The most obvious explanation for the differences in the community's and law enforcement agencies' reactions to the two gangs is that one group of boys was "more delinquent" than the other. Which group was more delinquent? The answer to this question will determine in part how we explain the differential responses to these groups by the members of the community and, particularly, by law enforcement and school officials.

In sheer number of illegal acts, the Saints were the more delinquent. They were truant from school for at least part of the day almost every day of the week. In addition, their drinking and vandalism occurred with surprising regularity. The Roughnecks, in contrast, engaged sporadically in delinquent episodes. While these episodes were frequent, they certainly did not occur on a daily or even a weekly basis.

The difference in frequency of offenses was probably caused by the Roughnecks' inability to obtain liquor and to manipulate legitimate excuses from school. Since the Roughnecks had less money than the Saints, and teachers carefully supervised their school activities, the Roughnecks' hearts may have been as black as the Saints', but their misdeeds were not nearly as frequent.

There are really no clear-cut criteria by which to measure qualitative differences in antisocial behavior. The most important dimension is generally referred to as the "seriousness" of the offenses.

If seriousness encompasses the relative economic costs of delinquent acts, then some assessment can be made. The Roughnecks probably stole an average of about $5.00 worth of goods a week. Some weeks the figure was considerably higher, but these times must be balanced against long periods when almost nothing was stolen.

The Saints were more continuously engaged in delinquency but their acts were not for the most part costly to property. Only their vandalism and occasional theft of gasoline would so qualify. Perhaps once or twice a month they would siphon a tankful of gas. The other costly items were street signs, construction lanterns, and the like. All of these acts combined probably did not quite average $5.00 a week, partly because much of the stolen equipment was abandoned and presumably could be recovered. The difference in cost of stolen property between the two groups was trivial, but the Roughnecks probably had a slightly more expensive set of activities than did the Saints.

Another meaning of seriousness is the potential threat of physical harm to members of the community and to the boys themselves. The Roughnecks were more prone to physical violence; they not only welcomed an opportunity to fight; they went seeking it. In addition, they fought among themselves frequently. Although the fighting never included deadly weapons, it was still a menace, however minor, to the physical safety of those involved.

The Saints never fought. They avoided physical conflict both inside and outside the group. At the same time, though, the Saints frequently endangered their own and other people's lives. They did so almost every time they drove a car, especially if they had been drinking. Sober, their driving was risky; under the influence of alcohol it was horrendous. In addition, the Saints endangered the lives of others with their pranks. Street excavations left unmarked were a very serious hazard.

Evaluating the relative seriousness of the two gangs' activities is difficult. The community reacted as though the behavior of the Roughnecks was a problem, and they reacted as though the behavior of the Saints was not. But the members of the community were ignorant of the array of delinquent acts that characterized the Saints' behavior. Although concerned citizens were unaware of much of the Roughnecks' behavior as well, they were much better informed about the Roughnecks' involvement in delinquency than they were about the Saints'.

◈ Visibility

Differential treatment of the two gangs resulted in part because one gang was infinitely more visible than the other. This differential visibility was a direct function of the economic standing of the families. The Saints had access to automobiles and were able to remove themselves from the sight of the community. In as routine a decision as to where to go to have a milkshake after school, the Saints stayed away from the mainstream of community life. Lacking transportation, the Roughnecks could not make it to the edge of town. The center of town was the only practical place for them to meet since their homes were scattered throughout the town and any noncentral meeting place put an undue hardship on some members. Through necessity the

Roughnecks congregated in a crowded area where everyone in the community passed frequently, including teachers and law enforcement officers. They could easily see the Roughnecks hanging around the drugstore.

The Roughnecks, of course, made themselves even more visible by making remarks to passersby and by occasionally getting into fights on the corner. Meanwhile, just as regularly, the Saints were either at the café on one edge of town or in the pool hall at the other edge of town. Without any particular realization that they were making themselves inconspicuous, the Saints were able to hide their time-wasting. Not only were they removed from the mainstream of traffic, but they were almost always inside a building.

On their escapades the Saints were also relatively invisible, since they left Hanibal and traveled to Big Town. Here, too, they were mobile, roaming the city, rarely going to the same area twice.

◈ Demeanor

To the notion of visibility must be added the difference in the responses of group members to outside intervention with their activities. If one of the Saints was confronted with an accusing policeman, even if he felt he was truly innocent of a wrongdoing, his demeanor was apologetic and penitent. A Roughneck's attitude was almost the polar opposite. When confronted with a threatening adult authority, even one who tried to be pleasant, the Roughneck's hostility and disdain were clearly observable. Sometimes he might attempt to put up a veneer of respect, but it was thin and was not accepted as sincere by the authority. School was no different from the community at large. The Saints could manipulate the system by feigning compliance with the school norms. The availability of cars at school meant that once free from the immediate sight of the teacher, the boys could disappear rapidly. And this escape was well enough planned that no administrator or teacher was nearby when the boys left. A Roughneck who wished to escape for a few hours was in a bind. If it were possible to get free from class, downtown was still a mile away, and even if he arrived there, he was still very visible. Truancy for the Roughnecks meant almost certain detection, while the Saints enjoyed almost complete immunity from sanctions.

◈ Bias

Community members were not aware of the transgressions of the Saints. Even if the Saints had been less discreet, their favorite delinquencies would have been perceived as less serious than those of the Roughnecks.

In the eyes of the police and school officials, a boy who drinks in an alley and stands intoxicated on the street corner is committing a more serious offense than is a boy who drinks to inebriation in a nightclub or a tavern and drives around afterwards in a car. Similarly, a boy who steals a wallet from a store will be viewed as having committed a more serious offense than a boy who steals a lantern from a construction site.

Perceptual bias also operates with respect to the demeanor of the boys in the two groups when they are confronted by adults. It is not simply that adults dislike the posture affected by boys of the Roughneck ilk; more important is the conviction that the posture adopted by the Roughnecks is an indication of their devotion and commitment to deviance as a way of life. The posture becomes a cue, just as the type of the offense is a cue, to the degree to which the known transgressions are indicators of the youths' potential for other problems.

Visibility, demeanor, and bias are surface variables which explain the day-to-day operations of the police. Why do these surface variables operate as they do? Why did the police choose to disregard the Saints' delinquencies while breathing down the backs of the Roughnecks?

The answer lies in the class structure of American society and the control of legal institutions by those at the top of the class structure. Obviously, no representative of the upper class drew up the operational chart for the police which led them to look in the ghettos and on street corners—which led them to see the demeanor of lower-class youth as troublesome and that of upper-middle-class youth as tolerable. Rather, the procedures simply developed from experience—experience with irate and influential upper-middle-class parents insisting that their son's vandalism was simply a prank and his drunkenness only a momentary "sowing of wild oats"—experience with cooperative or indifferent, powerless, lower-class parents who acquiesced to the laws' definition of their son's behavior.

◈ Adult Careers of the Saints and the Roughnecks

The community's confidence in the potential of the Saints and the Roughnecks apparently was justified. If anything, the community members underestimated the degree to which these youngsters would turn out "good" or "bad."

Seven of the eight members of the Saints went on to college immediately after high school. Five of the boys graduated from college in four years. The sixth one finished college after two years in the army, and the seventh spent four years in the air force before returning to college and receiving a B.A. degree. Of these seven college graduates, three went on for advanced degrees. One finished law school and is now active in state politics, one finished medical school and is practicing near Hanibal, and one boy is now working for a Ph.D. The other four college graduates entered submanagerial, managerial, or executive training positions with larger firms.

The only Saint who did not complete college was Jerry. Jerry had failed to graduate from high school with the other Saints. During his second senior year, after the other Saints had gone on to college, Jerry began to hang around with what several teachers described as a "rough crowd"—the gang that was heir apparent to the Roughnecks. At the end of his second senior year, when he did graduate from high school, Jerry took a job as a used car salesman, got married, and quickly had a child. Although he made several abortive attempts to go to college by attending night school, when I last saw him (ten years after high school) Jerry was unemployed and had been living on unemployment for almost a year. His wife worked as a waitress.

Some of the Roughnecks have lived up to community expectations. A number of them were headed for trouble. A few were not.

Jack and Herb were the athletes among the Roughnecks and their athletic prowess paid off handsomely. Both boys received unsolicited athletic scholarships to college. After Herb received his scholarship (near the end of his senior year), he apparently did an about-face. His demeanor became very similar to that of the Saints. Although he remained a member in good standing of the Roughnecks, he stopped participating in most activities and did not hang out on the corner as often.

Jack did not change. If anything, he became more prone to fighting. He even made excuses for accepting the scholarship. He told the other gang members that the school had guaranteed him a "C" average if he would come to play football—an idea that seems far-fetched, even in this day of highly competitive recruiting.

During the summer after graduation from high school, Jack attempted suicide by jumping from a tall building. The jump would certainly have killed most people trying it, but Jack survived. He entered college in the fall and played four years of football. He and Herb graduated in four years, and both are teaching and coaching in high schools. They are married and have stable families. If anything, Jack appears to have a more prestigious position in the community than does Herb, though both are well respected and secure in their positions.

Two of the boys never finished high school. Tommy left at the end of his junior year and went to another state. That summer he was arrested and placed on probation on a manslaughter charge. Three years later he was arrested for murder; he pleaded guilty to second degree murder and is serving a 30-year sentence in the state penitentiary.

Al, the other boy who did not finish high school, also left the state in his senior year. He is serving a life sentence in a state penitentiary for first degree murder.

Wes is a small-time gambler. He finished high school and "bummed around." After several years he made contact with a bookmaker who employed him as a runner. Later he acquired his own area and has been working it ever since. His position among the bookmakers is almost identical to the position he had in the gang; he is always around but no one is really aware of him. He makes no trouble and he does not get into any. Steady, reliable, capable of keeping his mouth closed, he plays the game by the rules, even though the game is an illegal one.

That leaves only Ron. Some of his former friends reported that they had heard he was "driving a truck up north," but no one could provide any concrete information.

◈ Reinforcement

The community responded to the Roughnecks as boys in trouble, and the boys agreed with that perception. Their pattern of deviancy was reinforced, and breaking away from it became increasingly unlikely. Once the boys acquired an image of themselves as deviants, they selected new friends who affirmed that self-image. As that self-conception became more firmly entrenched, they also became willing to try new and more extreme deviances. With their growing alienation came freer expression of disrespect and hostility for representatives of the legitimate society. This disrespect increased the community's negativism, perpetuating the entire process of commitment to deviance. Lack of a commitment to deviance works the same way. In either case, the process will perpetuate itself unless some event (like a scholarship to college or a sudden failure) external to the established relationship intervenes. For two of the Roughnecks (Herb and Jack), receiving college athletic scholarships created new relations and culminated in a break with the established pattern of deviance. In the case of one of the Saints (Jerry), his parents' divorce and his failing to graduate from high school changed some of his other relations. Being held back in school for a year and losing his place among the Saints had sufficient impact on Jerry to alter his self-image and virtually to assure that he would not go on to college as his peers did. Although the experiments of life can rarely be reversed, it seems likely in view of the behavior of the other boys who did not enjoy this special treatment by the school that Jerry, too, would have "become something" had he graduated as anticipated. For Herb and Jack outside intervention worked to their advantage; for Jerry it was his undoing.

Selective perception and labelling—finding, processing, and punishing some kinds of criminality and not others—means that visible, poor, nonmobile, outspoken, undiplomatic "tough" kids will be noticed, whether their actions are seriously delinquent or not. Other kids, who have established a reputation for being bright (even though underachieving), disciplined, and involved in respectable activities, who are mobile and moneyed, will be invisible when they deviate from sanctioned activities. They'll sow their wild oats—perhaps even wider and thicker than their lower-class cohorts—but they won't be noticed. When it's time to leave adolescence most will follow the expected path, settling into the ways of the middle class, remembering fondly the delinquent but unnoticed fling of their youth. The Roughnecks and others like them may turn around, too. It is more likely that their noticeable deviance will have been so reinforced by police and community that their lives will be effectively channelled into careers consistent with their adolescent background.

READING 23

Rosenhan's is a classic study of labeling and mental illness. Eight sane adults simulated symptoms of psychosis and gained admission to 12 mental hospitals. Once admitted, they immediately stopped simulating symptoms and waited to be judged sane and discharged. Their hospitalization averaged 19 days but ranged from a low of 7 days to a high of 52 days. In that time, staff treated the "pseudopatients" like nonpersons or like children and handed out more than 2,000 pills. At release, each of the pseudopatients was diagnosed with schizophrenia "in remission"; none was judged to be sane. The article is quite powerful and persuasive, but it is not without its critics. Robert Spitzer (1976) published two reaction pieces following "On Being Sane in Insane Places," and he too is quite persuasive, arguing,

Source: Rosenhan, David L. (1973). On being sane in insane places. *Science, 179,* 250–258. Reprinted by permission of the American Association for the Advancement of Science.

among other things, that (1) "sane" and "insane" are legal, not psychiatric, terms, and therefore, it is unreasonable to expect psychiatrists to find someone "sane." In fact, the term used, "schizophrenia in remission," is a rarely used term and actually fits the facts as they were brought to the hospitals. (2) The patients (although faking it) gave the doctors all the signs of schizophrenia, which, in general, simply does not "just go away." Spritzer argues that the responses by hospital staff were actually remarkably good, given that they were deceived in the first place. Still, Rosenhan's study is a classic and provides the reader with a great deal to think about. As you read this study, think about the power of labels and how hard they can be to overcome. Would you volunteer to be a pseudopatient in a study like this? Why or why not? How would it affect how others view you? How do you think it might affect your self-image?

On Being Sane in Insane Places*

David L. Rosenhan

If sanity and insanity exist, how shall we know them?

The question is neither capricious nor itself insane. However much we may be personally convinced that we can tell the normal from the abnormal, the evidence is simply not compelling. It is commonplace, for example, to read about murder trials wherein eminent psychiatrists for the defense are contradicted by equally eminent psychiatrists for the prosecution on the matter of the defendant's sanity. More generally, there are a great deal of conflicting data on the reliability, utility, and meaning of such terms as "sanity," "insanity," "mental illness," and "schizophrenia" [1]. Finally, as early as 1934, Benedict suggested that normality and abnormality are not universal [2]. What is viewed as normal in one culture may be seen as quite aberrant in another. Thus, notions of normality and abnormality may not be quite as accurate as people believe they are.

To raise questions regarding normality and abnormality is in no way to question the fact that some behaviors are deviant or odd. Murder is deviant. So, too, are hallucinations. Nor does raising such questions deny the existence of the personal anguish that is often associated with "mental illness." Anxiety and depression exist. Psychological suffering exists. But normality and abnormality, sanity and insanity, and the diagnoses that flow from them may be less substantive than many believe them to be.

At its heart, the question of whether the sane can be distinguished from the insane (and whether degrees of insanity can be distinguished from each other) is a simple matter: do the salient characteristics that lead to diagnoses reside in the patients themselves or in the environments and contexts in which observers find them? . . . [T]he belief has been strong that patients present symptoms, that those symptoms can be categorized, and, that the sane are distinguishable from the insane. More recently, however, this belief has been questioned. . . . [T]he view has grown that psychological categorization of mental illness is useless at best and downright harmful, misleading, and pejorative at worst. Psychiatric diagnoses, in this view, are in the minds of the observers and are not valid summaries of characteristics displayed by the observed [3–5].

Gains can be made in deciding which of these is more nearly accurate by getting normal people (that is, people who do not have, and have never suffered, symptoms of serious psychiatric disorders) admitted to psychiatric hospitals and then determining whether they were discovered to be sane and, if so, how. If the sanity of such pseudopatients were always detected, there would be prima facie evidence that a sane individual can be distinguished from the insane context in which he is found. . . . If, on the other hand, the sanity of the pseudopatients were never discovered, serious difficulties would arise for those who support traditional modes of

---

*Some text and accompanying endnotes have been omitted. Please consult the original source.

psychiatric diagnosis. Given that the hospital staff was not incompetent, that the pseudopatient had been behaving as sanely as he had been outside of the hospital, and that it had never been previously suggested that he belonged in a psychiatric hospital, such an unlikely outcome would support the view that psychiatric diagnosis betrays little about the patient but much about the environment in which an observer finds him.

This article describes such an experiment. Eight sane people gained secret admission to 12 different hospitals [6]. Their diagnostic experiences constitute the data of the first part of this article; the remainder is devoted to a description of their experiences in psychiatric institutions. . . .

◈ Pseudopatients and Their Settings

The eight pseudopatients were a varied group. One was a psychology graduate student in his 20's. The remaining seven were older and "established." Among them were three psychologists, a pediatrician, a psychiatrist, a painter, and a housewife. Three pseudopatients were women, five were men. All of them employed pseudonyms, lest their alleged diagnoses embarrass them later. Those who were in mental health professions alleged another occupation in order to avoid the special attentions that might be accorded by staff, as a matter of courtesy or caution, to ailing colleagues [7]. With the exception of myself (I was the first pseudopatient and my presence was known to the hospital administrator and chief psychologist and, so far as I can tell, them alone), the presence of pseudopatients and the nature of the research program was not known to the hospital staffs [8].

The settings were similarly varied. In order to generalize the findings, admission into a variety of hospitals was sought. The 12 hospitals in the sample were located in five different states on the East and West coasts. Some were old and shabby, some were quite new. Some were research-oriented, others not. Some had good staff–patient ratios, others were quite understaffed. Only one was a strictly private hospital. All of the others were supported by state or federal funds or, in one instance, by university funds.

After calling the hospital for an appointment, the pseudopatient arrived at the admissions office complaining that he had been hearing voices. Asked what the voices said, he replied that they were often unclear, but as far as he could tell they said "empty," "hollow," and "thud." The voices were unfamiliar and were of the same sex as the pseudopatient. . . .

Beyond alleging the symptoms and falsifying name, vocation, and employment, no further alterations of person, history, or circumstances were made. The significant events of the pseudopatient's life history were presented as they had actually occurred. Relationships with parents and with spouse and children, with people at work and in school, consistent with the aforementioned exceptions, were described as they were or had been. Frustrations and upsets were described along with joys and satisfactions. These facts are important to remember. If anything, they strongly biased the subsequent results in favor of detecting sanity, since none of their histories or current behaviors were seriously pathological in any way.

Immediately upon admission to the psychiatric ward, the pseudopatient ceased simulating any symptoms of abnormality. In some cases, there was a brief period of mild nervousness and anxiety, since none of the pseudopatients really believed that they would be admitted so easily. Indeed, their shared fear was that they would be immediately exposed as frauds and greatly embarrassed. Moreover, many of them had never visited a psychiatric ward; even those who had, nevertheless had some genuine fears about what might happen to them. Their nervousness, then, was quite appropriate to the novelty of the hospital setting, and it abated rapidly.

Apart from that short-lived nervousness, the pseudopatient behaved on the ward as he "normally" behaved. The pseudopatient spoke to patients and staff as he might ordinarily. Because there is uncommonly little to do on a psychiatric ward, he attempted to engage others in conversation. When asked by staff how he was feeling, he indicated that he was fine, that he no longer experienced symptoms. He responded to instructions from attendants, to calls for medication (which was not swallowed), and to dining-hall instructions. Beyond such activities as were available to him on the admissions ward, he spent his time writing down his observations about the ward, its patients, and the staff. Initially these notes were written "secretly," but as it soon became clear that no one much cared, they were subsequently written on standard tablets of paper in such public places as the dayroom. No secret was made of these activities.

The pseudopatient, very much as a true psychiatric patient, entered a hospital with no foreknowledge of when he would be discharged. Each was told that he would have to get out by his own devices, essentially by convincing the staff that he was sane. The psychological stresses associated with hospitalization were considerable, and all but one of the pseudopatients desired to be discharged almost immediately after being admitted. They were, therefore, motivated not only to behave sanely, but to be paragons of cooperation. That their behavior was in no way disruptive is confirmed by nursing reports, which have been obtained on most of the patients. These reports uniformly indicate that the patients were "friendly," "cooperative," and "exhibited no abnormal indications."

◈ The Normal Are Not Detectably Sane

Despite their public "show" of sanity, the pseudopatients were never detected. Admitted, except in one case, with a diagnosis of schizophrenia [9], each was discharged with a diagnosis of schizophrenia "in remission." The label "in remission" should in no way be dismissed as a formality, for at no time during any hospitalization had any question been raised about any pseudopatient's simulation. Nor are there any indications in the hospital records that the pseudopatient's status was suspect. Rather, the evidence is strong that, once labeled schizophrenic, the pseudopatient was stuck with that label. If the pseudopatient was to be discharged, he must naturally be "in remission"; but he was not sane, nor, in the institution's view, had he ever been sane.

The uniform failure to recognize sanity cannot be attributed to the quality of the hospitals. . . . Nor can it be alleged that there was simply not enough time to observe the pseudopatients. Length of hospitalization ranged from 7 to 52 days with an average of 19 days. The pseudopatients were not, in fact, carefully observed, but this failure clearly speaks more to traditions within psychiatric hospitals than to lack of opportunity.

Finally, it cannot be said that the failure to recognize the pseudopatients' sanity was due to the fact that they were not behaving sanely. While there was clearly some tension present in all of them, their daily visitors could detect no serious behavioral consequences—nor, indeed, could other patients. It was quite common for the patients to "detect" the pseudopatients' sanity. . . . "You're not crazy. You're a journalist, or a professor [referring to the continual note-taking]. You're checking up on the hospital." While most of the patients were reassured by the pseudopatient's insistence that he had been sick before he came in but was fine now, some continued to believe that the pseudopatient was sane throughout his hospitalization [10]. The fact that the patients often recognized normality when staff did not raises important questions.

Failure to detect sanity during the course of hospitalization may be due to the fact that . . . physicians are more inclined to call a healthy person sick . . . than a sick person healthy. . . . The reasons for this are not hard to find: it is clearly more dangerous to misdiagnose illness than health. Better to err on the side of caution, to suspect illness even among the healthy.

But what holds for medicine does not hold equally well for psychiatry. Medical illnesses, while unfortunate, are not commonly pejorative. Psychiatric diagnoses, on the contrary, carry with them personal, legal, and social stigmas [11]. It was therefore important to see whether the tendency toward diagnosing the sane insane could be reversed. The following experiment was arranged at a research and teaching hospital whose staff had heard these findings but doubted that such an error could occur in their hospital. The staff was informed that at some time during the following 3 months, one or more pseudopatients would attempt to be admitted into the psychiatric hospital. Each staff member was asked to rate each patient who presented himself at admissions or on the ward according to the likelihood that the patient was a pseudopatient. . . .

Judgments were obtained on 193 patients who were admitted for psychiatric treatment. All staff who had had sustained contact with or primary responsibility for the patient—attendants, nurses, psychiatrists, physicians, and psychologists—were asked to make judgments. Forty-one patients were alleged, with high confidence, to be pseudopatients by at least one member of the staff. Twenty-three were considered suspect by at least one psychiatrist. Nineteen were suspected by one psychiatrist and one other staff member. Actually, no genuine pseudopatient (at least from my group) presented himself during this period.

The experiment is instructive. It indicates that the tendency to designate sane people as insane can be reversed when the stakes (in this case, prestige and diagnostic acumen) are high. But what can be said of the 19 people who were suspected of being "sane" by one psychiatrist and another staff member? Were these people truly "sane?" . . . There is no way of knowing. But one thing is certain: any diagnostic process that lends itself so readily to massive errors of this sort cannot be a very reliable one.

◈ The Stickiness of Psychodiagnostic Labels

Beyond the tendency to call the healthy sick—a tendency that accounts better for diagnostic behavior on admission than it does for such behavior after a lengthy period of exposure—the data speak to the massive role of labeling in psychiatric assessment. Having once been labeled schizophrenic, there is nothing the pseudopatient can do to overcome the tag. The tag profoundly colors others' perceptions of him and his behavior.

From one viewpoint, these data are hardly surprising, for it has long been known that elements are given meaning by the context in which they occur. . . . Once a person is designated abnormal, all of his other behaviors and characteristics are colored by that label. Indeed, that label is so powerful that many of the pseudopatients' normal behaviors were overlooked entirely or profoundly misinterpreted. Some examples may clarify this issue.

Earlier I indicated that there were no changes in the pseudopatient's personal history and current status beyond those of name, employment, and, where necessary, vocation. Otherwise, a veridical description of personal history and circumstances was offered. Those circumstances were not psychotic. How were they made consonant with the diagnosis of psychosis? Or were those diagnoses modified in such a way as to bring them into accord with the circumstances of the pseudopatient's life, as described by him?

As far as I can determine, diagnoses were in no way affected by the relative health of the circumstances of a pseudopatient's life. Rather, the reverse occurred: the perception of his circumstances was shaped entirely by the diagnosis. A clear example of such translation is found in the case of a pseudopatient who had had a close relationship with his mother but was rather remote from his father during his early childhood. During adolescence and beyond, however, his father became a close friend, while his relationship with his mother cooled. His present relationship with his wife was characteristically close and warm. Apart from occasional angry exchanges, friction was minimal. The children had rarely been spanked. Surely there is nothing especially pathological about such a history. . . . Observe, however, how such a history was translated in the psychopathological context, this from the case summary prepared after the patient was discharged.

> This white 39-year-old male . . . manifests a long history of considerable ambivalence in close relationships, which began in early childhood. A warm relationship with his mother cools during his adolescence. A distant relationship to his father is described as becoming very intense. Affective stability is absent. His attempts to control emotionality with his wife and children are punctuated by angry outbursts and, in the case of the children, spankings. And while he says that he has several good friends, one senses considerable ambivalence embedded in those relationships also. . . .

The facts of the case were unintentionally distorted by the staff to achieve consistency with a popular theory of the dynamics of a schizophrenic reaction [12]. Nothing of an ambivalent nature had been described in relations with parents, spouse, or friends. . . . Clearly, the meaning ascribed to his verbalizations (that is, ambivalence, affective instability) was determined by the diagnosis: schizophrenia. An entirely different meaning would have been ascribed if it were known that the man was "normal."

All pseudopatients took extensive notes publicly. Under ordinary circumstances, such behavior would have raised questions in the minds of observers, as, in fact, it did among patients. Indeed, it seemed so certain that the notes would elicit suspicion that elaborate precautions were taken to remove them from the ward each day. But the precautions proved needless. The closest any staff member came to questioning these notes occurred when one pseudopatient asked his physician what kind of medication he was receiving and began to write down the response. "You needn't write it," he was told gently. "If you have trouble remembering, just ask me again."

If no questions were asked of the pseudopatients, how was their writing interpreted? Nursing records for three patients indicate that the writing was seen as an aspect of their pathological behavior. . . . Given that the patient is in the hospital, he must be psychologically disturbed. And given that he is disturbed, continuous writing must be a behavioral manifestation of that disturbance, perhaps a subset of the compulsive behaviors that are sometimes correlated with schizophrenia.

One tacit characteristic of psychiatric diagnosis is that it locates the sources of aberration within the individual and only rarely within the complex of stimuli that surrounds him. Consequently, behaviors that are stimulated by the environment are commonly misattributed to the patient's disorder. For example, one kindly nurse found a pseudopatient pacing the long hospital corridors. "Nervous, Mr. X?" she asked. "No, bored," he said.

The notes kept by pseudopatients are full of patient behaviors that were misinterpreted by well-intentioned staff. Often enough, a patient would go "berserk" because he had, wittingly or unwittingly, been mistreated by, say, an attendant. A nurse coming upon the scene would rarely inquire even cursorily into the environmental stimuli of the patient's behavior. Rather, she assumed that his upset derived from his pathology, not from his present interactions with other staff members. . . . [N]ever were the staff found to assume that one of themselves or the structure of the hospital had anything to do with a patient's behavior. One psychiatrist pointed to a group of patients who were sitting outside the cafeteria entrance half an hour before lunchtime. To a group of young residents he indicated that such behavior was characteristic of the oral-acquisitive nature of the syndrome. It seemed not to occur to him that there were very few things to anticipate in a psychiatric hospital besides eating.

A psychiatric label has a life and an influence of its own. Once the impression has been formed that the patient is schizophrenic, the expectation is that he will continue to be schizophrenic. When a sufficient amount of time has passed, during which the patient has done nothing

bizarre, he is considered to be in remission and available for discharge. But the label endures beyond discharge, with the unconfirmed expectation that he will behave as a schizophrenic again. Such labels, conferred by mental health professionals, are as influential on the patient as they are on his relatives and friends, and it should not surprise anyone that the diagnosis acts on all of them as a self-fulfilling prophecy. Eventually, the patient himself accepts the diagnosis, with all of its surplus meanings and expectations, and behaves accordingly [5].

. . . .

 ## Powerlessness and Depersonalization

Eye contact and verbal contact reflect concern and individuation; their absence, avoidance and depersonalization. The data I have presented do not do justice to the rich daily encounters that grew up around matters of depersonalization and avoidance. I have records of patients who were beaten by staff for the sin of having initiated verbal contact. During my own experience, for example, one patient was beaten in the presence of other patients for having approached an attendant and told him, "I like you." Occasionally, punishment meted out to patients for misdemeanors seemed so excessive that it could not be justified by the most radical interpretations of psychiatric canon. Nevertheless, they appeared to go unquestioned. Tempers were often short. A patient who had not heard a call for medication would be roundly excoriated, and the morning attendants would often wake patients with, "Come on, you m——f——s, out of bed!"

Neither anecdotal nor "hard" data can convey the overwhelming sense of powerlessness which invades the individual as he is continually exposed to the depersonalization of the psychiatric hospital. . . .

Powerlessness was evident everywhere. The patient is deprived of many of his legal rights by dint of his psychiatric commitment [13]. He is shorn of credibility by virtue of his psychiatric label. His freedom of movement is restricted. He cannot initiate contact with the staff, but may only respond to such overtures as they make. Personal privacy is minimal. Patient quarters and possessions can be entered and examined by any staff member, for whatever reason. His personal history and anguish is available to any staff member (often including the "grey lady" and "candy striper" volunteer) who chooses to read his folder, regardless of their therapeutic relationship to him. His personal hygiene and waste evacuation are often monitored. The [toilets] may have no doors.

At times, depersonalization reached such proportions that pseudopatients had the sense that they were invisible, or at least unworthy of account. Upon being admitted, I and other pseudopatients took the initial physical examinations in a semipublic room, where staff members went about their own business as if we were not there.

On the ward, attendants delivered verbal and occasionally serious physical abuse to patients in the presence of other observing patients, some of whom (the pseudopatients) were writing it all down. Abusive behavior, on the other hand, terminated quite abruptly when other staff members were known to be coming. Staff are credible witnesses. Patients are not.

A unbuttoned her uniform to adjust her brassiere in the presence of an entire ward of viewing men. One did not have the sense that she was being seductive. Rather, she didn't notice us. A group of staff persons might point to a patient in the dayroom and discuss him animatedly, as if he were not there.

One illuminating instance of depersonalization and invisibility occurred with regard to medications. All told, the pseudopatients were administered nearly 2100 pills. . . . Only two were swallowed. The rest were either pocketed or deposited in the toilet. The pseudopatients were not alone in this. Although I have no precise records on how many patients rejected their medications, the pseudopatients frequently found the medications of other patients in the toilet before they deposited their own. As long as they were cooperative, their behavior and the pseudopatients' own in this matter, as in other important matters, went unnoticed throughout.

Reactions to such depersonalization among pseudopatients were intense. Although they had come to the hospital as participant observers and were fully aware that they did not "belong," they nevertheless found themselves caught up in and fighting the process of depersonalization.

. . . .

◈ The Consequences of Labeling and Depersonalization

Whenever the ratio of what is known to what needs to be known approaches zero, we tend to invent "knowledge" and assume that we understand more than we actually do. We seem unable to acknowledge that we simply don't know. The needs for diagnosis and remediation of behavioral and emotional problems are enormous. But rather than acknowledge that we are just embarking on understanding, we continue to label patients "schizophrenic," "manic-depressive," and "insane," as if in those words we had captured the essence of understanding. The facts of the matter are that we have known for a long time that diagnoses are often not useful or reliable, but we have nevertheless continued to use them. We now know that we cannot distinguish insanity from sanity. It is depressing to consider how that information will be used.

Not merely depressing, but frightening. How many people, one wonders, are sane but not recognized as such in our psychiatric institutions? How many have been needlessly stripped of their privileges of citizenship, from the right to vote and drive to that of handling their own accounts? How many have feigned insanity in order to avoid the criminal consequences of their behavior, and, conversely, how many would rather stand trial than live interminably in a psychiatric hospital—but are wrongly thought to be mentally ill? How many have been stigmatized by well-intentioned, but nevertheless erroneous, diagnoses? . . . [P]sychiatric diagnoses are rarely found to be in error. The label sticks, a mark of inadequacy forever.

Finally, how many patients might be "sane" outside the psychiatric hospital but seem insane in it—not because craziness resides in them, as it were, but because they are responding to a bizarre setting, one that may be unique to institutions which harbor nether people? Goffman [4] calls the process of socialization to such institutions "mortification"—an apt metaphor that includes the processes of depersonalization that have been described here. And while it is impossible to know whether the pseudopatients' responses to these processes are characteristic of all inmates—they were, after all, not real patients—it is difficult to believe that these processes of socialization to a psychiatric hospital provide useful attitudes or habits of response for living in the "real world."

. . . .

◈ References and Notes

1. P. Ash, *J. Abnorm. Soc. Psychol.* **44**, 272 (1949); A. T. Beck, *Amer. J. Psychiat.* **119**, 210 (1962); A. T. Boisen, *Psychiatry* **2**, 233 (1938); N. Kreitman, *J. Ment. Sci.* **107**, 876 (1961); N. Kreitman, P. Sainsbury, J. Morrisey, J. Towers, J. Scrivener, ibid., p. 887; H. O. Schmitt and C. P. Fonda, *J. Abnorm. Soc. Psychol.* **52**, 262 (1956); W. Seeman, *J. Nerv. Ment. Dis.* **118**, 541 (1953). For an analysis of these artifacts and summaries of the disputes, see J. Zubin, *Annu. Rev. Psychol.* **18**, 373 (1967); L. Phillips and J. G. Draguns, ibid., **22**, 447 (1971).

2. R. Benedict, *J. Gen. Psychol.* **10**, 59 (1934).

3. See in this regard H. Becker, *Outsiders: Studies in the Sociology of Deviance* (Free Press, New York, 1963); B. M. Braginsky, D. D. Braginsky, K. Ring, *Methods of Madness: The Mental Hospital as a Last Resort* (Holt, Rinehart & Winston, New York, 1969); G. M. Crocetti and P. V. Lemkau, *Amer. Sociol. Rev.* **30**, 577 (1965); E. Goffman, *Behavior in Public Places* (Free Press, New York, 1964); R. D. Laing, *The Divided Self: A Study of Sanity and Madness* (Quadrangle, Chicago, 1960); D. L. Phillips, *Amer. Sociol. Rev.* **28**, 963 (1963); T. R. Sarbin, *Psychol. Today* **6**, 18 (1972); E. Schur, *Amer. J. Sociol.* **75**, 309 (1969); T. Szasz, *Law, Liberty and Psychiatry* (Macmillan, New York; 1963); *The Myth of Mental Illness: Foundations of a Theory of Mental Illness* (Hoeber Harper, New York, 1963). For a critique of some of these views, see W. R. Gove, *Amer. Sociol. Rev.* **35**, 873 (1970).

4. E. Goffman, *Asylums* (Doubleday, Garden City, N.Y., 1961).

5. T. J. Scheff, *Being Mentally Ill: A Sociological Theory* (Aldine, Chicago, 1966).

6. Data from a ninth pseudopatient are not incorporated in this report because, although his sanity went undetected, he falsified aspects of his personal history, including his marital status and parental relationships. His experimental behaviors therefore were not identical to those of the other pseudopatients.

7. Beyond the personal difficulties that the pseudopatient is likely to experience in the hospital, there are legal and social ones that, combined, require considerable attention before entry. For example, once admitted to a psychiatric institution, it is difficult, if not impossible, to be discharged on short notice, state law to the contrary notwithstanding. I was not sensitive to these difficulties at the outset of the project, nor to the personal and situational emergencies that can arise, but later a writ of habeas corpus was prepared for each of the entering pseudopatients and an attorney was kept "on call" during every hospitalization. I am grateful to John Kaplan and Robert Bartels for legal advice and assistance in these matters.

8. However distasteful such concealment is, it was a necessary first step to examining these questions. Without concealment, there would have been no way to know how valid these experiences were; nor was there any way of knowing whether whatever detections occurred were a tribute to the diagnostic acumen of the staff or to the hospital's rumor network. Obviously, since my concerns are general ones that cut across individual hospitals and staffs, I have respected their anonymity and have eliminated clues that might lead to their identification.

9. Interestingly, of the 12 admissions, 11 were diagnosed as schizophrenic and one, with the identical symptomatology, as manic-depressive psychosis. This diagnosis has a more favorable prognosis, and it was given by the only private hospital in our sample. On the relations between social class and psychiatric diagnosis, see A. B. Hollingshead and F. C. Redlich, *Social Class and Mental Illness: A Community Study* (Wiley, New York, 1958).

10. It is possible, of course, that patients have quite broad latitudes in diagnosis and therefore are inclined to call many people sane, even those whose behavior is patently aberrant. However, although we have no hard data on this matter, it was our distinct impression that this was not the case. In many instances, patients not only singled us out for attention, but came to imitate our behaviors and styles.

11. J. Cumming and E. Cumming, *Community Ment. Health* **1**, 135 (1965); A. Farina and K. Ring, *J. Abnorm. Psychol.* **70**, 47 (1965); H. E. Freeman and O. G. Simmons, *The Mental Patient Comes Home* (Wiley, New York, 1963): W. J. Johannsen, *Ment. Hygiene* **53**, 218 (1969); A. S. Linsky, *Soc. Psychiat.* **5**, 166 (1970).

12. For an example of a similar self-fulfilling prophecy, in this instance dealing with the "central" trait of intelligence, see R. Rosenthal and L. Jacobson, *Pygmalion in the Classroom* (Holt, Rinehart & Winston, New York, 1968).

13. D. B. Wexler and S. E. Scoville, *Ariz. Law Rev.* **13**, 1 (1971).

CHAPTER 9

Marxist and Conflict Theories of Deviance

Sandy was born in 1941. She realized she was a lesbian in her late teens but did not tell anyone of her feelings for many years. It wasn't easy being gay in the late 1950s and 1960s. Gays and lesbians were discriminated against legally and socially. Men and women were driven from their schools and towns if it was suspected they were gay. Government hearings (the McCarthy hearings) persecuted individuals who were suspected of being gay. Police harassed and arrested individuals who were suspected of being gay.

On June 28, 1969, in New York City's Greenwich Village, a riot broke out in response to a police raid on a bar suspected of catering to gays and lesbians. Sandy was 28 at the time and could hardly believe that there were people in New York rioting over these raids. She had lived with the fear that someone might suspect she was a lesbian for a long time and was amazed that other individuals were so open with their feelings. These riots, called the Stonewall riots, became known as the start of the gay rights movement.

Over the years, Sandy slowly came out to her friends and family. Some did not understand her feelings and were cruel and judgmental, but many were supportive, and she surrounded herself with a close group of loved ones and built a satisfying life for herself. She met an amazing woman when she was 34 and became more active in the gay rights movement, attending protests and advocating for social acceptance and legal equality.

As the years passed, Sandy saw that many individuals came to accept gays and lesbians. She saw pop culture embrace gays and lesbians in many ways. In many cities, she felt accepted enough to openly acknowledge her relationship with her partner, but this was not the case everywhere in the United States, and she waited a long time for the right to legally marry her partner. Recently, the law has been a significant place in which the right to marry for same-sex couples has played out.

- Domestic partnerships were established in many states, allowing same-sex couples some of the rights of married couples, such as health care, while still not allowing them to marry.

(Continued)

(Continued)

- Several states signed bills that made same-sex marriage legal, but those laws were challenged by voters and in court. One of the most famous cases was in California, where the right to marry was allowed, only to be overturned by Proposition 8.

- In 2013, the Supreme Court declined to uphold the ban on same-sex marriages in California that had been enacted with Proposition 8. On that same day, the Court overturned the federal Defense of Marriage Act (DOMA; enacted in 1996), which declared that marriage was a union between one man and one woman and that the states did not have to acknowledge a same-sex union. (Up until the passage of this act, states were required to acknowledge a marriage legally obtained in any state and offer the rights and privileges of marriage to that couple.) These Court decisions meant that the legality and acceptance of same-sex marriage became a decision for each state to make individually.

- Then, on June 26, 2015, the Supreme Court ruled in *Obergefell v. Hodges* that the fundamental right to marry is guaranteed to people of the same sex, and states are not allowed to ban that right.

- Since this Supreme Court decision, there have been varying reactions. Some conservative lawmakers argue that the law is not final and that it can be overturned or ignored. (While another case can be brought before the Supreme Court that may affect this decision, it is *not* the case that the Supreme Court decision can be ignored. The Supreme Court has the final say on law in the United States.) Some individuals have argued that because of their religious beliefs, they should not have to issue marriage licenses because it violates their religious freedom. (State courts and the U.S. Court of Appeals have not supported the argument.)

- Finally, in many areas, the fight for the rights for same-sex couples has moved into new territory. Most recently, there have been charges of discrimination when it comes to allowing same-sex couples to foster or adopt children (Hanna, 2015). In addition, LGBTQ individuals can still be discriminated against in the areas of work and housing.

Now in her 70s, Sandy is excited she can finally marry her longtime partner. She remembers the challenges she has faced throughout her lifetime—the social and legal discrimination against her. She knows in many ways that her sexuality is becoming more accepted, but she also sees the ways that she is still made to feel deviant. And she worries if there are other ways the law might be used to support discrimination against her as a lesbian.

◈ Introduction

Perhaps one of the most striking ways that deviance textbooks have changed over the past 30 years is that many early textbooks on deviance had a chapter discussing homosexuality as a deviant act. Some groups in society still argue that homosexuality is a "deviant lifestyle" (for the most part, these groups are conservative religious groups), but the idea that gays and lesbians are deviant is waning. Advocacy groups are increasing, and the gay rights movement has been very successful in the fight for social acceptance and equal rights. A discussion of deviance in a textbook today that focused on gays and lesbians would not focus on the "lifestyle" as deviant but might instead focus on the discourse, the changing attitudes, and the constantly changing legal rights as well as the implication of these changes. This study of deviance might ask the following questions: What arguments do opponents of homosexuality make? What arguments do advocates of gays and lesbians make? How do these groups use the law to support their arguments? Under what conditions do these arguments "win" or "lose"? These questions help illustrate the **social**

construction of deviance and the social construction of gays and lesbians from a group uniformly accepted as deviant to a group growing in social acceptance that has strong, vocal advocates.

This chapter presents the perspectives of the Marxist and conflict theories. While the theorists discussed in this chapter do not always agree on all the tenets of their theories, these theories come from the same social constructionist or relativist perspective and so are often discussed together. There are two general ways in which these theories differ from each other. The first is their definition of power. Marxists focus on the political economy and the capitalist system in their analyses of power and conflict (Moyer, 2001), whereas conflict theorists have traditionally expanded their definitions of power beyond a singular focus on the capitalist system. The second difference between the two is the policy implications that stem

▲ **Photo 9.1** Marxist and conflict theories examine why certain laws, such as marriage laws, are written and who may or may not benefit from such laws.

from the theories. Marxists tend to advocate for a revolutionary overthrow of the capitalist system as the only way to solve power differentials and conflict, while conflict theorists are more open to reforms that do not advocate revolution (Bohm, 1982). Both theories operate from a macro perspective, meaning that they focus on structural issues, institutions, and group behaviors, not on individual behavior or experiences. Much of the focus of these theories is on the creation and maintenance of laws that benefit one group over another (Liska & Messner, 1999). For a book on deviance, then, we might say that Marxist and conflict theorists are interested in why and how some groups are defined as deviant and how their behavior, now defined as deviant, gets translated into illegal behavior through application of the law.

At the center of this perspective is the acknowledgment that conflict exists (especially in a capitalist society), and this conflict arises from power differentials in society. These theories focus on two questions: (1) Why are certain groups more likely to be considered deviant? And (2) why are some actions, which many might consider harmful, not considered deviant or criminal? These questions have implications for what is often studied using the various theories that make up this perspective—as you will see from the discussions in this chapter, a variety of social phenomena, including same-sex marriage, the effects of the abolition of slavery on prison populations, and workplace misconduct, can be evaluated from Marxist and conflict perspectives. The rest of this chapter explores the theories that make up the Marxist and conflict perspectives.

◈ Development of Marxist Theory

The best place to start any discussion of Marxist and conflict theories is with Karl Marx (and his colleague Friedrich Engels) (Marx, 1867/1992, 1885/1993; Marx & Engels, 1848/1961). Marx was not a criminologist, and he did not study crime or deviance to any extent. In fact, while criminologists claim him as a key theorist in the field, communication studies, economics, political science, and sociology all make formal claims, too. At the core of Marxist theory is a focus on the capitalist system as one that creates conflict, inequality, and power differentials. Some argue that because the capitalist system is central to Marxist thought, such phenomena as the conflict surrounding same-sex marriage cannot be adequately explained by this theory. However, Turk (2002) argues that much capitalist conflict is diversionary in nature, designed to keep the "workers" focused on issues that keep them divided, rather than uniting to fight for their rights against capitalists. "To leftists, particularly those inspired by Marxism, class, racial and other forms of discrimination are promoted by the 'ruling class' to keep the workforce divided, thus more easily controlled" (Turk, 2002, p. 312). In other words, an emotional and heated conflict over same-sex marriage and other rights of the LGBTQ community could benefit capitalism by diverting attention away from issues those in power do not want to discuss and by dividing the working class on a social issue, thus making it harder for them to come together to fight the powerful when the need arises. As we examine Marxist and conflict theories, think about how this conflict may benefit the capitalist system and/or the ruling class.

Conflict

Marx, writing during the Industrial Revolution in Europe, argued that society could best be understood by its "social relationships" (Meyer, 1963), and given the era he was writing in, Marx argued that the fundamental basis of society was "class conflict." In other words, he saw capitalism as creating a conflict between the social relationships of the owners of the means of production (the bourgeoisie) and the laborers (the proletariat). This conflict would arise because to maximize profits, the bourgeoisie needed to keep costs down. Since labor is one of the most significant costs in business, owners must maximize their profits by paying laborers as little as possible. Marx argued that since the laborer was the actual creator of a given product, that laborer was the true owner of the profits from its creation. Therefore, laborers should earn the full price of the product (maximize their earnings). Laborers' maximization of their wages comes in direct conflict with the bourgeoisie's maximization of profit.

Marx went on to argue that a struggle for power—namely, **conflict**—arises as both groups try to maximize their advantage. In the short run, according to Marx, the bourgeoisie would win because they have the control over the means of production and communication. But in the long run, Marx believed, the proletariat would win. He believed that capitalism had sown the seeds of its own destruction, and as soon as proletarians understood the exploitive nature of capitalism, they would rise up and overthrow the system.

Dialectical Materialism

Marx based much of his philosophy about social relationships, conflict, and the workings of society on the concept of **dialectical materialism**. In many respects, this concept is the reason that Marxist and conflict theories fall under the heading of relativist theories. Marx believed that reality existed in the "material world." The material world had a meaning or reality separate from the meaning that individuals gave it (Mayo, 1960)—or, more specifically, the material world is important, separate from ideas, and for our ideas to have importance, we must put them into action. He also believed in the "dialectic," which, in its simplest form, means a negotiation of contradictions. He believed that nature (the material world) was full of contradictions (conflict) and that through a process of negotiating those contradictions, we could arrive at a new reality. Mayo (1960) explains this process as the thesis, antithesis, and synthesis of an idea (or reality). Using our legal history of the right to marry as an example, we can say that there has been heated debate in this country over the right of gays and lesbians to marry. The thesis of this idea may be "gays and lesbians have the right to marry," the antithesis of this reality may be "gays and lesbians do not have the right to marry," and from these contradictions came the synthesis "gays and lesbians may have civil unions but may not marry." This synthesis became the new thesis, and the process started all over again.

Marxism and the Creation of Law and Deviance

While Marx was not a criminologist, he spent a fair amount of time writing about the importance of the law. He never gave a specific definition of the law (Cain, 1974), but he did discuss how it was used to maintain the status quo (keep the bourgeoisie in power). Marx saw the law as the instrument used to support the ideology of capitalism. That is to say, he believed that the function of the law in a capitalist society was to maintain capitalism. For Marx, this meant that the law might be used to control the proletariat, but it was also used to settle disputes that might arise among the bourgeoisie because disputes weakened the power of the bourgeoisie and, ultimately, the power of the capitalist system (Cain, 1974).

The function of the law, according to Marx and Engels, was to obscure real power by offering power, on paper, to everyone equally (Cain, 1974; Marx & Engels, 1957). In other words, Marx believed that by emphasizing the rationality of the law and the recourse for everyone to use the law equally, the fact that, in practice, everyone does not have the power to use the law equally could be overlooked. In fact, this could be not only overlooked but actively ignored—if everyone has the right to use the law, then it becomes the *individual's responsibility* to use the law. Equality on paper means we can ignore inequality in practice.

At the beginning of the 20th century, William Bonger, a Dutch scholar, built upon Marxist ideas and explicitly related them to the topic of crime in his book *Criminality and Economic Conditions* (1916). He forwarded the idea that capitalism is a system in which business owners are encouraged to dominate and take advantage of the others in society—the workers and the consumers—in order to make a profit. Bonger claimed that capitalism basically tears apart the social fabric by making people, especially capitalists, inclined to egotism, or selfishness. According to Bonger, crime, especially economic crime, is to be expected in a system that dehumanizes and pits people against one another in the name of profit. In order to minimize criminal activity, he stated that a large step would have to be taken—a redistribution of wealth that took all people's needs into account and a shared ownership of the means of production (i.e., a shift to socialism). These proposed measures would be ones that would shift the societal emphasis on domination to one focused on cooperation.

In the 1960s and 1970s, many radical or conflict criminologists picked up on the work of Bonger and his predecessors, as well as the work of labeling theorists, and focused on the role of the economy and class conflict in the production of law and crime (e.g., Beirne, 1979; Chambliss, 1964, 1969, 1975; Chambliss & Seidman, 1971; Hall, Critcher, Jefferson, Clarke, & Roberts, 1978; Platt, 1974; Schwendinger & Schwendinger, 1970; S. Spitzer, 1975; I. Taylor, Walton, & Young, 1973; Turk, 1969, 1976a, 1976b, 1977).

Steven Spitzer (1975, 1983) did expand on traditional Marxist thought to develop a theory of deviance. He argued that capitalism was changing to advanced (or monopoly) capitalism. Monopoly capitalism was likely to promote two realities. The first was that as capitalism advanced, it would become more efficient. This efficiency would make it more likely that some capitalists would fail (as monopolies became stronger); these failed capitalists would fall into the laborer class, and this ever-growing class would become less and less useful as fewer laborers became needed to do the same work. The second was that advanced capitalism would promote increased levels of education needed to do the more advanced work of the economy. This education would create a more thoughtful population that was likely to criticize the system. Spitzer called these two populations "problem populations" and argued that capitalists (those in power) would see these two groups as "social junk" (the unneeded laborers) and "social dynamite" (those critical of the system). These problem populations would need to be controlled (most likely through criminalization—creating laws

© Shutterstock/eyeidea

▲ **Photo 9.2**   Spitzer argues that as monopoly capitalism grows, "problem populations" will develop. One of those problem populations is "social dynamite"— a group willing to protest those in power.

(vertical credit) © Stephen Strathdee (sharply_done)/iStockphoto

▲ **Photo 9.3** The Occupy Wall Street protests that started in the fall of 2011 are an excellent example of what many might call "the social dynamite"—individuals who are protesting the status quo and perceived sources of power in the United States (and the world).

focused on their status or behaviors) when the populations became too big, too organized, or unresponsive to informal social control (for example, family or school) (Liska & Messner, 1999).

We might argue, then, that one of the ways in which Marxist theory can help explain deviance is in the use of deviance to control certain groups for the benefit of the capitalist system. As Marx said, the power of the capitalists comes from their ability to control both the means of production and *communication*. If laborers live under a **false consciousness** that does not allow them to understand or acknowledge their oppression and exploitation, then the bourgeoisie can manipulate them by labeling behaviors or groups that are dangerous to capitalism as deviant. Much of this labeling can be communicated through the media. In our example, if same-sex marriage can be labeled as deviant and harmful, then the capitalist system and

ruling class may benefit in two ways: (1) The focus is taken off of harmful and deviant behaviors that the ruling class may be engaged in, and (2) the workers will be divided over the issue of same-sex marriage, thus weakening their own connection to other workers. While same-sex marriage may not be harmful to capitalism, promoting it as a deviant practice benefits capitalism by diverting attention away from harms (deviance) produced by capitalism and keeping individuals or groups who would benefit from banding together to fight the harms of the system divided over a diversionary issue (same-sex marriage).

DEVIANCE IN POPULAR CULTURE

Examples of conflict theory and its focus on power abound in popular culture. Here we offer recommendations for a few films and television segments that you might watch; we think you will find it quite easy to apply general ideas from the conflict perspective to these specific cases.

Documentary films such as Michael Moore's *Capitalism: A Love Story* or *The Corporation* give an inside—and often critical—look at big business in the United States. Moore, in particular, juxtaposes the greed of corporations against the human suffering their actions may cause. Moore's ideas are compatible with a Marxist perspective; for a broader view of issues of power in the United States, you might watch one or more of the following:

Murder on a Sunday Morning—A documentary following the case of a 15-year-old African American male who is arrested for the murder of an elderly woman after an eyewitness places him near the scene of the crime. This film gives you a chance to question whether race still matters in our criminal justice system and how it might play out.

North Country—A woman goes to work in a Minnesota steel mine and is harassed, verbally abused, and assaulted by her male coworkers. When she decides to file a lawsuit for sexual harassment, she faces resistance from both men and women in the community.

Serial—From two producers of *This American Life*, this podcast follows a story or "mystery" over numerous installments. The first season followed the 1999 murder of Hae Min Lee and her ex-boyfriend, Adnan Masud Syed, accused and consequently found guilty of her death. Many questions arise about the handling of Syed's case. The first season is an examination of what happens after someone is murdered and someone is accused. The second season is focusing on Sergeant Bowe Bergdahl, the soldier held for five years by the Taliban and now facing court-martial charges for desertion.

What Would You Do?—This series from ABC News offers a number of experimental vignettes in which actors stage scenes about hate crimes or "shopping while black," and cameras watch to see how the people witnessing the interaction will react. Many of the scenarios deal with race and ethnicity, and the reactions of the public can be directly related to the readings in this chapter. In one vivid example, a group of white boys vandalized a car in a neighborhood park as many people passed them by; few reacted or called the police. The producers then switched it up and had a group of black boys vandalize the car in the same park; in this case, there were more calls to the police and more suspicion. Most telling of all, while the white boys vandalized the car, a stranger called 911 not about the vandals but about two African American young men who were sleeping in their car in the parking lot. You can watch these vignettes online at abcnews.go.com; most run less than 15 minutes, and several provide concrete examples of conflict and labeling theories in action.

◈ Development of Conflict Theory

While Marx did not spend much time focusing on crime or deviance, his work has been expanded by a series of criminologists who focused specifically on the law and, thus, definitions of crime and deviance. We have already discussed Spitzer, who remained fairly true to the Marxian fundamentals of economic structure and social class. The following theorists focused on what some have called culture conflict. At its most basic, this expansion allows that there may be more groups in conflict than just the bourgeoisie and proletariat. As you will see, each of these theorists examines the impact that conflict, culture, values, and/or power have on the creation and implementation of the law.

Gusfield

Gusfield (1967, 1968) examined the legislation of morality—the use of law to control behaviors that did not necessarily create victims (prostitution, drug use, gambling, and homosexuality). He argued that law has two functions: instrumental and symbolic. The instrumental function of law is one in which the behavior of individuals is proscribed; the law tells individuals what actions they can and cannot engage in, and agents of the law enforce those rules by arresting individuals who break the law. This is important but not nearly as important as the symbolic function of the law for our understanding of culture conflict, power differentials, and the imposition of deviance in society.

The symbolic function of law does not rely on enforcement or action but instead "invites consideration" (Gusfield, 1967, 1968) of what is considered moral by a society. "In a pluralistic society these defining and designating acts can become political issues because they support or reject one or another of the competing and conflicting cultural groups in the society" (Gusfield, 1968, p. 57). In other words, a law that supports the cultural beliefs of one group over another suggests that those beliefs are the moral, normative beliefs of society as a whole. The process of creating that law becomes the political process of supporting that group. More so than even the enforcement of that law, the ability of the cultural group to claim that its beliefs are supported by law is what is important.

Applying the symbolic function of law to the continued struggles for and against same-sex marriage shows the importance of these laws in justifying the beliefs of both proponents and opponents of this legislation. Opponents of same-sex marriage are most often socially and religiously conservative. Laws that ban same-sex marriage are seen to support a socially and religiously conservative agenda. Beyond the specific prohibition that two people of the same sex may not marry, these bans give strength to general cultural beliefs in social conservatism, making the whole movement stronger in areas well beyond the issue of same-sex marriage. In contrast, proponents of same-sex marriage are generally more socially and religiously progressive. Laws that support same-sex marriage are evidence of a progressive agenda that advocates for equality under the law for all groups. Laws that support same-sex marriage, then, also further other legal arguments for equality and thus strengthen the cultural beliefs of socially and religiously progressive groups.

Vold

George Vold expanded on Marxist and conflict theories by developing a theory of group conflict in his 1958 book *Theoretical Criminology*. Vold describes the process by which individuals become a part of a particular group and how the relationships between various groups develop as they compete for space, resources, and power.

The Creation and Maintenance of "the Group"

Vold (1958) argues that individuals are "group-involved beings" (p. 203) who both influence and are influenced by the groups of which they are a part. Individuals become a part of their groups because of similar interests with other group members. The more similarity between the interests and loyalties of its members, the stronger the group. Groups are created because of the needs of group members; groups that cannot fulfill these needs are disbanded while groups that can fulfill them flourish and become stronger. Old groups are disbanded when they can no longer further their cause, and new groups form with the onslaught of new interests or needs.

Society, then, is made up of constant interaction between these various groups. Groups jockey for position and power in relation to the other groups and, through the "social process," gain and/or lose status relative to their counterparts. What is most important about this part of Vold's theory is that groups are in a constant state of action as they fight for the interests of their constituents.

Conflict arises between groups when their interests and needs overlap. Groups that do not have overlapping interests and needs are less likely to develop a conflicted relationship with one another. When interests and needs overlap, there is the danger of one group replacing the other (or groups can perceive this danger as their worlds encroach on each other). The goal of all groups, then, becomes to not be replaced, disbanded, or abandoned. In other words, the goal of all groups is to maintain the interests and serve the needs of the group and to flourish in the face of other groups.

Vold argues that when conflicts between groups arise and groups are threatened by the competing interests of other groups, individuals increase loyalty to their group. And the harder one must fight for her or his respective group, the more loyal that person becomes. "Nothing promotes harmony and self-sacrifice within the group quite as effectively as a serious struggle with another group for survival" (Vold, 1958, p. 206).

Vold's ideas about the creation and maintenance of a group can be applied to our example of same-sex marriage. We can argue that both same-sex groups and conservative religious groups are struggling for control of the definition of marriage (the interests and needs of both groups overlap on the issue of marriage). It could easily be argued that both groups have increased their solidarity and group member loyalty as the fight over same-sex marriage has intensified and that this power struggle or conflict has increased the membership of both groups. For example, many people who are not gay or lesbian themselves now identify with the cause of marriage equality and support gay and lesbian groups, counting themselves as members even though, as heterosexuals, they already have the right to marry.

The Use of the Law to Maintain Interests

According to Vold, the law becomes a way for groups to maintain their interests and protect themselves. Sometimes this process is a negotiation between two competing groups in which the political process develops a compromise that both sides can live with. Vold used the example of liquor laws to illustrate this compromise. If we see two groups—those who believe in prohibition as one group and the liquor industry as the other—we can see that the prohibition group would like to see liquor outlawed, whereas we can imagine that the liquor industry would prefer to have no restrictions on the selling and use of alcohol. Liquor laws—rules about where, when, and how alcohol can be sold—can then be seen as a way to compromise between these groups. We can also see this as an example of Marx's dialectical materialism, in which prohibition may be the thesis, the selling of liquor with no restriction may be the antithesis, and liquor laws may be the synthesis of the competing ideas.

However, law can also be understood as the tool that more powerful groups can use to maintain their interests and service their needs. Vold argued that those groups that were powerful enough to control the law were also powerful enough to codify their values into law. This control means that certain groups who are in conflict with the values of the most powerful group(s) are more likely to be deemed criminal because they are more likely to have values and engage in behaviors that are in conflict with the power group. Vold argued that this is how crime and deviance come about.

Turk

Turk (1969, 1976a, 1976b), like Vold, focused on the use of law as a socially controlling agent. He saw law as a resource that groups struggled to control. Groups who had the power to control the law had the power to criminalize (or make deviant) groups who did not have that power. He argued that laws were more likely to be enforced when they represented cultural values or were being enforced on subjects who had very little power (Liska & Messner, 1999).

The Use of the Law as a Socially Controlling Agent

In discussing his belief of "law as power" (p. 279), Turk (1976a) argued that the resources that groups marshal go beyond just the economic resources that are often focused on in Marxist and conflict theories. Turk conceptualized five types of resource control (or power):

> These are (1) control of the means of direct physical violence, i.e., war or police power; (2) control of the production, allocation, and/or use of material resources, i.e., economic power; (3) control of decision-making processes, i.e., political power; (4) control of definitions of and access to knowledge, beliefs, values, i.e., ideological power; and (5) control of human attention and living-time, i.e., diversionary power. (Turk, 1976a, p. 280)

Police power means that if a group controls the law, it is often justified in using force or violence (i.e., the police) when other groups are not. For example, the police may forcefully carry protesters away from a rally or protest, but the individuals protesting may not in any way use force against the police or counterprotesters. Turk (1976a) was interested in how and to what extent "economic power was enhanced or eroded by the law" (p. 280). For example, he saw the use of tax laws to protect the economic gains of the wealthy as an example of the law protecting and enhancing the resource of economic power for a certain group. Political power means that the law serves the purpose of organizing and supporting the political system. For example, the law supports the two-party system in the United States that benefits the Democrats and Republicans at the expense of those not associated with either party. Ideological power is supported by the law in two important ways. First, given that the law is the central tenet of political order, it legitimates itself (creates an ideological understanding of the importance and rightness of itself) by its very existence. Second, the law is used to both deny the rightness of certain ideas and to legitimate others that justify the overall ideology of groups in power. Finally, diversionary power means that the law can be used to divert the attention of groups and individuals from more pressing concerns. For example, encouraging our preoccupation with street crime is an excellent tactic to divert attention away from other harms that might be more far-reaching. Turk argued that the law is less likely to be used as a consensus-building negotiator of problems and is more likely to be the ultimate purveyor of power and manipulator of resources.

Quinney

While Quinney has written over many decades, spanning many theories, his work with Marxist and conflict theories took place during a similar time as Turk's—the 1960s and 1970s. Quinney's (1963, 1970, 1991) work has ranged from positivist to relativist (Einstadter & Henry, 1995), with important works theorizing Marxist, conflict, and finally peacemaking criminologies (which you will read about in the next chapter). In his work *The Social Reality of Crime*, Quinney (1970) puts forth a theory of the law that offers an explanation for the social construction of crime.

Process

While Quinney does not mention dialectical materialism in his discussion of process, it is easy to see the Marxian philosophy in his work. He argues that most work on crime, to this point in time, has been static (instead of dynamic). This static worldview has a strong impact on how we view deviance and crime. Quinney (1970) believes that this static view means that deviance and crime rest in the realm of the pathological. In other words, our definition of deviance and crime is normative—it cannot and does not change with our understanding of the world. He argues that our social relationships and, thus, our understanding of the world is a *process*. Because it is a process, our understanding of the world changes as the process evolves.

Conflict and Power

Quinney (1970) also believes that conflict is inevitable in society and that "society is held together by force and constraint and is characterized by ubiquitous conflicts that result in continuous change" (pp. 9–10). This view of society links conflict and power very closely because it assumes that coercion is needed to keep society functioning. Namely, coercion is needed for one group to impose its beliefs or values on the society as a whole. Only those groups with sufficient power to coerce the whole will be able to impose their will.

Theory: The Social Reality of Crime

In Quinney's (1970) book, he outlined six propositions describing what he called the "social reality of crime" (p. 3). These propositions are as follows:

Proposition 1 (definition of crime): Crime is a definition of human conduct that is created by authorized agents in a politically organized society. In other words . . . crime is a definition of behavior that is conferred on some persons by others.

Proposition 2 (formulation of criminal definition): Criminal definitions describe behaviors that conflict with the interests of the segments of society that have the power to shape public policy.

Proposition 3 (application of criminal definition): Criminal definitions are applied by the segments of society that have the power to shape the enforcement and administration of criminal law.

Proposition 4 (development of behavior patterns in relation to criminal definitions): Behavior patterns are structured in segmentally organized society in relation to criminal definitions, and within this context persons engage in actions that have relative probabilities of being defined as criminal.

Proposition 5 (construction of criminal conceptions): Conceptions of crime are constructed and diffused in the segments of society by various means of communication.

Proposition 6 (the social reality of crime): The social reality of crime is constructed by formulation and application of criminal definitions, the development of behavior patterns related to criminal definitions, and the construction of criminal conceptions. (pp. 15–23)

Our example of same-sex marriage legislation can be evaluated using several of Quinney's propositions. The same-sex marriage debate was played out in a very political manner in California, with the right to marry or not marry being decided in several ballot measures over an extended period of time. While various state polls suggested that a majority of Californians were not opposed to same-sex marriage, a constitutional ban on same-sex marriage was enacted with the passage of Proposition 8 on November 4, 2008. The passage of that constitutional amendment, then, effectively defined same-sex marriage as deviant (or not legally allowed, like heterosexual marriage), thus illustrating the abilities of one group to define another group's actions as deviant and not sanctioned by the law. Then, on June 26, 2013, the Supreme Court ruled that DOMA was unconstitutional and that those supporting Proposition 8 did not have standing to challenge a lower court decision that Proposition 8 was unconstitutional (because the state of California chose not to defend the proposition). These Court decisions meant that the decision of whether same-sex marriage was legal was passed to each state individually (thus ensuring that the argument got played out over and over again) and that in California, because a lower court had deemed that Proposition 8 was unconstitutional, it was legal. Then, while states across the country were experiencing their own fights over same-sex marriage, the Supreme Court agreed to hear the *Obergefell v. Hodges* case, which made same-sex marriage legal at the federal level, thus ensuring it was legal in each state.

Chambliss

In his article "Toward a Political Economy of Crime," Chambliss (1975) argues that the question, "Why do some individuals become involved with criminal behavior, while others do not?" (p. 165) is meaningless because, as he puts it, "everyone commits crime" (p. 165). In fact, much of Chambliss's (1964, 1975, 1978, 1999; Chambliss & Seidman, 1971) work focuses on the corrupt behavior and policies of *the state* (police, bureaucrats, politicians). Given that he focuses on the state, many might put his work under Marxist theory (indeed, the following excerpt detailing his paradigm of crime and criminal law is Marxian), and Chambliss does focus significantly on the corruption of the capitalist system. However, his works go beyond an analysis of the owners of the means of production and laborers, and for this reason, we have chosen to discuss him under conflict theory.

The following propositions highlight the most important implications of a Marxian paradigm of crime and criminal law.

A. On the content and operation of criminal law

   1. Acts are defined as criminal because it is in the interests of the ruling class to so define them.

   2. Members of the ruling class will be able to violate the laws with impunity while members of the subject classes will be punished.

   3. As capitalist societies industrialize and the gap between the bourgeoisie and the proletariat widens, penal law will expand in an effort to coerce the proletariat into submission.

B. On the consequences of crime for society

1. Crime reduces surplus labor by creating employment not only for the criminals but for law enforcers, locksmiths, welfare workers, professors of criminology and a horde of people who live off of the fact that crime exists.

2. Crime diverts the lower classes' attention from the exploitation they experience, and directs it toward other members of their own class rather than towards the capitalist class or the economic system.

3. Crime is a reality which exists only as it is created by those in the society whose interests are served by its presence.

C. On the etiology of criminal behavior

1. Criminal and non-criminal behavior stem from people acting rationally in ways that are compatible with their class position. Crime is a reaction to the life conditions of a person's social class.

2. Crime varies from society to society depending on the political and economic structures of society.

3. Socialist societies should have much lower rates of crime because the less intense class struggle should reduce the forces leading to and the functions of crime. (Chambliss, 1975, pp. 152–153)

While our example of same-sex marriage is not about criminalization per se, it does illustrate several of Chambliss's propositions. Opponents to same-sex marriage spent significant amounts of time and money diverting the attention of the general public ("No on Prop 8," 2008). Opponents argue that children should only be raised in households where a father and mother (as opposed to father/father or mother/mother) are present and that society in general is threatened by same-sex marriage because if same-sex marriage remains legalized, "our children" will be exposed to its existence in the public schools. As it has been argued that same-sex marriage threatens the hegemonic control of a patriarchal society, it serves the interests of capitalists in general to oppose same-sex marriage. Same-sex marriage is thus presented as a deviant idea or practice that would harm groups everyone should want to keep safe: families and children.

◈ Applications of Marxist and Conflict Theories

A significant number of studies have used conflict theory to examine racial discrimination in the law and/or justice system (Blalock, 1967; Bridges & Crutchfield, 1988; Chamlin, 2009; Leiber & Stairs, 1999; Percival, 2010). One of the ways these studies have used this theory is by arguing that the perceived threat of minority individuals (in many cases, racial minorities) will increase the likelihood of social control of that group. In other words, as a given minority population increases in size, the perceived threat to the ruling population also increases. Blalock (1967), in his power-threat hypothesis, argued that the relationship between minority threat and social control would be curvilinear. (That is to say, as the minority size increases, so would social control, *to a certain point*, and then, at a tipping point—in his argument, as the minority group reaches 50% of the population—the increase in minority size would actually likely lead to a decrease in formal social control.) This curvilinear relationship has been partially supported in more than one study (Greenberg, Kessler, & Loftin, 1985; Jackson & Carroll, 1981), although support depends on both geography and historical time period.

Payne and Welch (2010) studied the discipline practices of 294 public schools and also supported conflict theory through a racial-threat hypothesis. They argued that schools are mirroring the get-tough policies of the criminal justice system even though delinquency is decreasing. They found that while most schools have a range of responses to bad behavior (from punitive to restorative), schools set in disadvantaged, urban locations with a disproportionate student population of color (black and Latino) are more likely to use punitive forms of discipline and less likely to use restorative forms of discipline.

Another contemporary study has used the ideas of conflict theory to predict perceptions of injustice among people of color—in this instance, black and Latino youth (Hagan, Shedd, & Payne, 2005). Many have argued that one of the detrimental effects of increased conflict and, thus, increased social control on any minority group (e.g., people of color, women, gays, lesbians) is that this leads to perceptions of injustice and a delegitimization of the justice system (see Cole, 1998). Hagan et al. (2005) argue that there is a comparative nature to exploitation and social control in that disadvantaged social groups can compare their disadvantage with other groups. They find that it is indeed the case that both black and Latino youth compare their disadvantage with one another and with white youth and that this comparative disadvantage does lead to increased perceptions of injustice at the hands of the criminal justice system. Hagan et al. (2005) conclude that "it is a possible further irony . . . that efforts to make city schools safer through increased deployment of the police may have the unintended consequence of alienating the students who are ostensibly being protected" (p. 400).

Writing in 1901, the African American scholar W. E. B. Du Bois vividly documented the way blacks and whites were historically dealt with by the criminal justice system in the South. Because slaves were literally property owned by whites prior to the Civil War, they had little to do with the criminal justice system. Misbehavior was generally dealt with by their owners and/or informal groups of whites who worked to keep blacks from associating, and the criminal justice system focused primarily on whites. As Du Bois put it, the system was "lenient in theory and lax in execution" (p. 83). Following the war, owners lost power, but a more formal illegal group, the Ku Klux Klan, emerged. More importantly, however, because whites so believed in the slave system and were convinced that freed slaves would not work as they had before, a new criminal justice system emerged "to restore slavery in everything but in name" (p. 84). New laws were passed, and the courts now became focused on African Americans. The convict lease system emerged, with the labor of blacks being sold to the highest bidder. The conditions were abysmal. The unintended consequences of the changes were to make the criminal justice system appear less legitimate and therefore ineffective. Du Bois concluded with some statistics documenting the poor governmental support for the criminal justice system in the South; there was little need as the convict lease system was a "money maker," but it was a deplorable system that remained problematic (Du Bois, 1901).

◈ Critiques of Marxist and Conflict Theories

There are numerous critiques of Marxist and conflict theories (for thorough and surprisingly different critiques, see Bohm, 1997; Kubrin et al., 2009; Liska & Messner, 1999). In general, it has been argued that in dismissing **social consensus**, Marxist and conflict theorists ignore that some laws seem to protect the interests of everyone (e.g., homicide or rape laws) (Liska & Messner, 1999). We might argue, however, that this critique is something of a straw man since so many laws (1) do not seem to protect the interests of everyone or (2) are differentially enforced on certain groups. It has also been argued that both perspectives are just that, perspectives, more than they are theories. In other words, they are hard to test, and theorists have been more focused on the theorizing than the "empirical inquiry" (Kubrin et al., 2009, p. 239). Those who argue this see the empirical inquiry as necessary to move the theory forward—without it, theory cannot be refined. There are those who go further with this critique and argue that these theories not only lack empirical evidence but, in many ways, are not theories but political statements about how the world works and how it should work (Akers & Sellers, 2004; Kubrin et al., 2009; Liska & Messner, 1999).

A critique specific to conflict theory (in which Marxist theory is held up as a "better" theory) is that conflict theory has not identified how power is established (Bohm, 1997). In other words, Marxist theory has very strictly and specifically linked the construction of power and conflict to the capitalist system, the mode of production, exploitation in general, and the creation of a ruling class that exploits a laborer class. Conflict theory, on the other hand, while it has expanded the discussion of power, has not explained where that power comes from. Why do some groups control more power than others? And how is that power conferred? A critique specific to Marxist theory is that the theory has not specified how laborers will lose their false consciousness; while there is general discussion, there are no testable propositions about how laborers come to be aware of their exploitation and then act on this awareness.

What do these and the many other critiques mean for the theories? Well, in many ways, they mean that the theories are robust and still stimulate discussion and use. They also mean that there is much room for continued work—work that focuses attention on the creation and maintenance of deviance, that is empirically testable, and that sharpens the direction of the theories as more data are analyzed. Next, we will examine a sample of contemporary studies that spring from Marxist or conflict theory.

◈ Explaining Deviance in the Streets and Deviance in the Suites: The Cases of Shoplifting and Employees Locked in the Workplace

Both discussions below stem from the underlying act of theft. In a capitalist society, one of the behaviors commonly focused on as harmful is the taking of property from individuals or businesses. Our example of deviance in the streets, then, is shoplifting, and one response to the notion of employee shoplifting—physically locking employees in the workplace—is our example of deviance in the suites.

Shoplifting

According to the FBI and the Uniform Crime Reports (UCR), shoplifting, a subcategory of larceny, is "the theft by a person (other than an employee) of goods or merchandise exposed for sale" (Federal Bureau of Investigation, 2004, p. 32). In 2010, there were approximately 6,185,000 larceny-thefts reported in the United States; 17.2% of these (approximately 925,000) were incidences of shoplifting (Federal Bureau of Investigation, 2011) (see Figure 9.1). Between 2009 and 2010, reports of shoplifting decreased 7.1%. These figures, however, are from the UCR, the data of which come from "crimes known to police" or arrest statistics. Both underestimate the amount of crime that exists. According to the National Association for Shoplifting Prevention (NASP; 2013) and the National Epidemiologic Survey on Alcohol and Related Conditions (Shteir, 2011), between 9% and 11% of the U.S. population has shoplifted. It is estimated that, on average, the loss from a single shoplifting event in 2009 was $178, up from $104 in 1990. The NASP estimates that more than $13 billion is lost to shoplifting in a single year.

Shoplifting has been presented in three manifestations: (1) as a crime, (2) as a disease, and (3) as a form of protest (Shteir, 2011). The most popular manifestation of shoplifting is as a crime. (As we have seen, it is categorized as a type of larceny.) It has contributed to increases in technological surveillance, including closed-circuit television, electronic article surveillance, radio frequency identification, and metal detectors. In addition to technological surveillance, many stores use loss prevention personnel, uniformed guards, and exit inspections. Shoplifting has also been characterized as a disease, much like alcoholism. Shoplifting Anonymous groups have been started, and many argue that shoplifting is an addiction that cannot be controlled. Finally, shoplifting has been presented as a form of protest against the establishment, corporations, and capitalism. Abbie Hoffman, an activist of the anti-establishment movement, wrote a book titled *Steal This Book* (1971, 2002) in which he advocates for the counterculture movement and for fighting against the government and corporations. The first section of the book focuses on how to acquire things such as food, clothing, transportation, land, entertainment, money, dope, and medical care for free.

Solomon and Ray (1984, p. 1076) identified eight rationalizations (that they referred to as irrational beliefs) of shoplifters: (1) If I am careful and smart, I will not get caught; (2) even if I do get caught, I will not be turned in; (3) even if

I am prosecuted, the punishment will not be severe; (4) the merchants deserve what they get; (5) everybody, at some time or another, has shoplifted; therefore, it is OK for me to do it; (6) shoplifting is not a major crime; (7) I must have the item I want to shoplift, or if I want it, I should have it; and (8) it is OK to shoplift because the merchants expect it.

Shoplifting and Conflict Theory

Conflict theory would not be used to explain why an individual might shoplift (unless it was focusing on Hoffman's argument that shoplifting is a political statement aimed as a protest against the capitalist system). Instead, it could be used to explain why one group is targeted and accused of shoplifting more than another group. Since the events of September 11, 2001, considerable concern and debate has been raised over racial profiling, especially the profiling of people from the Middle East in airports. In the 1990s, concerns arose (and continue to be discussed) over racial profiling by the police, who, in some cases, seem to target persons of color in traffic stops. This phenomenon is sometimes referred

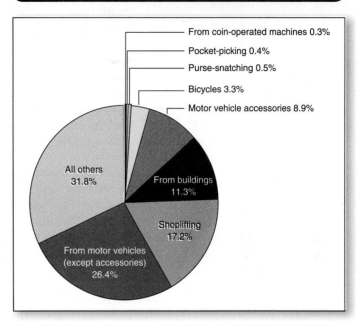

Figure 9.1   Larceny-Theft Percentage Distribution, 2010

- From coin-operated machines 0.3%
- Pocket-picking 0.4%
- Purse-snatching 0.5%
- Bicycles 3.3%
- Motor vehicle accessories 8.9%
- All others 31.8%
- From buildings 11.3%
- Shoplifting 17.2%
- From motor vehicles (except accessories) 26.4%

Source: Federal Bureau of Investigation. (2011). *Crime in the United States, 2010.* U.S. Department of Justice. Retrieved from http://www.fbi.gov/about-us/cjis/ucr/crime-in-the-u.s/2010/crime-in-the-u.s.-2010/property-crime/larcenytheftmain

Note: Due to rounding, the percentages may not add to 100.0.

to as "driving while black" (DWB). Shaun Gabbidon (2003) examined another source of targeting—"shopping while black," or SWB. The concern is with store employees and private security officers who racially profile black shoppers. Borrowing from conflict theory, Gabbidon argues that the power differential in class and race leads to racial profiling. Using key terms such as false arrest, shoplifting, and racial profiling in the LexisNexis Legal Research database, he focused on 29 clear-cut cases of racial profiling in retail settings from 1967 to 2002. Although he used only a relatively small number of cases, they are very interesting ones, and it is likely that the practice is much larger since the vast majority of unpleasant encounters between employees and shoppers probably do not make it to court or even to the attention of the police. This is an excellent example of the transitory nature of the definition of deviance. In most of these cases, these individuals were engaged in the same behaviors as the white shoppers—examining and/or paying for merchandise—yet the organizational policies of the stores, the perceptions of store clerks, and the color of the shoppers' skin meant they were treated as deviants instead of customers.

Employees Locked in the Workplace

There have been numerous incidents of fire exits, back doors, or all exits of a workplace being locked during or after business hours so that employees do not have free and clear access to leave. We will discuss two examples of this.

The first example is the Hamlet fire. On September 3, 1991, a fire broke out at Imperial Food Products, a food-processing plant in Hamlet, North Carolina, that processed chicken for restaurants. The one-story structure, built from bricks and cinder blocks, had housed the processing plant for 11 years (P. Taylor, 1991). The fire broke out

© nojustice/iStockphoto

▲ **Photo 9.4** While locking exit doors when employees or the public are present is illegal, businesses have been found to do just that to address theft concerns, with often disastrous results.

in or near a 25-foot deep-fat-fryer vat around 8:20 a.m. In addition to the fire in the vat, nearby gas lines in the ceiling also ignited (Haygood, 2002). Thick smoke from the oil fire and ignited insulation quickly filled the building. Because the building did not have many interior walls, there were few barriers to the smoke and heat from the fire.

Although the front doors were unlocked, the back doors were kept padlocked and the windows boarded up, allegedly to prevent theft, vandalism, and other crimes. Those closest to the front of the building escaped the fire, but heavy smoke and heat kept many of the other workers from being able to get to the front of the plant. Twenty-five people died in the fire—some huddled near the padlocked back door, others trapped in a walk-in freezer where they had taken refuge. In addition to the 25 dead, 54 were injured. Some of the injuries were extremely severe and included burns; blindness; and smoke inhalation that led to respiratory disease and neurological and brain damage (Emergency Response and Research Institute, 1991).

The owner of the plant, Emmett Roe; Roe's son, who was the operations manager; and the plant manager were charged with non-negligent manslaughter. But only Emmett Roe was found guilty after he entered into a plea agreement for 25 counts of involuntary manslaughter. His sentence was 19 years and 11 months, but he served slightly less than four years (Haygood, 2002; Riley, 1995).

The second example is the Walmart and Target lock-ins. According to Walmart workers, in some locations, the company policy was to lock the doors after hours (Greenhouse, 2004). In 2004, reports surfaced that in many of these lock-in stores, there were no keys on site to unlock the doors, effectively holding workers prisoner until management arrived to unlock the doors in the morning. Although the stores all had working fire exits, workers reported that they were told that the fire exits were not to be used unless there was a "real emergency," such as a fire, and even though workers had been hurt and severely ill in some of these lock-in stores, they were told they would lose their jobs if they complained or used the fire exits to leave the store. When asked about this policy, a Walmart spokesperson said the company told all its employees to use common sense and that if an employee was hurt, "he was clearly capable of walking out a fire door anytime during the night" (Greenhouse, 2004, n.p.).

Walmart confirmed that about 10% of their stores had a policy of locking the doors at night (Greenhouse, 2004), and in 2004, it changed the policy to require a manager with a key to be on site during the night shift. Walmart said this policy was in place for stores in high-crime areas in order to keep the stores and employees safe. However, former store managers said that the reason for the lock-ins was to prevent shrinkage (thefts by employees or outsiders) and to increase efficiency by making sure no one went outside to smoke or leave the premises for a long break.

As recently as early 2013, Target has also been accused of locking in their employees overnight (Eidelson, 2013). Complaints were filed with the Occupational Safety and Health Administration (OSHA) on behalf of 25 workers with three janitorial services that contract with Target. In these instances, a Target manager was on the premises with a key, but if a worker needed to leave the building for any reason, the manager had to be tracked down, which was not always a quick task. OSHA requires that employees be "able to open an exit route door from the inside at all times without keys, tools, or special knowledge" (Kennedy, 2013, n.p.). However, there is evidence of these rules being broken by Target and other companies.

Workplace Lock-ins and Conflict Theory

We can use Chambliss's propositions on the content and operation of criminal law to examine workplace lock-ins.

- *Acts are defined as criminal because it is in the interest of the ruling class to so define them.* The mere assumption that workers are thieves means that business owners can treat them as such. In the Walmart and Target cases above, it was not the employees working on any given night that were accused of shoplifting, and even if one or more employees on any given shift *was* stealing from the organization, the lock-in policy was not exercised on just those employees. *All* employees on the shift were locked in. By both suggesting to management that workers cannot be trusted and must be locked in *and* suggesting to the public that the lock-in policies are established to keep employees working in high-crime neighborhoods safe, the company benefits twice from the policy. First, employee power is decreased by stigmatizing them as alleged criminals, and second, company power (in the form of good press) is increased by suggesting that companies care about the well-being of employees beyond the basic employer–employee relationship.

- *Members of the ruling class will be able to violate the laws with impunity, while members of the subject classes will be punished.* While both of these instances of locking in employees are known because the company deviance was uncovered, the punishment that these companies (or management in these companies) experienced was not as severe as the harm they inflicted. For example, while the employees at the chicken-processing plant experienced the trauma of a fire, injuries, and, in some cases, death, one of the three owners of the company served four years in prison for this tragic event. While Walmart and Target employees have also been locked in (although no one died, there were reports of bodily harm), the companies merely experienced the filing of complaints with OSHA that could end in a civil penalty (most likely a fine) if they were found to have violated OSHA policy. This means that all employees on these night shifts were punished for the suspected behavior of a few (although if there was evidence against any individual employee, that employee would have been fired and arrested for theft) while a majority of owners escaped any punishment at all.

◈ Ideas in Action: Racial Impact Statements

Racial impact statements have existed since 2008, when Iowa governor Chet Culver signed legislation requiring that all proposed legislation affecting sentencing, probation, or parole be evaluated for its likelihood to impact racial disparity in the criminal justice system. Other states soon followed with similar legislation. According to Mauer (2009),

> The premise behind racial impact statements is that policies often have unintended consequences that would be best addressed prior to adoption of new initiatives. In this sense they are similar to fiscal and environmental impact statements. Policy makers contemplating new construction projects or social initiatives routinely conduct such assessments, which are now widely viewed as responsible mechanisms of government. . . . Racial impact statements are particularly important for criminal justice policy because it is exceedingly difficult to reverse sentencing policies once they have been adopted. (p. 19)

One of the most obvious public policies that could have benefitted from a racial impact statement is the crack cocaine mandatory-sentencing policies that significantly impact black Americans disproportionate to their use of crack cocaine. Even though it is common to critique this policy and acknowledge its unequal application, the policy has not been overturned. Politicians fear appearing soft on crime if they overturn any criminal justice policy. Racial impact statements are intended to stop such disparity-producing legislation before it gets enacted and becomes exceedingly hard to change.

Racial Impact Statements and Conflict Theory

Racial impact statements are a useful example of the type of legislation that extends from the tenets of conflict theory. Given that conflict theorists explore the effects of power differentials on the creation and maintenance of laws, a public policy that is designed to critique proposed legislation and specifically examine it for its effects on groups (people of color) that have traditionally had less power in relation to the criminal justice system extends from these theoretical propositions. A further examination of this legislation from the conflict perspective would explore the success of racial impact statements in changing or limiting policies that would disproportionately affect communities of color.

NOW YOU . . . USE THE THEORY

In April 2010, Arizona enacted SB 1070, the toughest immigration bill in existence, into law. This law requires police officers to detain people they "reasonably suspect" are undocumented and verify their status. It also makes it a misdemeanor to not carry papers proving one's immigration status. Finally, it allows individuals to sue public agencies that they think are not enforcing the law. The law is so controversial that its enactment was postponed while the courts determined its constitutionality. Subsequently, in 2012, the Supreme Court upheld portions of the law and struck down others.

In October 2010, National Public Radio (NPR) uncovered a direct link between SB 1070 and the largest private prison corporation in the nation. The law was written by Russell Pearce, a state senator in Arizona, but it was written with considerable help from a group called the American Legislative Exchange Council (ALEC). ALEC comprises legislators and members of major corporations such as Reynolds Tobacco, ExxonMobil, the National Rifle Association, and the Corrections Corporation of America (CCA). Pearce and the CCA both sit on the board of ALEC.

The CCA, according to company documents, anticipates a significant portion of their future profits will come from supplying private prison services to Immigration and Customs Enforcement.

When asked if both the state senator and the CCA were at the same meeting in which the legislation was crafted, Michael Hough, staff director of ALEC, is quoted as saying, "Yeah. That's the way it's set up. It's a, you know, it's a public–private partnership. And that's how it's set up, so that—we believe both sides, businesses and lawmakers should be at the same table, together" (L. Sullivan, 2010).

There is nothing illegal about what Pearce or the CCA did in cocrafting the legislation. However, the partnership was not made public.

Use Marxist and/or conflict theory to comment on ALEC, the partnership between Pearce and the CCA, SB 1070, and the impact of SB 1070 on legal immigrants, undocumented workers, and the state of immigration policy in the United States.

Source: Facts of this case were taken from NPR.org (L. Sullivan, 2010).

◈ Conclusion

The importance of Marxist and conflict theories in the study of deviance cannot be denied. As some of the first theories to take a relativist (or social constructionist) perspective on deviance, they allow us to question how deviance is defined and used to maintain positions of power in society. While the earliest tenets of these theories focused solely on the impact of the capitalist system on power, group structure, and group conflict, later iterations of the theory have shifted from a sole focus on capitalism to one that examines other power differentials—most notably, power differentials among racial groups and the ways in which legislation and agents of social control (the police) are used to control these groups. While these critical analyses may make some people (and groups) uncomfortable, they are necessary for a better understanding of deviance and society.

EXERCISES AND DISCUSSION QUESTIONS

1. As Reiman and Leighton (2009) wrote, "The rich get richer and the poor get prison." How might a Marxist or conflict theorist explain this sentence? Discuss a specific theorist.

2. Given the global recession that began in 2008, using Marxist and conflict theories, predict the trends we may see in legislation and incarceration in the United States.

3. Using the concept of dialectical materialism, trace the history of marijuana legislation in the United States.

4. Give an example of controlling "problem populations" through the creation and maintenance of deviance. How is deviance used to control this population?

5. This chapter used same-sex marriage legislation as an example of the struggle of competing groups to control the law and avoid deviant labels. Give another example of a group, its interests, and its struggle for power and how legislation is/was used to negate this power.

6. Identify a specific law in your town, city, or state and critique its creation using Marxist or conflict theory. In other words, why was it created, and who does it benefit?

KEY TERMS

Conflict

Dialectical materialism

False consciousness

Social consensus

Social construction

READING 24

This short piece from *The Communist Manifesto* may be unsettling to students—certainly the term *communism* has not held a very positive connotation in American culture, and a reading touting its virtue may come across as inconsistent (at the very least) with core American values. But it is important to recognize the background and context behind the writings of Marx and Engels. Take the introductory lines "The history or all hitherto existing society is the history of class struggles. Freeman and slave, patrician and plebeian, lord and serf, guild-master and journeyman, in a word, oppressor and oppressed." Hence, historically, conflict was endemic to society, and within capitalism, they saw horrific problems based on class that needed to be changed for a better outcome for all—long working hours in dangerous and unhealthy conditions, machinery taking over the jobs of many, and lower wages to make more wealth for the powerful. In a very different way than most theories of deviance that view the vast

Source: Marx, K., & Engels, F. (1848). *The communist manifesto.* Many editions. Many publishers.

majority of deviance stemming from a small minority of persons who don't follow conventions, these conflict theorists see the deviance coming from the top down—the master (bourgeois) suppressing the suppressed (proletariat). Historically, they argue that the powerful control and alienate the less powerful, and it is only through class struggle and revolution that major changes in society are made. In this way, Marx has been labeled a "functionalist" recognizing the need for social change for the better. Indeed, Marx is seen by many as an optimist, with eyes open to a better society with more equalitarian social relations.

The Communist Manifesto

Karl Marx and Friedrich Engels

A specter is haunting Europe—the specter of communism. All the powers of old Europe have entered into a holy alliance to exorcise this specter: Pope and Czar, Metternich and Guizot, French Radicals and German police-spies.

Where is the party in opposition that has not been decried as communistic by its opponents in power? Where the opposition that has not hurled the branding reproach of communism, against the more advanced opposition parties, as well as against its reactionary adversaries?

Two things result from this fact.

I. Communism is already acknowledged by all European powers to be itself a power.

II. It is high time that Communists should openly, in the face of the whole world, publish their views, their aims, their tendencies, and meet this nursery tale of the specter of communism with a Manifesto of the party itself.

To this end, Communists of various nationalities have assembled in London, and sketched the following Manifesto, to be published in the English, French, German, Italian, Flemish, and Danish languages.

◈ I. Bourgeoisie and Proletarians

The history of all hitherto existing society is the history of class struggles.

Freeman and slave, patrician and plebeian, lord and serf, guild-master and journeyman, in a word, oppressor and oppressed, stood in constant opposition to one another, carried on an uninterrupted, now hidden, now open fight, a fight that each time ended, either in a revolutionary reconstitution of society at large, or in the common ruin of the contending classes.

In the earlier epochs of history, we find almost everywhere a complicated arrangement of society into various orders, a manifold gradation of social rank. In ancient Rome we have patricians, knights, plebeians, slaves; in the Middle Ages, feudal lords, vassals, guild-masters, journeymen, apprentices, serfs; in almost all of these classes, again, subordinate gradations.

The modern bourgeois society that has sprouted from the ruins of feudal society has not done away with class antagonisms. It has but established new classes, new conditions of oppression, new forms of struggle in place of the old ones.

Our epoch, the epoch of the bourgeoisie, possesses, however, this distinctive feature: it has simplified the class antagonisms. Society as a whole is more and more splitting up into two great hostile camps, into two great classes directly facing each other: bourgeoisie and proletariat.

From the serfs of the Middle Ages sprang the chartered burghers of the earliest towns. From these burgesses the first elements of the bourgeoisie were developed.

The discovery of America, the rounding of the Cape, opened up fresh ground for the rising bourgeoisie.

The East-Indian and Chinese markets, the colonization of America, trade with colonies, the increase in the means of exchange and in commodities generally, gave to commerce, to navigation, to industry, an impulse never before known, and, thereby, a rapid development to the revolutionary element in the tottering feudal society.

The feudal system of industry, under which industrial production was monopolized by closed guilds, now no longer sufficed for the growing wants of the new markets. The manufacturing system took its place. The guild-masters were pushed to one side by the manufacturing middle class; division of labor between the different corporate guilds vanished in the face of division of labor in each single workshop.

Meantime the markets kept ever growing, the demand ever rising. Even manufacture no longer sufficed. Thereupon, steam and machinery revolutionized industrial production. The place of manufacture was taken by the giant, modern industry, the place of the industrial middle class, by industrial millionaires, the leaders of whole industrial armies, the modern bourgeois.

Modern industry has established the world market, for which the discovery of America paved the way. This market has given an immense development to commerce, to navigation, to communication by land. This development has, in its turn, reacted on the extension of industry; and in proportion as industry, commerce, navigation, railways extended, in the same proportion the bourgeoisie developed, increased its capital, and pushed into the background every class handed down from the Middle Ages.

We see, therefore, how the modern bourgeoisie is itself the product of a long development, of a series of revolutions in the modes of production and exchange.

Each step in the development of the bourgeoisie was accompanied by a corresponding political advance of that class. An oppressed class under the sway of the feudal nobility, an armed and self-governing association in the medieval commune. At first, an independent urban republic (as in Italy and Germany) or a taxable "third estate" of the monarchy (as in France), afterwards, in the period of manufacture proper, serving either the semi-feudal or the absolute monarchy as a counterpoise against the nobility, and, in fact, cornerstone of the great

monarchies in general, the bourgeoisie has at last, since the establishment of modern industry and of the world market, conquered for itself, in the modern representative State, exclusive political sway. The executive of the modern State is but a committee for managing the common affairs of the whole bourgeoisie.

The bourgeoisie, historically, has played a most revolutionary part.

The bourgeoisie, wherever it has got the upper hand, has put an end to all feudal, patriarchal, idyllic relations. It has pitilessly torn asunder the motley feudal ties that bound man to his "natural superiors," and has left remaining no other nexus between man and man than naked self-interest, than callous "cash payment." It has drowned the most heavenly ecstasies of religious fervor, of chivalrous enthusiasm, of philistine sentimentalism, in the icy water of egotistical calculation. It has resolved personal worth into exchange value, and in place of the numberless indefeasible chartered freedoms, has set up that single, unconscionable freedom— Free Trade. In a word, for exploitation, veiled by religious and political illusions, it has substituted naked, shameless, direct, brutal exploitation.

The bourgeoisie has stripped of its halo every occupation hitherto honored and looked up to with reverent awe. It had converted the physician, the lawyer, the priest, the poet, and the man of science into its paid wage-laborers.

The bourgeoisie has torn away from the family its sentimental veil and has reduced the family relation to a mere money relation.

The bourgeoisie has disclosed how it came to pass that the brutal display of vigor in the Middle Ages, which reactionaries so much admire, found its fitting complement in the most slothful indolence. It has been the first to show what man's activity can bring about. It has accomplished wonders far surpassing Egyptian pyramids, Roman aqueducts, and Gothic cathedrals. It has conducted expeditions that put in the shade all former Exoduses of nations and crusades.

The bourgeoisie cannot exist without constantly revolutionizing the instruments of production, and thereby the relations of production, and with them all social relations. Conservation of the old modes of production in unaltered form, was, on the contrary, the first condition of existence for all earlier industrial classes.

Constant revolutionizing of production, uninterrupted disturbance of all social conditions, everlasting uncertainty and agitation distinguish the bourgeois epoch from all earlier ones. All fixed fast-frozen relations, with their train of ancient and venerable prejudices and opinions are swept away, all newly formed ones become antiquated before they can ossify. All that is solid melts into air, all that is holy is profaned, and man is at last compelled to face with sober senses, his real conditions of life, and his relations with his kind.

The need of a constantly expanding market for its products chases the bourgeoisie over the whole face of the globe. It must nestle everywhere, settle everywhere, establish connections everywhere.

The bourgeoisie has through its exploitation of the world market given a cosmopolitan character to production and consumption in every country. To the great chagrin of reactionaries, it has drawn from under the feet of industry the national ground on which it stood. All old, established national industries have been destroyed or are daily being destroyed. They are dislodged by new industries, whose introduction becomes a life and death question for all civilized nations, industries that no longer work with indigenous raw material, but raw material drawn from the remotest regions, industries whose products are consumed, not only at home, but in every quarter of the globe. In place of the old wants, satisfied by the productions of the country, we find new wants, requiring for their satisfaction the products of distant lands and climes. In place of the old local and national seclusion and self-sufficiency, we have intercourse in every direction, a universal interdependence of nations. And as in material, so also in intellectual production. The intellectual creations of individual nations become common property. National one-sidedness and narrow-mindedness become more and more impossible, and from the numerous national and local literatures, there arises a world literature.

The bourgeoisie, by the rapid improvement of all instruments of production, by the immensely facilitated means of communication, draws all, even the most barbarian, nations into civilization. The cheap prices of its commodities are the heavy artillery with which it batters down all Chinese walls, with which if forces the barbarians' intensely obstinate hatred of foreigners to capitulate. It compels all nations, on pain of

extinction, to adopt the bourgeois mode of production; it compels them to introduce what it calls civilization into their midst, *i.e.,* to become bourgeois themselves. In one word, it creates a world after its own image.

The bourgeoisie has subjected the country to the rule of the towns. It has created enormous cities, greatly increased the urban population as compared with the rural, and thus rescued a considerable part of the population from the idiocy of rural life. Just as it has made the country dependent on the towns, so it has made barbarian and semi-barbarian countries dependent on the civilized ones, nations of peasants on nations of bourgeoisie, the East on the West. More and more the bourgeoisie continues to do away with the scattered state of population, means of production, and property. It has agglomerated population, centralized means of production, and concentrated property in a few hands. The necessary consequence of this was political centralization. Independent, or but loosely connected, provinces with separate interest, laws, government and systems of taxation, became lumped together into one nation, with one government, one code of laws, one national class-interest, one frontier and one customs-tariff.

The bourgeoisie, during its rule of scarcely one hundred years, has created more massive and more colossal productive forces than have all preceding generations together. The subjection of nature's forces to man and machinery; the application of chemistry to industry and agriculture; [the development of] steam-navigation, railways and electric telegraphs; the clearing of whole continents for cultivation; the canalization of rivers and the conjuring of whole populations out of the ground—what earlier century had even a presentiment that such productive forces slumbered in the lap of social labor?

We see then: the means of production and exchange, on whose foundation the bourgeoisie built itself up, were generated in feudal society. At a certain stage in the development of these means of production and exchange, the conditions under which feudal society produced and exchanged, the feudal organization of agriculture and manufacturing industry, in one word, the feudal relations of property became no longer compatible with the already developed productive forces; they became so many fetters. They had to be burst asunder. They were burst asunder.

Into their place stepped free competition, accompanied by a social and political constitution adapted to it and by the economical and political sway of the bourgeois class.

A similar movement is going on before our own eyes. Modern bourgeois society with its relations of production, exchange and property, a society that has conjured up such gigantic means of production and exchange, is like the sorcerer, who is no longer able to control the powers of the nether world whom he has called up by his spells. For many decades the history of industry and commerce has been but the history of the revolt of modern productive forces against modern conditions of production, against the property relations that are the conditions for the existence of the bourgeoisie and of its rule. It is enough to mention the commercial crises that by their periodic return put on its trial each time more threateningly, the existence of the entire bourgeois society. In these crises a great part not only of the existing products, but also of the previously created productive forces are periodically destroyed. In these crises there breaks out an epidemic that in all earlier epochs would have seemed an absurdity—the epidemic of overproduction. Society suddenly finds itself put back into a state of momentary barbarism. It appears as if a famine or a universal war of devastation had cut off the supply of every means of subsistence. Industry and commerce seem to be destroyed. And why? Because there is too much civilization, too much means of subsistence, too much industry, too much commerce. The productive forces at the disposal of society no longer tend to further the development of the conditions of bourgeois property. On the contrary, they have become too powerful for these conditions, by which they are fettered, and so soon as they overcome these fetters, they bring disorder into the whole of bourgeois society, endanger the existence of bourgeois property. The conditions of bourgeois society are too narrow to encompass the wealth created by them. And how does the bourgeoisie get over these crises? On the one hand by enforced destruction of a mass of productive forces; on the other, by the conquest of new markets, and by the more thorough exploitation of the old ones. That is to say, by paving the way for more extensive and more destructive crises, and by diminishing the means whereby crises are prevented.

The weapons with which the bourgeoisie brought feudalism to the ground are now turned against the bourgeoisie itself.

But not only has the bourgeoisie forged the weapons that bring death to itself; it has also called into existence the men who are to wield those weapons—the modern working class—the proletariat.

In proportion as the bourgeoisie, *i.e.,* capital, develops, in the same proportion the proletariat, the modern working class, develops—a class of laborers, who live only so long as they find work, and who find work only so long as their labor increases capital. These laborers, who must sell themselves piecemeal, are a commodity, like every other article of commerce, and are consequently exposed to all the vicissitudes of competition, to all the fluctuations of the market.

Owing to the extensive use of machinery and to the division of labor, work for the proletarians has lost all individual character, and, consequently, all charm for the workman. He becomes an appendage of the machine, and it is only the simplest, most monotonous, and most easily acquired knack that is required of him. Hence, the cost of production of a workman is restricted, almost entirely, to the means of subsistence that he requires for his maintenance and for the propagation of his race. But the price of a commodity, and therefore also of labor, is equal to its cost of production. In proportion, therefore, as the repulsiveness of the work increases, the wage decreases. Nay more, to the extent that the use of machinery and the division of labor increases, to the same extent the burden of toil also increases, whether by the prolongation of working hours, the increase of the work exacted in a given time or the increased speed of the machinery, etc.

Modern industry has converted the little workshop of the patriarchal master into the great factory of the industrial capitalist. Masses of laborers crowded into the factory are organized like soldiers. As privates of the industrial army they are placed under the command of a perfect hierarchy of officers and sergeants. Not only are they slaves of the bourgeois class and the bourgeois state; they are daily and hourly enslaved by the machine, by the supervisor, and, above all, by the individual bourgeois manufacturer himself. The more openly this despotism proclaims gain to be its end and aim, the more petty, the more hateful and the more embittering it is.

The less the skill and exertion of strength involved in manual labor (in other words, the more modern industry becomes developed), the more the labor of men is replaced by that of women. Differences of age and sex have no longer any distinctive social validity for the working class. All are instruments of labor, more or less expensive to use, according to their age and sex.

No sooner is the exploitation of the laborer by the manufacturer, so far, at an end, that he receives his wages in cash, than he is set upon by the other portions of the bourgeoisie, the landlord, the shopkeeper, the pawnbroker, etc.

The lower strata of the middle class—small tradespeople, shopkeepers, retired tradesmen, handicraftsmen and peasants—all these sink gradually into the proletariat, partly because their diminutive capital does not suffice for the scale on which modern industry is carried on and is swamped in the competition with the large capitalists, partly because their specialized skill is rendered worthless by new methods of production. Thus, the proletariat is recruited from all classes of the population.

The proletariat goes through various stages of development. With its birth begins its struggle with the bourgeoisie. At first the contest is carried on by individual laborers, then by the workers of a factory, then by the laborers of one trade in one locality, against the individual bourgeois who directly exploits them. They direct their attacks not against the bourgeois conditions of production, but against the instruments of production themselves; they destroy imported wares that compete with their labor, they smash to pieces machinery, they set factories ablaze, they seek to restore by force the vanished status of the workman of the Middle Ages.

At this stage the laborers still form an incoherent mass scattered over the whole country, and divided by their mutual competition. If they unite anywhere to form more compact bodies, this is not yet the consequence of their own active union, but of the union of the bourgeoisie, which, in order to attain its own political ends, is compelled to set the whole proletariat in motion, and is moreover yet, for a time, able to do so. At this stage, therefore, the proletarians do not fight their enemies, but the enemies of their enemies, the remnants of absolute monarchy, the landowners, the non-industrial bourgeois, the petty bourgeoisie. Thus

the whole historical movement is concentrated in the hands of the bourgeoisie; every victory so obtained is a victory for the bourgeoisie.

But with the development of industry the proletariat not only increases in number; it becomes concentrated in greater masses, its strength grows, and it becomes more aware of that strength. The various interests and conditions of life within the ranks of the proletariat are more and more equalized, in proportion as machinery obliterates all distinctions of labor, and nearly everywhere reduces wages to the same low level. The growing competition among the bourgeoisie and the resulting commercial crises, make the wages of the workers ever more fluctuating. The unceasing improvement of machinery, ever more rapidly developing, makes their livelihood more and more precarious. The collisions between individual workmen and individual bourgeois take more and more the character of collisions between two classes. Thereupon the workers begin to form combinations (trade unions) against the bourgeois; they join together in order to keep up the rate of wages; they form permanent associations in order to make provision beforehand for these occasional revolts. Here and there the contest breaks out into riots.

Now and then the workers are victorious, but only for a time. The real fruit of their battles lies, not in the immediate result, but in the ever-expanding union of the workers. This union is helped on by the improved means of communication that are created by modern industry and that place the workers of different localities in contact with one another. It was just this contact that was needed to centralize the numerous local struggles, all of the same character, into one national struggle between classes. But every class struggle is a political struggle. And that union, which took the burghers of the Middle Ages, with their miserable highways centuries to acquire, the modern proletarians, thanks to railways, achieve in a few years.

This organization of the proletarians into a class, and consequently into a political party, is continually being upset again by the competition between the workers themselves. But it continually re-emerges, stronger, firmer, mightier. It compels legislative recognition of particular interests of the workers, by taking advantage of the divisions among the bourgeoisie itself. Thus the ten-hours' bill in England was carried.

The sum of these collisions between the classes of the old society further, in many ways, the development of the proletariat. The bourgeoisie finds itself involved in a constant battle. At first with the aristocracy; later, with those portions of the bourgeoisie itself, whose interests have become antagonistic to the progress of industry; at all times, with the bourgeoisie of foreign countries. In all these battles it sees itself compelled to appeal to the proletariat, to ask for its help, and thus, to drag it into the political arena. The bourgeoisie itself, therefore, supplies the proletariat with its own elements of political and general education, in other words, it furnishes the proletariat with weapons for fighting the bourgeoisie.

Further, as we have already seen, entire sections of the ruling classes are, by the advance of industry, precipitated into the proletariat, or are at least threatened in their conditions of existence. These also supply the proletariat with fresh elements of enlightenment and progress.

Finally, in times when the class struggle nears the decisive hour, the process of dissolution going on within the ruling class (in fact, within the whole range of old society) assumes such a violent, glaring character, that a small section of the ruling class cuts itself adrift, and joins the revolutionary class, the class that holds the future in its hands. Just as, therefore, at an earlier period, a section of the nobility went over to the bourgeoisie, so now a portion of the bourgeoisie goes over to the proletariat, and in particular, a portion of the bourgeois ideologists, who have raised themselves to the level of comprehending theoretically the historical movement as a whole.

Of all the classes that stand face to face with the bourgeoisie today, the proletariat alone is a really revolutionary class. The other classes decay and finally disappear in the face of modern industry; the proletariat is its special and essential product.

The lower middle class, the small manufacturer, the shopkeeper, the artisan, the peasant—all these fight against the bourgeoisie, to save from extinction their existence as fractions of the middle class. They are therefore not revolutionary, but conservative. Nay more, they are reactionary, for they try to roll back the wheel of history. If by chance they are revolutionary, they are so only in view of their impending transfer into the

proletariat, they thus defend not their present, but their future interests, they desert their own standpoint to place themselves at that of the proletariat.

The "dangerous class," the social scum, that passively rotting mass thrown off by the lowest layers of the old society, may, here and there, be swept into the movement by a proletarian revolution; its conditions of life, however, prepare it far more for the part of a bribed tool of reactionary intrigue.

For the proletariat, the conditions of the old society are already virtually swamped. The proletarian is without property; his relation to his wife and children has no longer anything in common with the bourgeois family relations; modern industrial labor, modern subjection to capital, the same in England as in France, in America as in Germany, has stripped him of every trace of national character. Law, morality, religion, are to him so many bourgeois prejudices, behind which lurk in ambush just as many bourgeois interests.

All the preceding classes that got the upper hand sought to fortify their already acquired status by subjecting society at large to their conditions of appropriation. The proletarians cannot become masters of the productive forces of society, except by abolishing their own previous mode of appropriation, and thereby also every other previous mode of appropriation. They have nothing of their own to secure and to fortify; their mission is to destroy all previous securities for, and insurances of, individual property.

All previous historical movements were movements of minorities, or in the interest of minorities. The proletarian movement is the self-conscious, independent movement of the immense majority, in the interest of the immense majority. The proletariat, the lowest stratum of our present society, cannot stir, cannot raise itself, without the whole overlying strata of official society being sprung into the air.

Though not in substance, yet in form, the struggle of the proletariat with the bourgeoisie is at first a national struggle. The proletariat of each country must, of course, first of all settle matters with its own bourgeoisie.

In depicting the most general phases of the development of the proletariat, we traced the more or less veiled civil war raging within existing society, up to the point where that war breaks out into open revolution, and where the violent overthrow of the bourgeoisie lays the foundation for the sway of the proletariat.

Hitherto, every form of society has been based, as we have already seen, on the antagonism between oppressing and oppressed classes. But in order to oppress a class, certain conditions must be assured to it under which it can, at least, continue its slavish existence. The serf, in the period of serfdom, raised himself to membership in the commune, just as the petty bourgeois, under the yoke of feudal absolutism, managed to develop into a bourgeois. The modern laborer, on the contrary, instead of rising with the progress of industry, sinks deeper and deeper below the conditions of existence of his own class. He becomes a pauper, and pauperism develops more rapidly than population and wealth. And here it becomes evident that the bourgeoisie is unfit any longer to be the ruling class in society and to impose on society its own conditions of existence as an overriding

law. It is unfit to rule because it is incompetent to assure an existence to its slave within his slavery, because it cannot help letting him sink into such a state that it has to feed him, instead of being fed by him. Society can no longer live under this bourgeoisie. In other words, its existence is no longer compatible with society.

The essential condition for the existence, and for the sway of the bourgeois class is the formation and augmentation of capital; the condition for capital is wage labor. Wage labor rests exclusively on competition between the laborers. The advance of industry, that the bourgeoisie involuntarily promotes, replaces the isolation of the laborers, due to competition, by their revolutionary combination, due to association. The development of modern industry, therefore, cuts from under its feet the very foundation on which the bourgeoisie produces and appropriates products. What the bourgeoisie, therefore, produces, above all, is its own gravediggers. Its fall and the victory of the proletariat are equally inevitable.

READING 25

Writing in 1901, African American scholar W. E. B. Du Bois vividly documents the way blacks and whites were historically dealt with by the criminal justice system in the South. Because slaves were literally property owned by whites prior to the Civil War, they had little to do with the criminal justice system. Misbehavior was generally dealt with by their owners and informal groups of whites who worked to keeps blacks from associating, and the criminal justice system focused primarily on whites. As Du Bois puts it, the system was "lenient in theory and lax in execution." Following the war, owners lost power, but a more formal illegal group, the Klu Klux Klan, emerged. More important, however, because whites so believed in the slave system and were so convinced that freed slaves would not work as they had before, a new criminal justice system emerged "to restore slavery in everything but in name." New laws were passed, and the courts now became focused on African Americans, with the convict-lease system emerging where the labor of blacks was sold to "the highest bidder." The conditions were abysmal. The unintended consequences of the changes were to make the criminal justice system appear less legitimate and therefore ineffective. Du Bois concludes with some statistics documenting the poor governmental support for the criminal justice system in the South—there was little need as the convict-lease system was a "money maker" but a deplorable system that remains problematic.

Source: Du Bois, W. E. B. (1901). The spawn of slavery: The convict-lease system in the South. *The Missionary Review of the World, 14,* 737–745.

The Spawn of Slavery

The Convict-Lease System in the South

W. E. B. Du Bois

A modified form of slavery survives wherever prison labor is sold to private persons for their pecuniary profit.

—Wines

Two systems of controlling human labor which still flourish in the South are the direct children of slavery, and to all intents and purposes are slavery itself. These are the crop-lien system and the convict-lease system. The crop-lien system is an arrangement of chattel mortgages so fixed that the housing, labor, kind of agriculture and, to some extent, the personal liberty of the free black laborer is put into the hands of the landowner and merchant. It is absentee landlordism and the "company-store" systems united and carried out to the furthest possible degree. The convict-lease system is the slavery in private hands of persons convicted of crimes and misdemeanors in the courts. The objects of the present paper is to study the rise and development of the convict-lease system, and the efforts to modify and abolish it.

Before the Civil War the system of punishment for criminals was practically the same as in the North. Except in a few cities, however, crime was less prevalent than in the North, and the system of slavery could become criminals in the eyes of the law only in exceptional cases. The punishment and trial of nearly all ordinary misdemeanors and crimes lay in the hands of the masters. Consequently, so far as the state was concerned, there was no crime of any consequence among Negroes. The system of criminal jurisprudence had to do, therefore, with whites almost exclusively, and as is usual in a land of scattered population and aristocratic tendencies the law was lenient in theory and lax in execution.

On the other hand, the private well-ordering and control of slaves called for careful cooperation among masters. The fear of insurrection was ever before the South, and the ominous uprising of Cato, Gabriel, Vesey, Turner, and Toussaint made this fear an ever-present nightmare. The result was a system of rural police, mounted and on duty chiefly at night, whose work it was to stop the nocturnal wandering and meeting of slaves. It was usually an effective organization, which terrorized the slaves, and to which all white men belonged, and were liable to active detailed duty at regular intervals.

Upon this system war and emancipation struck like a thunderbolt. Law and order among the whites, already loosely enforced, became still weaker through the inevitable influence of conflict and social revolution. The freedman was especially in an anomalous situation. The power of the slave police supplemented and depended upon that of the private masters. When the masters' power was broken the patrol was easily transmuted into a lawless and illegal mob known to history as the Ku Klux Klan. Then came the first, and probably the most disastrous, of that succession of political expedients by which the South sought to evade the consequences of emancipation. It will always be a nice question of ethics as to how far a conquered people can be expected to submit to the dictates of a victorious foe. Certainly the world must to a degree sympathize with resistance under such circumstances. The mistake of the South, however, was to adopt a kind of resistance which in the long run weakened her moral fiber, destroyed respect for law and order, and enabled gradually her worst elements to secure an unfortunate ascendancy. The South believed in slave labor, and was thoroughly convinced that free Negroes would not work steadily or effectively. The whites were determined after the war, therefore, to restore slavery in everything but in name. Elaborate and ingenious apprentice and vagrancy laws were passed, designed to make the freedmen and their children work for their former masters at practically no wages. Some justification for these laws was found in the inevitable tendency of many of the ex-slaves to loaf when the fear of the lash was taken away. The new laws, however, went far beyond such justification, totally ignoring that large class of freedmen eager to work and earn property of their own, stopping all competition between employers, and confiscating the labor and liberty of children. In fact, the new laws of this period recognized the Emancipation Proclamation and the Thirteenth Amendment simply as abolishing the slave-trade.

The interference of Congress in the plans for reconstruction stopped the full carrying out of these schemes, and the Freedmen's Bureau consolidated and sought to develop the various plans for employing and guiding the freedmen already adopted in different places under the protection of the Union army. This government guardianship established a free wage system of labor by the help of the army, the striving of the best of the blacks, and the cooperation of some of the whites. In the matter of adjusting legal relationships, however, the Bureau failed. It had, to be sure, Bureau courts, with one representative of the ex-master, one of the freedman, and one of the Bureau itself, but they never gained the confidence of the community. As the regular state courts gradually regained power, it was necessary for them to fix by their decisions the new status of the freedmen. It was perhaps as natural as it was unfortunate that amid this chaos the courts sought to do by judicial decisions what the legislatures had formerly sought to do by specific law—namely, reduce the freedmen to serfdom. As a result, the small peccadillos of a careless, untrained class were made the excuse for severe sentences. The courts and jails became filled with the careless and ignorant, with those who sought to emphasize their new-found freedom, and too often with innocent victims of oppression. The testimony of a Negro counted for little or nothing in court, while the accusation of white witnesses was usually

decisive. The result of this was a sudden large increase in the apparent criminal population of the Southern states—an increase so large that there was no way for the state to house it or watch it even had the state wished to. And the state did not wish to. Throughout the South laws were immediately passed authorizing public officials to lease the labor of convicts to the highest bidder. The lessee then took charge of the convicts—worked them as he wished under the nominal control of the state. Thus a new slavery and slave-trade was established.

◈ The Evil Influences

The abuses of this system have often been dwelt upon. It had the worst aspects of slavery without any of its redeeming features. The innocent, the guilty, and the depraved were herded together, children and adults, men and women, given into the complete control of practically irresponsible men, whose sole object was to make the most money possible. The innocent were made bad, the bad worse; women were outraged and children tainted; whipping and torture were in vogue, and the death-rate from cruelty, exposure, and overwork rose to large percentages. The actual bosses over such leased prisoners were usually selected from the lowest classes of whites, and the camps were often far from settlements or public roads. The prisoners often had scarcely any clothing, they were fed on a scanty diet of corn bread and fat meat, and worked twelve or more hours a day. After was insufficient shelter; in one Georgia camp, as late as 1895, sixty-one men slept in one room, seventeen by nineteen feet, and seven feet high. Sanitary conditions were wretched, there was little or no medical attendance, and almost no care of the sick. Women were mingled indiscriminately with the men, both in working and sleeping, and dressed often in men's clothes. A young girl at Camp Hardmont, Georgia, in 1895, was repeatedly outraged by several of her guards, and finally died in childbirth while in camp.

Such facts illustrate the system at its worst—as it used to exist in nearly every Southern state, and as it still exists in parts of Georgia, Mississippi, Louisiana, and other states. It is difficult to say whether the effect of such a system is worse on the whites or on the Negroes. So far as the whites are concerned, the convict-lease system lowered the respect for courts, increased lawlessness, and put the states into the clutches of penitentiary "rings." The courts were brought into politics, judgeships became elective for shorter and shorter terms, and there grew up a public sentiment which would not consent to considering the desert of a criminal apart from his color. If the criminal were white, public opinion refused to permit him to enter the chain-gang save in the most extreme cases. The result is that even today it is very difficult to enforce the laws in the South against whites, and red-handed criminals go scot-free. On the other hand, so customary had it become to convict any Negro upon a mere accusation, that public opinion was loathe to allow a fair trial to black suspects, and was too often tempted to take the law into their own hands. Finally the state became a dealer in crime, profited by it so as to derive a new annual income for her prisoners. The lessees of the convicts made large profits also. Under such circumstances, it was almost impossible to remove the clutches of this vicious system from the state. Even as late as 1890 the Southern states were the only section of the Union where the income from prisons and reformatories exceeded the expense.[1] Moreover, these figures do not include the county gangs where the lease system is today most prevalent and the net income largest.

The effect of the convict-lease system on the Negroes was deplorable. First it linked crime and slavery indissolubly in their minds as simply forms of the white man's oppression. Punishment, consequently, lost the most effective of its deterrent effects, and the criminal gained pity instead of disdain. The Negroes lost faith in the integrity of courts and the fairness of juries. Worse than all, the chain-gangs became schools of crime which hastened the appearance of the confirmed Negro criminal upon the scene. That some crime and vagrancy should follow emancipation was inevitable. A nation can not systematically degrade labor without in some degree debauching the laborer. But there can be no doubt but that the indiscriminate careless and unjust method by which Southern courts dealt with the freedmen after the war increased crime and vagabondage to an enormous extent. There are no reliable statistics to which one can safely appeal to measure exactly the growth of crime among the emancipated slaves. About seventy per cent of all prisoners in the South are black; this, however, is in part explained by the fact that accused Negroes are still easily convicted and get long sentences, while whites still continue to escape the penalty of many crimes even among themselves. And yet allowing for all this, there can be no reasonable doubt but that there has arisen in the South since the war a class of black criminals, loafers, and ne'er-do-wells who are a menace to their fellows, both black and white.

Table 1   Income and Expense of State Prisons and Reformatories, 1890

	Earnings	Expense	Profit
New England	$299,735	$1,204,029	—
Middle States	71,252	1,850,452	—
Border States	597,898	962,422	—
Southern States[2]	938,406	890,452	$47,974
Central States	624,161	1,971,795	—
Western States	378,036	1,572,316	—

The appearance of the real Negro criminal stirred the South deeply. The whites, despite their long use of the criminal court for putting Negroes to work, were used to little more than petty thieving and loafing on their part, and not to crimes of boldness, violence, or cunning. When, after periods of stress of financial depression, as in 1892, such crimes increased in frequency, the wrath of a people unschooled in the modern methods of dealing with crime broke all bounds and reached strange depths of barbaric vengeance and torture. Such acts, instead of drawing the best opinion of these states and of the nation toward a consideration of Negro crime and criminals, discouraged and alienated the best classes of Negroes, horrified the civilized world, and made the best white Southerners ashamed of their land.

◇ What Has Been Done

Nevertheless, in the midst of all this a leaven of better things had been working and the bad effects of the epidemic of lynching quickened it. The great difficulty to be overcome in the South was the false theory of work and of punishment of wrong-doers inherited from slavery. The inevitable result of a slave system is for a master class to consider that the slave exists for his benefit alone—that the slave has no rights which the master is bound to respect. Inevitably this idea persisted after emancipation. The black workman existed for the comfort and profit of white people, and the interests of white people were the only ones to be seriously considered. Consequently, for a lessee to work convicts for his profit was a most natural thing. Then, too, these convicts were to be punished, and the slave theory of punishment was pain and intimidation.Given these ideas, and the convict-lease system was inevitable. But other ideas were also prevalent in the South; there were in slave times plantations where the well-being of the slaves was considered, and where punishment meant the correction of the fault rather than brute discomfort. After the chaos of war and reconstruction passed, there came from the better conscience of the South a growing demand for reform in the treatment of crime. The worst horrors of the convict-lease system were attacked persistently in nearly every Southern state. Back in the eighties George W. Cable, a Southern man, published a strong attack on the system. The following decade Governor Atkinson,

of Georgia, instituted a searching investigation, which startled the state by its revelation of existing conditions. Still more recently Florida, Arkansas, and other states have had reports and agitation for reform. The result has been marked improvement in conditions during the last decade. This is shown in part by the statistics of 1895; in that year the prisons and reformatories of the far South cost the states $204,483 more than they earned, while before this they had nearly always yielded an income. This is still the smallest expenditure of any section, and looks strangely small beside New England's $1,190,564. At the same time, a movement in the right direction is clear. The laws are being framed more and more so as to prevent the placing of convicts altogether in private control. They are not, to be sure, always enforced, Georgia having several hundreds of convicts so controlled in 1895 despite the law. In nearly all the Gulf states the convict-lease system still has a strong hold, still debauches public sentiment and breeds criminals.

The next step after the lease system was to keep the prisoners under state control, or, at least, regular state inspection, but to lease their labor to contractors, or to employ it in some remunerative labor for the state. It is this stage that the South is slowly reaching today so far as the criminals are concerned who are dealt with directly by the states. Those whom the state still unfortunately leaves in the hands of county officials are usually leased to irresponsible parties. Without doubt, work, and work worth the doing—*i.e.,* profitable work—is best for prisoners. Yet there lurks in this system a dangerous temptation. The correct theory is that the work is for the benefit of the criminal—for his correction, if possible. At the same time, his work should not be allowed to come into unfair competition with that of honest laborers, and it should never be an object of traffic for pure financial gain. Whenever the profit derived from the work becomes the object of employing prisoners, then evil must result. In the South today it is natural that in the slow turning from the totally indefensible private lease system, some of its wrong ideas should persist. Prominent among these persisting ideas is this: that the most successful dealing with criminals is that which costs the state least in actual outlay. This idea still dominates most of the Southern states. Georgia spent $2.38 per capita on her 2,938 prisoners in 1890, while Massachusetts spent $62.96 per capita on her 5,227 prisoners. Moreover, by selling the labor of her prisoners to the highest bidders, Georgia not only got all her money back, but made a total clear profit of $6.12 on each prisoner. Massachusetts spent about $100,000 more than was returned to her by prisoners' labor. Now it is extremely difficult, under such circumstances, to prove to a state that Georgia is making a worse business investment than Massachusetts. It will take another generation to prove to the South that an apparently profitable traffic in crime is very dangerous business for a state; that prevention of crime and the reformation of criminals is the one legitimate object of all dealing with depraved natures, and that apparent profit arising from other methods is in the end worse than dead loss. Bad public schools and profit from crime explain much of the Southern social problem. Georgia, Florida, and Louisiana, as late as 1895, were spending annually only $20,799 on their state prisoners, and receiving $80,493 from the hire of their labor.

Moreover, in the desire to make the labor of criminals pay, little heed is taken of the competition of convict and free laborers, unless the free laborers are white and have a vote. Black laborers are continually displaced in such industries as brick-making, mining, road-building, grading, quarrying, and the like, by convicts hired at $3, or thereabouts, a month.

The second mischievous idea that survives from slavery and the convict-lease system is the lack of all intelligent discrimination in dealing with prisoners. The most conspicuous and fatal example of this is the indiscriminate herding of juvenile and adult criminals. It need hardly be said the such methods manufacture criminals more quickly than all other methods can reform them. In 1890, of all the Southern states, only Texas, Tennessee, Kentucky, Maryland, and West Virginia made any state appropriations for juvenile reformatories. In 1895 Delaware was added to these, but Kentucky was missing. We have, therefore:

	1890	1895
New England	$632,634	$854,581
Border States	233,020	174,781
Southern States	10,498	33,910

And this in face of the fact that the South had in 1890 over four thousand prisoners under twenty years of

age. In some of the Southern states—notably, Virginia—there are private associations for juvenile reform, acting in cooperation with the state. These have, in some cases, recently received state aid, I believe. In other states, like Georgia, there is permissive legislation for the establishment of local reformatories. Little has resulted as yet from this legislation, but it is promising.

I have sought in this paper to trace roughly the attitude of the South toward crime. There is in that attitude much to condemn, but also something to praise. The tendencies are today certainly in the right direction, but there is a long battle to be fought with prejudice and inertia before the South will realize that a black criminal is a human being, to be punished firmly but humanely, with the sole object of making him a safe member of society, and that a white criminal at large is a menace and a danger. The greatest difficulty today in the way of reform is this race question. The movement for juvenile reformatories in Georgia would have succeeded some years ago, in all probability, had not the argument been used; it is chiefly for the benefit of Negroes. Until the public opinion of the ruling masses of the South can see that the prevention of crime among Negroes is just as necessary, just as profitable, for the whites themselves, as prevention among whites, all true betterment in courts and prisons will be hindered. Above all, we must remember that crime is not normal; that the appearance of crime among Southern Negroes is a symptom of wrong social conditions—of a stress of life greater than a large part of the community can bear. The Negro is not naturally criminal; he is usually patient and law-abiding. If slavery, the convict-lease system, the traffic in criminal labor, the lack of juvenile reformatories, together with the unfortunate discrimination and prejudice in other walks of life, have led to that sort of social protest and revolt which we call crime, then we must look for remedy in the sane reform of these wrong social conditions, and not in intimidation, savagery, or the legalized slavery of men.

◆ Notes

1. Bulletin No. 8, Library of State of New York. All figures in this article are from this source.

2. South Carolina, Georgia, Alabama, Mississippi, Louisiana, Texas, and Arkansas.

READING 26

In 1968, the Kerner Report concluded that we as a society were "moving toward two societies, one black, one white—separate and unequal" (National Advisory Commission on Civil Disorders, 1968). Embrick explores current race relations in the United States, paying special attention to the well-publicized killings of young black and brown men and women by police and, in some instances, vigilantes in recent years. Embrick concludes that little has changed between 1968 and 2015; the United States is still a society divided with considerable racial violence and oppression.

Two Nations, Revisited

The Lynching of Black and Brown Bodies, Police Brutality, and Racial Control in "Post-Racial" Amerikkka

David G. Embrick

Wrapped in plastic

Or closed casket for our troubles

Pressed in times

We busted like bubbles

With the police

This nation's peace sent here to run you

Now look at what this crooked world has come to . . .

. . .They don't give a fuck about us

While I'm kickin rhymes, getting to their children's minds

Now they give a fuck about us

They wanna see us die, they kick us every time we try

They don't give a fuck about us

—Tupac Shakur[1]

Source: Embrick, D. G. (2015). Two nations, revisited: The lynching of black and brown bodies, police brutality, and racial control in "post-racial" Amerikkka. *Critical Sociology, 41*(6), 835–843.

◈ Introduction

On 19 April 2015, 25-year-old Freddie Gray was pronounced dead after having sustained massive injuries to his larynx, vertebrae, and his spine where it was reported that it was 80 percent severed from his neck. Although the Baltimore authorities were quick at first to admit that the police did not follow procedure in both the immediate and timely medical care that Mr Gray needed and was denied, and were neglectful in Mr Gray's safety (i.e., failure to buckle Mr. Gray in the van as he was being transported to the police station), there continues to be silence and denial on the violence that Mr Gray was exposed to during his arrest. Ultimately, Freddie Gray's death was deemed a homicide and as I write this, a grand jury has indicted six officers with various counts of second-degree heart murder, involuntary manslaughter, and second-degree assault.[2] While many race and social justice scholars and activists have expressed relief with the outcome, some have clearly noted that this particular action represents only a start in terms of what needs to happen to adequately address illegal actions by the police,[3] and the institutional racism that runs rampant in the US criminal justice system and prison industrial complex.

Regardless of the ultimate outcome of these six police officers, they are outliers in a society that views police officers as legitimate in their authority and capacity to control black and brown bodies, bodies that are often viewed as less valuable to whites and whites' property. If this were untrue, how do we explain the consistent patterns of social inequalities that treat whites as victims and minorities as perpetrators? How do we explain that the six officers indicted in Mr Gray's death had bails set lower than Allen Bullock, the 18-year-old young man who turned himself in for vandalizing a Baltimore City police vehicle? If Mr Bullock were white instead of black, one wonders if he might have been applauded as a "reveler" looking to just have some rebellious fun against the police such as was seen during the 2014 New Hampshire pumpkin festival riot,[4] or the so-called "rallies" such as the one that occurred after University of Kentucky's loss in the 2015 March Madness tournament in which the looting, car-flipping, and fire incidences were calmly explained away as fans

"blowing off steam" (see Reeves, 2015). Indeed, how do we explain the sheer violence, dis[d]ain, and anger toward brown and black bodies—such as recently captured by Cleveland Police Officer Michael Brelo, who not only killed two black unarmed men who led police on a high-speed car chase in 2012, but who also felt it necessary to shoot Malissa Williams and Timothy Russell 49 times and at one point climbed on to the hood of their car and reloaded his gun in order to keep shooting after all of the other officers had already stopped firing (see Smith and Southall, 2015). Other Cleveland Police Officers must have felt similar to Brelo when they decided to kill 12-year-old Tamir Rice for brandishing a toy gun. As of this writing, no one has been charged in Tamir's death; Officer Michael Brelo was acquitted of manslaughter charges in May 2015.

The blatant disregard for black and brown bodies and racialized acts of social control is evident with the recent murders committed by police officers (or vigilantes) across the nation. Tanisha Anderson, Eric Garner, Rekia Boyd, Yvette Smith, Trayvon Martin, Michael Brown, Miriam Carey, Jonathan Ferrell, and Tamir Rice only represent a small number of blacks who have been killed at the hands of police in the US. Indeed, Mappingpoliceviolence.org reports that over 300 blacks were killed by police in 2014.[5] The murder of brown and black bodies and the frequencies in which they take place are not outlier accidental situations, nor are they reflective of the excuses that have come to be standard police responses to these situations—fear of personal safety. Rather, these murders point to the systemic and racialized ways in which murdering brown and black bodies have become normative practice in US society.

But it is not only the overt disregard for black and brown lives that should offend us, it is also the spectacle of racial oppression—for example, the fact that Michael Brown's body was left on the street for hours after he was killed by police officer Darren Wilson—that points to just how little has changed in American race relations since the days of Jim Crow. In fact, race scholars such as Michael Omi, Howard Winant, Eduardo Bonilla-Silva, Joe R. Feagin, Michelle Alexander, and countless others have noted that one could look at modern day race practices (and the need for racial spectacle) as old perfume repackaged in a new bottle. Thus, the legitimacy given to police agencies represents a rearticulation of slavery and Jim Crow era practices specifically designed to socially control people of color (Alexander, 2010; Bonilla-Silva, 2001). These modern day lynchings serve today in much the same way that they did in the past—as a way to illustrate and highlight white supremacy and emphasize minorities' place in a racialized social system. As people try to make sense of the escalation of police brutality and violence on poor people and people of color in a supposed era of colorblindness, one thing is clear—that social scientists and sociologists, in particular, have failed to take a central role in helping to reshape a nation that continues to control and punish minorities for the color of their skin and/or their non-European phenotype.

◈ **We Live in Two Nations**

This is our basic conclusion: Our nation is moving toward two societies, one black, one white—separate and unequal.

—National Advisory Commission
on Civil Disorders, 1968[6]

In 1968, President Lyndon B. Johnson established the National Advisory Commission on Civil Disorders (NACCD) to examine the 1967 race riots that were taking place in Los Angeles, Chicago, Newark, and Detroit that erupted in the mid-1960s. That report, also referred to as the Kerner Report after the chair of NACCD, Illinois Governor Otto Kerner, Jr, outlined in detail the deepening racial division between blacks and whites in the US that was directly related to existing structural inequalities that privileged whites: "What white Americans have never fully understood but what the Negro can never forget—is that white society is deeply implicated in the ghetto. White institutions created it, white institutions maintain it, and white society condones it" (1968: 1). The most famous line of the Kerner Report was their conclusion that the US is moving toward two separate and unequal societies, one black and one white. This report, while painstakingly to the point with race matters at the time, was certainly not groundbreaking news, at least not to social scientists such as Gunnar

Myrdal who outlined America's hypocrisy toward social justice in his 1944 book, *An American Dilemma: The Negro Problem and Modern Democracy*, or W.E.B. Du Bois (1903) who predicted the challenge of the 20th century would continue to be the problem of the color line. Nonetheless, the Kerner Report was instrumental for showcasing America's hypocrisy in its claim of being a global leader (and judge) of democracy and equality. Further, the report was instrumental in highlighting one of the top grievances[7] blacks had mentioned regarding consistent inequality in their cities that was largely ignored: police practices.

Andrew Hacker's notable 1992 book, *Two Nations: Black & White, Separate, Hostile, Unequal*, painted a picture of America 25 years after the publication of the Kerner Report. That picture was bleak, harsh, and yet reflected the reality of black and brown lives that was strikingly different from the lives of whites. Being black in America meant significantly more obstacles to economic, educational, or political success in comparison with their white counterparts. It also meant more resentment and animosity for blacks who became successful in their endeavors—and a questioning of the legitimacy of their success. And it meant increased surveillance of, and violence toward, minorities by state agencies and federal police agencies (Bonilla-Silva, 2001). Yet, for as much as whites seem to think that blacks have it made in the US, most whites would never trade their skin color with blacks.[8] The basic conclusion of Hacker's book was that the lives of minorities in the US in 1992 continued to be no different than what [was] outlined in the Kerner Report. And white responses to racial inequality in America has been one that exacerbates stereotypes in a way that ultimately leads to justifying the control of, and racial violence toward, black and brown bodies. Forty-seven years after the Kerner Report, where do we stand on race relations in the United States? Specifically, where do we stand on violence toward and control of black and brown bodies in our so-called era of colorblindness? And what are some thoughts we might consider moving forward?

Views on Race in the US

There is no denying that race continues to affect the lives of countless brown and black folks in America today—unless, of course, you are white. Although this statement may seem harsh, the truth of the matter is that 50 plus years after the passing of the Civil Rights Act of 1964 and over 150 years after the Emancipation Proclamation in 1863, many minorities say that race relations between whites and minorities have either not changed or have gotten worse.

The contrast between views on race relations in the US is most stark between blacks and whites. For example, according to the 2014 national survey conducted by the PEW Research Center, fewer blacks today than five years ago believe that blacks and whites get along "pretty well" or "very well," a drop from 76 percent to 64 percent (Lovelace, 2014). In contrast, whites are more optimistic regarding race relations these days (Wang, 2014). Blacks are also more skeptical of police shootings of minorities than whites and more likely to believe race to be a central factor in the shootings.[9] Whites are three times more likely than blacks to believe there will be fair investigations into any shootings of brown or black bodies by the police or white vigilantes. And three out of four blacks polled said they expect relations between minorities and the police will get worse in the coming year.

A 2015 Poll conducted by CNN/ORC found that 69 percent of minorities think that the US criminal justice system favors whites over blacks. This compares with 42 percent of whites who believed the same. In another question, when asked whether they believed that blacks have as good a chance as whites to get jobs for which they are qualified, whites (81 percent) were twice as likely as blacks (45 percent) to claim "as good a chance." The differences in views between whites and minorities continue to highlight the two worlds in which we live, where one group (whites) continues to be afforded more opportunities, dignities, and rights over other groups (minorities).

Violence Toward Minorities

The US has long had a fascination with black bodies. From days of slavery to the years of Jim Crow to the post–Civil Rights Era, black and brown bodies have been controlled and put on display as an affirmation of white superiority. This fixation is particularly notable when it comes to black male bodies. As Bonilla-Silva

(2001), Feagin (2006), and others have noted, the regulation of brown and black bodies—once the purview of slave overseers and night patrols, overt and violent racist organizations such as the Ku Klux Klan, and individual whites—has become largely replaced by state agencies such as the criminal justice system, and local and federal police (Marable, 1997).

In a US racialized social system, Bonilla-Silva (2001) argues that while the level of violence towards blacks and other minorities by the police has always been high, the phenomenal growth of police departments since the 1960s has allowed these state agencies to become the primary agents of social control of brown and black bodies. The media portrayal of minorities as violent perpetrators in need of social control allows for legitimation in many whites' eyes for extreme police brutality and mass incarceration as a new form of lynching for the 21st century (Alexander, 2010; Smith, 1995). The violence of police toward minorities is not a new phenomenon. It has been an ongoing issue in a US society that fears, loathes, and seeks control over minorities. Racial incidents of police brutality toward minorities today (e.g., Michael Brown, Eric Garner, Freddie Gray, Miriam Carey, etc.) mirror racial incidents just 25 years ago (e.g., Rodney King, Anthony Baez, Ahmed "Amadou" Diallo, etc.). Similar to Malissa Williams and Timothy Russell who were shot at 137 times by 13 Cleveland police officers (49 times by Officer Brelo alone), Ahmed "Amadou" Diallo, for instance, was shot at 41 times by New York police in 1999 while standing in front of his apartment building (Ruderman and Goodman, 2012). Like Williams and Russell, Diallo was unarmed.

Media Lies and Deceits

Contributing to whites' justification of violence toward brown and black bodies by both police and the larger criminal justice system is the media. No different than in the past, media not only continue to stereotype minorities as violent offenders that need to be controlled, they distort images and language in ways that provide privilege to whites who are almost always portrayed as innocent victims. Charles M. Blow, in a 2015 *New York Times* op-ed noted that calling protesters of the murder of Freddie Gray a "lynch mob" was a profound overreach and misuse of language that in no way resembled past (and present) violence toward minorities by whites. While not suggested directly by media (the term "lynch mob" was uttered by Baltimore police union president, Gene Ryan), the media no doubt added fuel to the fire with their 24 hour coverage of more angry protesters—protesters who represented only a small portion of the larger peaceful folks who attended protests across the nation against the brutality, murder, and injustice of police violence toward brown and black bodies. That blacks and other minorities continue to be stereotyped as violent (Embrick and Henricks, 2013; Entman and Rojecki, 2001; Stromberg, 2006) and therefore in need of control has direct consequences for minority lives as it justifies (in whites' eyes) police harassment and continued violence toward minorities (Alexander, 2010; Cole, 1999; Russell, 1998), even for what are typically phantom offenses (Russell, 1998). White perpetrators of crimes are almost never portrayed the same by media in comparison with minorities. A recent story by CNN (Kohn, 2015) was one of the few commentary published on double standards of coverage by media on events by race. For instance, media coverage on the deadly shootout by white biker gangs (or "biker clubs" as reported in some media outlets) in Waco, Texas in May 2015 failed, for the most part, to mention the race of the perpetrators, failed to make commentary on the white on white violence, and failed to discuss how whites were destroying their own communities. This might not be an issue except for the fact that such commentaries are almost always made about minorities. Once again white privilege allowed for what was arguably one of the most brutal and violent events in recent Texas history—in which nine people lost their lives and 170 were arrested—to disappear, unexamined.

The Burden of Black Women

The coverage of black and brown male bodies in the media stands in stark contrast with that of black and brown females. While there is no denying that we should be concerned by the brutal murders of Tamir Rice, Eric Garner, Michael Brown, Freddie Gray, and countless other minority men these past few years, one wonders about the media coverage of black and brown women who have also lost their lives at the hands of police officers.[10] Where is the news coverage of Tanisha Anderson

who found herself with her face slammed to the ground with a knee to her back by a police officer who was called by her mother to help with a mental episode she was having that day? Her death was ruled a homicide. Where was the extensive coverage of Miriam Carey, who had her one-year-old daughter in the car with her when she was shot at by US Secret Service and Capitol police officers? Or Shelly Frey, a 27-year-old black woman who was killed in 2012 by an off-duty sheriff's deputy after allegedly being caught stealing from a Walmart store. The fascination with black bodies is a long history of white supremacy that discards the humanity of both black men and women but has largely ignored violence toward black women while celebrating violence toward black men (Savali, 2014). In a white supremacist, capitalist, and patriarchal society, black women, and the violence toward them, are rendered invisible (Marable, 1997). The sexual degradation of black women and their unheard pleas are captured most vividly by W. E. B. Du Bois (2003: 75) in his originally titled poem, "The Burden of Black Women":

> And crying and sighing and crying again as a
> voice in the midnight cries,—But the burden
> of white men bore her back and the white
> world stifled her sighs.

Dying While Indigenous or Latino/a

Missing equally from media coverage is the police violence toward Indigenous Americans and Latino/a immigrants in the US. In the past 16 years, Indigenous Americans tied with blacks for the number of folks killed by police officers in America (see Cheney-Rice, 2015). While representing just over 10 percent of the black population in the US, this means that Indigenous Americans are being murdered at an alarming rate, yet one in which most folks remain unaware. Similarly, recent polls have found that a majority of Latino/as fear law enforcement officials, both Border Patrol and local police. The circumstances between the deaths of Indigenous, Latino/as and blacks are resoundingly similar. In fact, as protests were garnering media attention for the murders of Michael Brown and Eric Garner, 2014 came to be silently known as one of the [worst] times in recent history for Native Americans who have been subjugated historically to death and violence by a white supremacist state.[11] As reported in a recent CNN story (Moya-Smith, 2014), in comparison with other racial groups, Native Americans are the most likely group to be killed by police in America. And violence toward Latino/as by the police are routinely dismissed as Latino/as are often seen as "illegal" in the US and therefore criminal, and deserving of whatever punishment they receive—as seen in the case of Antonio Zambrano-Montes, a Mexican migrant worker who was unarmed when Pasco, Washington police officers shot and killed him on 10 February 2015 (see Planas, 2015). The violence toward Indigenous Americans and Latino/as in the US is nothing new. Since Europeans set eyes toward murdering Indigenous Americans for their resources in the 15th and 16th centuries (Berkhofer, Jr., 1978; Cornell, 1988), and used Latino/as as controlled labor (Montejano, 1987), both groups, similar to blacks in the US, have been cast as violent savages in need of control by whites. Both groups have been targets of extreme violence and continue to be cast as outsiders.

◈ Conclusion: Is There a "Real" Solution in Sight?

Being a minority in the US, for many brown and black folks, continues to mean living [in] a world different from whites. It means, as Toni Morrison once noted at the 1986 International PEN Congress, never feeling as if one were American (Haskins, 2002: 100). It means telling your children that they will not be fully accepted as equals in a world that privileges whites, and it means preparing them for a world in which they have to tread carefully for fear of their lives. In 2015 we ask ourselves again, echoing the question once posed by Martin Luther King, Jr., "where do we go from here?"

The struggles for justice and democratic transformation through peaceful means have only resulted in the deaths of more brown and black folks. When peaceful means have been shown to give little to no justice, whites become surprised and angry at minority protesters who fight back through anger of their own. Yet, this is not a new phenomenon; minorities have always fought back against their oppressors in various ways, some peaceful, some not (Fanon, 1963; Kelley, 2002;

Marable, 1997, 1999). In every era, whites have found ways to control minorities: through slavery, through Jim Crow laws, and now increasingly through state agencies. What do you do when police are given a free pass to murder brown and black bodies, are "caught" lying or trying to cover up their illegal actions, or whose actions when deemed inappropriate are often downplayed or ignored? How do you deal with a system in which police actions toward minorities are deemed legitimate in the eyes of most whites?

Recent race scholars have called for a new black power movement (Marable, 1997), or a new civil rights movement (Bonilla-Silva, 2003). Central to this movement needs to be the firm understanding that in order to deal with racial and ethnic inequalities today we need to understand the "new racism" of the racialized social system (Bonilla-Silva, 1997, 2001, 2003). That is, despite positive changes in the legal system stemming from the Civil-Rights Era, the racial practices and mechanisms that have kept Blacks and other minorities subordinated have become less overt and more covert, subtle and ambiguous (Bonilla-Silva, 1997; Bonilla-Silva and Lewis, 2000; Smith, 1995). Further, despite the political and legal gains minorities have achieved in the past 50 years, and despite the fact that we have a black president occupying the highest political office in the US, the reality is that conditions for many blacks, Latino/as, and Indigenous Americans have become worse. The call for a new civil rights movement needs to recognize the larger collective in the struggle for inequality and justice against police and state brutality. This includes not only the blacklivesmatter movement, but also the Latino/alivesmatter, NativeAmericanlivesmatter, and womenlivesmatter movements. The progress forward must be well organized and embracing of the fact the struggle for equality has always been a struggle over race, class, and gender matters in America. One thing is clear: police violence toward brown and black bodies are not new, we just keep acting as if they are.

◈ Notes

1. Shakur, Tupac (2002) They Don't Give a Fuck about Us. *Better Dayz*. Amaru, Tha Row. For more information on the album, see: http://www.allmusic.com/album/better-dayz-mw0000663367.

2. See *CNN Wire* (2015); see also Campbell (2015).

3. Although Baltimore police claimed that Freddie Gray was arrested for carrying an illegal weapon (switchblade), the State Attorney of Baltimore noted that the knife that Mr Gray was carrying was legal and therefore the police made an illegal arrest.

4. For more information, see Pearce (2014).

5. For more details on the individual cases, see: http://mapping policeviolence.org/

6. For the full report, see National Advisory Commission on Civil Disorders (1968).

7. Page 7 (Chapter 2) of the 1968 Kerner Report identified 12 major grievances from blacks that were divided into three distinct intensity levels. The most intense (level 1) included: police practices, unemployment and underemployment, and inadequate housing. Level 2 included: inadequate education, poor recreation facilities and programs, and ineffectiveness of the political structure and grievance mechanisms. Level 3 included: disrespectful white attitudes, discriminatory administration of justice, inadequacy of federal programs, inadequacy of municipal services, discriminatory consumer and credit practices, and inadequate welfare programs.

8. In Chapter 3, Hacker mentions a parable that was given to white students in which they woke up one day as a black man or woman. Students were then asked how much money they would need in order to be compensated for the change in skin tone. Most students suggested that $1m per year was not out of the ordinary.

9. For further information, see: http://www.people-press.org/2014/08/18/stark-racial-divisions-in-reactions-to-ferguson-police-shooting/

10. For a look at one of the few coverages on black women killed during police encounters, see: Abbey-Lambertz (2015).

11. Six Native Americans were reportedly killed by police in the last two months of 2014 alone. For more information, see: http://lastrealindians.com/six-native-americans-killed-by-police-in-last-two-months-of-2014/

◈ References

Abbey-Lambertz K (2015) The 15 black women were killed during police encounters. Their lives matter, too. *Huffington Post: Black Voices*, 13 February.

Alexander M (2010) *The New Jim Crow: Mass Incarceration in the Age of Colorblindness.* New York, NY: The New Press.

Berkhofer RF Jr (1978) *The White Man's Indian: Images of the American Indian From Columbus to the Present.* New York, NY: Vintage Press.

Blow CM (2015) 'Lynch mob': Misuse of language. April. *New York Times*, 27 April. Available (accessed 20 May 2015) at: http://www.nytimes.com/2015/04/27/opinion/charles-blow-lynch-mob-misuse-of- language.html?_r=0

Bonilla-Silva E (1997) Rethinking Racism: Toward a Structural Interpretation. *American Sociological Review* 62(3): 465–480.

Bonilla-Silva E (2001) *White Supremacy & Racism in the Post-Civil Rights Era.* Boulder, CO: Lynne Rienner Publishers.

Bonilla-Silva E (2003) *Racism without Racists: Color-Blind Racism & Racial Inequality in Contemporary America.* Lanham, MD: Rowman & Littlefield.

Bonilla-Silva E and Lewis AE (2000) 'This is a white country': The racial ideology of the Western nations of the world-system. *Sociological Inquiry* 70(2): 188–214.

Campbell A (2015) Grand jury indicts six officers in Freddie Gray Case. *The Huffington Post*, 21 May.

Cheney-Rice Z (2015) The police are killing one group at a staggering rate, and nobody is talking about it. *Identities.Mic*, 5 February. Available (accessed 5 May 2015) at: http://mic.com/articles/109894/the-police-are-killing-one-group-at-a-staggering-rate-and-nobody-is-talking-about-it

CNN Wire (2015) Freddie Gray's death deemed homicide; six officers face charges. 1 May. Available at: http://wtvr.com/2015/05/01/freddie-grays-death-deemed-a-homicide-six-officers-face-charges/

Cole D (1999) *No Equal Justice: Race and Class in the American Criminal Justice System.* New York, NY: The New Press.

Cornell S (1988) *The Return of the Native: American Indian Political Resurgence.* New York, NY: Oxford University Press.

Du Bois WEB (1903) *Souls of Black Folk.* Chicago, IL: A.C. McClurg.

Du Bois WEB (2003 [1920]) *Darkwater: Voices From Within the Veil.* New York, NY: Humanity Books.

Embrick DG and Henricks K (2013) Discursive colorlines at work: How epithets and stereotypes are racially unequal. *Symbolic Interaction* 36(2): 197–215.

Entman RM and Rojecki A (2001) *The Black Image in the White Mind: Media and Race in America.* Chicago, IL: The University of Chicago Press.

Fanon F (1963) *The Wretched of the Earth.* New York, NY: Grove Press.

Feagin JR (2006) *Systemic Racism: A Theory of Oppression.* New York, NY: Routledge.

Hacker A (2003 [1992]) *Two Nations: Black & White, Separate, Hostile, Unequal.* New York, NY: Scribner.

Haskins J (2002) *Toni Morrison: Telling a Tale Untold.* Brookfield, CT: Twenty-First Century Books.

Kelley RDG (2002) *Freedom Dreams: The Black Radical Imagination.* Boston, MA: Beacon Press.

Kohn S (2015) Waco coverage shows double standard on race. *CNN*, 18 May. Available (accessed 10 May 2015) at: http://www.cnn.com/2015/05/18/opinions/kohn-biker-shooting-waco/

Lovelace R (2014) Poll: African Americans think race relations have gotten worse since 2009. August. *National Review*, 26 August. Available (accessed 15 May 2015) at: http://www.nationalreview.com/corner/386336/poll-african-americans-think-race-relations-have-gotten-worse-2009-ryan-lovelace

Marable M (1997) *Black Liberation in Conservative America.* Boston, MA: South End Press.

Marable M (1999) *How Capitalism Underdeveloped Black America: Problems in Race, Political Economy, and Society.* Boston, MA: South End Press.

Montejano D (1987) *Anglos and Mexicans in the Making of Texas, 1836–1986.* Austin, TX: University of Texas Press.

Moya-Smith S (2014) Who's most likely to be killed by police? *CNN, U.S. Edition,* 24 December. Available (accessed 1 May 2015) at: http://www.cnn.com/2014/12/24/opinion/moya-smith-native-americans/

Myrdal G (1944) *An American Dilemma: The Negro Problem and Modern Democracy.* New York, NY: Harper and Brothers.

National Advisory Commission on Civil Disorders (1968) *Report of the National Advisory Commission on Civil Disorders.* New York, NY: Bantam Books.

Pearce M (2014) Riot breaks out at New Hampshire pumpkin festival. *Los Angeles Times,* 19 October.

Planas R (2015) Why the media pays less attention to police killings of Latinos. *Huffington Post: Latino Voices,* 24 February. Available (accessed 15 May 2015) at: http://www.huffingtonpost.com/2015/02/24/ police-killings-latinos_n_6739448.html

Reeves C (2015) Riots, looting & fires break out in Kentucky. Don't worry. It's mostly white kids. *Daily KOS,* 5 April. Available (accessed 15 May 2015) at: http://www.dailykos.com/story/2015/04/05/13 75772/-Riots-Looting-Fires-Break-Out-in-Kentucky-Don-t-Worry-It-s-Mostly-White-Kids

Ruderman W and Goodman JD (2012) Diallo's mother asks why officer who shot at her son will get gun back. *The New York Times,* 3 October. Available (accessed 10 May 2015) at: http://www.nytimes.com/2012/10/03/nyregion/amadou-diallos-mother-asks-why-officer-who-shot-at-her-son-will-get-gun-back.html

Russell KK (1998) *The Color of Crime: Racial Hoaxes, White Fear, Black Protectionism, Police Harassment, and other Macroaggressions.* New York, NY: New York University Press.

Savali KW (2014) Black women are killed by police, too. *Salon,* 24 August. Available (accessed 1 May 2015) at: http://www.salon.com/2014/08/24/black_women_are_killed_by_police_too_partner/

Smith RC (1995) *Racism in the Post-Civil Rights Era: Now You See It, Now You Don't.* New York, NY: State University of New York Press.

Smith M and Southall A (2015) Cleveland police officer acquitted of manslaughter in 2012 deaths. *The New York Times,* 23 May. Available (accessed 15 May 2015) at: http://www.nytimes.com/2015/05/24/us/michael-brelo-cleveland-police-officer-acquitted-of-manslaughter-in-2012-deaths.html

Stromberg F (2003) *Black Images in the Comics.* Korea: Fantagraphics Books.

Wang HL (2014) Whites more optimistic than blacks on race relations in U.S. *NPR,* 30 December. Available (accessed on 15 May 2015) at: http://www.npr.org/sections/codeswitch/2014/12/30/373934184/fact-checking-obamas-assessment-on-race

CHAPTER 10

Critical Theories of Deviance

In 2004, Little Rock, Arkansas, was voted the meanest city in United States by the National Coalition for the Homeless. What made Little Rock the meanest city toward the homeless? The city, at the time, "managed" the homeless population by ordering the police to engage in ongoing raids of the 27 homeless encampments found in the area. Police came into these encampments during the day, while the inhabitants were not there, and demolished the sites, often destroying the few belongings that inhabitants owned. While the mayor of Little Rock at the time (Jim Dailey) admitted that he did not know where the homeless were supposed to go, the police continued the raids, often without warning to the residents. The city justified the raids by calling the homeless panhandlers and petty thieves. While the homeless have been cast as common criminals by the city, there is no evidence this is the case. In fact, the fastest growing homeless population in the area was single women with children. At the time, only 75 shelter beds were available for homeless women (adapted from Rampona, 2004). And according to the National Coalition for the Homeless, since January 2013, 21 cities have successfully made it illegal to feed the homeless with at least 10 more as of October 2014 in the process of legislating against individuals and community groups feeding the homeless (Stoops, 2014).

◈ Introduction

The story above highlights an all-too-common problem for the homeless in the United States—the criminalization or stigmatization of their homeless plight. While many organizations—national and local, religious and secular—focus on helping the homeless through such means as soup kitchens, shelters, and "10-year plans" to eradicate homelessness, the major governmental response to homelessness in many cities is one of social control and banishment (Beckett & Herbert, 2010).

The deviance theories examined in this chapter are considered critical theories. In other words, they examine issues of deviance and crime from a perspective that questions the normative and status quo. While earlier theories in this book might look at the plight of homelessness and ask how someone becomes homeless or why the homeless are homeless—oftentimes focusing specifically on what many might consider individual flaws or propensities to engage in this "deviance"—these critical theories instead examine societal responses to homelessness, often from the perspective of those with less societal power (people of color or women) or those with nontraditional philosophies (peacemaking). In other words, just like Marxist/conflict theory in Chapter 9, the theories in this chapter will ask, What role does society play in the creation and maintenance of homelessness? Critical theories are wide-ranging, and we have chosen three—feminist theory, **critical race theory**, and peacemaking theory—that represent a variety of those theories. (Our choices are eclectic because they offer you an opportunity to see the vast ways we can start to think about deviance and social control.) Some argue that critical theories are just an extension of Marxist/conflict theories, and it is certainly the case that these critical theories developed because of the existence of those earlier theories, but each critical theory adds

▲ **Photo 10.1**   How do we address homelessness? The answer depends on the theory we are using to understand it.

something well beyond the theories in Chapter 9, and they are different enough to warrant their own chapter. While some of these theories are newer (for example, peacemaking does not have the body of empirical work that feminist theory does), they offer a way of looking at the world that broadens our understanding and discussion of deviance.

◈ Development of Feminist Criminology

Feminist criminology questions the status quo, most specifically the male-centered view that much of criminology takes. Feminist thought has a long, rich history in the United States, with feminist criminology emerging in the 1970s through the influential works of F. Adler (1975), R. J. Simon (1975), and Smart (1977). As with many of these critical perspectives, there is no single ideology but, rather, a diversity of feminist thought with ranging, often competing, viewpoints: **liberal feminism; radical feminism; Marxist feminism; socialist feminism; postmodern feminism** (Burgess-Proctor, 2006; Daly & Chesney-Lind, 1988; Tong, 1998); black feminism and critical race feminism (Burgess-Proctor, 2006); psychoanalytic feminism; gender feminism; existentialist feminism; global and multicultural feminism; and ecofeminism (Tong, 1998).

While a diverse set of theories falls under the feminist perspective, these theories all stem from the critique that criminological theories and theories of deviance prior to the introduction of feminist thought treated women in one of two ways: either as subsumed under the heading of "men," assuming that general theories of deviance could explain female deviance, or in a sexist manner, assuming that women were somehow "different" or "pathological" in their makeup and that their deviance stemmed from this pathology. Until the feminist perspective, none of the theories acknowledged the position of women in a patriarchal society and the structural oppression that women experienced in this society (Smart, 1977).

For the purposes of this overview, this chapter will highlight five branches of feminism that have produced much research on deviance and crime. Liberal feminism focuses on gender role socialization. The roles that women are socialized into are not valued as much as the roles into which men are socialized; in other words, nurturing roles such as teacher are not valued as much as competitive roles such as CEO. For this reason, liberal feminists focus on equal rights and opportunities, especially in education and the workplace, that would allow women to compete fairly with men. Liberal feminist scholars argue that women engage in deviance less because they are socialized in a manner that provides them fewer opportunities to deviate (Burgess-Proctor, 2006).

Radical feminism focuses on the sexual control of women, seeing their oppression as emerging from a social order dominated by men. Because of their emphasis on sexual control, radical feminists focus much of their theoretical insights on sex, gender, and reproduction (Tong, 1998) as well as—in the areas of crime and deviance—on domestic violence, rape, sexual harassment, and pornography (Burgess-Proctor, 2006).

Socialist feminism focuses on structural differences, especially those we find in the capitalist modes of production. Social feminists argue that both patriarchy and capitalism are oppressive forces for women and that until the patriarchal system and the class-based system are eradicated, there can be no equality for women (Tong, 1998).

Postmodern feminism may be closest to **peacemaking criminology** in that it questions the idea of a single "truth" or way of knowing and understanding. Postmodern feminists examine the social construction of such "accepted" ideas as crime and deviance (Burgess-Proctor, 2006). Even with their rich diversity, at the center of all of these strands of feminist thought is an emphasis on the oppression of women.

As Amanda Burgess-Proctor (2006) explained, in the 21st century, one of the most promising approaches to feminist theorizing is known as multicultural feminism. Multicultural feminists (e.g., Baca Zinn & Thornton Dill, 1996) build upon the work of Patricia Hill Collins (1990) and Kimberlé Crenshaw (1989, 1993) by putting the concept of intersectionality at the center of analysis of social issues.

Intersectionality is the idea that in order to truly understand the social experience of someone, you have to consider the ways in which they experience race, class, gender, age, sexuality, and ability—all of these variables simultaneously affect a person's experience of the world. By using this sophisticated conceptual lens, we can then better understand how a given person can be oppressed in some ways and be privileged in other ways; it allows for a nuanced investigation of our social reality (Burgess-Proctor, 2006).

Certainly, for a book on deviance and social control, one of the most central forms of oppression to be examined would be the criminal justice system and prison-industrial complex. Many feminist scholars have examined the effect of increasing social controls on the experiences of women. Between 1970 and 2001, the female prison population increased from 5,600 to 161,200 women (a 2,800% increase), even though for much of this time, crime rates were actually decreasing in the United States (Sudbury, 2005). Many have looked at this increase and tried to explain it with individual-level theories that focus on increasing female criminality, but feminist scholars argue that to really understand both the reasons behind such an exponential increase and the effect such an increase has on women and society, we must examine the business of criminalization that has made more behaviors deviant and punishments harsher over the past 30 years.

Feminist theories examine the label of deviant from the perspective of the outsider. Like conflict theory in Chapter 9 and critical race theory later in this chapter, feminist theory argues that the label of deviant is used to control women, especially poor women and women of color (Neve & Pate, 2005; Ogden, 2005). Instead of acknowledging a structural system of oppression that pays women less than men, does not adequately support childcare, and offers far fewer opportunities for women than men, the system criminalizes sexuality, makes the rules for welfare almost impossible to follow and then considers welfare fraud a crime punishable with five years in prison (Ogden, 2005), and labels women deviant for many behaviors they engage in as a means of survival (for example, running away and prostitution). Feminist theorists argue that the system itself must be changed instead of narrowly focusing on changing women's behavior.

Feminism and Homelessness

Feminist theorists have devoted themselves to the study of women and their experiences in the social world (Burgess-Proctor, 2006). Much of this research—on domestic violence, the physical and sexual abuse of teenagers, and the position of women in the economic system—can have a significant impact on our understanding of women and homelessness. Feminist theory would ask what it is about women's position in society that might affect their likelihood of becoming homeless and how this position affects them once they are homeless.

For example, patriarchal society normalizes the abuse of women. The fact that victimization of women is considered normal or acceptable means that many women are not helped in any systematic fashion. Women who want to escape abusive situations can quickly find themselves homeless. In addition, women who have no choice but to become homeless when they want to leave an abusive relationship are likely to delay or completely cancel their escape because homelessness presents its own hardships. These women are left with few alternatives.

Extensive research has documented the experience of teenage girls who run away from home (see Chesney-Lind & Shelden, 2003). These girls are often escaping very abusive families, and running away becomes a preservation technique, but our public policies for running away do not take into consideration the reasons why girls may be running away. These policies criminalize this behavior and treat the girls as deviants who need to be punished or "reformed" for leaving their families. Feminists have long argued that good public policy would acknowledge the oppressive social structure that exists and not hold young girls accountable for the systems of oppression they are subject to. In other words, public policy should not focus on labeling the girls as deviant for running away and becoming homeless but should instead focus on services and policies that stop physical and sexual abuse in the home and that offer girls who have been abused a safe haven—resources, affordable housing, educational and work opportunities, and counseling to make sense of their experiences.

DEVIANCE IN POPULAR CULTURE

This chapter introduces you to critical theories and peacemaking criminology. As with many theoretical perspectives, the ideas may become more clear and accessible to you if you can apply them to specific examples. Popular culture and films, once again, offer compelling real-life and fictional cases for you to watch and practice using these perspectives.

The Accused—This film is a fictional account of a young woman who is gang-raped in a bar. The victim's judgment and character are questioned when she decides to take the case to court. How would feminist theory view this case? From a peacemaking perspective, how might it have been better handled?

Crash—This popular film offers examples of racial prejudice and profiling from several different perspectives. Each character reveals his or her own biases throughout the film; some learn significant lessons as they interact in surprising ways, but every character feels the powerful effect of fear and racial discrimination. Each character eventually questions his or her belief system and the larger society we live in.

The Dhamma Brothers—This documentary explores the power of meditation in a maximum-security prison. The film takes you inside the Donaldson Correctional Facility in Alabama as inmates embark upon an emotionally and physically demanding program of silent meditation lasting 10 days and requiring 100 hours of meditation. Can such a program change these men, and can it change the larger culture of the prison? Is this a desirable outcome?

12 Years a Slave—This book and film follow the story of Solomon Northup's saga as a free black man who was kidnapped and sold into slavery in 1841. He spent the next 12 years enslaved to a cruel southern plantation owner named Edwin Epps. After 12 years, he was finally rescued with the help of northern friends. After returning home, he wrote the book detailing his life as a slave in the South.

(Continued)

(Continued)

Redemption—This is a made-for-television movie about the life of Stan "Tookie" Williams, founder of the Crips, who was nominated for the Nobel Peace Prize while on death row. Can a man who was convicted of terrible crimes turn his life around and be a role model for youth in the larger community? From his prison cell, Tookie Williams wrote a number of children's books speaking out against gang violence. Williams was executed by the state of California in 2005. Whether redemption was possible in his case is now an academic question, but it is one we would like you to consider.

Twitter—While the existence of Twitter might itself be an example of deviance (as many argue we have become obsessed with being known and followed), in several instances, it has also been used to release information that has been used to stand up to those in power. In a 2008 news story that brought Twitter into the light for many people, James Karl Buck, a UC Berkeley graduate student, tweeted the single word "arrested" when he was detained in Egypt. Some of his 48 followers told his school, the US Embassy, and the press, and he was released soon after. More recently, Twitter has been used by protesters, news organizations, and witnesses to document social movements like Black Lives Matter and the Arab Spring.

◈ Development of Critical Race Theory

Critical race theory is an extension of critical legal studies that came to prominence through the writings of legal scholars in the 1970s. Scholars of critical race theory were interested in explaining why the civil rights movement of the 1960s had stalled and why the advances in the 1960s and 1970s had come under attack (Crenshaw, Gotanda, Peller, & Thomas, 1995). These scholars offered a counterstory to the dominant, mainstream accounts of the events of the civil rights movement and the use of law as a tool of equality. According to Cornel West (1995), "Critical Race Theory . . . compels us to confront critically the most explosive issue in American civilization: the historical centrality and complicity of law in upholding white supremacy" (p. xi).

While the theory first began to coalesce among legal scholars, today it is used in the areas of communication, education, and sociology by an array of race scholars who are unified by two goals:

> The first is to understand how a regime of white supremacy and its subordination of people of color have been created and maintained in America, and, in particular, to examine the relationship between that social structure and professed ideals such as "the rule of law" and "equal protection." The second is a desire not merely to understand the vexed bond between law and racial power but to *change* it. (Crenshaw et al., 1995, p. xiii)

Challenging this idea of white supremacy and, thus, the belief that the white experience is the normative standard by which all other experiences are measured, critical race theorists argue that to understand law and racial exclusion, we must understand the experiences of people of color under this legal system. These scholars insist "that the social and experiential context of racial oppression is crucial for understanding racial dynamics, particularly the way that current inequalities are connected to earlier, more overt, practices of racial exclusion" (E. Taylor, 1998, p. 122). Critical race theory, then, can be used to examine the use of law to negate the experiences of discrimination and victimization of people of color while heightening the focus on deviance that may or may not exist in communities of color.

Critical legal scholars argue that the law is not "neutral" or "objective" in its creation or application and, instead, has been used overtly, when possible, and covertly, when necessary, to subordinate people of color (Crenshaw et al., 1995). Even in such arenas as affirmative action, a policy from the civil rights era designed to help people of color, the law has been used, in the end, to mute this effort (Aguirre, 2000; Crenshaw et al., 1995).

At its very foundation, critical race theory offers a unique position in the forum of legal critique by proposing that racism is an intricate and enduring pattern in the fabric of American life, woven into the social structure and social institutions of the modern day (Crenshaw et al., 1995). This is in direct contrast to most liberal legal and social scholars, who argue that racism and discrimination, in general, are sociopathic, anomalous acts that not only can be explained by individual evil behavior but also can be fixed through accepted legal practices (Fan, 1997). As Crenshaw et al. (1995) note,

> From its inception mainstream legal thinking in the U.S. has been characterized by a curiously constricted understanding of race and power. Within this cramped conception of racial domination, the evil of racism exists when—and only when—one can point to specific, discrete acts of racial discrimination, which is in turn narrowly defined as decision-making based on the irrational and irrelevant attribute of race. (p. xx)

One of the most important tenets of critical race theory may be its supposition that racial domination is at the center of much of today's legal and social decision-making—and that this domination is so routine, it is accepted as both legally and morally legitimate. Critical race scholars, in essence, argue that the "white" experience is so established as the "proper" experience that this viewpoint has been institutionalized as normative, and experiences or viewpoints that deviate from this are seen as harmful and therefore deviant.

Critical Race Theory and Homelessness

Critical race theory, then, is used to analyze the use of law and legal processes to maintain the status quo or "protect" a white, middle-class interpretation of the world in the face of poor communities and communities of color. This perspective can be used to examine the experiences of the homeless in general, focusing on how laws are used to socially control the homeless instead of helping them. An excellent, specific example of this can be seen in the experiences of the homeless, migrant populations, and Latino populations during the San Diego fire evacuations of 2007 (see American Civil Liberties Union [ACLU], 2007). According to a report published November 1, 2007, the evacuation process for many San Diegans was subject to extra scrutiny and social control for what appeared to be racially and class-motivated reasons.

On October 21, 2007, fires broke out in San Diego County that required the evacuation of thousands of residents. One of the main evacuation centers was Qualcomm Stadium in the city of San Diego. While the ACLU reports that volunteers at the evacuation center were meticulous in their help of those in need, in more than a few instances, law enforcement seemed to be working at cross-purposes with these volunteers. One such example was that on more than one occasion (and with only evacuees of color), law enforcement detained individuals after they had been given their supplies from volunteers and accused these individuals of looting the supplies or "taking too many supplies" for their needs. In a second example, law enforcement entered the evacuation center during the late evening and woke up evacuees, requesting that they show identification proving they were from official evacuation areas. This was especially harmful for evacuees who were homeless (but living on the streets in evacuated areas) because they had no documentation with an official address given that they were homeless. These evacuees were ordered to leave the evacuation shelter because it was assumed they were not "in need" of the services and were taking advantage of the situation by staying at the shelter. While volunteers repeatedly emphasized that the services were available for anyone who came to the facility, many of the evacuees were assumed to be there under false pretenses. The ACLU

© Stockbyte/Thinkstock

▲ **Photo 10.2** When a firestorm hit San Diego County, some individuals were treated as victims while others were treated as deviants. This treatment was often based on the individual's race/ethnicity.

(2007) report suggests that most, if not all, of those who were accused of unlawful behavior were the homeless or evacuees of color. In other words, white, middle-class evacuees were seen as deserving of help while the homeless or evacuees of color were not (by law enforcement, not volunteers).

Critical race theory, as a theory that emphasizes the importance of capturing individuals' stories and highlighting the experiences of everyone, not just those most visible or "deserving" of storytelling, allows for a more thorough examination of many experiences that usually go unnoticed or unrecorded. Certainly, during the firestorms of 2007 in San Diego County, the experiences of the homeless and evacuees of color were overlooked by most who focused on more visible evacuees. Critical race theory gives voice to individuals who may not have their stories told in more traditional settings.

◈ Development of Peacemaking

It is fitting to include peacemaking criminology as one of the theories in this chapter because one of its strongest proponents is Richard Quinney, the critical criminologist whose early work we read about in Chapter 9 under conflict theories. One might say that peacemaking theory (Pepinsky & Quinney, 1991; Quinney, 1995) is the contemporary extension of Quinney's work in conflict theory. Writing and theorizing with Hal Pepinsky, Quinney continued with this theory to critically examine not only our understanding of crime and deviance but also our understanding of how we come to know what we know. In other words, they critically examined criminology *and* criminologists as well.

According to the peacemaking philosophy, most criminology today is "warlike" because at its foundation, it advocates making war on crime. This war on crime is evidenced in two ways in traditional criminology: (1) through the us-versus-them philosophy that suggests that those who engage in crime are somehow different from the rest of society and (2) through advocating punishment as the primary means to stop crime (Pepinsky & Quinney, 1991). Pepinsky and Quinney (1991) argue that neither of these viewpoints has reduced criminal activity; in fact, both have increased the suffering of not only victims but offenders alike. According to Pepinsky and Quinney,

> There are basically two kinds of criminologists, those who think criminals are different from themselves and those who don't. You cannot separate a criminal's self-understanding from our understanding of the criminal. More than empathy, understanding requires our sympathy—allowing ourselves to feel the offender's pain and committing ourselves to trying to alleviate the pain for us both. (p. 303)

Peacemaking criminology, on the other hand, is focused on a different way of seeing and organizing the world: around compassion, sympathy, and understanding. Quinney (1991) defines this way of thinking:

> In other words, without inner peace in each of us, without peace of mind and heart, there can be no social peace between people and no peace in societies, nations, and in the world. To be explicitly engaged in this process, of bringing about peace on all levels, of joining ends and means, is to be engaged in peacemaking. (p. 10)

The peacemaking tradition has no single tenet or assumption, and it has many followers in both the academic world and the world of praxis (Pepinsky & Quinney, 1991). In 1991, Pepinsky and Quinney published the first book on the peacemaking perspective. They outline three substantive areas that flourish in the peacemaking tradition: religious, feminist, and critical. Peacemakers coming from a religious perspective focus on a variety of religious traditions, including Christianity, Buddhism, Hinduism, Islam, Judaism, and Native American traditions (Braswell, Fuller, & Lozoff, 2001). They look to these traditions to advocate a way of meeting those who might engage in harm not as enemies but as members of the community who need understanding. "It is rather that when violence happens, they [the Mennonites] choose to try to restore peace rather than to respond in kind. And once again, the method is the way" (Pepinsky & Quinney, 1991, p. 305).

In contrast, the feminist peacemaking tradition is broad and varied and hard to summarize in a short space. However, at its core, those working in this tradition are focused on a humane system of justice that acknowl-edges that women are placed at a disadvantage in a patriarchal society (Fuller & Wozniak, 2006). This patriarchy and, by definition, gendered power differences create an oppressive, warlike experience for women both within and beyond the criminal justice system. Finally, the critical tradition of peacemaking also includes a robust examination of societal power differences, including but not limited to gender, race, and class.

All three of these traditions have in common a belief that a different paradigm must be established for criminal justice—one that focuses on restoration and not retribution. Restorative justice, as a practi-cal method, advocates for the use of restorative practices or mediation between victims and offend-ers, offering victims a real opportunity to work through their victimization, often by playing a cen-tral role in the offender's justice experience. Many restorative justice practices are informed by the concept of reintegrative shaming (Braithwaite, 1989), the idea that the shaming of someone who has done wrong that is then followed by reintegra-tion of the wrongdoer into the fabric of his or her family or greater community is a powerful way of influencing the offender's future behavior. This type of shaming is thought to work best in settings in which the people being shamed are generally treated in positive and encouraging ways most of the time, and then, when they face disapproval about their acts, they are ashamed and feel bad.

The majority of the scholarly literature related to restorative justice addresses the particulars of restor-ative methods and/or the philosophical and theoreti-cal bases of restorative principles (e.g., Cragg, 1992; Messmer & Otto, 1992; Strang & Braithwaite, 2001;

▲ **Photo 10.3** Peacemaking theory suggests that we should help those with a "deviant" status, such as the homeless, instead of criminalizing them.

▲ **Photo 10.4** Peacemaking theory argues that we often "make war" on deviant behavior by criminalizing it.

Umbreit, 1994; M. Wright, 1996; Zehr, 1990). Also evident in the literature are the attendant critiques of statements of restorative theory and practice and discussions of the challenges facing restorative justice (e.g., Andersen, 1999; Ashworth, 1993; Hudson, 1998; LaPrairie, 1998; Minor & Morrison, 1996). These critiques echo long-standing concerns about informal justice expressed in the sociolegal literature (Abel, 1982; Merry, 1989)—namely, that the lack of formal authority involved in mediation and community dispute resolution practices may result in greater injustices than the very system it seeks to improve.

Peacemaking and Homelessness

Gregg Barak (1991) offers a peacemaking analysis of homelessness as a deviant status in the United States. At the core of his analysis is an argument that we must approach homelessness from a place of kindness and regard for those who have found themselves homeless. Most debates about homelessness have, at their core, an individualistic deficit model that suggests that those who are homeless are so because of individual problems or deficits of their character (they are lazy, like being homeless, are drug addicts, etc.). This characterization allows for treatment of the homeless that is warlike and inhumane.

For example, if we assume that individuals are homeless because of personal "problems" such as laziness or drug use, it is easy to also characterize the homeless as immoral and more likely to be dangerous. These characterizations lead to public policies that focus on (1) making the homeless invisible and (2) criminalizing the homeless and homelessness.

Public policies that focus on making homelessness invisible use tactics such as banishment (Beckett & Herbert, 2010) and loitering laws that make standing or sitting on public sidewalks against the law. While these policies, in the short run, may move the homeless to different parts of the city or to different cities altogether, they do nothing to alleviate the problem of homelessness or offer individuals who are homeless any hope of finding permanent affordable housing.

The example at the beginning of this chapter offers an even more warlike law enforcement practice of using sweeps to destroy the encampments of the homeless. In most instances, this means that these individuals lose the few possessions they have saved and can mean arrest if they are caught in the encampments during the sweep, although often sweeps are conducted during the day when the homeless are less likely to be on site. This practice does nothing to help those who are homeless find affordable housing. It does, however, exacerbate the feelings of alienation and helplessness that the homeless are likely to feel (Barak, 1991).

Peacemaking practices designed to help homelessness would not focus on an individual deficit model of homelessness but, instead, would focus on structural conditions that may lead to homelessness (Barak, 1991). For example, young women often run away from home because of physical, emotional, or sexual abuse they are experiencing in the home. Individuals and families often find themselves homeless because of market forces, such as the tightening of the low-income housing market, an increasing unemployment rate due to market fluctuations, or the globalization of the economy. Public policies that focus on offering services and places of refuge for young women who are abused or services for workers and families who have been affected by the structural conditions of the economy are more peaceful in nature. However, even these policies can be conducted in a warlike manner if the homeless are not treated as complete human beings and are made to "prove their worth" in order to receive these services.

For example, many social service agencies require that individuals take special classes to earn the "right" to receive their help. Individualized hoops that assume that the homeless are in need of extra education are still within a deficit model that places most of the blame for homelessness on the individual. A true peacemaking approach to homelessness would offer services and empathy without assuming that the homeless are different from those who enjoy stable housing. In other words, the homeless would not need to prove their worth while getting help.

◈ Critiques of Critical Theories

It may be unfair to lump the critiques of three such different critical theories as peacemaking, feminist theory, and critical race theory into one discussion, but it seems that one of the main critiques of all three theories is that *they do not see the world the way other theories see the world.* In other words, the very features that set these theories apart as unique or special are used to dismiss them. For example, Akers (1998) argued that peacemaking criminology was

> a utopian vision of society that calls for reforming and restructuring to get away from war, crime, and violence. . . . This is a highly laudable philosophy of criminal justice, but it does not offer an explanation of why the system operates as it does or why offenders commit crime. It can be evaluated on other grounds but not on empirical validity. (p. 183)

Moyer (2001) argued that the peacemaking perspective was in its infancy (compared with other crime and deviance theories) and pointed out that Akers offered no empirical evidence himself for his claims. Feminist criminology has often been criticized as reductionist (namely, reducing the discussion of crime to the single variable of gender)—a critique that is ironic given that one of the main reasons for the emergence of feminist criminology in the first place was the androcentric (male-centric) nature of both theory and research in the field of crime and deviance. Similarly, critical race theory is often criticized for "playing the race card" or essentially making race a singularly important predictor of experience in U.S. society (for a discussion of this critique, see Levit, 1999). In all of these criticisms, the common denominator is that the theories are denounced for critically analyzing the status quo.

◈ Explaining Deviance in the Streets and Deviance in the Suites: The Cases of Pornography and Illegal Governmental Surveillance

Both of the discussions of deviance below have the common thread of changing technology running through them. While changing technology has allowed for an explosion of opportunities in the pornography industry, offering exponential growth, it has also made both the surveillance of U.S. citizens and the exposing of those surveillance programs easier.

Pornography

Pornography is so diverse and its mediums so varied, it would be almost impossible to cover it comprehensively here. In many ways, it is an industry of contradictions. On the one hand, there is little known about it (for example, its true net worth and number of users); on the other hand, general estimates suggest that enough people are familiar with some form of pornography to suggest it is one of the worst-kept secrets on the planet. Adult videos, escort services, magazines, sex clubs, phone sex lines, cable and pay-per-view channels, Internet sites, and novelties have all been listed under the heading of pornography (although many might argue that this list ranges from the sex/pleasure industry to pornography). Of this list, the most revolutionary medium would be the Internet.

The Internet has made pornography "ubiquitous" (Ruvolo, 2011, n.p.). While it is estimated that in 1991 (before the Internet), there were fewer than 90 U.S. porn magazines, in the late 2000s, there were more than 2 million porn sites and more than 100 million individuals logging into them (Ogas & Gaddam, 2011, as discussed in Ruvolo, 2011). Pornhub, one of the largest online pornography sites, reported 18.35 billion visits in 2014

Is Erotica Pornography?

The question of whether literary erotica (sexually explicit romance novels) is pornography is one that the courts have recently weighed in on. The First Appellate District, Division Two, Court of Appeal of the State of California recently ruled on whether erotica violated the obscenity rules of the California prison system. They decided as follows:

> [The] San Francisco appeals court has ruled that a werewolf erotica novel must be returned to Andres Martinez, an inmate of Pelican Bay State Prison, after prison guards took it away from him on the grounds that it was pornography. Although the court grants that the novel in question, *The Silver Crown*, by Mathilde Madden, is "less than Shakespearean," it argues that the book nevertheless has literary merit and shouldn't be banned under prison obscenity laws. The court also notes that "the sex appears to be between consenting adults. No minors are involved. No bestiality is portrayed (unless werewolves count)." (Quinn, 2013, n.p.)

(individual users may have returned more than once and would have, then, been counted more than once), and more than 78.9 billion videos were viewed (Pornhub, 2014). In addition to the Internet making pornography much more accessible to the viewer, it has also made it much more accessible to the participant, with numerous sites devoted to "amateur" pornography.

The Internet has made pornography so ubiquitous that some argue it has overwhelmed its own prosecution (Ruvolo, 2011). While child pornography has been the focus of federal prosecution for many years, in 2005, Alberto Gonzales, then the attorney general, created the Obscenity Prosecution Task Force to focus on adult pornography because of concerns he had about the prevalence and ease of use of Internet pornography. In 2011, Attorney General Eric Holder disbanded the task force for several reasons, one of which was that there was too much porn to prosecute but also because the Internet had so blurred the lines between pornography and pop culture (Gerstein, 2011). Instead, all prosecutions of pornography (with that prosecution focused on child pornography) would again be handled through the U.S. attorneys' offices and the Child Exploitation and Obscenity Section of the Department of Justice's Criminal Division.

Pornography and Feminist Theory

There has been a continuing debate within feminist theory as to the advantages or disadvantages of pornography. Anti-porn feminism became popular in the 1970s with the work of Catharine MacKinnon and Andrea Dworkin. Anti-porn feminists argue that pornography subordinates women to men, making women second-class citizens (MacKinnon, 1984). According to MacKinnon (1984), pornography is a form of forced sex:

> Pornography is not harmless fantasy or a corrupt and confused misrepresentation of an otherwise natural and healthy sexuality. With the rape and prostitution in which it participates, pornography institutionalizes the sexuality of male supremacy, which fuses the erotization of dominance and submission with the social construction of male and female. . . . In pornography, women desire dispossession and cruelty. Men, permitted to put words (and other things) in women's mouths, create scenes in which women desperately want to be bound, battered, tortured, humiliated, and killed. Or, merely taken and used. This is erotic to the male point of view. (pp. 325–326)

MacKinnon was referring to pornographic films shown in theaters at the time she wrote this passage in 1984. However, she has since argued that in whatever form pornography exists, it still subjugates women and contributes to gender inequality (Ciclitira, 2004). Feminists who advocate a more pro-pornography viewpoint argue that anti-porn feminists are anti-sex, racist, and classist because they do not acknowledge the context of pornography. Focusing specifically on Internet pornography, these feminists argue that cybersex offers several opportunities: identity bending, improved access to sex education, opportunities for "safe" sex, increased opportunities for women and minorities to produce and distribute pornography, female access to pornography in the privacy of their homes, and the allowance of exploring differing sexualities. In other words, Internet pornography has increased the level of control and power that women can have over their own bodies, the image of their bodies, and the definition of sexuality, and it offers an opportunity for women to more fully participate in and enjoy pornography, if they so choose (Ciclitira, 2004).

Even those who may not go as far as to say that Internet pornography has all the benefits above argue that it at least allows greater access and more information for women.

> Crucially, pornography has become truly available to women for the first time in history. . . . This central mechanism of sexual subordination, this means of systematizing the definition of women as a sexual class, has now become available to its victims for scrutiny and analysis as an open public system. (as cited in Ruvolo, 2011, n.p.)

Illegal Government Surveillance

The U.S. government has been engaging in electronic surveillance of American citizens both abroad and in the country since at least 2001. Initial reports of electronic surveillance suggested that it was of communications outside the United States (although reports suggested that some of the monitoring was still of American citizens even if the communication may not have occurred in the United States). Later reports suggest that the surveillance did occur inside the United States as well. Both e-mails and phone conversations were monitored. The Bush administration initiated the first surveillance program, working with AT&T to collect a mass of e-mails and phone logs.

The surveillance program continued into the Obama administration, with whistleblower Edward Snowden, in 2013, reporting the partnership between the National Security Agency (NSA) and Verizon to collect telecommunications data on U.S. citizens in the United States without a warrant. Snowden, who was an employee of both the NSA and Central Intelligence Agency (CIA), handed over top-secret documents detailing the surveillance program to the U.K. newspaper *The Guardian*. Many of these documents "confirmed longstanding suspicions that NSA's surveillance in this country is far more intrusive than we knew" (Shane & Somaiya, 2013, n.p.).

The current program, referred to as PRISM, went into effect in 2007 and includes the collection of data from such providers as Microsoft, Google, Yahoo!, Facebook, PalTalk, YouTube, Skype, AOL, and Apple. The depth of data collection is staggering. The *Washington Post* reports the type of data that can be collected includes

> audio and video chats, photographs, e-mails, documents, and connection logs. . . . [Skype] can be monitored for audio when one end of the call is a conventional telephone, and for any combination of "audio, video, chat, and file transfers" when Skype users connect by computer alone. Google's offerings include Gmail, voice and video chat, Google Drive files, photo libraries, and live surveillance of search terms. (Gellman & Poitras, 2013, n.p.)

At issue is the violation of the Fourth Amendment, which stipulates that

> the right of the people to be secure in their persons, houses, papers, and effects, against unreasonable searches and seizures, shall not be violated, and no warrants shall issue, but upon probable cause, supported by oath or affirmation, and particularly describing the place to be searched, and the persons or things to be seized.

This means that according to the Constitution, the state should not be allowed to collect information without probable cause and a warrant describing what is, specifically, being searched for. There are several general arguments for whether or not the NSA collection of telecommunications data is a violation of the Fourth Amendment. First, some argue that it is not a violation because the Foreign Intelligence Surveillance Act (FISA) allows for electronic surveillance without a warrant when national security is an issue. However, FISA requires that the government get court approval (basically, a warrant) within seven days. Second, some argue that it is not a violation because the information is being collected by private companies (AT&T and Verizon, for example) and not the government. But these companies are being compelled by the government to give this information over, and FISA has released these companies from liability for providing this information to the government. Finally, some just argue that the violation of the Fourth Amendment is outweighed by the greater good of searching for terrorist activity.

A second issue involving the PRISM program and potential violations of the Fourth Amendment is whether Snowden should be considered a criminal or spy (he has been charged with theft and espionage) or a whistleblower for providing the top-secret documents and exposing the PRISM program. The Whistleblower Protection Program is conducted from the U.S. Department of Labor and

> enforces the whistleblower provisions of more than twenty whistleblower statutes protecting employees who report violations of various workplace safety, airline, commercial motor carrier, consumer product, environmental, financial reform, food safety, health insurance reform, motor vehicle safety, nuclear, pipeline, public transportation agency, railroad, maritime, and securities laws. Rights afforded by these whistleblower acts include, but are not limited to, worker participation in safety and health activities, reporting a work related injury, illness or fatality, or reporting a violation of the statutes. (U.S. Department of Labor, n.d.)

However, the program does not condone or allow for the breaking of laws in order to bring this information to light, which Snowden did when he provided top-secret documents to *The Guardian* to support his allegations. Some argue that these illegal activities (considered espionage by the U.S. government) were the reason the program was uncovered, and given that these actions uncovered other illegal activities, Snowden should not be held accountable for these actions.

> In GAP's view, Edward Snowden is a whistleblower. He disclosed information about a secret program that he reasonably believed to be illegal, and his actions alone brought about the long-overdue national debate about the proper balance between privacy and civil liberties, on the one hand, and national security on the other. Charging Snowden with espionage is yet another effort to retaliate against those who criticize the overreach of U.S. intelligence agencies under this administration. The charges send a clear message to potential whistleblowers: this is the treatment they can expect should they speak out about constitutional violations. (Government Accountability Project, 2013)

For his part, Snowden seems to believe that he will be held accountable for his actions, saying, "I understand that I will be made to suffer for my actions," but "I will be satisfied if the federation of secret law, unequal pardon and irresistible executive powers that rule the world that I love are revealed even for an instant" (Greenwald, MacAskill, & Poitras, 2013, n.p.). Snowden sought asylum in Russia, and as of 2015, Snowden has received a three-year residency permit from Russia (granted in 2014), meaning he can freely move about Russia. However, he is quoted as saying, "People say I live in Russia, but that's actually a little bit of a misunderstanding. I live on the Internet" (PEN America, 2015).

Illegal Surveillance and Critical Theories

Critical race theory, critical legal studies, and peacemaking criminology can all be used to examine the events surrounding PRISM and Snowden's leaking of information. Remember that critical race theory examines the use of law as a way to increase social control of certain groups—even laws that, on the surface, are theoretically meant to help those groups. In this instance, we might examine the language used to justify PRISM and NSA spying. On the one hand, it is a clear violation of the Fourth Amendment and introduces a level of social control of U.S. citizens in general that goes far beyond what one would expect. However, its very existence is used as a justification for keeping U.S. citizens safer in the "war on terror." U.S. citizens are asked to give up one form of safety—safety from a government that collects large amounts of information on them—in order to increase another form of safety—safety from terrorist threats.

Peacemaking criminology can now add to this analysis by examining how the argument for PRISM is framed as an assault on terrorism in which personal privacy is an acceptable casualty. In addition, peacemaking criminology can be used to examine the government reaction to Snowden. Those advocating a peacemaking perspective would argue that once Snowden uncovered PRISM, the government should have listened to the concerns of the public and at least negotiated, if not disbanded, PRISM outright because of its Fourth Amendment violations. Instead, the government has "made war" on Snowden, labeling him a traitor to the United States and charging him with espionage.

◈ Ideas in Action: Navajo Peacemaking and Domestic Violence

One of the stark differences between critical theories and more traditional theories of deviance and crime is the strong connection between the theoretical tenets of critical theories and advocating for public policy and social change. The Navajo focus on peacemaking is an excellent example of this.

The Navajo Nation, using the philosophy of peacemaking, led an effort during the 1980s and 1990s to reform Navajo law to better support the Navajo people. These changes included the following:

- The Peacemaking Division [was] established by the Navajo Judiciary in 1982

- In the 1990s, the Navajo Supreme Court began a strong effort to promote Peacemaking, receiving a federal grant to fund the payment of Peacemaking personnel

- Eliminating fines and incarceration for over 60 offences, requiring instead that courts use Peacemaking, security bonds, and/or community service

- Requiring that judges speak both Navajo and English, and have some knowledge of Navajo culture and tradition

- Navajo women having meaningful access to the political process (Coker, 2006, pp. 71–72)

Donna Coker (2006) examines the use of peacemaking practices in offering alternatives to how battered women receive just outcomes for their abuse. She situates this peacemaking philosophy in a feminist and critical race theory understanding of both battered women's and abusers' experiences. Coker's work offers an example of the intersections of three critical theories by showing how feminist, peacemaking, and critical race theories may come together to better inform our understanding of the experiences of battered women.

Coker (2006) argues that the feminist tradition advocates for safety and empowerment for abused individuals as well as changes in both cultural and political conditions that support violence toward women. In addition, the critical race perspective advocates for a deeper understanding of the choices that women may make while in abusive relationships. While conventional wisdom argues that the only way for a woman to make herself safe is to permanently leave an abusive partner, critical race scholars contend that this view does not acknowledge that for some women, the choice is not that simple. Women often resist domestic violence in a more complicated way than just "staying" or "leaving," and often, separating from an abusive partner may also mean leaving behind a community and cultural resources that are needed for survival. This focus on separation as the end goal can oftentimes leave the victim worse off than if she had stayed with her abuser. The peacemaking philosophy (also known as restorative justice) can offer alternatives to separation.

The peacemaking philosophy allows battered women to experience "horizontal" justice, which is focused on the process of solving the problem—including allowing a woman (and her family members) to confront her abuser, validate her feelings, and facilitate a solution that best fits her circumstances, rather than a "vertical" justice that focuses on coercion, power, and punishment and most often does not take the wishes of the woman into account.

Coker (2006) found that the peacemaking process was a fruitful avenue for seeking justice for battered women as long as the process made the safety of the women a priority and did not make forgiveness of the abuser a condition of the process.

NOW YOU . . . USE THE THEORY

Using feminist, critical race, and peacemaking theories, analyze the account below. According to the theories, what would be considered deviant in the story below? Why?

I am a middle-aged white woman from the East Coast and a town that was 99% white, who now lives in a barrio, an original neighborhood settled by Latino families residing in California for generations. The town incorporated in the early 1960s with a population of 19,000 and grew rapidly to over 80,000 by 2000. As an inland town built around agriculture, it lacks the same degree of good vibrations and laid-back atmosphere of stereotypical Southern California beach communities.

More than 75% of the households in this working-class town make less than $100,000. The Latino population is 47%, up from 38% in 2000. While the particulars of this increase are not clear, what is clear is that a large portion of that 47% live in the barrio area and have brought much to this town in terms of culture, economics, and opportunity.

Life in the barrio is richly textured. Mexican restaurants and corner stores flourish; families and friends gather in parks and yards to grill *carne asada* accompanied by *salsa fresco*. Pedestrians abound, with mothers walking their children to school, youth walking to high school, and people going to stores. There are always men and women waiting for the bus and commuter train. Many people work more than one job to make ends meet in the expensive living environment of California. Being part of this vibrant community and knowing my neighbors has made it clear that their hopes, dreams, and determination include working hard to prosper and to realize the American Dream for themselves and their families. Their hopes and dreams surely mirror immigrants who have come before.

In 2005, things began to erupt between the sheriffs and the community as three young Latino men met their death through the use of lethal force by the police. Shortly after that, in early 2006, the Minute Men descended upon the town to address what they saw as a problem with "illegals." The Minute Men continued their vigilance over the "illegal" problem, shoving cameras in people's faces, waving signs that dehumanized and criminalized immigrants, and winning over the politicians of the city and effectively diminishing the numbers of day laborers in the city.

Since that time period, law enforcement in the barrio has continued. Various strategies are used to enhance routine community patrols. These strategies include directed patrols, saturation patrols, Immigration Control and Enforcement (ICE) raids, speed traps, and sweeps of buses and transit stations. These are conducted primarily in the barrio area, with two checkpoints conducted in the parking lot of the county courthouse. In general, a checkpoint consists of pulling over about 1,000 cars, arresting several people, handing out numerous citations, and towing an average of 30 cars. In the entire year of 2008, for example, checkpoints garnered over 200 citations, 155 cars were impounded, and 15 were arrested for DUI. Unlicensed drivers, including immigrants without documents and cars that are not registered or insured, are impounded for 30 days. This results in approximately $1,500 fees for towing and storage. Unable to pay the impound fees, many people lose their cars.

When there are heavy patrols and checkpoints, the usually active sidewalks and stores of the city are empty. It does not take much to recognize when these are happening as there are always several black and whites in a very small area, about a square mile, for hours. I have had comments from visitors who witness this and ask about it. When I tell them about these activities, they always look in disbelief.

While these activities have become routine, their impact remains disturbing. It is never routine to see people walking away from cars that will be towed, carrying their belongings, groceries, children, and car seats. It is disheartening to see people who are simply living their lives—coming home from work, going to work, going to the doctors, delivering children to school and picking them up. It is difficult to know that parents are deported and their children left with family, friends, or to fend for themselves.

There is a weariness that comes with this much law enforcement and a great sadness to see people criminalized and treated in this manner. It has also created in me a distrust of law enforcement, in those who should be trusted to protect the community. Ultimately, given the increase in the size of the prison-industrial complex of this country, it begs the question of how things will be in the future if law enforcement strategies continue in this trajectory, meaning to target large groups and populations instead of individuals. Living in the barrio has created the realization of the mutuality of freedom—that individual freedom is dependent on and relative to the freedom of all people.

By Mary Jo Poole, January 16, 2011

◈ Conclusion

Much of the deviance research that exists makes fairly traditional assumptions about how we define deviance. From a traditional perspective, these definitions tend to favor whites, men, and the middle and upper classes. In other words, these groups end up defining what is considered acceptable or deviant behavior. The theories presented in this chapter question the status quo and offer a nontraditional definition of acceptable behavior. What this means is that our taken-for-granted assumptions about deviance are questioned and expanded, allowing for more diversity in our understanding of deviant behavior. Not only do these perspectives give voice to individuals who may be considered deviant but they also question the very makeup of society as we know it, suggesting that warlike, patriarchal, racist systems of oppression are what are truly deviant.

EXERCISES AND DISCUSSION QUESTIONS

1. Compare the experience of Muslim Americans after 9/11 with the experience of whites in America after Timothy McVeigh was captured for committing the Oklahoma City bombing in 1995. How would peacemaking criminology and critical race theory explain these different experiences?

2. Choose another structural deviance (like homelessness), and evaluate it using peacemaking, feminist, and critical race theories. What would each theory offer as a public policy to address this deviance?

KEY TERMS

Critical race theory

Feminist criminology

Liberal feminism

Marxist feminism

Peacemaking criminology

Postmodern feminism

Radical feminism

Socialist feminism

READING 27

In this article, Radosh uses Richard Quinney's peacemaking approach to think about women, especially mothers in prison. Radosh argues quite persuasively that we need to move toward a peacemaking approach as opposed to a deterrent or retributionist approach to dealing with a social problem as opposed to a social evil. She points to the fact that the vast majority of women and mothers in prison are there for nonviolent, low-level drug dealing (often as a secondary dealer for their boyfriends or husbands) and even simple possession of drugs. Their fate is due to their lack of education, resources, and support. Furthermore, women's involvement in crime is often due to past experiences and injustices (e.g., domestic violence, child physical and sexual abuse). The fact that some of these experiences were at the hands of males whose punishments were often fairly lenient adds to the injustices in the way females and mothers are dealt with by the criminal justice system. A key feature to think about here is how seriously punishing women for relatively nonserious crimes affects their children: clearly, it harms them. Finally, Radosh argues in line with peacemaking criminology that we need to provide support for the children of women convicted of crimes, not cause undue hardships on them by incarcerating nonviolent female offenders.

Source: Radosh, P. F. (2002). Reflections on women's crime and mothers in prison: A peacemaking approach. *Crime & Delinquency, 48,* 300–316. Reprinted with permission.

Reflections on Women's Crime and Mothers in Prison

A Peacemaking Approach

Polly F. Radosh

What is important in the study of crime is everything that happens before crime occurs. The question of what precedes crime is far more significant to our understanding than the act of crime itself. Crime is a reflection of something larger and deeper.

—Quinney (2000, p. 21)

Among my earliest memories of my childhood in upstate New York is learning to cut with scissors in the Irish Catholic school I attended for the first 9 years of my education. In this school, the nuns were very strict and required absolute attention and adherence to the rules and protocol of the classroom. All of the desks were in neat rows, students stood next to their desks with hands at their sides when called on the answer a question, and when the nun looked down each row of desks she wanted to see all papers aligned at the same angle on the desk and each student holding pencils, scissors, or other implements in exactly the same way. For most students the requirements were not too difficult to master, although there were always a few stray papers that shifted or children who held their pencils in defiance to the required norm, especially in the younger grades. Eventually, everyone adhered to the protocol and there was little correction needed by about the third grade. I had a problem for most of my early education, however, because I am left-handed. It was difficult to get my paper aligned at the appropriate angle on the desk, but eventually I did master this requirement. The biggest problem for me was learning to cut with scissors. The nuns could tolerate my writing with my left hand, but they would not provide left-handed scissors and I was not permitted to use my left hand to cut.

I learned to cut with my right hand because I was not permitted to use my left hand. I eventually mastered the skill completely and today I am perfectly competent in the use of right-handed scissors. I have so completely shifted away from my natural inclination that I am actually no longer able to maneuver my left hand to cut at all. I have transformed my innate preference for my left hand into an adaptation that is so complete that I am no longer able to revert back to my natural inclination, and now I must use right-handed scissors. I have many questions about my adaptation, however: What might I have been able to accomplish if I had been able to develop my natural talents? How has my adaptation shaped my thinking or my personality? What artistic masterpiece of cutting might I have produced if I had not been forced to shift to a more difficult means of achieving my cutting goals? Why was it so important that I conform? and What social, organizational, or human goal was accomplished by my conformity or punishment for nonconformity?

When I think of Richard Quinney's work, I think of my educational experience. There are several parallels to my experience and the effect that Quinney has had on my thinking about crime. First, I believe that his work helps to equip those of us who are metaphorically left-handed in a world of right-handed people with a pair of left-handed scissors. That is, he helps us to see the world as we are naturally inclined to see it, rather than as we are shaped by cultural convention or criminal justice protocol to see it.

This is especially true with his work on peacemaking criminology. From this perspective, crime is produced by factors that are out of the control of the individual, such as political, economic, or social structures that limit human potential. To address crime with violence or punishment will never solve the problem of crime because violence and punishment address only the outcome, not the source of crime. From Quinney's (1991) view, only "understanding, service, justice ... [which] flow naturally from love and compassion, from mindful attention to the reality of all that is" (p. 4) will solve the problem of crime. To focus on individual failings as the source of crime is myopic. To solve crime by punishing individual failings is unjust and will only create more suffering. What useful purpose is served by punishing, especially for those who violate laws that serve no useful social purpose? Punishing because a violator has broken the law, without attention to the social utility of the law or the good that could be accomplished by compliance, is to attend to the letter of the law and ignore the spirit of support and communal connection that law should engender. To enforce compliance without utilitarian goals is much like forcing left-handed people to cut with right-handed scissors. We can mold most people to conform to the norms, but some people have different backgrounds, experiences, or societal impairments that make conformity differentially more difficult.

Second, he helps us to understand that adherence to laws and protocol merely for the requirement of adherence does nothing to solve social problems, address crime, or eliminate suffering. The requirement in my school that I learn to adapt to a pair of right-handed scissors was a temporary handicap for me. I eventually adapted but the requirement did no lasting good and probably some harm to my developing skills. Quinney's insights into the criminal justice system show us that we often pay such strict attention to the requirements of control and punishment that we miss the meaning of crime. We address the expression of crime, but we ignore the causes of crime. Quinney's work teaches us that humane, nonjudgmental approaches to crime will help us to achieve a more humane society. Just as the goal of using scissors should be cutting, the goal of law should be social good. Intermediary, cumbersome, or painful obstacles to attaining the goal should be eliminated.

Third, rules, law, protocol, ordinances, and all of the other mechanisms we use to "keep peace" in our society are a means of preserving order, but we often become so focused on the rules that we have forgotten why the rules were important in the first place. Often the requirement of adherence to law is much more important that the harm that would be done by law violation. Learning to cut with my right hand was important only because it was a rule, not because it would improve my skills, make me a better person, or cause chaos in the classroom if I did not adhere to the rule. Such is the case with enforcement of many laws. With women's crime, in particular, adherence to the law is required because it is the law, not because it promotes social justice, public order, or a better quality of life.

From his 1970s work that articulated the effect of capitalistic structures on individual action to Quinney's current work on peacemaking, love, and existentialism, the underlying structures that shape social action have been a thematic concern in his explanations of crime. Actions are shaped by forces that go beyond free will or opportunity. Events, structures, systems of oppression, and power affect human choices and predicate personal interests. Events that precede crime are as important to understanding crime as are the actual criminal events. Quinney's work is like the use of the metaphorical "left-handed scissors"—it helps us to see that law has layers of meaning that are obscured when we focus merely on the act of law violation. The true meanings of law, the life experiences of the law violator, and underlying social inequities that produce crime are not addressed. Instead, the illegal act is addressed through punishment.

From my first reading of Quinney's work when I was a student in the 1970s, I have returned innumerable times to his writings as a touchstone for my own understanding of women's crime. In no other field of inquiry do his theories make more sense. Structure, oppression, economic exploitation, and marginalized social opportunity explain almost all of women's crime. Minor drug crimes committed by women, for example, draw sentences as long as, and sometimes longer than, serious male crime. Women's crime is defined as symbolically equivalent to serious men's crime, even when it is not. For many years I have returned to Quinney to help in my own understanding of this apparent injustice. It is not only patriarchy that explains this but also the defining structures of capitalism that allocate authority for criminal definitions in the hands of the powerful. Women, who lack significant social power, are defined as criminal through definitions created to verify the existing social order. Prevailing popular views about crime and criminals, as well as public criminal justice policies, legitimate the existing system as a reflection of justice. If we use the metaphorical "left-handed scissors," Quinney's work helps us to see that women's crime is a reflection of social injustice. When we see the world as it is rather than as we are conditioned to see it, women's crime has new meaning.

Women's crime is grounded in exploitation. Without exploitation there would not be crime. Nearly all of women's crime is related to sexual exploitation, abuse, poverty, and structural inequality. Quinney's most recent work, which explores the relationship between mature love and a world without crime, provides an especially clear lens with which to focus women's crime. A world without crime is one in which crime would not be possible because inner individual peace is reflected in peaceful coexistence (Quinney, 2000, p. 21). Crime is produced by human suffering. The connection between suffering and women's crime is widely acknowledged by academics as well as administrators of women's prisons. There is little dispute about the connections, but there is considerable disagreement about the most appropriate response to women's crime. A mature response would mean that we should move beyond the act of law violation and address the means by which the human needs of the law violator may be met. To focus on punishment of the offender ignores the fact that the crime reflects events that happened prior to the criminal action. The crime cannot be understood without attention to the prior experience, and punishment will do nothing to address the prior experience or to help the offender move beyond the pain that is reflected in crime.

◈ Contemporary Thinking About Crime

Quinney's summary of the criminal justice system in the United States, organized around the belief that those who commit crimes deserve their punishments, is as true today as it was when he published *Class, State, and Crime* in 1977 (p. 21). Modern thinking about crime says that it results from personal failures, lack of self-control, weakness, laziness, moral lapse, or other character flaws that inhibit self-restraint. Those who commit crimes should be willing to pay the penalties for their mistakes, given the widely know[n] "hard on crime" political ideology characterized by punitive sentencing strategies that have been well-known and highly publicized for more than 20 years. According to the predominant paradigm, one of the most important goals of criminal justice policy should be deterrence produced through sure, swift, and severe punishment. A second important goal is to restore "balance" through retribution or to ensure that the offender "pays" his or her debt to society by suffering the pains of imprisonment.[1]

◈ Women Offenders

Criminologists are in general agreement that across time and in all cultures, women's crime is less serious and less frequent than men's. Even with significant changes in sentencing and a rapid increase in the prison population in the United States in recent years, women's incarceration remains a small fraction of men's.

Both arrest patterns and incarceration trends indicated that almost all of women's crime in the 20th century has been concentrated in the area of low-level property or public order (prostitution) crime.[2] In the 1980s, an additional "feminine" crime surfaced, with changes in U.S. drug laws. In 1997, for example, 74% of women in federal and 35% in state prisons had been sentenced to prison for a drug crime (Mumola, 2000, p. 6). This compares with 67% of men in federal and 23% in state prisons who were incarcerated for drug crimes. About 72% of women under correctional supervision in jail, on probation, or in prison during the 1990s had committed a property, drug, or public order offense (Greenfield & Snell, 1999).

Women's involvement in drug crime is usually low-level dealing or delivery activities, although about 10% of federal and 15% of state female inmates have been incarcerated for possession (Mumola, 2000, p. 6). Limited economic circumstances motivate some nonusers of drugs to sell. Of those women incarcerated during the 1990s, only 40% indicated that they had been employed during the months prior to their arrest (compared to 60%

of men) and 30% were on welfare. Nearly 40% of those who were employed earned less than $600 per month (Greenfield & Snell, 1999, p. 8). Women with few economic alternatives, limited life skills, and great economic need often participate in the drug trade as a means of supplementing their income. Risk of detection is exacerbated by their low-level, high-visibility positions in the drug distribution network.

In addition to difficult economic circumstances, 60% of incarcerated women in state prisons indicated in surveys between 1995 and 1997 that they had been physically or sexually abused in the past (Greenfield & Snell, 1999, p. 1). Women who had spent some of their childhood in foster care or institutions indicated that they had been victims of sexual or physical abuse in 87% of cases. Of those who grew up in homes where parents abused alcohol or drugs, 76% reported prior abuse; and among those who lived in homes where a family member had been incarcerated, prior abuse was reported among 64% of female inmates. In about 95% of cases among all abused women in jail, on probation, or incarcerated in a federal or state prison, the perpetrator of the abuse was someone they knew, such as a relative, their mother's boyfriend, or a family friend (Greenfield & Snell, 1999, p. 3). Not surprisingly, 80% of those with a history of abuse were regular users of drugs at the time of their arrest (Greenfield & Snell, 1999, p. 3).

The life circumstances of incarcerated women help to explain much of their criminal behavior. Whereas many people who have lived in poverty or who have been victims of abuse do not commit crimes, the common thread of continuity that runs through the history of women's incarceration is that most women in prison share common life experiences. They are very likely to have been living in poverty, have experienced prior abuse by male friends and relatives, have had childhood experiences that included substance abuse by parents, have been sexually abused as children, and suffer with personal stress, trauma, and fear in many stages of their lives. According to the National Institute of Justice, the needs of women in prison are different from men and thus require different programming:

> Women in prison have some needs that are quite different from men's resulting in part from women's disproportionate victimization from sexual or physical abuse and in part from their responsibility for children. Women offenders are also more likely than men to have become addicted to drugs, to have mental illnesses, and to have been unemployed before incarceration. (Morash, Bynum, & Koons, 1998, p. 1)

Each of the special problems of female inmates may seem to be a separate issue, but they actually weave together into a complex set of problems that have been rarely addressed by the correctional system. Women whose life experiences have presented many overwhelming personal problems often seek relief in substances that ease their pain. Common backgrounds of poverty, physical and sexual abuse, and accompanying feelings of loss, betrayal, depression, and desperation spawn ongoing personal problems that are highly likely to result in recidivism if they are not addressed.

◈ Incarceration Patterns

The number of people incarcerated in U.S. prisons and jails has increased to unprecedented levels in the past two decades. In 1980 the national rate of incarceration was 139, but this had risen to 682 by mid-year 1999 (Beck, 2000, p. 2; Gilliard, 1993, p. 2). Table 1 illustrates some of the growth in incarceration rates since 1980.

Women represent a small overall proportion of the prison population, even though the percentage of women in prison is increasing faster than the percentage of men (Beck, 2000, p. 1). Regardless of the rapid increase in women's incarceration, men are still 16 times more likely to serve time in a state or federal prison (Beck, 2000, p. 4). The overall greater likelihood of men to serve time in prison has meant that for most of the 20th century, women's corrections received little attention. It was not until the number of women incarcerated began to rise in the early 1980s that researchers began to address either the patterns of women's incarceration or programming in women's prisons.

As research has articulated some of the unique characteristics of female inmates, patterns that differentiate women from men have become apparent. Female inmates, for example, are more likely to have

Table 1 Incarceration Trends, 1980–1999: Number and Rate[a] of Incarceration

Year	Total	Rate	Men		Women	
			Number	**Rate**	**Number**	**Rate**
1980	315,974	139	303,643	275	12,331	11
1985	480,568	202	458,972	397	21,296	17
1990	739,980	297	699,416	575	40,564	32
1995	1,085,363	411	1,021,463	796	63,900	48
1999[b]	1,860,520	682	1,246,362	897	87,199	57

Source: Adapted from Maguire and Pastore (1999, p. 490) and Gilliard (1993, p. 4).

a. The rate of incarceration is the number of people incarcerated for every 100,000 population.

b. Mid-year estimates.

been convicted of a nonviolent crime, have a prior history of physical or sexual abuse, be incarcerated for a drug offense, and have been the primary caretaker for their children prior to their incarceration.

Traditionally, women received longer sentences than men for the same offenses because female offenders often deviated significantly from expected gender role restrictions that required a higher degree of self-control and lifestyle restrictions than would be typical expectations for men. Studies of sentencing, for example, have indicated that women were sentenced longer than men for the same offense because it often appeared to judges that female offenders were "worse" than male offenders. Only a few women, by comparison to men, engaged in crime, which implied that such behavior by women was an especially abhorrent anomaly to typical "female behavior" (Lanagan & Dawson, 1993, p. 2; Parisi, 1982). Patriarchal definitions of women's "proper" nurturing roles affected judicial decision making in such a way that judges often believed that women's crime was not only law violation but also "unnatural." The subtle but widely dispersed belief that female criminals were "worse" than men translated into longer average sentences for women. Whereas all prisoners are serving longer sentences under new mandatory sentencing laws, much of the gender disparity in sentencing that had resulted in

lengthy prison terms for women prior to the mid-1980s has been significantly reduced.

Sentencing reform in the mid-1980s highlighted rational criteria in sentencing, which reduced the disparity between men's and women's sentences. Factors such as prior offense history, use of a weapon in commission of the crime, whether the offense was violent, and other criteria related to the characteristics of both the offense and the offender are now used to set the length of sentences under minimum mandatory guidelines. Women rarely commit violent crimes, and they have much lower rates of recidivism than men. As a result, women's sentences for index crimes are comparable to equally charged and convicted men.

Although objective criteria in sentencing are much more consistent than they were prior to sentencing reform, other gender differences in offending patterns, as well as gender-specific patterns related to sentencing, do work against women in drug cases. Women's involvement in the drug trade is usually at the lowest level of participation. Under federal drug conspiracy laws, participants with minor roles are sentenced as long, and often longer, than those with key roles in the distribution network. A woman who drives her boyfriend to make drug deals and waits in the car until after the deal is completed may end up serving a longer sentence than her boyfriend, who is the actual dealer. Drug convictions and sentencing rely very heavily on informant deals. The driver in the car would not have knowledge that would be beneficial to authorities and thus could not "deal" with prosecutors on her own behalf. Also, loyalty to boyfriends or husbands prevents many women from making deals, even when they have such knowledge. A review of more than 60,000 federal drug cases indicates that men are much more willing to sell out women to get a shorter sentence than women are likely to sell out men (Szalavitz, 1999, p. 43). Women are frequently convicted of drug crimes when they have had no involvement or very little knowledge of their boyfriend's involvement. Women, for example, have been convicted of "improper use of the telephone" or answering the phone for what later turned out to be a drug sale (Szalavitz, 1999, p. 43).

◈ Inmate Mothers

In 1999, there were about 87,000 women incarcerated in prisons and jails in the United States. This represents 6.5% of the prison population (Beck, 2000, p. 4). Although the exact percentage of female inmates with children is not known, most estimates indicate that about 80% have dependent children at the time that they are incarcerated (Watterson, 1996, p. 210; Williams, 1996, p. 80). In 1999, there were at least 126,100 children with mothers in prison, and the mean age for all children with parents in prison was 8 years (Mumola, 2000, p. 2).

There are many more children with fathers in prison than mothers, but incarcerated mothers are more likely to have been living with their children prior to incarceration (Mumola, 2000, p. 2).[3] Undoubtedly, the social and emotional trauma inherent in incarceration of a parent produces significant strain on all children with imprisoned parents, but the pain is especially significant for those whose families were broken by the incarceration of a parent. More than 60% of fathers in state prisons and more than half of those in federal prisons did not live with their children in the months before arrest. But about 60% of mothers in state prisons and 73% of those in federal prisons did live with their children before arrest (Mumola, 2000, p. 2).

In addition to the obvious stress created by separation, there are other concerns associated with incarceration of mothers. About 25% of incarcerated women are pregnant or have recently given birth at the time of their incarceration. Separation from a newborn infant creates additional stress, worry, and anxiety for an incarcerated mother. Their unique concerns are different from the typical worries of other parents who are separated from their children while in prison.

Most research on the effects of incarceration on parenting or on children have focused on the immediate issues related to stress, anxiety, maintaining strong family ties, and other programmatic concerns. The issue is much wider than the immediate needs of inmates or families, however. Factors related to the life histories and crimes of inmate mothers both explain incarceration patterns and influence post release family unity.

Although incarcerated women are not a monolithic group, their background characteristics are much more similar than those of incarcerated men. The overriding experience of abuse and very common pattern of substance abuse by female offenders are linked. Most incarcerated women enter prison with these problems. The fact that most also have dependent children means that many of the problems of female inmates also present problems for their children. To be effective, programming in women's prisons must address the unique characteristics of incarcerated women, as well as promote family growth and unity. Despite widespread recognition of the unique needs of female inmates, 39 states use the same classification instrument for men and women, in 7 states the male instrument is adapted for women, and only 3 states use a special instrument for female inmates (Mumola, 2000, p. 3). By most accounts, the special needs of female inmates are met with sporadic, inconsistent, inappropriate, or inadequate programming.

Women are very likely to return to their children after release from prison. Among the many differences between male and female inmates is an overriding concern among women for the welfare of their children while they are in prison and high anxiety about how they will provide for their children when they are released. Programming in women's prisons only sporadically addresses these concerns.

But by most accounts, programming for female inmates fails to address the issues that are most important for humanistic reasons and are most likely to reduce recidivism. As one administrator in the National Institute of Justice's survey of approaches to women's programming indicated, "Women who are victims of abuse tend to continue on as victims of abuse. Men on the other hand, tend to react to their own history of victimization by becoming abusers themselves" (Mumola, 2000, p. 10). And, as another prison administrator indicated in a private conversation, the most consistent pattern among all incarcerated women is that they "have been battered beyond belief."[4]

Female inmates have generally used more drugs and used them more frequently than men prior to their incarceration (Morash et al., 1998, p. 1). Drugs have provided a means of escape for most female inmates. Incarceration frequently provides their first opportunity to evaluate their own lives and the effects of their decisions on their children. Female inmates' needs are different from male inmates' and interrelated to both their prior history and their future parenting skills.

◈ Punishment, Women's Crime, and Parenting

Current punishment strategies that focus on instilling future goals of self-restraint, personal control, and moral strength through retribution for wrongful behavior are inadequate, illogical, and futile as a response to women's crime. The prior life experiences of incarcerated women dictate more humane and constructive approaches than characterize contemporary strategies. To use contemporary retribution models as a response to women's crime fails to recognize the prior precipitating experiences of women. Their crime does not fit the justice model for several reasons.

First, women's crime is generally nonviolent and low-level. It is often punished with serious prison time, not because of the inherent harmfulness of their criminal acts but because of their lack of power or knowledge with which to negotiate prosecutorial deals, especially in drug cases. The punishment does not fit either the crime or the offender.

Second, women's crime commonly reflects prior life experiences with men who clearly perpetrated serious criminal acts, such as childhood sexual molestation, rape, incest, and domestic violence. The fact that such offenders frequently were not prosecuted or punished cannot frame the defense of women in their current offense. Yet the underlying injustice inherent in societal tolerance of suffering on one level, while overreacting to less serious crime on another level, frames a basic violation of human rights. If the justice model, which applies a hard-on-crime strategy to combat women's drug crime, were applied evenly, the issues that frame women's incarceration would be different. The dismissal or trivial reactions to the more serious actions of prior male offenders who have abused and mistreated female offenders at earlier stages of their life, however, contributes to the profound feelings of inevitable loss and hopelessness that are graphic in the stories of female offenders. Women's crime does not fit the hard-on-crime justice model because the penalties are often especially hard-on-women's-crime. Whereas many men have been unduly sentenced to very long prison terms on the basis of this philosophy, the pattern among women is rather overwhelming.

Third, the punishment of women's relatively nonserious crime with the same vehemence with which serious male crime is addressed hurts children. Among the most consistent themes that run through the literature about inmate mothers is the intense sense of loss, betrayal, desperation, and hopelessness that accompanies their incarceration. Their children suffer the loss of their mother while the hard-on-crime political strategy publicizes justice and deterrence. Children and society would be better served by more reasonable, proportionate sentences or no punishment at all. To perpetuate injustice into the lives of children whose mothers have been incarcerated for their boyfriends' crimes, as is frequently the case with drug crime, is inhumane, counterproductive, and futile. Women who have been victimized through multiple stages of patriarchy, exploitation, and marginalized social opportunities need understanding, support, and many therapeutic services. Punishment is the least effective way to address their crime. Among women, crime is often an obvious symptom of their suffering at another level.

Fourth, in keeping with Quinney's basic principles of peacemaking, societal response to women's crime should accommodate the unique features of their offending patterns. Women's prior experiences of exploitation should be addressed in treatment. Children of women who have committed crimes should be supported with reasonable, positive opportunities for growth and development. Punishment does not serve this end.

◈ Prison Programs for Mothers

Mothers in prison have the same worries and concerns that all parents have about their children, but their inability to fulfill parental responsibilities for their children creates fear for their emotional and physical well-being, as well as great grief and anxiety over loss of involvement in their children's lives. Common backgrounds of abuse, high likelihood of drug involvement, and probable poverty also indicate that parenting and life-skill programs are essential for post release success. Drug addiction treatment and therapy that helps offenders deal with problems of past sexual abuse and family violence are especially critical because these factors are linked to women's criminal behavior, as well as to their parenting skills.

The most common programming options available for inmate mothers are those that allow for special visitation. The "Girls Scouts Beyond Bars" program, for example, has initiated girl scout troops in five states: Ohio, New Jersey, Missouri, Maryland, and Florida (Moses, 1995, p. 1). Girl scouts with incarcerated mothers may belong to special girl scout troops that meet in prison. The purpose of the program is to enhance parenting skills for the mother and maintain involvement of mothers in their daughters' lives.

Most states provide either regular or occasional special visitation for families of inmates. Ohio and Illinois, for example, allow children of inmates to camp on the grounds of the prison with their mothers on some weekends during the summer. Ohio runs a 3-day day camp where inmates interact with their children in the camp. Pennsylvania gives children a book that helps them understand the pain of separation from their mothers, and they provide in-home social work to caregivers of incarcerated mothers' children. The New York Department of Corrections provides for extended overnight visits with families at 18 prisons. They also provide transportation to the prisons and operate play areas and hospitality centers for families. Texas allows for weekly contact visits between mothers and their children.[5]

The most innovative and comprehensive programs are in New York, Nebraska, Illinois, and California. Each of these states has some variation of the prison nursery program that was started in the women's prison at Bedford Hills, New York, in 1901. Nebraska's program is patterned after the Bedford Hills program. In both of these programs, mothers who have been convicted of an offense that did not involve their children and who have less than 2 years of their sentence left to serve may keep their babies with them in prison. Counseling, support groups, parenting classes, substance abuse treatment, and employment preparation are integral components of both programs. California offers prisoner mother/infant programs, which are operated by private agencies under contract with the state, at six locations. Illinois contracts with a nonprofit agency to run the Women's Treatment Center, where inmates keep their children with them in a converted hospital (Christian, 2000; Ervin, 1998, p. 14; Lays, 1992, pp. 44–51).[6] Both the California programs and the Illinois treatment center include substance abuse treatment, occupational counseling, and support groups in their treatment strategies. Two additional states, Ohio and Vermont, are exploring the possibility of inmate nursery programs.

◈ Effectiveness of Mother-Infant Programs

Although comprehensive statistical analysis of four programs would not provide meaningful data, the success of mother-infant programs is accepted as definitive in those states that have funded these programs. The most common measures of success may give only vague insight into the utility of these programs, however. Recidivism, which measures the likelihood of reoffense among released inmates, is decidedly lower for women who participate in mother-infant programs. Women's recidivism is generally much lower than men's, but mother-infant programs claim a further reduction of 20% to 50% in recidivism. In other words, mothers who participate are not likely to return to prison (Christian, 2000; Ervin, 1998, p. 14; Lays, 1992, pp. 44–51).[7] Whether the recidivism results from the success of the programs or the selection of inmates who participate in the programs is less clear. Supporters of mother-infant programs claim that both the opportunity to interact with their infants in a controlled, supportive environment and the comprehensive counseling that accompanies these programs are what lead to their success.

The success of children whose lives are enhanced by their mothers' opportunity to participate in a mother-infant program are less easily studied. Researchers and advocates for more humane treatment of female prisoners have pointed out for many years that children of inmate mothers suffer tremendous loss and experience profound alteration of their lives. Critics may contend that mothers should have thought of these issues prior to committing the crime for which they were incarcerated. But the pervasive patterns of physical and sexual abuse, drug addiction, and emotional pain characteristic of female inmates prohibits the sort of reflective thinking that would have prevented their crime, regardless of how much they love their children. And wider structures of patriarchy and capitalism are not even imagined as sources of women's crime, by this reasoning. The result of more compassionate response to women's crime is that children who are connected in meaningful ways with their incarcerated mothers are less likely to feel abandoned, isolated, and lonely.

Prisoner programs that address the complex nature of women's confinement, which include treatment for emotional and substance abuse problems and help them to achieve purposeful child rearing, offer the most promise for post release success and successful parenting. Models available in Nebraska, New York, Illinois, and California may provide insight into the importance of strengthening family bonds for inmate mothers and their children.

 ## Conclusions

The horrifying, heartbreaking experiences that incarcerated mothers live with, or relive in prison, often overwhelm intentions for good parenting. Thus, prison programming that addresses only parenting skills or which narrowly focuses on specific occupational skills will fail to address the needs of incarcerated women. Comprehensive approaches that treat addiction, depression, occupational skills, and parenting offer the most [effective] options. Women's incarceration stems not only from a conviction for a specific crime but also from an array of social problems that affect women as a group and which permeate many facets of American culture. As Quinney told us, what has gone on before the crime tells us more than the act itself. The life patterns of incarcerated women poignantly illustrate Quinney's point. Humane, supportive, and therapeutic responses to female offenders would also address what has gone on before the criminal act.

Cultural devaluation of women results in exploitation, abuse, and mistreatment. The specific illustrations of the suffering of female victims are visible in the faces of incarcerated women. To ignore the cultural problems that give rise to women's crime is to blame the victims of abuse for their own abuse. In the short term, women who are empowered to control their own lives and avoid men who abuse and exploit them will be the most successful after release from prison. They will also be better mothers who may be able to break the cycles of abuse that are very commonly characteristic of their own lives and the lives of their mothers. In the long term, ending patriarchal exploitation and economic inequality and fostering humane, compassionate respect for human potential are essential to a peaceful society, and they are what will end women's crime.

Crime will continue until we end suffering. If we robotically adhere to laws and models of justice without understanding the sources of crime, we will not be able to end suffering. With Quinney's poignant explanations of what it takes to end suffering in mind, we must abandon the philosophy of punishment and find a means of supporting female offenders by responding to the sources of their suffering. In other words, we must find a means of cutting through the arbitrary rules to find the true meaning of the actions.

◈ Notes

1. Alternative perspectives are sometimes discussed, although they have found little representation in contemporary criminal justice policies. Liberal critics of contemporary trends suggest that education, investment in neighborhoods, community building, and jobs training could counter crime with positive alternatives. Those who offer solutions to crime in this venue stress the importance of investment in programs to improve the quality of life among those most vulnerable to crime. Poor neighborhoods, inadequately funded schools, hopelessness fostered by urban decay, and insufficient investment in those with the fewest social opportunities produce crime, from this perspective. Solutions require investment and commitment to improve. For discussion of the underlying philosophy of criminal justice policy, see Walker (2001, chap. 1).

2. See, for example, Steffensmeier and Allan (1996, pp. 459–487) and Messerschmidt (1986).

3. There are estimated to be 1.3 million children with fathers in prison.

4. Conversation with Jane Higgins in 1989, when she was warden of Dwight Correctional Facility in Dwight, Illinois.

5. See the Directory of Programs for Families of Inmates at http://www.fenetwork.org/Dir98/dir98f-n.html.

6. See the Directory of Programs for Families of Inmates at http://www.cdc.state.ca.us/program/mother.htm.

7. See the Directory of Programs for Families of Inmates at http://www.cdc.state.ca.us/program/mother.htm.

◈ References

Beck, A. J. (2000). Prison and jail inmates at midyear 1999. In *Bureau of Justice Statistics Bulletin*. Washington, DC: U.S. Government Printing Office.

Christian, S. E. (2000, January 25). Pregnant inmates get county help with MOM. *Chicago Tribune*, p. 1.

Ervin, M. (1998). A center for jailed mothers. *Progressive, 62*, 10.

Gilliard, D. K. (1993). Prisoners in 1992. In *Bureau of Justice Statistics Bulletin*. Washington, DC: U.S. Government Printing Office.

Greenfield, L. A., & Snell, T. L. (1999). Women offenders. In *Bureau of Justice Statistics Special Report*. Washington, DC: U.S. Government Printing Office.

Lanagan, P., & Dawson, J. (1993). Felony sentences in state courts, 1990. In *Bureau of Justice Statistics Bulletin*. Washington, DC: U.S. Government Printing Office.

Lays, J. (1992). Babies behind bars. *State Legislatures, 18*(5), 44–51.

Maguire, K., & Pastore, A. L. (Eds.). (1999). *Sourcebook of criminal justice statistics 1998* (U.S. Department of Justice Statistics, Bureau of Justice Statistics). Washington, DC: U.S. Government Printing Office.

Messerschmidt, J. (1986). *Capitalism, patriarchy, and crime: Toward a social feminist criminology*. Totowa, NJ: Rowman and Littlefield.

Morash, M., Bynum, T. S., & Koons, B. A. (1998). Women offenders: Programming needs and promising approaches. In *National Institute of Justice Research in Brief* (U.S. Department of Justice Office of Justice Programs). Washington, DC: U.S. Government Printing Office.

Moses, M. C. (1995). Keeping incarcerated mothers and their daughters together: Girl scouts beyond bars. In *National Institute of Justice Program Focus*. Washington, DC: U.S. Department of Justice.

Mumola, C. (2000). Incarcerated parents and their children. In *Bureau of Justice Statistics Special Report*. Washington, DC: U.S. Government Printing Office.

Parisi, N. (1982). Are females treated differently? In N. H. Rafter & E. A. Stanko (Eds.), *Judge, lawyer, victim, thief* (pp. 205–220). Boston: Northeastern University Press.

Quinney, R. (1977). *Class, state and crime: On the theory and practice of criminal justice*. New York: David McKay.

Quinney, R. (1991). The way of peace: On crime, suffering, and service. In H. E. Pepinsky & R. Quinney (Eds.), *Criminology as peacemaking* (pp. 3–13). Bloomington: Indiana University Press.

Quinney, R. (2000). Socialist humanism and the problem of crime: Thinking about Erich Fromm in the development of critical/peace-making criminology. In K. Anderson & R. Quinney (Eds.), *Erich Fromm and critical criminology: Beyond the punitive society* (p. 21). Urbana: University of Illinois.

Steffensmeier, D., & Allan, E. (1996). Gender and crime: Toward a gendered theory of female offending. *Annual Review of Sociology, 22*, 459–487.

Szalavitz, M. (1999, Winter). War on drugs, war on women. *On the Issues, 8*(1), 42–45.

Walker, S. (2001). *Sense and nonsense about crime and drugs: A policy guide* (5th ed.). Belmont, CA: Wadsworth.

Watterson, K. (1996). *Women in prison: Inside the concrete womb*. Boston: Northeastern University Press.

Williams, E. F. (1996, October). Fostering the mother-child bond in a correctional setting. *Corrections Today*, pp. 80–81.

READING 28

Myths about violence against women abound, but those employed or who volunteer to help those violently or sexually victimized are generally educated about those myths. In particular, those who provide support for victims of violence are taught to avoid "blaming the victim." In this study, the researchers interviewed 15 victim support volunteers (13 women and 2 men) who clearly have been trained that violent victimization is not the fault of the victim. They clearly know the "correct answer" to questions regarding victim blame is that "No, I don't think the victim's to blame. Only the aggressor" (p. 41). However, on more in-depth questioning, it becomes clear that these volunteers do, at least to some extent, perceive the victim to be responsible for the victimization. The authors clearly state that they do not "blame the volunteers" but recognize the need for further training.

"But Sometimes I Think . . . They Put Themselves in the Situation"

Exploring Blame and Responsibility in Interpersonal Violence

Suruchi Thapar-Björkert and Karen J. Morgan

 Introduction

In this article, we examine some of the processes and mechanisms through which prevalent ideological and social discourses of violence provide legitimacy to the imminent nature of domestic and sexual violence in the United Kingdom. Our article draws attention to the importance of understanding the social contexts and social worlds in which violence and victimization are understood and conceptualized. We argue that these social contexts inform understandings of those supporting victims of violence and thereby contribute to an ideologically dilemmatic situation between a culture of blame, on one hand, and a culture of responsibility, on the other. Drawing on empirical data, we highlight three key themes contributing to this culture of blame and responsibility: First, the burden of responsibility is placed on women for their victimization, and in doing so

it absolves the perpetrators from accepting accountability for their own actions. Second, victims of violence are often placed under surveillance and expected to conform to regulated behavior by perpetrators, by those from whom they seek help, and by society at large. Third, we suggest that certain unintentional institutional attitudes may not sufficiently challenge the prevalent discourses toward victims of violence.

The article is structured in the following way: First, we highlight the qualitative methodological approaches that inform the analyses of this article. Second, we provide a background to some of the key feminist debates on domestic and sexual violence. Given the vast amount of literature already available on the topic, in this article, we emphasize those issues that are most relevant to our analysis. Third, we examine some of the discursive frameworks that facilitate a culture of blame and responsibility in relation to

Source: Thapar-Björkert, S., & Morgan, K. J. (2010). "But sometimes I think . . . they put themselves in the situation": Exploring blame and responsibility in interpersonal violence. *Violence Against Women, 16*(1), 32–59. Reprinted with permission.

women experiencing violence. We believe that there is a dialectical relationship between society and discourse, with society (and culture) both being shaped by and simultaneously constituting discourse (Wodak, 1996, cited in Titscher, Meyer, Wodak, & Vetter, 2000, p. 146). This we will mainly analyze through the narratives of volunteers working for the U.K. charity, Victim Support (VS). Finally, we conclude by suggesting that a more thorough engagement with feminist research, traditions, and philosophy could lead to a reassessment of some institutional attitudes toward women experiencing violence.

◈ Method

Our focus for this article is the United Kingdom, and we will draw on discourses deployed by those with particular expertise of working with women victims of violence. We will specifically engage with the narratives of VS volunteers who operate through a network of local charities that provide support to crime victims throughout the United Kingdom.[1] For the research on which this article is based, a total 15 VS volunteers, aged between 22 and 65, were interviewed, 13 of whom were women and 2 were men—a reflection of the gender split among outreach support volunteers in the organization as a whole (VS, 2005). According to the 2001 Census, the geographical area in which most of the research was conducted has a population that is 97.6% White, 1.4% Asian or British Asian, 0.8% mixed race, 0.7% Black or Black British, and 0.5% Chinese or Other (National Statistics Online, 2001). During 2003/2004, the ethnic breakdown of VS volunteers in the area scheme in which the research was conducted was 92.9% White and 7.1% from Black and minority ethnic groups (VS, 2005). In the specific branch from which the volunteers who participated in the research were recruited, at the time of the research, the breakdown of volunteers was 100% White. Not surprisingly therefore, all the volunteers who participated in the research were White British. Suffice it to say, however, that those interviewed for the research are not intended to be seen as a representative sample of the United Kingdom as a whole but are rather intended to illustrate the type of attitudes prevalent within certain communities.

With the agreement of the relevant VS branch coordinator, the volunteers were approached by the second author who had herself worked as a VS volunteer for several years. All those approached had previously been met by the second author at various meeting and training events, although none of them was known well and the relationship with all of them was little more than that of casual acquaintance. At a volunteers' meeting, the second author talked a little about the research and made a general request for participants. However, to avoid the possibility that any of the volunteers may have felt compelled to agree to take part by the fact that the scheme coordinator was present at the meeting (see Tisdall, 2003), they were subsequently approached individually and in private. Of the 20 volunteers asked, all agreed to be interviewed. In practice, however, it was not possible to interview all those who agreed for a variety of reasons, such as illness, personal problems, and leaving VS.

All but two of the interviews were conducted in the volunteers' own homes (the remaining two were conducted in the second author's home). All volunteer-participants readily agreed that the interviews could be recorded with none expressing any concerns about confidentiality (although two did request that the recorder be switched off for a few minutes during their interview as they gossiped about colleagues). At the beginning of each interview, informed consent was obtained, with the nature of the research being explained and confidentiality issues discussed. It was reiterated that the participant was free to refuse to answer any questions, request that the recorder be turned off, and/or terminate the interview at any time.[2] None of the participants expressed concerns about any of these issues. However, it is not clear whether their particularly relaxed attitudes were due to the fact that they knew the second author was also a volunteer with VS and thus used to dealing with sensitive and confidential matters or because they felt that they were talking about others rather than anything particularly personal.

Furthermore, although the interviews with the volunteer-participants were intended to be comparatively loosely structured, it is problematic to refer unreflexively to unstructured interviews.[3] Nevertheless, these interviews, to a large extent, were driven by the participants and provided the freedom to explore any unexpected areas that arose throughout the discussion. The interview data were analyzed bearing in mind Ruthellen Josselson's (2004) reworking of Ricoeur's (1981) hermeneutics of faith, in which the central process involves understanding the research participants' narratives from his or her point of view rather than regarding them with suspicion.[4]

VS

Although VS operates as an independent organization, at the time of the research, it received the majority of its funds from the U.K. government's Home Office and the rest from private fund-raising, local council grants, or sources such as the European Commission or Lottery funding (VS, 2006). The issue of funding is an important one, not least from a feminist perspective. As Radford and Stanko (1996) note, "despite the commitment of some feminist volunteers within victim support, the philosophy of the national organization, Victim Support, is actively non-feminist" (p. 74). This has to be located within the wider political climate of support, whereby "respectable" groups such as VS are supported, often at the expense of "more radical, anti-racist and pro-feminist groups" such as Women's Aid and Rape Crisis (Williams, 1999, p. 388).[5] In fact, arguably, the Victim's Charter[6] maintains the government's policy of marginalizing "pro-feminist, anti-racist and single issue, self-help victims organisations by the simple expedient of ignoring their existence" (Williams, 1999, p. 394).

Victim Support's remit at the time the research was conducted involved offering a range of services to victims of crime:

- providing free and confidential, emotional, and practical help and advice;

- liaising with criminal justice agencies on behalf of victims;

- coordinating support from other agencies and community organizations;

- carrying out research and public education into issues affecting crime victims;

- lobbying government on behalf of crime victims and witnesses;

- providing support via the Witness Service (sister organization) to witnesses attending court (Crown or Magistrates' Courts) to give evidence;

- liaising with the Witness Service to provide a continuation of service and support for victims giving evidence (National Audit Office, 2002; VS, 2006).[7]

The majority of volunteers with the organization provide support to victims of a variety of incidents, ranging from burglary to the most serious violent crimes including domestic and sexual abuse. At the time the research on which this article draws was conducted, most of the work carried out by volunteers was outreach support—going out to see victims in their homes. More recently, however, there has been a shift toward providing helpline support with only victims of more serious crimes tending to receive personal visits.

The strength of the VS role and of particular relevance for this article, we suggest, is the fact that the volunteers may be seen as expert-amateurs. Although they lack professional involvement with victims, though some volunteers may of course have a relevant professional capacity in addition to their voluntary role (in their paid employment, for example, as social workers), they are provided with specialist training that is intended to highlight the problems and issues faced by victims of crime. Accordingly, the volunteers must be seen as somewhere between those who have little or no awareness of issues relating to victims of violence (other than the commonsense understandings acquired through routine social interactions) and those who have acquired knowledge through their own victimization. It should be pointed out, of course, that the motivation for some of the volunteers working with VS is the fact that they have themselves experienced some form of victimization. The rationale for the provision of support through volunteers is that they help to restore faith in the local community. The fact that their work is unpaid is seen as going some way toward redressing the balance as regards the harm the victim has had caused to them (Personal communication, VS trainer, March, 2003).

It is worth nothing that as compared to VS, victim advocacy (as it is called in the United States)[8] seems a more formal, proactive system of support. Dunn and

Powell-Williams (2007) suggest that victim advocacy in the United States has "recently become a profession in addition to a calling" (p. 978). It has therefore become increasingly professionalized, using paid staff rather than volunteers, unlike the explicitly volunteer-driven focus of VS. However, recent changes within VS in the United Kingdom have meant a greater emphasis on "advocacy," which is described as being "about taking action to help people say what they want, claim their rights, represent their interests and obtain the services they need" (VS, 2007, p. 60). Still, at present, the provision of an explicit advocacy service is not widespread within the organization.

McDermott and Garofalo (2004) discuss "follow-up advocacy" and "victim safety checks," which they say "involves intrusion into the lives of battered women who did not seek services" (p. 1255). This would not happen in the United Kingdom's VS system because support is never imposed on a victim who does not request it. VS volunteers may work with a victim of domestic violence irrespective of the fact that the police or other agencies are involved and would not seek to involve the wider criminal justice system without the victim's explicit agreement.[9]

◈ Contexts of Violence

The issues that inform the work of VS in the United Kingdom (and victim advocacy in the United States) have to be located within the broad interventions made by feminist research, which has increasingly questioned the gaps in the conceptualization and in the experience of violence.[10] Feminist interventions, we would argue, have pushed the debates forward in several key areas. First, while foregrounding familiarity as a central feature of domestic and sexual violence (Boateng, 1999; Maynard, 1993; Mezey & Stanko, 1996; Smart, 1989), the debates have broadened definitions of violence to incorporate a range of behaviors including emotional and psychological as well as physical abuse, thus shifting the focus away from the "battered woman" to look at "lesser" physical forms of abuse that damage women and children psychologically and which if not checked can set the stage for more extreme incidents (hooks, 1997, p. 282; also see Lamb, 1999; Loseke, 1999). For example, hooks (1997)

argues that an overfocus on forms of extreme physical violence leads to an acceptance of everyday physical abuse such as occasional hitting (also see Morgan & Thapar-Björkert, 2006). Second, they have highlighted not only the invisible and often insidious workings of male power and control within public and private spaces (cf. Corrin, 1996; Dobash & Dobash, 1997; Hester, Kelly, & Radford, 1996; Kelly, 1988, 1996; Maynard, 1993; Radford & Russell, 1992) but also the endemic and routine nature of violence (Stanko, 1985, 2003, 2006). Thus, it is not necessarily the tangible act of violence, which imposes a form of social control over women, but the "internalization through continual socialization" of the possibility of violence (Smart & Smart, 1978, p. 100). Third, many writers suggest that violence against women should be located in a broad sociostructural context. Pahl (1985) points out that violence against women can be legitimized by society at large to the extent that it becomes possible to deny that domestic violence takes place at all, or to claim that if it does happen, it is only applicable to "unusual or deviant couples" (p. 11). As Stanko (2006) argues, context governs how seriously we as a society respond to incidents of violence as (un) "acceptable" (p. 545). In fact, one of the pivotal premises of the Zero Tolerance Campaign against gendered violence in the United Kingdom was the need to "change societal attitudes towards . . . violence by making it socially unacceptable, and by challenging the norms . . . which . . . sustain it" (Cosgrove, 1996, p. 189). Fourth, debates suggest that mere theorizing is insufficient, and ideas and strategies produced as a result of investigations of women's experiences should inform as well as be informed through feminist activism (McLaughlin, 2003). This, it was argued, would also enable women who have been abused to say what they want and need (Hague & Mullender, 2006; Kelly, 1996). As Hague and Mullender (2006) note, "if services addressing domestic violence are to . . . effectively meet abused women's needs, then the views of those using them need to be heeded" (p. 568).

A part of the process of exposure has involved the explicit naming of violence and abuse by men to ensure that women's experiences of violation should not be left literally unspeakable (see Kelly, 1996). Thus, the necessity of a feminist approach that was characterized by consciousness raising and activism was emphasized. This tradition of consciousness raising coupled with the need for a sympathetic societal response led to the creation of the battered woman syndrome in the 1980s and 1990s in America (Loseke, 1992). This syndrome was viewed by many as a form of cultural compromise (Rothenberg, 2003) because although it enabled advocates to achieve their goals of public sympathy, it also created a homogenous construct of the battered woman. The "battered woman," a "long-suffering victim," and a "mainstay client of therapists" was absorbed by the "consuming public" (Lamb, 1999, p. 116). For example, Loseke (2001) argues that support groups in the United States, through their organizational practices, promulgate the identity of a battered woman even though women victims' lived realities are often at odds with the template of the formula stories (also see Kendrick, 1998).[11] She suggests that "women's talk about their lived realities often complicates, even subverts, the straightforward narratives of the formula story of wife abuse" (Loseke, 2001, p. 110). Institutionally preferred narratives, as Holstein and Gubrium (2000) claim, lead to an "institutionalization of the selves" (p. 16).

Building on these arguments our article focuses on the tension between institutional discourses and individual perception and how these can contribute to an understanding that sometimes violence is natural, normal, to be expected, and/or understandable. For example, specific discourses that imply that women are responsible for their victimhood are reflected in statements such as "she asked for it." Separating attitudes encapsulated in statements such as this from more professional attitudes of nonblame may not always be a straightforward or easy matter. We question, therefore, whether unintentionally judgmental attitudes to women victims of violence may not be inherent in the understandings of some of those engaged in combating the effects of violence, despite their genuine desire to provide support.

◈ Culture of Blame and Responsibility

In this article, our intention is not to deny the enabling and autonomy enhancing potential of institutional practices within statutory and voluntary organizations toward women who have experienced violence. However, we also want to acknowledge analyses that suggest that these institutions may fail some women (Westlund, 1999; see also Hague, 1998; Hague & Mullender, 2006; Malos, 2000).

Shouldering the Burden of Responsibility

Interventionist strategies for dealing with domestic abuse (such as the Duluth model in Minnesota in the United States) have alerted practitioners and activists dealing with all forms of interpersonal violence to the need for a coherent philosophical approach, which focuses on victim safety, holds offenders accountable, and eliminates victim blaming (Pence & MacMahon, 1999).

In relation to sexual violence particularly, it is argued that women are often blamed or seen as complicit in the sexual offenses against them (Berns, 2001; Corrin, 1996; Hague, 1998; Lamb, 1996; Lea, 2007; Maynard, 1993; Morgan, 2006). The attention and questioning therefore shifts toward the women rather than to men's violence. Thus an environment of victim blaming and normalization of violence is created in which women feel unable to report crimes of violence against them. As Bunch and Carrillo (1992) suggest, "women are socialized to associate their self-worth with the satisfaction of the needs and desires of others and thus are encouraged to blame themselves as inadequate or bad if men beat them" (p. 18). Women who are victims of male violence find "breaking the silence" stigmatizing because they are often perceived by others as "fallen women who have failed in the 'feminine' role" (hooks, 1997, p. 283).

Nancy Berns (2001) argues that political discourses on violence often shift the focus from abusers to the victims. She argues that the popular representation in, for example, newspapers, magazines, or television reports is responsible for constructing and reproducing images of domestic violence, which in turn influence the way individuals "construct their own conceptions of what is normal and acceptable" (p. 263; see also Berns & Schweingruber, 2007, p. 247). She refers to this perspective as patriarchal resistance and usefully highlights three implications in this resistance discourse: the normalization of intimate violence, the diversion of attention from men's responsibility in violence, and the distortion of women's violence.

Although we agree with Berns that the argument that men and women are equally violent is often used in "de-gender(ing)" the problem of domestic violence, it is still important to understand how both men and women are complicit in "gendering the blame" through the "refram[ing]" of discourses in such a way as to "obscur[e] men's violence while placing the responsibility on women" (Berns, 2001, p. 262). To illustrate our point, we will look at some of the ideas articulated by VS volunteers who, we suggest, are potentially uniquely placed to resist and challenge some of the perceptions and stereotypes relating to women victims of violence. The increased level of understanding acquired by the volunteers that places them in such a position was appreciated by at least some of the volunteers interviewed, as expressed here by Sally:

I think training and talking to people have opened my eyes to what goes on [in relation to victim blaming]. I mean I think perhaps people *that are on the outside* and don't have more information maybe don't see it quite that clearly. (Sally, VS volunteer; our emphasis)

As a result of their training, these volunteers see themselves as being in a position to help the victim come to them and thus to empower the victim, enabling him/her to continue with their lives. For example,

She gradually didn't need me. Which I was really pleased about. I mean I was glad when she said she didn't need me because I thought that was good. She's—she's moving forward, isn't she?

She's coping for herself. (Sally, VS volunteer)

And a little later into the same interview,

All their self-esteem is on the floor. So I put quite a lot of effort into telling them that they're not useless and that they really are perfectly good human beings, and you know when they tell me anything that was really good that they've done, I do sort of say "that was really good what you did. That was brilliant wasn't it?" ... Because it's horrendous the things they've come through. (Sally, VS volunteer)

Whereas in an interview with another volunteer,

Researcher: When you're with a victim, how do you know or when do you feel that—that it's been successful? That you've done a good job?

Yvonne: At the end, I feel. When you're saying "bye-bye." And then they've suddenly turned round and said "thanks, that's really helped me." And they're smiling and ... I think if they've smiled ... they're thinking about what I'm saying and that might just give them enough confidence to maybe to do something.... And then that ... would make me feel better. If I walked out and that lady was still—or that man—was still sat there with a solemn face, then I would think I haven't done it. I haven't got them to think the other way. They're still thinking that they're still in a bottomless pit. If I walked out and they looked happy, then I think they're thinking about this. It's just enough to give somebody that little bit of confidence to think they can step over it. And find their own way out. Somehow. (Yvonne, VS volunteer)

The VS volunteers aimed to make their clients feel "not useless" and help them out of a "bottomless pit." Similarly, Dunn and Powell-Williams (2007), in their interviews with domestic violence victim advocates in a midwestern state in the United States, also state that a central aspect of the advocates' work is to make clients realize they have choices because many come in feeling defeated.

In many respects, the relationship between the VS volunteer and the victim (or client) involves much the same forms of social interactions as those that may develop in research interviews that involve "differing aspects of social interaction such as power, friendship, reciprocity and shared understandings" (Birch & Miller, 2000, p. 190). The exact form of the volunteer/victim relationship is somewhat confused therefore, with a blurring of roles between counselor, friend, and various other positions in between. Most volunteers seemed clear that their role was to listen rather than to push for information. For example, Sally commented, "She didn't want to talk details and I wasn't probing. Because it's not what we do, is it?"

However, this blurring of boundaries has raised concerns in the past, with some VS volunteers feeing that they were being expected to take on too much of a counseling role, despite the fact that the majority are not trained counselors (Morgan, 2005). One of the workshops at the 1998 National Conference discussed whether VS is moving to a counseling role and whether it is appropriate. Key points to come out of the discussion were that VS volunteers

> provide an immediate, vital response and have a specific role to fulfil, which is not counseling. VS visitors provide a good listening ear, a non-judgemental lasting relationship, empowerment and confidentiality, and they help victims to make informed choices as well as practical information, liaison *[sic]* with other agencies, as well as possible referrals to counseling. (Victim Support Magazine, 1998, p. 7)[12]

Most of the volunteers recognized that to restore the victim's sense of self-worth, they should be encouraged and supported in avoiding the feelings of self-blame that affect many such victims. In other words, in keeping with the VS "non-blame" rhetoric, and as pointed out by one of the interviewees quoted below, the intention is to empower the victim to acknowledge that "the only person to blame for a crime is the perpetrator" (Spackman, 2000, p. 66):

> First of all you just have to let them talk. And then sort of suggest that perhaps it's not their fault and you know, if you really think about it, did you do anything wrong? So get their train of though actually working another way rather than let them sort of think that they're to blame all the time because that is very often what's been taken away from them—is the way to think for themselves . . . you're trying to help them get back upon that ladder and think for themselves. (Olive, VS volunteer)

Nevertheless, despite their training and their evident sincerity in supporting and encouraging women victims of violence, it could also be suggested that the volunteers struggle with the idea that perpetrators of violence are solely to blame for their actions. Statements of those interviewed indicated that some believe that there are occasions when women victims, to some extent, are accountable for what has happened to them. For example, women who transgress acceptable boundaries of dress, behavior, or femininity may be seen as complicit in what has happened to them—as individually responsible for their fate. Weaver (1998) notes that it has become apparent that "women are taught to believe it is their individual responsibility to restrict and censure their activities so as to avoid becoming the victim of [sexual violence]" (p. 262). As Emma (VS volunteer) stated, to avoid violence, "you've got to be careful now wherever you go and . . . like work your route out and know where you're going to go and all that sort of thing."

Although the VS volunteers are certainly not concerned with blaming the victims, they do seem to have taken on board the wider societal discourses of, to use Berns' (2001) term again, "patriarchal resistance" or "gendering" the blame. So, when directly asked about blame, the responses were as follows:

> No, I don't think the victim's to blame. Only the aggressor. (Olive, VS volunteer)

> No, I can't think of any reason [the victim is to blame]. No. (Ivy, VS volunteer)

> [The victim is] not to blame, no, no. (Emma, VS volunteer)

> Umm. Not really. No. Umm . . . (Sam, VS volunteer)

> I don't—no, I don't think there is any justifiable reason for a man to attack a woman physically or sexually. No, I couldn't justify that. Ever. (Sally, VS volunteer)

However, there were also statements that directly contradicted those quoted above:

> But sometimes I think . . . they put themselves in the situation. (Edna, VS volunteer)

No I don't think you can be blamed no. But I think you—you need to look after ourselves *[sic]* more. (Emma, VS volunteer)

So I—you know—I'm not a subscriber to the view that women do bring it on themselves, although sometimes I think people don't know when to stop and they don't know when to shut up! (Sally, VS volunteer)

These conflicting statements do not mean that the volunteers are attempting to be misleading about their attitudes, and it is certainly not our intention to suggest that there was any element of subterfuge in the volunteers' discourses. However, statements such as this do reveal that it is possible to share different, mutually incompatible ideologies, which have to be negotiated and managed (Van Dijk, 1997). We also believe that training that fails to take into account feminist perspectives may also fail to challenge traditional gender-role beliefs that "are more likely to attribute responsibility to the victim, whilst those holding less traditional [gender]-role beliefs are less likely to attribute responsibility to the victim" (Lea, 2007, p. 497). The training provided to VS volunteers and the resource pack made available to those supporting victims of domestic violence state that the volunteers should "make sure that the responsibility for the perpetrators' behaviour rests with them and is not made the responsibility of the service user [victim]." In other words, "if patterns of abuse arise, some people will assume that they are to blame . . . don't collude with these thoughts . . . [and] instead explain that no one is ever to blame for abuse" (VS, 2003, p. 23). However, there is no real attempt to address the roots of a victim-blaming culture and the way in which it may be sustained by patriarchy. Thus, although the volunteers may well see themselves as becoming more enlightened as illustrated by Sally's quote earlier in the article, it is apparent that this is insufficient to overcome entrenched beliefs.

These internal arguments or ideological dilemmas (Billig et al., 1988) may be revealed through discourse and discursive practices and arise from the contrary themes within common sense (Billig et al., 1988). Ideology, Billig et al. suggest, takes two forms, intellectual and lived. The former consists of a "system of

political, religious or philosophical thinking," whereas lived ideology is described as "society's way of life" (p. 27): in other words, the everyday aspects of life, including common sense, that govern everyday life. Intellectual ideological processes tend to be coherent formalize forms of thought, "an internally consistent pattern" that enables thoughts and values together to construct "total mental structure" (Billig et al., 1988, p. 29). So, in terms of the initial response of many of the volunteers interviewed, the conscious acceptance of the VS philosophy that "the victim is not to blame" forms part of the volunteer's intellectual ideology. However, a dilemma arises in respect to a commonsense understanding of the world. It makes sense, for example, for women to avoid walking alone at night in certain areas or that women should try not to wind up their partners when they know them to be potentially violent, particularly when the men have been drinking. Consequently, for VS volunteers, the tensions between the intellectual ideology (the nonblame rhetoric) and the lived ideology (the commonsense knowledge, reinforced by public discourse, that it is women's responsibility to avoid violence, rather than men's responsibility to avoid committing violence) results in the simultaneous possession of opposing views. Emma, as quoted above, for example, notes that women victims of violence are not to blame for their own victimization, but she continues,

But I think she's opening herself up to—you've got to be careful now wherever you go and umm you know they say like work your route out and know where you're going to go and all that sort of thing. (Emma, VS volunteer)

Women, therefore, have to plan where they go, consider possible dangers, and select the safest routes (see also Gardner, 1990; Morgan & Thapar-Björkert, 2006; Stanko, 1990). The volunteers' understanding that women should not be blamed and should be able to go where they want is therefore at odds with their commonsense knowledge of the world and its dangers for women.

Billig et al. (1988) see that ideological dilemmas as revealed through discursive practices illustrate that individuals do think about what they know. Indeed, it is through the possession of "opposing themes" that "ordinary people [are able] to find the familiar puzzling and therefore worthy of thought" (p. 143). Fairclough (1995) also points out that

> it is quite possible for a social subject to occupy institutional subject positions which are ideologically incompatible, or to occupy a subject position incompatible with his or her overt political or social beliefs and affiliations, without being aware of any contradiction. (p. 42)

So examining the volunteers' narratives in relation to the central question of whether they challenge or support discourses of blame and how far they are able to accept or refute the notion reveals, as noted above, a tension between the nonblaming rhetoric and commonsense understandings of the causes and consequences of violence against women.[13] Two themes that constituted these discourses were the role of alcohol in violence and the choice available to women victims to leave an abusive relationship.

Blame, alcohol, and lack of control. It is widely acknowledged among health and policy-related researchers that alcohol consumption can be a major contributor to intimate partner violence (Finney, 2004). However, it is also recognized that individual and societal beliefs that alcohol causes aggression can encourage violent behavior after drinking and the use of alcohol as an excuse for violent behavior (Field, Caetano, & Nelson, 2004). Often intoxication is invoked as a postoffense excuse (Ollett, 1994). Several of the volunteers referred to alcohol as a contributory feature in the escalation of violence. Volunteers referred to the way in which it apparently causes the drinker (apart from one reference, they all referred to the drinker being the perpetrator, rather than the victim) to somehow lose control, to become another type of person. Almost all of those who mentioned alcohol remarked on the fact that the drinkers were actually likeable people and that the alcohol seems to have changed some essential part of their nature. So, for example, Ray, who was particularly adamant that drink causes violence said,

> I personally know people who—meet them when they're sober and they're completely

different people to when they're drunk, you know? Or when they've got some alcohol in them. (Ray, VS volunteer)

Others, although perhaps not quite as adamant as Ray that alcohol is a major factor in violence, were still fairly forceful and yet still blamed the alcohol itself rather than the drinker.

> They're lovely when they're sober. I think drink's got lot to answer for. (Edna, VS volunteer)

> But that is often the result of drinks—or drugs and they're out of control. But they're not totally out of control because they still know what they're doing. But . . . they're not the same person that they are when they're sober or not on whatever it is they're on. And it alters their behavior and their character. (Sally, VS volunteer)

Consequently, it becomes possible to blame the alcohol rather than the individual for any loss of control. Finney (2004) suggests that "societal and individual beliefs about the links between alcohol and violence may encourage a person to drink to find courage to commit violent behaviour" (p. 5). It is possible, however, that men with a tendency to be violent may drink so as to provide themselves with a ready-made excuse for their behavior (Ollett, 1994, cited in Finney, 2004). This latter point seems also to be borne out by some of Jeff Hearn's (1998) research in which one of his interviewees claimed, "I did use alcohol as an excuse, like a vehicle, so that I could do it. To give me an excuse in my own head, saying 'Oh I've had a drink.' But it were an excuse for me to do it, that's all" (p. 141). Nancy Hirschmann (1997) supports these ideas and suggests that men's violence is not viewed as a choice:

> Men routinely blame their violence on alcohol, on women's nagging or deficiencies as wife and mother. And of course such men rarely see that they have chosen to subscribe to rigid sex roles that legitimize violence, but rather consider such values to be a factual account of the natural order of things. (p. 203)

As suggested from the volunteer discourses, these excuses seem to have become an integral part of the way society views violent behavior in general and men's violent behavior in particular. However, alongside the volunteers suggesting that men experience decreased self-control as a result of alcohol comes the idea that women need to adapt or modify their own behavior, whether or not they are the ones doing the drinking. In a potentially violent domestic situation, for example, this might mean that women need to avoid any form of nagging behavior. Thus,

> [It] was his drink thing you see? And she would just go on and on niggling him, until eventually he would umm I don't say he actually hit her but he sort of would throw [her] against the wall. (Edna, VS volunteer)

Whereas Yvonne, who had herself experienced a violent relationship, said,

> Well—the girl across the road, I mean she knew what was going on, and . . . she used to say to me "well don't speak to him when he's drunk, you know, and then he won't go back at you." And I said well, "yeah, probably I am winding him up then." But then I should have a right to say to him, "you're a drunken bastard" [laughter]. You know? . . . but at the start, he was drunk and of course I used to get on my high horse with him, and of course that would make it worse and then bop! But then you—I think you get to listen to the signs and you think, "well when he's drunk, you don't say nothing." (Yvonne, VS volunteer)

Despite learning to say nothing, however, the violence continued for 4 or 5 years until eventually Yvonne left him.

So, as Radford and Stanko (1996) suggest, domestic violence tends to be resented as "either a reflection of bad marital relations, personality disputes, or intoxication substances, not the manifestation of unequal power and a need to control" (p. 77). Also, the theme of

gaining and losing self-control, as Eisikovits and Buchbinder (1999) argue, become a "central motif in the metaphoric world of battered women . . . (where) her sense of survival is based on her sense of self-control over her and his violence" (p. 860). The woman shoulders the burden of controlling her partner's violence, by first controlling her own speech, actions, or demeanor.

"She went back." Whether women choose to stay, leave, or return has to be understood in terms of contextual factors and specific life circumstances that influence their decisions (see Baker, 1997; Barnett, 2000; Eisikovits & Buchbinder, 1999; Lempert, 1997). Often women are expected to adhere to a dominant cultural script that directs them to get away and stay away from their abusers (Baker, 1997). Although the volunteers appeared to try to understand and support women's choices, it was also apparent that they experienced dilemmas in relation to this. On one hand, they denied any attribution of blame (and actively sought to support the victim in avoiding this), yet they also revealed that they expected women to avoid any situation that could possibly be violent. This is amply illustrated by the following:

Researcher: Do you find it frustrating when they go back? Like this woman (client) who went back the first time?

Olive: No, no. Because I think, at the end of the day . . . you cannot tell people how to live their lives. You cannot do that. You've just got to be there for them. That is what you are there for. Just to help them and put them in the right direction for help. It has to be their decision at the end of the day. And I always said to her you know "whatever happens, you know, if, *if* you go back to [him], that is your decision" and umm that's what she did, as I said, she went back. But then she realized that it wasn't gonna work out and left again. [But at least then] it was her *final* decision. (Olive, VS volunteer; our emphasis)

However, as the interview proceeded, the same volunteer made the following comment regarding the well-publicized violence between the English ex-footballer, Paul Gascoigne, and his then wife, Sheryl:

> And I think she had a pretty raw deal . . . but on the other hand, so did he, because you [sic] knew he was violent, but again she kept going back for more, didn't she? And she married him *knowing how violent he was.* (Olive, VS volunteer; our emphasis)

It was evident from this narrative that to Olive, at least, Sheryl Gascoigne had to accept some responsibility for what happened to her. To make a women shoulder responsibility for abuse because she "went back for more," for not leaving the domestic situation, or for marrying the man (with a known history of violence) is problematic. It also suggests that there was a degree of consent in her abuse because the victim has the option of leaving the situation but chooses not to. In their research with domestic violence victim advocates in the United States, Dunn and Powell-Williams (2007) explore the tensions inherent in reconciling victim ideology with victim behavior. They argue that victim advocates help battered women to recognize their options and choose to leave. However, they argue that

> the language the advocates use inevitably places decision-making in the hands of the clients. It is the women, not their abusers, whom they expect . . . to make the changes and . . . the only choice the advocates see as appropriate, the only acceptable agency, is leaving the violent relationship. (Dunn & Powell-Williams, 2007, p. 993)

Looking at a similar issue but from the perspective of the victim, Phyllis Baker (1997) argues that often the dominant cultural script directs women to get away and stay away from their abusers, but in her own research she found that women victims felt that the script was too narrow and did not sufficiently reflect the complexities of their decision to stay with the abuser (Baker, 1997; also see Peled, Eisikovits, Enosh, & Winstok, 2000). In her article, "Feminism and Power," Ann Yeatman (1997)

argues that it is not so much a case of consent "but a complex psycho-dynamic process whereby battered women do not possess any sense of efficacious independent agency in the face of continuing presence of their abusive male partner," their agency being continuously eroded through physical force, unequal power relations, and "a need to control" (p. 150).

Despite the training received by these volunteers, there seemed on the part of some to be a failure to recognize the myriad and complex reasons for a woman remaining with, or returning to, a violent partner. For example, women may find it difficult to leave an abusive relationship because the perpetrators often isolate and undermine women, thus rendering them dependent. "Some women attempting to survive and cope in such circumstances may feel that staying with their violent partner will appease him and thus lessen the violence" (Hester, Pearson, & Harwin, 1998, p. 22). Often, of course, the victim may continue to have positive feelings for the abuser. Westlund (1999) points out that

> in between periods of high tension . . . life may take on a semblance of normality, giving the battered woman hope that future bouts of violence can be avoided and that the peace will hold. Women living in such conditions may even come to see their batterers as the bearers of mercy, the source of their happiness as well as their misery. (p. 1047)

Furthermore, as Dobash and Dobash (1992) note, women's reluctance to take action and to report the abusive men

> is often exacerbated by social, medical and legal institutions whose actions reveal a powerful legacy of policies and practices that explicitly or implicitly accept or ignore male violence and/or blame the victim and make her responsible for its solution and elimination. (p. 4)

So women victims are expected to "remove themselves from the situation":

> I mean nothing is excusable. But I think there are some women that really sort of, you know, irritate. Well it—it's just tension, isn't it? You

know tension will grow umm and women won't remove themselves from the situation. . . . Well I think some women goad men into turning violent. You know when they belittle them and . . . but this is people that are not *normally* violent. (Edna, VS volunteer; our emphasis)

This means that the victims are considered to be the ones who have to change their lives and adapt themselves to the domestic situation, the ones who have to look for a solution to their problem (e.g., of being irritating). In extreme circumstances, the woman is often obliged to move away from her home to live away from the aggressor, who normally continues to stay at home, at least in the beginning. An NCH Action for Children Survey in the United Kingdom pointed out that 58% of women did not want to leave home as opposed to 49% who said that they had no place to go to (Hester et al., 1998).

These attitudes enable male perpetrators to project their violence as rational and justified. In an in-depth study conducted with 33 domestically violent heterosexual men in the United States, Anderson and Umberson (2001) suggest that some men often depict their partner's acts as "irrational and hysterical" to "justify their own violence and present themselves as calm, cool and rational men" (p. 365). Men described actions such as "[I] grabbed her and threw her down" or "sat on her" as "nonviolence" and "controlled" as opposed to the "outrageous" behavior of their female partners. In addition, Anderson and Umberson argue that "respondents also shifted blame onto female partners by detailing faults in their partner's behaviors and personalities" (p. 367). Similarly, VS volunteers seemed to imply that if women exercised greater restraint over their own behavior, then situations where violence occurs could be avoided. Moreover, it gives legitimacy to men to exercise their "controlled" power to maintain the gendered patterns of behavior. An uncomfortable idea is that it appears as if the VS volunteers interviewed here assume the power that men exercise (or expect to have) is natural and if the status quo is disturbed (through nagging, for example), then women should feel responsible for the exercise of that power.

The narratives of these volunteers raise an important issue in relation to who blames whom. How volunteers position themselves within discourses of violence is important as they also feed back to interagency policy

forums. An ethos of blame/responsibility can be seen as contributing to a culture in which violence is normalized, sustained, and ultimately accepted by default. Also, an understanding of the analytically rigorous literature on sexual violence is right in suggesting that a patriarchal framework is useful to understand the persistence/existence of interpersonal violence and the ways in which men are implicated in sustaining patriarchal discourses.

Surveillance and Normalizing Judgments

This leads us to our next point that attitudes held by abusers as well as by some statutory and voluntary organizations can place women victims of violence through a regime of regulated behavior and gendered norms.[14] Andrea Westlund (1999), using Foucault's analysis of power in *Discipline and Punish: The Birth of the Prison* (1991),[15] argues that the techniques used to maintain power and control over women (experiencing sexual and domestic violence) are both premodern and modern forms of power. She illustrates her argument by looking at domestic violence within households and battered women's interaction and treatment with modern institutions (police, domestic violence shelters, courts, medical and psychiatric professions).[16] In cases of domestic violence, the power exercised over women by the "batterer/sovereign" is, Westlund (1999) claims, often "pre-modern" in that the techniques used are "intensely corporal and brutal and . . . are wielded in a personal and sporadic rather than an impersonal and meticulous manner" (p. 1045). Corporal punishment, sometimes particularly horrific, is exercised to redress perceived contempt for authority, as illustrated by one of the volunteers talking about a victim of domestic violence, to whom she had provided support:

> He didn't treat her very well. Kept her short of money and she had to basically—to get the money it was sexual favors to him . . . and she retaliated one day rather than take the beating, and so he poured petrol over her and set her alight. (Olive, VS volunteer)

Another research participant, Yvonne, the volunteer who had also been a victim, described an incident with her ex-husband, who was annoyed at his son using the telephone without his permission:

> He just [went up] to Ian [17-year-old son] and punched him in the face. Of course, I jumped up then, in front of Ian, as I had done so many times before. . . . And, of course, Ian then pushed me out the way . . . cos [my husband] went for me—and Ian said, "you're never gonna hit her again" and I thought, "this is father and son now fighting" and I thought, "this has got to stop, this has got to stop. I'm not having him hit his son over me." And that's all it was; he hit Ian so that he knew I was going to jump up so he could have a go at me then. (Yvonne, VS volunteer)

This narrative illustrates that corporal punishment can occur directly or indirectly against a loved one. In addition to this premodern form of corporal power, however, there is a degree of close surveillance, which is more akin to the power to be found in some modern institutions such as prisons (Westlund, 1999). This surveillance is not only imposed on battered women by their abusers but requires that they learn to "nicely comport themselves exactly as their oppressors would want," seeking to regain some control over their own lives by "concentrating on the micro-practices of everyday life" (MacCannell & MacCannell, 1993, p. 211). Furthermore, if she takes the help of professional services outside the household, she is often placed within "new and different sets of power relations" by these institutions and may be pathologized as mentally unstable and incapable of appraising her own situation (Westlund, 1999, pp. 1046–1049). Women are advised to "commit to" and work on their relationships, making it difficult for some women to recognize which behaviors they should or should not accept (Fraser, 2005, p. 15). This advice, although well meaning, may serve to reflect the more damaging aspects of societal opinion relating to gendered violence in reiterating the responsibility of the victim. For example, discussing sexual abuse, one of the volunteers commented on the advisability of women wearing certain clothing:

> If a woman was walking down the road, if she was dressed in a miniskirt and a tight top, is

she to blame? And you know if she was sort of raped or attacked or something I wouldn't say she was to blame. . . . Her wearing that wasn't the causal factor in her getting attacked . . . But had I sort of known her and was talking to her before she did that, I'd advise her not to do it, just because I'm aware even if she's not the causal factor, the causal factors are in place, they're out there. . . . So I think there's a certain sense of . . . perhaps *you have to take responsibility for your own safety.* (Sam, VS volunteer; our emphasis)

In relation to research and experience in both Britain and the United States, Dobash and Dobash (1992) argue that when women experiencing violence have sought professional help "they have often been blamed for the violence, asked to change their behaviour in order to meet their husband's demands, and had their own concerns and requests deflected or ignored" (p. 231). The police and refuge services are two agencies that are often involved in domestic cases (Malos, 2000). However, the growing acceptance of the police as a service provider, rather than a *force*—a term that more accurately connotes police monopoly of coercive powers—shows the tendencies of agencies to deny issues of structural power and inequality (Patel, 1999).

Even the very terms applied to women who have experienced such violence may be seen as an indication of the imposition of normalizing judgments. The rejection of the *victim* label by many of the organizations offering help and support to women and its replacement with *survivor* may impose unwanted subjectivities on those who are already feeling vulnerable and unsure of themselves. On one level, the replacement of victim with survivor is perfectly understandable as the former has become synonymous with blame, largely as a result of the work of the early victimologists (e.g., Von Hentig, 1948; Wolfgang, 1958). By using survivor, therefore, feminists and activists are seeking not only to challenge victim blaming but at the same time are stressing the resistance and coping strategies used by women and children and the extent to which they ensure their own survival (Kelly & Radford, 1996; Walklate, 2003). Furthermore, as Stanko (1985) points out, "in applying the term 'victim' . . . one implicitly separates victim from non-victim," and it is this separation that enables theorists to examine victims as a cohesive group to find defining characteristics (p. 13). As this culture of victim blaming has entered public consciousness, women who have been abused have become increasingly reluctant to identify themselves as victims. However, the alternative construction of survivor is also far from ideal for many women. Given the many difficulties faced by those forced to cope with sexual and/or domestic violence, and the high numbers killed through such acts, many feminists contend that women cannot and should not be portrayed either as "inevitable victims or as strong survivors for whom abuse has minimal consequences" (Kelly, Burton, & Regan, 1996, p. 82).

The position of many support agencies in referring to victim/survivor either as dichotomous positions or as different stages of the same situation tends to be unhelpful for those struggling to deal with their experiences. For those women who believe that they could be or should have been more proactive in dealing with what has happened to them, achieving survivor status may seem unattainable, leaving them feeling that they have failed somehow to respond in the way they feel society would expect them to respond. Kelly et al. (1996) make similar points, suggesting that the victim/survivor dichotomy places individuals in an either/or position that "misrepresents both material and emotional reality" (p. 91; also see Lamb, 1996, 1999). Walklate (2003) points out that although victim and survivor tend to be presented as opposed, they are not necessarily so, as it is, of course, as "possible to think in terms of an active or passive victim, as it is to identify an active or passive survivor" (p. 36). In addition, though, not only is it possible to criticize the dichotomous construction of victim/survivor but also that used most often by feminists and agencies working with women who have experienced domestic violence, the notion of the victim-to-survivor healing journey. This alternative chronological construction of victim to survivor, in its tendency to presume passivity during the victim stage, ignores the resistance and coping strategies that many women adopt during their abuse (see Kelly et al., 1996). We would like to suggest that the meanings of survivor-victim are ambiguous and context specific, and our intent here is not to resolve these dichotomous constructions (as

each category can carry elements of both strength and vulnerability) but to foreground women victims' own definitions of their situation.

Institutional Attitudes

Increasing structural pressures of state funding have led to a steady professionalization of services and an institutionalization of therapeutic vocabularies (Dunn & Powell-Williams, 2007; Eisikovits & Buchbinder, 1999; Kendrick, 1998; Lempert, 1997; Loseke, 2001). As a consequence, not only has there been a steady homogenization of women victims' diverse experiences but also increasingly institutional functioning has come to be privileged over individual needs (Loseke, 2001). Institutional files stand in for real people, which process women victims as data points (Pence, 2005; Pence & McMahon, 1999).

Often dissimilar events and situations are lumped together in a way that fits a "discursive environment (that) privileges stories featuring the centrality of dangerous violence" (Loseke, 2001, p. 114). This means that women victims are expected to include a theme of violence in their narratives, even though women might want to talk about marital infidelity, a nonappreciative husband and family, or problems related with alcohol abuse.

In our specific research with VS volunteers, we argue that institutional discourses can nurture embedded social norms that enable society to absolve itself of any collective responsibility for tackling interpersonal violence. This is highlighted in institutional texts such as safety advice literature, aimed specifically at women, which embodies institutional thinking.

Although there is unambiguous reference in literature provided by VS to the fact that "[r]ape and sexual assault, whether by a stranger or friend, is never the woman's fault" (VS, n.d.), at the same time the personal-safety information they distribute places emphasis on the need for women to "take care." In a participant observation (2003) of domestic violence training, a male trainee (in his late 50s) who was supported in his views by a female trainee (of a similar age) suggested that young girls and women wearing "revealing clothing" were problematic because culture is making sexuality another commodity—"something you can take."

The literature exacerbates women's fear of crime, not only subjecting women to a form of social control but also under the guise of common sense creates an implicit division between women who follow the advice and those who do not. Gardner (1990) notes that it is "women's alleged responsibility for their own victimization" that results in them having to become "streetwise" and to take a variety of precautions (p. 312). This, we would suggest, maintains the status quo by reiteration of the dominant position—that it is incumbent on women to take precautions rather than on men to take control (Morgan & Thapar-Björkert, 2006). Thus we would argue that any real change would also entail making a change in the institutional texts.

The purpose of writing this is not to suggest that professional services should be removed (in fact, rather the opposite), and we recognize the invaluable work conducted by the vast majority of professional organizations and individuals offering support to women who have experienced all forms of violence. We are suggesting, however, that some professional services are in danger of imposing a set of regulatory norms on women and children who have already been subjected to an external and internalized gaze.

◈ Conclusion

The persistence of interpersonal violence in the experiences of ordinary lives is one of the main reasons for reexploring some of the mechanisms through which women (and men) experience violence. Violence is not the responsibility of women or the result of an individual pathology but a problem of the entire society, particularly the norms and attitudes that harbor prejudices relating to women victims of violence. In reviewing some of the dominant discourses that create, nurture, and sustain violence, we argue that the culture of blame and responsibility disempowers women who experience domestic and sexual violence.

In this article, we have focused on VS in the United Kingdom and suggested that the volunteers are in a unique position to have a greater understanding of the range of harms encompassed by the term violence.

However, we argue that some volunteers, through no fault of their own, fail adequately to challenge discourses of blame in relation to women victims of violence because the dominant discourses of victim blame outweigh the new, less popular discourses of nonblame. Often in speech, counter theories are implicit rather than explicit, and the person expressing the discourse may not be aware of these counter-meanings in the way that a hypocrite would be (Billig et al., 1988). Thus although the organizational rhetoric, policies, and measures may provide immediate (and necessary) assistance to the victim, they fall short in addressing or changing wider social attitudes and thus providing permanent safety or genuine empowerment. The tensions between nonblame and responsibility as revealed by the volunteers appear to be part of a wider understanding of how women and men interact. Although there are problems in attributing certain discourses to patriarchal power alone, there does appear to be evidence of dominant discourses and prevalent ideologies, which are a potential source of ambiguity particularly when considering women's experiences of violence. The volunteers, explicitly faced with two opposing ideologies, are perhaps more likely to experience conflicting attitudes than most people and are therefore more likely to articulate their ideological dilemmas. The volunteers who participated in this research were attempting to reconcile the opposing discourses to which they were exposed and create a coherent schema. Perhaps, this reconciliation could have become easier if the volunteers had access to feminist discourse, which has historically encouraged a reflexive practice of the limits of our own approaches in dealing with victims of violence.

There is thus, we suggest, an urgent need for a steady and continuous change in the civic-political culture (broadly understood as a set of institutional, representational, and discursive values held by citizens and among citizens)—a change from the prevalent culture of resignation (Morgan, 2005, 2006). A culture of resignation only reiterates disempowering constructions of blame/responsibility, which do not completely map the complexity or plurality of violence toward women. Our focus should move away from a produced victim to social attitudes that may generate a victim.

◈ Notes

1. The network of affiliated charities known collectively as the National Association of Victim Support Schemes originated in Britain in 1973–1974 following the development of the Bristol Victims Support Scheme. Within 4 years, some 30 similar schemes had been set up, and by the late 1990s there were approximately 450 schemes operating throughout England and Wales (National Audit Office, 2002) with the National Office based in London.

2. The issue of obtaining informed consent is an ambiguous one. In conducting "feminist research," which was the intention here, we recognize that "knowledge production [is] . . . grounded in individual and collective experiences," and consequently at the outset of the research it is not always completely apparent where it will lead us (Miller & Bell, 2002, p. 54). So although it is extremely important to explain the research aims to the participants, the findings may not always correspond to the original research aims. Such was the case in the research, which was intended to examine attitudes to women victims of violence and yet which surprised us in revealing the extent to which these VS volunteers possessed simultaneous yet conflicting notions of who was deserving or undeserving of violence.

3. Collins (1998) points out that using a structured/unstructured dichotomy is ultimately unhelpful when talking about interviews, as the interview situation is always structured to some extent. Mason (2002) also noted that it is not possible to conduct a "structure-free interview not least because the agendas and assumptions of both interviewer and interviewee will inevitably impose frameworks for meaningful interaction" (p. 231).

4. Ricoeur's (1981) science of hermeneutics suggests that there are two types of interpretation, the hermeneutics of faith and the hermeneutics of suspicion. The former can be "construed as the restoration of a meaning addressed to the interpreter in the form of a message. This type of hermeneutics is animated by faith, by a willingness to listen," whereas the latter is "regarded as the demystification of a meaning presented to the interpretation in the form of a disguise. This type of hermeneutics is animated by suspicion, by a skepticism towards the given" (Thompson, 1981, p. 6).

5. At the time the empirical research was conducted (2003–2004) by the second author, VS was a network of affiliated charities, operating under an umbrella organization of Victim Support National Office. In 2003, the government announced plans to direct funding via local Criminal Justice Boards rather than directly to Victim Support (VS). And in May 2007, an extraordinary General Meeting of VS voted overwhelmingly (90%) in favor of creating a single charity, a process that is now underway (VS, 2007).

6. The Victim's Charter is a statement of service standards for victims of crime (Home Office, 2004) and is available on demand from the Home Office, VS, and police stations. Interestingly, the charter mentions only VS and its Witness Service but ignores organizations such as Women's Aid and Rape Crisis (see Williams, 1999).

7. The Home Office is currently reviewing the service provided to victims of crime in a series of moves that will impact the way in which VS and other organizations operate (see Criminal Justice System, 2005).

8. Victim advocates in the United States work in shelters and criminal justice settings such as the prosecutor's office, police department, and sheriff's office (see McDermott & Garofalo, 2004).

9. Unless the volunteer has reason to believe that children may be at risk, in which case a decision may be taken to involve social services.

10. We recognize that this experience is shaped by gender, race/ethnicity, religion, class, and sexuality, which are not separate systems of domination or axes of power but are mutually constitutive (Hill Collins, 1998; Mama, 1989). These social divisions can render women of color's experiences as qualitatively different from those of White women (Crenshaw, 1994).

11. Donileen Loseke (2001) argues that "formula stories are narratives about types of experience (such as wife abuse), involving distinctive types of characters (such as battered women and the abusive man)" (p. 107).

12. Both Victim Support National Office and the Home Office consider that "the involvement of members of the community, offering their time free of charge, was vital to the work. Victims did not necessarily want full-time paid professional counselors supporting them but local people" (House of Commons, 2003, p. 8). This means, however, that the quality and extent of service available can vary significantly from area to area, although there are significant moves underway to ensure that all areas reach the same high standards.

13. It is difficult to say how these views of VS workers were reflected in their practices with victims, but the second author observed several training sessions between volunteers, VS training staff, and trainers from external professional training organizations. In these situations, all of them upheld the principles of nonblame, active listening, and nonjudgmental support. All volunteers interviewed indicated a willingness to comply with these rules in practice.

14. Other research has recognized that institutions can be as "violent and intimidating as individuals" (Hanmer & Maynard, 1987, p. 5). For example, Amina Mama (1989) argues that multiagency responses in the United Kingdom to battered Black women (Asian, African and Caribbean), in particular, aggravate their suffering and isolation. Many Black women are often coerced into a relationship with social services, which adds "to their oppressions of violence, homelessness and racism by further disempowering rather than supporting the women" (Mama, 1989, p. 96). Also, in the British context, many women of African, Asian, and Caribbean descent would not access the "palliative" measures because of the stereotypes and preconceptions associated with their ethnicity (Mama, 1989, p. 24).

15. Michel Foucault in *Discipline and Punish* (1991) suggests that premodern power is characterized by using violence that is intensely corporal and brutal and wielded in a personal manner. Modern power is defined by using violence in a more anonymous, invisible, and lighter way. Disciplinary institutions and practices would follow this pattern, which is less violent and more invisible and diffuse but extremely invasive.

16. Different disciplines studying the problems associated with violence, such as medicine, psychology, psychiatry, and legal studies, have been redescribing women's abnormalities, pathologizing women who are victims of male dominance, created and supported at the same time by patriarchal cultures that allow female domination (Caplan, 1991).

◈ References

Anderson, K., & Umberson, D. (2001). Gendering violence: Masculinity and power in men's account of domestic violence. *Gender & Society, 15,* 358–380.

Baker, L. P. (1997). "And I went back": Battered women's negotiation of choice. *Journal of Contemporary Ethnography, 26,* 55–74.

Barnett, O. W. (2000). Why battered women do not leave, Part 1: External exhibiting factors within society. *Trauma, Violence and Abuse, 1,* 343–372.

Berns, N. (2001). Degendering the problem and gendering the blame: Political discourse on women and violence. *Gender & Society, 15,* 262–281.

Berns, N., & Schweingruber, D. (2007). "When you're involved, it's just different": Making sense of domestic violence. *Violence Against Women, 13,* 240–261.

Billig, M., Condor, S., Edwards, D., Gane, M., Middleton, D., & Radley, A. (1988). *Ideological dilemmas: A social psychology of everyday thinking.* London: Sage.

Birch, M., & Miller, T. (2002). Inviting intimacy: The interview as therapeutic opportunity. *International Journal of Social Research Methodology, 3,* 189–202.

Boateng, P. (1999, November 24–25). *Living without fear: An agenda for action.* Speech made at the Home Office Special Conference on Violence Against Women. Retrieved March 1, 2007, from http://www.homeoffice.gov.uk/dometsicviolence/pbspeech.htm

Bunch, C., & Carrillo, R. (1992). *Gender violence: A development and human rights issue.* Dublin, Ireland: Attic Press.

Caplan, P. (1991). How do they decide who is normal? The bizarre but true tale of the DSM process. *Canadian Psychology, 32,* 162–170.

Collins, P. (1998). Negotiation selves: Reflections on "unstructured" interviewing. *Sociological Research Online, 3.* Retrieved from November 2, 2009, http://www.socresonline.org.uk/3/3/2 .html

Corrin, C. (Ed.). (1996). *Women in a violent world: Feminist analyses and resistance across Europe.* Edinburgh, UK: Edinburgh University Press.

Cosgrove, K. (1996). No man has the right. In C. Corrin (Ed.), *Women in a violent world: Feminist analyses and resistance across Europe* (pp. 186–203). Edinburgh, UK: Edinburgh University Press.

Crenshaw, K. W. (1994). Mapping the margins: Intersectionality, identity politics and violence against women of color. In M. Fineman & R. Mykitiuk (Eds.), *The public nature of private violence* (pp. 93–121). New York: Routledge.

Criminal Justice System. (2005). *Rebuilding lives: Supporting victims of crime.* London: HMSO.

Dobash, R. E., & Dobash, R. P. (1992). *Women, violence and social change.* London: Routledge.

Dobash, R. E., & Dobash, R. P. (1997). Violence against women. In L. O'Toole & J. R. Schiffman (Eds.), *Gender violence: Interdisciplinary perspectives* (pp. 266–279). New York: New York University Press.

Dunn, L. J., & Powell-Williams, M. (2007). "Everybody makes choices": Victim advocates and the social construction of battered women's victimization and agency. *Violence Against Women, 13,* 977–1001.

Eisikovits, Z., & Buchbinder, E. (1999). Talking control: Metaphors used by battered women. *Violence Against Women, 5,* 845–868.

Fairclough, N. (1995). *Critical discourse analysis: The critical study of language.* London: Longman.

Field, C. A., Caetano R., & Nelson, S. (2004). Alcohol and violence related cognitive risk factors associated with the perpetration of intimate partner violence. *Journal of Family Violence, 19,* 249–253.

Finney, A. (2004). *Alcohol and intimate partner violence: Key findings from the research.* London: Home Office, Communication Development Unit.

Foucault, M. (1991). *Discipline and punish: The birth of the prison.* London: Penguin.

Fraser, H. (2005). Women, love, and intimacy "gone wrong": Fire, wind and ice. *Affiliate, 20*(1), 10–20.

Gardner, C. B. (1990). Safe conduct: Women, crime and self in public places. *Social Problems, 37,* 311–327.

Hague, G. (1998). Interagency work and domestic violence in the UK. *Women's Studies International Forum, 21,* 441–449.

Hague, G., & Mullender, A. (2006). Who listens? The voices of domestic violence survivors in service provision in the United Kingdom. *Violence Against Women, 12,* 568–587.

Hanmer, J., & Maynard, M. (Eds.). (1987). *Women, violence and social control.* London: Macmillan.

Hearn, J. (1998). *The violences of men: How men talk about and how agencies respond to men's violence to women.* London: Sage.

Hester, M., Kelly, L., & Radford, J. (Eds.). (1996). *Women, violence and male power.* Buckingham, UK: Open University Press.

Hester, M., Pearson, C., & Harwin, N. (1998). *Making an impact: Children and domestic violence. A reader.* Essex, UK: Barnardo's.

Hill Collins, P. (1998). It's all in the family: Intersections of gender, race and nation. *Hypatia, 13,* 62–82.

Hirschmann, N. J. (1997). Toward a feminist theory of freedom. In M. L. Shanley & U. Narayan (Eds.), *Reconstructing political theory: Feminist perspectives* (pp. 195–210). Cambridge, UK: Polity.

Holstein, J. A., & Gubrium, J. F. (2000). *The self we live by: Narrative identity in a post-modern world.* New York: Oxford University Press.

Home Office. (2004). *The Victim's Charter: A statement of service standards for victims of crime.* London: Criminal Justice System.

hooks, b. (1997). Violence in intimate relationships: A feminist perspective. In L. O'Toole & J. Schiffman (Eds.), *Gender violence: Interdisciplinary perspectives* (pp. 279–285). New York: New York University Press.

House of Commons, Committee of Public Accounts. (2003). *Helping victims and witnesses: The work of victim support* (Seventeenth Report of Session 2002–2003). London: Stationery Office Limited.

Josselson, R. (2004). The hermeneutics of faith and the hermeneutics of suspicion. *Narrative Inquiry, 14,* 1–28.

Kelly, L. (1988). *Surviving sexual violence.* Cambridge, UK: Polity.

Kelly, L. (1996). When does the speaking profit us? Reflections on the challenges of developing feminist perspective on abuse and violence by women. In M. Hester, L. Kelly, & J. Radford (Eds.), *Women, violence and male power: Feminist activism, research and practice* (pp. 34–49). Buckingham, UK: Open University Press.

Kelly, L., Burton, S., & Regan, L. (1996). Beyond victim or survivor: Sexual violence, identity, and feminist theory and practice. In L. Adkins & V. Merchant (Eds.), *Sexualizing the social: Power and the organization of sexuality* (pp. 77–101). Basingstoke, UK: Macmillan Press.

Kelly, L., & Radford, J. (1996). "Nothing really happened." The invalidation of women's experiences. In M. Hester, L. Kelly, & J. Radford (Eds.), *Women, violence and male power* (pp. 19–33). Buckingham, UK: Open University Press.

Kendrick, K. (1998). Producing the battered woman: Shelter politics and the power of feminist voice. In N. Naples (Ed.), *Community activism and feminist politics: Organizing across race, class and gender* (pp. 151–173). New York: Routledge.

Lamb, S. (1996). *The trouble with blame: Victims, perpetrators and responsibility.* Cambridge, MA: Harvard University Press.

Lamb, S. (1999). Constructing the victim: Popular images and lasting labels. In S. Lamb (Ed.), *New versions of victims: Feminists struggle with the concept* (pp. 108–139). New York: New York University Press.

Lea, J. S. (2007). A discursive investigation into victim responsibility in rape. *Feminism and Psychology, 17,* 495–514.

Lempert, L. B. (1997). The other side of help: Negative effects in the help-seeking processes of abused women. *Qualitative Sociology, 20,* 289–308.

Loseke, D. R. (1992). *The battered woman and shelters: The social construction of wife abuse.* Albany: State University of New York Press.

Loseke, D. R. (1999). *Thinking about social problems: An introduction to constructionist perspectives.* New York: Aldine de Gruyter.

Loseke, D. R. (2001). Lived realities and formula stories of "battered women." In J. F. Gubrium & J. A. Holstein (Eds.), *Institutional selves: Troubled identities in a post-modern world* (pp. 107–126). New York: Oxford University Press.

MacCannell, D., & MacCannell, J. F. (1993). Violence, power and pleasure: A revisionist reading of Foucault from the victim perspective. In C. Ramazanoğlu (Ed.), *Up against Foucault: Explorations of some tensions between Foucault and feminism* (pp. 203–238). London: Routledge.

Malos, E. (2000). Supping with the devil?: Multi-agency initiatives on domestic violence. In J. Radford, L. Harne, & M. Friedberg (Eds.), *Women, violence and strategies for action: Feminist research, policy and practice* (pp. 120–136). Buckingham, UK: Open University Press.

Mama, A. (1989). *The hidden struggle: Statutory and voluntary sector responses to violence against Black women in the home.* London: London Race and Housing Research Unit.

Mason, J. (2002). Qualitative interviewing: Asking, listening and interpreting. In T. May (Ed.), *Qualitative research in action* (pp. 225–241). London: Sage.

Maynard, M. (1993). Violence towards women. In D. Richardson & V. Robinson (Eds.), *Introducing women's studies: Feminist theory and practice* (pp. 99–122). London: Macmillan.

McDermott, J. M., & Garofalo, J. (2004). When advocacy for domestic violence victims backfires: Types and sources of victim disempowerment. *Violence Against Women, 10,* 1245–1266.

McLaughlin, J. (2003). *Feminist social and political theory: Contemporary debates and dialogues.* New York: Palgrave Macmillan.

Mezey, G., & Stanko, E. (1996). Women and violence. In K. Abel, M. Buszewicz, & E. Staples (Eds.), *Planning community mental health service for women: A multiprofessional handbook* (pp. 166–175). Routledge: London.

Miller, T., & Bell, L. (2002). Consenting to what? Issues of access, gatekeeping and "informed" consent. In M. Mauthner, M. Birch, & T. Miller (Eds.), *Ethics in qualitative research* (pp. 53–69). London: Sage.

Morgan, K. (2005). *Violence against women: The discursive construction of a culture of resignation.* Unpublished doctoral thesis, University of Bristol, UK.

Morgan, K. (2006). Cheating wives and vice girls: The construction of a culture of resignation. *Women's Studies International Forum, 29,* 489–498.

Morgan, K., & Thapar-Björkert, S. (2006). "I'd rather you'd lay me on the floor and start kicking me": Understanding symbolic violence in everyday life. *Women's Studies International Forum, 29,* 441–452.

National Audit Office. (2002, 23 October). *Helping victims and witnesses: The work of Victim Support (2001–2002)* (Report by the Comptroller and Auditor-General HC1212. Session 2001–2002). London: The Stationery Office.

National Statistics Online. (2001). *Neighbourhood statistics: Neighbourhood profile.* Retrieved 30 March, 2005, from http://www.neighbourhood.statistics.gov.uk/dissemination/AreaProfile2.do?tab=2

Ollett, B. (1994, April). *Alcohol and crime: A Women's Aid perspective: Causes of domestic violence.* Paper presented at the conference From Problems to Solutions: Alcohol and Crime, Carmarthen, UK.

Pahl, J. (Ed.). (1985). *Private violence and public policy: The needs of battered women and the response of the public services.* London: Routledge.

Patel, P. (1999). The multi-agency approach to domestic violence: A panacea or obstacle to women's struggles for freedom from violence. In N. Harwin, G. Hague, & E. Malos (Eds.), *The multi-agency approach to domestic violence: New opportunities, old challenges?* (pp. 172–190). London: Whiting and Birch.

Peled, E., Eisikovits, Z., Enosh, G., & Winstok, Z. (2002). Choice and empowerment for battered women who stay: Towards a constructivist model. *Social Work, 45,* 9–25.

Pence, E. (2005, March). *Violence against women: Coordinating activism, research and service provision conference.* Plenary at the ESRC seminar, University of Bristol, UK.

Pence, E., & McMahon, M. (1999). Duluth: A coordinated community response to domestic violence. In N. Harwin, G. Hague, & E. Malos (Eds.), *The multi-agency approach to domestic violence: New opportunities, old challenges?* (pp. 180–194). London: Whiting and Birch.

Radford, J., & Russell, D. E. H. (Eds.). (1992). *Femicide: The politics of woman killing.* Buckingham, UK: Open University Press.

Radford, J., & Stanko, E. A. (1996). Violence against women and children: The contradictions of crime control under patriarchy. In M. Hester, L. Kelly, & J. Radford (Eds.), *Women, violence and male power* (pp. 142–157). Buckingham, UK: Open University Press.

Ricoeur, P. (1981). *Hermeneutics and the human sciences.* Cambridge, UK: Cambridge University Press.

Rothenberg, B. (2003). "We don't have time for social change": Cultural compromise and the battered woman syndrome. *Gender & Society, 17,* 771–786.

Smart, C. (1989). *Feminism and the power of law.* London: Routledge.

Smart, C., & Smart, B. (1978). Accounting for rape: Reality and myth in press reporting. In C. Smart & B. Smart (Eds.), *Women, sexuality and social control* (pp. 10–23). London: Routledge.

Spackman, P. (2000). *Victim support handbook: Helping people cope with crime.* London: Hodder and Stoughton.

Stanko, E. A. (1985). *Intimate intrusions: Women's experience of male violence.* London: Routledge.

Stanko, E. A. (1990). When precaution is normal: A feminist critique of crime prevention. In L. Gelsthorp & A. Morris (Eds.), *Feminist perspectives in criminology* (pp. 171–183). Milton Keynes, UK: Open University Press.

Stanko, E. A. (Ed.). (2003). *The meanings of violence.* London: Routledge.

Stanko, E. A. (2006). Theorizing about violence: Observations from the Economic and Social Research Council's Violence Research Programme. *Violence Against Women, 12,* 543–555.

Thompson, J. B. (1981). Critical hermeneutics: *A study in the thought of Paul Ricoeur and Jürgen Habermas.* Cambridge, UK: Cambridge University Press.

Tisdall, E. K. M. (2003). The rising tide of female violence? Researching girls' own understanding and experiences of violent behavior. In R. M. Lee & E. A. Stanko (Eds.), *Researching violence: Essays on methodology and measurement* (pp. 137–153). London: Routledge.

Titscher, S., Meyer, M., Wodak, R., & Vetter, E. (2000). *Methods of text and discourse analysis.* London: Sage.

Van Dijk, T. A. (1997). Discourse as interaction in society. In T. A. van Dijk (Ed.), *Discourses as social interaction* (pp. 1–37). London: Sage.

Victim Support. (n.d.). *Rape and sexual assault: Information for women.* London: Author.

Victim Support. (2003). *Resource pack for supporting victims of domestic violence.* London: Victim Support National Office.

Victim Support. (2005). *Service Personnel and Equal Opportunities Survey report 2004.* London: Victim Support National Office, Research and Development Department.

Victim Support. (2006). *Victim and witness review: Annual report and accounts.* London: Author.

Victim Support. (2007). *Handbook on delivering Victim Support's enhanced services* (Interim version). London: Victim Support National Office.

Victim Support Magazine. (1998, autumn). London: Author.

Von Hentig, H. (1948). *The criminal and his victim.* New Haven, CT: Yale University Press.

Walklate, S. (2003). Can there be a feminist victimology? In P. Davies, P. Francis, & V. Jupp (Eds.), *Victimisation: Theory, research and policy* (pp. 28–45). Basingstoke, UK: Palgrave Macmillan.

Weaver, C. K. (1998). Crimewatch UK: Keeping women off the streets. In C. Carter, G. Branston, & S. Allan (Eds.), *News, gender and power* (pp. 248–262). London: Routledge.

Westlund, A. (1999). Pre-modern and modern power: Foucault and the case of domestic violence. *Signs, 24,* 1046–1066.

Williams, B. (1999). The Victim's Charter: Citizens as consumers of criminal justice services. *Howard Journal, 38,* 384–396.

Wodak, R. (1996). *Disorders of discourse.* London: Longman.

Wolfgang, M. E. (1958). *Patterns in criminal homicide.* Philadelphia: University of Pennsylvania Press.

Yeatman, A. (1997). Feminism and power. In M. L. Shanley & U. Narayan (Eds.), *Reconstructing political theory: Feminist perspectives* (pp. 144–157). Cambridge, UK: Polity.

READING 29

A 1975 Supreme Court decision makes stopping persons with a "Mexican appearance" for no other reason legal under the 4th Amendment. However, because the Immigration and Naturalization Service (INS) does not keep statistics on incidents of stopping and interrogating legal residents (false positives), there is little information on the extent to which Latino Americans are differentially treated and discriminated against by the agency of the criminal justice system. In an effort to describe the injustices Latino Americans (legal citizens and illegal residents) face, Mary Romero uses a case study approach and describes a 5-day immigration raid in the late 1990s known as the Chandler Roundup, which took place in Chandler, Arizona. More than 400 stops were documented, and she examined data on 91 complaints filed during the 5 days. All of the complainants were Latino or of Mexican descent. Several (14) were stopped more than once during the 5-day period. Nearly half of the complainants (42) were clearly not illegal immigrants. Only 33 outcomes for the 91 incidences were documented; 23 were detained, and only 3 of those were clear cases of illegal residence. Equally disconcerting is the way the "suspects" were treated, some handcuffed, while others were interrogated in a manner inconsistent with the way "white" people are typically stopped and questioned.

Racial Profiling and Immigration Law Enforcement

Rounding Up of Usual Suspects in the Latino Community

Mary Romero

"Where are you from?"

I didn't answer. I wasn't sure who the agent, a woman, was addressing. She repeated the question in Spanish, "¿De *dónde eres*?"

Without thinking, I almost answered her question—in Spanish. A reflex. I caught myself in midsentence and stuttered in a nonlanguage.

"¿*Dónde naciste*?" she asked again . . .

She was browner than I was. I might have asked her the same question . . .

"Are you sure you were born in Las Cruces?" she asked again.

I turned around and smiled, "Yes, I'm sure." She didn't smile back. She and her driver sat there for a while and watched me as I continued walking . . .

"Sons of bitches," I whispered, "pretty soon I'll have to carry a passport in my own neighborhood." . . . It was like a video I played over and over—memorizing the images . . . *Are you sure you were born in Las Cruces?* ringing in my ears. (Sáenz 1992: xii)

The personal and community cost of racial profiling to Mexican Americans who are treated as outside the law does not appear in official criminal justice statistics. Benjamin Alire Sáenz captured the racial-affront experience when Immigration and Naturalization Service (INS) agents use racial profiling; he emphasized the irony when Mexican-American INS agents interrogate other Mexican Americans about their citizenship. Citizenship appears embodied in skin color (that is, brown skin absent a police or border patrol uniform) serving as an indicator of illegal status. Carrying a bodily "figurative border" (Chang 1999), "Mexicanness"

Source: Romero, M. (2006). Racial profiling and immigration law enforcement: Rounding up of usual suspects in the Latino community. *Critical Sociology*, 32, 447–473.

becomes the basis for suspecting criminality under immigration law. Mexican Americans and other racialized Latino citizens[1] and legal residents are subjected to insults, questions, unnecessary stops, and searches. Surveillance of citizenship, relentless in low-income and racialized neighborhoods along the border and in urban barrios, increases the likelihood of discrimination in employment, housing, and education. Latinos (particularly dark complected, poor, and working class) are at risk before the law. The following article uses a case study approach to identify the use of racial profiling in immigration law enforcement; and to document the impact on US citizens and legal residents.

◈ Domestic Function of Immigration Policy

Conquest of the Southwest subliminally grafted Mexicans to "the American psyche as a 'foreigner,' even though the land had once belonged to Mexico" (Romero 2001:1091). Following the Mexican-American War, special law-enforcement agencies were established to patrol the newly formed border and to police Mexicans who remained in occupied territory, as well as later migrants across the border. The most distinct form of social control and domination used by the US in this occupation was the creation of the Texas and Arizona Rangers. Maintaining the interests of cattle barons in Texas, the Texas Rangers treated Mexicans living along the border as cattle thieves and bandits when they attempted to reclaim stolen property from cattle barons. Similarly, the Arizona Rangers protected capitalist interests by protecting strikebreakers against Mexican miners. Following a parallel pattern, the INS rarely raided the fields during harvest time and scheduled massive immigration roundups during periods of economic recession and union activity (Acuña 2000). Remembering the policing functions of the Texas and Arizona Rangers and the Border Patrol (including the current militarization at the border) is crucial in recognizing the social functions accomplished by racialized immigrant raids, sweeps, and citizenship inspections (Acuña 2000; Andreas 2000; Dunn 1996; Nevins 2002). Under Operation Wetback, for example, only persons of Mexican descent were included in the campaign

and thus were the only group to bear the burden of proving citizenship (Garcia 1980). Militarized sweeps of Mexicans maintained the community in "a state of permanent insecurity" in the 1950s; in response a petition was submitted to the United Nations charging the USA with violating the Universal Declaration of Human Rights (Acuña 2000:306).

A number of recent studies unveil the hypocrisy of US border policies that manage to allow enough undocumented immigrant labor in to meet employers' demands while at the same time increasing INS and Border Patrol budgets (Andreas 2000; Massey et al. 2002; Nevins 2002). Longitudinal studies comparing INS efficiency and increased budget prior to the 1986 Immigration Reform and Control Act (IRCA) to late-1990s immigration law reforms suggest that the cost of detaining unauthorized border crossers has increased (Massey et al. 2002). Immigration researchers (Chavez 2001; Massey et al. 2002) claim that we are paying for the illusion of controlled borders while politicians make a political spectacle, pandering to alarmist public discourse about a Mexican immigrant invasion, the breakdown of the US-Mexico border, and increased crime resulting from immigration (Chavez 2001). Operation Blockade and Operation Gatekeeper failed to deter extralegal immigration from Mexico. US employers continue to have access to a vulnerable, cheap labor force created by assigning workers an "illegal" status. The worst cost of these failed policies are the increasing loss of human lives as migrants are forced to cross the border in the most desolate areas of the desert (Cornelius 2001; Eschbach et al. 1999).

In what follows I demonstrate that more than "illusion" or "political capital' is gained. Meeting employers' demand for cheap labor while appearing to deter immigration includes a cost borne by Mexican Americans and other racialized Latinos. Immigration research tends to ignore the political, social, and economic costs paid by Mexican Americans and other Latinos who are implicated by immigration policies. Racialized citizens and legal residents become subjects of immigration stops and searches, and pay the cost of increased racism—sometimes in the form of hate crimes or the decrease of government funding and services to their communities (Chang and Aoki 1997; Johnson 1993; Mehan 1997). Both Operation Blockade and Operation

Gatekeeper provided impetus to anti-immigration policies that not only decreased public funding assisting low-income Latino communities in general (regardless of citizenship status) but also fueled racism and anti-affirmative action policies (Chavez 2001; Lee et al. 2001). This article explores the ways that immigration raids function as a policing practice to maintain and reinforce subordinated status among working-class US citizens and legal residents of Mexican ancestry.

◈ Critical Race Theory and Immigration Law Enforcement

Using a critical race theory framework, I examine racial- and class-based micro- and macro-aggressions that result from the use of racial profiling in immigration law enforcement. Citizens sharing racial and cultural similarities with "aliens" targeted by immigration law enforcement agents have been, and continue to be, treated as "foreigners" and denied equal protection under the law. Racialized immigration law enforcement not only places darker Mexican Americans at risk, but threatens members of the community who are bilingual speakers, have friends or family members who are immigrants, or who engage in certain cultural practices. Critical race theory "challenges ahistoricism and insists on a contextual/historical analysis of the law" (Matsuda et al. 1993:6). It aims to illuminate structures that create and perpetuate domination and subordination in their "everyday operation" (Valdez et al. 2002:3). Applying a critical race theory perspective to immigration, legal scholar Kevin Johnson (2002:187) argues that, "exclusions found in the immigration laws effectuate and reinforce racial subordination in the United States." A history of immigration laws based on racial exclusions reinforces stereotypes the Mexicans and other third-world immigrants are inferior and "alien" (Hing 1997; Johnson 1997). Conceptualizing racial profiling practices in immigration law enforcement as micro- and macro-aggressions—a petit apartheid—helps recognize the discriminatory functions that policing and inspections have on citizenship participation and the rights of Mexican Americans, Mexican immigrants, and other racialized Latinos, particularly the poor and working class.

Building on the work of psychologist Chester Pierce, critical race theorists have found the concept of micro-aggressions useful in describing the form of policing common in communities of color: "subtle, stunning, often automatic, and non-verbal exchanges which are 'put downs' of blacks by offenders" (Pierce et al. 1978:66).[2] In her research on race and crime, Katheryn Russell distinguished between racial assaults on a personal level or micro-aggressions, and "face group affronts" or macro-aggressions. The latter type of affront is "not directed toward a particular Black person, but at Blackness in general" and may be made "by a private individual or official authority" (Russell 1998:139). Macro-aggressions reinforce stereotypes of racialized groups "either criminals, illiterates, or intellectual inferiors" (Russell 1998:140).[3] Dragan Milovanovic and Katheryn K. Russell (2001:vii) argued that both micro- and macro-aggressions work as "a cycle which sustains hierarchy and harms of reductions and repression." "Harms of reduction occur when offended parties experience a loss in their standing . . . or restriction, preventing them from achieving a desired position or standing" (Henry and Milovanovic 1999:7–8). Harms of reduction and repression are detrimental because "they belittle, demean, ridicule or subordinate on the one hand, and on the other, they limit access to equal opportunities and fair dealings before the law" (Milovanovic and Russell 2001:xvi).

Daniel Georges-Abeyie's (2001:x) theoretical paradigm of grand and petit apartheid links current practices of racial profiling with other "negative social factors and discretional decision-making by both criminal justice agents and criminal justice agencies." Georges-Abeyie's theoretical work outlines a continuum of petit apartheid discriminatory practices ranging from the covert and informal to the overt and formal. Petit apartheid has been used to explain racial profiling in the war against drugs (Campbell 2001; Covington 2001), regulating and policing public space (Bass 2001; Ferrell 2001b), under-representation of persons of color interested in law enforcement (Ross 2001) and the use of racial derogation in prosecutors' closing arguments (Johnson 2001).

Petit apartheid relates to concerns about struggles over access to urban public space, freedom of movement, the processes of capital investment, political decision-making, and policing first theorized by Henri Lefebvre (1996 [1968]) and others (see Caldeira 2000; Ferrell 2001a; Harvey 1973, 1996; Holston 1999; Mitchell 2003). Images and perceptions of public space are used to encourage, discourage, or prohibit use and movement. Exclusionary models of public life are most noted for privileging middle-class consumers. Surveillance, stops, and searches maintain a landscape of suspicion and reinforce white, middle-class citizens' suspicions of racial minorities and protect their access to public space. When citizenship is racially embodied though law-enforcement practices that target Mexican-American neighborhoods and business areas, then Henri Lefebvre's (1996 [1968]: 174) statement about urban space is actualized: "The right of the city manifests itself as a superior form of rights: right to freedom, to individualization in socialization, to habitat and to inhabit."

Immigration law enforcement assists such exclusionary use of urban public spaces and limits freedom of movement. However, the INS is in the position of having to negotiate an adequate flow of undocumented labor to meet urban capitalist needs while maintaining the appearance of controlling immigration. Consequently, immigration law enforcement in US cities is not structured around systematic or random checking of identification but rather a pattern of citizenship inspection that maintains the landscape of suspicion. Given the class and racial segregation perpetuated by exclusive residential zoning, the INS targets ethnic cultural spaces marked by Mexican-owned businesses, agencies offering bilingual services, and neighborhoods with the highest concentration of poor and working-class Latinos. Within these areas, INS agents engage in "typing" suspected aliens (Heyman 1995; Weissinger 1996) that embodies a "figurative border" (Chang 1999). In the process of typing Mexicans as suspects, Americans are "whitened."

The 1975 Supreme Court decision that "Mexican appearance" "constitutes a legitimate consideration under the Fourth Amendment for making an immigration stop" (Johnson 2000:676) legalized micro- and macro-aggressions inflicted upon Mexican Americans. Micro- and macro-aggressions, as well as petit apartheid, are experienced by Mexican Americans when they are caught within a racially profiled dragnet in which

INS agents operate with unchecked discretion. Harms of reduction and repression occur when Latinos are subjected to racially motivated (and frequently class-based) stops and searches and race-related INS abuse (Arriola 1996–97; Benitez 1994; Lazos 2002; Vargas 2001). Micro-aggressions are racial affronts on a personal level, experienced when an individual Mexican American is stopped and asked to prove citizenship status; macro-aggressions are group affronts because they are directed towards "Mexicanness" in general. Macro-aggressions target dark complexions and physical characteristics characterized as "Mexican" or "Latino;" speaking Spanish, listening to Spanish music, shopping at Mexican-owned businesses, or any other cultural practices bring on racially motivated stops.

◈ The Case of the Chandler Roundup

INS data provide statistics on the number of individuals apprehended but the agency does not collect data on the number of individuals stopped and searched who were citizens or legal residents. Consequently, the impact of racialized immigration law enforcement on communities of color is rarely visible in legal reporting procedures. However, every once in awhile, community protests against raids gain sufficient media attention to require public officials to respond by conducting investigations into allegations of law-enforcement wrongdoings. In these rare instances it becomes possible to uncover "more covert, hidden forms of discrimination" (Georges-Abeyie 2001:xiv) in the documentation of civil-rights or human-rights violations. Formal investigations reveal the group and communities targeted and the ways that public and private space is regulated under the auspices of immigration law enforcement. These institutional practices are "relations of ruling" and unravel the everyday management of social control and domination (Smith 1990, 1999).

In order to identify micro- and macro-aggressions and petit apartheid accomplished by immigration raids, I analyzed data from two official investigations into a five-day immigration raid in Chandler, Arizona. The raid was the third of its kind conducted by the Chandler Police during the summer of 1997 (Fletcher 1997). The immigration sweep came to be known as the "Chandler Roundup," reinforcing both the cowboy legacy of law enforcement in Mexican-American communities and the notion that Mexicans are "strays." On July 27, 1997, the Chandler Police Department and Border Patrol agents from Casa Grande Station and the Tucson area began a five-day immigration raid as a joint operation in the most highly populated Latino section of the city. Over the five days, 432 suspected undocumented Mexicans were arrested. The Chief Patrol Agent's *Summary Report of the Border Patrol Operations in Chandler, AZ* cited in the Arizona Attorney General's report (Office of the Attorney General Grant Wood 1997:15–7) outlined the daily activities as follows:

Day 1—July 27, 1997: "Within three hours . . . more than 75 arrests out of approximately 100 contacts" were made through "casual contacts . . . along the streets in and around public areas." A total of 83 arrests were made that day (82 Mexicans and 1 Guatemalan).

Day 2—July 28, 1997: The target area was "expanded to one square mile of the downtown Chandler area" and "nearly all contacts occurred outside dwellings" and "the exceptions were the result of specific information or probable cause." On this day, they arrested 102 Mexicans.

Day 3—July 29, 1997: Working with Chandler Police between 4:00 AM and 8:00 AM, they arrested 69 (ethnicity not noted). Bicycle patrols working public areas and trailer parks arrested an additional 49.

Day 4—July 30, 1997: A total of 77 illegal aliens were arrested.

Day 5—July 31, 1997: 52 arrests were made.

Immigrant advocates and Mexican-American residents in Chandler began organizing and held several community meetings with the police chief, Chandler City Council members, and the State Attorney General's staff. As a consequence of the public outcry, the investigations and lawsuits that followed produced government documentation of law-enforcement practices that detail the use of micro- and macro-aggressions towards Mexican Americans and other Latinos racially profiled as criminal, unauthorized, or extralegal. The primary focus of the investigations was police misconduct and violation of civil rights. A secondary issue concerned the role of local police departments participating in joint operations with the INS.

The State Attorney General's office immediately responded to complaints and began collecting eyewitness accounts from individuals willing to be interviewed. The Office of the Attorney General Grant Woods issued a report, *Results of the Chandler Survey,* in December 1997. Data collected and analyzed in the report included: minutes of meetings with the Latino community in Chandler, interviews with citizens and legal residents stopped during the five-day operation, minutes of City Council Meetings with community members, newspaper articles, memoranda between city officials, review of Chandler Police radio dispatch audio tapes, police field notes, and witness testimonies. The Attorney General's report is organized into the following sections: background information,[4] summary of the survey,[5] summary of the Commission on Civil Rights Reports, and an evaluation of claims of civil-rights violation and recommendations.

The following summer, the City of Chandler paid for an independent investigation (Breen et al. 1998). The final product was the three-volume report. Volume I, *Report of Independent Investigation Into July 1997 Joint Operation Between Border Patrol and Chandler Police Department,* includes a mission statement, narrative[6] and summaries of interviews conducted with public officials.[7] Volume II, *Complainants,* is the independent investigators' direct response to the descriptive accounts of civil-rights violations documented in the Office of the Attorney General's *Survey*. Incidents reported in Volume II include only complaints formally filed with the Chandler Police, the Office of the Attorney General, or the Mexican Consultant's office. Volume III, *Appendices to Report of Independent Investigation,* includes four maps (the Tucson sector of the Border Patrol, Chandler and Vicinity, Area of Operation Restoration, and areas covered in the joint operation), excerpts from policy and procedure handbooks,[8] a survey of policies regarding illegal aliens in 14 cities in border states, a survey of how media learned of the 1997 joint operation, the Chandler Police Department's Community-Oriented Policing Programs; and 89 records of Border Patrol Forms I-213 (Deportable Alien) produced during the Joint Operation.

The summary section of each report differs in the perspective taken. In the State Attorney General's report, *Results of the Chandler Survey,* the construction of immigration as a problem in Chandler is presented from the community's perspective and supported by official documents whereas the *Report of Independent Investigation Into July 1997 Joint Operation Between Border Patrol and Chandler Police Department* privileges the INS and police's documentation of a growing immigration problem and presents the "roundup" as the official response. Witness accounts cited in the *Survey* were collected immediately following the five-day immigration sweep. Each of the civil-rights violations from witness accounts noted in the Attorney General's report was investigated a year later by the independent investigators; however, only those violations corroborated by police officers' interviews, field notes, or arrest records were deemed legitimate in the *Report of Independent Investigation.* Defining validity with criteria that privileged police interviews and records (as well as INS official documentation) assured that the independent investigators' report minimized the violation of civil rights and was more favorable to the Chandler Police Department than was the Attorney General's report.

This study is an analysis of the official reports. While these data were obtained from legal documents constructed within a specific political, social, and economic context, the variety of documents produced presents diverse perspectives, including interested community members, citizens and legal residents stopped and searched, police officers participating in the raid, and City Council members. Clearly, the data analyzed do not include a complete profile of all the stops that were made during the five-day operation. However, the two reports provide a rare insight into strategically planned immigration law enforcement targeting low-income areas highly populated by Mexican Americans.

Complainants (Volume II of the *Report of Independent Investigation)* contained the following data: a profile of the type of individuals stopped and searched, activities by these individuals that warranted "reasonable suspicion," the type of documents these individuals are expected to carry, and the outcomes of stops. A few of the complaints include a brief summary of the incident in question. Not all complaints recorded by the government officials are complete, but as documentary practices of agencies of control, the data reveal everyday processes of ruling apparatus in low-income Latino communities (Smith 1990, 1999). Although only 71 individuals made formal complaints, 91 complaints were filed because each incident was documented as a separate complaint—a number of individuals were stopped more than once. I coded each of the 91 complaints, looking for patterns of immigration enforcement, including ethnicity of complainant, age, citizenship status, sex, activity engaged in at the time of the stop, request for identification, and outcomes of the stop.

Narratives are also an important source of data for identifying micro- and macro-aggressions and petit apartheid restricting citizenship rights, freedom of movement, and use of public and private urban space. Two types of narratives were coded. First, the narrative of the reports itself. This included setting up the story of the Chandler Roundup (what is the context selected as background information to the raid?), an explanation of Mexican immigration requiring a joint operation between Chandler Police Department and INS (how is the problem defined?), and, the justification for using racial profiling (why were low-income Mexican Americans stopped and searched?). The second type of narrative appears in the Attorney General's Report. These are summaries of witness accounts and detailed descriptions of incidents documented by the police in their radio-dispatch reports. Witness accounts were coded for verbal and non-verbal racial affronts against individuals and against "Mexicanness" in general. Radio-dispatch reports were coded for incidents of racial profiling and regulation of movement and activity. In order to explore micro- and micro-aggressions and the existence of processes and structures of petit apartheid in immigration raids, witness accounts and police records were coded for discriminatory practices ranging from the covert and informal to the overt and formal.

My analysis focuses first on identifying the distinct differences in each report for explaining the occurrence of a Joint Operation between the Chandler Police and the INS. I begin with the *Report of Independent Investigation*'s narration of Mexican immigration as a problem requiring the immediate attention of the Chandler Police. Next, I contrast this with the community's depiction of Mexican immigration as a problem constructed by the Chandler City Council's urban-renewal project, Operation Restoration. I then turn to a quantitative analysis of data from the complaints complied in Volume II of the *Report of Independent Investigation*. A qualitative analysis of witness accounts from the Attorney General's Report follows. Here, I analyze the ways that citizenship is policed and the impact this form of policing has on freedom of movement and use of urban space.

◈ Narrating Mexican Immigration as a Problem

Considering that the USA acquired Arizona as a result of the Mexican-American War, and that the Chandler area is the homeland of the Tohono O'Odham Nation, the version of history narrated in the *Report of Independent Investigation*'s (Breen et al. 1998:1) is clearly biased and self serving: "Chandler, Arizona is a city of about 160,000 that has blossomed in slightly more than a century from a seed planted by Alexander Chandler, who came to Arizona in 1887 as territorial veterinary surgeon." The first mention of Mexicans in the narrative describes their presence as workers and Anglos as employers:

> In the first years after the town's founding, cotton became the crop of choice for central Arizona farmers. These were the years of the Mexican Revolution, and thousands of Mexicans streamed northward to escape the violence spawned by it. Labor-intensive cotton farming provided a way for those fleeing the revolution to earn a living. Thus began a marriage between Chandler and those of Hispanic heritage that has lasted till the present day. (Breen et al. 1998:1)

This seeming "marriage" involved Mexicans providing the labor and Americans (read whites) providing the land from which the cotton was to be harvested. Mexican presence is also noted during WWII in reference to the Bracero Program: "the Arizona Farm Bureau approved the importation of Mexican workers, who found themselves harvesting cotton alongside German prisoners of war in the labor-starved market" (Breen et al. 1998:2).

The narrative continues by describing the "streams" that turn into the present "hordes" of Mexican immigrants entering the area. "Ron Sanders, chief patrol agent for the Border Patrol's Tucson sector, calls Chandler 'the most notorious hub for alien smuggling in the United States of America'" . . . until "literally thousands" of illegal aliens were in Chandler (Breen et al. 1998:2). INS intelligence in Dallas is the source for citing Chandler "as a major smuggling area as far south as Honduras and El Salvador" (Breen et al. 1998:2). The narrative continues with a litany from a handful of growers who complained about garbage, use of water, stolen fruit, and violence. To reinforce immigration as a social problem, the report lists six "homicides allegedly committed by illegal aliens" dating back to 1982 (Breen et al. 1998:10). In 1997, the Casa Grande Border Patrol station began targeting operations in groves. According to the Chandler Police, complaints about harassment of citizens and an increase in crime led to a series of joint actions in the summer of 1997. No doubt the federal government's Operations Gatekeeper, Hold-the-Line, and other steps in militarizing the USA-Mexico border, gave local authorities in Chandler tacit approval to engage in the Joint Operation.

However, the Attorney General's *Survey* argues that another chain of events led up to the Joint Operation. Based on community protests voiced at meetings and interviews given to the media, the beginning of the "immigration problem" is not dated to the founding of the city but rather to the City of Chandler's 1995 urban-renewal project, Operation Restoration. City Council members began Operation Restoration by creating a task force to study issues affecting residents. The Neighborhood Empowerment Team conducted several mail-in surveys and held neighborhood meetings. Their final report found that residents were concerned about broken streetlights, uncollected garbage, trash in the streets, and unkempt alleys. From its inception,

Operation Restoration targeted four older neighborhoods in the city located next to the newly developed downtown area. The targeted areas had the highest percentage of Latinos and low-income residents in the City. Claiming the Joint Operation was about redevelopment, City Council member Martin Sepulveda argued that the Mayor's dream of transforming Chandler into "'The jewel of the East Valley' would push out poor Hispanics" (Office of the Attorney General 1997:5). Operation Restoration was perceived by the Mexican-American community as urban renewal to create high-income real estate and zoning for strip malls, which would dislocate residents and raise land value beyond the reaches of local businesses.

In response to the community's accusation that the immigration sweep was a Mexican-American removal program, the *Report* stated that the Chandler Police involvement was merely "to undertake intensive zoning code enforcement and . . . step up patrol of the area" (Breen et al. 1998:14). Although the independent investigators acknowledged that the Neighborhood Empowerment Team's report was limited to repairing and cleaning the surrounding area, they accepted the police department's claim that the Joint Operation with INS was conducted as their part in implementing Operation Restoration. Since Operation Restoration had already targeted "the downtown redevelopment zone, ranging from an eight-block to a four square mile area," using similar parameters for the roundup was justified and did not discriminate against Latinos.

The Attorney General's Office refuted this claim and argued that the Task Force's final report did not include reference to, or recommendations about undocumented immigrants. Importantly, the Office of the Attorney General (1997:14) found that the area targeted for the raid was "without specific articulated criminal activity." Drawing from community meetings, the Attorney General's *Survey* includes the community standpoint primarily from Latinos. They perceived the redevelopment of the downtown area as the major incentive behind the raid. Operation Restoration became a defining moment in their memory of Chandler's history when "Mexicanness" was perceived as undesirable, even as cheap labor.

The careful selection of terms used in the documents evokes associations, meanings, and images

supporting political spectacle (Edelman 2001). In order to establish undocumented Mexican immigration as an increasingly dangerous problem, the independent investigators erased Mexican Americans (and the Tohono O'Odham people) from local history. Restricting Mexican presence to discussions of "immigrants," "laborers," and "criminals" made American citizens of Mexican ancestry invisible. The terms "streams" and "hordes" found in the *Independent Investigation Report* in reference to the movement of people crossing the USA-Mexico border is consistent with the alarmist terminology noted by a number of immigration scholars (Chavez 2001; Santa Ana 2002). Mexican Americans are not mentioned in the *Report* as citizens or as long-term residents in the area but rather in the non-human category of "alien" (Johnson 1997). In the *Report,* Mexican Americans are always referred to in the present tense and only as "Hispanic." Mexican is always used as a term for the unauthorized, extralegal, or undocumented.

 ## Policing Citizenship, Movement and the Use of Urban Space

The policing of citizenship by the Chandler Roundup exemplified procedures used to determine status and urban spaces that require regulation. The focus on policing was the redevelopment area targeted under Operation Restoration; that is, the cultural space inhabited by the large Latino population, low-income residents, and a commercial area serving a Spanish-speaking clientele. However, the image of citizenship visible in the discretionary stops suggests that beyond geography, the landscape of suspicion was embodied in particular behavior and appearance. Complaints made against the Chandler Police make visible the type of persons suspected as unauthorized and thus requiring surveillance. Requests for various types of identification reveal surveillance and restraint of movement in public areas. Embedded in witness accounts are the aesthetics of authority that enforce exclusionary use of public urban space, remaking the Mexican cultural space into white space. The material consequences of policing reinforce the vulnerability of undocumented workers in the local economy; place low-income, racialized citizens at risk before the law; and legitimate discriminatory behavior towards persons under surveillance.

◈ Complainants Analysis

Analysis of the data in the 91 complaints indicates specific patterns of racial and ethnic typing used in the Joint Operation. Data show that cultural and class behavior or activity was only monitored in targeted locations. The dominant feature of identifiable complainants was their racial ethnic background; all were of Mexican ancestry or Latino.[9] Fourteen of the complainants were stopped more than once during the five-day raid. Complainants ranged in age from 16 to 75; 49 were male and 22 were female. The majority of males were between 18 and 39 years old and the majority of females were between the ages of 30 and 49. Complaints for 42 complainants contained the following information: 11 were US citizens of Mexican ancestry, 15 were Latino legal residents, 1 was a permanent resident, 3 had work permits, 1 had a green card, and 11 were undocumented. There is no documentation in the reports or in the newspaper coverage of a white person stopped during the raid. Ironically, one newspaper quoted a blond, blue-eyed, undocumented Irish immigrant employed at a local law firm as stating that she had never been asked to show proof of her citizenship status: "I don't have to worry. I blend in very well" (Amparano 1997:A1).

The phrase "driving while black" became familiar in debates over racial profiling, similarly the experience of "walking/driving/biking/standing while brown" is common for Mexican Americans in the vicinity of an immigration raid or during national sweeps, such as Operation Wetback in 1954 (Calavita 1992) or Operation Jobs in 1995 (US Attorney General Report 1995). The activities recorded in the complaints are accurately captured in the media's initial reporting of Mexican Americans' experience during the five-day immigration raid: "As they walked down sidewalks, drove cars or walked outside their homes" they were stopped by the police (Amparano 1997). Based primarily on interviews with police officers assigned to the target area during the operation (few Border Patrol agents agreed to be interviewed), the independent investigators found that illegal aliens were arrested in residential areas, in front of stores

(especially the local Circle K), in trailer courts, and driving between 4:00 and 6:00 AM (the time many workers are traveling to construction sites during the summer).

The wide net that was cast made it inevitable that citizens and legal residents would be stopped by the police. The complaints indicate that, when proof of citizenship status was requested by law-enforcement agents, 33 of the 91 were driving, 24 were walking in their neighborhood or to a nearby store, 17 were at home, 10 were shopping (most were approached in the parking lot or in front of stores), 3 were riding bikes, and 2 were using public telephones. Significantly, only 2 were approached at their place of employment, suggesting the tacit desire to protect employers from possible sanctions. Specific activities are significant when class-based racial profiling is occurring. As in most urban areas, being a pedestrian is a sign of poverty. Middle and upper classes rarely walk or bike in Arizona heat unless they are engaged in exercise and dressed in special "work-out" clothes. They might be observed walking if a leashed dog is attached to their bodies. Using a public telephone is a similar sign of poverty when most homes in the US have several phones as well as cell phones.

After the stops were made, investigators documented only 33 outcomes for the 91 incidents. Of the 33 outcomes documented in the complaints, 23 were detained. Three of the people detained were illegal and twenty were legal. Four of those detained were handcuffed, including one US citizen. The period that the 23 were detained ranged from five minutes to four hours. Some of those detained for long periods of time reported that they stood in the 100+ degree weather common in July. After they showed proof of legal status, three complainants were issued citations for minor traffic violations (e.g., a rolling stop at a stop sign, a broken windshield, a missing headlamp, or a turn into the wrong lane).

Eighty-six claims involved law enforcement agents requesting proof of citizenship status. However, the kinds of documents requested were inconsistent, at times vague, and confusing to US citizens who had never been stopped before—51 incidents involved officers requesting to see the person's "papers" or *"papeles,"* 2 incidents involved requests for immigration papers, 13 incidents requested drivers license, 9 were asked to show "an identification," 10 were asked specifically for their green cards, and 1 officer requested to see "a card." Birth certificates, Social Security cards, green cards, or driver licenses were produced by the claimants before the police allowed them to leave. In some cases, particularly for children and adolescents, family members assisted in obtaining documents.

◈ Witness Accounts Analysis

Based on the writings of immigration-critical race legal scholars (i.e., Benitiez 1994; Chang and Aoki 1997; Johnson 2000, 2004; Vargas 2001), I identified five patterns of immigration law enforcement that placed Mexican Americans at risk: (1) discretionary stops based on ethnicity and class; (2) use of intimidation to demean and subordinate persons stopped; (3) restricting the freedom of movement of Mexicans but not others in the same vicinity; (4) reinforced stereotypes of Mexican as "alien," "foreign," inferior and criminal; and (5) limited access to fair and impartial treatment before the law. Recurring expressions that witnesses used to describe stops and searches were pain and humiliation, frightened, fearful, nervous, scared, embarrassed, violated, and mortified. Witness accounts offer descriptive narratives of the micro- and macro-aggressions occurring in immigration law enforcement.

Embedded in all the accounts is the recognition that they were stopped, questioned, and inspected by the police because their physical appearance was classified by law enforcement agents as "Mexican" and, thus, they were assumed to be unauthorized to be in the US. Skin color is used in the everyday immigration law-enforcement practice of operationalizing "reasonable suspicion":

> T was stopped and questioned by Chandler police and INS/Border Patrol when he stopped at a Circle K . . . The Chandler Police were stopping every "Mexican-looking" person as they entered or exited the store. "Non Mexican-looking" people entered and exited without being stopped. (Office of Attorney General Wood 1997:22)

An excerpt from witness account "D" demonstrates community members' recognition of INS and police officers' "discretion," as well as their power to violate civil rights.

> All the people shopping at this shopping center appeared to be Hispanic and many were being stopped and questioned by the officers. D and his uncle were conversing in Spanish and leaving the store with a package when they were approached by a Chandler police officer and an INS/Border Patrol agent on bicycles. The INS/Border Patrol agent asked them in Spanish for their papers. The uncle, who had just become a United States citizen, had his citizenship papers with him and showed those to the officer. D had only a social security card and a driver's license . . . D took his wallet from his pocket to get his identification; the INS/Border Patrol officer then asked him for the wallet and examined everything in it. D feared that if he did not give the officer his wallet he would be arrested. Neither officer wrote any information down or kept anything from the wallet. No explanation was given for the stop (Office of Attorney General Wood 1997:21).

Although "D" is a US citizen, he understood that he does not have the same rights as whites and has limited access to fair dealings before the law. He was intimidated by the INS officer extending the citizenship inspection beyond his driver's license and Social Security card and into his personal belongings without a search warrant or a basis for probable cause.

"U" provided a description of an incident involving a person who questioned stops without probable cause and police discretion.

> U has a permit to work in the United States and is here legally . . . he and his cousin stopped at a Circle K . . . While they were parking their car, they were approached by a Chandler police officer on a bicycle who asked, in Spanish, for their papers. The cousin said that the police had no right to ask for papers and the Chandler police officer asked if they wanted him to call Immigration. They said yes and INS/Border patrol agents soon appeared. The cousin showed the agents his papers but U did not have his on him and

when he showed them his social security card, there was a discrepancy in the computer and they were told the number had been canceled. The INS/Border Patrol agent said "I'm tired of this, everybody lies and says they have papers when they don't." The officers put U in handcuffs, searched him and took him to the Chandler Police Station where he was detained. He asked them to give him a chance to call his home and have his wife bring his papers but they refused. He was held until about 11:30 (from 7 p.m.) until his cousin and his wife brought his papers to the police station. U was afraid that the Chandler police were going to take his green card away, or that he was going to be separated from his family. (Office of Attorney General Wood 1997:23)

"U" assumed protection and rights that his work permit grants and distinguished between city police officers and the INS. However, his attempt to assert his rights resulted in the use of excessive force and he was treated like a violent criminal requiring physical restraint. His account points to extensive discretionary power given to immigration law enforcement; the incident exemplified intimidation, excessive force, and the lack of probable cause in the police stop.

Since the downtown redevelopment zone targeted in the roundup was not completely racially segregated, discretionary stops of persons of Mexican ancestry who appear to be poor or working class became visible. Public areas like stores, phone booths, and gas stations produced a spectacle for white gaze and allowed the immigration inspectors to employ stereotypes of Mexicans as foreign, alien, and criminal. However, appearances of class and citizenship can be deceiving as the following witness testimony reveals.

C is the highest ranked left handed golfer in Arizona. C is a large, dark completed, Hispanic, and native born Arizonan . . . Returning from a golf match in July, he stopped . . . for a cold drink and saw Chandler police officers talking to different people of apparent Mexican descent. At the time he was wearing an old tee shirt and a baseball cap. As he tried to exit the market, he was barred exit by a Chandler Police officer who asked if he was a local, if he had papers, and whether he was a citizen. C told the officer that he was a citizen and was leaving and the officer told him "No, you are not." C then walked around the officer and went over to his car which was a 1997 Acura. The officer followed him but when he saw what car he was driving, permitted him to drive off. . . . (Office of Attorney General Wood 1997:21)

Clearly "C" assumed "class privilege," challenging the officer's attempt to stop and search without probable cause. This account demonstrates the significance of class in immigration law enforcement. Once middle- and upper-middle-class status is identified by officers, police are less likely to violate civil rights.

In response to the extraordinary policing, community members avoided public areas. Witnesses reported that elderly neighbors feared the police, asking for assistance in obtaining food and medication so they could remain home, behind closed doors. Law enforcement agents' treatment of Mexicans thus deterred civic participation and shaped the field of action that Latinos perceived as available to them (Davis et al. 2001; Nelson 2001). By the fifth day of the operation, the community avoided local grocery stores and gas stations that had been heavily patrolled by the police and INS. Mexican shop owners complained that they lost revenue during the raid because their customers feared shopping in the area. In the absence of people in the streets and shopping areas, the police developed alternative strategies that included homes and construction sites.

Alongside stores with the largest number of Latino customers, the second major target areas were apartment complexes and trailer courts occupied by low-income Mexican Americans and Mexican immigrants. In a newspaper interview with a Chandler police officer, the claim was made that they did not bust "down doors in search of illegal immigrants." Witness accounts provide a counter narrative. Not only were neighborhoods in the targeted area searched house by house but apartment and trailer court managers assisted Chandler Police by identifying residents of Mexican descent. The following testimony describes the intimidation and demeaning actions used by law enforcement agents.

On July 28, 1997, at approximately 11 P.M., B and his family were sound asleep in a trailer owned by his brother-in-law . . . The family was wakened by a loud banging on the front door and bright lights shining through the windows. When B looked around, he saw two Chandler police officers, with an INS/Border patrol agent behind them. All officers were bicycle officers. The officers demanded to be allowed into the trailer and when B asked if they had the right to come in, he was told "We can do whatever we want, we are the Chandler Police Department. You have people who are here illegally." Although B denied that there were any undocumented aliens there, the officers insisted on entering the trailer, rousing everyone from bed. The family members were all in their sleep clothes, but the officers refused to allow them to dress. None of the children were United States citizens, and except for the brother-in-law, all the rest were legal aliens; the brother-in-law had entered the country legally but his visa had expired and he was in the process of getting it renewed. When the officers discovered that the brother-in-law did not have proper papers, they called a Chandler Police Department back up vehicle and took him away in a patrol car. B attempted to give his brother-in-law street clothes when the officers were taking him away, but the officers would not allow this and took him away in his sleep clothes. He was later readmitted to the United States with the renewed visa he had been awaiting. The others were detained in the trailer for approximately ninety minutes; they were not searched but they were questioned even after they showed the papers demonstrating that they were legally in the United States. The police told B that they had spoken with the park manager and he had given them permission to search the trailers, had given them a map, and had marked on the map where Hispanic residents lived. The four children involved in this incident are still fearful when someone knocks at the door of the trailer, and continue to be nervous when they see police officers on the street. . . . Most

of the police visits occurred between 10 p.m. and 11 p.m. and were precipitated by police banging on doors and windows and shining lights through the windows. . . . Every night someone else was taken away. (Office of Attorney General Wood 1997:19–20)

Home searches conducted in the presence of children serve as powerful socialization, teaching them about their lack of rights, inferior status, and unequal access to protection under the law. For many children, the house searches were probably their first encounter with a police officer, and they witnessed their parents, grandparents, and other family elders humiliated and treated as criminals. Witnessing stops and searches serves as an important lesson for children that the law distinguishes between family and neighbors on the basis of immigration status rather than criminal activity that harms others. Unlike stops made at shopping centers, house-to-house searches conducted on private property concealed civil and human rights violations from public view.

In addition to the house-to-house searches conducted, apartment complexes and trailer courts were also targeted for traffic enforcement. Several officers' interview summaries acknowledged that, outside of special D.U.I. enforcement, the Chandler Roundup was the first time they used traffic enforcement with a spotter. Vehicles leaving specific housing units that appeared to contain "migrant workers" were followed. Several officers reported that they "were to follow them and if probable cause was established" the vehicle was stopped. Officers were "instructed to issue a citation for the probable cause in case there was a question in reference to the stop." A summary of radio-dispatch transcripts for July 29, 1997, demonstrated that laborers driving to work were targeted as vehicles left apartment complexes housing low-income Mexican Americans and Mexican immigrants:

The vehicles were described by make, model and/or color, as well as direction of travel. A total of forty-three (43) vehicles were specially singled out in a two hour period of time from 4:00 to 6:00 A.M. The officers identified seven (7) vehicles because of known violations of law warranting a stop. However, of the remaining thirty-six (36) vehicles called in, seven (7) calls describing vehicles were made despite the officers stating that there was no probable cause to believe that violations of the law had occurred. The other twenty-nine (29) vehicles were singled out without articulation of what, if any, violation of law may have been observed by the reporting officer. (Office of Attorney General Wood 1997:10)

Both the *Survey* and *Report* note that the Chandler Roundup extended to construction sites and permission from supervisors at the construction sites was obtained before entering the area to question employees. Even though the police arrested undocumented workers at construction sites, neither report cited employers' violation of the law. IRCA includes employer sanctions designating penalties for employers who hire immigrants not authorized to work in the United States. While citizenship and movement of laborers were clearly documented in both reports, there is a glaring absence of enforcement of employers' compliance with IRCA. Although questioning workers at a construction site resulted in 52 arrests, no employer suffered legal sanctions for IRCA violations. Nowhere in the Attorney General's *Survey,* or in the independent investigator's *Report,* is there a mention of employers at construction sites being investigated.

◈ Conclusion

While legal scholars, civil rights advocates, and the general public denounced federal law enforcement practices towards Muslims and persons of Middle-Eastern descent under the Patriot Act, racialized immigration stops and searches, abuse, and harassment are ongoing processes honed over a century of citizenship inspections of Mexicans. Immigration policing is based on determining that citizenship is visibly inscribed on bodies in specific urban spaces rather than "probable cause." In the Chandler Roundup, official investigations found no evidence that stops and searches were based on probable cause of criminal activity. The conclusion drawn by the Attorney General's investigation underscores the harms of micro- and macro-aggressions and the use of petit apartheid:

. . . there were no other warrants, charges, or holds for these individuals that in any way indicated other criminal activity or that required extraordinary security or physical force. The issue raised by this type of treatment is not whether the arrest and deportation is legal, but whether human beings are entitled to some measure of dignity and safety even when they are suspected of being in the United States illegally. (1997:28–9)

The Chandler Roundup fits into a larger pattern of immigration law-enforcement practices that produce harms of reduction and repression and place Mexican Americans at risk before the law and designate them as second-class citizens with inferior rights. Latino residents in Chandler experienced racial affronts targeted at their "Mexicanness" indicated by skin color, bilingual speaking abilities, or shopping in neighborhoods highly populated by Latinos. During immigration inspections, individuals stopped were demeaned, humiliated, and embarrassed. Stops and searches conducted without cause were intimidating and frightening, particularly when conducted with discretionary use of power and force by law enforcement agents.

Like other metropolitan areas surrounding Phoenix, Chandler depends heavily upon low-wage, non-union, undocumented Mexican workers for their tourism and construction industries. These powerful business interests are influential at the state level, and cooperative efforts are made to assure seasonal labor needs are met. Both official investigations into the Chandler Roundup demonstrate complete disregard for enforcing sanctions of employers under IRCA. Yet the ability to clearly identify the everyday work patterns of immigrants and to use these circumstances to arrest immigrants as undocumented workers indicate that employers operate with complete immunity to IRCA provisions. The case of the Chandler Roundup demonstrates how INS enforcement practices not only favor and protect employers' access to an exploitable labor force, but remove or relocate workers as specific industries' needs warrant. Enforcement is structured specifically at eliminating and relocating undocumented workers from areas no longer relevant to the local economy or redevelopment plans. The Chandler Roundup was intended to remove a low-income population to allow for urban renewal, by creating a hostile environment for citizens, violating their civil rights through immigration law enforcement employing micro- and macro-aggressions. Racialized immigration stops establish, maintain, and reinforce second-class citizenship and limit civil, political, economic, and cultural rights and opportunities. In urban barrios, the costly enterprise of selected stops and searches, race-related police abuse, and harassment results in deterring political participation, in identifying urban space racially, in classifying immigrants as deserving and undeserving by nationalities, and serves to drive a wedge dividing Latino neighborhoods on the basis of citizenship status.

◈ Notes

1. Unlike the census categories, which make a distinction between race and ethnicity for the category "Hispanic," and restricting race to black and white, law enforcement clearly uses the ethnic descriptors of Mexican and Hispanic to identify an individual's physical characteristics. Therefore, this study makes a distinction between Latinos who can racially pass as white and those who are socially constructed (but nevertheless have real consequences) as racially distinct from whites or blacks (Romero 2001).

2. An example is assuming that a Mexican American cannot speak English or that she is the secretary, rather than a faculty member in the department.

3. Richard J. Herrnstein and Charles Murray's (1994) claims of Blacks' mental inferiority espoused in their book, *The Bell Curve,* is a prime example of a macro-aggression that has received an extensive news coverage.

4. Background information is based on media coverage from local newspapers, community meetings, and the minutes from Chandler City Council Meeting[s].

5. The summary of the survey includes a detailed description of the Chandler Redevelopment Initiative developed by the City Council. The survey describes the Initiative's efforts and its connection to the joint operation carried out in areas with the highest concentration of Latino residents; INS protocols for joint operation; description of day-to-day activities based on Border Patrol documents; summary of witness accounts regarding children and schools, home contacts, and contacts around businesses, because these were areas that the police and public officials claimed were not included in the raid; and descriptions of the types of request made for the proof of citizenship.

6. The narrative offers a history of the City of Chandler and describes the development of immigration issues as a social problem

that led to the joint operation. A description of the operation and the aftermath of community meetings, complaints, and lawsuits is also included.

7. Interviews were conducted with the police who participated in the joint operation, supervisors and officers involved with processing illegal aliens, Border Patrol agents, City Council members, and Chandler city officials.

8. Excerpts describe the duties of city officials and the Chandler Police Department, a summary of line of authority in the city, and a description of the structure and duties of the US Border Patrol.

9. Citizenship status in not recorded for 29 complainants (involved in 41 stops).

◈ References

ACUÑA, RODOLFO

2000 *Occupied America.* New York, NY: Longman.

AMPARANO, JULIE

1997 "Brown Skin: No Civil rights? July Sweep on Chandler Draws Fire." *Arizona Republic* August 15:B1.

ANDREAS, PETER

2000 *Border Games, Policing the U.S.-Mexico Divide.* Ithaca, NY: Cornell University Press.

ARRIOLA, ELVIA R.

1996–97 "LatCrit Theory, International Human Rights, Popular Culture, and the Faces of Despair in INS Raids." *University of Miami Inter-American Law Review* 28:245–62.

BASS, SANDRA

2001 "Out of Place: Petit Apartheid and the Police." Pp. 43–54 in *Petit Apartheid in the U.S. Criminal Justice System, The Dark Figure of Racism,* edited by Dragan Milovanovic and Katheryn Russell. Durham, NC: Carolina Academic Press.

BENITEZ, HUMBERTO

1994 "Flawed Strategies: The INS Shift from Border Interdiction to Internal Enforcement Actions." *La Raza Law Journal* 7:154–79.

BREEN, THOMAS, SERGIO MURETA, AND JOHN WINTERS

1998 *Report of Independent Investigation Into July 1997 Joint Operation Between Patrol and Chandler Police Department.* Vol. I, II, and III, Chandler, Arizona: The City of Chandler.

CALAVITA, KITTY

1992 *Inside the State, The Bracero Program, Immigration, and the I.N.S.* New York, NY: Routledge.

CALDEIRA, TERESA P. R.

2000 *City of Walls: Crime, Segregation, and Citizenship in São Paulo.* Berkeley, CA: University of California Press.

CAMPBELL, JACKIE

2001 "Walking the Beat Alone: An African American Police Officer's Perspective on Petit Apartheid." Pp. 15–20 in *Petit Apartheid in the U.S. Criminal Justice System, The Dark Figure of Racism,* edited by Dragan Milovanovic and Katheryn Russell. Durham, NC: Carolina Academic Press.

CHANG, ROBERT S.

1999 *Disoriented: Asian Americans, Law, and the Nation-State.* New York, NY: New York University Press.

CHANG, ROEBRT S. AND KETIH AOKI

1997 "Centering the Immigrant in the Inter/National Imagination." *California Law Review* 85:1395–1447.

CHAVEZ, LEO R.

2001 *Covering Immigration, Popular Images and the Politics of the Nation.* Berkeley, CA: University of California Press.

CORNELIUS, WAYNE A.

2001 "Death at the Border: Efficacy and Unintended Consequences of US Immigration Control Policy." *Population and Development Review* 27(4):661–85.

COVINGTON, JEANETTE

2001 "Round Up the Usual Suspects: Racial Profiling and the War on Drugs." Pp. 27–42 in *Petit Apartheid in the U.S. Criminal Justice System, The Dark Figure of Racism,* edited by Dragan Milovanovic and Katheryn Russell. Durham, NC: Carolina Academic Press.

DAVIS, ROBERT C., EDNA EREZ, AND NANCY AVITABILE

2001 "Access to Justice for Immigrants who are Victimized: The Perspectives of Police and Prosecutors." *Criminal Justice Policy Review* 12(3):183–96.

DUNN, TIMOTHY J.

1996 *The Militarization of the U.S.-Mexico Border.* Austin, TX: CMAS Books, University of Texas at Austin.

EDELMAN, MURRAY

2001 *The Politics of Misinformation.* New York, NY: Cambridge University Press.

ESCHBACH, KARL, JACQUELINE HAGEN, NESTOR RODRIGUES, RÚBEN HERNÁNDEZ-LEÓN, and STANLEY BARILEY

1999 "Death and the Border." *International Migration Review* 33(2):430–54.

FERRELL, JEFF

2001a *Tearing Down the Streets: Adventures in Urban Anarchy.* New York, NY: Palgrave Macmillan.

2001b "Trying to Make Us a Parking Lot: Petit Apartheid, Culture Space, and the Public Negotiation of Ethnicity." Pp. 55–68 in *Petit Apartheid in the U.S. Criminal Justice System, The Dark Figure of Racism,* edited by Dragan Milovanovic and Katheryn Russell. Durham, NC: Carolina Academic Press.

FLETCHER, MICHAEL A.

1997 "Police in Arizona Accused of Civil Rights Violations; Lawsuit Cites Sweep Aimed at Illegal Immigrants." *Washington Post* August 20:A14.

GARCIA, JUAN RAMON

1980 *Operation Wetback: The Mass Deportation of Mexican Undocumented Workers in 1954.* Westport, CT: Greenwood Press.

GEORGES-ABEYIE, DANIEL E.

1990 "Criminal Justice Processing of Non-White Minorities." Pp. 25–34 in *Racism, Empiricism and Criminal Justice,* edited by Brian D. MacLean and Dragan Milovanovic. Vancouver, BC: The Collective Press.

HARVEY, DAVID

1973 *Social Justice and the City.* Baltimore, MD: John[s] Hopkins University Press.

1996 *Justice, Nature, and the Geography of Difference.* Oxford, UK: Blackwell.

HENRY, STUART AND DRAGAN MILOVANOVIC

1999 *Constitutive Criminology.* London: Sage Publications.

HERRNSTEIN, RICHARD J. AND CHARLES MURRAY

1994 *The B[e]ll Curve: Intelligence and Class Structure in American Life.* New York, NY: Free Press.

JEYMAN, JOSIAH McC.

1995 "Putting Power in the Anthropology of Bureaucracy: The Immigration and Naturalization Service and the Mexico-United States Border." *Current Anthropology* 36(2):261–87.

HING, BILL ONG

1997 *To Be An American.* New York, NY: New York University Press.

HOLSTON, JAMES (ED.)

1999 *Citizens and Citizenship.* Durham, NC: Duke University Press.

JOHNSON, KEVIN

1993 "Los Olvidados: Images of the Immigrant, Political Power of Noncitizens, and Immigrant Law and Enforcement." *Binghamton Young University Law Review* 1993:1139–1241.

1997 "Racial Hierarchy, Asian Americans and Latinos as 'Foreigners,' and Social Change: Is Law the Way to Go?" *Oregon Law Review* 76(2):347–67.

2000 "The Case Against Race Profiling in Immigration Enforcement." *Washington University Law Quarterly* 78(3):676–736.

2002 "Race and the Immigration Laws: The Need for Critical Inquiry." Pp. 187–98 in *Crossroads, Directions, and a New Critical Race Theory,* edited by Francisco Valdez, Jerome McCristal Culp, and Angela P. Harris. Philadelphia, PA: Temple University Press.

JOHNSON, SHERI LYNN

2001 "Racial Derogation in Prosecutors' Closing Arguments." Pp. 79–102 in *Petit Apartheid in the U.S. Criminal Justice System, The Dark Figure of Racism,* edited by Dragan Milovanovic and Katheryn Russell. Durham, NC: Carolina Academic Press.

LAZOS VARGAS, SYLVIA R.

2002 "'Latina/o-ization' of the Midwest: *Cambio de Colores* (Change of Colors) as *Agromaquilas* Expand into the Heartland." *Berkeley la Raza Law Journal* 13(113):343–68.

LEE, YUEH-TING, VICTOR OTTATI, AND IMTIAZ HUSSAIN

2001 "Attitudes Towards Illegal Immigration into the United States: California Proposition 187." *Hispanic Journal of Behavioral Sciences* 23(4):430–43.

LEFEBVRE, HENRI

1996 "The Right to the City." Pp. 63–181, in *Writings on Cities,* edited and translated by E. Kofman and E. Lebas. Oxford, UK: Blackwell.

MASSEY, DOUGLAS S., JORGE DURAND, AND NOLAN J. MALONE

2002 *Beyond Smoke and Mirrors: Mexican Immigration in an Era of Economic Integration.* New York, NY: Russell Sage Foundation.

MATSUDA, MARI J., CHARLES R. LAWRENCE III, RICHARD DELGADO, AND KIMBERLÈ W. CRENSHAW
1993 *Words That Wound: Critical Race Theory, Assaultive Speech, and the First Amendment.* Boulder, CO: Westview Press.

MEHAN, HUGH
1997 "The Discourse of the Illegal Immigration Debate: A Case Study in the Politics of Representation," *Discourse & Society* 8(2): 249–70.

MILOVANOVIC, DRAGAN AND KATHERYN RUSSELL (EDS.)
2001 *Petit Apartheid in the U.S. Criminal Justice System, The Dark Figure of Racism.* Durham, NC: Carolina Academic Press.

MITCHELL, DON
2003 *The Right to the City: Social Justice and the Fight for Public Space.* New York, NY: The Guilford Press.

NELSON, HILDE LINDEMANN
2001 *Damaged Identities, Narrative Repair.* Ithaca, NY: Cornell University Press.

NEVINS, JOSEPH
2002 *Operation Gatekeeper, The Rise of the "Illegal Alien" and the Making of the U.S.-Mexico Boundary.* New York, NY: Routledge.

Office of the ATTORNEY GENERAL GRANT WOOD
1997 *Results of the Chandler Survey.* Phoenix, State of Arizona.

PIERCE, CHESTER M., JEAN V. CAREW, DOAMA PIERCE-GONZALEZ, AND DEBORAH WILLIS
1978 "An Experiment in Racism: TV Commercials." Pp. 62–88 in *Television and Education,* edited by Chester Pierce. Beverly Hills, CA: Sage Publications.

ROMERO, MARY
2001 "State Violence, and the Social and Legal Construction of Latino Criminality: From Bandido to Gang Member." *Denver University Law Review* 78(4):1081–1118.

ROSS, LEE E.
2001 "African-American Interest in Law Enforcement: A Consequence of Petit Apartheid?" Pp. 69–78 in *Petit Apartheid*

in the U.S. Criminal Justice System, The Dark Figure of Racism, edited by Dragan Milovanovic and Katheryn Russell. Durham, NC: Carolina Academic Press.

RUSSELL, KATHERYN K.
1998 *The Color of Crime: Racial Hoaxes, White Fear, Black Protectionism, Police Harassment and Other Macroaggressions.* New York, NY: New York University Press.

SÁENZ, BENJAMIN ALIRE
1992 *Flowers for the Broken: Stories.* Seattle, WA: Broken Moon Press.

SANTA ANA, OTTO
2002 *Brown Tide Rising, Metaphors of Latinos in Contemporary American Public Discourse.* Austin, TX: University of Texas Press.

SMITH, DOROTHY E.
1990 *Texts, Facts, and Femininity: Exploring the Relations of Ruling.* New York, NY: Routledge.

1999 *Writing the Social: Critique, Theory, and Investigations.* Toronto, ON: The University of Toronto Press.

U.S. ATTORNEY GENERAL['S] OFFICE
1995 "Securing America's Borders," in 1995 annual Report of the Attorney General of the United States. Retrieved January 4, 2004 (http://www.usdoj.gov/ag/annualreports/ar95/chapter3.htm).

VALDEZ, FRANCISCO, JEROME McCRISTAL CULP, AND ANGELA P. HARRIS (EDS.)
2002 *Crossroads, Directions, and a New Critical Race Theory.* Philadelphia, PA: Temple University Press.

VARGAS, JORGE A.
2001 "U.S. Border Patrol Abuses, Undocumented Mexican Workers, and International Human Rights." *San Diego International Law Review* 2(1):1–92.

WEISSINGER, GEORGE
1996 *Law Enforcement and the INS, A Participant Observation Study of Control Agents.* New York, NY: University Press of America.

CHAPTER **11**

Social Control of Deviance

I will always be a felon...a felon is a term here, obviously it's not a bad term...for me to leave here, it will affect my job, it will affect my education...custody, it can affect child support, it can affect everywhere—family, friends, housing....People that are convicted of drug crimes can't even get housing anymore....Yes, I did my prison time. How long are you going to punish me as a result of it? And not only on paper, I'm only on paper for ten months when I leave here, that's all the parole I have. But that parole isn't going to be anything. It's the housing, it's the credit re-establishing...I mean even to go into the school to work with my child's class—and I'm not even a sex offender—but all I need is one parent who says, "Isn't she a felon? I don't want her with my child." Bingo. And you know that there are people out there like that.

—"Karen," discussing how being labeled a felon will
affect virtually every area of her life, from Manza and Uggen,
Locked Out (2006), p. 152. Copyright © 2006 by Oxford University Press, Inc.

◈ Introduction

The comments above illustrate some of the long-term effects that involvement in deviance can have on individuals, families, and communities. While much of this book so far has focused on different *causes* of deviant behavior, this chapter focuses on societal reactions to deviance and will look in more detail at a few of the varied forms that social control may take. We focused on these ideas a bit in Chapter 8, when looking at labeling theory, but here we offer ideas and examples from different contexts and reiterate the real and lasting consequences of social control.

Philosophers have suggested that human societies are possible because of the **social contract**; the idea is that individuals give up some personal freedoms and abide by general rules of conduct to live in a community and enjoy the protection and companionship of the group (Rousseau, 1987). If most in the group live by the social contract, what is to be done when an individual breaks the contract? How should the community or larger society react to the breach? Should the individual be punished? Once punished, should members of the community be responsible to help the offender reintegrate back into the community?

There are many different forms of social control. One basic distinction is between formal and informal controls. Formal social controls would include hospitalization in a mental ward or rehabilitation facility, expulsion from school, and all types of processing by the criminal justice system, including probation, parole, imprisonment, and fines. Informal controls are often just as powerful, but they are implemented by those around you—your family members, your church, or your peers. If you have ever been given the silent treatment or felt your parents' disappointment, you have experienced informal social control.

As suggested by the critical theorists in Chapter 10, social control and sanctions for deviant behavior are not meted out equally. Recent studies have made clear that the U.S. criminal justice system—and particularly our reliance on mass incarceration—disproportionately affects minorities and the poor and has long-lasting impact on the life chances and opportunities available to individuals, families, and whole communities (Alexander, 2010; Haney, 2010; Pager, 2007; Tonry, 2011; Wacquant, 2000).

◈ Medicalization of Deviant Behavior

We don't always think of medicine as an institution of social control, but just as legal definitions turn some acts into crimes, medical definitions are important in societal conceptions of what is deemed deviant and how such behavior should be managed. Medicalization is "a process by which nonmedical problems become defined and treated as medical problems, usually in terms of illnesses or disorders" (Conrad, 1992, p. 209). There are many examples of medicalized deviant behavior, including mental illness, hyperactivity in children, alcoholism, eating disorders, compulsive gambling, and addiction. It is important to remember that these are social constructions of deviance, and our definitions can and do change over time and vary across cultures.

Medical diagnoses of deviant behavior can have an enormous impact on individuals and communities. Daphne Scholinski's (1997) memoir, *The Last Time I Wore a Dress*, offers an individual perspective on what it is like to spend one's adolescent years in a series of mental hospitals. As a troubled teenage girl, Scholinski was diagnosed with gender identity disorder, which her doctor believed she had developed around the third grade: "He said what this means is you are not an appropriate female, you don't act the way a female is supposed to act" (p. 16).

Scholinski was 14 years old when she was admitted to her first mental hospital; she was released just after her 18th birthday, when her insurance and ability to pay for the treatment ran out. Looking back on the experience, she writes, "One million dollars my treatment cost. Insurance money, but still. Three years in three mental hospitals for girly lessons" (Scholinski, 1997, p. xi). While she was generally happy to be released from her last institution, she occasionally had doubts about her ability to survive and succeed in the community. She wrote, "Sometimes I wish I could return to the hospital. It's ridiculous, I know. But it's hard to figure out everything on my own. In the hospitals, I lost my ability to trust myself" (p. 196). The medicalized diagnosis and treatment of her behavior had undermined her sense of self-efficacy.

Medicalization can take many forms. On the extreme end, individuals can be institutionalized in mental hospitals and/or heavily medicated. They can also be compelled to enter counseling or to join self-help groups; once they admit they have a problem, they can begin working toward a "cure."

An article in a Florida newspaper (Laforgia, 2011) investigated the heavy doses of powerful drugs administered to children in state-operated jails and residential programs. These children were given a lot of antipsychotic medications, which temporarily control behavior but do little to provide meaningful treatment for incarcerated youth. These drugs can also cause suicidal thoughts and have harmful side effects. The reporter writes,

Overall, in 24 months, the department [Florida's Department of Juvenile Justice] bought 326,081 tablets of Seroquel, Abilify, Risperdal and other antipsychotic drugs for use in state-operated jails and homes for

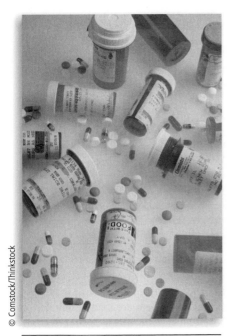

© Comstock/Thinkstock

▲ **Photo 11.1**   The medicalization of social control can include compelling individuals to take heavy doses of prescription drugs.

children. . . . That's enough to hand out 446 pills a day, seven days a week, for two years in a row, to kids in jails and programs that can hold no more than 2,300 boys and girls on a given day.

The changing definitions of deviance can clearly be seen in the field of medicalization. As Conrad (1992) explains, "A key aspect of medicalization refers to the emergence of medical definitions for previously nonmedical problems" (p. 223). While new categories of deviance emerge through medicalization, the process can also work in the opposite direction: Behaviors previously thought to be deviant can be "demedicalized." **Demedicalization** refers to the process in which problems or behaviors no longer retain medical definitions. A vivid example of demedicalization is homosexuality; if you read early textbooks on deviant behavior, you will often see homosexuality included as deviant behavior in need of treatment. Our conceptions of homosexuality changed in American society in the 1970s to the point that it is no longer defined as an illness (Conrad, 1992).

We hope that you can see that while it is often less blatant than the social control practiced by criminal justice agencies, the **medicalization of deviance** has a profound effect on individuals and communities. We now turn to a discussion of social control and surveillance by the criminal justice system.

◈ Policing, Supervision, and the Impact of Incarceration on Disadvantaged Populations and Communities

Several recent studies offer compelling insight into the way that poor and disadvantaged populations and communities are supervised and controlled. In their book *Banished*, Beckett and Herbert (2010) discuss how city laws and ordinances are used to control where and how populations can congregate. Using Seattle as a case study, they describe how individuals—often poor or homeless—may be arrested and then subsequently prohibited from entering or occupying areas associated with drug dealing or prostitution. Beckett and Herbert view banishment as

> an emerging and consequential social control practice . . . banishment is consequential, even more so than the civility codes that they increasingly supplant. Not only do these new tools enable banishment, they provide the police greater license to question and to arrest those who occupy public space. (p. 16)

In an ethnographic study of young African American men in Philadelphia, Alice Goffman (2009) shows how police surveillance, outstanding arrest warrants, and the status of being on probation can affect every part of "wanted" young men's lives. The risk of being captured makes such young men afraid to go to social service agencies; it compels them to keep moving and to stay "on the run" rather than find stable housing.

Alice Goffman (2009) explains the different ways these young men find to resist the formal social control of the state, but despite this, the constant threat and surveillance deeply affects their lives. Their partners are often frustrated by the lack of stability but, at times, also find they can control a particular young man by threatening to call the police on him. She explains why this population faces unique challenges in maintaining conforming relationships.

Young men who are wanted by the police find that activities, relations, and localities that others rely on to maintain a decent and respectable identity are transformed into a system that the authorities make use of to arrest and confine them. The police and the courts become dangerous to interact with, as does showing up to work or going to places like hospitals. Instead of a safe place to sleep, eat, and find acceptance and support, mothers' homes are transformed into a "last known address," one of the first places the police will look for them. Close relatives, friends, and neighbors become potential informants. (A. Goffman, 2009, p. 353)

Todd Clear (2007) focuses on communities burdened by high incarceration rates, describing certain disadvantaged neighborhoods as "prison places." He explains the impact of unstable, imprisoned populations as they contribute to social disorganization (the theory described in Chapter 5) in the larger communities:

Incarceration can operate as a kind of "coercive mobility," destabilizing neighborhoods by increasing levels of disorganization, first when a person is removed to go to prison, then later when that person reenters the community. In high-incarceration neighborhoods, the processes of incarceration and reentry create an environment where a significant portion of residents are constantly in flux. (p. 73)

Clear (2007) argues that these prison places suffer distinct disadvantages and that the effect of incarceration is felt far beyond the lives of the individual inmates: "The concentration of imprisonment of young men from disadvantaged places has grown to such a point that it is now a bedrock experience, a force that affects families and children, institutions and businesses, social groups and interpersonal relations" (p. 3).

Michelle Alexander (2010) goes even farther and suggests that mass incarceration be considered "the new Jim Crow." She claims,

Rather than rely on race, we use our criminal justice system to label people of color "criminals" and then engage in all the practices we supposedly left behind. Today it is perfectly legal to discriminate against criminals in nearly all the ways that it was once legal to discriminate against African Americans. Once you're labeled a felon, the old forms of discrimination—employment discrimination, housing discrimination, denial of the right to vote, denial of educational opportunity, denial of food stamps and other public benefits, and exclusion from jury service—are suddenly legal. As a criminal, you have scarcely more rights, and arguably less respect, than a black man living in Alabama at the height of Jim Crow. We have not ended racial caste in America; we have merely redesigned it. (p. 2)

The Black Lives Matter movement suggests that many community members are heeding Alexander's and others' call to action to create a new social movement to challenge mass incarceration and dismantle the current caste system, replacing it with a more equitable and respectful system of justice.

▲ **Photo 11.2**   Alice Goffman's research offers a look into the lives of "wanted" young men—those who are on probation or have warrants out for their arrest. Resisting the formal social control of the state often keeps them on the run.

DEVIANCE IN POPULAR CULTURE

There are many representations of institutions of social control in popular culture. In the chapter on labeling theory, we recommended the films *One Flew Over the Cuckoo's Nest* and *Girl, Interrupted*. While those films are good examples for labeling, they also show the role of mental hospitals as formal institutions for social control. Prisons are another popular setting for films and television shows or documentaries. Watch one or more of the following to get an inside glimpse at social control of deviance:

The Shawshank Redemption—A classic prison film that tells the fictional story of how an innocent man survives decades in prison. In the character of Brooks, we see a clear example of how a man can be "institutionalized" after living the majority of his adult life in prison—when he is finally paroled, how will he adapt? If you have not seen *The Shawshank Redemption*, it is definitely worth your time.

Girlhood—A documentary featuring Shanae and Megan, two teenage girls with troubled histories who have committed violent crimes. The filmmaker met them while they were incarcerated in the Waxter Juvenile Facility in Baltimore and follows them both in the facility and when they are released and reunited with their mothers. By focusing on these two young women, this documentary gives human faces to larger issues of abuse, neglect, and social control.

Lockup—An MSNBC series that travels the country to take viewers inside a wide range of prisons, jails, and juvenile facilities. By watching several episodes, you can begin to get a sense of the similarities these total institutions share as well as the differences in how inmates are treated.

Little Children—This fictional film is about life in the suburbs and includes a plotline about a convicted (and registered) sex offender who has just returned from prison to live with his mother. The community's nearly hysterical reaction to his presence among them provides a memorable example of both informal and formal social control.

Orange Is the New Black—Based on Piper Kerman's book about her experience in a federal correctional facility, the television series takes some dramatic license in its portrayal of a women's prison but also brings up interesting issues of gender, race, and social class in America's prisons.

◈ Total Institutions

Perhaps the most severe form of social control (other than the death penalty) is **institutionalization** in a prison, jail, juvenile correctional facility, or mental hospital. Sociologist Erving Goffman (1961) characterized such facilities as **total institutions**. He explained the defining characteristics of total institutions as follows:

A basic social arrangement in modern society is that the individual tends to sleep, play, and work in different places, with different co-participants, under different authorities, and without an over-all rational plan. The central feature of total institutions can be described as a breakdown of the barriers ordinarily separating these three spheres of life. First, all aspects of life are conducted in the same place and under the same single authority. Second, each phase of the member's daily activity is carried on in the immediate company of a large batch of others, all of whom are treated alike and required to do the same thing together. Third, all phases of the day's activities are tightly scheduled, with one activity leading at a prearranged time into the next, the whole system of activities being imposed from above by a system of explicit formal rulings and a body of officials. Finally, the various enforced activities are brought together into a single, rational plan purportedly designed to fulfill the official aims of the institution. (pp. 5–6)

As described, total institutions include prisons, jails, juvenile correctional facilities, mental hospitals, rehabilitation facilities, nursing homes, boarding schools, army barracks, monasteries, and convents. While some total institutions are entered into voluntarily, others—including prisons and secure hospitals—represent society's strongest reaction to or sanction for deviant behavior. If you take the time to watch films such as *One Flew Over the Cuckoo's Nest* or *Girl,*

▲ **Photo 11.3** Incarceration in a prison or other correctional facility is one of the most severe forms of social control. How do you think years of living in cells such as these affects the individuals?

Interrupted, you can get a small sense of what it might feel like to be deemed mentally ill and a threat to yourself and/ or the larger society.

Once confined in a total institution, it can be extremely difficult to make the transition back into the community. After spending months and years in the relative isolation of a prison, mental hospital, or other total institution, individuals may become institutionalized (or "prisonized" as Clemmer [1940/1958] so aptly phrased it) to at least some extent. They may become so used to the structure and routine of the facility that they lose the confidence and capability to exist independently in the outside world.

◈ Correctional Facilities and the Purposes of Punishment

While this book is not about the criminal justice system, it is useful to at least briefly examine the different rationales for formal social control and punishment. Criminologists generally differentiate between several philosophies or purposes of punishment; by understanding the purpose, we can often make better sense of why the particular sanctions are used. Hagan (1985, pp. 288–289) offers seven purposes of criminal sanctions: (1) restraint or incapacitation, (2) individual or specific deterrence, (3) general deterrence, (4) reform or rehabilitation, (5) moral affirmation or symbolism, (6) retribution, and (7) restitution or compensation.

Correctional facilities reside near the deep end of social control and are used primarily for incapacitation—to hold offenders in a contained space away from the rest of society. Punishing those individuals who act outside of the accepted range of behavior also serves the function of moral affirmation or symbolism; when an offender is caught and sanctioned, the boundaries of the community are clearly tested, set, and reaffirmed (Erikson, 1966). If individuals find the reality of incapacitation unpleasant enough, they may be prevented from committing further deviant acts; this is the idea behind specific deterrence. If punishing one individual harshly enough keeps others from committing similar crimes, general deterrence has been achieved. Retribution is punishment as a form of payment for the harm done; this view is best represented in the expressions "an eye for an eye" or "a life for a life." Restitution is repayment for damage or harm, and rehabilitation generally involves an effort to treat the offender in order to make him or her more capable of living as a conforming citizen.

◈ Gresham Sykes and the Pains of Imprisonment

In *The Society of Captives*, a classic work on life inside a maximum-security prison, Gresham Sykes (1958) offers a sociological view of prison culture and how time spent in prison affects both inmates and staff. He outlines five central **pains of imprisonment**, highlighting the fact that the costs of confinement are both physical and psychological. The pains of imprisonment are described as follows:

▲ **Photo 11.4**   Gresham Sykes writes about the pains of imprisonment. Which do you think would be hardest to adapt to?

Deprivation of liberty—Confined to the claustrophobic world of the prison, the isolation cuts deep. "The mere fact that the individual's movements are restricted, however, is far less serious than the fact that imprisonment means that the inmate is cut off from family, relatives, and friends, not in the self-isolation of the hermit or the misanthrope, but in the involuntary seclusion of the outlaw . . . what makes this pain of imprisonment bite most deeply is the fact that the confinement of the criminal represents a deliberate, moral rejection of the criminal by the free community" (p. 65).

Deprivation of goods and services—Inmates are without most of their personal possessions. "The inmate population defines its present material impoverishment as a painful loss" (p. 68).

Deprivation of heterosexual relationships—In male prisons, the inmate is "figuratively castrated by his involuntary celibacy" (p. 70). Sykes makes clear that living with only members of your own sex can be damaging to inmates' self-image and identity.

Deprivation of autonomy—Every significant movement an inmate makes is controlled by others; inmates must abide by others' decisions and submit with enforced respect and deference. Treating adult offenders in this way may make the inmates feel like helpless children.

Deprivation of security—Sykes quotes an inmate: "The worst thing about prison is you have to live with other prisoners" (p. 77). Individual inmates are likely to be tested by other inmates and may have to engage in physical fights for their own safety, sanity, and possessions.

◈ Juvenile Correctional Facilities

Juvenile correctional facilities—often called training schools or reform schools—are quite similar to adult prisons. After committing a crime and being adjudicated delinquent or convicted of the offense, the youth are sentenced to confinement. Incarcerated youth experience the same pains of imprisonment as their adult counterparts, but juvenile institutions generally have more of a focus on rehabilitation, so there is more emphasis on education and programming (such as therapy groups for anger management, victim empathy, or drug and alcohol issues).

Juvenile correctional facilities are the last stop and are often the last chance in the juvenile justice system for delinquent youth. If a youth commits another offense after being released from a juvenile facility, he or she often faces adult prison, punishment, and a permanent criminal record.

Historically, juvenile facilities were used as a sort of catchall for troubled youth, housing serious delinquents alongside status offenders (whose acts would not be crimes if they were committed by adults) and dependent and neglected children who needed help in meeting their basic needs. While grouping these children and adolescents all in one place made basic supervision and care possible, it also caused many problems as younger and weaker children were victimized by peers and staff members (Bartollas, Miller, & Dinitz, 1976; Feld, 1977), and all were branded with a delinquent label once they returned to the community.

In the 1970s, the ideas of labeling theory were taken seriously, and states were encouraged to deinstitutionalize status offenders and noncriminal youth. Juvenile correctional facilities now generally house the most serious delinquents in the state. While this once seemed like a harsh placement—particularly when compared with community options such as group homes or foster care—the comparison has now shifted. Youth incarcerated in juvenile facilities may be the lucky ones, especially when compared with youth tried and convicted as adults who will spend a significant portion of their lives in adult prisons.

The push and pull between punishment and treatment can be clearly viewed in juvenile correctional facilities as states struggle with trying to balance public fear and possibilities for rehabilitating wayward youth. The lessons juvenile correctional facilities intend to teach and those that young men and women in confinement actually learn while serving their sentences can be quite different (Inderbitzin, 2006). Knowing that nearly all juvenile offenders will return to the community within months or years, it is worth exploring what they are actually learning while they are incarcerated and thinking about what skills and coping mechanisms we would like them to gain before emerging from the institution.

◈ Reentry: Challenges in Returning to the Community After Time in an Institution

Reentering society after time spent in any total institution is a shock to the system and requires adjustment by the individual, his or her family, and the larger community. As the statement that opened this chapter clearly shows, individuals with a felony record face an especially difficult time in coping with the stigma of their conviction and trying to overcome the numerous obstacles felons must overcome in building new lives.

These problems are shared by an ever-increasing segment of the population. Figure 11.1 shows the growth of adult correctional populations over three decades; the numbers of people in prison and on probation are striking. If state laws and community practices close doors and take away opportunities for the millions of individuals involved with the criminal justice system, what message of social control are we sending? How should we expect these individuals to respond?

Prisoner reentry is a delicate process. While the many challenges faced by former inmates in rebuilding their lives are relatively clear, Maruna (2011) takes a wider view and describes the challenge to the larger society, observing, "Like the commission of a crime, the reintegration of the former outcast back into society represents a challenge to the moral order, a delicate transition fraught with danger and possibility" (p. 3).

For those who have been formally convicted of a crime, the repercussions can last a lifetime. The stigma of a felony conviction may lead to a "closing of doors" (Sampson & Laub, 1993, p. 124), negatively affecting employment opportunities, educational funding, housing, and the ability to vote alongside fellow community members. Marc Mauer (2005) provides a clear illustration of the potential **collateral consequences of imprisonment** for a felony conviction.

> An 18-year-old with a first-time felony conviction for drug possession now may be barred from receiving welfare for life, prohibited from living in public housing, denied student loans to attend college, permanently excluded from voting, and if not a citizen, be deported. (p. 610)

To better understand how felony convictions interact with race and affect the search for employment, Devah Pager (2007) designed an experimental study in which she sent out young men with matched credentials and fictional criminal records to apply for various entry-level jobs. Pager (2003) explains the process and her findings.

Jerome could have been any one of the hundreds of thousands of young black men released from prison each year who face bleak employment prospects as a result of their race and criminal record. Except in this case, Jerome happened to be working for me. He was one of four college students I had hired as "auditors" for a study of employment discrimination. His assignment was to apply for entry-level job openings throughout the Milwaukee metropolitan area, presenting himself as an ex-offender some of the times. For each job opening, a second black auditor also submitted an application, presenting equal educational qualifications, work experience and inter-personal skills. Everything was the same in the two cases except for the criminal record, which Jerome and the other auditor alternated presenting weekly. This one detail made a decisive difference.

After those applications in which Jerome reported a criminal record, Jerome was about one-third as likely to receive a call-back for an interview as was his equally qualified partner who presented no criminal record. Based on these results, a black ex-offender would have to apply for an average of 20 job openings to receive just one call-back—and that's just for an interview. Getting to a job offer would require still more effort and good fortune.

At the same time, I had a second pair of auditors—white students—applying to a separate set of job openings. The contrast between their outcomes and those of Jerome and his partner was striking. A white auditor who reported no criminal record was more than twice as likely to receive a call-back than a black auditor with no record. Indeed, the white applicant with a criminal record was more likely to receive a call-back than a black applicant without any criminal background. (p. 58)

While employers were generally reluctant to hire any ex-offenders, Pager and Quillian (2005) found that black ex-offenders were much less likely to be offered a job and a second chance than their white counterparts. Pager and Quillian's study is a strong example of using experimental methods to learn more about the obstacles convicted offenders face; the fact that African American males were given significantly fewer opportunities clearly shows how race and a criminal label interact to close doors and diminish individuals' life chances.

Felon Disenfranchisement

As we have illustrated, felony convictions and the stigma of incarceration limit individuals' opportunities for employment and housing. A more formal consequence of a felony conviction is "civil death," or the loss of the right to vote in local and national elections. **Felon disenfranchisement** varies by state, but most states have at least some limits in place whereby those who have committed felony offenses lose the right to participate in democratic elections. In most states, currently incarcerated felons are not allowed to vote from prison or jail. States are split as to whether parolees and probationers living in the community are allowed to vote, and some states ban ex-felons from ever voting again. For the most updated and comprehensive overview of felon voting rights, check out the website of The Sentencing Project (www.sentencingproject.org), which includes an interactive map with information available for every state.

Christopher Uggen and Jeff Manza have spent the past decade studying felon disenfranchisement, estimating the scope and number of individuals affected as well as the impact on communities and elections. Uggen, Manza, and Thompson (2006, p. 283) further estimate that there now exists a "felon class" of more than 16 million felons and ex-felons in the United States; these individuals represent 7.5% of the adult population, 22.3% of the black adult population, and 33.4% of the black adult male population. In other words, a full one-third of African American men in the

Figure 11.1 Adult Correctional Populations, 1980–2013

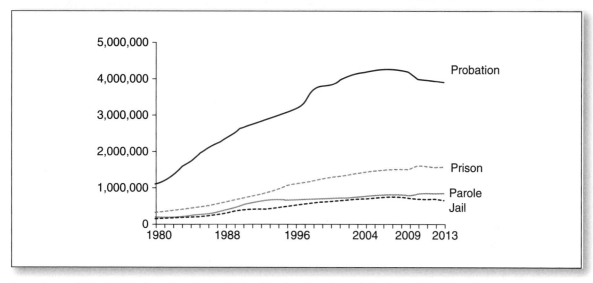

Source: Bureau of Justice Statistics Correctional Surveys. Retrieved from http://www.bjs.gov/index.cfm?ty=kfdetail&iid=487

United States have serious criminal records and have their rights restricted, even though they have "paid their debt to society." In interviews with incarcerated felons and ex-felons, Manza and Uggen (2006) found that the right to vote did indeed matter to the individuals affected; their interviewees felt the sting of being classified as "less than the average citizen" (p. 155) even as they were still expected to pay taxes and work in the communities that denied them a voice.

◈ Public Fear and Social Control: The Case of Sex Offenders

The social control of sex offenders offers an extreme example of public fear and widespread panic over a particular offense and group. Despite relatively low recidivism rates, sex offenders are arguably the most feared and demonized of all criminals. All 50 states have adopted sex offender registration and notification laws, and more than 20 states allow involuntary **civil commitment** of sexual predators, whereby sex offenders can be held indefinitely, even after completing their criminal justice sentences (Harris & Lurigio, 2010).

Online registries and mandatory registration make it easy for community members to learn about convicted sex offenders living—or attempting to find housing—in their midst. It opens the possibility for harassment of the offenders and, in extreme cases, murder by overzealous vigilantes. Local residency laws severely restrict where sex offenders may live, stipulating, for example, that they must stay 2,500 feet away from schools, parks, and playgrounds. A story in *Newsweek* highlighted the desperate circumstances some sex offenders face under such restrictions, suggesting that the offenders are treated as pariahs and essentially banned from entire cities. Faced with such restrictions, one group of approximately 70 sex offenders settled under the Julia Tuttle Causeway, a six-lane bridge in Miami with no running water or sewage system (Skipp, 2009). Some individuals lived at the Julia Tuttle camp for years until it was ultimately disbanded.

Clearly, as a society, we must learn to balance public fear and public safety with individual rights. Have individuals forfeited their rights forever once they are convicted of a crime? Or should those rights (and opportunities) be restored once they have served their mandated sentences? Are redemption and reintegration possible? These are complicated questions that we must continue to grapple with and explore. As Maruna (2011) explains,

> Criminal sanctions, for the most part, end very badly. Indeed, by most accounts, they do not end at all. Except for a very fortunate few who have their offenses formally forgiven through pardons or other legal means, individuals with felony records can remain permanently stigmatized, excluded from employment, educational and social opportunities, on the grounds of something they did many years or decades earlier. (p. 5)

◈ Collateral Consequences: Effects on Communities and Families

> If prisons affected no one except the criminals on the inside, they would matter less. But, after thirty years of penal population growth, the impact of America's prisons extends far beyond their walls. By zealously punishing lawbreakers—including a large new class of nonviolent drug offenders—the criminal justice system at the end of the 1990s drew into its orbit families and whole communities. These most fragile families and neighborhoods were the least equipped to counter any shocks or additional deprivations. (Western, 2006, p. 11)

Just as police surveillance and supervision is concentrated among poor and predominantly minority neighborhoods, incarceration is concentrated among poor, often minority men and women from disorganized areas. This affects not only the imprisoned individuals but also their family members and the larger community. Todd Clear (2007) explains the impact as follows:

> The way these young people cycle through our system of prisons and jails, then back into the community, leaves considerable collateral damage in its wake. Families are disrupted, social networks and other forms of social support are weakened, health is endangered, labor markets are thinned, and—more important than anything else—children are put at risk of the depleted human and social capital that promotes delinquency. After a certain point, the collateral effects of these high rates of incarceration seem to contribute to more crime in these places. (p. 175)

On any given day, approximately 1.5 million children have a parent serving time in a state or federal prison (Mumola, 2000). Mass incarceration in the United States affects literally millions of family members who come into prisons to visit their loved ones even as they deal with depleted resources and troubled surroundings at home.

Meagan Comfort (2003, 2008) describes the "secondary **prisonization**" women experience in "the tube," or the visitor waiting area at San Quentin. She calculated that approximately 95% of the visitors to the men's prison were women, and even though they were legally innocent of any crimes, they were subject to marginalization and their own pains of imprisonment due to their extended contact with the correctional facility. Comfort offers a detailed description of the rules and dress code of the prison, the women who arrive hours in advance and then wait patiently or resentfully to be allowed into the visiting room to see their loved ones, and the humiliating treatment these women often receive at the hands of correctional officers processing them into and out of the institution. While prisoners experience the pains of imprisonment, Comfort makes clear that their visitors also suffer from the contaminative contact of the prison.

In another article, Comfort (2002) explores how these women work to prevent the institutionalization of their loved ones while they are in the prison. Comfort explains that the visitors move important life and family events into the prison's visiting room so that fathers, boyfriends, and husbands can maintain involvement and strengthen family ties. San Quentin allows family visits where prisoners and their guests can spend nearly two days together in bungalows on the prison grounds. The women dip into their savings and plan carefully to purchase the approved ingredients to make memorable meals for their partners, who can, in that moment, escape prison food if not prison supervision.

In addition to intimate visits and special meals and celebrations in the prison visiting room, Comfort also describes weddings held within the prison (2002, 2008), happy days for the brides despite the bleak setting. She suggests that the women involved with prisoners essentially fight for the sanity and souls of their men by reminding them of their families and their humanity. "Wives, fiancées, and girlfriends of inmates strive to bridge the distance between the outside world and their loved one: unable to bring him home, they bring home to him through the relocation of intimate activities inside the penitentiary walls" (Comfort, 2002, p. 492).

◈ Explaining Deviance in the Streets and Deviance in the Suites: Considering How Money Can Matter in Local Jails

In some states and under some circumstances, money can help ease the pain if you are facing a jail sentence. In California, the Fremont detention center near San Francisco acts as a pay-to-stay prison, allowing healthy, nonviolent offenders without gang affiliations to stay in one of Fremont's cells for $155 per night and a one-time $45 fee. The detention center, which is rarely full, can make more than $140 per night in profit from such stays (Watson, 2013). Fremont officials claim that it is just a jail with no special treatment or benefits; their residents get the same food, blankets, and amenities as those at other jails. The main advantage is that Fremont it is a smaller, quieter facility, and its detainees will not have to interact with the full population of the county jail.

In 2007, the *New York Times* reported the following on pay-to-stay jails:

> For roughly $75 to $127 a day, these convicts—who are known in the self-pay parlance as "clients"—get a small cell behind a regular door, distance of some amplitude from violent offenders and, in some cases, the right to bring an iPod or computer on which to compose a novel, or perhaps a song.
>
> Many of the overnighters are granted work furlough, enabling them to do most of their time on the job, returning to the jail simply to go to bed (often following a strip search, which granted is not so five-star).
>
> The clients usually share a cell, but otherwise mix little with the ordinary nonpaying inmates, who tend to be people arrested and awaiting arraignment, or federal prisoners on trial or awaiting deportation and simply passing through. (Steinhauer, 2007, n.p.)

By contrast, today's jails and prisons are also serving as the new asylums for the country's mentally ill who cannot afford treatment, medication, private hospitals, and much-needed psychiatric care (Fields & Phillips, 2013). The National Institutes of Health estimates that one in four American adults suffers from a diagnosable mental illness in any given year but that nearly two thirds of inmates in local jails were diagnosed or treated for mental health problems. Many mentally ill inmates commit minor crimes that land them in jail for brief sentences. While in the facility, they may be diagnosed, treated, and given a small supply of medication upon their release. The medication often runs out before they can get treatment in the community, and many end up back in jail in a continuing cycle. The *Wall Street Journal* illustrated the beginning of this pattern with the story of Steven Dorsey:

> Mr. Dorsey, 48, was a part-time worker at a janitorial supply company, but his hours had dried up in recent months, and he lost his job. Mr. Dorsey, who said he had been diagnosed as bipolar and schizophrenic, had felt lucky to be placed in a group home. He had to leave, though, after Medicaid turned him down for benefits, he said.

He ended up living on the streets, occasionally scrounging in dumpsters for food scraps. . . .

"I didn't have a way of eating or sleeping," says Mr. Dorsey. Voices told him to "steal what you need." He ended up in jail after allegedly lifting a sandwich and a toothbrush from a convenience store. A sheriff's spokesman said he was charged with retail theft under $300. (Fields & Phillips, 2013, n.p.)

A *Frontline* documentary called *The Released* (Navasky & O'Connor, 2009) offers a vivid and disturbing look into the lives of men who suffer from serious mental illness and find themselves in and out of jail. In jail, these men are medicated and often get their symptoms under control; they may feel like they are again capable of living in the community. But once they are released, they have a limited supply of medication, and many of them struggle to find housing and stability. Once the medication runs out, they are frequently rearrested and brought to jail for new crimes.

So here we see again how social class and privilege matter in one's treatment in our communities and criminal justice system. If you are fortunate enough to be able to afford psychiatric treatment and proper medication, you are much less likely to end up in jail in the first place. If, however, jail is unavoidable, you may be able to pay your way into a nicer facility and serve your time as pleasantly as possible.

◈ Ideas in Action: College Programs in Prisons

While social control of deviance is often about sanctions and punishment, social control, in its many forms, can also be focused on prevention of future deviant and criminal acts and the rehabilitation of offenders. College programs in prison are an excellent example of rehabilitative programming in a secure facility. Education has long been shown to be one of the most effective correctional interventions to decrease recidivism. The largest ever meta-analysis of studies of correctional education showed that prisoners who participated in correctional education programs had 43% lower odds of returning to prison than inmates who did not. The study also found that prison education programs are cost-effective, suggesting that a $1 investment in prison education can reduce incarceration costs by $4 to $5 during the first three years after release, which is when those leaving prison are most likely to return (Davis, Bozick, Steele, Saunders, & Miles, 2013).

Even when convicted offenders are incarcerated and incapacitated for the duration of their sentences, they may still be able to learn new skills and to find new direction for their lives. College programs operating within correctional facilities generally receive no public funding and are made possible through private grants, individual sponsorship, and hours donated by faculty and volunteers around the country. Below, we offer examples of several of the most successful college prison programs operating in the United States.

The Bard Prison Initiative (BPI; n.d.) is a division of Bard College that offers incarcerated men and women the chance to enroll in academic programs and earn degrees from Bard College. The program offers a liberal arts curriculum, and incarcerated students are held to the exact same standards as undergraduates on campus. The BPI website explains its success and its goals in this way:

As the largest program of its kind in the United States, BPI enrolls nearly 300 incarcerated men and women across a full spectrum of academic disciplines, and offers over 60 courses each semester. By 2013, Bard granted nearly 300 degrees to BPI participants and enrolled more than 700 students. . . . With the help of a significant private grant, the Consortium for the Liberal Arts in Prison was created to support other innovative college-in-prison programs throughout the country. Wesleyan University in Connecticut, Grinnell College in Iowa, Goucher College in Maryland, and the University of Notre Dame and Holy Cross College in Indiana have now established programs, and the Consortium plans to establish programs in as many as ten more states within the next five years. (paras. 2, 4)

The Prison University Project (n.d.) was formed to support the College Program at San Quentin. Currently, more than 20 college courses are offered each semester in San Quentin, and more than 300 students are enrolled. All faculty working in the program are volunteers, and there are more than 100 faculty, teaching assistants, and tutors guiding classes and studies in the prison.

The Bedford Hills College Program at Marymount Manhattan College (n.d.) offers courses leading to an associate of arts degree in social science and a bachelor of arts degree in sociology at the Bedford Hills Correctional Facility, a New York State maximum-security prison for women. In a unique twist, the Bedford Hills College Program is now an extension campus of Marymount Manhattan College; students in both locations take the same core courses for the sociology major as well as a wide variety of electives. The Bedford Hills College Program involves more than 175 students per semester, and students who have already earned their bachelor's degrees serve as mentors and tutors. Annually, more than 200 women register for college courses. As of 2011, the Bedford Hills College Program has graduated 142 students.

The Inside-Out Prison Exchange Program, started by Lori Pompa at Temple University (n.d.) in Philadelphia, brings college students into correctional facilities to share classes with prisoners for a full term. "Inside" and "outside" students read the same books, do the same assignments, and work collaboratively on class projects. Throughout the term, students engage in extensive dialogue, helping everyone involved to see beyond labels and to value each individual class member's contributions. Classes cover any number of topics and disciplines, including sociology, criminal justice, literature, philosophy, nursing, and drama; no matter what the specific subject matter, students who participate in the classes are exposed to a deep, transformative learning experience. Inside-Out requires intensive, hands-on training for prospective instructors, and all participants must agree to follow the program's strict rules in order to ensure Inside-Out's continued success and growth. At this point, more than 400 potential instructors have completed the Inside-Out training, and more than 10,000 students have been part of more than 300 distinct classes. Inside-Out classes have been held in more than 25 states; the program has begun offering classes in Canada, and the network is rapidly growing.

The Prison-to-College Pipeline is one of the newest prison college programs, developed at John Jay College in New York in 2011. The Prison-to-College Pipeline is a small program (involving only about 25 male prisoners by 2013) with big goals:

> The program has three components: 1) offering college credit courses, 2) a re-entry program that works with Osborne Association, an organization that helps parolees gain housing, jobs and continue their education, 3) a learning exchange program where John Jay students volunteer to study with the prisoners. (Stern, 2013, n.p.)

NOW YOU . . . THINK ABOUT SOCIAL CONTROL

We have explored myriad forms of deviance in this book: police misconduct, drug use, corporate misconduct, prostitution, and making "war" on various behaviors, to name a few. What we can probably conclude by these disparate behaviors, issues, and perspectives is that deviance is often in the eye of the beholder. While one person might define the homeless person as deviant, many others might define a society that does not have enough safety nets for those in need—thus allowing homelessness—as deviant.

(Continued)

(Continued)

In the same vein, social control of "deviants" takes on many faces. Some of this social control is informal, while much of it has been formalized, leading to an explosion in both regulations and prison populations.

Given what you have learned about deviants, deviance, and theory in this book, what should be the relationship between deviance and social control? If we asked you to build a better vision of social control, what would your philosophy be? What behaviors would you focus on? What behaviors would you allow? Would you focus on informal or formal social control? On individuals or groups? On making peace or war? Why?

◈ Conclusion

In this chapter, we have given you a quick glimpse into some specific forms of social control of deviant behavior. Much more could be and has been written on the topic, but we chose to keep it simple and highlight some current practices that show the challenges of effectively controlling deviant behavior without creating widespread damage to individuals, families, and communities.

We would like to point out, too, that reactions to deviant behavior and efforts at social control are constantly evolving. For example, because prison populations soared for several decades, states are now looking for more creative—and less expensive—responses to criminal behavior. As a result, the number of prisoners held in state and federal facilities decreased slightly in 2014, a welcome change in trend. "Ban the Box" campaigns have sprung up around the country, encouraging states and counties to eliminate the box on employment and housing forms that asks whether the applicant has a criminal conviction or criminal record. In addition, some progress has been made in efforts to restore voting rights to felons, with current research suggesting that the benefits of civic reintegration of ex-offenders far outweigh the potential risks (Uggen & Inderbitzin, 2010). What changes will be next?

In the next chapter, you will read about deviant careers and career deviance. While most theories and books on deviant behavior focus on how individuals enter deviance, we think it is just as interesting and important to examine how the majority of individuals change their life trajectories and, sooner or later, find a way to exit deviance.

EXERCISES AND DISCUSSION QUESTIONS

1. Do you think deviance and social control are necessary to society? What functions do they serve? Which of the purposes of punishment do you think best fit our current criminal justice system? Why do you think so?

2. Should we be concerned about the institutionalization of prisoners? Why, or why not? What might be done to prevent institutionalization and prisonization?

3. Felony records disqualify individuals from a number of different types of jobs that are not necessarily related to the type

of crime committed. Do you think this is a fair practice? Why, or why not? What do you think would be appropriate guidelines in terms of felony convictions and employment?

4. Check out the interactive map on The Sentencing Project's website (http://www.sentencingproject.org/map/map.cfm). How does your state compare with others and the national average in terms of corrections populations, corrections expenditures, and felon disenfranchisement? Are you surprised by any of this information?

5. Do you think persons convicted of felony offenses should be able to vote in local and national elections? What restrictions, if any, do you think would be appropriate? What are the laws in your state?

6. Should sex offenders be treated differently than other violent offenders? Does the community have a right to know and perhaps even dictate where they live and work? Do you think civil commitment of sex offenders is appropriate?

KEY TERMS

Civil commitment

Collateral consequences of imprisonment

Demedicalization

Felon disenfranchisement

Institutionalization

Medicalization of deviance

Pains of imprisonment

Prisonization

Social contract

Total institutions

READING 30

This article takes readers inside a cottage for violent offenders in one state's end-of-the-line juvenile correctional facility. Inderbitzin spent hundreds of hours in the cottage interacting with both the adolescent inmates and the staff members charged with their supervision and care. The goal of the article is to contrast the lessons the institution intended to impart to its "residents" with the life lessons the young men actually learned during their incarceration. She begins by using her observations and interviews to help the reader understand what it is like to be a juvenile behind bars, identifying the "pains of imprisonment," discussed largely in the adult corrections literature but less often a major concern in the juvenile justice literature. Pains of incarceration are many, and much of it focuses on the loss of autonomy and poor living environments. Inderbitzin makes the very interesting point that because these youth were basically raising themselves prior to their arrest and incarceration and had possessed a great deal of autonomy, the period of incarceration literally stunted the transition to adulthood. Clearly, the institution intended to promote education, basic work proficiencies, "life-skills, anger management, victim empathy and cultural literacy." Indeed, many of the staff worked hard in these areas despite the low quality of the resources and unique backgrounds of the youth, which presented many challenges to their stated intentions. The youth did learn some important things from the staff, and there was evidence that the boys trusted some staff more than others and garnered various lessons and emotional support from them. Alternatively, by many accounts, it was too little and too late. The boys also learned from the other youth in the cottage, including lessons about keeping quiet and staying in their place until they earned the right to speak out. There were also elements of a "crime school" so commonly perceived in prisons for youth and adults. The picture painted is bleak but not insurmountable. As you read the article, think about whether you believe "training schools" or juvenile prisons are an effective way for society to respond to serious delinquents. Are there other viable options?

Source: Inderbitzin, M. (2006). Lessons from a juvenile training school: Survival and growth. *Journal of Adolescent Research, 21*(1), 7–26.

Lessons From a Juvenile Training School

Survival and Growth

Michelle Inderbitzin

There are those who believe that the idea of a separate justice system for juveniles, after more than a century in existence, has outgrown its usefulness. They argue that as long as young offenders commit serious crimes, they should be prepared to face the consequences; indeed, it seems that "recent reforms in juvenile justice have placed the notion of youth itself on trial" (Grisso & Schwartz, 2000, p. 5). In spite of such arguments, however, the juvenile justice system continues its mission, and those who speak on its behalf espouse the ideals of rehabilitation and the malleability of youth.

The central question in this article concerns the function and utility of juvenile training schools as institutions of social control and as agents of change for adolescent inmates. More specifically, I examine one such institution in light of the rhetoric surrounding reform schools and the reality of daily life within the institution's walls and then evaluate its effectiveness based on the lessons learned by young offenders who serve a portion of their adolescence there. After spending a significant percentage of their lives confined to a juvenile correctional facility, what do young offenders think they have learned? What will they take away from their time in the institution? How will they have changed?

More than two decades ago, apparently the best that could be said for juvenile institutions was that "at least some training schools do not have as damaging an effect on juveniles as do prisons" (Haskell & Yablonsky, 1982, p. 446). In the 1970s, Massachusetts, under the helm of Jerome Miller, took a bold step and attempted to deinstitutionalize virtually all of the juvenile offenders in the state. At that time, reform schools ("an old-fashioned but honest name," according to Miller, 1998, p. xvii) were thought to do more harm than good, and Miller managed to close down all such institutions and replace them with alternative programs and placements in the community. Proponents of deinstitutionalization argued that the negative lessons learned and the stigma associated with incarceration far outweighed any benefit for individuals in the system (Miller, 1998). In addition, studies from that era report conditions in state training schools that today would certainly be viewed as unacceptable: Cottage "parents" frequently used physical means to punish the boys in their care—striking, shaking, and shoving them (Weber, 1961); boys were housed in the "tombs," an extreme form of isolation and were not allowed to speak while in their cottage living unit (Feld, 1999; Miller, 1998); and younger and weaker boys were regularly victimized by their tougher counterparts (Bartollas, Miller, & Dinitz, 1976; Feld, 1977; Polsky, 1962).

During the past two decades, the United States has made a clear movement to get tough on juvenile crime, and the sentencing of juvenile offenders has become increasingly punitive (Feld, 1999). As such, the categories of comparison have drastically changed. In the 1960s and 1970s, when compared to deinstitutionalization and community alternatives, juvenile correctional facilities were often viewed as the strictest of punishments for juvenile offenders—the last resort for the state's most incorrigible youth. These days, the possibilities for punishment have shifted to the point that reform schools now seem to be the kinder, gentler option—the two alternatives facing serious juvenile offenders are now generally confinement in juvenile correctional facilities or confinement in adult prisons.

The past two decades have also witnessed a relative dearth of ethnographic studies on training schools. The heyday of studies of the inmate culture and the inner workings of training schools seemed to be in the 1960s and 1970s (Bartollas et al., 1976; Feld, 1977; Polsky, 1962; Weber, 1961; Wooden, 1976). In fact, some researchers have suggested that interest in the conditions of training schools in the United States has fallen to such a degree that it is hard to make meaningful comparisons

(Chesney-Lind & Shelden, 2004, p. 224). The findings from the earlier works were overwhelmingly negative, and the authors painted dark pictures of juvenile institutions. Feld (1998), in reviewing the evidence some 20 years after his own sociological study of state training schools, concludes: "Evaluations of training schools, the most common form of institutional treatment for the largest numbers of serious and chronic delinquents, report consistently negative findings. . . . They constitute the one extensively evaluated and clearly ineffective method to treat delinquents" (Feld, 1998, p. 237).

Bortner and Williams (1997) conducted one of the more recent, in-depth studies of a model program operating in two juvenile prisons. The model program they describe was created in response to a class-action lawsuit against Arizona's system of juvenile corrections. In much the same way earlier research condemned practices in state training schools as damaging to young inmates, the lawsuit suggested that Arizona's juvenile correctional facilities were punitive, coercive, and inhumane (Bortner & Williams, 1997, p. x). The model treatment program sought to provide youths the skills necessary to succeed in society, emphasizing accountability, responsibility, mutual respect, and personal efficacy. It offered a new goal and vision for society's treatment of delinquent youth. The innovative program was never fully implemented and ultimately came to be viewed as a failure. Although the changes did not last, Arizona's experiment with new programming in juvenile correctional facilities provides at least one example of thinking outside of the prison box in treating young offenders.

Interestingly, some recent studies (Forst, Fagan, & Vivona, 1989; Lane, Lanza-Kaduce, Frazier, & Bishop, 2002) suggest that the juvenile offenders themselves found their time in the "deep end" of juvenile corrections to be their most helpful or productive placement. Lane et al. (2002) describe deep end juvenile programs as residential commitment facilities that are the most restrictive in the state, with more physical security, closer supervision, and longer periods of confinement than other programs and facilities (p. 433). In interviews, the youths cited a combination of available programming, caring staff members, and smaller populations as making their time in juvenile correctional facilities a better experience in their perception than the more punitive jails

and prisons where they were incarcerated alongside generally older, stronger, more criminal adults. In addition, sanctions earlier in the more "shallow end" of the juvenile system, including probation, day programs, and short-term placements in low-risk, least restrictive residential programs, proved to have little effect on the young offenders; the shorter sentences did not give them enough time away from their lives to become fully immersed in the programming.

Developmental psychologists argue that:

> adolescence in modern society is an inherently transitional time during which there are rapid and dramatic changes in physical, intellectual, emotional, and social capabilities . . . other than infancy, there is probably no period of human development characterized by more rapid or pervasive transformations in individual competencies. (Steinberg & Schwartz, 2000, p. 23)

Because they work primarily with adolescents, juvenile justice agencies have the potential to exert enormous influence over the rapidly changing lives of their captive populations. As such, it seems we should pay particular attention to the treatment of adolescent offenders.

Although little research is being conducted inside training schools and juvenile institutions, there is now a great deal of attention being paid to issues of prisoner reentry (Altschuler & Brash, 2004) as increasing numbers of inmates are released from correctional facilities to return to their communities. This is an especially interesting dilemma for juvenile offenders who are literally becoming men behind bars; most will leave the juvenile prisons and training schools where they served their sentences as legal adults with virtually no safety nets in place (Furstenberg, Rumbaut, & Settersten, 2005).

Arnett (1998) makes the point that "the transition to adulthood is characterized not by a single event but by an extended process of preparation for the challenges and responsibilities of adult life" (p. 311). Young Americans identify three main criteria for the transition to adulthood: accepting responsibility for one's self, making independent decisions, and becoming financially independent (p. 295). One question of interest is whether this transition to adulthood is stunted or accelerated by incarceration in a juvenile correctional facility. Because many young offenders were largely living on their own and supporting themselves while still teenagers in the community, I would argue that the transition to adulthood was accelerated for them prior to their confinement. During their incarceration, however, when adolescent inmates' responsibilities and ability to make decisions are severely limited, the transition to adulthood is likely stunted.

For most American young people, "Emerging adulthood is a time of looking forward and imagining what adult life will be like, and what emerging adults imagine is generally bright and promising. . . . Whatever the future may actually hold, during emerging adulthood, hope prevails" (Arnett, 2004, p. 206). This point brings up a second question of particular interest for adolescent inmates: Does hope manage to prevail for a particularly troubled population of emerging adults, incarcerated young men, most of whom are minority males who grew up poor, living with troubled families in disadvantaged neighborhoods? Going inside juvenile institutions and listening to the young inmates as they pass through different stages of their confinement is an important step in answering such questions.

Evaluating the current state of juvenile justice, Van Vleet (1999) argued that "get-tough measures . . . have returned much of the youth corrections system to the training school mentality that was largely abandoned during the decades of deinstitutionalization" (p. 204). He goes on to describe incarceration in a juvenile correctional facility as "punishment with treatment components added on" (pp. 209–210). The availability of and the quality of treatment components is one important difference between juvenile and adult institutions; given their younger, developing populations, juvenile correctional facilities tend to be more focused on rehabilitation than are adult prisons (Altschuler & Brash, 2004) and are better able to utilize approaches grounded in developmental knowledge (Scott, 2000).

In the current study, I sought to find out—from the ground level—what is happening in juvenile correctional facilities, to discover how serious juvenile offenders experience incarceration in a state training school. To do so, I focused on the following questions: What lessons does the institution attempt to teach its population of adolescents and emerging adults? What lessons are the inmates actually learning? What, ultimately, will these young offenders take with them back into the community? Are training schools still a viable response for violent juvenile offenders?

◈ Method

The training school in this study houses the state's most serious problem children still held under the jurisdiction of the juvenile justice system. The population of chronic and violent male offenders in this juvenile prison ranges in age from 15 to 20. Most of them have done time and served sentences in other juvenile institutions, and this facility was often their last stop in the juvenile system. If they committed further crimes, they would face adult consequences.

The maximum-security institution in this study is very much a juvenile prison. As Bortner and Williams (1997) point out in their own study of a juvenile prison in Arizona: "The special language of juvenile justice denies the realities of prison conditions. . . . It is impossible to ignore the level of control, the razor wire, electronic gates, and the harsh and punitive nature of these institutions, historically and currently" (pp. xvi–xvii). Likewise, the institution in this study has a razor wire fence surrounding the perimeter, a full-time security staff, and locked rooms within locked living units. At the time of this study, there were about 200 boys sentenced to this training school. Based on his offense type, each was assigned to a cottage living unit that would be his home during his incarceration. The boys would attend school, work in the institution, go to recreation at the gym, and eat their meals in the institution's cafeteria, but each night they would return to their cottage. In attempting to see long-term interactions and deeper layers of meaning, I chose to focus on the "Blue" cottage, a cottage housing a population of 18 to 26 violent offenders at any given time and widely regarded as home to the toughest offenders in the toughest training school in the state.

The ethnographic data for this study were gathered through observations during a period of approximately 15 months. During the course of the study, I averaged approximately one visit per week, generally staying for 7 or 8 hours at a time. I often chose to visit and observe on Saturdays and afternoons or evenings when the boys would be out of school and spending time in the cottage. Most of the time, I simply hung out in the cottage, watching, listening, and interacting with the *residents* (the school's preferred term for its inmates) and the staff members.

In response to the boys' initial cynicism about talking to an outsider, I chose not to do formal interviews, preferring instead to gather information through less intrusive means—conversing informally, listening to the residents and the staff members, asking questions, and paying attention to the interactions in the cottage. In my role as a researcher, I went from being an outsider to being a welcome diversion; within a few months, many of the boys looked forward to my visits as they helped to break the monotony of their daily lives. This gave me an opportunity to have ongoing discussions with the boys and the staff members; I was able to ask the same question in different ways and at various times, and I was able to follow up questions and conversations weeks and months later as circumstances changed and the boys went through different phases of their sentences. After each visit, I took extensive field notes detailing events, conversations, and my own thoughts; the field notes were then the data for analysis.

This case study of a single cottage of violent offenders may not have been representative of the larger institution, let alone representative of juvenile corrections more generally. Yet, the body of research on training schools—and, to some extent, adult prisons—largely fit the reality of life in this cottage. It rang true enough that I came away convinced that inmate cultures share at least some universal issues. The present study is offered, then, as a supplement to the classic pieces on prison culture (Goffman, 1961; Irwin, 1970; Sykes, 1958) and as a glimpse into life inside a modern day training school. Ultimately, I wanted to find out how serious young offenders experienced punishment in the state's end-of-the-line juvenile institution. This article is one part of the answer; it is a recounting of lessons I learned in spending time attempting to delve beneath the rhetoric while witnessing the patterns of daily life in the Blue cottage. To protect the identity of young men who hope to have better futures, all names have been changed.

Results

One of the primary goals of this study was to understand the effect of time inside the institution on the individuals, to closely examine the experiences, the adaptations, and the survival strategies of residents in the Blue cottage. The focus of this article is on the lessons that the boys learned during their incarceration. Some of the lessons were abstract, some were concrete, some physical, some mental. Some the institution tried to teach, others were the inescapable result of the experience of incarceration. I will begin by discussing the pains of imprisonment and how the young offenders learned to deal with them. I will then move to lessons in conformity the institution intended, informal lessons learned from cottage staff members and other inmates, lessons learned in relation to family and friends, and lessons learned over time. Finally, I will discuss the lessons that the broader society can learn about training schools and their effect on young offenders.

Learning to Deal With the Pains of Imprisonment

The first lesson all of the boys had to learn is one with which inmates have been dealing for generations: learning to survive the daily frustrations and challenges inherent in the structure of the institution. A defining aspect of the residents' lives in the juvenile prison was their indignation over losing liberties, what Sykes (1958) calls "pains of imprisonment." TJ, a 20-year-old African American, expressed how much he hated doing time in the institution and how the loss of liberty grated on him. He explained that he hated the fact that he had to pound on his locked door to get out to go to the bathroom, how everyone else controls your life when you are locked up. His feelings fit perfectly with Sykes and Messinger's (1960) discussion of the deprivation of autonomy:

> Rejected, impoverished, and figuratively castrated, the prisoner must face still further indignity in the extensive social control exercised by the custodians. The many details of the inmate's life, ranging from the hours of sleeping to the route to work and the job itself,

are subject to a vast number of regulations made by prison officials. The inmate is stripped of his autonomy; hence, to the other pains of imprisonment we must add the pressure to define himself as weak, helpless, and dependent. (Sykes & Messinger, 1960, pp. 14–15)

The young inmates had to ask permission to shave, to shower, to make phone calls, to get paper and a pencil, to send letters. In discussing the deprivation of liberty, Sykes (1958) makes the point that treating inmates like helpless children poses a severe threat to their self-image. This becomes an interesting question when dealing with juvenile inmates who have never experienced full acceptance into the adult world. The oldest inmates—those who had reached the age of 19 or 20—felt the threat most acutely, but many of the boys in the cottage had basically been independent and on their own for some time before being incarcerated, so the restrictions still stung. It may be that when dealing with a population of juvenile offenders, the deprivation of autonomy is less severe than it is for adults, but such treatment may pose more damage in the long term to self-concepts that are not yet fully formed.

In addition to the loss of many small privileges and most of their autonomy, the residents also chafed at the loss of privacy. Because few of them were assigned to rooms by themselves, they often had to deal with irritating roommates. I heard many complaints about roommates—some were told to me in conversation, others were taken to the staff in the hopes of changing the situation. Sometimes the issue was about race or age—African American residents did not want to room with White residents; older residents did not want to room with immature boys (although by state law, children younger than 18 could not be placed in a room with those older than 18). The complaints of the residents were wide ranging: Some were disgusted by the "funky" smells generated by their roommates, and at least one unpopular roommate was known for wetting his bed. Others complained about having to "play counselor" for their roommates and having to listen to their problems at all hours. And some roommates, they said, were just plain annoying—talking all the time or asking too many questions. The real issue, it seemed, was the lack of privacy.

As Sykes (1958) points out in discussing the pains of imprisonment and particularly the deprivation of goods and services: "There are admittedly many problems in attempting to compare the standard of living existing in the free community and the standard of living which is supposed to be the lot of the inmate in prison" (p. 67). Although times have changed enough that these inmates did not have to go through all of the degradation and mortification ceremonies that Sykes (1958) and Goffman (1961) describe, they were, on their entrance, stripped of most of their own possessions and given state-issue replacements of basic necessities.

The boys frequently expressed their annoyance at having to live with what they deemed inferior products. When Tony, a 20-year-old Latino, was about to be transferred out of the institution to a group home, one small privilege that he was excited about was the opportunity he would have to choose and to purchase nice soap. The residents were even skeptical about some of the treats that the institution provided. For example, cottages often ordered pizzas from a local restaurant on Friday nights. Tony said that the pizza was often "skunky"; he believed that the restaurant, knowing that the institution would likely order pizza on Fridays, probably saved all of their old, unused crusts for the institution's order. Although he had no proof that the restaurant did this, his belief was strong. The residents' complaints about the quality of the products provided by the institution generally fell on deaf ears.

The food at the institution was described by both staff members and residents as "all starch," filling but also fattening and not as healthy as it could be. The Latino boys particularly complained that the food was bland and never had enough spices, seeming to agree with Sykes' (1958) point that "a standard of living can be hopelessly inadequate, from the individual's perspective, because it bores him to death" (p. 68). Even the staff regularly made fun of the food, one of them warning me not to eat there unless I was "starving to death." Perhaps because the food offered subsistence and little else, the boys often begged staff members to give them their desserts or to share with them whatever snacks or treats they might have brought in from the outside. Individuals would ask the staff members who served as their counselors to bring them in something "eatable" for their birthdays, graduations, or other special occasions. When they were lucky enough to get candy or food from their families, the boys were often generous in sharing their stashes with friends and others in the cottage.

Along with different and better food, the residents were very eager for something, anything different to do to relieve the monotony of their days and nights in the institution. They would often try to convince the staff to rent movies or video games for them. One night, I witnessed an interaction where a resident, Alex, and the cottage supervisor played a game of pool with the stakes being that the supervisor would rent Alex a video game if he won. With such motivation, Alex played a great game of pool, and the supervisor was compelled to rent him a game during the next week. The boys were also eager for magazines, catalogues, or different books to read, particularly because, as one young man expressed to me, "The library here doesn't have shit." On occasions when I would bring my laptop computer to the cottage, the boys would beg me to bring it out and then would line up to play card games or checkers on the computer and would stand back and offer advice to the person currently playing. They always treated the computer with the utmost respect, encouraging me to bring it in on my next visit.

Lessons the Institution Intended: School, Life Skills, Work

Among the lessons that the institution hoped to transmit to its residents were basic life skills and conforming attitudes. Boys younger than 18 were required to attend school in the institution, working toward the completion of their high school diploma or a GED. Most of the inmates of the training school were severely behind academically; their time inside essentially forced them to at least go through the motions of attending school. Once they earned a diploma or GED, their opportunities for formal education essentially ended. The only way that a motivated student could take college courses was if he or his family could afford to finance correspondence or distance learning courses. For most of the boys in this study, this was not a realistic possibility. Although they could not further their education while in the institution, the cottage staff members did encourage young men who would be getting out soon to consider attending community college. They spent a good deal of time with interested individuals showing them how to fill out applications for financial aid, advising them on courses, and helping them get their paperwork in order.

As part of their programming, each cottage was responsible for conducting classes on topics such as life skills, anger-management, victim empathy, and cultural literacy. Although they had virtually no training to do so, cottage staff members were expected to lead the classes and attempt to impart knowledge the young men would need when returning to the community. The institution provided photocopied notebooks of ideas for lessons, but the quality of the classes varied widely, largely dependent on the skill, commitment, and creativity of the staff member in charge. The connection of some of the materials to the reality of the boys' lives was highly questionable.

Several meetings were centered around videotaped programs: The drug and alcohol group viewed a fairly generic video on a White female's addiction, and the cultural literacy group was shown a tabloid-style video that advanced a conspiracy theory about the death of Jesus. The staff member in charge gave an awkward introduction to the video, saying, "Don't get mad; it's just a viewpoint. Be open-minded," but he failed to make it relevant to the topic of the class or the boys' lives.

The life skills class was a better example of tailoring the curriculum to the population. In it, the staff member, Luke, led frank discussions about sex and birth control and about paying bills and managing money. He tried to teach the residents how to plan their finances and arranged for them each to have a "checking account" for the money in their institutional accounts. It turned out to be more challenging than the staff had predicted, however, because the boys kept lending each other checks and messing up their accounts.

Along with a high school education and the competencies learned in their treatment groups, the boys also learned basic work skills and what would be expected of them as employees. Nearly all of the boys performed some sort of work in the institution. Some worked in the kitchen, some in the laundry, some in maintenance. Two jobs that were particularly sought after were helping out the staff in the gym for recreation and driving staff members and guests around the campus in a small golf cart or tram. All of the jobs paid the same minimal amount ($1 an hour at the end of the study), but the work itself was considered an important part of the learning experience for inmates. It taught them characteristics that would be expected in a job in the community: to show up on time, to perform their assigned duties, and to cooperate with authority figures.

Lessons Learned
From Cottage Staff Members

In their daily interactions with the juvenile offenders, the Blue cottage staff members strove to model prosocial behaviors in the hopes that the boys would learn conforming attitudes and behaviors. They hoped to offer them a glimpse of another set of values, another lifestyle they could choose. In addition, they worked to be consistent in their dealings with the young men in the cottage so that none of the individuals would feel singled out for unjust treatment.

The boys learned about consequences both big and small during their time in the cottage and the larger institution. They saw the long-term consequences of their crimes as the days of their confinement added up to months and years. They learned about short-term consequences for their behavior in their dealings with the cottage staff who sanctioned them for their bad behavior and rewarded them for positive steps. For many of the boys, it was the first time they had ever been so closely monitored and held accountable for their actions. It was often the first time an adult had taken a real interest in what they were doing and what they were thinking.

Although they did the best they could with limited resources and difficult circumstances, staff members feared their intervention might come too late for many of the young men in the cottage. For example, one night after spending nearly 2 hours individually counseling a boy named Andre, a staff member, Luke, told me that he wished he could do a lot more to give these kids a chance. He explained that Andre "did not get much socialization" from his mother; he remembered sleeping on the yard as a very small child, waiting for his mother to come home. Luke said that when he asked Andre how he will raise his own children, "he knew how it should be" and he spoke of how he would "consequent" his own

children to teach them responsibility for their actions. Although Andre knew how things "should" be, he never really learned how to behave himself. Luke said that Andre understood all of this, but he was learning to behave while incarcerated, which Luke believed was "fucked up." As Andre's counselor, Luke put a great deal of time and effort into trying to help him and teach him before he returned to the community.

Along with the prosocial skills that were modeled, the boys learned other skills from the staff members who essentially served as their surrogate parents, coaches, big brothers, and counselors during their time in the cottage. Staff members taught them to play chess and cribbage, showed them how to improve their athletic skills, and encouraged them in their artistic endeavors. They spent a lot of time talking to the boys about their friends and their families, helping them to make concrete plans for their return to the community.

Two examples illustrate the range of the lessons imparted by the cottage staff. In the first, a young man was involved in an assault within the institution. With new criminal charges being filed, he could no longer stay in the juvenile justice system, and he was to be transferred to an adult institution. Before his transfer, the cottage supervisor went over to the lockdown unit where he was being temporarily held to spend some time talking to him, advising him "how not to get killed in prison." On an entirely different level, cottage staff members were reminded of the youth of some of their charges as they watched them grow, their bodies filling out and maturing during their incarceration. Without family members around to guide them into manhood, many of the boys sought help and advice from the more trusted staff members. Such guidance was poignantly illustrated when I witnessed Luke patiently teach a young man how to shave his face for the first time.

Lessons Learned
From Other Inmates

At least as important as the lessons learned from the staff members and from the programming provided by the institution were the lessons the young offenders learned from their fellow inmates. Peer pressure and one's peer group standing are at least as important for institutionalized juveniles as they are for children in other populations (Preveaux, Ray, LoBello, & Mehta, 2004); in fact, the influence of peers is likely magnified in a total institution (Goffman, 1961) where your peers are your only public.

One of the first things new boys learned was to keep their mouths shut until they had proven themselves to the other members of the Blue cottage. This was clearly illustrated at dinner one night when I sat with a group of boys, and they told me that a particularly quiet individual was "too young to have any say yet" and he had to "sit and take it and be quiet." The boys who had "big mouths" and did not learn this quickly enough found that there was often a physical price to be paid as tougher inmates with longer tenure in the cottage taught them a lesson they would not soon forget. There were several instances throughout this study where I would notice fresh bruises or black eyes on one of the inmates, and I was told that individual had been "taken down a notch." The consensus in the cottage was generally that the boy had deserved the beating he got, if not more.

Along with learning how and when to keep their mouths shut, the boys in the cottage also had to learn to get along with others. They were virtually never alone, and so they had to find a way to compromise and to live in relative peace. They learned to be a little more tolerant. Rival gang members had to share the same space in the Blue cottage and learn to put their vendettas on hold. They learned who, if anyone, to trust.

The institution did have some elements of the "crime school" that correctional facilities are feared to be. The young inmates grew tougher as they grew older, and some became more criminally sophisticated; they spent a great deal of their time and energy trying to think of ways to be better criminals. Many of the boys in Blue had a history of selling drugs, and they thought if they were smarter in their actions and slow to turn to violence, they could return successfully to the drug market to make their money. Those individuals were quick to point out that they had not been caught and punished for selling drugs; most were in the institution for robbery or assault or some other act of violence.

As one example, Marco, a 19-year-old Latino, was incarcerated for being the "trigger man" on a drive-by shooting. As he neared the end of his sentence, Marco vowed that he was finished with gang violence, telling me: "I'm not putting in anymore work, though . . . no more drive-bys." He did intend to sell drugs when he was back in the community, but he had thought carefully about how to reduce the risk. He said that he would not take a lot of risks and would not be a visible dealer out on the street corner. Instead, he planned to make his deals with a pager; with a pager, he said, "you know who is calling you, and you can arrange to meet in a safe place." He also said that he would not carry the drugs in plastic baggies, because "baggies are used to prove intent to sell/deliver," which would carry a longer, more severe sentence.

In addition to thinking about ways to earn money while staying out of prison, Marco spent some of his time in the institution trying to figure out ways to beat the system; although he enjoyed writing for the training school's student newspaper, he also went to considerable effort forging a GED certificate. It was clear that he was smart and skilled enough to earn his GED legitimately, but he chose instead to try to forge it. Although it was a very good effort, the forgery was ultimately detected.

The residents of Blue also learned lessons from their day-to-day interactions. They learned to negotiate with each other and with staff members for small privileges. They learned how to fight verbal battles and to take or deflect teasing when it was aimed at them. In their attempts to stave off boredom, they improved their skills at video games, card games, pool, cribbage, and chess. After being soundly beaten at the cottage's two video games, one of the boys called Alex a "video game addict." Alex responded simply: "What else is there to do but play video games and watch TV?" A few of the boys exercised their creativity by writing poetry and raps and drawing pictures. Some took on leadership roles and learned how to teach their own hard-won conforming skills to others. Ultimately, from each other, the inmates learned how to survive their time in the institution.

Lessons Learned in Relation to Family and Friends

An important and sometimes painful lesson for the young men in this study was learning how to manage long distance relationships with friends and families, including their own children. Throughout their sentences, they learned who would be there for them and what loyalty really means in tough times. In combating their loneliness and frustration, it was important for the residents to feel that their friends in the community remembered them and cared what happened to them. A couple of the boys expressed their contempt for fair-weather friends. They made the point that people who they had not heard from the whole time they were locked up suddenly started calling them again as they were about to get out. They said that they were suddenly acting like their best friends, acting like nothing had changed after basically ignoring them for most of the time they were incarcerated. The residents prized loyalty and no longer valued such inconsistent friends.

In maintaining relationships throughout their sentences, the telephone and the mail served as important lifelines for the residents (Sykes, 1958). Phone calls and visits provided the boys a chance to keep in contact with the outside world. Yet, even that contact was severely restricted as mail was scanned and sometimes censored by staff members as they checked it both coming in and going out of the institution. Letters with gang references or veiled threats were confiscated. The number of telephone calls made by each of the boys was also carefully monitored and regulated by cottage staff members. Although there was more flexibility with incoming calls, the institution was far from most of their hometowns, and the boys' long distance calls out were generally limited to 5 minutes.

The phone and the mail were particularly important for communicating with girls. Many of the boys had met their current girlfriends while locked up. Friends shared their pictures of girls with each other, they shared their phone calls from girls with each other, and they sometimes even shared girls with each other, passing numbers and addresses to their friends, "like a pen pal," one of the young men suggested with a knowing laugh. The boys were well aware of who was receiving how many phone calls from girls, and they often teased each other about juggling girls or about how they hadn't been getting many phone calls at all lately.

Some of the boys had more serious, long-term relationships with girls "on the outs." Many of the young men (perhaps a third of the boys in the cottage at any given time) were already fathers. Although there were differing levels of involvement with their children and "my baby's mom," they all seemed to take a certain amount of pride in their paternity, and most said that they hoped to be good fathers and be there for their kids

as they grew up. TJ and Marco, particularly, spoke often of their young daughters and proudly showed off Polaroid pictures and tattoos of their daughters' names and images. Many of their plans for the future centered around doing whatever was necessary to provide better lives for their little girls.

The residents' relationships with their girlfriends went through many ups and downs during their time in the institution. On one of my visits, the cottage supervisor told me that it had been a pretty quiet week and that a lot of the boys were having "girl problems" and were fighting with their girlfriends. He mentioned a few of the residents by name and said that he had heard them "crying on the phone" to their girls. Especially acute was the frustration that these boys felt on hearing rumors about their girlfriends seeing other men and not being able to confront them face-to-face. When I asked Alex one day, "What's up with your girl?" his response illustrated the general frustration and lack of efficacy the young inmates often felt when he said: "What's up with her? You know as much as I do. Nothing I can do about it while I am in here." The residents sometimes came to me for a female perspective, something clearly lacking in the male institution, but the seeds of doubt were easily planted and difficult to remove. Troubled teenagers to begin with, the young men in the Blue cottage faced a formidable challenge in dealing with and maintaining relationships from inside the institution.

Lessons Learned Over Time

Some lessons were simply the result of being locked up for months and years in a juvenile correctional institution. Whether they liked it or not, the young men in the Blue cottage were forced to learn patience. Much of their time was spent waiting. Their daily lives were filled with waiting to be let out of their rooms, waiting to be allowed to shower, waiting to go to meals or recreation, waiting to be escorted to school or their jobs, waiting to use the phone, waiting for their next visit. Even watching television was a lesson in waiting. They would see advertisements for a new movie and would express their excitement over seeing the film, but the reality was that many of them would not be able to see that movie for years. They would see beautiful women on television and know that it would be months or years before sex with their girlfriends was a possibility. Ultimately, one thing their sentences taught all of the boys in the cottage was to find a way to endure the waiting and to survive their own impatience.

Finally, their time in the institution offered these young men a chance to reflect on their lives and their place in the world. It gave them the opportunity to really think about who they were before their incarceration, who they were turning into during their time in confinement, and who they wanted to be when they got out and grew up. Even in the confines of a juvenile correctional facility, "Emerging adulthood is arguably the period of the life course when the possibility for dramatic change is greatest" (Arnett, 2004, p. 190). Although not all of the boys took full advantage of the opportunity for such introspection, some clearly did. TJ, for example, made the comment that his 22-year-old unemployed brother should rob a bank and get locked up for 2 to 3 years; he thought it would give him a chance to get his life together because "prison gives you perspective."

◈ Discussion: Lessons Learned About Training Schools

Bartollas et al. (1976) concluded their study on a juvenile training school nearly 30 years ago with this dire message:

> This is certainly not the first, nor is it likely to be the last, in a long series of books, monographs, and articles which indict the juvenile correctional system as anti-therapeutic, anti-rehabilitative, and as exploitative and demeaning of keepers and kept alike. The juvenile correctional institution, not unlike any other total institution, is or can be more cruel and inhumane than most outsiders ever imagine. . . . The juvenile institution is a culmination of the worst features of a free society. (p. 259)

Juvenile institutions are clearly not a panacea for the problems of juvenile delinquency, but as I argued earlier, they look better or worse depending on what we compare them to. Currently, violent adolescents who are considered a danger to the community are generally sentenced to one of two options: training schools or adult prisons. With prison as the alternative, training

schools appear to do less harm to the young offenders in their midst (Austin & Irwin, 2001), or as Feld (1998) suggests: "Despite extensive judicial findings of deplorable conditions of confinement, juvenile correctional facilities probably remain less harsh or abusive than most adult prisons" (p. 234).

Conditions of confinement were not, in fact, deplorable in the training school in this study, but incarceration and the pains of imprisonment would leave significant marks on all of the young males, regardless. Although incarceration appears to be a turning point for some offenders who desist from crime, for nearly all who pass through a correctional facility, it adds to the cumulative disadvantage and the obstacles they will face on their release. Incarceration may weaken community bonds, contribute to school failure and unemployment, and ultimately increase the likelihood for adult crime (Laub & Sampson, 2003).

The rationale for a separate system for juveniles is the belief that there is something qualitatively different about adolescents and that they should not be intermingled with adult offenders. Although those youths who have committed serious and violent crimes are often viewed as beyond rehabilitation (Lipsey, 1999), those working in the juvenile justice system continue to profess hope for the rehabilitation and resocialization of the young offenders in their care (Caeti, Hemmens, Cullen, & Burton, 2003). Following the developmental perspective, they recognize that damage done by the criminal justice system carries long-term consequences that are nearly impossible to reverse (Steinberg & Schwartz, 2000). As such, allowing even serious delinquents to remain in the juvenile justice system helps to diminish those long-term consequences and reaffirms the belief that young offenders have a chance to be resocialized and pointed toward more conforming futures, that they are capable of learning valuable life lessons during their time in the juvenile system.

Most of the boys in the Blue cottage would serve relatively long sentences for their violent offenses. If resocialization was to occur while they were under the jurisdiction of the juvenile justice system, the end-of-the-line training school was generally their most stable placement, the place where they endured a state mandated time out from their lives and were encouraged to consider what they wanted their futures to hold.

In spending time with the adolescent inmates in this study, it was impossible to ignore the very fact of their youth. They were, for the most part, still boys literally growing up and maturing behind bars. There was still an air of invincibility and enthusiasm in many of the boys and young men in the Blue cottage; most had not yet fully committed to the convict world. They held on to at least some of their vulnerability and some hope for a better future. The juvenile system allowed them to make bad choices without necessarily throwing their lives away. As Feld (1996) explains: "One premise of juvenile justice is that youths should survive the mistakes of adolescence with their life chances intact" (pp. 425–426).

Compared to adult prisons, training schools such as the one in this study offer such young offenders a reprieve. They offer troubled adolescents one last opportunity to grow up a little, learn important lessons, and emerge from the institution with a chance to start their lives over. Many of them will cross the legal boundary into adulthood during their confinement; they enter the institution as boys and leave it as young men with new rights and responsibilities, facing their futures with both fear and hope. Emerging adulthood may hold particular promise for young men who are also emerging from juvenile prisons, for as Arnett (2004) has argued, "There is something about reaching emerging adulthood that opens up new possibilities for transformation for people who have had more than their share of adversity during their early years" (p. 205).

I heard again and again from individuals in this study, that "the system" cannot force anyone to change, that individuals have to want to change, they have to want to get out of "the life." The desire to change happened for some of the young men during their time in the Blue cottage as they matured and made strides toward becoming conforming adults. They are the success stories of the institution. In their efforts to overcome disadvantaged backgrounds and their own criminal histories, they provide an important lesson to the larger community by offering a compelling reason to strengthen the programming and opportunities in our juvenile correctional facilities and to continue giving adolescent offenders one last chance in the juvenile system.

 # References

Altschuler, D. M., & Brash, R. (2004). Adolescent and teenage offenders confronting the challenges and opportunities of reentry. *Youth Violence and Juvenile Justice, 2*, 72–87.

Arnett, J. J. (1998). Learning to stand alone: The contemporary American transition to adulthood in cultural and historical context. *Human Development, 41*, 295–315.

Arnett, J. J. (2004). *Emerging adulthood: The winding road from the late teens through the twenties.* New York: Oxford University Press.

Austin, J., & Irwin, J. (2001). *It's about time: America's imprisonment binge* (3rd ed.). Belmont, CA: Wadsworth.

Bartollas, C., Miller, S. J., & Dinitz, S. (1976). *Juvenile victimization: The institutional paradox.* New York: John Wiley.

Bortner, M. A., & Williams, L. M. (1997). *Youth in prison.* New York: Routledge.

Caeti, T. J., Hemmens, C., Cullen, F. T., & Burton, V. S., Jr. (2003). Management of juvenile correctional facilities. *The Prison Journal, 83*, 383–405.

Chesney-Lind, M., & Shelden, R. G. (2004). *Girls, delinquency, and juvenile justice* (3rd ed.). Belmont, CA: Wadsworth.

Feld, B. C. (1977). *Neutralizing inmate violence: Juvenile offenders in institutions.* Cambridge, MA: Ballinger.

Feld, B. C. (1996). Juvenile (in)justice and the criminal court alternative. In J. G. Weis, R. D. Crutchfield, & G. S. Bridges (Eds.), *Juvenile delinquency* (pp. 418–427). Thousand Oaks, CA: Pine Forge Press.

Feld, B. C. (1998). Juvenile and criminal justice systems' responses to youth violence. In M. Tonry & M. H. Moore (Eds.), *Youth violence* (pp. 189–261). Chicago: University of Chicago Press.

Feld, B. C. (Ed.). (1999). *Readings in juvenile justice administration.* New York: Oxford University Press.

Forst, M., Fagan, J., & Vivona, T. S. (1989). Youth in prisons and training schools: Perceptions and consequences of the treatment-custody dichotomy. *Juvenile and Family Court Journal, 40*, 1–14.

Furstenberg, F. F., Jr., Rumbaut, R. G., & Settersten, R. A., Jr. (2005). On the frontier of adulthood: Emerging themes and new directions. In R. A. Settersten Jr., F. F. Furstenberg Jr., & R. G. Rumbaut (Eds.), *On the frontier of adulthood: Theory, research, and public policy* (pp. 3–28). Chicago: University of Chicago Press.

Goffman, E. (1961). *Asylums.* New York: Anchor.

Grisso, T., & Schwartz, R. G. (2000). Introduction. In T. Grisso & R. G. Schwartz (Eds.), *Youth on trial: A developmental perspective on juvenile justice* (pp. 1–5). Chicago: University of Chicago Press.

Haskell, M. R., & Yablonsky, L. (1982). *Juvenile delinquency* (3rd ed.). Boston: Houghton Mifflin.

Irwin, J. (1970). *The felon.* Berkeley: University of California Press.

Lane, J., Lanza-Kaduce, L., Frazier, C. E., & Bishop, D. M. (2002). Adult versus juvenile sanctions: Voices of incarcerated youths. *Crime & Delinquency, 48*, 431–455.

Laub, J. H., & Sampson, R. J. (2003). *Shared beginnings, divergent lives: Delinquent boys to age 70.* Cambridge, MA: Harvard University Press.

Lipsey, M. W. (1999). Can intervention rehabilitate serious delinquents? *The Annals of the American Academy of Political and Social Science, 564*, 142–166.

Miller, J. G. (1998). *Last one over the wall: The Massachusetts experiment in closing reform schools* (2nd ed.). Columbus: Ohio State University Press.

Polsky, H. W. (1962). *Cottage six—The social system of delinquent boys in residential treatment.* New York: Russell Sage.

Preveaux, N. E., Ray, G. E., LoBello, S. G., & Mehta, S. (2004). Peer relationships among institutionalized juvenile boys. *Journal of Adolescent Research, 19*, 284–302.

Scott, E. S. (2000). Criminal responsibility in adolescence: Lessons from developmental psychology. In T. Grisso & R. G. Schwartx (Eds.), *Youth on trial: A developmental perspective on juvenile justice* (pp. 291–324). Chicago: University of Chicago Press.

Steinberg, L., & Schwartz, R. G. (2000). Developmental psychology goes to court. In T. Grisso & R. G. Schwartz (Eds.), *Youth on trial: A developmental perspective on juvenile justice* (pp. 9–31). Chicago: University of Chicago Press.

Sykes, G. M. (1958). *The society of captives: A study of a maximum security prison.* Princeton, NJ: Princeton University Press.

Sykes, G. M., & Messinger, S. (1960). The inmate social system. In R. A. Cloward (Ed.), *Theoretical studies in social organization of the prison* (pp. 5–19). New York: Social Science Research Council.

Van Vleet, R. K. (1999). The attack on juvenile justice. *The Annals of the American Academy of Political and Social Science, 564*, 203–214.

Weber, G. H. (1961). Emotional and defensive reactions of cottage parents. In D. R. Cressey (Ed.), *The prison: Studies in institutional organization and change* (pp. 189–228). New York: Holt, Rinehart & Winston.

Wooden, K. (1976). *Weeping in the playtime of others: America's incarcerated children.* New York: McGraw-Hill.

❖ ❖ ❖

READING 31

In this brief article, Bruce Western considers how mass incarceration in the United States has reconfigured civic life, arguing that the state has played an important role in amplifying rather than ameliorating inequality. To help to put a human face on these issues, Western details some of the challenges that a man named Peter faced in the first year after his release from prison, arguing that the future of citizenship for the poor depends, in part, on how much the insiders of American society can see of themselves in individuals like Peter.

*Incarceration, Inequality, and Imagining Alternatives**

Bruce Western

Citizenship is a public declaration of equality. Regardless of the inequalities that internally divide a society, citizens enjoy a common set of rights—perhaps to protest or vote or run for office. The content of citizenship rights has varied greatly across time and place. In the stylized history of T. H. Marshall (1950/1992), rights to speech and access to the courts were among the earliest pillars of citizenship, followed by rights to the franchise, and finally by rights to social welfare with the emergence of modern social policy.

Source: Western, B. (2014). Incarceration, inequality, and imagining alternatives. *ANNALS of the American Academy of Political and Social Science, 651*, 302.

*Some text has been omitted. Please consult the original source.

Marshall's account of the historical development of citizenship describes a virtuous circle in which the pool of citizens grows as the rights of citizenship become more extensive. Civil rights empower citizens to press for voting rights. Once the male working class was enfranchised in Europe, unions and labor parties set about expanding social rights embodied in the welfare state. In Marshall's account, universal education was the key breakthrough, but safety net programs, national health care, and public pensions could also be added to the list. . . .

The virtuous circle of citizenship—never fully developed in the United States to begin with—has been interrupted. The punitive turn in criminal justice policy amounts to a transformation of the quality of citizenship, in which the state plays an active role in deepening, not reducing, inequality. The virtuous circle turned vicious.

The vicious circle of mass incarceration has three main elements. First, incarceration deepens inequality because its negative social and economic effects are concentrated in the poorest communities. Deep race and class inequalities in incarceration are well documented. Recent cohorts of African American men are more likely to go to prison than to graduate from college with a four-year degree. In 2010, young black male dropouts were more incarcerated (37 percent) than employed (26 percent) (Western and Pettit 2009). It is among these men that we observe the reduced wages, impaired health, and family instability following time in prison. . . .

Second, much of the social and economic inequality associated with incarceration is invisible. Becky Pettit provides a detailed treatment of this in her book, *Invisible Men* (2012) . . . Our data systems are unsuited to measure populations that are significantly institutionalized. They skew our assessments of social inequality. Household surveys reporting on employment, wages, and educational attainment make the well-being of African Americans look artificially good because the poorest are uncounted. The invisibility of inequality associated with incarceration is also sustained in a related but different way. The experience of incarceration is so deeply stratified, its reality is confined to a small fraction of the population for whom

the prison has become ubiquitous. The lived experience of urban poverty has been transformed by the growth of the penal system, but this is largely unknown to the mainstream of American society whose relationship to criminal justice institutions looks much as it did before the prison boom.

Third, mass incarceration and its social and economic consequences contribute to a legitimacy gap between the poor and the rest of American society. In the mainstream perspective, incarceration and its accompanying socioeconomic disadvantage stems more from the criminal conduct of offenders than the policy choices of government officials. The institutions themselves are not questioned. This is the sense in which Marshall (1950/1992, 7) observed that "citizenship is the architect of legitimate social inequality." The inequalities arising under a citizenship regime are traced to the defects of individuals and not the institutions themselves. In poor, high-incarceration communities, criminal justice and other state institutions have become de-legitimated. . . .

These elements of the vicious circle—deeper and invisible inequalities combined with a widening legitimacy gap between the poor and the mainstream—make the social exclusion of mass incarceration intractable. Exclusion through incarceration further impoverishes poor communities and breeds cynicism about the civic institutions that might bring about change.

How can the vicious circle of mass incarceration be broken? Much of the political significance of incarceration lies in its intimate connection with extreme poverty. Because of its social and economic effects and because of the sense of injustice it fuels, incarceration adds mightily to the social distance between the poor and the affluent. Against this great social distance, the extension of citizenship is an act of imagination. Outsiders must be reconceived as insiders. For this to happen, the insiders must recognize something of themselves in the citizens to be.

In April 2012, a research team at Harvard University began a series of interviews with 135 men and women who were leaving prison and returning to neighborhoods in the Boston area. One of my first interviews was at a minimum security prison with Peter, an African American man in his 40s who had spent most of the last 15 years in prison. Peter had a long history of violence that was episodically associated with drinking and drug use. Throughout his life, he had dealt drugs, stolen cars, and gotten in fights. The first time we spoke, in prison, he was reluctant to share his social security number (which we use for record linkage to unemployment insurance) or many other personal details.

Over the following year, after his release, we saw in detail many of the challenges confronting those who leave prison. In the first week out, Peter applied to a community program for work clothes and a mass transit card. At first he divided his time between a friend's place and his older sister's crowded home that also housed her fiancé, daughter, and granddaughter. Over the months, Peter began to develop a relationship with two of his three children and their two mothers. Closer to one mother and her child than to the other, he seemed to focus more attention on his 10-year-old son, though he did what he could to buy them both clothes and school supplies. Peter was enrolled in the food stamps program and MassHealth, the Massachusetts Medicaid program. Each month he gave his $200 in food stamps to his sister, though his eligibility for that program has now expired and he is hoping to be reinstated. Through MassHealth, he attended mental health and substance abuse treatment. He also had a physical and visited the dentist.

Peter could not find work but did enroll in employment programs doing maintenance and operating machines. The programs paid less than minimum wage, but he thought it was important to get into a daily routine. For six months, he would rise at 5:00 a.m., start work at 6:30 a.m., and work through until 3:00 p.m. Every two weeks he would report to his probation officer and on weekends he would do community service in lieu of a $65-a-month probation fee. Peter gets from place to place by mass transit and walking, concerned that riding in a car with friends might get him arrested. (If the car is stopped by police, his probation status might come up and this might trigger a violation if others in the car have felony convictions or if drugs or guns are discovered.) He is yet to find a job, unable to move forward in the hiring process once his criminal record is disclosed.

With more interviews and phone calls, we learned a little of Peter's family history. He grew up in the Lennox Street projects, a public housing complex in Boston's South End. He was a runaway. Starting around the age of 12, he would leave the house for weeks at a time, living with friends, often drinking, using drugs, and getting in trouble. One of his earliest memories of serious violence was of a brawl at midnight between blacks and whites outside an Irish bar in the neighborhood of Mattapan. Peter was 12, and he and his uncle were involved in the fight. In that melee, Peter saw a white man stabbed to death, just outside the diner where we talked some 30 years later. At 13, Peter stole a car and drove it to New York and stayed there for a while. Shortly after, his father took him to live in Los Angeles, but they returned after about a year and Peter began to live with his mother.

Mass incarceration looks a lot like this. It is not just a burgeoning prison population but how American poverty has come to be lived. The poor do not just live below an income threshold. Low income accompanies the tightly correlated adversity of violence, addiction and mental illness, childhood trauma, school failure, labor market discrimination, housing instability, and family complexity. On top of all this, we have overlaid lengthy periods of penal confinement.

The future of citizenship for the poor depends a lot on how much the insiders of American society see of themselves in Peter. The totality of his life seems light years away. He is struggling now for sobriety, housing security, economic independence, and reconciliation with his children. Mass incarceration yields few degrees of freedom. Arrest and reincarceration are often close at hand. Can we imagine a citizenry that includes Peter as much as it includes the rest of society? If Peter's life circumstances are unfamiliar, he shares in a history that is thoroughly recognizable. The Lennox Street projects are one of the many large public housing complexes that formed much of the context for U.S. race relations over the last half century. His daily struggles to make ends meet and provide for his children are basic human challenges increasingly swamping the American middle class. Of course, the likelihood and consequences of failure for Peter are far greater, but the struggle is familiar.

So perhaps his place in a shared history and the effort he makes to find a righteous place in the world can close the social distance enough to help start a different conversation about prison policy, crime, and American poverty. Building such a conversation requires a detailed analysis of poverty as it is lived. Here we should acknowledge all the agency, effort, and creativity of those engulfed in the penal system, just as we emphasize the weighty constraint of social forces. This would seem to be a basic part of the project of humanization that might disrupt the vicious circle.

Peter has sold drugs, been on both sides of serious violence, and has been locked up for most of his adult life. For all that, he gets up at 5:00 a.m., looks for work or goes to programs, and meets his son after school. Street life, he says, is well behind him. Still, the future is hard to predict for poor men with long criminal histories. Could he once again wave a gun in someone's face, abandon his children, or relapse to addiction? Sure. A good part of Peter's humanity rests in that possibility, too.

 References

Burch, Traci. 2014. Effects of imprisonment and community supervision on neighborhood political participation in North Carolina. *The ANNALS of the American Academy of Political and Social Science*, 651.

Ewert, Stephanie, Bryan Sykes, and Becky Pettit. 2014. The degree of disadvantage: Incarceration and inequality in education. *The ANNALS of the American Academy of Political and Social Science*, 651.

Justice, Benjamin, and Tracey L. Meares. 2014. How the criminal justice system educates citizens. *The ANNALS of the American Academy of Political and Social Science*, 651.

Lee, Hedwig, Lauren C. Porter, and Megan Comfort. 2014. Consequences of family member incarceration: Impacts on civic participation and perceptions of the legitimacy and fairness of government. *The ANNALS of the American Academy of Political and Social Science*, 651.

Marshall,* T. H. 1950/1992. *Citizenship and social class.* London: Pluto.

Muller, Christopher, and Daniel Schrage. 2014. Mass imprisonment and trust in the law. *The ANNALS of the American Academy of Political and Social Science*, 651.

Pettit, Becky. 2012. *Invisible men: Mass incarceration and the myth of black progress.* New York, NY: Russell Sage Foundation.

Schnittker, Jason. 2014. The psychological dimensions and the social consequences of incarceration. *The ANNALS of the American Academy of Political and Social Science*, 651.

Western, Bruce, and Becky Pettit. 2009. Technical report on revised population estimates and NLSY79 analysis tables for the Pew Public Safety and Mobility Project. Unpublished manuscript, Harvard University, Cambridge, MA.

Wildeman, Christopher. 2014. Parental incarceration, child homelessness, and the invisible consequences of mass imprisonment. *The ANNALS of the American Academy of Political and Social Science*, 651.

CHAPTER 12

Deviant Careers and Career Deviance

I felt a little inferior at first, because I had no knowledge myself of nudist camps. . . . I started to enjoy myself, but I couldn't quite feel comfortable. In the nude. In front of a lot of people. A lack of confidence. By not having complete knowledge. I really didn't know what to expect.

—A soon-to-be nudist's first experience
at a nudist camp (From Weinberg, 1966, p. 20)

A really bad work day is, nobody's calling, [you're] stressed trying to pick from people that you kind of don't want to have over because you don't know them, they might be—they're probably not cops but it's not clear, because they either won't give their work number or they won't do something [else that is part of her screening process]—and trying to [decide] to see them or not to see them, since it's already pledged as a work day and not [a day off]. . . . Just sitting around and waiting is really one of the higher-level bad days, I think.

—A really bad day for an "elite prostitute" (From Lucas, 2005, p. 524)

I can if somebody says something to me that I don't like you know it doesn't bother me any more . . . it meant (after being saved) that I could literally get ease with myself and not jump up and beat the crap out of somebody or if somebody comes and gets something from me and didn't bring it back you know at a certain time I'd go and beat the crap out of them.

—An ex-offender previously incarcerated
in a state facility describing how being "saved" helped
keep him from violence in situations that would have provoked
him earlier (From Giordano, Longmore, Schroeder, & Seffrin, 2008, p. 117)

Introduction

The three stories above seem quite different. The first discusses a novice nudist's first experience at a nudist camp and how she felt as she entered a new deviant context and form of deviant behavior. The second is from an "elite prostitute" whose worst "working day" is where she is ambivalent about what work (i.e., clients) she will take. The final quote is from an ex-offender who believes that his spirituality helps prevent him from violence in situations when he normally would have "beaten the crap out of someone." What links these very different quotes is that they are from persons deemed deviant by much of society, but each of these people is at a different stage of a deviant life course. The first is entering a deviant lifestyle; the second, presumably, is actively involved in a deviant career; and the last one is desisting from a violent history. These are the themes of this chapter—how deviance changes over time and often has a beginning, a middle, and an end.

As the title of this chapter implies, a distinction can be made between deviant careers and career deviance. The term "deviant careers" implies an actual career: a job, room for possible advancement (or dismissal), "regular" pay, and possibly even taxes. In a deviant career, it is clear that there is work for money, a beginning to the career, and an end to the career (retirement, change in jobs, or death). The careers in question, however, are ones that are formally or informally sanctioned (socially, morally, or legally) or are typically disrespected by society—or at least certain segments of society. For simplicity's sake, examples might include dancers in strip clubs, sex workers in pornography, certain prostitutes, drug dealers and smugglers, and professional thieves, among others.

The notion of "career deviance" brings a different connotation. Our view of a career deviant is one who becomes involved in crime or other deviant behavior not so much as a career, per se, but as a sequence of deviant events that occur over time with a beginning and an end. The career can be very short, such as that of a rebellious youth who has a few run-ins with the law, or it could be a long-term pattern of sexual encounters with same-sex strangers in public restrooms. The major commonality about deviant careers and career deviance is time.

Many of the theories we have discussed are static in nature and attempt to distinguish deviants from conformists using any number of variables (e.g., social bonds, self-control, strains, or association with deviant peers). Thinking about deviance in terms of careers forces us to think longitudinally (over time) and brings up some very interesting questions that are not necessarily intuitive. Thinking longitudinally, we start to recognize that different factors may influence (1) the onset of deviance, (2) continuation or **escalation** of deviance, and (3) **desistance** from deviance (be it almost immediate or gradually over time). We also start thinking about whether deviants specialize in particular forms of deviance or are generalists, engaging in many forms of deviance given the opportunities available, and whether **specialization** or diversification changes over time.

DEVIANCE IN POPULAR CULTURE

The subject of deviant careers and career deviance has gained momentum in recent years as more and more scholars have focused on issues of desistance and community re-entry. As you learned in the last chapter, labeling is often an important factor in deviant careers; once labeled, it can be extremely difficult to get a job, rent an apartment, or lead a conforming lifestyle. Here we offer several examples of films that address this issue.

The Released—This PBS *Frontline* documentary (available to watch online) is about mentally ill inmates being released back into the community with no care or safety net. The filmmakers follow several men over an extended period of time and show their struggles trying to manage mental illness and survive in the community.

Tequila Sunrise—A popular fictional film from the 1980s starring Mel Gibson as a successful drug dealer trying to leave his illegitimate business and start a conforming one. In one memorable scene, Gibson's character tries to explain how difficult it can be to leave the drug-dealing scene, detailing a list of people that don't want him to quit, each for his or her own reasons.

The Woodsman—In this dark film starring Kevin Bacon, a convicted sex offender is released after 12 years in prison. The film follows his attempts to build a conforming and quiet life in the community.

Sherrybaby—After three years in prison, a drug addict with a troubled history struggles to reconnect with her young daughter. The strong performance by Maggie Gyllenhaal showcases the difficulty of trying to rebuild relationships and become a good mother.

◈ Development of a Deviant Careers and Career Deviance Approach

We raise this distinction between deviant careers and career deviance in part because of a very large debate in criminology, referred to by some as the "great debate" (Soothill, Fitzpatrick, & Brian, 2009, p. 14), that escalated in the 1980s and continues today. The debate is largely between those who believe that longitudinal research is too expensive and not necessary for a thorough understanding of criminal behavior and those who believe longitudinal designs are crucial. The former typically believe that the factors that affect criminal behavior are relatively static and that cross-sectional designs are perfectly appropriate to test theories and develop appropriate programs and policies. The latter believe that different factors may affect the **onset/initiation** of criminal behavior, its continuation and possible escalation, and the desistance process. This is not a trivial debate, and both sides have made important points. For example, it may seem "obvious" to many that knowing when different types of criminal behaviors begin, how long they persist across the life course, and when different types of offenders age out of crime is useful information. Indeed, several statistical analyses and reviews seem to support the conclusion that there are certain groups of offenders who consistently offend over time that could be incarcerated for long periods of time, thus resulting in significantly lower rates of crime (see Blumstein & Cohen, 1979; Farrington, Gallagher, Morley, Ledger, & West, 1985; Greenberg, 1985). Alternatively, others disagree and argue that similar factors affect criminal behavior whether it is early or late in the game. They seriously challenge the notion that high-risk groups can be identified early on and argue that most offenders age out of crime fairly early in the life course and that the "career criminal" paradigm is basically without merit (Gottfredson & Hirschi, 1986).

We bring this debate regarding career criminals and criminal careers to your attention because we feel that it is important that students have at least heard of the debate. For the student of the sociology of deviance (as opposed to criminal behavior) for whom this book was written, this is just one small tree in a huge forest. First, there are many forms of deviance that we have no interest in trying to stop, particularly through incarceration.

© Doug Menuez/Thinkstock

▲ **Photo 12.1** Marijuana can be experienced in very different ways, especially among novice users.

Second, the chronological age that people typically begin to engage in deviance may not be terribly interesting in itself. Alternatively, why some people become interested in a particular form of deviance or the circumstances under which they initiate the behavior is fascinating to most all of us. Why do people begin to use or sell drugs, turn tricks, enter a nudist colony, begin a career in pornography, become a compulsive consumer of porn, or any number of other deviant behaviors? Similarly, estimating the length of a deviant career may be somewhat interesting but probably not as interesting as studying how people live a deviant lifestyle, the challenges they face with conventional society, or the dangers inherent in many deviant careers. Finally and related, what pushes or pulls people out of careers of deviance? Indeed, the process of desistance—getting out of the business or "out of the life"—is one of the most interesting aspects of the sociological study of deviance.

◈ Getting Into Deviance: Onset of a Deviant Career

At a very general level, it doesn't take much to initiate many deviant acts. Sneaking a drink from the parents' liquor cabinet, stealing a cigarette from an unguarded purse, breaking into an unlocked home, or cheating on a spouse or partner after too much drinking is fairly easy given the opportunity, a little interest or motivation, or especially some encouragement. Becoming a serious underage drinker or smoker, a burglar, or a career cheater will likely take more effort. The entrances to deviant careers vary considerably depending on the behavior in question, so in this section of the book, we discuss several different forms of deviance to provide the reader with some idea of the complexities and tremendous variation in ways individuals get into a career of deviance.

Howard Becker (1953) presented a series of socially interactive stages that he argued one needed to go through to become a user of marijuana. He contended that to become a "marijuana smoker," one must (1) learn to smoke the drug properly, (2) feel the intoxicating "high" associated with smoking marijuana, and (3) come to understand the feeling of intoxication as pleasurable. That is, one needs to learn to take in the smoke and hold the smoke for some time to get enough THC (the active chemical in marijuana) to actually get intoxicated. He argued that even if enough THC is ingested, individuals don't always feel the high of the drug, and even when they do, they may not find it terribly enjoyable. More recent research supports Becker's theory but suggests that times have changed, at least to some extent. For example, most of Becker's research subjects did not get high their first time, but perhaps that was because of the quality of the marijuana in the 1950s versus the 1980s and 1990s. More recent research (Hallstone, 2002; Hirsch, Conforti, & Graney, 1990) shows that most first-timers do feel the effects of smoking pot, and some recall their very first experience as pleasant. However, the first experience is not always pleasurable and may in fact be quite negative physically (dry mouth, coughing, etc.) and emotionally. As one of Hallstone's (2002) respondents reported when asked if he enjoyed getting high the first time,

Umm . . . (emphatically) nooo! I was scared. I was very scared because not only could I not tell anybody, but um . . . I did not know if I was going to come down, how long it was going to last, and is my mom going to know. (p. 839)

Marijuana is clearly the most popular and widespread illegal drug in this country, although it is now legal in several states. A 2010 survey of eighth, tenth, and twelfth graders conducted by Monitoring the Future showed lifetime prevalence of marijuana use at 17%, 33%, and 44%, respectively. When asked about the availability of marijuana, 41% of eighth graders, 69% of tenth graders, and 83% of twelfth graders said that it would be fairly or very easy to obtain. Given the innocuous or even positive representation of marijuana in the media, few would be surprised that even "good kids" have experimented with the substance. Alternatively, consider what might be required for the initiation of harder, less "popular" drugs, such as heroin, which has been tried by around 1% of people. Or in line with a true deviant career, what is involved in becoming a drug dealer?

P. A. Adler and P. Adler (1983) studied a group of upper-level drug dealers and smugglers (of mostly marijuana and cocaine in a county in southwest California). They found three routes to becoming upper-level drug dealers and smugglers: low-level entry, middle-level entry, and smuggling, which was considered the highest level. People who started at the bottom, as it were, were largely heavy drug users who basically had to deal to support their own habits. Most low-level dealers stayed low-level dealers, not having the motivation and/or never developing the skills or the resources to make it into the middle level. The Adlers found that only about 20% of their upper-level dealer sample began as low-level dealers, and most of these dealers came from other parts of the country and had graduated into mid-level dealing before moving into the lucrative California market.

Middle-level entry was more common (about 75%) among their sample of upper-level dealers, and these dealers often came from other professions—some conventional and others on the seedier side. For example, one of the mid-level dealers was involved in a conventional real estate business but was laundering money through the business. Mid-level dealers had money and went in big, but they still had to learn the drug-trafficking trade, including "how to establish business connections, organize profitable transactions, avoid arrest, transport illegal goods, and coordinate participants and equipment" (P. A. Adler & P. Adler, 1983, pp. 198–199). These were largely entrepreneurs who wanted to make it to the top and found the social networks needed in the drug subculture to make that happen.

Only a small proportion of the smugglers (about 10%) got into smuggling on their own; even upper-level drug dealers didn't have the knowledge, skills, connections, equipment, and other resources to embark on their own smuggling operation. Rather, "most novice smugglers were recruited and trained by a sponsor with whom they forged an apprentice–mentor relationship" (P. A. Adler & P. Adler, 1983, p. 199). Through this relationship, the recruits learned the techniques, acquired resources, and, most importantly, made contacts, and they eventually branched out or, in some cases, took over the operation when someone retired from the business. This is clearly consistent with the differential association and social learning theories discussed in Chapter 6. It also brings up the notion of stratification within deviant careers. Just as there are hierarchies in conventional business (workers, supervisors and managers, upper administration, presidents, and owners), so too is there stratification in the world of deviant careers. Just as in conventional organizations, upward mobility is possible but not always easy.

Other research on entering the business of drug dealing, which examines the dealing of crack and meth, shows that it actually looks somewhat similar to that of these upper-level cocaine and marijuana dealers (see Dunlap, Johnson, & Manwar, 1994; Murphy, Waldorf, & Reinarman, 1990; VanNostrand & Tewksbury, 1997). Most research suggests that the motivations, techniques, and contacts need to be learned over the course of time for a full career to develop.

Truly getting into deviance often requires the acquisition of a deviant identity. As people come to define themselves as drinkers and smokers, they drink and smoke; it is part of their identity. Socially, drinkers are offered alcoholic beverages, and it is understood that when smokers walk outside, they are probably going for a cigarette. But how do deviant identities emerge? Penelope McLorg and Diane Taub (1987) provide an excellent example of how anorexics and bulimics move through a process from very conforming behavior to primary deviance to secondary deviance. Specifically, through participant observations of the self-help group BANISH (Bulimics/Anorexics in Self-Help), they conducted qualitative interviews with 15 participants and found that the women and men they studied started out quite conventionally. They had strong attachments to their families, did well in school, and internalized the cultural norm that slim is beautiful. They were rewarded when they lost weight, but like most dieters, they often were unable to maintain lowered weights, resulting in seemingly extreme behaviors to maintain desired weights. Here the anorexics and bulimics moved into a stage of primary deviance where they did not consider themselves anorexic or bulimic, their deviance was largely unknown to others, and the outcome of their behaviors was both psychologically and socially rewarding—they were slim and, therefore, more "beautiful." At some point, however, friends and family came to recognize compulsive behaviors surrounding food and exercise among the anorexics and evidence of bingeing and purging among the bulimics. As with many other forms of deviance, friends and families were resistant to labeling the behaviors problematic, and, among the anorexics, there was a great deal of denial when called out on their compulsive behaviors. In contrast, bulimics tended to know that bingeing and purging was abnormal and unhealthy and, when confronted, were more likely to admit that they were bulimic.

By the nature of McLorg and Taub's (1987) study design, all of the anorexics and bulimics were part of a self-help group designed to help those stigmatized as deviant regain a sense of normality. Their disorder, then, became a master status, something that provided a new identity that dramatically affected their lives.

Another article focusing on initiation involved "club drugs" and was conducted by Halkitis and Palamer (2008). They interviewed and surveyed a sample of gay ($n = 385$) and bisexual men ($n = 52$) in the early to mid-2000s over the course of a year about their club drug use. At the initial assessment, the majority of respondents (79%) had used cocaine in the previous four months (the time frame for most of the drug use questions). Similarly, a majority had used ecstasy (75%), methamphetamines (55%), and ketamine (55%). Just under a third (29%) had used GHB. A clear majority (59%) reported that cocaine was the first club drug they initiated, followed by ecstasy at 35%. Rarely was ketamine, methamphetamine, or GHB the first club drug initiated (5% reporting one of them to be the first). Interestingly, the most common second drug initiated was ecstasy, again at 35%. So if we combine the most common first and second club drug initiated, we get almost equal proportions for cocaine and ecstasy (74% and 75%, respectively).

Using these statistics, the authors developed a model that distinguished first initiation of various drugs compared with cocaine (the most commonly first initiated). They found that those who initiated ecstasy first tended to be older and tended to use more club drugs (i.e., they were polydrug users). Those who initiated ketamine first were also more likely to be polydrug users. Interestingly, those initiating methamphetamines first were indistinguishable from cocaine initiators on every variable available, including age, race/ethnicity, HIV status, sexual orientation, and polydrug use. Gay and bisexual men, like the general population, were more likely to use cocaine first, which is consistent with sequential theories. It is only after these initiating drugs that a difference in type of drug use emerges between this population and the general population.

What should be clear from this section is that getting into deviance takes many forms, and various stages of development are required in almost any career in deviance.

◇ Risk and Protective Factors for Onset

Over the past several decades, great concerns have arisen over the onset of certain forms of deviant behavior, including drug and alcohol use, violence, teen pregnancy, high-risk sexual behavior, and other problematic behaviors. Because of societal concern over these issues, a tremendous amount of literature has emerged attempting to find factors that are positively related to deviant involvement (risk factors). Intricately related is a line of research that attempts to find factors that minimize the deleterious effects of risk factors (protective factors). An overview of **risk** and **protective factors** for adolescent problem behaviors, developed by the Social Development Group at the University of Washington, is provided in Figure 12.1. Risk factors have been categorized under several domains, including (1) individual and peer factors (e.g., rebelliousness of the child and deviant peers); (2) school (e.g., lack of commitment to school); (3) family (e.g., family conflict and management problems); and (4) the community (e.g., availability of alcohol and drugs and economic deprivation). Protective

Figure 12.1 Risk and Protective Factor Framework

The following graph supports a public health model using a theoretical framework of risk reduction and protection enhancement. Developments in prevention and intervention science have shown that there are characteristics of individuals and their families and their environment (i.e., community neighborhood, school) that affect the likelihood of negative outcomes including substance abuse, delinquency, violence, and school dropout. Other characteristics serve to protect or provide a buffer to moderate the influence of the negative characteristics. These characteristics are identified as risk factors and protective factors. (Arthur, Hawkins, et al., 1994; Hawkins, Catalano, Miller, 1992).

	Risk Factors	Adolescent Problem Behaviors						Protective Factors	Social Development Model (SDM)
		Substance Abuse	Depression & Anxiety	Delinquency	Teen Pregnancy	School Drop-Out	Violence		
Domains	*Risk factors are characteristics of individuals, their family, school, and community environments that are associated with increases in alcohol and other drug use, delinquency, teen pregnancy, school dropout, and violence. The following factors have been identified that increase the likelihood that children and youth may develop such problem behaviors.*							*Factors associated with reduced potential for drug use are called protective factors. Protective factors encompass family, social, psychological, and behavioral characteristics that can provide a buffer for the children and youth. These factors mitigate the effects of risk factors that are present in the child or youth's environment.*	*SDM is a synthesis of three existing theories of criminology (control, social learning, and differential association). It incorporates the results of research on risk and protective factors for problem behaviors and a developmental perspective of age, specific problem, and prosocial behavior. It is based on the assumption that children learn behaviors.*
Community	Availability of alcohol/other drugs	✓					✓	Opportunities for prosocial involvement in community	
	Availability of firearms			✓			✓		
	Community laws and norms favorable to drug use, firearms, and crime	✓		✓			✓	Recognition for prosocial involvement	
	Transitions and mobility	✓	✓	✓		✓			
	Low neighborhood attachment and community disorganization	✓		✓			✓		
	Media portrayals of violence						✓		
	Extreme economic deprivation	✓		✓	✓	✓	✓		
Family	Family history of the problem behavior	✓	✓	✓	✓	✓	✓	Bonding to family with healthy beliefs and clear standards	
	Family management problems	✓	✓	✓	✓	✓	✓	Attachment to family with healthy beliefs and clear standards	
	Family conflict	✓	✓	✓	✓	✓	✓		
	Favorable parental attitudes and involvement in problem behaviors	✓		✓			✓	Opportunities for prosocial involvement / Recognition for prosocial involvement	
School	Academic failure beginning in late elementary school	✓	✓	✓	✓	✓	✓	Bonding and attachment to school / Opportunities for prosocial involvement	
	Lack of commitment to school	✓		✓	✓	✓	✓	Recognition for prosocial involvement	
Individual / Peer	Early and persistent antisocial behavior	✓	✓	✓	✓	✓	✓	Bonding to peers with healthy beliefs and clear standards	
	Rebelliousness	✓		✓		✓		Attachment to peers with healthy beliefs and clear standards	
	Friends who engage in the problem behavior	✓		✓	✓	✓	✓	Opportunities for prosocial involvement	
	Favorable attitudes toward the problem behavior (including low perceived risk of harm)	✓		✓	✓	✓		Increase in social skills	
	Early initiation of the problem behavior	✓		✓	✓	✓	✓		
	Gang involvement	✓		✓			✓		
	Constitutional factors	✓	✓	✓			✓		

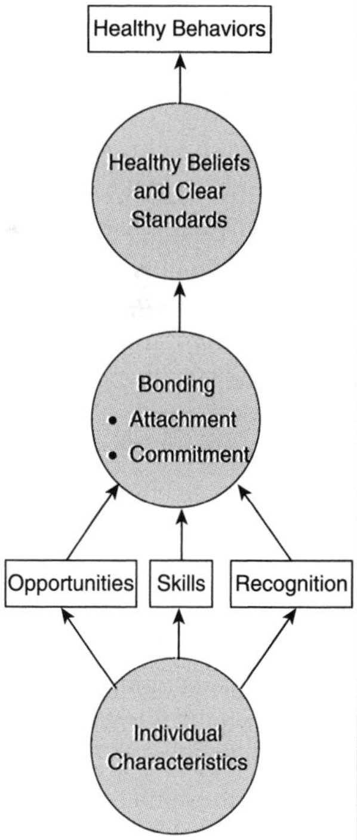

Social Development Model (SDM) diagram:

Healthy Behaviors → Healthy Beliefs and Clear Standards → Bonding (• Attachment • Commitment) ← Opportunities | Skills | Recognition ← Individual Characteristics

Source: The Substance Abuse and Medical Services Administration, U.S. Department of Health and Human Services. Retrieved from http://sde.state.ok.us/Schools/SafeHealthy/pdf/RiskProtectFactor.pdf

factors that mitigate the risk factors are also listed by domain. Protective factors are particularly important because they provide insights for developing effective policy and programs based on research evidence. So at the community level, we might encourage programs that provide opportunities for conventional involvement and rewards for doing good things in the neighborhood. High-risk families might be targeted and offered parent-training courses or social supports that help them manage daily life. There are obviously a number of school-based programs that encourage students to feel that they are a part of the institution and structured activities to make them committed to doing well in school. Similarly, we might encourage individual counseling or other programs (be they school or family based) to help young persons become attached to prosocial individuals (e.g., mentors) and institutions (the family or the school).

◈ Getting Out of the Game: Desistance From Career Deviance

If you think about most traditional theories of deviance, they have typically focused on two questions: (1) Why do people begin to engage in deviance, and (2) why does deviance persist (Paternoster & Bushway, 2009). For example, Hirschi's (1969) early social control theory, which we covered in Chapter 7, would say that deviance is fun, easy, and rewarding, and people are drawn toward it. Deviance is initiated because of a lack of the social controls (attachment, commitment, involvement, and beliefs) that usually prevent people from initiating deviance. Unless there is a significant change in social bonds (e.g., a good job or investment in school or marriage), deviance persists because bonds remain weak. His later theory with Gottfredson (Gottfredson & Hirschi, 1990), which focused on self-control, shares a similar perspective and, furthermore, insists that self-control is stable, and that is why deviance persists. Strain theorists (especially Agnew with his individual-level version), introduced in Chapter 4, suggest that initial deviance is a reaction to frustration and anger, and deviance persists because the structure of society means certain people remain in stressful conditions (Agnew, 2006). Finally, differential association and social learning theories, covered in Chapter 6, suggest that deviance emerges when definitions favorable to deviance outweigh definitions unfavorable to deviance. To the extent people are, for example, immersed in a subculture conducive to deviance, the deviance is likely to continue. This is the way these theories have typically been used. However, with the emergence of the **criminal career paradigm** or the **life course perspective**, introduced earlier in Chapter 7, people started to be much more concerned with the tail end of the deviant career and how and why criminals and other deviants desist.

Surely the theories above might be used to explain desistance. Social controls or bonds can emerge by entering a solid relationship such as marriage or obtaining stable employment (Sampson & Laub, 1993). Or one might escape situations that produce strain or develop skills to help deal with frustrating conditions (Agnew, 1997). Finally, people sometimes do change their social networks and, therefore, the definitions they are exposed to, enabling them to exit a deviant career (Akers, 1998). Indeed, social control, strain, and differential association theories have all been placed within a life course perspective and can be used to help explain the desistance process (Agnew, 2006; Sampson & Laub, 1995; Warr, 2002). Importantly, these theories have also been used to identify key concepts associated with several other theories and relate those ideas to desistance. For example, Peggy Giordano and her colleagues (Giordano, Longmore, Schroeder, & Seffrin, 2008) argue that "spirituality," a key component of many self-help and formal treatment programs as well as prison-based support groups, can be linked to desistance through social control, strain, and differential association theories. Spirituality can be linked to social control theory through the bond of "belief" as well as informal agents of social control that deviants may associate with because of newfound spiritual beliefs. Similarly, because of newfound spirituality, deviants may begin to disassociate with nonbelievers and begin to associate with believers who reinforce nondeviant definitions. Finally, spirituality and association with other believers may provide a source of social support that reduces frustrations and strains that earlier may have led to deviant involvement.

Giordano et al. (2008) interviewed incarcerated adolescents (half male and half female) in 1995 and again in 2003. Quantitative analyses of these data lend no support to the idea that spirituality (closeness to God and church attendance) was related to desistance. However, the sample size was fairly small, and it was therefore difficult to detect statistical significance. Indeed, few variables in this model were statistically significant.

Alternatively, in-depth qualitative interviews with 41 of the incarcerated youth seemed to suggest that spirituality was a strong "hook" for some offenders to change their lives and desist from criminal involvement. These qualitative comments were related to the theories discussed earlier. For example, spirituality often brought couples or parents and children together, increasing attachment and social control. Said one respondent, "Without Christ and the church we would never be together, and I mean we already know that. We prayed a lot and we know it's through prayer that we're together and our family's together" (Giordano et al., 2008, p. 119). Another

▲ **Photo 12.2** Can religion "save" people from a career in deviance?

references the bond of involvement: "If you would have told me ten years ago or say the last time I seen you, seven years ago that I would be singing in the choir regularly, going to church regularly I probably would have thought you were crazy" (p. 114). In terms of differential association and social learning, another said, "The things that preacher say from out of the Bible. I love that. He's just teaching you the ways to live. To live like the way God wants you to live right" (p. 114). Finally, referencing social support and ability to reduce strain, one interviewee stated, "I don't worry like I used to before. I know all things are in the Lord's hands and I know he takes care of me" (p. 117).

Spirituality can be seen as a "hook"—something that some involved in career deviance can grab hold of to help them use their own **human agency** to open doors out of the lifestyle they wish to exit. Spirituality is clearly something that will garner more theoretical and empirical attention as federal money is invested into faith-based approaches to reforming criminals and other deviants. Other "hooks," such as new relationships, occupations, and geographic moves away from "bad influences," are also likely to be carefully studied both quantitatively and qualitatively in the future.

Exiting a deviant career can be difficult. P. A. Adler and P. Adler's (1983) upper-level drug dealers and smugglers had a hard time "phasing out" of their careers because they had become accustomed to the "hedonistic and materialistic satisfactions the drug world provided" (p. 202) and, in fact, had a hard time finding legitimate jobs because they had been out of the lawful labor market for so long that they had few legal opportunities. The drug-using lifestyles of alcoholics and drug addicts are also difficult to leave. Recovery requires motivation, social support, and often treatment, and the process is frequently plagued by back-and-forth periods of abstinence and use (Brownell, Marlatt, Lichtenstein, & Wilson, 1986).

Recently, Lynda Baker and her colleagues reviewed several general and prostitution-specific models of change as well as the empirical literature on the specific barriers women face when exiting prostitution (Baker, Dalla, & Williamson, 2010, pp. 588–590). These barriers included the following:

1. Individual factors

    a. Self-destructive behavior and substance abuse

    b. Mental health problems

    c. Effects of trauma from adverse childhood

d. Psychological trauma/injury from violence

e. Chronic psychological stress

f. Self-esteem/shame and guilt

g. Physical health problems

h. Lack of knowledge regarding services

2. Relational factors

a. Limited conventional formal and informal support

b. Strained family relations

c. Pimps

d. Drug dealers

e. Social isolation

3. Structural factors

a. Employment, job skills, limited employment options

b. Basic needs (e.g., housing, poverty, economic self-sufficiency)

c. Education

d. Criminal record

e. Inadequate services

4. Societal factors

a. Discrimination and stigma

Through an analysis of previous models and the barriers that women face when exiting prostitution, the authors developed an integrated model that is described in Figure 12.2. The model focuses on prostitution but could also be used to understand exiting other deviant careers (drug dealing, drug and alcohol addiction, anorexia/bulimia, etc.). The first stage is immersion, and technically, this stage is not about change at all but precedes any inkling of leaving the business—that is, the woman is immersed in a lifestyle of prostitution. In the second stage, the woman becomes aware that things are not as they should be. Of course, at either part of this stage, there are the barriers listed above to leaving, and the woman could (and often does) return to the immersion stage. If the woman makes it past this stage, she enters the stage of deliberate planning and preparation. At this stage, attempts are made to contact informal social support (e.g., family and friends) as well as formal agents of social support, such as drug and alcohol treatment centers and homeless shelters. The initial exit period begins when the woman actively and behaviorally works to get out of the lifestyle. She may use informal contacts, such as family and friends, or she may invoke formal measures, such as counseling or drug treatment. Breaking through the barriers is critical at this stage, and human agency becomes especially important. At this point,

Some women may enter a drug treatment program, actively engaged and ready to change; they may rely on their support system (e.g., sponsors), internalize knowledge gained, and then apply newly acquired skills to their own lives. Others may begin a treatment program, fail to utilize available support or internalize knowledge and, therefore, be unable to make behavioral changes. These women will likely abandon the program prior to completion and eventually return to the sex industry. It is at this stage of the model that a woman's internal desire and motivation to exit are severely tested. (Baker et al., 2010, p. 592)

Figure 12.2   Baker, Dalla, and Williamson's (2010) Integrated Model of Exiting Prostitution

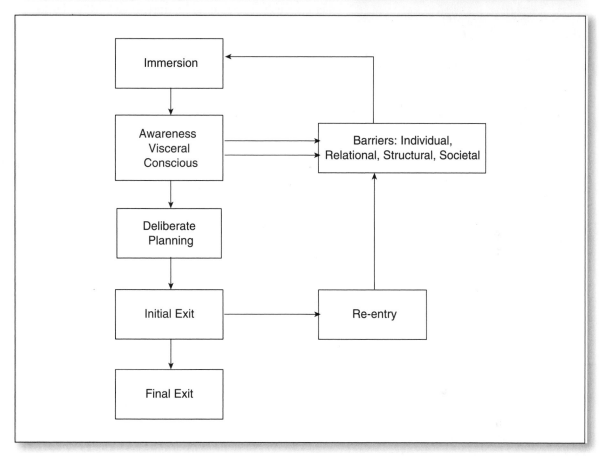

Source: Adapted from Baker et al. (2010).

In the former case, the woman may enter the final exit stage or she may not—she may reenter the business. In the latter case, the woman will almost always go back to prostitution, and in either case, there may be what Sanders (2007) termed "yo-yoing," where multiple attempts are made to exit the business and lifestyle. Baker and colleagues (2010) conclude that very often the final exiting stage comes after many attempts to leave a career in prostitution.

◈ Explaining Deviance in the Streets and Deviance in the Suites: Street Prostitutes Versus Elite Prostitutes

Living the life of a deviant can be exciting, challenging, difficult, taxing, demoralizing, frightening, upsetting, and a host of other adjectives, depending on the type of deviance and where in the deviant career we look. Consider the upper-level drug dealers discussed by P. A. Adler and P. Adler (1983) earlier. On one side, many dealers were drawn to the business because of the fun and excitement of the party and druggy lifestyle and the potential to make large

© RapidEye/iStock

▲ **Photo 12.3**   Sociological research shows the very different lives of elite sex workers and street prostitutes.

sums of money. On the other side, dealing and smuggling was real work with many risks, including the dangers of associating with other criminals (some not to be trusted) and getting busted by law enforcement. In this section, we describe two studies concerning the lives of very different types of sex workers: women who exchange sex for drugs and money in the streets and elite prostitutes who exchange sex for large sums of money and expensive material goods. The comparison sheds light on how class and power differentiate the deviant careers of those involved in different levels of prostitution.

Living with deviance on a daily basis can be physically and emotionally draining. A large body of research has developed describing the lives of street prostitutes and the stigma, social rejection, and abuses they face on a day-to-day basis (see Farley & Barkan, 1998; Hunter, 1993; Nixon, Tutty, Downe, Gorkoff, & Ursel, 2002). Recently, Jolanda Sallman (2010) reported on her interviews with 14 women recruited from a program that provided social services ("prostitution-specific services") to women in need. Because these women did not necessarily consider themselves to be "prostitutes" or "sex workers," she began each interview with the following:

I'm interested in learning as much as possible about what it's like to be a woman who has sex for material goods, such as money, drugs, shelter, or clothing. I'm particularly interested in hearing about your experience. It would be helpful for me if you would begin by describing a situation that stands out for you. (p. 149)

From these interviews, she derived five themes that provide insights into the daily lives of these women. First was living with the labeling and stigma by members of society (including conventional citizens, pimps, and the police), who viewed them as "whores," "dispensable," "garbage," and "less than human." Such devaluation led directly to the second theme that involved comments concerning the day-to-day living with violence. The prostitutes reported being kidnapped, raped, gang raped, beaten, and cut with knifes by pimps. Responses to these incidents of victimization showed clear evidence of their stigmatized and devalued status. One pimp immediately put a prostitute back on the street after she had been kidnapped and raped at knifepoint by a "john." The police response to rapes was equally demoralizing, as law enforcement officers seemed either not to believe a prostitute could be raped or to think that it was a good thing. The third theme involved living with discrimination, especially by the criminal justice system, which often denied the women's victimization or blamed them for it. The fourth theme involved how their experiences had altered their perceptions of themselves even after they had given up prostitution. That is, their own devalued sense of self (self-stigma) remained even after they stopped engaging in sex in exchange for drugs and money. A final and almost positive theme that Sallman (2010) unearthed in her interviews had to do with "resistance." She describes how some of the women refused to accept societal stigma and often lashed out at those who judged them negatively.

The research is clear that violence is prevalent in the working lives of both indoor and street prostitutes (Raphael & Shapiro, 2004), but compare the prior descriptions of street prostitution with the following analysis of the lives of 30 elite prostitutes interviewed by Ann Lucas (2005). The women she interviewed unanimously voiced positive sentiments regarding their profession. They found it lucrative and empowering in terms of interpersonal skills and boundary setting, and they often said it exposed them less to sexual harassment. These women felt very in control of their environments. According to one interviewee,

> I think that they think, a lot of times, that they've rented me for an hour so I should have to do anything they want to. I think, maybe, it takes them by surprise that I walk in and take charge of the situation, and I'm like, "OK, let's do this" and they can make suggestions but if I don't want to do something I'm not gonna do it. (p. 520)

For some of these women, prostitution was clearly a means to an end in terms of finance and lifestyle. Some "stressed their ability to be independent, to have control over their work and non-work lives, to be able to afford some indulgences, and to vary how much they worked each month" (Lucas, 2005, p. 526). Others stressed the non-sexual nature of their work, which often involved providing conversation and company to lonely men, some of them regulars. This is in contrast to other work that describes prostitutes as "exploitative, man-hating con artists; whether friendly or strictly professional, these women largely appreciated and respected their clients" (Lucas, 2005, p. 536).

The point of this comparison between drug-using street prostitutes and elite sex workers is not to generate debate about the morality and politics of prostitution, although there is plenty there to discuss. Rather, the point is to highlight massive differences in two seemingly similar deviant careers and how social class and power affect the lives of "deviant women" who exchange sex for material goods. This reiterates an emerging theme in this chapter—that just like social stratification in conventional careers, there is also important stratification in deviant careers. In a conventional organization, there are usually clear levels related to pay, power, flexibility, and other benefits. This is also the case in many deviant careers.

◈ Ideas in Action: Programs and Policy From a Career Deviance and Deviant Career Perspective

Although we did not use the term "policy," we certainly hinted at it in the beginning of this chapter when we discussed the "great debate." Basically, the debate was all about policy. On the one hand, some believe that longitudinal research is necessary and important. If we know the characteristics of persistent and serious offenders, we can incarcerate them, making the public feel safer and preventing needlessly lost lives, saving property, and maybe even saving costs to the criminal justice system if these are the primary offenders requiring the most attention from the police and court personnel. We have also briefly but more directly discussed policy as it relates to risk and protective factors. Here we would like to continue that discussion, although not by focusing on specific policies or programs that come from a deviant career and career deviance perspective because that would be a daunting task—indeed, one well beyond the scope of this small section. Instead, we will provide some policy-related issues to think about when working from a risk and protective-factor approach.

We first recommend thinking about the importance of the issue of concern. This is sometimes—but not always—a quantitative issue (e.g., the extent of the problem), though this argument is often used to push for policy and/or resources for programs. Probably most research proposals begin with some numbers regarding the extent of the problem that they want to research, and students are notorious for starting papers with "The crime (or juvenile delinquency or social problem x) is worse now than it has ever been," regardless of whether or not that is true. The nice thing about numbers is that they can help make an argument persuasive. Another nice thing about numbers is that they can be checked for accuracy and compared with others. "Wow! There sure is a lot of x going on, and it is very bad, but look how much y is going on, and it is bad, too." These are important general issues to think about when people are proposing programs and policy.

Clearly, there are also rare events or behaviors that warrant attention. Medical scientists study some of the rarest diseases, and billions are spent on space exploration, but compared with all of the problems we experience on Earth, at times, this seems questionable. Alternatively, people working at NASA are very smart and persuasive. Closer to home, homicide occurs far less often than marijuana use, but if given a voice, we may be more eager to put effort (time, energy, and money) toward reducing one over the other. The point here is that we need to consider the importance of an issue before developing programs and policies.

On a related note, although it is difficult to predict unintended consequences of policies and programs, remember the negative effects of various programs discussed in Chapter 3. It is also easy to think of the unintended consequences of large-scale policies developed in the past. While research does suggest that alcohol consumption probably went down during Prohibition (1919–1933), people who continued to drink became criminals (the crime rate almost by definition went up), organized crime rose to levels that never previously existed in this country, and a great deal of "bad" alcohol was produced and consumed, sometimes with serious health consequences. More recently, changes in drug seizure laws have led to police corruption as departments basically use money taken from citizens to fund their budgets. Furthermore, it is quite clear that these innocent citizens have little or no recourse as they are often threatened with more severe sanctions and/or having their children taken away if they complain. Stillman (2013) reports that

> in general, you needn't be found guilty to have your assets claimed by law enforcement; in some states, suspicion on a par with "probable cause" is sufficient. Nor must you be charged with a crime, or even be accused of one. Unlike criminal forfeiture, which requires that person be convicted of an offense before his or her property is confiscated, civil forfeiture amounts to a lawsuit filed directly against a possession, regardless of the owner's guilt or innocence. (p. 50)

Once a deviant issue has been defined as important and worthy of developing programs or policies for it, then we need to think about (1) where in the process we think we should focus and (2) what the risk and protective factors are that might be important in helping the situation. Regarding the former, we might think that preventing some form of deviance is most important. At that point, it is probably best to think about the population that should be the focus of a policy or program. One question that is raised a great deal these days is whether a program or policy should be universal or targeted (Hopkins et al., 2008). That is, should the program be delivered to the entire population or a targeted subset of that population? So for example, if the issue is drug abuse prevention, and you believe that the intervention would be best administered in the fifth grade, should the program be delivered to all fifth-graders (universally)? Only to males since they are at greater risk of drug use (targeted)? Or only to the students who have shown clear risk factors for drug use, such as feelings of alienation, parental drug use, or poor social skills (targeted)? There may be some subsets of a population where the risk is so small that the intervention would be a true waste of time and scarce resources, whereas for another group, the risk is so high that it makes much more sense to focus on that group. Of course, knowing in advance who is at greater risk is not always clear. Once we move past the prevention stage and focus on persistence/escalation or desistance, we are generally thinking about targeted programs, but where, when, and how we want to focus those programs may make them even more targeted. For example, do we want to focus on treatment for all heroin addicts, only those who have shown an interest in quitting, or those who are incarcerated so you have a captive audience?

Regarding the second issue, we have to ask what risk or protective factors are most likely to affect the problem and whether, even if we are sure which factors are most important, we can help to reduce the risk or increase protection. For both of these questions, we recommend relying on science. In terms of risk factors, we may think that a, b, or c is strongly and causally related to z, but science has often shown that common sense is wrong or overly simplified. Similarly, as we discussed in Chapter 3, doing things that sound good (e.g., the DARE program) may have no effect whatsoever and may actually have negative unintended consequences. In many cases, we do not have the abilities or resources we need, or there may be ethical or political constraints so that even if we "know" what would work, there is little or nothing we can do to resolve the problem. We hate to end on such a negative note, but these are important things to consider, and it is better to think them through as thoroughly as possible before making a potentially serious bad move.

NOW YOU . . . THINK ABOUT DEVIANT CAREERS

Individuals labeled as sex offenders are often assumed to be some of the most likely to become career offenders. For this reason, Megan's Law has mandated that sex offenders register with local law enforcement—making their status of sex offender public information. Government registry websites list these men and women by name and, oftentimes, address. However, over the years, the label of sex offender has been applied to a wide array of behaviors beyond those of rapists and child molesters. These behaviors include urinating in public, streaking, engaging in a consensual relationship with someone younger than age 18, and having consensual sex in a public place.

A report conducted by Robert Barnoski (2005) of the Washington State Institute for Public Policy tracked the recidivism rate of sex offenders released from Washington state prisons. Below are the rates (by year). Barnoski found that compared with all felony offenders, felony sex offenders had the lowest recidivism rates.

Year	5-Year Rate	Year	5-Year Rate
1986	6%	1993	8%
1987	7.5%	1994	6%
1988	7.5%	1995	4%
1989	6%	1996	3%
1990	7%	1997	2%
1991	8%	1998	3%
1992	6%	1999	3.7%

First, using the figures above, describe the recidivism rate of sex offenders. How do you think it compares with rates for other offenders? (You could actually do the research here to find an answer.) Now, using the understanding of deviant careers you've gained from this chapter, discuss the expected and actual recidivism rates for sex offenders. What does this mean for understanding sex offending as a deviant career? How might the broad set of behaviors defined as sex offenses and the public treatment of sex offenders affect our beliefs about the offenders' deviant careers?

◈ Conclusion

In this chapter, we have discussed deviant careers, meaning one's work is deviant, and career deviance, meaning a period of deviant behavior that has a beginning, a middle that might include escalation or specialization, and an end. We view this period of deviant behavior as a process. In fact, each stage of many deviant careers or career deviance can be viewed as a process. The obvious exception might be a quick, untimely death before one even considers exiting the career. We should note that in this chapter, we have focused on deviant behaviors that are criminal—or at least unhealthy (e.g., smoking, excessive drinking, and eating disorders)—cases where we felt most students would expect or hope to see an end to the behaviors. Many forms of deviance do not fit this model. Homosexuality is still considered deviant by many in our society, but most of us recognize that one's sexual orientation may not and should not change over time. As well, various mental and physical disorders and the behaviors that accompany them may not change greatly over the life course.

Still, the career paradigm does offer some useful insights into the initiation process, a better understanding of how people manage their deviant careers or career deviance, and useful knowledge of the process of desistance for many forms of deviance. A prestigious sociologist, Francis Cullen (2011), in his Sutherland Award address, lamented how the study of deviant careers became less popular with the rise of survey research so easily used in schools to study "delinquency." He described how static, cross-sectional research is now falling to the wayside (or at least that it should) and that we need to take a life course perspective, including longitudinal data collection, if we are to advance the study of crime and deviance. We agree that cross-sectional designs are limited, especially when it comes to studying career deviance and deviant careers, and we hope more longitudinal designs will emerge that are focused on noncriminal forms of deviance. However, it is the reemergence and popularity of the study of life course deviance that excites us, no matter what research design is used to address the issues in question.

EXERCISES AND DISCUSSION QUESTIONS

1. How might different factors influence people to initiate, persist in, and exit a deviant career?

2. Consider any deviant behavior that you have been involved in. What factors motivated you to initiate this behavior? If you persisted, what factors led you to do this? If you didn't persist, what factors motivated you to stop?

3. What deviant behaviors might best be explained from a life course perspective, and which ones probably can be explained from a static perspective?

4. Choose a theory from the list below, and describe how it might be particularly useful to employ from a deviant career and career deviance perspective. Would any of the theories not work well from such a perspective? Or might one work better than another? Why?

   a. Differential association and social learning

   b. Social control or bonding

   c. Self-control

   d. Labeling

   e. Conflict

   f. Critical theories (feminist, peacemaking, and critical race theory)

5. If you had to study just one aspect of deviance in the life course perspective (e.g., onset/initiation, persistence/escalation/specialization, or desistance), what would you study and why?

KEY TERMS

Criminal career paradigm	Human agency	Protective factors
Desistance	Life course perspective	Risk factors
Escalation	Onset/initiation	Specialization

READING 32

This is a clever article that uses Harry Potter's life to bring out several key themes of the life course perspective. For example, how did Harry grow out of a "dark and difficult" childhood so stable and normal? Was it the early love he was given as an infant? Was it the love and support he received as he entered the wizardry school? Or was there something simply "resilient" about Harry? Thiede Call and McAlpine illustrate several themes found in the life course perspective through J. K. Rowling books in a way that is accessible even to those not terribly familiar with the Harry Potter series.

Harry Potter and the
Wise and Powerful Life Course Theorist

Kathleen Thiede Call and Donna D. McAlpine

On July 31, in an unspecified year, in a small village called Godric's Hollow, in the United Kingdom, a baby was born to a mother and father who loved him.

In the next year, his parents were murdered by an evil, self-proclaimed dark lord—but the boy lived. He was left on the doorstep of his mother's sister and her husband, who appeared to feel some familial responsibility but no connection. We know very little about the next 10 years of his life except that he lived in a room under the stairs bereft of love and affection, bullied by his cousin, and teased at school for many reasons, including the odd lightning-bolt scar that marked his forehead. These years have perhaps been best characterized as "dark and difficult."

In her series of seven books, J.K. Rowling takes us through the adolescence of this Boy Who Lived, Harry Potter. These books became a world-wide phenomenon, topping both the children's and adult literature best-seller lists. Readers waited in long lines for each to be released at midnight and delighted in the new stories of Harry Potter's life set against the backdrop of his schooling at Hogwarts School of Witchcraft and Wizardry.

While the courses at Hogwarts seemed to cover every imaginable topic from Care of Magical Creatures to Potions, it's not clear that Harry or his contemporaries were ever exposed to life course theory.

That is a shame.

But we can *imagine* they were. Better yet, we can imagine that The Wise and Powerful Life Course Theorist meets Harry Potter and is both perplexed and pleased. Reflecting upon Harry's life, The Theorist might wrestle with how the teachings of life course theory make sense of Harry's story. And The Theorist might confront some doubts about whether such theories hold up in the life course of those born as wizards and witches.

A long history in the sociology of the life course demonstrates that our early beginnings shape our later experiences. The Life Course Theorist might predict that such a boy would grow up with attachment problems, alienation and delinquency issues, substance abuse problems, and a host of other difficulties that often (but not always) mark the lives of muggles (non-magical persons) who start life with extreme deprivation.

Source: Thiede Call, K., & McAlpine, D. D. (2008). Harry Potter and the wise and powerful life course theorist. *Contexts, 7*(3), 75–77.

But that was not the case. Harry emerges from his "dark and difficult" early life a good natured and well-adjusted boy, which seems nothing short of magical. Similarly fantastic is that Harry remains developmentally and academically "on track" with his peers, in spite of facing incredible adversities in each of the seven years the books chronicle his life.

Yet, we know he was deeply loved in his first year of life and that his entry into the wizarding world was marked by the appearance and ongoing presence of a cadre of loving and attentive adults, such as Professor Albus Dumbledore, Hogwarts groundkeeper Rubeus Hagrid, his best friend's mother Mrs. Molly Weasley, and godfather Sirius Black. Moreover, his athletic prowess on the Quidditch field and successful mastery over each adversity he faced boosted Harry's sense of competence. Both social support and self-efficacy are well-documented markers of resilience and essential to positive life course development. The Theorist stands once again reassured of the magic of life course theories.

Perhaps the most formidable challenge to The Wise and Powerful Life Course Theorist's paradigm is the prophecy made before Harry's birth revealing that his life path was "predetermined" or "destined" to culminate in a fight to the death against the dark lord who killed his parents, He Who Must Not Be Named (Lord Voldemort. There. We've said it.). The Theorist (who remains unnamed) would argue that the notion of a prophecy is inconsistent with a central tenet of life course theory, which professes that the course of one's life is dynamic, malleable, and shaped by historical context, and importantly, that one can act on and influence the course of history.

Upon closer inspection, however, the manner in which the prophecy is "fulfilled" over the course of seven books perfectly illustrates themes of choice and chance or agency and structure—themes central to sociology generally and the life course perspective specifically.

For example, early in the first book, *The Sorcerer's Stone,* we find Harry seated with the Sorting Hat upon his head. This magical chapeau assesses the wearer's personality and potential, and decides the house to which the wearer will be assigned for the next seven years. Harry and the Sorting Hat face the choice between courage and chivalry (as exemplified by the members of Gryffindor House) and ambition and cunning (the Slytherin House traits).

As we know, Harry's insistence on being placed in Gryffindor influences who he calls his closest friends and the messages he receives about what kind of person he is becoming. Yet, recognition that the Sorting Hat thought Slytherin a wise choice haunts Harry as he learns in *Chamber of Secrets,* book 2, that he shares his ability to speak Parseltongue, the language of snakes, with the founding wizard of Slytherin as well as that house's most infamous student—Tom Riddle, who later became Lord Voldemort.

Much of Harry's journey through adolescence is a struggle to reject the part of himself that links him to Lord Voldemort. Yet everything about Harry and his path is inextricably linked to the Dark Lord.

In choosing to believe a prophecy received by Professor Sybill Trelawney before Harry was even born (that a child would be born with the power to vanquish the Dark Lord), and in attempting to fulfill it by ending young Harry's life, the Dark Lord binds their lives together. Professor Dumbledore explains to Harry ". . . the prophecy does not mean you have to do anything! But the prophecy caused Lord Voldemort to mark you as his equal. . . . In other words, you are free to choose your way, quite free to turn your back on the prophecy! But Voldemort continues to set store by the prophecy. He will continue to hunt you . . . which makes it certain, really, that . . ." Harry would accept the prophecy and assume the role of Chosen One by seeking to avenge his parents' death and end Lord Voldemort's threat to both the wizard and muggle worlds.

The Life Course Theorist might also see power as the essential element in Harry's choices to "do good" and his repeated successes at battling the Dark Lord. Harry's power comes from his mother's love and Voldemort's choice to mark him as his equal. In the wizarding world, power is emblemized by one's wand—and the "wand chooses the wizard," wandmaker Mr. Ollivander explains. Thus, Harry's power chooses him—it is ascribed rather than achieved.

Although others in his school (including a girl named Hermione Granger) are more skilled in magic,

Harry has an advantage. Indeed, the world Harry inhabits echoes our own in terms of complex stratification structures that permit and constrain choices and clear pathways. His world is divided into muggles and wizards, with further divisions among wizards into Pure Bloods (two magical parents), Mud Bloods (no magical parent), Blood Traitors (sympathizers of those who are not magical), and Squibs (no magical powers despite being born to magical parents), followed by other magical creatures. In the wizarding world, perhaps none rank lower than house-elves, who are slaves to their masters. Harry's status as the Boy Who Lived perhaps made up for any stigma he may have experienced because he was only a Half Blood (his mother was muggle-born, his father a wizard).

Choices and possibilities are partially shaped by these power structures. One can't imagine, for example, that a house-elf who had all Harry's qualities (kindness, loyalty, bravery—qualities we find in the house-elf Dobby), but lacked status, would be able to make choices and survive the deeds that Harry and his friends accomplished: to find the Sorcerer's stone, help an innocent man escape (*Prisoner of Azkaban*), overpower Death Eaters (*Order of the Phoenix*), and so much more.

Part of the series' sociological and lay appeal is that it is set in the familiar backdrop of life course development. The books bring to life the agents of socialization and social pathways familiar to anyone experiencing, or having already experienced, the transition from adolescence into adulthood. Readers relate to or recall the drudgery of formal education; teachers looked up to (Professors Lupin and McGonagall) and disdained (Professors Snape and Umbridge); kindling close peer (Ron Weasley and Hermione) and romantic relationships (Cho Chang, Ginny Weasley); confronting bullies (Malfoy, Crabbe, and Goyle); befriending misfits (Luna Lovegood and Neville Longbottom); the angst of homework and

exams (O.W.L.s and N.E.W.T.s); the self-centered focus of the teenage years and the exhilaration that comes with discovering one's talents (flying, Quidditch); facing fear (Dementors) and adversity (deaths of loved ones); as well as learning about injustices in the world (prejudice toward "lesser creatures" such as muggles, house-elves, and centaurs).

Perhaps most importantly, through Harry's biography the Wise and Powerful Life Course Theorist might be reminded that adolescence and the transition to adulthood are more than a series of successfully negotiated markers (leaving school, getting a job, among others), they are a magical adventure. The essential transition for Harry and his friends involves establishing a degree of competence as they face the challenges of their particular historical period. In the end, they emerge as "adults" not because of their chronological age, but because they have found a place for themselves in the world and mastered their environment.

Life course theorists young and old (or adolescents, young adults, near adults, adults, near elderly, young-old, old-old, and the like) enjoy this action-packed series partly because it's filled with sociological, developmental, and life course–relevant references to struggles between structure and agency, isolation and connectedness, risk and resilience, power and vulnerability, good and evil, hallows and horcruxes, and life and death.

More than anything, though, these are the stories of the power (or the magic) of love—and its effects on our paths through adolescence. Despite some 4,000 pages devoted to describing these pathways for Harry and his friends, we still want more. J.K. Rowling has recently hinted there may be an eighth book in the series. It's probably too much to dare imagine it will finally be the tale of Harry Potter and the Wise and Powerful Life Course Theorist. But—if it were—picture the midnight lineups for first editions.

READING 33

Poverty and welfare may not come across as the most obvious forms of deviance, but those impoverished are often looked down upon and treated with suspicion or outright antagonism. Furthermore, as the authors of the following article point out, many associate those in poverty with a barrage of negative stereotypes often seen as deviant (e.g., homeless, lazy, criminals). Mark Rank points out that poverty across the life course is more normal that we might think. In fact, he provides convincing data that 59% of Americans will have spent at least a year living in poverty over their life course. It is not only marginalized populations that find themselves in poverty—it is "us." The article also discusses how we *have* framed the poverty issue and how we *should* frame it.

As American as Apple Pie

Poverty and Welfare

Mark R. Rank

For many Americans, the words poverty and welfare conjure images of people on the fringes of society: unwed mothers raising several children, inner-city black men, high school dropouts, the homeless, and so on. The media, political rhetoric, and often even the research of social scientists depict the poor as alien and often undeserving of help. In short, being poor and using welfare are perceived as outside the American mainstream.

Yet, poverty and welfare use are as American as apple pie. Most of us will experience poverty during our lives. Even more surprising, most Americans will turn to public assistance at least once during adulthood. Rather than poverty and welfare use being an issue of *them*, it is more an issue of *us*.

◈ The Risk of Poverty and Drawing on Welfare

Our understanding about the extent of poverty comes mostly from annual surveys conducted by the Census Bureau. Over the past three decades, between 11 and 15 percent of Americans have lived below the poverty line in any given year. Some people are at greater risk than others, depending on age, race, gender, family structure, community of residence, education, work skills and physical disabilities. (See sidebar, "Counting the Poor.")

Studies that follow particular families over time—in particular, the Panel Study of Income Dynamics (PSID), the National Longitudinal Survey (NLS), and the Survey of Income and Program Participation (SIPP)—have given us a further understanding of year-to-year changes in poverty. They show that most people are poor for only a short time. Typically, households are impoverished for one, two, or three years, then manage to get above the poverty line. They may stay above the line for a while, only to fall into poverty again later. Events triggering these spells of poverty frequently involve the loss of a job and its pay, family changes such as divorce, or both.

There is, however, an alternative way to estimate the scope of poverty. Specifically, how many Americans

Source: Rank, M. R. (2003). As American as apple pie: Poverty and welfare. *Contexts, 2*(3), 41–49.

COUNTING THE POOR

When President Johnson declared his War on Poverty in 1964, the United States had no official measure of the number of people who were poor. The official poverty line that was subsequently developed estimated the minimum amount of income necessary in order to purchase a basic "basket" of goods and services. If a family's income falls below that level, members in the household are counted as poor. The poverty line is adjusted for the size of the family and increased each year to keep up with the cost of living. For example, in 2001 the poverty line for a household of one was $9,039, for a household of four, $18,104, while for a household of nine or more it was $36,286.

experience poverty at some point during adulthood? Counting the number of people who are ever touched by poverty, rather than those who are poor in any given year, gives us a better sense of the scope of the problem. Put another way, to what extent is poverty a "normal" part of the life cycle?

My colleague Tom Hirschl and I have constructed a series of "life tables" built from PSID data following families for over 25 years. The life table is a technique for counting how often specific events occur in specific periods of time, and is frequently used by demographers and medical researchers to assess risk, say, the risk of contracting breast cancer after menopause. It allows us to estimate the percentage of the American population that will experience poverty at some point during adulthood. We also calculated the percentage of the population that will use a social safety net program—programs such as food stamps or Aid to Families with Dependent Children (AFDC, now replaced by the Temporary Assistance for Needy Families [TANF] program)—sometime during adulthood. Our results suggest that a serious reconsideration of who experiences poverty is in order.

Figure 1 shows the percentage of Americans spending at least one year living below the official poverty line during adulthood. It also graphs the percentage who

have lived between the poverty line and just 25 percent above it—what scholars consider "near poverty."

By the age of 30, 27 percent of Americans will have experienced at least one year in poverty and 34 percent will have fallen below the near-poverty line. By the age of 50, the percentages will have risen to 42 and 50 percent, respectively. And finally by the time Americans have reached the age of 75, 59 percent will have spent at least a year below the poverty line during their adulthood, while 68 percent will have faced at least a year in near poverty.

If we included experiences of poverty in childhood, these percentages would be even higher. Rather than an isolated event that occurs only among the so-called "underclass," poverty is a reality that a clear majority of Americans will experience during their lifetimes.

Measuring impoverishment as the use of social safety net programs produces even more startling results. Figure 2 draws on the same PSID survey to show the proportion of people between the ages of 20 and 65 who will use one of the major need-based welfare programs in the United States, including food stamps, Medicaid, AFDC, Supplemental Security Income, and other cash subsidies such as general assistance. By the time Americans reach the age of 65, approximately two-thirds will have, as adults, received assistance for at least a year, while 40 percent will have used a welfare program in at least five separate years. (Again, adding childhood experiences would only raise the rates.) Contrary to stereotypes, relying on America's social safety net is widespread and far-reaching.

Of course, people with disadvantages such as single parents or those with fewer skills will have even higher cumulative rates of poverty and welfare use than those shown in Figures 1 and 2. Yet to portray poverty as an issue affecting only marginalized groups is clearly a mistake.

◈ Why Is the Risk of Poverty So High?

Time. First, most discussions of poverty look at single years, or five or ten years at a stretch. The life table techniques employed in Figures 1 and 2 are based upon assessing the risk of poverty across a lifetime,

Figure 1   Cumulative Percent of Americans Who Have Experienced Poverty

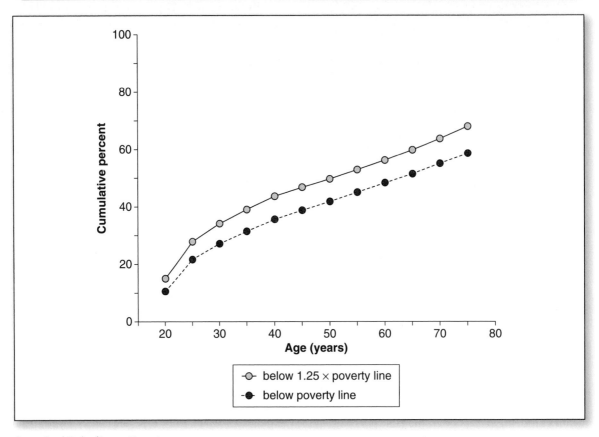

Source: Panel Study of Income Dynamics.

more than 50 years. Over so many years, individuals face many unanticipated events—households split up, workers lose their jobs, family members become sick, and so on—that become financial emergencies. The familiar saying of being "one paycheck away from poverty" is particularly apt. For example, it is estimated that families with average incomes have enough assets to maintain their standards of living for just over one month.

The Safety Net. A second reason poverty rates are so high is that there is little government help to tide households over during financial emergencies. Although most Americans will eventually rely on need-based

government aid (as shown in Figure 2), that assistance often fails to save them from poverty. Contrary to the rhetoric about vast sums being spent on public assistance, the American welfare system can be more accurately described as minimal. Compared to other Western industrialized countries, the United States devotes far fewer resources to assisting the economically vulnerable.

Most European countries provide a wide range of social and insurance programs that effectively keep families from falling into poverty. These include substantial cash payments to families with children. Unemployment assistance is far more generous in these countries than in the United States, often providing

Figure 2 Cumulative Percent of Americans Who Have Received Welfare

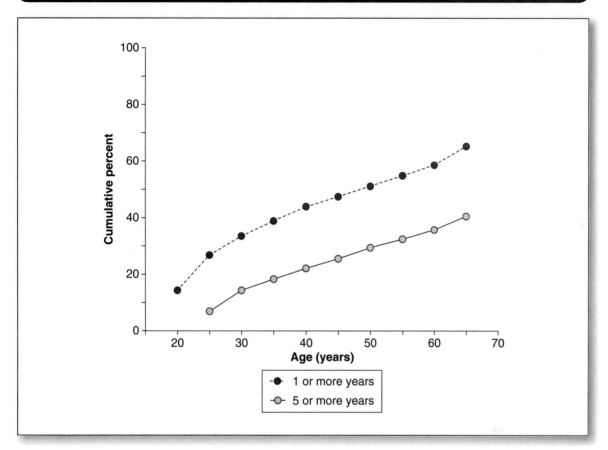

Source: Panel Study of Income Dynamics.

support for more than a year following the loss of a job. Furthermore, universal health coverage is routinely provided along with considerable support for child care.

These social policies substantially reduce the risk of poverty in Europe and Canada, while U.S. social policies—aside from programs specifically directed to aid the elderly—have reduced poverty modestly at best. As economist Rebecca Blank notes in *It Takes a Nation*, "the national choice in the United States to provide relatively less generous transfers to low-income families has meant higher relative poverty rates in the country. While low-income families in the United States work more than in many other countries, they are not able to make up for lower governmental income support relative to their European counterparts" (pp. 141–142).

Scholars who have used the Luxembourg Income Study (LIS), an international collection of economic surveys, have documented the inability of the American safety net to reduce the risk of poverty. For example, Finnish social scientist Veli-Matti Ritakallio has examined the extent to which cash assistance reduces poverty across eight European countries,

Canada, and the United States. European and Canadian programs reduce rates of poverty by an average of 79 percent from what they would have been absent the assistance. Finland, for instance, reduced the percentage of its residents who would have been poor from 33 percent down to 4 percent. In contrast, the United States was only able to reduce its percentage in poverty at any given time from 29 percent to 18 percent. As a result, the current rates of U.S. poverty are among the highest in the industrialized world.

The Labor Market. A third factor elevating the risk of American poverty across the life course is the failure of the labor market to provide enough jobs that pay well enough. During the past 30 years, the U.S. economy has produced increasing numbers of low-paying jobs, part-time jobs and jobs without benefits. For example, the Census Bureau estimated that the median earnings of workers who were paid hourly wages in 2000 was $9.91. At the same time, approximately 3 million Americans were working part-time because of a shortage of full-time jobs. As journalist Barbara Ehrenreich and others have shown, these jobs simply do not support a family. A higher percentage of the U.S. workforce falls into this low-wage sector than is true in comparable developed countries. For example, economist Timothy Smeeding and his colleagues have found that 25 percent of all American full-time workers could be classified as being in low-wage work (defined as earning less than 65 percent of the national median for full-time jobs). This was by far the highest percentage of the countries analyzed, with the overall average of non-U.S. countries falling at 12 percent.

In addition, there are simply not enough jobs to go around. Labor economist Timothy Bartik used several different approaches to estimate the number of jobs that would be needed to significantly reduce poverty in the United States. Even in the booming economy of the late 1990s, between 5 and 9 million more jobs were needed in order to meet the needs of the poor and disadvantaged.

To use an analogy, the demand for labor versus the supply of decent paying jobs might be thought of as an ongoing game of musical chairs. That is, the number of workers in the labor market is far greater than the number of jobs that pay a living wage. Using SIPP data for 1999, I estimated this imbalance as ranging between 9 percent and 33 percent, depending upon how poverty and labor market participation were defined. Consequently, between 9 and 33 percent of American household heads were either in non-living-wage jobs or looking for work. The very structure of the labor market ensures that some families will lose out at this musical chairs game and consequently will run a significant risk of poverty.

Some may point out that U.S. rates of unemployment are fairly low when compared to European levels. Yet Bruce Western and Katherine Beckett demonstrate that these lower rates are largely a result of extremely high rates of incarceration. By removing large numbers of American men from the labor force and placing them into the penal system (thus out of our musical chairs analogy altogether), unemployment rates are kept artificially low. When this factor is taken into account and adjusted for, U.S. unemployment rates fall more into line with those of Europe.

◈ Changing the Poverty Paradigm

A life course perspective shows us that Americans are highly susceptible to experiencing poverty first-hand. Understanding the normality of poverty requires us to rethink several of our most enduring myths. Assuming that most Americans would rather avoid such an experience, it becomes in our enlightened self-interest to ensure that we reduce poverty and establish an effective safety net. This risk-sharing argument has been articulated most notably by the philosopher John Rawls. As well as being charitable, improving the plight of those in poverty is an issue of common concern.

We are also beginning to recognize that, as a nation, we pay a high price for our excessive rates of poverty. Research shows that poverty impairs the nation's health, the quality of its workforce, race relations, and, of course, its future generations. Understanding the commonality of poverty shifts how we choose to think about the issue—from a distant concept of *them*, to an active reality of *us*. In addition, much of the public's resistance to assisting the poor and particularly those on welfare is the perception that the poor are often underserving of assistance, that their poverty arises from a lack of motivation, questionable morals, and so on. Yet my analysis suggests that, given its pervasiveness, poverty appears systemic to our economic structure. In short, we have met the enemy, and they are us. C. Wright Mills made a similar point about unemployment:

> When, in a city of 100,000, only one man is unemployed, that is his personal trouble, and for its relief we properly look to the character of the man, his skills, and his immediate opportunities. But when in a nation of 50 million employees, 15 million men are unemployed, that is an issue, and we may not hope to find its solution within the range of opportunities open to any one individual. The very structure of opportunities has collapsed. Both the correct statement of the problem and the range of possible solutions require us to consider the economic and political institutions of the society, and not merely the personal situation and character of a scatter of individuals.

So too with poverty. That America has the highest poverty rates in the Western industrialized world and that most Americans will experience poverty during their lifetimes has little to do with individual motivation or attitudes. Rather, it has much to do with a labor market that fails to produce enough decent paying jobs, and social policies that are unable to pull individuals and families out of poverty when unforeseen events occur. The United States has the means to alleviate poverty, and a range of models from other countries to borrow from. Allowing our policies to be mired in self-righteous moralism while millions of citizens suffer is unconscionable. It is time to shift the debate from one of blame, to one of justice and common concern.

◈ Recommended Resources

Bartik, Timothy H. "Poverty, Jobs, and Subsidized Employment." *Challenge* 45, 3 (2002): 100–111. An argument for the importance of labor demand policies that encourage job growth and improved wages for low-income workers.

Blank, Rebecca. *It Takes a Nation: A New Agenda for Fighting Poverty.* New York: Russell Sage Foundation, 1997. A review of the characteristics, nature and current strategies for addressing American poverty.

Ehrenreich, Barbara. *Nickel and Dimed: On (Not) Getting By in America.* New York: Henry Holt and Company, 2001. A first-hand account of trying to survive on low-wage work in three different settings.

O'Connor, Alice. *Poverty Knowledge: Social Science, Social Policy, and the Poor in Twentieth-Century U.S. History.* Princeton, NJ: Princeton University Press, 2001. O'Connor critiques the dominant social science emphasis in the past 40 years on analyzing individual attributes as the primary cause of poverty.

Patterson, James T. *America's Struggle Against Poverty in the Twentieth Century.* Cambridge, MA: Harvard University Press, 2000. An historical overview of American social policy directed at the alleviation of poverty.

Rank, Mark R. *One Nation, Underprivileged: How American Poverty Affects Us All.* New York: Oxford University Press, in press. A new perspective on understanding and addressing U.S. poverty.

Rank, Mark R. and Thomas A. Hirschl. "Rags or Riches? Estimating the Probabilities of Poverty and Affluence Across the Adult American Life Span." *Social Science Quarterly* 82, 4 (2001): 651–669. An examination of the likelihood that Americans will experience poverty or affluence at some point during their adulthood, which suggests a new conceptualization of social stratification.

Ritakallio, Veli-Matti. "Trends of Poverty and Income Inequality in Cross-national Comparison." *Luxembourg Income Study Working Paper*, No. 272. Maxwell School of Citizenship and Public Affairs, Syracuse University, Syracuse, New York, 2001. Ritakallio uses the Luxembourg Income Study to assess the effectiveness of government policy in reducing poverty among nine developed countries.

Smeeding, Timothy M., Lee Rainwater, and Gary Burtless. "U.S. Poverty in a Cross-national Context." Pp. 162–189 in *Understanding Poverty*, ed. Sheldon H. Danziger and Robert H. Haveman. Cambridge, MA: Harvard University Press, 2001. The authors compare the extent of poverty in the United States and other developed countries.

Western, Bruce, and Katherine Beckett. "How Unregulated Is the U.S. Market? The Penal System as a Labor Market Institution." *American Journal of Sociology* 104 (January 1999): 1030–1060. This study shows the role that incarceration plays in lowering overall U.S. unemployment rates.

READING 34

In this article, Ulmer and Spencer compare and contrast the most common positivist explanation of criminal and deviant careers with a less common but important approach—the symbolic interactionist approach. Drawing on three common themes (i.e., indeterminacy, stability, and change) and how the two approaches deal with these issues, the authors review both qualitative and quantitative research as well as the policy implications of the approaches. They conclude that an interactionist approach has much to offer the study of criminal/deviant careers.

The Contributions of an Interactionist Approach to Research and Theory on Criminal Careers

Jeffery T. Ulmer and J. William Spencer

Introduction

The concept of careers in crime and deviance has proved very useful in criminology for several decades. However, the term 'criminal career' is treated in different ways by two distinct approaches, with two different sets of ontological assumptions about human social behavior—a positivist approach (e.g. Blumstein et al., 1985, 1986, 1988) and a pragmatist/symbolic interactionist approach (Becker, 1963; Goffman, 1963; Adler and Adler, 1983; Best and Luckenbill, 1994).

Though contemporary positivist criminal careers literature recognizes the practical and methodological limits to predicting individual criminal career trajectories, there is insufficient recognition that these limits are not just of methodological importance but also of theoretical importance (for exceptions, see Gottfredson and Gottfredson, 1994; Maltz, 1994). We argue that symbolic interactionist conceptualizations of criminal careers, with their pragmatist ontological assumptions, offer much theoretical insight on indeterminacy in criminal careers, the dynamics of career phases and the notion of stability in criminal propensity, and the role of quantitative and qualitative methods in the study of

criminal careers. Symbolic interactionism emphasizes dialectics of continuity and change, and decisions and processes within situational opportunities and constraints which, in turn, are conditioned by social structural contexts. It posits that social constraints and opportunities, socialization, and even biology may influence, but never totally determine the contingencies and choices involved in criminal activity throughout the life course. Symbolic interactionism would therefore provide those using quantitative and qualitative research on both criminal careers and stable criminal propensities a theoretical framework that makes sense of individual level indeterminacy, stability, and patterned change in criminal activity over the life course.

In what follows we first review various recent directions in the positivist criminal career literature, including debates about its policy implications, the notion of stable criminal propensities, and methodological issues; and second, compare and contrast the ontological assumptions underlying symbolic interactionist approaches and positivist approaches to criminal careers, and review key exemplars of interactionist research on careers in crime and deviance. We conclude by outlining several ways in which an interactionist

Source: Ulmer, J. T., & Spencer, J. W. (1999). The contributions of an interactionist approach to research and theory on criminal careers. *Theoretical Criminology* 3(1), 95–124.

approach can contribute even more to research and theory on criminal careers, and briefly noting some policy implications of such an approach.

◇ Positivistic Conceptions of Criminal Careers

The positivist approach emphasizes the predictive modeling of the characteristics of criminal careers, such as onset, duration, frequency of offending, and exit. The approach has its roots in the research on crime in New York City by Avi-Itzhak and Shinnar (1973), who were trained in engineering and emphasized the importance of formal mathematical models for predicting criminal behavior. This approach, refined and expanded by Petersilia (1980) and Blumstein et al. (1986, 1988), defines criminal careers as 'the longitudinal sequence of offenses committed by an offender who has a detectable rate of offending during some period of time' (Blumstein et al., 1988: 2). Further, 'criminal careers are characterized during a lifetime by a beginning (onset or initiation), an end (dropout or termination), a duration (career length), and a frequency of offending (lambda)' (p. 2). Farrington (1987: 59) also points out that 'the criminal career approach has the great advantage of quantification.' Thus, this definition of criminal careers is couched in terms of sequences of discrete events to be quantitatively measured and predicted through statistical techniques.

Positivist criminal careers research addresses how offender characteristics, social environmental factors, and (in some studies) criminal justice interventions can predict onset, frequency, persistence, and exit from criminal activity over time. One of the most important tenets of this approach is that these different phases of criminal careers are potentially generated by distinct causal factors. In noting the practical importance of distinguishing between different aspects or phases of criminal careers, Blumstein et al. state:

> If offending is widespread throughout the population (high participation), with a large number of offenders committing crimes at low frequencies, participation is an appropriate target for crime control. If, however, participation in crime

is low and individual offending frequencies are high, then policies directed at high lambda offenders may be more suitable. (1988: 7)

Of particular interest is the identification of that small but troublesome proportion of 'persistent offenders' first identified in the cohort studies of Wolfgang and associates (see Wolfgang, 1958; Wolfgang et al., 1972, 1987). The famous longitudinal criminal careers studies by Blumstein and associates (Blumstein et al., 1985, 1986, 1988) exemplify this approach, and focus on identifying types of criminal careers and examining their distinct trajectories and determinants.

Positivist criminal careers research incorporates the logic of 'soft positivism' (see Blalock, 1989; Collins, 1989) and a probabilistic determinism, as used in stochastic statistical methods. The various kinds of statistical models found in the criminal careers literature exemplify this soft positivist logic: researchers attempt to predict events of criminal offending with varying degrees of error. This approach therefore recognizes that measurements are not isomorphic with reality due to measurement error, insufficiently complete data, model misspecification, and other measurement and modeling limitations (see Hanushek and Jackson, 1977: 12). Hence, there is a distinction in quantitative models of criminal careers between the 'true' and 'observed' values of parameters, or 'true' versus 'specified' causal models. For example, Farrington (1987: 59) distinguishes between 'true' and 'observed' individual crime rates: 'The actual number of offenses is related probabilistically to the recorded number because of measurement biases ... The major problem is to draw conclusions from measured rates about the true rate of offending.'

Sophisticated statistical modeling has been the methodological hallmark of both the Blumstein et al. (1986, 1988) criminal careers approach and the stable criminal propensity critique (discussed later). In their review of statistical techniques for modeling criminal careers, Osgood and Rowe (1994: 527) explain that determinism is probabilistic due to an indeterminate relation between 'the measured outcome and an underlying causal dimension.' Thus, they argue, probabilistic determinism must suffice in explaining and predicting criminal events over time since underlying causal variables may be unobservable (latent), and since observation and measurement are likely to be insufficiently precise (see also Rowe et al., 1990).

Specifically, positivist treatments of criminal careers tend to depict prediction error as a problem of insufficiently valid and reliable measurements, inappropriate modeling techniques, incompletely specified models, or all three. Thus, Gottfredson and Gottfredson (1986: 272–4) call for improvements in statistical prediction tools in criminal careers research, including improved reliability, validity of measurements, and modeling techniques, statistical bootstrapping, and better links between theory and model specification—most of which center on methodological/measurement issues. In addition, Blumstein et al. (1986: 114) state: 'In short, most of the evaluative research on preventative interventions is nondefinitive because of design problems, small sample sizes, inadequate follow-up periods, and inadequate randomization.' Further, Chaiken et al.'s (1993: 226–8) discussion of sources of error in predicting violence focuses solely on measurement issues, and states: 'by refining instruments that help assess violent persons probabilistically along several dimensions, behavioral and medical scientists can help shape practices that consider a variety of options for dealing with violent persons rather than a simple choice of two alternatives' (p. 284).

Criminal Careers Research and Criminal Justice Policy

A lively debate has occurred within the criminal careers literature on the role of predictive criminal careers research in crime policy. Some are very hopeful about its contribution to crime control. Behavioral prediction is, after all, a principal activity of the criminal justice system. Gottfredson and Gottfredson (1986, 1994) argue that criminal justice decision makers will predict the future behavior of offenders with or without the assistance of scientific research, and that society is better served by basing such predictions on the best data and research available. The language, findings, and assumptions of the positivist criminal careers literature suffuse the crime policy arena (Visher, 1995). Osgood and Rowe describe the uses of this research for crime policy:

> This approach has generated findings in the form of projections of rates of offending,

probabilities of desistance, and so forth, and often the projections are specific to instances, such as individuals recently convicted of a felony. Results in this form have proved useful for addressing policy issues, such as selective incapacitation, targeting prevention efforts, and sentencing strategies. As a result, the criminal career approach has been influential in the public policy arena. (1994: 519)

Individual level prediction has been central to discussions of selective incapacitation as part of what Feeley and Simon (1992: 458) call the 'new penology': 'Its objectives are to identify high-risk offenders and to maintain long term control over them while investing in shorter terms and less intrusive control over lower risk offenders' because of the need to allocate scarce correctional resources and manage offender populations. Some have hoped that prediction-oriented criminal careers research can contribute to the development of such proactive, predictive crime control policies.[1] Thus, Visher reviews criminal career research, its future, and what it offers criminal justice policy:

> the success of this strategy [classifying and targeting offenders] depends on the ability of the criminal justice system to identify career offenders accurately and early in their criminal careers. Better information needs to be gathered and made available to the criminal justice officials who arrest, prosecute, and sentence these offenders ... A multifaceted approach to crime control that reserves incapacitation for career offenders or for those offenders convicted of truly heinous crimes and expands the use of intermediate sanctions with other types of offenders is likely to be the most effective crime control strategy for the 1990s. (1995: 532–3)

Moreover, Farrington argues for empirical prediction-based criminal justice decision making with a medical-model analogy:

> Many illnesses can more easily and effectively be prevented than cured. One method of preventing the spread of diseases is through

quarantine. This clearly involves some costs to the individual who is isolated. However, it is felt that the benefits to the community of preventing diseases outweigh the costs to the individual of being quarantined. (1987: 89)

Chaiken et al. (1993: 229) argue that empirical correlations of violent behavior, even if they do not directly implicate causal processes, are useful for predicting behavior and classifying offenders: 'The absence of proved causal relationships does not mean that these correlates are useless for classifying and predicting violent behavior . . . noncausal correlates can provide bases for meaningful utilitarian classification and prediction.'[2]

The predictive limitations of criminal careers models are by now widely acknowledged by those involved in such research. Many of the prediction models in the criminal careers studies discussed above are 'wrong' (either predicting false positives or false negatives) 30 to 67 percent of the time (e.g. Blumstein et al., 1986; Farrington, 1987; Chaiken et al., 1993; Gottfredson and Gottfredson, 1994; see also review by Barnett et al., 1992). Such levels of prediction error are not surprising, and are not in themselves grounds for damning criticism. After all, positivist research on criminal careers, in general, does no worse at predicting behavior than research elsewhere in social science. The 'false positives' problem—when 'high risk' individuals are predicted to become criminal offenders or recidivists, but in fact do not—is an important and enduring one in the prediction and intervention in criminal careers (Moore, 1986; Farrington, 1987; Agnew, 1995a).

In his commentary on ethical issues that accompanies the Blumstein et al. (1986) volumes, Moore (1986) locates debates about predictive intervention—and the attendant problem of false positive predictions—within the distinction between deontological versus utilitarian ethical systems. While he cautions against a 'technocratic enthusiasm for prediction' (p. 352), he argues that a sharp distinction between these two ethical systems in terms of criminal justice policy is 'unfortunate' (p. 321). He notes the utilitarian argument that the key goal of the criminal justice system is to reduce crime and promote public security, and states:

In this utilitarian conception the concern about punishing people for predicted future offenses disappears entirely—unless the means seem so grossly unjust and so bizarre as to be repugnant to the community. Similarly, the concern for 'false positives' fades, but does not entirely disappear. (1986: 327, see also p. 321)

He goes on to advocate the further development of research-based predictive tests to identify small and distinctive groups of offenders, and argues that interventions targeted at these offenders would be acceptable if they stressed prior record.

Farrington (1987: 92) argues that false positive predictions, in and of themselves, need not prevent the utilitarian use of research-based predictive information in crime control policy, provided there is adequate consideration of the social costs and benefits of incorrect predictions, both of which, he suggests, should be quantified and weighed explicitly:

experience suggests that few well-designed prediction exercises will manage to keep both false positive and false negative rates below 50 percent. However, this need not necessarily prevent the use of prediction scores in criminal justice decision making . . . what matters is not the absolute false positive rate but the predictive efficiency of the score. (1987: 95)

He thus ties future individual level interventions such as selective incapacitation to future advances in criminal careers research methodology aimed at prospectively predicting persistent offenders.

However, other proponents of positivist criminal careers research remain more cautious—even skeptical—about applying predictive-based findings to the development of policies that try to predict and control the criminal career trajectories of individuals. As Blumstein et al. state:

We are not uncritical enthusiasts of the concepts of career criminals and selective incapacitation, but we do believe that these policy ideas can stimulate important research. The outcome of the debate over these policies, however, has little relevance for the value of research on criminal careers, the participation/ frequency distinction, or the longitudinal method, all of which rest on theoretical, methodological and other scholarly considerations. (1988: 32)

In addition, Gottfredson and Gottfredson (1994: 466) argue that 'the prediction of offenders' behavior is difficult, and we don't do it very well.' They also note that the only way to reduce the number of prediction errors is to develop more accurate prediction tools, and that perfect prediction is unrealistic due to existing measurement and methodological problems (pp. 467–8). Further, the same crimogenic conditions can produce different responses, and individuals' interpretations of, and responses to, conditions can also vary throughout the life course (Sampson and Laub, 1993; Maltz, 1994).

Critiques and Extensions of Criminal Careers Research

We wish to highlight three recent and important developments in the literature on positivist criminal careers research. The first two raise issues for stability and change in criminal behavior over time; the third has ontological implications for indeterminacy.

First, some scholars have noted that the criminal careers research of the 1970s and 1980s was unable theoretically to explain why different phases of criminal careers might exhibit distinct causal processes (see Tittle, 1988; Osgood and Rowe, 1994; Paternoster and Brame, 1997). In response, others have developed theories that combine the Blumstein et al. criminal careers framework with insights from life course and developmental research to explain differential patterns of earlier and later onset and desistance from crime (Moffitt, 1993; Patterson and Yoerger, 1993; see also Osgood and Rowe, 1994: 519; Paternoster and Brame, 1997: 51). As Nagin et al. summarize:

To varying degrees these theories emphasize some combination of the following arguments: The progression or trajectory of offending across ages will differ among individuals; the determinants of antisocial behavior are age graded and vary over the life course; antisocial behaviors themselves are sequenced; and time-stable individual differences have an enduring impact on antisocial behavior. (1995: 111)

Developmental and life-course perspectives offer useful theoretical extensions of criminal careers research. These perspectives take note of both the stability (persistence) and dynamic changes (onset and desistance) in offending during a person's life (Thornberry, 1995). Many of these perspectives are derived from more established theories such as social control, social learning, strain, and the like (e.g. Samspon and Laub, 1993; Agnew, 1995b; Matsueda and Heimer, 1997). These theories are founded on important meta-theoretical assumptions that are congruent with some of the pragmatist assumptions underlying interactionist theory, a point we return to later.

Second, criticism of the work of Blumstein and others emphasizes variation in a population in terms of a 'persistent, underlying criminal potential' (Nagin and Farrington, 1992: 236). This 'stable criminal propensity' approach disagrees neither with the above-mentioned concept of a criminal career as Blumstein et al. (1986) define it, nor with the observation that there are persistent patterns among individuals in their rates of criminal behavior over time (see Nagin and Land, 1993). Rather, the 'stable criminal propensity' position and the criminal careers position differ chiefly in that the propensity position rejects the claim that separate components of offending (onset, frequency, length, termination, etc.) reflect distinct causal domains, and should be analyzed separately (see Osgood and Rowe, 1994).

Instead, the stable propensity approach proposes that a single propensity underlies the full range of measures of crime (Greenberg, 1991; Osgood and Rowe, 1994). Drawing in part from the work of Wilson and Herrnstein (1985) and the sharp criticisms of Blumstein et al.'s (1986, 1988) work by Gottfredson and Hirschi (1990), this approach attempts to predict criminal activity over time based on population variations in stable, latent individual criminal propensities. As Osgood and Rowe (1994: 520) put it, 'the propensity position provides the baseline for gauging the need for the more complex criminal careers position.' This approach is exemplified by the studies of Rowe et al. (1990), Greenberg (1991), Nagin and Farrington (1992), and Osgood and Rowe (1994), all of which argue that latent, stable criminal propensities to some degree account for criminal behavior over the life course. The stable criminal propensity position also seeks to influence public policy by providing what are thought to be improved and more parsimonious predictions of criminal behavior over time (Osgood and Rowe, 1994).

Much recent work suggests that the stable criminal propensity position and the criminal careers approach, including its developmental theory variants, are not incompatible. Sampson and Laub's (1993) and Nagin et al.'s (1995) studies have shown that variations in criminal career trajectories are predicted by variations in social bonds throughout the life course as well as by indicators of stable criminal propensities. Further, Paternoster and Brame (1997) call for further research and theorizing of 'dynamic factors' in the life course that channel trajectories of criminal and conventional behavior. Their research findings support what they call a 'theoretical middle ground,' as exemplified by the work of Sampson and Laub (1993), between the stable criminal propensity position and the developmental criminal careers theory of Moffitt (1993). In addition, Nagin and Land (1993: 356–8) found mixed support for both 'latent-trait criminal propensity theory' and 'conventional' criminal careers theory (e.g. Blumstein et al., 1988).

These discussions of stability and change in criminal careers have also provided a link between positivist criminal careers research and research into biological influences on crime. That is, some posit that complex interactions between individual biological characteristics and social environments may enable explanations of how stable criminal propensities interact with 'environmental insults' in order to more completely explain crime over the life course and to predict it more accurately (Rowe et al., 1990: 244–5). Biology and social environments can interact to determine criminal careers, it is argued, in at least two ways (see Jeffery, 1978, 1996; Fishbein, 1990; Walters, 1992; Booth and Osgood, 1993; Chaiken et al., 1993):

1. certain environments are differentially favorable to the development of biological conditions or the expression of genetic characteristics that may be conducive to crime; or

2. social environments channel the expression of existing biological states or genetic characteristics in ways that are conducive to crime or conformity.

Osgood and Rowe (1994: 520) state that stable criminal propensity can be conceptualized as 'an amalgam of whatever factors are relevant to crime in an individual's personality, biological make-up, interpersonal relations, and position in the social structure.'[3]

Third, recent statistical methodologies employed by studies of criminal career dynamics and stable criminal propensities recognize individual level indeterminacy in modeling criminal behavior over time. These methodologies include Poisson regression methods (Rowe et al., 1990; Land, 1992; Nagin and Land, 1993), as well as general linear model alternatives (Osgood and Rowe, 1994). The Poisson and mixed-Poisson regression frameworks hold that an individual's age, measures of latent criminal propensity, and any other measures of social environmental factors do not determine the actual criminal behavior outcomes for individuals, but simply an individual rate of offending which incorporates a probability distribution of outcomes characterized by a Poisson process. Thus, the Poisson framework recognizes individual level indeterminacy to the extent that it recognizes the probabilistic relationship between latent variables (such as the 'true' rate of individual offending) and measured outcomes (such as the observed frequency of offenses) (see Land, 1992; Osgood and Rowe, 1994). Additionally, Osgood and Rowe (1994) incorporate similar assumptions of individual level indeterminacy in their general linear model alternatives to the Poisson framework. They summarize what they (and others) see as sources of indeterminacy in modeling criminal careers, and what this implies for the stable propensity and criminal careers positions:

> In our conceptual framework, indeterminacy stems from two separate sources. The first is a probabilistic relationship between the measured outcome and an underlying causal

dimension. [Second] It is because of this probabilistic relationship that the causal dimension is unobservable, or latent. In other words, we assume that even individuals with identical 'true' propensities to engage in crime differ in their observed offending due to innumerable random factors such as chance encounters of everyday life and error in detection or measurement. The propensity position can be defined by the assumption that a single, latent dimension determines all measures of offending. In contrast, the criminal career model implies that distinct latent causal dimensions underlie different measures. (1994: 527–8)

Indeterminacy in predicting criminal careers, stability and change in criminal careers, and the issue of what quantitative models of criminal careers and criminal propensity can and cannot tell us are not just technical and methodological issues, but also theoretical ones. The positivist criminal career literature, as well as its stable propensity critique, would greatly benefit from a careful consideration of the pragmatist ontological position, and the symbolic interactionist research on criminal careers that is based on it.

The symbolic interactionist approach provides a unique theoretical framework for understanding four interrelated sets of issues about criminal careers:

1. indeterminacy and reflexivity;

2. stability and change in criminal careers and criminal propensity;

3. the respective roles of quantitative and qualitative research in criminal careers; and

4. the implications of criminal careers research for policy.

In addition, attention to the interactionist framework can contribute to recent developmental (Moffitt, 1993) and life-course theories (Sampson and Laub, 1993; Agnew, 1995b) of criminal careers. Below, we discuss the interrelated notions of indeterminacy, stability, and change, and then the role of quantitative and qualitative research in the context of pragmatist ontological

assumptions. We then review several key exemplars of interactionist research on criminal and deviant careers and how they can contribute to further criminal careers research. In the conclusion, we discuss the implications of interactionist criminal careers research for policy.

◆ Interactionist Conceptions of Criminal Careers

Pragmatist Assumptions: Indeterminacy, Stability, and Change

Pragmatism and its sociological offspring, symbolic interactionism, offer a useful and sometimes underappreciated view of human social action in general (Maines, 1997), and of criminal activity in particular. Pragmatism depicts a dialectical process[4] in which human social behavior is partially determined and partially indeterminate (Dewey, 1896; Maines, 1989). Mead (1934: 330) describes the indeterminate, or emergent dimensions of behavior this way: 'Emergence [refers to] a certain environment that exists in its relationship to an organism, and in which new characters can arise by virtue of the organism.'

The pragmatist position does not reject the notion of stable, recurring patterns in social action, nor does it reject the goal of probabilistic explanation in a science of the social (Maines, 1989; Blumer, 1993). Rather, pragmatism insists that continuity and discontinuity are inseparable and mutually constituting phases of a dialectical process (Strauss, 1993: 42). The potential for novel, emergent, unpredictable trajectories of action is inherent in human social life, and thus the social sciences will never achieve highly precise predictions of behavior (Strauss, 1993). According to Shalin:

> there is a degree of indeterminacy endemic to any social whole . . . the outcome of each social encounter becomes a matter of probability. High as this probability might be, one cannot assume the outcome will follow the same pattern the next moment simply because it happened this way the moment before. (1986: 15)

This pragmatist notion of a dialectic of determinacy and indeterminacy, and continuity and discontinuity, applies to realms of both biophysical and social conditions. In his pragmatism-based action theory, Strauss (1993) argues that biological factors, the individual's biography, and the structuring of social environments influence and condition, but do not determine, future trajectories of action. In their dialogues with early behaviorist psychology, pragmatists such as William James, John Dewey, and G.H. Mead recognized a dialectical relationship between the biological and the social—as evidenced, for example, in their rejection of Cartesian mind/body dualism. Thus, pragmatism does not deny potential biological influences on behavior, but emphasizes that the role of both biological conditions and social environments, as well as their interaction, are characterized by a dialectical process of stability and emergence, determinacy and indeterminacy (see James, 1984: 342–3; Strauss, 1993). This means that even the kind of research that focuses on the interaction of social environments and biological factors envisioned by Fishbein (1990), Booth and Osgood (1993), and Jeffery (1996) cannot fully predict criminal career trajectories or completely identify stable criminal propensities.

As scientists of whatever field, we can investigate and discern stable patterns and regularities, and even make generalizable theoretical propositions, but individual level predictions will always to some degree be indeterminate—not just because of methodological limitations, but also because of the nature of human social activity. Pragmatism would thus allow researchers to make ontological and theoretical sense out of the individual level indeterminacy already acknowledged by the methodological strategies used by some contemporary studies of criminal careers, such as the Poisson regression framework.

Research Methods: Outcomes and Processes

Note, however, that this pragmatist position does not deny the value of quantification or statistical modeling per se. Various interactionists have repeatedly claimed that statistics and various qualitative methods are not in conflict with each other, but are mutually complementary phases of a division of labor in empirical research (Park, 1929; Blumer, 1969; Shalin, 1986). Blumer (1956, 1969) argued that measured variables do not exert agency, even though social scientists often

reify such variables and imbue them with agency in their reports of research. Instead, human beings exert agency in their interpretive actions and interactions within situational contexts. These processes and the social organizational contexts that condition them are what our variables actually measure, and variables are simply heuristic concepts that help us analyze and understand those processes and contexts. Further, quantified variables and statistical modeling are sufficient and useful for studying outcomes, or series of outcomes, of social processes and stable, obdurate contextual features that surround them. Qualitative methods such as ethnography, however, are better suited for the study of social processes themselves, which include social interaction processes, definitions of situations, decision-making processes, and contingencies and turning points in the life course (see Strauss, 1969), and the ways in which larger-scale contextual factors such as social structures are dealt with by social actors (Maines, 1982).

The positivist criminal career research tradition provides a set of techniques and quantitative strategies for studying aggregate and individual sequences of *outcomes* of criminal careers (recall, for example, that Blumstein et al., 1988 define criminal careers in terms of a series of discrete criminal events). The qualitative methodological strategies that usually (but not exclusively, see Hagan and Palloni, 1990; Matsueda, 1992) guide symbolic interactionist research on crime and criminal careers provide a way to capture and analyze the contextualized *processes* that produce the kinds of aggregate outcomes measured by quantitative criminal career models. Put differently, the qualitative strategies used by the symbolic interactionist exemplars of criminal career research we discuss later capture the processual conditions, interpretations, decisions, activities, and their consequences (see Hall, 1995) that lie behind the quantified variables used in quantitative criminal career models. As Carl Taylor (1947: 7) put it long ago: '[Qualitative] field studies . . . place flesh, blood, and nervous system on the skeleton of statistical information.' In fact, some quantitative students of crime and the life course have already recognized the value of such qualitative research. Sampson and Laub's (1993) reanalyses of the Gluecks' data, for example, include a laudable (though somewhat brief and truncated) analysis of their subjects' qualitative life histories.

Interactionist Research on Criminal Careers

The rich and long tradition of interactionist research on crime and deviance (e.g. Lemert, 1951; Becker, 1963; Stebbins, 1971; Schur, 1980; Steffensmeier, 1986; Hagan and Palloni, 1990; Best and Luckenbill, 1994) has been based on the following assumptions (see Lofland, 1969; Matza, 1969; Strauss, 1993):

1. People confront situations and act on the basis of their definitions of those situations.

2. Different probabilities of action are conditioned by the constraints and opportunities presented by situational contexts, and definitions of situations are influenced by an actor's biography and prior repertoires of action. Further, situational and biographical constraints can influence individuals' definitions and actions both with and without their awareness of those constraints.

3. However, behavior involves a dialectic of choice and constraint—the potential for novel choices and emergent lines of action is always present.

4. Situational contexts are set by, and actors' biographies are located within, larger arrangements of institutional organization and social structure.

Lofland outlined the foci of what he termed a 'situational' or interactionist approach:

[it] focuses upon successions of dependencies through time; upon ways in which prior conditions may or may not develop into succeeding conditions of a given outcome . . . upon ways in which alternatives may or may not be present, upon ways in which, and the degree to which, action may be constrained. In contrast, a static model leads easily to static statistical profiles of the 'characteristics' associated with an outcome. Or, more particularly, it may lead to profiling the characteristics of 'types of persons', such as Republicans, murderers or juvenile delinquents. (1969: 296)

According to Lofland, a situational approach takes 'the phenomenology of the actor rather seriously and (is) concerned with discovering and depicting it in its own terms' (p. 296). Lofland contrasts this focus to an approach which privileges the analyst's perspective. As opposed to other approaches focusing on explanatory variables which are spatio-[temporally] and conceptually remote from the behavior in question, interactionist approaches 'highlight explanatory variables whose operation is relatively *proximate* to that for which an account is being given' (p. 297; our emphasis), and these proximate factors are in turn linked to larger-scale patterns of social organization.

Interactionist models of deviant or criminal careers articulate closely with Lofland's situational approach. Criminal careers are conceptualized as a process comprising a sequence of steps or stages. However, in these models it is not just the attributes of each stage that are important, but the contingencies that facilitate or constrain movement from one stage to another. The nature of this process is often compared and/or contrasted with so-called respectable careers (see Best and Luckenbill, 1994: 230–1). Becker's (1963) *Outsiders* represents one of the most influential interactionist models of deviant careers. Borrowing from sociological studies of occupations, Becker conceptualized a deviant career as a 'sequence of movements from one position to another in an occupational system made by any individual who works in that system' (1963: 24). Based on this definition, Becker focused on the processes that comprise these sequences of movements, rather than (as in positivist models) measuring discrete sequences of outcomes. While recognizing that deviant careers could be short-lived, Becker, like Lemert (1951) before him, focused on those cases in which the actors made deviance a way of life and came to organize their identities around that pattern of deviant behavior.

In his model, Becker (1963) delineated four stages:

1. the commission of the first nonconforming act;

2. development of deviant vocabularies of motive, interests, and definitions;

3. public labeling and redefinition of the actor by the social audience and him/herself; and

4. movement into an organized deviant group.

Crucial throughout this process are deviant vocabularies of motive, neutralizations (Sykes and Matza, 1957), definitions and interests as they both account for, and are consequent to, emergent patterns of deviant behavior.

Becker's model reflects pragmatists' concern with the dialectic of choice and constraint. The social actor faces choices among alternative lines of action and these choices are variously constrained or facilitated by social structural forces. Constraints are exemplified in his discussion of how social reactions limit the possibilities for social interaction with conventional, as opposed to deviant, others (as Becker, 1963: 35 puts it, 'the treatment of deviants denies them the ordinary means of carrying on the routines of everyday life open to most people'). Alternatively, associations with deviant others can help facilitate the actor's choice to remain deviant.

Further, individual choices of lines of action can influence, in a dialectical fashion, the very forces or contingencies that condition later choices. Initial choices of deviant behavior could eventually result in constraints and restricted conventional opportunities conditioned by labeling and subsequent social reactions, invoking what Becker (1960) called 'unfitting processes.' It is important to remember, however, that these factors operate as *contingencies*, which are 'factors on which mobility from one position to another depends,' including both 'objective facts of social structure and changes in the perspectives, motivations and desires of the individual' (1963: 24). According to Becker:

> Apprehension may not lead to increasing deviance if the situation in which the individual is apprehended for the first time occurs at a point where he can still choose between alternative lines of action. Faced, for the first time with the possible ultimate and drastic consequences of what he is doing, he may decide that he does not want to take the deviant road and turn back. If he makes the right choice, he will be welcomed back into the conventional community; but if he makes the wrong move, he will be rejected and start a cycle of increasing deviance. (1963: 37)

Many interactionist analyses have focused on entry into, and exit from, criminal careers (Best and Luckenbill, 1994). Becker's analysis of marijuana smokers is an example of this focus, as is Levi's (1981) study of the 'hit man.' According to Levi (1981), independent professional killing—certainly a type of serious and potentially persistent criminal career—lacks most of the characteristics of other kinds of killing (e.g. those who work for organized syndicates or those who kill spontaneously) that can be used to justify the behavior. Instead, the contract, based as it is on the hit man's reputation for profit and skill, provides him with opportunities for various neutralizations and accounts. This, however, does not fully explain *entry* into the career of independent professional killing. According to Levi, the first killing-for-hire produces extremely negative emotional responses which the killer must somehow reframe (Goffman, 1974) or redefine in order to continue in this career track. In his analysis, Levi illustrates how the killer learns how to dissociate himself from the action by dissattending to personal or individual features of the victim. Such reframing is reminiscent of Becker's (1963) analysis of how first-time marijuana smokers learn how to disattend to the negative aspects of getting high. In both cases, the accomplishment of attention framing is a career *contingency*, the occurrence of which is indeterminate and problematic and which, when it does occur, facilitates further movement into a criminal career.

In his analyses of male ordinary property offenders, Shover (1983, 1996) has examined the contingencies which accompany exit from the later stages of criminal careers. Identifying age as a major explanatory variable, he argues that it is not the biological process of aging per se that explains exit from a career of property offending but 'the socially constructed and negotiated changes in perspectives which accompany aging' (1983: 210). Shover found four temporal contingencies or 'changes in definitions of oneself and significant others or patterns of events in one's life' (p. 210), including shifts in identity, an awareness of time becoming an exhaustive resource, changes in aspirations and goals, and growing tired of the relentless effects of incarceration. Property offenders also experience an interpersonal contingency that Shover defines as 'an objective change in one's social relationships or networks' (p. 210), typically involving a satisfying job or stable relationship with a woman.

As in other analyses of deviant careers, Shover found variability and unpredictability in the occurrence of, and interdependence among, these contingencies. In some cases, the occurrence of separate contingencies could not be isolated and, at times, contingencies occurred simultaneously. In many cases, temporal and interpersonal contingencies:

> interacted with or followed one another as part of a dynamic process, with one type preceding and increasing the probability of occurrence for the other(s). *Imposition of a rigid temporal and causal order on this process would violate its dynamic nature, and given our present state of knowledge, would be arbitrary and premature.* (1983: 214, our emphasis)

Shover's more recent work (1996) on persistent property offender careers also emphasizes how these offenders choose between structurally constrained alternatives at key turning points in their lives, and how these choices lead them down complicated roads of persistent and varied criminal activity, trying to 'go straight,' re-entry into crime, going straight once again, and so forth.

Best and Luckenbill (1994) have elaborated on earlier models of deviant careers, arguing that models like Becker's (1963) were too orderly, that deviant careers were more fluid and precarious and less structured than even Becker's model had allowed. For Best and Luckenbill (1994: 230), the metaphor of an escalator, 'suggesting mobility involving short passages, along visible, established routes'—used by Becker and Strauss (1956) to characterize organizational careers—is inappropriate for most criminal careers. Rather, Best and Luckenbill (1994: 231–2) use the metaphor of a 'walk through the woods—while some people take the pathways marked by their predecessors, others strike out on their own, some walk slowly, exploring before moving farther, while others run, caught up in the action.'

Best and Luckenbill build on Becker's and other interactionist models of deviance in other ways. Arguing that previous theory and research have focused on entry into, and exit from, deviant careers, their model specifies the *intermediate* stages of deviant careers. In doing so,

they argue that existing literature has necessarily oversimplified the middle part of deviant careers. More importantly, Best and Luckenbill's model specifies the ways that social organization influences the multiple points of decision making that accompany the numerous shifts possible during deviant careers. Like Becker's, Best and Luckenbill's model involves an actor who makes choices in the face of various constraints and opportunities. In each phase, the actor can continue engaging in deviant behavior or abandon the process altogether. In their model, however, deviant behavior can be a defensive reaction to outside or structural pressures, or it can simply represent a rewarding experience, or it can result from the rational choice among a variety of options.

Further, according to Best and Luckenbill (1994: 232), 'being deviant . . . involves a complex series of career shifts as individuals make their way through the deviant experience.' Such shifts may be horizontal, involving movement into parallel kinds of deviant activity such as a shift from heroin use to small-time burglary. Other shifts may be vertical, such as movement from small-time burglary to armed robbery. In the *preliminary* stage, actors assemble the necessary equipment, knowledge, skills, and motives required for an upcoming stage. In the *commission* stage, the actor carries out the new line of action, after which he/she assesses the meaning of the new experience. Upon deciding to continue this new line of action, he/she enters the *routine* stage, becoming familiar with the new activity, perhaps improving skills and developing interpretive frameworks for the experience. Finally, 'the deviant may become aware of additional options' (p. 232), thereby marking the last stage of one career shift as the first stage of another.

Adler and Adler's (1983) analysis of the middle phase of careers of upper-level drug dealers illustrates important aspects of Best and Luckenbill's model, and resonates with Shover's (1996) later work. As described by Adler and Adler, these careers are typically temporary as almost all of the dealers quit the business at some point. However, dealers who quit usually reentered the business at different levels of dealing or assumed different roles. Thus, these careers were marked by 'shifts and oscillations' in which any particular decision to leave or return could be the last one, or could be merely another step in a continuing pattern of phase-out or re-entry. In their analysis, Adler and Adler emphasize how dealers made decisions about retirement, re-entry, or career shifts in response to changing conditions in their lives:

> As dealers and smugglers aged in the career they became more sensitized to the extreme risks they faced. Cases of friends who were arrested, imprisoned, or killed began to mount. Many individuals became convinced that continued drug trafficking would inevitably lead to arrest. (1983: 536)

There are two features of Adler and Adler's analysis of retirement from drug dealing that deserve emphasis. First, rather than a predictable outcome of a linear process, retirement appears to be marked by indecision and changes of heart. It is never quite clear if any particular decision to retire is final. Second, this decision results from choices made by dealers as they attempt to adjust to changing contingencies in their lives. Some of these contingencies appear to facilitate retirement (e.g. mounting arrests of friends) while others facilitate remaining in the career.

Another valuable exemplar of the interactionist study of criminal careers is Steffensmeier's (1986) ethnography of the social world and career of fencing stolen goods. He describes several features that distinguish fences whose criminal careers are 'episodic, situational, and opportunistic' (p. 16) and those for whom fencing is a regular, long-term, and sustained business requiring significant skill, time, planning, and organization. Steffensmeier's ethnography focuses on the socialization, social organizational contexts, networks, skills, and career contingencies of a committed long-term business fence and his associates. In particular, his study describes in intricate detail:

1. the symbiotic relationships between fences and the conventional public;

2. the material and social rewards of a career in fencing; and

3. the objective contexts of opportunity and subjective definitions, attitudes, and rationalizations that make a 'successful' fencing career possible.

In a similar vein, Ulmer (1994) applied Michael Johnson's (1991) typology of commitment processes to deviant lines of action in order to critique and extend Stebbins's (1971) conceptualization of the role of negative social reaction and the potential entrenchment of commitment to criminal careers. Like Becker, Stebbins (1971) proposed a model of deviance in which sanctions can restrict some conventional lines of action and relationships and placement in deviant identities can result in the development of deviant self-concepts by actors. One key to Ulmer's application, and our discussion here, is the focus on the dialectic of social structural constraints and individual choice:

> Commitment [to a criminal career] is not solely a psychological experience, nor a condition of structurally forced behavior, but a dialectic process that encompasses the social organizational factors that produce commitments and the actor's interpretation and decision-making in the face of those factors. (Ulmer, 1994: 137)

Ulmer (1994) applies Johnson's (1991) three interrelated types of commitment to labeling processes and criminal careers contingencies. First, *structural commitment* 'derives from factors external to the individual that constrain action independently of personal and moral commitments' (Ulmer, 1994: 138–9). Second, *personal commitment* refers to 'choices based on one's desire to continue a line of action' based on personal attitudes and definitions of self (p. 138). Third, *moral commitment* involves self-constraint based on perceived obligations to others or internalized values that emphasize consistency in lines of action. At different points in criminal careers, structural and interactional contingencies arise to which the actor adjusts, reacts or resists. Consider the following propositions about the development of structural commitment to deviance (p. 149):

1. Restricted availability of conventional alternatives increases the attractiveness of deviant alternatives. Actors may thus adjust by continuing deviant activities and further exploring deviant opportunities and networks.

2. This adjustment, in turn, can lead to further reduction in the availability and attractiveness of conventional alternatives through unfitting processes.[5]

3. Adjustment to deviant identity placement conditions irretrievable investments in deviant activities and network relationships. These investments, in turn, further reduce the attractiveness of conventional alternatives.

Ulmer (pp. 149–50) also develops similar propositions about personal and moral commitment to deviance and their relationship to structural commitment processes.

Finally, Agnew (1995a) has recently argued that criminal behavior variously involves soft determinism, drift, or indeterminacy, depending on the biography, social context, and even biological states of individual actors. He defines five contextual conditions that alternatively foster determinacy, drift, and interdeterminacy in criminal behavior over time. Under some conditions individuals face strong constraints that channel them into criminal behavior or restrict them to conformity (soft determinism). Under other conditions individuals face relatively equal constraints and opportunities toward crime and conformity, and can *drift* into and out of criminal activity (see Matza, 1964). Under still other conditions, individuals can produce radically new and unpredictable lines of action—which might be criminal or conventional. Agnew argues that freedom of choice is greatest when individuals:

1. have a large number of behavioral options of both a criminal and conformist nature;

2. are aware of both the behavioral options in (1);

3. perceive as equal the biological, psychological, and social constraints for selection of the options in (1);

4. are under some pressure to make a choice between criminal and conformist behavioral options;

5. have the capacity and motivation to engage in self-directed behavior.

Agnew's arguments thus imply that such indeterminacy and drift make it impossible to predict criminal behavior trajectories with complete or even near-complete precision, no matter how rigorous the data or analytical techniques.

From Becker's (1963) early statement to more recent examples such as Shover's (1996), interactionist models of criminal careers have increased our understanding of the kinds of choices actors make and the kinds of social organizational factors that both constrain and facilitate those choices. Underlying all of this interactionist research on criminal careers is a dialectic of choice and constraint. As we have argued, positivist models emphasize the prediction of sequences of outcomes in criminal careers. In these models, the primary goal is identifying correlates of these career outcomes and inferring the causal factors at work. Further, the causal factors are also often distal, removed in time and space from the immediate context of action. On the other hand, interactionist models of criminal careers take seriously a dialectic of choice and constraint. From this perspective, the actor confronts larger social organizational arrangements in everyday life and makes choices that are variously facilitated and constrained by these arrangements. These choices pose consequences for the social context in which the actor is embedded that in turn facilitate and constrain subsequent choices. Accordingly, while in the aggregate criminal career patterns are probabilistically predictable, at the individual level criminal careers and the actions that they comprise are to some extent indeterminate, as Agnew (1995a) implies. The choices made by actors are, to a large extent, situational in nature and not amenable to precise prediction and control (for more on the need for situational analyses of crime and deviance, see McCarthy and Hagan, 1992).

◈ Contributions of Interactionist Models of Criminal Careers

Symbolic interactionism's emphasis on the dialectic of determinacy and indeterminacy, reflexivity, choice and constraint, the dialectic of stability and change, and the roles of quantitative and qualitative research contribute to our understanding of at least four key issues in the study of criminal careers. First, it emphasizes dialectics of determinacy and indeterminacy, as well as stability and change over the life course. This means that social actors reflexively confront problematic situations in the present, make decisions, and construct future lines of action by drawing on previously constructed definitions and interpretations, prior repertoires of action, and by accounting for and confronting previously mobilized constraints. All of these are sources of continuity, and to some extent determinacy in social behavior (see Blumer, 1993). However, actors always have the potential to adapt to present situations, constraints, and contingencies in creative, novel, or otherwise unpredictable ways, and this potential is a constant source of indeterminacy and change.

We argue that the kind of dialectic described by pragmatist ontology between stability and change lies behind the findings from the growing number of quantitative studies that find support for both the stable propensity position and the differential-cause criminal careers position, such as Sampson and Laub (1993), Nagin et al. (1995), and Paternoster and Brame (1997). On the one hand, continuities in criminal or conventional behavior over the life course would be expected when social structural environments present relatively stable constraints and opportunities, when individuals' prior socialization imparts relatively enduring attitudes, definitions, self-concepts, conventional social bonds (or lack thereof), and repertoires of action. Under such conditions, it would make sense to speak of stable criminal propensities. On the other hand, the work of Matza (1969), Adler and Adler (1983), Agnew (1995a, 1995b), Ulmer (1994) and Shover (1996), strongly suggests that various phases of criminal careers, and varying kinds of criminal careers, may be qualitatively different from one another. Different temporal dimensions of criminal careers, such as entry, frequency of offending, duration, and exit may entail different objective and subjective contingencies, constraints, and opportunities (Lofland, 1969), different kinds of problematic situations to be confronted by individuals, and different adaptations to those situations. This is what is meant, for example, by Adler and Adler's phrase 'shifts and oscillations' as a description of the careers of upper-level drug dealers. Thus, an

interactionist framework can make theoretical sense out of the debate between the notion of stable criminal propensities and the notion that different phases of criminal careers are potentially conditioned by different factors, providing the kind of 'theoretical middle ground' between them called for by Paternoster and Brame (1997).

Second, interactionist conceptualizations of criminal careers recognize the value of quantitative studies of the outcomes, or series of outcomes, of social activity. Our research cannot stop there, however. Our understandings of criminal careers must also be informed by qualitative data and analyses, such as those we discussed earlier, that can better investigate the action processes themselves as well as the proximal, situational contexts that encompass and condition them (see also McCarthy and Hagan, 1992). Research on criminal careers would therefore be improved by a methodological division of labor in which quantitative models of criminal career outcomes (including longitudinal sequences of outcomes) and qualitative studies of social processes and their situational contexts mutually sensitize one another.

Third, there are points of congruence between the meta-theoretical assumptions underlying both developmental/life course perspectives and symbolic interactionist perspectives that facilitate this division of theoretical and methodological labor. For example, Sampson and Laub's (1993) model stresses, and attempts to explain, both continuity and change in delinquent and criminal behavior over time. Further, they argue that the causal influences they found are bi-directional or reciprocal over the life course. For example, they quote (p. 235) Thornberry et al.:

> The initially weak bonds lead to high delinquency involvement, the high delinquency involvement further weakens the conventional bonds, and in combination both of these effects make it extremely difficult to reestablish bonds to conventional society at later ages. As a result, all of these factors tend to reinforce one another over time to produce an extremely high probability of continued deviance. (Sampson and Laub, 1993: 30)

Likewise, Agnew (1995b) speaks of an amplification loop involving reciprocal relations between causal factors. For example, in his model aggressive traits can result in aversive reactions from others (e.g. peers, adults) and these aversive reactions can reinforce those aggressive traits.

These kinds of reflexive relationships can help explain stability, as well as escalation, in criminal career trajectories. Best and Luckenbill's (1994) model focuses on the specific factors that produce this stability, examining the multiple decision points that occur within different social organizational contexts. Likewise, Steffensmeier (1986) showed how networks of relationships and organizational factors operated as career contingencies that produced continuity in criminal activity. However, at the same time, symbolic interactionism understands that subtle changes in decision making and interactive dynamics can introduce significant changes in these career trajectories. For example, while Adler and Adler (1983) showed how dealers become increasingly sensitized to the risks of the drug trade, they emphasized how this decision making resulted in both retirement *and* reentry.

At a theoretical level, developmental/life course theories typically assume, or infer, these interpretive and interactive processes, which are the *focus* of interactionist work. For example, in offering reasons why adolescents are more likely to view their environment as aversive, Agnew (1995b) talks of increasing egocentrism that is exacerbated by:

1. the belief that others are just as obsessed by behavior and appearance; and

2. the public nature of their social world, such as much of their negative treatment occurs before an audience.

In the first instance, interactionist theory and research draws our attention squarely to the interpretive processes that constitute the self. In the second instance, interactionism focuses on the interactive dynamics that constitute the 'front stage' behavior of social actors (Goffman, 1959).

Sampson and Laub (1993) also have a place for interpretive processes in understanding how contextual, structural factors indirectly affect delinquent behavior. Their use of qualitative narrative data to shed light on these processes, while admirable, fails to adequately conceptualize these processes. Consider their finding that formal sanctions effect delinquency through their effect on social bonds such as conventional employment. Their discussion of this finding does not address the specific interpretive and interactive processes which constitute this causal effect. Ulmer (1994), however, captures this idea in his use of Johnson's (1991) concept of structural commitment as a set of contingencies by which criminal sanctions can constrain conventional action and make continued delinquent or criminal behavior both structurally more available and subjectively more attractive.

Sampson and Laub (1993: 252) call for the 'need to identify subjective transitions in the life course independently of behavioral transitions.' These changes in how actors define, and adjust to, their social worlds have been the focus of each of the pieces of interactionist research we discussed earlier. For example, Adler and Adler's (1983) work serves as an exemplar here by privileging the actor's perspective, focusing on shifts in perceptions of self and situation through the life course. Likewise, Levi (1981) examined the complex interpretive process of reframing that conditioned the hit man's entrance into professional killing.

Finally, many discussions of the politics of crime have noted that constructing crime as an individual problem, to be solved by individual interventions, treatments, and control strategies, is more palatable in the contemporary American political climate than addressing social contexts, especially large-scale structural ones (see Schur, 1980; Skolnick, 1995). The assumption of the new penology, as Feeley and Simon's (1992) critique argues, is that policies regarding crime cannot realistically address social structures and contexts conducive to crime, but the criminal justice system can hope to predict the behavior of, classify, and manage individual offenders. Yet, as we noted, many adherents to the positivist study of criminal careers are quite wary of using such research findings for proactive prediction and control of individual offenders. They recognize the methodological limits of individual level prediction and the role of indeterminacy at the individual level, as the logic of the Poisson regression framework demonstrates. Many scholars who do such positivist research emphasize crime policies directed at social contexts, and distance themselves from policies like selective incapacitation or proactive medical-model treatment regimes (for example, see Blumstein, 1993; Gottfredson and Gottfredson, 1994). Pragmatist assumptions, and the various interactionist approaches to criminal careers discussed earlier, would provide criminal careers research with sound theoretical reasons why policies would do better to address the cultural, structural, community, and situational contexts within which conventional opportunities are constrained, criminal opportunities are relatively more available, and criminal choices are seen as more attractive (see also Stark, 1987).

An interactionist approach to criminal careers would support policies that take the dialectic of choice and constraint seriously. Policies that are serious about channeling individuals away from or out of criminal careers would be directed at the social structures, institutional contexts, communities, peer groups, and families that present the situational constraints and opportunities within which developmental processes take place, biographies unfold, and within which people make choices between conventional and criminal activity. These kinds of policies would address the availability and attractiveness of conventional and criminal learning and performance opportunities (Cloward, 1959; Ulmer, 1994) and the ways these are configured by larger-scale arrangements of community, institutional structure, and stratification.

There is a distinct irony here. Symbolic interactionism is often mischaracterized as a perspective that only applies to the micro-level realm of individual minds, behavior and interaction. However, the types of social policies it encourages are not individual level ones but ones aimed at the interrelationship between larger-scale social organization and situational contexts of action (see Maines and Morrione, 1990; Hall, 1995). This, by the way, is exactly the type of social reform efforts in the realms of education, poverty, urban land use, and crime developed and supported by the early pragmatists (see Shalin, 1986; Maines, 1997).

An interactionist view of human behavior and criminal careers would lead us even further away from the notion that scientific progress will bring us increasingly accurate ability to predict individuals' criminal behavior,

and that what we can predict, we can control. Instead, we would recognize that continuity and change are inseparable, and that biology, previous behavior and experience, and constraints and opportunities may influence, but never totally determine the contingencies and choices involved in criminal activity throughout the life course. This view, and the theoretical models and research programs that derive from it, provide an important complementary approach to the study of criminal careers.

◆ Notes

1. Hopes for incorporating criminal careers research findings into policies that target individual offenders are based on the kind of 'theory growth' model of cumulative scientific progress described and critiqued by Camic (1992) and Maines et al. (1996). That is, some scholars have argued that with continued and cumulative progress in terms of better social science, psychological, or perhaps biological data and more sophisticated statistical modeling techniques, criminal risk prediction will allow social control policies of more proactive individual level intervention. Such envisioned interventions could include selective incapacitation, selective psychological treatment regimes, and perhaps even drug or gene therapy (Jeffery, 1993; Katz and Chambliss, 1995; Visher, 1995).

2. They continue: 'the current state of knowledge is not even close to having an adequate understanding of the causes of violence that would be needed to classify violent offenders and to predict violence with great accuracy' (1993: 229). Exemplifying the positivist notion of cumulative scientific progress, they argue that advances in research can enable greater accuracy in prediction and classification in the future.

3. Three of the most compelling statements regarding the role of biological and/or genetic factors in stable criminal propensities, and the possibilities of using such information to aid criminal justice decision making come from Jeffery (1978, 1996) and Fishbein (1990). Both recognize potential ethical problems with such an approach, but both foresee the effective use of such information and interventions:

> Overall, evidence to suggest that biological conditions have a profound impact on the adaptive, cognitive, and emotional abilities of the individual is compelling . . . The capability to identify and predict the factors responsible for maladaptivity may eventually enable society to employ innovative methods of early detection, prevention, and evaluation. (Fishbein, 1990: 46)

Jeffery calls for a major interdisciplinary research effort that is not race, class, or gender-biased, but is directed at individual level intervention and prevention of crime.

Whether or not a given individual has a genetic predisposition to crime must be examined at the individual level, not at the social level in terms of categories such as race or class or gender . . . the prevention of criminal behavior must involve genetics, the neurosciences, psychopharmacology, and neuropsychiatry as well as biological criminology in a major interdisciplinary effort. (1996: 2–3)

4. Pragmatists and symbolic interactionists use the term 'dialectical' to refer to an ontological relationship in which two or more conditions, objects, or phenomena mutually constitute, define, constrain, and enable one another (see Perinbanayagam, 1991; Joas, 1993). For example, they see the individual, social interaction, and social organization as dialectically related in that each reciprocally enables, creates, and influences one another in an ongoing process that is characterized by both stable patterns and creative emergence (see Shalin, 1986).

5. 'Unfitting processes,' a term coined by Becker (1960), refers to processes by which an actor's choices in the present restrict the availability of alternative lines of action in the future.

◇ References

Adler, Patricia and Peter Adler (1983) 'Relations Between Dealers: The Social Organization of Illicit Drug Transactions', *Sociology and Social Research* 67(3): 260–78.

Agnew, Robert (1995a) 'Determinism, Indeterminism, and Crime: An Empirical Exploration', *Criminology* 33(1): 83–110.

Agnew, Robert (1995b) 'Stability and Change in Crime over the Life Course: A Strain Theory Explanation', in T. Thornberry (ed.) *Developmental Theories of Crime and Delinquency*, pp. 101–32. New Brunswick, NJ: Transaction.

Avi-Itzhak, Benjamin and Reuel Shinnar (1973) 'Quantitative Models in Crime Control', *Journal of Criminal Justice* 1: 185–217.

Barnett, Arnold, Alfred Blumstein, Jaqueline Cohen and David Farrington (1992) 'Not All Criminal Career Models Are Equally Valid', *Criminology* 30(1): 133–40.

Becker, Howard S. (1960) 'Notes on the Concept of Commitment', *American Journal of Sociology* 66: 32–40.

Becker, Howard S. (1963) *Outsiders*. New York: Macmillan.

Becker, Howard S. and Anselm Strauss (1956) 'Careers, Personality, and Adult Socialization', *American Journal of Sociology* 62: 253–63.

Best, Joel and David Luckenbill (1994) *Organizing Deviance*. Englewood Cliffs, NJ: Prentice-Hall.

Blalock, Hubert (1989) 'The Real and Unrealized Contributions of Quantitative Sociology', *American Sociological Review* 54(3): 447–60.

Blumer, Hebert 'Sociological Analysis and the "Variable"', *American Sociological Review* 19: 3–10.

Blumer, Hebert (1969) *Symbolic Interactionism*. Englewood Cliffs, NJ: Prentice-Hall.

Blumer, Hebert (1993) 'Blumer's Advanced Course on Social Psychology' (edited by L. Athens), in N. Denzin (ed.) *Studies in Symbolic Interaction*, pp. 163–93. Greenwich, CT: JAI Press.

Blumstein, Alfred (1993) 'Making Rationality Relevant', *Criminology* 31(1): 1–16.

Blumstein, Alfred, Jaqueline Cohen and David Farrington (1988) 'Criminal Career Research: Its Value for Criminology', *Criminology* 26(1): 1–35.

Blumstein, Alfred, Jaqueline Cohen, J. Roth and Christy Visher (1986) *Criminal Careers and 'Career Criminals'*, vols 1 and 2. Washington, DC: National Academy Press.

Blumstein, Alfred, David Farrington and Soumyo Moitra (1985) 'Delinquency Careers: Innocents, Desisters, and Persisters', in M. Tonry and N. Morris (eds) *Crime and Justice: A Review of Research,* vol. 6, pp. 187–220. Chicago, IL: University of Chicago Press.

Booth, Alan and D. Wayne Osgood (1993) 'The Influence of Testosterone on Deviance in Adulthood: Assessing and Explaining the Relationship', *Criminology* 31(1): 93–118.

Camic, Charles (1992) 'Reputation and Predecessor Selection: Parsons and the Institutionalists', *American Sociological Review* 57: 421–45.

Chaiken, J., M. Chaiken and W. Rhodes (1993) 'Predicting Violent Behavior and Classifying Violent Offenders', in A. Reiss and J. Roth (eds) *Understanding and Preventing Violence*, vol. 4, pp. 217–95. Washington, DC: National Academy Press.

Cloward, Richard (1959) 'Illegitimate Means, Anomie, and Deviant Behavior', *American Sociological Review* 24: 164–76.

Collins, Randall (1989) 'Sociology: Proscience or Antiscience?', *American Sociological Review* 54(1): 124–39.

Dewey, John (1896) 'The Reflex Arc Concept in Psychology', *The Psychological Review* 3: 363–70.

Farrington, David (1987) 'Predicting Individual Crime Rates', in D. Gottfredson and M. Tonry (eds) *Prediction and Classification: Criminal Justice Decision-Making*, pp. 53–101. Chicago, IL: University of Chicago Press.

Feeley, Malcolm and Jonathan Simon (1992) 'The New Penology: Notes on the Emerging Strategy of Corrections and Its Implications', *Criminology* 30(4): 449–74.

Fishbein, Diane (1990) 'Biological Perspectives in Criminology', *Criminology* 28(1): 27–72.

Goffman, Erving (1959) *The Presentation of Self in Everyday Life*. New York: Doubleday.

Goffman, Erving (1963) *Stigma: Notes on the Management of Spoiled Identity*. Englewood Cliffs, NJ: Prentice-Hall.

Goffman, Erving (1974) *Frame Analysis*. Boston, MA: Northeastern University Press.

Gottfredson, Michael and Travis Hirschi (1990) *A General Theory of Crime*. Stanford, CA: Stanford University Press.

Gottfredson, Stephen and Don Gottfredson (1986) 'Accuracy of Prediction Models', in A. Blumstein, J. Cohen, J. Roth and C. Visher (eds) *Criminal Careers and 'Career Criminals'*, vol. II, pp. 212–90. Washington, DC: National Academy Press.

Gottfredson, Stephen and Don Gottfredson (1994) 'Behavioral Prediction and the Problem of Incapacitation', *Criminology* 32(3): 441–74.

Greenberg, David (1991) 'Modeling Criminal Careers', *Criminology* 29(1): 17–46.

Hagan, John and Alberto Palloni (1990) 'The Social Reproduction of a Criminal Class in Working Class London', *American Journal of Sociology* 92: 265–99.

Hall, Peter (1995) 'The Consequences of Qualitative Analysis for Sociological Theory: Beyond the Microlevel', *The Sociological Quarterly* 36(2): 397–424.

Hanushek, Eric and John Jackson (1977) *Statistical Methods for Social Scientists*. New York: Academic Press.

James, William (1984) *Psychology: Briefer Course*. Cambridge, MA: Harvard University Press.

Jeffery, C. Ray (1978) 'Criminology as an Interdisciplinary Behavioral Science', *Criminology* 16(2): 149–69.

Jeffery, C. Ray (1993) 'Genetics, Crime, and the Cancelled Conference', *The Criminologist* 18(1): 1, 6–8.

Jeffery, C. Ray (1996) 'The Genetics and Crime Conference Revisited', *The Criminologist* 21(2): 1–3.

Joas, Hans (1993) *Pragmatism and Social Theory*. Chicago, IL: University of Chicago Press.

Johnson, Michael (1991) 'Commitment to Personal Relationships', in W. Jones and D. Perlman (eds) *Advances in Personal Relationships*, vol. 3, pp. 117–43. London: Jessica Kingsley.

Katz, Janet and William Chambliss (1995) 'Biology and Crime', in J. Sheley (ed.) *Criminology*, pp. 275–304. Belmont, CA: Wadsworth.

Land, Kenneth (1992) 'Models of Criminal Careers: Some Suggestions for Moving Beyond the Current Debate', *Criminology* 30(1): 149–55.

Lemert, Edwin (1951) *Social Pathology*. New York: McGraw-Hill.

Levi, Ken (1981) 'Becoming a Hit Man: Neutralization in a Very Deviant Career', *Urban Life* 10(1): 47–63.

Lofland, John (1969) *Deviance and Identity*. Englewood Cliffs, NJ: Prentice-Hall.

McCarthy, Bill and John Hagan (1992) 'Mean Streets: The Theoretical Significance of Delinquency Among Homeless Youths', *American Journal of Sociology* 98(3): 597–627.

Maines, David (1982) 'In Search of Mesostructure: Studies in the Negotiated Order', *Urban Life* 11: 267–79.

Maines, David (1989) 'Herbert Blumer and the Possibility of Science in the Practice of Sociology: Further Thoughts', *Journal of Contemporary Ethnography* 18: 160–77.

Maines, David (1997) 'Interactionism and Practice', *Applied Behavioral Science Review* 5(1): 1–8.

Maines, David and Thomas Morrione (1990) 'On the Breadth and Relevance of Blumer's Perspective: Introduction to his Analysis of Industrialization', in D. Maines and T. Morrione (eds) *Industrialization as an Agent of Social Change*, by H. Blumer, pp. xi–xxiv. New York: Aldine.

Maines, David, Jeffrey Bridger and Jeffery Ulmer (1996) 'Mythic Facts and Park's Pragmatism: On Predecessor Selection and Theorizing in Human Ecology', *The Sociological Quarterly* 37(3): 521–49.

Maltz, Michael (1994) 'Deviating from the Mean: The Declining Significance of Significance', *Journal of Research in Crime and Delinquency* 31(4): 434–63.

Matsueda, Ross (1992) 'Reflected Appraisals, Parental Labeling, and Delinquency: Specifying a Symbolic Interactionist Theory', *American Journal of Sociology* 97(6): 1577–611.

Matsueda, Ross and Karen Heimer (1997) 'Developmental Theories of Crime', in T. Thornberry (ed.) *Advances in Criminological Theory*, pp. 174–86. New Brunswick, NJ: Transaction.

Matza, David (1964) *Delinquency and Drift*. New York: Wiley.

Matza, David (1969) *Becoming Deviant*. Englewood Cliffs, NJ: Prentice-Hall.

Mead, George Herbert (1934) *Mind, Self, and Society*. Chicago, IL: University of Chicago Press.

Moffitt, Terrie (1993) 'Adolescence-limited and Life-course-persistent Antisocial Behavior: A Developmental Taxonomy', *Psychology Review* 100: 674–701.

Moore, Mark (1986) 'Purblind Justice: Normative Issues in the Use of Prediction in the Criminal Justice System', in A. Blumstein, J. Cohen, J. Roth and C. Visher (eds) *Criminal Careers and 'Career Criminals'*, vol. II, pp. 314–55. Washington, DC: National Academy Press.

Nagin, Daniel and David Farrington (1992) 'The Stability of Criminal Potential from Childhood to Adulthood', *Criminology* 30(2): 235–60.

Nagin, Daniel and Kenneth Land (1993) 'Age, Criminal Careers, and Population Heterogeneity: Specification and Estimation of a Nonparametric, Mixed Poisson Model', *Criminology* 31(3): 327–62.

Nagin, Daniel, David Farrington and Terrie Moffitt (1995) 'Lifecourse Trajectories of Different Types of Offenders', *Criminology* 33(1): 111–40.

Osgood, D. Wayne and David Rowe (1994) 'Bridging Criminal Careers, Theory, and Policy Through Latent Variable Models of Individual Offending', *Criminology* 32(4): 517–54.

Park, Robert E. (1929 [1952]) 'Sociology, Community, and Society', in E. Hughes (ed.) *The Collected Papers of Robert Ezra Park, Vol. II: Human Communities*, pp. 178–209. Glencoe, IL: Free Press.

Paternoster, Raymond and Robert Brame (1997) 'Multiple Routes to Delinquency? A Test of Developmental and General Theories of Crime', *Criminology* 35(1): 49–80.

Patterson, Gerald and Karen Yoerger (1993) 'Developmental Models for Delinquent Behavior', in S. Hodgins (ed.) *Mental Disorder and Crime*, pp. 94–121. Newbury Park, CA: Sage.

Perinbanayagam, Robert (1991) *Discursive Acts*. New York: Aldine.

Petersilia, Joan (1980) 'Criminal Career Research: A Review of Recent Evidence', in N. Morris and M. Tonry (eds) *Crime and Justice: An Annual Review of Research*, vol. 2, pp. 321–79. Chicago, IL: University of Chicago Press.

Rowe, David, D. Wayne Osgood and W. Alan Nicewander (1990) 'A Latent Trait Approach to Unifying Criminal Careers', *Criminology* 28(2): 237–70.

Sampson, Robert and John Laub (1993) *Crime in the Making: Pathways and Turning Points Through Life*. Cambridge, MA: Harvard University Press.

Schur, Edwin (1980) *The Politics of Deviance: Stigma Contests and the Uses of Power*. Englewood Cliffs, NJ: Prentice-Hall.

Shalin, Dmitri (1986) 'Pragmatism and Social Interactionism', *American Sociological Review* 51: 9–27.

Shover, Neal (1983) 'The Later Stages of Ordinary Property Offender Careers', *Social Problems* 31: 208–18.

Shover, Neal (1996) *Great Pretenders: Pursuits and Careers of Persistent Thieves*. Boulder, CO: Westview Press.

Skolnick, Jerome (1995) 'What Not to Do About Crime', *Criminology* 33(1): 1–16.

Stark, Rodney (1987) 'Deviant Places: A Theory of the Ecology of Crime', *Criminology* 25: 893–909.

Stebbins, Robert (1971) *Commitment to Deviance*. Westport, CT: Greenwood.

Steffensmeier, Darrell (1986) *The Fence: In the Shadow of Two Worlds*. Totowa, NJ: Rowman and Littlefield.

Strauss, Anselm (1969) *Mirrors and Masks: The Search for Identity*. San Francisco, CA: The Sociology Press.

Strauss, Anselm (1993) *Continual Permutations of Action*. New York: Aldine.

Sykes, Gresham and David Matza (1957) 'Techniques of Neutralization: A Theory of Delinquency', *American Sociological Review* 22: 664–70.

Taylor, Carl (1947) 'Sociology and Common Sense', *American Sociological Review* 12(1): 1–12.

Thornberry, Terence P. (1995) *Developmental Theories of Crime and Delinquency*. New Brunswick, NJ: Transaction.

Tittle, Charles (1988) 'Two Empirical Regularities (Maybe) in Search of an Explanation: Commentary on the Age/Crime Debate', *Criminology* 26(1): 75–85.

Ulmer, Jeffery (1994) 'Revisiting Stebbins: Labeling and Commitment to Deviance', *The Sociological Quarterly* 35(1): 135–57.

Visher, Christy (1995) 'Career Offenders and Crime Control', in J. Sheley (ed.) *Criminology*, pp. 515–34. Belmont, CA: Wadsworth.

Walters, Glenn (1992) 'A Meta-Analysis of the Gene-Crime Relationship', *Criminology* 30(4): 595–613.

Wilson, James Q. and Richard Herrnstein (1985) *Crime and Human Nature*. New York: Simon and Schuster.

Wolfgang, Marvin (1958) *Patterns in Criminal Homicide*. Philadelphia, PA: University of Pennsylvania Press.

Wolfgang, Marvin, R. Figlio and T. Sellin (1972) *Delinquency of a Birth Cohort*. Chicago, IL: University of Chicago Press.

Wolfgang, Marvin, T. Thornberry and R. Figlio (1987) *From Boy to Man, From Delinquency to Crime*. Chicago, IL: University of Chicago Press.

The open-access Study Study Site, available at
study.sagepub.com/inderbitzindeviance2e,
provides useful study materials including SAGE journal
articles and multimedia resources.

CHAPTER 13

Global Perspectives on Deviance and Social Control

A recent *USA Today* featured a short article on weird laws from around the world. While all are truly "weird," some appear to actually have a rational reason for their existence while others do not. For example, in Rome, it is illegal to eat or drink near landmarks, and in Greece, it is illegal to wear stiletto heels. While both these laws appear to be rather random, when explored, they make perfect sense. The laws are designed to preserve the ancient landmarks found in both places. It is fairly obvious that eating and drinking in historic places could lead to sticky walls or ruined artifacts, but stiletto heels may be just as dangerous. It turns out that the pressure from a thin stiletto heel is roughly equal to the pressure of an elephant walking in the same spot. Thailand and Canada both have laws that dictate how people treat or use their currency. In Thailand, it is illegal to step on the nation's currency. All currency in Thailand carries a picture of the king, and because the king is so revered, it is a great offense to treat the currency and thus the king disrespectfully. In Canada, it is illegal to use more than 25 pennies in a single transaction. Why? We're not quite sure, except there appears to be a strong feeling that the penny is worthless—the government has phased out the coin. Not to be outdone, the United States has its fair share of weird laws, too. In Washington State it is illegal to harass Bigfoot, Sasquatch, or any other undiscovered subspecies. In North Dakota, it is illegal to serve beer and pretzels at the same time at a bar or restaurant. And in Missouri, you can't ride in a car with an uncaged bear.

Sources: Sarkis, C. (2012, December 20). 10 weird laws from around the world. *USA Today*. Retrieved from http://www.usatoday.com/story/travel/destinations/2012/12/19/10-weird-laws-from-around-the-world/1779931; Dumb Laws. (2013). *The Dumb Network*. Retrieved from http://www.dumblaws.com/law/1917

◈ Introduction

It is fun to sit and ponder the weird laws that exist around the world, but there are two larger points to be made in a chapter on global perspectives on deviance and social control. First, there is no greater example of the relativist nature of deviance than examining the laws of a country or region. While it is unlikely anyone is getting into a car with an uncaged bear anytime soon, it is much more likely that beer and pretzels will be served at the same time, that stiletto heels will be worn, and that someone might mistreat the currency of a country. While some might engage in these acts knowing their behavior will be defined as deviant, it is our bet that a good number will have no clue that their actions are defined as deviant, at least by the laws in that country. Second, the responses to these forms of deviance are also relative. While it is true that the law says you cannot eat or drink near historic landmarks in Rome, it is rarely enforced, and while the authors have not had the pleasure of drinking a beer in North Dakota, we bet we could find at least one restaurant that would serve us a pretzel, too. None of us are willing to test the uncaged-bear law. As you will see in this chapter, there is much to be studied about global deviance and social control.

Most of this book is dedicated to how we think about, understand, describe, and explain deviance. In other words, most of this book is dedicated to a sociological and theoretical understanding of deviance. For this reason, this chapter is outside the norm (or, as some might say, deviant) in this book. We have chosen to include it because we believe that an analysis of global perspectives on deviance and social control helps us appreciate an examination of deviance by including perspectives we do not often experience. It also allows us the opportunity to apply those theories we have been discussing in the rest of the book. For this reason, you will see the structure of this chapter mirrors the structure of the book: First, we examine researching deviance globally, then we look at empirical tests of theories of deviance globally, and finally, we discuss social control in a global context.

◈ Researching Deviance Globally

For the undergraduate student of deviant behavior and especially those interested in deviance across the globe, research should always start with the work of others. There are a number of journals that purport to publish studies of crime and criminal justice outside the United States or internationally. Others focus on particular forms of deviance and make an effort to include research with an international or interdisciplinary focus. Thumbing through those journals, one will find some research outside the United States and some truly international research—that is, research that transcends borders. Alternatively, a great deal of research will be conducted by Americans and focus on American citizens. On its website, the journal *Deviant Behavior* (n.d.) purports to be

> the only journal that specifically and exclusively addresses social deviance. International and interdisciplinary in scope; it publishes refereed theoretical, descriptive, methodological, and applied papers. All aspects of deviant behavior are discussed, including: crime, juvenile delinquency, alcohol abuse and narcotic addiction, sexual deviance, societal reaction to handicap and disfigurement, mental illness, and socially inappropriate behavior. (para. 1)

While the journal is open to research from around the world and perhaps even actively strives to be international and interdisciplinary, a great many of the articles are written by U.S. researchers focused on American citizens. The next section discusses issues surrounding doing research outside of the United States.

◈ Trials and Tribulations Involved in Researching Deviance Across the Globe

Laws and official reporting and recording practices vary significantly across countries (Newman, 2008), thus making comparisons of deviance rates using official statistics problematic. That is, while official statistics may be very useful, they measure as much what officials do as how deviant individuals behave and the correlates of that behavior. This leaves many thinking that self-report measures may provide more valid information regarding deviance in other countries. While this may be true, there are definite problems collecting data regarding deviance in other countries and cultures, and many things must be considered in advance.

As with any scientific research, the research protocol must be approved by an institutional review board (IRB). As discussed in Chapter 3, while most IRBs support research, they have to make sure that certain procedures are followed, and this may become even more complex and problematic when one is proposing to do research outside the United States. First, the IRB will want evidence that the researcher has permission to do research in a foreign country. Some countries legally prohibit research. Indeed, the U.S. Department of Health and Human Services (n.d.) website provides "a listing of over 1,000 laws, regulations, and guidelines on human subjects' protections in over 100 countries and from several international organizations" (para. 1). IRBs will want documentation from public citizens, schools, or local officials showing that they understand the nature of the research and that they agree to allow the research to take place.

Second and most generally, an IRB will want to make sure that culturally appropriate procedures are in place to protect participants in the research activity. Although the researcher may (or indeed may not) know a great deal about the culture and local customs outside the United States, it is very likely that some IRB members will not be aware of the norms, customs, and beliefs that may offend research participants or their leaders, and the IRB will probably need to be educated in these regards before it can approve research. It would behoove a researcher, even one with a vast knowledge of a particular culture, to have an endorsement from another expert that the research will not cause offense or concern in the society in question.

A third issue is language. If the research involves in-depth interviews, the researcher or research team must know the language well enough to conduct the interviews. Usually, in-depth interviews do not follow a specific script, and the researcher will begin with only a set of key questions that he or she expects will change as more is learned about the specific issues being studied. This could become a slippery slope in studies of deviance because the research may go down a path that was not approved by an IRB and lead to problems. There is not much an IRB can do about this, but the researcher(s) would be required to let the IRB know if any adverse events occur.

When conducting survey research in a foreign country that speaks a language other than English, it is likely that the survey will need to be translated. Once again, IRB members will not likely speak the other language, and so they may want to have the survey translated, then back-translated, so that they know that what is being included in the translated document is consistent with the original. While this may be time-consuming and potentially expensive, it would appear to be the right thing to do and would ultimately make the results of the research more valid.

A fourth issue has to do with protected groups. There are several protected populations where special consideration must be given to the respondents' ability to provide consent to participate in research. For example, prisoners may feel compelled to do research if a guard is supplying the survey or even in the room when the researcher is asking for consent. Children are also an issue as they are not legally eligible to give consent. In the United States, the legal age of consent is 18, but it may be older or younger in other countries. This raises an interesting question. It may seem self-evident that if the legal age of consent in a country is older than 18, the local law should be followed. However, if the local law is younger than 18, do we follow local custom or U.S. regulations? Another issue that arises when studying children is parental consent. In the United States, parental consent is usually required to conduct research on children. But what if parental consent is culturally inappropriate in a particular society—for example, one in which tribal elders or other family members are responsible for the children? In any case, the person who needs to provide the consent, be it a parent or other person, must be provided with a request that is written in the language of the resident at such a level that he or she will understand the protocol (what is being asked of the child). This request should inform the consent giver that he or she does not have to allow the child to participate and/or can stop the research at any point without penalty. If a waiver of active parental permission is granted, a letter informing the parents of the research, written at a literacy level that would be understood by the parents, may be required and should be prepared and sent to them by the most expeditious method possible.

Finally, how the data will be kept anonymous or confidential must be specified. If and how the data will be handled by different individuals or agencies must be laid out. How the data might be transferred physically or electronically and how the information will be protected must be demonstrated. In some cases, it will be important to describe how the data will be analyzed and presented to the public so that concerns about disclosing individual information are minimized.

These are many issues to consider, and they may not seem all that relevant to undergraduate students. However, just because undergraduates may not be conducting their own actual research outside the United States, it does not follow that such issues should not be considered and discussed. Understanding the practical and ethical issues surrounding such research will help us to understand the limitations of other studies we come across, making us both more appreciative and skeptical of what we are reading or hearing about in class or in social media. The next section provides a quick look into a few alternatives available to study deviance in other countries.

DEVIANCE IN POPULAR CULTURE

Because many of us have not had the opportunity to travel around the world—or the misfortune to be held in a foreign prison—much of what we think we know about deviance and social control in a global context comes from popular culture. Here we have selected a few films that portray foreign cultures, deviance, crime, and prisons. What messages do you think these films share with their mainstream audiences? How do they shape perceptions of deviance and social control in countries around the world?

Brokedown Palace (1999)—Claire Danes and Kate Beckinsale play American high school friends vacationing in Thailand who, whether they intended to do so or were simply vulnerable victims, are caught smuggling drugs and sentenced to 33 years in a Thai prison. The film shows their adjustment to life in a prison in a foreign land and their attempts to find a way out.

Return to Paradise (1998)—Three friends meet on vacation in Malaysia, indulging in alcohol, drugs, and the beach. After two return to their lives in the United States, one is caught with a large amount of their shared hashish. In an interesting plot twist and moral question, if the others will return and accept responsibility and ownership of the drugs, they will all do shorter sentences in the Third World prison. Otherwise, the friend who was caught will be sentenced to death because the large amount has branded him a trafficker and earned him a death sentence.

City of God (2002)—A vivid film and story focusing on the City of God housing project, plagued by crushing poverty, violence, and gangs in the slums of Rio de Janeiro. The focus is on two boys growing up surrounded by and immersed in deviance, drugs, and weapons.

Trainspotting (1996)—Something of a cult favorite film about a group of heroin addicts in the Edinburgh drug scene, famous for its "Choose life" monologue. The film displays all kinds of deviant behavior, mixing humor with horrifying scenes. The plot details the main character's efforts to kick his habit.

Hunger (2008)—A film based on the true story of a 1981 hunger strike in which 10 Irish Republican Army prisoners died. The film focuses on inhumane prison conditions and highlights three different stories: the daily life of a prison guard, the IRA prisoners' refusal to bathe or wear prison clothes, and the hunger strike. The film pays special attention to Bobby Sands, who was the first prisoner to die.

◈ More Reasonable Strategies for Undergraduates to Study Deviance Outside the United States

Most students will not have the resources to directly study (e.g., go to the foreign country and conduct surveys or interviews) deviance outside the United States. There are several existing large-scale data sets for studying deviance across countries. Sometimes the focus is on the criminal justice system or reactions to deviance. For example, Interpol and the United Nations provide data on what crimes are known to the police across a large number of countries and also about how these crimes are handled—for example, the number or rates of arrests, prosecutions, and convictions. Alternatively, a number of data sets exist that use surveys to collect self-reported measures of crime, delinquency, or victimization across countries. While these titles highlight a criminological emphasis, note that these generic terms include numerous offenses that may or may not come to the attention of the police, and softer forms of deviant behavior that even if they came to the attention of authorities might provoke little or no reaction.

For example, the International Self-Reported Delinquency Study of 1992 (Junger-Tas, Marshall, & Ribeaud, 2003) focused on self-reported misbehavior and victimization among youth aged 12 to 15 in 13 countries. A follow-up of this project resulted in the Second International Self-Reported Delinquency Study (Enzmann & Podana, 2010), now expanded to 31 countries. Self-report items ranged from relatively minor forms of deviance (e.g., "Steal something from a shop or department store") to quite serious ones (e.g., "Intentionally beat someone up, or hurt him with a stick or knife, so bad that they had to see a doctor") (Enzmann & Podana, 2010, p. 183). Vazsonyi, Pickering, Junger, and Hessing (2001) developed the *normative deviance scale*, which was designed to measure noncriminal forms of lifetime deviance. They collected data from several countries, including the United States, Switzerland, Hungary, and New Zealand.

The following list highlights just a few data sets that are available through the International Consortium of Political and Social Research (see Chapter 3), which your university may be affiliated with. These data sets focus on deviance and social control internationally—or at least outside the United States.

- International Dating Violence Study, 2001–2006 (covering 32 countries)
- International Crime Victimization Survey, 1989–2000 (the 2000 wave covering 47 industrialized and developing countries)
- Correlates of Crime: A Study of 52 Nations, 1960–1984
- United Nations Surveys of Crime Trends and Operations of Criminal Justice Systems Series, Waves 1–10, 1970–2006
- Citizenship, Democracy, and Drug-Related Violence, 2011 (Mexico)
- Center for Research on Social Reality [Spain] Survey, December 1993: Attitudes and Behavior Regarding Alcohol, Tobacco, and Drugs
- Euro-Barometer 32: The Single European Market, Drugs, Alcohol, and Cancer, November 1989

In the following section, we describe how several theories developed in the United States have been tested in other countries.

◈ Empirical Tests of Theories of Deviance Globally

Studying deviance around the world is nothing new. Indeed, much anthropological work might be seen as the study of customs, attitudes, behaviors, and beliefs that modern Western society might find deviant. However, the sociological research focusing on the theories described in this book, most all carried out in the United States or in other developed Western societies, has only recently been empirically investigated outside the United States. This investigative extension might very likely stem from the seemingly audacious claim by Gottfredson and Hirschi (1990) that their general theory of crime could explain not only crime but other analogous behaviors (i.e., deviance) across all cultures and historical times; this claim led others to test Gottfredson and Hirschi's theory and other theories of deviance as well. In this chapter, we examine empirical evidence as it relates to a variety of theories of deviance and social control.

Empirical Tests of Gottfredson and Hirschi's General Theory of Deviance: Self-Control and Deviance in Other Countries

As discussed in Chapter 7, Gottfredson and Hirschi's (1990) general theory of crime, which focuses on the relationship between low self-control and crime and analogous behaviors (i.e., deviance), has been well researched, especially in the United States. Indeed, in the meta-analysis conducted by Pratt and Cullen (2000) they concluded that "with these caveats stated, the meta-analysis reported here furnishes fairly impressive empirical support for Gottfredson and Hirschi's theory" (p. 951). Interestingly, the meta-analysis, which was conducted nearly 10 years after Gottfredson and Hirschi first published their book, did not include empirical tests conducted outside the United States, presumably because they were not available to be included. Subsequent to the publication of the meta-analysis, there have been a number of important empirical tests of the relationship between self-control and deviant behavior outside the United States.

Cretacci and his colleagues published several studies examining self-control theory based on convenience samples collected in China (Cretacci, Fei Ding, & Rivera, 2010; Cretacci & Cretacci, 2012). In their most direct test of the theory, which focused on the relationship between self-control and deviance, they collected data from students ($n = 148$) in the law and social work departments at a Beijing university (Cretacci et al., 2010). Interestingly, the survey was administered in English. At least one of the authors, however, had interacted enough with the respondents to be confident that they could complete the relatively simple survey the researchers had designed. Deviance was measured with a 14-item scale asking about various forms of deviance. The study found support for Hirschi's (1969 and 2004) social control construct, which was significantly associated with lower levels of deviance.

Lu, Yu, Ren, and Marshall (2013) provide a more recent analysis using the Second International Self-Report Delinquency Study. The data came from a probability sample of seventh-, eighth-, and ninth-grade students from nine schools in five urban areas in the city of Hanzhou, China (the capital city of the Zhejiang Province). In this study, the self-report instrument was translated and pretested with exchange students at an American university. Two dependent variables measuring deviance were (1) minor "risky behaviors" (e.g., drinking and smoking); and (2) "delinquency" (e.g., fighting, carrying a weapon, vandalism). Self-control was measured with a shorter adaptation of Grasmick's scale, including the dimensions of "impulsivity, risk-seeking, self-centeredness, and temper" (Lu et al., 2013, p. 39). Social control measures included family and school bonding, school commitment, and beliefs. As in most studies conducted in the United States, the results supported the general theory of crime, showing self-control to be a significant and relatively robust predictor of both forms of deviance after controlling for a number of theoretically relevant variables (e.g., measures social control) and standard control variables (e.g., age and sex). Some support was also found for social control theory, especially as family bonding and beliefs appeared significant in at least two models. Given that this was a much more rigorous examination of the relationship between self-control and deviance, we conclude that Gottfredson and Hirschi's theory of deviance is indeed generalizable to China.

Self-control has been tested in other countries as well, by researchers such as Vazsonyi and his colleagues. One especially interesting study (Vazsonyi et al., 2001) involved a test of self-control theory among youths in America ($n = 2,213$), Switzerland ($n = 889$), Hungary ($n = 4,018$), and the Netherlands ($n = 1,315$). Deviance was measured with a 55-item normative deviance scale, with subscales including vandalism, alcohol and drug use, school misconduct, general deviance, theft, and assault. Self-control was measured with Grasmick's 24-item scale. The researchers found consistent support across countries for the general theory of crime in that self-control explained between 10% and 16% of the variation in the deviant behavior subscales and over 20% of the variation in the full measure of deviance. In another study using the same measures, Vazsonyi, Wittekind, Belliston, and Van Loh (2004) tested the theory among Japanese youth ($n = 334$), finding comparable outcomes to a U.S. sample of youth. In yet another study using similar measures but with the addition of family process measures related to social control (closeness, support, and monitoring), Vazsonyi and Klanjsek (2008) examined the relationship between self-control, social control, and deviance with more than 3,000 Swiss. They found at least some support for both Hirschi's social control theory and Hirschi's general theory of crime.

Özbay and Köksoy (2009) provided tests of self-control theory in the developing country of Turkey. They focused on predicted general violence and political violence among college students ($n = 974$) using a modified version of Grasmick's scale. Özbay and Köksoy (2009) found that low self-control was associated with a significantly greater likelihood of both forms of violence after controlling for a host of theoretically relevant variables (e.g., strain and criminal friends) and standard control variables (e.g., age and gender). In another article, Özbay (2008) examines the generalizability of self-control across gender. Using the same data set, the researcher finds that not only is self-control generalizable across males and females; the empirical evidence suggests that the theory is more generalizable than other theories, including bonding and strain theories.

We will conclude this section with a discussion of what is clearly the largest global test of Gottfredson and Hirschi's general theory. In "Self-Control in a Global Perspective," Rebellon, Straus, and Medeiros (2008) tested several aspects of the general theory within and across fully 32 nations spanning "all six humanly habitable continents" (p. 331) and including Western, non-Western, developed, and developing countries. The data came from the International Dating Violence Consortium, which collected it from college students in universities across the 32 countries. Straus and Medeiros developed a six-item scale to measure the six dimensions of self-control described by Gottfredson and Hirschi. These items included the following:

Self-Centered: I don't think about how what I do will affect other people.

Risk-Taking: I often do things that other people think are dangerous.

Temper: There is nothing I can do to control my feelings when my partner hassles me.

Preference for Physical: I often get hurt by the things that I do.

Impulsivity: I have trouble following the rules at work or in school.

Long-Term Consequences: I have goals in life that I try to reach.

For each question, respondents were asked to what extent they agreed or disagreed with the statement on a four-point scale (1 = "strongly disagree" to 4 = "strongly agree").

Criminal behavior included both property crime (stolen property worth more than $50 U.S. and stolen money from anyone, including family) and violent crime (physical attack of someone with intention of seriously harming them and hit or threatened to hit a nonfamily member). Each of the four items were conditioned in terms of age, so respondents were asked once if the event happened before they were 15 years old and then asked again if it had occurred after they were 15. Two scales were then created with four items each, measuring property and violent crime, respectively.

Given Gottfredson and Hirschi's emphasis on child rearing and emotional involvement of parents in children's lives in the development of self-control, the researchers also included an eight-item "parental neglect scale" that included items measuring direct control (e.g., parents making sure the respondent went to school) and social support (e.g., parent provided comfort). These measures allowed a pretty solid test of the general theory in that parental efforts could be correlated with self-control, which in turn could be related to criminal behavior.

The findings and results of the study are fairly clear and supportive of Gottfredson and Hirschi's theory. First, parental neglect was a significant predictor of self-control in all 32 countries, explaining between 15% and 39% of the variation in self-control. Second, self-control was significantly related to violent crime in all 32 countries, and self-control was significantly related to property crime in 28 of the 32 countries.

While the researchers found considerable support for Gottfredson and Hirschi's general theory of crime across both Western and non-Western nations, they do point out a few caveats. First, the measure of criminal peers was also found to be a relatively robust predictor of crime across nations. Second, even though self-control was largely associated with violence and property crime across countries, there was considerable variation in its predictive ability—that is, the effect of self-control was not constant across cultures, as predicted by the theory.

This study and the others described above, taken together, suggest that self-control is a relatively strong correlate of crime and deviance across more than 32 nations. Although empirical evidence is not perfectly consistent across countries, overall, there appears to be general support across various forms of deviance.

Testing Differential Association and Social Learning Theories Outside of the United States

Like social and self-control theories, tests of differential association and social learning theories have mostly been conducted in the United States. However, some recent efforts have moved beyond the confines of this country. Not far from the United States is the French- and English-speaking country to the north, Canada. There, Gallupe and Bouchard (2013) examined social learning theory and substance use through an investigation of party-going among adolescents in a large Canadian city. A total of 829 students were surveyed, and 411 of them reported on their behavior at a total of 775 parties. Three hundred sixty-one students reported on multiple parties, which allowed the researchers to investigate changes in party characteristics and how that affected substance use. The key social learning variable was reinforcement, and this was measured by the number of close friends who drank alcohol or used marijuana at the party and the amount of alcohol and marijuana these friends used. In both the cross-sectional and semilongitudinal analyses (change), reinforcement variables were found to be relatively strong predictors of both alcohol and marijuana use, thus showing support for differential association and social learning theories.

Moving across the ocean, we find that differential association and social learning theories have also been tested in Europe. By the year 2000, there had been only a few ethnographic and interview-based studies of youth deviance conducted in France and no systematic self-report studies, so Hartjen and Priyadarsini (2003) initiated a study to test theories in rural France, focusing heavily on differential association and social learning theory. They argued that France is a particularly interesting country to utilize self-reported methods because

> France appears to have an extremely benevolent and tolerant approach to misbehaving youth. Very few are ever incarcerated and, if so, not for very long. Every effort is made by officials from police to judges to divert misbehaving juveniles from official processing or punitive action. (Hartjen & Priyadarsini, 2003, p. 389)

With official counts of criminal sanctions being so low, self-report research is likely to detect much more deviant behavior and should be a better indicator of misbehavior. Hartjen and Priyadarsini surveyed male and female junior high and high school students ranging in age from 13 to 18 from three schools. All three schools were located in a single, ethnographically homogeneous, rural town in France.

The survey they used was based on the National Youth Survey, which was translated into French. They included two measures of delinquency—a total delinquency scale based on 50 items and a "petty delinquency" scale that included minor misbehaviors. Measures based on differential association and social learning theories included attitudes towards deviance [measured as negative attitudes towards deviance or prosocial attitudes], peer involvement [measured as positive peer involvement], exposure to delinquent peers, and an index of exposure to delinquent peers [created by combining peer involvement with exposure to delinquent peers]. (p. 393)

Positive peer involvement and prosocial attitudes were negatively related to both total and petty deviant behaviors among both males and females in the sample, whereas exposure to delinquent peers was positively related to both measures of deviant behavior among both groups. Interestingly, there were no differences in the effects of the differential association and social learning variables across gender, suggesting that the theory is generalizable and not unique to male or female respondents.

In one of the more impressive and truly international inquiries, Antonaccio, Botchkovar, and Tittle (2011) have tested several theories, including social learning theory, in three key cities in three European countries that have "exhibited widely publicized actions to preserve their unique national cultural patterns" (p. 1203). The cities were Athens, Greece; Nizhni Novgorod, Russia; and Lvov, Ukraine. In an effort to maintain causal order in a cross-sectional study, the researchers asked questions about the likelihood of committing violent and property crimes in the future and about past experiences reinforcing violent behavior and property crime (via social learning theory). They argue that using projected offending has been found to be as valid as using self-reports of prior deviant behaviors and comes as close to maintaining the causal ordering of the model as one can get with a cross-sectional design.

Under the supervision of the research team, trained local interviewers conducted face-to-face interviews with individuals from randomly selected households in Athens ($n = 400$), Lvov ($n = 500$), and Nizhni Novgorod ($n = 500$). In analyses of the data set as a whole (merging data from the three cities), they found that reinforcement was significantly associated with projections of both violent behavior and property crimes after controlling for a number of other variables. Indeed, reinforcement was the strongest predictor across models. Similarly, when the analyses were disaggregated by city (analyzed separately), the social learning measure of reinforcement was positively related to both property and violent crime projections. Again, in virtually all of the models, reinforcement was the strongest predictor.

Differential association and social learning theories have also been tested in Asian countries. Kim and her colleagues (Kim, Kwak, & Yun, 2010; Kim, Akers, & Yun, 2013), for example, have provided at least two tests of social leaning theory in South Korea, both focused on substance use. In the first study, they analyzed data from the Korea Youth Panel Survey, which was a longitudinal study of two cohorts (second-graders and junior high students) beginning in 2003 (Kim et al., 2013). They used the first two waves of data collected in 2003 and 2004. There was only minor attrition from the study (<10%), resulting in 3,188 student respondents. Substance use, the dependent variable, was measured with self-reported items indicating how often they had drunk alcohol or smoked cigarettes in the past year. Three concepts emerged that were most clearly derived from social learning theory: (1) a differential peer association measure based on six items indicating how many of their close friends engaged in delinquent activities, (2) differential association intensity indicated by a single item indicating how important one's reputation with deviant peers was, and (3) peer substance use measured with two items indicating how many close friends used tobacco and how many used alcohol. Interestingly, in a multivariate model, substance use was unrelated to substance use by peers and peer delinquency, but it was positively related to deviant peer intensity, increasing the odds of using substances by 21%. In this carefully collected data from a nationally represented sample of young South Koreans, we find only modest support for social learning theory. In fact, controls for parental attachment and supervision, usually associated with social control or bond theory, were more powerful predictors of substance abuse.

The second study (Kim et al., 2013) was more ambitious theoretically and empirically. In this study, Kim and colleagues attempted to test Akers's full social structure and social learning (SSSL) model to predict alcohol use. The data came from a self-report study of high school students in Busan, South Korea, a large metropolitan area in the southeast tip of the Korean Peninsula. Data were collected from just over 1,000 high school students. The data analyses clearly show support for the standard social learning theory. Kim and colleagues (2013) found that alcohol use increases when students

1. have a greater proportion of peers who use alcohol,

2. have fathers who use alcohol,

3. have definitions favorable to alcohol use, or

4. have a greater chance of imitating use of alcohol by behavioral models (p. 908).

Furthermore, they found that, consistent with Akers's SSSL theory, the effects of several of the structural-level variables, significant when only they were in the model, were mediated by the social learning variables. Specifically, the effects of population size, residential mobility, type of school, and religiosity were explained by social learning variables. Even the strong gender effect, which remains significant in the final model, is largely explained by the social learning variables. Given the more rigorous measurement of the key constructs and analyses conducted in the previous study, we believe the evidence lends considerable support for Akers's SSSL theory.

◈ A Global Perspective on Social Disorganization Theory

Social disorganization theory is clearly an American-born theory, rooted in the Chicago School of Sociology. Indeed, stemming from the original theoretical and empirical work by Shaw and McKay (1942/1969) in the early 1900s, work in this tradition continues to the present day (e.g., Sampson, 2012). Of course, the theory has been tested in other major U.S. cities, such as New York, Chicago, and St. Louis, among others. The theory was originally developed to explain neighborhood variation in delinquency and crime across relatively small macrounits, but there is clearly reason to believe that the same general structural characteristics (i.e., economic deprivation, population instability, and racial/ethnic heterogeneity) may operate at other levels to explain various forms of crime and deviance. For example, social disorganization theory has also been applied to schools, cities, and states within the United States. There is also reason to believe that social disorganization is a general macrolevel theory of crime that can be applied to other countries and across nations that vary in levels of informal social control.

Recently, several efforts to test the theory at the neighborhood level in other countries have been published, and it appears that social disorganization has the potential to explain levels of deviant behavior outside the United States. In the next section, we describe studies that focus on neighborhood-level analyses across cities outside the United States.

Tests of Social Disorganization in Cities Outside the United States

Breetzke (2010) argues that South Africa provides an excellent setting to test social disorganization theory. He states that

the recent political history of South Africa is inherently intertwined with social disorganization and community fragmentation. While a few examples may exist elsewhere, no other country in the world has endured such a direct and sustained attack on the social fabric of its society through state laws and policies aimed at enforcing and accentuating spatio-social segmentation. (p. 447)

To test social disorganization theory in this context, Breetzke collected data in the city of Tshwane, one of the six largest metropolitan areas in South Africa. The level of analysis was the census-defined suburb, with the number of households in each suburb ranging from 150 to 300.

Three years of violent crime data (2001–2003), including "murder, attempted murder, sexual offenses, assault with the intent to cause grievous bodily harm and common assault," were culled from the Crime and Information Analysis Centre (Breetzke, 2010, p. 448). Address-based data were geocoded and aggregated to the suburb level.

These were matched with other 2001 census measures, including ethnic heterogeneity, socioeconomic deprivation, family disruption, and residential mobility (Breetzke, 2010, p. 448). Several of these variables were quite different in nature from those found in the United States or had potentially different meanings from our understanding in the West. For example, in addition to unemployment (a common measure used in tests of social disorganization theory in the United States), the measure of socioeconomic disadvantage included "type of dwelling, source of water, toilet facilities, refuse or rubbish removal, and energy or fuel for lighting, heating and cooking" (Breetzke, 2010, p. 448). These items are largely irrelevant in industrialized developed nations and were specifically designed by the United Nations Development Programme to assess socioeconomic development in South Africa. Interestingly, given the heterogeneous nature of the country, there was plenty of room to measure various forms of racial and ethnic heterogeneity (as the country has four official racial groups and nine distinct ethnic groups) and linguistic heterogeneity (as the country has eleven official languages). The authors chose to focus simply on the percentage black, given the history of apartheid that segregated "Black African, Colored, Asian, or Indian" individuals who were viewed as nonwhites (Breetzke, 2010, p. 448).

Results were mixed. On the one hand, consistent with social disorganization theory, both measures of socioeconomic deprivation (unemployment and the deprivation index) were statistically and positively related to rates of violent crime. Similarly, residential mobility (the percentage of the population that had moved in the past five years) was positively related to the rate of violent crime. However, the percentage of the suburb characterized as black or nonwhite actually trended in a negative direction and was not statistically significant. This was also the case for the percentage of female-headed households. The race finding is particularly interesting given the history of South Africa and its policy of total segregation. One would think with this shift in policy that desegregated communities would have higher violent crime rates. There may be something statistically odd going on here, but not enough information was provided on the distribution of this variable to comment further. However, given the heterogeneous nature of the country, more work should look at finer measures of racial/ethnic and linguistic heterogeneity.

The fact that the percentage of households headed by women was unrelated to violent crime might be explained by the measurement of the variable. Black South Africans often work far from home and are gone for long periods of time, even though their household census designation is in the home. Thus, because two of the empirical inconsistencies with social disorganization theory may have to do with poor measurement and statistical anomalies, we suggest that the bulk of the evidence supports the predictive ability of social disorganization, at least across suburbs of Tshwane, South Africa.

Moving to Asia, L. Zhang, Messner, and Liu (2007) studied household burglary victimization across neighborhoods in Tianjin, China. The results were interesting and, while somewhat different from what researchers have found in the West, in some ways still supportive of social disorganization theory. First, inconsistent with social disorganization theory, poverty was unrelated to burglary, and residential stability was positively associated with burglary. The former may have something to do with the lack of attractive targets in impoverished neighborhoods canceling out the safer but wealthier neighborhoods. The latter seems somewhat intractable given the various possibilities. Alternatively, collective efficacy was, as expected, negatively associated with burglary, as was the presence of formal agents of social control (the visibility of the police). The perceived effectiveness of neighborhood mediation groups was not a significant predictor of burglary, but this may reflect the amount of mediation going on. That is, if there are many problems, there may be more information to base judgment on (though mediation may appear less effective because there are many problems), but when there are few disputes, there is little to base judgment on. Given these concerns, perceptions of mediation groups may not be the best indicator of the semipublic control the researchers wanted to measure. These findings are supportive of newer versions of social disorganization theory that focus on collective efficacy (social cohesion and informal social control) and social control from the public sector (i.e., the police).

As mentioned, social disorganization theory has mostly been tested in the United States and mostly in urban areas. While a few empirical tests of social disorganization theory in rural areas of the United States have been conducted and have supported the theory (Osgood & Chambers, 2000), not much has been done outside the country.

However, Jobes, Barclay, and Weinand (2004) provided one such test in New South Wales, Australia. They obtained crime data from the New South Wales Bureau of Crime Statistics and census data from the Australian Bureau of Statistics for 123 local geographic areas. These are the smallest "municipal" units defined by the census and include, on average, fewer than 50,000 residents. Crime data included rates of assault, breaking and entering, malicious damage to property, and motor vehicle theft. The researchers collected 19 different measures from the census that fell under five dimensions of social disorganization theory: (1) low socioeconomic status (e.g., unemployment, poverty); (2) residential instability (e.g., living at a different address, living in own home); (3) ethnic heterogeneity (e.g., proportion indigenous); (4) family disruptions (e.g., divorce, sole parent); and (5) population size and density.

Across dimensions of crime, the social disorganization variables explained a good deal of the variation—between 20% and 45% across models. This is similar to analyses conducted in rural areas in the United States, suggesting that not only is the theory generalizable; its ability to explain variation is about the same across these two countries. Dimensions of social disorganization particularly predictive of the various crimes included measures of ethnic heterogeneity, residential instability, and family disruption.

Another study in Australia, though not directly testing social disorganization theory per se, does offer some insight on the predictors of indigenous violence among the Australian Aboriginals. Using the National Aboriginal and Torres Strait Islander Survey (NATSIS), Snowball and Weatherburn (2008) examined a number of theoretical explanations to assess violence among Aboriginals. This is a large survey, not specifically designed to test any one theory, but several items pertained to social disorganization. Given what was available and based on social disorganization theory, the authors expected that "violent victimisation would be higher amongst Indigenous Australians who:

- Are not socially involved in their communities
- Are sole parents
- Have high rates of geographic mobility (as measured by the number of times they moved house)
- Are member or have relatives who are member of the stolen generation" (p. 222)

With the exception of the first expectation, the results were largely supportive of social disorganization theory. In contrast to the researchers' expectations, Aboriginals who were involved in their communities were actually more likely to be victimized than those who were more socially isolated. This may have to do with the different environmental and social settings those in the community find themselves in. Alternatively, the odds of a sole parent being victimized were 39% higher than those with a partner, and the odds of members of the stolen generation (or having relatives who were members) being victimized were 71% higher than others. Finally, each additional geographic move increased the odds of being victimized by 33%. Although this is an individual-level examination of a macrolevel theory, the data seem to support social disorganization theory. Taken in total, we find significant support for social disorganization theory outside the United States and across several countries.

Cross-National Tests of Institutional Anomie Theory

In trying to understand the high rates of crime in the United States, Messner and Rosenfeld (2007a) argued that societies that value economic institutions (e.g., capitalism and the accumulation of wealth) over noneconomic institutions (e.g., education and the family) will have higher rates of crime. Several studies have examined their theory by analyzing subnational macrosocial units within the United States, including counties (Maume & Lee, 2003) and states (Chamlin & Cochran, 1995). Some support for the theory has been found.

A few studies have begun to investigate the merits of the theory using cross-national tests, which would seem to be the most appropriate test of the theory as it was originally developed to explain the high rates of crime in the

United States relative to other nations. Messner and Rosenfield (2007b) provided the first empirical test of their theory by linking it with the concept of **decommodification**—the movement away from pure market economies to ones that provide political institutions (such as the welfare state) to protect individuals from the harsh realities of pure capitalism. They argue that "a greater degree of decommodification indicates a lower level of economic dominance in this particular institutional interrelationship" (p. 1397). They created a measure of decommodification that reflects "the ease of access to welfare benefits, their income-replacement value, and the expansiveness of coverage across different statuses and circumstances" (pp. 1398–1399) across 45 nations. These nations varied widely, ranging from developed nations such as the United States and Japan to developing nations such as El Salvador and Sri Lanka. Messner and Rosenfield found support for their hypothesis that countries that have moved away from a pure market economy have lower homicide rates.

Savolainen (2000) extends this work by suggesting that a more "critical test of the institutional anomie theory should estimate the moderating effect of the institutional context on the relationship between economic inequality and serious crime, preferably at the cross-national level of analysis" (p. 1026). That is, other institutions should affect the strength of the relationship between economic inequality and crime. He found not only a direct effect of decommodification on homicide rates but also an interaction effect with measures of income inequality. Savolainen (2000) concludes that "nations that protect their citizens from the vicissitudes of market forces appear to be immune to the homicidal effects of economic inequality" (p. 1021).

Cochran and Bjerregaard (2012) provide the most recent cross-national test of institutional anomie theory with a new complex measure of structural anomie based on measures of economic freedom, wealth, and income inequality. Controlling for measures of other social institutions, such as the family (divorce rates), the polity (lack of voter turnout), and educational spending, they found that their measure of structural anomie was a robust predictor of both the homicide rate and rates of theft. Taken together, this emerging line of research suggests relatively strong support for institutional anomie theory in a cross-national setting.

Critical Collective Framing Theory and the Genocide in Darfur

While much of the sociological research to date has focused on what leads up to genocide (Gurr & Harff, 1994; Horowitz, 2001), the problem of defining genocide (Chirot & Edwards, 2003), typologies of genocide (Chirot & McCauley, 2006), and the disputed scales of genocide (Hagan, Schoenfeld, Palloni, Cook, & Massey, 2006), Hagan and Rymond-Richmond (2008) examined the genocide in Darfur from the perspective of critical collective framing theory. Their focus was on "the dehumanizing racial motivations and intentions that explain how a government mobilizes and collaborates in the ideological dehumanization and criminal victimization of a racial group" (p. 876). They found that, indeed, there was an emergence of collective racial motivation and intent with respect to the killings in Darfur that was indicated through the use of racial epithets preceding and during attacks.

> This dehumanization process placed black African groups in Darfur outside a bounded universe of moral obligation and left them vulnerable to targeted genocidal victimization. Treatment of groups as dehumanized and contemptible makes them vulnerable to displacement and destruction. We found compelling evidence that collective processes of racial motivation and intent influenced the severity of victimization across settlements, above and beyond this influence at the individual level, and that this collective frame mediated the concentration of attacks on densely settled areas and particular African groups. (Hagan & Rymond-Richmond, 2008, p. 895)

In other words, by framing a group as subhuman (deviant), it makes this group vulnerable to violence in general and, in the case of Darfur, genocide in particular.

◈ Social Control in a Global Context

Discussing social control in a global context is a daunting task. Just as there are many, many types of deviant acts depending on the cultural context, there are many different and varied reactions to human behaviors and statuses. Rather than attempt to give a comprehensive overview of the extreme differences in both informal and formal social control across the globe—a herculean, if not impossible, task—in this section, we offer a few examples of how perceived deviance is responded to in different cultural settings. We chose these few examples to illustrate that the systems in America are culturally specific and are not necessarily the best or only way to react to deviance. Our hope is that your curiosity will be sparked by these differences and you will pause to question and research social control as you continue your education.

When we think about social control, what often comes to mind is the reaction to an act—it might be a criminal act, a social faux pas, or the violation of a society's unwritten rules that trigger a reaction from the community. If you think back to what you learned about labeling theory (Chapter 8), however, you will recall that sometimes people are punished, oppressed, and sanctioned purely because of who they are. The following examples take two master statuses—that of being a woman and that of identifying as gay or as a gay rights activist—and show how simply existing within those statuses can lead to deadly consequences in some parts of the world.

Social Control of Girls and Women

▲ **Photo 13.1**   Malala Yousafzai was targeted by the Taliban and won a Nobel Peace Prize as a teenager for her courage in advocating for education for girls in Pakistan.

© Claude Truong-Ngoc/Wikimedia Commons; licensed under the Creative Commons Attribution-Share Alike 3.0 Unported license, https://creativecommons.org/licenses/by-sa/3.0/deed.en

The book *Half the Sky*, written by husband and wife journalist team Nicholas D. Kristof and Sheryl WuDunn (2009), vividly documents the oppression and control of women and girls across the globe. The authors focus their book on three particular kinds of abuse: "sex trafficking and forced prostitution; gender-based violence, including honor killings and mass rape; and maternal mortality, which still needlessly claims one woman a minute" (p. xxi).

Kristof and WuDunn tell stories of young girls in Cambodia, Nepal, Thailand, and Malaysia who were kidnapped, raped, and sold into brothels where they were regularly drugged, beaten, and forced to live as prostitutes and/or modern-day slaves. Girls who were brave enough and risked their lives to escape found no help from local police, who sent them back to the brothels (p. 7).

The authors go on to report on many different kinds of punishments and threats that women endure in other nations. Women perceived to be "loose" or "bad" in Pakistan had their faces destroyed by acid or had their noses cut off as a form of punishment (p. 75). Girls in Iraq were killed by family and religious leaders if it was believed they lost their virginity before marriage (p. 82). In Darfur, militia members gang-raped and mutilated women from African tribes, and the Sudanese government responded by punishing women who reported the rapes or sought medical attention (p. 83). In the Congo, rape was used as a terror tactic to control civilian populations; Congolese militia members raped women with sticks or knives and were known to fire their guns into women's and girls' vaginas (p. 84). A teenage soldier in Congo explained that rape was routine, saying if he and his fellow soldiers saw girls, it was their right to rape and violate them (p. 86).

As terrifying as it may be, some girls living in restrictive and punitive cultures take great risks to fight for better lives. Malala Yousafzai, a Pakistani schoolgirl, received widespread attention—both positive and negative—when she began speaking out against Taliban oppression when she was only 11 years old. She began her individual form of resistance by writing her thoughts and experiences in a blog, using a pseudonym to protect her identity; gradually, she became a more public figure and made media appearances advocating for education for girls. When she was just 14 years old, Malala was targeted and shot in the head and neck by a Taliban gunman while on the school bus home. In part because of her public persona and status as a martyr, she was fortunate enough to get specialized medical care and recover from her wounds.

In October 2014, Malala was awarded the Nobel Peace Prize; at 17 years old, she was the youngest person to ever receive the prize. She had won the European Union's highest human rights honor, the Sakharov Prize, the year before at the age of 16. Her bravery has been lauded by the international press, and she has inspired other young girls to fight against oppression and for education and opportunities. "I Am Malala" became the slogan for a campaign to demand global access to education for children. Malala herself continues to face threats from the Taliban; the goals she risks her life for may seem quite simple to those who grew up in the United States and accept such circumstances as their birthright. In Malala's words, "I hope that a day will come when the people of Pakistan will be free, they will have their rights, there will be peace, and every girl and every boy will be going to school" (quoted in Williams, 2013).

Social Control of Homosexuality

Although the United States continues grappling with evolving norms and attitudes around the issues of homophobia, the bullying of gay teens, and the legality and/or morality of gay marriage, simply being gay is not a crime, and threats and cruelty are not formally sanctioned. The same cannot be said in other countries. Homosexuality is illegal in most African countries, and homosexual acts are punishable by 14 years to life in prison in Uganda (T. Walsh, 2011). The Anti-Homosexuality Bill proposed in Uganda in 2009 included harsh sanctions for anyone engaging in gay sex or protecting the privacy of those who do. The bill featured the following provisions:

- Gays and lesbians convicted of having gay sex would be sentenced, at minimum, to life in prison.

- People who test positive for HIV may be executed.

- Homosexuals who have sex with a minor, or engage in homosexual sex more than once, may also receive the death penalty.

- The bill forbids the "promotion of homosexuality," which in effect bans organizations working in HIV and AIDS prevention.

- Anyone who knew of homosexual activity taking place but did not report it would risk up to three years in prison. (Ahmed, 2009, n.p.)

The Anti-Homosexuality Bill prompted an international reaction; European nations threatened to cut aid to Uganda if such laws were passed, and the bill was shelved. While the bill was not passed into law, harsh and deadly informal sanctions are still a real threat to gays and gay rights activists in Uganda. A Ugandan tabloid published a front-page story targeting the "top 100 homosexuals," complete with photographs and addresses of those on the list. David Kato, a gay rights activist, told reporters that he feared for his life after his name was published on the list; he was right to be afraid—within the year, Kato was bludgeoned to death in his home (Walsh, 2011).

Social Control of Crime: Extremes in Prison Conditions Internationally

Scandinavia has long been considered the gold standard in terms of creating and maintaining humane prisons that work to rehabilitate offenders and keep crime and incarceration rates low. Indeed, Scandinavian prisons were designed to be constructive and productive, built on the belief that a prison should not be a place of suffering, fear, and deprivation but instead should be one of redemption, learning, training, and cure, until ultimately, with the commitment to normalization, it replicated the conditions of the outside world rather than shutting it out (Pratt & Eriksson, 2011, p. 20).

Prisons in the United States vary markedly in their quality, and few compare favorably with prisons in Norway or Sweden. Yet there are basic minimum standards for the treatment of prisoners, with codified rules and written documentation that are part of "a culture of audit and control" (Birkbeck, 2011, p. 318). When documented standards are not met in the United States, litigation is a possibility, and the courts may step in to order changes. Many countries in Latin America and the developing world do not have this type of quality control, and prisons are often overcrowded, unsanitary, and unsafe. Here we offer comparison of prisons in Norway and prisons in Latin America to show these two extremes.

Norway: The Best Prisons in the World?

The goal of many Scandinavian prisons is to make life for prisoners as normal as possible. Loss of liberty is the primary punishment. Arne Nilsen, the governor or head of Bastøy Prison, located on an island of the same name, explained how his philosophy that a prison should be "an arena of developing responsibility" was put into practice.

> In closed prisons we keep them locked up for some years and then let them back out, not having had any real responsibility for working or cooking. In the law, being sent to prison is nothing to do with putting you in a terrible prison to make you suffer. The punishment is that you lose your freedom. If we treat people like animals when they are in prison they are likely to behave like animals. Here we pay attention to you as human beings. (quoted in James, 2013a)

The Norwegian penal system has no death penalty or life sentences; the maximum sentence that can be handed down in Norway is just 21 years. This maximum sentence can be extended only if the inmate is deemed to be an imminent threat to society (Sutter, 2012). With this sentencing structure, Norwegian society is forced to confront the fact that most prisoners, however heinous their crimes, will one day be released back into society (Hernu, 2011). In fact, more than 89% of Norway's sentences are for less than one year of confinement, as compared with U.S. federal prisons where only 2% of sentences are for one year or less (Sutter, 2012). The Norwegian Correctional Service "works with other government agencies to secure a home, a job and access to a supportive social network for each inmate before release; Norway's social safety net also provides health care, education and a pension to all citizens" (Benko, 2015).

Two examples—one of a closed prison and one of a more open and transitional prison—help to show Norway's commitment to rehabilitating and reintegrating all of its offenders, even those who have committed very serious crimes. Inmates may still suffer the pains of imprisonment (as discussed in Chapter 11), but they can gain skills, maintain contact with their families, and practice responsible and conforming living even while incarcerated.

Halden is Norway's most secure prison and its second largest, holding about 250 men. While Halden does have a 20-foot cement wall around the perimeter, security is not its defining feature. A reporter describes approaching Halden: "There were no coils of razor wire in sight, no lethal electric fences, no towers manned by snipers—nothing violent, threatening or dangerous. And yet no prisoner has ever tried to escape" (Benko, 2015). Life inside is meant to mimic a small village. Prison cells in Halden are similar to dorm rooms and have windows, adjoining bathrooms, and flat-screen televisions. Prisoners do their own laundry, purchase their own groceries, and cook their own meals, sharing waffles together on Sunday mornings as is common in most Norwegian homes (Benko, 2015). There is a two-bedroom house on the prison grounds where prisoners can host their families overnight. There are jogging trails, sports fields, and a recording studio (Adams, 2010).

Bastøy Prison in Norway looks virtually nothing like an American prison. While it might be compared to Alcatraz due to its location on a 1-square-mile island, Bastøy operates under a much different philosophy. Bastøy offers prisoners trust and responsibility, giving them the chance to become educated, learn new skills, work at varying jobs around the island, grocery shop and cook meals, live semi-independently in small houses around the island, and generally prepare themselves for their full transition back into the community upon their release. Prisoners farm and grow much of their own food, and families can share weekly visits in private rooms. Prisoners, including those convicted of serious violent crimes such as murder and rape, can apply for transfer to Bastøy from more traditional, close-custody prisons when they have five years left on their sentence and can show "determination to live a crime-free life on release" (James, 2013a). Most prisoners that come to Bastøy have served time in higher security prisons—such as Halden—in Norway; they recognize the privileges and relative freedom that Bastøy offers and view finishing their sentences there as a valued opportunity.

Bastøy, which holds approximately 120 male prisoners without the use of concrete walls, razor wire fences, or bars, is one of the cheapest prisons in Norway to run (James, 2013b). Inmates work 9 hours a day, earning approximately $10 per day. Guards work alongside them on a daily basis yet carry no weapons. At night, only a handful of corrections officers stay on the island with their charges. Correctional officers in Norway are highly trained in comparison to much of the rest of the world; it takes at least two years of practical and theoretical training to be a prison guard in Norway. Prisoner officer training in the United Kingdom, in comparison, lasts only six weeks.

The methods used in the Scandinavian prisons, especially those in Norway, appear to be working. The reoffending average across Europe is approximately 70% to 75%. In Denmark, Sweden, and Finland, the average is 30%. In Norway, it is 20%. The reoffending rate for those released from Bastøy Prison is just 16% and is the lowest in Europe (James, 2013a).

Prisons in Latin America

Prisons in Latin America tend to be characterized by mass overcrowding, filthy conditions, and the presence of powerful prison gangs. Supervision can be difficult as there are higher numbers of inmates per staff member, and there is very little technology to help with surveillance in Latin American prisons as compared with the United States (Birkbeck, 2011, p. 312). In such conditions, violence and chaos can rule the institutions. To show a sampling of violent death in Latin American prisons, *The Economist* reported in an article titled "A Journey Into Hell" (2012) that a jail fire in Honduras killed more than 350 inmates in 2012; during the same month, 44 inmates were murdered in a Mexican jail; and in Chile, 81 prisoners serving sentences of less than five years were killed in a fire started during a prison fight.

▲ **Photo 13.2**   While still somewhat isolated from the rest of society, Norway's island prison offers prisoners some freedom and responsibility, helping them prepare for the transition back to their home communities.

Lurigancho, Peru's largest prison, is considered to be one of the world's most dangerous. The inmates essentially run the institution while corrupt and outnumbered guards regularly accept bribes from both inmates and visitors alike. Inmates with resources can purchase food, drugs, nice clothing, conjugal visits, and influence over their fellow inmates. Those without resources are left to try to eke out a miserable existence within the prison's walls.

In Venezuela, penal confinement is prescribed for all felony convictions, and there is no possibility of sentencing to probation. While there are more avenues for parole and early release from prison (Birkbeck, 2011) than in the United States, inmates' time served in prison may turn into a *de facto* death penalty: Venezuela had more than 500 prison deaths in 2012 (Sanchez, 2013). Prisons in Latin America do have the potential benefit of more permissive visiting policies. In Mexico and Bolivia, for example, families and children may actually live in the prisons with their incarcerated parent(s) for an extended period of time. Visits are much less regimented and allow for significant mingling with members of the outside community, helping to ease the social isolation often experienced by prisoners. With the philosophy of internment—where detaining the offenders is the primary goal—what happens inside the facility is irrelevant; inmates must rely on self-government, for better or worse. There is little public scrutiny unless inmates escape or are killed in dramatic circumstances.

Social Control of Mental Illness

Communities both define and react to mental illness in very different ways. In many countries, there is not much of a safety net for those with mental illness. In China, for example, there is no national mental health law, and insurance rarely covers psychiatric care. Even when families and individuals are motivated to seek professional help, there are few educated psychiatrists to care for the population. The *New York Times* focused attention on a tragic case that illustrates the immensity of the problem:

> A Lancet study estimated that roughly 173 million Chinese suffer from a mental disorder. Despite government efforts to expand insurance coverage, a senior Health Ministry official said last June that in recent years, only 45,000 people had been covered for free outpatient treatment and only 7,000 for free inpatient care because they were either dangerous to society or too impoverished to pay.
>
> The dearth of care is most evident when it comes to individuals who commit violent crimes. For example, after Liu Yalin killed and dismembered an elderly couple cutting firewood in a Guangdong Province forest, he was judged to be schizophrenic and released to his brother. Unable to afford treatment, the brother flew Mr. Liu to the island province of Hainan, in the South China Sea, and abandoned him, a Chinese nongovernment organization, Shenzhen Hengping, said in a recent report.
>
> Last year, the tragedy was multiplied when—left without care or supervision—Mr. Liu killed and dismembered an 8-year-old Hainan girl. (LaFraniere, 2010, n.p.)

In poor countries, the government returns severely mentally ill people to their families, and the families are generally at a loss as to how to care for them. With few resources, information, or help available in their communities, families must sometimes resort to locking up and shackling relatives who pose a threat to themselves and others.

In Kenya, mentally ill family members are tied up daily by their relatives in order to keep them from running away or harming themselves. Family members are consumed with the task of caring for their mentally ill loved ones. They may find themselves entirely alone in their efforts, shunned by the community because of the unpleasant noise and stench. While one fourth of patients visiting Kenyan hospitals or clinics complain of mental health problems, the Kenyan government spends less than 1% of its health budget on mental health (McKenzie & Formanek, 2011).

Social Control and Reintegration: Restorative Justice

Howard Zehr, one of the early proponents of restorative justice, explains the basic principles of the concept as follows: Crime is a violation of people and of interpersonal relationships, violations create obligations, and the central obligation is to put right the wrongs (Zehr, 2002, p. 19). While he uses an American lens to discuss these principles, Zehr suggests that there are deep roots for the concept in many different cultures, expressed in different languages.

He writes, "Many cultures have a word that represents this notion of the centrality of relationships: for the Maori, it is communicated by *whakapapa*; for the Navajo, *hozho*; for many Africans, the Bantu word *Ubuntu*" (Zehr, 2002, pp. 19–20).

After spending a decade studying restorative justice, primarily in South Australia, Kathleen Daly found that there is little empirical evidence as to what actually happens in youth justice conferences and how participants feel about the process and outcomes. Daly argues that there is a complex definition and meaning of restorative justice.

> Restorative justice is not easily defined because it encompasses a variety of practices at different stages of the criminal process, including *diversion* from court prosecution, actions taken *in parallel* with court decisions, and meetings between victims and offenders *at any stage* of the criminal process (for example, arrest, pre-sentencing, and prison release). For virtually all legal contexts involving individual criminal matters, restorative justice processes have only been applied to those offenders who have *admitted* to an offence; as such, it deals with the penalty phase of the criminal process for admitted offenders, not the fact-finding phase. Restorative justice is used not only in adult and juvenile criminal matters, but also in a range of civil matters, including family welfare and child protection, and disputes in schools and workplace settings. (Daly, 2002, p. 57)

New Zealand's youth justice system, which emphasizes diversion, family involvement, and restorative justice principles, has been a model for other jurisdictions worldwide. From approximately 1990 to 2010, New Zealand dealt with most youth offenders—nearly 80% of apprehensions—through diversion rather than prosecution (Lynch, 2012). With the use of restorative justice, "the victim of the offence may be part of the process, giving him or her tangible power in the resolution of the offence. True participation by victims (and by the community) can reduce the public appetite for punitiveness" (Lynch, 2012, p. 512). Similarly, Bazemore (1998) advocates for a variation of restorative justice featuring a system of earned redemption that would allow offenders to earn trust back from the community by making amends to those they harmed.

In Africa, using the "ubuntu" principle, the goals of justice-making include the restoration of victims, the reintegration of the offender back into the community, and the restoration of relationships and social harmony undermined by the conflict. All stakeholders should have equal access and participation in the conflict resolution process (Elechi, Morris, & Schauer, 2010, p. 73); this process has the power to reinforce the values of the community. Elechi et al. (2010) argue that the African Indigenous Justice System is "an opportunity for the resocialization of community members and the relearning of important African values and principles of restraint, respect, and responsibility" (p. 74). Furthermore, when communities rely on themselves to solve problems, both individual and collective accountability may be improved as a result (p. 83).

Different cultures and individuals may embrace a wide variety of restorative justice principles and techniques, but what sets these efforts apart from the criminal justice system in the United States is the focus on the reparation of harm and the restoration of the offender, rather than on retribution for the harm caused.

◈ Explaining Deviance in the Streets and Deviance in the Suites: Human Trafficking: Crossing Boundaries and Borders

We have chosen to discuss **human trafficking** because it is a deviance that is both big business and found on the streets. While some human trafficking occurs across state or regional lines, a great proportion of it is transnational and global.

Human trafficking is a crime that "recognizes no race, gender, or national boundary" (S. X. Zhang, 2010, p. 15), although it is generally visited on the least powerful: children, women, and people of color. According to the Trafficking Victims Protection Act, human trafficking is "the act of recruiting, harboring, transporting, providing, or obtaining a person for compelled labor or commercial sex acts through the use of force, fraud, or coercion"

(U.S. Department of State, 2013, p. 29). While most envision that human trafficking means transporting a victim from one country to another, the official definition does not require the victim to be transported.

> Human trafficking can include but does not require movement. People may be considered trafficking victims regardless of whether they were born into a state of servitude, were transported to the exploitative situation, previously consented to work for a trafficker, or participated in a crime as a direct result of being trafficked. At the heart of this phenomenon is the traffickers' goal of exploiting and enslaving their victims and the myriad coercive and deceptive practices they use to do so. (U.S. Department of State, 2013, p. 29)

Children and adults who are victims of human trafficking are coerced into being soldiers, sold for hard labor or sex, or forced into domestic labor, prostitution, or marriage. Others find themselves working in mines, plantations, or sweatshops (United Nations Global Initiative to Fight Global Trafficking [UN.GIFT], 2008). Many initially go with their captors willingly because of promises of a better job or an escape from a hard life, only to be turned into slaves once they arrive at their new destination. These experiences are illustrated by the stories of three trafficking victims below.

> *Ximena:* "When you're a kid, it's easy to be deceived. Each Sunday when I walked down from the town, where my mum had a business, they would urge me to go with them, telling me that I would have a really good time, that it was better to go with them than to keep on working. On my 12th birthday, they came back for me. My mum was away at work, so I took the chance and escaped with them. . . . Five months later I regretted being there, but there was no chance of leaving. Besides, they told my mum that I was dead, that they had already killed me." (UN.GIFT, 2008, p. 2)

> *Luana:* "A friend of mine told me that a Spanish group was hiring Brazilian girls to work as dancers on the island of Lanzarote. My friend Marcela and I thought it was a good opportunity to earn money. We didn't want to continue working as maids. For a short while we only danced. But later they told us there had been too many expenses. And we would have to make some extra money." (UN.GIFT, 2008, p. 5)

> *Marcela:* "We were trapped by criminals and forced into prostitution in order to pay debts for the trip. We had up to 15 clients per night. The use of condoms was the client's decision, not ours. The criminals kept our passports and had an armed man in front of the 'disco' to make sure we never escaped. But a woman helped us. We went to the police and told everything." (UN.GIFT, 2008, p. 5)

According to the United Nations Global Initiative to Fight Human Trafficking (2008), human trafficking is a billion-dollar industry. The UN acknowledges, however, that our understanding of human trafficking is negligible; there is no broad agreement on how to count individuals that have been trafficked, and therefore, the estimates from various organizations often contradict each other. One organization estimates that at least 2.5 million people are victims of human trafficking, with an estimated 130,000 in sub-Saharan countries; 200,000 in countries with economies in transition; 230,000 in the Middle East or North Africa; 250,000 in Latin America and the Caribbean; 270,000 in industrialized countries; and more than 1.4 million in Asia and the Pacific (International Labour Organization, 2005). A second estimate suggests that at least 800,000 people are smuggled across national borders every year, with millions more trafficked in their own countries (U.S. Department of State, 2007). And the nongovernmental organization Free the Slaves estimates that there are between 21 and 30 million people in slavery globally (Free the Slaves, 2013).

The elusive nature of human trafficking is illustrated in the small number of human trafficking incidents that are investigated and confirmed in the United States, in comparison with the estimated number of human trafficking cases that are believed to exist. The U.S. Department of Justice reports that in the United States, just over 2,500 cases were investigated by federally funded human trafficking task forces between 2008 and 2010 (Banks & Kyckelhahn, 2011). And there were very few cases in which law enforcement could confirm the victim's characteristics (see Table 13.1).

Table 13.1 Victim Characteristics in Cases Confirmed to Be Human Trafficking by High Data Quality Task Forces, by Type of Trafficking

Victim Characteristic	Total[a]	Sex Trafficking	Labor Trafficking
Sex			
Male	49	27	20
Female	477	432	43
Age			
17 or younger	257	248	6
13–24	159	142	17
25–34	68	46	22
35 or older	27	12	15
Unknown	16	12	3
Race/Hispanic origin			
White[b]	106	102	1
Black/African American[b]	167	161	6
Hispanic/Latino origin	129	95	34
Asian[b, c]	26	17	9
Other[b, d]	35	23	11
Unknown	63	61	2
Citizenship			
U.S. Citizen/U.S. National	346	345	1
Permanent U.S. resident[e]	6	6	0
Undocumented alien[f]	101	64	36
Qualified alien[e]	19	1	15
Temporary worker	2	0	2
Unknown	50	41	9
Number of victims identified	527	460	63

Source: Banks, D., & Kyckelhahn, T. (2011). *Characteristics of suspected human trafficking incidents, 2008–2010.* Bureau of Justice Statistics. Washington, DC: U.S. Department of Justice. Retrieved from http://www.bjs.gov/content/pub/pdf/cshti0810.pdf

Note: Analysis restricted to cases opened and observed between January 2008 and June 2010 in high data quality task forces.

a. Includes cases of unknown trafficking type.

b. Excludes persons of Hispanic or Latino origin.

c. Asian may include Native Hawaiian and other Pacific Islanders or persons of East Asian or Southeast Asian descent.

d. Includes persons of two or more races.

e. Permanent residents and qualified aliens are legal residents in the U.S., but do not have citizenship.

f. Undocumented aliens reside in the U.S. illegally.

◈ Ideas in Action: What Can Be Done About Human Trafficking?

While the challenges to eradicate human trafficking are significant, at least many are known and can be addressed. The United Nations suggests that some of these challenges include the following:

- Lack of knowledge: there are still huge gaps in knowledge even about the extent of human trafficking and modern-day slavery.

- Lack of a national legal framework, policy, and capacity to respond: while human trafficking is acknowledged as a crime, there is little systematic legal response or public policy to address it.

- Limited protection of and assistance to victims: social service and law enforcement agencies need training in order to better identify and respond to victims of human trafficking.

- Limited international cooperation: as probably the best example of deviance or crime that crosses national borders, there is surprisingly less cooperation than one would hope between countries in identifying and stopping human trafficking. (UN.GIFT, 2008, p. 1)

Another challenge that has been identified involves the definition of human trafficking. Human trafficking laws in many countries require that the person accused of human trafficking be proven to have "bought or sold" another human being. But the reality is that most human trafficking victims are never bought or sold in the traditional sense. Because no transaction occurs and no money changes hands, the vast majority of human trafficking victims are not acknowledged or protected by such laws. Broadening language in countries that rely on the provision of buying and selling individuals would mean that more offenders would be prosecuted and more victims acknowledged (U.S. Department of State, 2013).

Finally, S. X. Zhang (2010) makes five suggestions for public policies to address human trafficking:

1. Law enforcement should focus on disruption tactics that make the business of human trafficking harder to sustain.

2. Increase the financial cost to the business of human trafficking; a legal outcome should be asset forfeiture for anyone found guilty of human trafficking.

3. Law enforcement agencies, medical providers, and social services providers need to be systematically educated on how to recognize trafficking victims.

4. Engage in a campaign that increases public awareness of the existence of human trafficking and that reaches victims of trafficking and makes them aware of who they can contact for help.

5. Effect an increase in political will measured by resource allocation that will secure and offer long-term solutions to human trafficking.

NOW YOU . . . THINK ABOUT GLOBAL DEVIANCE

It is often easy to pass judgment on other countries for their beliefs and practices, and in most instances when we are passing judgment, we are implicitly or explicitly defining those practices as deviant. It is your turn to explore and critique these differences.

1. Choose a country.

2. Find a practice or behavior that the laws in your chosen country or individuals in the country define as deviant that the United States or individuals in the United States would be less likely to define as deviant.

3. Find a practice or behavior that laws in the United States or individuals in the United States define as deviant that your chosen country or individuals in the country would be less likely to define as deviant.

4. Find a practice or behavior that is defined as deviant in both your chosen country and the United States.

5. Why is it that these practices or behaviors may or may not be defined as deviant? Does it matter who engages in the practice for it to be defined as deviant? Who benefits from these definitions of deviance or nondeviance? Why might this behavior be deviant in one country and not in another?

◆ Conclusion

We hope you have enjoyed this exploration into the many, many forms of deviance and the varied ways that societies first define deviance and then react to such acts or characteristics. While we understand that we may be considered deviant ourselves due to our years focusing on the topic, we find all of this material so fascinating that we have devoted our careers to studying it, researching our favorite theories and subtopics, and writing this textbook to share with you. Whether you choose to join us in a career related to deviance, crime, delinquency, or mental health or whether you can simply now check this off your list of required classes, we hope that after reading this book, you will bring a lingering curiosity and a more complex understanding of the causes of and reactions to deviant behavior into all of your future endeavors.

EXERCISES AND DISCUSSION QUESTIONS

1. You are part of a research team that will be studying human trafficking links between China, Mexico, and the United States. Explain the research challenges and issues you will need to be aware of as you plan your study.

2. Choose a country whose prison system has not been discussed in this chapter. Research its forms of social control. Compare and contrast these forms of social control with the U.S. prison system.

KEY TERMS

Decommodification   Human trafficking

READING 35

We started our book with a look at the social construction of extreme body modification as deviance. We end our book with an examination of the moral panic constructed around the British media's focus on forced marriage. This panic constructs forced marriage as a problem that threatens Britain's social order. Anitha and Gill argue that forced marriage should be examined as another form of violence against women, not necessarily a threat to the British establishment.

A Moral Panic?

The Problematization of Forced Marriage in British Newspapers

Sundari Anitha and Aisha K. Gill

◈ **Introduction**

The specific forms of violence experienced by minority ethnic women had long been neglected both in the academic literature and in policy debates in the United Kingdom that have focused on violence perpetrated by partners and ex-partners. However, over the last decade increasing attention has been directed to the different manifestations of violence against women (VAW). This includes violence perpetrated by (primarily though not exclusively) male relatives from the wider kin group rather than just the immediate family such as so-called honor-based violence, dowry violence, and forced marriage (FM). Understanding the forms of violence experienced by minority ethnic women requires an approach that takes account of the continuities between different forms of gender-based violence while also addressing the specificity of particular forms of violence such as FM.

The UK government (HM Government, 2008) defines FM as

> a marriage in which one or both spouses do not (or in the case of some adults with learning or physical disabilities, cannot) consent to the marriage and duress is involved. Duress can include physical, psychological, financial, sexual and emotional pressure. (p. 10)

However, it is important to recognize that consent and coercion are not binaries; the social context within which consent is constructed is crucial to understanding coercive constraints. Consent and coercion can be better conceptualized as two ends of a continuum between which lie degrees of gendered socio-cultural expectations, control, persuasion, pressure, threat, and force (Anitha & Gill, 2009).

Unlike with "mainstream" forms of domestic violence, there is no official data on the prevalence of FM across European Union Member States (Rude-Antoine, 2005); there is a similar gap in our knowledge about the extent of FM in Canada, the United States, and Australia. However, FM has garnered significant media attention in recent years in a number of European states, though the American, Australian, and Canadian media have only recently begun to give prominence to stories concerning FM. Meanwhile, media debates in Europe have informed policy initiatives to address this problem; countries including Norway, Denmark, Sweden, Germany, and the

---

Source: Anitha, S., & Gill, A. K. (2015). A moral panic? The problematization of forced marriage in British newspapers. *Violence Against Women, 21*(9), 1123–1144.

United Kingdom have recently created a specific offense associated with forcing someone into marriage rather than strengthen the existing criminal code that is applicable in the case of "mainstream" forms of VAW (Bredal, 2005; Rude-Antoine, 2005; Tzortzis, 2004).

This recent upsurge of interest contrasts starkly with the fact that FM and early marriage have been the subject of campaigning by women's groups for several decades in these and other parts of the world. In Afghanistan, sub-Saharan Africa, Iraq, and rural China, where bride-price traditions lead many poverty-stricken families to "marry off" their daughters at a young age, women's groups have supported policies and campaigns discouraging early marriage; they have also called for a minimum age for marriage to be established or, where such provisions already exist, for more stringent enforcement of existing laws and policies (Hague & Thiara, 2009). Algeria, Bangladesh, Jordan, Iraq, Malaysia, Morocco, and Turkey are among the countries that have raised the minimum age for marriage to combat FM. In most of these countries, the minimum age is now 18.

This article examines the representation of FM in British newspapers to illuminate (a) how this form of VAW is constructed by the media and (b) what sort of policy solutions these constructions both suggest and exclude.

◈ The Problematization of FM

Foucault's (1985) concept of problematization directs attention to the ways in which a problem comes to be framed and the implications of this framing for how the "development of a given into a question . . . transform[s] a group of obstacles and difficulties into problems to which the diverse solutions will attempt to produce a response" (Foucault, 2000, p. 118). By using this concept to "unpack" the construction of FM in British media discourses, the article aims (a) to examine the underlying and often implicit assumptions behind the construction of FM as a "problem" and (b) to understand how this problematization of FM influences policy responses to it.

Analyses of media representations of crime and criminal justice policy have drawn attention to the framing processes whereby journalists use notions of selectivity and salience to organize their material in news reports (Entman, 1993; Reese, 2001). Framing

determines not only how media content is shaped but also how it is contextualized in terms of the points of reference and latent structures of meaning that underlie the construction of particular media accounts. This simultaneously reflects and influences public perception of the issues at stake (McQuail, 2005).

Research indicates that print and television media have accorded disproportionate and increasing attention to crime over the past four decades, focusing especially on individual criminal incidents and their victims, rather than on patterns of crime or possible causal factors (Beckett & Sasson, 2000; Reiner, Livingstone, & Allen, 2003). Benedict (1992) and Shoemaker and Reese (1996) have identified the core socio-political and practical factors that affect the framing of news stories about crimes against women; these include conceptions of "what sells," journalistic traditions, racism, sexism, class prejudices, sources' biases, and organizational pressures and constraints. Mirroring press coverage of crime in general, reporting on VAW has increased since the 1980s; however, media representations of VAW and its victims continue to reflect dominant societal attitudes toward women and, thus, serve to perpetuate gender inequalities (Berns, 2004; Meyers, 1997). Media accounts of domestic violence typically exclude the concept of male accountability and focus on victims, who are (a) celebrated for having the courage to leave abusive relationships, (b) accused of instigating their abuse, or (c) held responsible for not escaping their predicament (Berns, 2004). Berns (2004) warns that although some of these frames have helped to foster support for victims through the development of legislation and the funding of shelters, they have not helped to "develop public understanding of the social context of violence and may impede social change that could prevent violence" (p. 3).

The crucial role of the media as an agent of moral indignation has been explored through the sociological concept of moral panic, which was developed in the 1970s by Young (1971), Cohen (1972), Cohen and Young (1973), and Hall (1978) to explain the processes involved in creating concern about a social problem that is disproportionate to the reality of the problem; this, in turn, serves to create a discursive space aimed at encouraging a shift in legal and social codes. The concern generated in a moral panic revolves around the identification of a specific threat that has the potential to destroy important social values, norms, and regulations. The identification of such a threat often catalyzes "a demand for greater social regulation or control and a demand for a return to 'traditional' values" (Thompson, 1998, pp. 8–9). Thompson (1998) notes that "in complex modern societies [a moral panic] seldom develops as a straightforward upsurge of indignation . . . there is a 'politics of social problems' or to put it another way, they are 'socially constructed'" (p. 12); hence, moral panic reflects, and often reinforces, prevailing power relations.

In Cohen's (1972) early conceptualization, the collective action that a moral panic triggers is marked by "mass hysteria, delusion and panics" (p. 11) that serve to focus public anxieties and fears on a specific category of deviants identified as "folk devils" (Cohen, 1972). Thus, the key ingredient in the emergence of a moral panic is the creation or intensification of hostility toward a particular group, category, or cast of characters. The "discovery" of the group seen as threatening or harmful to the sanctity of society as a whole is accompanied by a simultaneous oppositional repositioning of the rest of society as defenders of the society's moral values. Thus, Rohloff (2008) points to the importance of changes in relative power ratios between groups not only as key to understanding the broader context within which moral panics develop, but also as potential triggers of moral panic.

Moral panic has traditionally been attributed to media and public formulations of the actions and practices of marginalized groups. Seldom have the actions of dominant groups come under similar media scrutiny, demonstrating the centrality of unequal power relations in moral panic. The concept of moral panic therefore has not been associated with media coverage or academic study of VAW. The absence of the concept of moral panic in the study of VAW was evident when a search for the term *moral panic* yielded one article each in the journals *Violence Against Women, Journal of Interpersonal Violence,* and *Trauma, Violence and Abuse.* A similar search yielded over 100 articles in *British Journal of Criminology* and 21 articles in *Criminology.* One exception to this trend was when public anxiety was invoked and fueled by parts of the American media through sustained newspaper reports

about "sexting" in 2008–2009, which has since been characterized as moral panic (Cumming, 2009; Lumby & Funnell, 2011). The key concerns that informed these debates were the regulation of teenage sexuality and the preservation of idealized constructs of childhood, rather than any possible concern about the gendered nature of sexual coercion in young people's intimate relationships. In other words, this moral panic did not view the issue as centered on the prevalence of VAW. Cohen's (2002, 2011) recent reflections on whether there can ever be a "good" moral panic (i.e., a folk devil that deserves such a reputation) is ideally suited to analyzing reporting on VAW should the issue ever become the focus of a sustained media outrage.

It is important to examine the media's representation of particular crimes, and the groups they affect, because such representations shape the construction of these crimes as problems requiring a policy response (Franklin, 1999; Rochefort & Cobb, 1994). However, it is difficult to assess the precise impact of media representations of crime on broader attitudes because many people choose which newspaper to read on the basis of existing views, not vice versa. Although concerns about the impact of media framings on individuals' attitudes to social issues are long-standing, this remains a complex subject and no definitive conclusions have been reached (Barker & Petley, 2001; Gauntlett, 1998). However, the link between media representations and policy making is more amenable to empirical scrutiny.

We do not deny that FM constitutes a form of VAW or that it deserves both media attention and public policy initiatives for its prevention and eradication. Indeed, the authors have long been part of campaigns and worked with organizations seeking to address such forms of violence affecting minority ethnic women in the United Kingdom. In this article, our focus is on the nature of media representations of FM in the United Kingdom and the ways in which this representation of FM opens discursive spaces for particular types of policy debates that suggest specific, often ill-advised, "solutions" to FM over other potentially more effective ones. These issues are illuminated through (a) quantitative analysis of news reporting on FM over a 10-year period, (b) qualitative mapping of dominant themes and concepts in newspaper articles on FM, and (c) textual analysis of a sub-sample of articles. The following four sections explore the key findings and the methods used to gather and analyze the data.

◈ Data and Method

Four national newspapers were analyzed to explore how news reporting on FM developed between 2001 and 2010 and how the problem of FM was articulated during this time. Both conservative and liberal editorial perspectives were examined: the *Daily Telegraph* (including the *Sunday Telegraph*) is a right-of-center broadsheet, the *Guardian* (and the *Observer*) is a left-of-center broadsheet, the *Daily Mail* (including the *Mail on Sunday*) is a right-of-center middle-brow newspaper, and the *Sun* (and the *News of the World*) is a right-wing tabloid. The selection of a 10-year time period and a wide range of editorial perspectives allowed for quantitative analysis of the extent of reporting on FM and qualitative analysis of a large set of textual data. This provided a representative overview of media reporting on FM in Britain during the first decade of the 21st century.

LexisNexis (an electronic database of legal documents and archive of publications in periodicals, including all major journals, magazines, and newspapers) was used as a search tool to identify all the relevant news reports from the period. All stories generated by the terms *forced marriage, forced marriages*, and *forced + marriage* were examined. These searches also identified news reports that used the term *forced into an arranged marriage*; these were included in the data set. The search generated a total of 367 relevant articles. As LexisNexis does not provide any contextual information (e.g., regarding the placement of articles in editions) or accompanying pictures, these factors did not form part of the analysis. However, online comments posted by readers in response to some of the longer articles published on the newspapers' websites afforded some preliminary observations about the reception of these articles, including whether the underlying framing devices were visible to readers. A detailed study that tests these observations about the reception of media discourses on FM would be a useful contribution to existing debates on media effects.

Figure 1   Newspaper Reporting on Forced Marriage

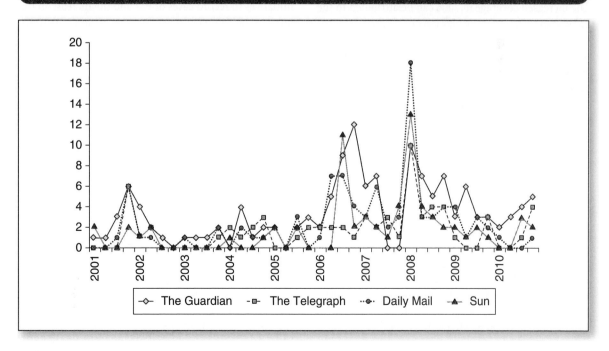

◈ General Trends in Newspaper Reporting on FM

General trends in news reports on FM were mapped by collating the number of articles published on FM in the four newspapers over the 10-year period. This demonstrated the development of the media's interest in FM and illuminated variations over time. Meanwhile, the comparison of the coverage offered by different media outlets afforded an opportunity to examine whether there was significant diversity or homogeneity between papers with regard to the extent of their coverage of FM and whether this changed over time.

The number of articles about FM published per quarter between January 2001 and December 2010 indicates an overall shift from lower levels of reporting in the early years of the decade to a sustained increase since 2006 (see Figure 1). There are three clear peaks in newspaper reporting on FM: mid-2001 to mid-2002, 2006 to mid-2007, and in 2008. The first of these periods was marked by increased coverage/mentions of FM in the context of debates on Britishness and cultural difference following the publication of the Cantle Report (2001–2002) on the urban disturbances in Burnley, Oldham, and Bradford in the summer of 2001. The increased coverage in 2006 can be attributed to the Labour government's consultation on whether the act of forcing someone to marry should be made a criminal offense and the subsequent decision against criminalization. Following this consultation, media coverage remained high as the government went on to announce that specific civil remedies would be created to prevent FMs (i.e., through Forced Marriage Protection Orders) and to assist victims when a marriage has already taken place (i.e., via the other remedies available under the Forced Marriage [Civil Protection] Act 2007). The 2008 peak can be attributed to two high-profile cases of FM that occurred in the same year that these civil remedies came into force. In January 2008, an inquest was held into the then unsolved death of 17-year-old Shafilea Ahmed, whose body was found in a Lake District river a few months after she refused an arranged marriage. Later that year, significant media attention was directed toward Humayra Abedin, a doctor whose parents tried to force her into marriage and held her captive in Bangladesh until she was freed by a court order.

The four newspapers' coverage of FM follows similar trends, with similar peaks and troughs. However, every quarter shows some reporting on FM and, during the last 5 years, a relatively consistent level of reporting. The *Guardian* has the most consistently high coverage, while the *Sun* moves from very low levels of reporting in the early 2000s to higher rates in the later years of the decade.

In addition to the increasing levels of reporting over the last 10 years, FM has frequently been reported as a growing problem. Research commissioned by policymakers (Kazimirski, Keogh, Smith, & Gowland, 2009; Khanum, 2008) offers wide-ranging estimates of the number of cases in the United Kingdom; there is no media consensus on the issue, but newspaper reports suggest that there are between 3,000 and 10,000 cases per year (Taylor, 2008; Slack, 2008). One report even suggests that there could be as many as 17,500 cases per year (Lyons, 2008). However, it is only recently that statistics on FM have begun to be collated by the police and other statutory agencies. A widespread *perception* that this is a growing problem has been created through newspaper headlines such as "Tenfold rise in forced marriages in four years" (Daily Mail Reporter, 2009a). Given the historic lack of documentation, both recent initiatives to record cases of FM and the increase in the number of women reporting such crimes may have been (mis)represented by the media as indicating that FM is a growing problem.

The recent "newsworthiness" of FM is surprising given that the media have historically been less inclined to report on FM than on mainstream forms of domestic violence, just as they were more likely to report on sensational homicides rather than those arising from domestic violence (Peelo, Francis, Soothill, Pearson, & Ackerley, 2004). Abdela (2008) has noted the disproportionate headline coverage in British newspapers of street stabbings involving young people, while stories about women killed by current or past intimates tend to receive little coverage. Knife crime involving adolescents is often represented as a social problem through discursive strategies such as the "tallying up" of the number of deaths that year as each new murder is reported. Meanwhile, domestic homicides are generally represented as unrelated crimes, and so no such toll is recorded. Thus, the media tends to represent VAW as a private rather than social harm (Berns, 2004; Meyers, 1997). In this context, it is curious that FM has come to occupy center stage in media discourses on VAW in the United Kingdom.

◈ Representing FM

The two authors coded the full text of each article to identify two core themes or concepts for each article. Coding a year's worth of articles for each of the four newspapers yielded the initial set of codes; additional ones were created during the subsequent analysis of all the articles. At the end of the process, the researchers met to discuss discrepancies in their coding to reach consensus on how each article should be coded. This process yielded 24 themes and concepts (see Figure 2a and 2b). These can be grouped into seven broad categories: (a) articles about the judicial disposition or policing of a specific case; (b) articles on individual victims and/or perpetrators that centered on the characteristics of victims and/or perpetrators, a theme found in many previous analyses of newspaper reporting on domestic violence (Wosniak & McCloskey, 2010); (c) reports that outlined policy and legislative developments; (d) reports on practical measures, including service provision, aimed at addressing FM and helping victims; (e) articles seeking to estimate the scale of the problem in the United Kingdom; (f) articles on prevention (a small, but defined subset); and (g) articles on the context, nature, and causes of FM. The last category included articles that discussed FM within the broader context of VAW or wide-ranging debates on community cohesion, multiculturalism, speaking English at home, immigration, Muslims/Islam, and minority communities and their culture and traditions, including arranged and transnational marriage.

The seven categories were not mutually exclusive. Indeed, some categories tended to overlap. For example, some articles reporting on particular cases of FM contained a brief factual outline of recent policy developments; others comprised longer features based on interviews with victims/survivors. During the coding process, the researchers decided to utilize two codes for each article to take account of such overlaps.

The overwhelming majority of articles fell under the final category on the context, nature, and causes of FM. Although articles in this category often offered the least detailed discussions of FM, examined collectively they illuminated the most common way of framing the issue. The contexts and causes that garnered most media attention were those that coupled FM with the following themes: Muslims and Islam, the problem of multiculturalism and/or the need for community cohesion, immigration issues, and issues concerning cultural traditions. Although FM was discussed as a form of VAW, it was more likely to be in the context of so-called honor-based crimes than as part of broader discussions about VAW or domestic violence.

Meanwhile, service provision for victims was rarely discussed. An article in the *Mail on Sunday* (2002) about FM and the lack of refuge spaces was a rare exception. Not one article found in the study detailed men's experience of FM or discussed FM in the context of disability or sexual orientation. Prevention and preventive education received little attention across all papers, with comparatively more coverage in the *Telegraph*. All the newspapers paid comparable attention to victims and perpetrators, policy issues, and particular cases of FM.

A detailed qualitative reading of a sample of 16 articles per year, drawn from across the four publications, enabled a closer examination of prominent themes in the construction of the "problem" of FM and especially the representation of victims and perpetrators. This also allowed for an in-depth analysis of how these constructions open up certain discursive spaces for policy debates and practical developments while foreclosing others.

◈ Framing FM as a Cultural Problem

This section examines the three main framing devices used to construct FM and the implications of these frames. The first frame concerns the portrayal of victims of FM. The second concerns perpetrators and their motives. The third revolves around the construction of FM with regard to assumptions about the contexts in which FM occurs and discussions about the causes of the problem and possible responses to it. Together, these frames convey broad messages about the nature of the "problem" and how it might be tackled.

Figure 2a Themes and Concepts in Newspaper Articles on Forced Marriage

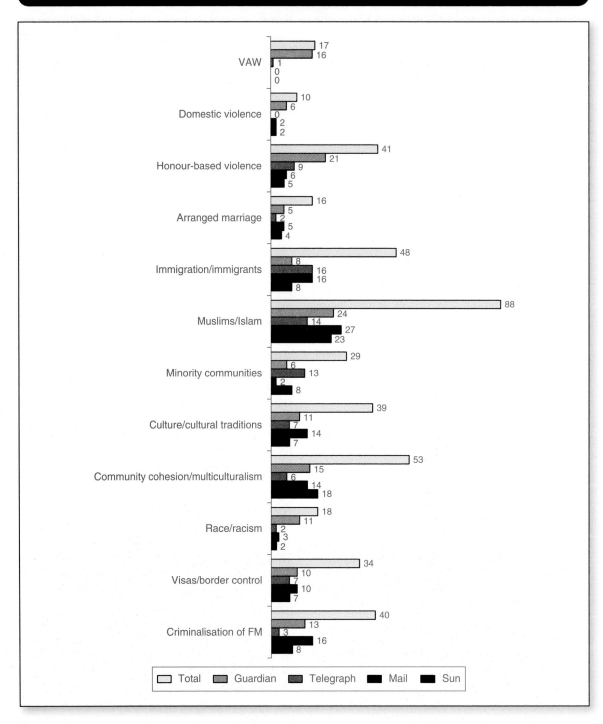

Figure 2b Themes and Concepts in Newspaper Articles on Forced Marriage

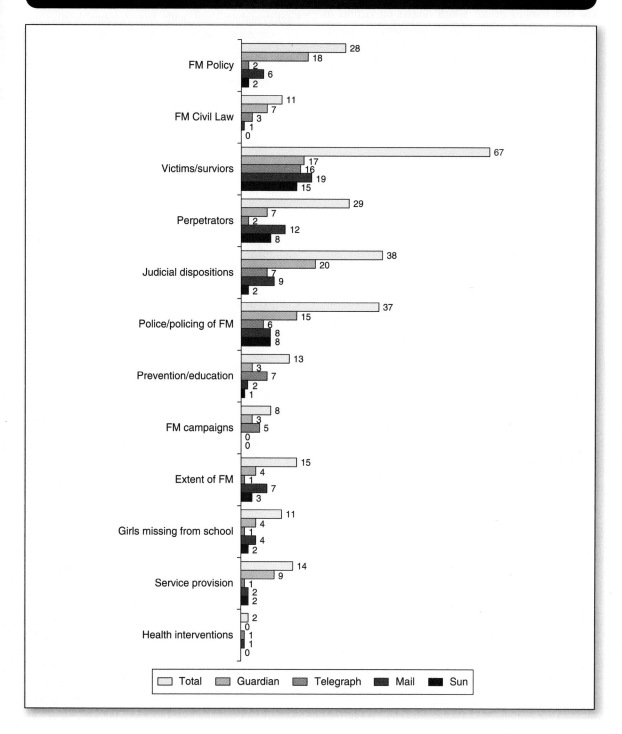

Representing Victims

The first framing device, which centers on victims of FM, was most commonly found in news reports on individual cases and in longer articles, especially "survivor narratives"; these were most likely to be found in weekend editions or special supplements (e.g., the *Daily Mail's* "Femail" or the *Sun's* "Sun Woman"). Most described the victim's experiences of FM (or the threat of FM), and then gave an account of how the victim escaped the threat/marriage, especially when this involved the police or the courts. Reports of this kind were primarily based on interviews with victims and, in some cases, on interviews with the agencies and professionals supporting the woman or working on her case; a number also discussed the relevant court proceedings.

Critically, the women at the center of these articles were portrayed as lacking in agency—as already and always victims of a deterministic culture (Narayan, 1997; Razack, 2004)—and/or as having made the journey from being victims of a deterministic culture to survivors who had distanced themselves from all aspects of their "former" culture. Women's accounts of surviving coercive marriages or the threat of a FM were marshaled into narratives about how these women had reconfigured themselves through their struggles. These narratives were framed by the concept of otherness and often harnessed Orientalist tropes of the absolute cultural difference between victims' former patriarchal communities and the liberated mainstream Western communities into which they had escaped. In a photograph of survivors of FM that accompanied a cover-story on the topic in the *Observer* (Seal & Wiseman, 2009), all the women were dressed in black clothes of European design, an image that emphasized the survivors' distance from their original communities. In this article, one survivor, Sanghera, is quoted as saying, "My father didn't leave his traditions behind at Heathrow" (Seal & Wiseman, 2009). The framing—and indeed, selection—of these narratives reinforces the commonplace view that migrants should abandon their cultural traditions, which are represented as the key cause of FM, to assimilate to Western cultural norms, which are unequivocally represented as privileging gender equality. In a celebratory account of a woman who survived FM, and then went on to marry her White boyfriend,

the *Daily Mail* lauded the woman's courage thus: "Today, she prides herself on being a thoroughly modern Englishwoman—and with her fashionably-streaked hair, elegantly-painted nails and designer wardrobe of must-have designs, she looks every inch the part" (Cable, 2006).

Survivors of FM speak out about their experiences to recover their voices, to make visible what has been rendered invisible, and to raise awareness about the problem (Ali, 2008; Sanghera, 2007, 2009). While recognizing the courage of these women, it is important to question why only some narratives are accorded space by the mainstream media. For example, Humayra Abedin, the doctor whose case occupied the front pages when she was rescued from a FM imposed by her parents in December 2008, was criticized for not denouncing her parents, whose actions she condemned but for whom she still professed love.

Constructing Perpetrators and Their Motives

The second framing device was primarily found in accounts of perpetrators' motivations that focused on family conflict or "culture clash"; as a rule, articles that used this framing device constructed FM as an inevitable feature of traditional Asian culture, rather than as a form of VAW. Articles that used this frame frequently described perpetrators' motives as stemming from the desire to help a relative or friend to immigrate to the United Kingdom on a spousal visa or to prevent the victim making an "unsuitable match." However, the most commonly reported explanation of perpetrators' motives revolved around cultural beliefs. For instance, in sentencing a woman to 3 years in prison for coercing her two daughters to marry their cousins in Pakistan, Judge Clement Goldstone, QC, stated that "those who choose to live in this country and who, like you, are British subjects, must not abandon our laws in the practice of those beliefs and that culture" (Narain, 2009).

These representations of FM are permeated with discursive strategies associated with moral panic. Perpetrators of FM were labeled deviants and the problem of FM seen as pervasive among such deviants—in this case, among all Muslims. In contrast, reports about domestic violence in White communities generally do not construct the problem as particularly widespread or, indeed, particularly disrespectable (Berns, 2004). In discussing preventive education, an editorial in the *Telegraph* (Telegraph View, 2009) argued that "While domestic violence is certainly an appalling problem, the evidence suggests that it is not a widespread one." Despite persistently high rates of domestic violence, the problem is usually cast as an aberration in White communities. Perhaps not surprisingly, the sole exception to such a representation is its reporting within working class communities, capturing the all too common "exoticization" of this issue in terms of both class and ethnicity (Yuval-Davis, 2006). Meanwhile, specific forms of domestic violence common in minority communities tend to be depicted as the norm in these "deviant" communities (Anthias, 2013). Thus, whereas "mainstream" forms of domestic violence are generally represented through discourses focused on the pathology of the individual perpetrator, the majority of the news stories analyzed in this study used a framing device centered on the cultural difference of perpetrators of FM and their very normality within the context of what was constructed as the social norm for their community.

Reporting on a study commissioned by the Home Office to document FM in Luton, Taylor (2008) criticized specific minority communities for perpetuating "a wall of silence" around FM, despite the fact that Black and minority ethnic women's groups have campaigned on FM, so-called honor-based violence, and VAW for many years. In contrast, the broad cultural norms and attitudes that foster tolerance toward gender-based violence are rarely evoked in reports on "mainstream" forms of domestic violence (Berns, 2004).

Constructing FM as a Cultural Problem

The third frame was particularly evident in news reports in which FM was coupled with the issues of immigration, minority communities (particularly Muslims), Britishness, the failure of multiculturalism, and/or the need for community cohesion. Such reporting peaked in the aftermath of the 2001 disturbances in Oldham, Burley, and Bradford with the publication of the Cantle report (2001–2002) about these events.

Newspaper reports of this nature continue to appear on a regular basis, particularly in right-wing tabloids like the *Sun* and in the *Daily Mail*. Statements made by David Blunkett, the Labour Party's former Home Secretary in 2001–2002, on the need for immigrants to learn English to integrate into British society, and the former Labour Home, Justice and Foreign Secretary Jack Straw's criticism of the full-face veil in 2006 were widely reported in articles that invoked FM as a marker of cultural difference.

Similarly, FM is regularly invoked in discussions about the threat to "Britishness" posed by alternate marriage practices, including both arranged marriages and transnational marriages that enabled one party to immigrate to the United Kingdom (Doughty, 2004). The construction of an underlying moral problem and a folk devil that requires social control responses was evident in a headline from 2007: "End Arranged Marriages to Unite Britain" (Blunkett, 2007). Articles of this nature argued that stricter regulation of immigration was needed to curb FM: "If it is important to control the influx of migrants to preserve the stability of our society, it is even more important to ensure that those who come here learn to share with us a common sense of values" (Hastings, 2005).

There were three main types of news coverage about FM that used this frame. This included newspaper reporting that stigmatized immigrant communities in general, and Muslim immigrant men in particular, by constructing FM as a purely cultural problem and paying little regard to its connection with other forms of VAW. In the second type of article, the media blamed British multiculturalism, associating this with a fear of appearing racist in the face of cultural problems such as FM. Indeed, the persistence of FM was often perceived to be symptomatic of the failure of multiculturalism, a sign that attempts to "appease" Muslims/immigrants/minority communities are pervasive in policy and practice. Many articles that adopted this stance called for policy responses focused on cultural assimilation. The third type of coverage was far less common. In articles of this sort, FM was constructed as either a form of VAW or a specific (cultural) manifestation of a broader problem of VAW. Some articles that constructed FM in this manner were also critical of multiculturalism, arguing that it often results in a neglect of specific manifestations of VAW within minority communities and, therefore, welcomed the current attention to this problem. This position was primarily articulated by women's groups, including many who were critical of the culturalization of FM within media and policy debates as well as those who welcomed the recent media and policy focus on this issue.

The representation of FM was far from uniform across the different newspapers. For instance, an overwhelming majority of articles in the *Daily Mail* and the *Sun* fell under the first two categories discussed above, as did a significant proportion of the articles in the *Telegraph*. Articles in the *Guardian* were more likely both to offer critical commentaries on the issues involved and to represent FM as a (culturally) specific form of VAW, though the first two approaches did inform a significant minority of articles in the paper. On the whole, the majority of media reporting on FM characterized it as a cultural problem.

The media's framing of FM contributes to the perception that culturally specific forms of violence are more abhorrent than "normal" domestic violence and, hence, that they are rightfully subject to a media-driven moral crusade. These forms of VAW are "endemic abuse[s] of the worst kind" according to Wayne Ives, former Head of the Forced Marriage Unit (Beckford, 2008). Singling out FM as a particularly barbaric form of VAW not only trivializes "mainstream" forms of domestic abuse but also locates FM in an othered, unchanging, pre-modern world (Fernandez, 2009). These representations are not unique to the British media. Winter, Thompson, and Jeffreys, writing about the formulation of the term *harmful traditional practices* by the United Nations (a victory of sorts for campaigners who sought recognition for the gendered harms that the United Nations had hitherto been silent on), criticized the assumption that the "metropolitan centres of the West contain no 'traditions' or 'culture' harmful to women, and that the violence which does exist there is idiosyncratic and individualized rather than culturally condoned" (2002, p. 72).

Framing FM and forms of VAW that primarily occur in minority communities as more dangerous than mainstream forms of domestic violence also informs debates about possible solutions to these problems. Women's groups have been critical of successive governments' focus on criminal justice responses to

what these groups perceive to be a larger social problem; indeed, the lack of attention to developing effective prevention strategies has been described as the "weakest part of the UK responses to VAW" (Coy, Lovett, & Kelly, 2008, p. 6). However, in November 2009, when domestic violence education was proposed as one possible response to VAW, a number of British newspaper articles were highly critical of this approach. Articles in right-wing newspapers sought to minimize both the prevalence of domestic violence and the need for preventive education in mainstream communities while stressing that domestic violence in minority communities (particularly FM and so-called honor-based crimes) were the "real" problems. According to these articles, these specific forms of VAW required preventive initiatives designed to tackle minority communities' problematic cultures. A 2009 article with the headline "Honour Based Violence Is Biggest Problem Facing Women" (Whitehead, 2009) cited David Green, the director of Civitas (an independent think tank), who argued that the strategy was "skirting around the edges" of the real problem:

> One of the dangers of having lessons to teach everyone from a certain age that it is wrong to use violence against women is that it implies that men are all a potential menace but that is not the problem we face. If you asked what is the biggest problem that women as a whole or particular women have at present, I would say the biggest problem is faced by women from ethnic minorities who are subject to routine violence.

Since acts of VAW in majority communities are perceived to result from the pathology of individual perpetrators (Berns, 2004), government attempts to tackle domestic violence have centered on punishing offenders through criminal justice responses. Viewing cases of violence against minority ethnic women through the lens of "harmful cultural practices" (Narayan, 1997; Razack, 2004; Volpp, 2000) has resulted in responses centered on bringing about changes in specific communities through "modernizing" these communities' sociocultural values, norms, and traditions—or, failing that, through using stricter immigration controls ostensibly aimed at defending minority women's rights. In responding to an article on FM in the online edition of the *Daily Mail*, one reader argued that, "If they choose to live by other laws/customs that are not deemed respectable in British society, then they should be on the first plane back to their home land" (Daily Mail Reporter, 2009b). Thus, the framing of "mainstream" forms of domestic violence as separate and distinct from FM constructs these problems and their potential solutions in specific ways, eliding discussion of the fact that VAW occurs in all sections of British society.

◈ From *a* Cultural Problem to *the* Problematic Culture

The frames discussed above are also evident in policy debates on FM, shaping the range of policy solutions that are discussed. In 2006, Anne Cryer (then Labour MP for Keighley) presented a memorandum to the Home Affairs Select Committee on Immigration Control outlining the problems, including FM and domestic violence, that she routinely dealt with in the course of her constituency work with minority communities. The memorandum referred to the "question mark regarding immigration on the back of a marriage of convenience" (Cryer, 2006, p. 3.5b) and framed the problem in terms of the "ghettoisation" of particular communities due to their lack of integration into mainstream British society (2006, p. 3.5f). Cryer cited consanguineous marriage, FM, and some immigrants' inability to speak English as "tragic problems [that] are facilitated by intercontinental marriages which, in turn, are facilitated by weak immigration control and spouse entry" (2006, p. 3.5h). Critically, the broader problem of VAW is afforded no place in Cryer's discussion or in the solutions centered on tighter immigration controls that she puts forward.

Reporters and policymakers have long identified FM as an issue concerning minority ethnic British women being forced into transnational marriages with men seeking to enter the United Kingdom on spousal visas. Following moves by other European Union countries to use border control measures in the name of tackling FM (Bredal, 2011), in March 2007, Liam Byrne (then Labour Minister for Immigration) announced proposals to raise the age of entry for spouses born outside the European Economic Area from 18 to 21. The press release about this move argued that it was expected to result in 3,000 fewer people entering Britain each year, though the potential impact on efforts to prevent FM could not be estimated (Ford, 2007). Prior to raising the minimum age of entry for spouses, the Home Office commissioned independent research on the possible impact of this change. The study raised concerns that this (a) could be perceived as discriminatory; (b) might violate human rights principles; (c) would not eradicate FM, as this affects people of all ages; and (d) would penalize those who genuinely wished to marry (Hester et al., 2006). The Home Office chose to ignore these findings; indeed, it was only following an application under the Freedom of Information Act that the Home Office released the full report (Yeo, 2009). In the end, the Supreme Court overturned the decision to raise the minimum age.

The Labour Government's decision to ignore the recommendations of the research it had commissioned, and also the advice of some women's groups working on the issue, is closely connected to its framing of the problem of FM. Viewing FM as a signifier of cultural difference suggests that eradicating or minimizing cultural heterogeneity through immigration control measures, and community cohesion strategies aimed at settled minority communities, will offer effective solutions to FM. Writing about Norwegian family reunification law and FM policy, Myrdahl (2010) argues that romance-based marriage has become central to constructions of the national subject, rendering some Norwegian citizens simultaneously invisible as national subjects and hyper-visible as objects of national management, irrespective of concerns about the potential for abuse within a specific marriage. In Britain too, FM, arranged marriage, and consanguineous marriage are often "lumped together" as markers of cultural difference that are contrasted with the norm of romance-based marriage. This serves to reinforce the boundaries of the nation in what Berlant refers to as the "privatisation of citizenship" (cited in Gedalof, 2007, p. 91).

Since 9/11, the problematization of ethnic differences has increasingly come to be articulated through rhetoric centered on the cultural incompatibility of immigrant communities. The notion of a normative form of "Britishness" places the onus on immigrant communities to adapt their cultural values and traditions to make them more like those of mainstream society (Gedalof, 2007). In these discourses, cultural incompatibility between minority and mainstream communities is attributed to the modes of cultural reproduction deployed by immigrant communities. Indeed, transnational marriages are often explicitly blamed for the persistence of immigrant cultures. Here, the problem of FM becomes uncoupled from issues of coercion and, through a focus on transnational marriages, comes to be posited as a "problem of continuous migration" (Migration Watch UK, 2009, p. 1). Bredal (2011) discusses a similar process behind the formulation of policies elsewhere in Europe whereby FM is constructed as a phenomenon that is "almost the same as" transnational arranged marriage or consanguineous marriage. These issues often supplant FM as the core theme in media reports and policy debates ostensibly about FM.

◈ Conclusion

Analysis of the media reporting of FM reveals the three dimensions of "discursive construction" identified by Critcher (2009, p. 30) as central to the typology of a moral panic: a perceived threat to moral order, the potential for social control in the form of new legislation on FM as well as enhanced immigration controls, and the oppositional ethical reconceptualization of the mainstream majority as defenders of the rights of women from minority communities.

How useful is the concept of moral panic in understanding the problematization of FM within British newspaper reporting? In addition, how productive is this moral panic for tackling the very real problem of FM? Does it constitute a "good" moral panic as some women's groups in the United Kingdom suggest? To apply the concept of moral panic, sociologists have adopted an apparently rational position that is actually representative of a broader affective attitude. It is one based on a voice that is grounded in "an attitude of knowing disbelief" (Garland, 2008, p. 21) toward the media and public construction of an issue as an urgent problem requiring a solution. The notion of a disproportionate and perhaps unhelpful overreaction to what, in some cases, might be a matter worthy of concern is

central to the concept of moral panic. However, the difference between panic and concern is not always clear-cut; indeed, this has been the subject of many debates about whether a given case qualifies as a moral panic (Critcher, 2003). Cohen's (2002, p. 2011) recent formulation of the notion of a "good moral panic" implicitly suggests the existence of a bad moral panic. As such, it offers opportunities to make explicit the affective positioning of those who attribute moral panic (i.e., sociologists) where this had previously been elided.

Another dimension of the moral panic debate concerns the consequences of such an attribution, particularly in terms of its usefulness in addressing the problem in question. As discussed above, the current moral panic about FM, as driven by British newspaper reporting, has significant consequences in terms of how the problem of FM is perceived and what policy responses to it are debated.

The prevailing construction of FM harnesses the protective role of the British state as a reformed patriarchy seeking to rescue minority ethnic women from their oppressive cultures. Through these discourses, the non-coercive marriage practices of Black and minority ethnic communities are also constructed as problematic in that they are perceived as (a) signifiers of minority ethnic women's passivity, (b) impediments to community cohesion, and (c) part of a broader immigration "problem." Thus, the key consequence of the media's framing of FM has been the rationalization of tighter immigration control measures and policy developments that privilege cultural assimilation.

Scholars and women's groups working with minority ethnic women in Britain are divided as to how best to understand and address the problem of FM. There are many women's groups in the United Kingdom, including Karma Nirvana and Ashiana, who have contributed to the recent media debates on FM and have been supportive of the Coalition government's policy initiatives on FM, including the recent criminalization of FM. From their perspective, any attention to this issue constitutes a "good" moral panic, as it helps save lives and acts as a corrective to the historic neglect by the media and the state of violence affecting minority ethnic women generally. Opponents to criminalization, however, tend to hold that the framing of FM in current news reporting does constitute a panic in that it is a disproportionate reaction when compared with the lack of attention given to other forms of VAW. Moreover, opponents of criminalization argue that it is a bad moral panic in that the solutions it fosters are, at best, ineffective and, at worst, centered on enhancing immigration controls rather than protecting women from violence. Despite their differences, advocates of both perspectives share a common identification of FM as an urgent problem that requires an immediate and effective policy response.

Where there is specificity in women's experience of violence, there is an urgent need to recognize, understand, and respond to that specificity. However, we argue that the recent media outrage about violence against minority ethnic women has not given rise to a better understanding of the ways in which intersections of gender, class, race, cultural norms, religious traditions, heteronormativity, migratory history, and state policies shape the nature and forms of violence that these women face. Nor have the recent media debates aided the development of context-specific solutions to the problem in the form of targeted service provision and preventive measures. The current problematization of FM by the British media mainly serves to restrict discursive spaces for policy debates and hinders attempts to respond to FM as part of broader coordinated responses to VAW.

◈ References

Abdela, A. (2008, November 25). Stop looking the other way. *The Guardian*. http://www.theguardian.com/commentisfree/2008/nov/25/domestic-violence-gender

Ali, S. (2008). *Belonging*. London, England: John Murray.

Anitha, S., & Gill, A. (2009). Coercion, consent and the forced marriage debate in the UK. *Feminist Legal Studies*, *17*, 165–184.

Anthias, F. (2013). *The tropes of "diversity" governmentality: A significant face of contemporary racisms*. Paper presented at University of Roehampton, March 2013. London, England.

Barker, M., & Petley, J. (Eds.). (2001). *Ill effects: The media/violence debate*. London, England: Routledge.

Beckett, K., & Sasson, T. (2000). *The politics of injustice: Crime and punishment in America*. Thousand Oaks, CA: Pine Forge Press.

Beckford, M. (2008, November 21). Forced marriage cases up by 80pc this year as investigators find parents using "bounty hunters." *Daily Telegraph*. http://www.telegraph.co.uk/news/uknews/3496442/Forced-marriage-cases-up-by-80pc-this-year-as-investigators-find-parents-using-bounty-hunters.html

Benedict, H. (1992). *Virgin or vamp: How the press covers sex crimes*. New York: Oxford University Press.

Berns, N. (2004). *Framing the victim: Domestic violence, media and social problems*. Hawthorne, NY: Aldine de Gruyter.

Blunkett, D. (2007, August 8). End arranged marriages to unite Britain. *The Sun*.

Bredal, A. (2005). Arranged marriages as a multicultural battle field. In M. Mette-Anderson, Y. Lithman, & O. Sernhede (Eds.), *Youth, otherness, and the plural city: Modes of belonging and social life* (pp. 75–106). Gothenburg, Sweden: Daidalos.

Bredal, A. (2011). Border control to prevent forced marriages: Choosing between protecting the women and protecting the nation. In A. Gill & S. Anitha (Eds.), *Forced marriage: Introducing a social justice and human rights perspective* (pp. 90–112). London, England: Zed Books.

Cable, A. (2006, June 9). A forced marriage? I'd rather kill myself. *Daily Mail*. http://www.dailymail.co.uk/femail/article-389831/A-forced-marriage-Id-kill-myself.html

Cohen, S. (1972). *Folk devils and moral panics*. London, England: MacGibbon & Kee.

Cohen, S. (2002). Moral panics as cultural politics. In S. Cohen (Ed.), *Folk devils and moral panics* (3rd ed., pp. vii–xxxvii). London, England: Routledge.

Cohen, S. (2011). Whose side are we on? The undeclared politics of moral panic theory. *Crime Media Culture*, *7*, 237–243.

Cohen, S., & Young, J. (Eds.). (1973). *The manufacture of news*. London, England: Constable.

Coy, M., Lovett, J., & Kelly, L. (2008). *Realising rights, fulfilling obligations: A template for an integrated strategy on violence against women for the UK*. London, England: End Violence Against Women.

Critcher, C. (2003). *Moral panics and the media*. Buckingham, UK: Open University Press.

Critcher, C. (2009). Widening the focus: Moral panics as moral regulation. *British Journal of Criminology*, *49*, 9–30.

Cryer, A. (2006). *Select Committee on Home Affairs: Additional written evidence. Memorandum submitted by Ann Cryer MP*. Retrieved from http://www.publications.parliament.uk/pa/cm200506/cmselect/cmhaff/775/775awe11.htm

Cumming, P. (2009, May 26). *Children's rights, children's voices, children's technology, children's sexuality*. Congress of the humanities and social sciences, Carleton University, Ottawa, Ontario, Canada. Retrieved from http://www.yorku.ca/cummingp/research.html

Daily Mail Reporter. (2009a, December 6). Fear being branded racist and of offending minorities hampers social workers' action over forced marriage. *Daily Mail*. http://www.dailymail.co.uk/news/article-1233660/Fear-branded-racist-offending-minorities-hampers-social-workers-action-forced-marriage.html

Daily Mail Reporter. (2009b, July 2). Ten-fold rise in forced marriages in just four years. *Daily Mail*. http://www.dailymail.co.uk/news/article-1196955/Ten-fold-rise-forced-marriages-just-years.html

Doughty, S. (2004, September 22). Arranged marriages double in a decade. *Daily Mail*, p. 17.

Entman, R. (1993). Framing: Toward clarification of a fractured paradigm. *Journal of Communication, 43*, 51–58.

Fernandez, S. (2009). The crusade over the bodies of women. *Patterns of Prejudice, 43*, 269–286.

Ford, R. (2007, March 29). Visa rules will raise marriage age to 21. *The Times.* http://www.thetimes.co.uk/tto/news/uk/article1914281.ece

Foucault, M. (1985). *The use of pleasure: The history of sexuality* (Vol. 2.). London, England: Penguin.

Foucault, M. (2000). Polemics, politics and problematizations: An interview with Michel Foucault. In P. Rabinow (Ed.), *Essential works of Michel Foucault 1954–84. Ethics: Subjectivity and truth* (Vol. 1, pp. 111–120). London, England: Penguin.

Franklin, B. (Ed.). (1999). *Social policy, the media and misrepresentation.* London, England: Routledge & Kegan Paul.

Garland, D. (2008). On the concept of moral panic. *Crime Media Culture, 4*, 9–30.

Gauntlett, D. (1998). Ten things wrong with the media "effects" model. In R. Dickinson, R. Harindranath, & O. Linné (Eds.), *Approaches to audiences: A reader* (pp. 120–30). London, England: Arnold.

Gedalof, I. (2007). Unhomely homes: Women, family and belonging in UK discourses of migration and asylum. *Journal of Ethnic and Migration Studies, 33*, 77–94.

Hague, G., & Thiara, R. (2009, March). Bride-price, poverty and domestic violence in Uganda. *British Academy Review*, issue 15. http://www.britac.ac.uk/pubs/review/15/index.cfm

Hall, S. (1978). *Policing the crisis: Mugging, the state and law and order.* London, England: Macmillan.

Hastings, M. (2005, March 22). Immigration. *Daily Mail*, p. 12.

Hester, M., Chantler, K., Gangoli, G., Ahmed, B., Burman, E., Sharma, S., et al. (2006). *Forced marriage: The risk factors and the effect of raising the minimum age for a sponsor, and of leave to enter the UK as a spouse or fiance(e).* Bristol, UK: University of Bristol.

HM Government. (2008). *Multi-agency practice guidelines: Handling cases of forced marriage.* London, England: Forced Marriage Unit.

Kazimirski, A., Keogh, P., Smith, R., & Gowland, S. (2009). *Forced marriage: Prevalence and service response.* London, England: Natcen.

Khanum, N. (2008). *Forced marriage, family cohesion and community engagement.* Luton, UK: Equality in Diversity.

Lumby, C., & Funnell, N. (2011). Between heat and light: The opportunity in moral panics. *Crime Media Culture, 7*, 277–291.

Lyons, J. (2008, February 10). 17,500 forced to wed. *The News of the World.*

No room at the refuge for Asian families in fear. (2002, June 9). *Mail on Sunday.* http://www.highbeam.com/doc/1G1-87164270.html

McQuail, D. (2005). *McQuail's mass communication theory* (5th ed.). London, England: Sage.

Meyers, M. (1997). *News coverage of VAW: Engendering blame.* Thousand Oaks, CA: Sage.

Migration Watch UK. (2009). *Immigration and marriage: The problem of continuous migration.* Guildford, UK: Author.

Myrdahl, E. (2010). Legislating love: Norwegian family reunification law as a racial project. *Social and Cultural Geography, 11*, 103–116.

Narain, J. (2009, May 22). Muslim mother who forced her school-age daughters to marry their cousins is jailed for 3 years. *Daily Mail.* http://www.dailymail.co.uk/news/article-1185589/Muslim-mother-forced-school-age-daughters-marry-cousins-jailed-3-years.html

Narayan, U. (1997). *Dislocating cultures: Identities, traditions, and third-world feminism.* New York: Routledge.

Peelo, M., Francis, B., Soothill, K., Pearson, J., & Ackerley, E. (2004). Newspaper reporting and the public construction of homicide. *British Journal of Criminology, 44*, 256–275.

Razack, S. (2004). Imperilled Muslim women, dangerous Muslim men and civilised Europeans: Legal and social responses to forced marriages. *Feminist Legal Studies, 1*, 256–275.

Reese, S. (2001). Prologue—Framing public life: A bridging model for media research. In S. D. Reese, H. Gandy Jr., & A. E. Grant (Eds.), *Framing public life: Perspectives on media and our understanding of the social world* (pp. 7–31). Mahwah, NJ: Lawrence Erlbaum.

Reiner, R., Livingstone, S., & Allen, J. (2003). From law and order to lynch mobs: Crime news since the Second World War. In P. Mason (Ed.), *Criminal visions: Media representations of crime and justice* (pp. 13–32). Cullompton, UK: Willan Publishing.

Rochefort, D., & Cobb, R. (Eds.). (1994). *The politics of problem definition.* Lawrence, KS: University Press of Kansas.

Rohloff, A. (2008). Moral panics as decivilising processes: Towards an Eliasian approach. *New Zealand Sociology, 23*, 66–76.

Rude-Antoine, E. (2005). *Forced marriages in Council of Europe member states: A comparative study of legislation and political initiatives.* Strasbourg, France: Council of Europe.

Sanghera, J. (2007). *Shame.* London, England: Hodder & Stoughton.

Sanghera, J. (2009). *Daughters of shame.* London, England: Hodder & Stoughton.

Seal, R., & Wiseman, E. (2009, January 11). Abducted. Abused. Raped. Survived. *The Observer.* Retrieved November 4, 2012 from http://www.guardian.co.uk/world/2009/jan/11/british-asian-forced-marriages

Shoemaker, P., & Reese, S. (1996). *Mediating the message: Theories of influence on mass media content.* New York: Longman.

Slack, J. (2008, March 11). More than 3,000 Asian children vanishing from school and "forced into arranged marriages." *Daily Mail.* http://www.dailymail.co.uk/news/article-530295/More-3-000-Asian-children-vanishing-school-forced-arranged-marriages.html

Taylor, M. (2008). Victims of forced marriages could total 4,000, says study. (2008, March 11). *The Guardian.* http://www.theguardian.com/world/2008/mar/11/gender.communities

Telegraph View. (2009, November 26). This is no way to curb domestic violence. *The Daily Telegraph.* http://www.telegraph.co.uk/comment/telegraph-view/6655761/This-is-no-way-to-curb-domestic-violence.html

Thompson, K. (1998). *Moral panic.* London, England: Routledge.

Tzortzis, A. (2004). *Europe tackles forced marriage.* Retrieved from http://www.csmonitor.com/2004/0121/p07s01-woeu.html

Volpp, L. (2000). Blaming culture for bad behavior. *Yale Journal of Law and the Humanities, 12,* 89–116.

Whitehead, T. (2009, November 26). Honour based violence is biggest problem facing women. *The Telegraph.* http://www.telegraph .co.uk/news/uknews/law-and-order/6655561/Honour-based-violence-is-biggest-problem-facing-women.html

Winter, B., Thompson, D., & Jeffreys, S. (2002). The UN approach to harmful traditional practices. *International Feminist Journal of Politics, 4,* 72–94.

Wosniak, J. A., & McCloskey, K. A. (2010). Fact or fiction? Gender issues related to newspaper reports of intimate partner homicide. *Violence Against Women, 16,* 934–952.

Yeo, C. (2009). Raising the spouse visa age. *Journal of Immigration Asylum and Nationality Law, 23,* 365–370.

Young, J. (1971). The role of the police as amplifiers of deviance. In S. Cohen (Ed.), *Images of deviance* (pp. 27–61). Harmondsworth, UK: Penguin.

Yuval-Davis, N. (2006). Intersectionality and feminist politics. *European Journal of Women's Studies, 13,* 193–209.

READING 36

Chirot and Edwards examine the reasons for genocide, arguing that not all genocides stem from the same causes. Instead, they suggest that genocides have varying causes, from cold-blooded calculation to realistic fears to instincts for revenge to ideologies for purification. Understanding these causes helps us better figure out how to stop genocides in the future.

Making Sense of the Senseless

Understanding Genocide

Daniel Chirot and Jennifer Edwards

Skeletal bodies clutching barbed-wire fences, the expressionless faces of the recently tortured and starved—the pictures that emerged from Yugoslavia in the 1990s were frighteningly reminiscent of Nazi concentration camps. In 1994, the images of thousands of bloated bodies filling the rivers of Rwanda, of men and women pleading not to be abandoned, and of their hacked up corpses a day later conjured images of the Rape of Nanking (1937–38). There, the Japanese army systematically tortured, raped, and killed 300,000 Chinese in six weeks. In Rwanda, 800,000 were killed while the world watched on satellite television.

The inevitable comparisons of these recent atrocities to those of the past, most notably the Holocaust, are highly controversial. Classifying an event as a genocide can be used to legitimate the claims of survivors or as justification for reprisals against perpetrators. Therefore, several questions about genocide should be considered:

Source: Chirot, D., & Edwards, J. (2003). Making sense of the senseless: Understanding genocide. *Contexts, 2*(2), 12–19.

- How successful does an attempted "cleansing" of a group need to be to warrant classification as genocide?

- Does a certain number or percentage of a population need to be killed?

- Does the intent of the perpetrators make any difference?

- Should the term genocide be reserved for the murder and expulsion of religious or ethnic minority groups or can political dissidents or enemies in war be victims of genocide?

Although burdened with issues of morality and politics, these questions are critical to understanding why (and when) genocides occur. The usual, narrow definition delimits genocide as a rare event produced by religious or racial ideologues. As such, we often overlook important similarities between the infamous large-scale attempts at extermination and the lesser-known, less successful, and smaller-scale mass murders. When we expand our definition, however, we discover that there are several important distinctions in the types of motivation and justifications political leaders give when committing genocidal acts. These differences can help us to better understand and anticipate genocide.

◈ Defining Genocide

Scholars vary widely in how they define and, thus, explain genocide—a term coined only in 1944 in response to the Holocaust. For some, genocide lies at the end of a continuum of violence. It may be a byproduct or the culmination of a violent civil war or even of a state's attempt to control a recalcitrant population. It is a step beyond massacres, mass murder or the violence of war.

For others, genocide is a distinct and rare event unlike other episodes of mass violence. The United Nations originally defined it as an attempt to destroy "in whole or in part, a national, ethnic, racial or religious group." If genocide is distinct from other types of violence, it requires its own unique explanation. This has led many to view genocide, like its name, as a peculiarly modern phenomenon. Zygmunt Bauman, for

example, sees genocide as the product of large governmental bureaucracies combined with pseudo-scientific ideas and utopian visions of modern totalitarian states, such as Nazi Germany and Soviet Russia.

If genocide is defined too narrowly, as something that exists only on the scale of the Holocaust, Rwanda, or the killing of almost 1 million Armenians in 1915 by the Ottoman Empire, then it is rare and hard to explain. Defined too broadly, however, it can devolve into a purely political label to even cover what some call "cultural genocide," which includes voluntary assimilation. To better understand them, genocidal acts should be defined more simply, in a way that sidesteps the political disputes raised by claims that certain groups have been subjected to genocide. We define genocide as politically motivated mass murder. Importantly, this definition encompasses variations in murder, from "first degree," or intentional and premeditated killing, to negligent or reckless "manslaughter."

> Genocides are politically motivated mass murders perpetrated by elites or agents of the government that kill a substantial portion of a targeted population, combatants and non-combatants alike, regardless of their age or gender. Both mass murders that were planned ahead of time, as in the Holocaust, Rwanda, or Armenia, and those that were the byproduct of mass expulsions, such as the Cherokees' eviction from the southeast to Oklahoma in 1838, are included. Genocidal events may be on a large scale, or on a smaller scale, when only one particular community is targeted and most of its population is killed.

Because the model cases have been interpreted as ethnic—the Holocaust, Rwanda, and Yugoslavia—that is how most people think of genocide, as the effort by one ethnic group to wipe out another. But genocides have also included the attempted destruction of peoples because of their religion, ideology, economic class, or merely because of the region in which they lived. Ethnicity and nationalism have been the major issues in 20th-century cases, but class and region played a major role in the mass political murders perpetrated by Stalin and the Khmer Rouge, and religion has been critical in cases such as the slaughter of several thousand Muslims by Hindu activists in Gujarat, India, in 2002, and the killing of hundreds of thousands of Muslims and Hindus during the partitioning of Pakistan and India in 1947. The best way to begin making sense of such events is to distinguish types of genocide according to the motivations of the political elites who order and condone them. In the end, genocides are not, as so many would like to believe, the products of sick minds or diseased societies. With such distinctions, we can begin to predict the likelihood of genocide by studying the pronouncements of political elites, the circumstances in which they come to power and their ideological commitments.

◈ The Varieties of Genocide

We identify four basic types of genocide based on the rationale and objectives of the perpetrators. Any particular case can fall into more than one type—perpetrators can have more than one motive—but these distinctions help us interpret past cases and weigh the likelihood of future ones.

Convenience

Sometimes it is simply expedient to kill all of an enemy population. Julius Caesar did not hesitate to exterminate recalcitrant tribes in Gaul, though he much preferred to have them cooperate. William the Conqueror wanted Anglo-Saxon peasants alive after his conquest of England to work for him and his lords, and he was willing to co-opt Anglo-Saxon lords if they submitted. But when Yorkshire continued to resist, he killed most of its population, burning villages and crops. This eliminated what could have become the focus of a more widespread uprising.

Strong resistance is not necessary to provoke genocidal killings or expulsions. The Cherokee in the southeastern United States worked hard to adapt themselves to white rule, but their lands were coveted, especially once gold was discovered there. In 1838–39 they were expelled to Oklahoma, despite a Supreme Court ruling that the seizure of their lands was illegal. Historical demographer Russell Thornton estimates that because of this forced ethnic cleansing, about 20 percent of the 16,000 expelled Cherokees died of hunger, privation, and disease on the "Trail of Tears," and perhaps up to 50 percent died, if deaths from disease immediately after resettlement are counted. This was genocide purely for the sake of greed and convenience.

Killing large numbers of civilians as part of a calculated strategy in war may also be genocidal, even if the ultimate aim is only to force a surrender. While different than the deliberate extermination of a whole people, it still comes under the definition we are using—the mass killing of non-combatants. Some of Genghis Khan's mass murders in the 13th century were similar to the American strategy of dropping nuclear weapons on Japan: surrender or face complete annihilation.

Revenge

Genocidal acts are rarely based entirely on simple, cold, unemotional calculations. Caesar claimed it was to preserve his "prestige" that he ordered the extermination of the Eburons, whose king he felt had betrayed a prior treaty. Genghis Khan was equally outraged by the treachery of the city of Herat when he ordered its several hundred thousand inhabitants slaughtered. Herat had previously surrendered, but then revolted against his rule. The fire bombings of civilian cities by the Americans and British during World War II (the most notorious case was Dresden, in 1945, where there were no obvious military or industrial targets) were meant to end the war, but also carried a strong element of vengefulness.

The desire for revenge, however, can go much further and provoke genocidal slaughters that have no conceivable military purpose. In 1904 the Herero in the German colony of Southwest Africa (today's Namibia) revolted and defeated a small German army. The infuriated Kaiser Wilhelm II sent a large force to this essentially worthless territory (before the event, the Germans were trying to get rid of it by selling it to the British) and explicitly ordered that the Herero be exterminated. They were shot, herded into the desert to starve, or put into concentration camps where they died. Of 80,000 Herero, at least 60,000 perished. Militarily, this was entirely unnecessary, but the commanding German general had ordered that not even women or children were to be spared.

The Rape of Nanking in 1937–38 was also a matter of revenge. Though the intent was to avenge the stiff resistance of the defending Chinese army, the victims were the civilians of Nanking. The Japanese army, obsessed with "honor," felt humiliated by the "inferiors," much as the Germans had in Southwest Africa. They salvaged their wounded pride by genocidal retribution, even though the Japanese warrior code demanded that non-combatants be treated better than enemy soldiers.

Despite the horror of these examples, from the viewpoint of the perpetrators, these mass murders were in some way retributive justice and, in that sense, "rational." The Japanese and German military believed, as had Caesar, that to forego revenge would incite further acts of resistance and convince the world that their armies were weak.

Fear

The examples so far were genocidal acts carried out against weak enemies and inflicted on mostly helpless populations. There are, however, many genocidal episodes that result from fear—whether real or imagined. Fear can quickly escalate and provoke mass murder by a group, clan, tribe, or nation that feels it must save itself from destruction by another. Deadly ethnic riots, for example, are usually instigated by leaders who invoke such fears.

In Yugoslavia, political elites bent on creating strong, separate Croatian and Serbian states manipulated fear of other ethnic groups. There had been ethnic tensions before World War II, mass killings in a complex civil war, and growing economic competition and insecurity in the 1970s and 1980s. But when ethnic entrepreneurs stirred up memories of past killings and strategically linked them to contemporary murders, they set off the genocidal wars and ethnic cleansings of the 1990s. The historical memories behind the fears were largely fabricated, and as Anthony Oberschall has shown, before this critical turn the various ethnic groups had gotten along well. Unfortunately, the new waves of killings and counter-killings reinforced these dubious historical memories and made them increasingly real.

Stalin's war against the Kulaks (prosperous peasants), 8 million of whom died, was based on an explicit fear that a rural middle class would obstruct socialism.

It hardly mattered that there was no distinct Kulak class, only some peasants who had done relatively well. Kulaks, just average peasants in good farming areas who were unhappy about giving up their produce for nothing, were starved, killed, or deported to camps where they died of privation and overwork.

Sometimes, of course, fears are grounded in reality. When the Ottoman Empire unleashed its genocide against the Armenians in 1915, it was desperately struggling to survive as an ally of Germany in World War I. Some Armenian nationalists were collaborating with the Empire's enemy Russia and sought to establish an Armenian state in a large part of Anatolia. The Ottoman authorities believed that if they did not rid themselves of this menace they would themselves face destruction. They used mass expulsion and extermination as "defensive" tactics. When the Hutu regime in Rwanda committed genocide in 1994, it was in response to a serious (and ultimately successful) invasion of Rwanda by Tutsi refugees, aided by Uganda, who aimed to overthrow the existing power structure. In both cases, the genocides were preceded by years of mistrust, killings, and increasing fear.

Even realistic fears do not justify genocides that wipe out mostly innocent bystanders. But we have to take into account both how fear motivates political elites and also how those elites deliberately manipulate fear among their followers. Had Western leaders followed the political maneuvering and statements of leading political figures in Rwanda in 1993, they would not have been taken by surprise at what happened. Gérard Prunier, a French expert on Africa, claims that Western governments did know what was happening, but deliberately chose to downplay this information because they believed their electorates would be unwilling to bear the costs of intervention.

Purification

There is a special, more insidious fear that also motivates genocide: the fear of pollution. It is the most difficult to explain because it depends on deep cultural beliefs that portray a group as a moral danger that demands extermination. Notorious among ideologues of pollution in the 20th century are Hitler and Stalin, although they were not the first.

The Catholic-Protestant Wars in 16th century France killed some 750,000 people and gave us the term "massacre." Though they were the result of a complex mixture of economic, political, and dynastic causes, there was a genuinely theological component to these wars. The urge to purify Catholicism of the stain of heresy was at the heart of the worst killing. Catholic mobs repeatedly felt it necessary not only to kill Protestants, but also to burn their possessions and mutilate their bodies in order to purify the land. The genital mutilation of men and cutting open of pregnant Protestant women was part of this ritual of purification.

The Bible contains many genocidal episodes, and whether these actually happened or not, the mere fact that they are found in a holy text indicates that God may demand such extreme purification. For example, the Lord commanded Joshua's men to kill "both men and women, young and old, oxen, sheep, and asses, with the edge of the sword" after the fall of Jericho. Subsequently, one of the main causes given for Israel's downfall was its failure to exterminate all of the Canaanites.

The major totalitarian ideologues of the 20th century had their own utopian views of the world that called for the cleansing of polluting elements. For Adolf Hitler, utopia would result from the triumph of a healthy, racially pure Aryan nation. All of civilization's ills were ascribed to racial mixing and weakness. This is why Jews, the ultimate carriers of racial pollution, had to be exterminated, along with gypsies, homosexuals, the mentally retarded, and eventually, Slavs. As historian Christopher Browning has explained, the bitter scholarly disputes of the 1970s and 1980s about whether or not Hitler's ideology, or structural conditions and political contingencies were responsible for the Holocaust is resolved by the fact that without Hitler's vision of a racially pure utopia the Holocaust would have been inconceivable.

In one of the major genocides of recent times, 500,000 to 1 million suspected Communists were killed in Indonesia in 1965–1966. In East Java, where some of the worst episodes occurred, this was the culmination of a long class war in the countryside. Not only were whole families massacred, but torture and mutilation, much of it of a sexual nature, were also common. The military wanted to be rid of Communists for political reasons, but the killings also arose from the murderous frenzy stirred by fear of religious pollution. Muslim activists carried out most of the killing, destroying infidels to restore the natural order.

Similarly, the Cambodian Communists' destruction of one-quarter of their population was committed in pursuit of a classless, racially pure Khmer utopia. Non-Khmers, especially Vietnamese, were the first to be killed; those influenced by Western or Vietnamese ways followed. Here also the killers sought to wipe out a polluting influence they feared.

◈ Looking Ahead

Mass political murder follows its own "logic," and we can only understand it if we follow the logic. Genocides are not specifically modern, but when they are controlled by modern states they tend to be more thorough and bloodier than pre-modern genocides. There will be more genocides in the future unless we learn to recognize their symptoms and are prepared to intervene.

Understanding the different sources of genocide gives us one tool. Sociology contributes by distinguishing among the causes that lead to genocidal acts. Today, public opinion can restrain genocides of convenience, such as the deaths of the Cherokees; such acts are no longer acceptable. We can foresee how the demands of war in a place like Chechnya might lead to genocidal acts by the Russians trying to keep control of that strategic province. But seemingly irrational fears can still lead to genocidal policies. Leaders who deliberately stoke a sense of fear and a thirst for revenge greatly increase the likelihood that their followers will extract terrible retributions. When it comes to the ideologies of purification, however, all we can do is to recognize these and warn the world. The religious absolutists, the ethnic and nationalist chauvinists, and the utopian ideologues, who are all prepared to eliminate whole classes of people to create a perfect world are all unlikely to change their opinions because of their genocidal implications—Osama Bin Laden is only the most recent example of these. Understanding the distinctions among the various motivations for genocide—however disturbing—is an important first step toward preventing them.

Recommended Resources

Bauman, Zygmunt. *Modernity and the Holocaust.* Ithaca: Cornell University Press, 1989. A clear, if controversial, sociological explanation of the thesis that modernity is responsible for genocide.

Browning, Christopher R. *The Path to Genocide.* Cambridge: Cambridge University Press, 1992. These essays by Browning, a leading Holocaust historian, lay out a balanced and thorough explanation of how the mass murders in World War II Germany came about.

Chirot, Daniel. *Modern Tyrants.* Princeton: Princeton University Press, 1996. Explains how 20th-century tyrants have come to power, and why they caused so many millions of deaths.

Horowitz, Donald L. *The Deadly Ethnic Riot.* Berkeley: University of California Press, 2001. A political scientist shows under what conditions ethnic tensions have led to murderous violence throughout the world.

Naimark, Norman M. *The Fires of Hatred: Ethnic Cleansing in 20th Century Europe.* Cambridge, MA: Harvard University Press, 2001. A historian's account of five major cases, it offers a disconcerting view of vicious ethnic nationalism.

Oberschall, Anthony. "From Ethnic Cooperation to Violence and War in Yugoslavia," in D. Chirot and M.E.P. Seligman, eds., *Ethnopolitical Warfare: Causes, Consequences, and Possible Solutions.* Washington: American Psychological Association Press, 2001, pp. 119–150. Oberschall's field work in the former Yugoslavia is a superb study of how this multiethnic society fell apart.

Prunier, Gérard. *The Rwanda Crisis: History of a Genocide.* New York: Columbia University Press, 1997. This is the best explanation of the 1994 Rwanda genocide, told by one of France's foremost scholars of Africa.

❖ ❖ ❖

READING 37

Rudrappa explores the business of transnational surrogacy in India. She examines how the garment industry, in which workers are paid barely subsistence wages, is directly tied to the surrogacy market in which female garment workers and former garment workers extract more value from their bodies by carrying babies for prospective parents in such countries as the United States.

India's Reproductive Assembly Line

Sharmila Rudrappa

"If you asked me two years ago whether I'd have a baby and give it away for money, I wouldn't just laugh at you, I would be so insulted I might hit you in the face," said Indirani, a 30-year-old garment worker and gestational surrogate mother. "Yet here I am today. I carried those twin babies for nine months and gave them up." Living in the southern Indian city of Bangalore, married at 18, and with two young children of her own, she had delivered twins a month earlier for a Tamil couple in the United States.

I met Indirani when she was still pregnant and living in a dormitory run by Creative Options Trust for Women, Bangalore's only surrogacy agency at the time. COTW works with infertility specialists who rely on

Source: Rudrappa, S. (2012). India's reproductive assembly line. *Contexts, 11*(2), 22–27.

the Trust to recruit, house, care for, and monitor surrogate mothers for their clients. Straight and gay couples arrive from all over India and throughout the world to avail themselves of Bangalore's expertise in building biological families. Indirani and other mothers introduced me to 70 other surrogates they had gotten to know through their line of work. Some of them, including Indirani herself, double as recruiting agents, bringing new laborers into Bangalore's reproductive assembly line.

India is emerging as a key site for transnational surrogacy, with industry profits projected to reach $6 billion in the next few years, according to the Indian Council for Medical Research. In 2007, the *Oprah* show featured Dr. Nayna Patel in the central Indian town of Anand, Gujarat, who was harnessing the bodies of rural Gujarati women to produce babies for American couples. Subsequent newspaper articles and TV shows, as well as blogs by users of surrogacy, popularized the nation as a surrogacy destination for couples from the United States, England, Israel, Australia and to a lesser extent Italy, Germany, and Japan.

The cities of Anand, Mumbai, Delhi, Hyderabad, and Bangalore have become central hubs for surrogacy due to the availability of good medical services, inexpensive pharmaceuticals, and, most importantly, cheap and compliant labor. The cost of surrogacy in India is about $35,000–40,000 per baby, compared to the United States, where it can run as high as $80,000, which makes it particularly appealing to prospective parents. It is working class women who make India's reproductive industry viable. In Bangalore, the garment production assembly line is the main conduit to the reproduction assembly line, as women move from garment factories, to selling their eggs, to surrogacy.

Indirani's life typifies that of other women in Bangalore's garment factories. Paid low wages, she works intermittently in one of the city's many garment factories. She quit when she became pregnant, and joined the line again when her two children attended school, taking time away when she was sick, or to care for sick family members. Bangalore's reproduction industry affords women like her the possibility of extracting greater value from their bodies once they have been deemed unproductive workers in garment factories. Because of its life affirming character, Indirani and others see surrogacy, however exploitative, as a more meaningful and creative option than factory work.

◆ Disposable Workers

The popular understanding is that women who have large debt burdens and are destitute opt to become surrogate mothers. But while they are in debt, the 70 mothers I met were not among the poorest in Bangalore. Many were part of dual or multiple income households, and tended to be garment workers who earn more than the average working woman in the city.

Former surrogate mothers, who also work as recruiting agents, have extensive networks among women in prime reproductive age in their own extended families, and among neighbors and friends who work as maids, cooks, street sweepers, or construction workers. Because cuts in food, education, and medical subsidies due to state divestment, along with volatile markets and global financial crises, lead to unsteady factory work and low wages, their greatest recruiting success is among garment workers.

Like garment workers in sweatshops across the world, women in Bangalore are underpaid and overworked. In order to meet short production cycles set by global market demands, they work at an inhumanely fast pace, with few or no breaks. They frequently suffer from headaches, chest pain, ear and eye pain, urinary tract infections, and other health problems. Sexual harassment and abuse are rampant on the production line. The supervisors, almost all men, castigate women in sexually derogatory terms when they do not meet production quotas, and often grope the women as they instruct them on how to work better. "Sometimes," says Indirani, "I wouldn't take a lunch break when pieces piled up. I didn't want to be shamed in front of everyone. I would go to any length to avoid calling the supervisor's attention to me."

Indirani earned $100 to $110 monthly, depending upon her attendance, punctuality, and overtime hours. Frequently, she and her co-workers were unable to meet the inordinately high production targets and were required by supervisors to stay past regular working hours to meet their quotas. "Playing" catch-up, however, did not necessarily result in overtime pay. Indirani's husband became suspicious if her paycheck did not reflect her overtime hours. He wondered whether she was really at the factory, or whether she was cavorting with another man. Indirani, like many of the women I interviewed, reported that she felt debased at work and at home.

Prior research on Bangalore's female garment workers suggests that they work an average of 16 hours a day in the factory and at home doing laundry, cooking, taking care of children, and commuting to work. Working in the factory all day, and then returning home to complete household tasks was absolutely exhausting. Indirani's friend Suhasini, who was also a surrogate mother, avoided garment work altogether. Her mother, sister, and other women family members had worked the line, and she knew it was not what she wanted for her life. "But I need money," she told me. "For us," she says, "surrogacy is a boon." She describes Mr. Shetty, who started COTW, as "a god to us." When I met her again in December 2011, Suhasini was receiving hormonal injections so that she could be a surrogate mother for a second time.

For much of her working life Indirani has been intermittently employed in one of Bangalore's many garment factories. She quit when pregnant, and joined the line again when her two children attended school. She also stopped factory work when she was sick, or had to care for sick family members. From the perspective of the garment factories, when Indirani is healthy she is a valuable worker for the firm. But during her pregnancies and illnesses, or when she has to attend to her family's needs, she loses her value as a worker, and the company replaces her. She is, as anthropologist Melissa Wright calls it, a "disposable worker." Upon recovering her health, or managing family chores efficiently, Indirani cycles back into the garment factory again, this time miraculously having regained her value for the production process. Over her working life, Indirani has shifted from being valuable, to becoming an undesirable worker who must seek other forms of employment to help support her family.

◈ Making Babies

Indirani and her auto-rickshaw worker husband have struggled for much of their married life to make ends meet, and to support their small children. Indirani's husband did not earn much money. He rented his vehicle from an acquaintance, and the daily rental and gasoline costs cut significantly into the household income. So Indirani and he decided to borrow money from her cousin to purchase an auto-rickshaw of their own. Their troubles worsened when they were unable to pay back the loan, and the cousin would often arrive at their door, demanding his money and screaming expletives at them. He would come to the factory on payday and take Indirani's entire paycheck. She said, "I'd work hard, facing all sorts of abuse. And at the end of it I wouldn't even see any money. I felt so bad I contemplated suicide." When a friend at work suggested that she sell her eggs to an agency called COTW for approximately $500, Indirani jumped at what she perceived as a wonderful opportunity. After "donating" her eggs, Indirani decided to try surrogacy; she became pregnant with twins on her first attempt.

When I asked Indirani whether the hormonal injections to prepare her for ova extraction, and subsequently for embryo implantation, were painful or scary, she avoided answering directly. "*Aiyo akka,*" she said. "When you're poor you can't afford the luxury of thinking about discomfort." When I told her about the potential long-term effects of hyperovulation, she shrugged. Her first priority was getting out of poverty; any negative health threats posed by ova extraction or surrogacy were secondary.

Indirani did not find surrogacy to be debasing work. She earned more money as a reproduction worker than she did as a garment worker, and found the process much more enjoyable. She was exhausted physically and emotionally working as a tailor in the factory and then cleaning, cooking, and taking care of her family. Upon getting pregnant, however, Indirani lived in the COTW dormitory. At first she missed her family, often wondering what her children were doing. Was her mother-in-law taking care of them? "I was in a different place surrounded by strangers," she recalled. But soon she began to like the dormitory. She didn't have to wake up by 5 am to prepare meals for the family, pack lunches for everyone, drop the children off at the bus stop so they could get to school, and then hop onto the bus herself to get to the garment factory. Instead, she slept in, and was served breakfast. She had no household obligations and no one made demands on her time and emotions. Surrogacy afforded her the luxury of being served by others. She did not remember a time in her life when she felt so liberated from all responsibilities.

◈ Surveillance and Sisterhood

As she got to know the other women in the COTW dormitory, Indirani began to feel as though she was on vacation. For Indirani and many of the surrogate mothers I interviewed, it was easier to talk with the friends they made in COTW than with childhood friends and relatives; they felt they had more in common with one another. Through the surrogacy process, many women told me, they lost a baby but gained sisters for life.

Indirani's husband brought the children over to visit on some weekday evenings, and her daughter stayed overnight with her on weekends. Her older sister Prabha, also a garment worker who was similarly strapped for cash, joined her at COTW two months after Indirani arrived, becoming a gestational surrogate for a straight, white couple. Like most surrogates, she had no idea where they were from, or where her contract baby would live.

Noting the closed circuit cameras that monitored the mothers' every move in the dormitory, I asked how they felt about them. Indirani said they didn't bother her; in fact, most of the mothers did not register the cameras' presence. While this initially surprised me, I soon realized that they were accustomed to surveillance in their everyday lives. Living under the gaze of relatives and inquisitive neighbors, and housed in one- or two-room homes where it was common for six to eight households to share a bathroom, notions of privacy were quite foreign. Surveillance at the dormitory was benign in comparison to the surveillance and punishment meted out for supposed infractions on the garment shop floor, where long conversations with teammates, taking a few minutes of rest, or going on breaks were all curtailed. In comparison, surveillance at COTW, designed to check on whether the women were having sex with their men-folk who visited the facilities, seemed relatively banal.

The surrogate mothers delivered their babies through caesarian surgeries between the 36th and 37th week of gestation in order to conform to the scheduling needs of potential parents. Indirani was initially fearful of going under the knife, but she saw many mothers survive caesarians and was no longer anxious. In the end, she found the caesarian method of delivering the twins she had carried easier than the vaginal births of her own two children.

The $4000 Indirani earned was far less than the $7000 the surrogacy agency charged for the children. While she was legally entitled to a larger amount because she carried twins, Indirani made no more money than those mothers pregnant with singletons. Her take-home pay actually ended up being less than $4000 after she paid the recruiting agent $200 and bought small, obligatory gifts for the COTW staff who cared for her during her pregnancy. Indirani had the option of staying on in the dormitory for up to two months after delivering her twins, but like all the mothers I interviewed, she chose not to do so because COTW charged for post-natal care, and for food and board. She could not afford to lose her hard-earned money on what she perceived as a luxury, so she returned home within days of delivery to all the household work that waited. Within a week of returning home, her remaining earnings went directly to her cousin, the moneylender. Still, knowing her debts were paid off gave her peace of mind.

Indirani claimed she does not feel any attachment to the twins she carried. "They were under contract. I couldn't bring myself to feel anything for them," she told me. "They were never mine to begin with, and I entered into this knowing they were someone else's babies." It is hard enough for her to take care of her own two children, she said. "Why do you think I'm going through all this now? What would I do with two more? They are burdens I cannot afford." On the other hand, some mothers professed deep attachments to the babies they had given up. Roopa, a divorced mother who gave birth to a baby girl three years ago, always celebrated her contract baby's birthday. "June 21st *akka*," she said, "I cook a special meal. My daughter doesn't know why we have a feast, but it's my way of remembering my second child. I still cry for that little girl I gave away. I think about her often. I could never do this again."

❖ Life Out of Waste

Regardless of how they felt about the babies they had given up, the women almost all said they derived far more meaning from surrogacy than they did working under the stern labor regimes of the garment factory. In our conversations, time and again, women described the many ways they are deemed worthless in the garment factory. Their labor powers exhausted, their sexual discipline suspect, their personal character under question, they are converted to waste on the shop floor—until they are eventually discarded. On the other hand, Bangalore's reproduction industry, they said, gave them the opportunity to be highly productive and creative workers once more.

Indirani contrasted the labor processes in producing garments and producing a baby: the latter was a better option, she said. "Garments? You wear your shirt a few months and you throw it away. But I make you a baby? You keep that for life. I have made something so much bigger than anything I could ever make in the factory." Indirani observed that while the people who wore the garments she'd worked on would most probably never think about her, she was etched forever in the minds of the intended parents who took the twins she bore.

Indirani and the other mothers I met did not necessarily see selling eggs or surrogacy as benign processes. Nor did they misread their exploitation. However, given their employment options and their relative dispossession, they believed that Bangalore's reproduction industry afforded them greater control over their emotional, financial, and sexual lives. In comparison to garment work, surrogacy was easy.

Surrogacy was also more meaningful for the women than other forms of paid employment. Because babies are life-affirming in ways garments are obviously not, surrogacy allowed women to assert their moral worth. In garment work their sexual morality was constantly in question at the factory and at home. At the dormitory, in contrast, they were in a women-only space, abstaining from sex, and leading pure, virtuous lives.

Through surrogacy, Indirani said, she had built a nuclear family unit and fulfilled one infertile woman's desire to be a mother. In the process, she had attempted to secure the future of her own family and her own happiness. As a garment worker Indirani felt she was being slowly destroyed, but as a surrogate mother she said she was creating a new world. She was ready to go through surrogacy once again to earn money for her children's private schooling. The last time we met in December 2011, Indirani asked me, "If anyone you know wants a surrogate mother, will you think of me? I want to do this again."

❖ Recommended Resources

Haimowitz, Rebecca and Vaishali Sinha. *Made in India* (2010). This is a feature length documentary film on surrogacy in India, which explains the organization of the industry through the journey of one American couple to an Indian surrogate.

Pande, Amrita. "Commercial Surrogacy in India: Manufacturing a Perfect Mother-Worker," *Signs* (2010) 35: 969–992. This is an account of surrogate mothers living in dormitories in Anand, India.

Teman, Elly. *Birthing a Mother: The Surrogate Body and the Pregnant Self.* (University of California Press, 2010). The book documents the relationships between straight women and their surrogates in Israel, where assisted reproductive technologies are subsidized for heterosexual couples.

Wright, Melissa. *Disposable Women and Other Myths of Global Capitalism.* (Routledge, 2006). An anthropological description of how women in the global south are seen as bad workers, and yet their work is crucial to multinational companies' profits.

The open-access Study Study Site, available at **study.sagepub.com/inderbitzindeviance2e**, provides useful study materials including SAGE journal articles and multimedia resources.

Glossary

Age–crime curve: an observed relationship between the likelihood to engage in crime and age. The relationship is low in the early childhood and adolescent years, peaks in late adolescence, and then declines as individuals age out of adolescence.

Anomie: a state of normlessness where society fails to effectively regulate the expectations or behaviors of its members.

Attachment: "emotional" component of the social bond that says individuals care about what others think.

Belief: component of the bond in social control theory that suggests the stronger the awareness, understanding, and agreement with the rules and norms of society, the less likely one will be to deviate.

Body modification: includes piercings, scarification, extreme tattooing, and reconstructive and cosmetic surgery.

Broken windows theory: basically the notion that social and physical disorder lead to greater disorder and other forms of crime and deviance.

Central business district: the commercial area of a city where most of the business activity occurs.

Civil commitment: a process whereby offenders, particularly sex offenders, who are perceived to be a risk to the community can be held indefinitely after completing the sentences handed down by the criminal justice system.

Collateral consequences of imprisonment: damages, losses, or hardships to individuals, families, and communities due to incarceration of some members.

Collective efficacy: conditions of some neighborhoods or groups where there is trust, cohesion, and a willingness to act for the common good.

Commitment: "rational" component of the social bond that says individuals weigh the costs and benefits of their behavior.

Concentric zones: a model of urban cities, generally consisting of and moving out from the central business district, the zone in transition, zone of the working class, residential zone, and commuter zone.

Conflict: a theoretical perspective that considers how society is held together by power and coercion for the benefit of those in power (based on social class, gender, race, or ethnicity).

Conflict subcultures: from Cloward and Ohlin's theory—conflict subcultures develop in disorganized neighborhoods where young people are deprived of both conventional and illegitimate opportunities; frustration and violence are defining characteristics.

Content analysis: involves reviewing records of communication and systematically searching, recording, and analyzing themes and trends in those records.

Covert observation: refers to public observation where the researcher does not let the human subjects under study know that he or she is a researcher and that they are being studied.

Criminal career paradigm: a view that there are some criminals who offend at high rates across their life courses.

Criminal subcultures: from Cloward and Ohlin's theory—criminal subcultures develop in poor neighborhoods where there is some level of organized crime and illegitimate opportunity for young people growing up in the area.

Critical conception: the conception of deviance that critiques the existing social system that creates norms of oppression.

Critical race theory: a theoretical perspective that examines the use of law, the legal order, and institutions in maintaining white privilege and supremacy.

Cross-sectional designs: involves data that are collected at only one point in time, such as a survey distributed in a classroom.

Cultural deviance theory: a theory emphasizing the values, beliefs, rituals, and practices of societies that promote certain deviant behaviors. Related, subcultural explanations emphasize the values, beliefs, rituals, and practices of subgroups that distinguish them from the larger society.

Decommodification: the movement away from pure market economies to ones that provide political institutions (such as the welfare state) to protect individuals from the harsh reality of pure capitalism.

Definitions: attitudes, values, orientations, rationalizations, and beliefs related to legal and moral codes of society.

Deinstitutionalization: encourages keeping offenders or the mentally ill in the community, to the extent that doing so is a reasonable option. The idea is that there is less disruption, labeling, and stigma if the individuals can be treated outside of prisons, mental hospitals, juvenile facilities, and so on.

Demedicalization: occurs when behaviors are no longer assigned or retain medical definitions. As one example, homosexuality was once defined as a form of mental illness, but it has been demedicalized and is no longer considered a medical issue.

Desistance: the process of ending a deviant career or career in deviance. This can be abrupt (e.g., "quitting cold turkey") or a gradual process (e.g., a self-help recovery process in which individuals alternate between periods of use and abstinence).

Dialectical materialism: the belief that nature (the material world) is full of contradictions (conflict) and that through a process of negotiating those contradictions, we can arrive at a new reality.

Differential association: social interactions with deviant as opposed to conventional others.

Differential location in the social structure: social and demographic characteristics of individuals that define or influence their position or role in the larger social structure (e.g., age, sex, and socioeconomic status).

Differential reinforcement: the balance of rewards and punishments (anticipated and/or actual) that follow from deviant behaviors.

Differential social location in groups: one's position or role in the social groups he or she is part of.

Elite deviance: criminal and deviant acts committed by large corporations, powerful political organizations, and individuals with prestige and influence; may result in physical harm, financial harm, or moral harm.

Escalation: some deviant behaviors accelerate or intensify over time, such as persistent drug use that may increase in frequency or quantity.

Ethics in research: much effort has gone into the ethical implications of researching human subjects, which can be quite complex when studying deviant behavior. Generally, the subject should be asked if he or she consents to participate and his or her confidentiality should be protected.

Ethnography: the study and recording of human society and subcultures.

Experiments: often considered the "gold standard" in research, experimental designs generally require subjects to be randomly assigned to a treatment or control condition.

External control: formal controls that society places on an individual to keep him or her from engaging in crime or deviance.

False consciousness: laborers' lack of awareness of the exploitation they are experiencing at the hands of the owners of the means of production and capitalism.

Felon disenfranchisement: the loss of the right to vote in local and national elections after conviction for a felony offense; laws vary by state.

Feminist criminology: a theoretical perspective that defines gender (and sometimes race and social class) as a source of social inequality, group conflict, and social problems.

Field research: generally involves getting out into the environment and studying human behavior as it exists in the "real world."

Folkways: everyday norms that do not generate much uproar if they are violated.

General strain theory (GST): Robert Agnew's version of strain theory; suggests that strain at the individual level may result from the failure to achieve valued goals and also from the presence of negative relations or stimuli.

Human agency: the capacity of people to make choices that have implications for themselves and others.

Human subjects: living persons being observed for research purposes.

Human trafficking: the illegal movement of people, usually for the purposes of forced labor or sexual exploitation.

Imitation: observing behavior and reenacting modeled behavior in actuality or in play.

Individual efficacy: an individual's ability to achieve specific goals.

Institutional anomie theory: from Messner and Rosenfeld— argues that the major institutions in the United States, including the family, school, and political system, are all dominated by economic institutions; the exaggerated emphasis on monetary success leads to crime and deviance.

Institutionalization/prisonization: when individuals who have been confined to a prison, mental hospital, or other total institution become so used to the structure and routine of the facility that they lose the confidence and capability to exist independently in the outside world.

Institutional review board: an independent group that reviews research to protect human subjects from potential harms of the research.

Internal control: rules and norms exercised through our conscience.

Involvement: component of the social bond that suggests the more time spent engaged in conforming activities, the less time available to deviate.

Laws: the strongest norms because they are backed by official sanctions (or a formal response).

Liberal feminism: focuses on gender role socialization and the roles that women are socialized into.

Life course perspective: a theoretical perspective that considers the entire course of human life (through childhood, adolescence, adulthood, and old age) as social constructions that reflect the broader structural conditions of society.

Longitudinal data: comes from a series of observations of the same phenomena over time.

Looking-glass self: concept from Charles Horton Cooley, who suggests that individuals define themselves at least in part based on social interactions and the perceptions of others.

Low self-control: the inability of an individual to refrain from impulsive behavior designed to increase immediate gratification.

Marxist feminism: focuses on explaining the oppression of women through capitalism and the capitalist system.

Master status: a status that proves to be more important than most others.

Medicalization of deviance: a process by which nonmedical problems and behaviors become defined and treated as medical conditions; examples might include mental illness, hyperactivity, alcoholism, and compulsive gambling.

Mores: "moral" norms that may generate outrage if broken.

Nonintervention: the policy of avoiding intervention and action for as long as possible. For example, labeling theorists often suggest we should tolerate some level of minor deviance and misbehavior before taking official action and labeling individuals deviant.

Normative conception: the conception of deviance that assumes there is a general set of norms of behavior, conduct, and conditions on which all individuals can agree.

Norms: rules of behavior that guide people's actions.

Onset/initiation: the beginning of a career in deviance; this career can be short- or long-lived.

Operationalization: refers to the process that a researcher uses to define how a concept is measured, observed, or manipulated in a study.

Overt observation: refers to studies in which the researcher makes human subjects aware that they are being observed.

Pains of imprisonment: as described by Gresham Sykes, the pains of imprisonment include deprivation of liberty, deprivation of goods and services, deprivation of heterosexual relationships, deprivation of autonomy, and deprivation of security.

Parental efficacy: parents' ability to control their children's behavior through parent–child attachment, rules, supervision, and social support.

Participant observation: research activity where the researcher is actively involved in the behaviors being studied. For example, a recovering alcoholic researcher might study the behaviors of others in AA meetings.

Pathologizing: a deficit or problem-based approach to deviance that focuses on the individual as medically or psychologically abnormal.

Peacemaking criminology: a theoretical perspective focused on the belief that there must be a new way of seeing and organizing the world around compassion, sympathy, and understanding.

Physical deviance: generally thought to be of two types: (1) violating norms of what people are expected to look like and (2) physical incapacity or disability.

Physical disorder: condition of some neighborhoods with high levels of, for example, litter, graffiti, vandalism, and "broken windows."

Polygamy: a subculture in which men are allowed and encouraged to take multiple wives.

Population turnover: also referred to as residential instability and often measured as the percentage of the population that did not reside in the neighborhood five years earlier.

Positive deviance: a concept that is still under debate but generally understood as intentional behaviors that depart from community norms in honorable ways.

Positivist perspective: a deterministic approach that focuses on "factual" knowledge acquired through observation and measurement.

Postmodern feminism: questions the idea of a single "truth" or way of knowing and understanding.

Poverty: a lack of resources or financial well-being.

Prevention programs: any number of programs and policies geared at keeping individuals away from crime and deviance and on a conforming path.

Primary deviance: common instances where individuals violate norms without viewing themselves as being involved in a deviant social role.

Prisonization. *see* Institutionalization/prisonization.

Protective factors: factors that reduce the impact of risk factors and protect or prevent individuals from turning to crime or deviance. Protective factors are not simply the opposite of risk factors.

Pure observation: form of study in which participants do not see the researcher or even know they are being observed.

Quasi-experimental designs: whereas experimental designs generally require random assignment to a treatment or control condition, quasi-experiments usually relax this requirement.

Racial/ethnic heterogeneity: refers to a mixture of different races and ethnicities in a given area.

Radical feminism: focuses on the sexual control of women, seeing their oppression as emerging from a social order dominated by men.

Rehabilitation programs: programs that are focused on changing individual behavior after an individual has already engaged in deviant behavior.

Reinforcement: an act or thing that strengthens or encourages a behavior.

Reintegrative shaming: a reaction to deviant behavior that views the offender as a good person who has done a bad deed; this process encourages repair work and forgiveness rather than simply labeling the individual as a bad person.

Relative deprivation: perspective suggesting that socioeconomic inequality has a direct effect on community crime rates.

Relativist conception: assumes that the definition of deviance is constructed based on interactions with those in society.

Residual rule breaking: deviance for which there exists no clear category—acts that are not crimes yet draw attention and make the societal audience uncomfortable.

Response rate: the number of people in a survey divided by the number of people in the defined sample.

Restorative justice: typically involves bringing victims, offenders, and community members together in a mediated conference where the offenders take responsibility for their actions and work to restore the harm they have caused, often through restitution to the victim and service to the community.

Retreatist subcultures: from Cloward and Ohlin's theory; similar to Merton's adaptation of retreatism, a subculture revolving around drug use, drug culture, and relative isolation from the larger society.

Risk factors: factors that place certain individuals at greater risk for engaging in deviant (often unhealthy) behaviors.

Sample: a group of people taken from a larger population and studied or surveyed.

Scientific method: analysis and implementation of a rigorous, replicable, and objective strategy to gain information about our world.

Secondary data: data collected by other researchers that may be used or reanalyzed by another researcher.

Secondary deviance: when an individual engages in deviant behavior as a means of defense, attack, or adjustment to the problems created by reactions to him or her.

Self-fulfilling prophecy: once an individual is labeled, that individual's self-conception may be altered, causing him or her to deviate and live up to the negative label.

Self-injury: harming oneself by cutting, burning, branding, scratching, picking at skin or reopening wounds, biting, hair pulling, and/or bone breaking.

Sexual deviance: largely determined by community, culture, and context, sexual deviance may include exotic dancers, strippers, sex tourism, anonymous sex in public restrooms, bisexuality, online sexual predators, prostitutes, premarital chastity, and many others.

Social bonds: bonds to conformity that keep individuals from engaging in socially unacceptable activities.

Social cohesion: neighborhoods characterized by positive social interaction, trust, and a sense of community.

Social consensus: general agreement by the group.

Social construction: subjective definition or perception of conditions.

Social constructionist conception: assumes that behaviors or conditions are not inherently deviant but that they become so when the definition of deviance is applied to them.

Social contract: the process by which individuals give up some personal freedoms and abide by general rules of conduct in order to live in a community and enjoy the protection and companionship of the group.

Social disorder: conditions of some neighborhoods with high levels of, for example, unmonitored youth misbehaving, drug dealers, people openly and illegally using alcohol or other drugs, and fighting.

Social disorganization theory: neighborhoods that lack the ability to control delinquent youth and other potentially problematic populations.

Social structure: organization of society, often hierarchical, that affects how and why people interact and the outcomes of those interactions.

Socialist feminism: focuses on structural differences, especially those we find in the capitalist modes of production.

Sociological imagination: the ability to see the link between our personal lives and experiences and our social world.

Specialization: a primary interest and focus on one form of deviant behavior (e.g., marijuana use) to be contrasted with "generality of deviance" (e.g., drug use, theft, and violent behaviors).

Status frustration: a concept from Albert Cohen, suggesting the strain that working-class boys feel when measured against middle-class standards they have trouble meeting.

Stigma: a mark of deviance or disgrace; a negative label or perceived deviance often leads to stigma that may then reduce an individual's life chances.

Strain: lack of opportunities for conventional success may lead to strain, which can manifest in anger, frustration, and deviance.

Structural impediments: obstacles on the road to conforming success—for example, lack of education, poor access to legitimate careers, and so on.

Subcultures: a distinct group within the larger culture that has its own subset of norms, values, behaviors, or characteristics.

Supervision: a process in which an individual's actions are either directly or indirectly known by (usually) a parent or guardian.

Suppression: the act of inhibiting, restraining, or stopping something, such as an activity or a behavior, by authority or force.

Survey: a form of research in which participants are asked a question or questions in order for the researchers to gather information.

Symbolic interactionism: a microlevel, relativist sociological perspective that is focused on individuals and the meanings they attach to objects, people, and interactions around them.

Theoretically defined structural variables: measures based on social theories of deviance such as anomie or strain, social disorganization, or patriarchy, among others.

Theory: a set of assumptions and propositions used for explanation, prediction, and understanding.

Total institutions: institutions such as prisons, jails, and mental hospitals in which all aspects of life are conducted in the same place, in the company of a group of others, and with tightly scheduled activities that are closely supervised and monitored.

Trajectory: a series of linked states or patterns under some domain of behavior. For example, students reading this book are likely to be in an educational trajectory, seeking a degree in higher education.

Transition: a turning point within a long-term trajectory, such as dropping out of school, divorce, or desistance from a particular form of deviant behavior.

Zone in transition: an area of a city that usually borders the central business district. The name comes from the notion that the poorest groups (often recent immigrants) are forced to live there, and as they secure financial stability, they move out, so it is an area in transition between different populations.

References

Abel, R. (1982). The contradictions of informal justice. In R. Abel (Ed.), *The politics of informal justice: Vol. 1. The American experience* (pp. 267–320). New York, NY: Academic Press.

Adams, W. L. (2010, July 12). Sentenced to serving the good life in Norway. *Time.com*. Retrieved from http://content.time.com/time/magazine/article/0,9171,2000920-1,00.html

Adler, F. (1975). *Sisters in crime: The rise of the new female criminal.* New York, NY: McGraw-Hill.

Adler, P. A. (1993). *Wheeling and dealing: An ethnography of an upper-level drug dealing and smuggling community* (2nd ed.). New York, NY: Columbia University Press.

Adler, P. A., & Adler, P. (1983). Shifts and oscillations in deviant careers: The case of upper-level drug dealers and smugglers. *Social Problems, 31*(2), 195–207.

Adler, P. A., & Adler, P. (2007). The demedicalization of self-injury: From psychopathology to sociological deviance. *Journal of Contemporary Ethnography, 36*(5), 537–570.

Adler, P. A., & Adler, P. (2012). Self-injury in cyberspace. *Contexts, 11*(1), 58–61.

Agnew, R. (1985). Social control theory and delinquency. *Criminology, 23,* 47–61.

Agnew, R. (1992). Foundation for a general strain theory of crime and delinquency. *Criminology, 30*(1), 47–87.

Agnew, R. (1997). Stability and change in crime over the life course: A strain theory explanation. In T. P. Thornberry (Ed.), *Developmental theories of crime and delinquency, advances in criminological theory* (Vol. 7) (pp. 101–132). New Brunswick, NJ: Transaction.

Agnew, R. (2006). *Pressured into crime: An overview of general strain theory.* Los Angeles: Roxbury.

Aguirre, A., Jr. (2000). Academic storytelling: A critical race theory story of affirmative action. *Sociological Perspectives, 43*(2), 319–339.

Ahmed, S. (2009, December 8). Why is Uganda attacking homosexuality? *CNN.com.* Retrieved from http://www.cnn.com/2009/WORLD/africa/12/08/uganda.anti.gay.bill/

Akers, R. L. (1985). *Deviant behavior: A social learning approach* (3rd ed.). Belmont, CA: Wadsworth.

Akers, R. L. (1996). Is differential association/social learning cultural deviance theory? *Criminology, 34*(2), 229–247.

Akers, R. L. (1998). *Social learning and social structure: A general theory of crime and deviance.* Boston, MA: Northeastern University Press.

Akers, R. L., & Cochran, J. K. (1985). Adolescent marijuana use: A test of three theories of deviant behavior. *Deviant Behavior, 6*(4), 323–346.

Akers, R. L., & Sellers, C. (2004). *Criminological theories: Introduction, evaluation, and application* (4th ed.). Los Angeles, CA: Roxbury.

Alexander, M. (2010). *The new Jim Crow: Mass incarceration in the age of colorblindness.* New York, NY: New Press.

American Civil Liberties Union (ACLU). (2007). *Firestorm: Treatment of vulnerable populations during the San Diego fires.* San Diego, CA: Author.

Andersen, C. (1999). Governing aboriginal justice in Canada: Constructing responsible individuals and communities through "tradition." *Crime, Law & Social Change, 31,* 303–326.

Anderson, E. (1999). *Code of the street: Decency, violence & the moral life of the inner city.* New York, NY: W. W. Norton.

Anderson, G., Hussey, P., Frogner, B., & Waters, H. (2005). Health spending in the United States and the rest of the industrialized world. *Health Affairs, 24,* 903–914.

Anderson, L., Snow, D. A., & Cress, D. M. (1994). Negotiating the public realm: Stigma management and collective action among the homeless. *Research in Community Sociology, 1,* 121–143.

Antonaccio, O., Botchkovar, E. V., & Tittle, C. R. (2011). Attracted to crime: Exploration of criminal motivation among respondents in three European cities. *Criminal Justice & Behavior, 38*(12), 1200–1221.

Arthur, M. W., Briney, J. S., Hawkins, J., Abbott, R. D., Brooke-Weiss, B. L., & Catalano, R. F. (2007). Measuring risk and protection in communities using the Communities That Care Youth Survey. *Evaluation & Program Planning, 30*(2), 197–211.

Ashworth, A. (1993). Some doubts about restorative justice. *Criminal Law Forum, 4,* 277–299.

Atkinson, M. (2011). Male athletes and the cult(ure) of thinness in sport. *Deviant Behavior, 32*(3), 224–256.

Atkinson, M., & Young, K. (2008). *Deviance and social control in sport.* Champaign, IL: Human Kinetics.

Baca Zinn, M., & Thornton Dill, B. (1996). Theorizing difference from multiracial feminism. *Feminist Studies, 22*, 321–331.

Bader, C. D. (2008). Alien attraction: The subculture of UFO contactees and abductees. In E. Goode & D. A. Vail (Eds.), *Extreme deviance* (pp. 37–65). Thousand Oaks, CA: Pine Forge Press.

Baker, L. M., Dalla, R. L., & Williamson, C. (2010). Exiting prostitution: An integrated model. *Violence Against Women, 16*(5), 579–600.

Bandura, A., Caprara, G.-V., & Zsolnai, L. (2000). Corporate transgressions through moral disengagement. *Journal of Human Values, 6*(1), 57–64.

Banks, D., & Kyckelhahn, T. (2011). *Characteristics of suspected human trafficking incidents, 2008–2010*. Washington, DC: Bureau of Justice Statistics. Retrieved from http://www.bjs.gov/content/pub/pdf/cshti0810.pdf

Barak, G. (1991). Homelessness and the case for community-based initiatives: The emergence of a model shelter as a short-term response to the deepening crisis in housing. In H. E. Pepinsky & R. Quinney (Eds.), *Criminology as peacemaking* (pp. 47–68). Bloomington: Indiana University Press.

Bard Prison Initiative. (n.d.). What we do. Retrieved on March 4, 2016, from http://bpi.bard.edu/what-we-do

Barlow, H. D., & Decker, S. H. (2010). *Criminology and public policy: Putting theory to work*. Philadelphia, PA: Temple University Press.

Barnoski, R. (2005). *Sex offender sentencing in Washington state: Does community notification influence recidivism rates?* (Document No. 05-08-1202). Olympia: Washington State Institute for Public Policy.

Bartollas, C., Miller, S. J., & Dinitz, S. (1976). *Juvenile victimization: The institutional paradox*. New York, NY: John Wiley.

Bates, K. A., & Swan, R. S. (2010). You CAN get there from here, but the road is long and hard: The role of public, private and activist organizations in the search for social justice. In K. A. Bates & R. S. Swan (Eds.), *Through the eye of Katrina: Social justice in the United States* (2nd ed., pp. 439–450). Durham, NC: Carolina Academic Press.

Bazemore, G. (1998). Restorative justice and earned redemption: Communities, victims, and earned reintegration. *American Behavioral Scientist, 41*(6), 768–813.

Becker, H. S. (1953). Becoming a marihuana user. *American Journal of Sociology, 59*(3), 235–242.

Becker, H. S. (1973). *Outsiders*. New York, NY: Free Press. (Original work published 1963)

Beckett, K., & Herbert, S. (2010). *Banished: The new social control in urban America*. Oxford, UK: Oxford University Press.

Beirne, P. (1979). Empiricism and the critique of Marxism on law and crime. *Social Problems, 26*, 373–385.

Bender, K., Thompson, S. J., McManus, H. H., Lantry, J., & Flynn, P. M. (2007). Capacity for survival: Exploring strengths of homeless street youth. *Child & Youth Care Forum, 36*(1), 25–42.

Bendle, M. F. (1999). The death of the sociology of deviance? *Journal of Sociology, 35*, 42–59.

Benko, J. (2015, March 26). The radical humaneness of Norway's Halden Prison. *New York Times*. Retrieved from http://www.nytimes.com/2015/03/29/magazine/the-radical-humaneness-of-norways-halden-prison.html?_r=0

Bennett, T., Holloway, K., & Farrington, D. (2006). Does neighborhood watch reduce crime? A systematic review and meta-analysis. *Journal of Experimental Criminology, 2*(4), 437–458.

Benson, M. L., Wooldredge, J., & Thistlethwaite, A. B. (2004). The correlation between race and domestic violence is confounded with community context. *Social Problems, 51*(3), 326–342.

Bentham, J. (1970). *An introduction to the principles of morals and legislation* (J. H. Burns & H. L. A. Hart, Eds.). London, UK: Athlone Press. (Original work published 1789)

Berg, M. T., & Rengifo, A. F. (2009). Rethinking community organization and robbery: Considering illicit market dynamics. *Justice Quarterly, 26*, 211–237.

Bernard, T., Snipes, J., & Gerould, A. (2009). *Vold's theoretical criminology*. Oxford, UK: Oxford University Press.

Bernasco, W., & Block, R. (2009). Where offenders choose to attack: A discrete choice model of robberies in Chicago. *Criminology, 47*(1), 93–130.

Birkbeck, C. (2011). Imprisonment and internment: Comparing penal institutions north and south. *Punishment & Society, 13*(3), 307–332.

Black, A. (2005, October 7). Unnecessary surgeries exposed. Why 60% of all surgeries are medically unjustified and how surgeons exploit patients to generate profits. Retrieved from http://www.naturalnews.com/012291.html

Blalock, H. M., Jr. (1967). *Toward a theory of minority group relations*. New York, NY: John Wiley.

Blevins, K. R., & Holt, T. J. (2009). Examining the virtual subculture of johns. *Journal of Contemporary Ethnography, 38*(5), 619–648.

Blumstein, A., & Cohen, J. (1979). Estimation of individual crime rates from arrest records. *Journal of Criminal Law and Criminology, 70*, 561–585.

Boeringer, S., Shehan, C. L., & Akers, R. L. (1991). Social context and social learning in sexual coercion and aggression: Assessing the contribution of fraternity membership. *Family Relations, 40*, 558–564.

Bohm, R. M. (1982). Radical criminology: An explication. *Criminology, 19*, 565–589.

Bohm, R. M. (1997). *A primer on crime and delinquency*. Belmont, CA: Wadsworth.

Bonger, W. A. (1916). *Criminality and economic conditions*. Boston, MA: Little, Brown.

Brait, E. (2015, July 31). Portland's bridge-hangers and 'kayaktivists' claim win in Shell protest. *The Guardian*. Retrieved from http://www.theguardian.com/business/2015/jul/31/portland-bridge-shell-protest-kayaktivists-fennica-reaction

Braithwaite, J. (1989). *Crime, shame and reintegration*. Melbourne, Australia: Cambridge University Press.

Braithwaite, J. (2000). Shame and criminal justice. *Canadian Journal of Criminology, 42*(3), 281–298.

Braithwaite, J. (2002). Setting standards for restorative justice. *British Journal of Criminology, 42*, 563–577.

Braithwaite, J., & Mugford, S. (1994). Conditions of successful reintegration ceremonies: Dealing with juvenile offenders. *British Journal of Criminology, 34*(2), 140–171.

Braswell, M. C., Fuller, J., & Lozoff, B. (2001). *Corrections, peacemaking, and restorative justice: Transforming individuals and institutions.* Cincinnati, OH: Anderson.

Breetzke, G. (2010). Modeling violent crime rates: A test of social disorganization in the city of Tshwane, South Africa. *Journal of Criminal Justice, 38*(4), 446–452.

Bridges, G., & Crutchfield, R. (1988). Law, social standing, and racial disparities in imprisonment. *Social Forces, 66*, 699–724.

Broidy, L. (1995). Direct supervision and delinquency: Assessing the adequacy of structural proxies. *Journal of Criminal Justice, 23*, 541–554.

Brownell, K. D., Marlatt, G., Lichtenstein, E., & Wilson, G. T. (1986). Understanding and preventing relapse. *American Psychologist, 41*(7), 765–782.

Browning, C. R. (2002). The span of collective efficacy: Extending social disorganization theory to partner violence. *Journal of Marriage and Family, 64*(4), 833–850.

Burgess, R. L., & Akers, R. L. (1966). A differential association reinforcement theory of criminal behavior. *Social Problems, 14*, 128–147.

Burgess-Proctor, A. (2006). Intersections of race, class, gender, and crime: Future directions for feminist criminology. *Feminist Criminology, 1*(1), 27–47.

Bursik, R. J., Jr. (1988). Social disorganization and theories of crime and delinquency: Problems and prospects. *Criminology, 26*(4), 519–551.

Cain, M. (1974). The main theme of Marx' and Engels' sociology of law. *British Journal of Law and Society, 1*(2), 136–148.

Campbell, D. T., & Stanley, J. C. (1963). *Experimental and quasi-experimental designs for research.* Chicago, IL: Rand McNally College.

Campos, R. (2012). Graffiti writer as superhero. *European Journal of Cultural Studies, 16*(2), 155–170.

Cancino, J. M. (2005). The *utility of social capital and collective efficacy*: Social control policy in nonmetropolitan settings. *Criminal Justice Policy Review, 16*(3), 287–318.

Capaldi, D. M., Kim, H. K., & Owen, L. D. (2008). Romantic partners' influence on men's likelihood of arrest in early adulthood. *Criminology, 46*(2), 267–299.

Castle, T., & Hensley, C. (2002). Serial killers with military experience: Applying learning theory to serial murder. *International Journal of Offender Therapy and Comparative Criminology, 46*(4), 453–465.

Cernkovich, S. A., & Giordano, P. C. (1987). Family relationships and delinquency. *Criminology, 20,* 149–167.

Chambliss, W. J. (1964). A sociological analysis of the law of vagrancy. *Social Problems, 12*(1), 67–77.

Chambliss, W. J. (1969). *Crime and the legal process.* New York, NY: McGraw Hill.

Chambliss, W. J. (1973, November/December). The Roughnecks and the Saints. *Society,* 24–31.

Chambliss, W. J. (1975). Toward a political economy of crime. *Theory and Society, 2*, 149–170.

Chambliss, W. J. (1978). *On the take: From petty crooks to presidents.* Bloomington: Indiana University Press.

Chambliss, W. J. (1999). *Power, politics, and crime.* Boulder, CO: Westview.

Chambliss, W. J., & Seidman, R. B. (1971). *Law, order and power.* Reading, MA: Addison-Wesley.

Chamlin, M. B. (2009). Threat to whom? Conflict, consensus, and social control. *Deviant Behavior, 30*, 539–559.

Chamlin, M. B., & Cochran, J. K. (1995). Assessing Messner and Rosenfeld's institutional anomie theory: A partial test. *Criminology, 33*(3), 411–429.

Chappell, A., & Lanza-Kaduce, L. (2010). Police academy socialization: Understanding the lessons learned in a paramilitary-bureaucratic organization. *Journal of Contemporary Ethnography, 39*(2), 187–214.

Chesney-Lind, M. (1988). Girls and status offenses: Is juvenile justice still sexist? *Criminal Justice Abstracts, 20*, 144–165.

Chesney-Lind, M. (1997). *Female offenders: Girls, women, and crime.* Thousand Oaks, CA: Sage.

Chesney-Lind, M., & Shelden, R. (1998). *Girls, delinquency, and juvenile justice* (2nd ed.). Pacific Grove, CA: Brooks/Cole.

Chesney-Lind, M., & Shelden, R. (2003). *Girls, delinquency and juvenile justice.* Belmont, CA: Wadsworth.

Chirot, D., & Edwards, J. (2003). Making sense of the senseless: Understanding genocide. *Context, 2*(2), 12–19.

Chirot, D., & McCauley, C. (2006). *Why not kill them all? The logic and prevention of mass political murder.* Princeton, NJ: Princeton University Press.

Ciclitira, K. (2004). Pornography, women, and feminism: Between pleasure and politics. *Sexualities, 7*, 281–301.

Clear, T. R. (2007). *Imprisoning communities: How mass incarceration makes disadvantaged neighborhoods worse.* New York, NY: Oxford University Press.

Clemmer, D. (1958). *The prison community.* New York, NY: Holt, Rinehart & Winston. (Original work published 1940)

Clinard, M. B., & Meier, R. F. (2010). *Sociology of deviant behavior.* Belmont, CA: Wadsworth.

Cloward, R. (1959). Illegitimate means, anomie, and deviant behavior. *American Sociological Review, 24*(2), 164–176.

Cloward, R., & Ohlin, L. (1960). *Delinquency and opportunity: A theory of delinquent gangs.* New York, NY: Free Press.

Cochran, J. K., & Bjerregaard, B. (2012). Structural anomie and crime: A cross-national test. *International Journal of Offender Therapy & Comparative Criminology, 56*(2), 203–217.

Cohen, A. K. (1955). *Delinquent boys: The culture of the gang.* New York, NY: Free Press.

Coker, D. (2006). Restorative justice, Navajo peacemaking, and domestic violence. *Theoretical Criminology, 10*, 67–85.

Cole, D. (1998). *No equal justice: Race and class in the American criminal justice system.* New York, NY: New Press.

Collins, P. H. (1990). *Black feminist thought: Knowledge, consciousness, and the politics of empowerment.* New York: Routledge.

Cooley, C. H. (1902). *Human nature and the social order.* New York, NY: Scribner's.

Comfort, M. L. (2002). "Papa's house": The prison as domestic and social satellite. *Ethnography, 3*(4), 467–499.

Comfort, M. L. (2003). In the tube at San Quentin: The "secondary prisonization" of women visiting inmates. *Journal of Contemporary Ethnography, 32*(1), 77–107.

Comfort, M. L. (2008). *Doing time together: Love and family in the shadow of the prison.* Chicago, IL: University of Chicago Press.

Conrad, P. (1992). Medicalization and social control. *Annual Review of Sociology, 18*, 209–232.

Cragg, W. (1992). *The practice of punishment: Towards a theory of restorative justice.* London, UK: Routledge.

Crenshaw, K. (1989). Demarginalizing the intersection of race and sex: A black feminist critique of antidiscrimination doctrine, feminist theory, and antiracist politics. *University of Chicago Legal Forum, 14*, 538–554.

Crenshaw, K. (1993). Mapping the margins: Intersectionality, identity politics, and violence against women of color. *Stanford Law Review, 43*, 1241–1299.

Crenshaw, K., Gotanda, N., Peller, G., & Thomas, K. (1995). Introduction. In K. Crenshaw, N. Gotanda, G. Peller, & K. Thomas (Eds.), *Critical race theory: The key writings that formed the movement* (pp. xiii–xxii). New York, NY: New Press.

Cretacci, M., & Cretacci, N. (2012). Enter the dragon: Parenting and low-self control in a sample of Chinese high school students. *Asian Journal of Criminology, 7*(2), 107–120.

Cretacci, M. A., Fei Ding, M. L., & Rivera, C. J. (2010). Traditional and bond measures of self-control and their impact on deviance among Chinese University students. *International Journal of Criminal Justice Sciences, 5*(1), 220–238.

Cullen, F. T. (2011). Beyond adolescent-limited criminology: Choosing our future—The American Society of Criminology 2010 Sutherland Address. *Criminology, 49*(2), 287–330.

Cullen, F. T., & Agnew, R. (2006). *Criminological theory: Past to present: Essential readings* (3rd ed.). New York, NY: Oxford University Press.

Cullen, F. T., & Agnew, R. (2011). *Criminology theory: Past to present: Essential readings* (4th ed.). New York, NY: Oxford University Press.

Cullen, F. T., & Messner, S. F. (2007). The making of criminology revisited: An oral history of Merton's anomie paradigm. *Theoretical Criminology, 11*(5), 5–37.

Daly, K. (2002). Restorative justice: The real story. *Punishment & Society, 4*(1), 55–79.

Daly, K., & Chesney-Lind, M. (1988). Feminism and criminology. *Justice Quarterly, 5*, 497–538.

Daniel, M. (2006, April 17). Suspect had three guns on bus. *Boston Globe.* Retrieved from http://www.boston.com/news/local/massachusetts/articles/2006/04/17/suspect_had_three_guns_on_bus/

Davenport, C. (2015, December 12). Nations approve landmark climate accord in Paris. *New York Times.* Retrieved from http://www.nytimes.com/2015/12/13/world/europe/climate-change-accord-paris.html

Davies, S., & Tanner, J. (2003). The long arm of the law: Effects of labeling on employment. *Sociological Quarterly, 44*(3), 385–404.

Davis, L. M., Bozick, R., Steele, J. L., Saunders, J., & Miles, J. N. V. (2013). *Evaluating the effectiveness of correctional education: A meta-analysis of programs that provide education to incarcerated adults.* Santa Monica, CA: Rand Corporation.

Defy Ventures. (n.d.). Defy Ventures website. Retrieved from http://defyventures.org

DeJong, W. (1987). A short-term evaluation of project DARE (Drug Abuse Resistance Education): Preliminary indications of effectiveness. *Journal of Drug Education, 17*, 279–294.

DeKeserdy, W., Ellis, D., & Alvi, S. (2005). *Deviance and crime: Theory, research and policy.* Cincinnati, OH: Anderson.

Deviant Behavior. (n.d.). Aims & scope. Retrieved from http://www.tandfonline.com/action/journalInformation?show=aimsScope&journalCode=udbh20#.VryrmMfGCAY

Dishion, T. J., Patterson, G. R., & Kavanagh, K. A. (1992). An experimental test of the coercion model: Linking theory, measurement, and intervention. In J. McCord & R. E. Tremblay (Eds.), *Preventing antisocial behavior: Interventions from birth through adolescence* (pp. 253–282). New York, NY: Guilford Press.

Downing, S. (2009). Attitudinal and behavioral pathways of deviance in online gaming. *Deviant Behavior, 30*(3), 293–320.

Du Bois, W. E. B. (1901). The spawn of slavery: The convict-lease system in the South. *Missionary Review of the World, 14*, 737–745.

Dumb Laws. (2013). The Dumb Network. Retrieved from http://www.dumblaws.com/law/1917

Dunlap, E., Johnson, B., & Manwar, A. (1994). A successful female crack dealer: Case study of a deviant career. *Deviant Behavior, 15*, 1–25.

Durkheim, É. (1951). *Suicide.* New York, NY: Free Press. (Original work published 1897)

Eddy, J. M., & Chamberlain, P. (2000). Family management and deviant peer association as mediators of the impact of treatment condition on youth antisocial behavior. *Journal of Consulting and Clinical Psychology, 68*(5), 857–863.

Edwards, M. L. (2010). Gender, social disorganization theory, and the locations of sexually oriented businesses. *Deviant Behavior, 31*(2), 135–158.

Eidelson, J. (2013, January 25). Workers tell OSHA they were locked inside Target stores overnight. *The Nation.* Retrieved from http://www.thenation.com/blog/172426/ohsa-charges-workers-were-locked-inside-target-stores-overnight#axzz2Y3PU7d8m

Einstadter, W., & Henry, S. (1995). *Criminological theory: An analysis of underlying assumptions.* Fort Worth, TX: Harcourt Brace College Publishers.

Einwohner, R. L. (2003). Opportunity, honor, and action in the Warsaw ghetto uprising of 1943. *American Journal of Sociology, 109*(3), 650–675.

Elechi, O. O., Morris, S. V. C., & Schauer, E. J. (2010). Restoring justice (ubuntu): An African perspective. *International Criminal Justice Review, 20*(1), 73–85.

Elliot, D. S., & Menard, S. (1996). Delinquent friends and delinquent behavior: Temporal and developmental patterns. In J. D. Hawkins (Ed.), *Delinquency and crime: Current theories* (pp. 28–67). New York, NY: Cambridge University Press.

Ellsworth-Jones, W. (2013, February). The story behind Banksy. *Smithsonian.* Retrieved from http://www.smithsonianmag.com/arts-culture/The-Story-Behind-Banksy-187953941.html?c=y&page=1

Emergency Response and Research Institute. (1991, September 4). Fire violations kill twenty-five in chicken plant. Retrieved from http://web.archive.org/web/20061205035348/http://emergency.com/nc-fire.htm

Empey, L. T., & Erickson, M. L. (1972). *The Prove Experiment: Evaluating community control of delinquency.* Lexington, MA: Heath.

Empey, L. T., & Lubeck, S. G. (1971). *The Silverlake Experiment: Testing delinquency theory and community intervention.* Chicago, IL: Aldine.

Ennett, S. T., Tobler, N. S., Ringwalt, C. L., & Flewelling, R. (1994). How effective is drug abuse resistance education? A meta-analysis of project DARE outcome evaluations. *American Journal of Public Health, 84,* 1394–1401.

Environmental Protection Agency. (2011). Climate change, basic info. Retrieved from http://www.epa.gov/climatechange/basicinfo.html

Enzmann, D., & Podana, Z. (2010). Official crime statistics and survey data: Comparing trends of youth violence between 2000 and 2006 in cities of the Czech Republic, Germany, Poland, Russia, and Slovenia. *European Journal on Criminal Policy & Research, 16*(3), 191–205.

Erikson, K. T. (1966). *Wayward puritans: A study in the sociology of deviance.* New York, NY: Macmillan.

Fahey, S., & LaFree, G. (2015). Does country-level social disorganization increase terrorist attacks? *Terrorism & Political Violence, 27*(1), 81–111. doi:10.1080/09546553.2014.972156

Fairbanks, A. M. (2012). Seeking arrangement: College students using "sugar daddies" to pay off loan debt. *Huffington Post.* Retrieved from http://www.huffingtonpost.com/2011/07/29/seeking-arrangement-college-students_n_913373.html?page=1

Fan, S. (1997). Immigration law and the promise of critical race theory: Opening the academy to the voices of aliens and immigrants. *Columbia Law Review, 97*(4), 1202–1240.

Farley, M., & Barkan, H. (1998). Prostitution, violence, and posttraumatic stress disorder. *Women and Health, 27*(3), 37–49.

Farrington, D. (1986). Age and crime. *Crime and Justice, 7,* 189–250.

Farrington, D., Gallagher, B., Morley, L., Ledger, R., & West, D. J. (1985). *Cambridge study in delinquent development: Long-term follow-up, first annual report to the Home Office.* Cambridge, UK: Cambridge University Press.

Federal Bureau of Investigation. (2004). *Uniform Crime Reporting handbook.* Washington, DC: Author. Retrieved from http://www2.fbi.gov/ucr/handbook/ucrhandbook04.pdf

Federal Bureau of Investigation. (2011). *Crime in the United States, 2010.* Washington, DC: Author. Retrieved from http://www.fbi.gov/about-us/cjis/ucr/crime-in-the-u.s/2010/crime-in-the-u.s.-2010/property-crime/larcenytheftmain

Feld, B. C. (1977). *Neutralizing inmate violence: Juvenile offenders in institutions.* Cambridge, MA: Ballinger.

Ferguson, K. M., Bender, K., Thompson, S., Maccio, E. M., Xie, B., & Pollio, D. (2011). Social control correlates of arrest behavior among homeless youth in five U.S. cities. *Violence and Victims, 26,* 648–668.

Ferrell, F., & Hamm, M. S. (1998). *Ethnography at the edge: Crime, deviance, and field research.* Boston, MA: Northeastern University Press.

Fields, G., & Phillips, E. E. (2013, September 25). The new asylums: Jails swell with mentally ill. *Wall Street Journal.* Retrieved from http://online.wsj.com/article/SB10001424127887323455104579012664245550546.html

Finley, R. (2013, February). A guerrilla gardener in South Central LA. *TED Talk.* Retrieved from http://www.ted.com/talks/ron_finley_a_guerilla_gardener_in_south_central_la

Fleisher, M. S. (1995). *Beggars and thieves: Lives of urban street criminals.* Madison: University of Wisconsin Press.

Free the Slaves. (2013). About slavery. Retrieved from http://www.freetheslaves.net/page.aspx?pid=348

Fremont Arts Council. (2010). Fremont Solstice Parade. Retrieved from http://fremontartscouncil.org/events/summer-solstice-parade

Fremont Fair. (2010). Fremont Fair homepage. Retrieved from http://www.fremontfair.org

Frericks, P., Maier, R., & de Graaf, W. (2009). Toward a neoliberal Europe? Pension reforms and transformed citizenship. *Administration & Society, 41,* 135–157.

Frieswick, K. (2012, May 29). Ex-cons launching lives as entrepreneurs. *Inc.com.* Retrieved from http://www.inc.com/magazine/201206/kris-frieswick/catherine-rohr-defy-ventures-story-of-redemption.html/3

Fuller, J., & Wozniak, J. F. (2006). Peacemaking criminology: Past, present, and future. In F. T. Cullen, J. P. Wright, & K. R. Blevins (Eds.), *Taking stock: The status of criminological theory* (pp. 251–276). New Brunswick, NJ: Transaction.

Gabbidon, S. L. (2003). Racial profiling by store clerks and personnel in retail establishments: An exploration of "shopping while black." *Journal of Contemporary Criminal Justice, 19*(3), 345–364.

Gallupe, O., & Bouchard, M. (2013). Adolescent parties and substance use: A situational approach to peer influence. *Journal of Criminal Justice, 41*(3), 162–171.

Gastil, R. D. (1971). Homicide and a regional culture of violence. *American Sociological Review, 36,* 412–437.

Gellman, B., & Poitras, L. (2013, June 6). U.S., British intelligence mining data from nine U.S. Internet companies in broad secret program. *New York Times*. Retrieved from http://www.washingtonpost.com/investigations/us-intelligence-mining-data-from-nine-us-internet-companies-in-broad-secret-program/2013/06/06/3a0c0da8-cebf-11e2-8845-d970ccb04497_story.html

Gerstein, J. (2011, April 16). Eric Holder accused of neglecting porn fight. *Politico*. Retrieved from http://www.politico.com/news/stories/0411/53314.html

Ghosh, B. (2012, August 11). Tag, you're it—Graffiti artists can't stop. *SF Gate*. Retrieved from http://www.sfgate.com/art/article/Tag-you-re-it-graffiti-artists-can-t-stop-3781992.php

Giordano, P. C., Longmore, M. A., Schroeder, R. D., & Seffrin, P. M. (2008). A life-course perspective on spirituality and desistance from crime. *Criminology, 46*(1), 99–132.

Glueck, S., & Glueck, E. (1950). *Unraveling juvenile delinquency.* Cambridge, MA: Harvard University Press.

Goffman, A. (2009). On the run: Wanted men in a Philadelphia ghetto. *American Sociological Review, 74*, 339–357.

Goffman, E. (1961). *Asylums.* Garden City, NY: Anchor Books.

Goffman, E. (1963). *Stigma: Notes on the management of spoiled identity.* Englewood Cliffs, NJ: Prentice Hall.

Goode, E. (1991). Positive deviance: A viable concept? *Deviant Behavior, 12*(3), 289–309.

Goode, E. (2005). *Deviant behavior* (7th ed.). Upper Saddle River, NJ: Pearson Education.

Goode, E. (2008a). *Deviant behavior* (8th ed.). Upper Saddle River, NJ: Pearson Prentice Hall.

Goode, E. (2008b). The fat admirer. In E. Goode & D. A. Vail (Eds.), *Extreme deviance* (pp. 80–90). Thousand Oaks, CA: Pine Forge Press.

Gottfredson, M., & Hirschi, T. (1986). The true value of lambda would appear to be zero: An essay on career criminals, criminal careers, selective incapacitation, cohort studies and related topics. *Criminology, 24*, 213–234.

Gottfredson, M. R., & Hirschi, T. (1990). *A general theory of crime.* Stanford, CA: Stanford University Press.

Gourley, M. (2004). A subcultural study of recreational ecstasy use. *Journal of Sociology, 40*(1), 59–74.

Gove, W. R. (1975). The labeling theory of mental illness: A reply to Scheff. *American Sociological Review, 40*, 242–248.

Government Accountability Project. (2013). GAP statement on the espionage charge filed against Edward Snowden. Retrieved from http://www.whistleblower.org/blog/44-2013/2804-gap-statement-on-the-espionage-charge-filed-against-edward-snowden

Gowan, T., & Whetstone, S. (2012). Making the criminal addict: Subjectivity and social control in a strong-arm rehab. *Punishment & Society, 14*(1), 69–93.

Greenberg, D. (1985). Age, crime, and social explanation. *American Journal of Sociology, 91*, 1–21.

Greenberg, D. F., Kessler, R. C., & Loftin, C. (1985). Social inequality and crime control. *Journal of Criminal Law and Criminology, 76*, 684–704.

Greene, J. M., Ennett, S. T., & Ringwalt, C. L. (1999). Prevalence and correlates of survival sex among runaway and homeless youth. *American Journal of Public Health, 89*(9), 1406–1409.

Greene, J., Ringwalt, C., Kelley, J., Iachan, R., & Cohen, Z. (1995). *Youth with runaway, throwaway, and homeless experiences . . . Prevalence, Drug Use, and Other At-Risk Behaviors.* Washington, DC: Family and Youth Services Bureau.

Greenhouse, S. (2004). Workers assail night lock-ins by Wal-Mart. *New York Times*. Retrieved from http://www.nytimes.com/2004/01/18/us/workers-assail-night-lock-ins-by-wal-mart.html?pagewanted=all&src=pm

Greenwald, G., MacAskill, E., & Poitras, L. (2013, June 9). Edward Snowden: The whistleblower behind the NSA surveillance revelations. *The Guardian* (London). Retrieved from http://www.guardian.co.uk/world/2013/jun/09/edward-snowden-nsa-whistleblower-surveillance

Greenwood, P. W. (1992). Substance abuse problems among high-risk youth and potential interventions. *Crime and Delinquency, 38*, 444–458.

Griffin, C., Bengry-Howell, A., Hackley, C., Mistral, W., & Szmigin, I. (2009). "Every time I do it I absolutely annihilate myself": Loss of narratives (self-)consciousness and loss of memory in young people's drinking. *Sociology, 43*(3), 457–476.

Grinberg, E. (2010, February 11). No longer a registered sex offender, but the stigma remains. CNN.com. Retrieved at http://www.cnn.com/2010/CRIME/02/11/oklahoma.teen.sex.offender/index.html

Gunter, W. D. (2008). Piracy on the high speeds: A test of social learning theory on digital piracy among college students. *International Journal of Criminal Justice Sciences, 3*(1), 54–68.

Gunther, A. (2011, October 3). Greening our food deserts from the ground up. *Huffington Post*. Retrieved from http://www.huffingtonpost.com/andrew-gunther/la-green-grounds_b_993247.html

Gurr, T. R., & Harff, B. (1994). *Ethnic conflict in world politics.* Boulder, CO: Westview Press.

Gusfield, J. (1967). Moral passage: The symbolic process of public designations of deviance. *Social Problems, 15*(2), 1785–1788.

Gusfield, J. (1968). On legislating morals: The symbolic process of designating deviance. *California Law Review, 56*(1), 54–73.

Haas, H., Farrington, D. P., Killias, M., & Sattar, G. (2004). The impact of different family configurations on delinquency. *British Journal of Criminology, 44*(4), 520–532.

Hackney, S. (1969). Southern violence. *American Historical Review, 74*, 906–925.

Hagan, J. (1985). *Modern criminology: Crime, criminal behavior, and its control.* New York, NY: McGraw-Hill.

Hagan, J. (1989). *Structural criminology.* New Brunswick, NJ: Rutgers University Press.

Hagan, J., Gillis, A. R., & Simpson, J. (1985). The class structure of gender and delinquency: Toward a power-control theory of common delinquent behavior. *American Journal of Sociology, 90*, 1151–1178.

Hagan, J., Gillis, A. R., & Simpson, J. (1990). Clarifying and extending power-control theory. *American Journal of Sociology, 95*(4), 1024–1037.

Hagan, J., & Rymond-Richmond, W. (2008). The collective dynamics of racial dehumanization and genocidal victimization in Darfur. *American Sociological Review, 73*(6), 875–902.

Hagan, J., Schoenfeld, H., Palloni, A., Cook, K. S., & Massey, D. S. (2006). The science of human rights, war crimes, and humanitarian emergencies. *Annual Review of Sociology, 32*, 329–349.

Hagan, J., Shedd, C., & Payne, M. R. (2005). Race, ethnicity, and youth perceptions of criminal injustice. *American Sociological Review, 70*, 381–407.

Hagan, J., Simpson, S., & Gillis, A. R. (1987). Class in the household: A power-control theory of gender and delinquency. *American Journal of Sociology, 92*(4), 788–816.

Halcon, L. L., & Lifson, A. R. (2004). Prevalence and predictors of sexual risks among homeless youth. *Journal of Youth and Adolescence, 33*(1), 71–80.

Halkitis, P. N., & Palamar, J. J. (2008). Multivariate modeling of club drug use initiation among gay and bisexual men. *Substance Use and Misuse, 43*, 871–879.

Hall, S., Critcher, C., Jefferson, T., Clarke, J., & Roberts, B. (1978). *Policing the crisis.* London, UK: Macmillan.

Hallstone, M. (2002). Updating Howard Becker's theory of using marijuana for pleasure. *Contemporary Drug Problems, 29*, 821–845.

Hamm, M. S. (2004). Apocalyptic violence: The seduction of terrorist subcultures. *Theoretical Criminology, 8*(3), 323–339.

Hammer, H., Finkelhor, D., & Sedlak, A. J. (2002). *Runaway/thrownaway children: National estimates and characteristics.* Washington, DC: Office of Juvenile Justice and Delinquency Prevention. Retrieved from https://www.ncjrs.gov/pdffiles1/ojjdp/196469.pdf

Haney, L. A. (2010). *Offending women: Power, punishment, and the regulation of desire.* Berkeley: University of California Press.

Hanna, J. (2015, December 11). Top Kansas welfare official rejects anti-gay criticism. *Kansas City Star.* Retrieved from http://www.kansascity.com/news/article49294645.html

Hanson, R. K., Letourneau, E. J., Olver, M. E., Wilson, R. J., & Miner, M. H. (2012). Incentives for offender research participation are both ethical and practical. *Criminal Justice & Behavior, 39*(11), 1391–1404.

Harcourt, B. (2001). *The illusion of order.* Cambridge, MA: Harvard University Press.

Harris, A. J., & Lurigio, A. J. (2010). Introduction to special issue on sex offenses and offenders: Toward evidence-based public policy. *Criminal Justice and Behavior, 37*(5), 477–481.

Hartjen, C. A., & Priyadarsini, S. S. (2003). Gender, peers, and delinquency. *Youth & Society, 34*(4), 387.

Hayes, T. A. (2010). Labeling and the adoption of a deviant status. *Deviant Behavior, 31*, 274–302.

Hayes-Smith, J., & Whaley, R. B. (2009). Community characteristics and methamphetamine use: A social disorganization perspective. *Journal of Drug Issues, 39*, 547–576.

Haygood, W. (2002). Still burning: After a deadly fire, a town's losses were just beginning. *Washington Post.* Retrieved from http://web.archive.org/web/20061208182200/http://www.fedlock.com/public_relations/Still_Burning.htm

Haynie, D. L. (2002). Friendship networks and delinquency: The relative nature of peer delinquency. *Journal of Quantitative Criminology, 18*(2), 99–134.

Heimer, K., & Matsueda, R. L. (1994). Role-taking, role commitment, and delinquency: A theory of differential social control. *American Sociological Review, 59*(3), 365–390.

Herman-Kinney, N. J., & Kinney, D. A. (2013). Sober as deviant: The stigma of sobriety and how some college students "stay dry" on a "wet" campus. *Journal of Contemporary Ethnography, 42*(1), 64–103.

Hernu, P. (2011, July 25). Norway's controversial "cushy prison" experiment—could it catch on in the UK? *Mail Online.* Retrieved from http://www.dailymail.co.uk/home/moslive/article-1384308/Norways-controversial-cushy-prison-experiment—catch-UK.html#ixzz2i10120Gy

Higgins, G. E., Tewksbury, R., & Mustaine, E. E. (2007). Sports fan binge drinking: An examination using low self-control and peer association. *Sociological Spectrum, 27*(4), 389–404.

Hinton, S. E. (1967). *The outsiders.* New York, NY: Penguin.

Hirsch, M. L., Conforti, R. W., & Graney, C. J. (1990). The use of marijuana for pleasure: A replication of Howard Becker's study of marijuana use. *Journal of Social Behavior and Personality, 5*, 497–510.

Hirschfield, P. (2008). The declining significance of delinquent labels in disadvantaged urban communities. *Sociological Forum, 23*(3), 575–601.

Hirschi, T. (1969). *Causes of delinquency.* Berkeley: University of California Press.

Hirschi, T., & Gottfredson, M. R. (1995). Control theory and life-course perspective. *Studies on Crime Prevention, 4*(2), 131–142.

Hochman, D. (2013, May 3). Urban gardening: An Appleseed with attitude. *New York Times.* Retrieved from http://www.nytimes.com/2013/05/05/fashion/urban-gardening-an-appleseed-with-attitude.html?pagewanted=all&_r=0

Hochstetler, A., Copes, H., & DeLisi, M. (2002). Differential association in group and solo offending. *Journal of Criminal Justice, 30*(6), 559–566.

Hoffman, A. (1971). *Steal This Book.* New York, NY: Pirate Editions (Grove Press).

Hoffman, A. (2002). *Steal This Book.* New York, NY: Four Walls Eight Windows.

Holt, T. J., & Copes, H. (2010). Transferring subcultural knowledge on-line: Practices and beliefs of persistent digital pirates. *Deviant Behavior, 31*(7), 625–654.

Homeboy Industries. (2012). The Homeboy Museum: Thursday, May 10, 2012. Retrieved from http://www.homeboystories.blogspot.com

Homeboy Industries. (2013a). Home. Retrieved from http://www.homeboyindustries.org

Homeboy Industries. (2013b). What we do. Retrieved from http://www.homeboyindustries.org/what-we-do

Hopkins, R. B., Paradis, J., Roshankar, T., Bowen, J., Tarride, J., Blackhouse, G., & Longo, C. J. (2008). Universal or targeted screening for fetal alcohol exposure: A cost-effectiveness analysis. *Journal of Studies on Alcohol & Drugs, 69*, 510–519.

Horowitz, D. (2001). *The deadly ethnic riot.* Berkeley: University of California Press.

Hudson, B. (1998). Restorative justice: The challenge of sexual and racial violence. *Journal of Law and Society, 25*(2), 237–256.

Huiras, J., Uggen, C., & McMorris, B. (2000). Career jobs, survival jobs, and employee deviance: A social investment model of workplace misconduct. *The Sociological Quarterly, 41*(2), 245–263.

Humphreys, L. (1970). *Tearoom trade: Impersonal sex in public places.* Chicago: Aldine.

Hunt, P. M. (2010). Are you kynd? Conformity and deviance within the jamband subculture. *Deviant Behavior, 31*(6), 521–551.

Hunter, S. K. (1993). Prostitution is cruelty and abuse to women and children. *Michigan Journal of Gender & Law, 1*, 91–104.

Inderbitzin, M. (2006). Lessons from a juvenile training school: Survival and growth. *Journal of Adolescent Research, 21*, 7–26.

Inderbitzin, M. (2007). Inside a maximum-security juvenile training school: Institutional attempts to redefine the American dream and normalize incarcerated youth. *Punishment & Society, 9*(3), 235–251.

Inderbitzin, M., & Boyd, H. (2010). William J. Chambliss. In K. Hayward, S. Maruna, & J. Mooney (Eds.), *Fifty key thinkers in criminology* (pp. 203–208). New York, NY: Routledge.

International Labour Organization. (2005). *A global alliance against forced labour.* Geneva, Switzerland: International Labour Office.

Irvine, C. (2008, October 27). Tattooed leopard man leaves hermit lifestyle behind. *The Telegraph.* Retrieved from http://www.telegraph.co.uk/news/newstopics/howaboutthat/3265474/Tattooed-Leopard-Man-Leaves-hermit-lifestyle-behind.html

Jackson, P., & Carroll, L. (1981). Race and the war on crime: The sociopolitical determinants of municipal police expenditures in 90 non-southern cities. *American Sociological Review, 46*, 390–405.

Jacobellis v. Ohio, 378 U.S. 184, 197 (1964).

James, E. (2013a). The Norwegian prison where inmates are treated like people. *The Guardian.* Retrieved from http://www.theguardian.com/society/2013/feb/25/norwegian-prison-inmates-treated-like-people

James, E. (2013b). Bastoy: The Norwegian prison that works. *The Guardian.* Retrieved from http://www.theguardian.com/society/2013/sep/04/bastoy-norwegian-prison-works

Jang, S. J., & Smith, C. A. (1997). A test of reciprocal causal relationships among parental supervision, affective ties, and delinquency. *Journal of Research in Crime and Delinquency, 34*, 307–337.

Janus, M., Burgess, A., & McCormack, A. (1987). Histories of sexual abuse in adolescent male runaways. *Adolescence, 22*, 405–417.

Jencks, C. (1994). *The homeless.* Cambridge, MA: Harvard University Press.

Jensen, G. F. (2007). The sociology of deviance. In C. D. Bryant & D. L. Peck (Eds.), *The handbook of 21st century sociology* (pp. 370–379). Thousand Oaks, CA: Sage.

Jobes, P. C., Barclay, E., & Weinand, H. (2004). A structural analysis of social disorganisation and crime in rural communities in Australia. *Australian and New Zealand Journal of Criminology, 37*(1), 114–140.

Johnson, R. E. (1986). Family structure and delinquency: General patterns and gender differences. *Criminology, 24*, 65–84.

Jones, A. L. (1998). Random acts of kindness: A teaching tool for positive deviance. *Teaching Sociology, 26*(3), 179–189.

A journey into hell. (2012, September 22). *The Economist.* Retrieved from http://www.economist.com/node/21563288

Junger, M., & Marshall, I. H. (1997). The interethnic generalizability of social control theory: An empirical test. *Journal of Research in Crime and Delinquency, 34*, 79–112.

Junger-Tas, J., Marshall, I. H., & Ribeaud, D. (2003). *Delinquency in an international perspective: The International Self-Report Delinquency Study.* Monsey, NY: USA Criminal Justice Press, 2003.

Kaufman, J. G., & Widom, C. S. (1999). Childhood victimization, running away, and delinquency. *Journal of Research in Crime and Delinquency, 36*(4), 347–371.

Kempf-Leonard, K., & Johansson, P. (2007). Gender and runaways: Risk factors, delinquency, and juvenile justice experiences. *Youth Violence and Juvenile Justice, 5*, 308–327.

Kennedy, B. (2013). Why do companies still lock workers inside? China's deadly factory fire joins an ever-growing list of examples in which employees have no means of escape despite workplace laws. *MSN Money.* Retrieved from http://money.msn.com/now/post.aspx?post=d8522b07-db76-4a0f-b8f5-b0b1c2392923

KFMB-News 8. (2010). Man flashes undercover cop during sting operation at Lake Murray. Retrieved from http://www.cbs8.com/global/story.asp?s=12842252

Kim, E., Akers, R. L., & Yun, M. (2013). A cross-cultural test of social structure and social learning: Alcohol use among South Korean adolescents. *Deviant Behavior, 34*(11), 895–915. doi:10.1080/01639625.2013.782-787

Kim, E., Kwak, D. H., & Yun, M. (2010). Investigating the effects of peer association and parental influence on adolescent substance use: A study of adolescents in South Korea. *Journal of Criminal Justice, 38*, 17–24.

Kipke, M. D., Unger, J. B., O'Connor, S., Palmer, R. F., & LaFrance, S. R. (1997). Street youth, their peer group affiliation and differences according to residential status, subsistence patterns, and use of services. *Adolescence, 32*(127), 655–669.

Klein, J. D., & St. Clair, S. (2000). Do candy cigarettes encourage young people to smoke? *British Medical Journal, 321*, 362.

Kobrin, S. (1959). The Chicago Area Project. *Annals of the American Academy of Political and Social Science, 322*, 20–29.

Kokaliari, E., & Berzoff, J. (2008). Nonsuicidal self-injury among nonclinical college women: Lessons from Foucault. *Affilia: Journal of Women and Social Work, 23*(3), 259–269.

Kornhauser, R. R. (1978). *Social sources of delinquency: An appraisal of analytic models.* Chicago, IL: University of Chicago Press.

Kotlowitz, A. (1988). *There are no children here: The story of two boys growing up in other America.* New York, NY: Anchor.

Krakauer, J. (1996). *Into the wild.* New York, NY: Anchor.

Kristof, N. D., & WuDunn, S. (2009). *Half the sky: Turning oppression into opportunity for women worldwide.* New York, NY: Vintage Books.

Krohn, M. D. (1999). On Ronald L. Akers' social learning and social structure: A general theory of crime and deviance. *Theoretical Criminology, 3*(4), 437–493.

Krohn, M. D., & Akers, R. L. (1977). An alternative view of the labeling versus psychiatric perspectives on societal reaction to mental illness. *Social Forces, 56*(2), 341–361.

Krohn, M. D., & Massey, J. (1980). Social control and delinquent behavior. *Sociological Quarterly, 21,* 529–543.

Kubrin, C. E. (2008). Making order of disorder: A call for conceptual clarity. *Criminology & Public Policy, 7*(2), 203–213.

Kubrin, C. E., Stucky, T. D., & Krohn, M. D. (2009). *Researching theories of crime and deviance.* New York, NY: Oxford University Press.

Laforgia, M. (2011, May 21). Huge doses of potent antipsychotics flow into state jails for troubled kids. *Palm Beach Post.*

LaFraniere, S. (2010, November 10). Life in shadows for mentally ill in China. *New York Times.* Retrieved from http://www.nytimes.com/2010/11/11/world/asia/11psych.html? pagewanted=all&_r=0

Langman, L. (2013). Occupy: A new social movement. *Current Sociology, 61*(4), 510–524.

Lankenau, S. E. (1999). Panhandling repertoires and routines for overcoming the nonperson treatment. *Deviant Behavior, 20*(2), 183–206.

Lanza-Kaduce, L., Capece, M., & Alden, H. (2006). Liquor is quicker. *Criminal Justice Policy Review, 17*(2), 127–143.

LaPrairie, C. (1998). The "new" justice: Some implications for aboriginal communities. *Canadian Journal of Criminology, 40*(1), 61–79.

Laub, J. H., & Sampson, R. J. (1988). Unraveling families and delinquency: A reanalysis of the Gluecks' data. *Criminology, 26,* 355–379.

Lefkowitz, B. (1997). *Our guys: The Glen Ridge rape and the secret life of the perfect suburb.* Berkeley: University of California Press.

Leiber, M. J., & Stairs, J. M. (1999). Race, contexts, and the use of intake diversion. *Journal of Research in Crime and Delinquency, 36*(1), 56–86.

Leiber, M., Mack, K., & Featherstone, R. (2012). Family structure, family processes, economic factors, and delinquency: Similarities and differences by race and ethnicity. *Youth Violence and Juvenile Justice, 7*(2), 79–99.

Lemert, E. (1951). *Social pathology.* New York, NY: McGraw-Hill.

Levit, N. (1999). Critical of race theory: Race, reason, merit, and civility. *Georgetown Law Journal, 87,* 795.

Liazos, A. (1972). The poverty of the sociology of deviance: Nuts, sluts, and preverts. *Social Problems, 20,* 103–120.

Link, B. G., Phelan, J. C., Bresnahan, M., Stueve, A., & Pescosolido, B. A. (1999). Public conceptions of mental illness: Labels, causes, dangerousness, and social distance. *American Journal of Public Health, 89*(9), 1328–1333.

Liska, A. E., & Messner, S. F. (1999). *Perspectives on crime and deviance* (3rd ed.). Englewood Cliffs, NJ: Prentice Hall.

Lowenkamp, C. T., Cullen, F. T., & Pratt, T. C. (2003). Replicating Sampson and Groves's test of social disorganization theory. *Journal of Research in Crime and Delinquency, 40*(4), 351–373.

Lu, Y., Yu, Y., Ren, L., & Marshall, I. (2013). Exploring the utility of self-control theory for risky behavior and minor delinquency among Chinese adolescents. *Journal of Contemporary Criminal Justice, 29*(1), 32–52.

Lucas, A. M. (2005). The work of sex work: Elite prostitutes' vocational orientations and experiences. *Deviant Behavior, 26*(6), 513–546.

Luhman, R. (2002). *Race and ethnicity in the United States: Our differences and our roots.* Fort Worth, FL: Harcourt College.

Lynch, N. (2012). Playing catch-up? Recent reform of New Zealand's youth justice system. *Criminology & Criminal Justice, 12*(5), 507–526.

Maass, A., Cadinu, M., Guarnieri, G., & Grasselli, A. (2003). Sexual harassment under social identity threat: The computer harassment paradigm. *Journal of Personality and Social Psychology, 85*(5), 853–870.

MacKinnon, C. (1984). Not a moral issue. *Yale Law & Policy Review, 2,* 321–345.

Madden, M., & Lenhart, A. (2009). *Teens and distracted driving: Texting, talking and other uses of the cell phone behind the wheel.* Washington, DC: Pew Internet and American Life Project. Retrieved from http://pewinternet.org/Reports/2009/Teens-and-Distracted-Driving.aspx

Mantsios, G. (2010). Making class invisible. In D. Newman & J. O'Brien (Eds.), *Sociology: Exploring the architecture of everyday life readings* (8th ed., pp. 236–241). Thousand Oaks, CA: Pine Forge Press.

Manza, J., & Uggen, C. (2006). *Locked out: Felon disenfranchisement and American democracy.* New York, NY: Oxford University Press.

Martin, D. (2002). Spatial patterns in residential burglary: Assessing the effect of neighborhood social capital. *Journal of Contemporary Criminal Justice, 18*(2), 132–146.

Martin, J., & O'Hagan, M. (2005, August 30). Killings of 2 Bellingham sex offenders may have been by vigilante, police say. *Seattle Times.* Retrieved from http://community.seattletimes.nwsource.com/archive/?date=20050830&slug=sexoffender30m

Maruna, S. (2011). Reentry as a rite of passage. *Punishment & Society, 13*(1), 3–28.

Marx, K. (1992). *Capital: Volume 1: A critique of political economy.* London, UK: Penguin. (Original work published 1867)

Marx, K. (1993). *Capital: Volume 2: A critique of political economy.* London, UK: Penguin. (Original work published 1885)

Marx, K., & Engels, F. (1957). *The holy family.* London, UK: Lawrence and Wishart.

Marx, K., & Engels, F. (1961). *The communist manifesto.* In A. P. Mendel (Ed.), *Essential works of Marxism* (pp. 13–44). Toronto, Canada: Bantam. (Original work published 1848)

Marymount Manhattan College. (n.d.). Bedford Hills College Program. Retrieved from http://www.mmm.edu/academics/bedford-hills-college-program.php

Matsueda, R. L. (1992). Reflected appraisals, parental labeling, and delinquency: Specifying a symbolic interactionist theory. *American Journal of Sociology, 97*(6), 1577–1611.

Mauer, M. (2005). Thinking about prison and its impact in the twenty-first century: Walter C. Reckless Memorial Lecture. *Ohio State Journal of Criminal Law, 2,* 607–618.

Mauer, M. (2009). Racial impact statements: Changing policies to address disparities. *Criminal Justice, 4,* 19–22.

Maume, M. O., & Lee, M. R. (2003). Social institutions and violence: A sub-national test of institutional anomie theory. *Criminology, 41*(4), 1137–1172.

Mayo, H. B. (1960). *Introduction to Marxist theory.* New York, NY: Oxford University Press.

McCarthy, B., Hagan, J., & Woodward, T. S. (1999). In the company of women: Structure and agency in a revised power-control theory of gender and delinquency. *Criminology, 37,* 761–788.

McCleary, R., & Tewksbury, R. (2010). Female patrons of porn. *Deviant Behavior, 31*(2), 208–223.

McCord, J. (1978). A thirty-year follow-up of treatment effects. *American Psychologist, 33,* 284–289.

McCormack, A., Janus, M., & Burgess, A. W. (1986). Runaway youths and sexual victimization: Gender differences in adolescent runaway populations. *Child Abuse & Neglect, 10,* 387–395.

McKenzie, D., & Formanek, I. (2011, February 25). Kenya's mentally ill locked up and forgotten. CNN.com. Retrieved from http://www.cnn.com/2011/WORLD/africa/02/25/kenya.forgotten.health/index.html

McLorg, P. A., & Taub, D. E. (1987). Anorexia nervosa and bulimia: The development of deviant identities. *Deviant Behavior, 8*(2), 177–189.

Meisner, J. (2013, April 14). Sister escaped "Trigger Town," but bleak fate snared brother. *Chicago Tribune.* Retrieved from http://articles.chicagotribune.com/2013-04-14/news/ct-met-brother-sister-trigger-town-20130414_1_grammar-school-drugs-family-friend

Menardi, R. (2013, May 9). Catherine Rohr helps former felons defy odds, start businesses. *Silicon Prairie News.* Retrieved from http://www.siliconprairienews.com/2013/05/catherine-rohr-helps-former-felons-defy-odds-start-businesses

Meranze, M. (2009, August 24). California's crisis: Coming to a neighborhood near you. *Huffington Post.* Retrieved from http://www.huffingtonpost.com/michael-meranze/califor nias-crisis-coming_b_267461.html

Merry, S. E. (1989). Myth and practice in the mediation process. In M. Wright & B. Galaway (Eds.), *Mediation and criminal justice: Victims, offenders, and community* (pp. 239–250). London, UK: Sage.

Merton, R. K. (1938). Social structure and anomie. *American Sociological Review, 3*(5), 672–682.

Merton, R. K. (1957). *Social theory and social structure* (Rev. and enlarged ed.). Glencoe, IL: Free Press.

Merton, R. K. (1964). Anomie, anomia, and social interaction: Contexts of deviant behavior. In M. B. Clinard (Ed.), *Anomie and deviant behavior.* New York, NY: Free Press.

Messmer, H., & Otto, H.-U. (Eds.). (1992). *Restorative justice on trial: Pitfalls and potentials of victim–offender mediation: International research perspectives.* Amsterdam, Netherlands: Kluwer.

Messner, S. F., & Rosenfeld, R. (2007a). *Crime and the American Dream* (4th ed.). Belmont, CA: Wadsworth.

Messner, S. F., & Rosenfeld, R. (2007b). Political restraint of the market and levels of criminal homicide: A cross-national application of institutional-anomie theory. *Social Forces, 75,* 1393–1416.

Mestrovic, S. G., & Lorenzo, R. (2008). Durkheim's concept of anomie and the abuse at Abu Ghraib. *Journal of Classical Sociology, 8*(2), 179–207.

Meyer, A. G. (1963). *Marxism: The unity of theory and practice.* Ann Arbor: University of Michigan Press.

Milkman, R. (2012). Revolt of the college-educated millennials. *Contexts, 11*(2), 12–21.

Miller, J. G. (1998). *Last one over the wall* (2nd ed.). Columbus: Ohio State University Press.

Mills, C. W. (2000). *The sociological imagination.* Oxford, UK: Oxford University Press. (Original work published 1959)

Miner, H. (1956). Body ritual among the Nacirema. *American Anthropologist, 58*(3), 503–507.

Minor, K., & Morrison, J. T. (1996). A theoretical study and critique of restorative justice. In B. Galaway & J. Hudson (Eds.), *Restorative justice: International perspectives* (pp. 117–133). Monsey, NY: Criminal Justice Press.

Mitchell, K. (2001). Transnationalism, neo-liberalism, and the rise of the shadow state. *Economy and Society, 30*(2), 165–189.

Moffitt, T. E. (1993). "Life-course-persistent" and "adolescence-limited" antisocial behavior: A developmental taxonomy. *Psychological Review, 100,* 674–701.

Moffitt, T. E. (2003). Life-course-persistent and adolescence-limited antisocial behavior: A 10-year research review and a research agenda. In B. B. Lahey, T. E. Moffitt, & A. Caspi (Eds.), *Causes of conduct disorder and juvenile delinquency* (pp. 49–75). New York, NY: Guilford.

Moffitt, T. E. (2006). Life-course-persistent versus adolescence-limited antisocial behavior. In D. Cicchetti & D. Cohen (Eds.), *Developmental psychopathology* (2nd ed., pp. 570–598). New York, NY: John Wiley.

Monk-Turner, E., Edwards, D., Broadstone, J., Hummel, R., Lewis, S., & Wilson, D. (2005). Another look at handwashing behavior. *Social Behavior and Personality: An International Journal, 33*(7), 629–634.

Monroe, J. (2004). Getting a puff: A social learning test of adolescents smoking. *Journal of Child & Adolescent Substance Abuse, 13*(3), 71–83.

Monto, M. A., Machalek, J., & Anderson, T. L. (2013). Doing art: The construction of outlaw masculinity in a Portland, Oregon, graffiti crew. *Journal of Contemporary Ethnography, 42*(3), 259–290.

Moore, M. D., & Sween, M. (2015). Rural youth crime: A reexamination of social disorganization theory's applicability to rural areas. *Journal of Juvenile Justice, 4*(1), 47–63.

Morash, M. (1999). On Ronald L. Akers' social learning and social structure: A general theory of crime and deviance. *Theoretical Criminology, 3*(4), 437–493.

Moyer, I. L. (2001). *Criminological theories: Traditional and nontraditional voices and themes.* Thousand Oaks, CA: Sage.

Moynihan, C. (2013, January 28). In "Occupy," well-educated professionals far outnumbered jobless, study finds. *New York Times.* Retrieved from http://cityroom.blogs.nytimes.com/2013/01/28/in-occupy-well-educated-professionals-far-outnumbered-jobless-study-finds/?ref=occupywallstreet

Mudge, S. (2008). The state of the art: What is neo-liberalism? *Socio-Economic Review, 6,* 703–731.

Muftic, L. R. (2006). Advancing institutional anomie theory: A microlevel examination connecting culture, institutions, and deviance. *International Journal of Offender Therapy and Comparative Criminology, 50*(6), 630–653.

Mui, H. Z., Sales, P., & Murphy, S. (2014). Everybody's doing it: Initiation to prescription drug misuse. *Journal of Drug Issues, 44*(3), 236–253. doi:10.1177/0022042613497935

Mumola, C. J. (2000). *Incarcerated parents and their children* (Bureau of Justice Statistics Special Report, NCJ 182335). Washington, DC: Bureau of Justice Statistics.

Murphy, S., Waldorf, D., & Reinarman, C. (1990). Drifting into dealing: Becoming a cocaine seller. *Qualitative Sociology, 13,* 321–343.

National Advisory Commission on Civil Disorders. (1968). *Report of the National Advisory Commission on Civil Disorders.* New York, NY: Bantam Books.

National Association for Shoplifting Prevention. (2013). National Learning & Resource Center: Shoplifting statistics. Retrieved from http://www.shopliftingprevention.org/WhatNASPOffers/NRC/PublicEducStats.htm

National Health Care Anti-Fraud Association. (2010). *The problem of health care fraud.* Washington, DC: Author. Retrieved from http://www.nhcaa.org

Navasky, M. (Producer/Director), & O'Connor, K. (Producer/Director). (2009). *The Released* [Motion picture]. Boston: Frontline and Mead Street Films, 2009. Retrieved from http://www.pbs.org/wgbh/pages/frontline/released

Neff, J. L., & Waite, D. E. (2007). Male versus female substance abuse patterns among incarcerated juvenile offenders: Comparing strain and social learning variables. *Justice Quarterly, 24*(1), 106–132.

Netter, S. (2010, September 16). Student's body modification religion questioned after nose piercing controversy. ABC News. Retrieved from http://abcnews.go.com/US/students-body-modification-religion-questioned-nose-piercing-controversy/story?id=11645847&page=1

Neve, L., & Pate, K. (2005). Challenging the criminalization of women who resist. In J. Sudbury (Ed.), *Global lockdown: Race, gender, and the prison-industrial complex* (pp. 19–34). London, UK: Routledge.

Newman, G. (2008). *Comparative deviance: Perception and law in six cultures.* Piscataway, NJ: Transaction Press.

Nixon, K., Tutty, L., Downe, P., Gorkoff, K., & Ursel, J. (2002). The everyday occurrence: Violence in the lives of girls exploited through prostitution. *Violence Against Women, 8,* 1016–1043.

No on Prop. 8. (2008, September 18). *San Diego Union-Tribune.* Retrieved from http://www.sandiegouniontribune.com/uniontrib/20080918/news_lz1ed18top.html

Nye, F. I. (1958). *Family relationships and delinquent behavior.* New York, NY: John Wiley.

Office of Community Planning and Development. (2014). *The 2013 Annual Homeless Assessment Report (AHAR) to Congress.* Washington, DC: U.S. Department of Housing and Urban Planning.

Ogas, O., & Gaddam, S. (2011). *A billion wicked thoughts: What the Internet tells us about sexual relationships.* New York, NY: Penguin Group.

Ogden, S. (2005). The prison-industrial complex in indigenous California. In J. Sudbury (Ed.), *Global lockdown: Race, gender, and the prison-industrial complex* (pp. 57–66). London, UK: Routledge.

O'Hagan, M., & Brooks, D. (2005, September 7). Man says he'll plead guilty to killing sex offenders. *Seattle Times.* Retrieved from http://community.seattletimes.nwsource.com/archive/?date=20050907&slug=sexoffender07m

Orcutt, J. D. (1983). *Analyzing deviance.* Chicago, IL: Dorsey.

Osgood, D. W., & Chambers, J. M. (2000). Social disorganization outside the metropolis: An analysis of rural youth violence. *Criminology, 38*(1), 81–115.

O'Shea, T. C. (2006). Physical deterioration, disorder, and crime. *Criminal Justice Policy Review, 17,* 173–187.

Özbay, Ö. (2008). Self-control, gender, and deviance among Turkish university students. *Journal of Criminal Justice, 36*(1), 72–80.

Özbay, Ö., & Köksoy, O. (2009). Is low self-control associated with violence among youths in Turkey? *International Journal of Offender Therapy & Comparative Criminology, 53*(2), 145–167.

Pager, D. (2003). Blacks and ex-cons need not apply. *Contexts, 2*(4), 58–59.

Pager, D. (2007). *Marked: Race, crime, and finding work in an era of mass incarceration.* Chicago, IL: University of Chicago Press.

Pager, D., & Quillian, L. (2005). Walking the talk? What employers say versus what they do. *American Sociological Review, 70*, 355–380.

Park, K. (2002). Stigma management among the voluntarily childless. *Sociological Perspectives, 45*(1), 21–45.

Paternoster, R., & Bushway, S. (2009). Desistance and the "feared self": Toward an identity theory of criminal desistance. *Journal of Criminal Law and Criminology, 99*(4), 1103–1156.

Patterson, G. R., & Dishion, T. J. (1985). Contributions of families and peers to delinquency. *Criminology, 23*, 553–573.

Patterson, G. R., Dishion, T. J., & Bank, L. (1984). Family interaction: A process model of deviancy training. *Aggressive Behavior, 10*(3), 253–267.

Payne, A., & Welch, K. (2010). Modeling the effects of racial threat on punitive and restorative school discipline practices. *Criminology, 48*, 1019–1062.

Payne, B. (2013). *White-collar crime: The essentials*. Thousand Oaks, CA: Sage.

PEN America. (2015, November 10). *Secret sources: Whistleblowers, national security & free expression*. Retrieved from http://www.pen.org/event/2015/10/22/secret-sources-whistleblowers-national-security-and-free-expression

Pepinsky, H., & Quinney, R. (1991). *Criminology as peacemaking*. Bloomington: Indiana University Press.

Peralta, R. L., & Steele, J. L. (2010). Nonmedical prescription drug use among US college students at a Midwest university: A partial test of social learning theory. *Substance Use & Misuse, 45*(6), 865–887.

Percival, G. L. (2010). Ideology, diversity, and imprisonment: Considering the influence of local politics on racial and ethnic minority incarceration rates. *Social Science Quarterly, 91*, 1063–1082.

Perez-McCluskey, C., & Tovar, S. (2003). Family processes and delinquency: The consistency of relationships by ethnicity and gender. *Journal of Ethnicity in Criminal Justice, 1*, 37–61.

Petts, R. J. (2009). Family and religious characteristics' influence on delinquency trajectories from adolescence to young adulthood. *American Sociological Review, 74*(3), 465–483.

Piquero, A. R., Daigle, L. E., Gibson, C., Leeper Piquero, N., & Tibbetts, S. G. (2007). Research note: Are life-course-persistent offenders at risk for adverse health outcomes? *Journal of Research in Crime and Delinquency, 44*, 185.

Platt, T. (1974). Prospects for a radical criminology in the United States. *Crime and Social Justice, 1*, 2–10.

Ploeger, M. (1997). Youth employment and delinquency: Reconsidering a problematic relationship. *Criminology, 35*(4), 659–675.

Pornhub. (2014). 2014 year in review. Retrieved from http://www.pornhub.com/insights/2014-year-in-review

Porter, B. E., & England, K. J. (2000). Predicting red-light running behavior: A traffic safety study in three urban settings. *Journal of Safety Research, 31*, 1–8.

Pratt, J., & Eriksson, A. (2011). "Mr. Larsson is walking out again". The origins and development of Scandinavian prison systems. *Australian & New Zealand Journal of Criminology, 44*(1), 7–23.

Pratt, T. C., & Cullen, F. T. (2000). The empirical status of Gottfredson and Hirschi's general theory of crime: A meta-analysis. *Criminology, 38*(3), 931–964.

Prison Entrepreneurship Program. (n.d.). Prison Entrepreneurship Program website. Retrieved from http://www.prisonentrepreneurship.org

Prison University Project. (n.d.). About us. Retrieved from http://www.prisonuniversityproject.org/about-us

Pruitt, M. V. (2008). Deviant research: Deception, male Internet escorts, and response rates. *Deviant Behavior, 29*(1), 70–82.

Pruitt, M. V., & Krull, A. C. (2011). Escort advertisements and male patronage of prostitutes. *Deviant Behavior, 32*(1), 38–63.

Quinn, A. (2013). Book news: Inmate fights for his right to read werewolf erotica. *The Two-Way: Breaking News From NPR*. Retrieved from http://www.npr.org/blogs/thetwo-way/2013/06/13/191237331/book-news-inmate-fights-for-his-right-to-read-werewolf-erotica?sc=ipad&f=1008

Quinney, R. (1963). Occupational structure and criminal behavior: Prescription violation by retail pharmacists. *Social Problems, 11*, 179–185.

Quinney, R. (1970). *The social reality of crime*. Boston, MA: Little, Brown.

Quinney, R. (1995). Socialist humanism and the problem of crime: Thinking about Erich Fromm in the development of critical/peacemaking criminology. *Crime, Law, and Social Change, 23*, 147–156.

Quinney, R. (1991). The way of peace: On crime, suffering, and service. In H. E. Pepinsky & R. Quinney (Eds.), *Criminology as peacemaking* (pp. 3–13). Bloomington: Indiana University Press.

Rampona, J. (2004, November 28). What happens to the homeless? Criminalizing the necessary and life-sustaining actions of homeless people adds to the burden of living in constant exposure to the elements. *Arkansas Democrat-Gazette*.

Rankin, B. H., & Quane, J. M. (2002). Social contexts and urban adolescent outcomes: The interrelated effects of neighborhoods, families, and peers on African-American youth. *Social Problems, 49*(1), 79.

Rankin, J. H., & Kern, R. M. (1994). Parental attachments and delinquency. *Criminology, 32*, 495–515.

Rankin, J. H., & Wells, L. E. (1990). The effect of parental attachments and direct controls on delinquency. *Journal of Research in Crime and Delinquency, 27*, 140–165.

Raphael, J., & Shapiro, D. L. (2004). Violence in indoor and outdoor prostitution venues. *Violence Against Women, 10*(2), 126–139.

Rebellon, C. J., Straus, M. A., & Medeiros, R. (2008). Self-control in global perspective. *European Journal of Criminology, 5*(3), 331–361.

Reed, M. D., & Rountree, P. W. (1997). Peer pressure and adolescent substance use. *Journal of Quantitative Criminology, 13*(2), 143–180.

Reiling, D. M. (2002). The "simmie" side of life: Old Order Amish youths' affective response to culturally prescribed deviance. *Youth & Society, 34*(2), 146–171.

Reiman, J., & Leighton, P. (2009). *The rich get richer and the poor get prison: Ideology, class, and criminal justice* (9th ed.). Englewood Cliffs, NJ: Prentice Hall.

Reitman, J. (2013, December 4). Snowden and Greenwald: The men who leaked the secrets: How two alienated, angry geeks broke the story of the year. *Rolling Stone.* Retrieved from http://www .rollingstone.com/politics/news/snowden-and-greenwald-the-men-who-leaked-the-secrets-20131204

Rhodes, K. W., Orme, J. G., Cox, M. E., & Buehler, C. (2003). Foster family resources, psychosocial functioning, and retention. *Social Work Research, 27*(3), 135–150.

Ridley, J. (2015, October 29). The storm isn't over yet for Ashley Madison cheaters. *New York Post.* Retrieved from http://nypost .com/2015/10/29/the-storm-isnt-over-yet-for-ashley-madison-cheaters

Riley, N. (1995). Hamlet: The untold tragedy. *Organica News.* Retrieved from http://web.archive.org/web/20070107011410/ http://www.organicanews.com/news/article.cfm?story_id=103

Robinson, M. M., & Murphy, D. (2009). *Greed is good: Maximization and elite deviance in America.* Lanham, MD: Rowman & Littlefield.

Rogers, T. (2011, August 28). Why do college students love getting wasted? *Salon.* Retrieved from http://www.salon.com/2011/08/ 28/college_drinking_interview

Ronai, C. R., & Ellis, C. (1989). Turn-ons for money: Interactional strategies of the table dancer. *Journal of Contemporary Ethnography, 18,* 271–298.

Rosenbaum, D. P. (2007). Just say no to DARE. *Criminology & Public Policy, 6*(4), 815–824.

Rosenfield, S. (1997). Labeling mental illness: The effects of received services and perceived stigma on life satisfaction. *American Sociological Review, 62*(4), 660–672.

Rosenhan, D. L. (1973). On being sane in insane places. *Science, 179,* 250–258.

Rosenthal, E. (1994). Irked by Medicare limits, doctors ask elderly to pay up. *New York Times.* Retrieved from http://www.nytimes .com/1994/02/15/nyregion/irked-by-medicare-limits-doctors-ask-elderly-to-pay-up.html?pagewanted=all&src=pm

Rothe, D. L., & Kauzlarich, D. (2010). State-level crime: Theory and policy. In H. D. Barlow & S. Decker (Eds.), *Crime and public policy: Putting theory to work* (2nd ed., pp. 166–187). Philadelphia, PA: Temple University Press.

Rothe, D. L., & Mullins, C. W. (2009). Toward a criminology for international criminal law: An integrated theory of international criminal violations. *International Journal of Comparative and Applied Criminal Justice, 3*(1), 97–118.

Rousseau, J. (1987). *The basic political writings* (D. A. Cress, Trans.). Indianapolis, IN: Hackett Publishing Company.

Rowe, D. C. (2002). *Biology and crime.* Los Angeles, CA: Roxbury.

Rubington, E. S., & Weinberg, M. S. (2008). *Deviance: The interactionist perspective.* Englewood Cliffs, NJ: Prentice Hall.

Rutter, M., & Giller, H. (1984). *Juvenile delinquency: Trends and perspectives.* London, UK: Guilford.

Ruvolo, J. (2011, May 20). The Internet is for porn (so let's talk about it). *Forbes.* Retrieved from http://www.forbes.com/sites/julieru volo/2011/05/20/the-internet-is-for-porn-so-lets-talk-about-it

Sallman, J. (2010). Living with stigma: Women's experiences of prostitution and substance use. *Affilia, 25,* 146–159.

Sampson, R. (1999). On Ronald L. Akers' social learning and social structure: A general theory of crime and deviance. *Theoretical Criminology, 3*(4), 437–493.

Sampson, R. J. (2012). *Great American city: Chicago and the enduring neighborhood effect.* Chicago, IL: Chicago University Press.

Sampson, R. J., & Groves, W. B. (1989). Community structure and crime: Testing social-disorganization theory. *American Journal of Sociology, 94*(4), 774–802.

Sampson, R. J., & Laub, J. H. (1993). *Crime in the making: Pathways and turning points through life.* Cambridge, MA: Harvard University Press.

Sampson, R. J., & Laub, J. H. (1994). Urban poverty and the family context of delinquency: A new look at structure and process in a classic study. *Child Development, 65,* 523–541.

Sampson, R. J., & Laub, J. H. (1995). Understanding variability in lives through time: Contributions of life-course criminology. *Studies on Crime and Crime Prevention, 4*(2), 143–158.

Sampson, R. J., & Raudenbush, S. W. (2004). Seeing disorder: Neighborhood stigma and the social construction of "broken windows." *Social Psychology Quarterly, 67,* 319–342.

Sampson, R. J., Raudenbush, S. W., & Earls, F. (1997). Neighborhoods and violent crime: A multilevel study of collective efficacy. *Science, 277,* 918–924.

Sanchez, F. (2013, April 2). Venezuela prison deaths: 591 detainees killed country's jails last year. *Huffington Post.* Retrieved from http://www.huffingtonpost.com/2013/01/31/venezuela-prison-deaths_n_2593736.html

Sanders, T. (2007). Becoming an ex-sex worker. *Feminist Criminology, 2*(1), 74–95.

Sarkis, C. (2012, December 20). 10 weird laws from around the world. *USA Today.* Retrieved from http://www.usatoday.com/story/ travel/destinations/2012/12/19/10-weird-laws-from-around-the-world/1779931

Savolainen, J. (2000). Inequality, welfare state, and homicide: Further support for the institutional anomie theory. *Criminology, 38*(4), 1021–1042.

Scarce, R. (2008). Earth First! Deviance inside and out. In E. Goode & D. A. Vail (Eds.), *Extreme deviance* (pp. 177–188). Thousand Oaks, CA: Pine Forge Press.

Scheff, T. J. (1966). *Being mentally ill: A sociological theory.* Chicago, IL: Aldine.

Schlossman, S., & Sedlak, M. (1983). The Chicago Area Project revisited. *Crime and Delinquency, 29,* 398–462.

Scholinski, D. (with Adams, J. M.). (1997). *The last time I wore a dress: A memoir.* New York, NY: Riverhead Books.

Schur, E. M. (1973). *Radical non-intervention: Rethinking the delinquency problem.* Englewood Cliffs, NJ: Prentice Hall.

Schur, E. M. (1983). *Labeling women deviant: Gender, stigma and social control.* Philadelphia, PA: Temple University Press.

Schwendinger, H., & Schwendinger, J. (1970). Defenders of order or guardians of human rights? *Issues in Criminology, 5,* 123–157.

Seddon, T. (2005). Paying drug users to take part in research: Justice, human rights and business perspectives on the use of incentive payments. *Addiction Research & Theory, 13*(2), 101–109.

Segall, L. (2015, September 8). Pastor outed on Ashley Madison commits suicide. *CNN Money.* Retrieved from http://money .cnn.com/2015/09/08/technology/ashley-madison-suicide

Shane, S., & Somaiya, R. (2013, June 16). New leak indicates U.S. and Britain eavesdropped at '09 world conferences. *New York Times.* Retrieved from http://www.nytimes.com/2013/06/17/world/ europe/new-leak-indicates-us-and-britain-eavesdropped-at-09- world-conferences.html?_r=0

Sharpe, E. B. (2005). Urban morality issues incidents in ten cities, 1990–2000. Retrieved from http://www.icpsr.umich.edu/icpsr web/ICPSR/studies/3735?author%5B0%5D=Sharp%2C+ Elaine+B.&paging.startRow=1

Shaw, C. A., & McKay, H. (1969). *Juvenile delinquency in urban areas.* Chicago, IL: University of Chicago Press. (Original work published 1942)

Shteir, R. (2011). *The steal: A cultural history of shoplifting.* New York, NY: Penguin Press.

Silver, E. (2000). Extending social disorganization theory: A multilevel approach to the study of violence among persons with mental illness. *Criminology, 38*(4), 1043–1074.

Simmons, J. L. (1965). Public stereotypes of deviants. *Social Problems, 13*(2), 223–232.

Simon, D. R. (2008). *Elite deviance* (9th ed.). New York, NY: Pearson Education.

Simon, R. J. (1975). *The contemporary woman and crime.* Rockville, MD: National Institute of Mental Health.

Simons, R. L., Simons, L., Burt, C., Brody, G. H., & Cutrona, C. (2005). Collective efficacy, authoritative parenting, and delinquency: A longitudinal test of a model integrating community and family level processes. *Criminology, 43*(4), 989–1029.

Singer, E., & Ye, C. (2013). The use and effects of incentives in surveys. *Annals of the American Academy of Political & Social Science, 645*(1), 112–141.

Skipp, C. (2009, July 25). A bridge too far. *Newsweek.* Retrieved from http://www.newsweek.com/2009/07/24/a-bridge-too-far.html

Skogan, W. (1990). *Disorder and decline: Crime and the spiral of decay in American neighborhoods.* New York, NY: Free Press.

Skogan, W. (2015). Disorder and decline: The state of research. *Journal of Research in Crime & Delinquency, 52*(4), 464–485. doi:10.1177/0022427815577836

Smart, C. (1977). Criminological theory: Its ideology and implications concerning women. *British Journal of Sociology, 28,* 89–100.

Snowball, L., & Weatherburn, D. (2008). Theories of indigenous violence: A preliminary empirical assessment. *Australian & New Zealand Journal of Criminology, 41*(2), 216–235.

Sokol-Katz, J., Dunham, R., & Zimmerman, R. (1997). Family structure versus parental attachment in controlling adolescent deviant behavior: A social control model. *Adolescence, 32,* 199–216.

Solomon, G. S., & Ray, J. B. (1984). Irrational beliefs of shoplifters. *Journal of Clinical Psychology, 40*(4), 1075–1077.

Soothill, K., Fitzpatrick, C., & Brian, F. (2009). *Understanding criminal careers.* Cullompton, UK: Willan.

Spitzer, R. L. (1976). More on pseudoscience in science and the case for psychiatric diagnosis: A critique of D. L. Rosenhan's "On being sane in insane places" and "The contextual nature of psychiatric diagnosis." *Archives of General Psychiatry, 33*(4), 459–470.

Spitzer, S. (1975). Towards a Marxian theory of deviance. *Social Problems, 22,* 638–651.

Spitzer, S. (1983). Marxist perspectives in the sociology of law. *Annual Review of Sociology, 9,* 103–124.

Spreitzer, G. M., & Sonenshein, S. (2004). Toward the construct definition of positive deviance. *American Behavioral Scientist, 47*(6), 828–847.

Stark, R. (1987). Deviant places: A theory of the ecology of crime. *Criminology, 25*(4), 893–909.

Steffensmeier, D. J., Allan, E. A., Harer, M. D., & Streifel, C. (1989). Age and the distribution of crime. *American Journal of Sociology, 94*(4), 803–831.

Steinhauer, J. (2007, April 29). For $82 a day, booking a stay in a 5-star jail. *New York Times.* Retrieved from http://www.nytimes .com/2007/04/29/us/29jail.html?pagewanted=all&_r=1&

Stern, G. M. (2013, September 30). John Jay College tries to help prisoners turn lives around. *New York Business Journal.* Retrieved from http://www.bizjournals.com/newyork/news/2013/09/30/ john-jay-college-tries-to-help.html?page=all

Stiles, B. L., & Clark, R. E. (2011). BDSM: A subcultural analysis of sacrifices and delights. *Deviant Behavior, 32*(2), 158–189.

Stillman, S. (2013, August 12–19). A reporter at large: Taken. *New Yorker,* 49–61.

Stoops, M. (2014). *Share no more: The criminalization of efforts to feed people in need.* Washington, DC: National Coalition for the Homeless.

Strang, H., & Braithwaite, J. (2001). *Restorative justice and civil society.* Cambridge, UK: Cambridge University Press.

Sudbury, J. (Ed.). (2005). *The global lockdown: Race, gender, and the prison-industrial complex.* London, UK: Routledge.

Sullivan, L. (2010, October 28). Prison economics help drive Arizona immigration bill. NPR. Retrieved from http://www.npr.org/ templates/transcript/transcript.php?storyId=130833741

Sullivan, M. L. (1989). *"Getting paid": Youth crime and work in the inner city.* Ithaca, NY: Cornell University Press.

Sumner, W. G. (1906). *Folkways: A study of the sociological importance of usages, manners, customs, mores, and morals.* Boston, MA: Ginn & Company.

Sutherland, E. H. (1934). *Principles of criminology.* Philadelphia, PA: Lippincott.

Sutherland, E. (1940). White-collar criminality. *American Society of Criminology, 5,* 1–12.

Sutherland, E. H. (1947). *Principles of criminology* (4th ed.). Philadelphia, PA: Lippincott.

Sutherland, E. H. (1949b). *White collar crime.* New York, NY: Holt, Rinehart & Winston.

Sutter, J. D. (2012, May 24). Welcome to the world's nicest prison. CNN. Retrieved from http://www.cnn.com/2012/05/24/world/ europe/norway-prison-bastoy-nicest/index.html

Sykes, G. M. (1958). *The society of captives.* Princeton, NJ: Princeton University Press.

Sykes, G. M., & Matza, D. (1957). Techniques of neutralization: A theory of delinquency. *American Sociological Review, 22*(6), 664–670.

Szalavitz, M. (2012, September 28). College binge drinking: How bad is the problem really? *Time.* Retrieved from http://healthland .time.com/2012/09/28/college-binge-drinking-how-bad-is-the-problem-really/

Tannenbaum, F. (1938). *Crime and the community.* Boston, MA: Ginn.

Taylor, E. (1998). A primer on critical race theory. *Journal of Blacks in Higher Education, 19,* 122–124.

Taylor, I., Walton, P., & Young, J. (1973). *The new criminology.* New York, NY: Harper Torchbooks.

Taylor, P. (1991). Fire at chicken processing plant kills 25: Disaster: Witnesses say locked doors added to death toll at North Carolina facility that had never been inspected for safety; 49 workers hurt. *Los Angeles Times.* Retrieved from http://articles.latimes .com/1991-09-04/news/mn-1562_1_chicken-processing-plant

Temple University. (n.d.). The Inside-Out Prison Exchange Program. Retrieved from http://www.insideoutcenter.org/index.html

Thio, A. (2009). *Deviant behavior.* New York, NY: Allyn & Bacon.

Thompson, W. E., Harred, J. L., & Burks, B. E. (2003). Managing the stigma of topless dancing: A decade later. *Deviant Behavior, 24*(6), 551–570.

Thornberry, T. P., Lizotte, A. J., Krohn, M. D., Farnworth, M., & Sung Joon, J. (1994). Delinquent peers, beliefs, and delinquent behavior: A longitudinal test of interactional theory. *Criminology, 32*(1), 47–83.

Tong, R. P. (1998). *Feminist thought: A more comprehensive introduction.* Boulder, CO: Westview.

Tonry, M. (2011). *Punishing race: A continuing American dilemma.* New York, NY: Oxford University Press.

Traub, S. H., & Little, C. B. (1985). *Theories of deviance* (3rd ed.). Itasca, IL: F. E. Peacock.

Tuggle, J., & Holmes, M. (1997). Blowing smoke: Status politics and the Shasta County smoking ban. *Deviant Behavior, 18*(1), 77–93.

Turk, A. T. (1969). *Criminality and legal order.* Chicago, IL: Rand McNally.

Turk, A. T. (1976a). Law as a weapon in social conflict. *Social Problems, 23,* 276–291.

Turk, A. T. (1976b). Law, conflict and order: From theorizing toward theories. *Canadian Review of Sociology and Anthropology, 13*(3), 282–294.

Turk, A. T. (1977). Class, conflict, and criminalization. *Sociological Focus, 10,* 209–220.

Turk, A. T. (2002). Crime causation: Political theories. In J. Dressler (Ed.), *Encyclopedia of crime and justice* (2nd ed.). New York, NY: Macmillan References USA.

Tyler, K. A., Hoyt, D. R., Whitbeck, L. B., & Cauce, A. M. (2001). The impact of childhood sexual abuse on later sexual victimization among runaway youth. *Journal of Research on Adolescence, 11*(2), 151–176.

Uggen, C., & Inderbitzin, M. (2010). The price and the promise of citizenship: Extending the vote to non-incarcerated felons. In N. A. Frost, J. D. Freilich, & T. R. Clear (Eds.), *Contemporary issues in criminal justice policy: Policy proposals from the American Society of Criminology Conference* (pp. 61–68). Belmont, CA: Cengage/Wadsworth.

Uggen, C., Manza, J., & Thompson, M. (2006). Citizen, democracy, and the civic reintegration of criminal offenders. *Annals of the American Academy of Political and Social Science, 605,* 281–310.

Umbreit, M. (1994). *Victim meets offender: The impact of restorative justice and mediation.* Monsey, NY: Criminal Justice Press.

United Nations Global Initiative to Fight Human Trafficking. (2008). *Human trafficking: An overview.* United Nations Office on Drugs and Crime. Retrieved from http://www.ungift.org/docs/ungift/ pdf/knowledge/ebook.pdf

University of Delaware. (2013). University of Delaware copyright guidelines: Students, faculty, and staff. Retrieved from http:// www.udel.edu/it/security/copyright

U.S. Department of Health and Human Services. (n.d.). International compilation of human research standards. Retrieved March 4, 2016, from http://www.hhs.gov/ohrp/international/intlcom pilation/intlcompilation.html

U.S. Department of Labor. (n.d.). The Whistleblower Protection Programs. Retrieved from http://www.whistleblowers.gov

U.S. Department of State. (2007). *Trafficking in persons report 2007.* Retrieved from http://www.state.gov/g/tip/rls/tiprpt/2007

U.S. Department of State. (2013). *Trafficking in persons report 2013.* Retrieved from http://www.state.gov/documents/organization/ 210737.pdf

Van Voorhis, P., Cullen, F. T., Mathers, R. A., & Garner, C. C. (1988). The impact of family structure and quality on delinquency: A comparative assessment of structural and functional factors. *Criminology, 26,* 235–261.

Vander Ven, T. (2011). *Getting wasted: Why college students drink too much and party so hard.* New York, NY: NYU Press.

VanNostrand, L.-M., & Tewksbury, R. (1997). The motives and mechanics of operating an illegal drug enterprise. *Deviant Behavior, 20,* 57–83.

Vaughan, D. (2004). Theorizing disaster: Analogy, historical ethnography, and the Challenger accident. *Ethnography, 5*(3), 315–347.

Vazsonyi, A. T., & Klanjsek, R. (2008). A test of self-control theory across different socioeconomic strata. *Justice Quarterly, 25*(1), 101–131.

Vazsonyi, A. T., Pickering, L. E., Junger, M., & Hessing, D. (2001). An empirical test of a general theory of crime: A four-nation comparative study of self-control and the prediction of deviance. *Journal of Research in Crime & Delinquency, 38*(2), 91–131.

Vazsonyi, A. T., Wittekind, J. C., Belliston, L. M., & Van Loh, T. D. (2004). Extending the general theory of crime to "the East": Low self-control in Japanese late adolescents. *Journal of Quantitative Criminology, 20*(3), 189–216.

Venkatesh, S. (2008). *Gang leader for a day: A rogue sociologist takes to the streets.* New York, NY: Penguin Books.

Veysey, B. M., & Messner, S. F. (1999). Further testing of social disorganization theory: An elaboration of Sampson and Groves's "community structure and crime." *Journal of Research in Crime and Delinquency, 36*(2), 156–174.

Vold, G. B. (1958). *Theoretical criminology.* New York, NY: Oxford University Press.

Wacquant, L. (2000). The new "peculiar institution": On the prison as surrogate ghetto. *Theoretical Criminology, 4,* 377–389.

Walsh, A. (2000). Behavior genetics and anomie/strain theory. *Criminology, 38*(4), 1075–1107.

Walsh, T. (2011, January 27). Ugandan gay rights activist bludgeoned to death. CNN. Retrieved from http://www.cnn.com/2011/WORLD/africa/01/27/uganda.gay.activist.killed/index.html

Warner, B. D., & Pierce, G. L. (1993). Reexamining social disorganization theory using calls to the police as a measure of crime. *Criminology, 31*(4), 493–517.

Warr, M. (1993). Parents, peers, and delinquency. *Social Forces, 72,* 247–265.

Warr, M. (2002). *Companions in crime: The social aspects of criminal conduct.* Cambridge, UK: Cambridge University Press.

Watson, B. (2013, August 6). Fremont's pay-to-stay jail offers a more pleasant prison experience. DailyFinance. Retrieved from http://www.dailyfinance.com/2013/08/06/freemont-calif-offers-pay-to-stay-nicer-jail-cells

Weeks, A. H. (1958). *Youthful offenders at Highfield.* Ann Arbor: University of Michigan Press.

Weinberg, M. S. (1966). Becoming a nudist. *Psychiatry: Journal for the Study of Interpersonal Processes, 29,* 15–24.

Weinberg, M. S., Williams, C. J., & Pryor, D. W. (2001). Bisexuals at midlife: Commitment, salience, and identity. *Journal of Contemporary Ethnography, 30*(2), 180–208.

Wells, L. E., & Rankin, J. H. (1988). Direct parental controls and delinquency. *Criminology, 26,* 263–285.

West, C. (1995). Foreword. In K. Crenshaw, N. Gotanda, G. Peller, & K. Thomas (Eds.), *Critical race theory: The key writings that formed the movement* (pp. xi–xii). New York, NY: New Press.

West, S. L., & O'Neal, K. K. (2004). Project DARE outcome effectiveness revisited. *American Journal of Public Health, 94,* 1027–1029.

Western, B. (2006). *Punishment and inequality in America.* New York, NY: Russell Sage Foundation.

Whaley, R., Smith, J. M., & Hayes-Smith, R. (2011). Teenage drug and alcohol use: Comparing individual and contextual effects. *Deviant Behavior, 32*(9), 818–845.

Williams, C. J. (2013, October 7). Malala's year: Shot for defying Taliban, now considered for Nobel. *Los Angeles Times.* Retrieved from http://www.latimes.com/world/world now/la-fg-wn-malala-yousafzai-taliban-20131007,0,876137.story

Wilson, J. Q., & Kelling, G. (1982). Broken windows: The police and neighborhood safety. *Atlantic Monthly, 249,* 29–38.

Wolfgang, M. E., & Ferrcuti, F. (1967). *The subculture of violence: Towards an integrated theory in criminology.* Beverly Hills, CA: Sage.

Wright, E. R., Gronfein, W. P., & Owens, T. J. (2000). Deinstitutionalization, social rejection, and the self-esteem of former mental patients. *Journal of Health and Social Behavior, 41*(1), 68–90.

Wright, J., & Cullen, F. T. (2001). Parental efficacy and delinquent behavior: Do control and support matter? *Criminology, 39*(3), 677–705.

Wright, M. (1996). *Justice for victims and offenders: A restorative response to crime* (2nd ed.). Winchester, UK: Waterside Press.

Yip, A. K. T. (1996). Gay Christians and their participation in the gay subculture. *Deviant Behavior, 17*(3), 297–318.

Zehr, H. (1990). *Changing lenses: A new focus for crime and justice.* Scottsdale, PA: Herald Press.

Zehr, H. (2002). *The little book of restorative justice.* Intercourse, PA: Good Books.

Zhang, L., Messner, S. F., & Liu, J. (2007). A multilevel analysis of the risk of household burglary in the city of Tianjin, China. *British Journal of Criminology, 47*(6), 918–937.

Zhang, S. X. (2010). *Sex trafficking in a border community: A field study of sex trafficking in Tijuana, Mexico.* San Diego, CA: San Diego State University.

Index

About the Authors

Michelle Inderbitzin primarily studies prison culture, juvenile justice, and transformative education. She is co-editor of the book *The Voluntary Sector in Prisons: Encouraging Personal and Institutional Change,* and she has published papers in *Punishment & Society, Journal of Adolescent Research, The Prison Journal, Journal of Offender Rehabilitation, International Journal of Offender Therapy and Comparative Criminology,* and *Criminology & Public Policy.* Dr. Inderbitzin earned her PhD in sociology from the University of Washington and has been a faculty member at Oregon State University since 2001. Along with her on-campus classes on crime and deviance, she regularly teaches classes and volunteers in Oregon's maximum-security prison for men and state youth correctional facilities.

Kristin A. Bates is a professor of criminology and justice studies in the Department of Sociology at California State University San Marcos. Her research focuses on racial, ethnic, and gender inequality in criminal justice policies. She is currently involved in a study examining the community impact of civil gang injunctions. She is co-editor of the book *Through the Eye of Katrina: Social Justice in the United States,* now in its second edition, as well as co-author of *Juvenile Delinquency in a Diverse Society.* Dr. Bates earned her PhD in sociology from the University of Washington in 1998.

Randy R. Gainey is a professor in the Department of Sociology and Criminal Justice at Old Dominion University. His research focuses on racial and ethnic disparities in sentencing decisions, alternatives to incarceration, neighborhood characteristics and crime, and quantitative methodologies. He is co-author of two other books: *Family Violence and Criminal Justice: A Life-Course Approach,* now in its third edition, and *Drugs and Policing.* His articles have recently appeared in *Criminology, Justice Quarterly, Theoretical Criminology, The Prison Journal, The Journal of Criminal Justice,* and *The Journal of Crime and Justice.* Dr. Gainey earned his PhD in sociology at the University of Washington.